Carroll D. Wright

Industrial Depressions

First annual Report of the US Commissioner of Labor

Carroll D. Wright

Industrial Depressions
First annual Report of the US Commissioner of Labor

ISBN/EAN: 9783337176020

Printed in Europe, USA, Canada, Australia, Japan

Cover: Foto ©ninafisch / pixelio.de

More available books at **www.hansebooks.com**

THE FIRST ANNUAL REPORT

OF THE

COMMISSIONER OF LABOR,

MARCH, 1886.

INDUSTRIAL DEPRESSIONS.

WASHINGTON:
GOVERNMENT PRINTING OFFICE.
1886.

CONTENTS.

	Page.
LETTER OF TRANSMITTAL	5
INTRODUCTION	11
CHAPTER I.—MODERN INDUSTRIAL DEPRESSIONS	15
Great Britain, 1837–86	16
France, 1837–86	35
Belgium, 1837–86	44
Germany, 1837–86	49
The United States, 1837–78	55
CHAPTER II.—THE INDUSTRIAL DEPRESSION IN THE UNITED STATES, 1882–86	65
The Extent of the Depression	65
Alleged Causes of the Present Depression	76
Falling Prices	79
Machinery and Over-production	80
The Variation in the Cost of Production	90
The Variation in the Rates of Wages	141
Speculative Railroad Building	242
Crippled Consuming Power, or Under-consumption	243
Tariff Inequalities	250
Miscellaneous	252
CHAPTER III.—THE MANUFACTURING NATIONS CONSIDERED AS A GROUP IN RELATION TO THE PRESENT DEPRESSION	254
CHAPTER IV.—SUGGESTED REMEDIES FOR DEPRESSIONS	264
The Restriction of Land Grants to Corporations	271
The Restriction of Immigration	271
The Enactment of Laws to Stop Speculation	273
The Establishment of Boards of Arbitration to Settle Industrial Difficulties	274
The Contraction of Credit	276
A Sound Currency	276
Commercial and Mercantile Conditions	276
The Distribution of Products	277
Profit-sharing	279
The Organization of Workmen; of Employers	286
CHAPTER V.—SUMMARY	290
Contemporaneousness and Severity of Depressions	290
Causes	291
Remedies	292
APPENDIX A.—Occupations, with Number and Wages of Employés, by Industries	295
APPENDIX B.—Earnings and Expenses of Wage Receivers in Europe	411
APPENDIX C.—Synopsis of Labor Legislation in the United States	457

LETTER OF TRANSMITTAL.

DEPARTMENT OF THE INTERIOR, BUREAU OF LABOR,
Washington, D. C., March 17, 1886.

SIR: I have the honor to submit herewith the first annual report relating to the information collected and collated by the Bureau of Labor.

The Bureau of Labor was established by act of Congress, approved June 27, 1884, which provided for the appointment of a Commissioner of Labor by the President, and a Chief Clerk, to be appointed by the honorable Secretary of the Interior, and such employés as might be necessary to conduct the work of the Bureau. No officers were appointed, however, until January, 1885, when, under a commission received from the President, I assumed the duties of Commissioner of Labor January 31, and February 3 Mr. Oren W. Weaver was appointed Chief Clerk. The policy under which it seemed to me best that the operations of the Bureau should be conducted was submitted February 4 in a communication to the Secretary of the Interior, the features of which policy need not be restated. March 11 I submitted for your approval an outline of the first year's work of the Bureau. This outline related to the collection of information relative to industrial depressions, the investigation comprehending a study of their character and alleged causes, whether contemporaneous in the great producing countries of the world, and whether, as to duration, severity, and periodicity, they have been similar in such countries. The outline also comprehended the collection of data relating to the variation of wages in different countries and in different parts of this country, in the cost of living in the same localities, and the cost of production, and, in fact, all such alleged causes of industrial depressions as might offer opportunity for illustration through classified facts. The suggested remedies for such depressions were also comprehended in the outline. March 17, a year ago to-day, you did me the honor to approve this outline of work, when I entered at once upon preparations for carrying it out. Unavoidable circumstances prevented the several agents of the Bureau getting to their respective fields of operations prior to June 1, as an average date of the commencement of our work. It will therefore be observed that the first year's work of the Bureau has been carried through in less than ten months.

The countries comprehended in the investigation other than our own were Great Britain, France, Belgium, Germany, and, to some extent, Switzerland and Italy. Five agents were employed in the foreign countries and fifteen in this, and to those who remained in the field and carried out their instructions I am under the greatest obligation for the faithfulness and the assiduity with which they performed the duties assigned to them. The results of the investigation relating to industrial depressions are not as complete as I could wish to have them, yet they are far more complete than I had any right to expect them to be. The difficulties attending an investigation of the magnitude of the one projected are great indeed. In fact, a line of work more difficult than that selected could hardly have been adopted. The statistical illustrations of the various features of industrial depressions as presented herein, unless otherwise stated, are the results of original inquiry, and these statistical illustrations, taken in connection with others, which are all from most trustworthy sources and from highest authorities, constitute a grouping of facts relative to conditions claiming the fullest attention, which, so far as I am aware, is novel not only in the grouping but in the extent of their influence. The agents of the Bureau have, as a rule, been met with courtesy and a desire to furnish the information sought; yet it should be distinctly understood that if the manufacturers of any locality miss comparative data in the construction of tables on cost of production, or other tables of great intrinsic value to them, the lack is due to their own failure or that of their associates to give the information required. If the tables on wages and cost of production do not present complete comparative data, the lack of completeness is due entirely to the apprehension of manufacturers that the information required would do them some harm, or to their positive refusal to furnish such information. As it is, these tables comprehend about forty industries, seven hundred and fifty-nine establishments, and about one hundred and fifty thousand employés. Of the seven hundred and fifty-nine establishments, one hundred and eighty-nine reported wages only, one hundred and seventy-seven cost of production only, and three hundred and ninety-three both wages and cost of production. It is seen then that wages were reported for five hundred and eighty-two establishments, and that the average number of employés for each establishment was two hundred and fifty-six.

The organic law of the Bureau provides that the Commissioner of Labor "shall collect information upon the subject of labor, its relation to capital, the hours of labor, and the earnings of laboring men and women, and the means of promoting their material, social, intellectual, and moral prosperity," * * * and he "shall annually make a report in writing to the Secretary of the Interior of the information collected and collated by him, and containing such recommendations as he may deem calculated to promote the efficiency of the Bureau." With this statutory instruction before me, and in accordance with my own inclination, the matter presented herewith is largely statistical, whether presented in the text of the work or in tabular form. Theoretical discussion has been avoided so far as possible. When speaking of certain influences resulting from the evolution of industrial forces, it is quite impossible to keep entirely outside of theoretical lines, nor is it always desirable, for the conclusions of one who has had the preparation of a report of this kind, and the opportunity to study closely the relations of all the facts presented, should, if impartially stated, have some value, even if they approach a theoretical basis.

Fifteen States in the Union have bureaus with similar duties to those assigned to this office. These State bureaus have been established as follows and in the following order: Massachusetts Bureau of Statistics of Labor, 1869; Pennsylvania Bureau of Industrial Statistics, 1872; Connecticut Bureau of Labor Statistics, 1873 (discontinued 1875, reestablished 1885); Ohio Bureau of Labor Statistics, 1877; New Jersey Bureau of Statistics of Labor and Industries, 1878; Missouri Bureau of Labor Statistics and Inspection, 1879; Illinois Bureau of Labor Statistics, 1879; Indiana Bureau of Statistics and Geology, 1879; New York Bureau of Labor Statistics, 1883; California Bureau of Labor Statistics, 1883; Michigan Bureau of Labor and Industrial Statistics, 1883; Wisconsin Bureau of Labor Statistics, 1883; Iowa Bureau of Labor Statistics, 1884; Maryland Bureau of Statistics of Labor, 1884; Kansas Bureau of Labor and Industrial Statistics, 1885. These bureaus are located at the capitals of the States named, and their publications are becoming widely known for the valuable contributions which they make to economic science and literature. They are bureaus distinctly American in their character, although some of the European Governments are now contemplating the establishment of kindred offices.

The law establishing this Bureau, as quoted, calls for such recommendations as may be deemed calculated to promote the efficiency of the office. The comprehensiveness of the law precludes any recommendation as to the range of work which may be undertaken, but I would recommend that the Bureau be given authority to publish specific reports, independently of its annual reports, whenever, in the judgment of the Secretary of the Interior, such special reports might be of value to the public—as, for instance, it might be wise to investigate promptly some great industrial movement and make report thereon—but such a report, delayed until the publication of the annual report of the information collected by the Commissioner, would lose its value. It should follow the collection of the special facts, and at once, in order to possess public value.

I have been fortunate in having the services of Mr. Oren W. Weaver as Chief Clerk of the Bureau. Mr. Weaver brought to the service of the Bureau not only excellent native capacity and ability for its peculiar work, but ten years' practical experience in statistical duties, and my thanks are cordially extended to him.

With the keenest appreciation of your own generous coöperation in the work of the Bureau, and of the kindly confidence which you have always extended to me in the critical work of organizing and carrying out the delicate duties of an office constituted on the basis of the Bureau of Labor,

I am, very respectfully, your obedient servant,

CARROLL D. WRIGHT,
Commissioner.

Hon. L. Q. C. LAMAR,
Secretary of the Interior.

INDUSTRIAL DEPRESSIONS.

INTRODUCTION.

The depressions with which the present generation is familiar belong to the age of invention and of organized industry. Whether these depressions are necessary concomitants of present industrial conditions may be a mooted question, but it is certain that they come with such conditions, and that many features of them must pass away when out of the present status of industrial forces there shall be evolved a grander industrial system, a system which must be as much grander than the present as the present is grander than that out of which it was evolved. Industrial depressions must not be confused with commercial crises and panics, notwithstanding the effects of one reach into the other; that is, a commercial and financial crisis may take place without immediately producing any industrial depression, although generally, if the effects of such commercial or financial crisis continue for any great length of time, the industries must be involved to a greater or less extent. The present industrial depression is the first of its kind as an entirety, as will appear from the facts to be stated. History is full of accounts of crises of various descriptions, resulting from various causes. Back of the age of rapid transportation, stagnation in any industrial sense might result from various natural causes, such as floods, famines, earthquakes, or from great political catastrophes, or from long and expensive and exhausting wars, but not through the causes which are potent in producing modern depressions; but the regularity and contemporaneity which characterize commercial, financial, and industrial disturbances belong to modern history, and are not seen in the past. Of old, stagnations, when occurring, lasted through long periods. The people might be suffering from depression of some form through a quarter, or a half, or a whole century, and then would come a generation of comparative prosperity. In modern times we have, in the place of the long reaches of the past, short, sharp, and frequent disturbances in the business world; but whether in the olden or in the modern times, the reality of the depressed periods was aggravated by apprehension, and it is therefore never quite safe to assume that contemporaneous accounts of depressed periods are accurate. The fears of men, the apprehension of direful results, the imagination, all these help to enlarge the reality and to cause the effects of a disturbance to be more widely felt. As instances in the past, it is necessary to refer to but two authorities. Richard Hakluyt, in his "Discourse Concerning Western Planting," written in the year 1584 for the purpose of urging the settlement of this western world, after referring to the discoveries of the French, uses the following language:

"But wee, for all the statutes that hitherto can be devised, and the sharpe execution of the same in poonishinge idle and lazye persons, for wante of sufficient occasion of honest employmente, cannot deliver our commonwealthe from multitudes of loyterers and idle vagabondes. Truthe it is, that throughe our longe peace and seldome sicknes (twoo singular blessinges of Almightie God), wee are growen more populous than ever heretofore; so that nowe there are of every arte and science so many, that they can hardly lyve one by another, nay rather they are readie to eate upp one another; yea many thousandes of idle persons are within this realme, which, haviuge no way to be sett on worke, be either mutinous and seeke alteration in the state, or at leaste very burdensome to the commonwealthe, and often fall to pilferinge and thevinge and other lewdnes, whereby all the prisons of the lande are daily pestered and stuffed full of them, where either they pitifully pyne awaye, or els at lengthe are miserably hanged, even xx[ti] at a clappe oute of some one jayle."

The other writer to which reference is made is Sir William Petty, the author of the famous "Political Arithmetick, or a Discourse Concerning the Extent and Value of Lands, People, Buildings," etc., published in 1691. Sir William recapitulates the fears of many concerning the welfare of England, as follows:

"That the Rents of Lands are generally fall'n; that therefore, and for many other Reafons, the whole Kingdom grows every Day poorer and poorer; that formerly it abounded with Gold, but now there is a great fcarcity both of Gold and Silver; that there is no Trade nor Employment for the People, and yet that the Land is under-peopled; that Taxes have been many and great; that *Ireland* and the Plantations in *America* and other Additions to the Crown, are a Burthen to *England;* that *Scotland* is of no Advantage; that Trade in general doth lamentably decay; that the *Hollanders* are at our heels, in the race of Naval Power; the *French* grow too faft upon both, and appear fo rich and potent, that it is but their Clemency that they do not devour their Neighbors; and finally, that the Church and State of *England*, are in the fame Danger with the Trade of *England;* with many other difmal Suggeftions, which I had rather ftifle than repeat."

Sir William undertook to disabuse the public mind of the fears which he recites. These statements are interesting and valuable at the beginning of this report upon industrial depressions, for they teach us to beware of imaginary conditions, to seek leading and direct causes, to study contributory causes, to eliminate remote and incidental causes, to give true value to suggested remedies, and to avoid being led to false conclusions.

Under the investigation undertaken by the Bureau the aim has been to group important facts, so far as possible in the time at its command, bearing upon modern industrial depressions. No necessity exists for studying any species of crises existing back of fifty years ago, because the regularity with which depressions and crises occur is apparent during that period, and because, too, the accompaniments of the depressions back of that did not involve the modern industrial conditions. No more important and no more vital question could have been selected for the first work of the Bureau of Labor, for the labor question, in a primary sense, stands for the contest between the two elements of production, labor and capital, relative to the share of the profits of production to be allotted to each. Any occurrence, whether of a commercial, financial, or industrial nature, resulting either in a decrease of profits to either labor or capital, or in causing serious fluctuation or inequality in the distribution of such profits, becomes in the largest sense one of the most important features of the labor question. So, while the present investigation was begun during the most serious period of the last industrial depression and closes with all the prospects of the early dawn of prosperity, the information gathered is of permanent value and importance.

The first work, then, is to classify the crises and depressions of the past fifty years for the great producing countries of the world, and to determine how far such crises have been contemporaneous, how far like causes have produced like results, to determine the nature of the present industrial depression as compared with the crises occurring during the period under consideration, and then to take up the various leading and contributory causes of the present depression and to consider such agencies as may be invoked to modify the severity or shorten the duration of future depressions. The Bureau has addressed itself to this work without the conceit of expecting to evolve any economic law relative to the cause or causes of depressions, or to lay down in any dogmatic way any positive remedial solution of such depressions.

CHAPTER I.

MODERN INDUSTRIAL DEPRESSIONS.

1837 - 1886.

A panic or a crisis is usually short, sharp, and decisive in its results. A depression is a condition which has duration of time attending it. Panics and crises may occur without a resulting industrial depression, as has been the case many times, and an industrial depression of much severity may occur without producing a financial or commercial crisis or panic, although financial conditions are always more or less disturbed during the continuance of an industrial depression. The terms crises, panics, and depressions are used under these distinctions.

As already stated, the features of regularity and contemporaneousness of crises and depressions have been apparent since the commencement of this century. Crises and panics, with more or less of industrial depression accompanying them, have occurred in various countries, but there were not such strong connecting influences and facts and associated conditions as have been observed during the past fifty years. The present investigation, then, has been directed, in a preliminary way, to those panics and depressions which have occurred within the period named, they involving nearly all of the phases and conditions which have been developed since the century opened.

The consideration of crises and depressions for one country alone would be very incomplete. The great producing nations of the world, Great Britain, France, Belgium, Germany, and the United States, have been so closely allied in industrial conditions that they really constitute a group of nations which should be considered, integrally and as a whole, in any logical study of panics and depressions. Other states and countries have been more or less involved in all the panics and depressions which have occurred in the countries named, but the great leading influences which are observable in all depressions and panics belong to one or more, or all, of the states mentioned. The grouping of facts, therefore, which constitute the body of this report will, in the main, relate to the great manufacturing countries, with only incidental mention of others.

In stating the facts as they have been found by the agents of the Bureau, many terms are used which are capable of varied application—some even are of doubtful meaning when considered metaphysically, but all such terms are used in this report in their common acceptation; as, for instance, the term "over-production" is used to indicate that condition of a locality, state, or country when more goods have been produced than are sufficient to meet the ordinary demand. Whether there is any such thing as over-production in the broadest metaphysical sense does not concern the matters in hand. "Cost of production," another expression which invites critical discussion, has been used in accordance with its simplest meaning; that is, in this report it relates simply to the cost so far as labor, material, and the other positive elements of production are concerned. "Under-consumption," which is often erroneously used as another term for over-production, only from a different point of view, means, so far as this investigation is concerned, the incapacity of a people, through crippled power, temporarily, from any cause, to consume what they would in a normal condition be able to consume. It is therefore seen, with these brief statements, that metaphysical definitions are not to be applied to the use of terms having a commonly-accepted meaning.

The best treatment of panics and depressions as they have occurred, with their nature, alleged causes, attendant conditions, and other features, seems to be by years or periods, taking up each country involved in turn.

GREAT BRITAIN.

1837.—For several years prior to the industrial depression of 1837 there had been a general overtrading with America and China on the part of English merchants, such overtrading having been facilitated by the expansion of the Bank of England issues and by a large increase in banking facilities consequent upon the formation of a large number of joint-stock banks. During these years unprecedented importations of cotton and tea were made, and large amounts of English capital had been invested in American securities. Through this division and absorption of capital there occurred a stringency in the money market, and the contraction of the issues of the Bank of England precipitated a financial panic in the latter part of the year 1836. The consequent pressure for money led to numerous failures in the American and East Indian trades, and there was a decline of 50 per cent. in the price of cotton and silk in the spring of 1837. In contrast to the decline in the value of other commodities, the price of provisions advanced so largely that when decreased employment occurred in the manufacturing districts the cost of living for wage earners had been greatly augmented. When the period of greatest depression occurred wheat steadily increased in price, as shown by the following figures of the prices of wheat per imperial quarter in each of the years from 1835 to 1839, inclusive: 1835, $9.44; 1836, $11.70; 1837, $13.40; 1838, $15.44; 1839, $16.92. The price of wheat was higher in 1839 than it had been at any ime since 1819. The industrial depression and period of commercial discredit continued through the five years succeeding 1837, prosperity having been much retarded by the poor crops of 1838 and 1839, which necessitated large exports of gold to pay for foreign grain. The industrial depression of this period does not seem to have affected savings banks unfavorably, either as to the number of depositors or amount, of deposits the total number of depositors in savings banks under trustees in the United Kingdom and the total amount of deposits, including interest, being for the year ending November 20, 1830, 427,830 depositors, and $70,161,292.80 the total amount of deposits. For the year ending November 20, 1837, the total number of depositors was 636,066, and the total amount of deposits, including interest, $96,195,272. There was a decrease in the number of depositors for amounts exceeding $1,000, but such had been the case for more than a decade prior to 1837, and the decrease in that year was smaller than usual. November 20, 1838, the total number of depositors had risen to 703,529, and the total amount of deposits, including interest, to $107,261,184, and the increase in both number of depositors and amount of deposits steadily continued in about the same ratio as that between 1830 and 1838 until the end of the year 1846.

The industrial depression, by many writers, was attributed, first, to competition or the attempts among manufacturers to undersell each other, by which they reduced wages to a low average; second, to the state of the currency and banking system, which afforded at one time undue facilities to overtrading, and, again, caused fatal revulsions in trade, conditions which aided in the reduction of wages below their natural level; third, to the corn laws, as keeping up the price of bread by the exclusion of foreign corn, thus giving a monopoly to land-owners and forcing the foreign capitalist to resort to manufacture instead of agriculture, on account of the corn laws preventing an exchange of produce, and enabling foreign manufacturers, from the cheapness of food abroad and its dearness in Great Britain, to undersell the British manufacturer, results leading to the transfer of cotton manufacture to America and the continent of Europe; fourth, to the faulty methods of manufacture by which large quantities of materials were stolen to such an extent that the sales of goods made from stolen raw material were made at such low rates as to seriously interfere with prices; fifth (and this many writers deemed the principal cause), to the superabundance of weavers, ascribed to the influx of Irish and others into the textile trades, to the necessity the weavers were under to increase their incomes by putting their children at an early age to the looms, to the effects of combinations in keeping weavers from entering into other trades, and to the application of machinery to many fabrics formerly wrought by hand.

The industrial depression beginning in 1837 was the result of financial and commercial causes, the industries becoming involved subsequently, and it lasted until the year 1843.

1847.—During 1843 the great dullness in trade which had existed from the time of the panic of 1837 commenced to disappear. A spirit of renewed enterprise was engendered, and notably manifested itself in the direction of railroad construction. December 31, 1842, there were 1,857 miles of railroad in operation in the United Kingdom. The following table shows the additional miles opened in the United Kingdom in each of the years from January 1, 1843, to December 31, 1852; also the amount of paid-up capital invested in railroads from December 31, 1843, to December 31, 1852, with the gross amounts of the paid-up capital on the respective dates:

RAILROADS OPENED IN THE UNITED KINGDOM, 1843–52.

Year ending December 31—	Miles opened.	Year ending December 31—	Miles opened.
1843	95	1848	1,182
1844	196	1849	904
1845	293	1850	590
1846	595	1851	269
1847	909	1852	246

Paid-up capital invested December 31, 1843	$314,547,801 00
Capital invested from January 1, 1844, to December 31, 1852	953,447,424 00
Total amount invested December 31, 1852	1,267,995,225 60

For several years prior to 1847 the error of 1835 and 1836, of excessive importations of cotton, was repeated. In 1846 there was a failure of the potato crop and a partial failure of the wheat crop, necessitating an importation of grain to the value of $150,000,000. In 1847 the results of a bad harvest were much more serious than would be the case at the present time. The price of wheat rapidly increased from August, 1846, to May, 1847, but when the apprehension of a failure in the crop of the following year was dispelled the price of wheat declined. The average price of wheat per quarter (8 bushels, or 560 pounds) in each year from 1846 to 1850, inclusive, was as follows:

AVERAGE PRICE OF WHEAT PER QUARTER IN GREAT BRITAIN, 1846–50.

Year.	Price per quarter.
1846	$13 14
1847	16 66
1848	12 12
1849	10 08
1850	9 72

The contraction in the Bank of England circulation from September, 1846, to September, 1847, amounted to $14,050,000, the circulation on the respective dates being: September, 1846, $107,325,000; September, 1847, $93,275,000. January 14, 1847, the Bank of England raised its rate of discount from 3 to $3\frac{1}{2}$ per cent., and January 21 to 4 per cent., and finally to 5 per cent. April 8 following. The stringency of the money market continued to increase, until October 25 of that year the rate of discount was raised to 8 per cent.; many failures occurred in September, October, and November, and the year 1847 closed in great gloom. The commercial crisis of 1847 and the suspension of the bank act at once ended the period of industrial prosperity. The abundant crops on the Continent in the year 1847 and the partial repeal of the corn laws in 1846 stimulated the importation of wheat in large quantities, and the prices of this cereal continued to decline for several years, the average price per quarter in 1851 being the lowest since 1780. All other forms of enterprise except that of railroad building were almost at a standstill from 1846 to 1849. As the year 1849 advanced there was a revival of the foreign trade, and this, coupled with the low rate of discount of the Bank of England, which November 22, 1849, dropped to $2\frac{1}{2}$ per cent., together with the depreciated price of many raw materials and the low cost of food, developed great activity in every department of trade. The discoveries of gold in California in 1849, and afterwards in Australia resulted in a demand for shipping and for manufactured goods, and a consequent general rise in prices and wages took place in the years 1851 to 1853. The exports from the United Kingdom doubled in value in five years, and manufacturers and wage earners enjoyed the prosperity resulting from the favorable influences of the gold discoveries, free trade, and rapid transportation. Owing, however, to the excessive and reckless shipments of commodities to the sparsely settled gold regions, many of which shipments did not pay the cost of carriage, a large number of failures took place in the United States, in Australia, and in England in 1854, which, with the declaration of war against Russia, created a stringency in the money market, and an increase in the rates of the Bank of England discounts, the rate June 2, 1853, being $2\frac{1}{2}$ per cent. and June 11, 1854, $5\frac{1}{2}$ per cent. Trade continued to be prosperous, however, until 1857, the anticipations of a general financial panic not being realized in 1854. The depression of 1847 was much more unfavorable to savings banks, both in regard to the number of depositors and amounts of deposits, than was the case during the depression of 1837. The following table shows the total number of depositors and the total amount of deposits, including interest, in the savings banks under trustees in the United Kingdom on the 20th of November of each year from 1846 to 1856, inclusive:

DEPOSITORS AND DEPOSITS IN SAVINGS BANKS UNDER TRUSTEES IN THE UNITED KINGDOM, 1846-56.

Year ending November 20—	Number of depositors.	Amount of deposits with interest.
1846	1,108,546	$161,734,281 60
1847	1,096,086	154,409,918 40
1848	1,037,422	144,565,300 80
1849	1,087,909	147,073,396 80
1850	1,113,585	149,799,945 60
1851	1,161,696	150,823,656 00
1852	1,209,934	164,268,048 00
1853	1,260,377	171,593,928 00
1854	1,278,439	172,491,019 20
1855	1,305,397	175,218,704 00
1856	1,342,232	177,112,070 40

It will be seen from the foregoing table that the decrease in the total number of depositors and total amounts of deposits in savings banks under trustees in 1847 and 1848 was as follows:

DECREASE IN DEPOSITS IN SAVINGS BANKS UNDER TRUSTEES IN THE UNITED KINGDOM.

Year.	Depositors decreased.	Amount of deposits decreased.
1847	12,460	$7,324,363 20
1848	38,664	9,844,616 60

1857.—The favorable influences which inaugurated the return to prosperity in 1849 were not destined to continue for a protracted period. The cheap rates for money which ruled from 1849, together with the general prosperity of the country, led to great speculation and expansion of credit. The cost of food also increased in anticipation of war with France, and wheat, the price of which in 1851 averaged $9.26 per imperial quarter, averaged $12.78 per imperial quarter in 1853, and under the influence of the Crimean war the price was $17.28 in 1854 and $17.94 in 1855, the average, $17.94, in 1855 being the highest price since 1818. The rates of the Bank of England discounts were violently affected during the period of the war. September 13, 1855, the rate was 3½ per cent., and October 18 following the minimum rate had reached 6½ per cent., the average rate for 1855 being 4¼ per cent., and for 1856 5¾ per cent., and for 1857 6¾ per cent. The importations of cereals suddenly increased from $84,042,000 in 1855 to $110,589,225.60 in 1856, and the exports of gold and silver and specie to pay for food imports increased from $119,288,625.60 in 1856 to $161,121,446.40 in 1857. When specie is exported the rate of discount increases, credit contracts, and distrust spreads. The Bank of England rate of discount steadily advanced from 5½ per cent. July 16 to 10 per cent. November 9, 1857, and this financial crisis abruptly ended the period of industrial prosperity. There had been a very gradual lowering of wages from 1854 to 1857, but in sympathy with the decline in the price of food, and the adverse financial condition of the country, there was a fall of about 25 per cent. in wages during 1858. Notwithstanding the fact that almost every industry in the United Kingdom was severely affected by the depression which followed the financial panic of 1857, railroad construction was not materially curtailed, the comparatively low prices of labor and materials which ruled from 1853 to 1864 being a great incentive to continued construction. The following table shows the miles of railroad opened in the United Kingdom in each year from January 1, 1853, to December 31, 1864, inclusive, also the amount of paid-up capital invested in railroads during this period, and the gross amounts of paid-up capital on the respective dates:

RAILROADS OPENED IN THE UNITED KINGDOM, 1853-63.

Year ending December 31—	Miles opened.	Year ending December 31—	Miles opened.
1853	350	1859	460
1854	368	1860	431
1855	282	1861	432
1856	375	1862	636
1857	329	1863	771
1858	503		

Paid-up capital invested January 1, 1853 .... $1,297,995,225 66
Capital invested from January 1, 1853, to December 31, 1863 .... 671,240,624 00

Total amount invested December 31, 1863 .... 1,969,235,849 60

In most branches of trade the period from January, 1853, to July, 1857, inclusive, was a fairly prosperous one, the industrial depression being most severely felt during the latter part of 1857 and throughout 1858. In some branches of industry and in the iron-manufacturing trades there were local and short, spasmodic ameliorations even during the latter period; but the years 1859 and 1860 were decidedly prosperous ones in almost every branch of industry.

1866.—The period from January, 1861, to May, 1866, was fraught with many changes, the trade of Great Britain as a whole, however, being quite satisfactory, even though the leading industry, cotton manufacturing, was completely prostrated and the persons employed therein reduced to the direst distress. This period covered what is known as the "cotton famine," which lasted from the latter part of 1861 until 1864, and was caused by the American civil war, and it constituted one of the most distressing periods of depression and consequent suffering, so far as the cotton industry is concerned, that has ever occurred in the annals of any industry. Of course many other industries suffered through sympathy. The rapid decline in the imports of raw cotton into the United Kingdom from the United States after the blockade of the Southern ports is shown by the following figures: 1861, 819,500,528 pounds; 1862, 13,524,224 pounds; 1863, 6,394,080 pounds. In the latter part of 1862 nearly 300,000 spinners, weavers, and other classes of operatives employed in cotton mills were thrown out of work and reduced ultimately to the severest poverty, many even to starvation.

Stimulated by low wages, comparatively light taxation, domestic peace, and general prosperity, there had been a reckless over-production in all branches of the cotton-manufacturing trades prior to the period under consideration. The condition of the British cotton trade in 1861 was similar to what it is at the present time. Manufacturers had pushed their goods into Bombay, into Calcutta, and, in fact, into every obtainable market, and after overstocking all their customers abroad had repeated the same process at home, so that by the autumn of 1861 it became necessary for many manufacturers to stop production; not, then, so much from a lack of raw material as from a lack of demand for the manufactured product. The cotton famine consequently inured to the benefit of manufacturers and saved the Manchester trade from a severe crisis. The period of greatest suffering in the cotton-manufacturing districts was during the last three months of 1862, after which time the number of persons requiring public relief rapidly diminished. The influence of the times from 1857 to 1866 on deposits is shown in the following table, which includes the total amounts of deposits, with interest, in the savings banks under trustees in the United Kingdom November 20 in each of the years named:

SAVINGS BANKS UNDER TRUSTEES IN THE UNITED KINGDOM, 1857-65.

Year ending November 20—	Number of depositors.	Amount of deposits with interest.
1857	1,336,580	$178,034,678 40
1858	1,408,584	173,827,785 60
1859	1,506,776	187,180,204 80
1860	1,585,778	198,040,166 40
1861	1,609,852	199,423,080 00
1862	1,558,189	194,703,066 23
1863	1,555,089	196,854,478 60
1864	1,492,251	188,530,545 60
1865	1,457,567	184,531,238 90

The interruption of the cotton industry itself, however, did not produce any great effect on the general prosperity of the country. The continuance of the cotton distress, the demand for money for speculative purposes, and the drain of bullion to Egypt, India, Brazil, and other countries to pay for cotton imports caused the rate of the Bank of England discounts to advance from 3 per cent. May 16, 1863, to 8 per cent. in December following, and although the rate of discount continued to fluctuate most violently throughout the year 1864, even reaching 9 per cent. in May and in September, still a general financial panic was avoided, and from 9 per cent. September 8, 1864, the rate of discount gradually fell to 3 per cent. June 16, 1865. The years from October 3, 1862, to the close of 1865 formed a period of excessive speculation in railroad and other securities, and is particularly memorable for the formation of a large number of joint-stock companies, the whole number registered in the United Kingdom for 1862 being 165; for 1863, 790; for 1864, 997, and for 1865, 1,034. In the formation of these joint-stock companies, having a total nominal capital of $3,070,195,072.40, which was about 40 per cent. in excess of the entire paid-up capital of all the railroads in the United Kingdom at the end of 1865, the country became pledged during the short period of three years and three months to the dangerous act of converting an enormous amount of floating into fixed capital. When so much surplus capital had been absorbed by the new schemes, the market for the shares became depressed under the influence of continuous sales of stocks, and this fact, coupled with the great fluctuations in the price of raw cotton and the consequent loss to manufacturers, contributed to keep the money market in an unsettled condition, especially during the last quarter of the year 1865.

The closing of the American war brought large orders from the United States for all classes of manufactured goods, and this condition was followed by an increase in the rates of wages, so that in almost every industry except the cotton trade the year 1865 was one of much activity. The year 1866, however, opened with an exceedingly unsatisfactory condition of the money market, the minimum rate of discount of the Bank of England being 8 per cent. in January of that year. Speculation and over-investment in new enterprises brought Great Britain in this year to a crisis. A series of failures commenced in February, and although there was a temporary lowering of the rate of discount to 6 per cent. March 15, still there were so many causes at work contributing to an unsatisfactory condition of credit in the early part of 1866 that the bank rate of discount advanced May 3 to 7 per cent., May 8 to 8 per cent., May 11 to 9 per cent., and May 12 to 10 per cent. The failure of Messrs. Overend, Gurney & Co. precipitated a general financial panic, and for fourteen weeks, from May 12, 1866, the minimum rate of discount of the Bank of England ruled at 10 per cent.

The outbreak of the German war disorganized trade upon the Continent, and in the United Kingdom the cattle-plague, troubles in Ireland, a deficient harvest, and a general election contributed to bring about an industrial depression which greatly impaired the purchasing capacity of a very great body of people.

Some of the causes of industrial depressions arise from failure of crops, epidemics in pastoral industry, cholera, and kindred checks to population and commercial intercourse, unproductive mining and manufacturing adventures, undue expansion and subsequent collapse of commercial credit, caution arising from reasonable anticipation of war or great political changes, periods of exhaustion which soon follow the close of actual wars, failure of banking institutions, railroad, and other corporations to meet their obligations to the money-lending public. No one of the causes enumerated would probably have been sufficient to bring about an industrial depression in 1866; but when a large number of these causes suddenly arose contemporaneously with a deficiency in the American cotton crop and a bad harvest throughout Western Europe, it is not surprising that there was precipitated a great and general financial panic, and that a most distressing industrial depression immediately followed. Prices in most trades during 1866 suffered a severe reduction, averaging about 20 per cent. Wages were generally reduced from 10 to 15 per cent., and the decline in wages continued throughout 1867, and as the cost of food had been augmented by the deficiency of the crops—the potato crop being the worst since 1845–46—much distress resulted.

In financial matters the year 1867 was one of decided retrenchment, which greatly aggravated the almost hopeless condition of the numerous joint-stock companies which had been so recklessly organized and foisted upon the general public in the prosperous times from October, 1862, to January 1, 1866.

The price of wheat averaged $11.98 per quarter in 1866, $15.46 per quarter in 1867, and $15.30 per quarter in 1868. A good wheat crop in 1868, however, and the large foreign importations of wheat, made food cheaper in 1869 than it had been for several years, the average price of wheat per quarter in 1869 being $11.56, and the cheapening of the cost of food, the low rates ruling for money during that year, and a feeling of greater confidence which followed the successful termination of the Abyssinian expedition, gave trade a more favorable turn.

During the summer of 1869 a rise of 5 per cent. in the wages of the persons employed in the iron trades took place, and this increase was followed in February, 1870, by a further advance of 10 per cent. in wages.

The iron ship-building trades, however, suffered disastrously from 1864, through intervening years, to 1870, and the cotton industry also suffered, especially in 1869, from the increasing competition and the high price of raw materials, which resulted in a diminution of profits to manufacturers and in the closing of many of the less modern mills.

There was a recovery of activity in 1870 and an expansion of trade throughout the year, during the latter part of which the decline in the price of raw cotton ameliorated the condition of that industry, and in general the year was a prosperous one in all the trades.

The sudden outbreak of the Franco-German war in July, 1870, caused a flurry in financial circles, and the Bank of England advanced its rate of discount from a minimum of 3½ per cent. July 21, to 6 per cent. August 4; but by September 29 the rate had fallen to 2½ per cent. Prices and wages in all branches of trades continued to increase to an unparalleled extent, and in February, 1873, the highest price ever paid for Scotch pig-iron was recorded at $33.12 per ton, $30.96 having been touched in August, 1872. As an example of the increase in wages during 1872 and 1873 it may be stated that a miner's wages in Scotland averaged $1.08 per day in 1871, $1.74 per day in 1872, and $2.04 per day in 1873. The average price per ton of Scotch pig-iron in each of the years from 1866 to 1872, inclusive, was as follows:

PRICE OF SCOTCH PIG-IRON, 1866-72.

Year.	Price per ton.
1866	$14 53
1867	12 84
1868	12 06
1869	12 78
1870	13 08
1871	14 14
1872	24 44

The following table shows the additional number of miles of railroad opened in the United Kingdom in each of the years from January 1, 1864, to December 31, 1872, inclusive; also the amount of paid-up capital invested in railroads during that period, and the gross amounts of paid-up capital on the respective dates:

RAILROADS OPENED IN THE UNITED KINGDOM, 1864-72.

Year ending December 31—	Miles opened.
1864	467
1865	500
1866	565
1867	393
1868	381
1869	a417
1870	a392
1871	(b)
1872	438

Amount of paid-up capital invested January 1, 1864	$1,940,235,849 60
Capital invested from January 1, 1864, to December 31, 1872	791,191,411 20
Total amount of paid-up capital invested December 31, 1872	2,731,427,260 80

a Number of miles constructed.
b The length of line open for traffic at the end of 1868 was 14,628 miles, and at the end of 1871 the length was 15,376 miles.

The total number of joint-stock companies registered in the United Kingdom from January 1, 1866, to December 31, 1872, inclusive, and the total nominal share capital, were as follows:

JOINT-STOCK COMPANIES IN THE UNITED KINGDOM, 1866-72.

Year ending December 31—	Number of companies.	Nominal share capital.
1866	762	$368,759,150 40
1867	479	151,031,913 60
1868	461	175,332,909 60
1869	475	a578,116,408 80
1870	595	183,011,395 20
1871	821	333,735,910 80
1872	1,116	638,598,696 00

a In this year (1869) a company was registered with a nominal capital of $500,000,000; but its paid-up capital appears at no time to have exceeded $1,000.

The following statement shows the violent fluctuations to which cotton yarns were subjected during the period from July, 1867, to December, 1872, numbers 32 and 50 twist being selected as standards, and the average monthly market price in Manchester, England, being given:

VARIATION IN MARKET PRICE OF COTTON YARNS IN GREAT BRITAIN, 1867-72.

Months.	Number 32 twist.						Number 50 twist.					
	1867.	1868.	1869.	1870.	1871.	1872.	1867.	1868.	1869.	1870.	1871.	1872.
	Cts.	Cts.	Cts.	Cts.	Cts.	Cts.	Cts.	Cts.	Cts.	Cts.	Cts.	Cts.
January	......	22⅛	30½	28¾	24⅛	28	......	26⅞	36	35½	28½	39
February	......	25⅞	30⅛	30⅛	22¾	29¾	......	31	36	35½	29	44
March	......	27½	28⅝	29⅞	23	29¼	......	35	35½	33⅝	28½	40¼
April	......	33	30	30⅜	23¼	29½	......	40	36	34½	29¼	40½
May	......	30½	29⅜	29	23	29	......	39	34½	34½	30	40
June	......	29	28⅝	30⅛	24⅜	29⅞	......	37	35	34¼	32	39
July	29	27½	25¼	31⅞	26⅛	28	38⅝	35	37	32¾	33¾	36¾
August	27⅛	25¾	23⅜	32⅝	25¾	26¾	35⅝	32	39	30⅝	33	34½
September	24⅞	25¼	25	30⅛	26⅛	26¼	31¼	32	37	30⅜	33⅞	33¼
October	22⅞	25⅜	24	28¼	26⅛	26¼	27⅝	31	34	29¼	34⅞	33¼
November	22⅜	26⅜	24⅜	28⅝	25⅜	26½	26⅞	31	33½	29⅞	34¼	34
December	21⅛	26⅞	24¼	29½	27	27	25⅛	30½	34½	28¾	36¼	36

The following table shows the total number of depositors and the total amounts of deposits, including interest, in the savings banks under trustees in the United Kingdom November 20 in each of the years from 1866 to 1872, inclusive:

SAVINGS BANKS UNDER TRUSTEES IN THE UNITED KINGDOM, 1866-72.

Year ending November 20—	Number of depositors.	Amount of deposits with interest.
1866	1,398,391	$173,854,901 84
1867	1,385,782	175,363,276 80
1868	1,371,844	176,967,681 60
1869	1,377,872	180,261,808 80
1870	1,384,756	182,104,777 00
1871	1,404,078	182,404,774 40
1872	1,425,147	191,067,131 48

The following table shows the number of accounts remaining open at the close of each year; also the amount, inclusive of interest, standing to the credit of all open accounts at the close of each year from 1862 to 1872, inclusive, in post-office savings banks in the United Kingdom:

POST-OFFICE SAVINGS BANKS IN THE UNITED KINGDOM, 1862-72.

Year ending December 31—	Number of depositors.	Amount of deposits with interest.
1862	178,495	$8,156,460 80
1863	310,669	16,211,904 00
1864	470,858	23,986,990 40
1865	611,364	31,326,720 00
1866	746,254	38,981,040 00
1867	854,983	46,790,059 20
1868	965,154	55,909,044 00
1869	1,085,785	64,910,203 20
1870	1,183,153	72,475,600 20
1871	1,303,492	81,720,019 20
1872	1,442,448	92,728,027 20

1873.—The three years immediately preceding 1873 were years of the greatest commercial activity. The extraordinary demands upon British manufacturers, owing to the enforced suspension of production in France and Germany during the progress of the Franco-German war, led to an enhancement in the price of labor and raw materials. It was during this period that British trade attained its greatest prosperity. The defeat of France, and the exaction from her of an enormous indemnity by Germany, resulted in the imposition of onerous taxes, which crippled the industries of the former country. A vast impulse to the financial and trade enterprise of Great Britain thus ensued. The iron ship-building industry was in a most prosperous condition, the demand for cotton and woollen manufactures constantly increased, and the augmenting demand for every description of iron resulted in general prosperity, not only in that, but also in the coal trade. Labor was very generally employed at remunerative rates; but December 1, 1872, notice was given of a reduction in wages of 10 per cent. in the coal and iron trades in South Wales, which resulted in immediately throwing out of employment some 65,000 colliers, miners, and iron workers. This strike continued for a period of eleven weeks, being kept alive by a strong organization of the trades unions, which distributed in that period a sum of $200,000. The loss of wages, however, amounted to $4,000,000.

The year 1873 opened with other premonitions of coming financial and labor troubles. The enormous demand for all classes of manufactures had carried prices and wages to an unsafe height. The Bank of England discounts, however, continued to fall during the first quarter of the year. March 25 the minimum rate was $3\frac{1}{2}$ per cent., but by June 17 following it had reached 7 per cent. It afterward rapidly declined to 3 per cent. August 21 of the same year. This condition was fed by the reaction caused by the partial recovery of Germany and France from the effects of the Franco-Prussian war, and by this reaction, or suffering under its effects, Great Britain was in a condition to receive great harm from the commercial crisis in the United States in September, 1873, which effects also reached in succession various countries of Europe, Asia, and South America. The Bank of England rate of discount rapidly advanced from a minimum rate of 4 per cent. September 25, 1873, to 9 per cent. November 1 following. This precipitated a financial panic, the immediate effect of which was to depress wages and prices in every branch of industry. A vast transference of floating to fixed capital had taken place in the extension of railroads in the United States and in all other parts of the world, and the concurrent rise of wages, price of materials, and coal had so enhanced the working expenses of all these railroads as to more than absorb the natural increase in traffic receipts. The decline in wages and the prices of commodities continued through the years 1874, 1875, 1876, and 1877.

The persons employed in the iron, coal, and iron ship-building trades were not satisfied to allow a natural fall in wages, and many disputes occurred, which resulted in a great loss of time and production. In the course of the year 1874 the wages of iron workers were reduced 35 per cent. The year 1875 was one of even greater distress and stringency than the preceding; the business failures of this year, amounting to about $250,000,000, returned not more than 10 per cent. on the average out of the liabilities. The monetary uncertainty was greatly heightened during the year 1875 by a fall in the price of silver, consequent upon its demonetization by Germany and an increased production on the Pacific coast, the product of that section being $46,000,000 in 1874 and $56,000,000 in 1875. The successions of poor harvests in the six years from 1873 to 1879 led to increasingly great distress in the agricultural sections. The very poor wheat crop of 1876 required large supplies to be purchased abroad, but the lower prices of meat and other necessaries somewhat alleviated the prevailing distress.

In 1877 the iron trade suffered, not only from the slackness in respect to the demand for manufactured materials, but from the fact that cheapened steel was steadily supplanting the former metal and aggravating the losses of those who had investments in iron plants.

The political uncertainties in Europe and Asia, such as the Russo-Turkish war and the trouble between India and Afghanistan, caused much disquiet in commercial circles throughout the whole of the year 1878. The failure of the City of Glasgow Bank was followed by many other banking failures, and a period of gloom ensued. Great losses were incurred in almost every branch of business, and in the coal and iron trade especially failures were numerous, consequent upon the general fall of prices.

In the latter part of the year 1879 trade was quickened by increased orders from the United States, which resulted in raising the price of most commodities. The embarrassed condition of the cotton industry, over which ruin had seemed to be impending, improved at the close of the year.

The depressed state of trade during 1877, 1878, and 1879 caused reductions to the extent of 20 per cent. to be made in the wages of persons employed in cotton spinning and weaving, but through improved trade in 1880 and 1881 there was an advance in this industry of 10 per cent. There was a general revival of trade in all industries during the years 1880 and 1881, but the quickening of business during these two years led to large over-production in almost every important branch of industry, and this over-production was continued through the years 1882 and 1883, and resulted in the serious and general depression of 1884.

1884.—The present prolonged depression of trade in Great Britain is largely owing to the succession of bad agricultural seasons, coupled with large over-production in nearly all the leading manufactures, and with the practical insolvency of many of the minor money-borrowing states of Europe and the American continent, which, having obtained large loans of money from England, have defaulted in the payment of both interest and principal. Great Britain is becoming increasingly dependent upon other nations for her food supplies. Almost a million acres, as is shown by the following table, formerly devoted to the growing of wheat, have gone out of cultivation since 1870. The following table shows the total wheat acreage of Great Britain in each of the years from 1870 to 1884, inclusive:

WHEAT ACREAGE OF GREAT BRITAIN, 1870-84.

The increase in the imports of the leading articles of food consumption since 1870 has been very great indeed. In payment for her food Great Britain has been reducing her holding of United States Government bonds and railroad mortgages, and a similar decrease has also taken place in her holding of Russian and other European bonds, and these foreign countries have in some instances increased their interests in British funds. The increased facilities which have arisen for procuring food supplies have not been followed in the same ratio by opportunities for selling or exchanging British manufactures. The abundant import of wheat from America, from Russia, and from India has reduced the price of this cereal to a lower point than has been reached since 1762.

The land system of Great Britain is also proving very detrimental to the agricultural interests, for the reason that land in rural districts is owned by a very small and constantly-decreasing number of persons, many of whom are so burdened that it is impossible for them to do justice to the land or improve it. The people of Great Britain appear to be becoming more and more divorced from the soil, and their knowledge of agriculture does not now compare favorably with that of the peasantry of some other nations of Europe. The class of men, formerly so numerous in Great Britain, who cultivated their own land is now almost extinct, and the agricultural laborers are entirely severed from any permanent interest in the land. The effects of the land laws are to force the people to abandon the soil, thereby greatly depressing the home trade and manufacturing interests by curtailing the demands of the rural population. In the face of the decline in the price of wheat and the evil effects of the land laws, it is probable that there will be a still further reduction in the wheat acreage in Great Britain.

The following table shows the average gazette prices of British wheat per imperial quarter (8 imperial bushels, or 560 pounds) for each of the years from 1870 to 1884, inclusive:

GAZETTE PRICES OF BRITISH WHEAT, 1870-84.

Years.	Prices.
1870	$11 26
1871	13 60
1872	13 68
1873	14 06
1874	13 36
1875	10 84
1876	11 08
1877	13 62
1878	11 14
1879	10 54
1880	10 64
1881	10 88
1882	10 82
1883	9 98
1884	8 56

The currency question, so far as it relates to bimetallism, is also an alleged element in the present depression. British enterprise and commerce with silver-using countries, it is asserted, are hampered in consequence of recent monetary changes adversely affecting the price of silver in Europe, and the consequent appreciation of gold and the depreciation in value of all commodities.

The total value of the cotton manufactures of Great Britain is, roughly speaking, $400,000,000. Of these manufactures there are exported about $300,000,000, of which about $150,000,000 go to silver-using countries. Thus it appears that one-half of all the cotton exports are sent to countries where they are not sold for money, but bartered for silver—a commodity which must afterward be sold for gold in order to become money to the vendors. Recent events make it probable that gold will continue to become dearer, and as a consequence silver must become cheaper, and Lancashire men fear they must face a declining value in that for which nearly one-half of their cotton manufactures are exchanged.

Silver has depreciated in value from two causes, one of which was the action of the Latin Monetary Union, and another the large recent production of the metal. Its value has been upheld mainly by the action of the United States, and there is so much that is artificial in its position that it is not possible to ascertain its probable future. It is partly from this uncertainty that the entire cotton industry of Great Britain suffers. The present depression in cotton manufacture in Great Britain is, however, chiefly due to over-production. The rapidly-increasing profitableness of cotton spinning and weaving in past times led to a considerable increase in the number of mills in England, and an excessive expansion of the producing capacity. Had there been a slower multiplication of cotton mills, or, in other words, a natural increase in the producing capacity, there would probably have been a decline in the price of the raw material and fewer fluctuations in the rates of wages.

The planters and cotton operators have so far largely been benefited by the excessive competition of the mill owners in extending their power of production without reference to the real wants of their markets.

For numerous reasons the cotton trade deserves, in the present industrial crisis, a very careful investigation. It affords, in all its phases, the most flagrant example of over-production, and consequently the best promise of determining the question whether over-production is or is not an evil to both capital and labor.

The facilities for manufacturing, owing to the rapid formation of joint-stock companies, are in no case more markedly illustrated than in the case of the Oldham Spinning Companies. Whereas borrowing powers in most public companies are limited and regulated by amount of paid-up capital, no limit whatever is placed by act of Parliament upon the borrowing powers of the Oldham limited concerns. They have the power to borrow as much money as they possess ability to persuade lenders to advance, and they can then proceed to mortgage the mill, machinery, stock, and even the very book debts. If it be said that this is an undoubted right, and that the open loans are upon short notice of repayment, it still must be apparent that the money can only be repaid to a limited extent, as a large portion of it is in the plant or working capital, and, in times of borrowing, cotton spinning has been developed to that point at which the percentage of profit is extremely small and the margin between the price of the raw material and the price of the manufactured yarn is so narrow as to make its production extremely hazardous to the capital invested.

The following tables show the average prices in Manchester, England, from January, 1873, to March, 1885, inclusive, of numbers 32 and 50 twist cotton yarn:

VARIATION IN MARKET PRICE OF COTTON YARNS IN GREAT BRITAIN, 1873-85.

Month.	Number 32 twist.												
	1873.	1874.	1875.	1876.	1877.	1878.	1879.	1880.	1881.	1882.	1883.	1884.	1885.
	Cents.	Cents.	Cents.	Cents.	Cents.	Cents.	Cents.	Cents.	Cents.	Cents.	Cents.	Cents.	Cents.
January	27	24	22¾	21¼	21½	18½	16	20⅞	19¾	19⅝	17⅜	17¼	17
February	27	23⅛	22¾	20¼	19¾	18	15½	23	19⅛	19	17¼	17⅛	16⅝
March	27	23⅛	23	19¼	18½	17½	15⅝	22⅝	18¼	19⅛	16⅞	17⅞	16⅞
April	26⅝	23½	23	19	18	16⅝	17	21	17¾	19⅝	16¾	17¼	......
May	26⅜	24	22⅝	17⅜	17⅛	16½	18¼	19½	17⅛	19	17¼	17⅞	......
June	26⅜	23⅛	22¼	17¼	18⅛	17⅜	18¾	19	17⅜	19¼	17	17⅝	......
July	25¾	23¼	21¾	16¼	18¾	17¾	17⅞	19	18	19⅞	16½	17⅞	......
August	25¼	22¾	21⅝	17¼	17½	18	17½	18¼	18⅝	19¾	16⅝	17	......
September	24¾	22½	21¾	17	17¼	17½	18	18¼	18⅞	19	16½	17	......
October	24¾	22¼	21¼	17½	18½	16½	18¼	18¾	18⅛	18½	16⅞	16⅜	......
November	24	22¼	21	19¼	18	16½	19¼	18¼	18½	18	17	16¾	......
December	24	22½	21⅛	19¾	18¼	15¾	20¼	19⅞	18⅞	17¼	16⅞	17	......

Month.	Number 50 twist.												
	1873.	1874.	1875.	1876.	1877.	1878.	1879.	1880.	1881.	1882.	1883.	1881.	1885.
	Cents.	Cents.	Cents.	Cents.	Cents.	Cents.	Cents.	Cents.	Cents.	Cents.	Cents.	Cents.	Cents.
January	36¼	32	29¾	29	26¼	23½	23¼	26½	25⅞	23¼	24¾	23⅝	21⅜
February	36½	31¾	30	28¼	26⅛	23¼	23	29¾	25	23⅞	25¼	23½	21⅛
March	36½	31	30¼	27¼	25	23	22⅝	29½	23¾	21½	25	23⅝	20⅞
April	36¼	31	30⅛	26¾	23¾	23	23¾	28½	23	25	25½	24	......
May	35½	31	30	25½	23	22½	25	27¼	22¼	25⅞	26	24	......
June	34½	31	29½	24	23½	23¼	25	26¼	22½	27	25¼	23⅞	......
July	34	30	29	22½	23½	24½	24½	24¾	23⅛	28¼	24¾	23¼	......
August	34	29½	29	23	23	26	24	24¼	23½	29½	24¾	22¾	......
September	34¼	29¼	20¼	22⅛	23½	24¾	21	24	23¾	28	24⅛	22⅞	......
October	34	29⅛	20	22⅝	24	23¼	21	24¼	23¾	26	23¾	21¾	......
November	33¼	29⅛	28¾	24¾	23½	22¾	24¾	24½	24¼	25½	23½	21⅞	......
December	32½	29⅛	28¾	25¼	23¼	23	20	25½	20⅞	24¾	23¼	21¼	......

The depression in the British iron trade is largely owing to the fact that the United States, Germany, Belgium, France, and Russia have of late years very largely curtailed their purchases of pig-iron from Great Britain; consequently the area of consumption to which British manufacturers can look for a market is greatly diminished, and competition has been sharpened by the fact that the countries which were previously Great Britain's best customers are at times supplying the English home market with manufactured iron, and also successfully competing with English makers for the trade of other markets. The export of rails from

Great Britain has largely decreased since 1883, and the decline is especially noticeable with South America, the only checks to the ruinous decline in exports to foreign countries being the increased demand from the colonies, especially from India and British North America. The merchant-iron trades, with the exception of the tin-plate branch, have also greatly suffered in consequence of the diminished foreign demand. The lower royalties, rents, and railroad charges make Germany and Belgium severe competitors with England in the iron trade, and the competition of Belgium is becoming especially noticeable in the large quantities of rolled-iron beams and other forms of manufactured iron which are now being imported into Great Britain.

As another example of the cause of the present depression, the iron ship-building trade may be mentioned as second only to cotton in prominence. During the prosperous period subsequent to 1879 the mercantile marine had been earning large profits, averaging from 25 to 30 per cent. interest on capital in steamers and sailing vessels, and in consequence of these not uncommonly large dividends an immense amount of capital was invested in the shipping trade. New fleets and lines of merchant steamers have been built, equipped, and placed upon the old ocean routes. This severe competition, together with the falling off of the world's trade, reduced freights to a ruinously low figure, with the result that vessels in many instances have been worked, even though they failed to pay expenses, and other vessels have been laid up at a considerable loss to their owners. The demand for shipping shares during the period from 1879 through 1883 was so great that shipping companies were organized and managed in many of the inland towns of Great Britain.

The year 1884 will be long remembered as a most disastrous one in the history of iron ship-building. At no time since this important industry came into existence has a collapse so sudden, so widespread, and so injurious in its effects been witnessed. The effects of this depression were not confined to a single district, but extended over the Clyde, Tyne, Wear, Tees, Humber, Mersey, and Thames. Many thousands of workingmen have been dismissed from lack of work, and in numerous cases the ship-building yards have been totally closed.

As has been previously stated, the depression in the woollen manufacturing industries of Great Britain is not so severe as in all other largely developed trades. The conservative manner in which the woollen trade has been developed, and the fact that manufacturers depend upon receiving positive orders before producing large quantities of any pattern, have prevented serious over-production and consequent distress. A very small increased demand in the woollen industry would probably make it at the present time the most flourishing branch of British trade.

The trades centering at Birmingham, such as the hardware and tool-making industries, and the manufacture of fowling-pieces, are probably the most depressed of any in Great Britain, and the result has been to throw out of employment a very large number of workingmen, among whom there is more suffering than is the case in any other manufacturing district. The depression in the trades named is largely owing to the severe competition of the United States in the production of tools, light hardware, and clocks, and also in the competition of Belgium in the manufactured-iron trade, and of Germany in the manufacture of iron, iron nails, etc.

The following table shows the miles of railroad opened in the United Kingdom in each of the years from January 1, 1873, to December 31, 1884, inclusive; also, the amount of paid-up capital invested in railroads during that period, and the gross amounts of paid-up capital on the respective dates:

RAILROADS OPENED IN THE UNITED KINGDOM, 1873-84.

Year ending December 31—	Miles opened.	Year ending December 31—	Miles opened.
1873	262	1879	362
1874	367	1880	237
1875	209	1881	242
1876	214	1882	282
1877	205	1883	224
1878	256	1884	183

Amount of paid-up capital invested January 1, 1873	$2,731,427,260 80
Capital invested from January 1, 1873, to December 31, 1884	1,116,801,700 80
Total amount of paid-up capital invested December 31, 1884	3,848,228,961 60

The following statement shows the number of miles of railroad in England and Wales, Scotland, and Ireland at the end of the year 1884:

MILES OF RAILROAD IN THE UNITED KINGDOM IN 1884.

Divisions.	Miles.
England and Wales	13,340
Scotland	2,999
Ireland	2,525
Total	18,864

The total number of joint-stock companies registered in the United Kingdom during the period from January 1, 1873, to December 31, 1884, inclusive, and the total nominal share capital, were as follows:

JOINT-STOCK COMPANIES IN THE UNITED KINGDOM, 1873-84.

Year ending December 31—	Number of companies.	Nominal share capital.
1873	1,234	$729,871,416 00
1874	1,241	530,592,302 40
1875	1,172	395,746,464 00
1876	1,066	231,907,608 00
1877	990	320,640,892 80
1878	886	325,731,480 00
1879	1,034	362,720,625 60
1880	1,302	808,638,345 60
1881	1,581	1,011,415,953 60
1882	1,632	1,222,772,788 80
1883	1,766	804,864,897 60
1884	1,541	664,758,854 40

The following table shows the total number of accounts remaining open and the total amounts of deposits, including interest, in the savings banks under trustees in the United Kingdom on November 20 in each of the years from 1873 to 1884, inclusive:

SAVINGS BANKS UNDER TRUSTEES IN THE UNITED KINGDOM, 1873-84.

Year ending November 20—	Number of depositors.	Amount of deposits, with interest.
1873	1,445,489	$194,524,085 04
1874	1,463,560	199,042,424 04
1875	1,479,193	203,463,917 42
1876	1,493,401	207,761,261 80
1877	1,509,817	212,345,603 00
1878	1,515,725	212,428,272 58
1879	1,506,714	210,229,466 82
1880	1,519,805	210,074,688 00
1881	1,532,486	211,861,705 52
1882	1,552,983	214,140,387 14
1883	1,566,184	215,008,124 82
1884	1,582,474	220,036,258 02

The following table shows the number of accounts remaining open at the close of each year, and the amount, inclusive of interest, standing to the credit of all open accounts at the close of each year, from 1873 to 1884, inclusive, in the post-office savings banks of the United Kingdom:

POST-OFFICE SAVINGS BANKS IN THE UNITED KINGDOM, 1873-84.

Year ending December 31—	Number of depositors.	Amount of deposits, with interest.
1873	1,556,645	$101,605,195 00
1874	1,668,733	111,155,851 20
1875	1,777,103	120,899,256 00
1876	1,702,574	129,580,440 00
1877	1,791,240	137,955,633 60
1878	1,892,756	145,975,502 40
1879	1,988,477	153,658,243 20
1880	2,184,972	161,926,257 60
1881	2,607,612	173,733,576 00
1882	2,858,976	187,387,540 80
1883	3,105,642	200,490,278 40
1884	3,333,675	214,914,110 40

This account of the industrial depressions of Great Britain has been made quite extensive because so many of the conditions which have resulted in panics and depressions there are found in other countries, and because, again, Great Britain has been and is the leading manufacturing country in the world. The results of her enterprise have produced certain conditions, however, which are found existing in the other countries involved in this investigation, which bring all these countries to an industrial state never before experienced, and which mark the present period as an epoch in industrial development. This condition will be brought out in the proper place.

FRANCE.

1837.—M. Clement Juglar, in treating of commercial and other crises, insists that the causes of depressions must be sought not in the troubles and revolutions of the time, but in the increase of speculation and of production. Referring to the period under discussion, it seems to be the opinion of the writer mentioned and of other eminent French authorities that the general liquidation necessary to a revival of commerce produces crises, and that such crises are the true test of the soundness of commercial houses, these crises being caused by, or this necessity of liquidation being founded on the fact that many have engaged in enterprises beyond their means and necessarily succumb, while others, robust enough to resist all financial storms and freed from the obstacle of imprudent speculation, recommence the course of their operations with a new vigor. A manufacturer, the writer says, whose products are in demand, cannot be wise enough to limit production to the demand, for, by the natural force of circumstances, he is compelled to extend his operations so long as the demand continues. When suddenly speculation is arrested, production which has been commenced and carried on upon a grand scale must be lessened, wages must be reduced, and laborers thrown out of employment. Confidence gave credit, and the facilities which it procured warranted operation on a large scale without exciting much solicitude as to prices; but through the difficulty of exchanges specie reserves were drawn upon, and crises consequently occurred, business transactions were arrested, suspensions began, and credit completely disappeared. This condition, however, in the period named in France, was not prolonged for many months, but then followed the period of liquidation, which lasted for two years or more, during which languor of trade, which was limited entirely to cash operations, prevented speculative production. The former continued increase of prices was followed by a rapid fall, so that every trade which depended upon credit for its principal support was partially arrested. The principal cause of these embarrassments was the exaggeration of exterior and interior commerce, resulting from the inflation of prices by speculation. It was found, under such conditions, impossible to dispose of productions at constantly-increasing cost while exchanges were embarrassed. Under such circumstances merchandise was offered for sale under rapidly-falling values. Such decline amounted in a few months to 25 or 30 per cent., thus completely effacing at once the increase of years. Credit tumbled to the ground, premiums disappeared, stocks no longer found purchasers, liquidation became necessary, and losses were suffered where fortunes had been expected.

1847.—The crisis of 1847–48 was a purely financial one, no question existing or being raised as to an excess of manufactured products. There was a scarcity of capital, and consequent difficulties of discounts and the disappearance of coin. The first cause of the evil of the year, as it appeared to the people, arose from the inclemency of the season, from which resulted a deficit in crops; and inundations, which, by destroying property, resulted in partial poverty. Had bad crops been peculiar to France their influence would not have been so great, but sufferings of a similar kind occurred in other countries and had their influence, which was strengthened by speculation in France enhanced by the foreign capital consequently attracted thither. Whatever crisis occurred at this period antedated the political events of 1848, and might be regarded as a contributory cause of such events rather than as a consequence. Other influential causes in producing the panic of this period were the exaggeration of Government expenses, the maintenance of an armed peace, and an over-investment in railroads and other great enterprises. French opinion (a) is that the crisis was first felt in England, then in Russia and Germany, France resisting its influence for a long time, the power to do this being attributed to national wealth and the nation's metallic currency. The modern system of industry had not taken such deep root in France at this time as to be materially affected.

1856-57.—Prior to this period there had been a very rapid increase in the mileage of railroads built, and railroad shares were to an exaggerated extent floated on the market. Many attributed the crisis of this period to the natural effect of war. France had found it necessary to borrow $300,000,000, and all through Europe similar loans had been negotiated to meet the needs of the situation. All this money was used in the payment of sterile expenses and to carry on unproductive labors. The industrial enterprises of France had been carried beyond proper limits, while bad crops contributed their influence. Many believed the crisis to have originated in Germany, this country having multiplied its industrial enterprises with insufficient capital, and being obliged to call foreign capital to its aid. The German financial crisis reacted on French markets by raising the rate of discount and reducing prices generally. The change of relationship between gold and silver also was alleged as a contributory cause of the panic; but in general the depression in France for the period of 1856-57 was almost wholly the result of financial difficulties, feverish speculation, war expenses, etc. Some authorities consider that the financial crisis in the United States contributed largely toward producing that of France, through the suspension of numerous banks. One of the authorities of the time, M. Baudrillart, in November, 1857, expressed himself as follows:

"In virtue of the economic solidarity which exists between nations, the crisis originating in the United States has propagated itself with a rapidity and to an extent without parallel. The whole of Europe has felt the blow. England, as a result of its vast and important relations with the United States, has suffered sooner and worse than any other country. The affairs of England with the United States amount to an annual

---

a M. Horace Say.

sum of $200,000,000, and it is well known that the United States, in purely commercial transactions, is always enormously indebted to England. Besides, the capital of the United States which has been recently withheld from European enterprises has been engaged to the extent of $400,000,000 or $450,000,000 in the railroads and banks of the United States. Consequently many important failures in London."

The same authority considers among the causes of the crisis in the United States, excess in enterprises, abuse of speculation, and the free banking system, while a prominent financial publication of the time gives as the reason of the American crisis a bear speculation audaciously organized in the principal cities of the United States against all investments, the cause of the success of this speculation having been the fault committed by railroad companies in the constitution and repartition of their capital, a great many of the railroad bonds being issued for short periods, and falling due in 1857; that American speculators, recognizing this fault, attempted to injure the credit of the companies involved, so that it would be impossible for them to meet their engagements, and that in this the speculators succeeded, and the railroad companies could neither pay their obligations nor renew them. The same authority states that while French capital was not engaged in American enterprises, the commerce of France with the United States was important, and the consumption of such a market being restrained reflected seriously upon French industry. Other authorities, contemporaneous with those just referred to, did not believe that the French crisis was the result of the one in America, but that every crisis results from a want of equilibrium between production and consumption, and that such equilibrium can be destroyed in two ways, by excess of production or by diminution of consumption, and that France was in the latter condition. These authorities took the ground that too many railroads had not been built in France, but that traffic had ceased to develop, owing to a want of commercial activity. Crippled consumption was attributed to the long agricultural crisis resulting from the bad crops of the few years previous to the period under consideration. From all sources it is safe to conclude that the crisis in France in 1856–57 was like the crises in other countries, and was the result of financial difficulties, and that the United States cannot be considered the source of the generally-prevailing monetary disturbances of the period.

1866-67.—The crisis of this period was largely agricultural in its nature, and it was variously attributed to the amount of money devoted to the maintenance of an armed peace, to the increase in taxation, to the investment of savings in unproductive enterprises, to high rates of wages, and to the low prices of grain and other agricultural products resulting from excessive production. The suspension of a great bank in London caused a temporary monetary panic and affected many establishments. M. Garnier considered that the cause of the difficulty in London was a development of financial speculations following a series of prosperous years, and the formation of many stock companies, and then the interruption of these affairs by political occurrences in Europe. The immediate apparent cause of the crisis was the failure of Overend, Gurney & Co. M. Juglar, before quoted, considers that the crisis in England of the period named was neither a monetary nor a commercial one; that the market, encumbered by the paper of many commercial enterprises, had been surprised by the war measures of Italy and Prussia, and the suspension of several large establishments. He also attributes the cause of the crisis in London to the formation of a large number of limited liability companies. M. Reybaud, of the Institute of France, and a very high authority, stated in December, 1867, that the causes of the crisis were the failures of credit, troubles of circulation, and the excessive oscillations in the price of merchandise, and the scarcity of grain. The industries of France, however, were not involved to such an extent as to justify one in designating the period of 1866–67 as one of great industrial depression. Whatever depression existed industrially was secondary to financial difficulties.

1873–78.—Excessive speculation again comes in as one of the leading causes of the crisis of 1873, resulting in an industrial depression which lasted until 1878. The payment of the French indemnity, as stated under Germany, resulted in a speculative fever in Germany, and its influences were widely felt. The best authorities considered the crisis not only a bourse panic but a general one, resulting from the exaggeration of enterprises and the fever of speculation caused by the previous great issue of paper money. The recent war troubles and the changes resulting therefrom, of course, had a direct and largely controlling influence in the financial and industrial troubles of France during the period named. The war between Austria and Prussia and that between Germany and France, resulting in an enormous increase in national armaments, must have been potent causes, and yet the situation of France was in many respects better than that of any other nation, because it was her period of self-denial and of saving. Contemporary French writers were fond, however, of attributing the crisis principally to the United States and Germany, alleging that in the United States the protective tariff had encouraged enterprises of all kinds—mines, factories, railroads, etc.—while the increase of the cost of production here had prevented protected industries from finding a market abroad. However potent the last reason may have been, with the facts of the Franco-German war and the baneful financial influences following, it is hardly correct to say that the European difficulties of this period arose in the United States—a theory, however, which has found general acceptance in all countries involved in the general crisis of 1873.

The industrial depression resulting from the financial difficulties in France and other countries continued until 1878, and was a result of financial panics rather than of purely industrial causes, the industries being involved in the matter secondarily, as in the previous periods.

1882-86.—France has experienced during this period the same difficulties that have arisen in the other nations given to mechanical production. She has sought to equip her industries to an extent which would enable her to supply her home market, and thus become independent of other nations. The fact that this period was not ushered in by any exciting financial panic has caused great inquiry as to the influences which have led to the prevailing depression. In 1884 a commission was appointed by the French Chamber of Deputies to report on the condition of industrial and agricultural laborers in France, and this commission secured much valuable evidence as to the causes of the industrial depression prevailing at the time, and which has not yet ceased. It was shown that consumption had not kept pace with industrial production under the stimulating influences of French legislation. Excessive cost of transportation, the want of protection, competition with foreign nations paying less wages to a class of laborers who can support themselves at less expense, and the excessive increase in manufacturing establishments, were alleged as the most potent causes of the depression in France, and the complicated questions of over-production and crippled consumption have troubled the French people the same as the peoples of other nations; for producers, seeing their resources diminished and their incomes decreased, have been compelled to lessen their consumption, and in the same way the laboring classes, as the result of the reduction of wages, have consumed and expended less. High taxes have an unfavorable influence on wages and industry, for, as French authorities consider, while these matters influence all classes of citizens, they more particularly affect the commercial and industrial classes. The tax burdens of France resulting from the disasters of 1870-71 have not yet passed away, in their estimation, and while French manufacturers have been seeking to supply the home demand, in which they have met with great success, the burden of taxation has placed them in a position of inferiority as compared with some of their foreign competitors. The French complain much of American competition, and say that while the United States is, as yet, one of the most important markets for Parisian products, the American manufacturers begin to compete with them in their markets of exportation and sometimes even in their own home markets. Many authorities consider that one reason of French depression is that French machinery is, in part, somewhat superannuated, and that the new industries which are created in other countries are furnished with new and perfected machinery, which places the French producers at a disadvantage. The excessive cost of railroad transportation has had a serious influence in the present depression.

M. Corbon, of the French Government, is authority for the following statement:

"There are two distinct sorts of crises, the one temporary and the other persistent and profound. The temporary crisis may be attributed to two causes: First, the excessive production of things which are not of the first necessity, and for which there is an insufficient demand.

All Europe and even America have produced an enormous quantity of these articles. Then there has been an excess of unproductive enterprises, and particularly in France. In Paris and in all the important cities an enormous expenditure in labor and capital has been incurred for embellishments which, good in themselves but not having been opportunely made, have contributed to determine the crisis."

The same senator states that foreign competition may be considered as a persistent cause of the present depressed condition of France.

M. André Lyonnais, a prominent representative of the workingmen, and recently elected a member of the Chamber of Deputies, thinks that while the depression is general, it is felt to a greater degree in France for the reason that the workmen are not well organized, and that employers are still less organized. He states that England supports a crisis better than France, because, in the first place, the workmen and the employers of England are better organized; and, in the second place, because England can avail herself of a much more extended market; that if the French produce in enormous proportions, they cannot always be their own consumers, and that France must consequently seek consumers in foreign countries. The same authority considers France suffering from inferior means of transportation.

A very wide consideration, however, of the utterances of the best authorities, and of the present condition of the French industries, discloses no other prominent causes of depression peculiar to France alone—causes that are not operating or have not operated in producing the general depression prevailing in all countries devoted to mechanical pursuits. These general causes are more fully set forth in Chapter III, relating to the general industrial situation of the countries involved in this investigation. It is the first depression of its kind that has appeared in French industrial history, and is not one of those crises which present themselves periodically, and which are caused or ushered in by financial panics.

The general and the special question, so far as France is concerned, is very well summed up by M. Dietz-Monnin, president of the Chamber of Commerce of Paris:

"A depression in business affects other nations, and it results from general causes. These are the unproductive expenses resulting from an armed peace; the excess of production by the parallel development in industry in every country; the propensity to speculate; the competition between the productions of every country on the globe, as a result of the rapidity of communication and of the facility of transportation. As regards France, the particular causes of the depression in her industries may be attributed, above all, to the bad crops, and to the phylloxera; to the considerable taxes resulting from the war; to the reconstitution of our means of defense; to the excessive extension of public works of all kinds; to numerous enterprises commenced, and not yet finished; to the financial crisis, the effects of which are still felt, principally in the industries of luxury; to the maintenance of certain taxes imposed provisionally after the war, and which have not yet been removed, owing to the constant increase in public expenses."

The course of production in steel, pig-iron, and other iron since 1874 is shown in the following tables:

PRODUCTION AND AVERAGE MARKET PRICE OF PIG-IRON IN FRANCE, 1874–83.

[NOTE.—In this table 1,000 kilograms (2,205 pounds) are considered a ton.]

Years.	Tons of pig-iron.		Average market price.	
	Raw pig-iron.	Pig-iron "moulded in first fusion."	Pig-iron.	Muck-bar iron.
1874	1,328,000	88,000	$22 80	$39 00
1875	1,373,000	75,000	20 60	39 00
1876	1,337,000	98,000	18 60	35 80
1877	1,402,000	105,000	17 80	34 60
1878	1,429,000	92,000	16 00	32 64
1879	1,326,000	74,000	15 60	35 40
1880	1,631,000	94,000	17 00	37 60
1881	1,798,000	88,000	17 00	35 80
1882	1,939,000	100,000	17 00	37 00
1883	1,987,000	82,000	15 40	30 80

PRODUCTION AND AVERAGE MARKET PRICE OF MERCHANT IRON IN FRANCE, 1874–83.

[NOTE.—In this table 1,000 kilograms (2,205 pounds) are considered a ton.]

Years.	Tons produced.				Average market price.	
	Rails.	Sheet-iron.	Other.	Total.	Sheet-iron.	Other.
1874	161,000	116,000	581,000	858,000	$76 00	$56 40
1875	119,000	124,000	627,000	870,000	69 40	51 20
1876	82,000	128,000	627,000	837,000	65 40	46 00
1877	60,000	129,000	695,000	884,000	61 80	43 20
1878	52,000	132,000	659,000	843,000	58 60	40 60
1879	40,000	137,000	680,000	857,000	60 80	40 80
1880	42,000	155,000	769,000	966,000	65 40	42 80
1881	28,000	168,000	830,000	1,026,000	67 00	41 60
1882	27,000	163,000	883,000	1,073,000	65 40	42 80
1883	19,000	151,000	809,000	979,000	63 80	40 40

PRODUCTION AND AVERAGE MARKET PRICE OF STEEL IN FRANCE, 1874–83.

[NOTE.—In this table 1,000 kilograms (2,205 pounds) are considered a ton.]

Years.	Average market price per ton of Bessemer and Martin steel.	Tons produced.			
		Bessemer and Martin steel.		Other steel.	Total.
		Rails.	Other.		
1874	$58 20	154,000	28,000	27,000	209,000
1875	51 80	178,000	45,000	33,000	256,000
1876	48 00	181,000	30,000	31,000	242,000
1877	47 20	184,000	56,000	29,000	269,000
1878	43 40	231,000	52,000	30,000	313,000
1879	43 20	254,000	53,000	26,000	333,000
1880	43 60	280,000	80,000	29,000	389,000
1881	41 80	303,000	91,000	28,000	422,000
1882	39 80	336,000	97,000	25,000	458,000
1883	37 40	391,000	108,000	23,000	522,000

The following table shows the production of coal, iron, and steel in France for each year since 1829. There are slight discrepancies between the amounts given for the years since 1873 and those given on the preceding page, but these are not sufficient to invalidate its general usefulness. It may be here stated, once for all, that errors or discrepancies found in tables taken from published documents should not be charged to this Bureau.

YEARLY PRODUCTION OF COAL, IRON, AND STEEL IN FRANCE, 1829–83.

[NOTE.—In this table 1,000 kilograms (2,205 pounds) are considered a ton.]

Years.	Tons of coal consumed.	Tons produced.			
		Coal.	Pig-iron.	Merchant iron.	Steel.
1829	2,289,000	1,741,000	217,000	153,000	
1830	2,493,000	1,862,000	266,000	148,000	
1831	2,301,000	1,760,000	224,000	141,000	5,000
1832	2,520,000	1,962,000	225,000	143,000	5,000
1833	2,736,000	2,057,000	236,000	152,000	6,000
1834	3,214,000	2,489,000	260,000	177,000	6,000
1835	3,288,000	2,506,000	284,000	209,000	6,000
1836	3,814,000	2,841,000	308,000	210,000	5,000
1837	4,091,000	2,980,000	331,000	224,000	6,000
1838	4,304,000	3,113,000	347,000	234,000	7,000
1839	4,180,000	2,994,000	350,000	231,000	7,000
1840	4,256,000	3,003,000	347,000	237,000	8,000
1841	4,979,000	3,410,000	377,000	263,000	8,000
1842	5,203,000	3,592,000	389,000	284,000	8,000
1843	5,293,000	3,692,000	422,000	309,000	10,000
1844	5,486,000	3,782,000	427,000	315,000	16,000
1845	6,343,000	4,202,000	478,000	342,000	12,000
1846	6,608,000	4,469,000	522,000	360,000	13,000
1847	7,648,000	5,153,000	591,000	376,000	12,000
1848	6,095,000	4,060,000	472,000	270,000	7,000
1849	6,405,000	4,049,000	414,000	243,000	9,000
1850	7,225,000	4,433,000	405,000	246,000	11,000
1851	7,376,000	4,465,000	415,000	254,000	14,000
1852	7,058,000	4,903,000	522,000	301,000	18,000
1853	9,422,000	5,937,000	660,000	450,000	22,000
1854	10,856,000	6,827,000	771,000	511,000	24,000
1855	12,293,000	7,453,000	849,000	557,000	22,000
1856	12,896,000	7,925,000	923,000	568,000	19,000
1857	13,149,000	7,991,000	992,000	559,000	25,000
1858	12,893,000	7,352,000	871,000	530,000	23,000
1859	13,262,000	7,641,000	864,000	533,000	23,000
1860	14,270,000	8,369,000	898,000	532,000	30,000
1861	15,402,000	9,395,000	966,000	631,000	38,000
1862	16,274,000	10,317,000	1,090,000	734,000	47,000
1863	16,513,000	10,707,000	1,156,000	770,000	37,000
1864	17,491,000	11,201,000	1,212,000	792,000	41,000
1865	18,522,000	11,652,000	1,203,000	769,000	40,000
1866	20,057,000	12,234,000	1,260,000	819,000	38,000
1867	20,160,000	12,533,000	1,229,000	776,000	46,000
1868	20,011,000	13,330,000	1,235,000	813,000	80,000
1869	21,432,000	13,509,000	1,380,000	903,000	110,000
1870	18,830,000	13,179,000	1,178,000	830,000	94,000
1871	18,860,000	13,240,000	859,000	667,000	86,000
1872	23,233,000	16,100,000	1,217,000	883,000	141,000
1873	24,702,000	17,479,000	1,381,000	760,000	150,000
1874	23,417,000	16,907,000	1,415,000	712,000	208,000
1875	24,657,000	16,956,000	1,448,000	745,000	256,000
1876	24,472,000	17,011,000	1,435,000	837,000	241,000
1877	24,144,000	16,804,000	1,506,000	884,000	269,000
1878	24,555,000	16,960,000	1,521,000	849,000	313,000
1879	25,332,000	17,110,000	1,400,000	857,000	333,000
1880	28,846,000	18,804,000	1,725,000	965,000	389,000
1881	29,444,000	19,765,000	1,886,000	1,026,000	422,000
1882	31,025,000	20,604,000	2,039,000	1,073,000	458,000
1883	32,439,000	21,334,000	2,069,000	979,000	522,000

MILES OF RAILROAD IN OPERATION AND MILES BUILT EACH YEAR IN FRANCE, 1840-84.a

Year.	Miles in operation at end of year.	Increase.	Year.	Miles in operation at end of year.	Increase.	Year.	Miles in operation at end of year.	Increase.
1840	271		1855	3,459	554	1870	10,904	414
1841	357	86	1856	3,875	416	1871	b10,766	b138
1842	374	17	1857	4,663	788	1872	11,120	354
1843	517	143	1858	5,433	770	1873	11,576	456
1844	519	2	1859	5,672	139	1874	11,919	343
1845	551	32	1860	5,900	228	1875	12,339	420
1846	825	274	1861	6,320	420	1876	12,687	348
1847	1,143	318	1862	6,934	614	1877	13,112	425
1848	1,387	244	1863	7,524	590	1878	13,839	727
1849	1,782	395	1864	8,155	631	1879	14,228	389
1850	1,879	97	1865	8,477	322	1880	14,839	611
1851	2,220	341	1866	9,074	597	1881	15,787	948
1852	2,417	197	1867	9,809	735	1882	16,455	668
1853	2,538	121	1868	10,200	391	1883	16,965	510
1854	2,905	367	1869	10,590	390	1884	18,417	c1,452

a In a few instances an irreconcilable discrepancy, not large, exists between the columns of "Miles in operation", etc., and "Increase".
b Decrease caused by the cession of Alsace and Lorraine.
c Certain conventions negotiated between France and the various railroad companies, which went into effect in 1883, provided for a considerable extension of the railroad system, the Government of France guaranteeing a dividend on the additional stock issued.

DEPOSITORS AND DEPOSITS IN SAVINGS BANKS IN FRANCE, 1835-83.

Year.	Number of depositors at end of year.	Amount. Deposited during year.	Amount. Due depositors at end of year.	Year.	Number of depositors at end of year.	Amount. Deposited during year.	Amount. Due depositors at end of year.
1835	258,000	$7,720,000	$12,352,000	1860	1,215,000	$31,073,000	$72,568,000
1836	276,000	11,001,000	19,528,000	1861	1,302,000	31,652,000	77,586,000
1837	377,000	10,808,000	20,458,000	1862	1,379,000	31,652,000	81,832,000
1838	267,000	14,282,000	28,178,000	1863	1,471,000	33,775,000	86,271,000
1839	310,000	14,861,000	33,007,000	1864	1,554,000	33,775,000	89,166,000
1840	351,000	17,949,000	37,056,000	1865	1,644,000	35,989,000	95,149,000
1841	426,000	23,739,000	47,478,000	1866	1,749,000	38,021,000	101,904,000
1842	500,000	27,020,000	57,707,000	1867	1,845,000	39,951,000	110,010,000
1843	572,000	28,564,000	67,550,000	1868	1,968,000	45,355,000	121,976,000
1844	687,000	30,108,000	75,656,000	1869	2,050,000	51,917,000	132,012,000
1845	684,000	27,085,000	75,849,000	1870	2,079,000	33,968,000	121,976,000
1846	728,000	27,599,000	70,533,000	1871	2,021,000	16,019,000	103,834,000
1847	} 712,000	24,318,000	65,234,000	1872	2,020,000	30,108,000	99,395,000
1848				1873	2,079,000	34,354,000	103,255,000
1849	586,000	19,107,000	14,282,000	1874	2,170,000	37,635,000	110,589,000
1850	584,000	18,914,000	20,827,000	1875	2,365,000	51,917,000	127,380,000
1851	611,000	18,721,000	29,994,000	1876	2,625,000	53,989,000	148,417,000
1852	754,000	19,143,000	47,864,000	1877	2,868,000	60,206,000	166,550,000
1853	855,000	27,792,000	55,970,000	1878	3,173,000	79,516,000	190,083,000
1854	865,000	21,616,000	52,303,000	1879	3,507,000	86,850,000	222,915,000
1855	890,000	23,160,000	52,303,000	1880	3,841,000	90,324,000	247,040,000
1856	939,000	24,318,000	53,448,000	1881	4,064,000	86,078,000	271,358,000
1857	970,000	22,907,000	53,654,000	1882	4,321,000	143,592,000	333,785,000
1858	1,041,000	25,090,000	59,830,000	1883			
1859	1,125,000	28,178,000	65,234,000				

BELGIUM.

1837.—The periods of crises correspond quite nearly to those in England. Situated as this country is in its relations to Germany and France, when either of these latter countries is affected Belgium is quite sure to feel its influence. The crisis of 1837 was due largely to financial causes, and it was quite severe. It lasted during 1837 and the most of 1838, the industries of the state being incidentally involved. It has been impossible to obtain detailed facts of interest and value regarding the depression of this year.

1848.—The crisis of 1848 was coincident with revolutionary outbreaks throughout a large part of Europe. Its causes were chiefly financial, and, like the crisis of 1837, it was distinguished by a violent contraction of business and a cessation of speculative enterprises, due to the stringency of the money market. The results of the crisis extended into the next year, really causing a depression, which was severe, and enormous losses occurred.

1855-56.—The Crimean war—in which England, France, Turkey, and Russia were actively engaged, while Prussia, Austria, and Italy stood prepared for an emergency—affected Belgium. A crisis occurred in 1855, which was sharp and severe, and which operated more or less unfavorably upon trade and industry throughout 1855-56 and the greater part of 1857. It is noticeable that but little is heard of over-production as a factor in the crises prior to this date, or even in that of the date under consideration. England, Belgium, and France were the chief producing nations, and other European countries played but a subordinate part. Prussia, prior to 1859, was industrially an unimportant state, as compared with the three just named; so Belgium, in the crisis of 1855-56, and through 1857, suffered in a way quite unknown to her German neighbors.

1864.—The crisis of this year, commonly known as the "cotton crisis," affected the cotton and linen industries, causing a stagnation in the former, owing to the restricted supply of raw material during the latter part of the American war and an abnormal development of the linen business, since linen goods absorbed for nearly two years the ordinary market for cottons. Linen manufacturing, therefore, was immensely overdone, and this industry has in later years felt severely the results of the unhealthy stimulus of the cotton famine.

1873.—Belgium suffered from the general European disturbances, and the crisis of 1873, resulting in a depression which lasted until 1878 or 1879, characterized by all the circumstances and conditions affecting other countries, although there were short intervening periods of prosperity in some branches of trade. In the opinion of M. Georges de Laveleye, editor of the Moniteur des Intérêts Matériels, of Brussels, the chief characteristic of this long-depressed period was the accumulation of an enormous amount of money, which remained unemployed, whereby the value of the public funds was raised and the revenues of capital lowered. He accounts for the fact that this enormous accumulation of capital, or rather money, remained inert and unattracted by new enterprises, by showing that a definitive stage of industry never before reached had then come about—viz., that the industrial activity of the last half century had resulted in fully equipping the civilized countries of the world with economic tools, and that the work of the future must necessarily be repair rather than construction. With this unique and predominant feature, no basis therefore existed for exact comparison of this with the crises of 1837, 1848, and 1855–56, in each of which periods there had been over-production, an abuse of credit, and a general disproportion between engagements undertaken and resources available for prosecuting them. In former crises credit had vanished quickly, and there had been a series of commercial and financial failures, violent contraction of business, and curtailment of new enterprises and of those already in progress. Preceding crises had not been of long duration, yet quite long enough to give the overstocked market time to work off surplus stocks of paper and merchandise, and to establish an equilibrium between engagements in progress and circulating capital and credit, resulting in industrial and commercial progress. New enterprises presented themselves which found favor with the public, and the play of credit was renewed after periods of forced calm. The progress of these preceding crises was always the same, the coming storms ushered in by huge undertakings of industrial speculation, and made evident by the scarcity of credit and the disappearance of disposable capital, and these conditions continued through the period of quiet, while old undertakings were liquidated and stocks of cash reconstituted. The crisis beginning in Belgium, as in other countries, in 1873, resulting in a depression which lasted until 1878 or 1879, presented new phases, capital steadily accumulating and a marked disproportion existing between new enterprises and available resources, a feature directly the opposite of any which appeared in preceding crises.

The crises of the bourses in 1873, breaking up foreign loans generally, seized all who possessed movable capital, that is, the capitalists of England, France, Holland, and Belgium, and in other countries such banks and financial institutions as existed, not from credit, but by giving credit. Unconsciously all these lenders of capital and credit sought for the return of their loans, called them in, and blamed themselves with having given too much confidence to foreigners. It is said that certain bankers, essentially wise and versed in monetary affairs, hold it advisable periodically to "see again their money," and to satisfy this desire they do not hesitate to interrupt an enterprise full of promise, give up lucrative relations, and reap before the harvest is fully ripe. It is generally admitted that those who have acted on this policy have never had cause to regret their action, for although at times they may have missed some profit which they might have made, they have more often escaped traps which would have led to ruin. It is also true in the period from 1873 to 1878 that what some did from wisdom or prudent custom, the great majority did from fear, and the whole of lending Europe wished "to see again its money," or, if miscalculations had been made, what remained of its money. Those who held foreign paper realized on it without regard to loss; those who made profit from their funds actively employed in foreign industries or enterprises retired therefrom, and those who had foreign accounts relinquished their operations. Every foreign account of credit was reclaimed and balanced. From these conditions followed different conditions of exchange and the unimportance of commerce in international paper. The result was that the countries and houses which worked with the aid of the credit and the capital of others saw their resources curtailed. Those who could stand of themselves under the storm found themselves under the obligation of discontinuing works already commenced, to suspend hoped-for progress, to reduce production, to balance their affairs, and, in a word, to renounce all that was possible beforehand, but which became impossible without the funds furnished by others. This was done under force and compulsion, but the borrowers did not attach great importance to the conditions referred to. "The trouble will pass," the borrowers thought, and the very fact that they were able to stand, to remain in the field, they expected would cause in a short time a return of the capital they so much needed and desired. This hope, however, was not justified, for the lending countries, England, France, Holland, and other countries accustomed to speculate with their surplus capital, were determined to bring their money into their coffers again, notwithstanding the deception and devices necessary to accomplish this result. Nor were the lending forces content with bringing their money back. They were deceived by the enchantment, for the sight of their treasures fascinated them and caused them to forget that the function of money was to circulate and to produce again in circulation. Instead of making their capital productive, they preferred to keep it in their own hands, at the cost of a vast sacrifice of interest; so it went either to accumulate the reserve and deposits in the banks, or was offered at a low price for immediate and indisputable sureties. The interest on deposits became one-fourth of 1 per cent., and first-class commercial paper was discounted at three-fourths of 1 per per cent. and 1 per cent. Everything which was sure, maturing early, and always capable of being realized upon, was abundantly aided with resources resulting from the great amount of capital which had been recalled from foreign countries. The result of these conditions was, on the part of the borrowing countries, a stoppage of works, of progress, and of business, and on the part of the lending countries a plethora of disposable capital, with hardly any avenue at home for its remunerative employment. This excess of capital in the leading countries operated in lowering the cost of production and prices as well. The foreign loans called in seriously crippled the powers of consumption in some of the best markets of the exporting nations. Belgium, being, like England, a great exporting nation, in this state of affairs could not help suffering, and thus the financial difficulties resulted in a long-continued depression, involving the industries of the state, and it was not until 1879 that there came much relief, when the revival of her iron industries enabled her to break partially, if not wholly, the depression.

1882.—The partial revival in 1879, just referred to, was of short duration, but it had the effect of bringing capital of a fixed nature into activity. Belgium has been an industrial country for many years, and the products of her industry have long since passed the limit of domestic consumption. Like England, her economic prosperity has depended largely upon her export trade, and the very same causes which have operated to restrict the market and depress the trade of the former, in particular the hostile tariffs of neighboring countries, have also affected the latter. These conditions are the result of features common to all manufacturing countries, and to avoid repetition will be discussed in an appropriate chapter comprehending such features for all the countries under consideration.

The following tables exhibit the course of trade in Belgium for some of the leading industries:

PRODUCTION, VALUE, ETC., OF COAL IN BELGIUM, 1831-88.

[NOTE.—In this table 1,000 kilograms (2,205 pounds) are considered a ton.]

Years.	Average wages yearly.	Employés.		Quantity produced.		Value of product at mine.	Market price per ton.
		Number.	Tons.	Tons per employé.			
1831	$72	29,000	2,305,016	79	$4,012,400	$1 74
1832	66	28,000	2,280,833	81	3,893,000	1 71
1833	75	28,300	2,551,405	89	4,337,000	1 71
1834	81	28,598	2,436,875	85	4,192,400	1 72
1835	90	28,589	2,638,731	92	5,002,200	1 85
1836	102	28,937	3,074,461	106	7,667,400	2 49
1837	114	33,222	3,228,507	97	8,458,000	2 62
1838	120	37,108	3,260,271	88	8,562,800	2 63
1839	115	37,047	3,479,161	94	9,024,800	2 59
1840	110	39,150	3,929,963	100	9,268,600	2 36
1841	105	37,629	4,027,767	107	8,502,200	2 11
1842	103	39,902	4,111,463	104	7,607,600	1 84
1843	98	37,503	3,982,274	106	7,235,400	1 82
1844	99	38,490	4,415,240	115	7,968,800	1 79
1845	105	41,359	4,919,156	119	9,429,800	1 92
1846	107	45,488	5,037,402	111	9,484,000	1 87
1847	105	48,817	5,661,459	116	10,461,000	1 85
1848	92	44,777	4,862,694	109	8,233,800	1 69
1849	90	46,131	5,251,843	114	6,098,800	1 50
1850	93	47,949	5,820,588	121	9,291,200	1 60
1851	98	49,500	6,233,517	126	9,013,400	1 60
1852	101	51,873	6,795,254	131	10,614,000	1 56
1853	114	54,204	7,172,687	132	12,497,600	1 73
1854	133	62,194	7,947,742	128	17,171,600	2 17
1855	149	70,960	8,409,330	118	20,809,400	2 46

PRODUCTION, VALUE, ETC., OF COAL IN BELGIUM, 1831-83—Concluded.

Year.	Employés. Average wages yearly.	Number.	Quantity produced. Tons.	Tons per employé.	Value of product at mine.	Market price per ton.
1856	$143	73,585	8,212,410	112	$21,091,800	$3 57
1857	141	72,577	8,383,002	116	20,094,200	2 39
1858	143	73,850	8,925,714	121	20,675,400	2 32
1859	146	77,290	9,160,702	119	20,801,200	2 27
1860	145	78,232	9,610,895	123	21,425,400	2 23
1861	145	81,675	10,057,163	123	22,003,000	2 19
1862	138	80,302	9,935,645	124	20,897,000	2 10
1863	140	79,187	10,345,330	131	20,957,400	2 03
1864	143	79,779	11,158,336	140	22,110,800	1 98
1865	157	83,368	11,840,703	144	24,779,200	2 09
1866	173	86,721	12,774,662	147	30,206,400	2 36
1867	178	90,339	12,755,822	137	31,650,600	2 48
1868	161	89,382	12,298,589	138	26,774,200	2 18
1869	166	89,924	12,942,894	144	27,223,200	2 10
1870	176	91,993	13,697,118	149	29,727,000	2 17
1871	173	94,286	13,733,176	146	30,760,600	2 24
1872	209	98,863	15,658,948	158	41,711,800	2 66
1873	271	107,902	15,778,401	146	67,527,400	4 38
1874	237	109,631	14,669,029	134	48,182,000	3 28
1875	233	110,720	15,011,331	136	45,908,000	3 06
1876	206	108,543	14,329,578	132	38,633,800	2 71
1877	167	101,343	13,938,523	138	30,591,400	2 20
1878	168	99,632	14,899,175	150	29,564,200	1 98
1879	162	97,714	15,447,292	158	28,099,000	1 88
1880	184	102,930	16,866,698	161	33,936,000	2 01
1881	186	101,351	16,873,951	166	32,740,800	1 94
1882	185	104,701	17,590,989	170	35,179,200	2 00
1883	201	106,252	18,177,754	171	36,955,600	2 00

PRODUCTION AND VALUE OF IRON AND STEEL IN BELGIUM, 1840-1883.

[NOTE.—In this table 1,000 kilograms (2,205 pounds) are considered a ton.]

Year.	Iron ore.		Pig-iron.			Merchant iron.			Steel.		
	Tons.	Value.	Blast furnaces.	Tons.	Value.	Establishments.	Tons.	Value.	Establishments.	Tons.	Value.
1840	191,912	$283,883									
1845	304,544	704,519	56	134,563	$2,812,065	240	75,081	$4,110,588	1	82	$4,956
1850	299,272	465,664	41	144,452	2,232,789	263	89,924	3,618,540	2		
1855	852,134	1,781,297	71	294,270	6,598,677	263	171,013	8,304,627	2	47	12,159
1860	809,176	1,495,486	51	319,934	5,078,849	206	271,890	10,573,407	4	3,172	162,837
1865	1,018,231	1,897,096	56	470,707	7,145,705	209	426,225	15,459,381	4	3,061	234,852
1867	603,829										
1868	519,740										
1869	628,049										
1870	654,332	1,120,452	48	565,224	7,962,955	294	580,560	20,803,611	2	9,563	468,480
1871	607,272										
1872	749,781										
1873	503,565										
1874	527,050										
1875	365,044	660,662	42	540,473	7,869,718	286	540,513	20,402,072	3	47,200	2,725,982
1876	268,266										
1880	253,409	301,875	36	608,684	7,194,340	281	575,435	19,145,650	2	90,096	3,411,803
1882	208,867	307,111	33	726,046	8,454,982				4	329,273	8,376,972
1883	215,670	282,150	36	783,433	8,599,386				4	331,106	7,706,148

GERMANY.

1837.—Germany, meaning by Germany all that now constitutes the German Empire, could not at this time be called a great manufacturing nation. Prussia was making considerable progress, as were some of the states of Germany, but it was not until 1859 that she could feel that she was taking rank among the great manufacturing nations. Prussia and the German states, therefore, in 1837 simply suffered from the financial shock of that year which affected other countries. Extended credits, speculation in some directions, and the general financial disturbances of the Continent had their influence on German financial and commercial affairs.

1847-48.—The crisis of this period belonged to that of revolutionary outbreaks, and was entirely financial and commercial in its features, the industries of the country being but slightly involved.

1855-56.—Prussia and the other German states were involved in the financial panics of this period although not participants in the Crimean war. Germany was not of sufficient importance as a manufacturing state to be in a position to take such benefits as a neutral power as might have been the case had she been generally engaged in production, and therefore did not have the experience usual under such circumstances of passing through a period of great industrial activity to be followed by one of stagnation. The Austro-Italian war, in which Prussia participated, caused local disturbances in Germany.

In 1864 the cotton industry felt the effects due to the scarcity of raw cotton, caused by the American war, as did other nations of Europe engaged in manufacturing cotton goods. Germany also suffered a brief depression resulting from the Prusso-Austrian war, and again in 1870 and 1871 a crisis was caused by the great Franco-German contest; but while suffering from these varied brief disturbances since 1857, no long-continued general industrial depression prevailed.

1873-79.—Germany became thoroughly involved in the crisis of 1873, and the depression of her industries resulted from such crisis; but there were other causes than those belonging to other countries which aggravated the depression in Germany. Since 1870 Germany has entered the lists as an industrial competitor on foreign ground, and she has consequently sought a wider market than her own territory. She was therefore in a condition in 1873 to be greatly injured by the disturbances in monetary affairs which took place everywhere. The cost of production of the principal articles of staple goods of the market reached so high a point that the consumption was crippled.

In 1871 German unity, the poetic dream of centuries, became an accomplished fact. The people felt proud of the Empire, and also felt that they must do something worthy of their high position in the world. This purely psychological stimulus was nurtured by the possession of ample means to carry out grand ideas. Germany had become one of the strongest political communities of the world, and her people determined that she should also be one of the first-rate industrial powers. Five milliards of francs in gold had been received from France as an indemnity for losses by the war, and the German Government took the opportunity to pay off its obligations; money became plenty, even superfluously abundant; the field of industry was yielding enormous profits, and the German people argued that their great opportunity to become a nation permanently wealthy had arrived. The whole country swallowed the deceptive bait and entered vigorously into great industrial, financial, and public undertakings. Old establishments were deceived by high prices and lured by lenders of capital into enlarging the capacity of their works. One Silesian firm of iron manufacturers informed the agent of the Bureau that early in 1872 a well-known Breslau bank sent an agent begging it to negotiate a loan at 1 per cent. to enlarge its establishment. The offer was accepted, and ever since the firm has absorbed its profits in paying off the debt. Manufacturers, instead of laying by their enormous profits, applied them to enlarging their facilities for production. Almost everybody of any means, or if they had enterprise and could secure credit, were engaged in some sort of speculation, and of course thrift and economy were laid aside. It is impossible to estimate the enormous sums lost through joint-stock enterprises. The joint-stock companies, however, soon became odious in public estimation, so that designating a man as a director of a joint-stock company was considered so great an insult that it excited the strongest antagonism. In Prussia alone, in 1872, 493 new joint-stock companies were founded, with an aggregate capital of $362,082,381; while during the first six months of 1873, 194 were established, with an aggregate capital of $118,963,586. In the latter part of 1873 the crash came. Great fortunes melted away, industry was stagnated, and Germany was in a far worse condition industrially than ever before. Purely artificial and weak institutions went to the wall, while strong ones gathered up the fragments that remained. The result was that German industry was stagnated completely until 1879, when a slight revival took place, but only for a short time. She has been laboring under the heavy burden of excessive means of production, created under the influences of what the Germans now call "the unfortunate war indemnity."

It is interesting to note, however, the fact that in the great excitement of 1872–73 the increase of railroad mileage in Germany was not beyond the normal rate. The great sums of money then in the country were mostly invested in manufacturing and purely speculative enterprises instead of in the development of railroads.

1882-86.—After the brief and slight reaction of 1879, which lasted two or three years, Germany found that she had not recovered from the effects of the disasters of 1873; yet many features have attended this period which did not attend that following 1873, for the present period is one purely of industrial depression, primarily; while the preceding period had the usual inception, resulting from financial and commercial causes. The general features, however, which have accompanied the present period of industrial depression in Germany belong to other countries in almost the same degree, and need not be recited in this chapter; but the statistics of savings banks, of railroad building, and of some of the prominent industries of Germany are properly stated at this point:

SAVINGS BANKS IN PRUSSIA, 1839-81.

Year.	Number.		Deposits at end of year.
	Savings banks.	Depositors.	
1839	85	....	$4,338,826
1840	94	....	4,872,689
1841	103	....	5,490,224
1842	116	....	6,367,957
1843	129	....	7,100,820
1844	143	....	8,093,402
1845	157	....	8,946,586
1846	173	....	10,016,407
1847	197	....	11,224,532
1848	213	....	10,242,110
1849	220	201,714	11,822,976
1850	234	278,147	12,937,575
1851	243	309,029	14,703,439
1852	246	339,112	16,486,551
1853	263	375,180	18,854,251
1854	285	397,913	20,832,211
1855	323	423,542	23,054,931
1856	365	463,431	25,705,000
1857	405	515,826	29,293,744
1858	453	557,697	31,911,488
1859	462	594,986	32,330,706
1860	471	613,782	36,027,231
1861	478	676,101	40,661,609
1862	483	739,353	47,366,064
1863	494	806,528	53,448,836
1864	504	864,131	58,479,991
1865	517	919,513	63,749,209
1866	525	900,408	64,524,297
1867	542	927,931	68,655,580
1868	548	983,857	74,296,588
1869	917	1,358,641	112,231,849
1870	932	1,391,970	117,964,820
1871	945	1,551,539	137,723,884
1872	950	1,700,111	163,976,391
1873	963	1,907,954	199,064,702
1874	983	2,061,109	234,962,448
1875	1005	2,209,101	266,744,228
1876	1020	2,371,632	290,674,236
1877	1080	2,512,019	300,418,086
1878	1157	2,661,382	319,367,515
1879	1174	2,760,302	351,481,244
1880	1190	2,936,055	369,102,952
1881	1203	3,091,564	406,375,157

SAVINGS BANKS IN SAXONY, 1845-80.

Year.	Amount.		Year.	Amount.	
	New deposits.	Deposits withdrawn.		New deposits.	Deposits withdrawn.
1845	$583,449	$425,926	1871	$9,845,782	$7,472,617
1850	1,359,911	861,119	1872	13,940,009	8,927,708
1855	2,481,256	2,184,950	1873	17,161,613	10,250,330
1860	4,156,572	3,314,516	1874	20,015,200	12,275,321
1865	6,416,699	5,514,944	1875	19,167,602	14,211,962
1866	6,074,039	6,047,456	1876	19,146,827	16,460,326
1867	6,582,624	6,568,224	1877	17,778,446	17,440,614
1868	7,903,988	6,280,195	1878	18,435,558	17,725,045
1869	8,413,581	6,992,994	1879	19,875,747	18,000,314
1870	8,166,742	7,026,275	1880	20,875,443	18,746,382

CLASSES OF DEPOSITORS IN SAVINGS BANKS IN SAXONY, 1845-81.

Having in bank—	1845.		1850.		1855.		1860.		1865.	
	Number.	Per cent.	Number.	Per cent.	Number.	Per cent.	Number.	Per cent.	Number.	Per cent.
Under $15	24,679	42.77	39,781	41.97	74,953	41.71	115,802	41.51	149,589	37.94
$15 to $37	15,426	26.73	24,244	25.58	42,298	23.54	63,514	22.77	85,421	21.67
$37 to $75	10,309	17.87	18,043	19.04	32,133	17.88	45,671	16.37	65,466	16.61
$75 to $150	5,057	8.76	9,188	9.79	21,265	11.83	36,235	12.99	57,561	14.60
Over $150	2,236	3.87	3,531	3.72	9,056	5.04	17,722	6.36	36,197	9.18
Total	57,707	100.00	94,787	100.00	179,705	100.00	278,944	100.00	394,234	100.00

Having in bank—	1870.		1875.		1880.		1881.	
	Number.	Per cent.	Number.	Per cent.	Number.	Per cent.	Number.	Per cent.
Under $15	181,279	38.14	232,501	31.68	298,460	32.81	323,178	33.72
$15 to $37	99,320	20.90	145,356	19.80	161,205	17.72	170,005	17.74
$37 to $75	74,487	15.67	116,969	15.94	135,857	14.93	139,137	14.51
$75 to $150	67,087	14.12	112,776	15.37	134,729	14.81	140,795	14.69
Over $150	53,099	11.17	126,319	17.21	179,527	19.73	185,344	19.34
Total	475,272	100.00	733,951	100.00	909,787	100.00	958,549	100.00

It is curious to see the remarkable increase of the number of depositors since 1870, and to note that this increase has been proportionally far greater in that class which have deposits of more than $150. This illustrates one of the unique features of the present depression, viz., plenty of money in the banks, with low prices prevailing at the same time.

While the percentage of the whole of the lowest class of depositors has decreased from 42.77 in 1845 to 33.72 in 1881, that of the highest class has increased from 3.87 in 1845 to 19.34 in 1881.

There is in Germany at present a growing agitation in favor of the institution of postal savings banks on the same basis as in England and Belgium. The majority of savings banks in Germany are municipal institutions, managed by directors appointed by the town councils. A moderate per cent. is paid to depositors and the remaining profits above the expenses of management are applied to local improvements—the institution of water and gas works, street paving, etc. In this way many improvements have been made which might never have been accomplished if the money had come directly from the tax-payers. The opponents of the postal savings bank scheme make strong use of this argument.

The steady progress of production and of railroad-building in Germany is well illustrated by the four tables following:

PRODUCTION OF PIG-IRON IN GERMANY, 1863–82.

[NOTE.—In this table 1,000 kilograms (2,205 pounds) are considered a ton.]

Years.	Tons.	Value.	Years.	Tons.	Value.
1863	812,600	$17,009,622	1873	2,240,600	$59,170,870
1864	904,700	18,210,570	1874	1,906,200	38,847,036
1865	988,200	20,018,894	1875	2,029,400	34,789,650
1866	1,046,900	20,509,650	1876	1,846,400	27,332,158
1867	1,113,600	20,142,892	1877	1,932,700	26,503,414
1868	1,264,400	22,111,628	1878	2,147,600	27,270,516
1869	1,413,000	24,927,882	1879	2,226,600	26,789,776
1870	1,391,100	25,314,870	1880	2,729,000	38,886,820
1871	1,536,700	30,215,766	1881	2,914,000	39,020,050
1872	1,988,400	52,917,390	1882	3,380,800	46,578,504

PRODUCTION OF COAL IN GERMANY, 1848–82.

[NOTE.—In this table 1,000 kilograms (2,205 pounds) are considered a ton.]

Years.	Tons.	Value.	Years.	Tons.	Value.
1848	5,800,985	$7,017,716	1871	37,855,100	$58,206,232
1853	10,770,756	13,883,746	1872	42,324,400	77,627,032
1857	14,867,121	22,373,367	1873	46,145,200	104,308,736
1862	20,600,677	23,135,408	1874	46,647,100	101,486,770
1863	22,306,200	20,955,414	1875	47,803,100	79,580,060
1864	25,612,900	28,110,180	1876	49,550,400	71,901,560
1865	28,552,800	31,394,494	1877	48,229,900	60,168,534
1866	28,172,900	34,706,584	1878	50,510,900	57,685,250
1867	30,802,900	37,476,670	1879	53,470,700	57,341,340
1868	32,879,200	39,459,686	1880	59,118,100	67,205,250
1869	34,444,000	42,087,206	1881	61,640,500	69,109,012
1870	34,003,000	44,170,420	1882	65,378,200	72,855,570

MILES OF RAILROAD (STATE AND PRIVATE) IN OPERATION IN THE GERMAN EMPIRE AT THE CLOSE OF EACH YEAR, 1835–81.

Years.	Miles.	Years.	Miles.	Years.	Miles.
1835	3.72	1851	4,012.02	1867	$10,203.09
1836	3.72	1852	4,329.33	1868	10,617.06
1837	12.46	1853	4,656.94	1869	11,299.41
1838	87.11	1854	4,943.07	1870	12,130.50
1839	162.75	1855	5,108.06	1871	13,125.27
1840	340.32	1856	5,640.01	1872	13,963.82
1841	512.31	1857	5,893.59	1873	14,789.10
1842	664.45	1858	6,312.53	1874	15,807.02
1843	901.83	1859	6,896.75	1875	17,317.28
1844	1,184.75	1860	7,212.27	1876	18,034.56
1845	1,428.72	1861	7,471.49	1877	18,778.62
1846	2,135.15	1862	7,832.89	1878	19,429.06
1847	2,771.77	1863	8,238.18	1879	20,518.46
1848	3,196.59	1864	8,599.46	1880	20,900.88
1849	3,470.19	1865	9,105.94	1881	21,289.71
1850	3,747.46	1866	9,674.85		

MILES OF RAILROAD (STATE AND PRIVATE) IN OPERATION IN THE KINGDOM OF PRUSSIA AT THE CLOSE OF EACH YEAR, 1838–81.

Years.	Miles.	Years.	Miles.	Years.	Miles.
1838	21.51	1853	2,699.17	1868	5,969.76
1839	52.04	1854	2,829.08	1869	6,154.37
1840	105.95	1855	2,948.65	1870	6,770.02
1841	222.27	1856	3,373.79	1871	7,440.37
1842	311.37	1857	3,717.64	1872	8,019.45
1843	524.08	1858	4,672.57	1873	8,495.92
1844	658.68	1859	4,001.70	1874	9,138.55
1845	819.70	1860	4,198.33	1875	10,021.47
1846	1,292.76	1861	4,311.91	1876	10,463.91
1847	1,707.72	1862	4,529.22	1877	10,771.57
1848	1,949.34	1863	4,741.63	1878	11,275.32
1849	2,025.04	1864	4,844.24	1879	11,907.17
1850	2,265.65	1865	4,985.00	1880	12,194.84
1851	2,343.53	1866	5,429.89	1881	12,423.87
1852	2,555.20	1867	5,740.33		

The German bimetallists hold pronounced views relative to the cause of the low prices which have in general prevailed in Germany, as elsewhere, since 1873. The fact that low prices are not confined to the province of industry alone, but relate to raw material as well as the products of labor, has been seized upon by them as a proof of their theory that low prices have been caused by the appreciation of gold in consequence of the displacement of silver as a coincident monetary unit. They point to the enormous increase in the volume of business during the last twenty years, and the small relative increase in the absolute amount of gold, in terms of which this wonderful new volume of business must be measured. A fall of prices, they argue, is a consequence of these phenomena; a restoration of silver by means of a strong monetary union composed of the leading commercial countries would, in their opinion, result in an advance in prices. While those who hold different views upon the real cause of the depression concede that the increase of products has been relatively much greater than the increase of the supply of gold, they point to the coincident fact that one of the peculiar factors of the present depression, differing in this respect from all preceding, is that there has been at no time a scarcity of money; that, in fact, there has been a plethora of money, and a very slight demand for it. The rates of interest and discount have been uniformly low. If there had been a scarcity of money, resulting from a scarcity of gold, or an insufficient new supply of gold to measure the increased volume of business, the very opposite of this—that is, the rise of the rates of interest and discount—should naturally have taken place. A very important point neglected by the German bimetallists in this discussion is the vast increase of the credit system which has taken place contemporaneously with the increase in production. With this extension the importance of coin as a medium of exchange has diminished. The sum of exchanges affected by the Reichsbank in Germany in 1874 was $101,388,000; in 1884, $6,267,730,000. The annual sum of the world's exchanges affected by the credit system is more and more doing away with the necessity for the actual movement of coin.

THE UNITED STATES.

1837.—The depression of 1837 was the result of financial troubles. The expansion of credit brought the train of evils of this period. There were many circumstances which seemed to aggravate the difficulties of the time, but they were mostly of a financial nature. Speculation, unsatisfactory financial condition of the country, inflation of the currency, unnatural extension of the system of internal improvements, short crops, overtrading, extension of credits—all these contributed their influence in causing a crisis, and the crisis, aggravated, grew into an industrial depression, although wages were not materially affected and the volume of production and of general business were kept remarkably steady. The influence of the distribution of the surplus revenue did much to aggravate the depression of the period under consideration. This surplus gave foreign investors confidence in the credit of the states, and many of them borrowed money for the prosecution of improvements. Men were taken from productive and put to work in non-productive undertakings, as the result of the existence of a credit based upon the knowledge of the large surplus in the treasury of the country. The natural result of the transfer of labor from productive to non-productive enterprises was the cessation of the production of the commodities of life. Great importations necessarily followed, calling for large shipments of specie to foreign countries. These conditions existed until the crash came, and then came the aggravation resulting from the distribution of the surplus itself.

Governor Thomas, of Maryland, in his message of December 27, 1842, used the following significant language:

"Nothing has influenced more fatally the evil councils by which so many of the states have become involved than the delusive expectations—rekindled constantly as fast as they are quenched—of pecuniary largesses from the national treasury for state purposes. The distribution law (miscalled the deposit act), which beggared the general government, whilst but few of the recipients of its bounties have been enriched, caused a most unfortunate revolution in public feeling, if not in public opinion. The possession of that fund, stimulating as it did the wildest speculations, destroyed at once all those salutary restraints found in the habits of the people and the conditions and powers of their local governments. An inexhaustible fountain of wealth, it was believed, had been opened, which was to flow in perennial streams into the state treasuries. State legislators, it was thought, were no longer to be limited in their operations, or abridged in their expenditures, by the amount of revenue they might be emboldened to take directly by taxes from the pockets of the people. A new source of supply was to come through the breach made in the federal constitution. Private property was to be obtained for public purposes by a less perceptible, because more circuitous, route. High tariffs were to be levied to supply not only the demands of the national treasury, but, in conjunction with the land sales, to furnish a surplus for distribution after that deposited was exhausted. Under the influence of these and similar delusions, the large and oppressive debt of Maryland has been contracted."a

The depression resulting from the crisis of 1837 continued with more or less severity for four or five years.

1847.—After the effects of the financial disturbances of 1837 had passed away a reasonable degree of prosperity was experienced, and then came many changes in the tariff. Prices became reduced, not entirely through the influence of tariff changes, for there were coöperating causes, but certainly there was a decline in prices after the increase of duties in 1841.b In 1843 imports began to increase. The revival of trade, which came with the reaction, brought the country to a state of considerable prosperity. In 1846 came another change in the tariff, and much agitation and discussion followed. Apprehension arose, fluctuation of prices ensued, imports largely increased, and the shipment of gold to foreign countries increased accordingly. The industries of the country became affected in the way of prices and profits, although the general business of the country in volume was not seriously involved. The years 1847 and 1848 passed with sufficient depression, however, to constitute those years a period of stagnation. The Mexican war had but little if any influence upon the commercial or industrial features of this period.

1857.—The industrial depression of 1857-58 was incidental to the financial panic. Wages were not affected to any great extent, nor was the volume of business. The total commerce of the country rose to a very high point in 1857, and fell more than $100,000,000 from that point in 1858, but rose again in 1859. Speculation, extension of credit, and all the usual accompaniments of financial disturbances ushered in the period. The only extensive investigation that has been observed relative to this period was made by a committee of the Boston Board of Trade, appointed at the annual meeting in January, 1858, "to make a deliberate and thorough investigation into the causes of the recent monetary difficulties and mercantile embarrassments, with a view to the adoption of such remedies as the nature of the case will allow." This committee made its report in April, 1858. The committee, disclaiming, all political and partisan bias, considered among the causes of the disturbances the effects of the tariff of 1846, but they remarked:

"The injurious effects of this measure have, doubtless, been materially modified by peculiarly marked events; such as the famine in Ireland, demanding an extraordinary export of breadstuffs from the United States, and by the discovery of the rich and extensive gold mines of California, by which many hundred millions of gold have been rapidly added to the currency of the world."

The committee concluded that the discovery of gold in California and Australia were events to be placed among the first and most influential

---

a History of the Surplus Revenue of 1837; by Edward G. Bourne. G. P. Putnam's Sons, New York, 1885.
b Financial History of the United States; Bolles, page 445.

causes which, by their excessively stimulating character, had a tendency to produce the commercial embarrassments of the period. This committee, which was composed of gentlemen well known in mercantile and manufacturing circles, after referring to these two great causes as stated, makes some most valuable suggestions as to the general causes of the financial troubles of 1857, and these are so interesting that they are given quite at length, as follows:

"We include the production of the gold mines of Australia, because, from the intimate relations and sympathy between the commerce of England and her colonies and that of the United States the trade of Australia is as open to our ships as to theirs. Some of the effects of these discoveries, together with the nearly cotemporaneous discovery of the vast deposits of guano in the Chincha Islands, made so opportunely to meet the necessities of agriculture, were immediately shown in a sudden and unparalleled stimulus to commerce. As if by the power of magic, the style and model of the ships soon after built were almost entirely changed, the genius of the naval architect was exercised to its utmost power, and a splendid fleet of clippers, of large class, of symmetrical proportions, and of hitherto unrivaled speed, were brought into service, contributing largely to the increase of tonnage in the United States, which increase from the year 1846 to 1856 amounted to 2,309,567 tons, or nearly 92 per cent.

"Many of these ships having carried large and remunerative freights from the Atlantic cities to San Francisco, proceeded to China, Manila, and to India, for return freights to the United States or to England, and by their own competition were compelled to accept rates so low as to encourage those merchants already engaged in the India and China trade to import much more freely than before, and also to induce others to embark in that branch of business. Commerce with other ports in the Pacific was also rapidly extended, and the sudden and unprecedented increase in tonnage was only equaled by a somewhat corresponding development and extent of trade with the Pacific, the East Indies and Australia. The transfer, within a short time, of a large amount of labor from the United States to the gold mines and to other departments of industry in California, caused a rise in the price of labor. The influx of gold changed existing values of property and induced an excessive expansion of bank loans and issues, as well as of individual credit. This was followed by a spirit of speculation and of overtrading, which steadily increased, until the prices of nearly all kinds of property had reached a point too unnatural to be permanently maintained.

"This extraordinary impulse to commerce was continued and sustained by the war in the Crimea, which required a large amount of tonnage for the transport service; and although British vessels were more generally thus employed, yet a larger 'carrying trade,' from India and China to Great Britain, remained to be prosecuted by American vessels. The withdrawal by England and France of a vast amount of capital and of productive labor from the ordinary channels of commerce to carry on the war could not fail to create an unfavorable influence on the financial condition of those countries, and by our intimate relations with them, on ours also. Coincident with and immediately following the preceding marked and peculiar events, the great staple productions of this country, as well as imported merchandise, affected by some of the causes already named, bore prices which required a much larger capital to represent than formerly. This was especially true of cotton, the price of which was also enhanced by moderate crops for several consecutive years, by an over-stimulated condition of the manufacturing interests, here and in Europe, and by the employment of more spindles than was required to meet the demand of consumers.

"Another and by no means unimportant cause was the recent short crop of sugar in Louisiana, which led to unusually large importations of that article from those foreign countries to which the exports of the United States are of comparatively small value. High prices, speculation and absorption of capital followed, creating a balance of trade against this country, so far as it concerns that branch of business to be paid in specie.

"Again, the abuse of the credit system has been one of the most potent causes, not only of producing the recent sad commercial embarrassments, but of bringing them to a disastrous crisis, and of leading to a general prostration of business. Under that abuse, we include first, and as being more influential than is generally admitted, the absorption of a vast amount of actual capital in railroads, and the creation of an immense floating debt, sustained in many cases at high rates of interest, and constituting a heavy item in our foreign debt.

"No intelligent and reflecting mind can doubt that the railroads in the United States have advanced and will continue to promote the material interests of the country in a degree not easily overestimated. But it must be admitted that far too many rival lines have been constructed and that a great amount of capital and labor have thus been injudiciously appropriated. The immense foreign debt of the United States may, we think, be regarded in some degree as the abuse of credit. By foreign debt we mean not only balances due from the merchants of America to those of Europe, but also investments of foreign capital in American securities. This cannot have existed without more or less unfavorable influence on our finances.

"The cotton and woollen manufacturing corporations of this commonwealth and in some of the adjacent states, established by the enterprise of some of our most intelligent and worthy fellow-citizens, and which have done so much to develop the industry and to promote the interests of the whole community, we think should bear some share of the general charge of the abuse of credit. The system of conducting their business with entirely inadequate capital, as has been done in some instances, may have been the result of unforeseen and, to some extent, unavoidable circumstances; but we cannot doubt that it has had an injurious effect on public credit.

"These effects might have been materially modified by purchases of stock in limited quantity, proportionable to the deficiency of capital and means. Indeed, to us it seems evident that the policy of the proprietors of those cotton manufacturing establishments which have not a sufficient amount of active capital, by purchasing (as they have done) cotton early in the season, and a large portion of the stock required for the whole year, amounting in the aggregate to many millions of dollars, and on terms almost equal to cash by the time the cotton arrived at the mill, with the practice of selling their fabrics on credit of six, of eight, and even of twelve months, and this by borrowing money often at high rates of interest, had the effect to absorb a vast amount of the monied capital of this State, and it seems to us should be regarded as an abuse of credit.

"Again, such a policy placed a great amount of cash facilities at the disposal of the cotton producers in the early part of the cotton season, and thus contributed largely to their ability and to that of speculators to raise and to maintain prices far too high for the interest of the whole community. It is estimated that the cotton manufacturers of the Northern States have required, for a few years past, about one-fifth part of the average crop of cotton raised in the United States, which, if taken at the average production of the last three years, is about 600,000 bales; and, at the assumed average cost of ten cents per pound, amounts to not less than $25,000,000 annually. The purchases of so large proportion of the year's stock by the manufacturers in the United States (which have often been made to a considerable extent previous to 1st of January), have had no inconsiderable effect on the finances of the Northern States, by causing a large accumulation of cash funds in the New York City banks. These banks, for several years past, have been the collection agents between the South and the North, and especially as it relates to Massachusetts, since her banks have been prohibited from allowing interest on deposits of individuals.

"The consignment of cotton to New York merchants under advance has created a large amount of funds from that source in New York for the time being, however the ultimate balance may have been between the North and South. May not this fact, added to the effects of the policy of the manufacturers, as before described, and the known practice of the New York banks in making extensive demand loans, based on these deposits, in a measure explain the reasons for the sudden contraction of their loans just preceding the late suspension of specie payment? Having continued the reduction of loans after the cessation of specie shipments to Europe, may it not have been for the purpose of fortifying themselves against their Southern depositors, who, when confidence was shaken and a panic existed, were as likely to draw specie as were their city depositors?

"We believe it will be generally conceded that the too liberal and excessive issues of foreign 'letters of credit' is another abuse of the credit system, and that this, in connection with the causes already mentioned, did much to encourage importations of merchandise from Europe and India to an extent very far beyond all former precedent, leading to the accumulation of stocks of East India produce, and of European goods also, in violation of the great law of supply and demand and to a consequent decline in prices.

"The holding of these immense stocks long before they were required for consumption contributed largely toward creating a balance of trade against the United States to be met in specie. Especially is this true, so far as regards the trade with India, China, and Manila, since our exports to those countries are of little value as compared with our importations from them.

"Another instance of abuse of credit may be seen in the business policy pursued by many, and perhaps we may be justified in saying by a majority, of those engaged in mercantile pursuits. An inordinate desire either for rapid accumulation of wealth or for means to sustain extravagant expenditure, or, in some instances, an excessive spirit of enterprise, induced the transaction of business of too great magnitude in proportion to the actual capital and available means. This, with the practice of giving long, indiscriminate, and too widely extended credit, often placed large amounts of property in the hands of inexperienced and enterprising merchants, who possessed superficial knowledge of business, were ignorant of sound principles of finance, and were often tempted into speculations and into such investments as placed beyond their reach the very resources which ought to have been paid to their creditors to sustain their confidence. The whole community, so far as this system of credit generally prevailed, became peculiarly exposed and sensitive to the first serious disturbing element in commerce, and consequent curtailment of credit and decline in prices of the staple commodities of the country. This, we think, was clearly illustrated in the late commercial embarrassments which existed between the Atlantic cities and the interior of this country."

They supplemented the causes, as stated in this long abstract, with a review and criticism of banking systems, of demand loans, of faulty exchange, and of other matters which naturally grow out of a vicious credit system. The conclusions of this committee have been given at considerable length because they seem to embody, so far as research can develop, the accepted facts relating to the great crash of 1857.

The rates of wages do not seem to have been much affected during this period, although there were many stoppages and many laborers worked on short time. The volume of business preserved its status to a wonderful degree, yet the period has passed into history as one of the severest depression that has occurred in this country. The revival of business came slowly, until the war gave activity to all branches of trade.

1867.—The year 1867 can hardly be called one of financial panics or industrial depression, although "hard times" apparently prevailed. The stimulation to all industries resulting from the war, the speculative enterprises undertaken, the extension of credits, and the slackening of production necessarily caused a reaction, and a consequent stagnation of business; but the period was hardly spoken of by business men as one of any particular hardship. People for awhile began to be conservative; but the impetus engendered by the war could not be overcome, and it was not until the crash of 1873 that the effects of undue excitement in all branches of trade and business were thoroughly realized.

1873-78.—The causes alleged for the disturbances in trade and industry during this period are very numerous. The United States felt the results of German overtrading and over speculation as reflected through Great Britain, and these and other exterior influences, combined with ample causes of our own, without looking abroad, caused the financial crises of 1873. There had been a period of excessive speculation, especially in railroads and real estate; large failures following that of Jay Cooke, inflation of the currency, high protective tariff, large immigration, and the unnatural stimulus given to industry by the war, brought the monetary affairs of the country to a crisis, resulting in general distrust, fall of prices, apprehension, and all the train of evils which follow such crises. The result was an industrial depression, lasting until the latter part of 1878, and this industrial depression was far more severe than any that preceded it or that which has followed it. This depression was so great, and the disturbances resulting from it of such varied and distressing ramifications, that it stimulated the study of panics and depressions to a greater extent than any preceding period. The period was, however, like most of those that had preceded it, so far as character was concerned, being ushered in by financial disturbances, and they followed in turn by industrial depressions. The causes alleged for the crisis and depression which followed them, as remarked, were varied indeed. Two Congressional committees, one under the chairmanship of the Hon. Hendrick B. Wright, of Pennsylvania, and the other under the chairmanship of Hon. Abram S. Hewitt, of New York, were appointed, with special instructions to investigate the causes of the depression. Later on, the Senate Committee on Education and Labor, under the chairmanship of Hon. Henry W. Blair, made a wide investigation of the affairs of labor and capital, and many of the witnesses who testified before this committee undertook to give the causes of the depression existing from 1873 to 1878. The volumes constituting the testimony taken before these three committees have been carefully examined, and the causes of industrial depressions as given by the various witnesses classified. These alleged causes constitute a most interesting feature in the history of industrial depressions, and they are given in classified and alphabetical form, as follows:

CAUSES OF DEPRESSIONS AS ELICITED BY COMMITTEES OF CONGRESS.

Administrations—
   change in the policies of.
Agitators—
   undue influence of.
Business enterprises—
   stoppage of, by panic.
Capital—
   influx of foreign.
   aggressive inroads of.
   excessive conversion of circulating, into fixed.
   centralization of.
   interests of, not identical with those of labor.
   small capitalists swallowed up by larger ones.
   manipulations of the money power.
   combinations of.
   undue accumulation of.
Cigar factories—
   tenement house.
Confidence—
   want of.
Consumption—
   under.
Corporations—
   land grants to.
Corruption—
   in municipal governments.
Credits—
   expansion of.
Crises—
   commercial.

Currency—
   contraction of.
   inflation of.
   agitation of.
   fluctuations of.
   depreciation of.
   deficient volume of the.
   withdrawal of, from circulation for speculation.
   inflation of the, followed by contraction.
   destruction of the.
   faulty legislation regarding.
   conversion of the Government, into interest-bearing bonds.
   losses of creditors during the depreciation of, and of debtors during the appreciation of.
   losses of workingmen by goods rising sooner than their wages during the depreciation of, and wages falling before goods during the appreciation of.
   suspension of specie payments.
   over-issue of irredeemable paper money.
   distrust of paper money.
   disturbed value of gold and silver.
   resumption of specie payment.
   changing the measure of the value of money.
   fraud of the finance system.
   borrowing depreciated money by Government and individuals.

Currency—Continued.
    demonetization of silver.
    remonetization of silver.
    issue of greenbacks.
    refunding act.
    passage of resumption act in 1875.
    solution of the labor question turns entirely on the circulation of.

Debts—
    contraction of.
    contraction of large foreign, prior to 1874.

Demand—
    want of.

Depression—
    prolonged by want of fixed policy for return to specie payment.

Destitution—
    caused by sickness.

Education—
    lack of.
    common school, not practical.
    too exclusively intellectual.
    indifference to.
    defects of system of.
    want of technical training.
    want of industrial schools.
    economic ignorance.

Electricity—
    great utilization of the power of.

Employment—
    want of.

Extravagance—
    induced by credit.
    of dress.
    in Government expenses.

Fashions—
    in dress, devotion to.

Food—
    adulteration of.

Franchises—
    Government not receiving enough for.

Girls—
    want of training of, for future duties.

Goods—
    importation of.

Immigration—
    immigration of Chinese.

Income tax—
    repeal of the.

Indebtedness—
    national and other.

Indolence—
    instinctive and widespread.

Indulgences—
    harmful.

Intemperance.

Interest—
    too high rates of.

Invention—
    the great development of.

Knowledge and wealth—
    lack of material.

Labor—
    inefficiency of.
    thriftlessness of.
    lack of interest of the laborer in his work.
    lack of combining power of.
    too small wages to.
    unadjustment of.
    competition of.
    two many hours of.
    handicapped by legislation.
    surplus of, in cities.
    unjust taxation of.
    coolie.
    convict.
    female.
    child.
    cheap imported.
    want of economy of.
    interests of, not identical with those of capital.
    improvident and misdirected efforts of laboring classes.
    social differences between the laboring classes and capitalists.
    neglect of laboring men by the aristocracy.

Laws—
    bankrupt.
    conspiracy.
    land.
    navigation.
    patent.
    trustee.
    relative to the guardianship of children.
    want of homestead exemption.

Legislation—
    class.
    faulty.
    privileged.
    withholding franchise from women.

Machinery—
    improper use of.
    labor-saving.

Miscalculation.

Mismanagement—
    financial.

Monopoly—
    land.
    telegraph.
    news.
    railroad.
    interest.
    invention.
National debt—
    paying the, before the development of the industries of the country.
Necessaries of life—
    speculation in the.
Non-producers—
    too many.
Panic of 1873.
Passes—
    free.
Produce exchange—
    fluctuations in.
Production—
    planless.
    over.
Products—
    competition of, in market.
Profits—
    unequal division of.
Railroads—
    speculation in.
    pools of.
    war of rates of.
    excessive freight rates of.
    excessive building of.
    land grants to.
    fictitious values in.
    reformed system of.
Reaction.
Revenue—
    faulty collection of.
Sanitary conditions—
    bad.
Speculative era—
    collapse from.
Speculation.
Steam—
    great utilization of the power of.
Stimulation—
    artificial.
Stocks—
    watered.
Systems—
    monetary.
    competitive.
    educational.
    contract.
    Government contract.
    truck.
    credit.
    national banking.
    political, perversion of.
    wage.
    financial, erroneous.
    social, erroneous.
Tariff—
    protective.
    restrictive.
    agitation of.
    improperly adjusted.
    unjust discrimination of.
    changes of.
Taxation—
    indirect.
    needless.
    unequal.
    over, of land.
    over, of labor.
    under, of incomes.
    under, of capital.
    bonanza farms escaping.
    capitalists escaping.
Telegraph—
    high rates of.
Tobacco.
Values—
    expanded.
War—
    absorption of capital by.
    destruction of property during.
Work—
    piece.

The foregoing causes, in their variety, in their contradictory character, and in their extent, show how thoroughly the depression impressed itself on men's minds. They also teach the difficulty of crystallizing into any formula those features of an industrial depression which can be considered as constituting any economic law.

The industrial depression of 1873–78 was very severe in extent and duration, although, like all other depressions, there was much apprehension to be added to the reality. As an instance of this, it was currently said, and generally believed, although the source of the information was never given, that there were at least 3,000,000 mechanics out of employment in the United States, and that the state of Massachusetts alone had at least 300,000 mechanics out of employment. An investigation conducted in June, 1878, and repeated in November of the same year, through all the towns and cities of the commonwealth named, showed the number of people out of employment who desired to be employed, and who would have been employed had it not been for the depression, to be about 29,000 (a) instead of 30,000. The absurdity of the statement of 300,000 being out of employment, in consideration of the fact that there were only about 318,000 in the state ordinarily engaged at that time in mechanical industries, stood unchallenged for nearly a year; yet the depression was severe, indeed, and the remarkable industrial activity which preceded it extended its influence over into the period of depression in which the country now finds itself. Activity was restored in the latter part of 1878, and continued, with more or less prosperity accompanying it, until 1882.

1882-86.—The depression for this period came in gradually and without the usual accompainments of financial panics and crises. It is the real period under investigation, and there are so many facts, features, and conditions to be considered, that its elements properly form the subject for a separate chapter.

---

a In June the number was 28,508, and in November of the same year, 23,000.

CHAPTER II.

THE INDUSTRIAL DEPRESSION IN THE UNITED STATES, 1882-86.

The Extent of the Depression.—It is easy, from observation, to understand that an industrial depression exists, but difficult to determine to what extent it prevails. When the agents of the Bureau left their field-work a far different feeling was noticeable from that existing in the summer when they entered upon the collection of information. From their observations, and other sources from which it has been possible to form conclusions, it is undoubtedly true that out of the total number of establishments, such as factories, mines, etc., existing in the country, about 5 per cent. were absolutely idle during the year ending July 1, 1885, and that perhaps 5 per cent. more were idle a part of the time; or, for a just estimate, $7\frac{1}{2}$ per cent. of the whole number of such establishments were idle or equivalent to idle during the year named. According to the census of 1880, there were, in round numbers, 255,000 such establishments, employing upwards of 2,250,000 hands. If the percentage stated above is correct, and it is believed to be approximately so, then there were possibly 19,125 establishments idle or equivalent to idle, and 168,750 hands out of employment, so far as such establishments were concerned, during the year considered. The percentage stated, if erroneous at all, is probably too large, because the idle establishments were to a large extent small and poorly equipped. In some industries the percentage of idle establishments would be much greater than the average given, while in other industries the percentage given is much too large. Applying this percentage, however, to the whole number of people employed in all occupations in the United States, which in 1880 was 17,392,099, there might have been 1,304,407 out of employment; but this is a number evidently too large, because it applies to all occupations—those engaged in agriculture, professional and personal service, trade and transportation, mechanical and mining industries, and manufactures. The percentage should be applied only to those engaged in agriculture, trade and transportation, mechanical and mining industries, and manufactures. There were engaged in these four great branches, as shown by the census of 1880, 13,317,861 persons. Applying the percentage arrived at ($7\frac{1}{2}$ per cent.), we obtain a total of 998,839 as constituting the best estimate of the possibly unemployed in the United States during the year ending July 1, 1885 (meaning by the unemployed those who, under prosperous times, would be fully employed, and who during the time mentioned were seeking employment), that it has been possible for the Bureau to make. It is probably true that this total (in round numbers 1,000,000), as representing the unemployed at any one time in the United States, is fairly representative, even if the laborers thrown out of employment through the cessation of railroad building be included.

This estimate exhibits the extreme possibility of non-employment at the worst point of the depression, but it should be remembered that even in so-called prosperous times there are from two to two and one-half per cent. of the forces considered out of employment. Prosperity often shifts employment from one class to another.

A million of people out of employment, crippling all dependent upon them, means a loss to the consumptive power of the country of at least $1,000,000 per day, or a crippling of the trade of the country of over $300,000,000 per year. The earnings of the people involved in the classes named above would not be far from $600 each per annum, representing total earnings of $7,990,716,600. Six hundred dollars has been taken as an average income for the number used, because, according to the best estimates, this constitutes a fair average—$400 as an average for those working for wages, and $1,000 for those who were working on salary. The constituent parts of the total number lead to the conclusion that $600, taking all into consideration, is a fair average. It is also probably nearly true that the potential 1,000,000 out of employment could not earn more than $1 each per day for the subsistence of themselves and families. The wage earnings, then, of the million that should be fully employed are crippled one-half, or to the extent of over $300,000,000 per annum, a sum sufficient to cause a reaction in business and a general curtailment of expenses, from which result apprehension and timidity among all classes. It is curious to observe, however, that while the severity of the depression causes a crippling to the extent of several hundred millions of dollars per year of the consuming power of the people, the volume of business transacted is not crippled comparatively to any such extent.

The popular idea of the severity of the present depression would lead one to suppose that all branches of business were severely stagnated, and that failures were the order of the day. An examination of some of the principal commercial and industrial facts available teaches the error of popular opinion in this respect. The following table exhibits the failures in the United States for twenty-nine years; that is, from 1857 to 1885, inclusive. The figures prior to 1866 are not as trustworthy as one could wish, but since then they are quite complete; at least they are sufficiently so to convey a fair idea of the relative losses by bad debts and disorganized business for the years named.

FAILURES IN THE UNITED STATES, 1857–85.[a]

Years.	Number.	Liabilities.		Years.	Number.	Liabilities.	
		Amount.	Average.			Amount.	Average.
1857	4,932	$291,750,000	$59,154+	1872	4,069	$121,056,000	$29,750+
1858	4,225	95,749,000	22,662+	1873	5,183	228,499,000	44,086+
1859	3,913	64,394,000	16,456+	1874	5,830	155,239,000	26,627+
1860	3,676	79,807,000	21,710+	1875	7,740	201,060,000	25,968+
1861	6,993	207,210,000	29,631+	1876	9,092	191,117,786	21,020+
1862	1,652	23,049,000	13,952+	1877	8,872	190,669,936	21,491+
1863	495	7,899,900	15,959+	1878	10,478	234,383,132	22,369+
1864	520	8,579,000	16,498+	1879	6,658	98,149,053	14,741+
1865	530	17,625,000	33,254+	1880	4,735	65,752,000	13,886+
1866	1,505	53,783,000	35,736+	1881	5,582	81,155,932	14,538+
1867	2,780	96,666,000	34,771+	1882	6,738	101,517,564	15,070+
1868	2,608	63,694,000	24,422+	1883	9,184	172,874,172	18,823+
1869	2,799	75,054,054	26,814+	1884	10,968	226,343,427	20,636+
1870	3,546	88,242,000	24,884+	1885	10,637	124,220,321	11,678+
1871	2,915	85,252,000	29,245+				

[a] Through the courtesy of R. G. Dun & Co., of New York. The statistics for the years 1862 to 1865, owing to the war, do not comprehend the failures for the Southern states. They are incomplete also for the years prior to the war, but the table contains the most trustworthy data otherwise obtainable.

By the foregoing table of failures it will be seen that during the year 1885 there were 10,637, involving $124,220,321 of liabilities, or an average liability of $11,678. While the number of failures for 1884 was but little more than the number for 1885, the total amount of liabilities was very nearly double, and the average liability for each failure $20,636. It will also be observed that the total amount of liabilities for 1885 was less than the amount of liabilities for either of the years 1857, 1861, 1873, 1874, 1875, 1876, 1877, 1878, 1883, or 1884. These certainly are very significant facts, when the great increase in the bulk of business transacted is taken into consideration, and they show conclusively that, while there has been widespread depression, the facts as to actual business disasters, so far as amount is concerned, or even average liability, for the year 1885, present an exceedingly satisfactory exhibit.

If from failures we turn to production, we shall find still more gratifying results. The two tables following show the production of Bessemer steel ingots and the production of rails, in net tons of 2,000 pounds, for the United States from 1874 to 1885, inclusive: [a]

PRODUCTION OF BESSEMER STEEL INGOTS IN THE UNITED STATES, 1874-85.

Year.	Tons of 2,000 pounds produced in—			
	Pennsylvania.	Illinois.	Other States.	Total.
1874	85,625	62,492	43,816	191,933
1875	148,374	136,356	90,787	375,517
1876	258,452	171,963	95,581	525,996
1877	328,599	111,299	120,689	560,587
1878	426,481	179,500	126,245	732,226
1879	514,165	250,980	163,827	928,972
1880	643,894	304,614	254,665	1,203,173
1881	844,501	375,763	318,893	1,539,157
1882	933,631	397,436	365,383	1,696,450
1883	1,014,396	273,325	336,906	1,654,627
1884	1,041,484	339,068	170,043	1,510,595
1885	1,109,034	366,659	226,064	1,701,757

[a] The Commercial and Financial Chronicle, February 13, 1886, page 200.

PRODUCTION OF STEEL AND IRON RAILS IN THE UNITED STATES, 1874-85.

Year.	Bessemer steel.	Open-hearth steel.	Total steel.	Iron rails, all kinds.	Total iron and steel.
	Tons of 2,000 pounds.				
1874	144,044	....	144,944	584,469	729,413
1875	290,863	....	290,863	501,649	792,512
1876	412,461	....	412,461	467,168	879,629
1877	432,169	....	432,169	352,540	704,709
1878	550,398	9,307	559,705	322,890	882,685
1879	683,964	9,149	693,113	420,160	1,113,273
1880	954,460	13,615	968,075	193,762	1,461,837
1881	1,330,302	25,217	1,355,519	488,581	1,844,100
1882	1,438,155	22,765	1,460,920	227,874	1,688,794
1883	1,286,554	9,186	1,295,740	64,054	1,360,694
1884	1,116,621	2,670	1,119,291	25,560	1,144,851
1885	1,074,607	1,400	1,076,007	14,692	1,090,699

By the first of the foregoing tables it will be seen that the product of Bessemer steel ingots for 1885 was larger than for any preceding year, the increase over 1884 alone being 161,162 tons. The table showing the production of rails exhibits a decrease of the total production, but this is owing to the cessation of railroad enterprises. It also shows the increasing use to which steel is put, because, by examining these two tables, we see that there is an increase in the production of steel ingots and a decrease in the production of steel rails.

The statistics of railroad building are interesting in this connection. We give the following table of the number of miles of railroad constructed and in operation in the United States each year from 1830 to 1885, inclusive:

MILES OF RAILROAD IN OPERATION AND MILES BUILT EACH YEAR IN THE UNITED STATES, 1830-85.a

Year.	Miles in operation.	Increase.	Year.	Miles in operation.	Increase.
1830	23	....	1858	26,968	2,465
1831	95	72	1859	28,789	1,821
1832	229	134	1860	30,635	1,846
1833	380	151	1861	31,286	651
1834	633	253	1862	32,120	834
1835	1,098	465	1863	33,170	1,050
1836	1,273	175	1864	33,908	738
1837	1,497	224	1865	35,085	1,177
1838	1,913	416	1866	36,801	1,716
1839	2,302	389	1867	39,250	2,449
1840	2,818	516	1868	42,229	2,979
1841	3,535	717	1869	46,844	4,615
1842	4,026	491	1870	52,914	6,070
1843	4,185	159	1871	60,293	7,379
1844	4,377	192	1872	66,171	5,878
1845	4,633	256	1873	70,268	4,097
1846	4,930	297	1874	72,385	2,117
1847	5,598	668	1875	74,096	1,711
1848	5,996	398	1876	76,808	2,712
1849	7,365	1,369	1877	79,088	2,280
1850	9,021	1,656	1878	81,717	2,629
1851	10,982	1,961	1879	86,463	4,746
1852	12,908	1,926	1880	93,349	6,876
1853	15,360	2,452	1881	103,145	9,796
1854	16,720	1,360	1882	114,713	11,568
1855	18,374	1,654	1883	121,454	6,741
1856	22,016	3,642	1884	125,379	3,825
1857	24,503	2,487	1885	....	2,866

a The statistics of railroad-building as given in this table are from Poor's Manual, and are approximately correct. The compiler of that manual has found considerable difficulty in harmonising statements from year to year, but has on the whole been fairly successful.

It will be noticed by the foregoing table that just previous to the financial panics of 1857, 1873, and 1882 there was an immense increase in the mileage of railroads constructed in the United States, and that, in the years following, there was a very notable decrease in the number of miles built annually.

The total production of pig-iron since 1870 and its distribution in each year between furnaces using anthracite coal, bituminous coal, and charcoal as fuel, is shown in the following table: *a*

YEARLY PRODUCTION OF PIG-IRON, ACCORDING TO FUEL USED IN THE UNITED STATES, 1870–85.

Year.	Tons of 2,000 pounds.			
	Anthracite.	Charcoal.	Bituminous.	Total.
1870	930,000	365,000	570,000	1,865,000
1871	956,608	385,000	570,000	1,911,608
1872	1,369,812	500,587	984,159	2,854,558
1873	1,312,754	577,620	977,904	2,868,278
1874	1,202,144	576,557	910,712	2,689,413
1875	908,046	410,990	947,545	2,266,581
1876	794,578	308,649	990,009	2,093,236
1877	934,797	317,843	1,061,945	2,314,585
1878	1,092,870	293,399	1,191,092	2,577,361
1879	1,273,024	358,873	1,438,978	3,070,875
1880	1,807,651	537,558	1,950,205	4,295,414
1881	1,734,462	638,838	2,268,264	4,641,564
1882	2,042,138	697,906	2,438,078	5,178,122
1883	1,885,596	571,726	2,689,650	5,146,972
1884	1,580,453	458,418	2,544,742	4,580,613
1885	1,454,390	399,844	2,675,635	4,529,869

It is interesting to mark the change in prices of pig-iron for a series of years, and this is shown in the next table of prices of No. 1 anthracite foundery pig-iron in Philadelphia, since 1870: *a*

AVERAGE MONTHLY PRICES FOR PIG-IRON (NO. 1 ANTHRACITE, AT PHILADELPHIA), 1870–85.

Year.	Price per ton of 2,240 pounds.				
	Opening.	Highest.	Lowest.	Closing.	Average.
1870	$36½	$36½ Jan.	$31½ Dec.	$31½	$33½
1871	30⅝	37½ Nov.	30⅝ Jan.	37½	35⅝
1872	37	53¾ Sept.	37 Jan.	47⅝	48⅞
1873	46½	48¾ Mar.	32½ Dec.	32⅝	42¾
1874	32	32 Jan.	24 Dec.	24	30½
1875	25¾	27 Mar.	23¼ Dec.	23¼	25¼
1876	23¼	23½ Jan.	21½ Dec.	21½	22½
1877	20¾	20¾ Jan.	18 Aug.	18	18⅞
1878	18¼	18¼ Jan.	16½ Nov.	17	17⅝
1879	17½	30¼ Dec.	17½ Jan.	30¼	21⅝
1880	40	41 Feb.	23 June.	25	28½
1881	25	26 Mar.	24 June.	26	25¼
1882	26	26¼ Oct.	23½ Apr.	25¾	25¾
1883	25	25 Jan.	21 June.	21	22⅜
1884	20½	20¼ Jan.	18½ Dec.	18½	19⅝
1885	18	18½ Oct.	17½ June.	18¼	18

a The Commercial and Financial Chronicle, January 30, 1886.

The total production of coal for the years 1882, 1883, 1884, and 1885 was as follows:

PRODUCTION OF BITUMINOUS COAL IN THE UNITED STATES, 1882-85.

States.	Tons produced in—			
	1885.	1884.	1883.	1882.
Pennsylvania	25,000,000	24,000,000	24,000,000	22,000,000
Illinois	9,791,874	10,101,000	10,508,790	9,115,650
Ohio	6,750,000	9,000,000	8,230,000	9,450,000
Iowa	3,600,000	3,903,450	3,881,300	3,127,100
West Virginia	3,250,000	3,100,000	2,805,560	2,000,000
Missouri	1,500,000	2,500,000	2,250,000	2,000,000
Maryland	2,860,000	2,765,000	2,206,170	1,294,300
Indiana	1,000,000	2,260,000	2,560,000	1,976,470
Alabama	2,225,000	2,000,000	1,400,000	800,000
Kentucky	1,600,000	1,550,000	1,650,000	1,300,000
Colorado	1,400,000	1,334,270	1,000,000	948,000
Tennessee	1,100,000	1,200,000	1,000,000	850,000
Kansas	1,283,500	1,100,000	850,000	750,000
Wyoming Territory	766,500	1,000,000	700,000	631,000
Indian Territory	481,800	400,000	175,000	150,000
Virginia	630,000	350,000	225,000	100,000
New Mexico Territory	300,000	350,000	250,000	146,400
Washington Territory	281,572	307,000	260,000	225,000
Utah Territory	136,000	250,000	250,000	250,000
California	90,000	157,000	200,000	200,000
Georgia	170,000	200,000	200,000	175,000
Arkansas	547,000	150,000	75,000	50,000
Michigan	150,000	135,000	135,000	130,000
Texas *a*	125,000	125,000	100,000	
Oregon	43,000	60,000	60,000	30,000
Montana Territory	185,000	75,000	50,000	30,000
Dakota Territory	26,000	32,000	50,000	
Idaho Territory *b*	10,000	20,000	10,000	
Total	65,308,246	68,424,720	65,081,820	57,728,920

a For year ending June 30, 1885.   *b* Estimated.

If to the above the official figures of the production of anthracite coal be added, we have the total production of coal:

PRODUCTION OF ANTHRACITE AND BITUMINOUS COAL IN THE UNITED STATES, 1882-85.

	Tons produced in—			
	1885.	1884.	1883.	1882.
Anthracite, Pennsylvania	31,623,529	30,718,293	31,793,027	29,120,196
Bituminous, as above	65,308,246	68,424,720	65,081,820	57,728,920
Total	96,931,775	99,143,013	96,874,847	86,849,116

The aggregate production of coal last year was over 2,000,000 tons less than in 1884, larger than the production in 1883, and more than 10,000,000 tons greater than the production in 1882. Iron and coal are the great directing materials which indicate the welfare or the progress of other industries.

In the examination of the boot and shoe industry of Massachusetts, the following table becomes instructive: a

PRODUCTION OF BOOTS AND SHOES IN MASSACHUSETTS, 1859-85.

Years.	Cases.	Years.	Cases.
1859	684,708	1873	1,336,553
1860	648,539	1874	1,390,428
1861	497,777	1875	1,449,180
1862	507,812	1876	1,521,295
1863	568,836	1877	1,758,025
1864	569,263	1878	1,648,724
1865	718,660	1879	1,959,577
1866	822,750	1880	2,263,890
1867	918,965	1881	2,307,731
1868	1,010,859	1882	2,413,531
1869	1,343,203	1883	2,568,033
1870	1,250,201	1884	2,487,322
1871	1,306,398	1885	2,633,075
1872	1,451,596		

It is shown by this table that the shipment of boots and shoes from Massachusetts for the year 1885 was larger than for any previous year. If we consult the volume of business done, we shall find figures which indicate that accompanying real depression there is a vast deal of apprehension.

The following table of imports and exports of merchandise since 1835 is exceedingly interesting and instructive, in showing how the volume of business, so far as commerce is concerned, is preserved: b

VALUE OF IMPORTS AND EXPORTS OF MERCHANDISE OF THE UNITED STATES, 1835-85.

Year ending—	Exports.			Imports.	Exports and imports.	Excess of exports.	Excess of imports.
	Domestic.	Foreign.	Total.				
Sept. 30—							
1835	$100,459,481	$14,756,321	$115,215,802	$136,764,295	$251,980,097		$21,548,493
1836	106,570,942	17,767,762	124,338,704	176,579,154	300,917,858		52,240,450
1837	94,280,895	17,162,232	111,443,127	130,472,803	241,915,930		19,029,676
1838	95,560,880	9,417,690	104,978,570	95,970,288	200,948,858	$9,008,282	
1839	101,625,533	10,626,140	112,251,673	156,490,056	268,748,629		44,245,283
1840	111,660,561	12,008,371	123,668,932	98,258,706	221,927,638	25,410,226	
1841	103,636,236	8,181,235	111,817,471	122,957,544	234,775,015		11,140,073
1842	91,799,242	8,078,753	99,877,995	96,075,074	195,953,069	3,802,924	
June 30—							
1843c	77,686,354	5,139,335	82,825,689	42,433,464	125,259,153	40,392,225	
1844	99,531,774	6,214,058	105,745,832	102,604,606	208,350,438	3,141,226	
1845	98,455,390	7,584,781	106,040,111	113,184,322	219,224,433		7,144,211
1846	101,718,042	7,865,206	109,583,248	117,914,065	227,497,313		8,330,817
1847	150,574,844	6,166,754	156,741,598	122,424,349	279,165,917	34,317,249	
1848	130,203,709	7,986,806	138,190,515	148,638,044	286,829,159		10,448,129
1849	131,710,081	8,641,091	140,351,172	141,206,199	281,557,371		855,027
1850	134,900,233	9,475,493	144,375,726	173,509,526	317,885,252		29,133,800
1851	178,620,138	10,295,121	188,915,259	210,771,429	399,686,688		21,856,170
1852	154,931,147	12,053,084	166,984,231	207,440,398	374,424,629		40,456,167
1853	189,869,162	13,620,120	203,489,282	263,777,265	467,266,547		60,287,983
1854	215,328,300	21,631,260	236,959,560	297,623,039	534,582,599		60,663,479

a Boston Daily Globe, January 1, 1886.
b From the report on the commerce and navigation of the United States, Bureau of Statistics, Treasury Department, Washington, December 1, 1885.
c Nine months, from September 30, 1842, to June 30, 1843.

VALUE OF IMPORTS AND EXPORTS OF MERCHANDISE, ETC.—Concluded.

Year ending—	Exports.			Imports.	Exports and imports.	Excess of exports.	Excess of imports.
	Domestic.	Foreign.	Total.				
June 30—							
1855	$192,751,135	$26,158,368	$218,909,503	$257,808,708	$476,718,211		$38,899,205
1856	266,438,051	14,781,372	281,219,423	310,432,310	591,651,733		29,212,887
1857	278,906,713	14,917,047	293,823,760	348,428,342	642,252,102		54,604,582
1858	251,351,033	20,660,241	272,011,274	263,338,654	535,349,928	$8,672,620	
1859	278,392,080	14,509,971	292,902,051	331,333,341	624,235,302		38,431,290
1860	316,242,423	17,333,634	333,576,057	353,616,119	687,192,176		20,040,062
1861	204,899,616	14,654,217	219,553,833	289,310,542	508,864,375		69,756,709
1862	179,644,024	11,026,477	190,670,501	189,356,677	380,027,178	1,313,824	
1863	186,003,912	17,060,535	203,064,447	243,335,815	447,300,262		39,371,368
1864	143,504,027	15,333,961	158,837,988	316,447,283	475,285,271		157,609,295
1865	136,940,248	20,089,055	166,029,303	238,745,580	404,774,883		72,716,277
1866	337,518,102	11,341,420	348,859,522	434,812,066	783,671,588		85,952,544
1867	279,786,809	14,719,332	294,506,141	395,761,096	690,267,237		101,254,955
1868	260,389,900	12,562,909	281,052,809	357,436,440	638,389,339		76,483,541
1869	275,166,697	10,951,000	286,117,697	417,506,379	703,624,076		131,388,582
1870	376,616,473	16,155,295	392,771,768	435,958,408	828,730,170		43,186,640
1871	428,398,008	14,421,270	442,820,178	520,223,684	963,043,862		77,403,506
1872	428,487,131	16,000,455	444,177,560	626,595,077	1,070,772,663		182,417,491
1873	505,033,439	17,446,483	522,479,922	642,136,210	1,164,616,132		119,656,288
1874	569,433,421	16,849,019	586,283,040	567,406,342	1,153,689,382	18,876,698	
1875	499,284,100	14,158,611	513,442,711	533,005,436	1,046,448,147		19,562,725
1876	525,582,247	14,802,424	540,384,671	460,741,190	1,001,125,861	79,643,481	
1877	589,670,224	12,804,996	602,475,220	451,323,126	1,053,798,346	151,152,094	
1878	680,709,268	14,156,498	694,865,766	437,051,532	1,131,917,298	257,814,234	
1879	698,340,790	12,098,651	710,439,441	445,777,775	1,156,217,216	264,661,666	
1880	823,946,353	11,092,305	835,038,658	667,954,746	1,503,503,404	167,683,912	
1881	883,925,947	18,451,399	902,377,346	642,664,628	1,545,041,974	259,712,718	
1882	733,239,732	17,302,525	750,542,257	724,639,574	1,475,181,831	25,902,683	
1883	804,223,632	19,015,770	823,239,402	723,180,914	1,547,920,316	100,058,488	
1884	724,964,852	15,548,757	740,513,609	667,697,693	1,408,211,302	72,815,916	
1885	726,682,946	15,506,809	742,189,755	577,527,329	1,319,717,084	164,662,426	

With here and there a year showing a sudden fall either in exports or imports, the general tendency, as shown by the table, is upward. It shows a great temporary increase of imports prior to periods of depression and a falling off in subsequent periods, but always with a reacting tendency; and, so far as steadiness is concerned, the commerce of the United States compares quite favorably with that of the United Kingdom and of France, as shown by the following table, by which the per cent. of increase since 1860 is seen to be for Great Britain 83, for France 80, and for the United States 105.

VALUE OF IMPORTS AND EXPORTS FOR THE UNITED KINGDOM, FRANCE, AND THE UNITED STATES, 1860-84.

Years.a	Imports and exports.		
	United Kingdom.	France.	United States.
1860	$1,825,191,648	$1,129,062,368	$687,192,176
1861	1,835,242,420	1,118,438,496	508,864,375
1862	1,907,108,888	1,158,051,808	380,027,178
1863	2,169,589,984	1,316,440,648	447,300,262
1864	2,372,768,090	1,426,585,276	475,285,271
1865	2,364,117,140	1,482,121,774	404,774,883
1866	2,599,668,619	1,581,820,626	783,671,588
1867	2,438,046,743	1,550,466,000	690,267,237
1868	2,542,670,269	1,553,211,606	639,389,339
1869	2,591,290,862	1,557,727,718	703,624,070
1870	2,663,620,718	1,353,587,776	828,730,170
1871	2,990,903,111	1,407,669,190	963,043,662
1872	3,257,063,082	1,602,201,212	1,070,772,663
1873	3,320,374,085	1,829,550,942	1,164,616,132
1874	3,249,523,447	1,776,194,636	1,153,689,382
1875	3,190,243,321	1,804,264,608	1,046,448,147
1876	3,075,293,695	1,840,783,358	1,001,125,861
1877	3,147,485,288	1,740,396,662	1,053,798,340
1878	2,989,270,011	1,791,008,262	1,131,917,298
1879	2,977,204,200	1,917,186,874	1,156,217,216
1880	3,395,084,677	2,087,786,898	1,503,593,404
1881	3,377,863,266	2,086,784,390	1,545,041,974
1882	3,502,324,287	2,087,903,694	1,475,181,831
1883	3,563,877,370	2,033,885,544	1,547,020,316
1884	3,338,351,609	(b)	1,408,211,302

a The commercial year of Great Britain and France is the calendar year. That of the United States ends June 30.
b No data.

The decrease of imports or of exports, as shown by the tables given, is observed through prices. A true way of measuring the volume of business would be through the quantities, by units, for the different articles imported and exported. This, of course, would involve much space, and it is impossible to present such data; but, bearing in mind that there has been a great decline in prices, the values given in the foregoing tables indicate that there has not been any great decline in the volume of business itself. This decline in prices of the leading domestic commodities, as given by Mr. Switzler, Chief of the Bureau of Statistics of the Treasury Department, in his annual report for 1885, is exhibited in the following table, relating to the average currency prices in New York, from 1847 to 1884, inclusive:

AVERAGE CURRENCY PRICES OF COTTON AND COTTON GOODS IN NEW YORK, 1847-84.

Years.	Middling cotton per pound.	Price per yard.				
		Standard sheetings.	Standard drillings.	Bleached sheetings.	Standard prints.	64 by 64 print cloths.
1847	$0.1121	$0.0828	$0.0834	$0.1496	$0.1183	$0.0601
1848	.0803	.0078	.0083	.1421	.1017	.0435
1849	.0755	.0091	.0090	.1421	.0933	.0458
1850	.1234	.0787	.0797	.1496	.1002	.0519
1851	.1214	.0708	.0775	.1473	.1050	.0459
1852	.0950	.0096	.0770	.1450	.1050	.0470
1853	.1102	.0792	.0793	.1450	.1050	.0015
1854	.1097	.0796	.0784	.1500	.1056	.0581
1855	.1039	.0764	.0777	.1500	.0980	.0511
1856	.1030	.0759	.0810	.1500	.0950	.0536
1857	.1351	.0890	.0904	.1500	.1010	.0598
1858	.1223	.0825	.0870	.1500	.0950	.0560
1859	.1208	.0850	.0882	.1542	.0950	.0567
1860	.1100	.0873	.0892	.1550	.0950	.0544
1861	.1301	.1000	.0058	.1533	.0971	.0533
1862	.3129	.1855	.1894	.2100	.1440	.0981
1863	.6721	.3604	.3341	.3533	.2124	.1520
1864	1.0150	.5207	.5302	.4835	.3325	.2342
1865	.8358	.3804	.3733	.4058	.2900	.4024
1866	.4320	.2431	.2514	.4590	.2115	.1413
1867	.3159	.1828	.1879	.3521	.1658	.0912
1868	.2485	.1679	.1649	.2065	.1383	.0818
1869	.2901	.1619	.1649	.2470	.1400	.0830
1870	.2398	.1458	.1498	.2250	.1241	.0714
1871	.1695	.1300	.1364	.2083	.1102	.0741
1872	.2210	.1427	.1514	.2066	.1200	.0788
1873	.2014	.1331	.1413	.1941	.1137	.0669
1874	.1795	.1142	.1175	.1804	.0975	.0557
1875	.1546	.1041	.1112	.1512	.0871	.0533
1876	.1208	.0885	.0871	.1358	.0706	.0410
1877	.1182	.0810	.0846	.1246	.0677	.0438
1878	.1122	.0780	.0765	.1100	.0609	.0344
1879	.1084	.0797	.0757	.1102	.0625	.0393
1880	.1151	.0851	.0851	.1274	.0741	.0451
1881	.1203	.0851		.1274	.0700	.0395
1882	.1150	.0845		.1295	.0650	.0376
1883	.1188	.0832		.1293	.0610	.0360
1884	.1088	.0728		.1046	.0600	.0336

The decline of prices in other matters is more accurately demonstrated in the following table relating to articles of domestic product, the export price in currency being given for the years indicated:

EXPORT PRICE IN CURRENCY OF DOMESTIC PRODUCTS, 1855-85.

Year ending June 30—	Indian corn per bushel.	Wheat per bushel.	Wheat flour per barrel.	Cotton per pound.	Leather per pound.	Mineral oils, refined, per gallon.	Bacon, hams, per pound.	Lard per pound.	Pork, salted, per pound.	Beef, salted, per pound.	Butter per pound.	Cheese per pound.	Eggs per dozen.	Starch per pound.	Sugar, refined, per pound.	Tobacco, leaf, per pound.
				Cts.	Cts.	Cts.	Cts.	Cts.	Cts.	Cts.	Cts.	Cts.	Cts.	Cts.	Cts.	Cts.
1855	$0.746	$1.853	$8.339	9.5	25.9	(b)	9.2	10.3	8.9	(b)	19.0	10.1	(b)	(b)	8.8	(b)
1856	.601	1.520	6.972	12.6	28.5	(b)	12.7	9.3	(b)	(b)	18.0	10.3	(b)	(b)	11.7	(b)
1857	.601	1.428	6.073	12.6	28.5	(b)	10.8	12.8	9.7	(b)	18.9	10.0	(b)	(b)	11.7	(b)
1858	.684	1.015	5.503	11.7	24.2	(b)	9.3	11.5	8.0	(b)	17.0	9.0	(b)	(b)	11.2	(b)
1859	.709	.949	5.943	11.8	24.2	(b)	10.5	11.5	8.1	(b)	16.4	9.1	(b)	(b)	9.5	(b)
1860	.726	.984	5.035	10.9	23.9	(b)	8.9	11.3	5.0	4.2	15.0	10.1	(b)	(b)	9.1	(b)
1861	.648	1.231	5.700	11.1	20.5	(b)	9.7	10.0	5.0	(b)	15.2	10.3	(b)	(b)	8.9	(b)
1862	.558	1.142	5.640	23.3	21.9	20.4	7.7	8.4	4.8	6.3	15.6	8.0	(b)	(b)	10.0	(b)
1863	.657	1.207	6.461	58.4	26.8	17.9	8.5	10.2	5.5	6.0	19.1	10.0	(b)	(b)	11.2	(b)
1864	.820	1.330	7.103	82.4	35.2	52.5	11.0	11.6	8.4	8.5	20.3	11.6	(b)	9.1	14.4	(b)
1865	1.310	1.950	10.414	76.4	40.2	74.2	22.9	20.5	10.8	9.0	33.8	22.0	(b)	0.8	20.1	(b)
1866	.850	1.410	6.427	42.7	29.5	54.2	16.7	19.0	15.9	14.7	33.3	16.6	31.1	9.6	10.4	15.4
1867	1.000	1.276	9.848	30.1	34.0	35.9	12.9	14.6	13.2	12.2	24.1	15.1	35.8	8.5	10.6	10.6
1868	1.180	1.910	10.059	19.2	24.3	29.4	12.6	14.0	11.4	11.9	28.1	13.7	29.9	8.4	14.2	11.1
1869	.970	1.300	7.731	25.0	(b)	35.6	15.4	17.8	14.1	9.9	28.4	16.1	(b)	8.6	13.5	11.8
1870	.925	1.289	6.112	23.5	28.5	30.5	15.7	16.6	13.2	7.3	29.3	15.5	39.6	8.2	12.6	11.3
1871	.750	1.316	6.594	14.9	25.3	23.7	11.4	13.2	11.0	8.7	21.5	13.8	28.5	6.6	13.2	9.2
1872	.606	1.473	7.141	19.3	23.7	24.9	6.0	10.1	7.9	7.0	19.4	11.7	20.4	5.0	12.6	10.3
1873	.617	1.312	7.565	18.5	25.3	23.5	8.8	9.2	7.8	7.7	21.1	13.0	26.5	5.3	11.6	10.0

a Including Sea Island.   b No data.

THE EXTENT OF THE DEPRESSION.

EXPORT PRICE IN CURRENCY OF DOMESTIC PRODUCTS, 1855-85—Concluded.

Year ending June 30—	Indian corn per bushel.	Wheat per bushel.	Wheat flour per barrel.	Cotton per pound. a	Leather per pound.	Mineral oils, refined, per gallon.	Bacon, hams, per pound.	Lard per pound.	Pork, salted, per pound.	Beef, salted, pound.	Butter per pound.	Cheese per pound.	Eggs per dozen.	Starch per pound.	Sugar, refined, per pound.	Tobacco, leaf, per pound.
				Cts.	Cts.	Cts.	Cts.	Cts.	Cts.	Cts.	Cts.	Cts.	Cts.	Cts.	Cts.	Cts.
1874	$0.719	$1.428	$7.146	15.4	25.2	17.5	9.6	9.4	8.2	8.2	25.0	13.1	22.0	6.6	10.4	9.6
1875	.847	1.124	6.601	15.0	26.0	14.1	11.4	13.7	10.1	8.7	23.7	13.5	25.6	5.9	10.8	11.3
1876	.672	1.242	6.208	12.9	20.3	14.4	12.1	13.3	10.6	8.7	23.9	12.6	28.0	5.4	10.7	10.4
1877	.587	1.169	6.479	11.8	23.9	21.1	10.8	10.9	9.2	7.5	20.6	11.8	25.9	5.2	11.6	10.2
1878	.562	1.338	6.358	11.1	21.8	14.4	8.7	8.8	6.8	7.7	18.0	11.4	15.8	4.7	10.2	8.7
1879	.471	1.068	5.252	9.9	20.4	10.9	7.0	7.0	5.7	6.3	14.2	8.9	15.5	4.2	8.5	7.8
1880	.543	1.243	5.878	11.5	23.3	8.7	6.7	7.4	6.2	6.4	17.1	8.5	16.5	4.3	9.0	7.6
1881	.552	1.113	5.669	11.2	22.0	10.3	8.2	9.3	7.7	6.5	19.8	11.1	17.2	4.7	9.2	8.3
1882	.668	1.185	6.149	11.4	20.9	9.1	10.0	11.6	9.0	8.5	19.4	11.0	10.3	4.8	9.7	8.5
1883	.684	1.127	5.956	10.8	23.6	8.8	11.2	11.8	10.0	9.9	18.5	11.2	20.9	4.0	9.2	8.3
1884	.611	1.066	5.588	10.5	20.6	9.2	10.2	9.5	7.9	7.6	18.2	10.3	21.2	4.5	7.1	9.1
1885	.540	.862	4.897	10.0	19.8	8.7	9.4	7.9	6.3	7.5	16.8	9.3	21.5	4.0	6.4	9.0

a Including Sea Island.

The statistics of savings banks offer indicative but not conclusive evidence in the same direction. These statistics are those reported from some fifteen states and territories by the Comptroller of the Currency. They are not full and complete, yet as far as they go they show the constant progress of deposits and the constant increase in the number of depositors:

EXHIBIT OF SAVINGS BANKS IN THE UNITED STATES, 1873-85.

Years.	Number of depositors.	Amount of deposits.	Average to each depositor.
1873-74	2,188,619	$759,954,175	$347 23
1874-75	2,306,182	849,581,633	354 56
1875-76	2,414,952	892,785,553	369 69
1876-77	2,395,314	866,218,306	361 63
1877-78	2,400,785	879,897,425	366 50
1878-79	2,268,707	802,490,298	353 72
1879-80	2,335,582	819,106,973	350 71
1880-81	2,528,749	891,961,142	352 73
1881-82	2,710,354	966,797,081	356 70
1882-83	2,876,438	1,024,856,787	356 29
1883-84	3,015,151	1,070,294,955	355 06
1884-85	3,071,495	1,095,172,147	350 50

The foregoing tables are sufficient to indicate two things: That while, as shown, the extent of the existing industrial depression involves a crippling of the wage-receivers of the country, and a consequent crippling of the consuming power of the people, the volume of business has been fairly well preserved—at least not reduced to any such extent as is indicated by the crippling of the consuming power—and that prices have constantly fallen. Along with these two features there has been a constant diminishing of profits until many industries have been conducted with little or no margin to those managing them, and a great lowering of wages in general. Some industries, of course, have been badly crippled temporarily, experiencing a few months of severe stagnation until a temporary removal of the glut in the market brought them up again; but, on the whole, the volume of business of the country during the depressed period has been fairly satisfactory.

With these statements indicating the extent of the depression and the influence it has had upon the business of the country, it is well to consider as fully as possible the causes which are alleged as having produced the depression.

Alleged Causes of the Present Depression.—In searching, whether in Europe or America, for the causes of the industrial disease which has affected the manufacturing world since 1882, it is interesting to note how fully trade, profession, or calling influences opinions given. Bankers and merchants are likely to give as the absolute cause of depressions some financial or commercial reasons; clergymen and moralists largely incline to assert that social and moral influences, united with providential causes, produce the industrial difficulties which afflict nations; manufacturers incline to give industrial conditions, labor legislation, labor agitation, the demands of the workingmen, over-production, and various features of the industrial system, as causes; while the workingmen attribute industrial diseases to combinations of capital, long hours of labor, low wages, machinery, and kindred causes. The politician feels that changes in administration, the non-enactment of laws that he desires, tariffs or the absence of tariffs, are the chief influencing causes of industrial disturbances. The fact that, as a rule, one's opinion can be foreseen by knowing his calling in life, vitiates to a large extent the value of causes alleged; yet when all classes unite upon a few prominent reasons, and those reasons can be illustrated by facts, it becomes possible to consider the alleged causes of industrial depressions with a fair degree of intelligence and with conclusions that have sufficient soundness in them to indicate partial remedial agencies. The agents of the Bureau, in searching for information as to the origin, course, and progress of industrial depressions, gathered the suggestions of those men most experienced in the chief lines of business of the countries involved in this investigation. These alleged causes are classified and shown in the following alphabetical list:

CAUSES OF DEPRESSIONS AS GATHERED BY AGENTS OF THE BUREAU.

Acts that startle money-lenders, causing them to withdraw funds and refuse loans.
Administration—
    change of.
Agricultural products—
    low prices for.
Apprentice system—
    abolition of the.
Banks—
    failure of.
    fear of adverse legislation relative to.
    too liberal lending by.
Banking system—
    erroneous.
Business—
    lack of comprehension of details of.

Capital—
    absorption of, by corporations.
    aggressiveness of.
    attitude of, *versus* labor.
    concentration of, in banking and discounting centres, instead of geographical ones.
    concentration of small interests in larger ones.
    dead, invested in railroads.
    farming on borrowed.
    presence of foreign.
    relation between, and labor lost.
    syndicates and pools formed by capitalists and manufacturers to control labor.
    timidity of.

ALLEGED CAUSES OF THE PRESENT DEPRESSION.

Capital—Concluded.
    too much, invested in manufactures.
    too much, invested in railroads.
Caste—
    absence of.
Children—
    employment of.
Competition.
Confidence—
    want of.
Congress—
    unfavorable and reckless legislation in.
Corners.
Corporations—
    creation of large.
    monopoly of.
    natural resources of the country in the hands of.
Credits—
    extended commercial.
Credit system.
Crops—
    small.
Currency—
    agitation of the silver question.
    coinage of the silver dollar.
    contraction of the.
    decrease of gold.
    dishonest.
    distrust of the silver dollar.
    faulty financial system.
    inflation of the.
    not increased in proportion to the uses.
    over-issue of paper money.
    scarcity of.
    uncertain value of the silver dollar.
    uncertainty of the future monetary standard.
    unequal value of gold and silver.
    want of, to pay the debts of the country when due.
Demand—
    decrease of home.
Democratic party in power.
Depressions are mental diseases.
Economy—
    enforced, of the laboring people.
    increased public and private.
    want of, by the working people.
Emigration—
    lack of, to the public lands.
Education—
    too much, and indiscriminate.

Elections—
    presidential.
Enterprises—
    investments in unproductive.
Goods—
    inattention to quality manufactured.
    under-valuation of, at custom houses.
Government—
    want of confidence in.
Idleness—
    enforced.
Immigration—
    too much, of the poorer class.
Immorality.
Importation of what should be manufactured at home.
Industries—
    establishment of, before required.
Industrial system—
    erroneous.
Industrial plants—
    enlargement of.
Interest—
    high rates of, charged the producing classes.
Labor—
    attitude of, *versus* capital.
    concentration of, in cities.
    foreign contract.
    inadequate means for distributing the proceeds of.
    prison.
    surplus of.
    unequal distribution of wages among different classes of.
Land—
    cultivating too many acres of, with too little labor.
Laws—
    natural.
    labor.
Living—
    extravagant.
    false manner of.
    variation in the cost of.
Machinery—
    labor-saving.
Margins—
    dealing in.
Markets—
    manipulation of, by speculators.
    want of foreign.
    want of, for home products.

Manufactures—
    efforts of manufacturers to supply the inordinate fancy and demand of the public for splendid articles.
    increase of.
Monopoly—
    land.
Over-production.
Party policy—
    Exaggerating the effects of.
Paupers—
    importation of.
Political campaigns—
    reaction after.
Political distrust.
Prices—
    inflation of.
    reduction of, to cost of production.
Production—
    uneven.
    variation in the cost of.
    want of adjustment between, and consumption.
Prosperity—
    reaction from.
Railroads—
    decreased building of.
    overbuilding of.
    too much capital invested in.
Rents—
    higher.
Republican party—
    extravagance of.
Securities—
    selling valueless.
Speculation—
    engaging in, rather than productive industries.

Steel—
    introduction of Bessemer.
Strikes.
Tariff—
    abuse of system of, among importers.
    discussions of the.
    discussions on the, in Congress.
    excessive.
    fear of Congressional action relative to the.
    high, protective.
    legislation on the.
    low rate of.
    mode of collecting duties on imported machinery.
    protective policy of the.
    reduction of the.
    revisions of the.
    unequal duties of the.
    unjust.
    want of proper construction of the.
    want of proper protection.
Taxation—
    enormous.
    unequal.
Tonnage duties—
    manner of determining.
Trading—
    the overdoing of.
Traffic—
    liquor.
Under-consumption.
Wages—
    reduction of.
    variation in the rates of.
Wage system—
    failure of the.
War.
Wealth—
    consolidation of.

The foregoing list, under analysis, is easily classified into three great divisions: First, leading or direct causes, such as over-production, cost of production, influence of machinery, crippling of the consumptive power, etc.; second, contributory causes, such as transportation, distribution, exchanges, commercial systems, etc.; and third, remote, indirect, and trivial causes. Such classification would relate to the influence of alleged causes or of their importance relative to their results. A second classification might be made, involving simply character of causes, as: First, providential, involving those causes which come from natural phenomena—floods, disasters, earthquakes, etc.; second, social and moral causes, such as speculative ideas, lack of integrity, lack of confidence in government, etc.; third, political, such as political changes, discussion of commercial systems, legislation, etc.; fourth, commercial and mercantile, such as railroad-building, improvements, systems of taxation, traffic, etc.; fifth, financial, such as banking systems, credit, currency, interest, etc.; sixth, industrial and mechanical, involving overproduction, displacement of labor by machinery, wages, variation in wages, cost of production, hours of labor, etc. The long list of causes given above will readily shape itself in any one's mind in accordance with these two classifications. It is not necessary that the power and influence of what are denominated providential causes be discussed, nor is it necessary that those which might be classed under remote, indirect, and trivial should be allowed to take up any time or space, but to those which are leading and to some of those which are contributory, and which occupy the largest place in men's minds, and especially to those causes regarding the influence of which the Bureau has been able to collect any illustrating facts, not only time but space should be given.

Falling Prices.—One of the chief positive causes, as alleged, which produce depressed periods is a fall in prices. It matters not what causes the fall. It may arise from a lack of demand or from too great a supply, or it may be the result of a general tendency or of improved methods of production; but whatever the cause, the first influence of a fall in prices is an apprehension of loss.

Dr. Robert Giffen (a), chief statistician of the British Board of Trade, in a very able discussion of the influence of low prices upon depressions, comes to the conclusion that it is clearly unnecessary to assign any other cause for the gloom of the last few years, and he cites that just before the beginning of the existing depression, the first symptoms of which were discernable in England about the end of 1882 or the beginning of 1883, there had been a period of prosperity and rising prices, though for a comparatively short time. The period of depression which had lasted from 1873 to 1879 suddenly came to an end; there was a general boom in the produce markets and a recovery of tone in business, which continued for two or three years; but at the end of 1882 prices began to fall, production and foreign trade fell off, and since then there has been in Great Britain a steady outcry from the market-place about depression, which has been echoed and re-echoed in political circles, and, as Dr. Giffen says, in a somewhat "unintelligent manner, with more than usual emphasis laid on the assumption, so common at such times, that depression is itself an uncommon and bewildering phenomenon, instead of being the most natural thing in the world, and that the present depression is the worst on record and the beginning of the end of British industrial greatness." Dr. Giffen's language might be used as American entirely and not be out of place; but in quoting so eminent an authority, who backs up his statements with so many facts, it is not necessary to quote the facts themselves, so far as the cause alleged is concerned. Along with low prices there must be, of course, reduced wages, low interest, and small profits. Low prices work to the

---

a "Trade Depression and Low Prices," in the Contemporary Review, June, 1885.

great advantage of those living on invested funds at permanent rates of interest, because one dollar in a depressed period to such parties has a purchasing power enhanced to the degree of the low prices. It is during such periods that fixed capital is tempted to become active. Surrendered estates are bought at low figures, properties are secured at bargains, and while the parties securing the great bargains are apt to utter the loudest complaints, and thereby keep up the apprehensive features of the depression, they contribute toward the restoration of business activity; so, while low prices may be regarded as one of the chief and one of the leading causes, if not the leading cause, of industrial depressions, the influence of the cause is sure to react upon itself and bring about an activity through example, the effect of which is felt in various directions.

Machinery and Over-production.—Machinery—and the word is used in its largest and most comprehensive sense—has been most potent in bringing the mechanically-producing nations of the world to their present industrial position, which position constitutes an epoch in their industrial development. The rapid development and adaptation of machinery in all the activities belonging to production and transportation have brought what is commonly called over-production, so that machinery and over-production are two causes so closely allied that it is quite difficult to discuss the one without taking the other into consideration. That labor-saving machinery, so called, but which more properly should be called labor-making or labor-assisting machinery, displaces labor temporarily cannot successfully be denied. All men of sound minds admit the permanent good effects of machinery; but the permanent good effects of it do not prevent the temporary displacement of labor, which displacement, so far as the labor displaced is concerned, assists in crippling the consuming power of the community. A few illustrations relative to the displacement of labor by the introduction of machinery, if of no value in themselves, are of historic value in preserving the growth of industrial systems and the changes which come with them, and are therefore given in this chapter. It has been very difficult to gather positive information illustrating points so thoroughly apparent; yet the Bureau has been able, and from original sources largely, to bring together a mass of facts relating to the temporary displacement of labor and to conditions of industry and of society which would exist without the presence of power machinery. These illustrations show positively the influence of inventions in bringing about industrial depression.

In the manufacture of agricultural implements new machinery during the past fifteen or twenty years has, in the opinion of some of the best manufacturers of such implements, displaced fully 50 per cent. of the muscular labor formerly employed; as, for instance, hammers and dies have done away with the most particular labor on a plow. The proprietors of an extensive establishment in one of the Western States has furnished the Bureau with the following table:

DISPLACEMENT OF MUSCULAR LABOR BY MACHINERY IN THE MANUFACTURE OF AGRICULTURAL IMPLEMENTS.

Department.	Number of employés—			Proportion.
	Required with machinery.	That would be required without machinery.	Displaced by machinery.	
Engine	60	540	480	1 to 9
Boiler	70	210	140	1 to 3
Foundry	110	165	55	1 to 1½
Wood working	60	300	240	1 to 5
Setting up	50	50		1 to 1
Blacksmiths	45	90	45	1 to 2
Machinists	45	405	360	1 to 9
Erecting room	35	70	35	1 to 2
Paint shop	30	30		1 to 1
Teamsters	10	20	10	1 to 2
Pattern making	5	40	35	1 to 8
Draft room	15	150	135	1 to 10
Tool room	10	10		1 to 1
Shipping and stock	30	30		1 to 1
Lumber	10	10		1 to 1
Bolt and nut	5	5		1 to 1
Belt	7	14	7	1 to 2
Watch	3	6	3	1 to 2
	600	2,145	1,545	1 to 3.57

By this table it is shown that in the establishment cited 600 employés are doing the work which under former conditions would have required 2,145 employés, a displacement of 1,545.

In the manufacture of small-arms, where 1 man, by manual labor, was formerly able to "turn" and "fit" 1 stock for a musket in 1 day of 10 hours, 3 men now, by a division of labor and the use of power machinery, will turn out and fit from 125 to 150 stocks in 10 hours. By this it is seen that 1 man individually turns out and fits the equivalent of 42 to 50 stocks in 10 hours as against 1 stock in the same length of time by manual labor, a displacement of 44 to 49 men in this one operation.

In brick-making improved devices displace 10 per cent. of the labor, while in manufacturing fire-brick 40 per cent. has been displaced, and yet in some concerns, in manufacturing various kinds of bricks, no displacement has occurred.

The manufacture of boots and shoes offers some very wonderful facts in this connection. In one large and long-established manufactory in one of the Eastern states the proprietors testify that it would require 500 persons working by hand processes to make as many women's boots and shoes as 100 persons now make with the aid of machinery, a displacement of 80 per cent. In another class of the same industry the number of men required to produce a given quantity of boots and shoes has been reduced one-half. In another locality, and on another quality of boots, being entirely for women's wear, where formerly a first-class workman could turn out 6 pairs in one week, he will now turn out 18 pairs. A well-known firm, engaged in manufacturing boots and shoes in the West states that in the grade of goods manufactured by it, it would take 120 persons working by hand to produce the amount of work done in its factory by 60 employés, and the hand-work would not compare in workmanship and appearance, as expressed by the concern, by 50 per cent. Goodyear's sewing machine for turned shoes, with 1 man, will sew 250 pairs in 1 day. It would require 8 men working by hand to sew the same number. By the use of King's heel-shaver or trimmer 1 man will trim 300 pairs of shoes a day, where it formerly took 3 men to do the same. One man, with the McKay machine, can handle 300 pairs of shoes per day, while, without the machine, he could handle but 5 pairs in the same time. In nailing on heels, by the use of machinery, 1 man and a boy can heel 300 pairs of shoes per day. It would require 5 men to do this by hand. In finishing the bottoms of shoes, 1 man with a sand-papering machine can handle 300 pairs; while it would require 4 men to do the same by hand. A large Philadelphia firm, engaged in the manufacture of boys' and children's shoes, states—and the foreman of the establishment corroborates the evidence—that the introduction of new machinery within the past thirty years has displaced about six times the amount of hand labor required, and that the cost of the product has been reduced one-half. On another grade of goods, manufactured in Maine, the facts collected by the agents of the Bureau show that 1 man can now do the work which twenty years ago required 10 men.

The broom industry has felt the influence of machinery, the broom sewing machine facilitating the work to such extent that each machine displaces 3 men. One large broom-manufacturing concern, in 1870, employed 17 skilled men to manufacture 500 dozen brooms per week. In 1885, with 9 men and the use of machinery, the firm turned out 1,200 dozen brooms weekly. Thus, while the force is reduced in this one establishment nearly one-half, the quantity of brooms sewed is much more than doubled.

In the construction of carriages and wagons, a foreman of fifty years' experience testifies that the length of time it took a given number of skilled workmen, working entirely by hand, to produce a carriage of a certain style and quality was equal to 35 days of one man's labor, while now 1 man produces substantially the same style of carriage in 12 days.

In the manufacture of carpets, some of the leading manufacturers in the country, and men of the largest experience, consider that the improvement in machinery in the past thirty years, taking weaving, spinning, and all the processes together, have displaced from ten to twenty times the number of persons now necessary. In spinning alone it would take by the old methods from seventy-five to one hundred times the number of operatives now employed to turn out the same amount of work, while in weaving there would be required at least ten times the present number. A carpet-measuring machine has been invented which brushes and measures the product at the same time. By the use of this device 1 operator will accomplish what formerly required 15 men.

In the manufacture of clothing, where all cutting was formerly done by hand, much of it is now done by the use of dies. In cutting out hats and caps, a man working improved cutters is able to cut out a great many thicknesses at once, and he does six times the amount of work with such a machine as could formerly be done by 1 man in the old way. The same is true to a certain extent in cutting out garments. On the whole, in an establishment for the manufacture of hats of a medium grade, 1 man does the work now of 3 formerly, and the product is far superior to that produced in the olden times. In the manufacture of some kinds of hats, especially soft and stiff hats, experienced men consider that there has been a displacement in the proportion of 9 to 1.

The cotton goods industry offers, perhaps, as striking an illustration as any of the apparent displacement of labor, a Delaware house considering that the displacement has been 17 per cent. outside of motive power. By a hand-loom a weaver used to weave from 60 to 80 picks per minute in weaving a cloth of good quality, with 20 threads of twist to each one-quarter square inch. A power-loom now weaves 180 picks per minute of the same kind of cloth. Even in power machinery, a weaver formerly tended but 1 loom. Now 1 weaver minds all the way from 2 to 10 looms, according to the grade of goods. In a large establishment in New Hampshire, improved machinery, even within ten years, has reduced muscular labor 50 per cent. in the production of the same quality of goods. In another line of goods manufactured in the same state machinery has displaced labor to the amount of one-third the number of operatives formerly required. In the days of the single-spindle hand-wheel, 1 spinner, working 56 hours, could spin 5 hanks of number 32 twist. In England, at the present time, with 1 pair of self-acting mules, having 2,124 spindles, 1 spinner, having the assistance of 2 boys, will produce 55,098 hanks of number 32 twist in the same time, when the mules are running at the moderate rate of 3 stretches in $45\frac{3}{4}$ seconds. It is quite generally agreed that there has been a displacement, taking all processes of cotton manufacture into consideration, in the proportion of 3 to 1. The average number of spindles per operative in the cotton mills of this country in 1831 was 25.2. It is now about 72, an increase of 185 per cent. Along with this increase of the number of spindles per operative there has been an increase of product per operative of 145 per cent., so far as spinning is concerned. In the olden time in this country a fair adult hand-loom weaver wove from 42 to 48 yards of common shirting per week. A weaver, tending 6 power looms in a cotton factory of to-day, would produce 1,500 yards a week.

In the manufacture of flour there has been a displacement of nearly three-fourths of the manual labor necessary to produce the same product.

In the manufacture of furniture from one-half to three-fourths only of the old number of persons is now required.

In the glass industry no particular improvements have been made by which labor has been displaced to any material extent. What improvements have been introduced increase the product in some features slightly, and have improved the quality. In the manufacture of glass jars and some kinds of bottles the introduction of machinery has, however, caused a displacement in the proportion of 6 to 1, and in polishing plate glass there has been a large displacement, and also in the grinding department of plate glass manufacture.

In leather-making, in some grades of morocco, there has been an apparent displacement of perhaps 5 per cent., and in the manufacture of patent leather nearly 50 per cent.

In the lumber business, 12 co-laborers with a Bucker machine, will dress 12,000 staves. The same number of men, by hand processes, would dress but 2,500. In many departments of lumber manufacturing there has been much displacement of labor.

A saving of about 25 per cent. is made in the manufacture of machines and machinery over the hand methods. By the introduction of screw-cutting and boring machines in brass-finishing shops, a given number of hands will secure 40 per cent. greater production. A pneumatic moulding machine has reduced the number of employés for a given quantity of product.

In the production of metals and metallic goods, long-established firms testify that machinery has decreased manual labor $33\frac{1}{3}$ per cent. A great saving has been made in the production of pig-iron during the last half century, Pittsburgh producers placing the saving at 20 per cent. over the simple country furnace. By the use of improvements and inventions during the past ten or fifteen years in hammers used in the manufacture of steel, there has been a displacement of employés in the proportion of nearly 10 to 1. A first-class journeyman can make from 600 to 1,000 two-pound tin cans per day by hand process. By the use of machinery he can make from 2,000 to 2,500 per day. In making lard pails, a machine is in use by which 1 man, with 1 boy as tender, can produce as much as was formerly produced by 10 skilled men. In 1876, certain kinds of tinware were made by the old processes by the gross, a skilled workman making a gross in about one and a half days. By the use of improved machinery the workman can now turn out five times as much product in the same time. In the manufacture of bread-boxes, what was done in 1876 by 13 men and women working together, is now accomplished by 3 men.

One boy, running a planing-machine in turning wood-work for musical instruments and materials, does the work of 25 men. In the manufacture of sounding-boards, 15 men can turn out 5,000 boards per month, or 278 per day, where a good man formerly could make but 4 in a day by the old method.

MACHINERY AND OVER-PRODUCTION. 85

A mining company in Missouri have 100 miners, getting out 200 tons of coal per day. They have 2 machines, which, with 14 men, mine 40 tons per day. If 100 men without machines get out 200 tons per day, 1 man will get out 2 tons per day, or 52 tons per month. If 14 men with 2 machines get out 40 tons per day, 1 man with machine will get out 2$\frac{6}{7}$ tons per day, or 74$\frac{2}{7}$ tons per month. Therefore, 1 man with a machine gets out 22$\frac{2}{7}$ tons per month more than the man without a machine. This, worked out fully, shows that the machine displaces 6 men, on the basis of the employment of 100 miners without machines and 14 miners with machines. In a phosphate mine in South Carolina 10 men accomplish with machinery what 100 men handle without in the same time. In the Hocking Valley mining coal by machines is experimental at present. In one place, however, mining machines, employing about 160 men, produce in a month's work about the same amount of coal that 500 men will produce by hand, working the same number of days.

The oil industry in Pennsylvania has been affected a good deal by inventions. In the early days of petroleum every barrel of the liquid had to be hauled from the wells to the railroads, sometimes a distance of ten or fifteen miles. The railroads then carried it to distant parts of the country or to the seaboard to be refined and shipped abroad, the cost of all this transportation being from $1 to $3 per barrel. All this work is now done by the National Transit Company, controlled by the Standard Oil Company. When a well is completed, the pipe line's agent connects the well in a few minutes with the main line's tanks. The producer or the owner of the well pays nothing for having his oil transported through the pipe lines, but pays 50 cents per day storage for every 1,000 barrels he has in the tanks of the company, and the consumer or refiner pays 20 cents per barrel upon the receipt of the oil for transportation, so far as Pittsburgh and vicinity are concerned, while the receiver for New York and distant places pays something more. Some of the producing territory is quite remote, and 10 barrels per day would be a very liberal average to allow for a team of horses to transport to the railroads. On this basis the pipe lines displace 5,700 teams of horses and double that number of men in handling the oil, the production of the country being placed at 57,000 barrels per day.

It is very difficult to get at the exact displacement of labor in the manufacture of paper, but a machine now used for drying and cutting, run by 4 men and 6 girls, will do the work formerly done by 100 persons, and do it very much better. This is the testimony of one of the leading houses, while another states that the apparent displacement by machinery is illustrated by the fact that 6 men can now produce as much per day on a given sample as 100 men could produce in 1800 of an approximate grade. A well-known firm in New Hampshire states that by the aid of machinery it produces three times the quantity, with the same number of employés, that it did twenty years ago. In the manufacture of wall-paper the best evidence puts the displacement in the proportion of 100 to 1.

In pottery, in South Carolina, the product is ten times greater by machine processes than by muscular labor; while in the better grades of pottery, as produced in New Jersey, there has been little or no displacement.

In the manufacture of railroad supplies there has been a displacement of 50 per cent. of the labor formerly required, while in some features of the manufacture of cars there has been a displacement of three times the labor now employed. This is the testimony of several well-known firms.

There has been a displacement of 50 per cent. in the manufacture of rubber boots and shoes.

In the manufacture of saws, experienced men consider that there has been a displacement of 3 men out of 5. Ten years ago grinding was done by hand. Now it is done by machinery.

In silk manufacture, 40 per cent. represents the displacement, according to some authorities, in the general manufacture, while in weaving there has been a displacement of 95 per cent., and in winding of 90 per cent.

A large soap-manufacturing concern very carefully estimates the displacement of labor in its works at 50 per cent.

Tobacco manufacturing now requires in Illinois but one-eighth the former force of laborers to produce a given quantity. There has been a great displacement of labor in the manufacture of cigars, but the exact ratio of displacement has not been ascertained.

In making trunks there has been a displacement of, perhaps, 5 per cent.

In building vessels an approximate idea of the relative labor displacement is given as 4 or 5 to 1—that is, four or five times the amount of labor can be performed to-day by the use of machinery in a given time that could be done under old hand methods.

In making wine in California a crushing machine has been introduced with which 1 man can crush and stem 80 tons of grapes in a day, this representing an amount of work formerly requiring 8 men. It would require 4 hand-crushers, with 2 men at each, to accomplish this amount of work.

In wooden goods, 1 man with a machine does the work formerly done by 3 men on hand lathes.

In woollen goods, in the carding department modern machinery has reduced muscular labor 33 per cent.; in the spinning department, 50 per cent., and in the weaving department, 25 per cent. This is during the past few years only, while generally improved machinery in spinning and weaving departments together has displaced 20 times the hand labor formerly employed, and in other departments from 5 to 10 times. In some kinds of spinning 100 to 1 represents the displacement, nearly all concerns agreeing that the displacement during the last ten to twenty years has been 25 per cent. An establishment in Indiana has worked out the displacement of muscular labor by machinery very carefully and in the following ratio: In weaving woollens, 1 machine equals 6 persons; in spinning, 1 machine equals 20 persons; in twisting, 1 machine equals 15 persons; in picking, 1 machine equals 40 persons, and in carding, 1 set of patent carders will turn out more in 1 day than the old carders would in 1 week. Other houses engaged in the manufacture of the same kind of goods give the same figures.

Very many other features of manufacturing might be cited were the facts necessary for the illustration of this topic. In box making, in all the processes of the manufacture of books and newspapers, in jewellery, and in fact in nearly every department of production, statements as positive and emphatic as those made for the industries examined might be secured. There are one or two general illustrations, however, of the most striking nature, which may be considered the epitome of the influence of steam and of power machinery.

The mechanical industries of the United States are carried on by steam and water power representing, in round numbers, 3,500,000 horsepower,(a) each horse-power equaling the muscular labor of 6 men; that is to say, if men were employed to furnish the power to carry on the industries of this country, it would require 21,000,000 men, and 21,000,000 men represent a population, according to the ratio of the census of 1880, of 105,000,000. The industries are now carried on by 4,000,000 persons, in round numbers, representing a population of 20,000,000 only. There are in the United States 28,600 locomotives. b To do the work of these locomotives upon the existing common roads of the country and the equivalent of that which has been done upon the railroads the past year would require, in round numbers, 54,000,000 horses and 13,500,000 men. The work is now done, so far as men are concerned, by 250,000, representing a population of 1,250,000, while the population required for the number of men necessary to do the work with horses would be 67,500,000. To do the work, then, now accomplished by power and power machinery in our mechanical industries and upon our railroads would require men representing a population of 172,500,000, in addition to the present population of the country of 55,000,000, or a total population, with hand processes and with horse-power, of 227,500,000, which population would be obliged to subsist on present means. In an economic view the cost to the country would be enormous. The present cost of operating the railroads of the country with steam-power is, in round numbers, $502,600,000 per annum; but to carry on the same amount of work with men and horses would cost

---

a United States Census, 1880.

b These calculations as to the horse and man power necessary to perform the work of the railroads of the country are based upon a very careful estimate from trustworthy data made by Hon. Edward Appleton, a well-known civil engineer, late of the Massachusetts Board of Railroad Commissioners. Mr. Appleton's calculations have been substantially corroborated by others through independent estimates. His basis has simply been projected to cover the United States.

the country $11,308,500,000. These illustrations, of course, show the extreme straits to which a country would be brought if it undertook to perform its work in the old way. The figures are only interesting because a condition represented by them is utterly impossible. They are to a certain extent valuable to shew the enormous benefits gained by the people at large through the application of improved motive power. They illustrate, too, the extreme view of the displacement of labor, which, as already remarked, has been positive, and, it may well be said, to some extent permanent. Certainly, to the men individually involved, the displacement has been severe indeed. It is not necessary to show that all the effects of the introduction of power machinery have been to raise the standard of life wherever the introduction has. taken place. It is true that in those countries where machinery has been developed to the highest the greatest number of work people are engaged, and that in those countries where machinery has been developed to little or no purpose poverty reigns, ignorance is the prevailing condition, and civilization consequently far in the rear. These statements are simply facts which common observation teaches. They could be easily illustrated by statistics.

The people at large, and especially those who work for wages, have experienced three great elements of progress along with the establishment of the factory system. In wages and in product the position is well illustrated in the cotton industry. The ratio of cost per pound for labor of common cotton cloth for the years 1828 and 1880 was as 6.77 to 3.31, wages for the same dates being as 2.62 to 4.84; the average consumption of cotton, which indicates the standard of life as well as any one item, was per capita of total population for the year 1831, 5.90 pounds, while in 1880 the consumption rose to 13.91 pounds, this being exclusive of exports.. In Great Britain in 1883 the consumption, exclusive of exports, was 6.62 pounds per capita, and in 1880, 7.75 pounds. Working time has been decreased on an average 12 per cent., while luxuries have become necessaries, and, to a very large extent, placed within the reach of people of small means. All these points are too familiar to require restatement. They are simply used as illustrative; and yet, if the question should be asked, has the wage-worker received his equitable share of the benefits derived from the introduction of machinery, the answer must be no. In the struggle for industrial supremacy in the great countries devoted to mechanical production it probably has been impossible for him to share equitably in such benefits. That he has shared greatly as a consumer is true. Much of the saving in production through the apparent and temporary displacement of labor has been applied in raising the quality and perfecting the style of the products. His greatest benefit has come through his being a consumer. In very many instances the adult male has been obliged to work at a reduced wage, because, under improved machinery, women and children could perform his work, but the net earnings of his family stand at a higher figure than of old. It is also true that while labor has been displaced apparently in many directions and in many industries, machinery has brought new occupations, especially to women. In the introduction of the telephone, errand boys to some extent were displaced from their regular work, but the vast army necessary to carry on the telephone system is much larger than any possible displacement. This is true in so many directions that this one illustration suffices. The apparent evils resulting from the introduction of machinery and the consequent subdivision of labor have to a large extent, of course, been offset by advantages gained; but it must stand as a positive statement, which cannot successfully be controverted, that this wonderful introduction and extension of power machinery is one of the prime causes, if not the prime cause, of the novel industrial condition in which the manufacturing nations find themselves.

The direct results, so far as the present period is concerned, of this wonderful and rapid extension of power machinery are, for the countries involved, over-production, or, to be more correct, bad or injudicious production; that is, that condition of production of things the value of which depends upon immediate consumption, or consumption by that portion of the population of the world already requiring the goods produced. If England, the United States, France, Belgium, and Germany unitedly produce more cotton goods than can be sold to their regular customers or in the world among people that use cotton goods, over-production exists, and it does not matter that the millions of human beings who do not consume and who do not desire cotton goods are unsupplied. So far as the factories and the operatives of the countries concerned are to be taken into consideration there does exist a positive and emphatic over-production, and this over-production could not exist without the introduction of power machinery at a rate greater than the consuming power of the nations involved and of those depending upon them demand; in other words, the over-production of power machinery logically results in the over-production of goods made with the aid of such machinery, and this represents the condition of those countries depending largely upon mechanical industries for their prosperity. Crippled consuming power, ordinarily known as under-consumption, may result from over-production, producing lower prices, or from other causes not connected with production in the ordinary sense. Some of these features are considered separately.

An influential cause in producing the condition of things recited as to the abnormal increase of machinery and the development of industrial enterprises has been the facility with which stock companies could be organized. In fact, the modern system of carrying on great works by stock companies has done much toward producing in all countries the bad industrial conditions under which the present generation is laboring. Formerly individual capital and individual enterprise constituted the moving power back of industrial development, and only men of considerable means, or two or three such men under copartnership arrangement, could undertake any very great enterprise, such as the building of great factories, the opening of mines, and undertakings in other directions; but now, under the modern system, when old partnership houses and family proprietors are adopting the joint-stock company basis for action, and many men of small means can contribute to the common stock of a great company, the inducement to push undertakings becomes speculative to a large extent. The depositors in savings banks, where such institutions exist, become indirectly associated with the very concerns they often condemn, and depend for their dividends on their deposits upon the welfare of such corporations. Legislatures have in very many, if not all, of the States of the Union greatly facilitated the organization of such companies through the provisions of general laws, while some have been reckless enough to allow such organizations to be created without regard to the actual capital invested or property owned. The result has been an abnormal organization of capital and of interests aimed at the development of the industries of the country. Material, labor, capital have been over-consumed, and to such an extent that over-production stands for over-consumption.

The Variation in the Cost of Production.—The question of the cost of production, especially so far as the labor cost relative to other elements of production is concerned, necessarily enters into the consideration of the causes and effects of industrial depressions, not that such depressions are caused by differences which may exist in the cost of producing a given article in different localities to any material extent; still it is often alleged that such differences are influential in producing a disturbance in the prices of things, and to the extent of such disturbance constitutes a remote cause of depressions. One of the most difficult tasks an investigator into economic conditions sets for himself is to ascertain the relation of the different elements in the cost of producing articles of consumption where more than one class of raw material enters into the production. The obstacles in the way are more than those which come from disinclination on the part of producers to state definitely all the cost elements involved; obstacles are met with even when the freest disposition exists to give such information. The manufacture of a given unit may require certain expenses through the remoteness of operations from the source of supplies, from condition of living, from cost of plant, from variation in the processes of manipulation, and from other conditions. It is true that if the actual facts relating to such cost of production could be ascertained beyond dispute in various localities, a wide variation would be shown; yet it is also true that the endeavor of all engaged in the production of a given unit to reduce the elements of cost to the lowest possible terms secures an approximate uniformity in the cost of making such unit where conditions are fairly the same. So it was with a view of ascertaining how great this variation is in communities having like conditions or substantially like conditions, and in communities remote from each other with dissimilar conditions, that the facts given in the following table were gathered. This table must be considered to a large extent tentative, because in some measure incomplete; yet it shows clearly what might be accomplished if a uniform disposition on the part of producers could be met with. It was not to be expected in the first work of the Bureau that manufacturers everywhere would freely give information in the publication of which there might be caused an apprehension of injury to be received; but when it is considered that establishments have not hesitated to furnish the required information, and when it is known that no harm results to any industry through the publication of such information, it is to be hoped that in the future work of the Bureau no obstacle will be placed in its way by those most interested in giving full information freely and accurately.

The first table presented gives the labor cost, the material cost, the administrative cost, and the total cost of the production of the articles described. There are two columns comprehending administrative cost, entitled "Administrative" and "Other." These two columns were made necessary from the fact that some establishments gave administrative cost by itself, meaning the expenses of management, and the "Other" comprehending insurance, taxes, interest, depreciation, etc. In such cases the two elements are separated; but in many cases, while proprietors were willing to give the labor and material cost, they preferred, through some motives of their own, to give administrative cost and the other elements together. Should it be desired to ascertain the wages paid or the number of persons engaged in each occupation in an establishment this can be seen by reference to the table "Occupations, with Number and Wages of Employés, by Industries," Appendix A, page 295. With reference to this table and the one showing cost of production it may be stated that 759 establishments are represented in the two. Of this number, 189 reported wages only, 177 cost of production only, and 393 both wages and cost of production. Thus, wages were reported for 582 establishments, covering 149,182 employés, an average of 256 employés to each establishment. The summarizing of this long, detail table of wages is exhibited in the five tables, pages 143 to 226. The table on cost of production is so full in itself, so far as details are concerned, that no analysis of it seems to be necessary, each industry being grouped by itself, and all the states or countries from which information was obtained relative to the cost of production being brought together; as, for instance, under "Metals and Metallic Goods," all the establishments, wherever situated, manufacturing such goods are placed under that title. This enables one to examine the relative cost of production in different localities with ease, and any text analysis would simply be a restatement of the facts given compactly in the table itself.

COST OF PRODUCTION.

NOTE.—The establishment numbers correspond to those in the table on page 295, Appendix A, showing number of employés and wages, except as noted below. See explanation of table, page 91.

AGRICULTURAL IMPLEMENTS.

Establishment No.	State.	Description of unit.
a583	Ohio	One 10-horse power thrasher with wagon and stacker
13	...do	One medium thrasher with wagon and stacker
14	...do	One first-class hand-dump hay-rake
15	...do	One first-class hand-dump hay-rake
16	...do	One first-class self-dump hay-rake
14	...do	One first-class self-dump hay-rake
15	...do	One first-class self-dump hay-rake
11	...do	One combined mowing and reaping machine with self-raking attachment.
10	...do	One combined mowing and reaping machine
10	...do	One mowing machine
11	...do	One mowing machine
15	...do	One lawn mower
10	...do	One harvesting and binding machine
15	...do	One first-class hay-tedder
13	...do	One 10-horse-power traction farm engine
6	Kentucky	One light plough
17	Ohio	One chilled-iron plough, weighing 105 pounds
a584	...do	One chilled-iron plough, weighing 115 pounds
a584	...do	One chilled-iron sulky plough, weighing 350 pounds
18	...do	One steel sulky plough, weighing 350 pounds
17	...do	One steel plough, weighing 105 pounds
a584	...do	One combination, iron and steel plough, weighing 105 pounds
a584	...do	One steel plough, weighing 105 pounds
20	Pennsylvania	One centre-lever plough
7	Maine	One scythe
8	New York	One farm hoe

ARMS AND AMMUNITION.

Establishment No.	State.	Description of unit.
21	Massachusetts	One double-action revolver, 38-caliber

ARTISANS' TOOLS.

Establishment No.	State.	Description of unit.
22	Indiana	One 72-inch circular saw
22	...do	One 10-inch circular saw
22	...do	One cross-cut saw, 6½ feet in length
22	...do	One small cross-cut saw

BOOTS AND SHOES.

Establishment No.	State.	Description of unit.
a585	Massachusetts	One pair men's stoga boots
a586	Illinois	One pair men's first-class stoga boots
a586	...do	One pair men's second-class stoga boots
a587	Ohio	One pair men's second-class stoga boots
a586	Illinois	One pair men's first-class calf boots
a586	...do	One pair men's second-class calf boots
a586	...do	One pair men's first-class kip boots
a586	...do	One pair men's second-class kip boots
68	Ohio	One pair men's hand-pegged, farmers' kip boots
68	...do	One pair men's hand-pegged domestic calf boots
a587	...do	One pair men's hand-pegged domestic calf boots
a588	...do	One pair men's first-class machine-sewed domestic calf boots
a587	...do	One pair men's first-class machine-sewed domestic calf boots
a588	...do	One pair men's first-class hand-sewed domestic calf boots
68	...do	One pair men's machine-sewed French calf boots
68	...do	One pair men's first-class hand-sewed French calf boots
a588	...do	One pair men's first-class hand-sewed French calf boots
68	...do	One pair men's hand-pegged French kip boots
a588	...do	One pair men's machine-sewed kip boots
a587	...do	One pair men's first-class double-soled wired or pegged kip boots
a589	Massachusetts	One pair men's boots
a587	Ohio	One pair men's common machine-sewed domestic calf button boots

a The wages of employés in this establishment were not reported; therefore the number will not be found in the wage table, Appendix A.

VARIATION IN THE COST OF PRODUCTION.

COST OF PRODUCTION.

NOTE.—The establishment numbers correspond to those in the table on page 295, Appendix A, showing number of employés and wages, except as noted below. See explanation of table, page 91.

AGRICULTURAL IMPLEMENTS.

Amount of unit cost.					Per cent. of unit cost.				Establishment No.
Labor.	Materials.	Administration.	Other.	Total.	Labor.	Materials.	Administration.	Other.	
$150.00000	$150.00000	....	$50.00000	$350.00000	42.86	42.86	....	14.28	a583
89.42000	92.14000	....	30.31000	217.87000	41.04	42.29	....	16.67	12
2.00000	8.00000	....	2.50000	12.50000	16.00	64.00	....	20.00	14
2.50000	9.15000	....	3.25000	14.90000	16.77	61.41	....	21.82	15
2.40000	10.00000	....	2.75000	15.15000	15.84	66.01	....	18.15	16
2.40000	9.60000	....	3.00000	15.00000	16.00	64.00	....	20.00	14
3.00000	10.50000	....	4.00000	17.50000	17.14	60.00	....	22.86	15
24.00000	38.00000	$13.00000	13.00000	88.00000	27.27	43.18	14.77	14.78	11
20.40000	17.02000	....	14.36000	51.78000	39.41	32.87	....	27.62	10
10.20000	8.41000	....	7.18000	25.79000	39.55	32.61	....	27.84	10
12.12000	19.00000	....	13.22000	44.34000	27.33	42.84	....	29.83	11
1.25000	1.80000	....	1.00000	4.05000	30.87	44.44	....	24.69	15
30.60000	25.53000	....	21.54000	77.67000	39.40	32.87	....	27.73	10
6.00000	14.00000	....	5.00000	25.00000	24.00	56.00	....	20.00	15
159.44000	315.50000	....	95.00000	570.00000	27.97	55.36	....	16.67	13
1.83000	1.96000	.42000	.10000	4.31000	42.46	45.47	9.75	2.32	6
2.50000	2.50000	....	1.00000	6.00000	41.66	41.67	....	16.67	17
2.00000	2.00000	....	3.00000	7.00000	28.57	28.58	....	42.85	a584
8.00000	8.00000	....	6.00000	22.00000	36.36	36.37	....	27.27	a584
8.00000	12.00000	....	6.00000	26.00000	30.77	46.16	....	23.07	18
3.75000	4.00000	....	1.00000	8.75000	42.86	45.71	....	11.43	17
2.00000	3.00000	....	3.00000	8.00000	25.00	37.50	....	37.50	a584
3.50000	3.50000	....	3.00000	10.00000	35.00	35.00	....	30.00	a584
2.27000	2.30000	.50000	.20000	5.27000	43.08	43.64	9.49	3.79	20
.12800	.19300	....	....	.32100	39.88	60.12	....	....	7
.11082	.10406	.01500	.03778	.27726	43.21	37.75	5.41	13.63	8

ARMS AND AMMUNITION.

$3.60000	$0.40000	$0.12000	$2.25000	$6.37000	56.51	6.29	1.88	35.32	21

ARTISANS' TOOLS.

$34.00000	$66.00000	....	$25.00000	$125.00000	27.20	52.80	....	20.00	22
.42000	.25000	....	.16000	.83000	50.60	30.12	....	19.28	22
1.00000	1.80000	....	.70000	3.50000	28.57	51.43	....	20.00	22
.40000	.50000	....	.22000	1.12000	35.71	44.64	....	19.65	22

BOOTS AND SHOES.

$0.45000	$1.65000	....	$0.05000	$2.15000	20.93	76.74	....	2.33	a585
.47417	1.99083	....	.24500	2.71000	17.50	73.46	....	9.04	a586
.40250	1.56250	....	.19166	2.15666	18.66	72.45	....	8.89	a586
.70000	1.37000	....	.14000	2.21000	31.67	61.99	....	6.34	a587
.59083	2.51417	....	.30834	3.41334	17.31	73.66	....	9.03	a586
.52500	1.90417	....	.24167	2.67084	19.66	71.20	....	9.05	a586
.55334	2.07583	....	.20017	2.89834	19.09	71.62	....	9.29	a586
.50250	1.67583	....	.21067	2.30500	20.98	69.97	....	9.05	a586
.75000	1.50000	....	.25000	2.50000	30.00	60.00	....	10.00	68
.80000	1.75000	....	.25000	2.80000	28.57	62.50	....	8.93	68
.75000	1.50000	....	.25000	2.50000	30.00	60.00	....	10.00	a587
1.25000	2.25000	....	.35000	3.85000	32.47	58.44	....	9.09	a588
.92000	1.75000	....	.30000	2.97000	30.98	58.92	....	10.10	a587
2.25000	2.25000	....	.45000	4.95000	45.45	45.46	....	9.09	a588
1.00000	2.25000	....	.35000	3.60000	27.78	62.50	....	9.72	68
3.00000	2.25000	....	.50000	5.75000	52.17	39.13	....	8.70	68
2.25000	3.25000	....	.55000	6.05000	37.19	53.72	....	9.09	a588
.75000	2.00000	....	.25000	3.00000	25.00	66.67	....	8.33	68
.75000	1.75000	....	.25000	2.75000	27.27	63.64	....	9.09	a588
.92000	1.75000	....	.30000	2.97000	30.98	58.92	....	10.10	a587
.41667	1.50000	....	.33333	2.25000	18.52	66.67	....	14.81	a589
.75000	1.15000	....	.15000	2.05000	36.58	56.10	....	7.32	a587

94   REPORT OF THE COMMISSIONER OF LABOR.

COST OF PRODUCTION—Continued.

NOTE.—The establishment numbers correspond to those in the table on page 295, Appendix A, showing number of employés and wages, except as noted below. See explanation of table, page 91.

BOOTS AND SHOES—Continued.

Establishment No.	State.	Description of unit.
a587	Ohio	One pair men's medium grade machine-sewed domestic calf button boots.
25	Illinois	One pair men's first-class machine-sewed domestic calf button boots.
25	...do	One pair men's first-class hand-sewed domestic calf button boots.
68	Ohio	One pair men's machine-sewed calf button boots.
68	...do	One pair men's hand-sewed calf button boots.
68	...do	One pair men's machine-sewed kip laced boots.
a588	...do	One pair men's first-class machine-sewed French calf button boots.
a588	...do	One pair men's first-class hand-sewed French calf button boots.
a587	...do	One pair men's first-class hand-sewed French calf button boots.
29	Maryland	One pair men's hand-sewed Congress boots.
29	...do	One pair men's McKay machine-sewed Congress boots.
30	...do	One pair men's McKay machine-sewed Congress boots.
30	...do	One pair men's hand-sewed calf button boots.
29	...do	One pair men's Goodyear machine-sewed calf button boots.
50	New Jersey	One pair men's hand-sewed French calf shoes.
40	Massachusetts	One pair men's hand-sewed slippers.
a590	Ohio	One pair women's common Curaçoa kid button boots.
591	...do	One pair women's common Curaçoa kid button boots.
67	...do	One pair women's medium grade Curaçoa kid button boots.
a592	...do	One pair women's medium-grade Curaçoa kid button boots.
66	...do	One pair women's medium-grade Curaçoa kid button boots.
65	...do	One pair women's medium-grade Curaçoa kid button boots.
a593	Illinois	One pair women's medium-grade Curaçoa kid button boots.
a594	...do	One pair women's medium-grade Curaçoa kid button boots.
a595	...do	One pair women's medium-grade Curaçoa kid button boots.
a591	Ohio	One pair women's medium-grade Curaçoa kid button boots.
a590	...do	One pair women's first-class Curaçoa kid button boots.
a592	...do	One pair women's first-class Curaçoa kid button boots.
a593	Illinois	One pair women's first-class Curaçoa kid button boots.
a597	...do	One pair women's first-class Curaçoa kid button boots.
a594	...do	One pair women's first-class Curaçoa kid button boots.
a595	...do	One pair women's first-class Curaçoa kid button boots.
a591	Ohio	One pair women's first-class Curaçoa kid button boots.
59	New York	One pair women's Curaçoa kid button boots.
60	...do	One pair women's Curaçoa kid button boots.
a597	Illinois	One pair women's first-class French kid button boots.
57	New York	One pair women's straight-grain kid button boots.
41	Massachusetts	One pair women's kid button boots.
53	New York	One pair girl's Tampico kid button boots.
a590	Ohio	One pair women's common pebbled-goat button boots.
a596	...do	One pair women's medium grade pebbled-goat button boots.
a592	...do	One pair women's medium-grade pebbled-goat button boots.
66	...do	One pair women's medium-grade pebbled-goat button boots.
65	...do	One pair women's medium-grade pebbled-goat button boots.
a593	Illinois	One pair women's medium-grade pebbled-goat button boots.
a594	...do	One pair women's medium-grade pebbled-goat button boots.
a595	...do	One pair women's medium-grade pebbled-goat button boots.
a591	Ohio	One pair women's medium-grade pebbled-goat button boots.
a593	Illinois	One pair women's first-class pebbled-goat button boots.
a597	...do	One pair women's first-class pebbled-goat button boots.
a594	...do	One pair women's first-class pebbled-goat button boots.
a595	...do	One pair women's first-class pebbled-goat button boots.
27	Maryland	One pair women's pebbled-goat button boots.
29	...do	One pair women's pebbled-goat button boots.
28	...do	One pair women's pebbled-goat button boots.
58	New York	One pair women's pebbled-goat button boots.
61	...do	One pair women's pebbled-goat button boots.
62	...do	One pair women's pebbled-goat button boots.
70	Pennsylvania	One pair women's pebbled-goat button boots.
52	New York	One pair girls' pebbled-goat button boots.
a592	Ohio	One pair women's medium-grade calf button boots.
65	...do	One pair women's medium-grade calf button shoes.
54	New York	One pair women's first-class domestic calf button boots.
63	...do	One pair women's domestic calf button boots.
51	...do	One pair girl's domestic calf button boots.
55	...do	One pair girl's domestic calf button boots.
64	...do	One pair girl's domestic calf button boots.
56	...do	One pair girl's domestic calf button boots.
42	Massachusetts	One pair women's grained-leather button boots.
a585	...do	One pair women's sandals.
34	...do	One pair children's ankle-tie shoes.
32	...do	One pair infants' soft sole four-button shoes.

a The wages of employés in this establishment were not reported; therefore the number will not be found in the wage table, Appendix A.

VARIATION IN THE COST OF PRODUCTION.

COST OF PRODUCTION—Continued.

NOTE.—The establishment numbers correspond to those in the table on page 295, Appendix A, showing number of employés and wages, except as noted below. See explanation of table, page 91.

BOOTS AND SHOES—Continued.

Amount of unit cost.					Per cent. of unit cost.				Establishment No.
Labor.	Materials.	Administration.	Other.	Total.	Labor.	Materials.	Administration.	Other.	
$1.01000	$1.44000	....	$0.22000	$2.67000	37.83	53.93	....	8.24	a587
.89000	1.87000	....	.31500	3.07500	28.94	60.61	....	10.25	25
1.78000	2.11500	....	.31500	4.19000	42.00	50.48	....	7.52	25
.70000	1.40000	....	.20000	2.30000	30.43	60.87	....	8.70	68
2.20000	1.40000	....	.30000	3.90000	56.41	35.90	....	7.09	68
.50000	1.20000	....	.15000	1.85000	27.03	64.87	....	8.10	68
1.00000	2.25000	....	.30000	3.55000	28.16	63.38	....	8.46	a588
2.00000	2.50000	....	.45000	4.95000	40.41	50.50	....	9.09	a588
2.10000	1.57000	....	.20000	3.87000	54.26	40.57	....	5.17	a587
1.90000	1.73000	....	.60000	4.23000	44.02	40.89	....	14.19	29
.95000	1.73000	....	.48000	3.16000	30.06	54.75	....	15.19	29
1.10000	1.90000	....	.48000	3.48000	31.61	54.60	....	13.79	30
2.10000	2.15000	....	.68000	4.93000	42.60	43.61	....	13.70	30
1.02500	1.73000	....	.50000	3.25500	31.49	53.15	....	15.36	29
2.00000	b3.75000	....	....	5.75000	34.78	65.22	....	....	50
.30000	.60000	....	.12000	1.02000	29.41	58.83	....	11.70	49
.70000	.90000	....	.07000	1.67000	41.92	53.89	....	4.19	a590
.57000	1.07000	....	.16000	1.80000	31.67	59.44	....	8.89	a591
.65000	1.25000	....	.05000	1.95000	33.33	64.11	....	2.56	67
.70000	1.30000	....	.20000	2.20000	31.82	59.09	....	9.09	a592
.50000	1.10000	....	.25000	1.85000	27.03	59.46	....	13.51	66
.57000	1.34000	....	.04000	1.95000	29.23	68.72	....	2.05	65
.65000	1.17000	....	.07000	1.89000	34.39	61.91	....	3.70	a593
.51500	1.07000	....	.11000	1.69500	30.38	63.13	....	6.49	a594
.60000	1.24000	....	.16000	2.00000	30.00	62.00	....	8.00	a595
.60000	1.25000	....	.18000	2.03000	29.56	61.58	....	8.86	a591
.93000	1.26750	....	.25000	2.44750	38.00	51.79	....	10.21	a596
.80000	1.85000	....	.25000	2.90000	27.59	63.79	....	8.62	a592
.72000	1.28000	....	.07000	2.07000	34.78	61.84	....	3.38	a593
.75000	1.65000	....	.25000	2.05000	28.31	62.26	....	9.43	a597
.73500	1.52500	....	.16000	2.42000	30.37	63.02	....	6.61	a594
.70000	1.55000	....	.25000	2.50000	28.00	62.00	....	10.00	a595
.65000	1.75000	....	.18000	2.58000	25.19	67.83	....	6.98	a591
.50760	.70000	$0.09150	.01560	1.31470	38.61	53.24	6.96	1.19	59
.52129	.74800	.07015	.04055	1.37999	37.77	54.21	5.08	2.94	60
.85000	2.40000	....	.33000	3.58000	23.74	67.04	....	9.22	a597
.62313	1.10000	.00193	.06129	1.78645	34.89	61.57	.11	3.43	57
.38000	.80000	....	.12000	1.30000	29.23	61.54	....	9.23	41
.56800	.93900	.03310	.10260	1.04300	34.61	57.13	2.01	0.25	53
.70000	.77333	....	.07000	1.54333	45.36	50.11	....	4.53	a590
.60500	.78000	....	.15000	1.53500	39.42	50.81	....	9.77	a596
.59000	1.01000	....	.18000	1.78000	33.15	56.74	....	10.11	a592
.50000	1.00000	....	.25000	1.75000	28.58	57.14	....	14.28	06
.55000	1.10000	....	.04000	1.09000	32.54	65.10	....	2.36	65
.65000	1.07500	....	.07000	1.79500	36.21	59.89	....	3.90	a593
.47500	.97000	....	.10000	1.54500	30.74	62.78	....	6.48	a594
.50000	1.18000	....	.12000	1.75000	28.57	64.57	....	6.86	a595
.54000	1.02000	....	.16000	1.72000	31.40	59.30	....	9.30	a591
.71000	1.17000	....	.07000	1.95000	36.41	60.00	....	3.59	a593
.70000	1.20000	....	.20000	2.10000	33.33	57.15	....	9.52	a597
.62866	1.01750	....	.11416	1.75832	35.04	57.87	....	6.49	a594
.50000	1.34000	....	.16000	2.00000	25.00	67.00	....	8.00	a595
.74000	.90000	....	.25000	1.89000	39.15	47.62	....	13.23	27
.68000	1.06040	....	.17000	1.89040	34.91	56.09	....	9.00	20
.76000	.96920	....	.25000	1.97920	38.40	48.97	....	12.63	28
.59140	.99800	.09810	.01470	1.70220	34.74	58.63	5.76	.87	58
.59030	.97100	.03600	.13790	1.73520	34.02	55.95	2.07	7.96	61
.59170	1.00000	.03580	.06260	1.69010	35.01	59.17	2.12	3.70	62
.58000	.97700	.05000	.05000	1.65700	35.00	58.96	3.02	3.02	70
.67230	.66000	.04800	.04700	1.42730	47.10	46.24	3.36	3.30	52
.70000	1.13000	....	.20000	2.03000	34.48	55.67	....	9.85	a592
.48000	1.20000	....	.04000	1.72000	27.90	69.77	....	2.33	65
.60868	1.23000	.12111	.05332	2.01111	30.17	61.16	6.02	2.65	54
.57525	.80000	.03333	.02382	1.48240	40.10	55.85	2.33	1.60	03
.53400	.79000	.06600	.01700	1.43700	37.10	54.97	4.60	3.27	51
.61160	.68000	.02292	.02100	1.33618	45.77	50.90	1.71	1.62	55
.58970	.77400	.04070	.09050	1.49490	39.45	51.78	2.72	6.05	64
.62630	.66000	.06704	.02730	1.38064	45.36	47.80	4.86	1.98	56
.25500	.70000	....	.03000	.98500	25.89	71.07	....	3.04	42
.07000	.22000	.01000	....	.30000	23.33	73.33	3.34	....	a585
.21000	.23500	....	....	.40500	45.16	54.84	....	....	34
.05400	.08500	....	.03000	.16900	31.95	50.30	....	17.75	32

b All expenses except labor are included in this amount.

COST OF PRODUCTION—Continued.

Note.—The establishment numbers correspond to those in the table on page 295, Appendix A, showing number of employés and wages, except as noted below. See explanation of table, page 91.

BOOTS AND SHOES—Concluded.

Establishment No.	State.	Description of unit.
31	Massachusetts	One pair infants' soft sole four-button shoes
32	...do	One pair infants' hard sole four-button shoes
31	...do	One pair infants' hard sole four-button shoes
69	Pennsylvania	One pair youths' leather-tipped shoes

BRICKS.

74	Delaware	One thousand common bricks
a598	Georgia	One thousand common bricks
a599	Tennessee	One thousand common bricks

CARPETINGS.

84	Connecticut	One yard extra superfine ingrain carpet (weighing 21 ounces to the yard)
95	Pennsylvania	One yard ingrain carpet
94	...do	One yard worsted velvet carpet
89	Massachusetts	One yard tapestry brussels carpet
91	New York	One yard (eight wire) tapestry brussels carpet
91	...do	One yard moquette carpet
a600	Maine	One square yard floor oil cloth
a601	New Jersey	One yard oil cloth (50 inches wide, enameled duck)

CARRIAGES AND WAGONS.

103	Illinois	One first-class hand-made leather-top top buggy
100	...do	One first-class hand-made leather-top top buggy
a602	...do	One first-class hand-made leather-top top buggy
101	...do	One first-class hand-made leather-top top buggy
a603	Ohio	One first-class hand-made leather-top top buggy
a604	...do	One first-class hand-made leather-top top buggy
a605	...do	One first-class hand-made leather-top top buggy
a606	...do	One first-class hand-made leather-top top buggy
a607	...do	One first-class hand-made leather-top top buggy
105	...do	One first-class leather-top top buggy
102	Illinois	One ordinary leather-top top buggy
103	...do	One first-class machine-made top buggy
106	Ohio	One first-class machine-made top buggy
97	Connecticut	One top buggy, with side bar
101	Illinois	One first-class hand-made phæton
100	...do	One first-class hand-made phæton
a603	Ohio	One first-class hand-made phæton
a605	...do	One first-class hand-made phæton
a606	...do	One first-class hand-made phæton
a607	...do	One first-class hand-made phæton
106	...do	One first-class machine-made phæton
103	Illinois	One first-class hand-made canopy top surrey wagon
101	...do	One first-class hand-made canopy top surrey wagon
a602	...do	One first-class hand-made canopy top surrey wagon
100	...do	One first-class hand-made canopy top surrey wagon
a603	Ohio	One first-class hand-made canopy top surrey wagon
a605	...do	One first-class hand-made canopy top surrey wagon
a607	...do	One first-class hand-made canopy top surrey wagon
102	Illinois	One first-class machine-made without-top surrey wagon
96	Connecticut	One first-class five-glass landau
99	...do	One first-class five-glass landau
98	...do	One first-class five-glass landau
100	Illinois	One first-class five-glass landau
97	Connecticut	One first-class cabriolet
96	...do	One first-class cabriolet
a602	Illinois	One first-class hand-made two-wheeled road cart
102	...do	One first-class machine-made two-wheeled road cart
100	...do	One first-class spring wagon
102	...do	One first-class spring wagon
104	New Jersey	One first-class Berlin coach

a The wages of employés in this establishment were not reported; therefore the number will not be found in the wage table, Appendix A.

VARIATION IN THE COST OF PRODUCTION.

COST OF PRODUCTION—Continued.

NOTE.—The establishment numbers correspond to those in the table on page 295, Appendix A, showing number of employés and wages, except as noted below. See explanation of table, page 91.

BOOTS AND SHOES—Concluded.

Amount of unit cost.					Per cent. of unit cost.				Establishment No.
Labor.	Materials.	Administration.	Other.	Total.	Labor.	Materials.	Administration.	Other.	
$0.04500	$0.05500	....	$0.00750	$0.10750	41.86	51.16	....	6.98	31
.06750	.08500	....	.03000	.18250	36.99	46.58	....	16.43	32
.06750	.06500	....	.00750	.14000	48.21	46.43	....	5.36	31
.13100	.35550	....	.19740	.68390	19.15	51.98	....	28.87	69

BRICKS.

$6.80000	$0.25000	....	....	$7.05000	96.45	3.55	....	....	74
3.45000	.45000	....	....	3.90000	88.46	11.54	....	....	a598
3.50000	1.00000	....	....	4.50000	77.78	22.22	....	....	a599

CARPETINGS.

$0.14000	$0.43000	....	$0.05000	$0.62000	22.58	69.36	....	8.06	84
.06100	.13250	$0.00500	.01000	.20850	29.26	63.55	2.40	4.79	95
.48100	.80000	....	.37000	1.65100	29.13	48.40	....	22.41	94
.14000	.48000	....	....	.62000	22.58	77.42	....	....	89
.14700	.41020	.00700	.00400	.56820	25.87	72.19	1.24	.70	91
.35000	.53210	.05000	.00900	.94110	37.19	56.54	5.31	.96	91
.05020	.20980	....	....	.26000	19.31	80.69	....	....	a600
.05000	.07000	....	....	.12000	41.67	58.33	....	....	a601

CARRIAGES AND WAGONS.

$119.00000	$112.50000	....	$15.00000	$246.50000	48.27	45.64	....	6.09	103
68.50000	76.50000	....	21.90000	166.90000	41.04	45.84	....	13.12	100
91.00000	120.60000	....	10.00000	221.60000	41.06	54.42	....	4.52	a602
83.00000	110.00000	....	20.00000	213.00000	38.97	51.64	....	9.39	101
96.70000	107.85000	....	40.84000	245.39000	39.40	43.95	....	16.65	a603
94.00000	105.00000	....	15.00000	214.00000	43.93	49.07	....	7.00	a604
75.00000	103.00000	....	15.00000	193.00000	38.86	53.37	....	7.77	a605
58.00000	76.68000	....	30.57000	165.25000	35.10	46.40	....	18.50	a606
70.00000	80.00000	....	22.50000	172.50000	40.58	46.38	....	13.04	a607
21.50000	73.00000	....	8.50000	103.00000	20.87	70.88	....	8.25	105
15.50000	71.00000	....	4.50000	91.00000	17.03	78.02	....	4.95	102
18.00000	74.30000	....	12.80000	105.10000	17.69	70.65	....	11.66	106
97.20000	121.01000	....	43.61000	261.83000	37.12	46.21	....	16.67	97
135.00000	140.00000	....	25.00000	300.00000	45.00	46.67	....	8.33	104
77.50000	92.00000	....	19.00000	188.50000	41.11	48.81	....	10.08	100
115.50000	124.65000	....	48.03000	288.18000	40.08	43.25	....	16.67	a603
81.00000	110.00000	....	15.00000	206.00000	39.32	53.40	....	7.28	a605
58.16000	88.82000	....	36.70000	183.70000	31.67	48.35	....	19.98	a606
75.00000	85.00000	....	24.00000	184.00000	40.76	46.20	....	13.04	a607
21.25000	84.85000	....	14.00000	120.10000	17.69	70.65	....	11.66	100
120.00000	122.60000	....	25.00000	267.60000	44.84	45.82	....	9.34	103
113.00000	110.00000	....	25.00000	248.00000	45.56	44.36	....	10.08	101
99.00000	133.00000	....	18.00000	250.00000	39.60	53.20	....	7.20	a603
75.00000	72.00000	....	21.15000	168.15000	44.60	42.82	....	12.58	100
120.00000	114.00000	....	48.80000	282.80000	42.43	40.31	....	17.26	a603
84.00000	106.00000	....	15.00000	205.00000	40.97	51.71	....	7.32	a605
80.00000	80.00000	....	24.00000	184.00000	43.48	43.48	....	13.04	a607
17.50000	36.50000	....	4.00000	58.00000	30.17	62.93	....	6.90	102
284.00000	476.00000	....	100.00000	860.00000	33.02	55.35	....	11.63	96
237.00000	503.00000	....	115.00000	855.00000	27.72	58.83	....	13.45	99
339.15000	312.98000	....	130.42000	782.55000	43.34	39.99	....	16.67	98
320.00000	429.00000	....	118.00000	867.00000	36.91	49.48	....	13.61	100
183.50000	246.84000	....	86.06000	516.40000	35.53	47.80	....	16.67	97
184.00000	262.00000	....	50.00000	500.00000	37.60	52.40	....	10.00	96
24.00000	37.50000	....	2.00000	63.50000	37.79	59.06	....	3.15	a602
8.75000	18.00000	....	1.25000	28.00000	31.25	64.29	....	4.46	102
41.00000	30.00000	....	10.00000	81.00000	50.62	37.04	....	12.34	100
15.00000	33.80000	....	4.00000	52.80000	28.41	64.01	....	7.58	.02
335.00000	300.00000	....	90.00000	725.00000	46.21	41.38	....	12.41	104

COST OF PRODUCTION—Continued.

NOTE.—The establishment numbers correspond to those in the table on page 295, Appendix A, showing number of employés and wages, except as noted below. See explanation of table, page 91.

CLOCKS AND WATCHES.

Establishment No.	State.	Description of unit.
108	Illinois	One average watch-movement.
109	Ohio	One average watch-movement.

CLOTHING.

Establishment No.	State.	Description of unit.
a608	Illinois	One suit common all-wool cassimere.
a609	...do	One suit common all-wool cassimere.
a610	...do	One suit common all-wool cassimere.
a611	...do	One suit common all-wool cassimere.
a612	...do	One suit common all-wool cassimere.
a613	Ohio	One suit common all-wool cassimere.
a614	...do	One suit common all-wool cassimere.
a615	...do	One suit common all-wool cassimere.
a608	Illinois	One suit medium all-wool cassimere.
a609	...do	One suit medium all-wool cassimere.
a610	...do	One suit medium all-wool cassimere.
a611	...do	One suit medium all-wool cassimere.
a612	...do	One suit medium all-wool cassimere.
a613	Ohio	One suit medium all-wool cassimere.
a614	...do	One suit medium all-wool cassimere.
a615	...do	One suit medium all-wool cassimere.
a608	Illinois	One suit fine all-wool cassimere.
a609	...do	One suit fine all-wool cassimere.
a610	...do	One suit fine all-wool cassimere.
a611	...do	One suit fine all-wool cassimere.
a612	...do	One suit fine all-wool cassimere.
a613	Ohio	One suit fine all-wool cassimere.
a614	...do	One suit fine all-wool cassimere.
a615	...do	One suit fine all-wool cassimere.
a609	Illinois	One suit union cassimere.
a610	...do	One suit union cassimere.
a611	...do	One suit union cassimere.
a612	...do	One suit union cassimere.
a613	Ohio	One suit union cassimere.
a614	...do	One suit union cassimere.
a615	...do	One suit union cassimere.
a608	Illinois	One suit Middlesex flannel.
a609	...do	One suit Middlesex flannel.
a610	...do	One suit Middlesex flannel.
a611	...do	One suit Middlesex flannel.
a612	...do	One suit Middlesex flannel.
a613	Ohio	One suit Middlesex flannel.
a614	...do	One suit Middlesex flannel.
a616	...do	One suit Middlesex flannel.
a617	...do	One suit Middlesex flannel.
a615	...do	One suit Middlesex flannel.
a618	...do	One suit Middlesex flannel.
a608	Illinois	One suit medium worsted.
a609	...do	One suit medium worsted.
a610	...do	One suit medium worsted.
a611	...do	One suit medium worsted.
a612	...do	One suit medium worsted.
a613	Ohio	One suit medium worsted.
a614	...do	One suit medium worsted.
a615	...do	One suit medium worsted.
a608	Illinois	One suit fine worsted.
a609	...do	One suit fine worsted.
a610	...do	One suit fine worsted.
a611	...do	One suit fine worsted.
a612	...do	One suit fine worsted.
a614	Ohio	One suit fine worsted.
a615	...do	One suit fine worsted.
a618	...do	One suit fine worsted.
a613	...do	One suit fine worsted.
a617	...do	One suit medium Riverside worsted.
a616	Illinois	One suit fine Riverside worsted.
a609	...do	One suit medium satinet.
a610	...do	One suit medium satinet.
a611	...do	One suit medium satinet.
a612	...do	One suit medium satinet.

a The wages of employés in this establishment were not reported. Therefore the number will not be found in the wage table, Appendix A.

VARIATION IN THE COST OF PRODUCTION.

COST OF PRODUCTION—Continued.

NOTE.—The establishment numbers correspond to those in the table on page 295, Appendix A, showing number of employés and wages, except as noted below. See explanation of table, page 91.

CLOCKS AND WATCHES.

Amount of unit cost.					Per cent. of unit cost.				Establishment No.
Labor.	Materials.	Administration.	Other.	Total.	Labor.	Materials.	Administration.	Other.	
$4.16000	$0.93500	....	$0.55000	$5.64500	73.70	16.56	....	9.74	108
4.12000	1.87000	....	1.50000	7.49000	55.01	24.96	....	20.03	109

CLOTHING.

Labor.	Materials.	Administration.	Other.	Total.	Labor.	Materials.	Administration.	Other.	Estab. No.
$2.06000	$6.00000	....	$0.35000	$8.41000	24.50	71.34	....	4.16	a608
2.63000	6.87000	....	.10000	9.60000	27.40	71.56	....	1.04	a609
2.53000	6.87000	....	....	9.40000	26.91	73.09	....	....	a610
2.40000	8.22000	....	....	10.62000	22.60	77.40	....	....	a611
2.02500	7.67000	....	.30000	9.99500	20.26	76.74	....	3.00	a612
1.50000	7.80000	....	.30000	9.60000	15.62	81.25	....	3.13	a613
1.60000	7.65000	....	.59000	9.84000	16.26	77.74	....	6.00	a614
1.62000	7.40000	....	.48000	9.50000	17.05	77.90	....	5.05	a615
2.57500	8.25000	....	.35000	11.17500	23.04	73.83	....	3.13	a0-8
2.65000	9.41000	....	.10000	12.16000	21.79	77.39	....	.82	a609
2.63000	9.25000	....	....	11.88000	22.14	77.86	....	....	a610
2.75000	11.31000	....	....	14.06000	19.56	80.44	....	....	a611
2.45000	10.56000	....	.30000	13.31000	18.40	79.34	....	2.26	a612
1.75000	10.10000	....	.39000	12.24000	14.30	82.51	....	3.19	a613
1.80000	10.10000	....	.84000	12.74000	14.13	79.28	....	6.59	a614
1.69000	9.90000	....	1.05000	12.64000	13.37	78.32	....	8.31	a615
3.80000	15.50000	....	.35000	19.65000	19.34	78.88	....	1.78	a608
3.08000	12.86000	....	.10000	16.04000	19.20	80.18	....	.02	a609
3.10000	12.75000	....	....	15.85000	19.56	80.44	....	....	a610
3.10000	14.94000	....	....	18.04000	17.18	82.82	....	....	a611
2.87500	14.56500	....	.10000	17.54000	16.39	83.04	....	.57	a612
2.55000	13.80000	....	.84000	16.00000	15.01	81.22	....	3.77	a613
2.45000	13.80000	....	1.00000	17.25000	14.20	80.00	....	5.80	a614
2.17000	13.50000	....	1.50000	17.17000	12.64	78.62	....	8.74	a615
1.70000	4.13000	....	.10000	5.93000	28.67	69.64	....	1.69	a609
1.67000	4.13000	....	....	5.80000	28.79	71.21	....	....	a610
1.75000	5.50000	....	....	7.25000	24.14	75.86	....	....	a611
1.47500	4.80000	....	.25000	6.61500	22.30	73.92	....	3.78	a612
1.27000	4.20000	....	.31000	5.78000	21.97	72.67	....	5.36	a613
1.21000	4.30000	....	.22000	5.73000	21.12	75.04	....	3.84	a614
1.35000	4.20000	....	.33000	5.88000	22.96	71.43	....	5.61	a615
2.45000	6.45000	....	.35000	9.25000	26.49	69.73	....	3.78	a608
1.85000	6.42000	....	.20000	8.47000	21.84	75.80	....	2.36	a609
1.73000	6.10000	....	....	7.83000	22.10	77.90	....	....	a610
2.00000	7.45000	....	....	9.45000	21.16	78.84	....	....	a611
1.67500	6.95000	....	.10000	8.72500	19.20	79.66	....	1.14	a612
1.53000	6.45000	....	.21000	8.19000	18.68	78.76	....	2.56	a613
1.50000	6.80000	....	.50000	8.80000	17.05	77.27	....	5.68	a614
1.00000	6.50000	....	.59000	8.09000	18.41	74.80	....	6.79	a616
1.25000	6.05000	....	.29000	7.59000	16.47	79.71	....	3.82	a617
1.00000	6.30000	....	.63000	8.53000	18.76	73.85	....	7.39	a615
1.50000	5.80000	....	.75000	8.05000	18.63	72.05	....	9.32	a618
3.00000	11.25000	....	.35000	14.60000	20.55	77.05	....	2.40	a608
2.53000	6.67000	....	.10000	9.30000	27.20	71.72	....	1.08	a609
2.53000	6.60000	....	....	9.13000	27.71	72.29	....	....	a610
2.40000	8.02000	....	....	10.42000	23.13	76.97	....	....	a611
2.27500	7.77000	....	.25000	10.29500	22.10	75.47	....	2.43	a612
1.80000	6.86000	....	.25000	8.91000	20.20	77.00	....	2.80	a613
1.65000	5.86000	....	.42000	7.93000	20.80	73.90	....	5.30	a614
1.60000	6.88000	....	.68000	9.16000	17.47	75.11	....	7.42	a615
3.80000	14.50000	....	.35000	18.65000	20.38	77.74	....	1.88	a608
3.08000	10.72000	....	.10000	13.90000	22.16	77.13	....	.71	a609
3.08000	10.65000	....	....	13.73000	22.49	77.57	....	....	a610
3.45000	13.44000	....	....	16.89000	20.43	79.57	....	....	a611
3.02500	12.84000	....	0.30000	16.16500	18.71	79.43	....	1.86	a612
2.45000	11.55000	....	1.06000	15.06000	16.27	76.69	....	7.04	a614
2.40000	11.55000	....	1.33000	15.28000	15.71	75.59	....	8.70	a615
2.30000	10.30000	....	1.55000	14.15000	16.25	72.79	....	10.96	a618
2.45000	11.55000	....	.50000	14.50000	16.89	79.66	....	3.45	a613
2.20000	8.00000	....	.50800	10.70000	20.56	74.77	....	4.07	a617
3.00000	11.25000	....	1.09000	15.34000	19.55	73.34	....	7.11	a616
1.35000	2.47500	....	.10000	3.92500	34.39	63.06	....	2.55	a609
1.02000	2.42500	....	....	3.74500	35.24	64.76	....	....	a610
1.30000	3.12500	....	....	4.42500	29.38	70.62	....	....	a611
1.20000	2.75600	....	.20000	4.15500	28.88	66.31	....	4.81	a612

COST OF PRODUCTION—Continued.

NOTE.—The establishment numbers correspond to those in the table on page 295, Appendix A, showing number of employés and wages, except as noted below. See explanation of table, page 91.

CLOTHING—Concluded.

Establishment No.	State.	Description of unit.
a613	Ohio	One suit medium satinet
a614	do	One suit medium satinet
a615	do	One suit medium satinet
a008	Illinois	One suit fine cloth
a617	Ohio	One suit common jeans, wool-filled
a618	do	One suit common jeans, wool-filled
127	Pennsylvania	One yard medium grade jersey cloth
127	do	One medium grade women's jersey
127	do	One medium grade men's jersey coat
127	do	One medium grade women's jersey skirt
127	do	One medium grade jersey polo cap
128	do	One dozen round-crown stiff hats
111	New Jersey	One dozen men's soft felt hats
110	do	One dozen men's soft felt hats
a019	New Hampshire	One dozen women's ribbed hose
a019	do	One dozen girls' ribbed hose
130	Virginia	One dozen cotton knit under-shirts
125	New York	One dozen colored knit cotton under-garments
112	do	One dozen (9 pounds) colored knit cotton under-garments
122	do	One dozen (7.4 pounds) knit cotton under-garments
126	do	One dozen colored knit cotton and wool under-garments
120	do	One dozen colored knit cotton and wool under-garments
116	do	One dozen colored knit cotton and wool under-garments
119	do	One dozen colored knit cotton and wool under-garments
124	do	One dozen colored knit cotton and wool under-garments
121	do	One dozen colored knit cotton and wool under-garments
a620	do	One dozen colored knit cotton and wool under-garments
115	do	One dozen colored knit cotton and wool under-garments
118	do	One dozen (8.5 pounds) knit cotton and wool under-garments
113	do	One dozen (8.5 pounds) knit cotton and wool under-garments
a621	do	One dozen (8.5 pounds) colored knit cotton and wool under-garments
114	do	One dozen (6 pounds) colored knit women's woolen under-garments
123	do	One dozen (8.5 pounds) scarlet knit woolen under-garments
a622	do	One dozen (8 pounds) colored knit woolen under-garments

COAL, COKE, AND ORE.b

Establishment No.	State.	Description of unit.
a671	Ohio (Tuscarawas Valley district).	One ton (2,000 pounds) bituminous lump coal
a672	do	One ton (2,000 pounds) bituminous lump coal
a673	do	One ton (2,000 pounds) bituminous lump coal
142	do	One ton (2,000 pounds) bituminous lump coal
141	do	One ton (2,000 pounds) bituminous lump coal
140	do	One ton (2,000 pounds) bituminous lump coal
146	Ohio (Hocking Valley district).	One ton (2,000 pounds) bituminous lump coal
147	do	One ton (2,000 pounds) bituminous lump coal
a674	do	One ton (2,000 pounds) bituminous lump coal
146	do	One ton (2,000 pounds) bituminous lump coal
148	do	One ton (2,000 pounds) bituminous lump coal
149	do	One ton (2,000 pounds) bituminous lump coal
a675	Ohio (Connotton Valley district).	One ton (2,000 pounds) bituminous lump coal
a676	do	One ton (2,000 pounds) bituminous lump coal
a677	Ohio (Jackson County district).	One ton (2,000 pounds) bituminous lump coal
a678	do	One ton (2,000 pounds) bituminous lump coal
143	do	One ton (2,000 pounds) bituminous lump coal
a679	do	One ton (2,000 pounds) bituminous lump coal
a680	do	One ton (2,000 pounds) bituminous lump coal
a681	do	One ton (2,000 pounds) bituminous lump coal
144	do	One ton (2,000 pounds) bituminous lump coal
a082	do	One ton (2,000 pounds) bituminous lump coal
a683	do	One ton (2,000 pounds) bituminous lump coal
a684	do	One ton (2,000 pounds) bituminous lump coal

a The wages of employés in this establishment were not reported; therefore the number will not be found in the wage table, Appendix A.

b In Ohio and West Virginia the value of the screenings has been deducted to arrive at the net cost of a ton of coal. This deduction has been made in the column headed Other. The royalty, or amount paid to the owners of the land for the privilege of mining, varying from 5 to 40 cents per ton, is included, in all states, in the column headed Other.

VARIATION IN THE COST OF PRODUCTION.

COST OF PRODUCTION—Continued.

NOTE.—The establishment numbers correspond to those in the table on page 295, Appendix A, showing number of employés and wages, except as noted below. See explanation of table, page 91.

CLOTHING—Concluded.

Amount of unit cost.					Per cent. of unit cost.				Establishment No.
Labor.	Materials.	Administration.	Other.	Total.	Labor.	Materials.	Administration.	Other.	
$1.11000	$2.50000	....	$0.25000	$3.86000	28.76	64.76	....	6.48	a613
.95000	2.70000	....	.15000	3.80000	25.00	71.05	....	3.95	a614
1.18000	2.40000	....	.09000	3.67000	32.15	65.40	....	2.45	a615
5.75000	20.50000	....	.35000	26.60000	21.62	77.07	....	1.31	a009
.85000	2.48000	....	.02000	3.35000	25.37	74.03	....	.60	a617
1.30000	2.75000	....	.26000	4.31000	30.10	63.81	....	6.03	a618
.11306	.50780	....	.06004	.08240	16.66	74.41	....	8.93	127
.07120	.54310	$0.06250	.00800	.68480	10.39	79.31	9.13	1.17	127
1.01250	1.57500	....	.25800	2.84550	35.58	55.35	....	9.07	127
.10000	1.01400	....	.13200	1.24600	8.02	81.39	....	10.59	127
.01330	.05000	....	.01000	.07330	18.14	68.21	....	13.65	127
7.00000	9.00000	....	3.00000	19.00000	36.84	47.37	....	15.79	128
7.00000	7.00000	....	....	14.00000	50.00	50.00	....	....	111
6.75000	8.75000	....	....	15.50000	43.55	56.45	....	....	110
.80000	1.80000	....	.50000	3.10000	25.81	58.06	....	16.13	a619
.70000	1.05000	....	.30000	2.05000	34.15	51.22	....	14.63	a619
.53000	1.11800	.16600	.04000	1.85400	28.59	60.30	8.95	2.16	130
.76900	1.34050	....	.11210	2.22160	34.61	60.34	....	5.05	125
.90830	1.70140	....	.44430	3.14400	31.75	54.12	....	14.13	112
.44462	.92300	.04600	.15039	1.57301	28.26	58.08	2.92	10.14	122
1.17200	1.82430	....	.55210	3.54840	33.03	51.41	....	15.56	126
1.33290	1.59170	....	.21020	3.13480	42.52	50.77	....	6.71	120
1.49600	1.82000	....	.44700	3.76300	39.76	48.36	....	11.88	116
1.35010	2.15650	....	.45160	3.96720	34.26	54.35	....	11.39	119
1.21712	1.75840	....	.27850	3.25402	37.40	54.04	....	8.56	124
1.14410	1.93000	.31700	.44000	3.83110	29.86	50.38	8.27	11.49	121
1.61110	1.20000	.12310	.27650	3.21070	50.18	37.37	3.84	8.61	a620
1.55080	1.35000	.13400	.30590	3.34070	46.42	40.41	4.01	9.16	115
1.34290	1.72600	....	.44000	3.50890	38.27	49.19	....	12.54	118
1.22960	1.52420	....	.55090	3.30470	37.21	46.12	....	16.67	113
.99800	1.92300	....	.60060	3.51960	28.30	54.64	....	17.06	a621
1.02150	1.89550	....	.22000	3.14600	32.47	60.25	....	7.28	114
.92700	1.74000	....	.31670	2.98370	31.07	58.31	....	10.62	123
1.15240	2.34810	....	.41590	3.91640	29.42	59.96	....	10.62	a622

COAL, COKE, AND ORE. b

Labor.	Materials.	Administration.	Other.	Total.	Labor.	Materials.	Administration.	Other.	Establishment No.
c$0.75000	....	....	$0.49000	$1.24000	60.48	....	....	39.52	a671
c.75000	....	....	.45500	1.20500	62.24	....	....	37.76	a672
c.75000	....	....	.64000	1.39000	53.96	....	....	46.04	a673
c.75000	....	....	.39000	1.14000	65.79	....	....	34.21	142
c.75000	....	....	.46000	1.21000	61.98	....	....	38.02	141
c.75000	....	....	.49000	1.24000	60.48	....	....	39.52	140
.78330	....	$0.04960	.06960	.90750	88.86	....	5.47	7.67	146
.64000	....	.06750	.03000	.73750	86.78	....	9.15	4.07	147
.66410	....	.08480	.09500	.84390	78.69	....	10.05	11.26	a674
d1.01050	....	.04280	.07110	1.12440	89.87	....	3.81	6.32	146
d.03030	....	.04000	.05730	1.03450	89.93	....	4.53	5.54	148
d.91240	....	.03260	.09800	1.04300	87.48	....	3.13	9.39	149
.79000	....	....	.05000	.84000	94.05	....	....	5.95	a675
.79000	....	(e)	....	.79000	....	....	....	....	a676
c.50000	....	....	.44500	.94500	52.91	....	....	47.09	a677
e.50000	....	....	.31500	.81500	61.35	....	....	38.65	a678
c.50000	....	....	.26000	.76000	65.79	....	....	34.21	143
c.50000	....	....	.32000	.82000	60.98	....	....	39.02	a679
c.55000	....	....	.31500	.86500	63.58	....	....	36.42	a680
c.55000	....	....	.33500	.88500	62.15	....	....	37.85	a681
c.55000	....	....	.36000	.91000	60.44	....	....	39.56	144
c.55000	....	....	.28000	.83000	66.26	....	....	33.74	a682
b.55000	....	....	.28500	.83500	65.87	....	....	34.13	a683
b.55000	....	....	.39500	.89500	55.87	....	....	44.13	a684

c Mining only; other labor aside from mining included in column headed Other.
d Production for 1883 when the price of mining averaged 75 cents per ton (1885, 50 cents per ton).
e The value of the screenings equal the "other" expenses.

102 REPORT OF THE COMMISSIONER OF LABOR.

COST OF PRODUCTION—Continued.

NOTE.—The establishment numbers correspond to those in the table on page 295, Appendix A, showing number of employés and wages, except as noted below. See explanation of table, page 91.

COAL, COKE, AND ORE—Concluded.

Establishment No.	State.	Description of unit.
a685	Ohio (Jackson County district).	One ton (2,000 pounds) bituminous lump coal
150	Ohio (Sunday Creek Valley district).	One ton (2,000 pounds) bituminous lump coal
a686	...do	One ton (2,000 pounds) bituminous lump coal
a687	...do	One ton (2,000 pounds) bituminous lump coal
a688	...do	One ton (2,000 pounds) bituminous lump coal
a689	Pennsylvania (Pittsburg district).	One ton (2,000 pounds) bituminous lump coal
151	...do	One ton (2,000 pounds) bituminous lump coal
152	...do	One ton (2,000 pounds) bituminous lump coal
135	Maryland (Cumberland district).	One ton (2,240 pounds) run of mine bituminous coal
136	...do	One ton (2,240 pounds) run of mine bituminous coal
137	...do	One ton (2,240 pounds) run of mine bituminous coal
a690	Ohio (Mahoning Valley district).	One ton (2,000 pounds) run of mine bituminous coal
a691	Ohio (Ohio River district).	One ton (2,000 pounds) run of mine bituminous coal
a692	...do	One ton (2,000 pounds) run of mine bituminous coal
a693	Ohio (Bellaire district)	One ton (2,000 pounds) run of mine bituminous coal
a694	West Virginia (Ohio River district).	One ton (2,000 pounds) run of mine bituminous coal
161	...do	One ton (2,000 pounds) run of mine bituminous coal
a695	West Virginia (Wheeling district).	One ton (2,000 pounds) run of mine bituminous coal
a696	...do	One ton (2,000 pounds) run of mine bituminous coal
131	Great Britain	One ton run of mine bituminous coal
a697	Alabama	One ton (2,240 pounds) run of mine bituminous coking coal
153	Pennsylvania (Connellsville district).	One ton (2,000 pounds) run of mine bituminous coking coal
a698	...do	One ton (2,000 pounds) run of mine bituminous coking coal
159	West Virginia (New River district).	One ton (2,240 pounds) run of mine bituminous coking coal
a699	...do	One ton (2,240 pounds) run of mine bituminous coking coal
158	...do	One ton (2,240 pounds) run of mine bituminous coking coal
160	...do	One ton (2,240 pounds) run of mine bituminous coking coal
165	Virginia	One ton (2,240 pounds) block, lump coal
133	Indiana (Clay County district).	One ton (2,000 pounds) block, lump coal
134	Indiana (Evansville district).	One ton (2,000 pounds) block, lump coal
a700	Ohio (Mahoning Valley district).	One ton (2,000 pounds) block, lump coal
a701	...do	One ton (2,000 pounds) block, lump coal
a702	...do	One ton (2,000 pounds) block, lump coal
a703	...do	One ton (2,000 pounds) block, lump coal
a704	West Virginia (Kanawha Valley district).	One ton (2,240 pounds) gas coal
162	...do	One ton (2,240 pounds) gas coal
a705	...do	One ton (2,240 pounds) gas coal
163	...do	One ton (2,240 pounds) gas coal
164	...do	One ton (2,240 pounds) splint coal
165	...do	One ton (2,240 pounds) splint coal
a706	...do	One ton (2,240 pounds) splint coal
a707	...do	One ton (2,240 pounds) splint coal
a708	Germany	One thousand kilograms (2,205 pounds) coal
a709	...do	One thousand kilograms (2,205 pounds) coal
a710	Alabama	One ton (2,240 pounds) coke
153	Pennsylvania (Connellsville district).	One ton (2,000 pounds) coke
154	...do	One ton (2,000 pounds) coke
a711	West Virginia (New River district).	One ton (2,240 pounds) coke
a712	...do	One ton (2,240 pounds) coke
166	...do	One ton (2,240 pounds) coke
a713	Virginia	One ton (2,240 pounds) coke
139	Missouri	One ton iron ore
157	Virginia	One ton iron ore
156	...do	One ton iron ore
132	Great Britain	One ton iron ore (yielding 28 per cent.)

a The wages of employés in this establishment were not reported; therefore the number will not be found in the wage table, Appendix A.

VARIATION IN THE COST OF PRODUCTION.

COST OF PRODUCTION—Continued.

NOTE.—The establishment numbers correspond to those in the table on page 296, Appendix A, showing number of employés and wages, except as noted below. See explanation of table, page 91.

COAL, COKE, AND ORE—Concluded.

Amount of unit cost.					Per cent. of unit cost.				Establishment No.
Labor.	Materials.	Administration.	Other.	Total.	Labor.	Materials.	Administration.	Other.	
b. 50000	....	....	.30500	.80500	62.11	....	....	37.89	a685
c1.06500	....	....	.06700	1.13200	94.08	....	....	5.92	150
b. 40000	....	....	.24000	.64000	62.50	....	....	37.50	a686
b. 40000	....	....	.26000	.66000	60.60	....	....	39.40	a687
b. 40000	....	....	.22000	.62000	64.52	....	....	35.48	a688
b. 72400	....	....	.46100	1.18500	61.10	....	....	38.90	a689
.91500	....	....	.19500	1.11000	82.43	....	....	17.57	151
.89500	....	....	.23250	1.12750	79.38	....	....	20.62	152
.50000	....	$0.07000	.29000	.86000	58.14	....	8.14	33.72	135
.47000	....	.06000	.29000	.82000	57.31	....	7.32	35.37	136
.51000	....	.08000	.29000	.88000	59.30	....	6.98	33.72	137
.57000	....	....	.47500	1.04500	54.55	....	....	45.45	a690
b. 40000	....	....	.47500	.87500	45.71	....	....	54.29	a691
b. 40000	....	....	.37500	.77500	51.61	....	....	48.39	a692
b. 50000	....	....	.42500	.92500	54.05	....	....	45.95	a693
b. 40000	....	....	.41250	.81250	49.23	....	....	50.77	a694
b. 40000	....	....	.35000	.75000	53.33	....	....	46.67	161
b. 50000	....	....	.37500	.87500	57.14	....	....	42.86	a695
b. 50000	....	....	.50000	1.00000	50.00	....	....	50.00	a696
.67728	....	....	.19800	.87528	77.38	....	....	22.62	131
.74000	....	....	.20000	.94000	78.72	....	....	21.28	a697
.38450	....	....	.09000	.47450	81.03	....	....	18.97	153
.39400	....	....	.10300	.49700	79.28	....	....	20.72	a698
b. 40000	....	....	.35000	.75000	53.33	....	....	46.67	159
b. 40000	....	....	.40000	.80000	50.00	....	....	50.00	a699
b. 40000	....	....	.40000	.80000	50.00	....	....	50.00	158
b. 40000	....	....	.50000	.90000	44.44	....	....	55.56	100
1.36800	....	.15000	.20000	1.71800	79.62	....	8.73	11.65	155
1.05000	....	....	.15000	1.20000	87.50	....	....	12.50	133
.95000	....	.20000	.15250	1.30250	72.98	....	15.36	11.71	134
b. 75000	....	....	.87000	1.62000	46.30	....	....	53.70	a700
1.24000	....	.03500	.25000	1.52500	81.31	....	2.30	16.39	a701
1.33000	....	.05000	.19000	1.57000	84.71	....	3.19	12.10	a702
b. 68000	....	....	.88500	1.56500	43.45	....	....	56.55	a703
b. 55000	....	....	.44000	.99000	56.00	....	....	44.00	a704
b. 56000	....	....	.40000	.96000	58.33	....	....	41.67	162
b. 56000	....	....	.41000	.97000	57.73	....	....	42.27	a705
b. 56000	....	....	.44000	1.00000	56.00	....	....	44.00	163
b. 62500	....	....	.22500	.85000	73.53	....	....	26.47	164
b. 62500	....	....	.35000	.97500	64.10	....	....	35.90	165
b. 62500	....	....	.20000	.82500	75.76	....	....	24.24	a706
b. 62500	....	....	.35000	.97500	64.10	....	....	35.90	a707
.63200	....	....	.41200	1.04400	60.54	....	....	39.46	a708
.75000	....	.16000	.44000	1.35000	55.56	....	11.85	32.59	a709
.56000	$1.57000	....	.17000	2.30000	24.35	68.26	....	7.39	a710
.34680	.63260	.03000	.07000	1.07940	32.13	58.60	2.78	6.49	153
.31200	.66200	.03000	.08800	1.09200	28.57	60.62	2.75	8.06	154
.40000	1.42500	....	.10000	1.92500	20.78	74.03	....	5.19	a711
.39000	1.39500	....	.20000	1.98500	19.65	70.28	....	10.07	a712
.60000	1.20000	....	.10000	1.90000	31.58	63.16	....	5.26	166
.29000	2.58000	....	....	2.87000	10.10	89.90	....	....	a713
.83140	....	....	1.29280	2.12420	39.14	....	....	60.86	139
.65000	....	.10000	.50000	1.25000	52.00	....	8.00	40.00	157
1.22250	....	.15000	.61000	1.98250	61.66	....	7.56	30.78	156
.20126	....	....	.12000	.32126	62.65	....	....	37.35	132

b Mining only; other labor aside from mining included in column headed Other.
c Production for 1886 when the price of mining averaged 80 cents per ton (1885, 40 cents per ton).

COST OF PRODUCTION—Continued.

NOTE.—The establishment numbers correspond to those in the table on page 295, Appendix A, showing number of employés and wages, except as noted below. See explanation of table, page 91.

COOKING AND HEATING APPARATUS.

Establishment No.	State.	Description of unit.
175	Illinois	One square cooking range (base outside, oven shelves, back extension, shelf at top, cut feed, tin-lined oven doors, nickel trimmings and panels, polished edges, cast-iron ash-pan, and nickel towel-rack, weighing 260 pounds).
175	...do	One cooking range (low closet, incased enameled reservoir, cut feed, tin-lined oven doors, nickel trimmings and panels, polished edges, and nickel towel-rack, weighing 300 pounds).
175	...do	One cooking range (incased enameled reservoir and base, cut feed, tin-lined oven doors oven shelves, nickel panels and trimmings, polished edges, and nickel towel-rack, weighing 300 pounds).
176	Kentucky	One cooking stove (four holes, and weighing 326 pounds).
176	...do	One cooking stove (medium grade, four hole, No. 7, weighing 258 pounds).
176	...do	One cooking stove (common, four hole, No. 7, weighing 175 pounds).
176	...do	One cooking stove (common, four hole, No. 6, weighing 135 pounds).
178	Michigan	One cooking stove (first class, full trimmed, weighing 360 pounds).
178	...do	One cooking stove (medium grade, weighing 300 pounds).
190	Pennsylvania	One cooking stove (weighing 250 pounds).
175	Illinois	One base-burning heating stove (nickel railings, highly polished edges, and brass urn).
178	Michigan	One base-burning heating stove (first class, nickel trimmings, and weighing 390 pounds).
178	...do	One base-burning heating stove (weighing 305 pounds).
175	Illinois	One common heating stove (sliding door, grate, register, and foot rails)
a623	...do	One ton first-class, light base-burning heating stoves.
185	Ohio	One ton first-class heating stoves.
a624	...do	One ton first-class heating stoves.
188	...do	One ton first-class heating stoves.
184	...do	One ton first-class heating stoves.
189	...do	One ton first-class heating stoves.
191	West Virginia	One ton common heating stoves.
172	Illinois	One ton medium grade, light heating stoves.
a625	...do	One ton heating stoves.
186	Ohio	One ton heating stoves.
179	New York	One ton first-class cooking and heating stoves.
180	...do	One ton first-class cooking and heating stoves.
181	...do	One ton first-class cooking and heating stoves.
183	...do	One ton first-class cooking and heating stoves.
182	...do	One ton first-class cooking and heating stoves.
a626	Ohio	One ton first-class cooking and heating stoves.
167	Illinois	One ton medium grade cooking and heating stoves.
171	...do	One ton, run of foundery, light cooking and heating stoves.
169	...do	One ton, run of foundery, cooking and heating stoves.
173	...do	One ton cooking and heating stoves.
174	...do	One ton cooking and heating stoves.
168	...do	One ton cooking and heating stoves.
170	...do	One ton cooking and heating stoves.
187	Ohio	One ton cooking and heating stoves.
a623	Illinois	One ton first-class cooking stoves.
185	Ohio	One ton first-class cooking stoves.
a624	...do	One ton first-class cooking stoves.
188	...do	One ton first-class cooking stoves.
a627	...do	One ton first-class cooking stoves.
191	West Virginia	One ton first-class cooking stoves.
189	Ohio	One ton medium grade cooking stoves.
a628	...do	One ton common cooking stoves.
a625	Illinois	One ton cooking stoves.
186	Ohio	One ton cooking stoves.

COTTON GOODS.

a629	France	One yard sheeting (31¼ inches wide, 56 by 64, measuring 2.58 yards to the pound).
a629	...do	One yard sheeting (31¼ inches wide, 64 by 64, measuring 3.125 yards to the pound).
a630	Georgia	One yard sheeting (36 inches wide, 40 by 40, measuring 3.24 yards to the pound).
a630	...do	One yard sheeting (36 inches wide, 44 by 42, measuring 2.21 yards to the pound).

a The wages of employés in this establishment were not reported; therefore the number will not be found in the wage table, Appendix A.

VARIATION IN THE COST OF PRODUCTION.

COST OF PRODUCTION—Continued.

NOTE.—The establishment numbers correspond to those in the table on page 295, Appendix A, showing number of employés and wages, except as noted below. See explanation of table, page 91.

COOKING AND HEATING APPARATUS.

Amount of unit cost.					Per cent. of unit cost.				Establishment No.
Labor.	Materials.	Administration.	Other.	Total.	Labor.	Materials.	Administration.	Other.	
$3.70000	$3.60000	....	$1.80000	$9.10000	40.66	39.56	....	19.78	175
5.24000	5.50000	....	2.00000	12.74000	41.13	43.17	....	15.70	175
5.50000	6.50000	....	2.00000	14.00000	39.29	46.42	....	14.29	175
3.89000	3.74000	....	1.63000	9.26000	42.01	40.39	....	17.60	176
2.58000	2.96000	....	1.29000	6.83000	37.78	43.34	....	18.88	176
1.38000	1.80000	....	.87000	4.05000	34.07	44.45	....	21.48	176
1.20000	1.40000	....	.67000	3.27000	36.70	42.81	....	20.49	176
4.36000	5.56000	....	2.04000	11.96000	36.45	46.49	....	17.06	178
3.98000	4.72000	....	1.77000	10.47000	38.01	45.08	....	16.91	178
4.05000	4.63000	$1.43000	.85000	10.96000	36.95	42.24	13.05	7.76	190
4.44000	4.70000	....	1.60000	10.74000	41.34	43.76	....	14.90	175
6.74000	11.55000	....	3.74000	22.03000	30.59	52.43	....	16.98	178
5.12000	6.69000	....	2.41000	14.22000	36.00	47.05	....	16.95	178
2.25000	2.65000	....	1.40000	6.30000	35.71	42.07	....	22.22	175
56.40000	33.60000	....	30.00000	120.00000	47.00	28.00	....	25.00	a623
30.50000	33.50000	....	26.00000	90.00000	33.02	34.00	....	27.08	185
37.50000	36.00000	....	25.50000	99.00000	37.88	36.86	....	25.76	a624
33.00000	28.00000	....	29.00000	90.00000	36.67	31.11	....	32.22	188
35.00000	38.00000	....	22.00000	95.00000	36.84	40.00	....	23.16	184
31.00000	36.50000	....	13.80000	81.36000	38.10	44.86	....	17.04	189
30.00000	23.00000	....	18.00000	71.00000	42.26	32.39	....	25.35	101
42.00000	30.00000	....	18.00000	90.00000	46.67	33.33	....	20.00	172
36.02000	34.60000	....	13.85000	85.07000	43.04	40.08	....	16.28	a625
49.50000	24.50000	....	6.00000	80.00000	61.87	30.63	....	7.50	186
43.29684	29.00000	6.54000	3.38808	82.22492	52.66	35.27	7.95	4.12	179
42.00000	25.50000	4.63304	2.88000	75.01304	55.99	33.99	6.19	3.83	180
36.28131	30.00000	3.06000	5.70000	75.04131	48.36	39.98	4.08	7.58	181
53.31465	....	4.91303	2.95233	61.18001	87.14	....	8.03	4.83	183
42.14340	....	....	4.88351	47.02691	89.62	....	....	10.38	182
40.00000	40.00000	....	20.00000	100.00000	40.00	40.00	....	20.00	a626
30.00000	20.00000	....	20.00000	70.00000	42.86	28.57	....	28.57	167
20.00000	18.50000	....	12.00000	50.50000	39.61	36.63	....	23.76	171
46.00000	40.00000	....	24.00000	110.00000	41.82	36.36	....	21.82	169
35.00000	25.00000	7.00000	15.00000	82.00000	42.68	30.49	8.54	18.29	173
30.00000	30.00000	....	19.00000	79.00000	37.97	37.97	....	24.06	174
37.00000	30.00000	....	12.00000	79.00000	46.84	37.97	....	15.19	168
37.00000	27.00000	....	26.00000	90.00000	41.11	30.00	....	28.89	170
35.00000	31.65000	....	8.15000	74.80000	46.79	42.31	....	10.90	187
33.50000	34.00000	....	22.50000	90.00000	37.22	37.78	....	25.00	a623
31.50000	29.00000	....	26.00000	80.50000	36.42	33.53	....	30.05	185
34.50000	29.00000	....	25.50000	89.00000	38.76	32.59	....	28.65	a624
33.00000	27.00000	....	29.00000	89.00000	37.08	30.34	....	32.58	188
30.00000	29.00000	....	22.00000	81.00000	37.04	35.80	....	27.16	a627
35.00000	26.00000	....	19.00000	80.00000	43.75	32.50	....	23.75	101
31.00000	31.00000	....	8.06000	70.06000	44.25	44.25	....	11.50	189
24.00000	17.80000	....	11.80000	53.60000	44.78	33.21	....	22.01	a628
31.36000	29.35000	....	12.10000	72.81000	43.07	40.31	....	16.62	a625
40.34000	24.50000	....	6.00000	70.84000	56.95	34.59	....	8.46	186

COTTON GOODS.

Labor.	Materials.	Administration.	Other.	Total.	Labor.	Materials.	Administration.	Other.	Estab. No.
$0.00950	$0.04801	....	$0.00847	$0.06598	14.40	72.76	....	12.84	a629
.00950	.05346	....	.00847	.07143	13.30	74.84	....	11.86	a629
.00354	.03581	$0.00044	.00415	.04004	17.62	73.02	.90	8.46	a630
.01266	.05248	.00065	.00605	.07184	17.62	73.05	.91	8.42	a630

b Not including material.

COST OF PRODUCTION—Continued.

NOTE.—The establishment numbers correspond to those in the table on page 295, Appendix A, showing number of employés and wages, except as noted below. See explanation of table, page 91.

COTTON GOODS—Continued.

Establishment No.	State.	Description of unit.
a630	Georgia	One yard sheeting (36 inches wide, 44 by 42, measuring 3.08 yards to the pound).
234	New York	One yard sheeting (36 inches wide, 44 by 48, measuring 4.5 yards to the pound).
248	Virginia	One yard sheeting (36 inches wide, 44 by 48, measuring 4.08 yards to the pound).
247	...do	One yard sheeting (36 inches wide, 44 by 48, measuring 4.08 yards to the pound).
241	South Carolina	One yard sheeting (36 inches wide, 48 by 44, measuring 2.99 yards to the pound).
244	...do	One yard sheeting (36 inches wide, 48 by 44, measuring 3.01 yards to the pound).
246	Virginia	One yard sheeting (36 inches wide, 44 by 44, measuring 4 yards to the pound).
244	South Carolina	One yard sheeting (36 inches wide, 48 by 40, measuring 3.12 yards to the pound).
237	North Carolina	One yard sheeting (36 inches wide, 46 by 46, measuring 4.5 yards to the pound).
199	Georgia	One yard sheeting (36 inches wide, 50 by 50, measuring 4.01 yards to the pound).
199	...do	One yard sheeting (36 inches wide, 50 by 50, measuring 3.6 yards to the pound).
a631	Maine	One yard sheeting (36 inches wide, 52 by 52, measuring 3.93 yards to the pound).
a629	France	One yard sheeting (36 inches wide, 56 by 64, measuring 3.86 yards to the pound).
a630	Georgia	One yard sheeting (40 inches wide, 48 by 48, measuring 2.40 yards to the pound).
a630	...do	One yard sheeting (40 inches wide, 56 by 56, measuring 3.18 yards to the pound).
231	New York	One yard sheeting (40½ inches wide, 88 by 96, measuring 2.88 yards to the pound).
230	...do	One yard sheeting (36 inches wide, No. 22 yarn, measuring 3.6 yards to the pound).
230	...do	One yard sheeting (39 inches wide, No. 22 yarn, measuring 3.33 yards to the pound).
230	...do	One yard sheeting (40 inches wide, No. 31 yarn, measuring 3 yards to the pound).
230	...do	One yard sheeting (48 inches wide, No. 22 yarn, measuring 2.777 yards to the pound).
230	...do	One yard sheeting (58 inches wide, No. 22 yarn, measuring 2.5 yards to the pound).
230	...do	One yard sheeting (77 inches wide, No. 22 yarn, measuring 1.75 yards to the pound).
230	...do	One yard sheeting (86 inches wide, No. 22 yarn, measuring 1.538 yards to the pound).
230	...do	One yard sheeting (96 inches wide, No. 22 yarn, measuring 1.35 yards to the pound).
a632	Alabama	One yard sheeting (36 inches wide, measuring 3.29 yards to the pound)
a632	...do	One yard sheeting (31¼ inches wide, measuring 3.31 yards to the pound)
a633	Georgia	One yard sheeting (36 inches wide, measuring 3.75 yards to the pound)
a633	...do	One yard sheeting (36 inches wide, measuring 3.4 yards to the pound)
207	Maine	One yard sheeting (40 inches wide, measuring 3.80 yards to the pound)
211	Maryland	One yard sheeting (36 inches wide, measuring 2.84 yards to the pound)
214	Massachusetts	One yard sheeting (36 inches wide, measuring 2.84 yards to the pound)
218	...do	One yard sheeting (40 inches wide, measuring 3.5 yards to the pound)
215	...do	One yard sheeting (40 inches wide, measuring 3.5 yards to the pound)
217	...do	One yard sheeting (40 inches wide, measuring 3.5 yards to the pound)
216	...do	One yard sheeting (40 inches wide, measuring 3.5 yards to the pound)
226	New Hampshire	One yard sheeting (36 inches wide, measuring 2.85 yards to the pound)
a634	South Carolina	One yard sheeting (36 inches wide, measuring 2.85 yards to the pound)
238	North Carolina	One yard sheeting (36 inches wide, measuring 3 yards to the pound)
a635	South Carolina	One yard sheeting (36 inches wide, measuring 3 yards to the pound)
a634	...do	One yard sheeting (36 inches wide, measuring 4 yards to the pound)
193	Connecticut	One yard print cloth (28 inches wide, 64 by 64, measuring 7 yards to the pound.
a631	Maine	One yard print cloth (28 inches wide, 64 by 64, measuring 7 yards to the pound.
a636	...do	One yard print cloth (28 inches wide, 64 by 64, measuring 7 yards to the pound.

a The wages of employés in this establishment were not reported; therefore the number will not be found in the wage table, Appendix A.

VARIATION IN THE COST OF PRODUCTION.

COST OF PRODUCTION—Continued.

NOTE.—The establishment numbers correspond to those in the table on page 295, Appendix A, showing number of employés and wages, except as noted below. See explanation of table, page 91.

COTTON GOODS—Continued.

Amount of unit cost.					Per cent. of unit cost.				Establishment No.
Labor.	Materials.	Administration.	Other.	Total.	Labor.	Materials.	Administration.	Other.	
$0.00909	$0.03770	$0.00046	$0.00427	$0.05152	17.65	73.17	.89	8.29	a636
.00914	.02644	.00088	.00565	.04211	21.71	62.79	2.09	13.41	234
.00853	.02801	.00124	.00445	.04223	20.19	64.23	2.94	10.54	248
.00642	.02893	.00124	.00291	.04150	20.29	69.71	2.99	7.01	247
.00989	.03981	.00087	.00470	.05527	17.89	72.03	1.57	8.51	244
.00979	.03954	.00087	.00466	.05486	17.85	72.07	1.59	8.49	244
.00954	.03090	....	.00759	.04803	19.86	64.33	....	15.81	246
.00949	.03814	.00084	.00449	.05296	17.92	72.02	1.58	8.48	244
b .01690	.02460	.00290	.00580	.05020	33.67	49.00	5.78	11.55	237
.00755	.03109	.00072	.00305	.04241	17.80	73.81	1.70	7.19	199
.00933	.03463	.00080	.00340	.04816	19.37	71.91	1.66	7.06	199
.01320	.03522	....	.00145	.04997	26.42	70.68	....	2.90	a631
.90831	.04574	....	.00741	.06146	13.52	74.42	....	12.06	a629
.01126	.04667	.00057	.00541	.06391	17.62	73.02	.89	8.47	a630
.00882	.03659	.00045	.00423	.05009	17.60	73.06	.90	8.44	a630
.03434	.04630	.00220	.00350	.08634	39.77	53.63	2.55	4.05	231
.01945	.03490	.00108	.00908	.06451	30.15	54.10	1.67	14.08	230
.02100	.03770	.00110	.00980	.06960	30.17	54.17	1.58	14.08	230
.02600	.04660	.00130	.01210	.08600	30.23	54.19	1.51	14.07	230
.02520	.04524	.00132	.01176	.08352	30.17	54.17	1.58	14.08	230
.02800	.05026	.00146	.01307	.09279	30.18	54.16	1.57	14.09	230
.04000	.07180	.00209	.01867	.13256	30.18	54.16	1.58	14.08	230
.04550	.08168	.00283	.02123	.15124	30.09	54.00	1.87	14.04	230
.05180	.09299	.00271	.02417	.17167	30.17	54.17	1.58	14.08	230
.01114	.03587	.00074	.00271	.05046	22.08	71.08	1.47	5.37	a632
.01049	.03575	.00073	.00270	.04967	21.12	71.97	1.47	5.44	a632
.00613	.02925	.00104	.00294	.05936	15.58	74.31	2.64	7.47	a633
.00676	.03285	.00114	.00324	.04399	15.37	74.68	2.59	7.36	a633
.02010	.03390	....	.00740	.06140	32.74	55.21	....	12.05	297
.01610	.04094	.00500	.00106	.06340	25.87	64.57	7.89	1.67	211
.01206	.04317	....	.00614	.06227	20.81	69.33	....	9.86	214
.02474	.03969	....	.00462	.06905	35.83	57.48	....	6.69	218
.02229	.03820	....	.00314	.06363	35.03	60.03	....	4.94	215
.02497	.04043	....	.00318	.06858	36.41	58.95	....	4.64	217
.02572	.03963	....	.00449	.06984	36.83	56.74	....	6.43	216
.01269	.04300	.00046	.00300	.05915	21.45	72.70	.78	5.07	226
.00816	.04010	....	.00275	.05101	16.00	78.61	....	5.39	a634
.00937	.04101	.00096	.00414	.05548	16.89	73.92	1.73	7.46	238
.00794	.04132	....	.00255	.05181	15.33	79.75	....	4.92	a635
.00883	.02868	....	.0`414	.04165	21.20	68.86	....	9.94	a634
.00972	.01929	.00130	.00381	.03412	28.49	56.53	3.81	11.17	193
.00960	.02010	....	.00110	.03080	31.17	65.26	....	3.57	a631
.01110	.01740	....	.00150	.03000	37.00	58.00	....	5.09	a636

b The high labor cost of a yard of sheeting in this establishment is due to the fact that the mill is a new one which had been in operation only two months when visited by the agent of the Bureau, and the efficiency of the employés is less, therefore, than in those long established.

COST OF PRODUCTION—Continued.

NOTE.—The establishment numbers correspond to those in the table on page 295, Appendix A, showing number of employés and wages, except as noted below. See explanation of table, page 91.

COTTON GOODS—Continued.

Establishment No.	State.	Description of unit.
219	Massachusetts	One yard print cloth (28 inches wide, 64 by 64, measuring 7 yards to the pound.
220	....do	One yard print cloth (28 inches wide, 64 by 64, measuring 7 yards to the pound.
227	New Hampshire	One yard print cloth (28 inches wide, 64 by 64, measuring 7 yards to the pound.
245	Vermont	One yard print cloth (28 inches wide, 56 by 60, measuring 8 yards to the pound).
227	New Hampshire	One yard print cloth (30 inches wide, 68 by 72, measuring 6 yards to the pound).
201	Great Britain	One yard print cloth (32 inches wide, 64 by 64, measuring 8 yards to the pound).
227	New Hampshire	One yard print cloth (35 inches wide, 68 by 72, measuring 5 yards to the pound).
a637	Georgia	One yard shirting (30 inches wide, measuring 5.099 yards to the pound.
a633	..do	One yard shirting (31½ inches wide, measuring 4.6 yards to the pound.
a635	South Carolina	One yard shirting (31½ inches wide, measuring 3.61 yards to the pound.
233	New York	One yard shirting (30 inches wide, 88 by 96, measuring 3.02 yards to the pound).
208	Maine	One yard shirting (40 inches wide, number 32 yarn, measuring 3.36 yards to the pound).
a637	Georgia	One yard shirting (34½ inches wide, measuring 5.32 yards to the pound
198	....do	One yard cotton cloth (27 inches wide, 40 by 40, measuring 4.73 yards to the pound).
196	France	One yard cotton cloth (31½ inches wide, 56 by 64, measuring 3.125 yards to the pound).
198	Georgia	One yard cotton cloth (31½ inches wide, 48 by 46, measuring 3.65 yards to the pound).
198	....do	One yard cotton cloth (36 inches wide, 48 by 46, measuring 3.01 yards to the pound).
193	Connecticut	One yard cotton cloth (39 inches wide, 68 by 76, measuring 4.5 yards to the pound).
193	....do	One yard cotton cloth (39 inches wide, 80 by 72, measuring 4.25 yards to the pound).
193	....do	One yard cotton cloth (40 inches wide, 80 by 80, measuring 3.75 yards to the pound).
193	....do	One yard cotton cloth (44 inches wide, 68 by 76, measuring 3.95 yards to the pound).
193	....do	One yard cotton cloth (44 inches wide, 80 by 80, measuring 3.5 yards to the pound).
a637	Georgia	One yard cotton cloth (36 inches wide, measuring 4.079 yards to the pound).
a638	....do	One yard cotton cloth (measuring 3.03 yards to the pound)
232	New York	One yard cotton cloth (unbleached, 48 by 48 picks, measuring 5.11 yards to the pound).
a639	Alabama	One yard cotton cloth
a640	Georgia	One yard cotton cloth
a641	Louisiana	One yard cotton cloth
a642	Mississippi	One yard cotton cloth
194	Delaware	One pound cotton cloth (unbleached, number 33 yarn)
244	South Carolina	One yard drilling (27 inches wide, 42 by 40, measuring 4.74 yards to the pound).
a630	Georgia	One yard drilling (29 inches wide, 70 by 48, measuring 2.82 yards to the pound).
a630	...do	One yard drilling (30½ inches wide, 70 by 48, measuring 2.84 yards to the pound.
a634	South Carolina	One yard drilling (30½ inches wide, 70 by 48, measuring 2.84 yards to the pound).
a635	...do	One yard drilling (30½ inches wide, 72 by 44, measuring 2.9 yards to the pound).
244	....do	One yard drilling (30½ inches wide, 72 by 44, measuring 2.9 yards to the pound).
244	....do	One yard drilling (30½ inches wide, 48 by 43, measuring 3.7 yards to the pound).
198	Georgia	One yard drilling (31½ inches wide, 62 by 48, measuring 3.06 yards to the pound).
199	...do	One yard drilling (31½ inches wide, 72 by 50, measuring 3.01 yards to the pound.)
244	South Carolina	One yard drilling (36 inches wide, 72 by 44, measuring 2.39 yards to the pound).

a The wages of employés in this establishment were not reported; therefore the number will not be found in the wage table, Appendix A.

VARIATION IN THE COST OF PRODUCTION.

COST OF PRODUCTION—Continued.

NOTE.—The establishment numbers correspond to those in the table on page 295, Appendix A, showing number of employés and wages, except as noted below. See explanation of table, page 91.

COTTON GOODS—Continued.

Amount of unit cost.					Per cent. of unit cost.				Establishment. No.
Labor.	Materials.	Administration.	Other.	Total.	Labor.	Materials.	Administration.	Other.	
$0.01035	$0.01714	....	$0.00357	$0.03106	33.32	55.18	....	11.50	219
.01000	.01643	....	.00500	.03143	31.82	52.27	....	15.91	220
.00999	.01712	....	.00171	.02882	34.66	59.41	....	5.93	227
.01000	.01610	....	.00180	.02790	35.84	57.71	....	6.45	245
.01174	.01998	....	.00199	.03371	34.83	59.27	....	5.90	227
.00802	.01618	....	.00294	.02714	29.55	59.62	....	10.83	201
.01408	.02398	....	.00240	.04046	34.80	59.27	....	5.93	227
.00664	.02356	$0.00077	.00155	.03252	20.41	72.45	2.37	4.77	a637
.00499	.02428	.00084	.00249	.03260	15.31	74.48	2.58	7.63	a633
.00859	.08438	....	.00212	.04309	15.29	79.79	....	4.92	a635
.02710	.04870	.00130	.00510	.08220	32.97	59.25	1.58	6 20	233
.01979	.03869	....	.00512	.06360	31.12	60.83	....	8.05	208
.00635	.02243	.00054	.00149	.03081	20.61	72.80	1.75	4.84	a637
.00613	.02628	.00048	.00254	.03543	17.30	74.17	1.35	7.18	198
.00983	.05616	....	.00654	.07253	13.55	77.43	....	9.02	196
.00810	.03406	.00062	.00320	.04598	17.61	74.08	1.35	6.96	192
.00963	.04131	.00075	.00399	.05568	17.29	74.19	1.35	7.17	198
.01513	.03001	.00203	.00592	.05309	28.49	56.53	3.83	11.15	193
.01602	.03177	.00215	.00626	.05620	28.50	56.53	3.83	11.14	193
.01815	.03601	.00243	.00710	.06369	28.50	56.54	3.81	11.15	193
.01724	.03419	.00231	.00673	.06047	28.51	56.54	3.82	11.13	193
.01945	.03858	.00261	.00760	.06824	28.50	56.53	3.83	11.14	193
.00827	.02929	.00079	.00194	.04029	20.53	72.70	1.96	4.81	a637
.00802	.03465	....	....	.04267	18.80	81.20	....	....	a638
.01017	.02390	....	.00674	.04081	24.92	58.56	....	16.52	232
.00876	.02364	....	....	.03250	27.26	72.74	....	....	a639
.02000	.03500	....	....	.05500	36.36	63.64	....	....	a640
.01750	.03500	....	....	.05250	33.33	66.67	....	....	a641
.01099	.03731	....	....	.04830	22.75	77.25	....	....	a642
.11250	.12000	....	.01940	.25190	44.67	47.63	....	7.70	104
.00622	.02511	.00055	.00296	.03484	17.85	72.07	1.58	8.50	244
.00993	.04114	.00051	.00476	.05634	17.62	73.03	.90	8.45	a630
.00988	.04090	.00050	.00471	.05599	17.65	73.05	.80	8.41	a630
.00822	.04036	....	.00276	.05134	16.01	78.62	....	5.38	a634
.00817	.04275	....	.00264	.05356	15.26	79.81	....	4.93	a635
.01016	.04104	.00090	.00484	.05694	17.84	72.08	1.58	8.50	244
.00796	.03217	.00070	.00380	.04463	17.84	72.08	1.57	8.51	244
.00941	.04037	.00074	.00389	.05441	17.29	74.20	1.36	7.15	198
.01197	.04142	.00096	.00406	.05751	19.25	72.02	1.67	7.06	199
.01225	.04987	.00109	.00588	.06910	17.84	72.07	1.58	8.51	244

COST OF PRODUCTION—Continued.

NOTE.—The establishment numbers correspond to those in the table on page 295, Appendix A, showing number of employés and wages, except as noted below. See explanation of table, page 91.

COTTON GOODS—Concluded.

Establishment No.	State.	Description of unit.
a630	Georgia	One yard drilling (36¼ inches wide, 68 by 52, measuring 2.43 yards to the pound).
a630	...do	One yard drilling (37 inches wide, 70 by 48, measuring 2.36 yards to the pound).
a630	...do	One yard drilling (37 inches wide, 83 by 46, measuring 1.6 yards to the pound).
a630	...do	One yard drilling (46 inches wide, 70 by 42, measuring 2.002 yards to the pound).
a630	...do	One yard drilling (51 inches wide, 70 by 42, measuring 1.79 yards to the pound).
a630	...do	One yard drilling (58 inches wide, 70 by 42, measuring 1.58 yards to the pound).
a635	South Carolina	One yard drilling (26 inches wide, measuring 3.34 yards to the pound).
a635	...do	One yard drilling (30 inches wide, measuring 3.17 yards to the pound).
a632	Alabama	One yard drilling (measuring 3.15 yards to the pound).
a633	Georgia	One yard drilling (measuring 3.05 yards to the pound).
a630	...do	One yard duck (38 inches wide, 83 by 28, measuring 1.79 yards to the pound).
a630	...do	One yard duck (46 inches wide, 83 by 28, measuring 1.49 yards to the pound).
a630	...do	One yard duck (51 inches wide, 83 by 28, measuring 1.32 yards to the pound).
a630	...do	One yard duck (57 inches wide, 83 by 28, measuring 1.19 yards to the pound).
212	Maryland	One yard duck (28 by 36 picks, measuring 2 yards to the pound).
213	...do	One yard duck (22 by 36 picks, measuring 1 yard to the pound).
222	Massachusetts	One yard calico (64 by 64 picks, measuring 7 yards to the pound).
228	New Hampshire	One yard calico (64 by 64 picks, measuring 7 yards to the pound).
235	New York	One yard calico (64 by 64 picks, measuring 7 yards to the pound).
a643	Pennsylvania	One yard calico (64 by 64 picks, measuring 7 yards to the pound).
241	North Carolina	One yard plaid (27 inches wide, 40 by 40, measuring 4 yards to the pound).
239	...do	One yard plaid (27 inches wide, 44 by 44, measuring 4.25 yards to the pound).
240	...do	One yard plaid (27 inches wide, 44 by 44, measuring 4.58 yards to the pound).
249	Virginia	One yard plaid (27 inches wide, 44 by 44, measuring 4.25 yards to the pound).
243	Pennsylvania	One yard gingham (26¼ inches wide, 45 by 54, measuring 6.8 yards to the pound).
a629	France	One yard gingham (31¼ inches wide, 56 by 60, measuring 4.55 yards to the pound).
209	Maine	One yard gingham (measuring 6.12 yards to the pound).
195	Delaware	One pound colored family cloth.
227	Massachusetts	One pound nainsook check.
226	New Hampshire	One seamless cotton bag (having a capacity of two bushels, and weighing one pound).
a644	New York	One pair cotton blankets (the pair weighing 6 pounds).
a645	France	One pound cotton yarn, number 33 (English).
197	...do	One pound cotton yarn, number 32 (English).
a646	...do	One pound cotton yarn, number 32 (English).
203	Great Britain	One pound cotton yarn, number 40.
206	Italy	One pound cotton yarn, number 16 (English).
242	North Carolina	One pound cotton yarn, number 20, two-ply.
240	...do	One pound cotton yarn, number 19.
236	New York	One pound cotton hosiery yarn, numbers 10 to 30.

FOOD PREPARATION.a

272	Ohio	One barrel fancy family flour (roller process).
a647	...do	One barrel fancy family flour (roller process).
a648	...do	One barrel fancy family flour (roller process).
a649	...do	One barrel fancy family flour (roller process).
a650	...do	One barrel fancy family flour (roller process).

a The wages of employés in this establishment were not reported; therefore the number will not be found in the wage table, Appendix A.
b For printing only.

VARIATION IN THE COST OF PRODUCTION. 111

COST OF PRODUCTION—Continued.

NOTE.—The establishment numbers correspond to those in the table on page 295, Appendix A, showing number of employés and wages, except as noted below. See explanation of table, page 91.

COTTON GOODS—Concluded.

Amount of unit cost.					Per cent. of unit cost.				Establishment No.
Labor.	Materials.	Administration.	Other.	Total.	Labor.	Materials.	Administration.	Other.	
$0.01151	$0.04782	$0.00059	$0.00553	$0.06545	17.58	73.08	.90	8.45	a630
.01186	.04917	.00061	.00569	.06733	17.61	73.03	.91	8.45	a630
.01752	.07263	.00090	.00840	.09945	17.62	73.04	.90	8.44	a630
.01402	.05811	.00072	.00672	.07957	17.62	73.03	.90	8.45	a630
.01561	.06490	.00080	.00750	.08881	17.58	73.08	.90	8.44	a630
.01770	.07336	.00091	.00848	.10045	17.62	73.03	.90	8.44	a630
.00683	.03706	....	.00229	.04618	14.79	80.25	....	4.96	a635
.00752	.03905	....	.00241	.04899	15.37	79.71	....	4.92	a635
.01102	.03755	.00077	.00283	.05277	22.02	71.16	1.46	5.36	a632
.00724	.03650	.00127	.00351	.04861	14.90	75.27	2.61	7.22	a633
.01567	.06500	.00080	.00752	.08899	17.61	73.04	.90	8.45	a630
.01887	.07793	.00096	.00902	.10678	17.67	72.98	.90	8.45	a630
.02128	.08821	.00109	.01020	.12078	17.62	73.03	.90	8.45	a630
.02350	.09745	.00121	.01127	.13343	17.61	73.03	.91	8.45	a630
.01330	.06020	.00320	.01690	.09360	14.21	64.31	3.42	18.06	212
.03340	.12450	.00250	.01750	.17790	18.78	69.98	1.40	9.84	213
.02309	.01048	....	.00147	.04404	52.43	41.23	....	3.34	222
.01438	.02480	....	.00509	.04427	32.48	56.02	....	11.50	228
.01335	.02115	.00110	.00123	.03703	36.50	57.11	2.97	3.33	235
b.00520	.03000	.00100	.00300	.03920	13.27	76.53	2.55	7.65	a643
.01280	.03620	.00140	.00290	.05330	24.02	67.92	2.62	5.44	241
.00840	.03460	.00120	.00250	.04670	18.00	74.09	2.56	5.85	230
.00897	.03523	....	.00032	.04452	20.15	79.13	....	.72	240
.01579	.03053	.00251	.00167	.05050	31.27	60.45	4.97	3.31	249
.02153	.01648	.00370	.00648	.04819	44.68	34.20	7.67	13.45	243
.01424	.07813	....	.01339	.10576	13.46	73.88	....	12.66	a629
.02720	.02540	....	.00860	.06120	44.45	41.50	....	14.05	209
.08470	.16400	....	.03500	.28370	29.85	57.81	....	12.34	195
.09500	.18000	....	.02500	.30000	31.67	60.00	....	8.33	223
.04171	.12160	.00131	.00143	.16605	25.12	73.24	.78	.86	226
.35571	.76555	....	.06256	1.18382	30.05	64.67	....	5.28	a644
.02674	.14700	....	.03897	.21271	12.57	69.11	....	18.32	a645
.02525	.13160	....	.01945	.17645	13.48	70.24	....	10.28	197
.02727	.14700	....	.03449	.20876	13.06	70.42	....	16.52	a646
.01943	.12320	.00110	....	.14373	13.52	85.72	.76	....	203
.01930	.13160	....	.01261	.16351	11.81	80.48	....	7.71	206
.02030	.13410	....	.01300	.16740	13.77	77.41	....	8.82	242
.01861	.11518	.00418	.00380	.14177	13.13	81.24	2.95	2.68	240
.02410	.13197	.00250	.01780	.17637	13.66	74.83	1.42	10.09	230

FOOD PREPARATION.c

$0.11000	$4.20250	....	$0.52333	$4.83583	2.28	86.90	....	10.82	273
.19000	3.98000	....	.45000	4.62000	4.11	86.15	....	9.74	a647
.20000	4.02000	....	.50000	4.72000	4.24	85.17	....	10.59	a648
.25000	3.71250	....	.45000	4.41250	5.66	84.14	....	10.20	a649
.20000	4.01000	....	.46000	4.67000	4.28	85.87	....	9.85	a650

c In Ohio, Illinois, West Virginia, and Indiana the value of middlings, bran, etc., has been deducted from the material.

COST OF PRODUCTION—Continued.

NOTE.—The establishment numbers correspond to those in the table on page 295, Appendix A, showing number of employés and wages, except as noted below. See explanation of table, page 91.

FOOD PREPARATION—Concluded.

Establishment No.	State.	Description of unit.
263	Illinois	One barrel fancy family flour (roller process)
a651	...do	One barrel fancy family flour (roller process)
257	...do	One barrel fancy family flour (roller process)
278	West Virginia	One barrel fancy family flour (roller process)
272	Ohio	One barrel fancy family flour
274	...do	One barrel fancy family flour
254	Illinois	One barrel high-grade family flour (roller process)
258	...do	One barrel high-grade family flour (roller process)
256	...do	One barrel high-grade family flour (roller process)
255	...do	One barrel high-grade family flour (roller process)
260	...do	One barrel high-grade family flour (roller process)
257	...do	One barrel high-grade family flour (roller process)
261	...do	One barrel high-grade family flour (roller process)
262	...do	One barrel high-grade family flour (roller process)
264	Indiana	One barrel high-grade family flour (roller process)
266	Minnesota	One barrel high-grade family flour (roller process)
a652	Georgia	One barrel family flour
275	Ohio	One barrel dairy salt (280 pounds)
277	...do	One barrel dairy salt (280 pounds)
276	...do	One barrel dairy salt (280 pounds)
a653	West Virginia	One barrel dairy salt (280 pounds)

GLASS.

299	Ohio	One dozen cup-foot goblets
a654	...do	One dozen cup-foot goblets
298	...do	One dozen common goblets
a655	...do	One dozen plain blown glass tumblers
a656	...do	One gross flint pint flasks
301	Pennsylvania	One gross flint pint flasks
304	...do	One gross flint pint flasks
315	West Virginia	One gross flint pint flasks
a656	Ohio	One gross flint half-pint flasks
315	West Virginia	One gross flint half-pint flasks
293	New Jersey	One box (50 feet) 12 x 26 inches, single strength window-glass
295	Ohio	One box (50 feet) 8 x 10 inches, single strength window-glass
309	Pennsylvania	One box (50 feet) 12 x 28 inches, single strength window-glass
308	...do	One box (50 feet) 12 x 28 inches, single strength window-glass
a657	Belgium	One box (50 feet) average size, single strength window-glass
288	Illinois	One box (50 feet) average size, single strength window-glass
290	Ohio	One box (50 feet) average size, single strength window-glass
295	...do	One box (50 feet) average size, single strength window-glass
294	...do	One gross half-gallon Mason fruit jars (without trimmings)
280	Kentucky	One gross quart Mason fruit jars (without trimmings)
305	Pennsylvania	One gross quart Mason fruit jars (without trimmings)
300	...do	One gross flint 8-ounce Philadelphia oval bottles
302	...do	One gross flint 8-ounce Philadelphia oval bottles
303	...do	One gross flint 8-ounce Philadelphia oval bottles
306	...do	One gross quart beer bottles
307	...do	One gross quart beer bottles
292	New Jersey	One gross 2-ounce green glass prescription phials
230	...do	One gross 2-ounce green glass prescription phials
291	...do	One gross 4-ounce green glass prescription phials
a656	Ohio	One gross flint, 8-ounce, French, square prescription bottles
a656	...do	One gross flint, 16-ounce, French, square prescription bottles
312	Pennsylvania	One dozen No. 2, crimp-top, lime, lamp chimneys
311	...do	One dozen No. 2, plain, lime, lamp chimneys
310	...do	One square foot, quarter-inch plate glass
313	...do	One table set (sugar bowl and cover, butter dish and cover, cream jug and cover, and spoon glass)

JUTE GOODS.

317	New Jersey	One pound jute yarn, medium grade

a The wages of employés in this establishment were not reported; therefore the number will not be found in the wage table, Appendix A.

VARIATION IN THE COST OF PRODUCTION

COST OF PRODUCTION—Continued.

NOTE.—The establishment numbers correspond to those in the table on page 295, Appendix A, showing number of employés and wages, except as noted below. See explanation of table, page 91.

FOOD PREPARATION—Concluded.

Amount of unit cost.					Per cent. of unit cost.				Establishment No.
Labor.	Materials.	Administration.	Other.	Total.	Labor.	Materials.	Administration.	Other.	
$0.16000	$3.29500	....	$0.41750	$3.87250	4.13	85.09	....	10.78	263
.05500	3.72000	....	.38250	4.15750	1.32	89.48	....	9.20	a651
.15000	3.80000	....	.44000	4.39000	3.42	86.56	....	10.02	257
.25000	3.85000	....	.47000	4.57000	5.47	84.25	....	10.28	278
.20000	4.24000	....	.35000	4.79000	4.18	88.52	....	7.30	272
.16000	3.99000	....	.35000	4.50000	3.55	88.67	....	7.78	274
.20000	3.32000	....	.46500	3.98500	5.02	83.31	....	11.67	251
.12000	3.01300	....	.48000	3.61300	3.32	83.39	....	13.29	258
.20000	3.61000	....	.34000	4.15000	4.82	86.99	....	8.19	256
.10000	3.80000	....	.32000	4.22000	2.37	90.05	....	7.58	255
.18000	3.48750	....	.42000	4.08750	4.40	85.32	....	10.28	260
.12000	3.61600	....	.37000	4.10600	2.93	88.05	....	9.02	257
.20000	4.03000	....	.56000	4.79000	4.18	84.13	....	11.69	261
.20000	3.35000	....	.40000	3.95000	5.06	84.81	....	10.13	262
.20000	3.97000	....	.47000	4.64000	4.31	85.56	....	10.13	264
.14000	4.00000	$0.03000	.08000	4.25000	3.28	94.12	$0.71	1.89	266
.25000	5.20000	....	....	5.45000	4.59	95.41	....	....	a652
.16500	....	....	.45500	.62000	26.62	....	....	73.38	275
.14000	....	....	.48000	.62000	22.58	....	....	77.42	277
.17000	....	....	.52250	.69250	24.55	....	....	75.45	276
.17000	....	....	.56000	.73000	23.29	....	....	76.71	a653

GLASS.

Amount of unit cost.					Per cent. of unit cost.				Establishment No.
Labor.	Materials.	Administration.	Other.	Total.	Labor.	Materials.	Administration.	Other.	
$0.18500	b$0.22500	....	$0.03500	$0.44500	41.57	50.57	....	7.86	299
.17000	b.26000	....	....	.43000	39.53	60.47	....	....	a654
.10000	b.18000	....	....	.28000	35.71	64.29	....	....	298
.23000	b.20000	....	.10000	.53000	43.39	37.74	....	18.87	a655
.90000	b2.25000	....	.50000	3.65000	24.66	61.65	....	13.69	a656
1.45500	.67080	....	.99190	3.11770	46.67	21.52	....	31.81	301
1.54340	.93872	....	.06880	3.15092	48.98	29.79	....	21.23	304
1.08000	b2.02500	....	.54000	3.64500	29.63	55.55	....	14.82	315
.65000	b1.35000	....	.40000	2.40000	27.08	56.25	....	16.67	a656
.81000	b1.37500	....	.38000	2.56500	31.59	53.60	....	14.81	315
1.00000	.90000	....	.10000	2.00000	50.00	45.00	....	5.00	293
.94500	.58000	$0.12000	.29230	1.93730	48.78	29.94	6.19	15.09	295
1.15000	.43000	....	.55000	2.13000	53.99	20.19	....	25.82	3CP
1.09000	.42400	....	.68800	2.20200	49.50	19.26	....	31.24	308
.54000	.12500	....	.50000	1.16500	46.35	10.72	....	42.93	a657
1.48000	.29850	....	.56430	2.34280	63.17	12.74	....	24.09	288
1.40158	.33256	....	.43301	2.16715	64.68	15.34	....	19.98	296
1.12700	.58090	.12000	.29230	2.12080	53.17	27.39	5.66	13.78	295
1.50000	1.74000	....	2.46000	5.70000	26.31	30.53	....	43.16	294
2.55400	.88400	....	1.18300	4.62100	55.26	19.13	....	25.60	289
2.10000	1.15000	....	1.57000	4.82000	43.57	23.86	....	32.57	305
1.26000	.37200	....	.58700	2.21900	56.78	16.77	....	26.45	300
1.31000	.38100	....	.57500	2.26600	57.81	16.81	....	25.38	302
.97760	.44010	....	.59480	2.01250	48.57	21.87	....	29.56	303
3.10000	1.23000	....	1.60000	5.93000	52.28	20.74	....	26.98	306
2.35000	1.31300	....	1.65000	5.31300	44.23	24.71	....	31.06	307
.70000	.40000	....	....	1.10000	63.64	36.36	....	....	292
.78000	.40000	....	....	1.18000	66.10	33.90	....	....	290
.88000	.54000	....	.08000	1.50000	58.67	36.00	....	5.33	291
.85000	b1.35000	....	.25000	2.45000	34.70	55.10	....	10.20	a656
1.43000	b2.92000	....	.50000	4.85000	29.48	60.21	....	10.31	a656
.15500	.04710	....	.05200	.25410	61.00	18.54	....	20.40	312
.18000	.05000	....	.02000	.25000	72.00	20.00	....	8.00	311
.37070	.09450	.04750	.14840	.66110	56.07	14.29	7.19	22.45	310
.09000	.05500	....	.09000	.23500	38.30	23.40	....	38.30	313

JUTE GOODS.

Amount of unit cost.					Per cent. of unit cost.				Establishment No.
Labor.	Materials.	Administration.	Other.	Total.	Labor.	Materials.	Administration.	Other.	
$0.02000	$0.03750	....	....	$0.05750	34.78	65.22	....	....	317

b All other labor except skilled and all expenses except package are included in material.

COST OF PRODUCTION—Continued.

NOTE.—The establishment numbers correspond to those in the table on page 295, Appendix A, showing number of employés and wages, except as noted below. See explanation of table, page 91.

LEATHER.

Establishment No.	State.	Description of unit.
324	Delaware	One dozen Tampico morocco skins
323	...do	One dozen Tampico morocco skins
323	...do	One dozen East India morocco skins
329	Pennsylvania	One square foot Tampico morocco
329	...do	One square foot Patna morocco
329	...do	One square foot Curaçoa morocco
328	...do	One square foot Brazilian morocco
330	...do	One pound finished harness leather

LIQUORS AND BEVERAGES. *a*

334	Illinois	One barrel beer (31½ gallons)
333	...do	One barrel beer (31½ gallons)
335	...do	One barrel beer (31½ gallons)
b658	...do	One barrel beer (31½ gallons)
340	Ohio	One barrel beer (31½ gallons)
341	...do	One barrel beer (31½ gallons)
339	...do	One barrel beer (31½ gallons)
b659	...do	One barrel beer (31½ gallons)
b660	Pennsylvania	One barrel beer (31½ gallons)
b661	West Virginia	One barrel beer (31½ gallons)
b662	...do	One barrel beer (31½ gallons)
338	Illinois	One gallon high wine
b663	...do	One gallon high wine
b664	...do	One gallon high wine
336	...do	One gallon high wine
b665	...do	One gallon high wine
337	...do	One gallon high wine
b663	...do	One gallon rye whisky
b666	Ohio	One gallon rye whisky
b667	...do	One gallon rye whisky
342	...do	One gallon rye whisky
b666	...do	One gallon Bourbon whisky
b667	...do	One gallon Bourbon whisky
342	...do	One gallon sweet-mash Bourbon whisky

LUMBER.

346	Illinois	One thousand feet white-pine lumber
345	...do	One thousand feet white pine lumber
b668	New Hampshire	One thousand feet best pine lumber
349	West Virginia	One thousand feet poplar lumber
350	...do	One thousand feet poplar lumber
b669	...do	One thousand feet poplar lumber
b670	...do	One thousand feet poplar lumber
349	...do	One thousand feet white-oak lumber
350	...do	One thousand feet white-oak lumber
b669	...do	One thousand feet white-oak lumber
b670	...do	One thousand feet white-oak lumber
346	Illinois	One complete window-sash
346	...do	One pair complete window-blinds
346	...do	One pine panel door

MACHINES AND MACHINERY.

365	Pennsylvania	One sheeting loom
354	Illinois	One sewing-machine (two drawers, cover and drop-leaf, all attachments). *c*
b747	...do	One sewing-machine (two drawers, cover and drop-leaf, all attachments). *d*
b748	...do	One sewing-machine (two drawers, cover and drop-leaf, all attachments). *e*

a The revenue tax (92½ cents per barrel on beer and 90 cents per gallon on distilled liquors) and the value of refuse and the saving of tax on fractional gallons of spirits are not included.
b The wages of employés in this establishment were not reported; therefore the number will not be found in the wage table, Appendix A.

VARIATION IN THE COST OF PRODUCTION.

COST OF PRODUCTION—Continued.

NOTE.—The establishment numbers correspond to those in the table on page 295, Appendix A, showing number of employés and wages, except as noted below. See explanation of table, page 91.

LEATHER.

Amount of unit cost.					Per cent. of unit cost.				Establishment No.
Labor.	Materials.	Administration.	Other.	Total.	Labor.	Materials.	Administration.	Other.	
$2.00000	$14.42000	....	$1.08000	$17.50000	11.42	82.40	....	6.18	324
3.20000	13.00000	....	2.05000	18.25000	17.54	71.23	....	11.23	323
1.75000	6.50000	....	....	8.25000	21.21	78.79	....	....	329
.06000	.22800	$0.02000	....	.30800	19.48	74.03	....	6.49	329
.06000	.16800	.02000	....	.24800	24.19	67.74	....	8.07	329
.04500	.16800	.02000	....	.23300	19.31	72.10	....	8.59	329
.05500	.23700	....	.03460	.32660	16.84	72.57	....	10.59	328
.04100	.22120	....	.03400	.29620	13.84	74.68	....	11.48	330

LIQUORS AND BEVERAGES. c

$0.85700	$2.14860	....	$1.55270	$4.55330	18.82	47.08	....	34.10	334
.97000	2.35730	....	1.59500	4.92230	19.71	47.89	....	32.40	333
1.00000	2.52000	....	.81000	4.39000	24.15	57.40	....	18.45	335
1.20000	2.79000	....	1.24000	5.23000	22.94	53.35	....	23.71	a658
.08000	2.45000	....	.78500	4.21500	23.25	58.12	....	18.63	340
.91000	2.34000	....	.97000	4.22000	21.56	55.45	....	22.99	341
.92800	1.85700	....	.68600	3.47100	26.73	53.50	....	19.77	339
1.00000	3.00000	....	.75000	4.75000	21.05	63.16	....	15.79	a659
2.00000	2.30000	....	....	4.30000	46.51	53.49	....	....	a660
.90260	2.68000	....	.92400	4.48660	20.12	59.29	....	20.59	a661
.88000	2.34600	....	1.24000	4.46000	19.73	52.40	....	27.81	a662
.00550	.10170	....	.03050	.13770	3.99	73.86	....	22.15	338
.01000	.10950	....	.03320	.15270	6.54	71.71	....	21.75	a663
.01290	.10690	....	.03050	.15030	8.59	71.12	....	20.29	a664
.00880	.10240	....	.02470	.13590	6.47	75.35	....	18.18	336
.01500	.12750	....	.06500	.20750	7.23	61.45	....	31.32	a665
.00670	.09940	....	.02880	.13490	4.96	73.69	....	21.35	337
.01550	.17220	....	.07240	.26010	5.96	66.20	....	27.84	a663
.02000	.19000	....	.06000	.27000	7.40	70.38	....	22.23	a666
.01770	.18440	....	.04430	.24640	7.19	74.82	....	17.98	a667
.01000	.17000	....	.04210	.22210	4.50	76.55	....	18.95	342
.02000	.16750	....	.06000	.24750	8.08	67.69	....	24.23	a666
.01770	.14660	....	.04430	.20860	8.48	70.28	....	21.24	a667
.01000	.12720	....	.04300	.18020	5.55	70.58	....	23.87	342

LUMBER.

$2.23000	$11.50000	....	$0.60000	$14.33000	15.56	80.26	....	4.18	346
2.32000	11.50000	....	.75000	14.57000	15.92	78.93	....	5.15	345
5.00000	7.00000	....	....	12.00000	41.66	58.34	....	....	668
2.25000	7.50000	....	.75000	10.50000	21.43	71.43	....	7.14	349
3.00000	8.50000	....	.50000	12.00000	25.00	70.83	....	4.17	350
3.00000	8.00000	....	.75000	11.75000	25.53	68.09	....	6.38	a669
4.50000	8.50000	....	.50000	13.50000	33.33	62.97	....	3.70	a670
2.75000	7.25000	....	.75000	10.75000	25.58	67.44	....	6.98	349
3.25000	7.50000	....	.50000	11.25000	28.89	66.67	....	4.44	350
3.50000	7.00000	....	.75000	11.25000	31.11	62.22	....	6.67	a669
4.50000	7.00000	....	.50000	12.00000	37.50	58.33	....	4.17	a670
.06000	.30000	....	.01500	.37500	16.00	80.00	....	4.00	340
.15000	.40000	....	.02000	.57000	26.31	70.18	....	3.51	346
.18000	.90000	....	.06000	1.14000	15.79	78.95	....	5.26	346

MACHINES AND MACHINERY.

$20.80000	$23.25000	$3.00000	$1.00000	$48.05000	43.29	48.39	6.24	2.08	365
6.05000	6.33000	....	....	12.38000	48.87	51.13	....	....	354
3.10000	7.71650	....	....	10.81650	28.66	71.34	....	....	e747
2.55000	5.78500	....	....	8.33500	30.61	69.39	....	....	e748

c Twenty pounds of iron and steel.
d Twenty-seven pounds of iron and steel.
e Sixteen pounds of iron and steel.

REPORT OF THE COMMISSIONER OF LABOR.

COST OF PRODUCTION—Continued.

NOTE.—The establishment numbers correspond to those in the table on page 295, Appendix A, showing number of employés and wages, except as noted below. See explanation of table, page 91.

METALS AND METALLIC GOODS.

Establishment No.	State.	Description of unit.
360	Alabama	One ton run of furnace foundery pig-iron (Alabama ore)
386	Indiana	One ton run of furnace foundery pig-iron
399	New York	One ton run of furnace foundery pig-iron (New York ore)
413	Ohio	One ton run of furnace foundery pig-iron (Lake Superior ore)
405	...do	One ton run of furnace foundery pig-iron (Hocking Valley and Lake Superior ore).
409	...do	One ton run of furnace foundery pig-iron (Hanging Rock ore)
414	...do	One ton run of furnace foundery pig-iron (Hanging Rock ore)
a714	...do	One ton run of furnace foundery pig-iron (Hanging Rock ore)
a715	Ohio	One ton run of furnace foundery pig-iron (Mahoning Valley and Lake Superior ore).
408	...do	One ton run of furnace foundery pig-iron (Mahoning Valley and Lake Superior ore).
a716	...do	One ton run of furnace foundery pig-iron (Mahoning Valley and Lake Superior ore).
a720	Pennsylvania	One ton run of furnace foundery pig-iron
435	Tennessee	One ton run of furnace foundery pig-iron (Tennessee ore)
a717	...do	One ton run of furnace foundery pig-iron (Tennessee ore)
436	Virginia	One ton run of furnace foundery pig-iron (Virginia ore)
437	...do	One ton run of furnace foundery pig-iron (Virginia ore)
438	...do	One ton run of furnace foundery pig-iron (Virginia ore)
a718	West Virginia	One ton run of furnace foundery pig-iron (Lake Superior ore)
a719	...do	One ton run of furnace foundery pig-iron (West Virginia ore)
376	Great Britain	One ton run of furnace pig-iron b
392	Maryland	One ton number one foundery pig-iron
400	New York	One ton number one foundery pig-iron
377	Great Britain	One ton number three foundery pig-iron
a721	Belgium	One thousand kilograms (2,205 pounds) white pig-iron
a722	Germany	One thousand kilograms (2,205 pounds) white pig-iron
a723	Ohio	One ton Bessemer pig-iron
410	...do	One ton Bessemer iron
412	...do	One ton Bessemer iron
a724	Pennsylvania	One ton Bessemer iron
424	...do	One ton Bessemer iron
425	...do	One ton Bessemer iron
407	Ohio	One ton foundery pig-iron, soft, silvery (Ohio brown hematite ore)
406	...do	One ton foundery pig-iron, soft, silvery (Ohio brown hematite ore)
411	...do	One ton foundery pig-iron, soft, silvery (Ohio brown hematite ore)
a725	...do	One ton foundery pig-iron, soft, silvery (Ohio brown hematite ore)
a726	...do	One ton foundery pig-iron, soft, silvery (Ohio brown hematite ore)
a727	...do	One ton foundery pig-iron, soft, silvery (Ohio brown hematite ore)
a728	Germany	One thousand kilograms (2,205 pounds) mill pig-iron
a729	Pennsylvania	One ton number one mill pig-iron
426	...do	One ton number one mill pig-iron
425	...do	One ton low-grade mill pig-iron
a730	Ohio	One ton cold-blast charcoal pig-iron (Hanging Rock ore)
a731	...do	One ton cold-blast charcoal pig-iron (Hanging Rock ore)
391	Maryland	One ton hot-blast charcoal pig-iron
396	Missouri	One pound pig-lead
395	...do	One pound pig-lead
386	Indiana	One ton merchant bar-iron
388	Kentucky	One ton merchant bar-iron
401	New York	One ton merchant bar-iron
428	Pennsylvania	One ton merchant bar-iron
427	...do	One ton merchant bar-iron
a732	Tennessee	One ton merchant bar-iron
a733	Ohio	One ton all-puddled bar-iron, based sizes
a734	...do	One ton all-puddled bar-iron, based sizes
a735	...do	One ton all-puddled bar-iron, based sizes
a736	...do	One ton all-puddled bar-iron, based sizes
415	...do	One ton all-puddled bar-iron, based sizes
416	...do	One ton mixed-puddled bar-and-old-rail bar-iron, based sizes
a737	...do	One ton mixed-puddled bar-and-old-rail bar-iron, based sizes
a735	...do	One ton muck bar-iron
431	Pennsylvania	One ton pipe-iron
380	Kentucky	One ton bar and plate iron
a738	Ohio	One ton flange-iron boiler plate
a738	...do	One ton tank-iron boiler plate

a The wages of employés in this establishment were not reported. Therefore the number will not be found in the wage table, Appendix A.

b Seven per cent. hematite, 27 per cent. spiegeleisen, and 66 per cent. foundery.

VARIATION IN THE COST OF PRODUCTION.

COST OF PRODUCTION—Continued.

NOTE.—The establishment numbers correspond to those in the table on page 295, Appendix A, showing number of employés and wages, except as noted below. See explanation of table, page 91.

METALS AND METALLIC GOODS.

Amount of unit cost.					Per cent. of unit cost.				Establishment No.
Labor.	Materials.	Administration.	Other.	Total.	Labor.	Materials.	Administration.	Other.	
$1.87000	$6.92000	$0.36000	$2.34000	$11.49000	16.28	60.22	3.13	20.37	366
1.90000	10.90000	....	....	12.80000	14.84	85.10	....	....	386
1.54760	9.51630	.18960	.57670	11.82980	13.08	80.45	1.60	4.87	399
1.30500	12.68800	....	.81700	14.81000	8.81	85.68	....	5.51	413
2.00000	11.30000	....	.75000	14.05000	14.23	80.43	....	5.34	405
1.20000	10.15000	.15000	.37000	11.87000	10.11	85.51	1.27	3.11	409
1.50000	9.80000	.44000	.70000	12.44000	12.06	78.78	3.53	5.63	414
1.80000	11.95000	.50000	.50000	14.75000	12.20	81.02	3.39	3.39	a714
1.40000	12.17000	0.10000	1.50000	15.17000	9.23	80.22	.66	9.89	a715
1.25000	12.62000	....	.75000	14.62000	8.55	86.32	....	5.13	408
1.50000	13.00000	....	1.00000	15.50000	9.68	83.87	....	6.45	a716
2.00000	13.75000	.25000	....	16.00000	12.50	85.94	1.56	....	a720
1.88000	10.01000	....	.70000	12.63000	14.49	79.26	....	6.25	435
2.17000	10.82000	....	....	12.99000	16.71	83.29	....	....	a717
1.28200	9.01000	.23100	1.14100	11.66400	10.99	77.25	1.98	9.78	439
1.16950	10.47500	.54000	.50000	12.68650	9.21	82.57	4.27	3.95	437
1.11400	10.70000	.15000	.25200	12.21600	9.12	87.59	1.23	2.06	438
2.10000	13.32500	.31000	.79500	16.53000	12.70	80.61	1.88	4.81	a718
1.50000	10.95000	....	1.00000	13.45000	11.16	81.41	....	7.43	a719
.96842	10.90971	....	....	11.87813	8.16	91.84	....	....	376
2.48110	14.77310	....	....	17.25420	14.38	85.62	....	....	392
2.17000	13.92700	.25084	.04300	16.40764	13.29	84.89	1.56	.26	400
.01214	6.33206	....	.32000	7.26610	8.42	87.18	....	4.40	377
1.08000	8.38000	....	.88000	10.34000	10.45	81.04	....	8.51	a721
1.30000	10.36000	....	1.05000	12.71000	10.23	81.51	....	8.26	a722
1.58830	15.01470	.15000	.39500	16.65800	7.13	90.13	.90	1.84	a723
2.50000	14.90000	.50000	.50000	18.40000	13.59	80.98	2.71	2.72	410
2.50000	14.90000	....	1.00000	18.40000	13.59	80.98	....	5.43	412
1.22000	14.75800	.75000	....	16.72800	7.29	88.22	4.49	....	a724
1.14000	13.91000	.75000	.75000	16.55000	6.89	84.05	4.53	4.53	424
1.50000	13.86000	.75000	1.50000	17.61000	8.52	78.71	4.25	8.52	425
2.25000	10.06000	.50000	.00000	13.45000	17.02	74.80	3.72	4.46	407
2.10000	10.42000	.40000	.50000	13.42000	15.65	77.65	2.98	3.72	406
1.86000	10.07000	.33020	.50000	12.76000	14.58	78.90	2.59	3.93	411
1.95000	10.07000	.40000	.50000	12.92000	15.09	77.94	3.10	3.87	a725
2.00000	10.62000	.50000	.50000	13.62000	14.69	77.97	3.67	3.67	a726
2.04000	10.22000	....	.75000	12.97000	15.43	78.79	....	5.78	a727
1.30000	8.04000	....	1.09000	10.43000	12.46	77.09	....	10.45	a728
1.40000	10.50000	1.50000	1.00000	14.40000	9.72	72.92	10.42	6.94	a729
2.00000	11.97000	.40000	.58000	14.95000	13.38	80.07	2.67	3.88	426
1.50000	9.12000	.75000	1.50000	12.87000	11.66	70.86	5.83	11.65	425
3.00000	18.70000	1.00000	1.00000	23.70000	12.66	78.90	4.22	4.22	a730
3.00000	16.88000	1.00000	1.00000	21.88000	13.71	77.15	4.57	4.57	a731
3.45640	18.42860	....	....	21.88500	15.79	84.21	....	....	394
.01531	....	.00548	.01170	.03249	47.12	....	16.87	36.01	396
.01322	....	....	.01413	.02735	48.34	....	....	51.66	395
0.34000	21.65000	....	....	30.99000	30.14	69.86	....	....	383
10.71000	10.43000	....	1.24200	31.38200	34.13	61.91	....	3.96	388
10.21440	19.29072	1.12574	6.58147	37.22433	27.44	51.85	3.01	17.70	401
13.00000	18.00000	2.50000	4.50000	38.00000	34.21	47.37	6.58	11.84	428
12.00000	20.05000	1.42000	5.93000	39.40000	30.46	50.88	3.61	15.05	427
15.00000	15.00000	....	....	30.00000	50.00	50.00	....	....	a732
3.75000	c28.00000	....	3.25000	35.00000	10.71	80.00	....	9.29	a733
5.72000	c27.00000	....	1.75000	34.47000	16.59	78.33	....	5.08	a734
4.00000	c26.50000	....	3.00000	33.50000	11.94	79.11	....	8.95	a735
13.00000	15.00000	....	6.00000	34.00000	38.23	44.12	....	17.65	a736
13.00000	15.00000	....	7.00000	35.00000	37.14	42.86	....	20.00	415
3.75000	24.50000	....	3.25000	31.00000	12.09	77.42	....	10.49	416
7.00000	16.50000	....	6.50000	30.00000	23.33	55.00	....	21.67	a737
7.00000	17.25000	....	2.25000	26.50000	26.42	65.09	....	8.49	a735
12.20000	18.25000	2.00000	2.00000	34.51000	35.53	52.88	5.79	5.80	431
16.00000	19.00000	....	....	35.00000	45.71	54.29	....	....	389
12.50000	40.00000	....	4.50000	57.00000	21.93	70.18	....	7.89	a738
12.50000	c26.00000	....	4.50000	29.07000	60.47	....	....	10.46	a738

c Material is muck bar-iron.
d Material is steel ingots.

COST OF PRODUCTION—Continued.

NOTE.—The establishment numbers correspond to those in the table on page 295, Appendix A, showing number of employés and wages, except as noted below. See explanation of table, page 91.

METALS AND METALLIC GOODS—Concluded.

Establishment No.	State.	Description of unit.
385	Illinois	One ton small T-rails, six to twenty pounds
a732	Tennessee	One ton light T-rails and fish and angle plates
a738	Ohio	One ton shell-iron boiler plate
417	...do	One ton hoop, band, and cotton-tie iron
375	Delaware	One ton ordinary black sheet-iron
419	Ohio	One ton sheet and plate iron and steel (run of mill)
418	...do	One ton Bessemer steel rails and merchant iron (run of mill)
371	Belgium	One thousand kilograms (2,205 pounds) Bessemer steel rails, weighing 76.6 pounds to the yard.
402	New York	One ton Bessemer steel rails
369	Belgium	One thousand kilograms (2,205 pounds) Bessemer steel ingots
418	Ohio	One ton Bessemer steel ingots
370	Belgium	One thousand kilograms (2,205 pounds) Bessemer steel plates for vessels.
380	Great Britain	One ton Siemens process steel plates, bars, and axles, from the pig
a738	Ohio	One ton shell-steel plates
a738	...do	One ton tank-box steel plates
a738	...do	One ton fire-box steel plates
421	...do	One ton common spring steel
433	Pennsylvania	One ton tool steel
432	...do	One ton plough steel
a739	Massachusetts	One ton number twelve bright coppered wire
420	Ohio	One ton assorted sizes steel wire
429	Pennsylvania	One ton assorted sizes iron pipe
430	...do	One twelve-hundred-pound safe
436	Vermont	One hay, coal, and wagon scale, capacity three tons, platform 8 by 14 feet.
436	...do	One family scale, capacity 240 pounds, with brass scoop and double brass beam.
436	...do	One portable platform scale on wheels, capacity 400 pounds, platform 15 by 22 inches.
403	New York	One ton horseshoes
404	...do	One pound merchant brass
a740	...do	One locomotive head-light
a741	Illinois	One keg iron nails
384	...do	One keg iron nails
a742	Ohio	One keg iron nails
423	...do	One keg iron nails
a743	...do	One keg iron nails
a744	West Virginia	One keg iron nails
443	...do	One keg iron nails
422	Ohio	One keg iron and steel nails
a745	West Virginia	One keg iron and steel nails
a742	Ohio	One keg steel nails
a743	West Virginia	One keg steel nails
385	Illinois	One ton railroad spikes
a744	Massachusetts	One thousand sewing-machine needles

MUSICAL INSTRUMENTS.

448	New York	One first-class grand piano
446	...do	One first-class grand piano
448	...do	One first-class upright piano
446	...do	One first-class upright piano
448	...do	One first-class square piano
446	...do	One first-class square piano
449	...do	One second-class grand piano
449	...do	One second-class upright piano

OILS AND ILLUMINATING FLUIDS.

a745	Great Britain	One gallon illuminating oil made from shale
451	New York	One gallon linseed oil
453	Pennsylvania	One gallon refined kerosene oil (110° test)
452	...do	One gallon refined kerosene oil (110° test)

a The wages of employés in this establishment were not reported. Therefore the number will not be found in the wage table, Appendix A.

VALUATION IN THE COST OF PRODUCTION. 119

COST OF PRODUCTION—Continued.

NOTE.—The establishment numbers correspond to those in the table on page 295, Appendix A, showing number of employés and wages, except as noted below. See explanation of table, page 91.

METALS AND METALLIC GOODS—Concluded.

Amount of unit cost.					Per cent. of unit cost.				Establishment No.
Labor.	Materials.	Administration.	Other.	Total.	Labor.	Materials.	Administration.	Other.	
$6.34000	$17.35000	....	$5.10000	$28.79000	22.02	60.26	....	17.72	385
15.00000	15.00000	....	....	30.00000	50.00	50.00	....	....	a7:2
12.50000	30.00000	....	4.50000	47.00000	26.60	63.83	....	9.57	a739
15.30000	22.10000	....	6.82000	44.22000	34.60	49.98	....	15.42	417
21.00000	26.00000	$3.20000	22.80000	73.00000	28.77	35.61	4.39	31.23	375
21.80000	d27.00000	....	16.34000	65.14000	33.46	41.45	....	25.09	419
7.50000	d27.00000	....	4.85000	39.35000	19.06	68.61	....	12.33	418
1.27000	18.39000	....	2.68000	22.34000	5.69	82.32	....	11.99	371
7.57200	21.00000	....	2.57300	31.14500	24.31	67.43	....	8.26	402
1.10000	13.93000	....	2.50000	17.53000	6.27	79.47	....	14.26	369
2.50000	22.81000	....	1.95000	27.26000	9.17	83.67	....	7.16	418
1.95000	d20.41000	....	6.20000	28.56000	6.82	71.47	....	21.71	370
6.07840	13.87213	....	2.06592	22.01645	27.61	63.00	....	9.39	380
12.50000	b45.00000	....	4.50000	62.00900	20.16	72.59	....	7.25	a738
12.50000	b38.00000	....	4.50000	55.00000	22.73	69.09	....	8.18	a738
12.50000	b60.00000	....	4.50000	77.00000	16.24	77.92	....	5.84	a738
17.00000	18.00000	....	10.00000	45.00000	37.78	40.00	....	22.22	421
64.82700	61.25000	15.00000	5.00000	146.07700	44.37	41.93	10.27	3.43	433
25.42000	37.44000	6.82000	7.40000	77.08000	32.98	48.57	8.85	9.60	432
5.06000	42.24000	....	8.50000	56.70000	10.51	74.49	....	15.00	a739
15.50000	39.00000	....	9.89000	64.39000	24.07	60.57	....	15.36	420
16.04000	34.51000	2.00000	2.80000	55.75000	30.39	61.90	3.59	4.12	429
22.61000	43.20000	3.75000	2.00000	71.56000	31.60	60.37	5.24	2.79	430
6.74000	19.05000	....	3.37000	29.16000	23.11	65.33	....	11.56	436
2.20000	2.37000	....	1.10000	5.67000	38.80	41.80	....	19.40	436
2.88000	4.00000	....	1.44000	8.32000	34.61	48.08	....	17.31	436
11.50000	19.63000	.83000	8.10000	39.56000	29.07	49.62	.83	20.48	403
.02680	.11050	.00026	.01804	.15560	17.22	71.02	.17	11.59	404
24.44091	22.04536	5.64374	2.80567	54.93568	44.49	40.13	10.27	5.11	a740
.68400	.90200	....	.29700	1.88300	36.33	47.90	....	15.77	a741
.80250	1.21310	....	.34950	2.36510	33.93	51.29	....	14.78	384
1.05900	.96250	....	.48790	2.50940	42.20	38.36	....	19.44	a742
.93000	.75000	....	.31500	1.99500	46.62	37.59	....	15.79	423
.94000	.75000	....	.43000	2.12000	44.34	35.38	....	20.28	a743
.98210	.89270	....	.48750	2.36230	41.57	37.79	....	20.64	a744
1.03100	.94500	.05000	.38900	2.41500	42.69	39.13	2.07	16.11	443
.90310	.96720	....	.47290	2.34320	38.54	41.28	....	20.18	422
.73000	1.17500	....	.37500	2.28000	32.02	51.53	....	16.45	a745
.67570	b1.37450	....	.36150	2.41170	28.02	56.99	....	14.99	a742
.07000	b1.32000	....	.35200	2.34200	28.61	56.36	....	15.03	a743
7.88000	17.00000	....	6.90000	31.78000	24.79	53.49	....	21.72	385
5.00000	1.50000	....	1.00000	7.50000	66.67	20.00	....	13.33	a744

MUSICAL INSTRUMENTS.

$141.33000	$137.23000	....	$22.19000	$300.75000	46.99	45.63	....	7.38	448
161.00000	121.10000	....	19.04000	301.14000	53.47	40.21	....	6.32	446
104.47000	112.62000	....	20.67000	237.76000	43.94	47.36	....	8.70	448
119.00000	90.49000	....	15.58000	225.07000	52.87	40.21	....	6.92	446
104.47000	105.62000	....	20.67000	230.76000	45.27	45.77	....	8.06	448
119.00000	80.16000	....	15.58000	214.74000	55.41	37.33	....	7.26	446
75.78000	70.44000	$4.78000	15.54000	175.54000	43.16	45.26	2.73	8.85	449
57.34000	61.75000	4.10000	13.64000	136.83000	41.91	45.13	2.99	9.97	449

OILS AND ILLUMINATING FLUIDS.

$0.04010	$0.03260	....	$0.00990	$0.08260	48.55	39.47	....	11.98	a745
.02211	.41211	....	.02938	.46360	4.77	88.89	....	6.34	451
.00310	.03000	....	.03560	.06870	4.51	43.67	....	51.82	453
.00490	.03000	....	.03560	.07050	6.95	42.55	....	50.50	452

b Material is steel slabs.

COST OF PRODUCTION—Continued.

NOTE.—The establishment numbers correspond to those in the table on page 295, Appendix A, showing number of employés and wages, except as noted below. See explanation of table, page 91.

PAPER.

Establishment No.	State.	Description of unit.
456	Delaware	One pound newspaper paper
458	Maine	One pound newspaper paper
455	Delaware	One pound book paper
460	Massachusetts	One pound number one sized and super-calendered book paper
457	Delaware	One pound tinted pamphlet cover paper
463	Massachusetts	One pound engine-sized flat writing paper
464	....do	One pound writing paper, superfine, folded and flat, made from best number one. white rags, soft dried, and both antique and plate finish.
465	....do	One ream glazed, plated, and enameled paper.
b746	....do	One thousand white envelopes, 3½ by 6 inches, engine-sized, rag paper; the ream weight is on a basis of 22½ by 30, 50 pounds to 500 sheets.

PRINT WORKS.

470	Massachusetts	Printing one yard print-cloth (24½ inches wide, 64 by 64)
471	....do	Printing one yard cheap dress goods in fugitive colors (27 inches wide, 48 by 48, and measuring 8 yards to the pound).

RUBBER GOODS.

483	New Jersey	One case (24 pairs) light-weight women's rubber shoes
482	....do	One case (12 pairs) women's arctic rubber shoes
483	....do	One case (12 pairs) heavy-weight men's rubber shoes
482	....do	One case (12 pairs) men's arctic rubber shoes
484	....do	One pound rubber hose.

SILK.

485	Connecticut	One pound machine twist and sewing silk
490	New York	One pound spun silk
489	....do	One pound of silk yarn for manufacturers' and household use.
488	....do	One pound silk ribbon.
486	New Jersey	One yard gros-grain silk.

TOBACCO.a

499	Illinois	One pound smoking tobacco (long cut, best grade)
499	....do	One pound smoking tobacco (granulated, medium grade)
499	....do	One pound smoking tobacco (low grade, stem)
500	....do	One pound smoking tobacco (granulated)
503	Michigan	One pound smoking tobacco (granulated)
500	Illinois	One pound fine-cut chewing tobacco
499	....do	One pound fine-cut chewing tobacco
499	....do	One pound fine-cut chewing tobacco
501	Kentucky	One pound fine-cut chewing tobacco
503	Michigan	One pound fine-cut chewing tobacco
498	Illinois	One pound plug chewing tobacco
498	....do	One pound plug chewing tobacco
498	....do	One pound plug chewing tobacco
502	Kentucky	One pound plug chewing tobacco
504	Missouri	One pound plug tobacco
508	New York	One pound plug tobacco
511	North Carolina	One pound plug tobacco
510	....do	One pound plug tobacco
509	....do	One pound plug tobacco
520	Virginia	One pound plug tobacco
522	....do	One pound plug tobacco
525	....do	One pound plug tobacco
523	....do	One pound plug tobacco

b The wages of employés in this establishment were not reported. Therefore the number will not be found in the wage table, Appendix A.   a Including other expenses.

VALUATION IN THE COST OF PRODUCTION.

COST OF PRODUCTION—Continued.

NOTE.—The establishment numbers correspond to those in the table on page 295, Appendix A, showing number of employés and wages, except as noted below. See explanation of table, page 91.

PAPER.

Amount of unit cost.					Per cent. of unit cost.				Establishment No.
Labor.	Materials.	Administration.	Other.	Total.	Labor.	Materials.	Administration.	Other.	
$0.00670	$0.05340	....	....	$0.06010	11.14	88.86	....	....	456
.00634	.02623	....	$0.01309	.04566	13.88	57.45	....	28.67	458
.00753	.04399	....	.01602	.06754	11.15	65.13	....	23.72	455
.01169	.04385	....	.01063	.06617	17.67	66.27	....	16.06	460
.00750	c.08250	....	....	.09000	8.33	91.67	....	....	457
.01000	.04500	....	.02500	.08000	12.50	56.25	....	31.25	463
.02750	.05500	....	.03300	.11550	23.81	47.62	....	28.57	464
.80000	2.00000	$0.20000	....	3.00000	26.67	66.67	6.66	....	465
.05000	.65000	.10000	.15000	.95000	5.26	68.42	10.53	15.79	b746

PRINT WORKS.

Labor.	Materials.	Administration.	Other.	Total.	Labor.	Materials.	Administration.	Other.	Est. No.
$0.00470	$0.00860	....	$0.00290	$0.01620	29.01	53.08	....	17.91	470
.00300	.00350	....	.00243	.00893	33.59	39.20	....	27.21	471

RUBBER GOODS.

Labor.	Materials.	Administration.	Other.	Total.	Labor.	Materials.	Administration.	Other.	Est. No.
$0.80000	$6.90000	....	....	$7.70000	10.39	89.61	....	....	483
1.20000	7.30000	....	....	8.50000	14.12	85.88	....	....	482
1.60000	8.90000	....	....	10.50000	15.24	84.76	....	....	483
1.60000	8.90000	....	....	10.50000	15.24	84.76	....	....	482
.02040	.01840	....	....	.03880	52.58	47.42	....	....	484

SILK.

Labor.	Materials.	Administration.	Other.	Total.	Labor.	Materials.	Administration.	Other.	Est. No.
$0.85000	$4.00000	....	$0.80000	$5.65000	15.04	70.80	....	14.16	485
.30290	4.00000	....	.06450	4.45740	8.81	89.74	....	1.45	490
.27200	4.25850	....	.09740	4.62790	5.88	92.02	....	2.10	489
2.30580	4.05970	....	.53150	7.79700	29.57	63.61	....	6.82	488
.40000	.38000	....	....	.78000	51.28	48.72	....	....	486

TOBACCO.c

Labor.	Materials.	Administration.	Other.	Total.	Labor.	Materials.	Administration.	Other.	Est. No.
$0.15000	$0.30000	....	$0.05000	$0.50000	30.00	60.00	....	10.00	499
.05000	.15000	....	.02000	.22000	22.73	68.18	....	9.09	499
.02000	.00750	....	.01000	.03750	53.33	20.00	....	26.67	499
.02000	.08000	....	.04000	.14000	14.29	57.14	....	28.57	500
.03000	.10050	....	.02500	.15560	19.35	64.52	....	16.13	503
.02000	.13000	....	.05000	.20000	10.00	65.00	....	25.00	500
.05000	.25000	....	.07500	.37500	13.33	66.67	....	20.00	490
.04000	.09000	....	.04500	.17500	22.86	51.43	....	25.71	499
.05000	.20000	....	.05000	.30000	16.66	66.67	....	16.67	501
.05000	.20000	....	.02500	.27500	18.18	72.73	....	9.09	503
.05000	.23000	....	.03750	.31750	16.00	73.60	....	10.40	498
.04000	.14000	....	.02250	.21250	18.82	65.88	....	15.30	498
.03500	.07000	....	.02750	.13250	26.42	52.83	....	20.75	498
.04000	.22000	....	....	.26000	15.38	84.62	....	....	502
.02185	.24370	....	.00367	.26922	8.12	90.52	....	1.36	504
.04370	.12170	$0.00530	.01150	.18220	23.99	66.80	2.90	6.31	508
.01688	.17851	.00184	.11977	.32000	5.28	55.78	.51	37.43	511
.04850	.15770	.00210	.01940	.26500	18.30	59.50	3.55	18.66	510
.05130	.13070	.00750	.04450	.22580	22.72	53.45	3.32	20.51	509
.02539	.17852	.00304	.06629	.29324	8.66	60.88	1.04	29.42	520
.02970	.19000	.00520	.05120	.27610	10.76	68.82	1.88	18.54	522
.03890	.15720	.00430	.05340	.25380	15.33	61.94	1.69	21.04	525
.03577	.12914	.00524	.05106	.22211	16.10	58.14	2.36	23.40	523

cThe revenue tax, 8 cents per pound on chewing and smoking tobacco, and $3 per thousand on cigars, is not included in this table.

COST OF PRODUCTION—Continued.

NOTE.—The establishment numbers correspond to those in the table on page 295, Appendix A, showing number of employés and wages, except as noted below. See explanation of table, page 91.

TOBACCO—Concluded.

Establishment No.	State.	Description of unit.
524	Virginia	One pound plug tobacco
521	...do	One pound plug tobacco
492	Connecticut	One thousand five-cent cigars
496	Illinois	One thousand five-cent cigars
496	...do	One thousand five-cent cigars
497	...do	One thousand five-cent cigars
497	...do	One thousand five-cent cigars
493	...do	One thousand five-cent cigars
403	...do	One thousand five-cent cigars
494	...do	One thousand five-cent cigars
a749	...do	One thousand five-cent cigars
a749	...do	One thousand five-cent cigars
495	...do	One thousand five-cent cigars
495	...do	One thousand five-cent cigars
a750	...do	One thousand five-cent cigars
a750	...do	One thousand five-cent cigars
514	Ohio	One thousand five-cent cigars
514	...do	One thousand five-cent cigars
517	...do	One thousand five-cent cigars
517	...do	One thousand five-cent cigars
512	...do	One thousand five-cent cigars
512	...do	One thousand five-cent cigars
a751	...do	One thousand five-cent cigars
a751	...do	One thousand five-cent cigars
513	...do	One thousand five-cent cigars
a752	...do	One thousand five-cent cigars
a752	...do	One thousand five-cent cigars
515	...do	One thousand five-cent cigars
515	...do	One thousand five-cent cigars
516	...do	One thousand five-cent cigars
516	...do	One thousand five-cent cigars
a753	...do	One thousand five-cent cigars
a754	...do	One thousand five-cent cigars
a755	...do	One thousand five-cent cigars
519	Rhode Island	One thousand five-cent cigars
492	Connecticut	One thousand ten-cent cigars
496	Illinois	One thousand ten-cent cigars
497	...do	One thousand ten-cent cigars
403	...do	One thousand ten-cent cigars
494	...do	One thousand ten-cent cigars
a749	...do	One thousand ten-cent cigars
495	...do	One thousand ten-cent cigars
a750	...do	One thousand ten-cent cigars
514	Ohio	One thousand ten-cent cigars
517	...do	One thousand ten-cent cigars
512	...do	One thousand ten-cent cigars
a751	...do	One thousand ten-cent cigars
a752	...do	One thousand ten-cent cigars
515	...do	One thousand ten-cent cigars
516	...do	One thousand ten-cent cigars
519	Rhode Island	One thousand ten-cent cigars
518	Ohio	One thousand seed stogie cigars
a754	...do	One thousand seed stogie cigars
a756	West Virginia	One thousand seed stogie cigars
527	...do	One thousand seed stogie cigars
526	Virginia	One thousand cigarettes

WOOLLEN GOODS.

567	New York	One yard cassimere (54 inches wide and weighing 12½ ounces)
542	Illinois	One yard cassimere (54 inches wide and weighing 16 ounces)
539	Delaware	One yard cassimere (54 inches wide and weighing 16 ounces)
570	Pennsylvania	One yard cassimere (54 inches wide and weighing 16 ounces)
570	...do	One yard cassimere (54 inches wide and weighing 20 ounces)
540	Delaware	One yard cassimere (54 inches wide and weighing 24 ounces)
557	Massachusetts	One yard fine worsted cassimere (54 inches wide)
554	Maryland	One yard kersey cloth (27 inches wide and weighing 13 ounces)

a The wages of employés in this establishment were not reported; therefore the number will not be found in the wage table, Appendix A.

VARIATION IN THE COST OF PRODUCTION.

COST OF PRODUCTION—Continued.

NOTE.—The establishment numbers correspond to those in the table on page 295, Appendix A, showing number of employés and wages, except as noted below. See explanation of table, page 91.

TOBACCO—Concluded.

Amount of unit cost.					Per cent. of unit cost.				Establishment No.
Labor.	Materials.	Administration.	Other.	Total.	Labor.	Materials.	Administration.	Other.	
$0.02250	$0.13540	$0.00550	$0.04520	$0.20860	10.78	64.91	2.64	21.67	524
.02140	.13290	.00740	.04280	.20450	10.46	64.99	3.62	20.93	521
11.00000	4.00000	....	3.00000	18.00000	61.11	22.22	....	16.67	492
10.50000	10.00000	....	3.00000	23.50000	44.68	42.55	....	12.77	490
12.50000	14.00000	....	3.25000	29.75000	42.01	47.06	....	10.93	496
10.50000	8.50000	....	4.50000	23.50000	44.68	36.17	....	19.15	497
11.50000	13.00000	....	4.50000	29.00000	39.65	44.83	....	15.52	497
8.00000	12.00000	....	4.00000	24.00000	33.33	50.00	....	16.67	493
7.00000	7.00000	....	4.00000	18.00000	38.89	38.89	....	22.22	493
9.75000	10.50000	....	2.55000	22.80000	42.70	46.05	....	11.19	494
10.50000	11.00000	....	3.25000	24.75000	42.42	44.45	....	13.13	a749
9.00000	6.50000	....	3.25000	18.75000	48.00	34.67	....	17.33	a749
10.00000	9.50000	....	3.00000	22.50000	44.45	42.22	....	13.33	495
8.75000	6.00000	....	3.00000	17.75000	49.30	33.80	....	16.90	495
10.50000	11.20000	....	3.00000	24.70000	42.51	45.34	....	12.15	a750
9.00000	6.50000	....	3.00000	18.50000	48.65	35.14	....	16.21	a750
8.50000	6.00000	....	3.50000	18.00000	47.22	33.33	....	19.45	514
9.25000	10.00000	....	3.50000	22.75000	40.66	43.96	....	15.38	514
10.00000	7.30000	....	4.00000	21.30000	46.95	34.27	....	18.78	517
10.00000	10.25000	....	4.00000	24.25000	41.24	42.27	....	16.49	517
8.25000	6.00000	....	3.20000	17.45000	47.28	34.39	....	18.33	512
8.25000	8.50000	....	3.20000	19.05000	41.85	42.61	....	16.04	512
8.25000	5.00000	....	3.00000	16.25000	50.77	30.77	....	18.46	a751
8.25000	8.00000	....	3.00000	19.25000	42.86	41.56	....	15.58	a751
8.00000	7.00000	....	2.90000	18.50000	46.49	37.84	....	15.67	513
10.35000	10.96000	....	3.15000	24.46000	42.32	44.80	....	12.88	a752
9.35000	9.60000	....	3.15000	22.10000	42.14	43.67	....	14.19	a752
8.25000	13.00000	....	3.00000	24.25000	34.02	53.61	....	12.37	515
7.50000	7.00000	....	3.00000	17.50000	42.86	40.00	....	17.14	515
9.85000	11.75000	....	2.75000	24.35000	40.45	48.26	....	11.29	516
8.40000	8.25000	....	2.75000	19.40000	43.30	42.53	....	14.17	516
8.25000	8.50000	....	2.75000	19.50000	42.31	43.59	.?......	14.10	a753
8.50000	8.50000	....	3.25000	20.25000	41.97	41.98	....	16.05	a754
8.50000	8.00000	....	3.50000	20.00000	42.50	40.00	....	17.50	a755
10.50000	11.00000	....	3.50000	25.00000	42.00	44.00	....	14.00	519
18.25000	28.00000	....	6.00000	52.25000	34.92	53.59	....	11.49	492
16.50000	27.00000	....	4.50000	48.00000	34.37	56.25	....	9.38	496
15.50000	23.40000	....	4.50000	43.40000	35.71	53.92	....	10.37	497
15.00000	28.50000	....	4.00000	47.50000	31.58	60.00	....	8.42	493
15.00000	26.50000	....	2.55000	44.05000	34.05	60.16	....	5.79	494
15.50000	26.00000	....	3.75000	45.25000	34.25	57.46	....	8.29	a749
14.00000	26.00000	....	3.20000	43.20000	32.41	60.18	....	7.41	495
16.00000	25.75000	....	3.25000	45.00000	35.56	57.22	....	7.22	a750
12.50000	27.50000	....	4.00000	44.00000	28.41	62.50	....	9.09	514
13.50000	26.52000	....	4.50000	44.52000	30.32	59.57	....	10.11	517
11.00000	27.00000	....	3.75000	41.75000	26.35	64.67	....	8.98	512
12.25000	29.00000	....	3.00000	44.25000	27.68	65.54	....	6.78	a751
15.35000	25.55000	....	3.15000	44.05000	34.85	58.00	....	7.15	a752
12.50000	24.00000	....	3.00000	39.50000	31.65	60.76	....	7.59	515
14.50000	22.00000	....	3.00000	39.50000	36.70	55.70	....	7.60	516
14.25000	30.50000	....	4.75000	49.50000	28.80	61.01	....	9.59	519
3.25000	1.50000	....	.50000	5.25000	61.90	28.57	....	9.53	518
3.35000	1.75000	....	.90000	6.00000	55.83	20.17	....	15.00	a754
3.20000	1.60000	....	.47500	5.33500	61.11	29.99	....	8.90	a756
3.33000	2.12500	....	.54500	6.00000	55.50	35.41	....	0.09	527
1.06200	1.68900	....	.91170	3.66270	28.99	46.12	....	24.89	526

WOOLLEN GOODS.

$0.87064	$0.52739	$0.03575	$0.28177	$1.22555	30.24	43.85	0.292	22.99	567
.29000	.80000	....	.29000	1.38000	21.02	57.97	....	21.01	542
.29990	.68100	.00940	.21990	1.21020	24.78	56.27	.78	18.17	539
.22800	.97500	....	.15050	1.35350	16.84	72.04	....	11.12	570
.33660	1.09390	....	.17270	1.60320	20.09	68.24	....	10.77	570
.30000	.98600	....	.12000	1.41000	21.27	65.96	....	12.77	540
.60000	1.70000	....	.10000	2.40000	25.00	70.83	....	4.17	557
.06450	.26560	....	.04250	.37240	17.26	71.33	....	11.41	554

COST OF PRODUCTION—Concluded.

NOTE.—The establishment numbers correspond to those in the table on page 295, Appendix A, showing number of employés and wages, except as noted below. See explanation of table, page 91.

WOOLEN GOODS—Concluded.

Establishment No.	State.	Description of unit.
569	North Carolina	One yard kersey cloth (27 inches wide and weighing 11 ounces)
a757	Tennessee	One yard cloth
558	Connecticut	One yard ladies' cloth (54 inches wide and weighing 8 ounces)
552	Maine	One yard ladies' cloth (54 inches wide and weighing 8 ounces)
557	Connecticut	One yard tricot dress goods (36 inches wide and weighing 4 ounces)
549	Kentucky	One yard Kentucky jeans
548	do	One yard common jeans
548	do	One yard best quality jeans
544	Indiana	One yard best quality jeans
543	do	One yard half-wool jeans
a758	do	One yard half-wool jeans (70 picks)
545	do	One yard flannel (26 by 26 and weighing 4 ounces)
560	Massachusetts	One yard flannel (27 inches wide and weighing 4 ounces)
562	do	One yard flannel (27 inches wide and weighing 4 ounces)
563	Missouri	One yard flannel (27 inches wide and weighing 8 ounces)
561	Massachusetts	One yard flannel (weighing 2¼ ounces)
546	Indiana	One yard flannel (weighing 5 ounces)
544	do	One yard flannel (weighing 5 ounces)
553	Maine	One yard flannel
545	Indiana	One pair blankets (22 by 22 picks and weighing 5 pounds)
565	New Jersey	One pair blankets (68 by 78 inches and weighing 5 pounds)
573	Pennsylvania	One pair blankets (weighing 5 pounds)
563	Missouri	One pair blankets (pure woollen, 80 by 90 inches and weighing 8 pounds)
563	do	One pound yarn (one-fourth blood wool)
568	New York	One pound colored yarn
a750	do	One yard upholstering goods (wool and hair, and measuring one yard to the pound.)

a The wages of employés in this establishment were not reported; therefore the number will not be found in the wage-table, Appendix A.

VARIATION IN THE COST OF PRODUCTION.

COST OF PRODUCTION—Concluded.

NOTE.—The establishment numbers correspond to those in the table on page 295, Appendix A, showing number of employés and wages, except as noted below. See explanation of table, page 91.

WOOLEN GOODS—Concluded.

Amount of unit cost.					Per cent of unit cost.				Establishment No.
Labor.	Materials.	Administration.	Other.	Total.	Labor.	Materials.	Administration.	Other.	
$0.06770	$0.16640	$0.01110	$0.05060	$0.29580	22.88	56.27	3.75	17.10	569
.05000	.17000	....	....	.22000	22.72	77.28	....	....	a757
.09000	.30250	....	.10750	.50000	18.00	60.50	....	21.50	588
.10000	.34000	....	.08000	.52000	19.23	65.38	....	15.39	552
.08000	.22000	....	.07000	.37000	21.62	59.46	....	18.92	537
.05000	.13500	....	.04500	.23000	21.74	58.00	....	19.57	549
.05000	.13000	....	.01500	.19500	25.64	66.67	....	7.69	548
.10000	.20000	....	.02000	.32000	31.25	62.50	....	6.25	548
.08000	.16000	....	.02000	.26000	30.77	61.54	....	7.69	544
.06000	.12000	....	.02000	.20000	30.00	60.00	....	10.00	543
.04000	.11750	....	.02500	.18250	21.91	64.39	....	13.70	a758
.03000	.12000	....	.02000	.17000	17.65	70.59	....	11.76	545
.03000	.12876	....	.02457	.18333	16.36	70.24	....	13.40	560
.03420	.15500	....	.02770	.21690	15.77	71.46	....	12.77	562
.13000	.30000	.04600	.03000	.50600	25.69	59.29	9.09	5.93	563
.04000	.10500	....	.01000	.15500	25.81	67.74	....	6.45	561
.07000	.23000	....	.02000	.32000	21.87	71.88	....	6.25	546
.08000	.16000	....	.02000	.26000	30.77	61.54	....	7.69	544
.02640	.11500	....	.02920	.17060	15.47	67.41	....	17.12	553
0.35000	2.06000	....	0.10000	2.51000	13.95	82.07	....	3.98	545
.70000	2.00000	....	....	2.70000	25.93	74.07	....	....	565
.61300	2.40000	$0.20000	.12300	3.30600	18.05	72.44	5.91	3.60	573
1.60000	4.28000	.60000	.12500	6.60000	24.24	64.85	9.09	1.82	563
.11000	.43000	.05600	.01400	.61000	18.03	70.50	9.18	2.29	563
.06900	.35130	.00910	.01360	.44300	15.57	79.30	2.06	3.07	568
.57868	.29141	....	.10731	.97740	59.20	29.82	....	10.98	a759

126   REPORT OF THE COMMISSIONER OF LABOR.

In the preceding table the cost of production of staple articles in a administration, and other expenses being separately exhibited. In the these items of cost is made. First, an analysis of the labor cost of bringing out the expense for carding, cloth room, reeling and winding, separately reported. When not separately reported they are to be this are shown. The establishment numbers in the margin correspond A, page 295, so that they may be readily identified. Next an analysis iron, classed in the preceding table under metals and metallic goods. producing articles of glass. As an additional, and important, item of

COTTON GOODS—ANALYSIS OF LABOR COST.

NOTE.—The establishment numbers correspond to those in the preceding table, and also to those in the table on page 295, Appendix A, except as noted below.

Establishment No.	State.	Description of unit.
a630	Georgia	Sheeting, 36 inches wide, 40 by 40, and measuring 3.24 yards to the pound..
a630	...do	Sheeting, 36 inches wide, 44 by 42, and measuring 3.08 yards to the pound..
a630	...do	Sheeting, 36 inches wide, 44 by 42, and measuring 2.21 yards to the pound..
240	Virginia	Sheeting, 36 inches wide, 44 by 44, and measuring 4 yards to the pound....
247	...do	Sheeting, 36 inches wide, 44 by 48, and measuring 4.08 yards to the pound..
248	...do	Sheeting, 36 inches wide, 44 by 48, and measuring 4.08 yards to the pound..
234	New York	Sheeting, 36 inches wide, 44 by 48, and measuring 4.5 yards to the pound ..
109	Georgia	Sheeting, 36 inches wide, 50 by 50, and measuring 3.6 yards to the pound ..
190	...do	Sheeting, 36 inches wide, 50 by 50, and measuring 4.01 yards to the pound..
a630	...do	Sheeting, 40 inches wide, 48 by 48, and measuring 2.49 yards to the pound..
a630	...do	Sheeting, 40 inches wide, 56 by 56, and measuring 3.18 yards to the pound..
231	New York	Sheeting, 40½ inches wide, 88 by 96, and measuring 2.88 yards to the pound.
230	...do	Sheeting, 36 inches wide, number 22 yarn, and measuring 3.6 yards to the pound.
230	...do	Sheeting, 39 inches wide, number 22 yarn, and measuring 3.33 yards to the pound.
230	...do	Sheeting, 40 inches wide, number 31 yarn, and measuring 3 yards to the pound.
230	...do	Sheeting, 48 inches wide, number 22 yarn, and measuring 2.777 yards to the pound.
230	...do	Sheeting, 58 inches wide, number 22 yarn, and measuring 2.5 yards to the pound.
230	...do	Sheeting, 77 inches wide, number 22 yarn, and measuring 1.75 yards to the pound.
230	...do	Sheeting, 80 inches wide, number 22 yarn, and measuring 1.538 yards to the pound.
230	...do	Sheeting, 96 inches wide, number 22 yarn, and measuring 1.35 yards to the pound.
a632	Alabama	Sheeting, 31½ inches wide, and measuring 3.81 yards to the pound ....
211	Maryland	Sheeting, 36 inches wide, and measuring 2.84 yards to the pound.........
214	Massachusetts	Sheeting, 36 inches wide, and measuring 2.84 yards to the pound.........
226	New Hampshire	Sheeting, 36 inches wide, and measuring 2.85 yards to the pound.........
a634	South Carolina	Sheeting, 36 inches wide, and measuring 2.85 yards to the pound ....
238	North Carolina	Sheeting, 36 inches wide, and measuring 3 yards to the pound ....
a632	Alabama	Sheeting, 36 inches wide, and measuring 3.29 yards to the pound.........
a633	Georgia	Sheeting, 36 inches wide, and measuring 3.4 yards to the pound ....
a633	...do	Sheeting, 36 inches wide, and measuring 3.75 yards to the pound ....
a634	South Carolina	Sheeting, 36 inches wide, and measuring 4 yards to the pound ....
219	Massachusetts	Print cloth, 28 inches wide, 64 by 64, and measuring 7 yards to the pound.
227	New Hampshire	Print cloth, 28 inches wide, 64 by 64, and measuring 7 yards to the pound.
227	...do	Print cloth, 30 inches wide, 68 by 72, and measuring 6 yards to the pound.
201	Great Britain	Print cloth, 32 inches wide, 64 by 64, and measuring 8 yards to the pound.
227	New Hampshire	Print cloth, 35 inches wide, 68 by 72, and measuring 5 yards to the pound.
233	New York	Shirting, 36 inches wide, 88 by 96, and measuring 3.12 yards to the pound.
a637	Georgia	Shirting, 30 inches wide, and measuring 5.090 yards to the pound ....
a633	...do	Shirting, 31½ inches wide, and measuring 4.6 yards to the pound.........
a637	...do	Shirting, 34½ inches wide, and measuring 5.32 yards to the pound........
198	...do	Cotton cloth, 27 inches wide, 40 by 40, and measuring 4.73 yards to the pound.
198	...do	Cotton cloth, 31½ inches wide, 48 by 46, and measuring 3.65 yards to the pound.
198	...do	Cotton cloth, 36 inches wide, 48 by 46, and measuring 3.01 yards to the pound.
a637	...do	Cotton cloth, 36 inches wide, and measuring 4.079 yards to the pound ...

a The wages of employés in this establishment were not reported; therefore the number will not be found in the wage table, Appendix A.

VARIATION IN THE COST OF PRODUCTION. 127

large number of industries has been shown, the cost of labor, materials, following table a step forward is taken, and an analysis of some of producing one yard of fully described articles of cotton goods is shown, spinning, spooling, and weaving, in each instance where these were found combined in the column headed Other. Sixty-four examples of to those used in the preceding table and in the wage table, Appendix is made in 40 cases of the cost of material in the production of pig- Finally, an analysis is given in 13 cases of the cost of materials in information, the cost for fuel is also shown.

COTTON GOODS—ANALYSIS OF LABOR COST.

NOTE.—The establishment numbers correspond to those in the preceding table, and also to those in the table on page 296, Appendix A, except as noted below.

			Labor cost of one yard.					Establishment No.
Carding.	Cloth room.	Reeling and winding.	Spinning.	Spooling.	Weaving.	Other.	Total.	
$0.001296	b$0.000731	$0.000846	$0.001385	$0.000902	$0.003152	$0.000532	$0.008644	a630
.001303	b.000768	.000679	.001457	.000920	.003318	.000559	.009093	a630
.001896	b.001069	.000945	.002029	.001320	.004610	.000779	.012657	a630
.001440			.001980		.004500	.001620	.009540	246
.001715			.001959		.004132	.000614	.008420	247
.001495			.001888		.003751	.001306	.008530	248
.001795			.002099		.004401	.000845	.009140	234
.001443			.001628		.003576	.002085	.008332	199
.001320			.001463		.003210	.001558	.007551	199
.001686	b.000951	.000841	.001894	.001108	.004108	.000693	.011257	a630
.001322	b.000745	.000650	.001414	.000921	.003220	.000543	.008824	a630
.005151			.005837		.020108	.003247	.034343	231
.002990			.003420		.009660	.003380	.019450	230
.003190			.003682		.010315	.003813	.021000	230
.003950			.004553		.012730	.004767	.026000	230
.003828			.004418		.012378	.004576	.025200	230
.004252			.004910		.013752	.005086	.028000	230
.006076			.007013		.019647	.007264	.040000	230
.006910			.007976		.022340	.008274	.045500	230
.007868			.009081		.025444	.009407	.051800	230
.001350	.000380		.002190		.005110	.001460	.010490	a632
.002363			.002402	.000992	.005799	.004759	.016405	211
.002366			.002380	.000728	.004605	.002883	.012962	214
.001810	.000910		.001760	.000600	.001080	.003750	.012690	226
.001399			.001192	.000563	.003162	.001848	.008164	a634
.002130			.002660		.003940	.000640	.009370	238
.001060	.000380		.002210		.005120	.001470	.011140	a632
.001559	.000382		.001147		.002617	.001059	.006764	a633
.001413	.000347		.001040		.002374	.000956	.006130	a635
.001663			.001419	.000660	.003761	.001321	.008833	a634
.001280			.001800		.001570	.002700	.010350	219
.001500	.000170		.001699	.000870	.004230	.001530	.009990	227
.001730	.000200		.002000	.001010	.005010	.001790	.011740	227
.000690			.001080		.005760	.000490	.008020	201
.002080	.000240		.002380	.001220	.006020	.002140	.014080	227
.004000			.004100		.012500	.006300	.027100	233
.001324			.001256		.002567	.001489	.006636	a637
.001152	.000283		.000848		.001934	.000782	.004999	a633
.001278			.001184		.002459	.001426	.006347	a637
.001105			.000992	.000258	.002566	.001206	.006127	198
.001596			.001286	.000334	.003326	.001563	.008105	198
.001737			.001558	.000406	.004033	.001897	.009631	198
.001655			.001545		.003209	.001861	.008270	a637

b Labor cost of dye-house help is included in this.

COTTON GOODS—ANALYSIS OF LABOR COST—Concluded.

NOTE.—The establishment numbers correspond to those in the preceding table, and also to those in the table on page 295, Appendix A, except as noted below.

Establishment No.	State.	Description of unit.
a630	Georgia	Drilling, 29 inches wide, 70 by 48, and measuring 2.82 yards to the pound.
a630	...do	Drilling, 30½ inches wide, 70 by 48, and measuring 2.84 yards to the pound.
a634	South Carolina	Drilling, 30½ inches wide, 70 by 48, and measuring 2.84 yards to the pound.
108	Georgia	Drilling, 31½ inches wide, 62 by 48, and measuring 3.08 yards to the pound.
199	...do	Drilling, 31½ inches wide, 72 by 50, and measuring 3.01 yards to the pound.
a630	...do	Drilling, 30½ inches wide, 68 by 52, and measuring 2.43 yards to the pound.
a630	...do	Drilling, 37 inches wide, 70 by 48, and measuring 2.30 yards to the pound.
a630	...do	Drilling, 37 inches wide, 83 by 40, and measuring 1.6 yards to the pound.
a630	...do	Drilling, 46 inches wide, 70 by 42, and measuring 2 yards to the pound.
a630	...do	Drilling, 51 inches wide, 70 by 42, and measuring 1.79 yards to the pound.
a630	...do	Drilling, 58 inches wide, 70 by 42, and measuring 1.58 yards to the pound.
a632	Alabama	Drilling, measuring 3.15 yards to the pound.
a633	Georgia	Drilling, measuring 3.05 yards to the pound.
a630	...do	Duck, 38 inches wide, 83 by 28, and measuring 1.79 yards to the pound.
a630	...do	Duck, 46 inches wide, 83 by 28, and measuring 1.49 yards to the pound.
a630	...do	Duck, 51 inches wide, 83 by 28, and measuring 1.32 yards to the pound.
a630	...do	Duck, 57 inches wide, 83 by 28, and measuring 1.19 yards to the pound.
213	Maryland	Duck, 22 by 36, and measuring 1 yard to the pound.
212	...do	Duck, 28 by 36, and measuring 2 yards to the pound.
241	North Carolina	Plaid, 27 inches wide, 40 by 40, and measuring 4 yards to the pound.
249	Virginia	Plaid, 27 inches wide, 44 by 44, and measuring 4.25 yards to the pound.

METALS AND METALLIC GOODS—ANALYSIS OF COST OF MATERIAL.

Establishment No.	State.	Description of unit.
366	Alabama	One ton run of furnace foundery pig iron (Alabama ore).
399	New York	One ton run of furnace foundery pig iron (New York ore).
413	Ohio	One ton run of furnace foundery pig iron (Lake Superior ore).
405	...do	One ton run of furnace foundery pig iron (Hocking Valley and Lake Superior ore).
409	...do	One ton run of furnace foundery pig iron (Hanging Rock ore).
414	...do	One ton run of furnace foundery pig iron (Hanging Rock ore).
a714	...do	One ton run of furnace foundery pig iron (Hanging Rock ore).
a715	...do	One ton run of furnace foundery pig iron (Mahoning Valley and Lake Superior ore).
408	...do	One ton run of furnace foundery pig iron (Mahoning Valley and Lake Superior ore).
a716	...do	One ton run of furnace foundery pig iron (Mahoning Valley and Lake Superior ore.)
435	Tennessee	One ton run of furnace foundery pig iron (Tennessee ore).
a717	...do	One ton run of furnace foundery pig iron (Tennessee ore).
439	Virginia	One ton run of furnace foundery pig iron (Virginia ore).
437	...do	One ton run of furnace foundery pig iron (Virginia ore).
438	...do	One ton run of furnace foundery pig iron (Virginia ore).
a718	West Virginia	One ton run of furnace foundery pig iron (Lake Superior ore).
a719	...do	One ton run of furnace foundery pig iron (West Virginia ore).
392	Maryland	One ton number one foundery pig iron.
400	New York	One ton number two foundery pig iron.
377	Great Britain	One ton number three foundery pig iron.
a720	Pennsylvania	One ton run of furnace foundery pig iron.
a721	Belgium	One thousand kilograms (2,205 pounds) white pig iron.
a722	Germany	One thousand kilograms (2,205 pounds) white pig iron.
a723	Ohio	One ton Bessemer pig iron.
400	...do	One ton Bessemer pig iron.
a724	Pennsylvania	One ton Bessemer pig iron.
424	...do	One ton Bessemer pig iron.
425	...do	One ton Bessemer pig iron.

a The wages of employés in this establishment were not reported; therefore the number will not be found in the wage table, Appendix A.

COTTON GOODS—ANALYSIS OF LABOR COST—Concluded.

NOTE.—The establishment numbers correspond to those in the preceding table, and also to those in the table on page 295, Appendix A, except as noted below.

Carding.	Cloth-room.	Reeling and winding.	Spinning.	Spooling.	Weaving.	Other.	Total.	Establishment No.
$0.001490	b$0.000838	$0.000740	$0.001594	$0.001035	$0.003021	$0.000011	$0.009929	a620
.001479	b.000834	.000738	.001589	.001030	.003603	.000608	.009881	a630
.001408	....	....	.001201	.000566	.003183	.001659	.008217	a634
.001697	....	....	.001522	.000396	.003041	.001852	.005408	198
.001758	....	....	.001946	....	.004277	.003091	.011072	199
.001729	b.000975	.000845	.001632	.001204	.004210	.000711	.011506	a620
.001777	b.001002	.000885	.001901	.001237	.004328	.000730	.011860	a630
.002024	b.001480	.001308	.002808	.001828	.006392	.001078	.017518	a630
.002100	b.001184	.001046	.002246	.001462	.005115	.000863	.014016	a630
.002345	b.001322	.001131	.002505	.001633	.005742	.000063	.015011	a630
.002651	b.001494	.001321	.002842	.001846	.006467	.001089	.017700	a630
.002049	.000400	....	.003307	....	.005330	.001537	.011623	a632
.001737	.000126	....	.001279	....	.002918	.001180	.007240	a683
.002347	b.001325	.001171	.002512	.001635	.005721	.000064	.015675	a630
.002881	b.001588	.001419	.003013	.001961	.006859	.001157	.018869	a630
.003188	b.001797	.001589	.003410	.002210	.007764	.001311	.021278	a630
.003522	b.001985	.001755	.003767	.002452	.008577	.001447	.023505	a630
.007113	....	....	.008362	....	.010181	.007232	.033378	213
.002243	.000801	....	.004445	....	.004167	.002644	.013306	212
.001100	....	....	.002300	....	.008000	.001400	.012800	241
.001253	....	....	.002130	....	.009147	.003260	.015790	249

b Labor cost of dye-house help is included in this.

METALS AND METALLIC GOODS—ANALYSIS OF COST OF MATERIAL.

			Material.					Establishment No.
Charcoal.	Coal.	Coke.	Limestone.	Iron cinder.	Lake Superior ore.	Native ore.	Ore.	Total.	
....	....	$4 03	$0 32	....	....	$2 57	....	$6 92	366
....	$1 67	3 91	53	....	....	3 41	....	9 52	399
....	....	4 27	66	$0 81	$6 94	....	....	12 68	413
....	1 90	....	1 15	1 25	2 75	....	4 25	11 30	405
....	....	4 50	70	....	....	4 95	....	10 15	409
....	1 40	2 60	80	....	....	5 00	....	9 80	414
....	....	4 80	85	....	....	6 30	....	11 95	a714
....	....	4 16	56	....	4 30	3 15	....	12 17	a715
....	....	4 32	80	83	2 77	3 90	....	12 62	408
....	....	4 05	45	....	5 25	3 25	....	13 00	a716
....	10	5 27	85	....	....	4 29	....	10 01	435
....	3 60	1 91	25	....	....	5 06	....	10 82	a717
....	....	3 52	45	....	....	5 04	....	9 01	439
....	....	5 05	1 08	55	....	3 80	....	10 48	437
....	....	3 87	78	....	....	6 05	....	10 70	438
....	....	4 35	63	70	7 65	....	....	13 33	a718
....	....	3 08	1 00	....	....	6 87	....	10 95	a719
....	5 88	....	1 24	....	....	....	$7 65	14 77	392
....	5 13	....	75	....	....	....	8 04	13 92	400
....	....	2 70	40	....	....	....	3 23	6 33	377
....	....	3 50	50	....	9 75	....	....	13 75	a720
....	....	3 40	30	....	....	....	4 08	8 38	a721
....	....	2 83	67	....	....	....	6 86	10 36	a722
....	....	3 08	61	....	10 72	....	....	15 01	a723
....	....	5 10	72	....	9 08	....	....	14 90	410
....	1 91	2 56	54	....	....	....	9 75	14 76	a724
....	....	2 71	60	....	10 60	....	....	13 91	424
....	....	2 80	56	....	10 50	....	....	13 86	425

METALS AND METALLIC GOODS—ANALYSIS OF COST OF MATERIAL—Concl'd

NOTE.—The establishment numbers correspond to those in the preceding table, and also to those in the tables on page 295, Appendix A, except as noted below.

Establishment No.	State.	Description of unit.
407	Ohio	One ton foundery pig iron, soft, silvery (Ohio brown hematite ore).......
409	....do	One ton foundery pig iron, soft, silvery (Ohio brown hematite ore).......
411	....do	One ton foundery pig iron, soft, silvery (Ohio brown hematite ore).......
a725	....do	One ton foundery pig iron, soft, silvery (Ohio brown hematite ore).......
a726	....do	One ton foundery pig iron, soft, silvery (Ohio brown hematite ore).......
a727	....do	One ton foundery pig iron, soft, silvery (Ohio brown hematite ore).......
a728	Germany	One thousand kilograms (2,205 pounds) mill pig iron..................
420	Pennsylvania	One ton number one mill pig iron................................
425	....do	One ton low grade mill pig iron..................................
a730	Ohio	One ton cold-blast charcoal pig iron (Hanging Rock ore)............
a731	....do	One ton cold-blast charcoal pig iron (Hanging Rock ore)............
591	Maryland	One ton hot-blast charcoal pig iron...............................

a The wages of employés in this establishment were not reported; therefore the number will not be found in the wage table, Appendix A.

GLASS—COST OF FUEL AND ANALYSIS OF COST OF MATERIAL.

Establishment No.	State.	Description of unit.
288	Illinois	One box (50 feet) average size, single strength window glass ....
296	Ohio	One box (50 feet) average size, single strength window glass ....
308	Pennsylvania	One box (50 feet) 12 by 28 inches, single strength, window glass........
309	....do	One box (50 feet) 12 by 28 inches, single strength, window glass........
300	....do	One gross flint eight-ounce Philadelphia oval bottles....................
302	....do	One gross flint eight-ounce Philadelphia oval bottles....................
301	....do	One gross flint pint flasks.......................................
304	....do	One gross flint pint flasks.......................................
289	Kentucky	One gross quart Mason fruit jars (without trimmings) ....
305	Pennsylvania	One gross quart Mason fruit jars (without trimmings) ....
306	....do	One gross quart beer bottles......................................
307	....do	One gross quart beer bottles......................................
312	....do	One dozen number two, crimp top, lima, lamp chimneys..............

METALS AND METALLIC GOODS—ANALYSIS OF COST OF MATERIAL—Concl'd.

NOTE.—The establishment numbers correspond to those in the preceding table, and also to those in the table on page 295, Appendix A, except as noted below.

Charcoal.	Coal.	Coke.	Limestone.	Iron cinder.	Lake Superior ore.	Native ore.	Ore.	Total.	Establishment No.
....	$2 67	$1 30	$0 72	....	....	$5 37	....	$10 06	407
....	3 27	....	90	....	....	6 25	....	10 42	406
....	2 40	1 20	80	....	....	5 07	....	10 07	411
....	2 40	1 20	80	....	....	5 07	....	10 07	a725
....	4 67	....	1 00	....	....	4 95	....	10 62	a726
....	3 60	....	1 12	....	....	5 50	....	10 22	a727
....	....	2 23	52	....	....	....	$5 29	8 04	a728
....	....	3 15	1 32	....	....	7 50	....	11 97	426
....	....	3 00	1 12	....	....	5 00	....	9 12	425
$12 30	....	....	15	....	....	6 25	....	18 70	a730
10 80	....	....	25	....	....	5 83	....	16 88	a731
6 83	....	....	13	....	....	....	11 46	18 42	391

GLASS—COST OF FUEL AND ANALYSIS OF COST OF MATERIAL.

Arsenic.	Charcoal.	Cullet.	Lime.	Saltcake.	Sodaash.	Sand.	Other.	Total.	Fuel.	Establishment No.
$0.00880	$0.00880	$0.01990	$0.03330	$0.18220	....	$0.04550	....	$0.29850	$0.33660	288
.01970	.00770	.01440	.02868	.08430	$0.13090	.04688	....	.33256	.24200	296
.02000	.01000	....	.02700	.20000	.13200	.03500	....	.42400	.39800	308
.02000	.01000	....	.03000	.16000	.15000	.06000	....	.43000	.14000	309
....	....	....	.02000	....	.26400	.03500	$0.05300	.37200	.20700	300
....	....	....	.02000	....	.27000	.05000	.03500	.38100	.14500	302
....	....	....	.05000	....	.44700	.07000	.09780	.67080	.21600	301
....	....	....	.04880	....	.56840	.12152	.20000	.93872	.10000	304
....	....	.03900	.07200	....	.67300	.10000	....	.88400	....	286
....	....	....	.10000	....	.88000	.17000	....	1.15000	.32000	305
....	....	....	.13000	....	.90000	.20000	....	1.23000	.60000	306
....	....	....	.15000	....	.98100	.18200	....	1.31300	.35000	307
....	....	....	.00460	....	.03000	.00750	.00500	.04710	....	312

In securing information from foreign countries it sometimes occurred that the facts could not be ascertained in the same form as were those from the United States, and thus it was impossible to place such facts in the preceding table, as would have been desirable. Such information, however, being deemed of great value to the manufacturers of this country, it is given as secured, and the following tables, mostly drawn from official sources, show the various elements as designated in their headings:

COST OF SPINNING ONE POUND OF COTTON YARN IN ALSACE.

Numbers (English scale).	Expenses (not including cotton).				
	Labor.	Fuel.	Interest and depreciation.	Other.	Total.
16 and under	$0.01388	$0.00511	$0.01534	$0.00660	$0.04093
18 to 24	.01809	.00667	.02000	.00857	.05333
24 to 30	.02259	.00832	.02497	.01070	.06658
30 to 35	.02713	.01000	.02735	.01285	.07733
38	.03056	.00916	.02779	.01833	.08584
40	.03308	.00992	.02975	.01985	.09260
42	.03592	.01078	.03233	.02155	.10058
45	.04126	.01232	.03700	.02467	.11525
47	.04512	.01354	.04061	.02701	.12628
49	.04888	.01434	.04304	.02868	.13494
52	.05000	.01499	.04500	.02999	.13998
54	.05280	.01600	.04791	.03200	.14871
57	.05788	.01737	.05210	.03473	.16208
59	.06153	.01846	.05537	.03691	.17227
61	.06717	.02015	.06045	.04030	.18807
64	.07040	.02112	.06336	.04224	.19712
66	.07394	.02232	.06655	.04436	.20717
68	.07787	.02335	.07008	.04687	.21817
71	.08224	.02466	.07401	.04935	.23026
73	.08079	.02603	.08081	.05387	.25140
75	.09461	.02838	.08515	.05077	.26491
78	.00778	.02933	.08800	.05866	.27377
80	.10231	.03069	.09209	.06138	.28647
82	.10731	.03219	.09658	.06438	.30046
85	.11281	.03384	.10153	.06709	.31587
87	.12054	.03616	.10848	.07232	.33750
90	.12940	.03882	.11646	.07764	.36232
92	.13663	.04099	.12208	.08198	.38258
94	.14193	.04258	.12774	.08515	.39740
97	.14764	.04429	.13288	.08858	.41339
99	.15384	.04614	.13845	.09230	.43073
101	.15941	.04782	.14347	.09584	.44634
104	.16416	.04925	.14776	.09850	.45967
106	.16602	.04980	.14943	.09962	.46487
108	.17460	.05237	.15714	.10475	.48886
111	.17959	.05387	.16162	.10774	.50282
113	.18409	.05522	.16568	.11045	.51544
116	.19047	.05713	.17142	.11428	.53330
118	.19130	.05739	.17217	.11477	.53563
120	.20091	.06027	.18081	.12054	.56253
123	.20657	.06196	.18590	.12393	.57836
125	.21255	.06376	.19130	.12752	.59513
127	.22000	.06600	.19800	.13200	.61600
130	.22564	.06768	.20307	.13537	.63176
136	.24175	.07252	.21758	.14505	.67690
142	.25882	.07764	.23294	.15529	.72469
147	.27500	.08250	.24750	.16500	.77000
153	.29333	.08800	.26400	.17600	.82133
159	.31428	.09428	.28285	.18856	.87997
165	.33082	.09924	.29773	.19849	.92628
171	.34920	.10476	.31428	.20951	.97776
177	.36974	.11092	.33277	.22184	1.03527

VARIATION IN THE COST OF PRODUCTION.

COST OF SPINNING ONE POUND OF COTTON YARN IN ENGLAND.

Numbers (English scale).	Expenses (not including cotton).				
	Labor.	Fuel.	Interest and depreciation.	Other.	Total.
18 and under	$0.01267	$0.00148	$0.00820	$0.00551	$0.02786
18 to 24	.01664	.00193	.01064	.00717	.03638
24 to 30	.02054	.00242	.01328	.00894	.04518
30 to 35	.02468	.00290	.01597	.01074	.05429
38	.02596	.00305	.01679	.01130	.05710
40	.02811	.00330	.01818	.01224	.06183
42	.03052	.00359	.01975	.01328	.06714
45	.03494	.00410	.02267	.01521	.07686
47	.03835	.00450	.02481	.01669	.08435
49	.04064	.00477	.02630	.01769	.08940
52	.04249	.00499	.02750	.01849	.09347
54	.04533	.00532	.02933	.01963	.09961
57	.04920	.00579	.03183	.02141	.10823
59	.05218	.00615	.03357	.02276	.11466
61	.05709	.00671	.03706	.02486	.12572
64	.05984	.00704	.03872	.02604	.13164
66	.06285	.00740	.04067	.02735	.13827
68	.06619	.00778	.04282	.02881	.14560
71	.06989	.00821	.04523	.03043	.15376
73	.07632	.00897	.04938	.03322	.16769
75	.08042	.00946	.05208	.03500	.17691
78	.08311	.00978	.05378	.03618	.18285
80	.08697	.01023	.05627	.03785	.19132
82	.09121	.01072	.05902	.03970	.20065
85	.09589	.01128	.06204	.04178	.21094
87	.10245	.01204	.06629	.04459	.22537
90	.11000	.01293	.07117	.04788	.24198
92	.11614	.01366	.07515	.05055	.25550
94	.12063	.01419	.07806	.05250	.26538
97	.12549	.01475	.08120	.05463	.27607
99	.13076	.01538	.08461	.05691	.28766
101	.13550	.01593	.08768	.05897	.29808
104	.13987	.01641	.09029	.06074	.30731
106	.14112	.01660	.09131	.06143	.31046
108	.14841	.01745	.09602	.06460	.32648
111	.15204	.01796	.09877	.06644	.33581
113	.15648	.01840	.10125	.06811	.34424
116	.16189	.01905	.10475	.07047	.35616
118	.16260	.01913	.10521	.07077	.35771
120	.17077	.02009	.11050	.07433	.37569
123	.17558	.02065	.11360	.07642	.38625
125	.18067	.02120	.11690	.07864	.39747
127	.18700	.02200	.12100	.08140	.41140
130	.19178	.02256	.12409	.08348	.42191
136	.20548	.02417	.13205	.08944	.45204
142	.22000	.02588	.14234	.09578	.48398
147	.23374	.02750	.15124	.10174	.51422
153	.24933	.02933	.16133	.10859	.54852
159	.26714	.03142	.17284	.11628	.58768
165	.28119	.03307	.18186	.12239	.61851
171	.29682	.03491	.19206	.12920	.65299
177	.31435	.03696	.20335	.13680	.69146

The following table shows the wages paid per spindle, and the cost of coal, tallow, and oil per spindle, in the cotton-spinning mills located in the Oldham district, England. The time covered is for the quarter commencing March 28, 1885, and ending June 27, 1885, being twelve weeks of fifty-six and one-half hours each (short time being reduced to full time). The mills were engaged during the period stated on number 32 twist or its equivalent:

COST OF PRODUCING COTTON YARN (NUMBER 32 TWIST) AT OLDHAM, ENGLAND.

Items of cost.	Mill number one.	Mill number two.	Mill number three.
Labor cost per spindle during the twelve weeks	$0.164	$0.170	$0.171
Cost of coal, tallow, and oil per spindle during the twelve weeks	.026	.026	.030
Average cost of labor per spindle for three mills			$0.168+
Average cost of coal, tallow, and oil per spindle for three mills			.027+
Cost of cotton consumed per spindle (eleven pounds)			1.220
Depreciation of plant per spindle			.052
Average cost of carriage per spindle			.013
Total cost per spindle			1.480
Value of product per spindle (ten pounds, at 17 cents per pound)			1.700
Manufacturer's margin			.220

The above margin of 22 cents is for profit, interest, discount, brokerage, commissions, taxes, repairs, insurance, and incidental expenses, such as water, gas, roller leather, cloth, skip paper, skips, belting, lacing, engine packing, wrapping paper, twine, etc., also office expenses, etc., for the period of twelve weeks; on this basis there would be a margin for a year of 95½ cents. The above statement shows a fair working margin of profit in cotton spinning for medium counts, but owing to the fact that number 32 twist or its equivalent had to be marketed at considerably less than 17 cents per pound the majority of mills in the Oldham district closed the quarter ending June 27, 1885, either with loss or without profit. The mills selected for averaging the labor cost per spindle, and the coal, tallow, and oil cost per spindle, are fairly representative ones in the Oldham district. For the quarter ending June 27, 1885, one of these companies made no profit, one lost money, and one paid a small dividend. All the companies named are limited-liability organizations, and are economically managed. The machinery used in the mills named was made by representative firms. Self-acting mules were employed in each mill.

The following table shows the per cent. labor cost, etc., of producing number 32 twist, the L. M. American cotton being calculated at 11 cents per pound, and the selling price of the cotton yarn at 17 cents per pound, the wages being based on the prices paid in the Oldham district prior to the strike of July 20, 1885, which were list prices of January, 1876, less 10 per cent.:

ANALYSIS OF COST OF PRODUCING NUMBER 32 TWIST AT OLDHAM, ENGLAND.

Items.	Per cent.
Cotton	71.76
Labor cost	9.88
Depreciation	3.06
Coal, tallow, and oil	1.58
Carriage	.77
Profit, interest, etc., insurance, and incidental expenses	12.95
Total	100

If we take the product of number 32 twist to be 13 ounces avoirdupois per week per spindle, with self-acting mule frames, and the combined wages of a minder and his piecers to be $13.98 for one week, from a pair of mules containing 2,124 spindles, the labor cost of 10 pounds of number 32 twist in the spinning department will be 8.1 cents, which, divided by $1.70, the selling price of 10 pounds at 17 cents per pound, will give 4.76 per cent. for the labor cost for spinning.

The entire labor cost for spinning number 32 twist, as has been shown in the preceding table, is 9.88 per cent., which, less 4.76 per cent. for the spinning department, leaves 5.12 per cent. to cover the labor cost in the preparatory and power departments and the cost of management.

The above calculations clearly indicate that the percentage of labor cost in all departments of cotton spinning has been minimized to such an extent for medium counts of yarn that it bears but a small proportion to the value of the finished product.

In the Bolton and Manchester districts, where finer counts are spun, the labor cost, as well as the margin of profit, is larger than has been given for the Oldham district, where only coarse and medium counts of cotton yarn are produced.

A margin of 6 cents per pound between the raw material and number 32 cop twist is considered by British spinners very remunerative, and with such a margin a large return upon the capital invested is usually made; for in properly-managed modern mills number 32 cop twist can be produced and marketed on a margin of 4½ cents per pound without loss.

PRODUCTION, ETC., OF COAL IN FRANCE, 1853-83.

[NOTE.—In this table 1,000 kilograms (2,205 pounds) are considered a ton.]

Year.	Employés.				Production.			Labor cost per ton.
	Number.	Amount of wages.	Average wages of each.		Tons.	Tons per employé.		
			Yearly.	Daily.		Yearly.	Daily.	
1853	40,958	$4,756,871	$116	$0.42	5,937,000	144	.529	$0.80
1858	56,035	7,540,124	134	.49	7,352,000	131	.479	1.02
1861	65,610	9,094,932	138	.49	9,395,000	143	.512	.96
1864	77,342	11,196,895	144	.50	11,201,000	144	.501	.99
1866	79,909	12,195,863	152	.53	12,234,000	153	.533	.99
1869	84,494	13,718,054	162	.57	13,509,000	160	.568	1.01
1870	82,673	13,948,882	168	.58	13,179,000	159	.560	1.05
1872	91,899	17,391,809	189	.64	16,100,000	175	.588	1.08
1873	101,844	20,168,114	197	.66	17,479,000	171	.569	1.15
1874	102,985	21,015,963	204	.69	16,907,000	164	.554	1.24
1875	105,366	21,665,408	205	.69	16,956,000	161	.542	1.28
1876	107,567	21,262,617	196	......	17,101,000	158	......	1.24
1877	105,813	19,917,021	187	......	16,804,000	158	......	1.18
1878	103,056	19,441,083	187	......	16,960,000	164	......	1.14
1879	99,155	18,901,618	190	......	17,110,000	172	......	1.10
1880	103,921	20,913,094	201	......	18,804,000	180	......	1.11
1881	103,002	21,043,502	203	......	19,765,000	191	......	1.06
1882	108,300	22,355,160	212	.71	20,601,000	190	.643	1.08
1883	113,000	24,544,003	217	.74	21,334,000	196	.644	1.10

PRODUCTION OF COAL IN 1883, IN THE EIGHT LARGEST PRODUCING DISTRICTS IN FRANCE. a

[NOTE.—In this table 1,000 kilograms (2,205 pounds) are considered a ton.]

Departments.	Within the mines.			Outside the mines.		
	Employés.	Days worked.	Wages.	Employés.	Days worked.	Wages.
Allier	3,242	290	$0 73	1,676	292	$0 40
Aveyron	2,580	300	83	1,726	300	55
Gard	8,083	286	92	4,109	286	63
Loire	12,688	285	90	5,816	268	63
Nord	15,510	300	77	4,370	300	45
Pas-de-Calais	21,403	303	70	5,869	290	64
Saone-et-Loire	4,898	305	81	2,319	306	53
Tarn	1,294	240	72	713	241	58

Departments.	Within and outside the mines.					
	Total employés.	Tons produced.	Tons daily per employé.	Labor cost per ton.	Average price per ton.	Taxes in 1884.
Allier	4,918	950,000	.66	$0 93	$2 41	$20,073
Aveyron	4,306	826,000	.63	1 13	2 12	10,181
Gard	12,192	1,972,000	.53	1 52	2 45	33,770
Loire	18,504	3,586,000	.09	1 18	2 90	-120,102
Nord	19,880	3,789,000	.63	1 10	2 20	42,704
Pas-de-Calais	27,272	6,155,000	.75	1 02	2 24	139,263
Saone-et-Loire	7,217	1,381,000	.02	1 15	2 62	38,374
Tarn	2,007	325,000	.55	1 03	3 09	13,326

a There is a slight unexplainable difference between the figures here shown for Pas-de-Calais and what appear in the succeeding table.

PRODUCTION OF COAL IN 1883 IN THE DEPARTMENT OF PAS-DE-CALAIS, FRANCE.

[NOTE.—In this table 1,000 kilograms (2,205 pounds) are considered a ton.]

Mines.	Employés.						Production.	
	Within the mines.		Outside the mines.			Total.	Tons.	Tons annually per employé.
	Men.	Children.	Men.	Women.	Children.			
Douiges	1,096	177	177	55	14	1,477	272,000	184
Courrières	2,236	154	567	32	63	3,052	850,000	278
Lens and Douvein	3,122	352	891	186	17	4,568	1,170,000	256
Grenay	2,168	309	617	72	9	3,265	775,000	237
Noeux	2,233	234	539	62	40	3,108	735,000	236
Bruay	1,910	201	302	68	8	2,489	569,000	228
Marles	1,528	197	304	23	57	2,169	526,000	242
Terfay	826	84	174	42	9	1,125	187,000	166
Auchy-au-Bois	418	60	130	74	29	681	37,000	54
Fléchinelle	211	24	80	5	19	339	48,000	145
Liévin	1,180	201	353	87	4	1,824	452,000	247
Vendin	218	25	49	9	2	303	41,000	135
Mourchin	472	37	187	10	7	733	177,000	241
Carvin	805	69	183	11	7	1,075	178,000	165
Ostricourt	146	23	27	11	9	216	44,000	203
Courcelles-l'Lens	121	10	23	13	7	174	25,000	143
Hardinghen	380	28	127	5	24	573	61,000	106

PRODUCTION, ETC., IN 1883, IN FIVE COAL MINES IN FRANCE.

[NOTE.—In this table 1,000 kilograms (2,205 pounds) are considered a ton.]

Localities	Within the mines.			Outside the mines.		
	Employés.	Days worked.	Wages.	Employés.	Days worked.	Wages.
Champagne (Cantal)	375	280	$0.74	125	288	$0.51
Decize (Nièvre)	948	260	.79	512	300	.33
Carmaux (Tarn)	1,294	249	.72	713	241	.59
Montrelais (Loire Inf.)	124	205	.78	64	252	.41
St. Saurs (Deux Sèvres)	103	263	.65	62	253	.46

Localities.	Within and outside the mines.				Average price per ton.	Maximum working depth (feet.)	Average working depth (feet.)	Thickness of vein (feet.)
	Total employés.	Tons produced.	Tons daily per employé.	Labor cost per ton.				
Champagne (Cantal)	500	42,463	.30	$2 25	$2 90	525	262	17
Decize (Nièvre)	1,460	194,306	.47	1 27	2 60	2,037	607	12
Carmaux (Tarn)	2,007	325,480	.66	1 03	2 79	984	557	6
Montrelais (Loire Inf.)	188	19,243	.36	1 44	2 81	1,205	577	4
St. Saurs (Deux Sèvres)	165	22,092	.52	1 12	3 09	771	377	5

The following estimate as to the cost of production of a ton of coal in the north of France was given in testimony before the French Tariff Commission in 1877:

Wages:
Tunnelling and laying tracks	$0.565
Sundry labor inside mines	.530
Sundry labor outside of mines	.237
	1.332
Sundry material used	.604
Taxes on mines	.034
General expenses	.129
	2.099

The following extracts from testimony given before the French Tariff Commission in 1877 give a very fair idea of the explanation given by various mining experts and engineers to account for the greater cost of coal production in France as compared with other countries of Europe:

"The condition of the coal deposits in France is not so favorable as that of other countries, the galleries requiring a great quantity of timber for supports, and the coal being of a character that requires much manipulation to free it from foreign matter, from which causes results a production per workman much inferior to that in other countries.

"However, the daily wages of coal miners in other countries is but 3.75 francs per day, while the French miner is paid about 4.25 per day.

"When the foreign coal mines are compared with those of France, the conditions of inferiority are abundant. We find these conditions of inferiority not only in the geological condition which requires expensive works, but also in the greater cost of labor.

"In the first place, the greater facility of extraction in England must be considered. In France it is necessary to mine the coal at considerable depth, while certain English coal mines are worked by simple galleries.

"The influence of the difference which exists between the deposits of the two countries (France and England) is shown not only in the increased cost of labor, but also in the amount of materials necessary, and in the general expenses of working.

"In France the cost of the wood alone used in the support of the galleries is 20 cents per ton of coal mined, while in England it averages but one-fifth of that sum.

"The increased cost of labor outside of the mines is owing 'to the various manipulations rendered necessary at the mouth of the mines. In the north of France the deposits are thin and irregular. To work them it becomes necessary to break the rock which surrounds them, and the coal always contains some of this rock, which it requires much care and time to separate.'

"In the north of France, the galleries require to be braced with timbers their whole length, and frequently the timber supports are almost continuous."

COST OF PRODUCTION, ETC., IN 1883, OF IRON ORE IN FRANCE.

[NOTE.—In this table 1,000 kilograms (2,205 pounds) are considered a ton.]

Departments.	Mines.	Within the mines.			Outside the mines.			Within and outside the mines.			
		Employés.	Days worked.	Wages.	Employés.	Days worked.	Wages.	Total employés.	Tons produced.	Tons daily per employé.	Labor cost per ton.
Ardèche	6	776	285	$0 67	137	236	$0 48	913	187,985	.74	$0 86
Ariège	5	449	243	55	19	255	49	468	33,285	.24	1 88
Aveyron	2	52	300	77	13	310	54	65	63,500		
Isère	7	215	256	74	108	244	45	323	38,275	.47	1 38
Meurthe	31	2,090	275	1 01	380	284	68	2,470	1,717,111	2.51	38
Moselle					547	269	72		423,057	2.88	25

COST OF PRODUCTION, ETC., OF IRON ORE IN FRANCE, 1853-83.

[NOTE.—In this table 1,000 kilograms (2,205 pounds) are considered a ton.]

Years.	Employés.			Production.		Labor cost per ton.	Average price per ton.
	Number.	Amount of wages.	Average yearly wages.	Tons.	Tons yearly per employé.		
1853	15,684	$1,092,981	$65	3,318,000	211	$0 33	$0 63
1858	17,934	1,524,700	85	3,933,000	219	39	70
1861	16,577	1,769,810	107	3,893,000	234	45	73
1864	14,879	1,731,210	116	3,993,000	268	43	76
1866	12,263	1,547,860	126	3,790,000	309	41	70
1868	9,314	1,246,780	133	3,005,000	322	41	68
1869	9,987	1,429,480	142	3,461,000	347	41	69
1870	9,415	1,167,650	124	2,899,000	308	40	69
1871	7,295	936,050	128	2,009,000	275	47	76
1872	9,605	1,383,810	144	3,081,000	328	45	85
1873	11,386	1,858,500	163	3,051,000	261	61	
1874	10,044	1,634,710	163	2,516,000	250	65	1 14
1875	9,618	1,632,780	169	2,505,000	260	65	1 08
1876	9,296	1,555,580	167	2,393,000	257	65	1 08
1877	9,151	1,630,610	178	2,426,000	265	67	1 07
1878	8,468	1,455,220	172	2,469,000	292	59	99
1879	6,012	1,194,670	172	2,271,000	327	53	97
1880	8,044	1,456,720	180	2,874,000	357	51	99
1881	8,600	1,646,290	191	3,032,000	352	54	96
1882	9,438	1,821,920	193	3,467,000	367	52	94
1883	8,820	1,686,820	191	3,298,000	374	51	90

VARIATION IN THE COST OF PRODUCTION.

PRODUCTION OF ILLUMINATING GAS, COKE, AND TAR IN CERTAIN DEPARTMENTS OF FRANCE.a

[NOTE.—In this table 1,000 kilograms (2,205 pounds) are considered a ton.]

Departments.	Employés.			Production.						Average price.		
				Thousand feet gas.		Tons coke.		Tons tar.				
	Number.	Days worked.	Wages.	Yearly.	Yearly per employé.	Yearly.	Yearly per employé.	Yearly.	Yearly per employé.	Thousand feet of gas.	Ton of coke.	Ton of tar.
Bouches-du-Rhone	262	365	$0 92	530,550	2,025	35,000	133	2,600	9.9	$1 80	$7 72	$9 65
Gironde	700	365	58	600,100	857	53,000	75	4,800	6.8	1 09	5 79	9 65
Hérault	223	365	58	148,260	665	13,000	58	600	2.7	2 18	4 82	11 58
Loire	369	365	68	359,424	974	29,900	81	2,300	6.2	1 58	4 24	9 13
Loire Inférieure	260	365	68	240,040	923	10,000	38	1,000	3.8	1 37	7 72	13 51
Meurthe-et-Moselle	232	336	70	119,102	513	5,900	25	500	2.1	1 80	7 33	9 05
Nord	990	365	68	1,369,110	1,383	98,000	98	12,000	12.1	1 37	4 19	8 70
Pas-de-Calais	340	365	63	338,103	994	25,500	75	2,300	0.8	1 37	4 82	9 65
Rhone	428	360	1 25	585,274	1,368	50,200	117	5,200	12.1	1 31	8 68	9 20
Seine	3,813	365	1 60	9,742,976	2,555	663,700	174	57,700	15.1	1 37	5 31	13 99

a Two hundred and seven establishments are covered by this table, about 28 per cent. of the whole number.

PRODUCTION OF ROLLED IRON IN WESTPHALIA, GERMANY, 1878. a

Classification.	Hamm.						Nachrodt.			
	Pounds per employé daily.			Daily earnings.			Pounds per employé daily.		Daily earnings.	
	1869.	1873.	1878.	1869.	1873.	1878.	1873.	1878.	1873.	1878.
First puddler	3,350	3,300	3,498	$1 18	$1 34	$1 08	2,644	2,840	$1 33	$1 01
Second puddler	3,300	3,300	3,408	85	1 01	82	2,644	2,840	98	83
First heater	9,680	9,900	11,000	1 06	1 30	1 20	7,689	13,048	1 60	1 20
Second heater	9,680	9,900	11,000	58	76	79	7,689	13,648	1 11	87
Third heater	9,680	9,900	11,000	48	60	45				
Head roller	9,680	9,900	11,000	1 06	1 30	93	7,689	13,648	1 55	1 35
Rougher	9,680	9,900	11,000	68	85	59	7,689	13,648	1 13	87
Catcher	9,680	9,900	11,000	58	70	47	7,080	13,648	93	63
Hammerman	20,900	20,900	20,400	92	1 03	1 01			06	77
Hammerman's helper			26,400	41	48	46			48	39
Blacksmith				48	63	56			1 03	60
Laborer				44	53	46			60	44

Classification.	Lippstadt.						Werdohl.			
	Pounds per employé daily.			Daily earnings.			Pounds per employé daily.			Daily earnings.	
	1869.	1873.	1878.	1869.	1873.	1878.	1869.	1873.	1878.	1869.	1873.	1878.
First puddler	3,080	3,300	3,300	$1 18	$1 44	$1 04	2,200	1,870	2,750	$0 96	$0 98	$1 08
Second puddler	3,080	3,300	3,300	54	76	69	2,200	1,870	2,750	53	63	81
First heater	15,400	16,500	24,200	1 35	1 63	1 59	14,300	15,400	19,800	1 96	2 28	2 16
Second heater	15,400	16,500	24,200	53	1 26	69	14,300	15,400	19,800	96	1 35	1 40
Third heater	15,400	16,500	24,200	68	91	79	14,300	15,400	19,800	60	68	74
Roller	15,400	16,500	24,200	84	1 08	1 27	14,300	15,400	19,800	1 28	2 18	1 83
Rougher	15,400	16,500	24,200	93	1 18	1 06	14,300	15,400	19,800	72	1 20	1 30
Catcher	11,000	11,000	11,000	60	66	55	14,300	15,400	19,800	63	1 01	1 20
Hammerman				1 01	1 73	1 30	14,300	15,400	19,800	87	96	1 08
Hammerman's help				52	85	70	14,300	15,400	19,800	41	46	55
Blacksmith				44	68	54				60	70	72
Laborer				30	48	41				41	48	46

a It is asserted by prominent manufacturers and others in position to know that the wages in 1885 were substantially the same as in 1878.

COST OF PRODUCTION OF 1,000 KILOGRAMS (2,205 POUNDS) OF BAR IRON IN WESTPHALIA IN 1878.a

Items of expense.	Hamm.		Nachrodt.		Lippstadt.		Joint stock company.		Private firm.	
	Amount	Per cent	Amount	Per cent	Amount	Per cent	Amount	Per cent	Amount	Per cent
Coal	$2 44	7.96	$2 59	6.82	$2 63	7.69	$2 14	7.59	$2 02	9.06
Transportation of coal	1 23	4.02	1 35	3.56	1 90	5.56	53	1.88	1 07	3.70
Raw iron	16 13	52.64	18 63	49.05	17 59	51.45	17 26	61.23	14 17	49.00
Transportation of raw iron	1 08	3.53	1 61	4.23	1 63	4.77	82	2.91	1 82	6.29
Labor	5 69	18.57	7 73	20.36	5 01	14.65	4 86	17.24	5 60	19.36
Official charges	26	.85	52	1.37	49	1.43	12	.43	60	2.08
Ordinary expenses	2 16	7.05	2 12	5.58	1 85	5.41	1 08	3.83	1 71	5.91
Miscellaneous	69	2.25	1 95	5.14	1 90	5.56	81	2.87	1 33	4.60
Interest, etc	96	3.13	1 48	3.89	1 19	3.48	57	2.02		
Total	30 64	100.00	37 98	100.00	34 19	100.00	28 19	100.00	28 92	100.00

a It is asserted by prominent manufacturers and others in a position to know that the cost of production in 1885 was not very much different from what it was in 1878.

SHARE OF LABOR AND CAPITAL IN COAL MINING—PROVINCE OF HAINAULT, BELGIUM, 1860-83.

Year.	Cost of production.			Market price.	Profit.	Amount going to—		Per cent. going to—		Average yearly wages of employés.
	Labor.	Other.	Total.			Labor.	Capital.	Labor.	Capital.	
1860	$1 16	$0 89	$2 05	$2 31	$0 26	$1 16	$0 26	81.69	18.31	$146
1861	1 11	1 06	2 17	2 39	22	1 11	22	83.46	16.54	144
1862	1 02	85	1 87	2 10	23	1 02	23	81.60	18.40	136
1863	1 02	83	1 85	2 01	16	1 02	16	86.44	13.56	137
1864	98	79	1 77	1 97	20	98	20	83.05	16.95	139
1865	1 03	79	1 82	2 06	24	1 03	24	81.10	18.90	152
1866	1 11	87	1 98	2 36	38	1 11	38	74.50	25.50	171
1867	1 26	89	2 15	2 49	34	1 26	34	78.75	21.25	175
1868	1 12	86	1 98	2 14	16	1 12	16	87.50	12.50	157
1869	1 11	85	1 96	2 08	12	1 11	12	90.24	9.76	162
1870	1 14	87	2 01	2 14	13	1 14	13	89.76	10.24	169
1871	1 14	90	2 04	2 22	18	1 14	18	86.36	13.64	164
1872	1 29	91	2 20	2 64	44	1 29	44	74.57	25.43	203
1873	1 85	1 29	3 14	4 22	1 08	1 85	1 08	62.71	37.29	271
1874	1 73	1 20	2 93	3 21	28	1 73	28	86.07	13.93	231
1875	1 67	1 20	2 87	3 05	18	1 67	18	90.27	9.73	227
1876	1 51	1 10	2 61	2 64	03	1 51	03	98.05	1.95	200
1877	1 17	98	2 15	2 17	02	1 17	02	98.32	1.68	161
1878	1 08	87	1 95	1 96	01	1 08	01	99.09	.91	161
1879	1 00	83	1 83	1 84	01	1 00	01	99.01	.99	155
1880	1 08	84	1 92	1 96	04	1 08	04	96.43	3.57	177
1881	1 07	82	1 89	1 89		1 07		100.00		179
1882	1 06	79	1 87	1 95	08	1 06	08	93.10	6.90	185
1883	1 14	79	1 93	1 98	05	1 14	05	95.8	4.20	194

The following exhibit, drawn from official sources, is given as the average cost of production of a ton (2,205 pounds) of coal in Belgium. These figures represent the average cost for the whole country:

	Cost.	Per cent.
Labor	$1 05	60.45
Plant	34	19.70
Fuel	10	5.88
Other expenses	24	13.97
Total	1 73	100.00

One of the most important elements in the cost of production, after the actual wages paid, lies in the efficiency of labor; but the difficulties in the way of ascertaining the efficiency of labor are greater than those in the way of ascertaining the general cost of production, and is a task involving such wide and such scientific work that it could not be taken up by the Bureau during its first year. The true element of wages, also, can only be ascertained by the most careful analysis of the efficiency of labor in all directions. The attempt will be made, when opportunity offers, to make such an analysis. It will be seen from the foregoing tables that there is no American standard of the cost of producing a given unit of production, nor, in fact, can any absolute standard be obtained for other countries. On the other hand, it is true that an approximate standard can be obtained, not only to a large extent from the data presented, but with ample information a standard could be reached by which the cost of production could be very carefully and very satisfactorily graded. Many corroborating statements have been examined to test the validity of the figures given in the great industries like iron and textiles, and while in some cases there has been found some deviation from statements made in trades journals and in the facts and figures published by associations, no deviation sufficient to invalidate the statements made in the foregoing tables has been observed.

The Variation in the Rates of Wages.—If the reader will refer to Appendix A, he will find a table covering 582 manufacturing establishments, showing the number of persons engaged in each specific occupation in each establishment, with their daily rates of wages. The wages in nearly all cases were taken direct from the pay-rolls. The table is referred to in this connection since it forms the basis of the summaries which follow, they having been directly derived from it. These summaries bring out the chief points of value contained in the long detailed table. The first shows the number of adult employés and the average rates of daily wages of leading occupations in the industries named in the various states and countries covered by the investigation. The second table shows the average rates of daily wages for children and youth in the same industries and in the same states and countries. The third table shows the number of employés in each occupation of an industry for each state, and the percentage of employés in each occupation considered of the whole number of employés in each state and country, so far as the establishments investigated by the Bureau are concerned. The fourth summary brings out the number of employés in each industry, for each state and country involved, with the average rates of daily wages and the average running time, both daily and yearly, during the past year. In this summary the states where conditions are more nearly alike are placed together, forming geographical groups, each separated from the other by a white line. The fifth summary shows the total number of employés, average daily wages, and average daily and yearly working time for the industries involved for all the states covered. A casual examination of these summaries will show that any attempt to prove an American rate of wages must necessarily result in failure. There is no such thing as an American rate of wages.

VARIATION IN THE RATES OF WAGES.

SUMMARY OF SELECTED OCCUPATIONS, ADULTS.

AGRICULTURAL IMPLEMENTS.

NOTE.—This table is *not* a complete exhibit for industries or states, but covers only the principal occupations in establishments investigated. See detail table, Appendix A, page 295, whence derived.

Occupations and states.	Number of adult employés.		Average rates of daily wages.		Occupations and states.	Number of adult employés.		Average rates of daily wages.	
	Male.	Fem.	Male.	Fem.		Male.	Fem.	Male.	Fem.
BLACKSMITHS.					**LABORERS**—concluded.				
Illinois	219		$2 41		Kentucky	6		$1 20	
Indiana	12		2 11		Maine	7		1 25	
Kentucky	4		2 50		New York	2		1 60	
Ohio	176		2 15		Ohio	345		1 30	
Pennsylvania	8		2 50		Pennsylvania	39		1 33	
Total and average	419		2 29		Total and average	1,185		1 35	
BLACKSMITHS' HELPERS.					**MACHINISTS.**				
Illinois	3		1 40		Illinois	426		2 39	
Indiana	13		1 30		Indiana	4		2 12	
Kentucky	6		1 20		New York	1		3 00	
Ohio	85		1 41		Ohio	506		2 07	
Pennsylvania	8		1 75		Total and average	937		2 22	
Total and average	115		1 41		**MOULDERS.**				
FOREMEN.					Illinois	152		3 10	
Illinois	22		3 20		Indiana	181		1 75	
Indiana	16		2 39		Kentucky	8		2 00	
Kentucky	3		3 00		Ohio	102		2 51	
Maine	3		2 42		Pennsylvania	22		1 80	
New York	2		2 62		Total and average	465		2 39	
Ohio	29		3 60		**PAINTERS.**				
Pennsylvania	1		4 00		Illinois	138		2 09	
Total and average	76		3 14		Indiana	10		1 72	
GRINDERS.					Maine	3		1 50	
Illinois	80		2 03		Ohio	270		1 80	
Indiana	96		1 48		Pennsylvania	1		2 50	
Kentucky	15		1 60		Total and average	422		1 89	
Maine	12		1 75		**WOOD WORKERS.**				
New York	7		1 60		Illinois	80		1 59	
Ohio (grinders; grinders and polishers)	59		2 07		Indiana	14		1 34	
Total and average	269		1 80		Kentucky	4		2 50	
LABORERS.					Ohio	377		1 68	
Illinois	744		1 39		Total and average	475		1 66	
Indiana	42		1 15						

BOOTS AND SHOES.

	Male	Fem.	Male	Fem.		Male	Fem.	Male	Fem.
BEADERS.					**BOTTOMERS**—concluded.				
New York	55		1 59		New York	213		1 95	
					Ohio	225		2 43	
Total and average	55		1 59		Total and average	656		2 20	
BLOCKERS.					**BRUSHERS.**				
New York	17		2 26		New York	13		1 77	
Total and average	17		2 26		Total and average	13		1 77	
BOTTOMERS.					**BUFFERS.**				
Kentucky	20		2 50		California	6		1 46	
Maryland	34		1 67		Massachusetts	3		2 00	
Massachusetts	164		2 28						

SUMMARY OF SELECTED OCCUPATIONS, ADULTS—Continued.

BOOTS AND SHOES—Continued.

NOTE.—This table is not a complete exhibit for industries or states, but covers only the principal occupations in establishments investigated. See detail table, Appendix A, page 295, whence derived.

Occupations and states.	Number of adult employés. Male.	Number of adult employés. Fem.	Average rates of daily wages. Male.	Average rates of daily wages. Fem.	Occupations and states.	Number of adult employés. Male.	Number of adult employés. Fem.	Average rates of daily wages. Male.	Average rates of daily wages. Fem.
BUFFERS—concluded.					**EDGE TRIMMERS.**				
New York	27		$1 40		California	9		$1 83	
Pennsylvania	6		2 50		Maryland	2		2 25	
Total and average.	42		1 61		Massachusetts	30		2 45	
BURNISHERS.					New York	49		2 45	
California	13		1 98		Pennsylvania	8		3 49	
Illinois	6		3 00		Total and average.	98		2 48	
Maryland	7		1 50		**FITTERS.**				
Massachusetts	26		1 80		California	6		2 08	
New York	14		2 27		Illinois		60		$1 50
Pennsylvania	12		2 15		Kentucky	3	30	2 50	1 00
Total and average.	78		2 00		Maryland	7	128	1 75	89
BUTTON-HOLE MAKERS.					Massachusetts	36	60	2 22	1 33
California	8		1 53		New Jersey	25	60	2 25	1 66
New York		70		$1 04	New York	9		1 69	
Pennsylvania	3	9	1 60	78	Ohio	25	325	2 25	1 23
Total and average.	11	79	1 55	1 01	Pennsylvania	59		1 36	
BUTTON SEWERS.					Total and average.	170	683	1 88	1 23
California		1		1 37	**FOREMEN.**				
New York	4		1 50		California	6		5 00	
Pennsylvania		39		90	Maryland	8		3 12	
Total and average.	4	40	1 50	91	Massachusetts	13		3 04	
CHANNELLERS.					New York	70		2 43	
California	4		1 53		Ohio	3		3 00	
New York	26		1 68		Total and average.	100		2 74	
Total and average.	30		1 66		**HEELERS.**				
CLOSERS.					California	15		1 75	
New York	22	19	1 23	1 07	Illinois	10		2 17	
Pennsylvania	25		1 97		Maryland	2		1 50	
Total and average.	47	19	1 62	1 07	Massachusetts	45		2 03	
CUTTERS.					New York	30		1 51	
California	37		2 00		Pennsylvania	13		2 67	
Illinois	8		2 67		Total and average.	115		1 93	
Kentucky	4		2 33		**LABORERS.**				
Maryland	19		1 86		Massachusetts	17		1 31	
Massachusetts	376	24	1 96	89	New York	84		1 10	
New Jersey	25		2 50		Pennsylvania	38		1 33	
New York	338		2 28		Total and average.	139		1 19	
Ohio	40		2 56		**LASTERS.**				
Pennsylvania	28		2 18		California	77		1 58	
Total and average.	875	24	2 14	89	Illinois	8		2 25	
EDGE SETTERS.					Kentucky	6		2 00	
California	8		1 87		Maryland	20		1 59	
Maryland	3		1 55		Massachusetts	291		2 17	
Massachusetts	36		2 20		New York	219		2 34	
New York	19		2 60		Pennsylvania	110		1 92	
Pennsylvania	14		3 00		Total and average.	731		2 10	
					LEVELLERS.				
					Maryland	2		1 42	
					Massachusetts	9		1 78	
					New York	19		2 56	
Total and average.	80		2 38		Total and average.	30		2 25	

VARIATION IN THE RATES OF WAGES.

SUMMARY OF SELECTED OCCUPATIONS, ADULTS—Continued.

BOOTS AND SHOES—Concluded.

NOTE.—This table is *not* a complete exhibit for industries or states, but covers only the principal occupations in establishments investigated. See detail table, Appendix A, page 295, whence derived.

Occupations and states.	Number of adult employés.		Average rates of daily wages.		Occupations and states.	Number of adult employés.		Average rates of daily wages.	
	Male.	Fem.	Male.	Fem.		Male.	Fem.	Male.	Fem.
MEASURERS.					**SEWERS, M'KAY MACHINE.**				
New York	17		$1 80		Massachusetts	2		$2 55	
					New York	11		2 67	
Total and average	17		1 80		Total and average	13		2 66	
MOULDERS.					**SEWING-MACHINE OPERATORS.**				
Massachusetts	1		2 25		California	24	32	1 37	$1 50
New York	16		2 44		Massachusetts	78	352	1 78	1 49
					New York	9	988	1 77	1 28
Total and average	17		2 43		Pennsylvania	29	71	1 78	1 32
PACKERS.					Total and average	140	1,443	1 71	1 34
California	7		1 93		**SKIVERS.**				
Maryland	1		67		Massachusetts	4	7	1 87	1 14
Massachusetts	30		1 97		New York	29		1 65	
New York	1		1 08						
Ohio	3		1 50		Total and average	33	7	1 68	1 14
Pennsylvania	6		1 00		**TACKERS.**				
Total and average	48		1 79		Maryland	1		1 50	
					Massachusetts	6	9	1 73	1 04
SAND PAPERERS.					New York	33		1 95	
Maryland	2		1 07		Pennsylvania	4		1 10	
Massachusetts	7		1 75		Total and average	44	9	1 83	1 04
New York	13		1 39		**TURNERS.**				
Total and average	22		1 52		Maryland	2		1 33	
SEAM RUBBERS.					Massachusetts	4		2 00	
New York		15		$1 00	New York	25		1 51	
Pennsylvania	6		1 15		Pennsylvania	57		2 39	
Total and average	6	15	1 15	1 00	Total and average	88		2 10	
SEAT WHEELERS.					**VAMPERS.**				
					California	6		2 36	
					Massachusetts	11	2	2 09	1 75
New York	14		1 19		New York	62		1 73	
					Pennsylvania	14		1 90	
Total and average	14		1 19		Total and average	93	2	1 84	1 75

BROOMS.

	Male.	Fem.	Male.	Fem.		Male.	Fem.	Male.	Fem.
LABORERS.					**WINDERS.**				
New York	135		1 25		New York	98		1 70	
Total and average	135		1 25		Total and average	98		1 70	

CARPETINGS.

	Male.	Fem.	Male.	Fem.		Male.	Fem.	Male.	Fem.
CARDERS.					**COMBERS.**				
Massachusetts	13	30	88	72	New York	20	83	2 05	97
New York	34		1 54		Pennsylvania		5		1 16
Total and average	47	30	1 36	72	Total and average	20	88	2 05	98

12854 LAB——10

SUMMARY OF SELECTED OCCUPATIONS, ADULTS—Continued.

CARPETINGS—Continued.

NOTE.—This table is not a complete exhibit for industries or states, but covers only the principal occupations in establishments investigated. See detail table, Appendix A, page 295, whence derived.

Occupations and states.	Number of adult employés.		Average rates of daily wages.		Occupations and states.	Number of adult employés.		Average rates of daily wages.	
	Male.	Fem.	Male.	Fem.		Male.	Fem.	Male.	Fem.
DESIGNERS.					**LABORERS—concluded.**				
Great Britain	10		$1 39		New York	136		$1 24	
New York	37		3 86		Pennsylvania	400		1 25	
Total and average	47		2 94		Total and average	607		1 22	
DRAWERS.					**LOOM FIXERS.**				
New York	5	194	2 03	$1 03	Massachusetts	4		2 70	
Pennsylvania		30		90	New York	63		2 44	
					Pennsylvania	21		2 25	
Total and average	5	224	2 03	1 01	Total and average	88		2 40	
DRESSERS.					**MACHINISTS.**				
Massachusetts	6		1 75		Massachusetts	4		2 75	
New York	101		1 54		New York	83		2 19	
					Pennsylvania	16		2 25	
Total and average	107		1 55		Total and average	103		2 22	
DYERS.					**PRINTERS.**				
Connecticut	10		1 75						
Great Britain	9		87		Great Britain	25	7	1 13	$0 71
Massachusetts	125		1 08		Massachusetts	8		1 08	
New York	63		1 58		New York	254		1 73	
Pennsylvania	18		1 50		Pennsylvania	30		1 50	
Total and average	225		1 28		Total and average	317	7	1 65	71
ENGINEERS.					**SCOURERS.**				
Massachusetts	15		1 56		Massachusetts	28		1 11	
New York	12		2 60		New York	172		1 37	
Pennsylvania	1		1 66						
Total and average	28		2 08		Total and average	200		1 33	
FINISHERS.					**SETTERS.**				
Connecticut		10		1 25	Great Britain		21		75
Massachusetts	10	95	1 05	94	Massachusetts		14		1 40
New York	67		1 56		New York	91	356	1 99	1 40
					Pennsylvania	120		1 80	
Total and average	86	105	1 45	97	Total and average	211	391	1 88	1 36
FOREMEN AND OVERSEERS.					**SPINNERS, MULE.**				
Great Britain	6		1 97		Massachusetts	37		1 19	
New York	170		2 62		New York	124		1 26	
Total and average	176		2 60		Total and average	161		1 25	
HARNESS FIXERS.					**SPINNERS, OTHER.**				
New York	23		1 78		Massachusetts		102		64
Total and average	23		1 78		New York	299	302	1 14	1 07
INSPECTORS.					Pennsylvania		60		83
New York	26	29	1 60	1 12	Total and average	299	464	1 14	94
Total and average	26	29	1 60	1 12	**SPOOLERS.**				
LABORERS.					Massachusetts		12		92
					New York	62	244	1 25	90
Great Britain	8		85		Pennsylvania	4	80	85	83
Massachusetts	63		1 01		Total and average	66	336	1 23	88

VARIATION IN THE RATES OF WAGES. 147

SUMMARY OF SELECTED OCCUPATIONS, ADULTS—Continued.

CARPETINGS—Concluded.

NOTE.—This table is not a complete exhibit for industries or states, but covers only the principal occupations in establishments investigated. See detail table, Appendix A, page 295, whence derived.

Occupations and states.	Number of adult employés.		Average rates of daily wages.		Occupations and states.	Number of adult employés.		Average rates of daily wages.	
	Male.	Fem.	Male.	Fem.		Male.	Fem.	Male.	Fem.
TWISTERS.					**WEAVERS**—concluded.				
New York	8	229	$1 43	$1 29	Pennsylvania	615	......	$1 67	......
Pennsylvania	......	30	......	90	Total and average	1,221	1,321	1 58	$1 42
Total and average	8	259	1 43	1 25	**WINDERS.**				
WARPERS.					Great Britain	......	29	......	46
Massachusetts	15	......	1 26	......	Massachusetts	40	84	1 29	88
New York	28	......	1 55	......	New York	36	313	1 43	1 11
Pennsylvania	2	......	1 35	......	Pennsylvania	......	28	......	75
Total and average	45	......	1 45	......	Total and average	76	454	1 36	1 00
WEAVERS.					**WOOL SORTERS.**				
Connecticut	......	48	......	1 56	Massachusetts	28	3	1 78	1 68
Great Britain	116	......	1 36	......	New York	123	......	1 25	......
Massachusetts	64	359	1 53	1 51	Total and average	151	3	1 35	1 68
New York	426	914	1 53	1 38					

CARRIAGES AND WAGONS.

Occupations and states.	Male	Fem	Male $	Fem	Occupations and states.	Male	Fem	Male $	Fem
BLACKSMITHS.					**PAINTERS.**				
Connecticut	55	......	2 76	......	Connecticut	96	......	2 11	......
Illinois	52	......	2 37	......	Illinois	92	......	1 87	......
New Jersey	16	......	1 92	......	New Jersey	18	......	1 75	......
Ohio	70	......	2 16	......	Ohio	97	......	1 39	......
Pennsylvania	4	......	2 03	......	Pennsylvania	3	......	2 33	......
Total and average	197	......	2 36	......	Total and average	306	......	1 79	......
BLACKSMITHS' HELPERS.									
Connecticut	58	......	1 75	......	**TRIMMERS.**				
Illinois	37	......	1 41	......	Connecticut	73	......	2 48	......
Ohio	14	......	1 35	......	Illinois	52	......	2 10	......
Pennsylvania	6	......	95	......	New Jersey	6	......	2 25	......
Total and average	115	......	1 55	......	Ohio	8	......	2 50	......
					Pennsylvania	1	......	2 00	......
FOREMEN.					Total and average	140	......	2 33	......
Connecticut	3	......	3 81	......					
Illinois	11	......	3 68	......	**WOOD WORKERS.**				
Ohio	30	......	2 92	......	Connecticut (body makers)	80	......	2 43	......
Total and average	44	......	3 17	......	Illinois	73	......	3 13	......
LABORERS.					New Jersey (body makers)	10	......	2 50	......
Connecticut	12	......	1 20	......	Ohio (wood workers, body makers)	58	......	2 01	......
Illinois	12	......	1 48	......	Pennsylvania	4	......	1 91	......
Ohio	23	......	1 36	......	Total and average	225	......	2 22	......
Total and average	47	......	1 37	......					

REPORT OF THE COMMISSIONER OF LABOR.

SUMMARY OF SELECTED OCCUPATIONS, ADULTS—Continued.

CLOTHING.

NOTE.— This table is *not* a complete exhibit for industries or states, but covers only the principal occupations in establishments investigated. See detail table, Appendix A, page 295, whence derived.

Occupations and states.	Number of adult employés.		Average rates of daily wages.		Occupations and states.	Number of adult employés.		Average rates of daily wages.	
	Male.	Fem.	Male.	Fem.		Male.	Fem.	Male.	Fem.
BUTTON-HOLE MAKERS.					**LABORERS.**				
New York	......	18	......	$1 75	New Jersey	7	......	$1 50	......
Pennsylvania	......	15	......	1 17	New York	7	......	96	......
					Pennsylvania	24	......	1 31	......
Total and average	......	33	......	1 40	Virginia	3	......	1 25	......
					Total and average	41	......	1 28	......
BUTTON SEWERS.					**LAPPERS.**				
New York	......	9	......	75	New York	28	......	1 00	......
Total and average	......	9	......	75	Total and average	28	......	1 00	......
CUTTERS.					**LOOPERS.**				
New York	20	2	$1 97	1 00	New York	2	109	1 00	$0 81
Pennsylvania	15	17	1 03	86	Total and average	2	109	1 00	0 81
Total and average	35	19	1 57	87	**MENDERS.**				
ENGINEERS.					New York	......	80	......	88
New Jersey	2	......	3 25	......	Total and average	......	80	......	88
New York	8	......	1 48	......	**SEWING-MACHINE OPERATORS.**				
Pennsylvania	3	......	2 18	......					
Virginia	1	......	2 00	......	New York	......	180	......	92
Total and average	14	......	1 92	......	Total and average	......	180	......	92
FINISHERS.					**SPINNERS, MULE.**				
New Jersey	116	......	2 02	......	New York	31	......	1 26	......
New York	39	231	1 12	95	Virginia	7	......	1 50	......
Pennsylvania	136	......	1 70	......	Total and average	38	......	1 31	......
Virginia	4	27	2 50	75	**SPOOLERS.**				
Total and average	205	258	1 76	93	New York	2	6	1 12	87
FOREMEN.					Total and average	2	6	1 12	87
New Jersey	4	1	3 21	1 07	**TRIMMERS.**				
New York (foremen, overseers)	45	4	2 40	1 88	New Jersey	......	60	......	1 00
					New York	......	25	......	1 13
Total and average	49	5	2 47	1 84	Pennsylvania	......	120	......	85
HEMMERS.					Total and average	......	205	......	93
New York	......	38	......	82	**WASH-ROOM HANDS.**				
Total and average	......	38	......	82	New York	49	......	1 42	......
INSPECTORS.					Pennsylvania	9	......	1 00	......
New York	......	16	......	67	Total and average	58	......	1 35	......
Total and average	......	16	......	67	**WINDERS**				
KNITTERS.					New York	......	75	......	78
New York	1	77	1 75	1 07	Pennsylvania	......	6	......	75
Virginia	2	......	1 75	......	Total and average	......	81	......	78
Total and average	3	77	1 75	1 07					

VARIATION IN THE RATES OF WAGES.

SUMMARY OF SELECTED OCCUPATIONS, ADULTS—Continued.

COAL, COKE, AND ORE.

NOTE.—This table is not a complete exhibit for industries or states, but covers only the principal occupations in establishments investigated. See detail table, Appendix A, page 296, whence derived.

Occupations and states.	Number of adult employés.		Average rates of daily wages.		Occupations and states.	Number of adult employés.		Average rates of daily wages.	
	Male.	Fem.	Male.	Fem.		Male.	Fem.	Male.	Fem.
BLACKSMITHS.					**ENGINEERS**—concluded.				
Great Britain	3		$1 08		West Virginia (engineers; engineers, stationary, locomotive)	8		$1 73	
Indiana	16		1 69						
Maryland	6		1 93						
Missouri	1		2 31		Total and average	78		1 93	
Ohio	13		2 08						
Pennsylvania	19		2 41		**FIREMEN.**				
Virginia	4		1 95						
West Virginia	12		2 02		Great Britain	20		97	
					Maryland	1		1 70	
Total and average	74		2 01		Missouri	1		2 31	
BLACKSMITHS' HELPERS.					Ohio	8		1 44	
Great Britain	2		72		Virginia	3		1 04	
Maryland	5		1 48						
Missouri	1		1 93		Total and average	33		1 15	
Ohio	2		1 45						
Virginia	3		1 25		**LABORERS.**				
West Virginia	1		1 25						
					Great Britain	23		72	
Total and average	14		1 33		Indiana	91		1 00	
CARPENTERS.					Maryland	16		1 24	
					Missouri	18		1 50	
Maryland	5		1 74		Ohio	49		1 43	
Missouri	4		2 00		Pennsylvania	428		1 21	
Ohio	5		2 20		Virginia	235		1 04	
Pennsylvania	13		2 50		West Virginia	49		1 16	
Virginia	7		1 53						
West Virginia	12		1 85		Total and average	909		1 15	
Total and average	46		2 04		**MINE BOSSES.**				
DRIVERS.									
					Indiana	6		3 50	
Great Britain	11		62		Missouri	1		2 88	
Indiana	85		1 40		Ohio	13		2 86	
Maryland	83		1 60		Pennsylvania	20		2 25	
Missouri	7		2 00		Virginia	14		1 69	
Ohio	100		1 57		West Virginia	8		2 71	
Pennsylvania	106		1 66						
Virginia	7		75		Total and average	62		2 44	
West Virginia	96		1 49						
					MINERS.				
Total and average	495		1 52						
DUMPERS.					Great Britain	285		1 10	
					Indiana	1375		1 49	
Great Britain	4		96		Maryland	762		1 62	
Maryland	20		1 35		Missouri	239		1 58	
Ohio	17		1 40		Ohio	1055		1 75	
Pennsylvania	12		2 50		Pennsylvania	1855		1 90	
West Virginia	6		1 36		Virginia	113		1 23	
					West Virginia	662		1 69	
Total and average	59		1 60						
ENGINEERS.					Total and average	6346		1 67	
Great Britain (stationary)	1		1 12						
Indiana	26		2 12		**STABLEMEN.**				
Maryland	2		2 20						
Missouri	7		1 91		Great Britain	1		80	
Ohio (engineers; engineers, stationary, locomotive)	15		1 81		Maryland	7		1 39	
					Ohio	4		1 42	
Pennsylvania (engineers; engineers, stationary, locomotive)	5		1 91		Virginia	2		1 38	
					West Virginia	4		1 44	
Virginia	14		1 84		Total and averages	18		1 38	

SUMMARY OF SELECTED OCCUPATIONS, ADULTS—Continued.

COAL, COKE, AND ORE—Concluded.

NOTE.—This table is *not* a complete exhibit for industries or states, but covers only the principal occupations in establishments investigated. See detail table, Appendix A, page 295, whence derived.

Occupations and states.	Number of adult employés.		Average rates of daily wages.		Occupations and states.	Number of adult employés.		Average rates of daily wages.	
	Male.	Fem.	Male.	Fem.		Male.	Fem.	Male.	Fem.
TRACKLAYERS.					**WEIGHERS.**				
Great Britain	25		$0 90		Great Britain	5		$0 84	
Indiana	25		2 00		Indiana	15		1 73	
Maryland	10		1 88		Maryland	5		1 77	
Missouri	5		2 35		Missouri	1		2 31	
Ohio	21		1 73		Ohio	9		1 83	
Virginia	6		1 25		Pennsylvania	3		2 50	
West Virginia	26		1 72		West Virginia	7		1 87	
Total and average.	118		1 63		Total and average.	45		1 74	

COOKING AND HEATING APPARATUS.

Occupations and states.	Male.	Fem.	Male.	Fem.	Occupations and states.	Male.	Fem.	Male.	Fem.
BLACKSMITHS.					**JAPANNERS.**				
Illinois	2		1 62		Michigan	2		2 00	
Michigan	4		2 16		New York	9		1 84	
New York	14		1 91		Total and average.	11		1 87	
Ohio	1		1 75						
Pennsylvania	1		1 75		**LABORERS.**				
Total and average.	22		1 92		Illinois	41		1 43	
CARPENTERS.					Kentucky	13		1 77	
Illinois	2		2 25		Michigan	19		1 54	
New York	38		2 23		New York	383		1 33	
Ohio	4		2 12		Ohio	15		1 70	
West Virginia	1		2 00		Pennsylvania	10		1 35	
Total and average	45		2 21		West Virginia	13		1 25	
CUPOLA MEN.					Total and average.	494		1 37	
Illinois	16		2 09						
New York	13		1 81		**MACHINISTS.**				
Ohio	3		1 72		Illinois	10		2 00	
West Virginia	1		2 25		Michigan	5		2 38	
Total and average.	33		1 95		New York	5		2 29	
ENGINEERS.					Ohio	7		1 80	
Illinois	6		2 08		Total and average.	27		2 07	
Michigan	2		2 50						
New York	5		2 20		**MOULDERS.**				
Ohio	4		2 19		Illinois	267		3 05	
Pennsylvania	1		2 25		Kentucky	37		2 25	
West Virginia	1		1 75		Michigan	430		2 27	
Total and average.	19		2 17		New York	945		3 26	
FOREMEN.					Ohio	350		2 60	
Illinois	4		3 31		Pennsylvania	48		3 50	
Michigan	27		3 83		West Virginia	23		2 50	
New York	29		3 25		Total and average.	2100		2 88	
Ohio	9		3 49						
Pennsylvania	2		3 00		**MOUNTERS.**				
Total and average.	71		3 50		Illinois	54		1 86	
GRINDERS.					Kentucky	6		2 25	
Illinois	4		1 50		Michigan	151		1 89	
Michigan	51		1 26		New York	56		3 32	
New York	35		1 52		Ohio	142		2 19	
Total and average.	90		1 37		Pennsylvania	12		3 00	
					West Virginia	9		1 65	
					Total and average.	430		2 20	

VARIATION IN THE RATES OF WAGES. 151

SUMMARY OF SELECTED OCCUPATIONS, ADULTS—Continued.
COOKING AND HEATING APPARATUS—Concluded.

NOTE.—This table is *not* a complete exhibit for industries or states, but covers only the principal occupations in establishments investigated. See detail table, Appendix A, page 295, whence derived.

Occupations and states.	Number of adult employés.		Average rates of daily wages.		Occupations and states.	Number of adult employés.		Average rates of daily wages.	
	Male.	Fem.	Male.	Fem.		Male.	Fem.	Male.	Fem.
NICKEL PLATERS.					**POLISHERS**—concluded.				
Illinois	1	......	$2 25	......	New York	43	......	$2 58	......
Michigan	5	......	1 45	......	Ohio	13	......	1 43	......
New York	18	......	2 79	......	Total and average	155	......	2 06	......
Ohio	30	......	1 53	......	**TEAMSTERS.**				
Total and average	54	......	1 96	......	Michigan	16	......	1 52	......
PATTERN MAKERS.					New York	19	......	1 63	......
Illinois	12	......	3 21	......	Ohio	1	......	1 50	......
Michigan	49	......	2 27	......	Pennsylvania	1	......	1 50	......
New York	12	......	2 28	......	Total and average	37	......	1 58	......
Ohio	19	......	2 83	......	**TINSMITHS.**				
Pennsylvania	2	......	3 00	......	Michigan	12	......	1 94	......
West Virginia	1	......	2 25	......	New York	58	......	1 98	......
Total and average	95	......	2 52	......	Ohio	3	......	2 11	......
POLISHERS.					Total and average	73	......	1 98	......
Illinois	1	......	1 50	......					
Michigan	98	......	1 92	......					

COTTON GOODS.

Occupations and states.	Male.	Fem.	Male.	Fem.	Occupations and states.	Male.	Fem.	Male.	Fem.
BEAMERS.					**CARD GRINDERS.**				
Delaware	11	......	1 47	......	Connecticut	2	......	1 25	......
Great Britain	4	......	90	......	France	1	......	86	......
Maine	22	5	2 01	$1 48	Georgia	6	......	1 05	......
Maryland	14	......	79	......	Germany	8	......	82	......
Massachusetts	......	8	......	1 00	Great Britain	9	......	91	......
New York	2	......	1 25	......	Italy	9	......	63	......
North Carolina	10	......	1 18	......	Maine	28	......	1 35	......
Pennsylvania	12	......	2 00	......	Maryland	10	......	1 52	......
Virginia	3	......	83	......	Massachusetts	58	......	1 24	......
					New Hampshire	13	......	1 37	......
Total and average	78	13	1 50	1 18	New York	31	......	1 16	......
BLACKSMITHS.					North Carolina	10	......	1 01	......
					Pennsylvania	2	......	1 54	......
Georgia	2	......	1 60	......	Vermont	2	......	1 50	......
Maine	4	......	1 88	......	Virginia	7	......	1 07	......
Maryland	1	......	1 50	......	Total and average	196	......	1 19	......
Massachusetts	4	......	2 36	......	**CARD STRIPPERS.**				
New York	2	......	1 75	......	Connecticut	4	......	90	......
Total and average	13	......	1 93	......	Delaware	1	......	1 33	......
CARDERS.					Georgia	2	......	85	......
					Maine	20	......	85	......
Delaware	33	......	85	......	Massachusetts	58	6	92	$0 85
France	2	......	53	......	New Hampshire	11	......	96	......
Germany	23	......	57	......	New York	28	......	1 02	......
Great Britain	24	......	86	......	Vermont	2	......	1 00	......
Italy	32	......	38	......	Total and average	126	6	94	85
Maryland	30	32	71	70	**CLOTH-ROOM HANDS.**				
Massachusetts	87	86	1 20	75	Georgia	1	......	85	......
New Hampshire	47	103	96	90	Great Britain	1	......	1 20	......
New York	6	349	1 20	87	Maine	4	4	98	82
North Carolina	18	......	77	......	Massachusetts	16	11	1 34	76
South Carolina	42	......	85	......	New Hampshire	35	39	1 73	1 08
Virginia	7	......	77	......					
Total and average	357	660	80	85					

SUMMARY OF SELECTED OCCUPATIONS, ADULTS—Continued.

COTTON GOODS—Continued.

NOTE.—This table is *not* a complete exhibit for industries or states, but covers only the principal occupations in establishments investigated. See detail table, Appendix A, page 295, whence derived.

Occupations and states.	Number of adult employés.		Average rates of daily wages.		Occupations and states.	Number of adult employés.		Average rates of daily wages.	
	Male.	Fem.	Male.	Fem.		Male.	Fem.	Male.	Fem.
CLOTH-ROOM HANDS—concluded.					**FILLING HANDS.**				
South Carolina	7	.....	$1 00	.....	Connecticut	1	.....	$1 00	.....
					Maine	3	.....	1 14	.....
Total and average	64	54	1 48	$1 00	Massachusetts	20	.....	1 07	.....
DOFFERS.					New Hampshire	1	.....	42	.....
Connecticut	.....	4	.....	60	Virginia	1	.....	94	.....
Total and average	.....	4	.....	60	Total and average	26	.....	1 04	.....
DRAWERS.					**FIREMEN.**				
Connecticut	.....	9	.....	1 02	France	2	.....	74	.....
France	6	3	60	41	Georgia	2	.....	75	.....
Georgia	.....	5	.....	08	Germany	27	.....	73	.....
Great Britain	.....	30	.....	72	Great Britain	3	.....	93	.....
Italy	.....	27	.....	20	Italy	9	.....	54	.....
Maine	4	51	92	88	Maine	4	.....	1 38	.....
Maryland	.....	13	.....	73	Maryland	1	.....	1 25	.....
Massachusetts	.....	105	.....	91	Massachusetts	18	.....	1 31	.....
New Hampshire	3	10	80	77	New Jersey	1	.....	1 35	.....
New Jersey	.....	8	.....	70	New York	10	.....	1 40	.....
New York	.....	17	.....	68	North Carolina	4	.....	94	.....
North Carolina	.....	9	.....	56	Vermont	1	.....	1 50	.....
Virginia	.....	8	.....	55	Virginia	3	.....	1 07	.....
Total and average	13	301	77	77	Total and average	85	.....	1 00	.....
DRAWERS-IN.					**FOLDERS.**				
Great Britain	13	.....	81	.....	Connecticut	1	.....	1 33	.....
Maine	.....	6	.....	1 10	Georgia	3	.....	72	.....
Massachusetts	.....	55	.....	77	Germany	24	.....	42	.....
New York	.....	11	.....	93	Maine	3	.....	1 42	.....
North Carolina	6	.....	72	.....	Massachusetts	4	.....	86	.....
Vermont	.....	6	.....	90	New York	6	.....	1 29	.....
Virginia	.....	2	.....	92	North Carolina	1	.....	1 00	.....
					Vermont	1	.....	1 10	.....
Total and average	19	80	78	83	Virginia	1	.....	1 00	.....
DYERS.					Total and average	44	.....	73	.....
Delaware	6	.....	1 50	.....	**INSPECTORS.**				
Germany	182	.....	53	.....	Connecticut	.....	1	.....	$1 12
Maine	37	.....	1 19	.....	Maine	.....	54	.....	74
Massachusetts	43	.....	1 10	.....	Massachusetts	2	11	1 00	80
North Carolina	17	.....	75	.....	New Hampshire	1	.....	83	.....
Pennsylvania	10	.....	1 67	.....	New York	2	1	1 56	1 12
Virginia	7	.....	1 00	.....	Vermont	1	.....	1 50	.....
Total and average	302	.....	77	.....	Total and average	6	67	1 24	76
ENGINEERS.					**LABORERS.**				
Connecticut	1	.....	2 50	.....	Connecticut	2	.....	1 00	.....
France	2	.....	1 08	.....	Delaware	5	.....	1 27	.....
Georgia	1	.....	1 50	.....	France	2	.....	58	.....
Great Britain	6	.....	1 53	.....	Georgia	3	.....	85	.....
Italy	5	.....	66	.....	Germany	17	.....	77	.....
Maryland	3	.....	1 67	.....	Great Britain	15	.....	88	.....
Massachusetts	11	.....	2 04	.....	Italy	52	.....	45	.....
New Jersey	1	.....	2 00	.....	Maine	121	.....	1 06	.....
New York	6	.....	2 33	.....	Maryland	25	.....	1 06	.....
North Carolina	5	.....	1 40	.....	Massachusetts	127	.....	1 08	.....
Pennsylvania	2	.....	2 43	.....	New Hampshire	31	.....	1 28	.....
Vermont	1	.....	4 33	.....	New York	111	.....	1 06	.....
Virginia	1	.....	1 13	.....	North Carolina	2	.....	75	.....
					South Carolina	15	.....	85	.....
					Virginia	5	.....	96	.....
Total and average	45	.....	1 70	.....	Total and average	533	.....	0 99	.....

VARIATION IN THE RATES OF WAGES.

SUMMARY OF SELECTED OCCUPATIONS, ADULTS—Continued.

COTTON GOODS—Continued.

NOTE.—This table is not a complete exhibit for industries or states, but covers only the principal occupations in establishments investigated. See detail table, Appendix A, page 295, whence derived.

Occupations and states.	Number of adult employés.		Average rates of daily wages.		Occupations and states.	Number of adult employés.		Average rates of daily wages.	
	Male.	Fem.	Male.	Fem.		Male.	Fem.	Male.	Fem.
LAPPERS.					**PACKERS.**				
Connecticut	3	......	$0 90	......	Germany	8	......	$0 58	......
Great Britain	9	12	88	$0 60	Great Britain	6	......	68	......
Massachusetts	2	......	118	......	Maine	1	......	1 00	......
New Hampshire	4	......	88	......	Maryland	20	......	1 45	......
North Carolina	3	......	80	......	New York	3	......	1 15	......
					North Carolina	9	......	89	......
Total and average	21	12	0 90	60	Pennsylvania	2	......	2 18	......
LOOM FIXERS.					Virginia	8	2	1 10	$0 55
Delaware	2	......	1 40	......	Total and average	57	2	1 11	55
Italy	1	......	48	......	**PAINTERS.**				
Maryland	14	......	1 54	......					
Massachusetts	13	......	1 41	......	Georgia	1	......	1 00	......
New Jersey	6	......	1 50	......	Maine	7	......	1 73	......
New York	20	......	1 78	......	Massachusetts	19	......	1 44	......
North Carolina	10	......	1 22	......	New York	13	......	1 83	......
Vermont	5	......	1 50	......					
Virginia	5	......	1 32	......	Total and average	40	......	1 61	......
					PICKERS.				
Total and average	88	......	1 50	......	Germany	13	......	56	......
MACHINISTS.					Maine	27	......	90	......
Connecticut	2	......	1 50	......	Maryland	17	......	1 21	......
Georgia	3	......	1 47	......	Massachusetts	18	......	1 01	......
Great Britain	1	......	1 35	......	New Hampshire	12	......	92	......
Maine	22	......	1 83	......	New Jersey	3	......	1 25	......
Maryland	1	......	2 13	......	New York	20	......	1 08	......
Massachusetts	43	......	1 47	......	North Carolina	11	......	89	......
New Jersey	3	......	2 35	......	Pennsylvania	2	......	94	......
New York	28	......	1 94	......	Vermont	4	......	1 00	......
North Carolina	1	......	2 00	......	Virginia	8	......	94	......
Virginia	5	......	2 10	......					
					Total and average	135	......	96	......
Total and average	109	......	1 73	......	**RAILWAY HANDS.**				
OILERS.					Connecticut	......	1	......	63
Connecticut	1	......	96	......	Georgia	1	......	80	......
France	2	......	71	......	Virginia	1	1	70	55
Georgia	5	......	80	......					
Germany	2	......	78	......	Total and average	2	2	80	59
Great Britain	4	......	97	......	**REELERS.**				
Italy	13	......	45	......					
Maine	32	......	99	......	Italy	......	200	......	24
Massachusetts	70	......	93	......	Maine	5	......	2 21	......
New Hampshire	8	......	94	......	Massachusetts	......	2	......	75
New York	5	......	115	......	North Carolina	......	29	......	57
North Carolina	3	......	75	......	Pennsylvania	......	12	......	90
Vermont	1	......	90	......	Virginia	......	2	......	75
Total and average	146	......	90	......	Total and average	5	245	2 21	32
OVERSEERS.					**ROVERS.**				
Connecticut	5	......	2 57	......	Germany	4	......	61	......
France	5	......	90	......	Great Britain	25	102	80	61
Georgia	7	......	3 43	......	Maine	......	11	......	1 20
Great Britain	14	......	1 00	......	New Hampshire	14	2	65	96
Italy	6	10	72	25	New York	2	......	1 25	......
Maine	10	......	3 60	......	North Carolina	1	......	75	......
Maryland	20	......	2 18	......					
Massachusetts	68	......	2 85	......	Total and average	46	115	82	67
New Hampshire	30	......	4 15	......	**SCRUBBERS.**				
New York	51	......	2 50	......					
North Carolina	23	......	2 00	......	Germany	......	3	......	48
Pennsylvania	15	......	2 25	......	Maine	3	4	70	85
Vermont	5	......	2 75	......	Massachusetts	......	40	......	61
Virginia	22	......	1 87	......	New Hampshire	......	20	......	56
Total and average	296	10	2 68	25	Total and average	3	67	70	61

REPORT OF THE COMMISSIONER OF LABOR.

SUMMARY OF SELECTED OCCUPATIONS, ADULTS—Continued.

COTTON GOODS—Continued.

NOTE.—This table is not a complete exhibit for industries or states, but covers only the principal occupations in establishments investigated. See detail table, Appendix A, page 293, whence derived.

Occupations and states.	Number of adult employés.		Average rates of daily wages.		Occupations and states.	Number of adult employés.		Average rates of daily wages.	
	Male.	Fem.	Male.	Fem.		Male.	Fem.	Male.	Fem.
SECOND HANDS.					**SPEEDERS—concluded.**				
Connecticut	4	....	$1 45	....	Great Britain	....	29	....	$0 68
Georgia	6	....	1 49	....	Maine	....	9	....	92
Maine	39	57	1 70	$0 95	Maryland	....	31	....	88
Maryland	3	....	1 75	....	Massachusetts	2	166	$0 95	82
Massachusetts	94	....	1 77	....	New Hampshire	8	....	1 00	....
New Hampshire	51	....	2 02	....	New Jersey	....	20	....	90
New York	82	....	1 67	....	New York	....	52	....	83
North Carolina	3	....	78	....	North Carolina	....	41	....	60
Vermont	4	....	1 50	....	Pennsylvania	....	9	....	1 12
Virginia	5	....	1 25	....	Vermont	14	....	82	....
					Virginia	....	13	....	60
Total and average	291	57	1 70	95	Total and average	24	408	89	79
SECTION HANDS.					**SPINNERS, MULE.**				
Connecticut	5	....	1 42	....	Connecticut	15	....	1 62	....
Georgia	17	....	1 08	....	Delaware	1	....	2 50	....
Maine	100	....	1 54	....	France	7	....	96	....
Massachusetts	136	4	1 45	1 10	Georgia	8	....	85	....
New Hampshire	13	....	1 48	....	Germany	26	....	88	....
					Great Britain	172	....	1 57	....
Total and average	271	4	1 46	1 10	Italy	32	....	73	....
SLASHERS.					Maine	59	....	1 49	....
Connecticut	1	....	1 67	....	Massachusetts	2 74	....	1 25	....
Georgia	3	....	1 22	....	New Hampshire	32	....	1 43	....
Maine	13	....	1 45	....	New Jersey	14	....	1 40	....
Massachusetts	32	....	1 42	....	New York	1 57	....	1 32	....
New Hampshire	7	....	1 60	....	Vermont	12	....	1 20	....
New York	49	....	1 10	....					
North Carolina	3	....	97	....	Total and average	809	....	1 33	....
Vermont	2	....	1 20	....	**SPINNERS, OTHER.**				
Virginia	1	....	1 70	....	Germany	....	15	....	49
					Great Britain	....	6	....	58
Total and average	111	....	1 28	....	Maine	....	80	....	76
SLUBBERS.					Maryland	....	162	....	71
Connecticut	3	....	1 13	....	Massachusetts	....	389	....	79
Great Britain	....	32	....	68	New Hampshire	....	327	....	75
Maine	....	19	....	95	New York	403	244	88	61
Maryland	....	18	....	78	Pennsylvania	....	28	....	88
Massachusetts	....	32	....	90	South Carolina	....	80	....	65
New Hampshire	2	3	96	87					
New York	78	9	1 00	72	Total and average	403	1,337	88	72
North Carolina	....	19	....	60	**SPOOLERS.**				
Pennsylvania	....	2	....	1 12	Connecticut	....	18	....	60
Vermont	....	6	....	88	Delaware	....	3	....	66
Virginia	....	7	....	61	Maine	....	132	....	71
					Maryland	....	50	....	75
Total and average	83	147	1 01	78	Massachusetts	3	329	98	71
SPARE HANDS.					New Hampshire	....	116	....	66
Maine	3	2	1 10	1 16	New York	8	8	60	70
Massachusetts	8	13	99	1 00	North Carolina	....	50	....	55
New Hampshire	7	1	1 02	96	Pennsylvania	....	15	....	90
New York	3	....	1 08	....	Virginia	....	17	....	63
North Carolina	....	4	....	55					
Vermont	....	6	....	82	Total and average	11	744	77	69
Virginia	1	2	90	55	**SWEEPERS.**				
					Italy	....	7	....	20
Total and average	22	28	99	88	Massachusetts	....	13	....	60
SPEEDERS.									
Connecticut	....	18	....	1 01	Total and average	....	20	....	46
Germany	....	17	....	39					

VARIATION IN THE RATES OF WAGES.

SUMMARY OF SELECTED OCCUPATIONS, ADULTS—Continued.

COTTON GOODS—Concluded.

NOTE.—This table is not a complete exhibit for industries or states, but covers only the principal occupations in establishments investigated. See detail table, Appendix A, page 295, whence derived.

Occupations and states.	Number of adult employés.		Average rates of daily wages.		Occupations and states.	Number of adult employés.		Average rates of daily wages.	
	Male.	Fem.	Male.	Fem.		Male.	Fem.	Male.	Fem.
TRAMSTERS.					**WATCHMEN.**				
Georgia	1	.....	$1 05	.....	Connecticut	2	.....	$1 15	.....
Maine	8	.....	1 24	.....	France	1	.....	1 00	.....
Massachusetts	10	.....	1 18	.....	Georgia	6	.....	83	.....
New York	20	.....	1 85	.....	Germany	16	.....	52	.....
North Carolina	3	.....	93	.....	Italy	2	.....	48	.....
Vermont	2	.....	1 25	.....	Maine	15	.....	1 33	.....
Virginia	2	.....	85	.....	Maryland	3	.....	1 25	.....
					Massachusetts	31	.....	1 39	.....
Total and average	46	.....	1 45	.....	New York	21	.....	1 21	.....
TWISTERS.					North Carolina	6	.....	94	.....
Great Britain	8	.....	75	.....	Pennsylvania	4	.....	1 67	.....
Italy	6	79	67	$0 25	South Carolina	5	.....	1 10	.....
Maine	3	2	1 42	1 50	Virginia	4	.....	1 14	.....
Maryland	.....	28	.....	85					
Massachusetts	2	50	1 52	80	Total and average	116	.....	1 14	.....
New York	12	.....	1 15	.....	**WEAVERS.**				
Total and average	31	159	1 01	57	Connecticut	43	97	1 17	$0 95
WARPERS.					Delaware	.....	153	.....	82
Connecticut	.....	3	.....	86	France	.....	100	.....	54
France	5	.....	67	.....	Georgia	71	158	86	77
Georgia	3	2	1 00	65	Germany	.....	1,067	.....	46
Germany	.....	18	.....	49	Great Britain	.....	152	.....	90
Maine	14	16	1 07	91	Maine	731	568	1 11	1 10
Maryland	15	.....	1 30	.....	Maryland	14	279	84	85
Massachusetts	15	44	1 02	96	Massachusetts	391	2,006	1 13	93
New Hampshire	.....	13	.....	1 10	New Hampshire	241	1,500	1 07	99
New York	.....	14	.....	78	New Jersey	.....	130	.....	84
North Carolina	11	.....	1 05	.....	New York	235	1,169	1 10	93
Pennsylvania	5	.....	1 85	.....	North Carolina	100	208	75	76
Virginia	.....	5	.....	84	Pennsylvania	40	134	1 12	1 12
					South Carolina	91	.....	92	.....
Total and average	68	115	1 13	86	Vermont	65	50	1 00	82
					Virginia	25	201	1 10	79
					Total and average	2,047	7,972	1 07	87

FOOD PREPARATIONS.

	Male.	Fem.	Male.	Fem.		Male.	Fem.	Male.	Fem.
CLEANERS.					**FIREMEN.**				
Illinois	6	.....	1 86	.....	California	3	.....	2 50	.....
Indiana	2	.....	1 80	.....	Illinois	10	.....	1 89	.....
Missouri	2	.....	1 65	.....	Missouri	6	.....	2 28	.....
New Hampshire	1	.....	85	.....	Ohio	14	.....	1 52	.....
Total and average	11	.....	1 72	.....	Total and average	33	.....	1 86	.....
COOPERS.					**LABORERS.**				
Ohio	44	.....	1 22	.....	California	9	.....	1 50	.....
					Illinois	60	.....	1 53	.....
Total and average	44	.....	1 22	.....	Indiana	424	.....	1 50	.....
ENGINEERS.					Minnesota	108	.....	1 80	.....
California	18	.....	4 80	.....	Missouri	77	.....	1 40	.....
Illinois	19	.....	2 48	.....	Ohio	15	.....	1 58	.....
Indiana	3	.....	2 40	.....	West Virginia	1	.....	1 42	.....
Missouri	7	.....	2 90	.....	Total and average	700	.....	1 55	.....
Ohio	11	.....	1 72	.....	**MILLERS.**				
West Virginia	1	.....	2 00	.....	California	5	.....	4 00	.....
					Illinois	31	.....	3 01	.....
Total and average	59	.....	3 00	.....	Indiana	3	.....	3 60	.....
					Minnesota	83	.....	2 50	.....
					Missouri	12	.....	3 59	.....

SUMMARY OF SELECTED OCCUPATIONS, ADULTS—Continued.

FOOD PREPARATIONS—Concluded.

NOTE.—This table is *not* a complete exhibit for industries or states, but covers only the principal occupations in establishments investigated. See detail table, Appendix A, page 295, whence derived.

Occupations and states.	Number of adult employés.		Average rates of daily wages.		Occupations and states.	Number of adult employés.		Average rates of daily wages.	
	Male.	Fem.	Male.	Fem.		Male.	Fem.	Male.	Fem.
MILLERS—concluded.					**SWEEPERS.**				
New Hampshire	5		$3 00		Illinois	14		$1 54	
Ohio	12		2 52		Indiana	2		1 80	
West Virginia	2		2 70		Minnesota	50		1 62	
					Missouri	2		1 65	
Total and average	153		2 80		New Hampshire	1		1 25	
PACKERS.					Ohio	2		1 67	
California	2		3 50						
Illinois	24		1 76		Total and average	71		1 61	
Indiana	2		1 60		**TEAMSTERS.**				
Minnesota	28		2 00						
Missouri	4		1 82		California	6		2 91	
New Hampshire	2		1 65		Illinois	17		1 63	
Ohio	8		1 84		Indiana	2		2 00	
West Virginia	1		1 67		Ohio	4		1 25	
Total and average	71		1 91		Total and average	29		1 87	

FURNITURE.

Occupations and states.	Number of adult employés.		Average rates of daily wages.		Occupations and states.	Number of adult employés.		Average rates of daily wages.	
	Male.	Fem.	Male.	Fem.		Male.	Fem.	Male.	Fem.
CABINET MAKERS.					**LABORERS.**				
Indiana	143		1 59		Indiana	48		1 08	
Kentucky	27		1 80		Kentucky	8		1 13	
Michigan	118		1 88		Michigan	63		1 27	
Total and average	288		1 73		Total and average	119		1 18	
CARVERS.					**MACHINE MEN.**				
Kentucky	6		2 25		Indiana	187		1 55	
Michigan	31		2 33		Kentucky	32		1 50	
Total and average	37		2 31		Michigan	166		1 73	
ENGINEERS.					Total and average	385		1 63	
Indiana	2		2 91		**UPHOLSTERERS.**				
Michigan	5		2 55						
Total and average	7		2 65		Indiana	5		2 00	
FOREMEN.					Kentucky	5		1 50	
					Michigan	19		1 82	
Indiana	4		3 00						
Michigan	18		2 99		Total and average	29		1 79	
Total and average	22		2 99						

GLASS.

Occupations and states.	Number of adult employés.		Average rates of daily wages.		Occupations and states.	Number of adult employés.		Average rates of daily wages.	
	Male.	Fem.	Male.	Fem.		Male.	Fem.	Male.	Fem.
BLACKSMITHS.					**BLOWERS AND FINISHERS, BOTTLE AND CHIMNEY.**				
California	3		$3 00						
Kentucky	1		2 25		California (blowers)	28		4 33	
New Jersey	7		2 66		Kentucky (blowers)	20		4 00	
Ohio	3		2 41		New Jersey (blowers)	207		4 50	
Pennsylvania	11		2 33		Ohio	23		4 28	
West Virginia	1		2 25		Pennsylvania	403		4 42	
					West Virginia (blowers)	18		4 90	
Total and average	26		2 50						
					Total and average	699		4 44	
BLOWERS, WINDOW GLASS.					**CUTTERS.**				
Illinois	16		6 25		Illinois	6		5 55	
New Jersey	32		4 80		New Jersey	20		4 12	
Ohio	37		5 08		Ohio	15		4 64	
Pennsylvania	27		5 48		Pennsylvania	11		4 16	
Total and average	112		5 26		Total and average	52		4 45	

VARIATION IN THE RATES OF WAGES.

SUMMARY OF SELECTED OCCUPATIONS, ADULTS—Continued.

GLASS—Concluded.

NOTE.—This table is *not* a complete exhibit for industries or states, but covers only the principal occupations in establishments investigated. See detail table, Appendix A, page 295, whence derived.

Occupations and states.	Number of adult employés.		Average rates of daily wages.		Occupations and states.	Number of adult employés.		Average rates of daily wages.	
	Male.	Fem.	Male.	Fem.		Male.	Fem.	Male.	Fem.
ENGINEERS.					**MIXERS.**				
California	1		$2 50		California	3		$2 50	
New Jersey	8		1 50		Kentucky	1		3 00	
Ohio	1		1 66		New Jersey	11		1 87	
Pennsylvania	7		2 31		Ohio	5		1 76	
					Pennsylvania	28		1 98	
Total and average	17		1 90		West Virginia	2		1 66	
FILLERS-IN.					Total and average	50		1 97	
Ohio	2		2 00		**MOULD MAKERS.**				
Pennsylvania	13		1 90		Ohio	7		4 00	
Total and average	15		1 92		Pennsylvania	23		3 58	
FLATTENERS.					Total and average	30		3 68	
Illinois	4		6 25		**PACKERS.**				
New Jersey	10		4 64		California	8		2 25	
Ohio	9		5 35		Kentucky	1		2 25	
Pennsylvania	8		4 47		New Jersey	13		2 80	
					Ohio	10		1 55	
Total and average	31		5 01		Pennsylvania	74		1 92	
FOREMEN.					West Virginia	5		1 50	
Kentucky	1		3 00		Total and average	111		2 00	
New Jersey	1		4 87		**POT MAKERS.**				
Pennsylvania	9		4 00		California	2		3 00	
West Virginia	1		4 00		New Jersey	3		2 90	
Total and average	12		3 99		Pennsylvania	8		3 09	
GATHERERS.					Total and average	13		3 03	
Illinois	16		4 00		**PRESSERS.**				
New Jersey	40		2 99		Ohio	29		4 00	
Ohio	71		2 00		Pennsylvania	41		4 41	
Pennsylvania	173		2 47		Total and average	70		4 24	
Total and average	300		2 73		**TEAMSTERS.**				
LABORERS.					California	3		3 00	
California	15		1 75		Kentucky	1		1 25	
Kentucky	21		1 04		New Jersey	18		1 42	
New Jersey	36		1 20		Pennsylvania	13		1 82	
Ohio	40		1 92		West Virginia	2		1 66	
Pennsylvania	435		1 60		Total and average	37		1 70	
Total and average	553		1 50		**TEASERS.**				
LEERSMEN.					California	3		3 00	
New Jersey	10		2 48		Kentucky	2		1 40	
Ohio	4		1 75		Ohio	9		1 94	
Pennsylvania	17		1 80		Pennsylvania	39		1 96	
West Virginia	2		1 66		West Virginia	2		1 75	
Total and average	42		2 01		Total and average	55		1 99	
MASTER SHEARERS.					**WATCHMEN.**				
New Jersey	20		2 09		Kentucky	1		1 15	
Total and average	20		2 09		Ohio	1		1 50	
MASTER TEASERS.					Pennsylvania	12		1 69	
Ohio	2		4 50		West Virginia	1		1 66	
Pennsylvania	3		4 43						
Total and average	5		4 46		Total and average	15		1 64	

SUMMARY OF SELECTED OCCUPATIONS, ADULTS—Continued.

LEATHER.

NOTE.—This table is not a complete exhibit for industries or states, but covers only the principal occupations in establishments investigated. See detail table, Appendix A, page 295, whence derived.

Occupations and states.	Number of adult employés.		Average rates of daily wages.		Occupations and states.	Number of adult employés.		Average rates of daily wages.	
	Male.	Fem.	Male.	Fem.		Male.	Fem.	Male.	Fem.
BEAMSMEN.					**LABORERS**—concluded.				
California	30		$2 16		Delaware	37		$1 50	
Delaware	38		1 83		Pennsylvania	24		1 20	
Massachusetts	10		1 60						
Pennsylvania	45		2 07		Total and average	98		1 55	
Total and average	123		1 98		**SHAVERS.**				
FINISHERS.					Delaware	16		3 16	
California	1		2 06		Pennsylvania	17		3 40	
Delaware	184		1 72		Total and average	33		3 28	
Massachusetts	40		2 05		**TANNERS.**				
Pennsylvania	108		2 27		Delaware	30		1 67	
Total and average	333		1 94		Massachusetts	10		1 53	
LABORERS.					Pennsylvania	27		1 86	
California	37		1 83		Total and average	67		1 73	

LIQUORS AND BEVERAGES.

Occupations and states.	Number of adult employés.		Average rates of daily wages.		Occupations and states.	Number of adult employés.		Average rates of daily wages.	
	Male.	Fem.	Male.	Fem.		Male.	Fem.	Male.	Fem.
BREWERS AND MALSTERS.					**FOREMEN.**				
Illinois	64		$2 12		Illinois	7		$4 06	
Ohio	72		2 00		Ohio	1		2 00	
Pennsylvania	12		2 25		Pennsylvania	1		3 00	
Total and average	148		2 12		Total and average	9		3 70	
ENGINEERS.					**TEAMSTERS.**				
Illinois	9		2 89		Illinois	20		2 01	
Ohio	4		2 75		Ohio	45		2 18	
Total and average	13		2 85		Pennsylvania	4		2 00	
FIREMEN.					Total and average	69		2 12	
Illinois	22		1 95						
Ohio	4		2 08						
Total and average	26		1 97						

MACHINES AND MACHINERY.

Occupations and states.	Number of adult employés.		Average rates of daily wages.		Occupations and states.	Number of adult employés.		Average rates of daily wages.	
	Male.	Fem.	Male.	Fem.		Male.	Fem.	Male.	Fem.
BLACKSMITHS.					**MACHINISTS.**				
California	16		$3 32		California	68		$2 97	
Indiana	29		2 44		Indiana	373		2 44	
Kentucky	6		2 06		Kentucky	43		2 10	
Maine	2		2 25		Maine	10		2 50	
New Jersey	3		3 06		Massachusetts	170		2 27	
					New Jersey	65		2 35	
Total and average	56		2 75		Pennsylvania	275		1 86	
BOILER MAKERS.					Total and average	1,004		2 27	
California	32		3 30		**MOULDERS.**				
Indiana	114		2 01		California	48		3 39	
Total and average	146		2 30		Indiana	43		2 30	
CARPENTERS.					Kentucky	10		2 37	
California	7		2 00		Maine	18		2 38	
Indiana	7		2 28		New Jersey	30		2 64	
Total and average	14		2 63		Total and average	149		2 74	

VARIATION IN THE RATES OF WAGES.

SUMMARY OF SELECTED OCCUPATIONS, ADULTS—Continued.
METALS AND METALLIC GOODS.

NOTE.—This table is *not* a complete exhibit for industries or states, but covers only the principal occupations in establishments investigated. See detail table, Appendix A, page 205, whence derived.

Occupations and states.	Number of adult employés. Male.	Number of adult employés. Fem.	Average rates of daily wages. Male.	Average rates of daily wages. Fem.	Occupations and states.	Number of adult employés. Male.	Number of adult employés. Fem.	Average rates of daily wages. Male.	Average rates of daily wages. Fem.
BREAKERS.					**CINDERMEN.**				
Maryland (limestone, ore)	7	.....	$1 25	.....	Alabama	10	.....	$1 40	.....
New York (ore)	6	.....	1 33	.....	Maryland	4	.....	1 25	.....
Ohio (iron, limestone, ore)	39	.....	1 28	.....	New York	12	.....	1 26	.....
Pennsylvania (iron, ore)	18	.....	1 43	.....	Ohio	50	.....	1 45	.....
Tennessee (ore)	4	.....	90	.....	Pennsylvania	30	.....	2 03	.....
Virginia (ore)	4	.....	1 00	.....	Virginia	14	.....	1 07	.....
Total and average	78	.....	1 26	.....	Total and average	120	.....	1 52	.....
BRICKLAYERS.					**DRAG-OUTS.**				
					Delaware	2	.....	1 35	.....
Belgium (masons)	2	.....	59	.....	Great Britain	2	.....	1 20	.....
Great Britain (bricklayers, masons)	10	.....	1 20	.....	New York	8	.....	1 62	.....
Illinois (bricklayers, masons)	2	.....	3 90	.....	Ohio (drag-outs; drag-outs, butt, muck, plate)	32	.....	1 85	.....
Indiana (masons)	2	.....	1 75	.....	Pennsylvania (drag-outs; drag-outs, bar, 10-inch)	9	.....	1 39	.....
Kentucky	1	.....	3 50	.....					
New York (masons)	4	.....	2 61	.....	Total and average	53	.....	1 69	.....
Ohio (bricklayers, masons)	5	.....	3 20	.....	**ENGINEERS.**				
Pennsylvania (bricklayers, masons)	61	.....	3 03	.....	Alabama	2	.....	2 00	.....
Virginia (masons)	4	.....	3 00	.....	Belgium	5	.....	80	.....
West Virginia (masons)	2	.....	3 50	.....	California	1	.....	2 00	.....
Total and average	93	.....	2 78	.....	Delaware	2	.....	1 80	.....
CARPENTERS.					Great Britain	24	.....	1 01	.....
					Illinois	10	.....	2 34	.....
Belgium	4	.....	00	.....	Indiana	9	.....	2 00	.....
California	11	.....	3 14	.....	Kentucky	6	.....	1 86	.....
Great Britain	2	.....	1 04	.....	Maryland	8	.....	1 74	.....
Illinois	3	.....	1 83	.....	Missouri	21	.....	1 78	.....
Indiana	5	.....	2 07	.....	New York	35	.....	2 04	.....
Kentucky	1	.....	1 65	.....	Ohio	118	.....	1 82	.....
Maryland	1	.....	1 75	.....	Pennsylvania	93	.....	2 00	.....
Massachusetts	5	.....	2 25	.....	Tennessee	3	.....	1 75	.....
Missouri	15	.....	2 17	.....	Vermont	5	.....	2 30	.....
New York	8	.....	1 09	.....	Virginia	7	.....	1 77	.....
Ohio	21	.....	1 88	.....	West Virginia	2	.....	2 50	.....
Pennsylvania	43	.....	2 50	.....	Total and average	351	.....	1 85	.....
Virginia	14	.....	1 57	.....	**FILLERS.**				
Total and average	133	.....	2 16	.....	Alabama (top)	4	.....	1 50	.....
CATCHERS.					Belgium (bottom, top)	12	12	65	$0 32
					Great Britain (fillers; fillers, bottom, top)	74	.....	1 08	.....
Delaware	6	.....	1 77	.....	Indiana	10	.....	1 35	.....
Great Britain (muck, rail)	15	.....	1 22	.....	Maryland	21	.....	1 35	.....
Illinois (catchers; catchers, plate, slab)	8	.....	3 83	.....	New York (bottom, top)	38	.....	1 51	.....
Indiana	2	.....	3 75	.....	Ohio (fillers; fillers, bottom, top)	175	.....	1 30	.....
Kentucky (bar, plate, wheel)	3	.....	3 25	.....	Pennsylvania (fillers; fillers, bottom, top)	46	.....	1 54	.....
New York	28	.....	1 91	.....	Tennessee (bottom, top)	12	.....	1 13	.....
Ohio (catchers; catchers, bar, butt, muck, plate, 8-inch, 9-inch)	46	.....	2 48	.....	Virginia (fillers; fillers, bottom, top)	66	.....	1 13	.....
Pennsylvania (catchers; catchers, bar, muck, 8-inch, 10 inch)	a 22	.....	2 72	.....	Total and average	458	12	1 27	32
Virginia (catchers; catchers, guide)	40	.....	1 24	.....	**FIREMEN.**				
West Virginia (plate)	2	.....	2 50	.....	Alabama	5	.....	1 25	.....
					Belgium	11	.....	66	.....
Total and average	172	.....	2 09	.....	Great Britain	10	.....	80	.....
					Illinois	10	.....	1 70	.....

a This does not include establishment 428, (catchers not reported).

SUMMARY OF SELECTED OCCUPATIONS, ADULTS—Continued.

METALS AND METALLIC GOODS—Continued.

NOTE.—This table is *not* a complete exhibit for industries or states, but covers only the principal occupations in establishments investigated. See detail table, Appendix A, page 205, whence derived.

Occupations and states.	Number of adult employés.		Average rates of daily wages.		Occupations and states.	Number of adult employés.		Average rates of daily wages.	
	Male.	Fem.	Male.	Fem.		Male.	Fem.	Male.	Fem.
FIREMEN—concluded.					**HEATERS' HELPERS**—concluded.				
Indiana	6		$1 47		Illinois (heaters' helpers; heaters' helpers, plate, old rail)	24		$2 47	
Kentucky	3		1 50		Indiana	9		1 60	
Maryland	2		2 14		Kentucky	3		2 30	
Ohio	119		1 23		New York	42		1 85	
Pennsylvania	35		1 65		Ohio (heaters' helpers; heaters' helpers, bar, butt, plate, sheet, 8-inch)	140		1 71	
Virginia	5		1 27						
Total and average	206		1 29		Pennsylvania (heaters' helper; heaters' helpers, bar)	51		1 89	
FOREMEN.					Virginia (heaters' helpers; heaters' helpers, bar, guide, plate)	31		1 50	
Alabama	4		2 25		West Virginia (plate)	7		1 75	
Belgium	7		1 10		Total and average	321		1 77	
California	1		4 00		**HOOKERS-UP.**				
Delaware	1		4 00		Belgium	8		70	
Great Britain	16		2 45		Delaware	2		1 25	
Illinois	3		3 44		Illinois (hookers-up; hookers-up, plate, slab)	14		1 71	
Massachusetts	1		3 20		New York (hookers-up; hookers-up, tumble)	37		1 98	
Missouri	10		2 00		Ohio (hookers-up; hookers-up, bar, butt, muck, plate)	50		1 45	
New York	27		3 26		Pennsylvania	2		1 80	
Ohio (foremen, overseers)	49		3 65		West Virginia (plate)	2		1 50	
Pennsylvania	19		3 25		Total and average	115		1 60	
Vermont	13		3 50		**KEEPERS.**				
Virginia	8		2 41		Belgium	6		1 00	
Total and average	159		3 08		Great Britain	10		1 86	
HAMMERMEN.					Indiana	2		1 85	
Indiana	2		4 00		Maryland	9		1 50	
Kentucky	4		4 13		New York	6		1 70	
New York	7		2 75		Ohio	20		1 65	
Ohio	6		3 61		Pennsylvania	6		2 02	
Pennsylvania	40		2 95		Tennessee	2		1 80	
Total and average	59		3 11		Virginia	6		1 93	
HEATERS.					Total and average	67		1 68	
Belgium	6		1 40		**KEEPERS' HELPERS.**				
Delaware	2		3 00		Belgium	18		64	
Illinois (heaters; heaters, old rail, plate)	20		5 25		Great Britain	10		1 28	
Indiana	12		4 17		Indiana	2		1 40	
Kentucky (bar, bloom and scrap, 8-inch, 10-inch, plate, sheet, slot)	13		5 56		Maryland	9		1 25	
New York	42		4 03		New York	8		1 58	
Ohio (heaters; heaters, bar, butt, plate, sheet, 8-inch, 9-inch)	a 80		4 34		Ohio	32		1 34	
Pennsylvania (heaters; heaters, bar, 8-inch, 10-inch)	b 27		5 74		Pennsylvania	10		1 56	
Virginia (heaters; heaters, bar, guide, plate, 18-inch)	54		3 50		Tennessee	2		1 35	
West Virginia	7		4 50		Virginia	14		1 43	
Total and average	263		4 31		Total and average	105		1 26	
HEATERS' HELPERS.									
Belgium	12		85						
Delaware	2		1 70						

a Not including 7 heaters in establishment 427, wages being indefinite; also, 4 heaters in establishment 419.

b Not including heaters in establishment 528, number not reported.

VARIATION IN THE RATES OF WAGES.

SUMMARY OF SELECTED OCCUPATIONS, ADULTS—Continued.

METALS AND METALIC GOODS—Continued.

NOTE.—This table is *not* a complete exhibit for industries or states, but covers only the principal occupations in establishments investigated. See detail table, Appendix A, page 295, whence derived.

Occupations and states.	Number of adult employees.		Average rates of daily wages.		Occupations and states.	Number of adult employees.		Average rates of daily wages.	
	Male.	Fem.	Male.	Fem.		Male.	Fem.	Male.	Fem.
LABORERS.					**PILERS.**				
Belgium	65		$0 63		Great Britain (iron)	7		$1 08	
Delaware	12		1 11		Illinois (old rail)	4		1 30	
Great Britain	113		69		Kentucky (plate)	4		2 00	
Illinois	171		1 33		New York (iron)	6		1 42	
Indiana	153		1 30		Ohio (iron, plate)	a18		1 34	
Kentucky	142		1 27		Pennsylvania (iron)	12		3 00	
Maryland	102		1 02						
Massachusetts	18		1 20		Total and average	51		1 75	
Missouri	412		1 25		**PUDDLERS.**				
New Hampshire	100		1 25						
New Jersey	12		1 35		Delaware	6		2 50	
New York	1,459		1 19		Great Britain	240		2 43	
Ohio	1,161		1 08		Illinois	6		4 00	
Pennsylvania	1,936		1 20		Indiana	32		4 00	
Vermont	62		1 10		Kentucky	83		3 60	
Virginia	339		92		New York	185		2 84	
West Virginia	15		1 25		Ohio	108		3 46	
					Pennsylvania	318		3 47	
Total and average	6,272		1 15		Virginia	124		2 36	
MACHINISTS.					West Virginia	36		2 75	
Belgium	9		49		Total and average	1,138		3 02	
California	79		3 17						
Great Britain	2		1 08		**PUDDLERS' HELPERS.**				
Illinois	16		2 52		Delaware	6		1 30	
Indiana	19		2 11		Illinois	10		2 25	
Kentucky	1		2 50		Indiana	32		2 00	
Maryland	1		2 30		Kentucky	84		1 80	
Massachusetts	40		2 20		New York	168		1 51	
Missouri	3		2 50		Ohio	150		1 64	
New Hampshire	5		2 25		Pennsylvania	318		2 14	
New Jersey	4		2 00		Virginia	204		1 31	
New York	283		1 93		West Virginia	72		1 50	
Ohio	39		2 19						
Pennsylvania	181		2 35		Total and average	1,044		1 73	
Vermont	10		1 75		**ROLLERS.**				
Virginia	17		2 07		Belgium (rollers; roller, chief, second, third, fourth)	12		98	
Total and average	709		2 21		Delaware	8		2 45	
MILLWRIGHTS.					Great Britain (forge, rail)	3		3 04	
Great Britain	10		90		Illinois (rollers; rollers, plate, slab)	11		7 72	
Kentucky	1		5 00		Indiana (bar, guide, muck)	3		7 17	
New York	2		2 15		Kentucky (bar, muck, plate, sheet, 8-inch, 10-inch)	13		6 73	
Ohio	3		2 27						
Pennsylvania	3		3 63		New York (rollers; rollers, muck)	43		4 80	
Virginia	3		2 25		Ohio (rollers; rollers, bar, bloom, butt, hoop, guide, muck, plate, sheet, rod, 8-inch, 9-inch, 18-inch, 22-inch)	b50		6 91	
Total and average	22		1 94						
PATTERN MAKERS.									
Illinois	1		3 10		Pennsylvania (rollers; rollers, bar, muck, plate, 8-inch, 10-inch)	c17		5 85	
Indiana	2		2 25						
Kentucky	1		2 50		Virginia (rollers; rollers, bar, muck, guide, plate, 18-inch)	30		3 04	
Massachusetts	2		2 60						
New Hampshire	7		2 50						
New Jersey	4		2 40						
Pennsylvania	30		2 43						
Virginia	3		2 00						
Total and average	50		2 43						

a Not including 1 plate piler, with 4 assistants, in establishment 419, the wages of 4 of whom were not reported.
b Not including 8 rollers in establishment 417, also 1 roller in establishment 419, wages being indefinite
c Not including 6 rollers in establishment 433, and 5 in establishment 437.

SUMMARY OF SELECTED OCCUPATIONS, ADULTS—Continued.

METALS AND METALLIC GOODS—Concluded.

NOTE.—This table is not a complete exhibit for industries or states, but covers only the principal occupations in establishments investigated. See detail table, Appendix A, page 295, whence derived.

Occupations and states.	Number of adult employés.		Average rates of daily wages.		Occupations and states.	Number of adult employés.		Average rates of daily wages.	
	Male.	Fem.	Male.	Fem.		Male.	Fem.	Male.	Fem.
ROLLERS—concluded.					**SHEARMEN—concluded.**				
West Virginia (muck, plate)	4		$6 00		Ohio (shearmen; shearmen, muck, plate)	70		$1 52	
Total and average	194		5 25		Pennsylvania	32		2 55	
ROLLERS' HELPERS.					Virginia	4		1 10	
Belgium	8		60		West Virginia	1		8 00	
Illinois (plate)	4		4 20		Total and average	142		1 98	
Indiana	16		1 50		**STRAIGHTENERS.**				
Kentucky (rollers' helpers; rollers' helpers, bar, muck, plate, sheet, 8-inch)	44		2 10		Belgium	5		64	
					Great Britain	10		80	
					Kentucky	5		1 60	
New York	9		1 32		New York (straighteners; straighteners, cold bar)	26		2 00	
Ohio (rollers' helpers; rollers' helpers, bar, muck)	10		2 25		Ohio (cold-bar, hot-bar, 8-inch, 9-inch)	15		2 42	
Pennsylvania	31		2 10		Pennsylvania (straighteners; straighteners, cold-bar)	22		2 30	
West Virginia (muck, plate)	8		2 13						
Total and average	130		1 98		Total and average	83		1 99	
ROUGHERS.					**TEAMSTERS.**				
Great Britain (forge, rail)	15		1 41		Alabama	2		1 25	
Illinois	11		3 50		Illinois	3		1 60	
Indiana	6		3 75		Indiana	5		1 40	
Kentucky (bar, plate, sheet, 8-inch, 10-inch)	11		2 48		Kentucky (cart driver)	1		2 50	
New York	26		2 67		Maryland (cart drivers, teamsters)	11		1 25	
Ohio (roughers; roughers, bar, plate, 8-inch, 9-inch)	80		3 02		New Jersey	9		1 37	
					New York	5		1 10	
Pennsylvania (roughers; roughers, muck bar, 8-inch, 10-inch)	10		2 77		Ohio (cartdrivers, teamsters)	22		1 28	
					Pennsylvania (cart driver)	1		2 25	
Virginia (roughers; roughers, guide, 18-inch)	53		1 96		Virginia (cart drivers)	4		1 09	
Total and average	212		2 60		Total and average	63		1 32	
SHEARMEN.					**WHEELERS.**				
Belgium	1		1 20		Great Britain (coal, fettling, metal, slag)	46		99	
Illinois (shearmen; shearmen, plate)	7		3 64		New York (coal, coke, limestone)	37		1 35	
Indiana	4		4 00		Ohio (ash, coal, iron)	162		1 13	
Kentucky (shearmen; shearmen, plate)	13		1 86		Virginia	2		1 10	
New York	10		1 44		Total and average	247		1 13	

MUSICAL INSTRUMENTS AND MATERIALS.

SUMMARY OF SELECTED OCCUPATIONS, ADULTS—Continued.

PAPER.

NOTE.—This table is not a complete exhibit for industries or states, but covers only the principal occupations in establishments investigated. See detail table, Appendix A, page 295, whence derived.

Occupations and states.	Number of adult employés.		Average rates of daily wages.		Occupations and states.	Number of adult employés.		Average rates of daily wages.	
	Male.	Fem.	Male.	Fem.		Male.	Fem.	Male.	Fem.
CALENDERERS.					**LABORERS.**				
Delaware	6		$1 70		Delaware	17		$1 57	
Massachusetts	38	12	1 72	$1 30	Maine	20		1 25	
					Massachusetts	38		1 45	
Total and average	44	12	1 71	1 30	Oregon	15		1 75	
ENGINEERS.					Total and average	90		1 48	
California	1		4 00						
Delaware	12		1 82		**MACHINE TENDERS.**				
Maine	9		2 00		Delaware	42		1 63	
Massachusetts	7		2 93		Maine	13		2 19	
Oregon	5		2 25		Massachusetts	78		2 01	
					New Hampshire	30		2 00	
Total and average	34		2 24		Oregon	5		2 75	
FINISHERS.					Vermont	35		2 00	
Delaware	13		2 89		Total and average	203		1 96	
Maine	6	1	1 93	1 00					
Massachusetts	72	28	1 64	96	**RAG-ENGINE TENDERS.**				
New Hampshire	8		2 00		Delaware	19		1 84	
Oregon		5		1 75	Massachusetts	57		1 80	
Vermont	10		2 00		New Hampshire	30		1 50	
					Vermont	48		1 50	
Total and average	109	34	1 86	1 08	Total and average	154		1 65	
FOREMEN.									
California	1		3 00		**REPAIR HANDS.**				
Delaware	3		3 25						
Maine	1		4 00		Massachusetts	21		2 81	
Massachusetts	12		2 12		New Hampshire	10		2 00	
New Hampshire	5		2 70		Vermont	20		2 00	
Vermont	4		3 00						
Total and average	26		2 60		Total and average	51		2 34	

PRINT WORKS.

Occupations and states.	Male.	Fem.	Male.	Fem.	Occupations and states.	Male.	Fem.	Male.	Fem.
AGEING AND STEAMING HANDS.					**ENGRAVERS.**				
					Massachusetts	14		4 11	
Massachusetts	37		1 08		New Hampshire	4		4 28	
New Hampshire	25		1 23		New Jersey	25		2 00	
					Pennsylvania	19		3 33	
Total and average	63		1 14		Total and average	62		3 03	
BLEACHERS.					**FOREMEN.**				
Massachusetts	29		1 11		Massachusetts (overseers)	35		3 20	
New Hampshire	30		1 32		New Hampshire	1		4 16	
New Jersey	30		1 00		New York	2		3 00	
New York	7		1 17		Pennsylvania	20		4 00	
Total and average	96		1 15		Total and average	58		3 48	
COLORERS AND DYERS.					**PRINTERS.**				
					Massachusetts	23		4 40	
Massachusetts	100		1 18		New Hampshire	14		4 30	
New Hampshire	37		1 30		New Jersey	10		4 00	
New Jersey	40		1 25		Pennsylvania	14		4 10	
Total and average	177		1 23		Total and average	61		4 26	

SUMMARY OF SELECTED OCCUPATIONS, ADULTS—Continued.

TOBACCO.

NOTE.—This table is *not* a complete exhibit for industries or states, but covers only the principal occupations in establishments investigated. See detail table, Appendix A, page 295, whence derived.

Occupations and states.	Number of adult employés.		Average rates of daily wages.		Occupations and states.	Number of adult employés.		Average rates of daily wages.	
	Male.	Fem.	Male.	Fem.		Male.	Fem.	Male.	Fem.
BUNCH BREAKERS.					**LABORERS**—concluded.				
Illinois		59		$1 09	Ohio	7		$1 50	
New Jersey		20		75	Rhode Island	1		1 50	
Ohio	116	176	$1 27	1 22	Virginia	215		86	
Total and average	116	255	1 27	1 15	Total and average	309	35	99	$0 80
CIGAR MAKERS.					**LUMP MAKERS.**				
Connecticut	15		2 25		Kentucky	2		1 67	
Illinois	118	55	1 58	1 45	Missouri	69		1 88	
New Jersey	31	30	1 81	1 00	New York	2	6	1 67	1 33
Ohio	348	222	1 52	1 19	North Carolina	52		1 38	
Rhode Island	14		2 10		Virginia	326		1 15	
West Virginia	48		1 50						
Total and average	574	307	1 58	1 22	Total and average	451	6	1 29	1 33
CUTTERS.					**PACKERS.**				
					Connecticut	1		3 33	
Illinois	10		1 98		Illinois	33	15	2 17	83
Kentucky	3		1 50		Michigan	23		1 00	
Michigan	6		2 00		Missouri	6	30	2 00	1 10
Missouri	10		2 33		New Jersey	6		1 50	
New York	12		2 00		New York	5	50	2 00	1 33
North Carolina	24		67		North Carolina	50		60	
Virginia	25		1 00		Ohio	57	2	2 34	1 29
Total and average	90		1 39		Rhode Island	1		2 17	
DRESSERS.					Virginia		75		83
Illinois	12		1 73		West Virginia		2		60
Kentucky		6		1 20	Total and average	182	174	1 62	1 02
Michigan	12	4	1 50	1 00	**PRESSMEN.**				
Missouri	12		2 00		Illinois	17		1 50	
New York	2	3	2 00	1 33	Kentucky	5		1 56	
Total and average	38	13	1 76	1 16	Missouri	80		1 24	
ENGINEERS.					New York	5		2 00	
Illinois	1		2 50		North Carolina	16		1 12	
Missouri	2		3 91		Virginia	167		1 20	
New York	1		3 33		Total and average	290		1 33	
North Carolina	1		1 50		**STEMMERS.**				
Virginia	4		1 87		Kentucky		10		83
Total and average	9		2 52		Missouri	310	93		
FOREMEN.					New York		100		75
Illinois	7		2 97		North Carolina	2	3	60	45
Kentucky	3		2 50		Virginia		539		54
Michigan	5		2 00		Total and average	312	652	93	59
Missouri	7		2 75		**STRIPPERS.**				
New Jersey	1		2 00		Connecticut		4		79
North Carolina	21		2 25		Illinois		5		1 00
Ohio	11		2 86		Kentucky		6		1 00
Virginia	23		1 94		Rhode Island		4		1 00
West Virginia	1		2 50		Virginia		10		55
Total and average	79		2 35		Total and average		29		81
LABORERS.					**WRAPPERS.**				
Connecticut	1		2 00		Illinois	20		2 00	
Illinois	12		1 43		Kentucky	2	4	2 00	2 00
Kentucky	28		1 25		Missouri	24		96	
Michigan	4		1 25		North Carolina		53		67
Missouri		35		80	Virginia	1	41	80	76
New Jersey	5		1 13						
North Carolina	36		69		Total and average	47	98	1 44	76

VARIATION IN THE RATES OF WAGES.

SUMMARY OF SELECTED OCCUPATIONS, ADULTS—Continued.
WOOLLEN GOODS.

NOTE.—This table is not a complete exhibit for industries or states, but covers only the principal occupations in establishments investigated. See detail table, Appendix A, page 295, whence derived.

Occupations and states.	Number of adult employés.		Average rates of daily wages.		Occupations and states.	Number of adult employés.		Average rates of daily wages.	
	Male.	Fem.	Male.	Fem.		Male.	Fem.	Male.	Fem.
BURLERS.					**DYERS**—concluded.				
Connecticut		13		$0 69	Illinois	4		$1 35	
Indiana		2		75	Indiana	34		1 35	
Maryland		4		90	Iowa	1		1 50	
Massachusetts		4		1 15	Kentucky	15		1 39	
New Hampshire		30		90	Maine	4		1 44	
New York		66		70	Maryland	18		1 25	
North Carolina		1		50	Massachusetts	57		1 12	
Pennsylvania		129		97	Missouri	11		1 25	
					New Jersey	8		1 00	
Total and average		249		87	New York	40		1 16	
CARDERS.					North Carolina	4		75	
					Pennsylvania	49		1 28	
California	9		$1 75		Vermont	24		1 02	
Connecticut	15		1 20						
Delaware	10		1 42		Total and average	291		1 21	
Indiana	2		1 50		**ENGINEERS.**				
Iowa	3		1 25						
Kentucky	4	4	1 75	1 10	California	1		2 75	
Maine		5		70	Delaware	2		1 91	
Massachusetts	18	3	1 15	85	Illinois	1		2 88	
Missouri	17		1 25		Indiana	4		1 75	
New Hampshire		19		80	Iowa	1		3 00	
New Jersey	10	1	1 13	90	Kentucky	2		2 98	
New York	16		1 08		Maine	1		1 50	
Pennsylvania	10		2 65		Maryland	2		2 00	
Vermont	14		1 00		Massachusetts	4		1 94	
					Missouri	1		2 50	
Total and average	128	32	1 35	86	North Carolina	1		1 83	
DRAWERS-IN.					New Hampshire	1		3 00	
					New York	3		2 47	
Connecticut		2		1 17	Pennsylvania	3		2 42	
Delaware	2		1 25						
Indiana	3	7	92	62	Total and average	27		2 25	
Maryland		2		80	**FINISHERS.**				
Massachusetts		8		1 14						
New York	2	6	1 50	1 40	California	8		1 00	
					Connecticut	14		98	
Total and average	7	25	1 18	1 03	Delaware	6		1 54	
DRESSERS.					Great Britain	37		87	
					Illinois	9	14	1 40	$0 72
California	1		2 75		Indiana	10	1	1 29	1 21
Connecticut	6		1 37		Iowa	2	3	1 50	75
Indiana	3		1 53		Kentucky	1		1 43	
Maine	1		1 60		Maine	1		1 50	
Massachusetts	19	15	1 47	85	Massachusetts	51	10	99	82
New Hampshire	6		1 75		Missouri	9	13	2 00	2 00
New York	5		1 53		North Carolina	5	3	77	50
Pennsylvania	8		2 00		New Jersey	24	24	75	66
Vermont	4		1 23		New York	2		1 25	
					Pennsylvania	31		1 50	
Total and average	53	15	1 59	85					
DRIERS.					Total and average	210	68	1 12	96
					FIREMEN.				
Maine	1		1 10						
Massachusetts	11		1 00		California	1		1 50	
New Hampshire	2		1 15		Connecticut	3		1 67	
New York	20		1 00		Delaware	1		1 16	
Vermont	4		1 02		Indiana	4		1 50	
					Kentucky	2		1 60	
Total and average	38		1 06		Maine	1		1 50	
DYERS.					New Hampshire	2		1 56	
					New York	5		1 29	
California	4		1 87		North Carolina	1		85	
Connecticut	11		1 56		Pennsylvania	2		1 71	
Delaware	1		3 00		Vermont	2		1 40	
Great Britain	6		92						
					Total and average	24		1 46	

SUMMARY OF SELECTED OCCUPATIONS, ADULTS—Continued.

WOOLLEN GOODS—Continued.

NOTE.—This table is *not* a complete exhibit for industries or states, but covers only the principal occupations in establishments investigated. See detail table, Appendix A, page 295, whence derived.

Occupations and states.	Number of adult employés.		Average rates of daily wages.		Occupations and states.	Number of adult employés.		Average rates of daily wages.	
	Male.	Fem.	Male.	Fem.		Male.	Fem.	Male.	Fem.
FULLERS.					**MACHINISTS**—concluded.				
California	9		$1 22		Maine	2		$2 00	
Connecticut	5		1 18		Maryland	2		2 00	
Delaware	4		1 41		Massachusetts	6		1 96	
Indiana	13		1 11		Missouri	1		2 50	
Maine	2		1 50		New Hampshire	3		2 00	
Maryland	5		1 43		New York	7		2 18	
Massachusetts	18		1 03		Pennsylvania	4		2 41	
New Hampshire	8		1 25		Vermont	6		1 78	
New York	10		1 09						
Vermont	16		1 00		Total and average	40		2 13	
Total and average	88		1 14		**OVERSEERS.**				
GIGGERS.					California	3		3 29	
					Connecticut	8		2 48	
Delaware	3		1 23		Delaware (foremen, overseers)	4		2 55	
Maine	2		1 10		Illinois	8		2 52	
Massachusetts	40		97		Indiana	17		2 98	
New York	15		1 11		Iowa (foremen)	4		3 00	
Pennsylvania	20		1 50		Kentucky	10		3 09	
Vermont	22		1 10		Maine (foremen, overseers)	15		2 63	
Total and average	102		1 14		Maryland (foremen)	8		2 44	
LABORERS.					Massachusetts	38		2 66	
					Missouri	5		3 25	
California	6		1 00		New Hampshire	21		2 61	
Connecticut	1		1 25		New Jersey	18		2 50	
Delaware	15		1 30		New York (foremen, overseers)	19		2 90	
Indiana	18		1 03		North Carolina	5		1 85	
Iowa	3		1 50		Pennsylvania (foremen, overseers)	17		2 93	
Kentucky	15		1 32		Vermont	23		2 61	
Maine	30		1 20						
Maryland	4		1 25		Total and average	223		2 71	
Massachusetts	24		98		**PICKERS.**				
Missouri	3		1 25						
New Hampshire	35		1 20		Delaware	6		1 58	
New Jersey	12		1 00		Indiana	3		1 17	
New York	12		1 03		Kentucky	10		1 13	
Pennsylvania	61		1 37		Maine	3	1	1 21	$0 50
Vermont	1		1 10		Maryland	12	9	1 30	68
Total and average	249		1 21		Massachusetts	16		1 14	
LOOM FIXERS.					North Carolina	2		75	
California	1		1 75		New Jersey	18		1 00	
Connecticut	2		1 35		New York	8		1 14	
Delaware	5		2 15		Pennsylvania	50		1 00	
Great Britain	6		1 33		Vermont	13		1 02	
Indiana	6		1 74						
Kentucky	5		1 75		Total and average	141	10	1 09	66
Maine	3		1 70		**PRESSERS.**				
Maryland	2		1 75						
Massachusetts	10		1 99		Delaware	1		1 33	
North Carolina	4		82		Maine	1		1 35	
New Hampshire	6		1 90		Massachusetts	5		1 02	
New Jersey	12		1 88		New York	6		1 30	
New York	6		2 16		Vermont	5		1 12	
Pennsylvania	19		2 07						
Vermont	8		1 86		Total and average	18		1 17	
Total and average	95		1 96		**SCOURERS.**				
MACHINISTS.					California	1		1 00	
Connecticut	2		1 87		Delaware	2		1 33	
Delaware	1		3 00		Great Britain	7		80	
Illinois	1		2 12		Maine	3		1 20	
Indiana	5		2 50		Maryland	4		1 25	

VARIATION IN THE RATES OF WAGES. 167

SUMMARY OF SELECTED OCCUPATIONS, ADULTS—Concluded.

WOOLLEN GOODS—Concluded.

NOTE.—This note is *not* a complete exhibit for industries or states, but covers only the principal occupations in establishments investigated. See detail table, Appendix A, page 205, whence derived.

Occupations and states.	Number of adult employés.		Average rates of daily wages.		Occupations and states.	Number of adult employés.		Average rates of daily wages.	
	Male.	Fem.	Male.	Fem.		Male.	Fem.	Male.	Fem.
SCOURERS—concluded.					**SPOOLERS—concluded.**				
Massachusetts	16		$1 30		Pennsylvania	28	27	$1 25	$0 73
New York	22		1 15		Total and average	34	62	1 22	0 81
Pennsylvania	1		2 33		**TEAMSTERS.**				
Vermont	8		1 06		Connecticut	1		1 25	
Total and average	64		1 17		Delaware	3		1 50	
SECOND HANDS.					Maine	1		1 25	
Connecticut	6		1 25		Maryland	3		1 38	
Illinois	1		1 68		Massachusetts	4		1 59	
Indiana	6		1 55		New Hampshire	2		1 50	
Maine	13		1 48		New York	3		1 36	
Massachusetts	47		1 54		Pennsylvania	1		2 00	
New Hampshire	9		1 70		Vermont	4		1 22	
New York	8		2 31		Total and average	22		1 43	
Vermont	17		1 52		**TWISTERS.**				
Total and average	107		1 58		Delaware		3		0.75
SHEARERS.					Maine	1		0 80	
California	1		1 16		Massachusetts	4		1 38	
Delaware	1	2	1 33	$1 00	Missouri		4		1 00
Maine	2		1 25		Pennsylvania	25	2	1 00	60
Maryland	1		1 50		Total and average	30	9	1 04	0 82
Massachusetts	6		93		**WEAVERS.**				
New Hampshire	6		1 41		California	46		1 42	
New York	11		1 15		Connecticut		61		1 05
Pennsylvania	10		1 50		Delaware	57	35	1 71	1 36
Total and average	38	2	1 27	1 00	Great Britain	3	178	83	50
SPINNERS, MULE.					Illinois	28		1 52	
Connecticut	29		1 29		Indiana	14	167	1 08	1 01
Delaware	5		2 31		Iowa	2	15	1 25	1 20
Great Britain	12		88		Kentucky		260		79
Indiana	4		1 25		Maine	85	15	1 30	1 23
Iowa	1		1 25		Maryland	4	69	1 05	99
Maine	21		1 68		Massachusetts	161	340	1 28	1 16
Maryland	4		1 35		Missouri	17	7	1 50	1 50
Massachusetts	88		1 31		New Hampshire	50	45	1 50	1 50
Missouri	18		1 25		New Jersey	50	30	1 00	1 00
New Hampshire	18		1 75		New York	126	105	1 08	1 11
New York	27		1 45		North Carolina		17		75
North Carolina	3		1 25		Pennsylvania	736	150	1 85	1 33
Pennsylvania	35		1 74		Vermont	43	100	1 17	1 17
Vermont	44		1 30		Total and average	1422	1594	1 58	1 02
Total and average	309		1 42		**WOOL SORTERS.**				
SPINNERS, OTHER.					California	2		1 25	
California	6		1 00		Delaware	6		1 45	
Illinois	4	5	1 02	1 02	Great Britain	1		1 20	
Indiana	1	20	1 00	75	Illinois	3		1 92	
Iowa		3		75	Indiana	15		1 33	
Maine	4		1 00		Iowa	1		2 00	
Massachusetts		8		98	Kentucky	6		1 50	
New Jersey	18	6	1 00	1 00	Maine	9		1 58	
New York		14		1 00	Maryland	1		2 20	
Total and average	33	56	1 00	0 89	Massachusetts	24		1 81	
SPOOLERS.					Missouri	9		1 50	
Connecticut		9		73	New Hampshire	20		1 78	
Delaware		3		1 00	New Jersey	1	12	80	67
Indiana	1		1 50		New York	44		1 65	
Maine	5		1 00		North Carolina	2		1 00	
Maryland		9		1 00	Pennsylvania	27	13	1 51	75
New Hampshire		14		85	Vermont	16		1 77	
					Total and average	187	25	1 62	.71

SUMMARY OF SELECTED OCCUPATIONS, CHILDREN AND YOUTH.

AGRICULTURAL IMPLEMENTS.

NOTE.—This table is *not* a complete exhibit for industries or states, but covers only the principal occupations in establishments investigated. See detail table, Appendix A, page 295, whence derived.

Occupations and states.	No. of children and youth.	Average rates of daily wages.	Occupations and states.	No. of children and youth.	Average rates of daily wages.
GRINDERS.			Indiana	1	$0 50
Indiana	4	$0 53	Total and average	33	68
Total and average	4	53	**PAINTERS.**		
LABORERS.			Indiana	3	65
Illinois	32	68	Total and average	3	65

BOOTS AND SHOES.

Occupations and states.	No. of children and youth.	Average rates of daily wages.	Occupations and states.	No. of children and youth.	Average rates of daily wages.
FITTERS.			**SEWING-MACHINE OPERATORS.**		
Pennsylvania	32	50	Massachusetts	25	90
Total and average	32	50	Total and average	25	90
HEELERS.			**TACKERS.**		
Massachusetts	8	1 25	Massachusetts	1	1 10
Total and average	8	1 25	Total and average	1	1 10
PACKERS.			**VAMPERS.**		
Maryland	1	67	Massachusetts	1	75
New York	54	72			
Total and average	55	72	Total and average	1	75

CARPETINGS.

Occupations and states.	No. of children and youth.	Average rates of daily wages.	Occupations and states.	No. of children and youth.	Average rates of daily wages.
CARDERS.			**SPINNERS, OTHER.**		
Massachusetts	57	64	Massachusetts	9	60
Pennsylvania	80	75	New York	22	56
Total and average	137	70	Total and average	31	58
COMBERS.			**SPOOLERS.**		
Massachusetts	50	59	Massachusetts	10	66
Total and average	50	59	New York	54	78
DESIGNERS.			Total and average	64	76
New York	2	92	**TWISTERS.**		
Total and average	2	92	Massachusetts	21	70
LABORERS.			Total and average	21	70
Massachusetts	23	73	**WINDERS.**		
Total and average	23	73	Connecticut	20	65
SELLERS.			Great Britain	17	35
Great Britain	14	33	Massachusetts	30	80
			New York	50	65
Total and average	14	33	Total and average	117	65

SUMMARY OF SELECTED OCCUPATIONS, CHILDREN AND YOUTH—Cont'd.

CLOTHING.

NOTE.—This table is *not* a complete exhibit for industries or states, but covers only the principal occupations in establishments investigated. See detail table, Appendix A, page 295, whence derived.

Occupations and states.	No. of children and youth.	Average rates of daily wages.	Occupations and states.	No. of children and youth.	Average rates of daily wages.
BUTTON SEWERS.			**LOOPERS.**		
New York	53	$0 56	New York	20	$0 35
Total and average	53	56	Total and average	20	35
CARD BOYS.			**SEWING-MACHINE OPERATORS.**		
New York	60	60	Pennsylvania	41	41
Virginia	9	60	Total and average	41	41
Total and average	69	60			
FINISHERS.			**SPINNERS, OTHER.**		
New York	6	53	New York	56	87
Pennsylvania	50	53	Total and average	56	87
Virginia	26	50			
Total and average	82	52	**SPOOLERS.**		
			New York	7	67
KNITTERS.			Total and average	7	67
New York	9	56	**TRIMMERS.**		
Pennsylvania	36	50	New York	12	60
Virginia	17	52	Total and average	12	60
Total and average	62	51			
LAPPERS.			**WINDERS.**		
New York	4	65	New York	46	65
Total and average	4	65	Total and average	46	65

COOKING AND HEATING APPARATUS.

Occupations and states.	No. of children and youth.	Average rates of daily wages.	Occupations and states.	No. of children and youth.	Average rates of daily wages.
LABORERS.			**NICKEL PLATERS.**		
Illinois	12	75	Michigan	6	75
Michigan	3	60	Ohio	28	80
Total and average	15	72	Total and average	34	79
MOULDERS.			**PATTERN MAKERS.**		
Michigan	5	55	Michigan	4	74
Total and average	5	55	Total and average	4	74
MOUNTERS.			**POLISHERS.**		
Illinois	4	75	Michigan	3	75
Michigan	6	75	Total and average	3	75
Total and average	10	75			

SUMMARY OF SELECTED OCCUPATIONS, CHILDREN AND YOUTH—Cont'd.

COTTON GOODS.

NOTE.—This table is *not* a complete exhibit for industries or states, but covers only the principal occupations in establishments investigated. See detail table, Appendix A, page 295, whence derived.

Occupations and states.	No. of children and youth.	Average rates of daily wages.	Occupations and states.	No. of children and youth.	Average rates of daily wages.
BACK BOYS.			**DRAWERS-IN.**		
Connecticut	12	$0 35	Georgia	10	$0 55
Georgia	9	32	New York	5	58
Maine	79	38			
Massachusetts	137	43	Total and average	15	56
New Hampshire	29	39			
New York	149	34	**FILLING HANDS.**		
Total and average	415	38	Georgia	3	65
BEAMERS.			Maine	13	72
			Maryland	23	46
Georgia	1	75	Massachusetts	3	75
			New York	2	75
Total and average	1	75	North Carolina	5	38
BOBBIN BOYS.			Total and average	49	56
Georgia	5	44			
Great Britain	4	32	**FOLDERS.**		
Maine	17	70	Maryland	1	1 00
Maryland	6	40	Massachusetts	2	62
Massachusetts	1	72	New York	22	69
New York	99	38	Vermont	1	75
Total and average	132	43	Total and average	26	70
CARD STRIPPERS.			**INSPECTORS.**		
Georgia	4	50			
Maine	27	80	Virginia	2	75
Total and average	31	76	Total and average	2	75
CLOTH-ROOM HANDS.			**LABORERS.**		
Great Britain	7	60	Georgia	32	47
			New Hampshire	1	67
Total and average	7	60			
DOFFERS.			Total and average	33	48
Connecticut	11	57	**LAPPERS.**		
Georgia	19	35			
Germany	47	27	Maine	2	75
Great Britain	9	43	New York	20	50
Maine	137	46			
Maryland	55	38	Total and average	22	52
Massachusetts	230	58	**OILERS.**		
New Hampshire	43	62			
New York	86	40	Georgia	3	49
North Carolina	60	36	Maine	13	52
Pennsylvania	19	50	Maryland	10	50
Vermont	15	42	Massachusetts	18	50
Virginia	52	39	New York	1	62
			North Carolina	9	47
Total and average	763	47	Pennsylvania	3	90
DRAWERS.			Virginia	4	55
Delaware	1	06	Total and average	61	53
Georgia	13	48			
Italy	13	16	**PACKERS.**		
Maine	22	56			
Massachusetts	47	57	Maryland	2	60
New York	163	39	Massachusetts	3	73
North Carolina	3	57	North Carolina	1	40
Pennsylvania	2	67	Virginia	3	62
Total and average	264	44	Total and average	9	63

VARIATION IN THE RATES OF WAGES.

SUMMARY OF SELECTED OCCUPATIONS, CHILDREN AND YOUTH—Cont'd.

COTTON GOODS—Continued.

NOTE.—This table is *not* a complete exhibit for industries or states, but covers only the principal occupations in establishments investigated. See detail table, Appendix A, page 205, whence derived.

Occupations and states.	No. of children and youth.	Average rates of daily wages.	Occupations and states.	No. of children and youth.	Average rates of daily wages.
PICKERS.			**SPARE HANDS.**		
Georgia	8	$0 62	Germany	2	$0 25
Maine	15	85	Maine	29	71
New York	12	51	Maryland	9	54
North Carolina	2	30	Massachusetts	14	60
Virginia	2	47	New York	3	54
			Pennsylvania	5	75
Total and average	39	65	Virginia	7	54
QUILLERS.			Total and average	69	63
Maine	23	67	**SPEEDERS.**		
North Carolina	32	44			
Virginia	10	50	Great Britain	23	38
			Maryland	2	60
Total and average	65	53	New York	214	50
RAILWAY HANDS.			Virginia	13	52
Great Britain	2	39	Total and average	252	49
Maine	6	62	**SPINNERS, OTHER.**		
Maryland	6	66			
Massachusetts	12	56	Connecticut	28	43
New Hampshire	1	62	Delaware	66	60
North Carolina	4	56	Georgia	71	41
Virginia	3	67	Germany	24	25
			Great Britain	27	40
Total and average	34	59	Italy	44	16
REELERS.			Maine	178	51
Maine	1	72	Maryland	32	45
			Massachusetts	220	50
Total and average	1	72	New Hampshire	429	74
ROVERS.			New Jersey	30	60
Georgia	4	69	New York	1,108	36
Germany	54	31	North Carolina	162	46
Maine	33	49	Vermont	25	65
Maryland	1	75	Virginia	92	48
Massachusetts	50	54			
New York	183	50	Total and average	2,546	47
			SPOOLERS.		
Total and average	325	48			
SCRUBBERS.			Georgia	31	34
Maine	30	45	Italy	140	16
			Massachusetts	34	42
Total and average	30	45	New York	147	57
SECOND HANDS.			Virginia	13	44
New York	2	67	Total and average	365	38
			SWEEPERS.		
Total and average	2	67			
SLASHERS.			Connecticut	4	33
New York	1	87	Georgia	16	28
			Italy	4	16
Total and average	1	87	Maine	51	35
SLUBBERS.			Maryland	17	30
Maine	2	45	Massachusetts	11	46
New York	36	55	New Hampshire	9	46
Virginia	4	44	New York	10	50
			North Carolina	15	30
Total and average	42	53	Pennsylvania	2	50
			Vermont	6	42
			Virginia	8	35
			Total and average	153	35
			TWISTERS.		
			Delaware	2	43
			Maine	5	85
			Maryland	11	50

SUMMARY OF SELECTED OCCUPATIONS, CHILDREN AND YOUTH—Cont'd.

COTTON GOODS—Concluded.

NOTE.—This table is *not* a complete exhibit for industries or states, but covers only the principal occupations in establishments investigated. See detail table, Appendix A, page 295, whence derived.

Occupations and states.	No. of children and youth.	Average rates of daily wages.	Occupations and states.	No. of children and youth.	Average rates of daily wages.
TWISTERS—concluded.			WARPERS—concluded.		
New Hampshire	53	$0 66	Virginia	8	$0 50
New York	6	50			
North Carolina	14	52	Total and average	108	49
Total and average	91	62			
WARPERS.			WEAVERS.		
			New York	170	41
New York	88	48			
North Carolina	12	58	Total and average	170	41

FURNITURE.

CABINET MAKERS.			LABORERS.		
Michigan	6	50	Michigan	1	65
Total and average	6	50	Total and average	1	65
CARVERS.			MACHINE MEN.		
Michigan	6	67	Indiana	58	58
			Michigan	18	58
Total and average	6	67	Total and average	76	58

GLASS.

GATHERERS.			PACKERS.		
California	14	1 25	Kentucky	2	75
New Jersey	26	1 00			
Ohio	8	1 25	Total and average	2	75
Pennsylvania	29	98			
Total and average	77	1 06			

LEATHER.

FINISHERS.			SHAVERS.		
Delaware	46	65	Delaware	1	67
Total and average	46	65	Total and average	1	67

MACHINES AND MACHINERY.

MACHINISTS.		
Indiana	1	$1 00
Total and average	1	1 00

VARIATION IN THE RATES OF WAGES.

SUMMARY OF SELECTED OCCUPATIONS, CHILDREN AND YOUTH—Cont'd.

METALS AND METALLIC GOODS.

NOTE.—This table is *not* a complete exhibit for industries or states, but covers only the principal occupations in establishments investigated. See detail table, Appendix A, page 295, whence derived.

Occupations and states.	No. of children and youth.	Average rates of daily wages.	Occupations and states.	No. of children and youth.	Average rates of daily wages.
CART DRIVERS.			**LABORERS.**		
Virginia	2	$0 50	Pennsylvania	3	$0 75
Total and average	2	50	Total and average	3	75
KEEPERS' HELPERS.					
Ohio	2	1 15			
Total and average	2	1 15			

MUSICAL INSTRUMENTS AND MATERIALS.

Occupations and states.	No. of children and youth.	Average rates of daily wages.
FINISHERS AND FLY FINISHERS.		
New York	10	1 25
Total and average	10	1 25

PAPER.

Occupations and states.	No. of children and youth.	Average rates of daily wages.
FINISHERS.		
Massachusetts	1	48
Total and average	1	48

PRINT WORKS.

Occupations and states.	No. of children and youth.	Average rates of daily wages.	Occupations and states.	No. of children and youth.	Average rates of daily wages.
AGEING AND STEAMING HANDS.			**BLEACHERS**—concluded.		
New Hampshire	8	75	New Hampshire	25	82
Total and average	8	75	Total and average	56	73
			COLORERS AND DYERS.		
BLEACHERS.			Massachusetts	36	71
Massachusetts	31	65	Total and average	36	71

TOBACCO.

Occupations and states.	No. of children and youth.	Average rates of daily wages.	Occupations and states.	No. of children and youth.	Average rates of daily wages.
BUNCH BREAKERS.			**STEMMERS.**		
Ohio	50	33	North Carolina	61	32
			Virginia	333	34
Total and average	50	33	Total and average	394	34
DRESSERS.			**STRIPPERS.**		
Illinois	3	75	Illinois	168	47
			Kentucky	46	80
Total and average	3	75	Michigan	55	80
			Missouri	30	1 09
LABORERS.			New Jersey	10	66
North Carolina	4	40	North Carolina	53	45
Virginia	35	43	Ohio	126	48
			Virginia	85	45
Total and average	39	43	West Virginia	10	50
PACKERS.			Total and average	583	56
North Carolina	19	35	**WRAPPERS.**		
			Virginia	125	50
Total and average	19	35	Total and average	125	50

SUMMARY OF SELECTED OCCUPATIONS, CHILDREN AND YOUTH—Concluded.

WOOLLEN GOODS.

NOTE.—This table is not a complete exhibit of industries for states, but covers only the principal occupations in establishments investigated. See detail table, Appendix A, page 295, whence derived.

Occupations and states.	No. of children and youth.	Average rates of daily wages.	Occupations and states.	No. of children and youth.	Average rates of daily wages.
BURLERS.			**LABORERS.**		
Delaware	25	$0 61	Delaware	1	$0 50
Great Britain	30	44	Indiana	1	85
New York	19	62	Massachusetts	7	69
North Carolina	1	50	Vermont	1	50
Vermont	173	59	Total and average	10	67
Total and average	248	58	**PICKERS.**		
CARDERS.			Illinois	2	48
Connecticut	9	57	Maryland	4	80
Delaware	9	91	Vermont	1	55
Illinois	9	58	Total and average	7	67
Indiana	37	66	**PRESSERS.**		
Iowa	4	75	Vermont	15	79
Kentucky	25	66	Total and average	15	79
Maine	14	71	**SPINNERS, MULE.**		
Massachusetts	65	70	New York	11	75
New Jersey	6	45	Total and average	11	75
New York	25	70	**SPINNERS, OTHER.**		
North Carolina	4	44	Indiana	86	59
Vermont	3	61	Kentucky	48	62
Total and average	220	70	New Jersey	12	43
DRAWERS-IN.			New York	41	50
Delaware	2	50	Total and average	187	57
Indiana	3	74	**SPOOLERS.**		
Total and average	5	64	California	3	75
DRESSERS.			Delaware	6	50
Illinois	5	44	Indiana	7	50
Pennsylvania	10	67	Massachusetts	44	58
Total and average	15	59	New York	45	52
DRIERS.			Vermont	12	47
Connecticut	5	56	Total and average	117	55
Total and average	5	56	**TWISTERS.**		
DYERS.			Iowa	5	60
North Carolina	4	75	New York	67	62
Total and average	4	75	Total and average	72	62
FINISHERS.			**WEAVERS.**		
Great Britain	32	30	Massachusetts	5	50
Indiana	24	68	New Jersey	22	50
Kentucky	30	54	New York	2	81
Maryland	5	60	Total and average	29	52
North Carolina	7	64	**WOOL SORTERS.**		
Total and average	98	53	Indiana	5	77
FULLERS.			Kentucky	7	44
Indiana	6	65	Maryland	2	80
Total and average	6	65	Total and average	14	61
GIGGERS.					
New York	1	75			
Total and average	1	75			

SUMMARY OF EMPLOYÉS, WITH PER CENT.

AGRICULTURAL IMPLEMENTS.

NOTE.—This table is *not* a complete exhibit for industries or states, but covers only establishments investigated by the Bureau. See detail table, Appendix A, page 295, whence derived.

States and occupations.	Number of employés.				Per cent. of number of employés in each occupation of the whole number considered in the industry in the state.
	Adult male.	Adult female.	Children and youth.	Total.	
ILLINOIS.					
Blacksmiths	219			219	9.27
Blacksmiths' helpers	3			3	.13
Foremen	22			22	.93
Grinders	80			80	3.39
Laborers	744		32	776	32.85
Machinists	426			426	18.04
Moulders	152			152	6.43
Painters	138			138	5.84
Wood workers	80			80	3.39
All others	466			466	19.73
Total	2,330		32	2,362	100.00
INDIANA.					
Blacksmiths	12			12	1.90
Blacksmiths' helpers	13			13	2.05
Foremen	16			16	2.53
Grinders	96		4	100	15.80
Laborers	42		1	43	6.79
Machinists	4			4	.63
Moulders	181			181	28.59
Painters	10		3	13	2.05
Wood workers	14			14	2.22
All others	195		42	237	37.44
Total	583		50	633	100.00
KENTUCKY.					
Blacksmiths	4			4	8.70
Blacksmiths' helpers	6			6	13.04
Foremen	3			3	6.52
Grinders	15			15	32.61
Laborers	6			6	13.04
Moulders	8			8	17.39
Wood workers	4			4	8.70
Total	46			46	100.00
MAINE.					
Foremen	3			3	6.52
Grinders	12			12	26.09
Laborers	7			7	15.22
Painters	3			3	6.52
All others	21			21	45.65
Total	46			46	100.00
NEW YORK.					
Foremen	2			2	3.13
Grinders	7			7	10.93
Laborers	2			2	3.13
Machinist	1			1	1.56
All others	52			52	81.25
Total	64			64	100.00
OHIO.					
Blacksmiths	176			176	6.53
Blacksmiths' helpers	85			85	3.12

SUMMARY OF EMPLOYÉS, WITH PER CENT.—Continued.

AGRICULTURAL IMPLEMENTS—Concluded.

NOTE.—This table is *not* a complete exhibit for industries or states, but covers only establishments investigated by the Bureau. See detail table, Appendix A, page 295, whence derived.

States and occupations.	Number of employés.				Per cent. of number of employés in each occupation of the whole number considered in the industry in the state.
	Adult male.	Adult female.	Children and youth.	Total.	
OHIO—concluded.					
Foremen	29			29	1.08
Grinders, (grinders, grinders and polishers)	59			59	2.19
Laborers	345			345	12.80
Machinists	506			506	18.78
Moulders	102			102	3.79
Painters	270			270	10.02
Wood workers	377			377	13.09
All others	744		2	746	27.68
Total	2,693		2	2,695	100.00
PENNSYLVANIA.					
Blacksmiths	8			8	9.88
Blacksmiths' helpers	8			8	9.88
Foreman	1			1	1.23
Laborers	39			39	48.15
Moulders	22			22	27.16
Painter	1			1	1.23
All others	2			2	2.47
Total	81			81	100.00

BOOTS AND SHOES.

States and occupations.	Adult male.	Adult female.	Children and youth.	Total.	Per cent.
CALIFORNIA.					
Buffers	6			6	1.80
Burnishers	13			13	3.89
Button-hole makers	8			8	2.40
Button sewer		1		1	.30
Channellers	4			4	1.20
Cutters	37			37	11.08
Edge setters	8			8	2.40
Edge trimmers	9			9	2.69
Fitters	6			6	1.80
Foremen	6			6	1.80
Heelers	15			15	4.49
Lasters	77			77	23.05
Packers	7			7	2.10
Sewing-machine operators	24	32		56	16.77
Vampers	6			6	1.80
All others	68	7		75	22.45
Total	294	40		334	100.00
ILLINOIS.					
Burnishers	6			6	3.30
Cutters	8			8	4.39
Fitters		60		60	32.97
Heelers	10			10	5.49
Lasters	8			8	4.40
All others	90			90	49.45
Total	122	60		182	100.00
KENTUCKY.					
Bottomers	20			20	31.75
Cutters	4			4	6.35
Fitters	3	30		33	52.38
Lasters	6			6	9.52
All others					
Total	33	30		63	100.00

VARIATION IN THE RATES OF WAGES.

SUMMARY OF EMPLOYÉS, WITH PER CENT.—Continued.

BOOTS AND SHOES—Continued.

NOTE.—This table is *not* a complete exhibit for industries or states, but covers only establishments investigated by the Bureau. See detail table, Appendix A, page 295, whence derived.

States and occupations.	Number of employés.				Per cent. of number of employés in each occupation of the whole number considered in the industry in the state.
	Adult male.	Adult female.	Children and youth.	Total.	
MARYLAND.					
Bottomers	34			34	9.42
Burnishers	7			7	1.94
Cutters	19			19	5.26
Edge setters	3			3	.83
Edge trimmers	2			2	.56
Fitters	7	128		135	37.40
Foremen	8			8	2.22
Heelers	2			2	.55
Lasters	20			20	5.54
Levelers	2			2	.55
Packer	1		1	2	.55
Sandpaperers	2			2	.55
Tacker	1			1	.28
Turners	2			2	.55
All others	72	2	48	122	33.80
Total	182	130	49	361	100.00
MASSACHUSETTS.					
Bottomers	164			164	7.40
Buffers	3			3	.13
Burnishers	26			26	1.17
Cutters	376	24		400	18.05
Edge setters	36			36	1.62
Edge trimmers	30			30	1.35
Fitters	36	80		116	5.28
Foreman	13			13	.58
Heelers	45		8	53	2.38
Laborers	17			17	.77
Lasters	291			291	13.14
Levellers	9			9	.41
Moulder	1			1	.05
Packers	30			30	1.35
Sandpaperers	7			7	.32
Sewers, McKay machine	2			2	.09
Sewing-machine operators	78	352	25	455	20.54
Skivers	4	7		11	.50
Tackers	6	9	1	16	.72
Turners	4			4	.18
Vampers	11	2	1	14	.63
All others	385	86	46	517	23.34
Total	1,574	560	81	2,215	100.00
NEW JERSEY.					
Cutters	25			25	9.62
Fitters	25	60		85	32.69
All others	125		25	150	57.69
Total	175	60	25	260	100.00
NEW YORK.					
Beaders	55			55	1.01
Blockers	17			17	.59
Bottomers	213			213	7.38
Brushers	13			13	.45
Buffers	27			27	.94
Burnishers	14			14	.49
Button-hole makers		70		70	2.42
Button sewers	4			4	.14
Channellers	26			26	.90
Closers	22	19		41	1.43
Cutters	338			338	11.72

SUMMARY OF EMPLOYÉS, WITH PER CENT.—Continued.

BOOTS AND SHOES—Concluded.

NOTE.—This table is *not* a complete exhibit for industries or States, but covers only establishments investigated by the Bureau. See detail table, Appendix A, page 295, whence derived.

States and occupations.	Number of employés.				Per cent. of number of employés in each occupation of the whole number considered in the industry in the state.
	Adult male.	Adult female.	Children and youth.	Total.	
NEW YORK—concluded.					
Edge setters	19			19	.66
Edge trimmers	49			49	1.70
Fitters	9			9	.31
Foremen	70			70	2.42
Heelers	30			30	1.04
Laborers	84			84	2.91
Lasters	219			219	7.60
Levellers	19			19	.66
Measurers	17			17	.59
Moulders	16			16	.56
Packers	1		54	55	1.91
Sand-paperers	13			13	.45
Seam rubbers		15		15	.52
Seat wheelers	14			14	.49
Sewers, McKay machine	11			11	.38
Sewing-machine operators	9	988		997	34.58
Skivers	29			29	1.00
Tackers	33			33	1.14
Turners	25			25	.87
Vampers	62			62	2.15
All others	80	58	141	279	9.68
Total	1,538	1,150	195	2,883	100.00
OHIO.					
Bottomers	225			225	29.11
Cutters	40			40	5.17
Fitters	25	325		350	45.28
Foremen	3			3	.39
Packers	3			3	.39
All others	85		67	152	19.66
Total	381	325	67	773	100.00
PENNSYLVANIA.					
Buffers	6			6	.66
Burnishers	12			12	1.31
Button-hole makers	3	9		12	1.31
Button sewers		39		39	4.27
Closers	25			25	2.74
Cutters	28			28	3.07
Edge setters	14			14	1.53
Edge trimmers	8			8	.88
Fitters	59		32	91	9.97
Heelers	13			13	1.42
Laborers	38			38	4.16
Lasters	110			110	12.05
Packers	6			6	.66
Seam rubbers	6			6	.64
Sewing-machine operators	29	71		100	10.95
Tackers	4			4	.44
Turners	57			57	6.25
Vampers	14			14	1.58
All others	169	93	68	330	36.14
Total	601	212	100	913	100.00

VARIATION IN THE RATES OF WAGES. 179

SUMMARY OF EMPLOYÉS, WITH PER CENT.—Continued.

BROOMS.

NOTE.—This table is *not* a complete exhibit for industries or states, but covers only establishments investigated by the Bureau. See detail table, Appendix A, page 295, whence derived.

States and occupations.	Number of employés.				Per cent. of number of employés in each occupation of the whole number considered in the industry in the state.
	Adult male.	Adult female.	Children and youth.	Total.	
NEW YORK.					
Laborers	135			135	37.60
Winders	98			98	27.30
All others	126			126	35.10
Total	359			359	100.00
CARPETINGS.					
CONNECTICUT.					
Dyers	10			10	11.36
Finishers		10		10	11.36
Weavers		48		48	54.55
Winders			20	20	22.73
Total	10	58	20	88	100.00
GREAT BRITAIN.					
Designers	10			10	2.51
Dyers	9			9	2.26
Foremen and overseers	6			6	1.51
Laborers	8			8	2.01
Printers	25	7		32	8.04
Setters		31	14	35	8.79
Weavers	116			116	29.15
Winders		29	17	46	11.56
All others	51	4	81	136	34.17
Total	225	61	112	398	100.00
MASSACHUSETTS.					
Carders	13	30	57	100	6.38
Combers		50		50	3.19
Dressers	6			6	.38
Dyers	125			125	7.98
Engineers	15			15	.96
Finishers	19	95		114	7.28
Laborers	63		23	86	5.49
Loom fixers	4			4	.26
Machinists	4			4	.26
Printers	8			8	.51
Scourers	28			28	1.78
Setters		14		14	.89
Spinners, mule	37			37	2.36
Spinners, other		102	9	111	7.08
Spoolers		12	10	22	1.40
Twisters			21	21	1.34
Warpers	15			15	.96
Weavers	64	359		423	26.99
Winders	40	84	30	154	9.83
Wool sorters	29	2		31	1.98
All others	87	70	42	199	12.70
Total	556	769	242	1,567	100.00
NEW YORK.					
Carders	34			34	.40
Combers	20	83		103	1.18
Designers	37		2	39	.45

180 REPORT OF THE COMMISSIONER OF LABOR.

SUMMARY OF EMPLOYES, WITH PER CENT.—Continued.

CARPETINGS—Concluded.

NOTE.—This table is not a complete exhibit for industries or states, but covers only establishments investigated by the Bureau. See detail table, Appendix A, page 295, whence derived.

States and occupations.	Number of employés.				Per cent. of number of employés in each occupation of the whole number considered in the industry in the State.
	Adult male.	Adult female.	Children and youth.	Total.	
NEW YORK—concluded.					
Drawers	5	194	....	199	2.27
Dressers	101	....	....	101	1.15
Dyers	63	....	....	63	.72
Engineers	12	....	....	12	.14
Finishers	67	....	....	67	.77
Foremen and overseers	170	....	....	170	1.94
Harness fixers	23	....	....	23	.26
Inspectors	26	29	....	55	.63
Laborers	136	....	....	136	1.55
Loom fixers	63	....	....	63	.72
Machinists	83	....	....	83	.94
Printers	254	....	....	254	2.90
Scourers	172	....	....	172	1.96
Setters	91	356	....	447	5.11
Spinners, mule	124	....	....	124	1.42
Spinners, other	299	302	22	623	7.12
Spoolers	62	244	54	360	4.11
Twisters	8	229	....	237	2.71
Warpers	28	....	....	28	.32
Weavers	426	914	....	1,340	15.30
Winders	36	313	50	399	4.56
Wool sorters	123	....	....	123	1.40
All others	1,647	650	1,204	3,501	39.97
Total	4,110	3,314	1,332	8,756	100.00
PENNSYLVANIA.					
Carders	....	....	80	80	4.26
Combers	....	5	....	5	.27
Drawers	....	30	....	30	1.60
Dyers	18	....	....	18	.96
Engineer	1	....	....	1	.05
Laborers	400	....	....	400	21.27
Loom fixers	21	....	....	21	1.12
Machinists	16	....	....	16	.85
Printers	30	....	....	30	1.60
Setters	120	....	....	120	6.38
Spinners, other	....	60	....	60	3.19
Spoolers	4	80	....	84	4.47
Twisters	....	30	....	30	1.60
Warpers	2	....	....	2	.11
Weavers	615	....	....	615	32.70
Winders	....	28	....	28	1.49
All others	310	30	....	340	18.08
Total	1,537	263	80	1,880	100.00

CARRIAGES AND WAGONS.

CONNECTICUT.					
Blacksmiths	55	....	....	55	13.50
Blacksmiths' helpers	58	....	....	58	14.25
Foremen	3	....	....	3	.73
Laborers	12	....	....	12	2.95
Painters	96	....	....	96	23.59
Trimmers	73	....	....	73	17.94
Wood workers (body makers)	80	....	....	80	19.66
All others	30	....	....	30	7.38
Total	407	....	....	407	100.00

VARIATION IN THE RATES OF WAGES.

SUMMARY OF EMPLOYÉS, WITH PER CENT.—Continued.

CARRIAGES AND WAGONS—Concluded.

NOTE.—This table is *not* a complete exhibit for industries or states, but covers only establishments investigated by the Bureau. See detail table, Appendix A, page 205, whence derived.

States and occupations.	Number of employés.				Per cent. of number of employés in each occupation of the whole number considered in the industry in the state.
	Adult male.	Adult female.	Children and youth.	Total.	
ILLINOIS.					
Blacksmiths	52			52	13.98
Blacksmiths' helpers	37			37	9.95
Foremen	11			11	2.96
Laborers	12			12	3.22
Painters	92			92	24.73
Trimmers	52			52	13.98
Wood workers	73			73	19.62
All others	20		23	43	11.56
Total	349		23	372	100.00
NEW JERSEY.					
Blacksmiths	16			16	30.77
Painters	18			18	34.61
Trimmers	6			6	11.54
Wood workers (body makers)	10			10	19.23
All others	2			2	3.85
Total	52			52	100.00
OHIO.					
Blacksmiths	70			70	11.24
Blacksmiths' helpers	14			14	2.25
Foremen	30			30	4.82
Laborers	23			23	3.69
Painters	97			97	15.57
Trimmers	8			8	1.28
Wood workers (wood workers, body makers)	58			58	9.31
All others	278	45		323	51.84
Total	578	45		623	100.00
PENNSYLVANIA.					
Blacksmiths	4			4	18.18
Blacksmiths' helpers	6			6	27.27
Painters	3			3	13.64
Trimmer	1			1	4.55
Wood workers	4			4	18.18
All others			4	4	18.18
Total	18		4	22	100.00

CLOTHING.

NEW JERSEY.					
Engineers	2			2	.46
Finishers	116			116	26.48
Foremen	4			4	.91
Laborers	7			7	1.60
Trimmers		60		60	13.70
All others	198	36	15	249	56.85
Total	327	96	15	438	100.00
NEW YORK.					
Button-hole makers		18		18	1.04
Button sewers		9	53	62	3.57
Card boys			60	60	3.46

SUMMARY OF EMPLOYÉS, WITH PER CENT.—Continued.

CLOTHING—Concluded.

NOTE.—This table is *not* a complete exhibit for industries or states, but covers only establishments investigated by the Bureau. See detail table, Appendix A, page 296, whence derived.

States and occupations.	Number of employés.				Per cent. of number of employés in each occupation of the whole number considered in the industry in the state.
	Adult male.	Adult female.	Children and youth.	Total.	
NEW YORK—concluded.					
Cutters	20	2	....	22	1.27
Engineers	8	....	....	8	.46
Finishers	39	231	6	276	15.90
Foremen (foremen, overseers)	45	4	....	49	2.82
Hemmers	....	38	....	38	2.19
Inspectors	....	16	....	16	.92
Knitters	1	77	9	87	5.01
Laborers	7	....	....	7	.40
Lappers	28	....	4	32	1.84
Loopers	2	109	20	131	7.55
Menders	....	86	....	86	4.95
Sewing-machine operators	....	180	....	180	10.37
Spinners, mule	31	....	....	31	1.79
Spinners, other	....	....	56	56	3.23
Spoolers	2	6	7	15	.86
Trimmers	....	25	12	37	2.13
Wash-room hands	49	....	....	49	2.82
Winders	....	75	46	121	6.97
All others	169	125	61	355	20.45
Total	401	1,001	334	1,736	100.00
PENNSYLVANIA.					
Button-hole makers	....	15	....	15	1.76
Cutters	15	17	....	32	3.76
Engineers	3	....	....	3	.35
Finishers	136	....	50	186	21.83
Knitters	....	....	36	36	4.23
Laborers	24	....	....	24	2.82
Sewing-machine operators	....	....	41	41	4.81
Trimmers	....	120	....	120	14.08
Wash-room hands	9	....	....	9	1.06
Winders	....	6	....	6	.70
All others	343	17	20	380	44.60
Total	530	175	147	852	100.00
VIRGINIA.					
Card boys	....	....	9	9	7.97
Engineer	1	....	....	1	.89
Finishers	4	27	26	57	50.44
Knitters	2	....	17	19	16.81
Laborers	3	....	....	3	2.66
Spinners, mule	7	....	....	7	6.10
All others	14	....	3	17	15.04
Total	31	27	55	113	100.00

COAL, COKE, AND ORE.

GREAT BRITAIN.					
Blacksmiths	5	....	....	5	.45
Blacksmiths' helpers	2	....	....	2	.20
Drivers	11	....	....	11	1.64
Dumpers	4	....	....	4	.60
Engineer (stationary)	1	....	....	1	.15
Firemen	20	....	....	20	2.99
Laborers	23	....	....	23	3.43
Miners	285	....	....	285	42.54

VARIATION IN THE RATES OF WAGES.

SUMMARY OF EMPLOYÉS, WITH PER CENT.—Continued.
COAL, COKE, AND ORE—Continued.

NOTE.—This table is not a complete exhibit for industries or states, but covers only establishments investigated by the Bureau. See detail table, Appendix A, page 295, whence derived.

States and occupations.	Number of employés.				Per cent. of number of employés in each occupation of the whole number considered in the industry in the state.
	Adult male.	Adult female.	Children and youth.	Total.	
GREAT BRITAIN—concluded.					
Stableman	1			1	.15
Track layers	25			25	3.73
Weighers	5			5	.75
All others	136		154	290	43.28
Total	516		154	670	100.00
INDIANA.					
Blacksmiths	16			16	.97
Drivers	85			85	5.19
Engineers	26			26	1.58
Laborers	91			91	5.55
Mine bosses	6			6	.37
Miners	1,375			1,375	83.89
Track layers	25			25	1.58
Weighers	15			15	.92
All others					
Total	1,639			1,639	100.00
MARYLAND.					
Blacksmiths	6			6	.64
Blacksmiths' helpers	5			5	.53
Carpenters	5			5	.53
Drivers	83			83	8.88
Dumpers	20			20	2.14
Engineers	2			2	.22
Fireman	1			1	.11
Laborers	16			16	1.71
Miners	762			762	81.50
Stablemen	7			7	.75
Track layers	10			10	1.07
Weighers	5			5	.53
All others	5		8	13	1.39
Total	927		8	935	100.00
MISSOURI.					
Blacksmith	1			1	.30
Blacksmith's helper	1			1	.30
Carpenters	4			4	1.20
Drivers	7			7	2.09
Engineers	7			7	2.10
Fireman	1			1	.30
Laborers	18			18	5.39
Mine boss	1			1	.30
Miners	239			239	71.55
Track layers	5			5	1.50
Weigher	1			1	.30
All others	14		35	49	14.67
Total	299		35	334	100.00
OHIO.					
Blacksmiths	13			13	.93
Blacksmiths' helpers	2			2	.14
Carpenters	5			5	.36
Drivers	100			100	7.17
Dumpers	17			17	1.22

SUMMARY OF EMPLOYÉS, WITH PER CENT.—Continued.

COAL, COKE, AND ORE—Concluded.

NOTE.—This table is not a complete exhibit for industries or states, but covers only establishments investigated by the Bureau. See detail table, Appendix A, page 295, whence derived.

States and occupations.	Number of employés.				Per cent. of number of employés in each occupation of the whole number considered in the industry in the state.
	Adult male.	Adult female.	Children and youth.	Total.	
OHIO—concluded.					
Engineers (engineers; engineers, locomotive, stationary)	15			15	1.08
Firemen	8			8	.57
Laborers	49			49	3.51
Mine bosses	13			13	.93
Miners	1,055			1,055	75.62
Stablemen	4			4	.29
Track layers	21			21	1.51
Weighers	9			9	.65
All others	51		33	84	6.02
Total	1,362		33	1,395	100.00
PENNSYLVANIA.					
Blacksmiths	19			19	.53
Carpenters	13			13	.37
Drivers	106			106	2.97
Dumpers	12			12	.34
Engineers (engineers; engineers, locomotive, stationary)	14			14	.39
Laborers	428			428	12.00
Mine bosses	20			20	.56
Miners	1,855			1,855	52.03
Weighers	3			3	.09
All others	1,095			1,095	30.72
Total	3,565			3,565	100.00
VIRGINIA.					
Blacksmiths	4			4	.95
Blacksmiths' helpers	3			3	.72
Carpenters	7			7	1.67
Drivers	7			7	1.67
Engineers	5			5	1.20
Firemen	3			3	.72
Laborers	235			235	56.22
Mine bosses	14			14	3.35
Miners	113			113	27.03
Stablemen	2			2	.48
Track layers	6			6	1.44
All others	8		11	19	4.55
Total	407		11	418	100.00
WEST VIRGINIA.					
Blacksmiths	12			12	1.25
Blacksmith's helper	1			1	.10
Carpenters	12			12	1.25
Drivers	96			96	10.01
Dumpers	6			6	.63
Engineers (engineers; engineers, locomotive; stationary)	8			8	.83
Laborers	49			49	5.11
Mine bosses	8			8	.84
Miners	662			662	69.03
Stablemen	4			4	.42
Track layers	26			26	2.71
Weighers	7			7	.73
All others	45		23	68	7.09
Total	936		23	959	100.00

VARIATION IN THE RATES OF WAGES.

SUMMARY OF EMPLOYÉS, WITH PER CENT.—Continued.

COOKING AND HEATING APPARATUS.

NOTE.—This table is *not* a complete exhibit for industries or states, but covers only establishments investigated by the Bureau. See detail table, Appendix A, page 295, whence derived.

States and occupations.	Number of employés.				Per cent. of number of employés in each occupation of the whole number considered in the industry in the state.
	Adult male.	Adult female.	Children and youth.	Total.	
ILLINOIS.					
Blacksmiths	2			2	.33
Carpenters	2			2	.33
Cupola men	16			16	2.67
Engineers	6			6	1.00
Foremen	4			4	.67
Grinders	4			4	.67
Laborers	41		12	53	8.85
Machinists	10			10	1.67
Moulders	267			267	44.57
Mounters	54		4	58	9.69
Nickel plater	1			1	.17
Pattern makers	12			12	2.00
Polisher	1			1	.17
All others	102		61	163	27.21
Total	522		77	599	100.00
KENTUCKY.					
Laborers	13			13	23.21
Moulders	37			37	66.07
Mounters	6			6	10.72
All others					
Total	56			56	100.00
MICHIGAN.					
Blacksmiths	4			4	.21
Engineers	2			2	.10
Foremen	27			27	1.38
Grinders	51			51	2.61
Japanners	2			2	.10
Laborers	19		3	22	1.13
Machinists	5			5	.26
Moulders	430		5	435	22.30
Mounters	151		6	157	8.05
Nickel platers	5		6	11	.56
Pattern makers	49		4	53	2.72
Polishers	98		3	101	5.18
Teamsters	16			16	.82
Tinsmiths	12			12	.61
All others	351		702	1,053	53.97
Total	1,222		729	1,951	100.00
NEW YORK.					
Blacksmiths	14			14	.55
Carpenters	38			38	1.50
Cupola men	13			13	.51
Engineers	5			5	.21
Foremen	29			29	1.14
Grinders	35			35	1.38
Japanners	9			9	.85
Laborers	383			383	15.08
Machinists	5			5	.20
Moulders	945			945	37.20
Mounters	56			56	2.20
Nickel platers	18			18	.71
Pattern makers	12			12	.47
Polishers	43			43	1.69
Teamsters	19			19	.75
Tinsmiths	58			58	2.28
All others	348		510	858	33.78
Total	2,030		510	2,540	100.00

SUMMARY OF EMPLOYÉS, WITH PER CENT.—Continued.

COOKING AND HEATING APPARATUS—Concluded.

NOTE.—This table is not a complete exhibit for industries or states, but covers only establishments investigated by the Bureau. See detail table, Appendix A, page 295, whence derived.

States and occupations.	Number of employés.				Per cent. of number of employés in each occupation of the whole number considered in the industry in the state.
	Adult male.	Adult female.	Children and youth.	Total.	
OHIO.					
Blacksmith	1			1	.12
Carpenters	4			4	.47
Cupola men	3			3	.35
Engineers	4			4	.47
Foremen	9			9	1.05
Laborers	15			15	1.75
Machinists	7			7	.82
Moulders	359			359	41.94
Mounters	142			142	16.59
Nickel platers	30		28	58	6.77
Pattern makers	19			19	2.22
Polishers	13			13	1.52
Teamster	1			1	.11
Tinsmiths	3			3	.35
All others	167		51	218	25.47
Total	777		79	856	100.00
PENNSYLVANIA.					
Blacksmith	1			1	1.28
Engineer	1			1	1.28
Foremen	2			2	2.56
Laborers	10			10	12.82
Moulders	48			48	61.54
Mounters	12			12	15.39
Pattern makers	2			2	2.57
Teamster	1			1	1.28
All others	1			1	1.28
Total	78			78	100.00
WEST VIRGINIA.					
Carpenter	1			1	1.59
Cupola man	1			1	1.59
Engineer	1			1	1.59
Laborers	13			13	20.63
Moulders	23			23	36.51
Mounters	9			9	14.29
Pattern maker	1			1	1.58
All others	2		12	14	22.22
Total	51		12	63	100.00

COTTON GOODS.

CONNECTICUT.					
Back boys			12	12	3.99
Card grinders	2			2	.65
Card strippers	4			4	1.30
Doffers		4	11	15	4.87
Drawers		9		9	2.92
Engineer	1			1	.32
Filling hand	1			1	.32
Folder	1			1	.32
Inspector		1		1	.32
Laborers	2			2	.65
Lappers	3			3	.98
Machinists	2			2	.65
Oiler	1			1	.32
Overseers	5			5	1.62

VARIATION IN THE RATES OF WAGES.

SUMMARY OF EMPLOYÉS, WITH PER CENT.—Continued.

COTTON GOODS—Continued.

NOTE.—This table is *not* a complete exhibit for industries or states, but covers only establishments investigated by the Bureau. See detail table, Appendix A, page 295, whence derived.

States and occupations.	Number of employés.				Per cent. of number of employés in each occupation of the whole number considered in the industry in the state.
	Adult male.	Adult female.	Children and youth.	Total.	
CONNECTICUT—concluded.					
Railway hand		1		1	.32
Second hands	4			4	1.30
Section hands	5			5	1.62
Slasher	1			1	.32
Slubbers	3			3	.98
Speeders		18		18	5.85
Spinners, mule	15			15	4.87
Spinners, other			28	28	9.09
Spoolers		18		18	5.85
Sweepers			4	4	1.30
Trimmers		2		2	.65
Warpers		3		3	.98
Watchmen	2			2	.65
Weavers	43	97		140	45.46
All others	5			5	1.62
Total	100	153	55	308	100.00
DELAWARE.					
Beamers	11			11	3.33
Carders	33			33	10.00
Card stripper	1			1	.30
Drawer			1	1	.30
Dyers	6			6	1.82
Laborers	5			5	1.52
Loom fixers	2			2	.61
Spinner, mule	1			1	.30
Spinners, other			66	66	20.00
Spoolers		3		3	.91
Twisters			2	2	.61
Weavers		153		153	46.36
All others	22	2	22	46	13.94
Total	81	158	91	330	100.00
FRANCE.					
Carders	2			2	.79
Card grinder	1			1	.39
Drawers	6	3		9	3.54
Engineers	2			2	.79
Firemen	2			2	.79
Laborers	2			2	.79
Oilers	2			2	.79
Overseers	5			5	1.97
Spinners, mule	7			7	2.75
Warpers	5			5	1.97
Watchman	1			1	.39
Weavers		100		100	39.37
All others	41	57	18	116	45.67
Total	76	160	18	254	100.00
GEORGIA.					
Back boys			9	9	1.36
Beamer		1		1	.15
Blacksmiths	2			2	.30
Bobbin boys			5	5	.76
Card grinders	6			6	.91
Card strippers	2		4	6	.91
Cloth-room hand	1			1	.15
Doffers			19	19	2.87
Drawers		5	13	18	2.72

SUMMARY OF EMPLOYÉS, WITH PER CENT.—Continued.

COTTON GOODS—Continued.

NOTE.—This table is not a complete exhibit for industries or states, but covers only establishments investigated by the Bureau. See detail table, Appendix A, page 295, whence derived.

States and occupations.	Number of employés.				Per cent. of number of employés in each occupation of the whole number considered in the industry in the state.
	Adult male.	Adult female.	Children and youth.	Total.	
GEORGIA—concluded.					
Drawers-in			10	10	1.51
Engineer	1			1	.15
Filling hands			3	3	.45
Firemen	2			2	.30
Folders	3			3	.45
Laborers	3		32	35	5.29
Machinists	3			3	.45
Oilers	5		3	8	1.21
Overseers	7			7	1.06
Painter	1			1	.15
Pickers			8	8	1.21
Railway hand	1			1	.15
Rovers			4	4	.60
Second hands	6			6	.91
Section hands	17			17	2.56
Slashers	3			3	.45
Spinners, mule	8			8	1.21
Spinners, other			71	71	10.73
Spoolers			31	31	4.68
Sweepers			16	16	2.42
Teamster	1			1	.15
Warpers	3	2		5	.76
Watchmen	6			6	.91
Weavers	71	158		229	34.59
All others	47	38	31	116	17.52
Total	199	203	260	662	100.00
GERMANY.					
Carders	23			23	.95
Card grinders	8			8	.33
Doffers			47	47	1.95
Dyers	182			182	7.53
Firemen	27			27	1.12
Folders	24			24	.99
Laborers	17			17	.70
Oilers	2			2	.08
Packers	8			8	.33
Pickers	13			13	.54
Rovers	4		54	58	2.40
Scrubbers		3		3	.13
Spare hands			2	2	.08
Speeders		17		17	.70
Spinners, mule	26			26	1.08
Spinners, other		15	24	39	1.61
Warpers		18		18	.75
Watchmen	16			16	.66
Weavers		1,067		1,067	44.16
All others	546	24	249	819	33.81
Total	896	1,144	376	2,416	100.00
GREAT BRITAIN.					
Beamers	4			4	.35
Bobbin boys			4	4	.35
Carders	24			24	2.08
Card grinders	9			9	.78
Cloth-room hands	1		7	8	.69
Doffers			9	9	.78
Drawers		36		36	3.12
Drawers-in	13			13	1.13
Engineers	6			6	.52
Firemen	3			3	.26
Laborers	15			15	1.30

VARIATION IN THE RATES OF WAGES. 189

SUMMARY OF EMPLOYÉS, WITH PER CENT.—Continued.

COTTON GOODS—Continued.

NOTE.—This table is *not* a complete exhibit for industries or states, but covers only establishments investigated by the Bureau. See detail table, Appendix A, page 295, whence derived.

States and occupations.	Number of employés.				Per cent. of number of employés in each occupation of the whole number considered in the industry in the state.
	Adult male.	Adult female.	Children and youth.	Total.	
GREAT BRITAIN—concluded.					
Lappers	9	12		21	1.81
Machinist	1			1	.09
Oilers	4			4	.35
Overseers	14			14	1.21
Packers	6			6	.52
Railway hands			2	2	.17
Rovers	25	102		127	11.00
Slubbers		32		32	2.77
Speeders		29	23	52	4.50
Spinners, mule	172			172	14.89
Spinners, other		6	27	33	2.85
Twisters	8			8	.69
Weavers		152		152	13.16
All others	149	62	189	400	34.63
Total	463	431	261	1,155	100.00
ITALY.					
Carders	32			32	3.06
Card grinders	9			9	.86
Drawers		27	13	40	3.82
Engineers	5			5	.48
Firemen	9			9	.86
Laborers	52			52	4.97
Loom fixer	1			1	.10
Oilers	13			13	1.24
Overseers	6	10		16	1.53
Reelers		200		200	19.10
Spinners, mule	32			32	3.06
Spinners, other			44	44	4.20
Spoolers		140		140	13.37
Sweepers		7	4	11	1.05
Twisters	6	79		85	8.11
Watchmen	2			2	.19
All others	187	153	16	356	34.00
Total	354	476	217	1,047	100.00
MAINE.					
Back boys			79	79	2.37
Beamers	22	5		27	.81
Blacksmiths	4			4	.12
Bobbin boys			17	17	.51
Card grinders	28			28	.84
Card strippers	20		27	47	1.40
Cloth-room hands	4	4		8	.23
Doffers			137	137	4.10
Drawers	4	51	22	77	2.30
Drawers-in		6		6	.18
Dyers	37			37	1.10
Filling hands	3		13	16	.48
Firemen	4			4	.12
Folders	3			3	.09
Inspectors		54		54	1.62
Laborers	121			121	3.62
Lappers			2	2	.06
Machinists	22			22	.66
Oilers	32		13	45	1.35
Overseers	19			19	.57
Packer	1			1	.03
Painters	7			7	.21
Pickers	27		15	42	1.26
Quillers			23	23	.69
Railway hands			6	6	.18

SUMMARY OF EMPLOYÉS, WITH PER CENT.—Continued.

COTTON GOODS—Continued.

NOTE.—This table is not a complete exhibit for industries or states, but covers only establishments investigated by the Bureau. See detail table, Appendix A, page 295, whence derived.

States and occupations.	Number of employés.				Per cent. of number of employés in each occupation of the whole number considered in the industry in the state.
	Adult male.	Adult female.	Children and youth.	Total.	
MAINE—concluded.					
Reelers	5		1	6	.18
Rovers		11	33	44	.31
Scrubbers	3	4	30	37	.11
Second hands	39	57		96	2.88
Section hands	100			100	3.00
Slashers	13			13	.39
Slubbers		19	2	21	.63
Spare hands	3	2	29	34	1.02
Speeders		9		9	.27
Spinners, mule	59			59	1.77
Spinners, other		86	178	264	7.91
Spoolers		132		132	3.95
Sweepers			51	51	1.53
Teamsters	8			8	.24
Twisters	3	2	5	10	.30
Warpers	14	16		30	.90
Watchmen	15			15	.45
Weavers	731	568		1,299	38.90
All others	135	60	84	279	8.36
Total	1,486	1,086	767	3,339	100.00
MARYLAND.					
Beamers	14			14	1.25
Blacksmith	1			1	.09
Bobbin boys			6	6	.54
Carders	36	32		68	6.08
Card grinders	10			10	.89
Doffers			55	55	4.92
Drawers		13		13	1.16
Engineers	3			3	.27
Filling hands			23	23	2.06
Fireman	1			1	.09
Folder			1	1	.09
Laborers	25			25	2.24
Loom fixers	14			14	1.25
Machinist	1			1	.09
Oilers			10	10	.89
Overseers	20			20	1.79
Packers	20		2	22	1.97
Pickers	17			17	1.52
Railway hands			6	6	.54
Rover			1	1	.09
Second hands	3			3	.27
Slubbers		18		18	1.61
Spare hands			9	9	.81
Speeders		34	2	36	3.22
Spinners, other than mule		162	32	194	17.35
Spoolers		56		56	5.00
Sweepers			17	17	1.52
Twisters		28	11	39	3.49
Warpers	15			15	1.34
Watchmen	3			3	.27
Weavers	14	279		293	26.21
All others	35	28	61	124	11.09
Total	232	650	236	1,118	100.00
MASSACHUSETTS.					
Back boys			137	137	1.94
Beamers		8		8	.11
Blacksmiths	4			4	.06
Carders	87	86		173	2.46
Card grinders	58			58	.82

VARIATION IN THE RATES OF WAGES.

SUMMARY OF EMPLOYÉS, WITH PER CENT.—Continued.

COTTON GOODS—Continued.

NOTE.—This table is not a complete exhibit for industries or states, but covers only establishments investigated by the Bureau. See detail table, Appendix A, page 295, whence derived.

States and occupations.	Number of employés.				Per cent. of number of employés in each occupation of the whole number considered in the industry in the state.
	Adult male.	Adult female.	Children and youth.	Total.	
MASSACHUSETTS—concluded.					
Card strippers	58	6		64	.91
Cloth-room hands	16	11		27	.38
Doffers			230	230	3.26
Drawers		105	47	152	2.16
Drawers-in		55		55	.78
Dyers	43			43	.61
Engineers	11			11	.16
Filling hands	20		3	23	.33
Firemen	18			18	.26
Folders	4		2	6	.09
Inspectors	2	11		13	.18
Laborers	127			127	1.80
Lappers	2			2	.03
Loom fixers	13			13	.17
Machinists	43			43	.01
Oilers	70		18	88	1.25
Overseers	68			68	.97
Packers			3	3	.04
Painters	19			19	.27
Pickers	18			18	.26
Railway hands			12	12	.17
Reelers		2		2	.03
Rovers		9	50	50	.71
Scrubbers		40		40	.57
Second hands	94			94	1.34
Section hands	136	4		140	1.99
Slashers	32			32	.45
Slubbers		32		32	.45
Spare hands	8	13	14	35	.50
Speeders	2	166		168	2.38
Spinners, mule	274			274	3.89
Spinners, other		389	220	609	8.64
Spoolers	3	329	34	366	5.19
Sweepers		13	11	24	.34
Teamsters	10			10	.14
Twisters	2	50		52	.74
Warpers	15	44		59	.84
Watchmen	31			31	.43
Weavers	391	2,006		2,397	34.01
All others	321	701	196	1,218	17.28
Total	2,000	4,071	977	7,048	100.00
NEW HAMPSHIRE.					
Back boys			29	29	.81
Carders	47	193		240	6.66
Card grinders	13			13	.36
Card strippers	11			11	.31
Cloth-room hands	35	39		74	2.05
Doffers			43	43	1.19
Drawers	3	10		13	.36
Filling hand	1			1	.03
Inspector	1			1	.03
Laborers	31		1	32	.89
Lappers	4			4	.11
Oilers	8			8	.22
Overseers	36			36	1.00
Pickers	12			12	.33
Railway hand			1	1	.03
Rovers	14	2		16	.44
Scrubbers		20		20	.55
Second hands	51			51	1.42
Section hands	13			13	.36
Slashers	7			7	.19
Slubbers	2	3		5	.14

SUMMARY OF EMPLOYÉS, WITH PER CENT.—Continued.

COTTON GOODS—Continued.

NOTE.—This table is *not* a complete exhibit for industries or states, but covers only establishments investigated by the Bureau. See detail table, Appendix A, page 295, whence derived.

States and occupations.	Number of employés.				Per cent. of number of employés in each occupation of the whole number considered in the industry in the state.
	Adult male.	Adult female.	Children and youth.	Total.	
NEW HAMPSHIRE—concluded.					
Spare hands	7	1		8	.22
Speeders	8			8	.22
Spinners, mule	32			32	.89
Spinners, other		327	439	766	21.25
Spoolers		116		116	3.22
Sweepers			9	9	.25
Twisters			53	53	1.47
Warpers		13		13	.36
Weavers	241	1,500		1,741	48.29
All others	45	141	43	229	6.35
Total	622	2,365	618	3,605	100.00
NEW JERSEY.					
Drawers		8		8	3.28
Engineer	1			1	.41
Fireman	1			1	.41
Loom fixers	6			6	2.46
Machinists	3			3	1.23
Pickers	3			3	1.23
Speeders		20		20	8.19
Spinners, mule	14			14	5.74
Spinners, other			30	30	12.29
Weavers		130		130	53.28
All others	8		20	28	11.48
Total	36	158	50	244	100.00
NEW YORK.					
Back boys			149	149	2.23
Beamers	2			2	.03
Blacksmiths	2			2	.03
Bobbin boys			99	99	1.48
Carders	6	349		355	5.32
Card grinders	31			31	.46
Card strippers	28			28	.42
Doffers			86	86	1.29
Drawers		17	163	180	2.70
Drawers-in		11	5	16	.24
Engineers	6			6	.09
Filling hands			2	2	.03
Foremen	10			10	.15
Folders	6		22	28	.42
Inspectors	2	1		3	.05
Laborers	111			111	1.66
Lappers			20	20	.30
Loom fixers	26			26	.39
Machinists	28			28	.42
Oilers	5		1	6	.09
Overseers	51			51	.76
Packers	3			3	.05
Painters	13			13	.20
Pickers	20		12	32	.48
Rovers	2		183	185	2.77
Second hands	82		2	84	1.26
Slashers	49		1	50	.75
Slubbers	78	9	36	123	1.84
Spare hands	3		3	6	.09
Speeders		52	214	266	3.99
Spinners, mule	157			157	2.35
Spinners, other	403	244	1,108	1,755	26.30
Spoolers	8	8	147	163	2.45
Sweepers			10	10	.15
Teamsters	20			20	.30

VARIATION IN THE RATES OF WAGES.

SUMMARY OF EMPLOYÉS, WITH PER CENT.—Continued.

COTTON GOODS—Continued.

NOTE.—This table is *not* a complete exhibit for industries or states, but covers only establishments investigated by the Bureau. See detail table, Appendix A, page 295, whence derived.

States and occupations.	Number of employés.				Per cent. of number of employés in each occupation of the whole number considered in the industry in the state.
	Adult male.	Adult female.	Children and youth.	Total.	
NEW YORK—concluded.					
Twisters	12	....	6	18	.27
Warpers	....	14	88	102	1.53
Watchmen	21	....	....	21	.32
Weavers	235	1,169	170	1,574	23.59
All others	195	303	353	851	12.75
Total	1,615	2,177	2,880	6,672	100.00
NORTH CAROLINA.					
Beamers	10	....	....	10	1.03
Carders	18	....	....	18	1.85
Card grinders	10	....	....	10	1.03
Doffers	....	....	60	60	6.17
Drawers	....	9	3	12	1.23
Drawers-in	6	....	....	6	.61
Dyers	17	....	....	17	1.75
Engineers	5	....	....	5	.51
Filling hands	....	....	5	5	.51
Firemen	4	....	....	4	.41
Folder	1	....	....	1	.10
Laborers	2	....	....	2	.20
Lappers	3	....	....	3	.30
Loom fixers	16	....	....	16	1.65
Machinist	1	....	....	1	.10
Oilers	3	....	9	12	1.23
Overseers	23	....	....	23	2.37
Packers	9	....	1	10	1.03
Pickers	11	....	2	13	1.34
Quillers	....	....	32	32	3.29
Railway hands	....	....	4	4	.41
Reelers	....	29	....	29	2.99
Rover	1	....	....	1	.10
Second hands	3	....	....	3	.30
Slashers	3	....	....	3	.30
Slubbers	....	19	....	19	1.95
Spare hands	....	4	....	4	.41
Speeders	....	41	....	41	4.22
Spinners, other than mule	....	....	162	162	16.70
Spoolers	....	50	....	50	5.15
Sweepers	....	....	15	15	1.54
Twisters	....	....	14	14	1.44
Warpers	11	....	12	23	2.37
Watchmen	6	....	....	6	.61
Weavers	100	208	....	308	31.70
All others	12	11	7	30	3.09
Total	275	371	326	972	100.00
PENNSYLVANIA.					
Beamers	12	....	....	12	3.02
Card grinders	2	....	....	2	.50
Doffers	....	....	19	19	4.79
Drawers	....	....	2	2	.50
Dyers	10	....	....	10	2.52
Engineers	2	....	....	2	.50
Oilers	....	....	3	3	.76
Overseers	15	....	....	15	3.78
Packers	2	....	....	2	.50
Pickers	2	....	....	2	.50
Reelers	....	12	....	12	3.02
Slubbers	....	2	....	2	.50
Spare hands	....	....	5	5	1.26
Speeders	....	9	....	9	2.27
Spinners, other than mule	....	28	....	28	7.05

SUMMARY OF EMPLOYÉS, WITH PER CENT.—Continued.

COTTON GOODS—Continued.

NOTE.—This table is *not* a complete exhibit for industries or states, but covers only establishments investigated by the Bureau. See detail table, Appendix A, page 295, whence derived.

States and occupations.	Number of employés.				Per cent of number of employés in each occupation of the whole number considered in the industry in the state.
	Adult male.	Adult female.	Children and youth.	Total.	
PENNSYLVANIA—concluded.					
Spoolers		15		15	3.78
Sweepers			2	2	.50
Warpers	5			5	1.27
Watchmen	4			4	1.01
Weavers	40	134		174	43.83
All others	50	2	20	72	18.14
Total	144	202	51	397	100.00
SOUTH CAROLINA.					
Carders	42			42	14.38
Cloth-room hands	7			7	2.40
Laborers	15			15	5.14
Spinners, other than male		80		80	27.40
Watchmen	5			5	1.71
Weavers	91			91	31.17
All others	8	44		52	17.80
Total	168	124		292	100.00
VERMONT.					
Card grinders	2			2	.72
Card strippers	2			2	.72
Doffers			15	15	5.39
Drawers-in		6		6	2.15
Engineer	1			1	.36
Fireman	1			1	.36
Folder	1			1	.36
Inspector	1			1	.36
Loom fixers	5			5	1.78
Oiler	1			1	.36
Overseers	5			5	1.78
Pickers	4			4	1.43
Second hands	4			4	1.43
Slashers	2			2	.72
Slubbers		6		6	2.15
Spare hands		6		6	2.15
Speeders	14			14	5.02
Spinners, male	12			12	4.30
Spinners, other			25	25	8.96
Sweepers			6	6	2.15
Teamsters	2			2	.72
Weavers	65	50		115	41.22
All others	7	4	32	43	15.41
Total	129	72	78	279	100.00
VIRGINIA.					
Beamers	3			3	.50
Carders	7			7	1.17
Card grinders	7			7	1.17
Doffers			32	32	5.36
Drawers		8		8	1.34
Drawers-in		2		2	.33
Dyers	7			7	1.17
Engineer	1			1	.17
Filling hand	1			1	.17
Firemen	3			3	.50
Folder	1			1	.17
Inspectors			2	2	.33
Laborers	5			5	.83
Loom fixers	5			5	.83
Machinists	5			5	.83

VARIATION IN THE RATES OF WAGES.

SUMMARY OF EMPLOYÉS, WITH PER CENT.—Continued.

COTTON GOODS—Concluded.

NOTE.—This table is *not* a complete exhibit for industries or states, but covers only establishments investigated by the Bureau. See detail table, Appendix A, page 293, whence derived.

States and occupations.	Number of employés.				Per cent. of number of employés in each occupation of the whole number considered in the industry in the state.
	Adult male.	Adult female.	Children and youth.	Total.	
VIRGINIA—concluded.					
Oilers			4	4	.67
Overseers	22			22	3.68
Packers	8	2	3	13	2.18
Pickers	8		2	10	1.68
Quillers			10	10	1.68
Railway hands	1	1	3	5	.83
Reelers		2		2	.33
Second hands	5			5	.83
Slasher	1			1	.17
Slubbers		7	4	11	1.85
Spare hands	1	2	7	10	1.68
Speeders		13	13	26	4.35
Spinners, other than mule			92	92	15.41
Spoolers		17	13	30	5.04
Sweepers			8	8	1.35
Teamsters	2			2	.34
Warpers		5	8	13	2.18
Watchmen	4			4	.67
Weavers	25	201		226	37.86
All others	2	6	6	14	2.35
Total	124	266	207	597	100.00

FOOD PREPARATIONS.

States and occupations.	Adult male.	Adult female.	Children and youth.	Total.	Per cent.
CALIFORNIA.					
Engineers	18			18	16.36
Firemen	3			3	2.73
Laborers	9			9	8.18
Millers	5			5	4.55
Packers	2			2	1.82
Teamsters	6			6	5.45
All others	65		2	67	60.91
Total	108		2	110	100.00
ILLINOIS.					
Cleaners	6			6	2.98
Engineers	19			19	9.45
Firemen	10			10	4.98
Laborers	66			66	32.83
Millers	31			31	15.42
Packers	24			24	11.94
Sweepers	14			14	6.97
Teamsters	17			17	8.46
All others	14			14	6.97
Total	201			201	100.00
INDIANA.					
Cleaners	2			2	.31
Engineers	3			3	.46
Laborers	424			424	65.13
Millers	3			3	.46
Packers	2			2	.31
Sweepers	2			2	.31
Teamsters	2			2	.31
All others	121		92	213	32.71
Total	559		92	651	100.00

SUMMARY OF EMPLOYÉS, WITH PER CENT.—Continued.

FOOD PREPARATIONS—Concluded.

NOTE.—This table is *not* a complete exhibit for industries or states, but covers only establishments investigated by the Bureau. See detail table, Appendix A, page 295, whence derived.

States and occupations.	Number of employés.				Per cent. of number of employés in each occupation of the whole number considered in the industry in the state.
	Adult male.	Adult female.	Children and youth.	Total.	
MINNESOTA.					
Laborers	108			108	31.49
Millers	83			83	24.20
Packers	28			28	8.16
Sweepers	50			50	14.58
All others	74			74	21.57
Total	343			343	100.00
MISSOURI.					
Cleaners	2			2	1.67
Engineers	7			7	5.83
Firemen	6			6	5.00
Laborers	77			77	64.17
Millers	12			12	10.00
Packers	4			4	3.33
Sweepers	2			2	1.67
All others	10			10	8.33
Total	120			120	100.00
NEW HAMPSHIRE.					
Cleaner	1			1	11.11
Millers	5			5	55.56
Packers	2			2	22.22
Sweeper	1			1	11.11
All others					
Total	9			9	100.00
OHIO.					
Coopers	44			44	22.34
Engineers	11			11	5.58
Firemen	14			14	7.11
Laborers	15			15	7.61
Millers	12			12	6.09
Packers	8			8	4.06
Sweepers	2			2	1.02
Teamsters	4			4	2.03
All others	87			87	44.16
Total	197			197	100.00
WEST VIRGINIA.					
Engineer	1			1	16.67
Laborer	1			1	16.67
Millers	2			2	33.34
Packer	1			1	16.66
All others	1			1	16.66
Total	6			6	100.00

FURNITURE.

INDIANA.					
Cabinetmakers	143			143	25.26
Engineers	2			2	.35
Foremen	4			4	.71
Laborers	48			48	8.48

VARIATION IN THE RATES OF WAGES.

SUMMARY OF EMPLOYÉS, WITH PER CENT.—Continued.

FURNITURE—Concluded.

NOTE.—This table is *not* a complete exhibit for industries or states, but covers only establishments investigated by the Bureau. See detail table, Appendix A, page 295, whence derived.

States and occupations.	Number of employés.				Per cent. of number of employés in each occupation of the whole number considered in the industry in the state.
	Adult male.	Adult female.	Children and youth.	Total.	
INDIANA—concluded.					
Machine men	187		58	245	43.29
Upholsterers	5			5	.88
All others	119			119	21.03
Total	508		58	566	100.00
KENTUCKY.					
Cabinet makers	27			27	23.08
Carvers	6			6	5.13
Laborers	8			8	6.84
Machine men	32			32	27.35
Upholsterers	5			5	4.27
All others	39			39	33.33
Total	117			117	100.00
MICHIGAN.					
Cabinet makers	118		6	124	15.98
Carvers	31		6	37	4.77
Engineers	5			5	.64
Foremen	18			18	2.32
Laborers	63		1	64	8.25
Machine men	166		18	184	23.71
Upholsterers	19			19	2.45
All others	287		38	325	41.88
Total	707		69	776	100.00

GLASS.

CALIFORNIA.					
Blacksmiths	3			3	2.03
Blowers and finishers, bottle and chimney (blowers)	28			28	18.92
Engineer	1			1	.67
Gatherers			14	14	9.46
Laborers	15			15	10.14
Mixers	3			3	2.03
Packers	8			8	5.40
Pot makers	2			2	1.35
Teamsters	3			3	2.03
Teasers	3			3	2.03
All others	20		48	68	45.94
Total	86		62	148	100.00
ILLINOIS.					
Blowers, window-glass	16			16	38.10
Cutters	6			6	14.29
Flatteners	4			4	9.52
Gatherers	16			16	38.09
All others					
Total	42			42	100.00
KENTUCKY.					
Blacksmith	1			1	1.45
Blowers and finishers, bottle and chimney (blowers)	20			20	28.98

SUMMARY OF EMPLOYÉS, WITH PER CENT.—Continued.

GLASS—Continued.

NOTE.—This table is not a complete exhibit for industries or states, but covers only establishments investigated by the Bureau. See detail table, Appendix A, page 295, whence derived.

States and occupations.	Number of employés.				Per cent. of number of employés in each occupation of the whole number considered in the industry in the state.
	Adult male.	Adult female.	Children and youth.	Total.	
KENTUCKY—concluded.					
Foreman	1			1	1.45
Laborers	21			21	30.43
Mixer	1			1	1.45
Packers	1		2	3	4.35
Teamster	1			1	1.45
Tossers	2			2	2.90
Watchman	1			1	1.45
All others	1		17	18	26.09
Total	50		19	69	100.00
NEW JERSEY.					
Blacksmiths	7			7	.88
Blowers, window-glass	32			32	4.02
Blowers and finishers, bottle and chimney (blowers)	207			207	25.97
Cutters	20			20	2.51
Engineers	8			8	1.00
Flatteners	10			10	1.25
Foreman	1			1	.13
Gatherers	40		26	66	8.28
Laborers	36			36	4.51
Master shearers	29			29	3.64
Mixers	11			11	1.38
Packers	13			13	1.63
Pot makers	3			3	.38
Teamsters	18			18	2.26
All others	54		282	336	42.16
Total	489		308	797	100.00
OHIO.					
Blacksmiths	3			3	.52
Blowers, window-glass	37			37	6.45
Blowers and finishers, bottle and chimney	23			23	4.01
Cutters	15			15	2.61
Engineer	1			1	.18
Fillers-in	2			2	.35
Flatteners	9			9	1.57
Gatherers	71		8	79	13.76
Laborers	46			46	8.01
Leersmen	4			4	.70
Master tossers	2			2	.35
Mixers	5			5	.87
Mould makers	7			7	1.22
Packers	10			10	1.74
Pressers	29			29	5.05
Tossers	9			9	1.57
Watchman	1			1	.17
All others	91		201	292	50.87
Total	365		209	574	100.00
PENNSYLVANIA.					
Blacksmiths	11			11	.50
Blowers, window-glass	27			27	1.22
Blowers and finishers, bottle and chimney	403			403	18.17
Cutters	11			11	.50
Engineers	7			7	.32
Fillers-in	13			13	.59
Flatteners	8			8	.36
Foremen	9			9	.40
Gatherers	178		29	202	9.11

VARIATION IN THE RATES OF WAGES.

SUMMARY OF EMPLOYÉS, WITH PER CENT.—Continued.

GLASS—Concluded.

NOTE.—This table is not a complete exhibit for industries or states, but covers only establishments investigated by the Bureau. See detail table, Appendix A, page 295, whence derived.

States and occupations.	Number of employés.				Per cent. of number of employés in each occupation of the whole number considered in the industry in the state.
	Adult male.	Adult female.	Children and youth.	Total.	
PENNSYLVANIA—concluded.					
Laborers	435			435	19.61
Leersmen	17			17	.76
Master teasers	3			3	.13
Mixers	28			28	1.26
Mould makers	23			23	1.04
Packers	74			74	3.34
Pot makers	8			8	.36
Pressers	41			41	1.85
Teamsters	13			13	.58
Teasers	39			39	1.76
Watchmen	12			12	.54
All others	145	27	662	834	37.60
Total	1,500	27	691	2,218	100.00
WEST VIRGINIA.					
Blacksmith	1			1	1.16
Blowers and finishers, bottle and chimney (blowers)	18			18	20.93
Foreman	1			1	1.16
Leersmen	2			2	2.33
Mixers	2			2	2.33
Packers	5			5	5.81
Teamsters	2			2	2.33
Teasers	2			2	2.33
Watchman	1			1	1.16
All others	14		38	52	60.46
Total	48		38	86	100.00

LEATHER.

CALIFORNIA.					
Beamsmen	30			30	19.48
Finisher	1			1	.65
Laborers	37			37	24.03
All others	84		2	86	55.84
Total	152		2	154	100.00
DELAWARE.					
Beamsmen	38			38	9.50
Finishers	184		46	230	57.50
Laborers	37			37	9.25
Shavers	16		1	17	4.25
Tanners	30			30	7.50
All others	32	14	2	48	12.00
Total	337	14	49	400	100.00
MASSACHUSETTS.					
Beamsmen	10			10	8.00
Finishers	40			40	32.00
Tanners	10			10	8.00
All others	65			65	52.00
Total	125			125	100.00

SUMMARY OF EMPLOYÉS, WITH PER CENT.—Continued.

LEATHER—Concluded.

NOTE.—This table is *not* a complete exhibit for industries or states, but covers only establishments investigated by the Bureau. See detail table, Appendix A, page 205, whence derived.

States and occupations.	Number of employés.				Per cent. of number of employés of each occupation of the whole number considered in the industry in the state.
	Adult male.	Adult female.	Children and youth.	Total.	
PENNSYLVANIA.					
Beamsmen	45			45	16.66
Finishers	108			108	40.00
Laborers	24			24	8.80
Shavers	17			17	6.30
Tanners	27			27	10.00
All others	34	14	1	49	18.15
Total	255	14	1	270	100.00

LIQUORS AND BEVERAGES.

	Adult male.	Adult female.	Children and youth.	Total.	Per cent.
ILLINOIS.					
Brewers and maltsters	64			64	24.06
Engineers	9			9	3.38
Firemen	22			22	8.27
Foremen	7			7	2.63
Teamsters	20			20	7.52
All others	144			144	54.14
Total	266			266	100.00
OHIO.					
Brewers and maltsters	72			72	43.64
Engineers	4			4	2.42
Firemen	4			4	2.42
Foreman	1			1	.61
Teamsters	45			45	27.27
All others	39			39	23.64
Total	165			165	100.00
PENNSYLVANIA.					
Brewers and maltsters	12			12	11.77
Foreman	1			1	.98
Teamsters	4			4	3.92
All others	85			85	83.33
Total	102			102	100.00

MACHINES AND MACHINERY.

	Adult male.	Adult female.	Children and youth.	Total.	Per cent.
CALIFORNIA.					
Blacksmiths	16			16	2.89
Boiler makers	32			32	5.79
Carpenters	7			7	1.26
Machinists	68			68	12.27
Moulders	48			48	8.66
All others	320		63	383	69.13
Total	491		63	554	100.00
ILLINOIS.					
All others	97		20	117	100.00

VARIATION IN THE RATES OF WAGES.

SUMMARY OF EMPLOYÉS, WITH PER CENT.—Continued.

MACHINES AND MACHINERY—Concluded.

NOTE.—This table is *not* a complete exhibit for industries or states, but covers only establishments investigated by the Bureau. See detail table, Appendix A, page 295, whence derived.

States and occupations.	Number of employés.				Per cent. of number of employés in each occupation of the whole number considered in the industry in the state.
	Adult male.	Adult female.	Children and youth.	Total.	
INDIANA.					
Blacksmiths	29			29	3.86
Boiler makers	114			114	15.16
Carpenters	7			7	.93
Machinists	373		1	374	49.73
Moulders	43			43	5.72
All others	167		18	185	24.60
Total	733		19	752	100.00
KENTUCKY.					
Blacksmiths	6			6	5.00
Machinists	43			43	35.83
Moulders	10			10	8.33
All others	55		6	61	50.84
Total	114		6	120	100.00
MAINE.					
Blacksmiths	2			2	3.45
Machinists	10			10	17.24
Moulders	18			18	31.03
All others	23		5	28	48.28
Total	53		5	58	100.00
MASSACHUSETTS.					
Machinists	170			170	51.36
All others	161			161	48.64
Total	331			331	100.00
NEW JERSEY.					
Blacksmiths	3			3	1.91
Machinists	65			65	41.40
Moulders	30			30	19.11
All others	59			59	37.58
Total	157			157	100.00
PENNSYLVANIA.					
Machinists	275			275	58.39
All others	106		90	196	41.61
Total	381		90	471	100.00

METALS AND METALLIC GOODS.

ALABAMA.					
Cindermen	10			10	10.21
Engineers	2			2	2.04
Fillers (top)	4			4	4.08
Firemen	5			5	5.10
Foremen	4			4	4.08
Teamsters	2			2	2.04
All others	71			71	72.45
Total	98			98	100.00

SUMMARY OF EMPLOYÉS, WITH PER CENT.—Continued.

METALS AND METALLIC GOODS—Continued.

NOTE.—This table is *not* a complete exhibit for industries or states, but covers only establishments investigated by the Bureau. See detail table, Appendix A, page 395, whence derived.

States and occupations.	Number of employés.				Per cent. of number of employés in each occupation of the whole number considered in the industry in the state.
	Adult male.	Adult female.	Children and youth.	Total.	
BELGIUM.					
Carpenters	4			4	.47
Engineers	5			5	.59
Fillers (top, bottom)	12			12	1.41
Firemen	11			11	1.29
Foremen	7			7	.82
Heaters	6			6	.70
Heaters' helpers	12			12	1.40
Hookers-up	8			8	.94
Keepers	6			6	.70
Keepers' helpers	18			18	2.11
Laborers	65			65	7.61
Machinists	9			9	1.05
Masons	2			2	.23
Rollers (rollers; roller, chief, second, third, fourth)	12			12	1.41
Rollers' helpers	8			8	.94
Shearman	1			1	.12
Straighteners	5			5	.58
All others	511	33	119	663	77.63
Total	702	33	119	854	100.00
CALIFORNIA.					
Carpenters	11			11	2.54
Engineer	1			1	.23
Foreman	1			1	.23
Machinists	79			79	18.25
All others	341			341	78.75
Total	433			433	100.00
DELAWARE.					
Catchers	6			6	10.00
Drag-outs	2			2	3.33
Engineers	2			2	3.33
Foreman	1			1	1.67
Heaters	2			2	3.33
Heaters' helpers	2			2	3.33
Hookers-up	2			2	3.33
Laborers	12			12	20.00
Puddlers	6			6	10.00
Puddlers' helpers	6			6	10.00
Rollers	8			8	13.34
All others	11			11	18.34
Total	60			60	100.00
GREAT BRITAIN.					
Bricklayers (bricklayers, masons)	10			10	.87
Carpenters	2			2	.17
Catchers (muck, rail)	15			15	1.30
Drag-outs	2			2	.17
Engineers	24			24	2.08
Fillers (fillers; fillers, bottom, top)	74			74	6.41
Firemen	10			10	.87
Foremen	16			16	1.38
Keepers	10			10	.87
Keepers' helpers	10			10	.87
Laborers	113			113	9.79
Machinists	2			2	.17
Millwrights	10			10	.87
Pilers (iron)	7			7	.61
Puddlers	240			240	20.80
Rollers (forge, rail)	3			3	.26

VARIATION IN THE RATES OF WAGES.

SUMMARY OF EMPLOYÉS, WITH PER CENT.—Continued.

METALS AND METALLIC GOODS—Continued.

NOTE.—This table is *not* a complete exhibit for industries or states, but covers only establishments investigated by the Bureau. See detail table, Appendix A, page 295, whence derived.

States and occupations.	Number of employés.				Per cent. of number of employés in each occupation of the whole number considered in the industry in the state.
	Adult male.	Adult female.	Children and youth.	Total.	
GREAT BRITAIN—concluded.					
Roughers (forge, rail)	15			15	1.30
Straighteners	10			10	.87
Wheelers (coal, fettling, metal, slag)	46			46	3.98
All others	501	10	24	535	46.36
Total	1,120	10	24	1,154	100.00
ILLINOIS.					
Bricklayers (bricklayers, masons)	2			2	.29
Carpenters	3			3	.43
Catchers (catchers; catchers, plate, slab)	8			8	1.16
Engineers	10			10	1.45
Firemen	10			10	1.45
Foremen	3			3	.43
Heaters (heaters; heaters, old rail, plate)	20			20	2.89
Heaters' helpers (heaters' helpers; heaters' helpers, old rail, plate)	24			24	3.47
Hookers-up (hookers-up; hookers-up, plate, slab)	14			14	2.02
Laborers	171			171	24.71
Machinists	16			16	2.31
Pattern maker	1			1	.14
Pilers (old rail)	4			4	.58
Puddlers	6			6	.86
Puddlers' helpers	10			10	1.45
Rollers (rollers; rollers, plate, slab)	11			11	1.59
Rollers' helpers (plate)	4			4	.58
Roughers	11			11	1.59
Shearmen (shearmen; shearmen, plate)	7			7	1.01
Teamsters	3			3	.43
All others	252		102	354	51.16
Total	590		102	692	100.00
INDIANA.					
Carpenters	5			5	1.31
Catchers	2			2	.52
Engineers	9			9	2.36
Fillers	10			10	2.62
Firemen	6			6	1.57
Hammermen	2			2	.52
Heaters	12			12	3.14
Heaters' helpers	9			9	2.36
Keepers	2			2	.52
Keepers' helpers	2			2	.52
Laborers	153			153	40.05
Machinists	19			19	4.97
Masons	2			2	.52
Pattern makers	2			2	.52
Puddlers	32			32	8.38
Puddlers' helpers	32			32	8.38
Rollers (bar, guide, muck)	3			3	.79
Rollers' helpers	16			16	4.19
Roughers	6			6	1.57
Shearmen	4			4	1.05
Teamsters	5			5	1.31
All others	49			49	12.83
Total	382			382	100.00
KENTUCKY.					
Bricklayer	1			1	.16
Carpenter	1			1	.16
Catchers (bar, plate, sheet)	3			3	.49

SUMMARY OF EMPLOYÉS, WITH PER CENT.—Continued.

METALS AND METALLIC GOODS—Continued.

NOTE.—This table is *not* a complete exhibit for industries or states, but covers only establishments investigated by the Bureau. See detail table, Appendix A, page 295, whence derived.

States and occupations.	Number of employés.				Per cent. of number of employés in each occupation of the whole number considered in the industry in the state.
	Adult male.	Adult female.	Children and youth.	Total.	
KENTUCKY—concluded.					
Engineers	6			6	.96
Firemen	3			3	.48
Hammermen	4			4	.64
Heaters (bar, bloom and scrap, 8-inch, 10-inch, plate, sheet, slot)	13			13	2.09
Heaters' helpers	3			3	.48
Laborers	142			142	22.83
Machinist	1			1	.16
Millwright	1			1	.16
Pattern maker	1			1	.16
Pilers (plate)	4			4	.64
Puddlers	83			83	13.35
Puddlers' helpers	84			84	13.51
Rollers (bar, muck, plate, sheet, 8-inch, 10-inch)	13			13	2.09
Rollers' helpers (rollers' helpers; rollers' helpers, bar, muck, plate, sheet, 8-inch)	44			44	7.08
Roughers (bar, plate, sheet, 8-inch, 10-inch)	11			11	1.77
Shearmen (shearmen; shearmen, plate)	13			13	2.09
Straighteners	5			5	.80
Teamster (cart driver)	1			1	.16
All others	148		37	185	29.75
Total	585		37	622	100.00
MARYLAND.					
Breakers (limestone, ore)	7			7	2.99
Carpenter	1			1	.43
Cindermen	4			4	1.71
Engineers	8			8	3.42
Fillers	21			21	8.97
Firemen	2			2	.85
Keepers	9			9	3.85
Keepers' helpers	9			9	3.85
Laborers	102			102	43.59
Machinist	1			1	.43
Teamsters (teamsters, cart drivers)	11			11	4.70
All others	59			59	25.21
Total	234			234	100.00
MASSACHUSETTS.					
Carpenters	5			5	5.56
Foreman	1			1	1.11
Laborers	18			18	20.00
Machinists	40			40	44.44
Pattern makers	2			2	2.22
All others	24			24	26.67
Total	90			90	100.00
MISSOURI.					
Carpenters	15			15	1.46
Engineers	21			21	2.04
Foremen	10			10	.97
Laborers	412			412	40.04
Machinists	3			3	.29
All others	568			568	55.20
Total	1,029			1,029	100.00
NEW HAMPSHIRE.					
Laborers	100			100	53.48
Machinists	5			5	2.67

VARIATION IN THE RATES OF WAGES.

SUMMARY OF EMPLOYÉS, WITH PER CENT.—Continued.

METALS AND METALLIC GOODS—Continued.

NOTE.—This table is *not* a complete exhibit for industries or states, but covers only establishments investigated by the Bureau. See detail table, Appendix A, page 295, whence derived.

States and occupations.	Number of employés.				Per cent. of number of employés in each occupation of the whole number considered in the industry in the state.
	Adult male.	Adult female.	Children and youth.	Total.	
NEW HAMPSHIRE—concluded.					
Pattern makers	7			7	3.74
All others	75			75	40.11
Total	187			187	100.00
NEW JERSEY.					
Laborers	12			12	10.81
Machinists	4			4	3.00
Pattern makers	4			4	3.60
Teamsters	9			9	8.11
All others	82			82	73.88
Total	111			111	100.00
NEW YORK.					
Breakers (ore)	6			6	.15
Carpenters	8			8	.20
Catchers	28			28	.69
Cindermen	12			12	.30
Drag-outs	8			8	.20
Engineers	35			35	.87
Fillers (bottom, top)	38			38	.94
Foremen	27			27	.67
Hammermen	7			7	.18
Heaters	42			42	1.04
Heaters' helpers	42			42	1.04
Hookers-up (hookers-up; hookers-up, tumble)	37			37	.92
Keepers	6			6	.15
Keepers' helpers	8			8	.20
Laborers	1,459			1,459	36.15
Machinists	283			283	7.01
Masons	4			4	.10
Millwrights	2			2	.05
Pilers (iron)	6			6	.15
Puddlers	185			185	4.59
Puddlers' helpers	168			168	4.12
Rollers (rollers; rollers, muck)	43			43	1.07
Rollers' helpers	9			9	.22
Roughers	26			26	.65
Shearmen	10			10	.25
Straighteners (straighteners; straighteners, cold bar)	26			26	.65
Teamsters	5			5	.12
Wheelers (coal, coke, limestone)	37			37	.92
All others	1,214		255	1,469	36.40
Total	3,781		255	4,036	100.00
OHIO.					
Breakers (iron, limestone, ore)	39			39	.73
Bricklayers (bricklayers, masons)	5			5	.09
Carpenters	21			21	.39
Catchers (catchers; catchers, bar, butt, muck, plate, 8-inch, 9-inch)	46			46	.86
Cindermen	50			50	.94
Drag-outs (drag-outs; drag-outs, butt, muck, plate)	32			32	.60
Engineers	118			118	2.22
Fillers (fillers; fillers, bottom, top)	175			175	3.28
Firemen	119			119	2.23
Foremen and overseers	49			49	.92
Hammermen	6			6	.11

SUMMARY OF EMPLOYÉS, WITH PER CENT.—Continued.

METALS AND METALLIC GOODS—Continued.

NOTE.—This table is *not* a complete exhibit for industries or states, but covers only establishments investigated by the Bureau. See detail table, Appendix A, page 295, whence derived.

States and occupations.	Number of employés.				Per cent. of number of employés in each occupation of the whole number considered in the industry in the state.
	Adult male.	Adult female.	Children and youth.	Total.	
OHIO—concluded.					
Heaters (heaters; heaters, bar, butt, plate, sheet, 8-inch, 9-inch)	a80			80	1.50
Heaters' helpers (heaters' helpers; heaters' helpers, bar, butt, plate, sheet, 8-inch)	140			140	2.62
Hookers-up (hookers-up; hookers-up, bar, butt, muck, plate)	50			50	.94
Keepers	20			20	.38
Keepers' helpers	32		2	34	.64
Laborers	1,161			1,161	21.78
Machinists	39			39	.73
Millwrights	3			3	.06
Pilers (iron, plate)	b18			18	.34
Puddlers	108			108	2.03
Puddlers' helpers	150			150	2.81
Rollers (rollers; rollers, bar, bloom, butt, hoop, guide, muck, plate, sheet, rod, 8-inch, 9-inch, 18-inch, 22-inch)	c50			50	.94
Rollers 'helpers (rollers' helpers; rollers' helpers, bar, muck)	10			10	.19
Roughers (roughers; roughers, bar, plate, 8-inch, 9-inch)	80			80	1.50
Shearmen (shearmen; shearmen, muck, plate)	70			70	1.31
Straighteners (cold-bar, hot-bar, 8-inch, 9-inch)	15			15	.28
Wheelers (ash coal, iron)	162			162	3.04
Teamsters (teamsters, cart drivers)	22			22	.41
All others	2,109		260	2,459	46.13
Total	5,069		262	5,331	100.00
PENNSYLVANIA.					
Breakers (iron, ore)	18			18	.34
Bricklayers (bricklayers, masons)	61			61	1.15
Carpenters	43			43	.81
Catchers, (catchers; catchers, bar, muck, 8-inch, 10-inch)	d22			22	.41
Cindermen	30			30	.56
Drag-outs (drag-outs; drag-outs, bar, 10-inch)	9			9	.17
Engineers	93			93	1.75
Fillers (fillers; fillers, bottom, top)	46			46	.87
Firemen	35			35	.66
Foremen	19			19	.36
Hammermen	40			40	.75
Heaters (heaters; heaters, bar, 8-inch, 10-inch)	e27			27	.51
Heaters' helpers (heaters' helpers; heaters' helpers, bar)	51			51	.96
Hookers-up	2			2	.04
Keepers	6			6	.11
Keepers' helpers	10			10	.19
Laborers	1,936		3	1,939	36.48
Machinists	181			181	3.40
Millwrights	3			3	.06
Pattern makers	30			30	.56
Pilers (iron)	12			12	.23
Puddlers	318			318	5.98
Puddlers' helpers	318			318	5.98
Rollers (rollers; rollers, bar, muck, plate, 8-inch, 10-inch)	f17			17	.32

a Not including 7 heaters in establishment 417, wages being indefinite; also 4 heaters in establishment 850.
b Not including 1 plate piler in establishment 419, whose wages, as reported, were inseparably combined with those of his 4 assistants.
c Not including 8 rollers in establishment 417, also 1 roller in establishment 419, wages being indefinite.
d Not including establishment 428. Catchers not reported.
e Not including heaters in establishment 428; number not reported.
f Not including 6 rollers in establishment 433; 5 in establishment 432.

VARIATION IN THE RATES OF WAGES.

SUMMARY OF EMPLOYÉS, WITH PER CENT.—Continued.

METALS AND METALLIC GOODS—Continued.

NOTE.—This table is *not* a complete exhibit for industries or states, but covers only establishments investigated by the Bureau. See detail table, Appendix A, page 295, whence derived.

States and occupations.	Number of employés.				Per cent. of number of employés in each occupation of the whole number considered in the industry in the state.
	Adult male.	Adult female.	Children and youth.	Total.	
PENNSYLVANIA—concluded.					
Rollers' helpers	31			31	.58
Roughers (roughers; roughers, bar, muck, 8-inch, 10-inch)	10			10	.19
Shearmen	32			32	.60
Straighteners (straighteners; straighteners, cold-bar)	22			22	.41
Teamster (cart driver)	1			1	.02
All others	1,880		10	1,890	35.55
Total	5,303		13	5,316	100.00
TENNESSEE.					
Breakers (ore)	4			4	14.81
Engineers	3			3	11.11
Fillers (bottom, top)	12			12	44.45
Keepers	2			2	7.41
Keepers' helpers	2			2	7.41
All others	4			4	14.81
Total	27			27	100.00
VERMONT.					
Engineers	5			5	2.11
Foremen	13			13	5.48
Laborers	62			62	26.16
Machinists	10			10	4.22
All others	147			147	62.03
Total	237			237	100.00
VIRGINIA.					
Breakers (ore)	4			4	.26
Carpenters	14			14	.92
Catchers (catchers; catchers, guide)	40			40	2.03
Cindermen	14			14	.92
Engineers	7			7	.46
Fillers (fillers; fillers, bottom, top)	66			66	4.34
Firemen	5			5	.33
Foremen	8			8	.53
Heaters (heaters; heaters, bar, guide, plate, 18-inch)	54			54	3.56
Heaters' helpers (heaters' helpers; heaters' helpers, bar, guide, plate)	31			31	2.04
Keepers	6			6	.40
Keepers' helpers	14			14	.92
Laborers	339			339	22.32
Machinists	17			17	1.12
Masons	4			4	.26
Millwrights	3			3	.20
Pattern makers	3			3	.20
Puddlers	124			124	8.16
Puddlers' helpers	204			204	13.43
Rollers (rollers; rollers, bar, muck, guide, plate, 18-inch)	30			30	1.98
Roughers (roughers; roughers, guide, 18-inch)	53			53	3.49
Shearmen	4			4	.27
Wheelers	2			2	.13
Teamsters (cart drivers)	4		2	6	.39
All others	427		40	467	30.74
Total	1,477		42	1,519	100.00

SUMMARY OF EMPLOYÉS, WITH PER CENT.—Continued.

METALS AND METALLIC GOODS—Concluded.

NOTE.—This table is *not* a complete exhibit for industries or states, but covers only establishments investigated by the Bureau. See detail table, Appendix A, page 295, whence derived.

States and occupations.	Number of employés.				Per cent of number of employés in each occupation of the whole number considered in the industry in the state.
	Adult male.	Adult female.	Children and youth.	Total.	
WEST VIRGINIA.					
Catchers (plate)	2			2	.56
Engineers	2			2	.56
Heaters	7			7	1.96
Heaters' helpers	7			7	1.96
Hookers-up (plate)	2			2	.56
Laborers	15			15	4.19
Masons	2			2	.56
Puddlers	36			36	10.05
Puddlers' helpers	72			72	20.11
Rollers (muck, plate)	4			4	1.12
Rollers' helpers (muck, plate)	8			8	2.23
Shearman	1			1	.28
All others	175		25	200	55.86
Total	333		25	358	100.00

MUSICAL INSTRUMENTS AND MATERIALS.

States and occupations.	Adult male.	Adult female.	Children and youth.	Total.	Per cent.
MAINE.					
Box-room hands	2			2	5.00
Finishers (finishers, fly finishers)	10			10	25.00
Machinists	8			8	20.00
All others	20			20	50.00
Total	40			40	100.00
NEW HAMPSHIRE.					
Box-room hands (case makers)	5			5	20.83
Finishers (fly finishers)	3			3	12.50
All others	16			16	66.67
Total	24			24	100.00
NEW YORK.					
Bellymen	98			98	5.12
Box-room hands (box-room hands, case makers, carpenters)	167			167	8.72
Finishers (finishers, fly finishers)	152		10	162	8.46
Key makers	59			59	3.08
Machinists	23			23	1.20
All others	1,239	18	149	1,406	73.42
Total	1,738	18	159	1,915	100.00

PAPER.

States and occupations.	Adult male.	Adult female.	Children and youth.	Total.	Per cent.
CALIFORNIA.					
Engineer	1			1	2.86
Foreman	1			1	2.86
All others	33			33	94.28
Total	35			35	100.00

VARIATION IN THE RATES OF WAGES.

SUMMARY OF EMPLOYÉS, WITH PER CENT.—Continued.

PAPER—Concluded.

NOTE.—This table is *not* a complete exhibit for industries or states, but covers only establishments investigated by the Bureau. See detail table, Appendix A, page 295, whence derived.

States and occupations.	Number of employés.				Per cent. of number of employés in each occupation of the whole number considered in the industry in the state.
	Adult male.	Adult female.	Children and youth.	Total.	
DELAWARE.					
Calenderers	6			6	3.17
Engineers	12			12	6.35
Finishers	13			13	6.88
Foremen	3			3	1.59
Laborers	17			17	8.99
Machine tenders	42			42	22.22
Rag-engine tenders	19			19	10.45
All others	36	33	8	77	40.74
Total	148	33	8	189	100.00
MAINE.					
Engineers	9			9	6.61
Finishers	6	1		7	5.14
Foreman	1			1	.74
Laborers	20			20	14.71
Machine tenders	13			13	9.56
All others	44	31	11	86	63.24
Total	93	32	11	136	100.00
MASSACHUSETTS.					
Calenderers	38	12		50	5.35
Engineers	7			7	.75
Finishers	72	28	1	101	10.80
Foremen	12			12	1.28
Laborers	38			38	4.06
Machine tenders	78			78	8.34
Rag-engine tenders	57			57	6.10
Repair hands	21			21	2.25
All others	245	319	7	571	61.07
Total	568	359	8	935	100.00
NEW HAMPSHIRE.					
Finishers	8			8	3.81
Foremen	5			5	2.38
Machine tenders	30			30	14.29
Rag-engine tenders	30			30	14.29
Repair hands	10			10	4.76
All others	91	36		127	60.47
Total	174	36		210	100.00
OREGON.					
Engineers	5			5	11.11
Finishers		5		5	11.11
Laborers	15			15	33.33
Machine tenders	5			5	11.11
All others		10	5	15	33.34
Total	25	15	5	45	100.00
VERMONT.					
Finishers	10			10	4.95
Foremen	4			4	1.98
Machine tenders	35			35	17.33
Rag-engine tenders	48			48	23.76
Repair hands	20			20	9.90
All others	60	25		85	42.08
Total	177	25		202	100.00

SUMMARY OF EMPLOYÉS, WITH PER CENT.—Continued.
PRINT WORKS.

NOTE.—This table is *not* a complete exhibit for industries or states, but covers only establishments investigated by the Bureau. See detail table, Appendix A, page 295, whence derived.

States and occupations.	Number of employés.				Per cent. of number of employés in each occupation of the whole number considered in the industry in the state.
	Adult male.	Adult female.	Children and youth.	Total.	
MASSACHUSETTS.					
Ageing and steaming hands	37			37	5.01
Bleachers	29		31	60	8.12
Colorers and dyers	100		36	136	18.40
Engravers	14			14	1.89
Foremen (overseers)	35			35	4.74
Printers	23			23	3.11
All others	251	26	157	434	58.73
Total	489	26	224	739	100.00
NEW HAMPSHIRE.					
Ageing and steaming hands	25		8	33	7.22
Bleachers	30		25	55	12.03
Colorers and dyers	37			37	8.10
Engravers	4			4	.88
Foreman	1			1	.22
Printers	14			14	3.06
All others	190	59	64	313	68.49
Total	301	59	97	457	100.00
NEW JERSEY.					
Bleachers	30			30	14.63
Colorers and dyers	40			40	19.51
Engravers	25			25	12.20
Printers	10			10	4.88
All others	100			100	48.78
Total	205			205	100.00
NEW YORK.					
Bleachers	7			7	16.28
Foremen	2			2	4.65
All others	5	26	3	34	79.07
Total	14	26	3	43	100.00
PENNSYLVANIA.					
Engravers	19			19	2.51
Foremen	20			20	2.64
Printers	14			14	1.85
All others	293	65	346	704	93.00
Total	346	65	346	757	100.00

TOBACCO.

CONNECTICUT.					
Cigar makers (cigar makers, rollers)	15			15	71.43
Laborer	1			1	4.76
Packer	1			1	4.76
Strippers		4		4	19.05
Total	17	4		21	100.00

VARIATION IN THE RATES OF WAGES.

SUMMARY OF EMPLOYÉS, WITH PER CENT.—Continued.

TOBACCO—Continued.

NOTE.—This table is not a complete exhibit for industries or states, but covers only establishments investigated by the Bureau. See detail table, Appendix A, page 295, whence derived.

States and occupations.	Number of employés.				Per cent. of number of employés in each occupation of the whole number considered in the industry in the state.
	Adult male.	Adult female.	Children and youth.	Total.	
ILLINOIS.					
Bunch breakers		59		59	10.42
Cigar makers (cigar makers, rollers)	118	55		173	30.57
Cutters	10			10	1.77
Dressers	12		3	15	2.65
Engineer	1			1	.17
Foremen	7			7	1.24
Laborers	12			12	2.12
Packers	33	15		48	8.48
Pressmen	17			17	3.00
Strippers		5	168	173	30.57
Wrappers	20			20	3.53
All others	10	14	7	31	5.48
Total	240	148	178	566	100.00
KENTUCKY.					
Cutters	3			3	2.22
Dressers		6		6	4.44
Foremen	3			3	2.22
Laborers	28			28	20.74
Lump makers	2			2	1.48
Pressmen	5			5	3.71
Stemmers		10		10	7.41
Strippers		6	46	52	38.52
Wrappers	2	4		6	4.44
All others	7		13	20	14.82
Total	50	26	59	135	100.00
MICHIGAN.					
Cutters	6			6	3.80
Dressers	12	4		16	10.13
Foremen	5			5	3.16
Laborers	4			4	2.53
Packers	23			23	14.56
Strippers			55	55	34.81
All others	15		34	49	31.01
Total	65	4	89	158	100.00
MISSOURI.					
Cutters	10			10	1.05
Dressers	12			12	1.25
Engineers	2			2	.21
Foremen	7			7	.73
Laborers		35		35	3.66
Lump makers	69			69	7.21
Packers	6	30		36	3.76
Pressmen	80			80	8.36
Stemmers	310			310	32.39
Strippers			30	30	3.13
Wrappers	24			24	2.51
All others	322	20		342	35.74
Total	842	85	30	957	100.00
NEW JERSEY.					
Bunch breakers		20		20	19.42
Cigar makers (cigar makers, rollers)	31	30		61	59.22
Foreman	1			1	.97
Laborers	5			5	4.85
Packers	6			6	5.83

212 REPORT OF THE COMMISSIONER OF LABOR.

SUMMARY OF EMPLOYÉS, WITH PER CENT.—Continued.

TOBACCO—Continued.

NOTE.—This table is not a complete exhibit for industries or states, but covers only establishments investigated by the Bureau. See detail table, Appendix A, page 296, whence derived.

States and occupations.	Number of employés.				Per cent. of number of employés in each occupation of the whole number considered in the industry in the state.
	Adult male.	Adult female.	Children and youth.	Total.	
NEW JERSEY—concluded.					
Strippers			10	10	9.71
All others					
Total	43	50	10	103	100.00
NEW YORK.					
Cutters	12			12	5.31
Dressers	2	3		5	2.21
Engineer	1			1	.44
Lump makers	2	6		8	3.54
Packers	5	50		55	24.34
Pressmen	5			5	2.21
Stemmers		100		100	44.25
All others	12		28	40	17.70
Total	39	159	28	226	100.00
NORTH CAROLINA.					
Cutters	24			24	3.76
Engineer	1			1	.16
Foremen	21			21	3.29
Laborers	36		34	70	10.97
Lump makers	52			52	8.15
Packers	50		19	69	10.82
Pressmen	16			16	2.50
Stemmers	2	3	61	66	10.34
Strippers			53	53	8.31
Wrappers		53		53	8.31
All others	92	71	50	213	33.39
Total	294	127	217	638	100.00
OHIO.					
Bunch breakers	116	176	50	342	30.19
Cigar makers (cigar makers, rollers)	348	222		570	50.31
Foremen	11			11	.97
Laborers	7			7	.62
Packers	57	2		59	5.21
Strippers			126	126	11.12
All others	9	1	8	18	1.58
Total	548	401	184	1,133	100.00
RHODE ISLAND.					
Cigar makers (cigar makers, rollers)	14			14	63.63
Laborer	1			1	4.55
Packer	1			1	4.55
Strippers		4		4	18.18
All others			2	2	9.09
Total	16	4	2	22	100.00
VIRGINIA.					
Cutters	25			25	.90
Engineers	4			4	.14
Foremen	23			23	.83
Laborers	215		35	250	9.02
Lump makers	326			326	11.77
Packers		75		75	2.71
Pressmen	167			167	6.03
Stemmers		539	333	872	31.40

VARIATION IN THE RATES OF WAGES. 213

SUMMARY OF EMPLOYÉS, WITH PER CENT.—Continued.

TOBACCO—Concluded.

NOTE.—This table is *not* a complete exhibit for industries or states, but covers only establishments investigated by the Bureau. See detail table, Appendix A, page 295, whence derived.

States and occupations.	Number of employés.				Per cent. of number of employés in each occupation of the whole number considered in the industry in the state.
	Adult male.	Adult female.	Children and youth.	Total.	
VIRGINIA—concluded.					
Strippers	..	10	85	95	3.43
Wrappers	1	41	125	167	6.03
All others	41	76	650	767	27.68
Total	802	741	1,228	2,771	100.00
WEST VIRGINIA.					
Cigar makers (cigar makers, rollers)	48	..	..	48	78.69
Foreman	1	..	..	1	1.64
Packers	..	2	..	2	3.28
Strippers	..	..	10	10	16.39
All others	..	..	..	..	..
Total	49	2	10	61	100.00

WOOLLEN GOODS.

States and occupations.	Adult male.	Adult female.	Children and youth.	Total.	Per cent.
CALIFORNIA.					
Carders	9	..	..	9	8.74
Dresser	1	..	..	1	.97
Dyers	4	..	..	4	3.88
Engineer	1	..	..	1	.97
Finishers	8	..	..	8	7.77
Fireman	1	..	..	1	.97
Fullers	9	..	..	9	8.74
Laborers	6	..	..	6	5.83
Loom fixer	1	..	..	1	.97
Overseers	3	..	..	3	2.91
Scourer	1	..	..	1	.97
Shearer	1	..	..	1	.97
Spinners, other than mule	6	..	..	6	5.83
Spoolers	..	..	3	3	2.91
Weavers	46	..	..	46	44.66
Wool sorters	2	..	..	2	1.94
All others	1	..	..	1	.97
Total	100	..	3	103	100.00
CONNECTICUT.					
Burlers	..	13	..	13	6.10
Carders	15	..	9	24	11.26
Drawers-in	..	2	..	2	.94
Dressers	6	..	..	6	2.82
Driers	..	..	5	5	2.35
Dyers	11	..	..	11	5.16
Finishers	14	..	..	14	6.57
Firemen	3	..	..	3	1.41
Fullers	3	..	..	3	1.41
Laborer	1	..	..	1	.47
Loom fixers	2	..	..	2	.94
Machinists	2	..	..	2	.94
Overseers	8	..	..	8	3.76
Second hands	6	..	..	6	2.82
Spinners, mule	29	..	..	29	13.62
Spoolers	..	9	..	9	4.23
Teamster	1	..	..	1	.47
Weavers	..	61	..	61	28.63
All others	8	2	3	13	6.10
Total	109	87	17	213	100.00

SUMMARY OF EMPLOYÉS, WITH PER CENT.—Continued.

WOOLLEN GOODS—Continued.

NOTE.—This table is *not* a complete exhibit for industries or states, but covers only establishments investigated by the Bureau. See detail table, Appendix A, page 293, whence derived.

States and occupations.	Number of employés.				Per cent. of number of employés in each occupation of the whole number considered in the industry in the state.
	Adult male.	Adult female.	Children and youth.	Total.	
DELAWARE.					
Burlers			25	25	8.39
Carders	10		9	19	6.38
Drawers-in	2		2	4	1.34
Dyer	1			1	.34
Engineers	2			2	.67
Finishers	6			6	2.02
Fireman	1			1	.34
Fullers	4			4	1.34
Giggers	3			3	1.00
Laborers	15		1	16	5.37
Loom fixers	5			5	1.68
Machinist	1			1	.34
Overseers	4			4	1.34
Pickers	6			6	2.02
Presser	1			1	.34
Scourers	2			2	.67
Shearers	1	2		3	1.00
Spinners, mule	5			5	1.68
Spoolers		3	6	9	3.02
Teamsters	3			3	1.00
Twisters		3		3	1.00
Weavers	57	35		92	30.87
Wool sorters	6			6	2.01
All others	31		46	77	25.84
Total	166	43	89	298	100.00
GREAT BRITAIN.					
Burlers			30	30	5.88
Dyers	6			6	1.18
Finishers	37		32	69	13.53
Loom fixers	6			6	1.18
Scourers	7			7	1.37
Spinners, mule	12			12	2.35
Weavers	3	178		181	35.49
Wool sorter	1			1	.20
All others	109	46	43	198	38.82
Total	181	224	105	510	100.00
ILLINOIS.					
Carders			9	9	9.48
Dyers	4			4	4.21
Dressers			5	5	5.26
Engineer	1			1	1.05
Finishers	9	14		23	24.22
Machinist	1			1	1.05
Overseers	8			8	8.42
Pickers			2	2	2.11
Second hand	1			1	1.05
Spinners, other than mule	4	5		9	9.47
Weavers	28			28	29.47
Wool sorters	3			3	3.16
All others	1			1	1.05
Total	60	19	16	95	100.00
INDIANA.					
Burlers		2		2	.35
Carders	2		37	39	6.76
Drawers-in	3	7	3	13	2.25
Dressers	3			3	.52
Dyers	34			34	5.89

VARIATION IN THE RATES OF WAGES.

SUMMARY OF EMPLOYÉS, WITH PER CENT.—Continued.

WOOLLEN GOODS—Continued.

NOTE.—This table is not a complete exhibit for industries or states, but covers only establishments investigated by the Bureau. See detail table, Appendix A, page 295, whence derived.

States and occupations.	Number of employés.				Per cent. of number of employés in each occupation of the whole number considered in the industry in the state.
	Adult male.	Adult female.	Children and youth.	Total.	
INDIANA—concluded.					
Engineers	4			4	.69
Finishers	16	1	24	41	7.11
Firemen	4			4	.69
Fullers	13			19	3.29
Laborers	18		6	6	3.29
Loom fixers	6		1	6	1.04
Machinists	5			5	.86
Overseers	17			17	2.94
Pickers	3			3	.52
Second hands	6			6	1.04
Spinners, mule	4			4	.69
Spinners, other	1	20	86	107	18.58
Spoolers	1		7	8	1.38
Weavers	14	167		181	31.37
Wool sorters	15		5	20	3.46
All others	38		4	42	7.28
Total	**207**	**197**	**173**	**577**	**100.00**
IOWA.					
Carders	3		4	7	13.73
Dyer	1			1	1.96
Engineer	1			1	1.96
Finishers	2	3		5	9.81
Foremen	4			4	7.85
Laborers	3			3	5.88
Spinners, mule	1			1	1.96
Spinners, other		3		3	5.88
Twisters			5	5	9.80
Weavers	2	15		17	33.33
Wool sorters	1			1	1.96
All others	3			3	5.88
Total	**21**	**21**	**9**	**51**	**100.00**
KENTUCKY.					
Carders	4	4	25	33	6.82
Dyers	15			15	3.10
Engineers	2			2	.41
Finishers	1		30	31	6.40
Firemen	2			2	.41
Laborers	15			15	3.10
Loom fixers	5			5	1.03
Overseers	10			10	2.07
Pickers	10			10	2.07
Spinners, other than mule			48	48	9.92
Weavers		260		260	53.72
Wool sorters	6		7	13	2.69
All others	2	36	2	40	8.26
Total	**72**	**300**	**112**	**484**	**100.00**
MAINE.					
Carders		5	14	19	6.96
Dresser	1			1	.37
Drier	1			1	.37
Dyers	4			4	1.47
Engineer	1			1	.37
Finisher	1			1	.37
Firemen	1			1	.37
Fullers	2			2	.73
Giggers	2			2	.73
Laborers	30			30	10.99

SUMMARY OF EMPLOYÉS, WITH PER CENT.—Continued.

WOOLLEN GOODS—Continued.

NOTE.—This table is not a complete exhibit for industries or states, but covers only establishments investigated by the Bureau. See detail table, Appendix A, page 295, whence derived.

States and occupations.	Number of employés.				Per cent. of number of employés in each occupation of the whole number considered in the industry in the state.
	Adult male.	Adult female.	Children and youth.	Total.	
MAINE—concluded.					
Loom fixers	3			3	1.10
Machinists	2			2	.73
Overseers	15			15	5.49
Pickers	3		1	4	1.47
Presser	1	1		1	.36
Scourers	3			3	1.10
Second hands	13			13	4.76
Shearers	2			2	.73
Spinners, mule	21			21	7.69
Spinners, other	4			4	1.47
Spoolers	5			5	1.83
Teamster	1			1	.36
Twister	1			1	.36
Weavers	85	15		100	36.63
Wool sorters	9			9	3.30
All others	15	12		27	9.89
Total	226	33	14	273	100.00
MARYLAND.					
Burlers		4		4	1.60
Drawers-in		2		2	.80
Dyers	18			18	7.20
Engineers	2			2	.80
Finishers			5	5	2.00
Foremen	8			8	3.20
Fullers	5			5	2.00
Laborers	4			4	1.60
Loom fixers	2			2	.80
Machinists	2			2	.80
Pickers	12	9	4	25	10.00
Scourers	4			4	1.60
Shearer	1			1	.40
Spinners, mule	4			4	1.60
Spoolers		9		9	3.60
Teamsters	3			3	1.20
Weavers	4	69		73	29.20
Wool sorters	1		2	3	1.20
All others	23	8	45	76	30.40
Total	93	101	56	250	100.00
MASSACHUSETTS.					
Burlers		4		4	.27
Carders	18	3	65	86	5.75
Drawers-in		8		8	.54
Dressers	19	15		34	2.27
Driers	11			11	.74
Dyers	57			57	3.81
Engineers	4			4	.27
Finishers	51	10		61	4.08
Fullers	18			18	1.20
Giggers	40			40	2.68
Laborers	24		7	31	2.07
Loom fixers	10			10	.67
Machinists	6			6	.40
Overseers	38			38	2.54
Pickers	16		4	20	1.34
Pressers	5			5	.34
Scourers	16			16	1.07
Second hands	47			47	3.14
Shearers	6			6	.40
Spinners, mule	88			88	5.89
Spinners, other		8		8	.54

VARIATION IN THE RATES OF WAGES.

SUMMARY OF EMPLOYÉS, WITH PER CENT.—Continued.

WOOLLEN GOODS—Continued.

NOTE.—This table is *not* a complete exhibit for industries or states, but covers only establishments investigated by the Bureau. See detail table, Appendix A, page 295, whence derived.

States and occupations.	Number of employés.				Per cent. of number of employés in each occupation of the whole number considered in the industry in the state.
	Adult male.	Adult female.	Children and youth.	Total.	
MASSACHUSETTS—concluded.					
Spoolers			44	44	2.94
Teamsters	4			4	.27
Twisters	4			4	.27
Weavers	161	340	5	506	33.84
Wool sorters	24			24	1.61
All others	107	156	52	315	21.06
Total	774	544	177	1,495	100.00
MISSOURI.					
Carders	17			17	14.05
Dyers	11			11	9.09
Engineer	1			1	.83
Finishers	9	13		22	18.18
Laborers	3			3	2.48
Machinist	1			1	.82
Overseers	5			5	4.13
Spinners, mule	18			18	14.88
Twisters		4		4	3.31
Weavers	17	7		24	19.83
Wool sorters	9			9	7.44
All others	6			6	4.96
Total	97	24		121	100.00
NEW HAMPSHIRE.					
Burlers		30		30	8.24
Carders		19		19	5.22
Dressers	6			6	1.65
Driers	2			2	.55
Engineer	1			1	.27
Firemen	2			2	.55
Fullers	8			8	2.20
Laborers	38			38	10.44
Loom fixers	6			6	1.65
Machinists	3			3	.82
Overseers	21			21	5.78
Second hands	9			9	2.47
Shearers	6			6	1.65
Spinners, mule	18			18	4.95
Spoolers		14		14	3.84
Teamsters	2			2	.55
Weavers	50	45		95	26.10
Wool sorters	20			20	5.49
All others	49	15		64	17.58
Total	241	123		364	100.00
NEW JERSEY.					
Carders	10	1	6	17	5.21
Dyers	8			8	2.46
Finishers	24	24		48	14.73
Laborers	18			18	5.52
Loom fixers	12			12	3.68
Overseers	18			18	5.52
Pickers	18			18	5.52
Spinners, other than mule	18	6	12	36	11.04
Weavers	50	30	22	102	31.29
Wool sorters	1	12		13	3.99
All others	32		4	36	11.04
Total	209	73	44	326	100.00

SUMMARY OF EMPLOYÉS, WITH PER CENT.—Continued.

WOOLLEN GOODS—Continued.

NOTE.—This table is not a complete exhibit for industries or states, but covers only establishments investigated by the Bureau. See detail table, Appendix A, page 295, whence derived.

States and occupations.	Number of employés.				Per cent. of number of employés in each occupation of the whole number considered in the industry in the state.
	Adult male.	Adult female.	Children and youth.	Total.	
NEW YORK.					
Burlers		66	19	85	7.71
Carders	16		35	51	4.62
Drawers-in	2	6		8	.73
Dressers	5			5	.45
Driers	20			20	1.81
Dyers	40			40	3.63
Engineers	3			3	.27
Finishers	2			2	.18
Firemen	5			5	.45
Fullers	10			10	.91
Giggers	15			16	1.45
Laborers	12		1	12	1.09
Loom fixers	6			6	.54
Machinists	7			7	.63
Overseers	19			19	1.72
Pickers	8			8	.73
Pressers	6			6	.54
Scourers	22			22	1.99
Second hands	8			8	.73
Shearers	11			11	1.00
Spinners, mule	27		11	38	3.44
Spinners, other		14	41	55	4.99
Spoolers			45	45	4.08
Teamsters	3			3	.27
Twisters			67	67	6.07
Weavers	126	105	2	233	21.12
Wool sorters	44			44	3.99
All others	74	78	122	274	24.84
Total	491	269	343	1,103	100.00
NORTH CAROLINA.					
Burler		1		1	1.64
Carders			4	4	6.56
Dyers	4			4	6.56
Engineer	1			1	1.64
Finishers	4	3		7	11.47
Fireman	1			1	1.64
Loom fixers	4			4	6.55
Overseers	5			5	8.20
Pickers	2			2	3.28
Spinners, mule	3			3	4.92
Weavers		17		17	27.87
Wool sorters	2			2	3.28
All others	3		7	10	16.39
Total	29	21	11	61	100.00
PENNSYLVANIA.					
Burlers		129		129	5.75
Carders	10			10	.45
Dressers	8		10	18	.80
Dyers	49			49	2.18
Engineers	3			3	.13
Finishers	31			31	1.38
Firemen	2			2	.09
Giggers	20			20	.89
Laborers	61			61	2.72
Loom fixers	19			19	.85
Machinists	4			4	.18
Overseers	17			17	.76
Pickers	50			50	2.23
Scourer	1			1	.05
Shearers	10			10	.45
Spinners, mule	35			35	1.56

VARIATION IN THE RATES OF WAGES.

SUMMARY OF EMPLOYÉS, WITH PER CENT.—Continued.

WOOLEN GOODS—Concluded.

NOTE.—This table is not a complete exhibit for industries or states, but covers only establishments investigated by the Bureau. See detail table, Appendix A, page 295, whence derived.

States and occupations.	Number of employés.				Per cent. of number of employés in each occupation of the whole number considered in the industry in the state.
	Adult male.	Adult female.	Children and youth.	Total.	
PENNSYLVANIA—concluded.					
Spoolers	28	27		55	2.45
Teamster	1			1	.04
Twisters	25	2		27	1.20
Weavers	736	150		886	35.02
Wool sorters	27	13		40	1.78
All others	509	73	194	776	34.58
Total	1,646	394	204	2,244	100.00
VERMONT.					
Burlers			173	173	21.15
Carders	14		3	17	2.08
Dressers	4			4	.49
Driers	4			4	.49
Dyers	24			24	2.93
Firemen	2			2	.25
Fullers	16			16	1.96
Giggers	22			22	2.68
Laborers	1		1	2	.25
Loom fixers	8			8	.98
Machinists	6			6	.73
Overseers	23			23	2.81
Pickers	13		1	14	1.71
Pressers	5		15	20	2.45
Scourers	8			8	.98
Second hands	17			17	2.07
Spinners, mule	44			44	5.38
Spoolers			12	12	1.47
Teamsters	4			4	.49
Weavers	43	100		143	17.48
All others	134	30	91	255	31.17
Total	392	130	296	818	100.00

SUMMARY OF ALL EMPLOYÉS, WITH WAGES AND TIME, BY STATES.

NOTE.—This table is *not* a complete exhibit for industries or states, but covers only establishments investigated by the Bureau. See detail table, Appendix A, page 295, whence derived.

Industries and states.	Number of establishments.	Number of employés.				Average rates of daily wages.			Average running time.		Days the past year.
		Adult male.	Adult fem.	Children and youth.	Total.	Adult male.	Adult fem.	Children and youth.	Daily. Hours.	Minutes.	
AGRICULTURAL IMPLEMENTS.											
Maine....................	1	46	......	......	46	$1 76	......	......	9	......	300
New York	1	64	......	......	64	1 83	......	......	10	......	300
Pennsylvania	1	81	......	......	81	1 69	......	......	10	......	300
Kentucky................	1	46	......	......	46	1 81	......	......	10	......	275
Ohio	11	2,693	......	2	2,695	1 81	......	$0 80	10	......	261
Indiana	2	583	......	50	633	1 65	......	68	10	......	250
Illinois	3	2,330	......	32	2,362	1 99	......	68	10	......	270
ARMS AND AMMUNITION.											
Massachusetts	1	437	......	......	437	2 02	......	......	10	......	302
ARTISANS' TOOLS.											
Indiana	1	91	......	8	99	1 59	......	1 12	10	......	260
BOOTS AND SHOES.											
Massachusetts	19	1,574	560	81	2,215	2 00	$1 34	80	9	51	268
New York.............	14	1,538	1,150	195	2,883	1 98	1 25	74	10	......	300
New Jersey...........	1	175	60	25	260	2 40	1 66	58	10	......	300
Pennsylvania	2	601	212	100	913	1 96	1 33	68	10	......	245
Maryland	4	182	130	49	361	1 70	89	76	10	......	261
Kentucky................	1	33	30	......	63	2 39	1 00	......	10	......	235
Ohio	4	381	325	67	773	2 35	1 24	86	10	......	300
Illinois	1	122	60	......	182	2 40	1 50	......	10	......	275
California	2	294	40	......	334	1 81	1 47	......	10	......	270
BOXES.											
New York	1	57	......	......	57	2 40	......	......	10	......	300
Virginia	2	55	287	31	373	2 12	65	64	10	......	295
BRICK.											
New Hampshire	1	63	......	......	63	1 56	......	......			....
New Jersey	2	200	......	......	200	1 57	......	......			....
Delaware................	1	73	......	8	81	1 42	......	50			....
Missouri	1	125	......	......	125	1 39	......	......			..
BROOMS.											
New York	5	359	......	......	359	1 47	......	......	10	......	273
CARPETINGS.											
Massachusetts	4	556	769	242	1,567	1 31	1 14	65	10	......	300
Connecticut.............	1	10	58	20	88	1 75	1 51	65	10	......	300
New York.............	3	4,110	3,314	1,332	8,756	1 54	1 23	61	10	20	233
Pennsylvania	2	1,537	263	80	1,880	1 47	81	75	10	......	250
Great Britain............	2	225	61	112	398	1 20	62	40	10	......	....
CARRIAGES AND WAGONS.											
Connecticut..............	4	407	......	......	407	2 28	......	......	10	......	304
New Jersey	1	52	......	......	52	2 03	......	......	10	......	300
Pennsylvania	1	18	......	4	22	1 69	......	83	10	......	250

VARIATION IN THE RATES OF WAGES. 221

SUMMARY OF ALL EMPLOYÉS, WITH WAGES AND TIME, BY STATES—Continued.

NOTE.—This table is not a complete exhibit for industries or states, but covers only establishments investigated by the Bureau. See detail table, Appendix A, page 295, whence derived.

Industries and states.	Number of establishments.	Number of employés.				Average rates of daily wages.			Average running time.		
		Adult male.	Adult fem.	Children and youth.	Total.	Adult male.	Adult fem.	Children and youth.	Daily. Hours.	Minutes.	Days the past year.
CARRIAGES AND WAGONS—concluded.											
Ohio	2	578	45	......	623	$1 70	$1 15	......	10	......	300
Illinois	4	349	......	23	372	2 03	......	$0 76	10	......	302
CLOCKS AND WATCHES.											
Ohio	1	69	40	......	109	2 29	1 00	......	10	......	275
Illinois	1	712	355	......	1,067	1 98	1 67	......	10	......	....
CLOTHING.											
New York	15	401	1,001	334	1,736	1 50	90	62	11	......	299
New Jersey	2	327	96	15	438	2 16	1 08	84	10	......	300
Pennsylvania	3	530	175	147	852	1 60	88	43	10	......	303
Virginia	1	31	27	55	113	1 68	75	52	10	......	300
COAL, COKE, AND ORE.											
Pennsylvania	4	3,565	......	......	3,565	1 72	......	......	9	......	236
Maryland	3	927	......	8	935	1 61	......	70	11	......	227
Virginia	3	407	......	11	418	1 17	......	69	10	......	300
West Virginia	9	936	......	23	959	1 64	......	50	10	......	224
Ohio	11	1,362	......	33	1,395	1 73	......	66	9	42	204
Indiana	2	1,639	......	......	1,639	1 49	......	......	10	......	222
Missouri	2	299	......	35	334	1 68	......	75	10	......	....
Great Britain	2	516	......	154	670	1 02	......	52	9	30	....
COOKING AND HEATING APPARATUS.											
New York	5	2,030	......	510	2,540	2 46	......	74	10	......	300
Pennsylvania	1	78	......	......	78	3 03	......	......	10	......	....
West Virginia	1	51	......	12	63	1 97	......	1 25	10	......	256
Kentucky	1	56	......	......	56	2 14	......	......	10	......	250
Ohio	6	777	......	79	856	2 21	......	83	10	......	271
Illinois	9	522	......	77	599	2 41	......	81	10	......	272
Michigan	2	1,222	......	729	1,951	1 94	......	67	10	......	259
COTTON COMPRESSING.											
Arkansas	1	26	......	......	26	1 70	......	......	10	......	....
COTTON GOODS.											
Maine	3	1,486	1,086	767	3,339	1 23	98	51	11	......	308
New Hampshire	3	622	2,365	618	3,605	1 38	91	69	10	45	309
Vermont	1	129	72	78	279	1 15	84	50	11	......	230
Massachusetts	12	2,000	4,071	977	7,048	1 37	85	53	10	......	301
Connecticut	1	100	153	55	308	1 35	90	43	11	......	303
New York	7	1,615	2,177	2,880	6,672	1 23	86	41	11	4	298
New Jersey	1	36	158	50	244	1 44	84	60	10	......	300
Pennsylvania	1	144	202	51	397	1 27	1 00	64	10	......	302
Delaware	2	81	158	91	330	1 19	82	51	10	......	300
Maryland	4	232	650	236	1,118	1 32	79	45	11	......	302
Virginia	4	124	266	207	597	1 24	75	47	11	......	297
North Carolina	6	275	371	326	972	96	71	44	11	30	279
South Carolina	1	168	124	......	292	96	74	......	11	......	306
Georgia	2	199	203	260	662	1 02	75	43	11	30	310
France	2	76	160	18	254	69	54	32	11	30	300
Germany	1	896	1,144	370	2,410	60	40	32	12	......	303
Great Britain	5	463	431	261	1,155	1 17	73	45	10	......	300
Italy	1	354	476	217	1,047	46	25	17	12	......	372

SUMMARY OF ALL EMPLOYÉS, WITH WAGES AND TIME, BY STATES—Continued.

NOTE.—This table is not a complete exhibit for industries or states, but covers only establishments investigated by the Bureau. See detail table, Appendix A, page 295, whence derived.

Industries and states.	Number of establishments.	Number of employés.				Average rates of daily wages.			Average running time.		
		Adult male.	Adult fem.	Children and youth.	Total.	Adult male.	Adult fem.	Children and youth.	Daily.		Days the past year.
									Hours.	Minutes.	
ENGRAVING AND PRINTING.											
New Jersey	1	77	......	......	77	$3 36	......	......	11	......	308
FOOD PREPARATIONS.											
New Hampshire	1	9	......	......	9	2 27	......	......	12	......	275
West Virginia	1	6	......	......	6	2 03	......	......	11	......	300
Ohio	6	197	......	......	197	1 43	......	......	11	50	253
Indiana	2	559	......	92	651	1 72	......	$0 75	11	......	300
Illinois	10	201	......	......	201	1 92	......	......	12	......	266
Minnesota	1	343	......	......	343	2 07	......	......	12	......	313
Missouri	4	120	......	......	120	1 92	......	......	12	......	300
California	3	108	......	2	110	2 47	......	1 75	11	......	258
FURNITURE.											
Kentucky	1	117	......	......	117	1 51	......	......	9	......	253
Indiana	3	508	......	58	566	1 50	......	58	10	......	288
Michigan	4	707	......	69	776	1 66	......	58	10	......	291
GLASS.											
New Jersey	4	489	......	308	797	3 36	......	57	8	22	255
Pennsylvania	15	1,500	27	691	2,218	2 79	$1 85	64	9	9	263
West Virginia	1	48	......	38	86	3 04	......	59	10	......	258
Kentucky	1	50	......	19	69	2 38	......	51			
Ohio	6	365	......	209	574	3 10	......	58	10	......	204
Illinois	1	42	......	......	42	a5 29	......	......	10	......	240
California	1	86	......	62	148	2 82	......	77	10	......	230
JUTE GOODS.											
New York	1	119	177	106	402	1 49	79	57	10	......	302
New Jersey	1	20	62	45	127	1 37	85	59	10	......	300
California	1	22	62	62	146	2 04	1 00	59	10	30	300
LEATHER.											
Massachusetts	1	125	......	......	125	1 56	......	......	10	......	308
Pennsylvania	4	255	14	1	270	2 14	1 57	67	10	30	295
Delaware	3	337	14	49	400	1 81	1 13	65	10	......	288
California	4	152	......	2	154	2 06	......	1 83	10	......	300
LINEN.											
Belgium	1	256	560	......	816	52	40	......	12	30	....
Great Britain	1	130	599	......	729	73	37	......	10	......	302
LIQUORS AND BEVERAGES.											
Pennsylvania	1	102	......	......	102	1 60	......	......	10	......	300
Ohio	4	165	......	......	165	2 11	......	......	12	......	300
Illinois	6	226	......	......	226	2 12	......	......	11	40	302
LUMBER.											
Maine	1	95	......	......	95	1 82	......	......	10	30	....
West Virginia	2	35	......	......	35	1 22	......	......	10	......	300
Arkansas	1	29	......	......	29	1 78	......	......	10	......	291

a This average is for blowers, cutters, flatteners, and gatherers of a single establishment, other occupations not being reported.

VARIATION IN THE RATES OF WAGES.

SUMMARY OF ALL EMPLOYÉS, WITH WAGES AND TIME, BY STATES—Continued.

NOTE.—This table is *not* a complete exhibit for industries or states, but covers only establishments investigated by the Bureau. See detail table, Appendix A, page 295, whence derived.

Industries and states.	Number of establishments	Number of employés.				Average rates of daily wages.			Average running time.		
		Adult male.	Adult fem.	Children and youth.	Total.	Adult male.	Adult fem.	Children and youth.	Daily.		Days the past year.
									Hours.	Minutes.	
LUMBER—concluded.											
Illinois	2	591			591	$1 54			11		220
Michigan	1	84			84	1 69			11		175
MACHINES AND MACHINERY.											
Maine	1	53		5	58	2 01		$0 85	10		
Massachusetts	2	331			331	1 95			10		308
New Jersey	1	157			157	2 17			10		300
Pennsylvania	1	381		90	471	1 71		57	10		300
Kentucky	1	114		6	120	1 82		87	10		
Indiana	5	733		19	752	2 18		61	10		300
Illinois	1	97		20	117	1 76		73	10		285
California	3	491		63	554	2 61		84	10		300
METALS AND METALLIC GOODS.											
New Hampshire	1	187			187	1 49			10		
Vermont	1	237			237	1 86			10		300
Massachusetts	1	90			90	2 00					
New York	6	3,781		255	4,036	1 74		87	11		327
New Jersey	1	111			111	1 83			9		300
Pennsylvania	12	a5,303		13	5,316	1 86		69	10	10	267
Delaware	1	60			60	1 83			10		288
Maryland	3	234			234	1 24			12		301
Virginia	6	1,477		42	1,519	1 60		36	10	40	303
West Virginia	1	333		25	358	2 29		54	10		
Alabama	1	98			98	1 20			12		
Kentucky	3	585		37	622	2 19		64	10		221
Tennessee	1	27			27	1 37			12		350
Ohio	19	5,069		262	5,331	b1 75		72	11	9	284
Indiana	2	382			382	2 02			10		234
Illinois	2	590		102	692	2 56		69	10		251
Missouri	2	1,029			1,029	1 27			8		
California	3	433			433	2 52			10		290
Belgium	5	702	33	119	854	66	$0 33	32	11	6	
Great Britain	8	1,120	10	24	1,154	1 34	63	48	11		
MUSICAL INSTRUMENTS AND MATERIALS.											
Maine	1	40			40	1 53			10		308
New Hampshire	1	24			24	1 95			10		250
New York	5	1,738	18	159	1,915	2 12	1 50	69	10		300
OILS AND ILLUMINATING FLUIDS.											
New York	1	115			115	1 36			10		304
Pennsylvania	2	78			78	1 82			10		307
PAPER.											
Maine	2	93	32	11	136	1 68	87	70	12		
New Hampshire	1	174	36		210	1 62	1 00		12		
Vermont	1	177	25		202	1 68	75		12		

a Not including 2 shinglers and 11 rollers, whose wages as reported were inseparably combined with the wages of their helpers.

b In computing this average there were excluded 1 gutterman, 1 galvanizer, 4 heaters, 17 knobblers, 1 plate piler, and 1 plate roller, whose wages were inseparably combined with the wages of their helpers; also 7 heaters, 8 rollers, and 50 drag-outs and straighteners, whose wages were inexactly reported.

SUMMARY OF ALL EMPLOYÉS, WITH WAGES AND TIME, BY STATES—Continued.

NOTE.—This table is not a complete exhibit for industries or states, but covers only establishments investigated by the Bureau. See detail table, Appendix A, page 295, whence derived.

Industries and states.	Number of establishments.	Number of employés.				Average rates of daily wages.			Average running time.		
		Adult male.	Adult fem.	Children and youth.	Total.	Adult male.	Adult fem.	Children and youth.	Daily.		Days the past year.
									Hours.	Minutes.	
PAPER—concluded.											
Massachusetts	7	568	359	8	935	$1 57	$0 97	$0 73	11	26	300
Delaware	3	148	33	8	189	1 84	92	69	12		297
Oregon	1	25	15	5	45	2 05	1 25	87	12		
California	1	35			35	1 58			12		286
PRINT WORKS.											
New Hampshire	1	301	59	97	457	1 65	93	72	10		300
Massachusetts	2	480	26	224	730	1 78	95	74	10		
New York	1	14	26	3	43	1 66	83	87	11		300
New Jersey	1	205			205	1 32			10		300
Pennsylvania	1	346	65	346	757	1 66	90	57	10		
RAILROAD CONSTRUCTION.											
Vermont	1	105			105	1 57			10		
Virginia	1	288		14	302	1 77		70	10		300
North Carolina	2	129		17	146	1 57		53	10		300
Tennessee	1	37			37	1 60			10		
RUBBER.											
Massachusetts	1	625	600		1,225	1 85	1 16		10		300
New Jersey	3	544	344	118	1,006	1 52	1 00	1 04	10		295
SILK.											
Connecticut	1	19	80		99	1 78	99		10		300
New York	3	87	232	47	366	1 76	87	70	10	40	272
New Jersey	2	313	826	60	1,199	2 44	1 46	1 00	10		276
STONE.											
Maine	1	194			194	2 18			10		
TOBACCO.											
Rhode Island	1	10	4	2	22	2 07	1 00	1 25	10		300
Connecticut	1	17	4		21	2 30	79		10		300
New York	1	39	159	28	226	2 02	97	67	10		304
New Jersey	2	43	50	10	103	1 69	90	66	9	10	300
Virginia	7	802	741	1,228	2,771	1 11	60	53	10		300
West Virginia	1	49	2	10	61	1 52	60	50	10		300
North Carolina	3	294	127	217	638	1 02	60	39	10	30	294
Kentucky	2	59	26	50	135	1 43	1 13	79	10		305
Ohio	7	548	401	184	1,133	1 57	1 20	45	9	30	293
Illinois	8	240	148	178	566	1 75	1 17	49	9	45	289
Michigan	1	65	4	89	158	1 42	1 00	72	10		300
Missouri	2	842	85	30	957	1 28	93	1 00	10		
VESSELS.											
Maine	3	301			301	1 73			10		..
Delaware	2	2,275		62	2,337	1 77		70	10		300
WOODEN GOODS.											
Virginia	1	122		81	203	1 84		74	10		30

SUMMARY OF ALL EMPLOYÉS, WITH WAGES AND TIME, BY STATES—Concluded.

NOTE.—This table is not a complete exhibit for industries or states, but covers only establishments investigated by the Bureau. See detail table, Appendix A, page 295, whence derived.

Industries and states.	Number of establishments.	Number of employés.				Average rates of daily wages.			Average running time.		
		Adult male.	Adult fem.	Children and youth.	Total.	Adult male.	Adult fem.	Children and youth.	Daily.		Days the past year.
									Hours.	Minutes.	
WOODEN GOODS—concluded.											
Indiana	1	58	......	......	58	$2 13	......	......	10	......	300
California	1	103	......	......	103	2 45	......	......	10	......	275
WOOLLEN GOODS.											
Maine	4	226	33	14	273	1 42	$0 96	$0 71	11	......	....
New Hampshire	1	241	123	......	364	1 61	1 15	......	11	......	305
Vermont	1	392	130	296	818	1 31	1 11	50	11	......	270
Massachusetts	8	774	544	177	1,495	1 35	1 03	69	10	......	304
Connecticut	2	109	87	17	213	1 46	96	54	11	15	287
New York	3	491	269	343	1,103	1 38	94	61	10	40	291
New Jersey	1	209	73	44	326	1 21	83	50	10	......	300
Pennsylvania	4	1,646	394	204	2,244	1 65	1 10	70	10	......	278
Delaware	2	166	43	89	298	1 85	1 27	61	10	......	304
Maryland	1	93	101	56	250	1 47	93	50	11	......	302
North Carolina	1	29	21	11	61	1 07	70	43	11	30	300
Kentucky	2	72	300	112	484	1 60	79	60	11	......	310
Indiana	4	207	197	173	577	1 42	97	62	10	45	275
Illinois	1	60	19	16	95	1 85	80	52	10	30	300
Iowa	1	21	21	9	51	1 81	1 07	67	10	......	....
Missouri	1	97	24	......	121	1 53	1 69	......	10	......	200
California	1	100	......	3	103	1 45	......	75	10	......	300
Great Britain	1	181	224	105	510	88	48	43	10	......	....
MISCELLANEOUS.											
Maine	1	107	......	......	107	1 77	......	......	12	......	....
New Hampshire	1	10	......	19	29	1 29	......	83	10	......	....
Massachusetts	1	37	250	......	287	2 17	80	......	10	......	300
New Jersey	4	540	106	157	803	2 00	84	1 07	9	55	297
Great Britain	1	30	6	......	36	1 54	55	......	10	......	....

12854 LAB——15

SUMMARY OF ALL EMPLOYÉS, WITH WAGES AND TIME, BY INDUSTRIES.

NOTE.—This table is not a complete exhibit for industries or states, but covers only establishment investigated by the Bureau. See detail table, Appendix A, page 295, whence derived.

Industries.	Number of establishments.	Number of employés.				Average rates of daily wages.			Average running time.		Days the past year.
		Adult male.	Adult fem.	Children and youth.	Total.	Adult male.	Adult fem.	Children and youth.	Daily. Hours.	Minutes.	
Agricultural implements	20	5,843		84	5,927	$1 86		$0 09	9	57	271
Arms and ammunition	1	437			437	2 02			10		302
Artisans' tools	1	91		8	99	1 50		1 12	10		260
Boots and shoes	48	4,900	2,567	517	7,984	2 05	$1 24	75	9	56	278
Boxes	9	112	287	31	430	2 26		64	10		297
Brick	5	461		8	469	1 49		50			
Brooms	5	359			359	1 47			10		273
Carpetings (United States)	10	6,213	4,404	1,674	12,291	1 51	1 19	62	10	6	258
Carpetings (Great Britain)	2	225	61	112	398	1 20	62	40	10		
Carriages and wagons	12	1,404	45	27	1,476	1 93	1 15	77	10		298
Clocks and watches	2	781	395		1,176	2 00	1 60		10		275
Clothing	21	1,289	1,299	551	3,139	1 72	91	58	10	9	209
Coal, coke, and ore (United States)	34	9,135		110	9,245	1 64		66	9		229
Coal, coke, and ore (Great Britain)	2	516		154	670	1 02		52	9	30	....
Cooking and heating apparatus	25	4,736		1,407	6,143	2 28		72	10		269
Cotton compressing	1	26			26	1 70			10		
Cotton goods (United States)	48	7,211	12,056	6,596	25,863	1 26	87	48	10	58	297
Cotton goods (France)	2	76	160	18	254	69	54	32	11		300
Cotton goods (Germany)	1	896	1,144	376	2,416	60	46	32	12		303
Cotton goods (Great Britain)	5	463	431	261	1,155	1 17	73	45	10		300
Cotton goods (Italy)	1	354	476	217	1,047	48	25	17	12		292
Engraving and printing	1	77			77	3 36			11		308
Food preparations	28	1,543		94	1,637	1 86		77	11	45	258
Furniture	8	1,332		127	1,459	1 59		57	9	53	285
Glass	29	2,580	27	1,327	3,934	2 98	1 85	62	9	42	249
Jute goods	3	161	301	213	675	1 55	85	58	10	10	301
Leather	12	869	28	52	949	1 92	1 35	70	10	10	269
Linen (Belgium)	1	256	560		816	52	40		12	30	
Linen (Great Britain)	1	130	549		729	73	36		10		302
Liquors and beverages	11	493			493	2 01			11	38	301
Lumber	7	834			834	1 58			10	30	241
Machines and machinery	15	2,357		203	2,560	2 12		69	10		300
Metals and metallic goods (United States)	65	20,026		736	20,762	1 80		74	10	42	270
Metals and metallic goods (Belgium)	5	702	33	119	854	66	33	33	11	6	....
Metals and metallic goods (Great Britain)	8	1,120	10	24	1,154	1 35	63	48	11		
Musical instruments and materials	7	1,802	18	159	1,979	2 22	1 50	69	10		294
Oils and illuminating fluids	3	193			193	1 55			10		306
Paper	16	1,220	500	32	1,752	1 04	96	73	11	45	299
Print works	6	1,355	176	670	2,201	1 66	91	66	10	10	300
Railroad construction	5	559		31	590	1 68		61	10		300
Rubber	4	1,169	944	118	2,231	1 70	1 10	1 04	10		296
Silk	6	419	1,138	107	1,664	2 27	1 31	87	10	20	278
Stone	1	194			194	2 18			10		
Tobacco	30	3,005	1,751	2,035	6,791	1 33	85	53	9	50	296
Vessels	5	2,576		62	2,638	1 77		70	10		300
Wooden goods	3	283		81	364	1 90		74	10		292
Woollen goods (United States)	38	4,933	2,379	1,564	8,876	1 49	1 00	62	10	40	289
Woollen goods (Great Britain)	1	181	224	105	510	88	48	43	10		....
Miscellaneous (United States)	7	604	356	176	1,226	1 96	81	1 04	10	9	263
Miscellaneous (Great Britain)	1	30	6		36	1 54	55		10		
Totals	582	96,621	32,375	20,186	149,182						

As with facts relative to cost of production in foreign countries, so it has been in some degree with rates of wages in such countries. They were not obtained on a basis which enabled the Bureau to classify them in the preceding summaries; yet these rates, being obtained from the best possible sources and being authoritative, are of great value to employers and employés, and are therefore presented in the form in which they were secured, together with such explanatory matter as seems of value.

The system of payment for counts of yarn spun in Oldham is an equitable one, the prices being fixed in accordance with the circumstances of individual firms, and not on an inflexible scale. When an order is received at a mill for yarn which can be satisfactorily produced from an inferior grade of cotton, the manager puts it in, reduces speed, and pays the spinners a small increase in price. But should a manufacturer improve his machinery, or by the use of superior talent keep the machinery in first-class order, or by the use of superior grades of cotton be enabled to increase the speed of his mill without too severely taxing the spinners and piecers, he is granted a reduction. By this equitable system of payment employers are stimulated to constantly improve their machinery and keep it in good condition, and reap their rewards in increased production and diminished cost, thus gaining an important point over competitors in other localities who are hampered by a fixed scale of prices, and who consequently possess but little or no inducements to make improvements, as they would have to pay the same fixed price for their yarn as some neighboring mill using old-fashioned machinery.

Workmen in cotton-spinning mills were formerly paid by the length of yarn spun; but this method has been superseded by the weight system, as the length system was open to serious abuses owing to the manner in which the lengths of yarn were registered. It is now in turn alleged by the operative spinners that the weight system is sometimes unscrupulously abused by managers, and mills using the system are compelled to pay 5 per cent. additional to the computed weight to their operatives. A spinner spinning, say number 32, although averaging full on his counts, not infrequently drops to 31 or goes up to 33, which by the weight system makes a difference of from 75 cents to $1 per week in his wages. The number of turns per inch in the yarn and the weight of the doffing skips are also grounds for difference of opinion between operatives and employers, and not infrequently terminate in local strikes.

The Oldham method of payment for yarn spun gives general satisfaction to all concerned, and operatives in the Oldham district are in no way affected by the objectionable points in the weight system, for without regard to thickness or hardness the Oldham operatives are paid by length, which is registered by an indicator attached to the machines and with which it is not possible to tamper.

The places comprised in the Oldham district to which the Oldham list of wages applies are Chadderton, Hollinwood, Littleborough, Lees, Middleton, Oldham, Royton, Shaw, and Crompton and Waterhead, the whole containing in July, 1885, almost as many spindles as there are in United States. The standard list of wages and conditions was established in January, 1876, it being at that time agreed to by both employers and employed. This list only applies to the wages of operative spinners, but as that body has a powerful and complete organization of over five thousand members, other classes of hands are generally guided by its decisions. The trade depression of 1877-78-79 caused reductions to be made from this list amounting in all to 20 per cent. Improved trade in 1880 and 1881 restored 10 of this 20 per cent.[a] No change has been made in the list since 1881, so that wages stand at this time (July, 1885), at 10 per cent. less than the standard list.

October 22, 1877, a reduction of 5 per cent. was made from the list; and May 27, 1878, a further reduction to the same extent. Two other reductions, each of 5 per cent., the one November 29, 1878, and the other October 29, 1879, were also made.

On the other hand, two advances, each of 5 per cent., were made, the first February 9, 1880, and the second on the last making-up day in January, 1881, thus leaving a net reduction, since the list was framed in 1876, of 10 per cent. It does not follow that wages are less now than ten years ago, the workmen having derived some of the advantage of quicker speed in machinery, the maximum rate of speed being even not yet reached.

A mill running three draws in fifty seconds in 1876 is probably running three draws in forty-four seconds in 1885, so that on a pair of 1,200 spindle mules six seconds would mean an addition of $1 per week to a spinner's earnings, the work of the spinner being, however, considerably more arduous under present circumstances than it formerly was.

In the following table is shown the standard list of wages per week of fifty-five hours paid at Oldham, England, to operative spinners on self-acting mules, running three draws in fifty seconds, with 63-inch draw, for any counts, twist, or weft, each spinner having the care of two mules. The amounts shown for two piecers are the amounts for both, and not for each:

---

[a] By this is meant that one-half the loss was restored. Throughout what is said in this connection as to cut-down or advance in wages in the Oldham district, the per cents. must be taken in their familiar meaning and not in a strict arithmetical sense.

SPINNERS' WAGES AT OLDHAM, ENGLAND, 1885.[a]

Spindles to each mule.	Wages.			Percentage.		Spindles to each mule.	Wages.			Percentage.	
	One spinner.	Two piecers.	Total.	One spinner.	Two piecers.		One spinner.	Two piecers.	Total.	One spinner.	Two piecers.
432	$6 12	$2 76	$8 88	68.92	31.08	924	$7 76	$6 48	$14 24	54.40	45.51
444	6 16	2 76	8 92	69.06	30.94	936	7 80	6 48	14 28	54.62	45.38
456	6 20	2 76	8 96	69.20	30.80	948	7 84	6 48	14 32	54.75	45.25
468	6 24	2 76	9 00	69.34	30.66	960	7 88	6 48	14 36	54.87	45.13
480	6 28	2 76	9 04	69.47	30.53	972	7 92	6 48	14 40	55.00	45.00
492	6 32	2 76	9 08	69.60	30.40	984	7 96	6 48	14 44	55.12	44.88
504	6 36	2 76	9 12	69.74	30.26	996	8 00	6 48	14 48	55.25	44.75
516	6 40	2 76	9 16	69.87	30.13	1,008	8 04	6 58	14 62	54.90	45.01
528	6 44	2 76	9 20	70.00	30.00	1,020	8 08	6 72	14 80	54.59	45.41
540	6 48	3 24	9 72	66.67	33.33	1,032	8 12	6 72	14 84	54.72	45.28
552	6 52	3 24	9 76	66.80	33.20	1,044	8 16	6 72	14 88	54.84	45.16
564	6 56	3 24	9 80	66.94	33.06	1,056	8 20	6 72	14 92	54.96	45.04
576	6 60	3 24	9 84	67.07	32.93	1,068	8 24	6 96	15 20	54.21	45.79
588	6 64	3 48	10 12	65.61	34.39	1,080	8 28	6 96	15 24	54.33	45.67
600	6 68	3 48	10 16	65.76	34.24	1,092	8 32	6 96	15 28	54.45	45.55
612	6 72	3 48	10 20	65.88	34.12	1,104	8 36	6 92	15 28	54.71	45.29
624	6 76	3 48	10 24	66.02	33.98	1,116	8 40	7 20	15 60	53.85	46.15
636	6 80	3 84	10 64	63.91	36.09	1,128	8 44	7 20	15 64	53.96	46.04
648	6 84	3 84	10 68	64.05	35.95	1,140	8 48	7 20	15 68	54.08	45.92
660	6 88	3 84	10 72	64.18	35.82	1,152	8 52	7 20	15 72	54.20	45.80
672	6 92	3 84	10 76	64.31	35.69	1,164	8 56	7 92	16 48	51.96	48.06
684	6 96	4 80	11 76	59.18	40.82	1,176	8 60	7 92	16 52	52.06	47.94
696	7 00	4 80	11 80	50.32	40.68	1,188	8 64	7 92	16 56	52.17	47.83
708	7 04	4 80	11 84	59.46	40.54	1,200	8 68	7 92	16 60	52.29	47.71
720	7 08	4 80	11 88	59.60	40.40	1,212	8 72	8 64	17 36	50.23	49.77
732	7 12	5 28	12 40	57.42	42.58	1,224	8 76	8 64	17 40	50.34	49.66
744	7 16	5 28	12 44	57.56	42.44	1,236	8 80	8 64	17 44	50.46	49.54
756	7 20	5 28	12 48	57.69	42.31	1,248	8 84	8 64	17 48	50.57	49.43
768	7 24	5 28	12 52	57.83	42.17	1,260	8 88	8 64	17 52	50.69	49.31
780	7 28	6 00	13 28	54.82	45.18	1,272	8 92	8 64	17 56	50.80	49.20
792	7 32	6 00	13 32	54.96	45.04	1,284	8 96	8 64	17 60	50.91	49.09
804	7 36	6 00	13 36	55.00	44.91	1,296	9 00	8 64	17 64	51.02	48.98
816	7 40	6 00	13 40	55.22	44.78	1,308	9 04	8 76	17 80	50.80	49.20
828	7 44	6 24	13 68	54.39	45.61	1,320	9 08	8 76	17 84	50.90	49.10
840	7 48	6 24	13 72	54.52	45.48	1,332	9 12	8 76	17 88	51.01	49.99
852	7 52	6 24	13 76	54.65	45.35	1,344	9 16	8 76	17 92	51.12	48.88
864	7 56	6 24	13 80	54.78	45.22	1,356	9 20	8 76	17 96	51.23	48.77
876	7 60	6 24	13 84	54.91	45.09	1,368	9 24	8 76	18 00	51.33	48.67
888	7 64	6 24	13 88	55.04	44.96	1,380	9 28	8 76	18 04	51.44	48.56
900	7 68	6 24	13 92	55.18	44.82	1,392	9 32	8 76	18 08	51.55	48.45
912	7 72	6 24	13 96	55.30	44.70						

[a] In spinning pin cops spinners earn 24 cents a week more than these wages.

In cases where self-acting mules are run at a quicker speed than three draws in fifty seconds, with 63-inch draw for any counts of yarn, twist, or weft, one-half of the advantage of the difference arising from quicker speed is added to the total earnings. The amount of this increase may be seen in the table which follows. There would be a proportional increase for other lengths of draw:

INCREASE OF WAGES FOR QUICKER SPEED.

Spindles to each mule.	Wages increased.	Spindles to each mule.	Wages increased.	Spindles to each mule.	Wages increased.	Spindles to each mule.	Wages increased.
432	$0.090	720	$0.120	1,008	$0.145	1,248	$0.175
480	.090	708	.125	1,056	.150	1,296	.175
528	.095	816	.130	1,104	.150	1,344	.180
576	.100	864	.135	1,152	.155	1,392	.180
624	.105	912	.140				
672	.110	960	.145	1,200	.165		

The following clauses of the agreement between the employers, and operatives' associations explain the list and its applications and workings:

"Clause No. 1. The mode of calculating the length of yarn spun by self-acting mules to be as follows:

"From fifty-six and one-half hours shall be deducted, (a) an allowance of one and one-half hours per week for cleaning and accidental stoppages; (b) an allowance for doffing time, as follows: For each pair of mules of less than 720 spindles, five minutes; for each pair of mules of 720 spindles and less than 1,080, six minutes; for each pair of mules of 1,080 spindles and upward, seven minutes; number of doffings reckoned off one mule only; (c) an allowance of $2\frac{1}{2}$ per cent. for breakage.

"Clause No. 2. Mule indicators to be so constructed as to allow $2\frac{1}{2}$ per cent. for breakage.

"Clause No. 3. The above list of total earnings does not apply to firms using a low quality of cotton and waste, requiring more piecers, or to firms using a superior quality of cotton, requiring fewer piecers. In such cases, if any dispute should arise, arrangements must be made with the consent of the two committees.

"Clause No. 4. In case of a dispute arising on account of quick speed, or from bad work, the question shall be referred to the two secretaries, and in event of their failure to agree the dispute shall be referred to the two committees for a decision.

"Clause No. 5. If spinning number 24 and under, 24 cents to be added to the list of total earnings; but in cases of mules running three draws in fifty seconds, slower, 24 cents to be added for counts from numbers 24 to 21, inclusive; 48 cents for number 20 and all counts below.

"Clause No. 6. The above list of total earnings does not apply to double-decked mules, to odd mules, or to hand mules."

The conditions regulating extra work are as follows:

(1) If no bobbin-carrier is employed, 3 cents per 100 pounds of yarn weighed in to be added to the list; but if a hoist is in use and no bobbin-carrier employed, 2 cents per 100 pounds to be allowed.

(2) If minder is employed on double-decked mules, 36 cents per week to be added to total earnings.

(3) If minder is spinning from double rovings, 24 cents per week to be added to the list; this to apply where the mules are adapted with tin guides for double rovings, though not always working double rovings.

(4) Breaking out rovings or turning strings: (a) For mules up to 432 spindles, inclusive, 24 cents per pair of mules to be allowed; (b) for mules upward of 432 spindles, 1 cent per 12 spindles per pair to be added; (c) for breaking out double rovings, double the above rates to be paid.

(5) Tubing to be left for individual arrangement.

(6) For resetting or leveling up mules, minder, if he is required and in attendance, to be paid at the following rate: (a) For mules up to 672

VARIATION IN THE RATES OF WAGES. 231

spindles, inclusive, 10 cents per hour; (b) for mules from 684 to 912 spindles, inclusive, 11 cents per hour; (c) all larger mules, 12 cents per hour.

Piecers, if required and in attendance, to be paid their usual wages by the employer, an equivalent for the yarn spun on one mule while the other is being reset."

The following exhibit shows the manner in which the calculations from the list and conditions are made. Let us take the example of a pair of mules spinning number 32 twist, 3 draws in 48 seconds, 63-inch stretch, 2,000 spindles:

One week of factory time, in hours	56¼
Less for accidents, etc., in hours	1¼
Making spinning time, in hours	55
Which equals, in minutes	3,300
Deduct for doffing nine times off each mule, at six minutes each, minutes	54
Deduct for breakage 2½ per cent., which equals, in minutes	81
Total deduction, in minutes	135
Leaving, in minutes	3,165
Which equals, in seconds	189,900

$$\frac{189{,}900 \text{ seconds} \times 63 \text{ inches stretch} \times 3 \text{ draws} \times 2{,}000 \text{ spindles}}{840 \text{ yards} \times 36 \text{ inches} \times 48 \text{ seconds}} = 49{,}453 \text{ hanks.}$$

The list price is	$14.50000
Add for two seconds extra speed	.29000
Making the wages for 49,453 hanks	14.79000
Or for 1,000 hanks	.29910
Deduct 10 per cent., which is	.02991
Leaving as net wages for 1,000 hanks	.26919

Below is shown the standard prices paid per 1,000 hanks for spinning medium and fine counts of twist, weft, and reeled yarn or bastard twist on self-acting mules in Bolton, England, and neighborhood. The Bolton district to which these prices apply comprises Atherton, Bolton, Chorley, Reddish, and Tyldesley. The list is based on self-acting mules of 420 spindles, subject to a reduction of one-half of 1 per cent. for each additional 12 spindles. But from the whole list of prices there is now (July, 1885), a reduction of 5 per cent.

COST OF SPINNING TWIST IN THE BOLTEN DISTRICT, ENGLAND.

Numbers.	Wages for 1,000 hanks.	Numbers.	Wages for 1,000 hanks.	Numbers.	Wages for 1,000 hanks.	Numbers.	Wages for 1,000 hanks.
32	$0.3364	55 and 56	$0.4452	77 and 78	$0.5256	99 and 100	$0.5944
33 and 34	.3468	57 and 58	.4532	79 and 80	.5322	101 and 102	.6010
35 and 36	.3570	59 and 60	.4610	81 and 82	.5388	103 and 104	.6066
37 and 38	.3660	61 and 62	.4684	83 and 84	.5454	105 and 106	.6126
39 and 40	.3764	63 and 64	.4770	85 and 86	.5518	107 and 108	.6182
41 and 42	.3856	65 and 66	.4834	87 and 88	.5508	109 and 110	.6240
43 and 44	.3940	67 and 68	.4906	89 and 90	.5646	111 and 112	.6296
45 and 46	.4034	69 and 70	.4978	91 and 92	.5708	113 and 114	.6354
47 and 48	.4142	71 and 72	.5048	93 and 94	.5770	115 and 116	.6408
49 and 50	.4208	73 and 74	.5118	95 and 96	.5830	117 and 118	.6070
51 and 52	.4286	75 and 76	.5186	97 and 98	.5890	119 and 120	.6518
53 and 54	.4372						

COST OF SPINNING WEFT IN THE BOLTON DISTRICT, ENGLAND.

Numbers.	Wages for 1,000 hanks.	Numbers.	Wages for 1,000 hanks.	Numbers.	Wages for 1,000 hanks.	Numbers.	Wages for 1,000 hanks.
36	$0.3150	57 and 58	$0.4000	79 and 80	$0.4698	101 and 102	$0.5300
37 and 38	.3296	59 and 60	.4066	81 and 82	.4754	103 and 104	.5352
39 and 40	.3212	61 and 62	.4132	83 and 84	.4812	105 and 106	.5400
41 and 42	.3402	63 and 64	.4200	85 and 86	.4868	107 and 108	.5454
43 and 44	.3408	65 and 66	.4208	87 and 88	.4924	109 and 110	.5500
45 and 46	.3416	67 and 68	.4328	89 and 90	.4980	111 and 112	.5550
47 and 48	.3636	69 and 70	.4392	91 and 92	.5036	113 and 114	.5604
49 and 50	.3712	71 and 72	.4454	93 and 94	.5090	115 and 116	.5652
51 and 52	.3784	73 and 74	.4516	95 and 96	.5144	117 and 118	.5700
53 and 54	.3852	75 and 76	.4576	97 and 98	.5196	119 and 120	.5752
55 and 56	.3928	77 and 78	.4636	99 and 100	.5252		

COST OF SPINNING REELED YARN OR BASTARD TWIST IN THE BOLTON DISTRICT, ENGLAND.

Numbers.	Wages for 1,000 hanks.	Numbers.	Wages for 1,000 hanks.	Numbers.	Wages for 1,000 hanks.	Numbers.	Wages for 1,000 hanks.
34	$0.3264	55 and 56	$0.4190	77 and 78	$0.4946	99 and 100	$0.5600
35 and 36	.3360	57 and 58	.4266	79 and 80	.5010	101 and 102	.5654
37 and 38	.3450	59 and 60	.4328	81 and 82	.5070	103 and 104	.5708
39 and 40	.3542	61 and 62	.4404	83 and 84	.5132	105 and 106	.5762
41 and 42	.3628	63 and 64	.4480	85 and 86	.5192	107 and 108	.5816
43 and 44	.3712	65 and 66	.4550	87 and 88	.5246	109 and 110	.5870
45 and 46	.3796	67 and 68	.4616	89 and 90	.5312	111 and 112	.5922
47 and 48	.3888	69 and 70	.4684	91 and 92	.5372	113 and 114	.5978
49 and 50	.3960	71 and 72	.4750	93 and 94	.5430	115 and 116	.6030
51 and 52	.4034	73 and 74	.4816	95 and 96	.5486	117 and 118	.6084
53 and 54	.4112	75 and 76	.4880	97 and 98	.5542	119 and 120	.6132

The standard is $0.4208 per 1,000 hanks for number 50 twist, with 25.5 revolutions per spindle per inch of yarn on mules of 420 spindles each, one-half of 1 per cent. being deducted for each additional 12 spindles up to 800. Mules of 1¼-inch gauge spindles and over are considered "twist mules," and discount up to 800 spindles only. All counts below number 32 twist are paid the same price per 1,000 hanks.

The standard revolutions per spindle per inch of yarn for number 50 weft is 25.5, and is calculated in proportion to the price paid for number 50 twist on mules of the same size, one-half of 1 per cent. being deducted for each additional 12 spindles up to 900 only. Mules of 1¼-inch gauge spindles and below are considered "weft mules," and discount up to 900 spindles. All counts below number 36 weft are paid the same price per 1,000 hanks. An additional 5 per cent. is allowed above the list price when spinning "pin-cops wefts" on all mules over 1¼-inch gauge spindles.

The revolutions per spindle per inch of yarn for number 50 bastard twist, and the price for the same, are the medium between twist and weft of the same counts on mules of the same size, one-half of 1 per cent. being deducted for each additional 12 spindles up to 800 twist mules and 900 weft mules. All counts below number 34 bastard twist are paid the same price per 1,000 hanks.

VARIATION IN THE RATES OF WAGES. 233

There is a discount from these lists for every 12 spindles above 420. This is shown in the following table:

DISCOUNT FROM THE BOLTON LISTS.

Spindles.	Discount (per cent.)	Spindles.	Discount (per cent.)	Spindles.	Discount (per cent.)
432	5.0	588	7.0	744	13.5
444	1.0	600	7.5	756	14.0
456	1.5	612	8.0	768	14.5
468	2.0	624	8.5	780	15.0
480	2.5	636	9.0	792	15.5
492	3.0	648	9.5	804	16.0
504	3.5	660	10.0	816	16.5
516	4.0	672	10.5	828	17.0
528	4.5	684	11.0	840	17.5
540	5.0	696	11.5	852	18.0
552	5.5	708	12.0	864	18.5
564	6.0	720	12.5	876	19.0
576	6.5	732	13.0	888	19.5

The standard speed of the spindle for number 50 is 4,700 revolutions per minute, including backing off and putting up. If running below the standard speed for any count, the spinner receives two-thirds difference in price extra for loss entailed. If working above the standard speed, the spinner is paid the same price per 1,000 hanks as if working only standard speed.

The revolutions per spindle per inch of yarn on self-acting mules is shown in the next table, the standard for number 50 twist being 25.5, and for number 50 weft 22.5.

REVOLUTIONS PER SPINDLE PER INCH OF YARN ON SELF-ACTING MULES.

Numbers.	Twist.	Reeled yarn.	Weft.	Numbers.	Twist.	Reeled yarn.	Weft.
30	19.75	18.58	17.42	66	29.29	27.58	25.87
32	20.40	19.20	18.00	68	29.73	27.98	26.23
34	21.02	19.78	18.55	70	30.17	28.39	26.62
36	21.64	20.36	19.09	72	30.60	28.80	27.00
38	22.23	20.92	19.61	74	31.02	29.19	27.37
40	22.81	21.47	20.13	76	31.44	29.59	27.74
42	23.37	22.00	20.62	78	31.85	29.97	28.10
44	23.92	22.51	21.10	80	32.25	30.36	28.47
46	24.45	23.01	21.58	82	32.65	30.73	28.81
48	24.98	23.51	22.04	84	33.05	31.10	29.16
50	25.50	24.00	22.50	86	33.44	31.47	29.50
52	26.00	24.47	22.94	88	33.83	31.83	29.84
54	26.50	24.94	23.38	90	34.21	32.19	30.18
56	26.98	25.39	23.81	92	34.59	32.55	30.52
58	27.46	25.84	24.23	94	34.96	32.90	30.85
60	27.93	26.28	24.54	96	35.33	33.25	31.17
62	28.39	26.72	25.05	98	35.70	33.60	31.50
64	28.85	27.15	25.45	100	36.06	33.94	31.83

When working mules with single and double speeds an additional 5 per cent. is allowed. An additional 5 per cent. is allowed also when spinning on double-decked mules, but they discount for total number of spindles as if single mules. One cent per 1,000 spindles each mule is allowed for large cops. For pin cops one-fourth cent per pound of yarn is paid, weight of tubes being included and weighed in as yarn. The above prices are extra for spinning any count with tubes up to number 100 twist, reeled yarn or weft, 6 cents per doffing being added for every ten hanks of fine numbers above 100. Full-length tubes are paid for at double price. The prices paid for stripping creels on mules containing 500 spindles or less is 72 cents per pair. For mules with over 500 spindles 6 cents is allowed for each additional hundred. The prices on all counts are calculated in proportion to the revolutions per spindle per inch required in the yarn, all counts being paid for according to what they are set. No deductions are made from the foregoing prices for gas, broken bobbins, or for carriage of goods. The proportion of the total prices per 1,000 hanks to piecers is not so large in Bolton as in the Oldham district. In Bolton, as in Oldham, the spinner draws the money for yarn spun and pays his piecers and creeler, side piecers, youth, receiving about $2.25 per week, and little piecers or creelers $2.15 per week, of fifty-six and a half hours.

WAGES PER HOUR IN IRON MOULDING IN GREAT BRITAIN IN 1885.

Locality.	Wages per hour.			Rate for overtime.
	Highest.	Standard.	Lowest.	
Accrington	$0.150	$0.150	$0.150	Actual time to actual time and one-fourth.
Banbury		.124	.106	Actual time to actual time and one-fourth.
Barnsley		.150	.124	Actual time and one-fourth.
Barrow	.168	{ .15 .141 }	.141	Actual time and one-fourth.
Belfast	.168	.111	.124	Actual time and one-fourth.
Bilston	.133	.133	.115	Actual time to actual time and five-eighths.
Birkenhead	.168	.150	.159	Actual time and one-fourth.
Birmingham	.150	.150	.124	Actual time and one-eighth.
Blackburn	.168	.150	.106	Actual time and one-fourth.
Bolton	.168	.150	.141	Actual time and one-fourth.
Bradford		.141	.133	Actual time and one-eighth to actual time and one-fourth.
Bristol	.141	.133	.124	Actual time and one-eighth.
Burnley	.159	.150	.124	Actual time to actual time and one-fourth.
Burton		.141	.133	Actual time to actual time and one-fourth.
Bury	.150	.150	.106	Actual time and one-fourth.
Butterley	.141	.133	.111	Actual time to actual time and one-fourth.
Cardiff	.159	.111	.930	Actual time to actual time and one-fourth.
Carlisle		.133	.970	Actual time to actual time and one-fourth.
Chatham	.159	.146	.133	Actual time to actual time and one-fourth.
Chelsea	.199	.168	.139	Actual time and one-fourth.
Chester	.159	.150	.106	Actual time and one-fourth.
Chesterfield	.150	.133	.120	Actual time and one-fourth.
Cleckheaton	.141	.133	.115	Actual time to actual time and one-fourth.
Cork	.133	.124	.106	Actual time to actual time and one-fourth.
Crewe	.168	.141	.124	Actual time and one-fourth.
Darlington		.133	.128	Actual time and one-fourth.
Dartford	.177	.159	.116	Actual time and one-fourth to actual time and one-half.
Darwen Over		.159		Actual time and one-fourth.
Derby	.150	.141	.133	Actual time to actual time and one-fourth.
Devonport	.194	.159	.106	Actual time and one-fourth.
Dewsbury		.133	.124	Actual time.
Dublin		.150	.124	Actual time and one-fourth.
Dudley	.155	.133	.890	Actual time and one-fourth.
Dumfries		.120		Actual time and one-fourth.
East London	.185	.168	.150	Actual time and one-fourth.
Exeter	.133		.890	Thirteen cents per hour to actual time.
Gainsborough		.133	.124	Actual time and one-fourth.
Gloucester	.133		.115	Actual time and one-fourth to actual time and one-half.
Grantham		.133	.890	Actual time to actual time and one-fourth.
Greenwich		.168	.133	Actual time and one-fourth.
Halifax		.150	.124	Actual time to actual time and one-fourth.

WAGES PER HOUR IN IRON MOULDING IN GREAT BRITAIN IN 1885—Concluded.

Locality.	Wages per hour.			Rate for overtime.
	High-est.	Stand-ard.	Lowest.	
Hanley	$0.141	$0.141	$0.124	Actual time and one-fourth.
Hartlepool	.163		.128	Actual time and one-fourth.
Haslingden	.168	{.150 / .150}	.124	Actual time to actual time and one-fourth.
Heywood	.159	.159	.150	Actual time and one-fourth.
Huddersfield	.150	.141	.115	Actual time and one-fourth.
Hull	.190	.150	.100	Actual time and one-fourth to actual time and one-half.
Hyde	.168	.159	.159	20 cents to 32 cents per hour.
Ipswich		.133	.070	Actual time to actual time and one-fourth.
Lancaster	.150	.141	.133	Actual time to actual time and one-fourth.
Leamington	.133	.133	.106	Actual time to actual time and one-fourth.
Leeds	.141	.133	.106	Actual time to actual time and one-fourth.
Leicester	.150	.141	.120	Actual time.
Leigh	.155	.150		Actual time and one-fourth.
Lincoln	.141		.102	Actual time and one-fourth.
Little Bolton	.168	{.150 / .150}	.141	Actual time and one-fourth.
Liverpool	.177	.150	.133	16 cents to 20 cents per hour.
Llanelly	.141	.124	.800	Actual time and one-fourth.
London	.177	.168	.155	Actual time and one-fourth.
Macclesfield		.150	.106	Actual time to actual time and one-eighth.
Maidstone	.159	.141	.106	Actual time to actual time and one-fourth.
Manchester	.168	.168	.159	Actual time and one-fourth.
Mansfield		.141	.124	Actual time to actual time and one-fourth.
Middlesborough	.140	.133	.133	Actual time and one-fourth.
Newcastle	.177		.070	Actual time and one-fourth.
Newport		.133	.890	Actual time and one-half.
Northampton	.141	.133	.106	Actual time to actual time and one-fourth.
Nottingham	.150	.150	.124	Actual time and one-fourth.
Oldham	.168	{.150 / .150}	.141	Actual time and one-eighth to actual time and one-half.
Portsmouth	.194	.150	.133	Actual time to actual time and one-fourth.
Preston	.168	.150	.141	
Reading	.150	.133	.070	Actual time and one-eighth to actual time and one-fourth.
Retford	.141	.133	.106	Actual time to actual time and one-fourth.
Rochdale		.150	.124	Actual time to actual time and one-fourth.
Rotherham	.150		.106	Actual time and one-fourth.
Salford	.177	.168	.141	Actual time and one-fourth.
St. Helen's	.159	.150	.150	Actual time and one-fourth.
Sheffield	.168	.159	.159	Actual time and one-fourth.
Smithwick	.168	.150	.141	Actual time and one-fourth.
Southampton	.168		.890	Actual time to actual time and one-fourth.
Sowerby Bridge	.168	.150	.890	Actual time and one-fourth.
Stalybridge		.150	.124	Actual time and one-fourth.
Stockport		.150	.124	Actual time and one-fourth.
Stockton	.155	.133	.124	Actual time and one-fourth.
Stourbridge	.159	{.141 / .133}	.106	Actual time and one-fourth.
Sunderland	.185		.133	Actual time and one-fourth.
Swansea	.150		.106	Actual time to actual time and one-eighth.
Swindon	.155		.106	Actual time and one-fourth.
Todmorden		.150	.141	Actual time to actual time and one-fourth.
Trowbridge		.133	.890	Actual time to actual time and one-fourth.
Wakefield	.146	.141	.133	Actual time and one-fourth.
Warrington	.168	.150	.106	Actual time and one-fourth.
Wednesbury	.141	.133	.106	Actual time to actual time and one-fourth.
Widnes	.168	.159	.159	18 cents per hour.
Wigan	.168	.150	.159	18 cents per hour.
Woolwich	.185	.159	.133	Actual time and one-fourth to one-half.
Worcester		.141	.106	Actual time and one-fourth.
Workington	.177	.139	.115	Actual time.
York		.133	.115	Actual time to actual time and one-fourth.

WAGES PER HOUR IN THE MANUFACTURE OF MACHINERY IN BIRMINGHAM, ENGLAND, IN 1885.

Occupations.	Wages per hour (cents).	Occupations.	Wages per hour (cents).
Air-furnace men	12	Foremen, working	18 to 20
Anglesmiths	12 to 16	Grinders and glaziers	12 to 14
Apprentices	4 to 9	Holders-up	9 to 10
Boiler makers	13 to 14	Iron moulders	12 to 16
Borers	13 to 14	Laborers	to 8
Brass finishers	12 to 13	Millwrights	12 to 15
Brass moulders	14 to 15½	Painters	9 to 10
Carpenters	13	Pattern makers	13 to 16
Carters	8 to 9	Planers	10 to 12
Coppersmiths	13 to 15	Platers	14 to 17
Core makers and dressers (men)	11 to 12	Riveters	12 to 13
Core makers and dressers (lads and boys)	4 to 9	Rivet heaters (youth and boys)	4 to 5
Draughtsmen	25 to 57	Shapers	12 to 13
Drillers	9 to 10	Screwers	8 to 9
Engineers	12 to 14	Slotters	10 to 12
Engine fitters	12 to 14	Smiths' strikers	9 to 10
Firemen	9	Steam-hammer men	23 to 25
Fitters	14 to 16	Stokers	8 to 9
		Tinsmiths	12 to 13

DAILY WAGES, ORDINARY, MAXIMUM, AND MINIMUM, IN PARIS, FRANCE.

Occupations.	1844.			1853.			1860.		
	Ord.	Max.	Min.	Ord.	Max.	Min.	Ord.	Max.	Min.
Bakers	$0 77								
Blacksmiths	48			$0 70	$0 80	$0 65	$0 82	$1 06	$0 67
Butchers	58								
Carpenters	77			96			96		
Glaziers					77	68			
Hatters	58			68					
Joiners	58			68	77	63	84	91	68
Locksmiths	68			87	1 06	48	91	1 16	68
Masons				91		87			
Metal workers				96	1 06	58			
Painters				77					
Plumbers				77					
Printers	77			96	1 16	68	1 06	1 35	67
Shoemakers	48			58	06	48			
Stonecutters	77				91	87			
Tailors				58	68	58	87	96	77
Tanners	68				77	68	87	96	67

Occupations.	1871.			1875.			1881.			1882.		
	Ord.	Max.	Min.	Ord.	Max.	Min.	Ord.	Max.	Min.	Ord.	Max.	Min.
Bakers	$1 27	$2 04	$0 46	$1 28	$1 93	$0 65	$1 35	$1 93	$1 16	$1 44	$2 24	$1 22
Blacksmiths	96	1 06	82	97	1 06	77	1 16	1 35	1 08	1 16	1 35	1 06
Brewers	82	96	67	82	96	67	96	1 16	77	96	1 16	77
Butchers				1 16	1 35	06	1 16	1 35	96	1 16	1 35	96
Carpenters	1 16	1 35	1 06	1 16	1 25	1 06	1 51	1 54	1 49	1 74	1 93	1 54
Glaziers	1 06	1 06	96	1 01	1 16	96	1 06	1 09	96	1 06	1 16	1 01
Hatters	1 25	1 74	77	1 25	1 73	77	1 25	1 74	77	1 25	1 74	77
Joiners	96	1 06	87	97	1 06	87	1 35	1 54	1 16	1 35	1 54	1 32
Locksmiths	87	1 16	77	87	1 16	77	1 25	1 35	1 16	1 25	1 35	1 16
Masons	96	1 06	82	97	1 06	87	1 45	1 54	1 35	1 54	1 74	1 35
Metal workers	1 16	1 54	77	1 16	1 35	1 06	1 35	1 74	1 16	1 35	1 74	1 16
Painters	1 16	1 16	96	1 16	1 25	97	1 35	1 45	1 16	1 35	1 46	1 16
Plumbers				1 16	1 25	1 06	1 16	1 35	1 06	1 16	1 35	1 06
Printers	1 16	1 25	1 06	1 16	1 25	1 03	1 25	1 73	1 06	1 25	1 74	1 06
Shoemakers	67	1 16	48	67	1 16	48	68	1 16	48	67	1 16	48
Stonecutters	1 16	1 35	1 06	1 16	1 35	96	1 54	2 51	1 35	2 02	2 32	1 54
Tailors	96	1 54	58	60	78	48	96	1 54	58	96	1 54	58
Tanners	96	1 35	87	96	1 16	77	96	1 16	77	96	1 16	77

VARIATION IN THE RATES OF WAGES.

DAILY WAGES, ORDINARY, MAXIMUM, AND MINIMUM, IN PRINCIPAL CITIES OF FRANCE, NOT INCLUDING PARIS.

Occupations.	1853.			1857.			1871.		
	Ord.	Max.	Min.	Ord.	Max.	Min.	Ord.	Max.	Min.
Bakers	$0 37	$0 45	$0 31	$0 41	$0 51	$0 35	$0 56	$0 68	$0 46
Blacksmiths	37	45	32	42	50	35	54	64	44
Brewers	42	53	35	47	59	39	55	73	46
Butchers	33	40	27	38	46	31	50	61	42
Carpenters	42	51	37	49	60	43	64	77	55
Glaziers	40	48	32	43	53	36	56	67	50
Hatters	41	53	33	46	59	38	58	75	46
Joiners	39	47	33	44	55	38	55	69	46
Locksmiths	42	51	33	47	59	38	58	73	46
Masons	40	48	34	46	55	39	59	70	50
Metal workers	49	62	39	55	72	46	67	86	55
Painters	42						60	72	47
Plumbers	43						60	75	49
Printers	46	59	37	51	67	42	63	80	48
Shoemakers	32	43	25	34	50	29	48	65	38
Stonecutters	46	59	38	53	77	45	67	83	56
Tailors	38	48	30	42	54	34	55	72	42
Tanners	39	47	32	44	54	37	53	66	44

Occupations.	1875.			1881.			1882.		
	Ord.	Max.	Min.	Ord.	Max.	Min.	Ord.	Max.	Min.
Bakers	$0 64	$0 77	$0 52	$0 68	$0 80	$0 56	$0 68	$0 80	$0 56
Blacksmiths	57	71	48	62	76	54	63	77	55
Brewers	62	79	52	66	80	57	66	80	57
Butchers	53	64	46	60	73	50	60	73	51
Carpenters	70	85	58	75	90	64	76	90	64
Glaziers	57	69	48	61	73	52	62	74	53
Hatters	61	82	49	67	84	54	69	84	55
Joiners	61	75	52	67	81	56	68	82	58
Locksmiths	63	79	52	67	83	56	68	84	57
Masons	63	76	53	68	82	58	70	87	60
Metal workers	72	92	60	75	94	63	76	95	65
Painters	65	79	55	69	87	58	70	88	59
Plumbers	64	80	54	68	84	58	68	85	60
Printers	66	89	53	72	91	59	74	91	59
Shoemakers	52	69	41	59	76	48	59	76	48
Stonecutters	71	92	60	74	92	64	76	94	66
Tailors	60	78	48	62	70	50	63	80	51
Tanners	58	74	48	63	77	52	64	78	53

EMPLOYÉS AND AVERAGE FORTNIGHTLY WAGES IN SPINNING

Year.	Foremen.		Spinners.		Tiers, winders cylinder coverers, etc.		Care takers and winders.		Packers, oilers, firemen, watchmen, porters, laborers, etc.		Carding department.	
	No.	Fortnightly wages.	No.	Fortnightly wages.	No.	Fortnightly wages.	No.	Fortnightly wages.	No.	Fortnightly wages.	No.	Fortnightly wages.
1855	3	$3 50	45	$7 47	110	$1 89	34	$2 69	28	$4 08	55	$2 98
1856	4	8 38	50	7 50	124	2 02	36	2 70	30	4 06	60	3 23
1857	4	8 60	50	7 68	123	2 12	35	2 81	32	4 19	64	3 38
1858	4	8 85	49	7 37	114	2 17	34	2 80	30	4 30	61	3 58
1859	4	9 00	49	7 24	111	2 27	35	2 84	29	4 30	54	3 84
1860	4	9 00	49	7 57	114	2 52	39	2 97	30	4 65	60	3 86
1861	4	9 04	49	8 04	118	2 63	40	3 10	30	4 54	61	3 91
1862	4	9 18	40	7 94	118	2 59	42	3 08	27	4 69	64	3 94
1863	5	8 90	49	7 14	113	2 49	45	3 02	25	4 81	60	3 83
1864	6	8 80	45	7 07	117	2 72	52	3 25	25	5 00	69	3 95
1865	7	9 04	49	7 02	119	2 90	53	3 33	26	5 17	60	3 84
1866	9	9 16	41	7 43	125	3 10	52	3 56	20	5 52	61	3 94
1867	9	9 71	40	8 00	130	3 21	52	3 69	28	5 52	60	4 10
1868	9	9 87	41	8 13	120	3 48	54	3 74	32	5 55	63	4 38
1869	9	10 23	40	8 34	116	3 60	60	3 80	37	5 62	66	4 48
1870	9	10 55	36	8 15	107	3 60	53	3 83	61	5 36	67	4 73
1871	9	10 00	28	6 80	80	3 20	52	3 26	55	5 50	60	4 00
1872	9	11 10	30	9 08	84	4 27	55	4 39	66	6 00	70	5 20
1873	9	11 75	30	9 24	81	4 69	58	4 55	60	6 05	70	5 41
1874	10	11 76	32	9 37	85	4 87	57	4 82	60	6 49	70	5 47
1875	10	12 26	35	9 30	94	4 88	56	4 98	60	6 67	65	5 89
1876	10	12 60	35	9 40	83	5 42	60	4 99	64	6 67	70	6 12
1877	12	12 82	37	9 58	88	5 49	65	5 06	60	6 95	80	6 24
1878	13	12 74	40	9 24	101	5 30	66	5 21	63	6 84	85	6 43
1879	12	12 60	42	8 92	106	5 20	69	5 18	61	7 00	87	6 35
1880	12	12 16	43	9 82	106	5 20	70	5 20	65	6 82	89	6 33
1881 *a*	12	12 24	43	8 88	113	4 82	70	5 20	78	6 46	88	6 24
1882	12	12 44	41	8 78	119	4 80	69	5 10	78	6 34	83	6 26
1883	11	12 07	41	8 74	120	4 94	70	5 20	80	6 46	80	6 46
1884	9½	13 66	41	8 56	123½	4 87	71½	5 20	80½	6 56	81	6 44
1885	9	14 17	41	8 48	122	4 85	70	5 30	82	6 58	85	6 39

a Introduced ring spinning this year, for which women and girls only are employed. This accounts for gradual decrease of wages for spinners since.

VARIATION IN THE RATES OF WAGES.

AND CARDING COTTON IN THE RHINE DISTRICT OF GERMANY, 1855-85.

Machinists, carpenters, joiners, assistants.		Masons.		Total employés.	Fortnightly wages for all employés.	Days of labor.	Amount of annual wages.	Pounds of yarn spun.	Spindles.	Year.
No.	Fortnightly wages.	No.	Fortnightly wages.							
46	$6 10	5	$5 47	326	$3 79	306	$32,144 17	692,858.65	21,600	1855
56	6 49	12	4 88	372	4 01	315	40,269 66	822,308.58	21,300	1856
48	6 54	12	5 28	309	4 09	300	39,323 36	807,940.37	24,300	1857
47	6 82	9	5 65	347	4 20	305½	37,903 22	837,824.90	24,300	1858
50	6 51	13	5 40	345	4 26	304½	38,102 28	823,403.13	24,312	1859
63	7 01	19	5 56	378	4 58	295½	44,842 01	874,002.89	24,312	1860
56	6 72	16	5 75	374	4 57	304	44,570 17	1,019,697.03	24,312	1861
59	7 00	26	6 21	389	4 61	305	46,556 11	1,044,271.91	24,312	1862
50	7 00	18	5 20	365	4 37	303	41,437 29	961,365.34	24,300	1863
57	7 10	28	5 30	399	4 53	300½	46,900 88	1,128,580.31	27,200	1864
42	7 44	15	5 66	370	4 51	308	43,429 35	1,000,437.46	29,025	1865
36	7 42	14	5 68	364	4 64	317	45,504 58	1,346,853.53	33,150	1866
46	7 44	27	5 04	392	4 82	305	49,219 33	1,483,200.73	34,644	1867
58	7 82	35	5 56	412	5 14	305	55,028 38	1,589,797.11	35,340	1868
54	7 47	32	5 80	414	5 22	301½	54,108 71	1,723,381.22	35,340	1869
56	7 10	31	6 00	420	5 24	306	57,305 20	1,731,486.79	35,140	1870
45	6 30	18	6 50	347	4 76	346	42,941 13	1,067,709.39	30,230	1871
60	7 50	26	6 13	400	5 84	304½	60,075 84	1,553,880.08	33,107	1872
60	8 28	23	7 20	391	6 23	304½	63,295 93	1,587,482.38	32,670	1873
65	8 53	12	8 15	381	6 40	305	63,295 93	1,700,217.66	35,362	1874
50	8 31	10	8 74	380	6 51	305½	64,281 26	2,048,256.10	38,340	1875
54	8 82	18	8 59	304	6 83	317½	72,584 03	2,281,132.92	39,592	1876
54	9 06	14	9 24	410	6 95	305½	74,108 00	2,448,242.72	40,192	1877
64	9 09	20	9 04	452	6 98	305½	82,049 24	2,799,771.04	42,972	1878
56	8 84	12	9 63	445	6 80	304½	78,710 13	3,001,905.81	41,307	1879
53	8 94	10	10 29	448	6 77	304½	78,802 06	3,259,654.09	42,807	1880
53	9 12	12	9 27	469	6 61	300	80,472 17	3,406,049.35	42,372	1881
57	8 64	14	9 54	473	6 48	307	70,675 10	3,235,034.99	41,720	1882
50	8 65	10	10 40	462	6 55	304	78,719 12	3,430,490.75	41,635	1883
48½	8 80	14½	10 00	470	6 52	304	79,899 15	3,568,190.34	42,211	1884
52	8 80	13	10 32	442	6 58	306	81,058 42	3,660,805.28	42,401	1885

EMPLOYÉS AND AVERAGE FORTNIGHTLY WAGES IN WEAVING

Year.	Foremen and assistants.		Print weavers.		Moleskin weavers.		Winders, warpers, knitters, etc.		Brushers, sizers, and gluers.		Burlers, etc.	
	No.	Fortnightly wages.	No.	Fortnightly wages.	No.	Fortnightly wages.	No.	Fortnightly wages.	No.	Fortnightly wages.	No.	Fortnightly wages.
1855	3	$7 05	81	$2 17	37	$3 72	40	$2 51	20	$6 39	10	$1 72
1856	5	6 86	74	1 97	68	3 59	46	2 41	20	6 08	11	1 00
1857	5	7 28	58	2 10	101	3 76	41	2 49	19	5 56	5	2 82
1858	6	7 76	70	2 29	110	3 76	41	2 61	19	5 82	7	2 34
1859	7	8 16	130	3 11	114	3 79	38	3 04	18	6 20	11	3 02
1860	10	7 89	151	3 43	140	3 75	47	3 10	20	6 40	16	2 91
1861	13	8 43	170	3 76	191	3 60	61	3 20	24	6 60	21	2 71
1862	13½	8 74	216	3 42	195	3 71	62	3 24	26	6 67	23	2 92
1863	13	8 93	222	3 27	199	3 65	63	2 95	22	6 38	23	3 08
1864	14	8 78	211	3 14	194	3 69	62	3 17	14	6 69	24	3 25
1865	14	9 00	222	3 30	140	3 66	60	3 10	11	6 80	19	3 60
1866	12	9 92	222	4 00	181	4 54	60	3 56	11	6 67	23	3 70
1867	14	9 63	209	3 94	235	4 42	64	3 60	10	6 96	22	4 00
1868	17	9 60	208	4 01	298	4 26	69	3 72	9	7 36	22	4 17
1869	18	9 83	224	4 03	332	4 32	76	3 80	10	7 00	25	4 17
1870	18	10 16	220	4 11	330	4 45	80	3 77	9	6 84	30	3 68
1871	17	9 01	216	3 57	248	3 55	63	2 96	7	6 60	26	2.93
1872	18	9 87	263	4 79	205	4 61	73	3 98	9	7 85	33	3 48
1873	19	10 34	260	5 01	330	4 84	83	4 15	9	8 09	42	3 40
1874	21	10 06	268	5 27	317	4 86	72	4 30	11	8 00	42	3 46
1875	21	10 54	273	5 40	347	5 19	72	4 41	12	8 00	42	3 41
1876	20	10 74	270	5 26	345	5 41	72	4 71	12	8 10	46	3 36
1877	18	11 25	272	5 43	360	5 32	71	4 71	12	8 45	50	3 17
1878	20	11 17	310	5 34	374	5 38	76	4 60	13	8 56	47	3 34
1879	30	10 22	392	5 34	384	5 30	85	4 73	14	8 95	51	3 50
1880	34	10 13	453	5 43	400	5 35	95	4 70	14	9 29	53	3 62
1881	36	10 18	500	5 55	401	5 55	96	4 73	15	9 06	57	3 69
1882	36	10 17	511	5 32	394	5 50	95	4 81	15	9 31	57	3 69
1883	37	10 00	527	5 33	400	5 57	102	4 85	16	9 49	58	3 70
1884	38	10 24	530	5 47	413	5 80	100	5 04	16	9 74	57	3 75
1885	38	10 35	478	5 40	474	5 60	101	4 92	16	9 74	57	3 84

VARIATION IN THE RATES OF WAGES. 241

COTTON GOODS IN THE RHINE DISTRICT OF GERMANY, 1855-85.

Driers, dressers, etc.		Oilers, firemen, laborers, etc.		Total employés.	Fortnightly wages for all employés.	Days of labor.	Amount of annual wages.	Looms.	Pieces of cloth woven.	Year
No.	Fortnightly wages.	No.	Fortnightly wages.							
8	$1 97	5	$4 25	204	$3 05	306	$16,197 55	240	12,421	1855
15	1 79	5	4 66	244	2 96	309	18,855 30	276	12,301	1856
17	2 38	6	5 00	252	3 30	306	21,633 20	305	15,059	1857
13	3 14	8	5 64	274	3 43	305½	24,443 22	344	17,985	1858
14	2 93	11	6 06	343	3 65	305½	32,622 01	461	26,556	1859
18	2 94	14	6 20	416	3 81	318½	42,814 45	544	34,466	1850
20	3 37	16	6 00	516	3 90	304½	52,320 48	694	43,891	1861
18¼	3 84	17	6 31	571	3 85	306½	57,142 14	812	48,549	1862
19	3 85	19	6 14	580	3 70	301½	55,739 80	823	57,279	1863
22	3 60	19	6 27	560	3 70	304	53,802 84	815	57,769	1864
18	3 88	19	6 00	502	3 75	307½	48,886 64	736	45,085	1865
18	3 80	19	6 14	546	4 35	305	61,674 65	800	55,814	1866
20	4 01	20	6 15	604	4 36	304½	67,304 89	859	60,640	1867
25	4 32	23	6 21	671	4 37	304	76,257 42	982	64,420	1868
32	4 17	25	6 40	743	4 41	305¾	85,168 71	1,100	73,336	1869
35	4 10	25	6 19	747	4 46	318	90,163 44	1,093	76,416	1870
25	4 12	23	5 81	625	3 77	301	61,248 45	914	46,079	1871
28	5 03	30	6 67	740	4 82	304½	93,804 39	1,055	68,090	1872
26	5 05	33	6 77	813	5 00	304½	105,850 60	1,154	75,670	1873
21	5 22	37	7 02	789	5 17	304½	105,912 31	1,123	76,752	1874
24	5 06	39	7 13	830	5 33	305	114,026 97	1,141	82,359	1875
25	5 11	40	7 34	830	5 44	305½	117,559 79	1,153	87,060	1876
24	5 25	43	7 47	850	5 47	304½	120,857 61	1,149	89,235	1877
21	5 49	45	7 80	906	5 48	304½	129,142 39	1,223	96,269	1878
19	5 56	42	7 88	1,017	5 49	304½	144,978 09	1,390	113,094	1879
15	5 43	43	7 90	1,107	5 54	304½	159,417 22	1,523	124,257	1880
1	6 09	45	7 89	1,122	5 67	317½	176,224 22	1,621	142,476	1881
......	......	47	7 83	1,155	5 58	306½	167,631 61	1,650	134,112	1882
......	......	48	8 01	1,168	5 60	304	172,958 29	1,703	137,550	1883
......	......	49	7 78	1,203	5 78	304	180,562 74	1,761	135,222	1884
......	......	49	7 66	1,213	5 80	303	183,018 64	1,779	129,397	1885

12854 LAB——16

The influence of the cost of living in creating differences in the rates of wages should be considered in studying rates. When such influences are carefully observed it will be found that the variation in the rates of wages has but little weight in causing industrial depressions. Depressions disturb wages: wages do not create depressions; yet, as a remotely-disturbing cause in the matter of prices, the variation in the rates of wages has a legitimate place. In Appendix B, page 411, there is presented some exceedingly valuable data relative to cost of living and wages of work people in different countries in Europe. The data there given, however, are not of sufficient extent, or do not cover a sufficient number of industries or of occupations in industries, to warrant their presentation in tabular form, or to admit of any very valuable summaries being drawn therefrom. For this reason the facts relative to cost of living are given as individual "budgets" of family expenses in detail, and of family earnings. As budgets they are exceedingly valuable and thoroughly interesting. The Bureau has no such collection of budgets for the United States, because it has been contemplated to make a sufficient collection of facts relative to cost of living to enable the Bureau to ascertain to what extent climate may affect the rate of wages. The budgets given, however, offer most excellent opportunity, tentatively, to observe the variation in expenses, the differences in diet, the habits of life, and other elements affecting the standard of living in the several countries from which they were obtained, and when it is stated that all such budgets are the result of living among the people furnishing the facts, eating and lodging with them, during the past year, their value is readily seen.[a]

Speculative Railroad Building.—The statistics of railroad building, as heretofore given, show that just prior to periods of depression, especially the later periods, there has been an enormous extension of railroad building, a large part of which must be considered as speculative. When times are good and profits are large, those who are making the large profits seek to increase their wealth through speculative investments, and railroad building, since the days of the railroad, has been one of great attractiveness. The idea seems to take possession of men that by running a line into the wilderness business can be developed. The truth always comes at last, and the original investors pay heavy tuition bills, while those who buy up the railroad for a small percentage of its cost can afford to wait until business does dedevelop. If the effect of this was only felt by those who lose directly the damage to the community would be of no consequence; but as these projected, speculative lines have become of greater extent, and vast areas of territory are to be covered, the consumption of material and of labor has been of like proportions. It has been estimated by an eminent authority,[b] and the estimate has not been doubted, that, as-

---
[a] Such data were collected by Mr. Lee Meriwether, of Saint Louis, and by him kindly furnished to the Bureau of Labor.
[b] Mr. Edward Atkinson.

suming the railroads built in 1882 to have cost, with the equipment, an average of $30,000 per mile, more than 766,000 workmen of all classes must have been employed in connection with railroad building in that year, while in the building of the greatly-reduced mileage of 1883, with a reduction in wages, say, of 11 per cent., and of 16⅔ per cent. in the cost per mile, only 250,000 persons were employed; a great army of 516,000 men employed in all the ramifications of railroad building thus being discharged from railroad work in one year. Two railroad projects alone resulted in the discharge of nearly 20,000 men, who had been brought from Southern Europe for the very purpose of building the roads, so when discharged they must to a large degree have served to increase the idle class. If the estimates given above of the number of men discharged through cessation of railroad building during the last few years are sound, and there is every reason to believe they are fairly so, the effect must have been serious indeed. Probably a very large proportion of the half million men found other employment; perhaps all found something to do, but at greatly reduced rates and in a desultory way, so that their consuming power must have been crippled to a very serious degree, and the crippling of the consuming power of a body no larger than that referred to has its influence, which, combined with other influences that tend to cripple consuming power, involves the industries of a community. In this subject of excessive railroad building is more clearly shown than in any other direction what is sometimes called the over-consumption of labor and material. The vast quantities of steel and iron and all other material necessary for the equipment of speculative roads have been over-consumed, or consumed to no immediate purpose, and when that over-consumption ceases because it has been illegitimate, legitimate production suffers correspondingly, and what then is called over-production can be denominated bad production; but, of course, along with what may be denominated an over-consumption of iron in the direction specified there must have been an over-consumption of labor, that is, a consumption of labor that resulted in no immediate benefit, but in positive, immediate harm, because such a large proportion of the over-consumed labor was brought in from abroad, and after the cessation of the over-consumption could not readily assimilate itself with the industries or work of a depressed community.

The crippled consuming power arising from the over-construction of railroads is only one influence, however, in the great grouping of influences which tend to produce the economic condition known as under-consumption.

Crippled Consuming Power or Under-consumption.
Some of the causes which tend to cripple the consuming power of a large body of our people are remote indeed, and yet have a direct bearing upon the question in hand. Any disturbance in the monetary affairs of our country by which the purchasing power of money is decreased cripples the consuming power of the people, and when the

people, through apprehension or through real results, feel that their consuming power is crippled in ever so slight a degree, individual retrenchment begins, and corresponding stagnation follows. The same results are reached through a lowering of wages from any cause whatever. If manufacturers find their warehouses overstocked, there must take place a cessation of production or a lowering of wages, in either case the consuming power of the workers being crippled. Short crops will often, and usually, result in crippling the purchasing power of a large body of people; so, too, a very large crop which cannot be sold readily and at good prices reduces the consuming power of great communities. In mining and manufacturing districts where the truck system prevails there inevitably results a crippled consuming power of the operatives concerned. Some company stores, so-called, are of real benefit to the employés of the concerns owning such stores, but in order to be of benefit the company or the proprietors of the works must see that the stores are well stocked with supplies at the lowest market prices, and that the customers—their own employés—can purchase goods for cash at an advance simply large enough to pay expenses. An instance of such a store in Connecticut represents what is meant. A large manufacturing company in that state owns and runs a store for the benefit of its operatives. All goods are purchased for cash, at the lowest prices, and of the best qualities. The store is conducted on the basis of simply paying expenses and a very small percentage of margin over expenses, which margin is devoted to the support of a free library for the use of the operatives. The reverse of this is found in many mining districts of the country, where at the companies' stores the miners purchase their goods oftentimes at a higher price than they could purchase for elsewhere, and under duress; that is, in many localities employment depends partially upon taking goods out of the companies' stores. When wages are lowered this necessity becomes more apparent. Laws in several states have been passed aiming at the removal of the truck and company-store system, and in many places with success. There is yet, however, too much evasion of these laws, and much remains to be done in the future. Truck stores conducted in the interest of greed, and not of the men, are simply contributory influences in localities to the crippling of the consuming power of the work people.

One of the most serious causes tending to cripple the consumptive power of a people, and an influence which has been especially felt during the last four or five years, results from the cessation of railroad building. This matter, however, has been sufficiently treated under alleged causes of the depression and under the preceding heading.

The employment of contract labor of foreign importation, and rapid immigration generally, are features which have a positive influence in crippling consuming power. The influence of foreign immigration is best exhibited by the following table, showing the foreign population ten years of age and over, and the percentage engaged in agriculture at the last two census periods:

THE FOREIGN-BORN, TEN YEARS OF AGE AND OVER, ENGAGED IN AGRICULTURE, MANUFACTURES, ETC., IN 1870 AND 1880.

	1870.	1880.
Population, ten years of age and over	28,228,945	36,761,607
Foreign-born, ten years of age and over	5,307,887	6,401,301
Per cent. of foreign-born of total population (ten years and over)	18.80+	17.65+
Foreign-born engaged in agriculture	619,108	812,829
Foreign-born engaged in manufactures, mining, etc	929,581	1,225,787
Total foreign-born engaged in agriculture, manufactures, etc	1,548,689	2,038,616
Per cent. of foreign-born engaged in agriculture of total foreign-born	11.66+	12.52+
Per cent. of foreign-born engaged in manufactures of total foreign-born	17.51+	18.88+
Per cent. of foreign-born engaged in agriculture, manufactures, mining, etc., of total foreign-born	29.17+	31.40+

This table offers some points of interest and of value at the present time. For instance, it will be seen that there were 812,829 of the foreign-born population engaged in agriculture. By the census of 1880 the whole number of people engaged in agriculture in the United States was 7,670,493. Into the total number then engaged in agriculture there had been absorbed but 812,829 foreign-born; that is, the foreign-born constituted 10.6 per cent. of the whole number employed in agriculture. The total number employed in the country in manufactures, mechanical, and mining industries was 3,837,112. Into this number had been absorbed 1,225,787 of the foreign-born, or 32 per cent. of the whole number engaged in such industries. It will be seen at once that the tendency of immigrants is to assimilate with our mechanical industries. This increases the supply of labor in comparison to the demand, lowers wages, contributes to whatever over-production exists, and cripples temporarily the consuming power of the whole. The progress of immigration has been very steady. This is best shown by the following table: *a*

IMMIGRATION INTO THE UNITED STATES.

Years.	Immigrants.	Years.	Immigrants.	Years.	Immigrants.
1820	8,385	1844	78,615	*Fiscal year ending June 30—*	
1821	9,127	1845	114,371		
1822	6,911	1846	154,416	1867	298,967
1823	6,354	1847	234,968	1868	282,189
1824	7,912	1848	226,527	1869	352,768
1825	10,199	1849	297,024	1870	387,203
1826	10,837	1850	369,980	1871	321,350
1827	18,875	1851	379,466	1872	404,806
1828	27,382	1852	371,603	1873	459,803
1829	22,520	1853	368,645	1874	313,339
1830	23,322	1854	427,833	1875	227,498
1831	22,633	1855	200,877	1876	169,986
1832	60,482	1856	195,857	1877	141,857
1833	58,640	1857	246,945	1878	138,469
1834	65,365	1858	119,501	1879	177,826
1835	45,374	1859	118,616	1880	457,257
1836	76,242	1860	150,237	1881	669,431
1837	79,340	1861	89,724	1882	788,992
1838	38,914	1862	89,007	1883	599,114
1839	68,069	1863	174,524	1884	518,592
1840	84,066	1864	193,195	1885	395,346
1841	80,289	1865	247,453		
1842	104,565	1866	167,757	Total	13,110,233
1843	52,496				

a From the Report of the Bureau of Statistics, Treasury Department, Washington, D. C.

In examining this table one sees that prior to each period of depression since 1837 there has been a large increase in immigration, and following the inception of the depression a sharp falling off. As times became prosperous after each period, immigration has set in and been followed up to an abnormal degree, and as soon as prosperity ceased temporarily the foreign mechanic or laborer has remained at home. This constant artificial augmentation of the number of laborers during prosperous years has had its full share in bringing in the following period of depression. The Forty-eighth Congress, at the second session, enacted a law aimed at the restriction and prevention of the importation of foreign labor under contract, which will be found in the chapter on remedies. The effect of this law cannot be appreciated, if it has any effect, until the country reaches a period of prosperity and those engaged in industrial enterprises, railroad-building, etc., seek to gain the greatest possible advantage during the season of prosperity. At the present time the law is practically inoperative, because no desire exists to break its provisions. The agents of the Bureau were not able to learn of a widespread importation of labor under contract. The cases which have occurred have been local, and although accompanied by many aggravating features such importations have not involved industries as a whole.

It is undoubtedly true that during the past fifty years immigration has been of inestimable value as an element in American industrial progress, but it cannot be said now, and probably not to any great extent in the future, that America is the home of the oppressed of all nations. This advertisement will undoubtedly be withdrawn, as well as that other, that there is room enough in the United States for all. This would not be so if this country was not one of the great family of nations now given to mechanical production. So long as it was largely an agricultural country the advertisement worked its good, for it brought wealth and labor and the wealth that comes of labor. Immigration in the future will continue to bring the same elements. The trouble comes in too rapid immigration. No one would probably consider for a moment the propriety of preventing immigration, but it is a subject for wise consideration whether or not it may not be regulated by equitable legal provisions. The present practice certainly results in the freest possible importation of labor, which profits by the prosperity of the country and aids materially in bringing about a condition where profits are not only reduced to a small margin but labor finds its power to consume crippled. Many instances might be given to illustrate the ill effects of the inopportune importation of foreign labor—the employment of Hungarians in mining districts, the padrone system in some localities, and other features, not only of foreign contract labor, but of the employment of foreign labor which comes freely on a certain kind of solicitation to induce it. So far as the investigation in hand indicates, the employment of foreign labor under contract to take the places of dissatisfied home laborers has been a miserable failure for all parties concerned, except, perhaps, the parties imported. The contractor here has gained no advantage beyond a temporary one, and in a large proportion of cases has met with permanent disadvantage; the home laborer has been thrown out of employment or obliged to work on a crippled basis, and the consumer has not been able to secure products at any appreciable discount. To some extent the imported man has been benefited, for he has been able, by continuing his old style of living, to secure what were to him marvelous wages, and after saving a few hundred dollars felt that he could return to his old associations with a fund which, with little work, would enable him to live in comparative affluence. The conclusion is inevitable that the consuming power of many communities is crippled through rapid immigration, and whatever cripples communities in respect to their consuming capacity cripples all in any way affiliated with such communities.

The decrease of the public domain suitable for farming purposes has probably had something to do in preventing immigration in recent years. If so, it may be expected, with farming land at a higher price than formerly, that immigration will not be abnormal in the future; that is, immigrants will not come to this country in such large numbers as to influence in any material degree the stability of our industries. About three-fifths of the public domain already has passed out of the ownership of the Government, while the remaining two-fifths embraces a very large proportion of desert and mountain lands unfit for habitation. *a* The reduction of the area of available public lands is, of course, only a contributory cause of the decrease of immigration, because, as has just been seen, the number of the foreign-born absorbed in the agricultural classes is only about two-thirds as large as that absorbed in mechanical industries. It is in this latter respect that the effects of immigration are felt. It is probable that this country could, with benefit to all its industries, absorb from 200,000 to 250,000 new-comers annually, but a much larger number coming in can be considered as one of the precursors of depressed business.

The population of the United States directly and indirectly dependent upon the success of agriculture is, in round numbers, 26,000,000. Anything that causes the agriculturists of the country to apprehend a cessation of exports of food products cripples to a greater or less extent the consuming power of the population involved. Apprehension is one of the most potent factors in producing and continuing industrial depressions. If apprehension leads people to believe that there is to be stagnation, they immediately begin to practice a severer economy and almost to adopt parsimonious habits.

The opening of the Suez Canal has led to an increased development of the agricultural interests of India, and these interests have been so fully developed that at the present time the grain acreage of India is,

---

a Report of the Secretary of the Interior for the year ending June 30, 1885.

under artificial development, rapidly approaching the grain acreage of the United States, in India the wheat acreage being, in round numbers, 30,000,000, and in the United States 40,000,000.a The direct result of this Indian development has been an increase in the imports of Indian wheat by Western Europe and a decrease in the imports of American grain. So far as the United Kingdom is concerned, this condition is shown by the following English data:

IMPORTS OF WHEAT INTO GREAT BRITAIN AND IRELAND.

Year.	Wheat imported into Great Britain and Ireland—	
	From United States. (Cwts.)	From India. (Cwts.)
1880	36,190,814	2,201,515
1881	36,083,468	7,444,375
1882	35,137,173	19,001,005
1883	36,128,761	14,193,763
1884	22,641,050	21,001,412

These figures are borne out by those taken from the reports of the United States Bureau of Statistics. The following table shows the values of our exports of domestic merchandise to foreign countries during the years indicated, subdivided into products of agriculture, of manufacture, of mining, etc., and of specie:

VALUE, ETC., OF ALL PRODUCTS EXPORTED FROM THE UNITED STATES.

Year ending June 30—	Agriculture.		Manufactures.		Mining, forestry, fisheries, etc.		Total value.	Gold and silver.
	Value.	Per cent.	Value.	Per cent.	Value.	Per cent.		
1869	$256,560,972	81.14	$45,658,873	14.43	$14,022,588	4.43	$316,242,423	$56,946,851
1870	361,188,483	79.34	47,921,154	10.53	46,098,704	10.13	455,208,341	43,883,803
1875	430,306,570	76.95	75,755,432	13.55	53,175,636	9.50	559,237,638	83,857,129
1876	456,113,515	76.67	81,374,077	13.68	57,430,123	9.65	594,917,715	50,028,601
1877	459,734,148	72.63	88,007,773	13.91	85,238,963	13.46	632,980,854	43,134,738
1878	536,192,873	77.07	91,416,576	13.14	68,140,481	9.79	695,749,930	27,061,885
1879	546,476,703	78.12	80,117,215	12.74	63,944,824	9.14	699,538,742	17,555,035
1880	685,961,091	83.25	79,510,447	9.65	58,474,815	7.10	823,946,353	9,347,893
1881	730,394,943	82.63	89,219,380	10.10	64,211,624	7.27	883,925,947	14,226,944
1882	552,219,819	75.31	103,132,481	14.08	77,887,432	10.61	733,239,732	43,480,271
1883	619,269,449	77.00	111,890,001	13.91	73,064,182	9.09	804,223,632	21,623,181
1884	535,315,318	73.98	111,330,242	15.35	77,319,293	10.67	724,064,852	50,225,635
1885	530,172,966	72.96	117,259,810	16.14	79,250,170	10.90	726,682,946	24,376,110

a The wheat acreage of the United States in 1883 was 34,189,000; of India, 27,620,223. The acreage of the United States in 1884 was 39,475,885. The round figures, 30,000,000 and 40,000,000, are fairly representative of the wheat acreage of the two countries named at the present time.

VALUE OF LEADING AGRICULTURAL PRODUCTS EXPORTED FROM THE UNITED STATES.

Year ending June 30—	Raw cotton.	Breadstuffs.	Leaf tobacco.	Meats and dairy products.	Cattle, sheep, and hogs.	Total.
1860	$191,806,555	$24,422,310	$15,906,547	$16,934,363	$1,463,843	$250,533,418
1861	34,051,483	72,152,366	13,784,710	22,483,213	254,030	142,726,702
1862	1,180,113	84,183,754	12,325,356	37,198,672	255,181	135,142,076
1863	6,652,405	89,180,332	19,752,076	58,623,579	372,414	174,580,806
1864	9,895,854	62,400,606	22,845,936	51,379,801	243,665	147,765,862
1865	6,836,400	53,941,231	41,625,220	54,015,641	244,148	156,662,846
1866	281,385,223	41,249,054	29,456,145	29,658,730	426,305	382,770,457
1867	201,470,423	41,288,804	19,620,159	27,224,060	378,170	289,981,616
1868	152,820,733	69,024,059	23,298,823	31,078,598	432,566	276,254,779
1869	162,633,052	53,724,154	20,552,943	30,326,781	(a)	267,236,930
1870	227,027,624	72,250,933	21,100,420	30,992,305	724,933	352,096,215
1871	218,327,109	79,381,187	19,908,797	39,748,796	551,769	357,917,658
1872	180,684,505	84,586,273	24,136,166	64,306,139	1,193,464	354,906,637
1873	227,243,069	98,743,151	22,689,135	82,911,660	1,591,057	433,178,072
1874	211,223,580	161,198,864	30,390,181	83,511,275	2,936,429	489,269,329
1875	100,638,625	111,458,265	25,241,549	83,100,065	2,026,198	412,464,702
1876	192,650,262	131,181,555	22,737,383	92,325,308	1,951,846	440,855,354
1877	171,118,508	117,806,476	28,825,521	118,579,676	2,526,740	438,856,921
1878	180,031,484	181,777,841	24,803,165	124,845,137	4,497,576	515,955,203
1879	162,304,250	210,355,528	25,157,364	119,857,692	10,162,400	527,837,234
1880	211,535,905	288,036,835	16,379,107	132,488,201	14,657,931	663,297,970
1881	247,695,746	270,312,519	18,737,043	156,809,840	15,639,173	709,514,321
1882	199,812,644	182,670,528	19,067,721	122,020,530	8,913,656	532,485,079
1883	247,328,721	208,040,850	19,438,066	109,217,119	9,768,803	593,793,550
1884	197,015,204	162,544,715	17,785,760	114,353,788	19,333,121	511,012,588
1885	201,962,458	160,370,821	22,025,786	107,532,456	13,998,441	505,689,962

a Live animals not separately stated.

The facts as to wheat alone, relative to decreased exportations, are shown by the following table:

Year.	Value.	Year.	Value.
1878	$96,872,016	1882	$112,929,718
1879	130,701,079	1883	119,879,341
1880	190,546,305	1884	75,026,678
1881	167,698,485	1885	72,933,097

The facts shown in the foregoing tables are by no means startling. The fear, however, that Indian wheat and cotton and Egyptian cotton are rapidly taking the place of American wheat and cotton has caused producers to feel that the future has no prosperity for them. The reduction in the exportation of grain and cotton has been sufficient, however, to induce those immediately engaged in their production to curtail expenditures, and to this extent practically, and to a larger extent by apprehension; thus the consuming power of one-half of our population has been crippled in a measure. Whatever can remove this apprehension will aid in restoring prosperity.

It should, therefore, be understood that several things have contributed to the decrease of exportations in food products as well as the development of the wheat crop in India, such as the increased effort to stimulate the crops of Western Europe, and especially the increase in meat products, induced partly by industrial depression and partly through the desire of the countries of Western Europe to be more independent of America. Again, the restrictive measures of European countries as against American meats must be considered. While, therefore, the prospect from the influence of Indian development may cause serious consideration on this side the Atlantic, it is not probable that such development need to be considered as alarming. It has probably had its worst influence so far as crippling the consuming power of a large body of the population of the United States is concerned. The influence coming from cheap wheat is one of a mixed character. If it be argued that the lowering of the price of wheat and flour would be an advantage to the working classes of this country, it may be answered that this is true only in a small degree, for, as it has been seen, if the producers of food products do not get fair prices for such products their power to purchase is crippled correspondingly, and so the influence is felt in all directions. By short crops or reduced prices the agriculturist is precluded from buying the products of mechanical industries except in a limited degree. Thus the disturbing influences resulting from stimulated development of industrial interests abroad act in a contributory way to produce and continue American depression.

It not necessary in this connection to consider the differences in quality between American and Indian cotton and wheat, or the effect of short crops in America.

Tariff Inequalities.—Very many well-informed business men allege that high duties on imported goods constitute a serious disturbing influence in manufacturing, but they complain more of the inequalities in rates than of high or low rates of duty. An illustration of the existing inequalities is given in the following table relating to woollen and mixed goods manufactured at Leeds, England, or having Leeds as the point from which distribution begins. This table states the description of the goods; their width in inches, and the weight per yard of each kind; the price of the goods at the factory; the rate and the amount of duty per pound and ad valorem, and the total amount of duty levied under the compound rate; and also the per cent. which the total duty is of the price per yard at the factory in England:

TARIFF IRREGULARITIES.

PRICE PER YARD OF LEEDS (ENGLAND) WOOLLEN AND MIXED GOODS, DUTIES, ETC.

Name.	Width (inches).	Weight (ounces).	Price at factory.	Duty. Rate. Per pound.	Duty. Rate. Ad valorem (per cent.).	Duty. Amount. Per pound.	Duty. Amount. Ad valorem.	Duty. Amount. Total.	Per cent. of price at factory.	Cost in New York, not including packing, carriage to port, ocean freight, and insurance.
West of England broadcloth	60	17	$3.60	$0.35	40	$0.372	$1.440	$1.812	50.3	$5.412
Fine worsted trousering	28	11	1.62	.35	40	.241	.648	.889	54.9	2.509
Imitation sealskin (mohair and cotton)	50	31	4.50	.35	40	.678	1.800	2.478	55.0	6.978
West of England beaver	58	25	3.36	.35	40	.547	1.344	1.891	56.3	5.251
West of England all-wool Moscow	58	29	3.60	.35	40	.634	1.440	2.074	57.6	5.674
Fine worsted coating	58	24	2.88	.35	40	.525	1.152	1.677	58.2	4.557
Fine worsted trousering	28	12	1.42	.35	40	.263	.568	.831	58.5	2.251
Indigo blue Cheviot coating	58	28	2.40	.35	40	.612	.960	1.572	65.5	3.972
Low worsted coating (worsted face, woolen back, cotton warp)	50	24	.82	.18	35	.270	.287	.557	68.0	1.377
Low worsted trousering (woolen back)	28	11	.48	.24	35	.165	.168	.333	69.4	.813
Ottoman (worsted face, woolen back, cotton warp)	50	27	.82	.18	35	.304	.287	.591	72.0	1.411
Matelassé (worsted face, woolen back, cotton warp)	50	28	.84	.18	35	.315	.294	.609	72.5	1.449
Mantle cloth (worsted face, woolen back, cotton warp)	50	24	.68	.18	35	.270	.238	.508	74.7	1.188
Wool, fancy suiting	54	25	.94	.35	35	.547	.329	.876	93.2	1.816
Cotton-warp cloth	50	15	.54	.35	35	.328	.189	.517	95.7	1.057
Fancy coating	54	23	.78	.35	35	.503	.273	.776	99.5	1.556
Fancy Cheviot	54	25	.82	.35	35	.547	.287	.834	101.7	1.654
Wool, fancy suiting	54	22	.70	.35	35	.481	.245	.726	103.7	1.426
Diagonal Cheviot	54	25	.76	.35	35	.547	.266	.813	107.0	1.573
Common blue Cheviot coating	52	25	.72	.35	35	.547	.252	.799	111.0	1.519
Cotton-warp Moscow	52	35	.96	.35	35	.766	.336	1.102	114.8	2.062
Cotton-warp cloth	52	25	.64	.35	35	.547	.224	.771	120.5	1.411
Cotton-warp twilled Melton	50	10½	.42	.35	35	.361	.147	.508	121.0	.928
Cotton-warp Moscow	52	30	.74	.35	35	.656	.259	.915	123.6	1.655
Cotton-warp cloth	50	13	.32	.35	35	.284	.112	.306	123.7	.716
Fancy overcoating (cotton warp)	50	34	.82	.35	35	.744	.287	1.031	125.7	1.851
Cotton-warp reversible	50	31	.74	.35	35	.678	.259	.937	126.6	1.677
Fancy overcoating (cotton warp)	50	32	.76	.35	35	.700	.266	.966	127.0	1.726
Cotton-warp coating	50	17	.40	.35	35	.372	.140	.512	128.0	.912
Imitation sealskin (calf hair mixed with wool, cotton warp)	50	28	.56	.35	35	.612	.196	.808	144.3	1.368
Cotton-warp coating	50	23	.46	.35	35	.503	.161	.664	144.3	1.124
Cotton-warp Melton	50	13	.24	.35	35	.284	.084	.368	153.3	.608
Cotton-warp serge Melton	50	15½	.26	.35	35	.339	.091	.430	165.4	.690
Reversible diagonal (cotton warp)	50	29	.48	.35	35	.634	.168	.802	167.1	1.282
Reversible nap (cotton warp)	50	29	.44	.35	35	.634	.154	.788	179.1	1.228
Cotton-warp reversible	50	30	.45	.35	35	.656	.157	.813	180.7	1.263

This table is well worthy of careful study. In examining the figures given in the column headed "Price at factory," and the column headed "Per cent. of price at factory," which the total duty amounts to, the startling inequalities in the rate of duty to be paid in this country becomes apparent. The highest-priced goods named in the table is West of England broadcloth, worth $3.60 per yard in Leeds, the specific duty being 35 cents per pound and the ad valorem duty 40 per cent., making a total duty of 50.3 per cent. on the value at the factory. This is on a high grade of goods. In looking at the bottom of the table, the last entry is for cotton-warp reversible cloth, made in imitation of a better kind. It is worth but 45 cents per yard at the factory. The specific duty is the same as on the West of England broadcloth, 35 cents per pound; the ad valorem duty is 35 per cent. but the specific duty and the ad valorem duty together make the rate on the price at the factory 180.7 per cent. That is to say, the cheaper the goods at the factory the greater is the proportional increment of duty. The column headed "Per cent. of price at factory," which shows the percentage that the duty is of the factory price, brings this out clearly. By looking at this column it will be seen that this per cent. steadily increases from 50.3 on high-priced goods to 180.7 on low-priced goods. It is such glaring inequalities that cause apprehension in the minds of producers, and they constitute a valid cause of, or rather they are a legitimate influence in, causing a disturbance in values, and therefore corresponding depressions. The adjustment of rates of duty on manufactured goods should be in accordance with the labor cost of production, if duties are to be continued. It is fallacious to attempt to regulate rates of duty by rates of wages alone. The labor cost in production and all the other elements of production must be considered before an equitable schedule can be arranged. Until some such basis is adopted, the inequalities shown in the foregoing table will exist, although they may be shifted so far as products are concerned.

Miscellaneous.—Among the many causes named in the list as given at the beginning of this chapter and which many consider influential causes, but for which causes the agents of the Bureau found no supporting facts or illustrations, may be considered the national banking system. The banking system as it exists may have something to do with the stringency or plethora of the money market, but no facts have come to hand showing that it has in any way been instrumental in bringing about the present industrial depression. The same may be remarked relative to the silver question. What the silver question in the future may cause, whether prosperity or adversity, it cannot be alleged that in this depression it has had sufficient influence to produce the existing condition of things. It may have had some influence in the fluctuation of prices, but not as yet to a sufficient extent to cite the silver question as containing the important cause of or remedy for industrial depressions. Foreign capital may be a disturbing and contributory cause, but not a primary one. When capital in foreign countries cannot find profitable investment, and it seeks such profitable investment here at a time when manufacturing is overdone, then such capital aggravates the disease. Convict labor is a disturbing element, affecting the moral apprehension of large bodies of people, and thereby aids in irritating the public mind relative to depressions, but the labor of all the prisons in the country bears so small a proportion to the whole product of the country's industries that such labor cannot be considered as a prime or influential cause of depressions. The inadequate means of distributing the proceeds of labor has far more influence in producing depressions. Extravagant living and excessive parsimony have their contributory influence in producing and continuing periods of industrial depression. Occasionally men are found who consider the enactment or the existence of labor laws as a moving influence in creating and sustaining depressions, but it is difficult to see how such can be the case. A careful examination of all such laws enacted in the different States of the Union destroys the force of such a statement.*a* In the minds of consumers, trading in futures, corners, etc., is an influence productive of depressions; but while these things aggravate they cannot be said to cause such depressions. The same is true of strikes. Strikes usually come after a depression begins and just before the dawn of prosperity. They are accompaniments and not causes of depressions. The liquor traffic, as one of those causes which might be classed in the moral list and also among economic causes, is a thoroughly aggravating feature of all industrial conditions other than of prosperity, but intemperance cannot be said to cause industrial depressions. The reduction of wages follow so closely upon the opening of a depressed period that it is often considered a cause instead of an effect. Many workingmen consider the wage system as an obstacle to permanent prosperity, and that it is now, whatever it has been in the past, a failure. In so far as the wage system does not allow earnings to keep pace with the wants of the people, it is a contributing influence in the induction of depressions. As a system it will be treated more fully under remedies. The other causes alleged in the long list are those springing almost entirely from apprehension, and they have such slight effect, if any, that it would be impossible to illustrate their influence by any collection of data.

---

a See Appendix C for a digest of such laws.

CHAPTER III.

THE MANUFACTURING NATIONS CONSIDERED AS A GROUP IN RELATION TO THE PRESENT DEPRESSION.

It is apparent from the statistical illustrations given in the preceding chapters that the family of manufacturing states, Great Britain, France, Belgium, Germany, and the United States, if not also Austria, Russia, and Italy, are suffering from an industrial depression novel in its kind, and yet having characteristic features of similarity throughout the whole range of states. It seems to be quite true that in those states considered the volume of business and of production has not been affected disastrously by the depression, but that prices have been greatly reduced, wages frequently reduced, and margins of profits carried to the minimum range. Over-production seems to prevail in all alike without regard to the system of commerce which exists in either. What has brought all these states to the position in which they are found at the present time constitutes a most interesting and important question in economics, and one vitally affecting the wage-workers of the world. The wide study given to this matter has resulted in some conclusions entirely warranted by the facts, which may not be lacking in value, and not only the facts, but the results of the facts, are properly stated at this point.

If each of these great communities has reached an industrial condition involving phases common to all, there must be somewhere a line of reasons for such universal condition, and one should be able to develop the logical course of events which has brought such a wide range of states to an industrial epoch.

England, with generations of skill in mechanical employment, was the first to establish the factory system and institute a new industrial order of things, in which the division of labor became more and more an important factor.[a] She controlled also the exchange of the world. In her insular position she was able to make the world pay tribute to her by compelling the produce of the world to pass through her hands, either in kind or in settlement of balances. With these immense advantages, and having the control, too, of raw materials in abundance, it was natural that England should seek to supply the world with manufactured products. This she was able to do with the aid of her skill,

---

[a] The moral and industrial causes which led to the establishment of the factory system are fully outlined in a report on the "Factory System," by the writer, for the Tenth Census.

of her science, of rapid transportation, which she did much to develop, and of the vast capital which she possessed, enabling her to carry on great enterprises. So her ambition was natural and legitimate, and her great prosperity came to her without regard to any commercial system which she might have established, and in spite of commercial systems. Free trade became to her a necessity, because she sold to the world her manufactured products, and the world had few manufactured products to sell to her. With the constant increase of equipment to carry out her industrial policy, England at last found herself, on account of the course of other nations, with a plant altogether too large for the demands made upon her, and with a capacity sufficient to supply not only all her own home and colonial markets but a great share of the other markets of the world.

The United States, after the war of the Revolution, found that political freedom only had been secured as the result of the war. Industrially this country was under the control of Great Britain. It became essential to establish a commercial system, which it was thought would enable our industries to become gradually free from the industrial control of England. This policy has, with few interruptions, been pursued to the present time. Foreign producers of manufactured goods have gradually lost the American market, and the American producers have gradually found themselves in position to supply the home demand. Stimulated in this direction, the United States has gone on perfecting machinery, duplicating plant, crowding the market with products, until to-day this country is in the exact position of England, with productive capacity far in excess of the demand upon it, and her industries, as those of Great Britain, stagnated, the wages of labor reduced, prices lowered, and the manufacturers and merchants trying to secure an outlet for surplus goods. This condition has been reached under a system the reverse of that which has prevailed in England, and while stimulation has been enhanced by the system prevailing here, the condition has been reached in spite of it.

France, at first drawing her skilled workmen from England and tardy in the establishment of the factory system, at last concluded she ought to supply her own markets at least, and so began war on British industry. With a natural ambition to supply her own markets, she has carried the stimulation so far that she has not only secured the capacity to supply herself but has a vastly enhanced capacity, and is seeking to supply others. To-day France finds herself, through her policy, in precisely the same industrial situation that attends Great Britain and America.

Germany has followed the example of France and the United States, and with precisely the same results. Her commercial policy or system has been, of late years, the same as that of the United States, while Belgium has followed that of Great Britain, and yet all these nations now find themselves in sympathy in their distress, all seeking outlets for their surplus production. The scale of wages in the countries named is according to the following order, the highest first: The United States, Great Britain, France, Belgium, Germany. It is difficult to connect commercial systems with this scale of wages, and when the broad view is taken that each of these countries has overstocked itself with machinery and manufacturing plant far in excess of the wants of production, and when it is considered also that the present period of industrial depression is unique in its character, as not having been attended with financial and commercial crises and panics, financial matters having been only incidentally involved, and when it is considered further that the condition of these nations has been reached under both free trade and protective policies, and under a wide range of tariff restrictions, it is readily seen that the family of nations given to mechanical production have reached an epoch in their existence, and that commercial systems which might have been at one time, or under some circumstances, necessities, are now apparently only expediencies, to be used temporarily and not as permanent features of national progress. Historically, it must be admitted that the two great opposing systems of free trade and protection have played well their parts in the industrial development of nations; but the wisdom derived from the experience of all the nations in the race for industrial success should teach each that ultimately that system freest from restrictions will beget generally the best conditions. Meantime, expediency has its power, and must continue to exercise it until the evil resulting from changes can be met through the softening influences which come from contest and hardship. The struggle so far has had a strong influence in producing ever-recurring periods of depression. These considerations are shown to be valid through the information collected by the Bureau in all the countries involved. The opinions of some of the ablest men, of wide experience and of great opportunity, substantiate the grounds taken, among others, M. de Laveleye, already referred to; Dr. Arthur von Studnitz, of Dresden; M. Piermez, of Brussels; M. Jules Duckerts, of Verviers; Professors Emil de Laveleye and Trasenster of Liège; Herr Annecke, of Berlin; and Dr. Engel, of Berlin.

In England, Belgium, and France the railroads and canals that are really needed have been built. There remain only to be constructed feeding and competing lines, and experience shows that for such lines the revenue for the capital invested is not equal to nominal remuneration. In Holland the great works are completed; Amsterdam is united to the sea, international communications have been well established, and there are no longer urgent works to be undertaken, and the reward of capital to be invested now is not sufficient to tempt lenders. In Italy and Spain the great arteries are provided with railroads, while the products moved and the revenues derived from capital invested are notoriously inferior to what was expected. When this is the case there is no prospect of rival or subsidiary lines being constructed. Harbors and rivers are sufficiently developed, and warehouses, water and gas works, tramways, etc., are largely provided for. The Pyrenees and the Alps are tunnelled, and a sufficient network of international communication established. In England railroad building cannot be extended to a sufficient degree to absorb much capital or much labor. In Russia the principal lines of railroad have been built with the aid of the Government, and it is not likely that further construction will take place except for strategical purposes. Germany is provided with a full network of railroads, and the facilities for transportation are in excess of actual needs. Austria is in much the same condition as Germany, and Turkey also has as many railroads as can be used. In the United States the mileage of new railroads constructed has been out of all proportion to the increase of products to be carried.

The Suez Canal has been built, terrestrial and transoceanic lines of telegraph have been laid, and the merchant marine has been transformed from wood to iron. To-day the carrying service of nations, and especially of the great marine nation, England, is overstocked to a far greater extent than the industries. On all sides one sees the accomplished results of the labor of half a century. From a financial point of view, these accomplished results should always be good, but in many cases it is apparent that undertakings have proved deceptive and Governments become needy and some, as Egypt, insolvent. Whatever may have been the financial results, industry has been enormously developed, cities have been transformed, distances covered, and a new set of economic tools has been given in profusion to rich countries, and in a more reasonable amount to poorer ones. What is strictly necessary has been done oftentimes to superfluity. This full supply of economic tools to meet the wants of nearly all branches of commerce and industry is the most important factor in the present industrial depression. It is true that the discovery of new processes of manufacture will undoubtedly continue, and this will act as an ameliorating influence, but it will not leave room for a marked extension, such as has been witnessed during the last fifty years, or afford a remunerative employment of the vast amount of capital which has been created during that period. The market price of products will continue low, no matter what the cost of production may be. The day of large profits is probably past. There may be room for further intensive, but not extensive, development of industry in the present area of civilization. Outside of the area of a high state of industrial civilization, in China, Japan, India, Australia, Persia, and South Africa, there is a vast deal to be done, but this of necessity will be accomplished slowly, as these countries, not having the capital to make speculative movements, must depend upon the money-lending countries. Supplying themselves with full facilities for industries and commerce will give to each of the great nations of Europe and of America something to do, but the part of each in this work will be small and far from enough to insure more than temporary activity.

It may help to keep away stagnation and modify the severity and the duration of industrial depressions. There are very many influences, like the great expense of standing armies, of war and revolutions, and local features, so far as causes are concerned, which enter into the consideration of the industrial situation of the world so far as localities are specifically concerned. The present treatment only has to do with those things which seem to be common. The building of railroads and of ships, even in countries where the land is interlaced with roads and supplied with wharfs lined with shipping, must go on, because the waste needs repairing, and the great industrial work of supplying the world will furnish enough for all to do; but the brief review of the present industrial situation of the great communities involved indicates that statesmanship is required to establish such guards and checks in human affairs as shall lead to a safer and surer progress than that which has attended the past decade. In the consideration of suggested remedies and in the summary of this report facts will be brought out which will at least be suggestive of channels into which legislation, but more effectually public sentiment, may be directed. Certainly, with the aid of the wisdom of some of the best minds in Europe and America, and of men having the largest experience, these directions should have their influence.

One of the agents of the Bureau reports as the result of interviews had with leading economists in Europe the following as the predominant features of modern industrial development among the producing nations: (1) The influence of the increased facilities for transportation and international communication. (2) The steady progress of rising wages, contemporaneous with declining profits. (3) The enlargement of the circle of producing nations to such extent as to make the means of production far in excess of the needs of consumption. The factors responsible for this state of affairs are—

(*a*) The desire to participate in the large profits made by those first in the field.

(*b*) The continuous flow of precious metals after the discovery of the gold mines of California and Australia.

(*c*) The extension of the credit system, facilitating the advance of capital to those who knew the processes and secrets of manufacture, but who had not the ready money to commence business on their own account.

(*d*) The establishment of protective tariffs in most of the western European countries and the United States inducing sharp domestic competition and over-production.

(*e*) The abnormal stimulus given to industry in Germany by the accomplishment of German unity and by the payment by the Government of its domestic obligations from the war indemnity received from France.

The saving made in the cost of production by modern highly-developed systems of transportation has been very great. During the first half century railroads were built gradually, and their effect on the cost of transportation and production was gradual also; but beginning with 1869, the simplification of methods of communication between man and man, between town and town, between nation and nation, and between continent and continent, has progressed by leaps and bounds. Between 1869 and 1875 especially railroad building assumed enormous proportions, the total mileage of roads in Germany, for example, being more than doubled between 1869 and 1880. Side by side with extensive railroad building came great improvements in ocean transit and the construction of oceanic cables. The effect of these things has been felt more particularly in recent years, because of late they have come with phenomenal rapidity. The state control of railroads in Belgium and Germany, it is considered, has done much to prevent the waste of capital upon the construction of useless parallel lines merely for speculative purposes, from which the United States has suffered. State control has also had another important influence, namely, in making the unit assigned to transportation in the cost of production a fixed and unvarying quantity. In Germany the railroads yield a handsome revenue to the state, and while the rates charged for transportation are not excessive, they are not fixed at the lowest paying level. Accordingly much attention has been paid of late years to the development of internal water-ways, and generous appropriations have been made by some of the state governments, particularly of Saxony, Prussia, Bavaria, and Baden, for such purposes. The development of traffic on the rivers of Germany, particularly on the Elbe and the Rhine, has been very extensive during the past few years. The tonnage and loading capacity of interior shipping in Germany are much greater than those of sea shipping. Large companies have been formed, regular and prompt service has been instituted, and a great carrying trade developed. Much interest is manifested in the question of facilitating internal water transportation. An influential journal, *Das Schiff*, ably edited by Baron von Studnitz, is published at Dresden to further this object, and the project of uniting the Lower Elbe with the Rhine is seriously considered. The difference in rates between rail and water transportation is considerable. In Upper Germany alone it has made a difference of nearly 20 per cent. in the price of coal, and, of course, a corresponding reduction in the cost of production. This development of water transportation is due to two causes, an effort to offset the disappearance of railroad competition when the state assumed the management of railroads, and the necessity, after the imposition of the German tariff of 1879, of the importers using the cheapest possible means of transportation, that the price of their wares might be affected but little. In Germany, as in other countries, the great practical bearing which the wonderful extension of the means of transportation and communication has had upon industry is that it has infinitely enlarged the field of competition, which enlarged competition has reacted upon prices by depressing them, and upon itself in turn by creating a demand for further and more efficient means to lower again the cost of production. Of course the consumer has been able to possess himself more easily and at less cost of the articles of use or luxury than in former times.

Upon the phenomenon of the rise of wages side by side with the general decline of prices and profits in Germany, Dr. Barth, one of the highest economic authorities of that country, observes that "human labor has become more productive; by the same quantity of labor vastly more useful products are produced and exchanged to-day than even twenty years ago. The sum of all products of labor in which the world has to share or which the world is free to enjoy has not only absolutely but also relatively been largely increased, and the economical condition of mankind has been improved. This, of course, does not mean that all classes of mankind have profited equally by the change. Certainly, however, the wage-laborers are not the losers but the gainers by this change. Take a list of wages wherever you please, and you will always find wages to have advanced with rare interruptions during the last half century. Even where such an advance of wages is not found, the contemporaneous decline in the prices of commodities nevertheless amounts to an advance of wages. This constant increase in the value of labor constitutes an immense progress of civilization."

M. Piermez, a thoughtful Belgian banker and public man, in an examination of the present economic situation, asks the questions: "(1) Are we in the face of a general diminution of wealth? (2) Or is there only a change in its distribution?" Answering the first in the negative, he proceeds to show how the distribution has been modified so as to give a proportion of revenue relatively less to land and capital and greater to labor. Capital has greatly increased and will continue to increase, but probably not in such a rapid progress as heretofore and chiefly for these reasons: "(1) It is not likely that there will be again an economic progress comparable to that by which this century has changed the face of the whole world. (2) The accumulation of savings will tend to diminish in proportion as they are rendered less and less productive. (3) The lower classes, whose share in the world's distribution of wealth will continue to increase, save less than the upper classes. The average well-being of society increases with increase of wealth, and in the partition of this well-being a continually smaller share will go to those who live by wealth already acquired and a greater share to those who work. It will be still more difficult than it is to-day to live without working. Side by side with the fact of the increased reward of the wage-earner must be placed the great advance in the purchasing power of his wages. All the necessaries of life, food, clothing, heating, and lighting have been cheapened, and the tendency is for them to become cheaper still, that is, unless, in the case of the first-named article, the tariffs recently imposed in some European countries, Germany and France especially, the cost of food should remain normal or ascend. Laborers are feeling the effects of higher wages by eating more, clothing themselves better, and lodging in more wholesome houses. This, in return, reacts in making their labor more efficient and enables them to gain still more."

A prominent manufacturer of Mülhausen remarked that he would be glad to have his laborers earn twice as much as they did and consume more, as he would certainly be the gainer thereby and be placed in a better position to compete with English labor. This higher standard of living, he thought, makes it next to impossible to reduce the wages of labor to any great extent in periods of depression.

The theory of European manufacturers is that piece wages have contributed much to the efficiency of labor. In times of depression, when it has been necessary to lower the tariff of wages, it is a well-known fact that the aggregate earnings of laborers have been as great and sometimes even greater under this system than before the depression.

The best European authorities agree that the circle of producing nations has been so enlarged as to make the means of production far in excess of the needs of consumption. The influence of this condition was perhaps first felt in the progress of the crisis of 1873–78. No leading industry has experienced a prominent stimulation since that time except the iron industry, which was due almost entirely to the demand for railroad iron in the United States during the years 1879–82. Twelve years ago a blast furnace producing 50 tons of pig-iron in twenty-four hours was regarded as a good furnace. Now a blast furnace produces as much as 200 tons in the same time. This exemplifies the tendency to increase the means of production far beyond the needs of consumption, and this increase in the great family of producing nations has been far in excess of the increase of population. Excessive production, in the opinion of M. Jules Duckerts, of Belgium, is the reason which every European manufacturer will give first of all as the cause of the prevailing low prices, and he will add that this over-production has been a growth nourished by permanent and not transitory phases of the industrial development of the last half century.

Very many economists and manufacturers consider that the influence of the imposition of protective and prohibitory tariffs in Europe during the last few years cannot be overlooked in a view of the present industrial situation, for formerly England, Belgium, and France were the great producing nations for the rest of Europe, and then the United States commenced to manufacture for herself, and finally to a large extent shut out European products by the imposition of the war tariff. Next Germany entered the list as an industrial competitor on foreign ground, and since 1870 especially has sought a wider market than her own territory. She did not, however, sufficiently control the home market to suit herself, and so the German Government enacted a stringent tariff law in 1879. Either in retaliation for this measure, or to share in the world's ambition to become industrially great, probably from both influences, Russia, Italy, Austria, Turkey, and even Switzerland have since hedged themselves in behind strong customs barriers. Among nations so intimately related geographically and commercially, these measures, in the opinion of very many men able to judge, have had a double effect: First, they have injured the export trade of the great producing nations, and, second, they have induced excessive domestic competition within each nation's boundaries. Both these influences have contributed to further augment the means of production, inducing over-production, or, as it is often called in Europe, faulty production, and lower prices. The manufacturers of Germany in 1878 demanded the tariff as a panacea for the then existing depression. It was given them, but prices were not raised, except the price of iron temporarily, due to the great demand in the United States for railroad iron from 1879 to 1882, in which latter year prices returned to the level of 1878, and they are now at the bottom. All over Germany one hears the complaint that although there is a fair amount to be done in industrial enterprise, it is not worth while to do it. The retaliatory measures of Russia, Austria, and Italy have hurt German export trade exceedingly, but their full effects have not yet been felt. The Russian and Prussian Governments are now engaged in the conciliatory work of expelling one another's subjects from their respective territories, the one mainly because the Russian Pole outbids his German competitor in the demand for labor, and the other because when the tariff went into operation many Prussians invested capital in mines and iron works just across the Prussian border from Upper Silesia. The South German states are also proposing to pour oil on the troubled waters by raising an agitation for the expulsion of Italian cheap labor from their territory.

The German Government considers that by the tariff of 1879 she gained a home market, with the chief exceptions of the lower grades of iron, machinery, and the finer qualities of cotton yarn and woollen cloth. She has also gained over $33,000,000 as annual customs dues, and the use of a great deal of English capital invested in some of the best-paying branches of manufacture from which England is excluded by the tariff. The prices of commodities, from having been permanently raised, are as low as they can be, and the wages of labor have been in no general respect increased. Domestic competition more than supplies the demand of the home market, and Germany, instead of competing with England and Belgium on her own soil, must try strength with them in colonial fields, and she is now trying in several ways to find outlets for her surplus goods, to take the place of the neighboring markets from which she has been largely excluded. Her colonial policy has for its object the establishment of German colonies in Africa and in the Pacific islands which shall be politically and industrially dependent upon the

Fatherland, and also the establishment by subsidy of regular steamship lines to China, Australia, and the East. A beginning in this direction was made in October last by the endowment of 4,500,000 marks (nearly $1,080,000) annually upon the North German Lloyd Steamship Company for a regular bi-monthly service to Australia and China. Germany has been slow to see the advantage of England's splendid equipment for oceanic transportation, but necessity has at last given her instruction. Her policy also includes the improvement of the character of the articles offered by her for export, and the establishment of a huge commercial agency—the Export Bank—with branches throughout the world, the object of which is to furnish trustworthy information to merchants on the state of foreign markets, the solvency of consignees, etc. She also contemplates changes in the laws governing joint-stock companies, with the view of making them more substantial and with greater responsibility toward debtors.

Belgium, whose prosperity in linen, coal, iron, and glass depends so largely upon the export trade, is very injuriously affected by these changes of economic policy by her neighbors.

The conditions relating to Germany have been thus dwelt upon at considerable length in this chapter for the lessons they teach, and because many of the features attending German industrial development are common to so many other nations, and because they illustrate the endeavors of other nations to not only supply their own market with manufactured goods as against the world through various policies, but in addition to gain a profitable export trade. If all the producing nations of the world succeed in supplying themselves with manufactured products, as they are so largely doing and in so many cases have succeeded in doing, and then all seek the relief which comes from selling their surplus products at low rates to their neighbors, the world has indeed reached an industrial epoch, and governmental policies and the rules of political economy must be changed to meet the new conditions resulting from the arrival at a novel industrial period.

CHAPTER IV.

SUGGESTED REMEDIES FOR DEPRESSIONS.

Very many remedies have been suggested for depressions in the past. In a general way, the remedies are very largely theoretical and not capable of statistical illustration as to their value. The testimony given before the three Congressional committees which have investigated industrial depressions, their causes and remedies, developed a very large number of suggested remedies, of course relating to depressions back of the present one. These remedies are stated, alphabetically, as follows:

REMEDIES FOR DEPRESSIONS AS ELICITED BY COMMITTEES OF CONGRESS.

Abrogation of all treaties that interfere with the practical enforcement of the Monroe doctrine, so as to secure the removal of obstacles that prevent our control of the trade of the South and Central American countries.

Apprentices—
    limit the number of.

Arbitration and conciliation—
    establish boards of.

Armies—
    "industrialization" of.

Banks—
    abolish national.
    abolish savings.
    establish postal savings.
    establish a system of uniform protection to investors in savings.

Bonds, national—
    immediate payment of, with paper, to be a legal tender.

Capital—
    proper distribution of.
    equal distribution of profits between, and labor.
    remuneration of labor before.
    let Government fill for the people the position now filled by capitalists.

Children—
    protection of, against the avarice of parents.
    not to be employed under fourteen years of age.

Civil service—
    revision of the.

Coal—
    public ownership of.

Colonization.

Competition—
    necessary to prevent excessive charges in business enterprises.

Contract system—
    abolish the.

Corners—
    prohibition of.

Corporations—
    revoke the corporate charters of, where the functions conferred can be performed by states or the Federal Government.
    limit the profits of.
    no more grants to.
    give labor the means of acquiring ownership in.

Currency—
    sound.
    reform of.
    reduce the fictitious value of the.
    uniform value of the.
    steady value of the.
    confidence in the.
    establish public depositories of.
    no inflation or contraction of the.
    issue, until the purchasing power of a dollar in the United States is placed at the same figure it had when the debt was contracted.

SUGGESTED REMEDIES FOR DEPRESSIONS.   265

Currency—Concluded.
  no further legislation relative to the.
  no further legislation relative to the, for five years.
  return to a specie basis.
  reconstruct the circulating system.
  improve the national banking system.
  legalize free banking.
  legalize free coinage.
  issue silver certificates.
  issue paper money on the faith of the entire wealth of the United States.
  issue twenty millions in greenbacks, of equal value of gold.
  issue $58 per capita, and continue to do so as population increases.
  substitute greenbacks for national-bank notes.
  call in bonds, and issue greenbacks in their stead.
  take the management of the national finances out of the hands of the money ring.
  establish a single unit of value which shall be legal tender.
  make all coin legal tender for all debts, public and private.
  make paper money full legal tender.
  make the gold and silver dollar exchangeable at sub-treasuries.
  make bank notes payable in gold.
  make silver coin redeemable in gold.
  restore silver to its place as a money material.
  substitute national security for private credit.
  bring the money we have into its natural use, instead of having it capitalized.
  let business furnish its own circulating medium.
  create a paper for legal tender, and in the settlement of debts.
  unlimited coinage of silver.
  retire all promissory notes.

District of Columbia—
  establish a municipal government for the.

Education—
  industrial, Government to have supervision over.
  compulsory.
  mechanical.
  technical.

Education—Concluded.
  national.
  general, with national aid.
  legalize a system of, for the lower classes.
  give all healthy children the benefits of, from the age of six to sixteen years.
  Government to have supervision over.
  establish boards of.
  establish industrial schools and colleges.
  establish normal institutes.
  establish art schools.
  establish trade schools.
  educate the masses.
  create a greater interest in the common schools.
  liberal system of, for the lower classes.
  make the educational system more attractive.

Elective franchise—
  give the, to every male.
  give the, to females.

Good judgment, and hard work.

Government—
  reduce salaries of officers of the.
  abolish all unnecessary offices of the.
  make it do its own work.
  change the, from a political to an industrial.
  never to borrow money, nor pay interest.
  more stable.
  rigid economy of the.
  local self, with no Federal interference, by laws of a purely moral or religious nature.

Growth and progress of the nation no longer measured and held in check by the amount of gold taken out of the earth.

Health—
  establish boards of.

Hygiene—
  establish a department of.

House of Representatives—
  restrict the powers of the.

Immigration—
  prohibit.
  prohibit Chinese.
  prohibit foreign contract.
  withdraw all inducements held out to immigrants.

Importation—
  make what we need, and stop importing.
Interest—
  reduce the rates of.
  abolish the system of.
Internal improvements—
  increase.
  make liberal appropriations for.
  undertaken by state and Federal authority, at a hundred points within our jurisdiction.
Iron—
  public ownership of.
Justice to the great labor interests of the country.
Kindergartens—
  establish public.
Labor—
  equal distribution of profits between, and capital.
  more equal distribution of, among the people.
  to receive the benefits of labor-saving machinery.
  redistribution of.
  less machinery to be used in.
  equal wages to male and female laborers doing the same or equal work.
  state action relative to.
  home market for productions of.
  remuneration of, before capital.
  Government pay to be the standard of.
  diversified.
  productions of, to be divided among all.
  national aid to, in developing the natural resources of the country.
  earnings of, proportioned to employers' profits.
  employment given to all.
  loans to indigent, desiring the benefits of the homestead act.
  give employment to, after education.
  make six hours a legal day's work.
  legalize the standard of wages.
  reduce the hours of.
  reduce the working time of, until all find employment.
  increase the wages of.
  organization of.
  reduce the productive power of.
  aid surplus, to settle upon and occupy the public domain.
  legislation in favor of.
  legal protection to.

Labor—Concluded.
  establish a United States bureau of.
  establish state bureaus of.
  establish bureaus for the direction of surplus.
  elect directors of bureaus for the employment of surplus, in every trade, profession, and occupation, paying all the same, from President down; and allowing none but such directors to employ labor.
  establish a new system of industry.
Lands—
  allow no person more than he can economically use.
  allow settlers, quantities of only sufficient for their necessities.
  adjust transportation laws so people can settle on the public.
  aid the surplus of labor to settle upon the.
  break up bonanza farms.
  ground rents to be for public use.
  Government aid in securing.
  scientific instruction in the cultivation of.
  give to actual settlers only.
  rent school.
  rent, instead of selling.
  reclaim, fraudulently obtained.
  reclaim, from corporations that have not earned them.
  reclaim forfeited.
  restore forfeited, to the people.
  abolish private property in.
Laws—
  abolish bankrupt.
  abolish conspiracy.
  abolish discriminating.
  abolish homestead.
  abolish navigation.
  abolish tramp.
  abolish usury.
  abolish land, which give protection to titles not based on personal occupancy.
  abolish, for the collection of debt.
  enforce the eight hour.
  enact land, preventing the holding of great tracts by corporations and individuals, including foreign landlords.
  enact stringent, against fictitious values.

Laws—Concluded.
- enact, punishing bribery with disfranchisment.
- enact, prohibiting lawyers who are legislators from accepting retainers to influence legislation.
- enact, prohibiting officers of public companies from speculating in their own securities.
- enact, making gambling in the necessaries of life a conspiracy.
- enact, limiting the life of corporate charters in future to thirty years, and so far as can be done re-enact existing ones.
- enact, making employers liable for injuries to employés.
- enact, prohibiting the granting of licenses to prisons for the manufacture of cigars.
- enact, prohibiting unjust discrimination.
- enact, prohibiting free passes.
- enact equal, for all classes.
- enact, for the suppression of vice.
- enact, simplifying remedial justice in courts, and reducing expenses.
- enact, against communistic schemes.
- enact, against watering corporate stocks.
- enact, compelling the observance of contracts.
- enact, simplifying the whole legal system.
- enact, changing the tenure of land.
- enact apprentice.
- enact homestead.
- enact prohibition.
- revise the revenue, in the interests of American commerce, agriculture, and manufactures.
- revise the patent.
- repeal of all, that are a burden upon American shipping, and award ocean mail contracts to the lowest bidders among the owners of American vessels, after open competition.
- revoke corporate charters which confer functions like those of transportation, telegraphing, etc., which could be more efficiently and equitably performed by states and the Federal Government.

Legislation—
- wise.

Manufactures—
- establish a department of.

Markets—
- open foreign.

Military Academy—
- abolish the.

Mines—
- public ownership of.

Mississippi River—
- improvement of the.

Monopolies—
- check.
- destroy.

Moral suasion.

Naval School—
- abolish the.

Navigation—
- improve internal.

Navy—
- abolish the.

"Parcel post"—
- establishment of a.

Patents—
- freedom of, with a royalty system.

Petroleum wells—
- public ownership of.

Piecework—
- abolishment of.

Political contributions and expenditures—
- to be made public.

Prejudices—
- extermination of sectional and geographical.

President—
- restrict the powers of the.

Press—
- free.

Prison system—
- abolishment of the.

Private fortunes—
- limitation of.

Producing interests—
- regulate the.

Property—
- secure a fair and just distribution of.
- common ownership of.

Protection—
- protect the manufacturer in his production and the laborer in his labor.

Public debt—
- stop the sinking fund to pay the.

Public works—
  establish efficient boards of, under a comprehensive system and policy.
Public service—
  develop it upon the basis of capable and honest services, and not upon partisan favor.
Railroads—
  Government to have direction and supervision of, and of other corporations.
  not allowed to change transportation rates.
  add building of, telegraphing, and interstate commerce to the functions of the Government.
  regulate freight charges.
  stop jobs of.
  let all, be owned by Government.
  public ownership of.
  provide commissions (state and national) to see that railroad laws are enforced.
  let charges of, be regulated by competition.
Sanitary inspectors—
  increase the number of.
Sanitary reform—
  compelling.
Senate, United States—
  abolish the.
Ships and shipping—
  encourage ship-building.
  own our own ships and do our own shipping.
  foster shipping interests.
  subsidize steamboat lines.
Societies—
  organize benefit.
State—
  entire and absolute secularization of the, and of all laws, in order that the spiritual power may be free, and that bigotry and superstition shall not hinder the state in its normal duties.
Stockholders—
  give the minority some representation.
Tariff—
  abolish the.
  abolish the, on all things which are necessaries of life to the poor, either for consumption or as raw material for their labor.

Tariff—Concluded.
  reduction of the.
  gradual reduction of the.
  revision of the.
  protect by, all articles of the kind we can produce, equal to the difference between the cost of the foreign and domestic labor and capital necessary for their production.
  remit duty on imports entering into goods for export.
  establish a protective.
  establish a reasonable protective.
  establish an ad valorem.
  increase the, on works of art.
  increase the, on articles that have been discriminated against in the late revision of the.
  revenue to be sufficient to carry on the business of the Government, and to be so adjusted as to be the largest on goods in which labor was the largest share.
Taxation—
  abolish.
  abolish all internal, of the United States.
  abolish all, except of land.
  abolish all, except such as is necessary to carry on the Government.
  abolish indirect.
  abolish all, upon things that are necessaries of life to the poor, either for consumption or as raw material for their labor.
  substitute income, for all other.
  establish income.
  establish a progressive income.
  establish a graded income.
  make income the basis of.
  increase of, on capital.
  increase of, on rum and tobacco.
  decrease of, on labor.
  of foreign steamers.
  of all property equally.
  of Government bonds.
  of railroads.
  direct.
  less.
  raise the load of.
  double, on unimproved lands of private owners.
  exempt from, homestead to the amount of $2,000 and household property.

SUGGESTED REMEDIES FOR DEPRESSIONS. 269

Taxation—Concluded.
   adjust, so the tendency will be to make capital, rather than labor, bear the burden.
Telegraphs—
   to be owned by Government.
   establish a system of.
Telephones—
   to be owned by Government.
Trades unions—
   organization of.

Trades union—Concluded.
   given the right to charter.
Truck system—
   abolish the.
Vice-President—
   restrict the powers of the.
Wages—
   let labor have a voice in fixing.
Wealth—
   "moralization" of, both capital as accumulated labor and labor as the potentiality of wealth.

The agents of this Bureau, in carrying out their instructions, sought for remedies for the present depression. They met with representative men in all walks of life, who freely gave the results of their observations and business experience in their suggestions of measures, which, in their minds, would remedy depressions, or modify their severity or shorten their duration. Of course, among such suggested remedies, as among the causes which have been given in the proper chapter, are to be found many trivial suggestions, remote and theoretical, and whose bearing cannot be traced as having any influence in the premises. Many suggestions will also occur to those who read this report, outside of those recorded; but, as a rule, it will be found that the most of those which will occur to men's minds are, to a greater or less extent, involved in the remedies suggested herein. These remedies as stated to the Bureau are classified as follows:

REMEDIES FOR DEPRESSIONS AS GATHERED BY THE AGENTS OF THE BUREAU.

Commercial and mercantile—
   Open foreign markets.
   Open up foreign trade.
   Build ocean steamers for foreign trade.
   Encourage ship-building.
   Subsidize steamboat lines for foreign trade by Government.
   Foster and encourage trade with Mexico and South America.
   Abolish a protective tariff.
   Conservative action relative to the tariff.
   Judicious revision of the tariff.
   Less tariff legislation.
   Removal of tariff on raw material.
   Protection.
   An established tariff.
   Abolish the tariff.
   Abolish the tariff except in a very few cases.
   Free trade.

Commercial and mercantile—Concluded.
   Placing duties on articles demanding protection for the interest of the laboring classes.
   Invest the treasury surplus in internal improvements.
   Forbid the further building of railroads and telegraph lines except by consent of a railroad commission.
   Check the tendencies to overtrading.
   Increase public works.
   Change the navigation laws so as to allow Americans to own foreign-built ships.
   Reclaim public lands forfeited by railroads.
   Reclaim the cattle lands of Colorado, New Mexico, and Wyoming.
   Increase ocean transportation.
   Definite settlement of the tariff for a series of years.
   Reform in distribution.

Financial—
  Reduce taxation.
  Check the expansion of credit.
  Settlement of a world-standard of values, with fixed equivalents in gold and silver.
  Check legislative derangement of the currency.
  Return to greenback currency.
  Tax no man owning less than $5,000 and all owning more than that.
  Legislation that will prevent the consolidation of large bodies of capital.
  A sound currency.
  Equalize taxation by a system of nationalization of land.
  Abolish taxation on all articles except distilled, vinous, and fermented liquors, and tobacco.

Industrial—
  Coöperation.
  Erect central factories to compete with the sugar factories of Germany and France.
  Check tendencies to over-production.
  Manufacture goods on demand.
  Extend the system of profit-sharing.
  Reduce the hours of labor.
  Less production.
  More even production.
  Equalize supply and demand.
  Manufacturers to be content with less than 10 per cent.
  Organization of laborers.
  Organization of employers.
  Sliding scale.

Political—
  Let Government give attention to the individual needs of its citizens.
  Let Congress cease framing laws for the industrial interests of the country.
  Encouragement of the mail service by Congress.

Political—Concluded.
  Adoption of measures to aid and encourage agricultural interests.
  More frequent changes in party administrations.
  Electing men of better judgment to Congress.
  Less frequent meeting of Congress.
  Cease granting lands to corporations.
  Extension of the Presidential term.
  Abolishment of the "spoils system."
  Restrict immigration.
  Extend the system on which the Postal Department is managed to the more important industries.
  Fewer state and national elections.

Social and moral—
  Economy in all directions.
  Better education of the people.
  Enactment of laws to stop speculation.
  Economy and prudence.
  Put honest men in office.
  Well-defined classification of society.
  Educate men for specific duties or stations in life.
  Cessation of speculation.
  Self-improvement of the workingmen.
  Allow no man to own more land than he can use himself.
  Establish industrial schools.
  Harmonious action between labor and capital.
  Teach laborers and employers that the decrease of wages and profits means fewer luxuries.
  Honesty in all business transactions.
  Suppress gambling that is carried on in the necessaries of life.
  Time.
  Boards of arbitration to be created by legislation to settle differences between capital and labor by dividing the profits of the business, above interest, equally between them.

It is neither advisable nor possible to treat all the foregoing remedies extensively or to attempt to illustrate their value. A few, however, stand out prominently, and it may be profitable to consider such at some length, and in such treatment, as in the treatment of causes, purely theoretical and metaphysical suggestions are allowed to stand as such. The first suggested remedy in the foregoing list which attracts attention is that relating to—

The Restriction of Land Grants to Corporations.—
It has been shown under causes that three-fifths of the public domain has been exhausted or taken up, either by settlers or by grants to corporations, but to a very large extent by the latter, and that the remaining two-fifths is made up largely of undesirable lands. These being the facts, a halt should be made in freely granting lands to corporations, for however valuable such grants may be to the public interest in developing great lines of railroads, the result is that the lands constitute a basis to a greater or less extent for speculative purposes. Had a halt been made at an earlier period in our history it would have been well for the country. If there are to be no restrictions upon immigration, the Government should keep control of as large an amount of lands suitable for actual settlement as possible consistent with a progressive policy. So the remedy suggested, to "cease granting lands to corporations," has a practical bearing, and casual consideration takes such suggested remedy out of the realms of theory. Closely connected with this suggested remedy is the following:

The Restriction of Immigration.—Under causes the results of too free immigration have been pointed out. Legitimate voluntary immigration may be too rapid to enable a country developing its industries to assimilate labor from the outside; but when immigration becomes a subject of inducement, of contract, for the purpose of displacing a higher grade of labor, the result is indeed pernicious, and all the authority of law should be called in to prevent the continuance of the wrong. This Congress has undertaken to do, as will be seen by the following law:

AN ACT to prohibit the importation and migration of foreigners and aliens under contract or agreement to perform labor in the United States, its territories, and the District of Columbia.

Be it enacted by the Senate and House of Representatives of the United States of America in Congress assembled, That from and after the passage of this act it shall be unlawful for any person, company, partnership, or corporation, in any manner whatsoever, to prepay the transportation, or in any way assist or encourage the importation or migration of any alien or aliens, any foreigner or foreigners, into the United States, its territories, or the District of Columbia, under contract or agreement, parol or special, express or implied, made previous to the importation or migration of such alien or aliens, foreigner or foreigners, to perform labor or service of any kind in the United States, its territories, or the District of Columbia.

SEC. 2. That all contracts or agreements, express or implied, parol or special, which may hereafter be made by and between any person, company, partnership, or corporation, and any foreigner or foreigners, alien or aliens, to perform labor or service or having reference to the performance of labor or service by any person in the United States, its territories, or the District of Columbia previous to the migration or importation of the person or persons whose labor or service is contracted for into the United States, shall be utterly void and of no effect.

SEC. 3. That for every violation of any of the provisions of section one of this act the person, partnership, company, or corporation violating the same, by knowingly assisting, encouraging or soliciting the migratión or importation of any alien or aliens, foreigner or foreigners, into the United States, its territories, or the District of Columbia, to perform labor or service of any kind under contract or agreement, express or implied, parol or special, with such alien or aliens, foreigner or foreigners, previous to becoming residents or citizens of the United States, shall forfeit and pay for every such offense the sum of one thousand dollars, which may be sued for and recovered by the United States or by any person who shall first bring his action therefor including any such alien or foreigner who may be a party to any such contract or agreement, as debts of like amount are now recovered in the circuit courts of the United States; the proceeds to be paid into the treasury of the United States; and separate suits may be brought for each alien or foreigner being a party to such contract or agreement aforesaid. And it shall be the duty of the district attorney of the proper district to prosecute every such suit at the expense of the United States.

SEC. 4. That the master of any vessel who shall knowingly bring within the United States on any such vessel, and land, or permit to be landed, from any foreign port or place, any alien laborer, mechanic, or artisan, who, previous to embarkation on such vessel, had entered into contract or agreement, parol or special, express or implied, to perform labor or service in the United States, shall be deemed guilty of a misdemeanor, and on conviction thereof, shall be punished by a fine of not more than five hundred dollars for each and every such alien laborer, mechanic or artisan so brought as aforesaid, and may also be imprisoned for a term not exceeding six months.

SEC. 5. That nothing in this act shall be so construed as to prevent any citizen or subject of any foreign country temporarily residing in the United States, either in private or official capacity, from engaging, under contract or otherwise, persons not residents or citizens of the United States to act as private secretaries, servants, or domestics for such foreigner temporarily residing in the United States as aforesaid; nor shall this act be so construed as to prevent any person, or persons, partnership, or corporation from engaging, under contract or agreement, skilled workman in foreign countries to perform labor in the United States in or upon any new industry not at present established in the United States: *Provided*, That skilled labor for that purpose cannot be otherwise obtained; nor shall the provisions of this act apply to professional actors, artists, lecturers, or singers, nor to persons employed strictly as personal or domestic servants: *Provided*, That nothing in this act shall be construed as prohibiting any individual from assisting any member of his family or any relative or personal friend, to migrate from any foreign country to the United States, for the purpose of settlement here.

SEC. 6. That all laws or parts of laws conflicting herewith be, and the same are hereby, repealed.

Approved, February 26, 1885.

To undertake to regulate voluntary immigration is an exceedingly delicate matter. The policy of the Government in the past, the principles on which the United States Government is founded, and all the traditions of the country furnish arguments against any such regulation, and yet free, voluntary immigration may do the industries of the country great harm. If so, the past and its precedents should not influence the future and its good. As stated under "Causes," the industrial world having arrived at what may be called a crisis period through the rapid extension of machinery and the consequent over development of the industries of the world, makes the doctrine that the United States offers an asylum to the world somewhat dangerous, or, at least, renders it a doctrine now largely out of place. The constitution of the forces employed in the mechanical industries offers the sharpest argument in favor of wise regulation of immigration, for it will be remembered that 31.9 per cent. of all those employed in such industries in this country are of foreign birth, and however much foreign immigration has aided the development of railroad building, public works, rivers, and other enterprises, the industries have been obliged to assimilate labor faster than the demands for products have warranted. These statements are made with a thorough understanding of the great value which foreign citizens have brought to this country—value not only in their own labor, but in the aggregate wealth which has been brought with them— and as their assimilation as citizens with those of longer residence becomes more and more felt, the value of their presence becomes more and more enhanced. Their interest, however, is involved in this question of over-immigration.

The Enactment of Laws to Stop Speculation.— The effect that such laws would have, if they could be applied specifically, would be for the public good. The facility with which stock companies can be organized in most of the states, and the means which such companies offer for the aggregation of small sums into large capital for the purpose of developing great movements, have been referred to. Probably any laws which might prevent such employment of small sums would be pernicious in their effects, but it might be wise to consider whether existing laws have not been too loosely drawn, and whether they do not grant too great privileges in the way of watering stock and of launching enterprises upon the public that have not money or property back of them. It might be well to enact laws allowing no organization to put its stock upon the market unless the full value of its capital stock is paid in, either in the currency of the country or in absolute property. Many corporations are organized for the purpose of floating stock, and with a glowing prospectus the stock is floated. The result, under such circumstances, is disastrous to all engaged, and the morals of the community in which such transactions take place are more or less damaged. Certainly in this suggested remedy there may be found practical steps which can be taken. Under this head, too, would come the question of corners and trading in futures. The attempt to make any law which shall be efficacious in preventing men from engaging in the unholy work of speculation in food products especially, and in bringing pecuniary responsibility to operations in futures, will be found to tax the ingenuity of the law-maker. The difficulties in the way have been well stated by Justice Fenner, of the supreme court of Louisiana, in a recent decision, in which he presented the following points:

"(1) Sales of property for future delivery, with the bona fide intention and obligation to make actual delivery, are lawful contracts; but, if under the form of such a contract the real intent be merely to speculate upon the rise and fall of prices, and the goods are not to be delivered, but the contract to be settled on the basis of difference of prices, the transaction is a wager and is non-actionable.

"(2) In order to affect the contract the alleged illegal intent must have been mutual, and such intent by one party, not concurred in by the other, will not avail.

"(3) The law presumes lawful purpose until the contrary is proved, and when one party charges illegal intent the burden of proof is imposed upon him.

"(4) The validity of the contract depends upon the state of things existing at its date, and is not affected by subsequent agreements under which the parties voluntarily assent to a settlement on the basis of differences.

"(5) The mere fact that at the date of his contract the vendor had not the goods and had made no arrangements for obtaining them, and had no expectation of receiving them unless by subsequent purchase, does not suffice to impair the contract. The contrary doctrine once announced is now thoroughly overruled.

"(6) It follows that the failure to identify the particular goods sold does not affect the matter, because the sale is not of ascertained articles but of articles of a designated kind, quantity to be selected thereafter, which is a lawful contract when the obligations are reciprocal."

The difficulties so clearly stated by Justice Fenner arise every time the attempt is made to prevent corners by law. It is not probable that trading in futures and the making up of corners on food products, or on products of manufacture, create or bring about industrial depression, but they are often serious aggravating accompaniments of such depression, and as such should be regulated, if it is in the power of law so to do, and it is to be hoped that some efficient means may be found which shall destroy the ability of men to work public harm through such kinds of speculation.

The Establishment of Boards of Arbitration to Settle Industrial Difficulties.

—Industrial arbitration, and, in fact, all arbitration, is the result of high moral perception of right and wrong in the parties resorting to it. The laws of most states, if not all, offer facilities for the settlement of suits at law by sending the matter, on proper agreement of the parties involved, to a referee or referees, the decision of the referee or referees, when entered on the records of a court, having the binding force of a judgment by that court. To reach such a reference or arbitration, however, a party aggrieved brings an action in the ordinary way, by which the defendant is brought before a tribunal under the pains and penalties of law. The two parties then are before the court as parties, the defendant, brought there by the process of law served on him by an officer of the court, and he must appear or subject himself to judgment by default. When the two parties are before a court then the law allows them a more speedy way, if they elect, to settle their difficulties than by trial; that is, by submitting the matter to a referee or referees. The adjustment of industrial difficulties in this way could have but one result, which, although an indirect result, would have all the features of a direct judgment at law. If the employer or the employés in an industrial establishment, feeling that they have cause of complaint, either against the other, could summon the offending party in the way described before a board of arbitration or any tribunal which might be established for the purpose of settling the difficulty, and after a hearing of all the facts bearing upon the case by both sides, or of *ex parte* testimony in case the party summoned did not appear, a decision should be entered having any binding force whatever, even for a definite and clearly-defined period, such decision must of necessity carry with it a penalty for nonconformance. The condition of things then leaves the parties in the position, if an employer, of being obliged to manufacture goods under conditions established by law; that is, he must pay wages which the law directs or suffer the penalty; if an employé, he must accept the wages decreed by law, whether too low or otherwise, or incur the penalty imposed. This is simply establishing the rates of wages and prices of goods by law, and is a result which neither the employer nor the employé can for a moment desire, although, without looking to the logical results of a board having the powers designated, such a board is freely demanded as a solution of labor troubles and a remedy for industrial depressions. Now, industrial arbitration, in order to be successful in the least degree, must be purely voluntary on the part of those intending to submit their grievances to the decision of others. The disposition to submit points in controversy to the decision of parties outside of those immediately concerned is almost arbitration in itself, and the parties are not far apart in their opinions. The creation of a board of arbitration by law, for the sake of having convenient machinery ready by which parties can have their differences adjusted by the good offices of arbitrators, would undoubtedly facilitate the growth of the spirit of arbitration, and in this direction the suggested remedy has vital force; but boards of arbitration created by law must be so constituted as not to make them obstacles to industrial peace instead of helps in bringing the workingman and his employer to a higher plane and a better appreciation of each other. It is the highest moral sentiment in man which leads him into arbitration, and when he is possessed of such sentiment he should have every facility given him for its activity. Industrial arbitration has done much in England toward preventing strikes, for in those trades where the men are most thoroughly organized, and where they have adopted or established by voluntary action boards of arbitration, the fewest strikes occur. The English statute relating to the establishment of such boards has not, however, been resorted to in many instances. In fact, to-day it is almost a dead letter, but it stands on the statute book as the reflection of a moral sentiment, and as such has stimulated the growth of the idea of adjusting difficulties on clearly-constituted and well-defined rights and privileges of both parties to a controversy.

The Contraction of Credit.—A very potent cause in producing financial difficulties, resulting it may be in industrial depression—certainly in producing falling prices, the opening symptoms of industrial depression—is the great expansion of credit, and the remedy suggested by some of the bankers of the country of "checking the expansion of credit" has great force, but such check is exceedingly difficult of accomplishment. So far as law is concerned, the most direct way, probably, would be to make the collection of debts more difficult under legal process, thereby stimulating men to depend upon honorable action for the payment of debts and not upon the force of an execution. The difficulty is more in the way of free transaction of business than in practical legal obstacles.

A Sound Currency is often suggested as one of the remedies for industrial depressions, but industrial depressions have occurred with a sound currency existing as well as when the currency was demoralized in any way. The present industrial depression, novel in its completeness, as has been pointed out, not only originated but has progressed along with the existence of what popularly has been considered the finest banking system of the world, and with a currency as stable as coin. It cannot be denied, however, that both inflation and contraction disturb values, and thereby disturb industry, and certainly a sound currency is demanded by labor in order that the laborer may know the value of his earnings at all times, and it is demanded by the producer that he may calculate with reasonable accuracy the cost of production. So, while a sound currency might not prevent an industrial depression or remedy it after it had commenced, it is one of the regulating influences which help largely to modify the severity of any industrial depression. The discussion of purely financial crises or monetary disturbances would develop far different considerations.

Commercial and Mercantile Conditions.—Under this general classification many remedies have been suggested. They nearly all relate to the tariff, ocean transportation, foreign trade, navigation laws, and public works; but under none of the topics suggested in the above general classification of commercial and mercantile is there much if any opportunity for illustration, and the remedies suggested are very largely confined to theoretical views. Nearly all have some bearing on the question, and some an important bearing, but it is difficult to see how any of the features suggested under commercial and mercantile remedies could, if adopted, prevent an industrial depression, because industrial depressions occur under the conditions referred to in such suggestions. The general view under the chapter relating to the manufacturing nations of the world shows clearly the impossibility of preventing or remedying industrial depressions by the adoption of any of the suggestions under this head. The opening of foreign markets would, of course, relieve this country of its surplus goods, but its surplus would then increase, and the relative position of the United States to the other nations in the family of manufacturing units would remain substantially the same. The increase of ocean transportation at a time when the means of transportation in Great Britain are a burden to that country, would hardly remedy depressions in this or any other commercial or industrial nation. The continuance of a protective tariff, or the abolition of a protective tariff, in the light of the conditions of other countries where as severe or severer depressions prevail than in this, would not remedy the depression nor prevent it. The judicious revision of the tariff, regulating duties on a just and equitable basis, in so far as it removes apprehension and puts all interests on a fairer basis, would be a remedial measure. Nor can a definite settlement of the tariff for a long series of years be accomplished, because changes in condition vary the cost of production, and would disturb any schedule which might be adopted. So far as a wide study of this subject would indicate, it seems that if a tariff having any of the elements whatever of protection in it is to be sustained, it should, as suggested under causes, be adjusted on a basis of the cost of production. Such adjustment would bring stability, would relieve manufacturers of anxiety, would satisfy labor, and would keep the treasury supplied with funds. Practically these are the ends sought, it is presumed, by any adjustment of the tariff, or even by its abolition. Any adjustment on the basis of the cost of production would inevitably result in a constant enlargement of the free list, and in so far would have a moral effect in the community which could not be otherwise than healthful.

The Distribution of Products.—Reform in the methods of distributing supplies would, if rightly directed, bring great relief to consumers. Coöperation, in its distributive form, is suggested as a remedy in this respect; but coöperative distribution is only a half measure, because this method is organized, economized, and made effective for consumers almost entirely, and producers as such are not materially benefited. This has been the case in England, where the Rochdale system has been carried to such magnificent proportions. Under this system the societies, as purchasers, keenly appreciate and follow the rule adopted by the private trader, buying at the lowest possible competition prices, and in their transactions with producers making use of the same expedients as those employed in private trade to drive good bargains and thus swell profits for the benefit of their customers. The maxim that "goods well bought are half sold" is kept constantly in view, and the importance of keen and shrewd buying is so well understood that employés possessing the requisite ability in this direction are highly prized and liberally paid. To the producer, therefore, the system of coöperative distribution offers no special advantages; on the other hand, it tends to lower prices, and in so far as this is the result depression is aided, so that the work or progress resulting from coöperative distribution may react against consumers so far as they are producers; and the attempt to remove the middleman from the channels of trade fails. The coöperative stores pay competition prices and manufacture goods at the lowest possible labor cost, but its workmen, unless members of a coöperative store, can have no share in the profits. A recent writer indulges in the following criticism on the system:

"The coöperative wholesale society is a gigantic middleman; in its workshops it pays the lowest of competition wages; in the language of one of the workers in one of the shoe factories, 'the workmen have to work for what they can get; they know there is no true coöperation.' In its transactions with other producers it pays the lowest of competition prices; the profits made out of the retail prices are distributed amongst the members, labor is depressed. In short, it is as far from displaying a single feature of real coöperation as any private trader is who uses the weapons of competition and capitalism for his personal ends, regardless of the interests of others.

"The coöperative labor association, whose principal object is to recognize the combined interests of capital and labor in productive enterprise, is largely composed of members of the coöperative movement. In a conference just held, a resolution was passed asking 'the committee of the labor association to point out in a *fraternal* spirit to the wholesale coöperative society the grave injury they are doing to the cause of coöperation by their failure to carry out coöperative principles in their productive works, and to offer their services in placing the wholesale workshops upon a true coöperative basis.'" a

So far, then, as relates to removing the evils which it is alleged spring from competition in the distribution of supplies, coöperative societies in England have not yet conspicuously succeeded. This does not, of course, indicate failure, for but little has been attempted in this direction, and the criticism is only introduced here to show that coöperative distribution without the alliance of coöperative production in some form is only a half measure as a remedy for bad distribution. The worst features of the distribution of goods are to be found, of course, in the enhanced price paid for products on account of the existence of intermediate handling by middlemen. A man who weaves cloth for which he receives less than 4 cents a yard as a producer, may have to pay 75 cents a yard as a consumer, the profit to the retailer in such case being at least 25 cents a yard; that is, the retailer, for handling one yard of goods receives 25 cents compensation, where the weaver, for weaving that same yard of cloth received less than 4 cents compensation. This single illustration is sufficient to show how far distribution is at fault in matters of depression and as an obstacle to the best interests of wage-receivers. In the production of goods cost has been greatly reduced by wise distribution of raw material; in fact, such distribution has been almost entirely reformed. The right honorable Mr. Goschen, M. P., in an address before the Manchester Chamber of Commerce in

---

a Distribution Reform, by Thomas Illingworth. Cassell & Co.

June last, stated to his audience: "You all know that between Manchester and India there has been an elimination of a great many middlemen. Now, in London that is the case to a still more extraordinary extent. Let me tell you how the cotton trade, for instance, used to be conducted between New Orleans and the interior of Germany. The New Orleans man consigned his cotton to New York or to a New York house, the New York house consigned it to Liverpool, Liverpool to London, London to Hamburg, and Hamburg to spinners in the interior of Germany. But now the German spinner goes direct to New Orleans, the agent visits him in his home, and a number of intermediate profits and commissions are swept away." Mr. Goschen also makes a very wise remark when speaking of the comparatively small profits which have been made in manufacturing: "It is true of a great portion of the country (Great Britain) that trade in which profits have been small has been sound, and comparatively less has been lost by bad debts."

A careful examination in all directions, so far as production is concerned, whether of agricultural or manufactured products, leads clearly to the conclusion that production increases faster than population, so that one of the great economic problems in this matter is, not how shall production be made to keep pace with population, but how shall production be more equably distributed. Faulty distribution, then, and not over-production, is the truer term, but to the community involved over-production more clearly expresses the difficulty.

Coöperation, as applied to distribution, might remedy this difficulty by reducing the share secured by the party who handles the yard of cloth, but it would in no wise raise the amount received by the weaver for weaving the same goods; so that coöperation, in order to effect the best results to the two forces, the producer and the consumer, must join the two in the same transaction; that is, coöperation, in order to be complete, must, as a principle, surround production as well as consumption. As a partial remedial agency, coöperative distribution, when successful, is influential. Its completed relationship involves —

Profit-sharing.—This is not only an attractive but a most instructive theme. It is the whole principle of coöperation applied to the production of goods. Simple, pure coöperation cannot succeed when applied to manufacturing, for two reasons: First, under it the worker must wait till the last for the profits which may come to him in the place of wages, and if no profit comes his labor has gone for naught; on the other hand, the management would receive its share in salary at the outset, as a rule. In the second place, a score of men, operating on the simple basis of each doing a full day's work on some kind of production, cannot make such coöperation a success, because some out of the score will find themselves doing more than others, while those who produce less receive the same amount of profits. Human nature, individual development, skill, ambition, are opposed to such coöperation. The advantage the present system has over simple coöperative production is that wages are paid from the outset and management waits for its compensation till the goods are sold and the books balanced. These fundamental difficulties prevent simple coöperation from being considered seriously as a remedy for industrial depressions or of labor troubles. This is the crude popular conception of coöperation in production as a plan to get rid of the employer and the wage system. The workers under it are supposed to employ a manager to be subject to their will, and, if necessary, hire capital at usual rates of interest. Then, pooling their services, they are to divide among themselves whatever profit there may be after fixed charges are paid. This scheme is purely visionary and utterly impracticable. Workers cannot wait till an indefinite future for their reward, neither can they run the risk of getting no reward at all. They must be guaranteed something, to be paid at frequent intervals, and the only party that can so guarantee is the capitalist employer, who alone can run risks and wait indefinitely for rewards. The capitalist employer may be an association of the workers themselves, but it is none the less an employer, a moral personality, possessing all the powers over individual workers that an individual employer would have. The more efficient and prosperous members become inevitably the controlling power in the association, and they will not consent to divide profits irrespectively of the value of services or to guarantee employment to inefficient members. The valid idea in this crude conception of coöperation is that in the degree that workmen develop the necessary qualifications and acquire the requisite capital they may become self-employers, and that, whether as self-employers or otherwise, they should as workers participate in the profits of industry in proportion to their efficiency. This ideal is in process of realization through various forms of coöperative organization and profit-sharing. Industrial partnership instituted by capitalist employers, and coöperation instituted by capital-owning workmen, work toward the same result from different directions. Each has its own proper field, and each will probably acquire increasing prominence in social economy.[a]

What is known as industrial copartnership, involving profit-sharing and embodying all the vitality there is in the principle of coöperation, offers a practical way of producing goods on a basis at once just to capital and to labor, and one which brings out the best moral elements of the capitalist and the workman. This system has been tried in many instances, and nearly always with success. The leading experiments in Europe are well known, among them being the system adopted by Leclaire, a Parisian house painter; the methods in vogue with the Paris and Orleans Railway Company; the industrial partnership established by M. Godin at Guise, France; the experiments of Messrs. Briggs Brothers in Yorkshire, England, and other places. In the United States but little has been done in this direction, but wherever

[a] Cf. "Profit-sharing," Seventeenth Annual Report of the Massachusetts Bureau of Statistics of Labor.

the principle has been tried there have been three grand results: Labor has received a more liberal share for its skill, capital has been better remunerated, and the moral tone of the whole community involved raised. Employment has been steadier and more sure. The interest of all has been given for the general welfare. Each man feels himself more a man. The employer looks upon his employés in the true light, as associates. Conflict ceases and harmony takes the place of disturbances. Sometimes the experiments in profit-sharing have been abandoned for one cause or another, but so long as they have existed no strikes have occurred, and no labor troubles have been experienced. This feature, as a suggested remedy for industrial depressions, has so much in it of hope for the future that specimen articles of agreement, which have been adopted by manufacturing concerns, are printed for the benefit of all:

"First. On all orders executed during the year 1886, commencing January 1 ultimo, both capital and labor in proportion to the amounts or values contributed by each shall share in the net profits made on such orders during the year.

"Second. The net profits shall be determined in the following manner, viz: Out of the gross receipts, or from the capital employed shall be drawn, first, the wages of the men employed as journeymen, whether by day's work or piece-work, at the rates mutually agreed upon or otherwise established, which shall be paid monthly. Second, all other expenses of conducting the business, including superintendence, travelling expenses, clerk hire, taxes, insurance, and legal interest on the capital employed, shall then be deducted and paid out of the gross profits, and the balance remaining shall be treated as the net profits from which a dividend shall be declared and paid in manner and form as hereinafter provided.

"Third. The net profits having been determined, the entire amount shall be divided into three parts, one part to be appropriated and paid as a dividend to labor, one part to be appropriated and paid as a dividend to capital, and one-third to be reserved as a guarantee fund, to which fund shall be charged all losses by bad debts, or credits given for materials and labor during the year.

"Fourth. The labor dividend shall be made and paid before any dividend is paid to capital, and such payment shall be made at the end of each fiscal year, or as soon thereafter as the books can be written up, an inventory taken, and the net profits determined.

"Fifth. When the net profits have been determined as aforesaid, the same may be verified by a competent accountant or auditor, to be selected and agreed upon by the parties in interest; and when such accountant shall certify that the net profits have been correctly and fairly determined, then the dividends may be paid; but such accountant or auditor shall not be at liberty to disclose or make public any other facts concerning the business audited than a simple verification of the accounts and the sum total of the net profits for the year, available for the purpose of a dividend.

"Sixth. As the labor dividend is intended for labor only, no officer, superintendent, overseer, clerk, agent, or other employé drawing a salary, or however otherwise paid, nor any contractor or subcontractor, who, for their own account and profit, contract or agree for a "lump sum" to do and perform the whole or certain specific parts of the work upon a building, monument, or other structure, such work being outside of and not subject to an established or agreed bill of prices, either for day's work or piece-work, therefore no such officer, superintendent, clerk, apprentice, or contractor will participate in any dividend paid to labor as hereinbefore stated.

"Seventh. No workman who during the year shall have been discharged for good and sufficient cause, such as drunkenness, insubordination, bad workmanship, etc., or who leaves the employment of the company without the consent of the superintendent in writing, shall be entitled to participate in any dividend of profits for the year during which such discharge has taken place.

"Eighth. No workman shall be deprived of his dividend who has been discharged arbitrarily or without good cause, or who has been discharged for the reason that the superintendent has not sufficient orders in hand to justify his further employment.

"Ninth. The value of all labor contributed to the business for the year shall, for the purpose of a dividend, be treated as so much capital, which capital, having been returned to the laborer in the form of wages, is still entitled to a share of the profits in just proportion to the amount contributed during the year in which such profits are made.

"Tenth. The true value of all labor contributed as aforesaid shall be determined by the amounts earned, and credited to each workman as wages for labor performed during the year; and the dividend to each will be declared upon the exact amount thus earned and credited to his individual account. For example, suppose the entire amount of capital employed to be $100,000, and the entire amount paid for labor during the year to be $150,000. Such an amount of capital employed and wages paid ought, with the added cost of transportation and delivery, to insure an output of $400,000 and a net profit of $25,000. Of this amount one-third, or $8,333.33, would be credited to guarantee amount to provide for an assumed loss of about 2 per cent. on the entire output; the balance would remain for a dividend to capital and labor in proportion to their respective contributions, in this example: Two-thirds to capital, $6,666.67, and three-fifths to labor, $10,000, or 6.66 per cent. on each; thus the workman whose wages for the year amounts to $1,000 would have a dividend of $66.66, and he whose wages amounts to $600 would have $39.96. This dividend to labor would also be materially increased, owing to the fact that all those who take work by contract, superintendents, clerks, apprentices, etc., do not participate; so that if each man's labor be treated as so much capital contributed to the business, that capital is not only returned to its owner as wages at the end of each month, but at the end of the year it is again reckoned and rewarded with a high rate of interest.

"Eleventh. At the end of the year all outstanding accounts and bills receivable will be treated as good under the guarantee account, and therefore available in determining the net profits. If the guarantee account does not prove to be sufficient to cover the losses the amount must be made up by the stockholders, but when it is more than sufficient the surplus will belong to the stockholders.

"Twelfth. The control of the business must necessarily be in the hands of the stockholders. Men employed every day in mechanical labor cannot watch the markets, or possess the aptitude for business management on a large scale which is requisite to success; but they can do much in stopping the leaks caused by inefficient and bad workmanship.

"Thirteenth. All work done or money earned by the employment of machinery will be counted to the credit of labor and capital alike, and the profits made thereby will be subject to the same rule for distribution as for profits otherwise made.

"Fourteenth. No officer, director, or stockholder shall receive any salary or compensation, except for services actually rendered, and time actually spent in the service of the company, all of which shall be as fully stated as the amount of service contributed by any other person in the employment of the company.

"Fifteenth. The rate of wages per diem, the bill of prices for piece-work, and the number of hours to constitute a day's work shall be determined by mutual agreement on or before the 1st day of January in each year, and any disagreement which may arise during the year between the superintendent and workmen in regard to the same shall be settled by arbitration.

"Sixteenth. The rate of wages per diem and the bill of prices for piece-work shall not be reduced by the superintendent to affect any contract on hand, or taken upon the rate of wages or bill of prices prevailing at the time such contract was made, neither shall the rate of wages or bill of prices be advanced by the workmen to affect such contracts, and if so advanced the difference in cost by reason thereof may be adjusted in making up the dividends."

That inquirers may have the advantage of the experience of one of the oldest coöperative stock-associations in the country, the by-laws of the Somerset (Mass.) Foundery are given:

"ARTICLE 1. This company shall be known by the name and title of the Somerset Coöperative Foundery Company. The business of this company shall be the manufacturing of iron castings.

"ART. 2. The capital stock of this company shall consist of $15,000, divided into one hundred and fifty shares, of $100 each, and no person shall be permitted to hold an amount to exceed ten shares.

"ART. 3. All stock shall be paid for within thirty days from the time of subscribing, and no one shall be a member of this association or entitled to vote in its meetings until he shall have paid an amount equal to one share.

"ART. 4. The salary of the officers shall be fixed at the yearly meetings.

"ART. 5. The officers of this company shall consist of a president, treasurer, and of not more than thirteen directors, who shall be styled a board of managers; they shall also have a corporation clerk and foreman.

"ART. 6. The board of managers shall have power to make such prudential by-laws as they may deem proper for the management and disposition of the capital stock and business affairs of the company, not inconsistent with the laws of this state, as they may elect, and of the prescribing the duties of officers.

"ART. 7. It shall be the duty of the president to preside at all meetings of the directors and stockholders; he shall make and execute all contracts as directed by the board of managers; he shall be the authorized agent of the company, and his signature, when attested by the clerk, shall be the bond of the company.

"ART. 8. The clerk shall keep a correct record of the meetings of the stockholders and the board of managers; he shall be chairman of the finance committee, and perform such other duties as the board of managers may prescribe.

"ART. 9. The treasurer shall have charge of the funds of the company; he shall receipt for all money received by him, and deposit the same in such place as the board of managers may designate; before entering upon the duties of his office, he shall give bonds in the penal sum of $5,000 for the faithful performance of the duties of his office, said bonds to be acceptable to the board of managers.

"ART. 10. There shall be annual meetings of the stockholders for the choice of officers held on the second Monday in January of each year, and special meetings of the stockholders may be called by the president at any time by giving seven days' notice of the time, place, and object of the meetings, by mail or otherwise, to all the stockholders, and in the absence or inability of the president to perform the duties of his office, it shall be the duty of the clerk, upon the application of five or more of the stockholders of the company in writing, setting forth the object of the meeting, to notify the stockholders in the same manner prescribed by the president.

"ART. 11. The board of managers shall hold regular meetings at least once in each month, or when ordered by the president, for the transaction of any business that may require their attention; it shall require a majority of the board to constitute a quorum for business.

"ART. 12. There shall be such distribution of the profits or earnings of the association among the workmen, purchasers, and stockholders as shall be described by the by-laws, at such times as therein prescribed and as often as once in twelve months, provided that no distribution shall be declared and paid until a sum equal to at least 10 per cent. of the net profits shall be appropriated for a contingent or sinking fund, until there shall have accumulated a sum equal to 30 per cent. in excess of such capital stock.

"ART. 13. Members employed by this company shall conduct themselves properly, and for the interest of the company; failing to do so they subject themselves to dismissal by the foreman or superintendent, and they shall not be again employed without the consent of two-thirds of the board of managers.

"ART. 14. In taking apprentices, sons of stockholders shall have the preference.

"ART. 15. No member shall be considered a working member except he shall hold five shares, but may be employed by the agent or foreman.

"ART. 16. This company shall not be bound to redeem any share of its capital stock within two years of the date of its corporation, and then it shall require four months' notice from any stockholder desiring the redemption of stock, but the same may be transferred at any time by any person acceptable to the board of managers.

"ART. 17. Any member having shares to sell shall first offer them to the company.

"ART. 18. No person not a stockholder shall be eligible to office.

"ART. 19. These by-laws may be altered or amended at any regular meeting of the stockholders, but any alteration shall require a vote of two-thirds of the stockholders present."

The system of profit-sharing means just this: That the proprietor receives for the capital he invests the ruling rate of interest, as part of the legitimate expense of production. He puts in as his share, other than capital, his managerial skill, his business accomplishments, and his knowledge of the industry in which he is engaged. The men who work for him receive for their time and for the ordinary display of the skill required, the ordinary rate of wage. The workman also contributes, under profit-sharing or industrial copartnership, his liveliest interest, his best skill, and the care of tools and materials. For the skill, knowledge, and management of the proprietor, and for his being liable for the risks of the establishment, he is entitled to the larger share of profits under this system, while the workman, taking no risks of the enterprise beyond that of employment, is entitled to the smaller share of profits; but the two forces together arrange for a division of profits on some just and equitable basis. This system, simple in itself, humane in all its bearings, just in every respect to all the parties concerned, is the combination of all that is good in the wage system and all that is good in coöperation as applied to production. This compound system is becoming a necessity. Under it the workman receives something more than has been accorded to him on account of the improvements in machinery; he becomes a part of the individuality of the establishment; he is lifted to a higher scale; his intelligence, his moral character have weight in the establishment in proportion to his interest in it, and the whole concern has a better chance for prosperity, for weathering depressions, and for general happiness, than under the present wage system alone. It is this compound system as the outgrowth of the wage system, that was referred to in the introduction of this volume as being grander than the wage system. It is a pleasure to be able to state that the proprietors of many influential manufacturing establishments in this country are contemplating the organization of their establishments upon this basis. They see the success of the enterprises where this system already has been adopted, and are glad to follow in so just a path.

An indirect method of sharing profits is through benefits of various kinds, as insurance, schools, libraries, and beautiful surroundings, where such are maintained by employers out of their profits and enjoyed by employés as an addition to what their wages would purchase. Such participation helps to preserve the stability of labor, and has been offered to workmen by many proprietors and in different countries. The erection of healthful residences, which are rented to operatives at a low per cent. on cost, has been resorted to in many places. This is true of great productive establishments like the works of Herr Krupp, at Essen, in Rhenish Prussia; of several establishments at Mülhausen; of Saltaire, founded by Sir Titus Salt, in Yorkshire, England; of the efforts of Fairbanks Brothers, at Saint Johnsbury, Vt.; of the Ludlow Company, in Massachusetts; of the Willimantic Linen Works and the Cheney Brothers Silk Works, in Connecticut; and of Pullman, in Illinois. All such undertakings help the workman up in his surroundings, and he secures indirectly a participation in the profits of production outside and beyond his wages; yet these are not experiments at profit-sharing, as such, but they lead to profit-sharing, and surely indicate the results which might accrue when the principle is carried to a greater extent.

Many peculiar institutions illustrative of this idea may be found in Belgium, especially in the coal, iron, and woollen districts. Most of these are voluntary in their origin, except the "Caisse de Prévoyance en faveur des Ouvriers Mineurs," which is obligatory upon every one receiving a mining concession. The object of this and of the numerous "Caisses particulières de Secours" is to set aside a sum equal to a certain per cent. (generally 3 per cent.) of each member's wages for provision against accidents, sickness, death, and for pensions for disabled and aged workmen. Besides these there are municipal institutions for similar purposes, such as baths, industrial, technical, day, Sunday, and night schools, and schools to educate laborers' daughters to become good and thrifty housewives, and many good and useful institutions, all voluntary in their character and chiefly supported, in many cases entirely supported, by individual manufacturing establishments for the benefit of their own laborers. The beneficiary institutions of the establishments "Société Anonyme de Marceneille et de Couillet" and Société Anonyme des Charbonnages de l'Ouest de Mons" will well repay the study and challenge the commendation of the social philosopher. Similar efforts are made by the Baltimore and Ohio Railroad Company and other great corporations in the United States, varying only in their character. Such institutions cannot be too highly praised, and their effect is almost instantly noticeable in the *morale* and spirit of the workman toward his employers. They have an excellent influence, and add much to the hopefulness and cheerfulness of labor. The laborer who participates in these benefits feels that, notwithstanding the wide social gulf which separates him from his employer his employer at least cares something for him. The voluntary character of such institutions make them all the more effective. They are certainly stimulative of an active appreciation of the benefits to be derived from a more direct system of profit-sharing. It must be concluded that participation by workmen in profits in addition to wages is a true harmonizer of the interests of capital and labor. It does, in fact, identify the interest of the employé with the interest of the employer. It converts their dustrial association of employer and employés into a moral organism in which all the various talents, services, and desires of the component individuls are fused into a community of purpose and endeavor.a

The Organization of Workmen, of Employers.— Nearly all the remedies suggested under the class "industrial" might be treated under "organization." The suggested remedies other than cooperation and profit-sharing relate to checking the tendency to over-production, the manufacture of goods on demand only, less production, more even production, the equalization of supply and demand, and the reduction of the hours of labor. It is probable that none of these features or suggested remedies can be experienced without organization, and yet or-

---

a Cf. Profit-sharing, Seventeenth Annual Report Massachusetts Bureau of Statistics of Labor.

ganization at the present day seems to constitute the chief bugbear in the public mind. The organization of capital or of the employing forces frightens the labor forces, and in return the rapid organization of labor forces frightens capital, and yet these two kinds of organization are suggested as remedies for industrial depressions, and it is probably true that much importance can be attached to the suggestions. Many manufacturers have said, in the course of this investigation, that if the employers in any industry would combine under an organization that should have positive coherence there would be no difficulty, so far as that industry is concerned, in regulating the volume of production in accordance with the demand, and that with this regulation of supply on a scientific foundation there would be no opportunity for labor troubles or depressions to occur. Such men recognize the fact of the too large supply of power machinery relative to the demand for the products of such machinery. On the other hand, workingmen almost universally are of the opinion that if they could organize on a strong, comprehensive basis, and in such a way as to preserve the coherency of their forces, they could regulate the rates of wages so that there would be uniformity and stability in their rates and uniformity in the hours of labor. If these results of the organization of employers on one hand and the organization of workmen on the other could be secured, depressions would have but little effect, either in severity or in duration. The manufacturers, so far as all the facts which can be observed indicate, are correct in their position. The workmen would be correct in their position if they embodied the amount of production in their view. This many of them do. There cannot, then, be much to fear in the complete organization of the employers on one hand and employés on the other; in fact there is great hope in such complete organization, for when organization is complete on each side, each force must treat with the other through intelligent representatives, and such treatment would result in doing away with passion, with excitement, and all that comes of the endeavor of a great body of men to treat with the proprietors individually. In addition to such a result would come the opportunity to reduce manufacturing, so far as production relative to supply is concerned, to a science. Any one great industry, under complete organization, can be regulated by all the forces acting understandingly and together, and it is only through such organization that production can be wisely regulated on the basis of necessity to supply the market. Hours of labor, through complete organization, can become uniform so far as uniformity is desirable. The rates of wages cannot be governed to a very full extent, because the rates of wages depend upon so many conflicting conditions; yet under complete organization, with the employer and employé working to one end, the success of the whole could secure far greater stability to the rates of wages and far greater stability to employment itself than can be secured under the present system, or, it might be said, under the present want of system. There may be some theory in this consideration of what would be the resulst of complete organization, because no such complete organization exists; but the wisdom of many men, and those the most thoughtful among employers and employés, indicate the tendency of things, and these men have full faith that out of complete organization will come a better state of affairs than now exists. It was said under causes, in treating of machinery, that the workman had not yet received an equitable share of the results growing out of the free introduction of power machinery. Profit-sharing and organization of all the forces of industry would aid in securing a more just division of the profits of production, and one of the first advantages to be gained would be a reduction in the hours of labor, considered by many as the only solution for labor troubles and the great panacea for industrial depressions. Probably these ideas are extravagant as to the complete potency of a general reduction of the hours of labor, but it is certain that under the present conditions of manufacturing through the aid of machinery the hours of labor ought to be reduced, because the drafts on the human system necessary to enable machinery to be well operated is so much greater than under hand processes. The manufacturing world is doing all in its power to build up industrial schools. Evening schools are looked upon in great towns as among the chief blessings of the poor, but there is little use in the establishment of evening schools and all the auxiliaries of industrial education unless time is given for their use, and in such a way that the evening does not add to the fatigue of the day. Long hours of labor in the presence of power machinery and evening schools cannot well go hand in hand. The establishment of the hours of labor by law cannot bring any such benefit to the working masses as can come to them through a voluntary reduction of working time. Law so far, where hours of labor have been established by it, has followed the general reduction and not preceded it. The law has been the reflection of the public sentiment which said that the old time was too long. Under complete organization of labor and capital, as represented by the proprietor and the employés, the hours of labor could be adjusted on a basis far more satisfactory than by law.

Another benefit of such complete organization would be the enlargement of the freedom of contract. Much is said of the freedom of contract; that the workman has the same power to make contracts for his labor as the merchant has for the sale of his goods. This idea is purely fallacious, for the merchant need not sell his goods to-day, while the workman must his labor, and he is, as a rule, at the mercy of the purchaser instead of being free to keep his labor if he cannot get his price.

These are some of the features which would result, it is thought, from the fullest organization of the forces of industry, and it must be admitted by all that the results are to be desired.

The value of a sliding scale of wages, adjusted to meet the market price of products, has often been suggested as a remedy for disagreements as to rates of wages. Such a scale requires not only great intelligence to adjust it, but excellent moral attributes to enable both sides to abide by it. Whatever of value there is in the adoption of a sliding scale, and there is undoubtedly virtue in such a measure, would result in the highest benefits of which it is capable under such complete organization as that indicated.

Quality as well as quantity would be an element affected by thorough organization, and the community at large would reap a benefit equal to that brought to the workman and to the capitalist. The constant division of labor, as it has grown through the past century on the one hand, has stimulated the combination of industrial forces on the other, and this combination, resulting from the still finer subdivision of labor, may be confidently expected in the future.

There is no contest between labor and capital, nor between the laborer and capitalist as such, but there is a contest between the latter as to the profits of capital and wages of labor, or, in simple terms, as to the profits each shall receive for his respective investment, and this contest will continue so long as the purely wage system lasts. It is absurd to say that the interests of capital and labor are identical. They are no more identical than the interests of the buyer and seller. They are, however, reciprocal, and the intelligent comprehension of this reciprocal element can only be brought into the fullest play by the most complete organization, so that each party shall feel that he is an integral part of the whole working establishment.

12854 LAB——19

CHAPTER V.

SUMMARY.

The endeavor throughout this report has been to present facts truthfully and fairly as brought to the attention of the Bureau through its original investigation, and to present the spirit of the testimony offered, fearlessly and impartially. It is therefore fitting that the treatment of the subject of industrial depressions, but more especially of the present industrial depression, should be summarized, that the reader may have whatever benefit accrues to one in the closest contact with the whole material collected.

Contemporaneousness and Severity of Depressions.

It has been clearly shown that the depressions of the past in the manufacturing nations of the world have been nearly or quite contemporaneous in their occurrence. Summarized as to dates, the following table is deduced:

YEARS OF DEPRESSIONS.

Countries.	Years.										
The United States			1814	1818	1826		1837	1847	1857	1867	1873	1882
Great Britain	1803	1810	1815	1818	1826	1830	1837	1847	1857	1866	1873	1882
France	1804	1810	1813	1818	1826	1830	1837	1847	1856	1866	1873	1882
Belgium							1837	1848	1855	1864	1873	1882
Germany							1837	1847	1855		1873	1882

As to the severity of the present industrial depression and its duration, it can safely be asserted that the depression commenced early in 1882 and has continued until the present time. From the time the agents of the Bureau entered the field in prosecuting their investigations to the time they left it, a period of five or six months, there had been a marked change in the condition of business. At the present time (March, 1886), the effects of the depression are wearing away, and all the indications are that prosperity is slowly, gradually, but safely returning. The extent of the depression has not been so great as the popular mind has conceived it. An industrial depression is a mental and moral malady which seizes the public mind after the first influences of the depression are materially or physically felt. Falling prices, or any of the other influential causes by which an industrial depression is inaugurated, create apprehensiveness on the part of all classes, and the result is that the depression is aggravated in all its features. The severity of the present depression, while real and tangible, should be considered as in part moral in its influences. The nations particularly involved, in their relation to each other, and as to severity stand in the following order: Great Britain, the United States, Germany, France, Belgium. It is worthy of remark that in those countries where machinery has not been largely adopted the depression in its peculiar features, as shown between 1882 and 1886, has not been felt to any material extent. In connection with the order of nations just given it is interesting to note the order of the same countries with reference to other points. In the rate of wages and earnings the rank is as follows: The United States, Great Britain, France, Belgium, Germany; in regard to the introduction of machinery, Great Britain, the United States, Belgium, France, Germany; in regard to the cost of production, the United States, Great Britain, France, Belgium, Germany; in regard to the cost of living, the United States, Great Britain, France, Belgium, Germany; in regard to the standard of living and the condition of work people, the United States, Great Britain, Belgium, France, Germany; with reference to popular education, the United States, Belgium, Germany, Great Britain, France; efficiency of labor, the United States, Great Britain, Belgium, France, Germany. If Italy had been added in these gradings it would have been named last in every instance, and Spain would have come after Italy. Austria would have preceded Italy in nearly every case, but Austria and Spain have not been included in the investigation, and Italy only to a certain extent.

Causes.—The causes of the present depression, so far as the United States is concerned and as they have been alleged, are varied indeed. The most potent and those most susceptible of illustration have been given. A chain of causes, or rather a combination of coacting causes, has probably worked to produce the present industrial depression in this country. These causes might work in a legitimate track. Good crops in England and other countries of Western Europe have caused considerable decrease in the exports of American breadstuffs. This has been aggravated by increased supplies of wheat from India by the Suez Canal, and to some extent by short crops here. The prohibition fully or in part of American meats by some countries has resulted in an injury of the export trade in food products. These influences tend in some degree to cripple the consuming power of the larger part of the population of the United States. The influence of the loss of exports in these ways to the United States has been aggravated through the cessation of railroad building, whereby a large unproductive force has been thrown upon the resources of the country, and the consuming power of which force has been necessarily reduced. Rapid immigration has aggravated the accumulated influences by a surplus of labor, which, with the presence of too great a supply of machinery, has rendered over-production easy. The decrease in Europe of the consumption of American cotton, in connection with the corresponding decrease in the United States, has helped to cripple the consuming power in the regions given to cotton-raising and thrown on the labor market a considerable number of laborers in those regions, this crippling coming at the same time of the increased importations and large numbers of immigrants, the other influences affecting the East. Thus these wide-reaching and widely-separated causes, in their initial influence, have combined to make the industrial depression of the past few years a reality. These influences have received contributions from the various minor causes described, and so the ball has rolled until the period of readjustment set in, and now, as that period of readjustment is passing away, prosperity dawns on the country. The lessons to be learned from these causes are what have been denominated as—

Remedies.—Probably no human device or combination of devices can be instituted powerful enough to prevent the recurrence of financial and commercial crises and industrial depressions, but this should not prevent men seeking devices which will mitigate the severity or shorten the duration of such calamities. When it is considered that each great manufacturing nation of the world is struggling for industrial existence as against the fierce competition of every other nation engaged in like pursuits, some of the questions which seem to absorb the minds of individual employers and employés seem trivial indeed; yet it must not be assumed, nor can it be assumed with reason, that the workmen of the United States or their employers wish to cripple in any degree the implements of industry. Therefore it is well to consider those remedial agencies which have been suggested. Which of these agencies can be reduced to practice in any degree?

There is no universal panacea, no absolute remedy for depressions; but if the public, through sentiment or through its agents in the legislatures of the country, can stimulate any methods for the mitigation of the severity and the shortening of the duration of the industrial depressions, certainly the effort should be made. And first, what can be done by legislation? With a healthy public opinion behind it, the law-making power can prevent to a great degree the unholy speculation in food products. It can indulge in a conservative care in extending railroad building and in facilitating the organization of manufacturing corporations. It can restrict the grants of the public domain. It can enact uniform bankruptcy laws, extending the provisions of such laws so that the poor man indebted but a few hundred dollars shall be able to readjust his financial affairs as readily as the larger debtor. It can abridge the provisions of laws relating to the collection of debts, to the end that the credit system shall not be abused. It can regulate transportation on a just and uniform basis, to the end that the stockholder shall not be robbed by ruinous competition, and that the workman may calculate with some degree of certainty the cost of his living and the producer the cost of production, so far as transportation is concerned. It can see to it that the tariff shall be regulated on the basis of justice and science and not on a haphazard basis which affects only individual interests and oftentimes inflicts general harm. It can see that a stable currency be guaranteed, that the workman may know the purchasing power of his stipulated earnings. It can consider what reasonable and humane regulations may be adopted relative to immigration, and see to it that labor is not lowered either in standard or through earnings by the pernicious method of importations by contract; that every lawful endeavor be made to stimulate industrial education in all parts of the country; that the necessity shall be recognized of the industrial development of all parts of the land that there may result a legitimate increase in the consuming power of the people. It can stimulate the growth of the principle of industrial copartnerships through methods of profit-sharing by wise, permissive laws. Public sentiment can encourage the perfect organization of the forces involved, to the end that each shall treat with the other through representatives, and that production shall be regulated by the demand and not by the ill-advised eagerness of men to push their work individually, to the detriment of others; that there may come the universal adoption of shorter hours of labor, and demand that after capital and labor shall have received fixed and reasonable compensation, each for its investment, the net profits of production shall be divided under profit-sharing plans or methods, or through industrial copartnerships, to the end that all the forces of production shall be equally alive to mutual welfare. It can ask that the contracts of labor be as free as the contracts for commodities, under fair agreements for services rendered, to the end that the workman shall not be obliged to make contracts on terms not acceptable to him, and it can hold the party which declines to resort to the conciliatory methods of arbitration morally responsible for all the ill effects growing out of contest.

These remedial agencies or remedial methods, alleviatory in their design, are all possible by the reasonable acts of men. They are not chimerical schemes, but measures adapted to practical adoption. They demand simply a fair recognition of a part only of the truth bound up in the rule which insists that all men shall do unto others as they would have others do unto them.

APPENDIX A.

Occupations, with Number and Wages of Employés, by Industries.

NOTE.—This table is *not* a complete exhibit for industries or states, but covers only establishments investigated by the Bureau. See page 91, also summaries, pages 143 to 226. One or two leading articles made are mentioned for each establishment. For lack of space others are omitted.

Agricultural Implements (Ploughs), Illinois.—Estab. No. 1.

Time, 10 hours per day; — days the past year.

Occupations.	Number.		Daily wages.	
	Male.	Fem.	Male.	Fem.
Blacksmiths	100	......	$2 50	......
Foremen	2	......	3 50	......
Foremen	3	......	3 00	......
Foremen	2	......	2 50	......
Grinders	50	......	1 75	......
Laborers	125	......	1 30	......
Loaders	40	......	1 50	......
Moulders	25	......	2 75	......
Painters	50	......	1 75	......
Plough fitters	200	......	2 00	......
Polishers	15	......	3 00	......
Stockers	25	......	3 00	......
Wood workers	50	......	1 50	......

Agricultural Implements (Ploughs), Illinois.—Estab. No. 2.

Time, 10 hours per day; — days the past year.

Occupations.	Number.		Daily wages.	
	Male.	Fem.	Male.	Fem.
Blacksmiths	70	......	$2 40	......
Grinders	30	......	2 50	......
Laborers	50	......	1 25	......
Moulders	30	......	2 25	......
Painters	30	......	1 75	......
Plough fitters	15	......	2 25	......
Wood workers	30	......	1 75	......
Wood-workers' helpers	70	......	1 25	......

Agricultural Implements (Mowers, Reapers, Harvesters), Illinois.—Estab. No. 3.

Time, 10 hours per day; 270 days the past year.

Occupations.	Number.		Daily wages.	
	Male.	Fem.	Male.	Fem.
Blacksmiths	3	......	$4 00	......
Blacksmiths	3	......	3 75	......
Blacksmiths	4	......	3 00	......
Blacksmiths	2	......	2 50	......
Blacksmiths	9	......	2 25	......
Blacksmiths	11	......	1 87	......
Blacksmiths	14	......	1 50	......
Carpenters	3	......	4 00	......
Carpenters	4	......	3 50	......
Carpenters	5	......	3 00	......
Carpenters	8	......	2 50	......
Carpenters	13	......	2 25	......
Carpenters	26	......	2 00	......
Carpenters	33	......	1 75	......
Carpenters	7	......	1 50	......

Agricultural Implements (Mowers, Reapers, Harvesters), Illinois.—Estab. No. 3—Concl'd.

Time, 10 hours per day; 270 days the past year.

Occupations.	Number.		Daily wages.	
	Male.	Fem.	Male.	Fem.
Draughtsman	1	......	$4 00	......
Draughtsmen	2	......	2 75	......
Draughtsmen	2	......	2 25	......
Engineer	1	......	4 50	......
Engineer	1	......	2 25	......
Foreman	1	......	5 00	......
Foremen	2	......	4 50	......
Foremen	2	......	3 25	......
Foremen	7	......	3 00	......
Foremen	3	......	2 50	......
Laborers	3	......	2 25	......
Laborers	28	......	2 00	......
Laborers	35	......	1 75	......
Laborers	51	......	1 60	......
Laborers	136	......	1 50	......
Laborers	51	......	1 37	......
Laborers	234	......	1 25	......
Laborers	9	......	1 12	......
Laborers	11	......	1 00	......
Laborers	a16	......	75	......
Laborers	a14	......	60	......
Machinists	5	......	4 00	......
Machinists	4	......	3 50	......
Machinists	20	......	3 00	......
Machinists	135	......	2 70	......
Machinists	57	......	2 50	......
Machinists	69	......	2 25	......
Machinists	64	......	2 00	......
Machinists	27	......	1 75	......
Machinists	32	......	1 55	......
Moulders	32	......	4 00	......
Moulders	27	......	3 75	......
Moulders	6	......	3 50	......
Moulders	14	......	3 25	......
Moulders	14	......	3 00	......
Moulders	4	......	2 87	......
Painter	1	......	4 00	......
Painter	1	......	3 75	......
Painters	6	......	3 50	......
Painters	13	......	3 00	......
Painters	7	......	2 75	......
Painters	6	......	2 50	......
Painters	4	......	2 25	......
Painters	13	......	2 00	......
Painters	2	......	1 75	......
Painters	5	......	1 50	......
Pattern makers	3	......	3 00	......
Pattern makers	5	......	2 75	......
Pattern maker	1	......	2 50	......
Teamsters	2	......	1 75	......
Teamsters	3	......	1 62	......
Teamsters	2	......	1 50	......
Undesignated	1	......	2 50	......
Watchmen	3	......	2 00	......

a Youth.

REPORT OF THE COMMISSIONER OF LABOR.

OCCUPATIONS, WITH NUMBER AND WAGES OF EMPLOYÉS, BY INDUSTRIES—Cont'd.

NOTE.—This table is *not* a complete exhibit for industries or states, but covers only establishments investigated by the Bureau. See page 91, also summaries, pages 149 to 226.

AGRICULTURAL IMPLEMENTS (PLOUGHS), INDIANA.— ESTAB. No. 4.

Time, 10 hours per day; 250 days the past year.

Occupations.	Number.		Daily wages.	
	Male.	Fem.	Male.	Fem.
Apprentices	a2		$0 75	
Bean and handle makers	5		1 75	
Blacksmith	1		2 75	
Blacksmiths	3		2 50	
Blacksmith	1		2 25	
Blacksmiths	3		2 00	
Blacksmiths	4		1 70	
Blacksmiths' helpers	6		1 40	
Blacksmiths' helpers	5		1 25	
Blacksmiths' helpers	2		1 13	
Bolt cutter	a1		70	
Bolt cutters	a4		50	
Carpenters	2		2 00	
Carpenter	1		1 50	
Casting cleaners	6		1 38	
Cinder millers	4		1 25	
Core maker		a1		$0 90
Core makers		a7		65
Cupola heaters	2		2 00	
Cupola helpers	3		1 25	
Cupola men	3		1 50	
Engineer	1		3 00	
Firemen	3		1 03	
Fireman	1		1 38	
Fitter	1		2 15	
Fitters	2		1 65	
Fitters	2		1 50	
Fitter	1		1 40	
Fitter	1		1 25	
Foremen	4		3 00	
Foremen	3		2 50	
Foremen	5		2 25	
Foremen	2		2 00	
Foreman	1		1 75	
Foreman	1		1 65	
Gatekeeper	1		1 00	
Grinders	2		1 70	
Grinders	76		1 50	
Grinders	17		1 38	
Grinder	1		1 25	
Grinder	a1		60	
Grinders	a3		50	
Iron breakers	4		1 50	
Japanners	3		1 13	
Japanners	a2		45	
Laborers	3		1 30	
Laborers	37		1 15	
Laborers	2		1 00	
Laborer	a1		50	
Loaders	2		2 12	
Loaders	12		1 25	
Machinists	2		2 25	
Machinists	2		2 00	
Machinist's helper	1		1 50	
Mason	1		2 50	
Mason's helper	1		1 25	
Millers	3		1 25	
Moulders	2		2 00	
Moulders	16		1 78	
Moulders	143		1 63	
Moulder	1		1 15	
Oiler	1		1 50	
Oiler	1		1 15	
Oven girl		a1		80
Painter	1		2 25	
Painter	1		2 00	
Painters	4		1 75	
Painters	2		1 60	
Painter	1		1 50	

AGRICULTURAL IMPLEMENTS (PLOUGHS), INDIANA.— ESTAB. No. 4—Concluded.

Time, 10 hours per day; 250 days the past year.

Occupations.	Number.		Daily wages.	
	Male.	Fem.	Male.	Fem.
Painter	1		$1 25	
Painters	a3		65	
Pattern maker	1		3 00	
Pattern maker	1		2 38	
Pattern maker	1		2 25	
Pattern makers	5		2 00	
Pattern makers	2		1 63	
Pattern maker	1		1 50	
Point fitters	1		2 20	
Point fitter	4		1 75	
Point fitters	2		1 45	
Point fitter	1		1 35	
Point fitter	1		1 25	
Polishers	3		2 75	
Polishers	3		2 10	
Polishers	5		2 00	
Polishers	12		1 50	
Polishers	4		1 13	
Polishers	a4		52	
Sand mixer	1		1 50	
Shaper	1		1 75	
Stablemen	3		1 25	
Stone dresser	1		2 25	
Stone dresser	1		2 00	
Stone dresser	1		1 50	
Sulky fitter	1		1 75	
Sulky fitter	1		1 50	
Sulky fitters	7		1 25	
Sulky fitters	a2		1 00	
Sulky fitter	a1		55	
Teamster	1		1 50	
Teamsters	5		1 25	
Top-house man	1		2 00	
Top-house helper	1		1 25	
Undesignated	a2		45	
Watchmen	3		1 75	
Watchman	1		1 38	
Wood workers	5		1 50	
Wood workers	9		1 25	
Wood-worker's helper	a1		1 00	

AGRICULTURAL IMPLEMENTS (THRESHING MACHINES AND FARM ENGINES), INDIANA.—ESTAB. No. 5.

Time, 10 hours per day; — days the past year.

Occupations.	Number.		Daily wages.	
	Male.	Fem.	Male.	Fem.
Blacksmiths	3		$2 50	
Blacksmiths' helpers	3		1 40	
Boiler maker	1		3 33	
Boiler makers	4		1 50	
Carpenters	2		2 50	
Core maker	1		1 70	
Core makers	2		1 40	
Draughtsman	1		2 50	
Draughtsman	1		2 00	
Engineer	1		2 00	
Laborer	1		1 60	
Laborers	10		1 20	
Machinists	13		3 00	
Machinists' helpers	a10		83	
Moulders	4		3 00	
Moulders	15		2 50	
Moulders' helpers	a4		83	
Pattern maker	1		3 50	
Pattern makers	7		1 50	

a Youth.

OCCUPATIONS AND WAGES.

OCCUPATIONS, WITH NUMBER AND WAGES OF EMPLOYÉS, BY INDUSTRIES—Cont'd.

NOTE.—This table is *not* a complete exhibit for industries or states, but covers only establishments investigated by the Bureau. See page 91, also summaries, pages 143 to 226.

AGRICULTURAL IMPLEMENTS (PLOUGHS), KENTUCKY.—ESTAB. No. 6.

Time, 10 hours per day; 275 days the past year.

Occupations.	Number.		Daily wages.	
	Male.	Fem.	Male.	Fem.
Blacksmiths	4	......	$2 50	......
Blacksmiths' helpers	6	......	1 20	......
Foremen	3	......	3 00	......
Grinders	15	......	1 60	......
Laborers	6	......	1 20	......
Moulders	8	......	2 00	......
Wood workers	4	......	2 50	......

AGRICULTURAL IMPLEMENTS (PITCHFORKS), MAINE.—ESTAB. No. 7.

Time, 9 hours per day; 300 days the past year.

Occupations	Male	Fem	Male	Fem
Foreman	1	......	$2 75	......
Foreman	2	......	2 25	......
Grinders	12	......	1 75	......
Hammerman	1	......	1 50	......
Heel turner	1	......	2 25	......
Laborers	7	......	1 25	......
Painters	3	......	1 50	......
Platers	3	......	2 00	......
Polishers	6	......	1 75	......
Repair hand	1	......	1 75	......
Temperers	2	......	3 00	......
Welders	4	......	2 00	......
Welders' helpers	3	......	1 13	......

AGRICULTURAL IMPLEMENTS (HOES AND FORKS), NEW YORK.—ESTAB. No. 8.

Time, 10 hours per day; 300 days the past year.

Occupations	Male	Fem	Male	Fem
Engineer	1	......	$2 00	......
Finisher	1	......	2 40	......
Finishers	3	......	1 60	......
Foreman	1	......	3 00	......
Foreman	1	......	2 25	......
Grinders	7	......	1 60	......
Hammerman	1	......	3 60	......
Hammermen	2	......	2 40	......
Hammerman	1	......	2 00	......
Hammermen	3	......	1 60	......
Handle fitter	1	......	3 00	......
Handle fitters	10	......	1 80	......
Laborers	2	......	1 80	......
Machinist	1	......	3 00	......
Plater	1	......	2 40	......
Plater	1	......	1 75	......
Polishers	6	......	1 80	......
Polishers	6	......	1 40	......
Pressman	1	......	3 20	......
Pressman	1	......	2 40	......
Teamster	1	......	1 60	......
Temperer	1	......	2 00	......
Temperers	2	......	1 48	......
Undesignated	10	......	1 60	......

AGRICULTURAL IMPLEMENTS (MOWERS, REAPERS, HARVESTERS, BINDERS), OHIO.—ESTAB. No. 9.

Time, 10 hours per day; — days the past year.

Occupations	Male	Fem	Male	Fem
Blacksmiths	30	......	$2 40	......
Blacksmiths' helpers	25	......	1 40	......
Bolt and nut makers	21	......	1 54	......
Casting cleaners	22	......	1 62	......
Core makers	10	......	1 26	......

AGRICULTURAL IMPLEMENTS (MOWERS, ETC.), OHIO.—ESTAB. No. 9—Concluded.

Time, 10 hours per day; — days the past year.

Occupations.	Number.		Daily wages.	
	Male.	Fem.	Male.	Fem.
Cupola men	10	......	$1 42	......
Laborers	86	......	1 35	......
Machinists	201	......	1 95	......
Moulders	33	......	2 50	......
Moulders' helpers	13	......	1 65	......
Painters	68	......	2 16	......
Wood workers	144	......	1 69	......

AGRICULTURAL IMPLEMENTS (MOWERS, REAPERS), OHIO.—ESTAB. No. 10.

Time, 10 hours per day; 250 days the past year.

Occupations	Male	Fem	Male	Fem
Blacksmiths	58	......	$1 87	......
Laborers	17	......	1 35	......
Loaders	27	......	1 10	......
Machinists	100	......	1 73	......
Moulders and helpers	39	......	1 97	......
Painters	66	......	1 47	......
Watchmen	3	......	1 37	......
Wood workers	73	......	1 61	......

AGRICULTURAL IMPLEMENTS (MOWERS, REAPERS), OHIO.—ESTAB. No. 11.

Time, 10 hours per day; 200 days the past year.

Occupations	Male	Fem	Male	Fem
Blacksmiths	5	......	$1 00	......
Blacksmiths' helpers	5	......	1 50	......
Grinders and polishers	15	......	1 50	......
Laborers	15	......	1 30	......
Machinists	20	......	2 00	......
Moulders	10	......	2 50	......
Painters	5	......	1 50	......
Wood workers	20	......	1 75	......

AGRICULTURAL IMPLEMENTS (MOWERS, REAPERS, FARM ENGINES), OHIO.—ESTAB. No. 12.

Time, 10 hours per day; — days the past year.

Occupations	Male	Fem	Male	Fem
Blacksmiths	9	......	$2 50	......
Blacksmiths	18	......	2 00	......
Blacksmiths' helpers	35	......	1 40	......
Boiler makers	8	......	2 00	......
Boiler-makers' helpers	12	......	1 35	......
Carpenters	27	......	1 80	......
Carpenters	10	......	1 50	......
Fitters	24	......	2 50	......
Fitters	12	......	1 90	......
Foremen	13	......	4 00	......
Grinders and polishers	30	......	2 25	......
Laborers	102	......	1 30	......
Loaders	14	......	1 40	......
Machinists	21	......	2 75	......
Machinists	64	......	2 25	......
Machinists	20	......	1 80	......
Machinists' helpers	20	......	1 40	......
Painters	16	......	1 80	......
Painters	37	......	1 45	......
Setters-up	37	......	2 25	......
Setters-up helpers	8	......	1 40	......
Wood workers	24	......	1 90	......
Wood workers	16	......	1 60	......

OCCUPATIONS, WITH NUMBER AND WAGES OF EMPLOYÉS, BY INDUSTRIES—Cont'd.

NOTE.—This table is *not* a complete exhibit for industries or states, but covers only establishments investigated by the Bureau. See page 91, also summaries, pages 143 to 226.

AGRICULTURAL IMPLEMENTS (FARM ENGINES, THRESHERS), OHIO.—ESTAB. No. 13.

Time, 10 hours per day; 250 days the past year.

Occupations.	Number.		Daily wages.	
	Male.	Fem.	Male.	Fem.
Blacksmiths	15		$3 50	
Blacksmiths	15		2 00	
Blacksmiths' helpers	15		1 40	
Belt lacers	7		1 30	
Boiler makers	20		2 50	
Boiler makers	30		1 75	
Boiler-makers' helpers	20		1 35	
Bolt and nut makers	15		1 00	
Draughtsmen	10		2 60	
Erectors	10		3 50	
Erectors	15		1 65	
Foremen	5		4 00	
Foremen	5		3 50	
Foremen	2		2 50	
Foremen	2		2 00	
Laborers	102		1 25	
Loaders	10		1 40	
Lumbermen	5		1 30	
Machinists	20		3 50	
Machinists	15		3 00	
Machinists	35		2 00	
Machinists' helpers	20		1 40	
Moulders	30		2 37	
Moulders' helpers	40		1 40	
Painters	15		2 50	
Painters	15		1 50	
Pattern makers	10		2 50	
Setters-up	15		2 00	
Setters-up	18		1 40	
Teamsters	30		1 40	
Tool makers	5		1 75	
Watchmen	3		1 60	
Wood workers	15		2 00	
Wood workers	25		1 40	

AGRICULTURAL IMPLEMENTS (HAY RAKES, TEDDERS), OHIO.—ESTAB. No. 14.

Time, 10 hours per day; 300 days the past year.

Occupations.	Male.	Fem.	Male.	Fem.
Foreman	1		$3 50	
Laborers	4		1 25	
Machinists	10		1 75	
Moulders and helpers	10		1 90	
Painters	5		1 40	
Wood workers	12		1 80	

AGRICULTURAL IMPLEMENTS (HAY RAKES, TEDDERS), OHIO.—ESTAB. No. 15.

Time, 10 hours per day; — days the past year.

Occupations.	Male.	Fem.	Male.	Fem.
Blacksmiths	5		$1 75	
Iron workers	35		1 60	
Painters	10		1 75	
Wood workers	15		1 50	

AGRICULTURAL IMPLEMENTS (HAY RAKES, TEDDERS), OHIO.—ESTAB. No. 16.

Time, 10 hours per day; 250 days the past year.

Occupations.	Male.	Fem.	Male.	Fem.
Blacksmiths	9		$1 90	
Iron workers	23		1 77	
Laborers	6		1 42	
Moulders and helpers	12		1 87	
Painters	18		2 19	
Setters-up	19		1 62	
Wood workers	26		1 72	

AGRICULTURAL IMPLEMENTS (PLOUGHS), OHIO.—ESTAB. No. 17.

Time, 10 hours per day; — days the past year.

Occupations.	Male.	Fem.	Male.	Fem.
Blacksmiths	3		$1 75	
Engineer	1		1 50	
Grinders	2		1 75	
Laborers	3		1 25	
Moulders	4		2 40	
Painters	2		1 50	
Polisher	1		1 75	
Pattern maker	1		3 50	
Undesignated	a2		80	
Wood workers	3		1 75	

AGRICULTURAL IMPLEMENTS (PLOUGHS), OHIO.—ESTAB. No. 18.

Time, 10 hours per day; 275 days the past year.

Occupations.	Male.	Fem.	Male.	Fem.
Blacksmiths	5		$2 50	
Blacksmiths' helpers	5		1 50	
Dressers	5		2 50	
Foreman	1		2 50	
Grinders and polishers	10		2 50	
Laborers	4		1 50	
Moulders	15		3 00	
Moulders' helpers	15		1 50	
Painters	4		2 25	
Painters	4		1 50	
Pattern makers	3		2 50	
Plough fitters	10		2 00	
Stockers	5		2 50	

AGRICULTURAL IMPLEMENTS (PLOUGHS), OHIO.—ESTAB. No. 19.

Time, 10 hours per day; 300 days the past year.

Occupations.	Male.	Fem.	Male.	Fem.
Blacksmiths	4		$2 00	
Fitters	2		1 50	
Grinders	2		1 90	
Laborers	6		1 25	
Moulders	10		2 25	
Painters	5		1 90	
Polishers	2		1 90	
Wood workers	4		1 90	

a Youth.

OCCUPATIONS AND WAGES. 299

OCCUPATIONS, WITH NUMBER AND WAGES OF EMPLOYÉS, BY INDUSTRIES—Cont'd.

NOTE.—This table is not a complete exhibit for industries or states, but covers only establishments investigated by the Bureau. See page 91, also summaries, pages 143 to 226.

AGRICULTURAL IMPLEMENTS (PLOUGHS), PENNSYLVANIA.—ESTAB. No. 20.

Time, 10 hours per day; — days the past year.

Occupations.	Number.		Daily wages.	
	Male.	Fem.	Male.	Fem.
Blacksmiths	8		$2 50	
Blacksmiths' helpers	8		1 75	
Foreman	1		4 00	
Laborers	9		1 60	
Laborers	30		1 25	
Moulders	22		1 80	
Painter	1		2 50	
Plough makers	2		2 50	

ARMS AND AMMUNITION (REVOLVERS), MASSACHUSETTS.—ESTAB. No. 21.

Time, 10 hours per day; 302 days the past year.

Occupations.	Male.	Fem.	Male.	Fem.
Assemblers	24		$2 75	
Bench workers	20		2 75	
Bench workers	10		1 75	
Bench workers	10		1 50	
Carpenters	2		3 00	
Drillers	25		1 75	
Engineer	1		2 75	
Fireman	1		2 25	
Foreman	7		4 50	
Forgers	10		2 50	
Inspectors	25		3 00	
Machinists	3		4 00	
Machinists	22		3 25	
Milling men, hand	50		1 75	
Milling men, machine	150		1 40	
Platers	2		2 75	
Platers	5		1 75	
Polishers	9		2 50	
Polisher	1		2 00	
Profilers	40		2 00	
Stockers	15		2 75	
Yard hands	5		1 75	

ARTISANS' TOOLS (SAWS), INDIANA.—ESTAB. No. 22.

Time, 10 hours per day; 300 days the past year.

Occupations.	Male.	Fem.	Male.	Fem.
Engineer	1		$2 00	
Fireman	1		1 25	
Grinders	3		3 50	
Laborers	20		1 25	
Laborers	41		1 00	
Machinists	3		3 00	
Saw filers	10		2 00	
Saw makers	12		3 00	
Saw makers	a2		1 50	
Saw makers	a8		1 00	

BOOTS AND SHOES (MEN'S BOOTS AND SHOES), CALIFORNIA.—ESTAB. No. 23.b

Time, 10 hours per day; 270 days the past year.

Occupations.	Male.	Fem.	Male.	Fem.
Buffers	4		$1 25	
Burnishers	4		1 37	
Button sewer			1	$1 37

BOOTS AND SHOES (MEN'S BOOTS AND SHOES), CALIFORNIA.—ESTAB. No. 23—Concluded.

Time, 10 hours per day; 270 days the past year.

Occupations.	Male.	Fem.	Male.	Fem.
Button-hole makers	2		$1 25	
Channellers	3		1 37	
Cutter	1		3 00	
Cutters	12		1 37	
Dressers	5		1 25	
Edge setter	1		2 00	
Edge setters	2		1 50	
Edge trimmers	3		1 50	
Engineer	1		2 00	
Finishers	3		1 25	
Fireman	1		1 25	
Heelers	3		1 50	
Heelers	3		1 25	
Lasters	35		1 37	
Packers	3		1 50	
Pasters		2		$1 37
Pasters	5		1 25	
Porters	4		1 37	
Sewing-machine operators	24		1 37	
Sewer, McKay machine	1		1 50	
Treers	5		1 25	
Undesignated	5		1 00	
Vampers	2		2 58	

BOOTS AND SHOES (MEN'S AND WOMEN'S BOOTS AND SHOES), CALIFORNIA.—ESTAB. No. 24.

Time, 10 hours per day; 270 days the past year.

Occupations.	Male.	Fem.	Male.	Fem.
Buffers	2		$1 87	
Burnishers	9		2 25	
Button-hole makers	6		1 62	
Channeller	1		2 00	
Cutters	14		3 00	
Cutters	10		1 25	
Dressers	7		2 25	
Dressers	3		2 00	
Edge setters	5		2 00	
Edge trimmers	6		2 00	
Engineer	1		3 75	
Finishers	8		2 50	
Fitters	2		2 25	
Fitters	4		2 00	
Foremen	6		5 00	
Heelers	6		2 50	
Heelers	3		1 00	
Ironers		2		$1 37
Lasters	c42		1 75	
Nailers	8		1 62	
Packers	4		2 25	
Pasters		3		1 25
Porter	1		2 25	
Sewer, McKay machine	1		2 00	
Sewing-machine operators		32		1 50
Stampers	2		2 37	
Teamster	1		2 00	
Treers	5		3 00	
Vampers	4		2 25	
Watchman	1		2 00	

a Youth.
b Employés all Chinese, except one cutter, two vampers, two pasters, and one button sewer.
c Chinese.

300   REPORT OF THE COMMISSIONER OF LABOR.

OCCUPATIONS, WITH NUMBER AND WAGES OF EMPLOYÉS, BY INDUSTRIES—Cont'd.

NOTE.—This table is *not* a complete exhibit for industries or states, but covers only establishments investigated by the Bureau. See page 91, also summaries, pages 143 to 226.

BOOTS AND SHOES (MEN'S SHOES), ILLINOIS.—ESTAB. No. 25.

Time, 10 hours per day; 275 days the past year.

Occupations.	Number.		Daily wages.	
	Male.	Fem.	Male.	Fem.
Burnishers	6		$3 00	
Cutters	8		2 67	
Finishers	6		2 67	
Fitters		60		$1 50
Heelers	10		2 17	
In-seamers	30		2 33	
Lasters	8		2 25	
Rounders	8		2 50	
Sewers, hand	30		2 33	
Trimmers	10		2 50	
Treers	6		2 33	

BOOTS AND SHOES (WOMEN'S SHOES), KENTUCKY.—ESTAB. No. 26.

Time, 10 hours per day; 235 days the past year.

Occupations.	Male.	Fem.	Male.	Fem.
Bottomers	20		$2 50	
Cutters	4		2 33	
Fitters	3	30	2 50	$1 00
Lasters	6		2 00	

BOOTS AND SHOES (WOMEN'S AND GIRLS' SHOES), MARYLAND.—ESTAB. No. 27.

Time, 10 hours per day; 240 days the past year.

Occupations.	Male.	Fem.	Male.	Fem.
Burnishers	2		$1 83	
Cutters	6		1 67	
Edge setters	2		1 33	
Edge trimmer	1		2 50	
Edge trimmer	1		2 00	
Finisher	1		1 67	
Fitters		30		$0 83
Foremen	3		3 33	
Heeler	1		1 50	
Laster	1		2 00	
Lasters	7		1 67	
Sewers, Goodyear machine	3		2 50	
Shankers	3		1 67	
Shanker's helper	a1		50	
Undesignated	3		1 16	

BOOTS AND SHOES (MEN'S AND WOMEN'S SHOES), MARYLAND.—ESTAB. No. 28.

Time, 10 hours per day; 270 days the past year.

Occupations.	Male.	Fem.	Male.	Fem.
Bottomers	14		$1 92	
Cutters	2		1 85	
Cutters' helpers	a2		55	
Fitters		14		$1 16
Lasters	4		1 85	
Sewers, hand	9		1 33	

BOOTS AND SHOES (MEN'S AND WOMEN'S SHOES), MARYLAND.—ESTAB. No. 29.

Time, 10 hours per day; 270 days the past year.

Occupations.	Number.		Daily wages.	
	Male.	Fem.	Male.	Fem.
Bottomers	20		$1 50	
Burnishers	2		1 67	
Burnishers' helpers	a2		67	
Cutters	5		2 33	
Cutters' helpers	a4		92	
Engineer	1		2 00	
Edge setter	1		2 00	
Edge-setter's helper	a1		50	
Finishers	a2		83	
Fitters	4		2 00	
Fitters	3	44	1 42	$0 83
Fitters' helpers	a2		50	
Fitters' helpers	b2		42	
Foreman	1		5 00	
Heeler	1		1 50	
Heeler's helper	a1		50	
Lasters	8		1 33	
Levellers	2		1 42	
Packer	a1		67	
Sandpaperers	2		1 67	
Sewers, Goodyear machine	5		1 67	
Shankers	a3		83	
Shavers	2		1 67	
Sock liners		2		83
Tacker	1		1 50	
Trimmers	2		2 50	
Turners	2		1 33	

BOOTS AND SHOES (MEN'S SHOES), MARYLAND.—ESTAB. No. 30.

Time, 10 hours per day; 264 days the past year.

Occupations.	Male.	Fem.	Male.	Fem.
Burnishers	3		$1 50	
Cutters	6		1 67	
Cutters' helpers	a3		75	
Engineer	1		2 00	
Fitters		40		$0 92
Foremen	4		2 50	
Finishers	a25		83	
Sewers, hand	40		1 50	
Stock keepers	3		1 67	

BOOTS AND SHOES (INFANTS' SHOES), MASSACHUSETTS.—ESTAB. No. 31.

Time, 10 hours per day; — days the past year.

Occupations.	Male.	Fem.	Male.	Fem.
Cutters	4		$1 50	
Lasters	2		1 50	
Sewing-machine operators		20		$1 00

BOOTS AND SHOES (INFANTS' SHOES), MASSACHUSETTS.—ESTAB. No. 32.

Time, 10 hours per day; — days the past year.

Occupations.	Male.	Fem.	Male.	Fem.
Fitters	9		$1 50	
Sewing-machine operators c		40		$1 00

a Youth.   *b* Children.   *c* Bottoming done outside by contract.

OCCUPATIONS AND WAGES. 301

OCCUPATIONS, WITH NUMBER AND WAGES OF EMPLOYÉS, BY INDUSTRIES—Cont'd.

NOTE.—This table is *not* a complete exhibit for industries or states, but covers only establishments investigated by the Bureau. See page 91, also summaries, pages 143 to 226.

BOOTS AND SHOES (YOUTHS' SHOES), MASSACHUSETTS.—ESTAB. No. 33.

Time, 10 hours per day; 292 days the past year.

Occupations.	Number.		Daily wages.	
	Male.	Fem.	Male.	Fem.
Cutters	2	.....	$2 23	.....
Cutters	3	.....	2 05	.....
Cutter's helper	a1	.....	93	.....
Engineer	1	.....	2 50	.....
Finisher	1	.....	2 40	.....
Lasters	6	.....	1 97	.....
Packer	1	.....	2 23	.....
Sewing-machine operators	.....	8	.....	$1 20
Sewing-machine operators	3	.....	2 10	.....
Shankers	2	.....	2 23	.....
Undesignated	.....	3	.....	65
Undesignated	.....	a3	.....	68

BOOTS AND SHOES (WOMEN'S AND YOUTHS' SHOES), MASSACHUSETTS.—ESTAB. No. 34.

Time, 10 hours per day; 300 days the past year.

Occupations.	Male.	Fem.	Male.	Fem.
Cutter	1	.....	$1 25	.....
Heeler	1	.....	1 75	.....
Sewing-machine operators	.....	2	.....	$1 00
Undesignated	10	.....	1 25	.....

BOOTS AND SHOES (WOMEN'S SHOES), MASSACHUSETTS.—ESTAB. No. 35.

Time, 10 hours per day; — days the past year.

Occupations.	Male.	Fem.	Male.	Fem.
Bottomers	47	.....	$2 12	.....
Cutter	1	.....	1 50	.....
Cutters	.....	3	.....	$1 25
Cutters	29	.....	2 23	.....
Cutters	13	.....	.....	73
Cutters	8	.....	.....	1 02
Cutters	28	.....	1 83	.....
Cutters	5	.....	1 96	.....
Cutters' helpers	a5	.....	93	.....
Edge setters	5	.....	2 09	.....
Finishers	.....	a5	.....	67
Finishers	.....	6	.....	1 14
Finishers	31	.....	1 77	.....
Finishers	8	.....	1 35	.....
Heelers	17	.....	1 86	.....
Heelers' helpers	a4	.....	50	.....
Peggers and nailers	9	.....	1 35	.....
Sewing-machine operators	.....	46	.....	1 40
Sewing-machine operators	.....	a19	.....	93
Sewing-machine operators	4	.....	2 13	.....

BOOTS AND SHOES (WOMEN'S SHOES), MASSACHUSETTS.—ESTAB. No. 36.

Time, 10 hours per day; 282 days the past year.

Occupations.	Male.	Fem.	Male.	Fem.
Cutters	6	.....	$2 50	.....
Cutters	5	.....	2 25	.....
Cutters	2	.....	2 00	.....
Cutter	1	.....	1 50	.....
Dressers	.....	4	.....	$1 17

BOOTS AND SHOES (WOMEN'S SHOES), MASSACHUSETTS.—ESTAB. No. 36—Concluded.

Time, 10 hours per day; 282 days the past year.

Occupations.	Number.		Daily wages.	
	Male.	Fem.	Male.	Fem.
Dressers	9	.....	$1 92	.....
Edge setters	5	.....	1 74	.....
Edge trimmers	4	.....	2 15	.....
Engineer	1	.....	2 00	.....
Finishers	10	.....	2 10	.....
Foreman	1	.....	2 25	.....
Foreman	1	.....	2 50	.....
Foreman	4	.....	3 00	.....
Lasters	11	.....	1 79	.....
Machinists	2	.....	2 50	.....
Packer	1	.....	2 00	.....
Packer	1	.....	1 75	.....
Peggers	7	.....	2 25	.....
Sewing-machine operators	.....	19	.....	$1 51

BOOTS AND SHOES (WOMEN'S SHOES), MASSACHUSETTS.—ESTAB. No. 37.

Time, 10 hours per day; 242 days the past year.

Occupations.	Male.	Fem.	Male.	Fem.
Cutters	10	.....	$2 25	.....
Dressers	.....	2	.....	$1 50
Edge setter	1	.....	2 15	.....
Edge trimmers	2	.....	3 00	.....
Engineer	1	.....	2 50	.....
Finishers	2	.....	2 65	.....
Finisher	1	.....	2 50	.....
Finisher	1	.....	2 25	.....
Foremen	2	.....	3 00	.....
Heelers	2	.....	2 75	.....
Lasters	10	.....	2 10	.....
Levellers	2	.....	1 50	.....
Nailer	a1	.....	1 00	.....
Sewers, hand	8	.....	1 60	.....
Sewer, McKay machine	1	.....	2 60	.....
Sewing-machine operators	2	11	2 00	1 80
Shiver	1	.....	2 00	.....
Tackers	2	.....	2 70	.....
Treers	3	.....	1 85	.....

BOOTS AND SHOES (WOMEN'S SHOES), MASSACHUSETTS.—ESTAB. No. 38.

Time, 9 hours per day; — days the past year.

Occupations.	Male.	Fem.	Male.	Fem.
Cutter	1	.....	$2 75	.....
Cutters	10	.....	2 50	.....
Cutters	2	.....	2 00	.....
Edge setters	2	.....	2 60	.....
Edge trimmers	2	.....	2 65	.....
Engineer	1	.....	2 20	.....
Finishers	4	.....	2 75	.....
Fitters	.....	30	.....	$1 20
Heelers	4	.....	1 25	.....
Heelers	2	.....	2 60	.....
Heeler	1	.....	2 20	.....
Laborers	7	.....	1 75	.....
Lasters	16	.....	2 48	.....
Packer	1	.....	2 50	.....
Teamsters	1	.....	1 25	.....
Treers	7	.....	1 50	.....

a Youth.

REPORT OF THE COMMISSIONER OF LABOR.

OCCUPATIONS, WITH NUMBER AND WAGES OF EMPLOYÉS, BY INDUSTRIES—Cont'd.

NOTE.—This table is not a complete exhibit for industries or states, but covers only establishments investigated by the Bureau. See page 91, also summaries, pages 142 to 226.

BOOTS AND SHOES (WOMEN'S SHOES), MASSACHUSETTS.—ESTAB. No. 39.

Time, 10 hours per day; 285 days the past year.

Occupations.	Number.		Daily wages.	
	Male.	Fem.	Male.	Fem.
Burnishers	3	......	$2 44	......
Burnishers	8	......	1 75	......
Cutters	44	......	1 35	......
Cutters	30	......	1 87	......
Cutters	38	......	1 48	......
Dressers	......	5	......	$1 30
Edge trimmers	5	......	2 23	......
Finishers	32	......	2 10	......
Heelers	2	......	2 33	......
Lasters	00	......	2 13	......
Nailers	4	......	2 54	......
Packers	3	......	2 33	......
Peggers	6	......	2 37	......
Scourers	7	......	1 84	......
Sewing-machine operators	34	......	1 63	......
Stringers	......	5	......	79
Treers	16	......	1 60	......
Varnishers	......	3	......	1 11

BOOTS AND SHOES (MEN'S BOOTS AND SHOES), MASSACHUSETTS.—ESTAB. No. 40.

Time, 10 hours per day; — days the past year.

Occupations.	Male.	Fem.	Male.	Fem.
Cutters	3	......	$1 00	......
Edge setters	5	......	2 33	......
Finishers	2	......	2 62	......
Fitters	2	......	2 82	......
Heelers	4	......	2 33	......
Lasters	4	......	1 97	......
Packer	1	......	1 25	......
Paster	......	1	......	$1 42
Paster	......	a1	......	70
Sewing-machine operator	1	......	2 67	......
Sewing-machine operators	4	......	2 00	......
Sewing-machine operators	......	3	......	1 60
Sowers, hand	11	......	2 25	......
Treers	2	......	2 25	......

BOOTS AND SHOES (WOMEN'S BOOTS), MASSACHUSETTS.—ESTAB. No. 41.

Time, 10 hours per day; — days the past year.

Occupations.	Male.	Fem.	Male.	Fem.
Fitters	12	......	$2 50	......
Sewing-machine operators	......	50	......	$1 33

BOOTS AND SHOES (WOMEN'S SHOES), MASSACHUSETTS.—ESTAB. No. 42.

Time, 10 hours per day; — days the past year.

Occupations.	Male.	Fem.	Male.	Fem.
Bottomers	67	......	$2 23	......
Cutters	22	......	2 43	......
Fitters	......	25	......	$1 50
Packers	13	......	2 00	......
Sewing-machine operators	......	63	......	1 40

BOOTS AND SHOES (MEN'S AND WOMEN'S SHOES), MASSACHUSETTS.—ESTAB. No. 43.

Time, 10 hours per day; 290 days the past year.

Occupations.	Number.		Daily wages.	
	Male.	Fem.	Male.	Fem.
Burnishers	2	......	$2 00	......
Cutters	4	......	1 97	......
Cutters	7	......	2 37	......
Cutters	14	......	2 50	......
Edge setters	3	......	2 37	......
Edge trimmers	5	......	2 50	......
Engineer	1	......	3 00	......
Finishers	10	......	1 87	......
Finisher	a1	......	62	......
Finishers	......	5	......	$1 40
Foreman	1	......	3 33	......
Heel filer	......	1	......	1 17
Heeler	1	......	2 50	......
Lasters	34	......	2 25	......
Levellers	2	......	2 00	......
Nailer	1	......	2 50	......
Packer	1	......	3 00	......
Peggers	2	......	2 75	......
Sandpaperers	3	......	2 00	......
Sower, McKay machine	1	......	2 50	......
Sewing-machine operators	......	36	......	1 37
Tackers	......	2	......	1 25
Treers	10	......	1 80	......
Vampers	8	......	2 25	......

BOOTS AND SHOES (MEN'S AND WOMEN'S SHOES), MASSACHUSETTS.—ESTAB. No. 44.

Time, 10 hours per day; 240 days the past year.

Occupations.	Male.	Fem.	Male.	Fem.
Assorters	2	......	$2 75	......
Buffers	3	......	2 00	......
Burnisher	1	......	3 00	......
Cutters	11	......	2 25	......
Cutters	5	......	1 75	......
Cutters	2	......	1 50	......
Edge setters	2	......	2 50	......
Edge trimmers	2	......	2 50	......
Engineer	1	......	2 00	......
Heelers	2	......	2 25	......
Lasters	22	......	2 17	......
Nail stickers	a3	a3	75	$0 56
Packers	2	......	2 00	......
Peggers	2	......	2 50	......
Screw nailer	1	......	2 66	......
Sewing-machine operators	......	15	......	1 66
Shanker	1	......	2 50	......
Skiver	1	......	2 00	......
Stringers	......	2	......	1 50
Tackers	4	......	1 25	......
Tacker	......	1	......	1 25
Teamster	1	......	1 50	......
Treers	2	10	2 50	1 25

BOOTS AND SHOES (MEN'S BOOTS), MASSACHUSETTS.—ESTAB. No. 45.

Time, 8 hours per day; 293 days the past year.

Occupations.	Male.	Fem.	Male.	Fem.
Cutter	1	......	$2 50	......
Finishers	2	......	2 00	......
Fitters	2	......	1 75	......
Heeler	1	......	1 50	......
Lasters	2	......	1 50	......
Sewing-machine operators	3	......	1 50	......
Treer	1	......	2 50	......
Vamper	1	......	1 33	......

a Youth.

OCCUPATIONS AND WAGES.

OCCUPATIONS, WITH NUMBER AND WAGES OF EMPLOYÉS, BY INDUSTRIES—Cont'd.

NOTE.—This table is *not* a complete exhibit for industries or states, but covers only establishments investigated by the Bureau. See page 91, also summaries, pages 143 to 226.

BOOTS AND SHOES (MEN'S SHOES), MASSACHUSETTS.—ESTAB. No. 46.

Time, 10 hours per day; 281 days the past year.

Occupations.	Number.		Daily wages.	
	Male.	Fem.	Male.	Fem.
Assorters	4		$2 62	
Assorters	2		2 50	
Burnishers	4		2 00	
Cutters	14		2 50	
Cutters	3		2 25	
Cutters	5		2 00	
Cutters	9		1 50	
Cutters	5		1 25	
Dressers		2		$1 35
Edge setters	3		2 50	
Edge trimmers	6		2 50	
Edge varnishers		2		1 25
Engineer	1		2 25	
Eyeleters		2		1 50
Finishers		21		1 87
Finishers	2		1 87	
Finishers		2		1 50
Foremen	3		3 25	
Heelers	2		2 50	
Heelers	5		2 00	
Heel breaster	a1		87	
Heel-nail setters		a3		50
Lasters	45		2 25	
Leather splitters	2		1 50	
Levellers	2		1 50	
Machinist	1		2 75	
Nailer, machine	1		2 75	
Packers	2		2 25	
Pasters	a2		60	
Peggers, machine	2		2 75	
Scourers	5		2 25	
Screw nailers	2		2 75	
Sewing-machine operators	20		1 62	
Skivers	2		1 75	
Skivers		2		1 25
Treers	9		2 25	
Vamper	1		1 50	
Vamper	a1		75	
Watchmen	1		2 00	

BOOTS AND SHOES (MEN'S SHOES), MASSACHUSETTS.—ESTAB. No. 47.

Time, 10 hours per day; 250 days the past year.

Occupations	Male	Fem	Male	Fem
Cutters	15		$2 60	
Edge setters	10		2 16	
Engineer	1		3 00	
Fitters	6		2 65	
Foreman	1		3 67	
Heeler	1		2 50	
Heeler's helper	a1		50	
Lasters	8		2 50	
Leveller	1		2 50	
Leveller's helper	a1		50	
Pasters and finishers	1	8	2 00	$1 54
Sewers, hand	9		2 50	
Sewing-machine operator	1		3 33	
Sewing-machine operator	1		3 00	
Sewing-machine operator	1		2 50	
Sewing-machine operator		1		2 00
Sewing-machine operators		30		1 58
Stitchers, hand	7		2 83	
Vamper	1		2 16	

BOOTS AND SHOES (MEN'S BOOTS), MASSACHUSETTS.—ESTAB. No. 48.

Time, 10 hours per day; 278 days the past year.

Occupations.	Number.		Daily wages.	
	Male.	Fem.	Male.	Fem.
Assorter	1		$3 00	
Assorter	1		2 50	
Assorters	2		2 25	
Assorter	1		2 00	
Binder		1		$1 25
Box paperer	1		1 40	
Bottom stamper	1		1 50	
Burnishers	3		1 75	
Burnishers	5		1 50	
Cobbler	1		2 00	
Cutters	4		2 75	
Cutters	12		2 50	
Cutters	3		2 25	
Cutters	6		1 50	
Cutters	9		1 10	
Cutter	1		1 00	
Edge blacker	a4		1 00	
Edge trimmer	4		2 50	
Engineer	1		2 75	
Eyelet setters	a2		1 25	
Fitters	2		2 62	
Fitters	2		2 25	
Fitter	1		1 75	
Gilders	2		1 50	
Heel attachers	2		3 00	
Heel breaster	1		2 00	
Heel compresser	1		2 75	
Heel filer	1		1 75	
Heelers	a8		1 25	
Heel trimmers	2		2 00	
Inspector	1		2 00	
Laborers	10		1 00	
Last pullers	2		1 75	
Lasters	68		2 15	
Leather wetter	1		1 50	
Levellers	2		1 75	
Moulder	1		2 25	
Nailers, hand	4		2 00	
Nailers, shank	2		1 75	
Nailer, Standard machine	1		2 00	
Nailer, Union machine	1		2 00	
Nail stickers		4		60
Packers	4		1 25	
Peggers, hand	6		1 75	
Peggers, machine	3		2 50	
Sandpaperers	4		1 50	
Sewing-machine operators	4		1 75	
Sewing-machine operators		a6		80
Sewing-machine operators		2		1 25
Sewing-machine operators		6		1 50
Shanker	1		3 00	
Shank striper	1		2 00	
Shoe stringer		a1		80
Siders	7		2 00	
Skivers		2		1 25
Skivers		3		1 00
Sole layers	2		3 00	
Splitters, sole	2		1 75	
Splitter, row		1		1 00
Splitter, welt		1		1 00
Tacker	a1		1 10	
Tackers		2		1 00
Tackers		4		90
Treers	44		1 75	
Turners	4		2 00	
Turner, row		a1		80
Vamper		2		1 75
Watchman	1		2 00	

a Youth.

OCCUPATIONS, WITH NUMBER AND WAGES OF EMPLOYÉS, BY INDUSTRIES—Cont'd.

NOTE.—This table is not a complete exhibit for industries or states, but covers only establishments investigated by the Bureau. See page 91, also summaries, pages 143 to 226.

BOOTS AND SHOES (SLIPPERS), MASSACHUSETTS.—ESTAB. No. 49.

Time, 10 hours per day; 240 days the past year.

Occupations.	Number.		Daily wages.	
	Male.	Fem.	Male.	Fem.
Bottomers	50		$2 50	
Fitters		25		$1 33

BOOTS AND SHOES (MEN'S SHOES), NEW JERSEY.—ESTAB. No. 50.

Time, 10 hours per day; 300 days the past year.

Occupations.	Number.		Daily wages.	
	Male.	Fem.	Male.	Fem.
Apprentices	a25		$0 58	
Bottomers and finishers	125		2 50	
Cutters	25		2 50	
Fitters	25		2 25	
Fitters		60		$1 66

BOOTS AND SHOES (YOUTHS' SHOES), NEW YORK.—ESTAB. No. 51.

Time, 10 hours per day; 300 days the past year.

Occupations.	Number.		Daily wages.	
	Male.	Fem.	Male.	Fem.
Benders	9		$1 67	
Blockers	2		2 25	
Bottomers	35		1 92	
Brusher	1		2 00	
Buffers	2		1 44	
Buffers	2		1 33	
Burnisher	1		2 29	
Button markers		2		$1 00
Button-hole makers		15		1 17
Channeller	1		1 58	
Channellers	2		1 00	
Closers		7		1 04
Cutters	26		2 67	
Cutter	1		2 42	
Cutters	25		2 00	
Cutters	2		1 50	
Cutters' helpers	a10		67	
Edge setters	2		2 67	
Edge trimmers	7		2 50	
Elevator tender	1		1 67	
Fitter	1		1 67	
Foremen	2		3 00	
Foremen	2		2 50	
Heelers	4		1 50	
Laborers	23		1 25	
Lasters	35		2 50	
Lasters	2		1 50	
Levellers	3		2 67	
Measurer	1		1 50	
Moulder	1		2 67	
Pasters		5		1 00
Sandpaperer	1		1 33	
Scourers	2		1 00	
Screw nailer	1		2 67	
Seam rubber		1		1 00
Seat wheelers	2		1 17	
Sewers, McKay machine	3		2 67	
Sewing-machine operators		150		1 33
Sewing-machine operators		10		96
Sewing-machine operators		8		83
Skivers	2		1 67	
Stayers		2		1 17

BOOTS AND SHOES (YOUTHS' SHOES), NEW YORK.—ESTAB. No. 51—Concluded.

Time, 10 hours per day; 300 days the past year.

Occupations.	Number.		Daily wages.	
	Male.	Fem.	Male.	Fem.
Stock rollers	a2		$0 83	
Tacker	1		2 17	
Tackers	4		1 67	
Timekeepers	3		1 00	
Turners	2		1 50	
Undesignated	a1		96	
Undesignated	a3		67	
Undesignated		a20		$0 67
Vampers	11		1 75	

BOOTS AND SHOES (YOUTHS' SHOES), NEW YORK.—ESTAB. No. 52.

Time, 10 hours per day; 300 days the past year.

Occupations.	Number.		Daily wages.	
	Male.	Fem.	Male.	Fem.
Benders	5		$1 58	
Blockers	2		2 25	
Bottomers	19		1 62	
Brusher	1		2 00	
Buffer	1		1 44	
Buffer	1		1 33	
Burnisher	1		2 29	
Button-hole makers		10		$1 00
Button markers		2		1 00
Channeller	1		2 00	
Channeller	1		1 67	
Closers	5		1 00	
Cutters	17		2 33	
Cutters	17		2 17	
Cutter	1		1 50	
Cutters' helpers	a8		67	
Edge setter	1		2 67	
Edge-setters' helpers	2		1 16	
Edge trimmers	5		2 42	
Fitter	1		1 50	
Foremen	2		3 00	
Foreman	1		2 67	
Foremen	2		2 50	
Foreman	1		2 00	
Heelers	2		1 50	
Laborers	7		1 25	
Lasters	19		2 33	
Lasters	2		1 50	
Levellers	2		2 67	
Measurer	1		2 25	
Measurer	1		1 50	
Moulder	1		2 67	
Packers	a8		67	
Pasters		3		1 00
Sandpaperer	1		1 33	
Scourer	a1		83	
Screw nailer	1		2 50	
Seam rubber		1		1 00
Seat wheeler	1		1 17	
Sewers, McKay machine	2		2 67	
Sewing-machine operators		75		1 33
Sewing-machine operators		8		83
Skivers	2		1 67	
Tacker	1		2 25	
Tackers	3		2 00	
Timekeepers	2		91	
Turners	2		1 50	
Undesignated	a1		75	
Vampers	8		1 75	

a Youth.

OCCUPATIONS AND WAGES.

OCCUPATIONS, WITH NUMBER AND WAGES OF EMPLOYÉS, BY INDUSTRIES—Cont'd.

NOTE.—This table is *not* a complete exhibit for industries or states, but covers only establishments investigated by the Bureau. See page 91, also summaries, pages 143 to 226.

BOOTS AND SHOES (YOUTHS' SHOES), NEW YORK.—ESTAB. No. 53.

Time, 10 hours per day; 300 days the past year.

Occupations.	Number.		Daily wages.	
	Male.	Fem.	Male.	Fem.
Beaders	2		$1 50	
Blocker	1		2 29	
Bottomers	12		2 04	
Brusher	1		1 67	
Buffers	2		1 50	
Burnisher	1		2 25	
Button marker		1		$0 96
Channellers	2		1 67	
Closers		3		1 20
Cutters	7		2 33	
Cutters	8		2 17	
Cutters' helpers	a4		75	
Edge setter	1		2 67	
Edge-setters' helpers	2		1 17	
Edge trimmers	2		2 42	
Foremen	2		2 67	
Foreman	1		2 50	
Foremen	2		2 00	
Heelers	2		1 50	
Heelers' helpers	3		1 00	
Heelers' helpers	a2		79	
Laborers	2		1 00	
Lasters	11		2 37	
Laster	1		1 50	
Leveller	1		2 50	
Measurer	1		2 17	
Moulders	2		2 67	
Packers	a4		79	
Sandpaperer	1		1 42	
Scourers	a2		83	
Seam rubber		1		1 00
Seat wheeler	1		1 17	
Sewing-machine operators		38		1 33
Sewing-machine operators		9		1 15
Sewing-machine operators		4		1 00
Sewing-machine operators		3		83
Skivers	2		1 67	
Tacker	1		2 00	
Time-keeper	a1		92	
Turners	2		1 50	
Undesignated		2		75
Vampers	4		1 75	

BOOTS AND SHOES (WOMEN'S AND YOUTHS' SHOES), NEW YORK.—ESTAB. No. 54.

Time, 10 hours per day; 300 days the past year.

Occupations.	Number.		Daily wages.	
	Male.	Fem.	Male.	Fem.
Beader	1		$1 50	
Blocker	1		2 25	
Bottomers	10		2 08	
Brusher	1		1 67	
Buffer	1		1 48	
Burnisher	1		2 25	
Button marker		1		$0 96
Button sewer	1		1 50	
Channeller	1		1 67	
Cutters	12		2 33	
Edge setters	2		2 17	
Edge trimmer	1		2 50	
Edge trimmer	1		3 33	
Finishers		5		82
Foremen	3		2 50	
Foremen	3		2 00	
Heelers	2		1 50	
Lasters	8		2 46	
Leveller	1		2 46	

BOOTS AND SHOES (WOMEN'S AND YOUTHS' SHOES), NEW YORK.—ESTAB. No. 54—Concluded.

Time, 10 hours per day; 300 days the past year.

Occupations.	Number.		Daily wages.	
	Male.	Fem.	Male.	Fem.
Measurer	1		$1 96	
Packer	a1		92	
Sandpaperer	1		1 48	
Seat wheeler	1		1 29	
Sewing-machine operators	2		1 75	
Sewing-machine operators		30		$1 25
Sewing-machine operators		2		83
Skiver	1		1 67	
Skiver	1		1 00	
Tacker	1		2 00	
Timekeeper	1		92	
Turner	1		1 67	
Undesignated	1		83	

BOOTS AND SHOES (YOUTHS' SHOES), NEW YORK.—ESTAB. No. 55.

Time, 10 hours per day; 300 days the past year.

Occupations.	Number.		Daily wages.	
	Male.	Fem.	Male.	Fem.
Beaders	6		$1 58	
Blocker	1		2 25	
Bottomers	15		1 92	
Brusher	1		2 00	
Buffers	2		1 83	
Burnisher	1		2 29	
Button-hole maker		8		$1 00
Button markers		2		1 00
Channeller	1		2 00	
Channeller	1		1 67	
Closers	4		1 65	
Cutters	13		2 33	
Cutters	15		2 17	
Cutters' helpers	a5		67	
Edge setter	1		2 79	
Edge trimmers	3		2 42	
Fitter	1		1 50	
Foremen	3		2 67	
Foreman	1		2 50	
Foreman	1		2 00	
Heelers	2		1 50	
Laborers	5		1 29	
Lasters	15		2 83	
Laster	1		1 50	
Leveller	1		2 67	
Leveller's assistant	a1		75	
Measurer	1		2 00	
Measurer	1		1 50	
Moulder	1		2 07	
Packers	a6		67	
Pasters		2		1 00
Sandpaperer	1		1 33	
Scourers	a2		83	
Screw nailer, McKay machine	1		2 50	
Seam rubbers		8		1 00
Seat wheeler	1		1 17	
Sewing-machine operators		68		1 33
Sewing-machines operators		6		83
Sewer, McKay machine	1		2 07	
Skivers	3		1 67	
Tackers	3		2 00	
Timekeepers	a2		83	
Turners	3		1 50	
Undesignated	5		1 25	
Vampers	6		1 75	

a Youth.

OCCUPATIONS, WITH NUMBER AND WAGES OF EMPLOYÉS, BY INDUSTRIES—Cont'd.

NOTE.—This table is *not* a complete exhibit for industries or states, but covers only establishments investigated by the Bureau. See page 91, also summaries, pages 143 to 226.

BOOTS AND SHOES (YOUTHS' SHOES), NEW YORK.—ESTAB. No. 56.

Time, 10 *hours per day;* 300 *days the past year.*

Occupations.	Number.		Daily wages.	
	Male.	Fem.	Male.	Fem.
Beaders	8		$1 67	
Blockers	2		2 25	
Bottomers	27		1 92	
Brusher	1		2 00	
Buffers	2		1 44	
Buffers	2		1 33	
Burnisher	1		2 29	
Button-hole makers		12		$1 00
Button markers		2		1 00
Channellers	2		2 00	
Channeller	1		1 58	
Closers		6		1 04
Cutters	20		2 62	
Cutters	22		2 00	
Cutters	8		1 50	
Cutters' helpers	a9		67	
Edge setters	2		2 67	
Edge trimmers	7		2 50	
Fitter	1		2 00	
Fitter	1		1 67	
Foreman	1		3 00	
Foreman	1		2 75	
Foremen	2		2 50	
Heelers	4		1 50	
Lasters	27		2 42	
Lasters	2		1 50	
Levellers	3		2 67	
Measurer	1		1 50	
Moulder	1		2 67	
Packers	a10		67	
Pasters		4		1 00
Sandpaperer	1		1 33	
Scourers	a2		1 00	
Screw nailer	1		2 00	
Seam rubber		1		1 00
Seat wheelers	2		1 17	
Sewing-machine operators	8	125	2 00	1 33
Sewing-machine operators		17		83
Skivers	2		1 67	
Stayers		2		1 17
Stock rollers	a2		83	
Tacker	1		2 25	
Tackers	4		1 67	
Timekeepers	a2		62	
Turners	2		1 50	
Undesignated	1		2 00	
Vampers	10		1 76	

BOOTS AND SHOES (WOMEN'S BOOTS), NEW YORK.—ESTAB. No. 57.

Time, 10 *hours per day;* 300 *days the past year.*

Occupations.	Number.		Daily wages.	
	Male.	Fem.	Male.	Fem.
Beaders	4		$1 54	
Blocker	1		2 29	
Bottomers	13		1 83	
Brusher	1		1 67	
Buffers	2		1 33	
Burnisher	1		2 29	
Button-hole makers		5		$1 00
Button marker		1		1 00
Channeller	1		2 00	
Channeller	1		1 50	
Closers	4		1 25	
Cutters	21		2 33	
Cutters' helpers	a4		65	
Edge setter	1		2 63	
Edge-setters' helpers	3		1 17	
Edge trimmers	3		2 50	
Fitter	1		1 67	

BOOTS AND SHOES (WOMEN'S BOOTS), NEW YORK.—ESTAB. No. 57—Concluded.

Time, 10 *hours per day;* 300 *days the past year.*

Occupations.	Number.		Daily wages.	
	Male.	Fem.	Male.	Fem.
Foremen	2		$2 79	
Foreman	1		2 50	
Foremen	2		2 00	
Foreman	1		1 75	
Heelers	2		1 50	
Laborers	7		1 00	
Lasters	13		2 35	
Laster	1		1 67	
Leveller	1		2 46	
Measurer	1		2 42	
Measurer	1		1 50	
Moulders	2		2 62	
Packer	1		1 08	
Packers	a3		75	
Pasters		2		$1 00
Scourers	a2		83	
Screw nailer, McKay machine	1		2 67	
Seam rubber		1		1 00
Seat wheeler	1		1 33	
Sewing-machine operators		50		1 33
Sewing-machine operators		4		83
Sewer, McKay machine	1		2 79	
Skivers	3		1 67	
Tackers	2		2 00	
Timekeeper	1		83	
Turners	2		1 50	
Undesignated	a2		75	
Vampers	4		1 75	

BOOTS AND SHOES (WOMEN'S BOOTS), NEW YORK.—ESTAB. No. 58.

Time, 10 *hours per day;* 300 *days the past year.*

Occupations.	Number.		Daily wages.	
	Male.	Fem.	Male.	Fem.
Beader	2		$1 53	
Blocker	1		2 29	
Bottomers	12		1 92	
Brusher	1		1 67	
Buffer	1		1 46	
Buffer	1		1 33	
Burnisher	1		2 25	
Button-hole maker		5		$1 00
Button marker		1		1 00
Channeller	1		2 00	
Channeller	1		1 50	
Closers	9		1 24	
Cutter	1		2 50	
Cutters	13		2 29	
Cutters	3		2 18	
Cutters' helpers	a5		67	
Edge setters	1		2 67	
Edge-setter's helpers	2		1 17	
Edge trimmers	3		2 50	
Fitter	1		1 67	
Foremen	2		2 67	
Foreman	1		2 50	
Foremen	2		2 00	
Heelers	2		1 50	
Laborers	9		1 00	
Lasters	12		2 33	
Laster	1		1 50	
Leveller	1		2 50	
Measurer	1		1 50	
Moulders	2		2 67	
Packers	a4		79	
Pasters		2		1 00
Sandpaperer	1		1 33	
Scourers	a2		83	

a Youth.

OCCUPATIONS AND WAGES.

OCCUPATIONS, WITH NUMBER AND WAGES OF EMPLOYÉS, BY INDUSTRIES—Cont'd.

NOTE.—This table is *not* a complete exhibit for industries or states, but covers only establishments investigated by the Bureau. See page 91, also summaries, pages 143 to 226.

BOOTS AND SHOES (WOMEN'S BOOTS), NEW YORK.—ESTAB. No. 58—Concluded.
Time, 10 hours per day; 300 days the past year.

Occupations.	Number.		Daily wages.	
	Male.	Fem.	Male.	Fem.
Screw nailer	1		$2 67	
Seam rubber		1		$1 00
Seat wheeler	1		1 17	
Sewer, McKay machine	1		2 67	
Sewing-machine operators		36		1 33
Sewing-machine operators		19		1 25
Sewing-machine operators		4		83
Skivers	2		1 67	
Tacker	1		2 25	
Tacker	1		2 00	
Timekeepers	a2		83	
Turners	2		1 50	
Undesignated	5		1 00	
Undesignated	a2		92	
Undesignated	a3		67	
Vampers	4		1 67	
Watchman	1		1 00	

BOOTS AND SHOES (WOMEN'S BOOTS), NEW YORK.—ESTAB. No. 59.
Time, 10 hours per day; 300 days the past year.

Occupations.	Male.	Fem.	Male.	Fem.
Beaders	4		$1 58	
Blocker	1		2 25	
Bottomers	12		1 92	
Brusher	1		1 67	
Buffers	2		1 33	
Burnisher	1		2 29	
Button-hole makers		5		$1 00
Button marker		1		1 00
Channeller	1		2 00	
Channeller	1		1 50	
Closers	3		1 00	
Cutters	22		2 25	
Cutters' helpers	a4		67	
Edge setter	1		2 67	
Edge-setters' helpers	5		1 17	
Edge trimmers	3		2 42	
Fitter	1		1 67	
Foremen	3		2 67	
Foremen	2		2 25	
Heelers	2		1 50	
Laborers	5		1 00	
Lasters	12		2 33	
Laster	1		1 50	
Leveller	1		2 50	
Measurer	1		2 42	
Measurer	1		1 50	
Moulder	1		2 67	
Packers	a5		75	
Pasters		2		1 00
Sandpaperer	1		1 33	
Scourers	a2		75	
Screw nailer	1		2 67	
Seam rubber		1		1 00
Seat wheeler	1		1 17	
Sewing-machine operators		59		1 33
Sewing-machine operator		1		83
Sewer, McKay machine	1		2 67	
Skivers	2		1 67	
Tackers	2		2 00	
Timekeepers	2		83	
Turners	2		1 50	
Undesignated	5		1 08	
Vampers	4		1 67	

BOOTS AND SHOES (WOMEN'S BOOTS), NEW YORK.—ESTAB. No. 60.
Time, 10 hours per day; 300 days the past year.

Occupations.	Number.		Daily wages.	
	Male.	Fem.	Male.	Fem.
Beader	1		$1 50	
Blocker	1		2 25	
Bottomers	9		2 04	
Brusher	1		1 67	
Buffer	1		1 48	
Burnisher	1		2 25	
Button marker		1		$0 96
Button sewer	1		1 50	
Channeller	1		1 75	
Cutters	10		2 33	
Cutter	1		1 96	
Edge trimmers	2		2 33	
Errand boy	a1		75	
Finishers		4		80
Foremen	3		2 50	
Heeler	1		1 50	
Laborers	4		1 00	
Lasters	7		2 46	
Leveller	1		2 40	
Measurer	1		2 04	
Sandpaperer	1		1 50	
Scourer	1		1 08	
Scraper		1		83
Sewing-machine operator	1		1 33	
Sewing-machine operator		1		88
Sewing-machine operators		25		1 25
Skiver	1		1 67	
Tacker	1		2 00	
Timekeeper	a2		83	
Turner	1		1 67	
Undesignated	3		1 00	
Watchman	1		1 42	

BOOTS AND SHOES (WOMEN'S BOOTS), NEW YORK.—ESTAB. No. 61.
Time, 10 hours per day; 300 days the past year.

Occupations	Male.	Fem.	Male.	Fem.
Beaders	3		$1 54	
Blocker	1		2 29	
Bottomers	11		2 00	
Brusher	1		1 67	
Buffers	2		1 50	
Burnisher	1		2 25	
Button marker		1		$1 00
Channeller	1		2 00	
Channeller	1		1 70	
Closers	3		1 24	
Cutters	15		2 25	
Edge trimmers	2		2 50	
Edge setter	1		2 67	
Edge setters' helpers	2		1 17	
Foremen	3		2 50	
Foremen	2		2 00	
Heelers	2		1 50	
Heelers' helpers	a7		83	
Laborers	8		1 00	
Lasters	10		2 38	
Laster	1		1 50	
Leveller	1		2 50	
Measurer	1		2 33	
Moulders	2		2 66	
Packers	a3		79	
Sandpaperer	1		1 42	
Scourers	a2		83	
Screw nailer	1		2 67	
Seam rubber		1		1 00
Seat wheeler	1		1 17	
Sewing-machine operators		40		1 35

a Youth.

308 REPORT OF THE COMMISSIONER OF LABOR.

OCCUPATIONS, WITH NUMBER AND WAGES OF EMPLOYÉS, BY INDUSTRIES—Cont'd.

NOTE.—This table is *not* a complete exhibit for industries or states, but covers only establishments investigated by the Bureau. See page 91, also summaries, pages 143 to 226.

BOOTS AND SHOES (WOMEN'S BOOTS), NEW YORK.—ESTAB. No. 61—Concluded.

Time, 10 hours per day; 300 days the past year.

Occupations.	Number.		Daily wages.	
	Male.	Fem.	Male.	Fem.
Sewing-machine operators		3		$1 21
Sewing-machine operators		6		1 03
Sewing-machine operators		4		83
Sewer, McKay machine	1		$2 07	
Skivers	2		1 75	
Sweeper		1		70
Tackers	2		2 00	
Timekeeper	a1		87	
Turners	2		1 50	
Vampers	4		1 75	
Watchman	1		1 00	

BOOTS AND SHOES (WOMEN'S BOOTS), NEW YORK.—ESTAB. No. 62.

Time, 10 hours per day; 300 days the past year.

Occupations.	Number.		Daily wages.	
	Male.	Fem.	Male.	Fem.
Beader	1		$1 57	
Blocker	1		2 29	
Bottomers	9		2 08	
Brusher	1		1 67	
Buffer	1		1 46	
Burnisher	1		2 29	
Button marker		1		$0 98
Button sewer	1		1 50	
Channeller	1		1 00	
Cutters	13		2 29	
Cutter	1		2 00	
Edge setters	2		2 62	
Edge trimmers	2		2 46	
Foreman	1		2 67	
Foremen	2		2 50	
Foremen	2		1 96	
Heeler	1		1 50	
Laborers	5		1 00	
Lasters	8		2 50	
Laster	1		1 50	
Leveller	1		2 46	
Moulder	1		2 50	
Packers	a3		79	
Sandpaperer	1		1 46	
Scourer	1		1 00	
Seam rubber		1		1 00
Sewing-machine operators		41		1 33
Sewing-machine operators		2		83
Skiver	1		1 58	
Tacker	1		2 00	
Timekeeper	1		92	
Turner	1		1 50	
Undesignated	2		87	
Undesignated	a3	a3	71	65

BOOTS AND SHOES (MEN'S AND WOMEN'S SHOES), NEW YORK.—ESTAB. No. 63.

Time, 10 hours per day; 300 days the past year.

Occupations.	Number.		Daily wages.	
	Male.	Fem.	Male.	Fem.
Beaders	6		$1 58	
Blocker	1		2 25	
Bottomers	15		1 92	
Buffer	1		1 44	
Buffer	1		1 33	
Burnisher	1		2 29	
Button-hole makers		10		$1 00
Button markers		3		1 00

BOOTS AND SHOES (MEN'S AND WOMEN'S SHOES), NEW YORK.—ESTAB. No. 63—Concluded.

Time, 10 hours per day; 300 days the past year.

Occupations.	Number.		Daily wages.	
	Male.	Fem.	Male.	Fem.
Channeller	1		$2 00	
Channeller	1		1 67	
Closers		3		$1 00
Cutters	34		2 33	
Cutters' helper	a1		75	
Edge setters	2		2 62	
Edge-setters' helpers	2		1 17	
Edge trimmers	6		2 42	
Fitter	1		1 50	
Foreman	1		2 79	
Foremen	2		2 67	
Foreman	1		2 00	
Foreman	1		2 17	
Heelers	2		1 50	
Laborers	5		1 00	
Lasters	17		2 33	
Laster	1		1 50	
Leveller	1		2 42	
Leveller's assistant	a1		75	
Measurer	1		2 00	
Measurer	1		1 50	
Moulder	1		2 00	
Packers	a4		67	
Pasters		3		1 00
Sandpaperer	1		1 33	
Scourers	a2		83	
Screw nailer	1		2 50	
Seam rubbers		2		1 00
Seat wheeler	1		1 17	
Sewing-machine operators		72		1 33
Sewing-machine operators		6		83
Sewer, McKay machine	1		2 07	
Skivers	3		1 67	
Tacker	3		2 00	
Timekeeper	2		83	
Turners	2		1 50	
Vampers	7		1 75	

BOOTS AND SHOES (MEN'S AND WOMEN'S SHOES), NEW YORK.—ESTAB. No. 64.

Time, 10 hours per day; 300 days the past year.

Occupations.	Number.		Daily wages.	
	Male.	Fem.	Male.	Fem.
Beaders	2		$1 50	
Blocker	1		2 29	
Bottomers	11		2 08	
Brusher	1		1 67	
Burnisher	1		2 25	
Button sewer	1		1 50	
Channeller	1		1 67	
Cutters	15		2 29	
Edge setters	2		2 62	
Edge trimmers	2		2 50	
Foreman	1		2 67	
Foremen	2		2 50	
Foremen	2		3 00	
Heeler	1		1 33	
Heeler	1		1 50	
Laborers	4		1 00	
Lasters	10		2 42	
Laster	1		1 50	
Leveller	1		2 50	
Moulder	1		2 58	
Packers	a3		79	
Sandpaperer	1		1 42	
Scourer	1		1 00	
Seam rubber		1		$1 00
Seat wheeler	1		1 17	

a Youth.

OCCUPATIONS AND WAGES.

OCCUPATIONS, WITH NUMBER AND WAGES OF EMPLOYÉS, BY INDUSTRIES—Cont'd.

NOTE.—This table is not a complete exhibit for industries or states, but covers only establishments investigated by the Bureau. See page 91, also summaries, pages 143 to 226.

BOOTS AND SHOES (MEN'S AND WOMEN'S SHOES), NEW YORK.—ESTAB. No. 64—Concluded.

Time, 10 hours per day; 300 days the past year.

Occupations.	Number.		Daily wages.	
	Male.	Fem.	Male.	Fem.
Sewing-machine operators	3	50	$1 71	$1 33
Sewing-machine operators		3		83
Skivers	2		1 67	
Timekeepers	2		92	
Turner	1		1 50	
Tacker	1		2 00	
Undesignated	a10		83	

BOOTS AND SHOES (WOMEN'S SHOES), OHIO.—ESTAB. No. 65.

Time, 10 hours per day; — days the past year.

Occupations.	Male.	Fem.	Male.	Fem.
Apprentices	a15		$1 25	
Bottomers	175		2 50	
Cutters	20		2 75	
Fitters	25	230	2 25	$1 33
Fitters' helpers	a12		75	

BOOTS AND SHOES (WOMEN'S SHOES), OHIO.—ESTAB. No. 66.

Time, 10 hours per day; — days the past year.

Occupations.	Male.	Fem.	Male.	Fem.
Apprentices	a5		$0 58	
Bottomers and finishers	40		2 50	
Cutters	5		2 50	
Fitters		35		$1 17
Inkers and sorters		a15		50

BOOTS AND SHOES (WOMEN'S SHOES), OHIO.—ESTAB. No. 67.

Time, 10 hours per day; 300 days the past year.

Occupations.	Male.	Fem.	Male.	Fem.
Bottomers and finishers	30		$2 00	
Fitters		30		$0 85

BOOTS AND SHOES (MEN'S AND WOMEN'S SHOES), OHIO.—ESTAB. No. 68.

Time, 10 hours per day; — days the past year.

Occupations.	Male.	Fem.	Male.	Fem.
Apprentices	a20		$1 00	
Bottomers	50		2 17	
Cutters	15		2 33	
Foremen	3		3 00	
Fitters		30		$1 00
Packers	3		1 50	

BOOTS AND SHOES (YOUTHS' AND CHILDREN'S SHOES), PENNSYLVANIA.—ESTAB. No. 69.

Time, 10 hours per day; 240 days the past year.

Occupations.	Male.	Fem.	Male.	Fem.
Beaters-out	6		$3 10	
Beaters	33		1 25	
Buffers	6		2 50	

BOOTS AND SHOES (YOUTHS' AND CHILDREN'S SHOES), PENNSYLVANIA.—ESTAB. No. 69—Concluded.

Time, 10 hours per day; 240 days the past year.

Occupations.	Number.		Daily wages.	
	Male.	Fem.	Male.	Fem.
Burnishers	7		$2 10	
Button-hole makers	3		1 60	
Button sewers		39		$0 90
Closers	19		1 85	
Closers	6		2 35	
Corders	20		1 66	
Edge setters	14		3 00	
Finishers	15		2 80	
Fitters	30		1 64	
Fitters	29		1 95	
Fitters		a32		50
Heelers	6		2 90	
Laborers	20		1 40	
Laborers	3		1 25	
Lasters	68		1 78	
Packers	6		1 00	
Scourers	2		2 00	
Seam rubbers	6		1 15	
Sewers, McKay machine	7		3 25	
Sewing-machine operators	16		1 80	
Sewing-machine operators	10		1 50	
Sewer, Standard machine	1		2 60	
Stayers		14		90
Stitchers, lining	11		1 85	
Tackers	4		1 10	
Trimmers	7		2 05	
Trimmers	5		1 50	
Turners	35		2 60	
Vampers	14		1 90	

BOOTS AND SHOES (WOMEN'S SHOES), PENNSYLVANIA.—ESTAB. No. 70.

Time, 10 hours per day; 250 days the past year.

Occupations.	Male.	Fem.	Male.	Fem.
Burnishers	5		$2 23	
Button-hole makers		9		$0 78
Cutters	28		2 15	
Edge trimmers	6		3 49	
Finishers	21		2 30	
Finishers	10		2 75	
Heelers	2		2 68	
Heelers	5		2 38	
Laborers	15		1 25	
Lasters	42		2 24	
Pasters		79		88
Sewing-machine operators	3	71	2 65	1 32
Sewers, hand	17		2 06	
Shavers	5		2 85	
Sock liners	6		1 64	
Treers	3		1 64	
Turners	22		2 95	
Undesignated	a68		50	

BOXES (WOODEN BOXES), NEW YORK.—ESTAB. No. 71.

Time, 10 hours per day; 300 days the past year.

Occupations.	Male.	Fem.	Male.	Fem.
Box makers	27		$2 33	
Engineer	1		3 00	
Fireman	1		2 00	
Lumber handlers	6		2 00	
Planers	2		3 17	

a Youth.

OCCUPATIONS, WITH NUMBER AND WAGES OF EMPLOYÉS, BY INDUSTRIES—Cont'd.

NOTE.—This table is not a complete exhibit for industries or states, but covers only establishments investigated by the Bureau. See page 91, also summaries, pages 143 to 226.

BOXES (WOODEN BOXES), NEW YORK.—ESTAB. No. 71—Concluded.

Time, 10 hours per day; 300 days the past year.

Occupations.	Number.		Daily wages.	
	Male.	Fem.	Male.	Fem.
Sawyers	12	......	$2 00	......
Teamsters	6	......	2 00	......
Tonguers and groovers	2	......	2 17	......

BOXES (WOODEN BOXES), VIRGINIA.—ESTAB. No. 72.

Time, 10 hours per day; 300 days the past year.

Box makers	22	......	$3 00	......
Engineer	1	......	1 50	......
Foreman	1	......	3 50	......
Laborers	12	......	1 00	......
Sawyers	4	......	2 00	......
Sawyers	4	......	1 50	......
Sawyers' helpers	a4	......	75	......
Undesignated	a9	......	50	......

BOXES (PAPER PILL BOXES), VIRGINIA.—ESTAB. No. 73.

Time, 10 hours per day; 290 days the past year.

Box makers	......	147	......	$0 67
Box makers	......	140	......	63
Cutters	5	......	$2 00	......
Cutters' helpers	a16	......	70	......
Engineer	1	......	1 50	......
Foremen	2	......	2 00	......
Laborers	a2	......	50	......
Packers	2	......	1 75	......
Teamsters	1	......	75	......

BRICKS, DELAWARE.—ESTAB. No. 74.

Time, 10 hours per day; 175 days the past year.

Foreman	1	......	$3 33	......
Laborers	29	......	1 25	......
Moulders	6	......	2 37	......
Machine tenders	16	......	1 27	......
Off-bearers	6	......	1 00	......
Setters and burners	9	......	1 75	......
Undesignated	a8	......	50	......
Wheelers	6	......	1 33	......

BRICKS (FIRE BRICKS, TILES), MISSOURI.—ESTAB. No. 75.

Time, 10 hours per day; — days the past year.

Engineers	2	......	$3 25	......
Laborers	111	......	1 25	......
Pressers	2	......	2 25	......
Retort makers	4	......	2 50	......
Trap makers	3	......	2 00	......
Tile makers	3	......	2 50	......

BRICKS, NEW HAMPSHIRE.—ESTAB. No. 76.

Time, 10 hours per day; — days the past year.

Occupations.	Number.		Daily wages.	
	Male.	Fem.	Male.	Fem.
Burners	2	......	$4 23	......
Foreman	1	......	5 69	......
Moulders	6	......	2 42	......
Setters	6	......	1 42	......
Wheelers and carriers	48	......	1 27	......

BRICKS, NEW JERSEY.—ESTAB. No. 77.

Time, 10 hours per day; 175 days the past year.

Burners	2	......	$3 25	......
Clay grinders	2	......	1 75	......
Engineers	1	......	2 00	......
Laborers	101	......	1 50	......
Moulders	14	......	2 80	......
Pressers	11	......	2 00	......
Setters	3	......	3 00	......
Wheelers and tossers	6	......	1 75	......

BRICKS (FIRE BRICKS), NEW JERSEY.—ESTAB. No. 78.

Time, 10 hours per day; 175 days the past year.

Blacksmith	1	......	$2 12	......
Brick burners	3	......	1 50	......
Diggers	9	......	1 12	......
Engineer	1	......	2 12	......
Laborers	31	......	1 00	......
Moulders	5	......	1 62	......
Pipe pressmen	5	......	1 20	......
Pressers	2	......	1 20	......
Setters	2	......	1 50	......
Wheelwright	1	......	2 12	......

BROOMS, NEW YORK.—ESTAB. No. 79.

Time, 10 hours per day; 273 days the past year.

Foremen	3	......	$3 00	......
Foremen, assistant	2	......	1 67	......
Laborers	15	......	1 35	......
Laborers	17	......	1 26	......
Laborers	23	......	1 17	......
Packers	6	......	83	......
Sackers	2	......	1 37	......
Sewers	9	......	1 54	......
Sewers	2	......	1 30	......
Sizers	5	......	1 42	......
Sizers	8	......	1 12	......
Trimmer	1	......	1 50	......
Winders	17	......	1 75	......
Winders	19	......	1 67	......

a Youth.

OCCUPATIONS AND WAGES.

OCCUPATIONS, WITH NUMBER AND WAGES OF EMPLOYÉS, BY INDUSTRIES—Cont'd.

NOTE.—This table is *not* a complete exhibit for industries or states, but covers only establishments investigated by the Bureau. See page 91, also summaries, pages 143 to 226.

BROOMS, NEW YORK.—ESTAB. No. 80.
Time, 10 hours per day; 273 days the past year.

Occupations.	Number.		Daily wages.	
	Male.	Fem.	Male.	Fem.
Foremen	3		$3 00	
Foremen	2		1 75	
Laborers	15		1 83	
Laborers	40		1 21	
Packers	6		83	
Sackers	2		1 37	
Sewers	12		1 67	
Sewers	3		1 58	
Sewers	4		1 48	
Sewers	2		1 83	
Sizers	5		1 42	
Sizers	9		1 12	
Sorter	1		1 62	
Trimmer	1		1 50	
Winders	8		1 79	
Winders	22		1 71	
Winders	6		1 60	

BROOMS, NEW YORK.—ESTAB. No. 81.
Time, 10 hours per day; 273 days the past year.

Occupations.	Male.	Fem.	Male.	Fem.
Foreman	1		$3 00	
Foremen	2		2 67	
Foremen, assistant	2		1 67	
Laborers	6		1 25	
Packers	2		83	
Sewers	6		1 50	
Sizer	1		1 25	
Sizer	1		1 12	
Sorter	1		1 58	
Trimmer and sacker	1		1 42	
Winders	8		1 75	

BROOMS, NEW YORK.—ESTAB. No. 82.
Time, 10 hours per day; 273 days the past year.

Occupations.	Male.	Fem.	Male.	Fem.
Foreman	1		$3 00	
Foremen	3		1 75	
Laborers	5		1 33	
Laborers	5		1 20	
Packers	2		83	
Sacker	1		1 37	
Sizer	1		1 12	
Sizers	2		1 41	
Sewers	2		1 58	
Sewers	2		1 50	
Sewer	1		1 33	
Trimmer	1		1 50	
Winders	11		1 66	

BROOMS, NEW YORK.—ESTAB. No. 83.
Time, 10 hours per day; 273 days the past year.

Occupations.	Male.	Fem.	Male.	Fem.
Foreman	1		$3 00	
Foremen	2		1 75	
Laborers	4		1 33	
Laborers	5		1 21	
Packers	2		83	
Sewers	4		1 62	
Sewers	2		1 50	

BROOMS, NEW YORK.—ESTAB. No. 83—Concluded.
Time, 10 hours per day; 273 days the past year.

Occupations.	Male.	Fem.	Male.	Fem.
Sewer	1		$1 33	
Sizers	2		1 42	
Sorter	1		1 67	
Trimmer and sacker	1		1 50	
Winders	3		1 75	
Winders	4		1 60	

CARPETINGS (EXTRA SUPER INGRAIN), CONNECTICUT.—ESTAB. No. 84.
Time, 10 hours per day; 300 days the past year.

Occupations.	Male.	Fem.	Male.	Fem.
Dyers	10		$1 75	
Finishers		10		$1 25
Weavers		12		1 75
Weavers		36		1 50
Winders		a20		65

CARPETINGS (BRUSSELS), GREAT BRITAIN.—ESTAB. No. 85.
Time, 10 hours per day, 56½ hours per week; — days the past year.

Occupations.	Male.	Fem.	Male.	Fem.
Alterers	a38		$0 50	
Designers	7		1 41	
Designers' assistants	a4		42	
Dyers	9		87	
Dyers' helpers	a4		33	
Foremen	4		2 08	
Laborers	8		85	
Packers	5		77	
Repair hands	13		1 04	
Sizers	4		1 25	
Sizers' assistants	a3		37	
Stampers		4		$0 83
Stampers' assistants		a2		33
Undesignated	6		54	
Undesignated	5		42	
Weavers	62		1 46	
Winders		17		44
Winders		a7		37

CARPETINGS (TAPESTRY), GREAT BRITAIN.—ESTAB. No. 86.
Time, 10 hours per day, 56½ hours per week; — days the past year.

Occupations.	Male.	Fem.	Male.	Fem.
Color hands	a10		$0 37	
Color hands	a15		33	
Designers	2		1 33	
Designers' assistants	a5		33	
Foremen	2		1 75	
Printers	25	7	1 17	$0 71
Setters		21		75
Setters		a14		33
Undesignated	18		83	
Weavers	51		1 25	
Winders		12		50
Winders		a10		33

a Youth.

REPORT OF THE COMMISSIONER OF LABOR.

OCCUPATIONS, WITH NUMBER AND WAGES OF EMPLOYÉS, BY INDUSTRIES—Cont'd.

NOTE.—This table is *not* a complete exhibit for industries or states, but covers only establishments investigated by the Bureau. See page 91, also summaries, pages 143 to 226.

CARPETINGS (BRUSSELS, WILTON, AND INGRAIN), MASSACHUSETTS.—ESTAB. No. 87.

Time, 10 hours per day; — days the past year.

Occupations.	Number.		Daily wages.	
	Male.	Fem.	Male.	Fem.
Carders	a51	20	$0 64	$0 64
Combers	a36	a14	50	50
Cotton-room hands	a16	10	69	69
Dyers	100		1 00	
Engineers	12		1 20	
Finishers	7	48	92	92
Finishers	7	40	87	87
Laborers	46		1 00	
Rulers	1	11	1 03	1 07
Scourers	19		1 00	
Scrubbers		7		60
Section hands	50		1 29	
Spinners, mule	37		1 10	
Spinners, other	a0	82	60	60
Spoolers		12		92
Warpers	15		1 20	
Waste pickers	a3	5	60	60
Weavers	22	111	2 03	2 03
Weavers	21	111	1 55	1 55
Weavers	21	111	98	98
Winders	10	53	84	84
Wool sorters	19	3	1 68	1 68

CARPETINGS (BRUSSELS AND WILTON), MASSACHUSETTS.—ESTAB. No. 88.

Time, 10 hours per day; 300 days the past year.

Occupations.	Male.	Fem.	Male.	Fem.
Carders	13	10	$0 88	$0 88
Doffers		a12		50
Doublers		7		80
Dressers	4		2 00	
Dyers	13		1 40	
Engineers and repair hands	3		3 00	
Finishers	5	7	1 50	1 50
Laborers	4		1 33	
Laborers	8		90	
Spinners, other		20		80
Twisters		21		70
Undesignated	16		3 00	
Undesignated	a30		60	
Winder	1	3	1 50	1 50
Winders		28		90
Wool sorters	9		2 00	

CARPETINGS (TAPESTRY), MASSACHUSETTS.—ESTAB. No. 89.

Time, 10 hours per day; — days the past year.

Occupations.	Male.	Fem.	Male.	Fem.
Beamers	4		$1 50	
Color hands	a3		58	
Dressers	2		1 25	
Laborers	a3		58	
Pickers	5		1 10	
Printers	8		1 08	
Scourers	9		1 33	
Setters		14		1 40
Spoolers		a10		66
Weavers		26		1 33

CARPETINGS (BRUSSELS AND WILTON), MASSACHUSETTS.—ESTAB. No. 90.

Time, 10 hours per day; — days the past year.

Occupations.	Number.		Daily wages.	
	Male.	Fem.	Male.	Fem.
Card cutters	2		$1 70	
Dyers	12		1 40	
Laborers	5		1 00	
Laborers	a20		75	
Loom fixers	4		2 70	
Machinists	4		2 75	
Winders	20		1 70	
Winders	a30		80	

CARPETINGS (BRUSSELS AND MOQUETTE), NEW YORK.—ESTAB. No. 91.

Time, 10 hours per day; 100 days the past year.

Occupations.	Male.	Fem.	Male.	Fem.
Adjusters	2		$2 00	
Analyst	1		1 83	
Bankers	16	b15	85	54
Beamers	9		1 46	
Beamers	48		1 12	
Blacksmiths	7		2 33	
Blacksmiths' helpers	7		1 50	
Bobbin boys	b32		58	
Brushers	a6		75	
Carders	19		1 46	
Card boys	b76		50	
Card cleaners	3		1 25	
Card cleaner	1		1 00	
Card grinders	6		1 50	
Card writers	3		83	
Carpenters	4		2 00	
Carriers	49	b11	1 20	53
Carriers	18		1 42	
Color hands	a9		58	
Color hands	2		1 50	
Color hands	b80		50	
Color hands	2		2 00	
Combers	9	12	2 40	80
Designer	1		8 00	
Designer	1		6 66	
Designer	1		6 00	
Designer	1		4 00	
Designers	7		2 50	
Designer	3		1 67	
Doffers		a30		55
Doublers	27	20	1 15	1 23
Drawers		20		1 00
Dressers	67		1 50	
Drum strippers	18		1 50	
Dryers	17		1 30	
Dryers	a15		58	
Dyers	10		1 46	
Dye preparers	8		2 17	
Elevator tenders	8		1 85	
Elevator tenders	8		83	
Engineers	6		2 33	
Feeder's breaker	2		1 15	
Feeders	8		1 00	
Fillers		33		1 30
Finishers	3		1 50	
Finishers	5		1 95	
Firemen	6		1 20	
Floormen	218		1 43	
Foremen	120		2 21	
Hacklers	5		1 80	
Harness fixers	3		1 50	
Harness fixers	5		2 21	
Laborers	3		1 25	
Inspectors	17	12	1 37	1 08

a Youth. b Children.

OCCUPATIONS AND WAGES.

OCCUPATIONS, WITH NUMBER AND WAGES OF EMPLOYÉS, BY INDUSTRIES—Cont'd.

NOTE.—This table is *not* a complete exhibit for industries or states, but covers only establishments investigated by the Bureau. See page 91, also summaries, pages 143 to 226.

CARPETINGS (BRUSSELS AND MOQUETTE), NEW YORK.—ESTAB. No. 91—Concluded.

Time, 10 hours per day; 100 days the past year.

Occupations.	Number.		Daily wages.	
	Male.	Fem.	Male.	Fem.
Inspectors	4		$2 42	
Laborers	43		1 15	
Laborers	3		1 00	
Lappers	6		1 20	
Loom fixers	30		2 54	
Machinists	60		2 25	
Machinists' apprentices	a6		58	
Manglers	7		1 25	
Matchers	3		1 87	
Menders		17		$1 37
Measurers	3		2 00	
Oilers	7		1 28	
Oil extractors	154		88	
Overseers	5		4 00	
Pattern starters	10		2 60	
Pickers	4		1 50	
Picker feeders	8		1 00	
Printers	175		1 66	
Rulers		29		1 03
Scourers	36		1 50	
Scourers	5		1 40	
Scourers	49		1 36	
Scourers	22		1 10	
Scrapers		154		1 00
Scrubbers	7	21	1 00	89
Section hands	21		1 63	
Separator	1		1 90	
Separators		3		85
Setters	90		2 00	
Setters		134		1 12
Shearers	6		1 75	
Sizers	12		1 50	
Sizers	4		1 25	
Spare hands	11	12	1 05	89
Speckers		35		1 52
Spinners, mule	*100		1 20	
Spinners, other	31	200	1 00	1 00
Spoolers		48		1 12
Spoolers		154		87
Spoolers	a54		78	
Suction-fan tenders	7		1 25	
Sweepers	a25		68	
Teamsters	12		1 44	
Tinsmiths	4		2 17	
Twisters	6	20	1 50	1 00
Undesignated	a371		58	
Warpers	7		1 50	
Warpers	12		1 43	
Waste gatherers	a3		67	
Waste gatherers	a16		62	
Watchmen	12		1 50	
Weavers		358		1 32
Weavers	390		1 50	
Weighers	4		2 50	
Weighers	31		1 67	
Weighers	4		1 25	
Winders		65		1 12
Winders		12		92
Wipers	12		1 07	
Wire and reed fixers	4		1 50	
Wool boxers	3		1 25	
Wool sorters	81		1 20	
Yarn bleachers	8		1 25	
Yarn numberers	a16		75	
Yarn steamers	2		1 42	

CARPETINGS (BRUSSELS AND VELVET), NEW YORK.—ESTAB. No. 92.

Time, 11 hours per day; 300 days the past year.

Occupations.	Number.		Daily wages.	
	Male.	Fem.	Male.	Fem.
Bankers		a5		$0 50
Beamers	5	10	$2 00	1 00
Belt lacer	1		2 03	
Blacksmiths	4		2 17	
Bobbin boys	a30		69	
Breakers	4		1 46	
Card boys	a28		75	
Carders	12		1 46	
Card cleaners	12		1 25	
Card writers	3		90	
Carpenters	10		2 25	
Carriers	13		98	
Color hands	a45		84	
Color hands	10		1 40	
Color hand	1		2 00	
Color hands	3		2 00	
Combers	2	21	2 42	1 00
Cooper	1		1 50	
Coupler	1		2 25	
Designer	1		6 00	
Designer	1		5 00	
Designer	1		4 17	
Designers	9		3 00	
Designers	2		1 25	
Doffers		a90		54
Doubler	1	38	1 42	1 08
Doublers	7		1 03	
Drawers		97		1 02
Dressers	5		1 58	
Dressers	17		1 49	
Drumstrippers	7		1 50	
Dryers	3		1 17	
Dryers	20		1 20	
Dye preparer	1		2 42	
Dyers	15		1 25	
Engineer	1		5 83	
Engineer	1		2 50	
Engineer	1		1 70	
Feeders	8		1 40	
Finishers	55		1 50	
Finishers	2		1 96	
Firemen	9		1 54	
Foremen	2		4 00	
Foremen	12		2 50	
Foreman	1		2 33	
Foreman	1		2 00	
Harness fixers	3		2 29	
Harness fixers	4		1 50	
Harness fixers	4		1 00	
Inspector	1		1 37	
Inspectors	3	2	1 50	1 00
Laborers	20		1 51	
Laborers	43		1 24	
Lappers	5		1 46	
Loom fixers	11		2 17	
Loom fixers	5		1 75	
Machinists	14		1 88	
Matchers	4		2 00	
Measurers	3		2 00	
Menders		61		1 12
Oilers and carriers	17		1 51	
Oil extractors	45		1 17	
Overseers	9		6 00	
Overseer	1		3 00	
Painters	3		2 00	
Pattern makers	2		2 33	
Pattern starters	4		2 29	

a Youth.

OCCUPATIONS, WITH NUMBER AND WAGES OF EMPLOYÉS, BY INDUSTRIES—Cont'd.

NOTE.—This table is *not* a complete exhibit for industries or states, but covers only establishments investigated by the Bureau. See page 91, also summaries, pages 143 to 220.

CARPETINGS (BRUSSELS AND VELVET), NEW YORK.—ESTAB. No. 92—Concluded. Time, 11 hours per day; 300 days the past year.					CARPETINGS (BRUSSELS, VELVET, AND INGRAIN), NEW YORK.—ESTAB. No. 93. Time, 10 hours per day; 300 days the past year.				
	Number.		Daily wages.			Number.		Daily wages.	
Occupations.	Male.	Fem.	Male.	Fem.	Occupations.	Male.	Fem.	Male.	Fem.
Picker	10		$1 39		Bankers	a14		$0 70	
Piecers	4		98		Bankers		a3		$0 55
Pipe setters	2		2 00		Beamers	3		2 35	
Preparer	1		1 92		Beamers	2		2 00	
Printers	45		1 07		Blacksmith	1		3 00	
Reelers	7	13	1 40	$1 02	Blacksmith	1		2 15	
Reelers	a6		87		Bobbin boys	a5		65	
Repair hand	1		3 00		Bobbin sorter		1		1 15
Rollers	4		1 13		Carder	1		2 60	
Scourers	13		1 42		Carder	1		2 35	
Scourers	18		1 27		Carder	1		2 15	
Scourers	16		1 19		Card cleaners	6		1 80	
Scrapers	45		1 50		Card cutter		2		1 40
Scrapers	45		1 17		Card cutter		1		1 25
Scrubbers and spoolers		19		88	Card cutter		1		1 00
Section hands	28		1 98		Card lacers		2		80
Setters		100		1 67	Card setter	1		2 50	
Setters		42		1 25	Card tenders	2		1 30	
Setters	1		1 50		Card writers	2		1 75	
Shaders	2		2 30		Carpenters	5		2 44	
Shearers	9		1 70		Carriers	a9		70	
Shearers	4		1 48		Carriers	a3		60	
Sizers	3		1 50		Chainer		1		1 05
Spare hands		8		77	Chainer		1		98
Speckers		45		1 33	Cloth carriers	a5		50	
Spinners	75		1 25		Color hands	a6		55	
Spinners	88		1 17		Color hands	10		1 75	
Spinners	105		1 08		Color hand	1		2 30	
Spinners		a11		45	Color hands	34		1 10	
Spinners		22		77	Comber	1		3 30	
Spoolers	62	10	1 25	69	Comber	1		2 10	
Suction-fan tenders	2		1 37		Combers	7		1 30	
Sweepers		21		77	Combers		50		1 00
Teamsters	4		1 52		Cooper	1		1 75	
Timekeepers	a4		82		Designer	1		5 83	
Tinsmiths	2		2 25		Designers	3		4 80	
Twister	1		1 42		Designer	1		3 00	
Twisters		135		1 00	Designers	3		2 50	
Undesignated	3		2 00		Designer	1		1 67	
Undesignated	a108		67		Designer	a1		1 00	
Warpers	3		1 50		Designer	a1		83	
Warper	1		1 12		Doffer		a30		55
Watchmen	4		1 51		Doublers		16		1 60
Water-main tenders	3		1 48		Drawers	2		2 37	
Weavers		313		1 25	Drawers	3		1 80	
Weigher	1		2 67		Drawers		77		1 05
Weighers	17		1 37		Dressers	12		1 80	
Wheelwright	1		4 00		Drum strippers	5		1 70	..v..
Wheelwright	1		2 00		Dyers	38		1 75	
Winders	16		1 67		Engineer	1		3 50	
Winders	9	20	1 50	69	Engineers	2		2 20	
Winders		4		95	Feeders	a6		70	
Winder	1		1 40		Fillers	34		1 50	
Winders		17		1 03	Finisher	1		1 85	
Winders		31		1 07	Finisher	1		2 15	
Winders		27		1 02	Firemen	8		2 00	
Winders		35		1 12	Firemen	3		1 77	
Winders	10		1 00		Foreman	1		3 50	
Wire makers	4		1 75		Foremen	5		3 28	
Wire makers	9		1 29		Foremen	6		2 55	
Wire and reed fixers	4		1 40		Foremen	2		2 10	
Wire pilers	4		1 00		Foreman	1		2 00	
Wood turner	1		2 29		Frame stringers		10		80
Wool sorters	30		1 21		Giller	1		1 52	
Yarn bleachers	4		1 08		Hackler	1		2 50	
Yarn numberers	a12		75		Harness fixers	2		2 75	
Yarn steamers	3		1 50		Harness fixer	1		1 87	
					Harness fixer	1		1 20	
					Inspectors	1	11	2 60	1 30

a Youth.

OCCUPATIONS AND WAGES.

OCCUPATIONS, WITH NUMBER AND WAGES OF EMPLOYÉS, BY INDUSTRIES—Cont'd.

NOTE.—This table is not a complete exhibit for industries or states, but covers only establishments investigated by the Bureau. See page 91, also summaries, pages 143 to 226.

CARPETINGS (BRUSSELS, VELVET, AND INGRAIN), NEW YORK.—ESTAB. No. 93—Concluded.

Time, 10 hours per day; 300 days the past year.

Occupations.	Number.		Daily wages.	
	Male.	Fem.	Male.	Fem.
Inspector		1		$1 10
Laborers	27		$1 22	
Loom fixers	17		2 63	
Machinists	9		2 30	
Matcher	1		2 50	
Numberers	a2		50	
Oilers	11		1 08	
Overseer	1		7 00	
Overseer	1		5 00	
Overseers	2		4 00	
Painter	1		2 45	
Painter	1		2 10	
Pattern maker	1		2 90	
Pattern starter	1		2 75	
Pattern starter	1		2 02	
Pickers	26		1 48	
Piler, wire	1		1 43	
Pipe setter	1		2 25	
Printers	34		2 20	
Reeler	1		2 60	
Reelers		31		1 50
Rollers	2		1 50	
Scourers	13		1 75	
Scrapers	34		1 75	
Second hand	1		4 00	
Second hands	2		3 00	
Second hands	2		2 75	
Second hand	1		2 25	
Second hand	1		2 00	
Section hands	36		2 60	
Section hands	4		1 88	
Separators		14		89
Setters	1	80		1 60
Shader	1		3 00	
Shearers	4		1 99	
Sizers	2		1 80	
Speckers		22		1 68
Spinner, mule	1		2 50	
Spinners, mule	2		2 25	
Spinner, mule	1		1 95	
Spinners, mule	2		1 70	
Spinners, mule	17		1 33	
Spinner, mule	1		1 20	
Spinners, other		79		1 33
Spinners, other		2		85
Spinners, other		a11		68
Spoolers		32		80
Sweepers		12		80
Tinsmith	1		2 25	
Twisters		4		90
Twisters		70		1 50
Twister	1		1 00	
Undesignated	37		1 70	
Undesignated	1		1 50	
Undesignated	1		1 20	
Undesignated	42		1 00	
Undesignated	a15		65	
Undesignated	a27		71	
Undesignated	a45		58	
Warpers	2		2 50	
Warper	1		2 00	
Warper	1		1 80	
Warper	1		1 50	
Waste sorter		a1		55
Weavers	3		2 50	
Weavers	2		2 00	
Weavers	31	243	1 70	1 63
Weighers	3		2 31	
Weighers and numberers	6		93	
Winders		7		1 50

CARPETINGS (BRUSSELS, VELVET, AND INGRAIN), NEW YORK.—ESTAB. No. 93—Concluded.

Time, 10 hours per day; 300 days the past year.

Occupations.	Number.		Daily wages.	
	Male.	Fem.	Male.	Fem.
Winders		10		$1 46
Winders		a26		0 75
Winders		a24		0 55
Winders		26		1 30
Winders		9		1 60
Wire hand	1		$1 90	
Wire and reed hand	1		1 65	
Wire and reed hand	1		1 50	
Wool blender	1		2 10	
Wool dusters	2		1 27	
Wool sorters	9		1 80	
Yarn layers	4		1 60	
Yarn loopers	2		1 75	
Yarn numberers	3		80	

CARPETINGS (BRUSSELS, TAPESTRY, AND VELVET), PENNSYLVANIA.—ESTAB. No. 94.

Time, 10 hours per day; 250 days the past year.

Occupations.	Number.		Daily wages.	
	Male.	Fem.	Male.	Fem.
Carders	a80		$0 75	
Color hands	30		1 00	
Combers		5		$1 16
Doffers		30		50
Doublers	20		1 33	
Drawers		30		90
Dyers	18		1 50	
Dye and wool-house hands	200		1 25	
Laborers	400		1 25	
Loom fixers	21		2 25	
Machinists	16		2 25	
Oil extractors	30		1 00	
Printers	30		1 50	
Setters	120		1 80	
Scrapers	30		1 00	
Spinners, other than mule		60		83
Spoolers		80		83
Twisters		30		90
Weavers	36		2 00	
Weavers	110		1 50	
Weavers	186		1 80	
Weavers	186		1 66	

CARPETINGS (INGRAIN), PENNSYLVANIA.—ESTAB. No. 95.

Time, 10 hours per day; — days the past year.

Occupations.	Number.		Daily wages.	
	Male.	Fem.	Male.	Fem.
Engineer	1		$1 66	
Spoolers	4		85	
Warpers	2		1 35	
Winders		28		$0 75
Weavers	103		1 50	

CARRIAGES AND WAGONS, CONNECTICUT.—ESTAB. No. 96.

Time, 10 hours per day; 300 days the past year.

Occupations.	Number.		Daily wages.	
	Male.	Fem.	Male.	Fem.
Blacksmith	1		$3 60	
Blacksmiths	2		2 75	
Blacksmiths	2		2 00	
Blacksmiths' helpers	7		2 00	
Body makers	2		3 25	
Body makers	2		2 50	
Body makers	6		2 00	

a Youth

OCCUPATIONS, WITH NUMBER AND WAGES OF EMPLOYÉS, BY INDUSTRIES—Cont'd.

NOTE.—This table is *not* a complete exhibit for industries or states, but covers only establishments investigated by the Bureau. See page 91, also summaries, pages 143 to 226.

CARRIAGES AND WAGONS, CONNECTICUT.—ESTAB. No. 96—Concluded.

Time, 10 hours per day; 300 days the past year.

Occupations.	Number.		Daily wages.	
	Male.	Fem.	Male.	Fem.
Foreman	1		$4 17	
Foreman	1		3 25	
Painters	2		2 50	
Painters	2		2 00	
Painters	4		1 67	
Porter	1		2 00	
Trimmer	1		3 00	
Trimmers	3		2 50	
Trimmer	1		2 25	

CARRIAGES AND WAGONS, CONNECTICUT.—ESTAB. No. 97.

Time, 10 hours per day; 300 days the past year.

Occupations.	Male.	Fem.	Male.	Fem.
Blacksmiths	6		$3 50	
Blacksmiths	10		2 75	
Blacksmiths	9		2 50	
Blacksmiths	5		2 25	
Blacksmiths' helpers	6		2 00	
Blacksmiths' helpers	10		1 75	
Blacksmiths' helpers	9		1 50	
Blacksmiths' helpers	5		1 25	
Body makers	6		3 25	
Body makers	11		2 50	
Body makers	18		2 00	
Laborers	10		1 25	
Painters	5		3 25	
Painters	5		2 50	
Painters	10		2 00	
Painters	30		1 67	
Trimmers	9		3 00	
Trimmers	27		2 50	
Trimmers	9		2 25	
Wheelwrights	15		2 25	

CARRIAGES AND WAGONS, CONNECTICUT.—ESTAB. No. 98.

Time, 10 hours per day; 308 days the past year.

Occupations.	Male.	Fem.	Male.	Fem.
Blacksmiths	10		$3 25	
Blacksmiths	4		2 75	
Blacksmiths' helpers	14		2 00	
Body makers	30		2 50	
Finishers	5		2 50	
Laborers	2		1 50	
Machine men	4		2 50	
Painters	8		3 50	
Painters	22		2 00	
Sawyers	2		2 25	
Trimmers	5		3 00	
Trimmers	5		2 50	
Trimmers	5		2 00	
Wheelwrights	3		2 50	

CARRIAGES AND WAGONS, CONNECTICUT.—ESTAB. No. 99.

Time, 10 hours per day; 308 days the past year.

Occupations.	Male.	Fem.	Male.	Fem.
Blacksmiths	3		$2 50	
Blacksmiths	3		2 00	
Blacksmiths' helpers	7		1 50	
Body makers	2		3 00	
Body makers	3		2 50	

CARRIAGES AND WAGONS, CONNECTICUT.—ESTAB. No. 99—Concluded.

Time, 10 hours per day; 308 days the past year.

Occupations.	Number.		Daily wages.	
	Male.	Fem.	Male.	Fem.
Foreman	1		$4 00	
Painters	8		2 00	
Trimmers	8		2 00	

CARRIAGES AND WAGONS, ILLINOIS.—ESTAB. No. 100.

Time, 10 hours per day; 300 days the past year.

Occupations.	Male.	Fem.	Male.	Fem.
Apprentices	a10		$0 83	
Apprentices	a10		67	
Blacksmiths	5		2 17	
Blacksmiths' helpers	5		1 00	
Finishers	6		1 60	
Foreman	1		3 00	
Foremen	2		2 50	
Painters	6		2 00	
Trimmers	6		2 17	
Wood workers	10		1 67	

CARRIAGES AND WAGONS, ILLINOIS.—ESTAB. No. 101.

Time, 10 hours per day; 310 days the past year.

Occupations.	Male.	Fem.	Male.	Fem.
Blacksmiths	7		$3 00	
Blacksmiths	15		2 50	
Blacksmiths	5		2 25	
Blacksmiths' helpers	5		2 00	
Blacksmiths' helpers	8		1 60	
Blacksmiths' helpers	5		1 00	
Painter	1		3 00	
Painters	9		2 35	
Painters	16		2 00	
Painters	4		1 50	
Painters	10		1 00	
Trimmers	12		3 00	
Trimmers	3		2 25	
Trimmers	4		1 75	
Trimmers	10		1 15	
Wood workers	15		3 00	
Wood workers	5		2 50	
Wood workers	10		2 15	
Wood workers	6		1 62	
Wood workers	2		1 25	
Wood workers	6		1 00	

CARRIAGES AND WAGONS, ILLINOIS.—ESTAB. No. 102.

Time, 10 hours per day; 300 days the past year.

Occupations.	Male.	Fem.	Male.	Fem.
Apprentice	a1		$0 75	
Apprentice	a1		1 00	
Blacksmith	1		2 25	
Blacksmiths	2		2 00	
Blacksmiths' helpers	3		1 50	
Fitters	2		1 75	
Foremen	2		3 00	
Laborers	7		1 50	
Painters	3		2 00	
Painters	2		1 25	
Shippers	2		1 25	
Trimmer	1		1 75	
Trimmers	4		1 50	
Wood workers	2		2 25	
Wood workers	3		1 50	

a Youth.

OCCUPATIONS AND WAGES.

OCCUPATIONS, WITH NUMBER AND WAGES OF EMPLOYÉS, BY INDUSTRIES—Cont'd.

NOTE.—This table is *not* a complete exhibit for industries or states, but covers only establishments investigated by the Bureau. See page 91, also summaries, pages 143 to 226.

CARRIAGES AND WAGONS, ILLINOIS.—ESTAB. No. 103.

Time, 10 hours per day; 300 days the past year.

Occupations.	Number.		Daily wages.	
	Male.	Fem.	Male.	Fem.
Apprentice	61		$0 75	
Blacksmiths	11		2 25	
Blacksmiths	6		2 00	
Blacksmiths' helpers	5		1 75	
Blacksmiths' helpers	6		1 00	
Foremen	3		5 00	
Foremen	2		4 00	
Foreman	1		3 50	
Harness makers	2		2 75	
Harness makers	8		1 87	
Laborers	3		1 75	
Laborers	2		1 00	
Painters	3		2 87	
Painters	26		2 00	
Painters	10		1 62	
Painters	2		1 25	
Trimmers	2		2 87	
Trimmers	4		2 50	
Trimmers	4		2 12	
Trimmers	2		1 50	
Wood workers	3		3 25	
Wood workers	4		2 50	
Wood workers	7		1 87	

CARRIAGES AND WAGONS, NEW JERSEY.—ESTAB. No. 104.

Time, 10 hours per day; 300 days the past year.

Occupations.	Male.	Fem.	Male.	Fem.
Blacksmiths	16		$1 92	
Body makers	10		2 50	
Painters	18		1 75	
Trimmers	6		2 25	
Wheelwrights	2		2 50	

CARRIAGES AND WAGONS, OHIO.—ESTAB. No. 105.

Time, 10 hours per day; — days the past year.

Occupations.	Male.	Fem.	Male.	Fem.
Blacksmiths	7		$2 75	
Blacksmiths' helpers	14		1 35	
Foremen	4		3 00	
Gear finishers	5		1 80	
Laborers	8		1 35	
Painters	14		1 35	
Trimmers	8		2 50	
Varnishers	13		2 00	
Wood workers	9		2 60	
Wood-workers' helpers	9		1 35	

CARRIAGES AND WAGONS, OHIO.—ESTAB. No. 106.

Time, 10 hours per day; 300 days the past year.

Occupations.	Male.	Fem.	Male.	Fem.
Blacksmiths	63		$2 10	
Body makers	26		2 25	
Body makers	23		1 50	
Dash-frame makers	19		1 40	
Dash polishers			17	$1 15

CARRIAGES AND WAGONS, OHIO.—ESTAB. No. 106—Concluded.

Time, 10 hours per day; 300 days the past year.

Occupations.	Number.		Daily wages.	
	Male.	Fem.	Male.	Fem.
Finishers, varnish	13		$2 75	
Finishers, iron	22		1 30	
Finishers' helpers, varnish	12		1 75	
Foremen	5		3 33	
Foremen	17		3 00	
Foremen	4		2 00	
Gear workers	42		1 75	
Gear and wheel workers, bench	32		2 00	
Gear and wheel workers, machine	18		1 40	
Hangers	7		2 25	
Hangers helpers	37		1 35	
Laborers	15		1 37	
Painters	83		1 40	
Sewing-machine operators		28		$1 15
Teamsters	8		1 50	
Varnishers	21		2 00	
Varnishers' helpers	15		1 25	
Watchman	1		3 50	
Watchmen	4		2 50	

CARRIAGES AND WAGONS, PENNSYLVANIA.—ESTAB. No. 107.

Time, 10 hours per day; 250 days the past year.

Occupations.	Male.	Fem.	Male.	Fem.
Apprentices	4		$0 83	
Blacksmiths	4		2 03	
Blacksmiths' helpers	6		95	
Painters	3		2 33	
Trimmer	1		2 00	
Wood workers	4		1 91	

CLOCKS AND WATCHES (MOVEMENTS), ILLINOIS.—ESTAB. No. 108.

Time, 10 hours per day; — days the past year.

Occupations.	Male.	Fem.	Male.	Fem.
Balance makers	29	15	$1 73	$1 73
Dial makers	48	20	2 17	2 17
Engineers	2		2 50	
Engravers	14	2	2 23	2 23
Escapement makers	46	22	1 89	1 89
Finishers	108	22	2 40	2 40
Finishers, nickel	5		2 29	
Forge-room hands	12		1 45	
Gilders	14	19	1 41	1 41
Hand makers	1	3	3 00	1 70
Jewellers	59	18	1 54	1 50
Laborers	20		1 50	
Machinists	75		2 86	
Main-spring makers	20		1 93	
Motion hands	60	8	1 67	1 67
Pattern makers	18		2 20	
Platers	33	29	1 90	1 90
Staff turners	7		3 46	
Steel and screw hands	53	67	1 56	1 56
Stock-room hands	13	2	1 74	1 74
Train hands	66	128	1 47	1 47

a Youth.

318 REPORT OF THE COMMISSIONER OF LABOR.

OCCUPATIONS, WITH NUMBER AND WAGES OF EMPLOYÉS, BY INDUSTRIES—Cont'd.

NOTE.—This table is *not* a complete exhibit for industries or states, but covers only establishments investigated by the Bureau. See page 91, also summaries, pages 143 to 226.

CLOCKS AND WATCHES (MOVEMENTS), OHIO.—ESTAB. No. **109.**

Time, 10 *hours per day*; 275 *days the past year*.

Occupations.	Number.		Daily wages.	
	Male.	Fem.	Male.	Fem.
Blacksmith	1		$2 75	
Finishers	8		3 00	
Foremen	4		6 00	
Foremen, assistant	4		3 50	
Machinists	12		2 75	
Machine operators	40	40	1 50	$1 00

CLOTHING (HATS AND CAPS), NEW JERSEY.—ESTAB. No. **110.**

Time, 10 *hours per day*; 300 *days the past year*.

Occupations.	Male	Fem	Male	Fem
Blockers	4		$4 17	
Blowers	3		1 00	
Colorers	4		1 83	
Engineers	1		3 00	
Foreman	1		3 33	
Foreman	1		2 00	
Foremen	2		3 75	
Former	1		3 00	
Formers	9	a5	2 00	$0 83
Finishers	2		3 67	
Finishers	70		2 00	
Laborers	7		1 50	
Makers-up	70		2 33	
Overseer		1		1 67
Packers	7		2 50	
Pouncers	12		2 00	
Stiffener	1		3 33	
Trimmers		60		1 00

CLOTHING (HATS AND CAPS), NEW JERSEY.—ESTAB. No. **111.**

Time, 10 *hours per day*; 300 *days the past year*.

Occupations.	Male	Fem	Male	Fem
Blockers	4		$2 50	
Colorers	4		1 66	
Engineer	1		3 50	
Finishers	40		2 00	
Finishers	4		1 80	
Flangers	2		3 33	
Formers	15	20	2 50	$1 33
Formers	a8	7	83	1 00
Leatherers		8		1 00
Packer	1		2 50	
Polishers	6		2 50	
Porter	1		2 00	
Sizers	50		2 00	
Sizers	2		1 80	
Stiffener	1		3 00	
Stiffeners	a2		91	
Watchman	1		2 00	

CLOTHING (HOSIERY), NEW YORK.—ESTAB. No. **112.**

Time, 11 *hours per day*; 300 *days the past year*.

Occupations.	Male	Fem	Male	Fem
Brusher	1		$1 15	
Button sewers		a5		$0 59
Button-hole makers	7	4	1 70	1 70
Card boys	a4		62	
Card cleaner		1		1 50

CLOTHING (HOSIERY), NEW YORK.—ESTAB. No. **112**—Concluded.

Time, 11 *hours per day*; 300 *days the past year*.

Occupations.	Number.		Daily wages.	
	Male.	Fem.	Male.	Fem.
Cutter	1		$1 96	
Finishers		16		$0 91
Finishers		2		87
Hemmers		2		85
Inspectors		2		66
Knitters		4		87
Knitter		1		1 25
Lappers	2		1 00	
Loopers		10		79
Menders		7		74
Overseer	1		2 50	
Overseer	1		1 75	
Overseer	1		1 50	
Pressers and packers	9		1 63	
Second hand	1		1 25	
Sewing-machine operators		2		1 15
Sewing-machine operators		8		96
Sewing-machine operators		9		70
Spinners		a6		87
Spoolers		a1		87
Undesignated	3	a3	1 53	56
Winders		a7		62
Winder	a1		62	

CLOTHING (HOSIERY), NEW YORK.—ESTAB. No. **113.**

Time, 11 *hours per day*; 302 *days the past year*.

Occupations.	Male	Fem	Male	Fem
Button sewers		a2		$0 59
Button-hole maker		1		1 70
Card boys	a2		$0 62	
Card cleaner		1		1 33
Cutter	1		1 99	
Engineer	1		1 25	
Finishers		12		92
Finishers		2		87
Hemmers		2		85
Inspector		1		66
Knitters		6		1 25
Laborer	1		83	
Lappers	2		1 29	
Lapper	a1		87	
Loopers		5		79
Mender		1		74
Overseers	3		2 00	
Pressers and packers	3		1 63	
Second hand	1		1 50	
Sewing-machine operators		5		96
Sewing-machine operator		1		85
Sewing-machine operators		7		70
Spinners	6		87	
Spooler		1		87
Trimmer		1		1 87
Trimmer		a1		69
Undesignated	1		1 52	
Undesignated		a6		71
Wash-room hands	2		1 17	
Winders		a4		62

a Youth.

OCCUPATIONS AND WAGES.

OCCUPATIONS, WITH NUMBER AND WAGES OF EMPLOYÉS, BY INDUSTRIES—Cont'd.

NOTE.—This table is *not* a complete exhibit for industries or states, but covers only establishments investigated by the Bureau. See page 91, also summaries, pages 143 to 226.

CLOTHING (HOSIERY), NEW YORK.—ESTAB. No. **114.**

Time, 11 *hours per day*; 300 *days the past year.*

Occupations.	Number.		Daily wages.	
	Male.	Fem.	Male.	Fem.
Brusher	1	......	$1 15	......
Button sewers	......	a5	......	$0 59
Button-hole makers	......	1	......	2 97
Card boys	a4	......	75	......
Card cleaner	1	......	1 25	......
Cutter	1	......	2 30	......
Engineer	1	......	1 50	......
Finishers	......	15	......	1 24
Finishers	......	2	......	1 00
Hemmers	......	3	......	85
Inspector	......	1	......	1 00
Knitters	1	4	1 75	1 00
Lappers	2	......	1 12	......
Loopers	......	16	......	98
Menders	......	7	......	1 15
Overseers	3	......	3 00	......
Pressers and packers	8	......	1 62	......
Second hands	3	......	1 06	......
Sewing-machine operators	......	7	......	1 17
Sewing-machine operators	......	9	......	1 08
Sewing-machine operator	......	1	......	85
Spinners, mule	6	......	1 00	......
Spooler	1	......	1 25	......
Trimmers	......	a2	......	60
Trimmers	......	2	......	1 70
Undesignated	......	a2	......	75
Undesignated	......	2	......	1 67
Wash-room hands	3	......	1 50	......
Watchman	1	......	1 50	......
Winders	......	7	......	87

CLOTHING (HOSIERY), NEW YORK.—ESTAB. No. **115.**

Time, 11 *hours per day*; 302 *days the past year.*

Occupations.	Male	Fem	Male	Fem
Brushers	4	......	$1 15	......
Button sewers	......	a9	......	$0 59
Button-hole makers	......	2	......	1 70
Card boys	a6	......	62	......
Cutters	4	......	1 98	......
Finishers	......	30	......	92
Inspectors	......	2	......	67
Knitters	......	12	......	1 25
Lappers	6	......	1 00	......
Lappers	3	......	87	......
Loopers	......	16	......	79
Menders	......	25	......	95
Menders	......	8	......	85
Pressers and packers	4	......	1 62	......
Sewing-machine operators	......	10	......	79
Spinners, mule	3	......	1 21	......
Trimmers	......	3	......	83
Wash-room hands	10	......	1 53	......
Winders	......	13	......	75

CLOTHING (HOSIERY), NEW YORK.—ESTAB. No. **116.**

Time, 11 *hours per day*; 302 *days the past year.*

Occupations.	Male	Fem	Male	Fem
Brusher	1	......	$1 15	......
Button sewers	......	a4	......	$0 66
Button-hole makers	......	1	......	1 70

CLOTHING (HOSIERY), NEW YORK.—ESTAB. No. **116**—Concluded.

Time, 11 *hours per day*; 302 *days the past year.*

Occupations.	Number.		Daily wages.	
	Male.	Fem.	Male.	Fem.
Card boys	a3	......	$0 62	......
Cutter	1	......	1 98	......
Finishers	......	14	......	$0 92
Foremen	2	......	2 04	......
Hemmers	......	2	......	85
Inspector	......	1	......	66
Knitters	......	3	......	87
Knitter	......	1	......	1 21
Lappers	2	......	1 00	......
Loopers and seamers	......	14	......	79
Menders	......	11	......	95
Overseers	2	......	2 50	......
Pressers and packers	2	......	1 62	......
Spinners	a5	......	88	......
Spooler	1	......	1 00	......
Trimmers	......	a3	......	60
Undesignated	......	10	......	83
Undesignated	a9	a5	54	56
Undesignated	......	a8	......	37
Wash-room hands	7	......	1 53	......
Winders	......	a5	......	62

CLOTHING (HOSIERY), NEW YORK.—ESTAB. No. **117.**

Time, 11 *hours per day*; 300 *days the past year.*

Occupations.	Male	Fem	Male	Fem
Brusher	1	......	$1 15	......
Button sewers	......	a4	......	$0 59
Button-hole maker	......	1	......	1 67
Card boys	a5	......	62	......
Cutter	1	......	1 98	......
Finishers	......	17	......	92
Hemmers	......	2	......	85
Inspector	......	1	......	83
Knitters	......	5	......	1 25
Lappers	5	......	1 00	......
Loopers	......	9	......	75
Menders	......	14	......	95
Overseers	4	......	2 50	......
Pressers and packers	3	......	1 67	......
Sewing-machine operator	......	1	......	1 15
Sewing-machine operators	......	8	......	75
Spinners	a6	......	87	......
Trimmers	......	a3	......	58
Undesignated	9	a9	1 53	56
Winders	......	7	......	73

CLOTHING (HOSIERY), NEW YORK.—ESTAB. No. **118.**

Time, 11 *hours per day*; 302 *days the past year.*

Occupations.	Male	Fem	Male	Fem
Brusher	1	......	$1 15	......
Button sewers	......	a4	......	$0 59
Button-hole maker	......	1	......	1 70
Card boys	a3	......	62	......
Card cleaner	1	......	1 25	......
Cutter	1	......	1 98	......
Engineer	1	......	1 50	......
Finishers	......	14	......	92
Finisher	......	1	......	87
Foreman	1	......	1 50	......
Hemmers	......	2	......	85

a Youth.

320 REPORT OF THE COMMISSIONER OF LABOR.

OCCUPATIONS, WITH NUMBER AND WAGES OF EMPLOYÉS, BY INDUSTRIES—Cont'd.

NOTE.—This table is not a complete exhibit for industries or states, but covers only establishments investigated by the Bureau. See page 91, also summaries, pages 143 to 226.

CLOTHING (HOSIERY), NEW YORK.—ESTAB. No. 118—Concluded.

Time, 11 hours per day; 302 days the past year.

Occupations.	Number.		Daily wages.	
	Male.	Fem.	Male.	Fem.
Knitters	......	3	......	$0 87
Knitter	......	1	......	1 25
Loopers	......	8	......	79
Menders	......	5	......	74
Overseer	1	......	$3 00	......
Overseer	1	......	1 75	......
Pressers and packers	7	......	1 62	......
Second hand	1	......	1 75	......
Sewing-machine operator	......	1	......	96
Sewing-machine operators	......	8	......	70
Sewing-machine operators	......	4	......	1 15
Spinners	a5	......	87	......
Spooler	......	1	......	87
Trimmers	......	2	......	1 87
Undesignated	1	a4	1 53	56
Wash-room hands	2	......	1 17	......
Watchman	1	......	1 25	......
Winders	......	a5	......	67

CLOTHING (HOSIERY), NEW YORK.—ESTAB. No. 119.

Time, 11 hours per day; 302 days the past year.

Occupations.	Number.		Daily wages.	
	Male.	Fem.	Male.	Fem.
Brusher	1	......	$1 00	......
Button sewers	......	a3	......	$0 59
Button hole maker	......	1	......	1 70
Card boys	a3	......	62	......
Card cleaner	1	......	1 25	......
Cutter	1	......	1 98	......
Engineer	1	......	1 50	......
Finishers	......	14	......	92
Finisher	......	1	......	87
Hemmer	......	1	......	85
Inspector	......	1	......	66
Knitters	......	2	......	87
Knitter	......	1	......	1 25
Loopers	......	7	......	79
Menders	......	4	......	74
Overseer	1	......	3 00	......
Overseers	2	......	1 75	......
Overseer	1	......	1 50	......
Packers and pressers	6	......	1 63	......
Sewing-machine operator	......	1	......	1 15
Sewing-machine operators	......	6	......	70
Sewing-machine operators	......	4	......	96
Spinners	a4	......	87	......
Spooler	......	1	......	87
Trimmer	......	a1	......	60
Trimmer	......	1	......	1 70
Undesignated	1	a2	1 53	56
Wash-room hands	2	......	1 17	......
Watchman	1	......	1 25	......
Winders	......	a4	......	67

CLOTHING (HOSIERY), NEW YORK.—ESTAB. No. 120.

Time, 11 hours per day; 300 days the past year.

Occupations.	Number.		Daily wages.	
	Male.	Fem.	Male.	Fem.
Button sewers	......	a5	......	$0 50
Button-hole maker	......	1	......	1 70
Card boys	a4	......	$0 63	......

CLOTHING (HOSIERY), NEW YORK.—ESTAB. No. 120—Concluded.

Time, 11 hours per day; 300 days the past year.

Occupations.	Number.		Daily wages.	
	Male.	Fem.	Male.	Fem.
Cutters	2	......	$1 98	......
Finishers	......	14	......	$0 92
Hemmers	......	4	......	85
Inspector	......	1	......	67
Knitter	......	1	......	1 25
Knitters	......	2	......	92
Lappers	a3	3	58	......
Loopers and seamers	......	14	......	79
Overseers	2	......	2 50	......
Packers	4	......	1 58	......
Packers	2	......	1 33	......
Sewing-machine operators	......	11	......	96
Spinners	a5	......	87	......
Trimmers	......	4	......	63
Undesignated	10	48	1 53	80
Undesignated	......	a3	......	56
Wash-room hands	10	......	1 63	......
Winders	......	6	......	73

CLOTHING (HOSIERY), NEW YORK.—ESTAB. No. 121.

Time, 11 hours per day; 302 days the past year.

Occupations.	Number.		Daily wages.	
	Male.	Fem.	Male.	Fem.
Button sewers	......	a2	......	$0 66
Button-hole maker	......	1	......	1 70
Card boys	a2	......	$0 62	......
Cutter	1	......	1 98	......
Engineer	1	......	1 50	......
Finishers	......	11	......	92
Finisher	......	1	......	1 25
Hemmer	......	1	......	85
Inspector	......	1	......	66
Knitters	......	2	......	87
Knitter	......	1	......	1 25
Loopers	......	6	......	79
Menders	......	4	......	74
Overseer	1	......	3 00	......
Overseer	1	......	1 75	......
Overseer	1	......	1 50	......
Sewing-machine operators	......	5	......	70
Sewing-machine operators	......	3	......	96
Spinners	a4	......	87	......
Spooler	a1	......	87	......
Trimmer	......	1	......	1 87
Undesignated	......	a2	......	56
Wash-room hands	2	......	1 17	......
Watchman	1	......	1 25	......
Winders	......	a4	......	67

CLOTHING (HOSIERY), NEW YORK.—ESTAB. No. 122.

Time, 11 hours per day; 269 days the past year.

Occupations.	Number.		Daily wages.	
	Male.	Fem.	Male.	Fem.
Button sewers	......	a8	......	$0 88
Button-hole makers	......	2	......	1 54
Card boys	a7	......	51	......
Card cleaner	a1	......	77	......
Cutters	......	2	......	1 00
Dryer	1	......	85	......
Dyer	......	1	......	77
Engineers	2	......	1 54	......
Finishers	......	14	......	88
Finisher	......	a1	......	71
Fireman	1	......	1 23	......

a Youth.

OCCUPATIONS AND WAGES.

OCCUPATIONS, WITH NUMBER AND WAGES OF EMPLOYÉS, BY INDUSTRIES—Cont'd.

NOTE.—This table is *not* a complete exhibit for industries or states, but covers only establishments investigated by the Bureau. See page 91, also summaries pages 143 to 226.

CLOTHING (HOSIERY), NEW YORK.—ESTAB. No. 122—Concluded.

Time, 11 hours per day; 209 days the past year.

Occupations.	Number.		Daily wages.	
	Male.	Fem.	Male.	Fem.
Folder		1		$0 77
Forewoman		1		1 54
Hemmers		3		65
Inspectors		2		48
Knitters		6		62
Knitters		a7		50
Knitters		3		86
Laborer	1		$0 92	
Menders		3		73
Oiler	1		1 00	
Overseer	1		3 85	
Overseer	1		3 07	
Overseer	1		2 10	
Overseer	1		1 54	
Packer	1		1 00	
Picker	1		1 06	
Presser	1		1 15	
Ribber		1		1 15
Ribbers		3		1 04
Second hand	1		1 19	
Second hand		1		90
Second hand	1		77	
Sewing-machine operators		8		83
Spinners, mule	4		1 23	
Spinner, other	a1		71	
Sweepers	2		53	
Trimmer	1		92	
Turner	1		83	
Undesignated	2	5	53	53
Wash-room hands	1		1 19	
Wash-room hands	2		75	
Watchman	1		1 46	

CLOTHING (HOSIERY), NEW YORK.—ESTAB. No. 123.

Time, 11 hours per day; 300 days the past year.

Occupations.	Number.		Daily wages.	
	Male.	Fem.	Male.	Fem.
Button sewers		a6		$0 60
Button-hole makers		2		1 70
Card boys	a6		$0 62	
Card cleaners	2		1 25	
Cutters	2		1 98	
Engineer	1		1 50	
Finishers		28		91
Finishers		3		87
Hemmers		4		85
Inspector		1		66
Knitters		2		1 25
Knitters		4		87
Loopers		14		79
Menders		8		74
Overseer	1		1 75	
Overseer	1		1 50	
Pressers and packers	12		1 63	
Sewing-machine operators		2		1 15
Sewing-machine operators		8		96
Sewing-machine operators		12		70
Spinner, mule	1		1 75	
Spinners, other	a3		87	
Spoolers		2		87
Trimmers		2		1 25
Trimmers		a2		60
Undesignated	2		1 53	
Wash-room hands	2		1 17	
Watchman	1		1 25	
Winders		a8		67

CLOTHING (HOSIERY), NEW YORK.—ESTAB. No. 124.

Time, 11 hours per day; 300 days the past year.

Occupations.	Number.		Daily wages.	
	Male.	Fem.	Male.	Fem.
Carders	14		$1 76	
Card boys	b7		48	
Cutters	3		1 83	
Dry-room hands	2		1 00	
Finishers		18		$0 96
Hemmers		10		80
Knitters		7		1 28
Loopers		b20		35
Overseers	3		3 50	
Overseers		3		2 00
Pressers		3		96
Sewing-machine operators		23		80
Sewing-machine operators		2		1 08
Spinners, mule	7		1 15	
Spoolers	a6		64	
Undesignated	12		1 44	
Winders		30		80

CLOTHING (HOSIERY), NEW YORK.—ESTAB. No. 125.

Time, 11 hours per day; 300 days the past year.

Occupations.	Number.		Daily wages.	
	Male.	Fem.	Male.	Fem.
Carder	1		$1 00	
Carders	a5		67	
Finishers	25		1 25	
Finishers		a5		$0 50
Foremen	2		3 50	
Foremen	2		2 00	
Knitter	a1		83	
Knitter	a1		67	
Laborers	2		1 00	
Lapper	1		1 00	
Machinist	1		1 50	
Packers	a2		83	
Packer	a1		50	
Picker	1		1 00	
Second hands	2		1 25	
Spinners, mule	5		1 75	
Teamster	1		1 50	
Winders	a8		67	

CLOTHING (HOSIERY), NEW YORK.—ESTAB. No. 126.

Time, 11 hours per day; 300 days the past year.

Occupations.	Number.		Daily wages.	
	Male.	Fem.	Male.	Fem.
Button sewers		5		$0 83
Button-hole maker		1		1 67
Card boys	a4		$0 62	
Cutter	1		1 98	
Finishers		16		92
Hemmers		2		85
Inspector		1		67
Knitters		5		1 25
Laborers	3		1 00	
Loopers		18		79
Overseers	3		2 50	
Packers	3		1 62	
Packers	2		1 33	
Sewing-machine operator		1		1 15
Sewing-machine operators		13		95
Spinners	a6		87	
Trimmers		3		79

a Youth.   *b* Children.

OCCUPATIONS, WITH NUMBER AND WAGES OF EMPLOYÉS, BY INDUSTRIES—Cont'd.

NOTE.—This table is *not* a complete exhibit for industries or states, but covers only establishments investigated by the Bureau. See page 91, also summaries, pages 143 to 226.

CLOTHING (HOSIERY), NEW YORK.—ESTAB. No. 126—Concluded.

Time, 2 hours per day; 300 days the past year.

Occupations.	Number.		Daily wages.	
	Male.	Fem.	Male.	Fem.
Undesignated		3		$0 83
Undesignated		3		62
Wash-room hands	3		$1 53	
Winders		7		81

CLOTHING (KNIT GOODS, JERSEYS), PENNSYLVANIA.—ESTAB. No. 127.

Time, 10 hours per day; 300 days the past year.

Occupations.	Male.	Fem.	Male.	Fem.
Button-hole makers		15		$1 17
Cutters		2		1 00
Folders		a2		80
Knitters		a36		50
Machinist	1		$2 08	
Pressers		2		1 85
Sewing-machine operators		a41		41
Weavers	2		1 50	
Winders		6		75

CLOTHING (HATS, CAPS), PENNSYLVANIA.—ESTAB. No. 128.

Time, 10 hours per day; 300 days the past year.

Occupations.	Male.	Fem.	Male.	Fem.
Finishers	14		$1 89	
Laborers	6		1 25	
Sizers	14		1 37	
Trimmers		13		$0 97

CLOTHING (HATS, CAPS), PENNSYLVANIA.—ESTAB. No. 129.

Time, 10 hours per day; 308 days the past year.

Occupations.	Male.	Fem.	Male.	Fem.
Blockers	27		$2 75	
Brushers	4		1 50	
Carrotters	10		1 53	
Colorers	11		1 78	
Curlers	8		2 70	
Curlers' helper	a1		70	
Cutters	10	15	1 05	$0 84
Cutters	5		1 00	
Engineers	3		2 18	
Finishers	122		1 68	
Finishers		a50		53
Formers	19		1 53	
Formers	a17		54	
Laborers	18		1 33	
Packers	15		1 20	
Pluckers	30		1 06	
Pouncers	13		1 96	
Printers	3		1 25	
Repairers	20		2 60	
Shavers	6		2 14	
Sizers	155		1 35	
Trimmers		107		83
Undesignated	5	15	1 80	83
Wash-room hands	9		1 00	

CLOTHING (MEN'S UNDERCLOTHING), VIRGINIA.—ESTAB. No. 130.

Time, 10 hours per day; 300 days the past year.

Occupations.	Number.		Daily wages.	
	Male.	Fem.	Male.	Fem.
Bale opener	1		$1 20	
Back boys	a2		50	
Bleachers	7		1 50	
Card boys	a9		60	
Carders	3		2 00	
Engineer	1		2 00	
Finishers	4	27	2 50	$0 75
Finishers		a26		50
Fireman	1		1 50	
Knitters	2		1 75	
Knitters	a4	a19	60	50
Laborers	3		1 25	
Picker	1		1 40	
Picker	a1		45	
Spinners, mule	7		1 50	
Watchman	1		1 50	

COAL, COKE, AND ORE (COAL), GREAT BRITAIN.—ESTAB. No. 131.

Time, 10 hours per day; — days the past year.

Occupations.	Male.	Fem.	Male.	Fem.
Bankmen	6		$0 96	
Blacksmiths	2		1 14	
Blacksmiths' helpers	2		72	
Cart drivers	a3		60	
Coal cleaners (jiggers)	a26		60	
Drivers	a80		50	
Engineer, stationary	1		1 12	
Fillers	80		96	
Firemen	14		1 08	
Firemen	4		72	
Furnace men	2		72	
Furnace-men's helpers	a2		48	
Joiners	4		1 66	
Laborers	20		72	
Lampmen	3		68	
Machinist	1		1 24	
Miners	160		1 12	
Overseers (overlookers)	1		2 40	
Overseers (overlookers)	2		1 68	
Sawyers (timber)	3		96	
Track layers	25		90	
Trappers	a25		48	
Takers-off	a20		60	

COAL, COKE, AND ORE (IRON ORE), GREAT BRITAIN.—ESTAB. No. 132.

Time, 9 hours per day; — days the past year.

Occupations.	Male.	Fem.	Male.	Fem.
Bankman	1		$0 90	
Blacksmith	1		96	
Cartman	1		72	
Deputies	12		1 08	
Drivers	11		62	
Dumpers	4		96	
Engine plane men	4		74	
Engine wright	1		68	
Fan-engine men	2		96	
Firemen	2		72	
Greaser	1		48	
Hauling-engine man	1		96	
Joiner	1		96	
Laborers	3		72	

a Youth.

OCCUPATIONS AND WAGES.

OCCUPATIONS, WITH NUMBER AND WAGES OF EMPLOYÉS, BY INDUSTRIES—Cont'd.

NOTE.—This table is *not* a complete exhibit for industries or states, but covers only establishments investigated by the Bureau. See page 91, also summaries, pages 143 to 226.

COAL, COKE, AND ORE (IRON ORE), GREAT BRITAIN—ESTAB. No. **132**—Concluded.

Time, 9 hours per day; — days the past year.

Occupations.	Number.		Daily wages.	
	Male.	Fem.	Male.	Fem.
Miners	125	....	$1 08	......
On-setters	8	....	96	......
Ore cleaner	1	....	72	......
Pumpman	1	....	76	......
Stableman	1	....	80	......
Striker	1	....	50	......
Timber leaders	2	....	89	......
Trappers	a4	....	22	......
Tub cleaner	1	....	48	......
Weigher	1	....	1 00	......
Weighers	4	....	80	......
Winding-engine man	1	....	1 04	......

COAL, COKE, AND ORE (COAL), INDIANA.—ESTAB. No. **133**.

Time, 10 hours per day; 220 days the past year.

Occupations.	Male	Fem	Male	Fem
Blacksmiths	10	....	$1 80	......
Drivers	50	....	1 50	......
Engineers	20	....	2 00	......
Laborers	82	....	1 00	......
Miners b	1200	....	1 45	......
Track layers	18	....	2 00	......
Weighers	9	....	1 75	......

COAL, COKE, AND ORE (COAL), INDIANA.—ESTAB. No. **134**.

Time, 10 hours per day; 225 days the past year.

Occupations.	Male	Fem	Male	Fem
Blacksmiths	6	....	$1 50	......
Drivers	35	....	1 25	......
Engineers	6	....	2 50	......
Laborers	9	....	1 00	......
Mine boss	6	....	3 50	......
Miners c	175	....	1 75	......
Track layers	7	....	2 20	......
Weighers	6	....	1 70	......

COAL, COKE, AND ORE (COAL), MARYLAND.—ESTAB. No. **135**.

Time, 11 hours per day; 225 days the past year.

Occupations.	Male	Fem	Male	Fem
Blacksmiths	2	....	$1 90	......
Blacksmith's helper	1	....	1 50	......
Carpenters	3	....	1 70	......
Drivers	31	....	1 60	......
Dumpers	9	....	1 35	......
Engineer	1	....	2 25	......
Fireman	1	....	1 70	......
Furnace man	1	....	1 75	......
Laborers	6	....	1 35	......
Miners d	247	....	1 73	......
Stableman	2	....	1 33	......
Track layers	3	....	2 00	......
Undesignated	e8	....	70	......
Weighers	3	....	1 70	......

COAL, COKE, AND ORE (COAL), MARYLAND.—ESTAB. No. **136**.

Time, 11 hours per day; 230 days the past year.

Occupations.	Number.		Daily wages.	
	Male.	Fem.	Male.	Fem.
Blacksmiths	2	....	$1 90	......
Blacksmiths' helpers	2	....	1 35	......
Drivers	36	....	1 60	......
Dumpers	6	....	1 35	......
Furnace men	3	....	1 65	......
Laborers	3	....	1 35	......
Miners d	315	....	1 56	......
Stableman	1	....	1 54	......
Stablemen	2	....	1 29	......
Track layers	4	....	2 00	......
Weigher	1	....	2 00	......
Weigher	1	....	1 75	......

COAL, COKE, AND ORE (COAL), MARYLAND.—ESTAB. No. **137**.

Time, 11 hours per day; 227 days the past year.

Occupations.	Male	Fem	Male	Fem
Blacksmiths	2	....	$2 00	......
Blacksmiths' helpers	2	....	1 60	......
Brakeman	1	....	1 50	......
Carpenters	2	....	1 80	......
Drivers	16	....	1 60	......
Dumpers	5	....	1 35	......
Engineer	1	....	2 15	......
Laborers	7	....	1 10	......
Miners d	200	....	1 57	......
Stableman	1	....	1 67	......
Stableman	1	....	1 00	......
Track layers	3	....	1 60	......

COAL, COKE, AND ORE (COAL), MISSOURI.—ESTAB. No. **138**.

Time, 10 hours per day; — days the past year.

Occupations.	Male	Fem	Male	Fem
Blacksmith	1	....	$2 31	......
Blacksmith's helper	1	....	1 93	......
Drivers	7	....	2 00	......
Engineer	1	....	2 88	......
Fireman	1	....	2 31	......
Laborers	18	....	1 50	......
Miners, machine	14	....	2 46	......
Miners	100	....	1 88	......
Mine boss	1	....	2 88	......
Pumper	1	....	1 93	......
Teamster	1	....	1 03	......
Track layer	1	....	2 50	......
Track layers	4	....	2 31	......
Weigher	1	....	2 31	......

COAL, COKE, AND ORE (IRON ORE), MISSOURI.—ESTAB. No. **139**.

Time, 10 hours per day; — days the past year.

Occupations.	Male	Fem	Male	Fem
Carpenters	4	....	$2 00	......
Engineers	6	....	1 75	......
Machinists	12	....	2 75	......
Miners	125	....	1 25	......
Undesignated	e35	....	75	......

a Children.
b Miners receive 80 cents per ton of 2,000 pounds, block coal (sliding scale).
c Miners receive 77 cents per ton of 2,000 pounds, block coal.
d Miners receive 40 cents per ton of 2240 lbs.
e Youth.

324 REPORT OF THE COMMISSIONER OF LABOR.

OCCUPATIONS, WITH NUMBER AND WAGES OF EMPLOYÉS, BY INDUSTRIES—Cont'd.

NOTE.—This table is not a complete exhibit for industries or states, but covers only establishments investigated by the Bureau. See page 91, also summaries, pages 143 to 226.

COAL, COKE, AND ORE (COAL), OHIO.—ESTAB. No. 140.

Time, 10 hours per day; 211 days the past year.

Occupations.	Number.		Daily wages.	
	Male.	Fem.	Male.	Fem.
Blacksmith	1		$1 75	
Cagers	2		1 75	
Drivers	5		2 00	
Dumpers	4		1 35	
Engineers	2		1 75	
Firemen	2		1 60	
Laborers	4		1 35	
Mine boss	1		3 00	
Miners a	100		1 75	
Oiler	1		1 35	
Track layers	2		1 75	
Trappers	b5		55	
Trimmer	1		1 35	
Weigher	1		2 00	

COAL, COKE, AND ORE (COAL), OHIO.—ESTAB. No. 141.

Time, 10 hours per day; 208 days the past year.

Occupations.	Number.		Daily wages.	
	Male.	Fem.	Male.	Fem.
Blacksmith	1		$2 00	
Cager	1		1 50	
Drivers	5		1 75	
Engineer	1		1 85	
Engineer	1		1 50	
Firemen	3		1 35	
Laborers	4		1 35	
Mine boss	1		3 00	
Miners a	70		2 00	
Pumper, mine	1		1 85	
Pumper, mine	1		1 25	
Track layers	3		1 75	
Trappers	b5		60	
Weigher	1		1 75	

COAL, COKE, AND ORE (COAL), OHIO.—ESTAB. No. 142.

Time, 9½ hours per day; 230 days the past year.

Occupations.	Number.		Daily wages.	
	Male.	Fem.	Male.	Fem.
Blacksmith	1		$2 00	
Drivers	5		1 75	
Engineer	1		2 00	
Engineer	1		1 75	
Mine boss	1		3 00	
Miners a	60		2 00	
Topmen	3		1 35	
Track layers	2		1 75	
Trappers	b4		60	
Weigher	1		1 75	

COAL, COKE, AND ORE (COAL), OHIO.—ESTAB. No. 143.

Time, 9 hours per day; 190 days the past year.

Occupations.	Number.		Daily wages.	
	Male.	Fem.	Male.	Fem.
Blacksmith	1		$1 80	
Blacksmith's helper	1		1 40	
Drivers	13		1 35	
Engineer	1		1 65	
Laborers	15		1 30	
Mine boss	1		4 00	

COAL, COKE, AND ORE (COAL), OHIO.—ESTAB. No. 143—Concluded.

Time, 9 hours per day; 300 days the past year.

Occupations.	Number.		Daily wages.	
	Male.	Fem.	Male.	Fem.
Miners c	105		$1 54	
Stableman	1		1 00	
Track layers	3		1 65	
Trappers	b4		60	
Water hauler	1		1 50	
Weigher	1		1 60	

COAL, COKE, AND ORE (COAL), OHIO.—ESTAB. No. 144.

Time, 10 hours per day; 208 days the past year.

Occupations.	Number.		Daily wages.	
	Male.	Fem.	Male.	Fem.
Blacksmith	1		$1 75	
Drivers	3		1 35	
Mine boss	1		2 11	
Miners d	30		1 80	
Oiler	b1		50	
Pumper, mine	b1		50	
Pushers	4		1 35	
Slack hauler	1		1 25	
Track layer	1		1 35	
Trimmer	1		1 25	

COAL, COKE, AND ORE (COAL), OHIO.—ESTAB. No. 145.

Time, 9 hours per day; 206 days the past year.

Occupations.	Number.		Daily wages.	
	Male.	Fem.	Male.	Fem.
Cager	1		$1 35	
Drivers	4		1 35	
Dumper	1		1 25	
Engineer	1		1 60	
Mine boss	1		2 00	
Miners c	28		1 88	
Water hauler	1		1 85	
Weigher	1		1 60	

COAL, COKE, AND ORE (COAL), OHIO.—ESTAB. No. 146.

Time, 10 hours per day; — days the past year.

Occupations.	Number.		Daily wages.	
	Male.	Fem.	Male.	Fem.
Blacksmiths	2		$2 50	
Blacksmith	1		2 25	
Brakeman	1		1 50	
Carpenters	2		2 50	
Drivers	25		1 50	
Drivers, boss	2		2 00	
Dumpers	4		1 50	
Engineer, locomotive	1		2 50	
Engineer, stationary	1		2 00	
Furnace man	1		1 25	
Laborers	12		1 50	
Machinist	1		2 75	
Mine bosses	2		3 00	
Mine boss	1		2 50	
Miners e	160		1 75	
Slack hauler	1		1 50	
Teamster	1		1 50	
Track layers	4		1 75	
Trimmers	3		1 50	
Water hauler	1		2 00	

a Miners receive 75 cents per ton of 2,000 pounds, lump coal (Tuscarawas Valley district).
b Youth.
c Miners receive 50 cents per ton of 2,000 pounds, lump coal (Jackson County district).
d Miners receive 55 cents per ton of 2,000 pounds, lump coal (Jackson County district).
e Miners receive 50 cents per ton of 2,000 pounds, lump coal (Hocking Valley district).

OCCUPATIONS AND WAGES.

OCCUPATIONS, WITH NUMBER AND WAGES OF EMPLOYÉS, BY INDUSTRIES—Cont'd.

NOTE.—This table is *not* a complete exhibit for industries or states, but covers only establishments investigated by the Bureau. See page 91, also summaries, pages 143 to 226.

COAL, COKE AND ORE (COAL), OHIO.—ESTAB. No. 147.

Time, 10 hours per day; — days the past year.

Occupations.	Number.		Daily wages.	
	Male.	Fem.	Male.	Fem.
Blacksmith	1		$2 25	
Brakeman	1		1 32	
Carpenter	1		2 00	
Drivers	2		1 25	
Drivers	2		1 40	
Dumper	1		1 75	
Engineer	1		1 60	
Fireman	1		1 25	
Laborer	1		1 25	
Mine boss	1		2 50	
Miners *a*	51		1 20	
Track layer	1		2 00	
Track layer	1		1 40	
Track layer	1		1 25	
Trapper	*b*1		50	
Weigher	1		2 50	

COAL, COKE AND ORE (COAL), OHIO—ESTAB. No. 148.

Time, 10 hours per day; — days the past year.

Occupations.	Male.	Fem.	Male.	Fem.
Blacksmith	2		$2 00	
Drivers	13		1 40	
Dumper	1		1 50	
Mine boss	1		2 40	
Miners *c*	150		1 50	
Stableman	1		1 60	
Trimmers	3		1 50	
Water hauler	1		1 40	
Weigher	1		1 60	

COAL, COKE, AND ORE (COAL), OHIO.—ESTAB. No. 149.

Time, 10 hours per day; — days the past year.

Occupations.	Male.	Fem.	Male.	Fem.
Carpenters	2		$2 00	
Drivers	7		1 40	
Dumper	1		1 50	
Engineers	2		1 66	
Fireman	1		1 50	
Laborers	8		1 25	
Mine boss	1		2 66	
Miners *c*	126		1 50	
Stableman	1		1 25	
Track layer	1		1 75	
Trimmers	3		1 40	
Water hauler	1		1 40	
Weigher	1		1 66	

COAL, COKE, AND ORE (COAL), OHIO.—ESTAB. No. 150.

Time, 10 hours per pay; 180 days the past year.

Occupations.	Male.	Fem.	Male.	Fem.
Blacksmith	1		$2 00	
Blacksmith	1		2 25	
Blacksmith's helper	1		1 50	

COAL, COKE, AND ORE (COAL), OHIO.—ESTAB. No. 150—Concluded.

Time, 10 hours per day; 180 days the past year.

Occupations.	Number.		Daily wages.	
	Male.	Fem.	Male.	Fem.
Cagers	3		$1 80	
Drivers	3		2 25	
Drivers	3		2 05	
Drivers	8		1 80	
Dumpers	2		1 75	
Dumpers	3		1 50	
Engineer	1		2 25	
Engineer	1		1 75	
Fireman	1		1 50	
Laborers, skilled	3		2 25	
Laborers	4		1 55	
Mine boss	1		4 00	
Miners	175		*d*2 40	
Oilers	2		1 25	
Pumpers, mine	2		1 38	
Screeners	3		1 50	
Stableman	1		1 25	
Sump digger	1		2 05	
Track layer	1		2 25	
Track layer	1		2 05	
Trimmer	1		2 00	
Trimmers	2		1 75	
Trappers	*b*5		75	
Water haulers	*b*7		85	
Weighers	1		2 00	

COAL, COKE, AND ORE (COAL), PENNSYLVANIA.—ESTAB. No. 151.

Time, 10 hours per day; 200 days the past year.

Occupations	Male.	Fem.	Male.	Fem.
Blacksmiths	3		$2 50	
Blacksmiths	3		2 00	
Carpenters	3		2 50	
Drivers, boss	3		3 00	
Drivers	33		2 50	
Dumpers	12		2 50	
Engineer, locomotive	1		3 00	
Engineer, stationary	2		2 50	
Hitchers	9		2 25	
Hitchers' helpers	3		1 75	
Incline brakemen	3		2 80	
Loaders	3		2 75	
Mine bosses	3		3 00	
Miners *e*	660		2 45	
Oilers	18		2 00	
Pumpers, mine	6		2 50	
Weighers	3		2 50	

COAL, COKE, AND ORE (COAL), PENNSYLVANIA.—ESTAB. No. 152.

Time, 10 hours per day; 225 days the past year.

Occupations	Male.	Fem.	Male.	Fem.
Blacksmith	1		$2 25	
Drivers and laborers	50		1 70	
Mine bosses	2		3 00	
Miners *f*	140		2 20	

a Miners receive 40 cents per ton of 2,000 pounds, furnace coal (Hocking Valley district).
b Youth.
c Miners receive 50 cents per ton of 2,000 pounds, lump coal (Hocking Valley district).
d This is for 1883. The price of mining has since been reduced one-half (Sunday Creek Valley district).
e Miners receive 78 cents per ton of 2,000 pounds, lump coal (Pittsburgh district).
f Miners receive 76 cents per ton of 2,000 pounds, lump coal (Pittsburgh district).

OCCUPATIONS, WITH NUMBER AND WAGES OF EMPLOYÉS, BY INDUSTRIES—Cont'd.

NOTE.—This table is *not* a complete exhibit for industries or states, but covers only establishments investigated by the Bureau. See page 91, also summaries, pages 143 to 226.

COAL, COKE, AND ORE (COKE), PENNSYLVANIA.—ESTAB. No. **153.**

Time, 8 hours per day; 260 days the past year.

Occupations.	Number.		Daily wages.	
	Male.	Fem.	Male.	Fem.
Blacksmiths	12		$2 50	
Carpenters	10		2 50	
Chargers	61		1 44	
Drawers	420		1 60	
Drivers	70		1 20	
Engineers	8		1 66	
Foremen	10		2 72	
Forkers	176		1 44	
Laborers	400		1 20	
Levellers	61		1 44	
Mine bosses	11		2 00	
Miners *a*	790		1 52	
Yard bosses	12		2 00	

COAL, COKE, AND ORE (COKE), PENNSYLVANIA.—ESTAB. No. **154.**

Time, 8 hours per day; 260 days the past year.

Occupations.	Male.	Fem.	Male.	Fem.
Chargers	17		$1 44	
Drawers	158		1 60	
Engineers	3		1 76	
Foremen	5		2 72	
Forkers	69		1 44	
Laborers	125		1 20	
Levellers	17		1 44	
Mine bosses	4		2 00	
Miners *a*	265		1 52	
Yard bosses	5		2 00	

COAL, COKE, AND ORE (COAL), VIRGINIA.—ESTAB. No. **155.**

Time, 10 hours per day; 300 days the past year.

Occupations.	Male.	Fem.	Male.	Fem.
Blacksmith	1		$1 75	
Blacksmith's helper	1		1 00	
Carpenter	1		1 75	
Cleaners, coal	b25		50	
Drivers	b7		75	
Engineers	2		1 25	
Firemen	2		1 00	
Laborers	13		95	
Mine bosses	2		2 00	
Miners	26		1 75	
Miners	27		1 25	
Timbermen	6		1 25	
Track layers	6		1 25	

COAL, COKE, AND ORE (IRON ORE), VIRGINIA.—ESTAB. No. **156.**

Time, 10 hours per day; 300 days the past year.

Occupations.	Male.	Fem.	Male.	Fem.
Blacksmiths	2		$2 35	
Blacksmiths' helpers	2		1 38	
Carpenters	b5		1 67	
Engineer	1		3 20	
Foreman	1		3 00	
Harness repairer	1		1 92	
Machinist	1		1 45	
Mine bosses	3		1 67	
Mine boss	1		2 25	
Miners	220		1 05	
Stablemen	2		1 38	
Timbermen	2		2 00	

COAL, COKE, AND ORE (IRON ORE), VIRGINIA.—ESTAB. No. **157.**

Time, 10 hours per day; 300 days the past year.

Occupations.	Number.		Daily wages.	
	Male.	Fem.	Male.	Fem.
Blacksmith	1		$1 35	
Brakemen	3		1 00	
Carpenter	1		1 35	
Engineers	2		1 75	
Feeder	1		1 13	
Fireman	1		1 13	
Laborer	1		1 13	
Mine bosses	3		1 35	
Miners	60		1 00	
Teamster	1		90	
Water boys	b4		45	

COAL, COKE, AND ORE (COAL), WEST VIRGINIA.—ESTAB. No. **158.**

Time, 10 hours per day; 200 days the past year.

Occupations.	Male.	Fem.	Male.	Fem.
Blacksmiths	2		$2 00	
Drivers	16		1 60	
Drum runners	2		1 71	
Laborers	10		1 20	
Mine bosses	2		2 50	
Miners *c*	105		1 40	
Track layers	2		1 80	
Trappers	b2		50	
Weighers	2		1 80	

COAL, COKE, AND ORE (COAL), WEST VIRGINIA.—ESTAB. No. **159.**

Time, 11 hours per day; 240 days the past year.

Occupations.	Male.	Fem.	Male.	Fem.
Blacksmith	1		$2 25	
Carpenter	1		2 00	
Driver	1		1 60	
Drivers	3		1 45	
Drivers	4		1 25	
Laborers	5		1 10	
Mine boss	1		3 50	
Miners *c*	90		1 60	
Track layer	1		1 80	
Undesignated	b4		50	

COAL, COKE, AND ORE (COAL), WEST VIRGINIA.—ESTAB. No. **160.**

Time, 10 hours per day; 300 days the past year.

Occupations.	Male.	Fem.	Male.	Fem.
Blacksmith	1		$2 00	
Blacksmith's helper	1		1 25	
Drivers	5		1 40	
Drivers	b3		75	
Incline brakeman	b1		50	
Mine boss	1		3 00	
Miners *c*	52		1 20	
Teamster	1		1 50	

COAL, COKE, AND ORE (COAL), WEST VIRGINIA.—ESTAB. No. **161.**

Time, 9 hours per day; 200 days the past year.

Occupations.	Male.	Fem.	Male.	Fem.
Drivers	5		$1 00	
Laborers	5		1 10	
Miners *d*	30		1 50	
Track layer	1		1 25	

a This establishment mines its own coal. The miners receive 23½ cents per ton of 2,000 pounds run of mine coal (Connelsville district). *b* Youth. *c* Miners receive 40 cents per ton of 2,240 pounds run of mine coal (New River district). *d* Miners receive 40 cents per ton of 2,000 pounds run of mine coal (New River district).

OCCUPATIONS AND WAGES. 327

OCCUPATIONS, WITH NUMBER AND WAGES OF EMPLOYÉS, BY INDUSTRIES—Cont'd.

NOTE.—This table is not a complete exhibit for industries or states, but covers only establishments investigated by the Bureau. See page 91, also summaries, pages 143 to 226.

COAL, COKE, AND ORE (COAL), WEST VIRGINIA.—ESTAB. No. 162.

Time, 10 hours per day; 175 days the past year.

Occupations.	Number.		Daily wages.	
	Male.	Fem.	Male.	Fem.
Blacksmith	1		$2 00	
Coal cleaner	1		1 25	
Drivers	4		1 65	
Incline brakeman	1		1 25	
Mine boss	1		2 00	
Miners *a*	35		1 68	
Track layer	1		2 00	
Weigher	1		2 00	

COAL, COKE, AND ORE (COAL), WEST VIRGINIA.—ESTAB. No. 163.

Time, 10 hours per day; 240 days the past year.

Occupations.	Number.		Daily wages.	
	Male.	Fem.	Male.	Fem.
Blacksmith	1		$2 00	
Carpenter	1		1 50	
Drivers	6		1 50	
Laborers	5		1 25	
Mine boss	1		2 50	
Miners *a*	50		2 00	
Weigher	1		1 50	

COAL, COKE, AND ORE (COAL), WEST VIRGINIA.—ESTAB. No. 164.

Time, 10 hours per day; 300 days the past year.

Occupations.	Number.		Daily wages.	
	Male.	Fem.	Male.	Fem.
Blacksmiths	4		$2 00	
Captain, tug-boat	1		1 68	
Carpenters	6		2 00	
Carpenters	2		1 50	
Caulkers, boat	2		2 00	
Caulkers, boat	3		1 50	
Driver	1		2 25	
Drivers	12		1 75	
Drivers	12		1 50	
Drivers	10		1 25	
Dumper	1		1 90	
Engineer, locomotive	1		3 25	
Engineer, locomotive	1		1 75	
Engineers, locomotive	2		1 25	
Engineer, stationary	1		1 83	
Laborers	15		1 25	
Mine boss	1		3 25	
Mine boss	1		2 40	
Miners *b*	180		1 87	
Pumpers, boat	3		1 50	
River boss	1		2 00	
Stableman	1		2 00	
Stableman	1		1 25	
Track layers	3		2 00	
Track layers	8		1 75	
Track layers	6		1 50	
Trappers	*c*10		50	
Weighers	2		2 00	

COAL, COKE, AND ORE (COAL), WEST VIRGINIA.—ESTAB. No. 165.

Time, 10 hours per day; 163 days the past year.

Occupations.	Number.		Daily wages.	
	Male.	Fem.	Male.	Fem.
Blacksmiths	2		$2 00	
Carpenter	1		2 00	

COAL, COKE, AND ORE (COAL), WEST VIRGINIA.—ESTAB. No. 165—Concluded.

Time, 10 hours per day; 163 hours the past year.

Occupations.	Number.		Daily wages.	
	Male.	Fem.	Male.	Fem.
Carpenter	1		$1 75	
Caulker, boat	1		1 75	
Caulker, boat	1		1 50	
Drivers	2		1 75	
Drivers	12		1 50	
Drivers	3		1 37	
Dumpers	5		1 25	
Engineer	1		2 00	
Engineers	2		1 25	
Furnace man	1		1 25	
Inspector	1		2 00	
Miners *b*	120		1 87	
Oiler	1		1 25	
Pumper, boat	1		1 50	
Pumpers, boat	3		1 25	
River boss	1		1 75	
Screeners	3		1 87	
Screener	1		75	
Stablemen	2		1 25	
Track layer	1		2 00	
Track layer	1		1 75	
Track layers	2		1 62	
Trappers	*c*7		50	
Weigher	1		2 00	

COAL, COKE, AND ORE (COKE), WEST VIRGINIA.—ESTAB. No. 166.

Time, 10 hours per day; 200 days the past year.

Occupations.	Number.		Daily wages.	
	Male.	Fem.	Male.	Fem.
Chargers	2		$1 20	
Drawers	9		1 20	
Laborers	9		1 00	

COOKING AND HEATING APPARATUS (STOVES), ILLINOIS.—ESTAB. No. 167.

Time, 10 hours per day; 275 days the past year.

Occupations.	Number.		Daily wages.	
	Male.	Fem.	Male.	Fem.
Cleaners	2		$1 75	
Cupola men	2		1 50	
Engineer	1		2 50	
Grinders and polishers	4		2 00	
Mounters	5		2 00	
Moulders	22		3 75	
Pattern makers	3		3 50	

COOKING AND HEATING APPARATUS (STOVES), ILLINOIS.—ESTAB. No. 168.

Time, 10 hours per day; — days the past year.

Occupations.	Number.		Daily wages.	
	Male.	Fem.	Male.	Fem.
Carpenters and pattern makers	7		$2 00	
Cupola men	8		1 25	
Grinders and trimmers	18		1 25	
Moulders	75		3 25	
Mounters	23		1 50	
Porters	6		1 50	

a Miners receive 56 cents per ton of 2,240 pounds, gas lump coal (Kanawha Valley district).
b Miners receive 62½ cents per ton of 2,240 pounds, splint lump coal (Kanawha Valley district).
c Youth.

OCCUPATIONS, WITH NUMBER AND WAGES OF EMPLOYÉS, BY INDUSTRIES—Cont'd.

NOTE.—This table is *not* a complete exhibit for industries or states, but covers only establishments investigated by the Bureau. See page 91, also summaries, pages 143 to 226.

COOKING AND HEATING APPARATUS (STOVES), ILLINOIS.—ESTAB. No. **169**.

Time, 10 hours per day; 266 days the past year.

Occupations.	Number.		Daily wages.	
	Male.	Fem.	Male.	Fem.
Apprentices, moulders'	a8		$0 50	
Carpenters	2		2 25	
Cupola men	3		1 75	
Engineer	1		2 25	
Grinders	4		1 50	
Laborers	22		1 50	
Moulders	5		3 50	
Moulders	25		2 00	
Mounters	8		2 00	
Pattern fitters	3		2 75	
Pattern makers	3		4 00	
Watchman	1		1 75	

COOKING AND HEATING APPARATUS (STOVES), ILLINOIS.—ESTAB. No. **170**.

Time, 10 hours per day; 265 days the past year.

Occupations.	Male.	Fem.	Male.	Fem.
Moulders	26		$3 00	
Mounters	8		2 25	
Pattern makers	4		2 75	

COOKING AND HEATING APPARATUS (STOVES), ILLINOIS.—ESTAB. No. **171**.

Time, 10 hours per day; 280 days the past year.

Occupations.	Male.	Fem.	Male.	Fem.
Apprentices, moulders'	a2		$0 75	
Engineer	1		2 00	
Laborers	4		1 25	
Moulders	16		2 25	
Mounter	1		2 50	
Pattern maker	1		2 50	

COOKING AND HEATING APPARATUS (STOVES), ILLINOIS.—ESTAB. No. **172**.

Time, 10 hours per day; 270 days the past year.

Occupations.	Male.	Fem.	Male.	Fem.
Apprentices, moulders'	a7		$1 35	
Cleaners and grinders	3		1 50	
Carpenters and fitters	3		2 25	
Driller	1		2 00	
Engineer	1		2 25	
Foreman	1		4 00	
Foreman	1		2 25	
Melters	2		2 00	
Moulders	20		3 50	
Mounters	a4		75	
Nickel plater	1		2 25	
Nickel-platers' helpers	a4		65	
Pattern and flask man	1		2 00	
Watchman	1		1 40	

COOKING AND HEATING APPARATUS (STOVES), ILLINOIS.—ESTAB. No. **173**.

Time, 10 hours per day; 281 days the past year.

Occupations.	Number.		Daily wages.	
	Male.	Fem.	Male.	Fem.
Apprentices, moulders'	a10		$1 25	
Cupola men and laborers	20		1 33	
Foreman	1		4 00	
Grinders and trimmers	16		1 33	
Moulders	23		3 60	

COOKING AND HEATING APPARATUS (STOVES), ILLINOIS.—ESTAB. No. **174**.

Time, 10 hours per day; 270 days the past year.

Occupations.	Male.	Fem.	Male.	Fem.
Apprentices, moulders'	a5		$1 50	
Cupola men	3		1 75	
Engineer	1		2 00	
Laborers	10		1 33	
Moulders	17		3 50	
Mounters	4		2 00	

COOKING AND HEATING APPARATUS (STOVES, MACHINERY), ILLINOIS.—ESTAB. No. **175**.

Time, 10 hours per day; 270 days the past year.

Occupations.	Male.	Fem.	Male.	Fem.
Apprentices, moulders'	a10		$1 25	
Blacksmith	1		1 75	
Blacksmith	1		1 50	
Blacksmiths' helpers	2		1 25	
Cleaners	a5		1 00	
Cleaners	a10		75	
Engineer	1		1 50	
Flask makers	6		2 00	
Foreman	1		3 00	
Heater	1		1 75	
Laborers	5		1 50	
Machinists	10		2 00	
Moulders	38		2 50	
Mounters	5		2 25	
Pattern maker	1		2 50	
Pattern fitter	1		2 25	
Pattern fitter	1		2 00	
Polisher	1		1 50	
Undesignated	a12		75	
Watchman	1		1 25	
Yard men	2		1 85	

COOKING AND HEATING APPARATUS (STOVES), KENTUCKY.—ESTAB. No. **176**.

Time, 10 hours per day; 250 days the past year.

Occupations.	Male.	Fem.	Male.	Fem.
Laborers	7		$2 00	
Laborers	6		1 50	
Moulders	37		2 25	
Mounters	3		2 50	
Mounters	3		2 00	

a Youth.

OCCUPATIONS AND WAGES.

OCCUPATIONS, WITH NUMBER AND WAGES OF EMPLOYÉS, BY INDUSTRIES—Cont'd.

NOTE.—This table is *not* a complete exhibit for industries or states, but covers only establishments investigated by the Bureau. See page 91, also summaries, pages 143 to 226.

COOKING AND HEATING APPARATUS (STOVES), MICHIGAN.—ESTAB. No. 177.

Time, 10 hours per day; 258 days the past year.

Occupations.	Number.		Daily wages.	
	Male.	Fem.	Male.	Fem.
Apprentices, moulders'	a350		$0 70	
Blacksmiths	2		2 25	
Buffers	10		1 25	
Cleaners	6		1 25	
Cleaners	a6		60	
Crater	1		1 75	
Crater	1		1 13	
Designer	1		4 00	
Dipper and baker	1		1 25	
Dipper and baker	a1		75	
Dippers and bakers	a3		50	
Draughtsman	1		5 00	
Drillers	10		2 00	
Engineer	1		3 00	
Fallow-board makers	4		2 25	
Filers	2		3 00	
Filers	3		2 67	
Filers	4		2 12	
Filers	13		1 63	
Fireman	1		1 50	
Fitters	10		2 00	
Flask carriers	2		2 25	
Flask carriers	4		1 50	
Flask maker	1		2 00	
Flask makers	2		1 75	
Flask maker	1		1 00	
Foreman	1		6 00	
Foremen	2		4 50	
Foremen	3		4 00	
Foremen	2		3 25	
Foremen	3		3 00	
Foremen	3		2 25	
Grinders	20		1 25	
Inspectors	2		2 50	
Inspector	1		2 53	
Ladleman	1		1 50	
Millers	6		2 00	
Miller, cinder	1		1 50	
Miller, facing	1		1 50	
Machinist	1		2 88	
Machinist	1		2 50	
Melter	1		2 75	
Melters	16		1 50	
Melter	1		1 25	
Mica man	1		75	
Moulders	100		2 75	
Moulders	70		1 67	
Mounters	100		2 00	
Oiler	1		2 00	
Packer	1		2 50	
Packers	2		1 50	
Packers	4		1 33	
Packer	a1		50	
Pattern carrier	1		1 38	
Pattern maker	1		3 50	
Pattern makers	2		3 00	
Pattern makers	3		2 50	
Pattern makers	13		2 00	
Pattern maker	1		1 75	
Pattern makers	2		1 50	
Pattern maker	a1		1 00	
Pattern maker	a1		75	
Picklers	6		1 17	
Platers	a6		75	
Platers	a14		50	
Polishers	65		1 78	
Porter	1		2 88	
Porter	1		2 50	
Porter	1		1 88	
Porters	2		1 50	
Porters	2		1 33	
Repairers	2		1 75	
Repairer	1		1 50	

COOKING AND HEATING APPARATUS (STOVES), MICHIGAN.—ESTAB. No. 177—Concluded.

Time, 10 hours per day; 258 days the past year.

Occupations.	Number.		Daily wages.	
	Male.	Fem.	Male.	Fem.
Rod and bolt men	a3		$0 50	
Sawyer	1		2 00	
Stableman	1		2 00	
Striper	2		2 25	
Striper	1		1 00	
Sweeper	1		1 25	
Teamsters	3		1 33	
Teamsters	3		1 54	
Trimmer	1		2 00	
Trimmer	1		1 50	
Undesignated	5		1 30	
Washers	3		1 00	
Watchmen	3		2 00	
Waxer	1		1 00	
Weigher	1		1 00	
Wheel maker	1		2 00	
Wheelers and pilers	6		1 50	
Wrappers	a5		60	
Yard men	9		1 33	

COOKING AND HEATING APPARATUS (STOVES), MICHIGAN.—ESTAB. No. 175.

Time, 10 hours per day; 260 days the past year.

Occupations.	Number.		Daily wages.	
	Male.	Fem.	Male.	Fem.
Apprentices, moulders'	a250		$0 65	
Blacksmith	1		2 75	
Blacksmith	1		1 38	
Blacksmith's helper	1		1 00	
Blacksmith's helper	a1		60	
Buffer	1		1 75	
Buffer	1		1 38	
Buffers	9		1 25	
Buffer	1		1 13	
Buffers	2		75	
Cleaners and sweepers	2		1 12	
Craters	4		1 63	
Craters	2		1 30	
Craters	3		1 00	
Driller and cutter	1		1 00	
Drillers and cutters	a6		65	
Elevator tenders	2		1 00	
Engineer	1		2 00	
Filer	1		4 50	
Filers	11		3 00	
Filers	4		2 75	
Filers	6		2 20	
Filer	a1		88	
Filers	a5		60	
Finisher and packer	1		2 25	
Finishers and packers	3		2 00	
Finishers and packers	6		1 63	
Finishers and packers	5		1 15	
Finishers and packers	a15		75	
Fireman	1		1 38	
Flask makers	2		1 75	
Flask makers	6		1 40	
Foreman	1		6 50	
Foremen	2		5 25	
Foremen	6		4 25	
Foremen	4		2 90	
Grinder	1		2 00	
Grinders	30		1 25	
Heaters	2		2 25	
Heaters	6		1 75	
Heaters	2		1 63	
Heaters	32		1 40	
Heaters	11		1 25	
Japanner	1		3 00	

a Youth.

OCCUPATIONS, WITH NUMBER AND WAGES OF EMPLOYÉS, BY INDUSTRIES—Cont'd.

NOTE.—This table is not a complete exhibit for industries or states, but covers only establishments investigated by the Bureau. See page 91, also summaries, pages 143 to 226.

COOKING AND HEATING APPARATUS (STOVES), MICHIGAN.—ESTAB. No. 178—Concluded.

Time, 10 hours per day; 260 days the past year.

Occupations.	Number.		Daily wages.	
	Male.	Fem.	Male.	Fem.
Japanner	1		$1 00	
Japanner's assistant	a1		50	
Laborer	1		2 25	
Laborers	3		1 90	
Laborers	11		1 50	
Laborers	4		1 20	
Laborers	a3		60	
Machinist	1		3 00	
Machinists	2		1 75	
Moulder	1		4 00	
Moulders	252		2 25	
Moulders	7		1 60	
Moulders	a5		55	
Moulders' helpers	84		1 25	
Moulder and pattern maker	1		5 00	
Moulder and pattern maker	1		3 50	
Moulders and pattern makers	3		3 00	
Mounters	8		2 25	
Mounters	10		2 00	
Mounters	16		1 63	
Mounters	17		1 25	
Mounters	a6		75	
Nickel plater	1		1 75	
Nickel platers	4		1 38	
Nickel platers	a6		75	
Nickel trimmers	9		1 20	
Nickel trimmers	2		1 00	
Nickel trimmers	a5		75	
Nickel trimmers	a3		55	
Pattern maker	1		5 00	
Pattern maker	1		3 50	
Pattern makers	3		3 00	
Pattern maker	1		3 75	
Pattern makers	5		3 10	
Pattern makers	6		2 25	
Pattern makers	4		1 63	
Pattern makers	6		1 13	
Pattern makers	a2		60	
Polishers	31		2 25	
Polisher	1		1 50	
Polisher	1		1 25	
Polishers	a3		75	
Stove blackener	1		1 25	
Teamsters	5		1 80	
Teamsters	2		1 50	
Teamsters	3		1 25	
Tinsmiths	6		2 30	
Tinsmiths	2		2 10	
Tinsmith	1		1 75	
Tinsmith	1		1 50	
Tinsmiths	2		1 00	
Tinsmith's helper	a1		75	
Undesignated	a1		50	
Watchmen	2		2 13	
Watchmen	2		1 40	
Wheelers and cleaners	2		2 20	
Wheelers and cleaners	9		1 50	
Wheelers and cleaners	10		1 13	
Wheelers and cleaners	a5		75	
Wheelers and cleaners	a20		60	
Yard men	2		1 25	

COOKING AND HEATING APPARATUS (STOVES), NEW YORK.—ESTAB. No. 179.

Time, 10 hours per day; — days the past year.

Occupations.	Number.		Daily wages.	
	Male.	Fem.	Male.	Fem.
Carpenters	3		$2 00	
Carpenter	1		1 00	
Cupola man	1		1 50	
Cupola man	1		93	
Engineer	1		2 00	
Foreman	1		3 00	
Foreman	1		2 50	
Furnace man	1		1 25	
Grinder	1		1 50	
Japanner	1		1 25	
Laborers	2		1 55	
Laborer	1		1 25	
Mason	1		3 00	
Mason	1		2 60	
Melter	1		2 00	
Moulder	1		4 16	
Moulder	1		3 67	
Moulder	1		2 70	
Moulders	3		3 33	
Moulders	11		2 92	
Moulders	11		2 58	
Moulders	12		2 25	
Moulders	3		1 67	
Moulders	7		1 30	
Moulders' helpers	2		1 46	
Moulders' helpers	a2		75	
Moulders' helper	a1		50	
Mounter	1		5 08	
Mounters	2		4 58	
Mounter	1		4 00	
Mounters	5		2 00	
Mounters' helpers	6		1 25	
Mounters' helpers	a2		50	
Pattern fitter	1		1 58	
Pattern fitter	1		2 00	
Pattern fitter	a1		1 00	
Polisher	1		3 75	
Sand boys	a3		83	
Scratcher	1		4 58	
Stove blackener	1		1 25	
Teamster	1		1 50	
Teamsters	2		1 25	
Tinsmith	1		2 92	
Tinsmiths	5		2 00	
Tinsmiths' helpers	a3		83	
Watchman	1		1 75	

COOKING AND HEATING APPARATUS (STOVES, RANGES), NEW YORK.—ESTAB. No. 180.

Time, 10 hours per day; — days the past year.

Occupations.	Number.		Daily wages.	
	Male.	Fem.	Male.	Fem.
Apprentices	a250		$0 69	
Blacksmiths	5		1 83	
Blacksmiths' helpers	3		1 17	
Burnisher	1		1 50	
Carpenters	15		2 42	
Cleaners	3		1 12	
Cleaners	2		1 42	
Cupola men	2		2 16	
Derrick man	1		92	
Designer	1		5 00	
Draughtsmen	2		2 67	
Engineer	1		2 50	
Facers	2		3 00	
Filers	3		2 33	

a Youth.

OCCUPATIONS AND WAGES.

OCCUPATIONS, WITH NUMBER AND WAGES OF EMPLOYÉS, BY INDUSTRIES—Cont'd.

NOTE.—This table is *not* a complete exhibit for industries or states, but covers only establishments investigated by the Bureau. See page 91, also summaries, pages 143 to 226.

COOKING AND HEATING APPARATUS (STOVES, RANGES), NEW YORK.—ESTAB. No. 180—Concluded.

Time, 10 hours per day; — days the past year.

Occupations.	Number.		Daily wages.	
	Male.	Fem.	Male.	Fem.
Firemen	2		$1 75	
Fire-brick men	2		1 25	
Foreman	1		5 00	
Foremen	2		4 00	
Foremen	5		3 00	
Grinders	14		1 50	
Instructor	1		2 08	
Iron pilers	6		1 12	
Japanners	2		2 00	
Laborers	138		1 25	
Ladle men	4		1 50	
Machinist	1		2 33	
Menders	3		1 75	
Mica men	3		1 96	
Moulders, contractors	13		4 00	
Moulders	365		3 16	
Moulder	1		2 50	
Mounters, contractors	4		4 50	
Mounters	4		2 79	
Mounters	5		2 50	
Nickel fitters	3		2 25	
Nickel platers	4		2 79	
Oilers	2		1 50	
Packers	6		1 65	
Painters	2		2 00	
Pattern carriers	2		1 08	
Pattern fitters	6		1 25	
Pattern fitters	2		2 33	
Pattern fitters	4		2 00	
Pattern fitters	12		1 08	
Pattern maker	1		2 71	
Pattern makers	3		2 25	
Polisher	1		4 66	
Polishers	4		2 83	
Polishers	16		2 17	
Porters	2		1 50	
Rod and bolt men	3		1 67	
Sand and clay men	3		1 00	
Shippers	4		2 00	
Spruc chippers	2		1 50	
Stove blackeners	2		1 50	
Stove liners	4		2 33	
Tamper	1		2 29	
Teamsters	5		1 67	
Teamsters	3		1 50	
Tinsmiths	7		2 50	
Tinsmiths	11		1 79	
Watchmen	6		1 50	

COOKING AND HEATING APPARATUS (STOVES, RANGES), NEW YORK.—ESTAB. No. 181.

Time, 10 hours per day; — days the past year.

Occupations.	Number.		Daily wages.	
	Male.	Fem.	Male.	Fem.
Apprentices, moulders	a192		$0 77	
Blacksmiths	7		1 80	
Blacksmiths' helpers	5		1 16	
Burnisher	1		1 50	
Carpenters	8		2 50	
Carpenters	9		1 87	
Cleaners	6		1 37	
Cleaners	6		1 04	
Cupola man	1		1 66	
Cupola men	2		2 16	

COOKING AND HEATING APPARATUS (STOVES, RANGES), NEW YORK.—ESTAB. No. 181—Concluded.

Time, 10 hours per day; — days the past year.

Occupations.	Number.		Daily wages.	
	Male.	Fem.	Male.	Fem.
Derrick man	1		$1 25	
Designer	1		5 00	
Draughtsman	1		3 00	
Draughtsman	1		1 50	
Engineers	2		2 50	
Engineers	3		2 00	
Facers	2		2 00	
Fire-clay men	2		2 00	
Firemen	2		1 71	
Flask carriers	8		1 00	
Foreman	1		5 00	
Foreman	1		4 16	
Foremen	3		3 00	
Foremen	2		2 66	
Foremen	2		2 16	
Grinders	15		1 50	
Heaters	3		1 50	
Iron breakers	2		1 33	
Inspector	1		1 83	
Instructor	1		2 12	
Iron pilers	6		1 23	
Japanners	4		2 00	
Laborer	1		1 66	
Laborers	161		1 33	
Ladle men	4		1 50	
Machinist	1		2 25	
Melters	4		1 50	
Mica men	6		1 86	
Millwright	1		2 00	
Moulder	1		4 00	
Moulders, contractors	12		4 00	
Moulders	269		3 62	
Moulders	151		2 87	
Moulder	1		2 50	
Mounters, contractors	4		5 00	
Mounters, contractors	3		4 41	
Mounters	2		2 66	
Mounters	5		2 50	
Nickel platers	5		3 00	
Packers	7		1 58	
Painters	2		2 00	
Pattern carriers	4		1 08	
Pattern fitters	4		2 00	
Pattern fitters	8		1 28	
Pattern fitters	2		2 33	
Pattern fitters	20		1 00	
Pattern maker	1		3 00	
Pattern makers	4		1 81	
Polisher	1		4 33	
Polishers	15		2 30	
Repairer	1		1 50	
Rod and bolt men	4		1 66	
Sand and clay men	5		1 00	
Shippers	3		2 00	
Shippers' assistants	10		1 25	
Spruc chippers	2		1 50	
Spruc chippers	3		1 12	
Stove blackeners	2		1 50	
Stove liners	9		2 40	
Tamper	1		2 21	
Teamsters	4		1 75	
Teamsters	4		1 50	
Tinsmiths	9		1 95	
Tinsmiths	13		1 60	
Watchmen	7		1 50	
Weighers	2		1 66	

a Youth.

OCCUPATIONS, WITH NUMBER AND WAGES OF EMPLOYÉS, BY INDUSTRIES—Cont'd.

NOTE.—This table is *not* a complete exhibit for industries or states, but covers only establishments investigated by the Bureau. See page 91, also summaries, pages 143 to 226.

COOKING AND HEATING APPARATUS (STOVES, RANGES), NEW YORK.—Estab. No. 182.

Time, 10 hours per day; 300 days the past year.

Occupations.	Number.		Daily wages.	
	Male.	Fem.	Male.	Fem.
Apprentices	a53		$0 83	
Blacksmith	1		2 67	
Blacksmith's helper	1		1 58	
Carpenters	2		2 25	
Cupola men	2		2 33	
Designer	1		6 00	
Draughtsman	1		3 00	
Draughtsman	1		1 50	
Engineer	1		2 50	
Fireman	1		1 58	
Flask fixer	1		1 67	
Foreman	1		4 67	
Foreman	1		4 17	
Foremen	5		3 00	
Foreman	1		2 50	
Grate setter	1		1 58	
Grinder	1		1 87	
Grinders	2		1 67	
Heater	1		2 00	
Instructor	1		1 79	
Japanner	1		1 83	
Laborers	68		1 50	
Ladle men	2		1 67	
Machinists	2		2 33	
Melter	1		2 29	
Mica man	1		2 33	
Moulder	1		4 00	
Moulders	58		3 65	
Mounter	1		4 00	
Mounters	13		3 21	
Nickel platers	8		2 67	
Painter	1		2 00	
Pattern fitter	1		1 67	
Pattern fitter A	1		2 00	
Pattern fitter	1		1 71	
Pattern makers	2		2 33	
Polisher	1		2 67	
Polisher	1		1 96	
Sand and scrap men	15		1 14	
Scrubbers	4		1 29	
Sprue chipper	1		1 67	
Stove blackener	1		1 50	
Stove liners	2		2 29	
Tamper	1		2 25	
Teamsters	2		2 00	
Timekeepers	2		1 37	
Tinsmith	1		2 42	
Tinsmiths	7		2 25	
Watchman	1		1 50	
Watchman	1		1 21	
Weigher	1		3 00	
Weigher	1		1 50	

COOKING AND HEATING APPARATUS (STOVES, RANGES), NEW YORK.—Estab. No. 183.

Time, 10 hours per day; — days the past year.

Occupations.	Number.		Daily wages.	
	Male.	Fem.	Male.	Fem.
Blacksmith	1		$2 33	
Burnisher	1		1 50	
Cupola men	2		1 40	
Cupola men	2		1 67	
Draughtsman	1		3 00	
Elevator tender	1		1 42	
Facer	1		1 75	
Flask carrier	1		1 50	
Foreman	1		3 67	
Foreman	1		3 00	

COOKING AND HEATING APPARATUS (STOVES, RANGES), NEW YORK.—Estab. No. 183—Concl'd.

Time, 10 hours per day; — days the past year.

Occupations.	Number.		Daily wages.	
	Male.	Fem.	Male.	Fem.
Grinders	2		$1 50	
Iron breaker	1		1 50	
Iron piler	1		1 50	
Japanner	1		1.46	
Laborers	2		1 50	
Laborers	10		1 25	
Ladle men	2		1 67	
Machinist	1		2 30	
Melter	1		1 90	
Mica man	1		2 50	
Moulder	1		4 00	
Moulders	23		3 25	
Mounters	6		3 17	
Nickel plater	1		2 67	
Pattern fitter	1		4 00	
Pattern fitter	1		1 50	
Pattern fitter	1		1 92	
Pattern maker	1		3 00	
Polisher	1		4 00	
Polishers	2		3 00	
Porter	1		1 78	
Porters	2		1 42	
Porter	a1		83	
Rod and bolt man	1		1 75	
Sand and clay man	1		1 50	
Sprue chipper	1		1 58	
Stove blackener	1		1 46	
Stove liner	1		2 29	
Stove liner	1		1 79	
Sweeper	1		1 25	
Teamster	1		1 58	
Tinsmith	1		2 87	
Tinsmiths	3		2 00	
Tinsmiths' helpers	a2		65	
Watchmen	2		1 50	

COOKING AND HEATING APPARATUS (STOVES), OHIO.—Estab. No. 184.

Time, 10 hours per day; 275 days the past year.

Occupations.	Number.		Daily wages.	
	Male.	Fem.	Male.	Fem.
Carpenters	2		$2 25	
Engineer	1		3 00	
Laborers	12		1 75	
Moulders	24		2 90	
Moulders	40		2 40	
Moulders	21		2 00	
Mounters	45		1 91	
Pattern fitters	7		1 87	
Pattern makers	5		2 85	
Tinsmiths	3		2 11	

COOKING AND HEATING APPARATUS (STOVES), OHIO.—Estab. No. 185.

Time, 10 hours per day; 250 days the past year.

Occupations.	Number.		Daily wages.	
	Male.	Fem.	Male.	Fem.
Engineer	1		$2 25	
Melter	1		2 50	
Melter's helper	1		1 75	
Moulders	80		2 70	
Mounters	13		2 50	
Mounters' helpers	16		1 25	
Undesignated	41		1 87	

a Youth.

OCCUPATIONS AND WAGES. 333

OCCUPATIONS, WITH NUMBER AND WAGES OF EMPLOYÉS, BY INDUSTRIES—Cont'd.

NOTE.—This table is *not* a complete exhibit for industries or states, but covers only establishments investigated by the Bureau. See page 91, also summaries, pages 148 to 226.

COOKING AND HEATING APPARATUS (STOVES), OHIO.—ESTAB. No. 186.

Time, 10 hours per day; — days the past year.

Occupations.	Number.		Daily wages.	
	Male.	Fem.	Male.	Fem.
Apprentices, moulders	a4	......	$0 90	......
Cupola man	1	......	2 00	......
Laborers	3	......	1 50	......
Moulders	15	......	2 75	......
Mounters	4	......	1 95	......

COOKING AND HEATING APPARATUS (STOVES), OHIO.—ESTAB. No. 187.

Time, 10 hours per day; — days the past year.

Occupations.	Number.		Daily wages.	
	Male.	Fem.	Male.	Fem.
Apprentices, moulders	a10	......	$0 80	......
Carpenters	2	......	2 00	......
Cupola man	1	......	1 75	......
Cupola man	1	......	1 40	......
Engineer	1	......	1 50	......
Foremen	2	......	3 00	......
Moulders	25	......	2 75	......
Mounters	10	......	2 25	......
Pattern maker	1	......	3 33	......
Polishers	6	......	1 35	......

COOKING AND HEATING APPARATUS (STOVES), OHIO.—ESTAB. No. 188.

Time, 10 hours per day; 260 days the past year.

Occupations.	Number.		Daily wages.	
	Male.	Fem.	Male.	Fem.
Apprentices, moulders	a35	......	$0 93	......
Cupola men and laborers	64	......	1 53	......
Foremen	7	......	3 63	......
Moulders	139	......	2 54	......
Mounters	66	......	2 30	......
Nickel platers	30	......	1 53	......
Nickel platers	a26	......	80	......
Pattern fitters	15	......	1 70	......
Pattern makers	12	......	2 80	......
Polishers	7	......	1 50	......
Porters	5	......	1 47	......
Stove blackeners	2	......	1 38	......

COOKING AND HEATING APPARATUS (STOVES, MACHINERY), OHIO.—ESTAB. No. 189.

Time, 10 hours per day; 300 days the past year.

Occupations.	Number.		Daily wages.	
	Male.	Fem.	Male.	Fem.
Blacksmith	1	......	$1 75	......
Cupola men and cleaners	4	......	1 40	......
Engineer	1	......	2 00	......
Machinists	7	......	1 80	......
Machinists' helpers	a2	......	50	......
Moulders	15	......	3 00	......
Mounters	4	......	2 50	......
Painter	1	......	2 00	......
Pattern maker	1	......	2 50	......
Pump men	3	......	2 00	......
Shippers	2	......	1 50	......
Teamster	1	......	1 50	......
Watchman	1	......	1 00	......

COOKING AND HEATING APPARATUS (STOVES), PENNSYLVANIA.—ESTAB. No. 190.

Time, 10 hours per day; — days the past year.

Occupations.	Number.		Daily wages.	
	Male.	Fem.	Male.	Fem.
Blacksmith	1	......	$1 75	......
Engineer	1	......	2 25	......
Foremen	2	......	3 00	......
Laborers	10	......	1 35	......
Moulders	48	......	3 50	......
Mounters	12	......	3 00	......
Pattern makers	2	......	3 00	......
Teamster	1	......	1 50	......
Watchman	1	......	1 50	......

COOKING AND HEATING APPARATUS (STOVES), WEST VIRGINIA.—ESTAB. No. 191.

Time, 10 hours per day; 256 days the past year.

Occupations.	Number.		Daily wages.	
	Male.	Fem.	Male.	Fem.
Apprentices, moulders	a12	......	$1 25	......
Carpenter	1	......	2 00	......
Cupola man	1	......	2 25	......
Driller	1	......	1 66	......
Engineer	1	......	1 75	......
Filer	1	......	2 00	......
Laborers	13	......	1 25	......
Moulders	23	......	2 50	......
Mounters	9	......	1 65	......
Pattern maker	1	......	2 25	......

COTTON COMPRESSING, ARKANSAS.—ESTAB. No. 192.

Time, 10 hours per day; — days the past year.

Occupations.	Number.		Daily wages.	
	Male.	Fem.	Male.	Fem.
Band clippers	3	......	$1 50	......
Firemen	2	......	1 75	......
Return tiers	5	......	1 75	......
Sewers	6	......	1 75	......
Tiers	6	......	2 00	......
Truckmen	4	......	1 25	......

COTTON GOODS (PRINT CLOTH), CONNECTICUT.—ESTAB. No. 193.

Time, 11 hours per day; 303 days the past year.

Occupations.	Number.		Daily wages.	
	Male.	Fem.	Male.	Fem.
Back boys	a12	......	$0 35	......
Baler	1	......	1 00	......
Bobbin tender	1	......	1 50	......
Carpenter	1	......	1 75	......
Card grinders	2	......	1 25	......
Card strippers	4	......	90	......
Doffers	a6	4	60	$0 60
Doffers	a5	......	54	......
Drawer	......	1	......	75
Drawers	......	3	......	1 20
Drawers	......	5	......	90
Elevator tender	1	......	1 00	......
Engineer	1	......	2 50	......
Filling hand	1	......	1 00	......
Folder	......	1	1 33	......
Inspector	......	1	......	1 12
Laborers	2	......	1 00	......
Lappers	2	......	1 00	......
Lapper	1	......	71	......
Machinists	2	......	1 50	......
Oiler	1	......	96	......
Overseers	3	......	2 75	......

a Youth.

334   REPORT OF THE COMMISSIONER OF LABOR.

OCCUPATIONS, WITH NUMBER AND WAGES OF EMPLOYÉS, BY INDUSTRIES—Cont'd.

NOTE.—This table is *not* a complete exhibit for industries or states, but covers only establishments investigated by the Bureau. See page 91, also summaries, pages 143 to 226.

COTTON GOODS (PRINT CLOTH), CONNECTICUT.—ESTAB. No. 193—Concluded.

Time, 11 *hours per day;* 303 *days the past year.*

Occupations.	Number.		Daily wages.	
	Male.	Fem.	Male.	Fem.
Overseers	2		$2 67	
Overseer	1		2 00	
Railway hand		1		$0 58
Repair hand	1		2 83	
Second hands	2		1 50	
Second hand	1		1 42	
Second hand	1		1 38	
Section hands	5		1 42	
Slasher	1		1 67	
Slubber	1		1 20	
Slubbers	2		1 10	
Speeders		6		1 12
Speeders		12		95
Spinners, mule	8		1 80	
Spinners, mule	7		1 42	
Spinners, other	a7	a8	58	58
Spinners, other	b5	b8	26	26
Spoolers		16		60
Sweepers		b4		33
Trimmers		2		75
Warper		1		95
Warpers		2		82
Watchmen	2		1 15	
Weavers	43		c1 17	
Weavers		97		d95

COTTON GOODS (SHEETING), DELAWARE.—ESTAB. No. 194.

Time, 10 *hours per day;* 300 *days the past year.*

Occupations	Male	Fem	Male	Fem
Carder	1		$2 50	
Card stripper	1		1 33	
Drawer	a1		66	
Dresser	1		2 33	
Fly-frame tenders	6		91	
Laborer	1		1 33	
Loom fixers	2		1 40	
Measurer	1		1 40	
Picker	1		1 20	
Piecers and doffers		b19		$0 25
Repair hand	1		1 83	
Spinners, mule	1		2 50	
Spoolers		3		66
Twisters	a2		43	
Undesignated		2		66
Undesignated		b3		33
Weavers		36		76

COTTON GOODS (COLORED FAMILY CLOTH), DELAWARE.—ESTAB. No. 195.

Time, 10 *hours per day;* 300 *days the past year.*

Occupations	Male	Fem	Male	Fem
Beamers	11		$1 47	
Carders	33		85	
Dyers	6		1 50	
Finishers	6		1 00	
Laborers	4		1 25	
Mechanics	5		1 85	
Spinners		a66		$0 60
Weavers		117		84

COTTON GOODS (PRINT CLOTH), FRANCE.—ESTAB. No. 196.

Time, 11 *hours per day;* — *days the past year.*

Occupations.	Number.		Daily wages.	
	Male.	Fem.	Male.	Fem.
Drawers	5		$0 60	
Drawers' assistants	b5		20	
Engineer	1		1 20	
Fireman	1		80	
Oiler	1		80	
Overseers	4		1 00	
Sizers	2		1 08	
Sizers' assistants	2		62	
Undesignated	14		60	
Warpers	5		67	
Watchman	1		1 00	
Weavers		150		$0 54
Winders	10		50	

COTTON GOODS (YARN), FRANCE.—ESTAB. No. 197.

Time, 12 *hours per day;* 300 *days the past year.*

Occupations	Male	Fem	Male	Fem
Adjuster	1		$0 86	
Blowing-room hands	1	1	62	$0 45
Carders	2		53	
Card grinders	1		86	
Card strippers	4		60	
Drawers	1	3	96	41
Engineer	1		96	
Fireman	1		67	
Jack-frame tenders		6		60
Laborers	2		58	
Oiler	1		62	
Overseer	1		96	
Piecers	7		53	
Piecer	a1		40	
Spinners, mule	7		96	
Winders	a7	a5	43	20

COTTON GOODS (DRILLING), GEORGIA.—ESTAB. No. 198.

Time, 11½ *hours per day;* 310 *days the past year.*

Occupations	Male	Fem	Male	Fem
Back boys	b9		$0 32	
Balers	2		85	
Beamer	a1		75	
Bolt maker	1		1 50	
Blacksmith	1		1 70	
Bobbin boys	a4		47	
Brush boys	a3		55	
Card grinders	4		1 05	
Card strippers	2		85	
Carpenters	7		1 25	
Cloth-room hand	1		85	
Doffers	b11		30	
Drawers		a11		$0 48
Drawers-in		a10		55
Engineer	1		1 50	
Filling hands	a3		65	
Fireman	1		85	
Folders	2		70	
Fly-frame tenders		21		72
Laborers	2		85	
Laborers	a19		50	
Laborers	a3		32	
Machinists	2		1 70	

a Youth.
b Children.
c Estimated average wages. The agent's return gives 43 weavers (male), at 92 cents to $1.67 per day.
d Estimated average wages. The agent's return gives 97 weavers (female), at 83 cents to $1.20 per day.

OCCUPATIONS AND WAGES.

OCCUPATIONS, WITH NUMBER AND WAGES OF EMPLOYÉS, BY INDUSTRIES—Cont'd.

NOTE.—This table is not a complete exhibit for industries or states, but covers only establishments investigated by the Bureau. See page 91, also summaries, pages 143 to 226.

COTTON GOODS (DRILLING), GEORGIA.—ESTAB. No. 198—Concluded.

Time, 11¼ hours per day; 310 days the past year.

Occupations.	Number.		Daily wages.	
	Male.	Fem.	Male.	Fem.
Mason	1		$2 25	
Mixers	a3		75	
Oilers	5		80	
Oiler	b1		32	
Overseers	3		4 25	
Overseer	1		1 90	
Openers	a2		58	
Painter	1		1 00	
Pickers	a4		75	
Rovers	a3		75	
Second hand	1		1 70	
Second hand	1		1 50	
Second hand	1		1 25	
Section hands	10		1 15	
Slashers	2		1 25	
Spinners, mule	8		85	
Spinners, other	a6	a30	44	$0 44
Spoolers		b24		30
Stampers	2		70	
Stitchers	a3		55	
Sweeper	a1		40	
Sweepers	b14		27	
Teamster	1		1 05	
Tinsmith	1		1 05	
Undesignated	4		85	
Undesignated	9		70	
Undesignated	3		50	
Undesignated		a13		40
Warpers	3		1 00	
Watchmen	4		85	
Weavers	48	110	85	75
Winders	8		75	

COTTON GOODS (DRILLING), GEORGIA.—ESTAB. No. 199.

Time, 11¼ hours per day; 310 days the past year.

Occupations.	Number.		Daily wages.	
	Male.	Fem.	Male.	Fem.
Baler	1		$0 75	
Bander	1		65	
Blacksmith	1		1 50	
Bobbin boy	a1		30	
Card grinders	2		1 05	
Card strippers	a4		50	
Carpenters	2		90	
Doffers	a8		42	
Drawers	a2	5	50	$0 68
Fireman	1		65	
Folder	1		75	
Fly-frame tenders		17		58
Laborer	1		85	
Laborers	a10		47	
Machinist	1		1 00	
Oiler	a1		65	
Oiler	a1		50	
Overseer	1		4 25	
Overseer	1		3 40	
Overseer	1		1 70	
Pickers	a4		50	
Railway hands	1		80	
Rover	a1		50	
Scrubber	a1		50	
Second hand	1		2 00	
Second hands	2		1 25	
Section hands	3		70	
Section hands	4		1 20	
Slasher	1		1 15	
Spinners	a13	a22	37	37
Spoolers		a7		48

COTTON GOODS (DRILLING), GEORGIA.—ESTAB. No. 199—Concluded.

Time, 11¼ hours per day; 310 days the past year.

Occupations.	Number.		Daily wages.	
	Male.	Fem.	Male.	Fem.
Stamper	1		$0 75	
Stitcher	1		75	
Sweeper	b1		25	
Undesignated	1		95	
Undesignated	2		65	
Undesignated	a4		50	
Undesignated	b1		25	
Warpers		2		$0 65
Watchmen	2		80	
Weavers	23	48	87	82
Yarn carrier	a1		65	

COTTON GOODS (PRINT CLOTH, MOLESKIN), GERMANY.—ESTAB. No. 200.

Time, 12 hours per day; 303 days the past year.

Occupations.	Number.		Daily wages.	
	Male.	Fem.	Male.	Fem.
Back tenders (tambours)	23		$0 46	
Bleachers	18		54	
Bobbin winders		a80 24		$0 25
Calenderers	7		52	
Carders	23		57	
Card grinders	8		82	
Card makers	5		60	
Carpenters	9		88	
Carpenters	8		68	
Chemists	2		67	
Cleaners and oilers	11		68	
Doffers		a47		27
Drivers	8		75	
Driers	3		35	
Dyers	167		54	
Dyers	15		44	
Engineers and machinists	37		70	
Firemen	27		73	
Floor hands	15		51	
Folders	24		42	
Foremen	9		1 16	
Foremen	20		70	
Gas makers	2		50	
Greasers	11		58	
Harness repairer	1		80	
Joiners	8		79	
Laborers	17		77	
Locksmiths	6		90	
Masons	30		82	
Masons	20		60	
Measurers	10		65	
Oilers	2		78	
Openers and preparers	12		50	
Packers	8		58	
Pantographers	7		77	
Pickers	13		56	
Porters	2		51	
Preparers	29		42	
Printers	12		1 13	
Printer	1		75	
Rollers	63		46	
Rovers	4	a26	61	40
Rovers		a28		22
Scrubbers		8		48
Sizers	4		85	
Sizers	12		81	
Spare hands		a2		25
Speeders		17		39
Spinners, mule	26		88	

a Youth.   b Children.

OCCUPATIONS, WITH NUMBER AND WAGES OF EMPLOYÉS, BY INDUSTRIES—Cont'd.

NOTE.—This table is *not* a complete exhibit for industries or states, but covers only establishments investigated by the Bureau. See page 91, also summaries, pages 143 to 226.

COTTON GOODS (PRINT CLOTH, MOLESKIN), GERMANY.—ESTAB. No. **200**—Concluded.

Time, 12 hours per day; 303 days the past year.

Occupations.	Number.		Daily wages.	
	Male.	Fem.	Male.	Fem.
Spinners, other		15		$0 49
Spinners, other		a24		25
Steamers	9		$0 54	
Tenters	10		51	
Tinsmiths	12		80	
Twisters		35		40
Undesignated	a225		35	
Varnishers	3		56	
Warehouse men	21		54	
Warpers		10		59
Warpers		8		37
Washers	12		46	
Watchmen	16		52	
Weavers		401		48
Weavers		576		45
White-room hands	5		61	
Winders	60	49	45	34

COTTON GOODS (PRINT CLOTH), GREAT BRITAIN.—ESTAB. No. **201**.

Time, 10 hours per day; 300 days the past year.

Occupations.	Number.		Daily wages.	
	Male.	Fem.	Male.	Fem.
Beamers	4		$0 90	
Bobbin boys	a4		32	
Card clothiers	1		80	
Creelers		a3		$0 45
Doffers	a7		37	
Drawers		3		64
Engineers	2		1 20	
Fireman	1		88	
Grinders and strippers, card	3		85	
Intermediates		2		82
Lappers		2		55
Machinist	1		1 35	
Machinist's helper	a1		32	
Oiler	1		84	
Overseers (overlookers)	3		1 52	
Overseers (overlookers)	5		1 44	
Rovers		9		66
Scutchers	3		63	
Slubbers		3		75
Spinners, mule	9		1 48	
Spinners, other		a27		40
Tenters		b29		22
Twisters	5		64	
Undesignated	2		1 40	
Warehouse men	5		72	
Weavers		152		90
Winders		19		54

COTTON GOODS (SHEETING), GREAT BRITAIN.—ESTAB. No. **202**.

Time, 10 hours per day; — days the past year.

Occupations.	Number.		Daily wages.	
	Male.	Fem.	Male.	Fem.
Bobbin tenders	2		$0 64	
Card feeders	a2		54	
Card grinders	7		92	
Card grinders	2		88	
Cloth-room hand	1		1 20	
Cloth-room hands	a7		60	

COTTON GOODS (SHEETING), GREAT BRITAIN.—ESTAB. No. **202** c—Concluded.

Time, 10 hours per day; — days the past year.

Occupations.	Number.		Daily wages.	
	Male.	Fem.	Male.	Fem.
Doffers	a2		$0 65	
Doubler		a1		$0 41
Drawers		11		75
Drawers-in	3		1 27	
Drawer-in	1		86	
Engineers	2		1 48	
Foreman	1		1 80	
Foremen	2		1 17	
Foreman	1		1 08	
Foremen, assistant	3		94	
Laborers	13		87	
Lappers		3		52
Mixer	1		1 17	
Mixer	1		88	
Mixers	2		75	
Oiler	1		1 07	
Openers	2		60	
Rovers		17		67
Slubbers		10		70
Speeders		9		66
Spinners, mule	42		1 75	
Spinners, other		6		58
Sweepers	b4		13	
Tapers	3		1 60	
Taper	1		1 40	
Twister	1		1 02	
Twisters	2	4	90	62
Warpers	8		74	
Warpers	3		58	
Watchman	1		88	
Winders		39		50

COTTON GOODS (YARN), GREAT BRITAIN.—ESTAB. No. **203**.

Time, 10 hours per day; — days the past year.

Occupations.	Number.		Daily wages.	
	Male.	Fem.	Male.	Fem.
Bobbin carrier	1		$1 15	
Can tenders		3		$0 56
Card clothier	1		1 28	
Carders	2		1 04	
Carders	6		92	
Carders	4		76	
Drawers		9		72
Engineer	1		1 80	
Fireman	1		96	
Laborer	1		1 15	
Laborer	1		80	
Lapper	1		96	
Lappers	1	4	72	64
Mixers	1	2	92	73
Mixers	2		72	
Oiler	1		1 00	
Overseer (overlooker)	1		2 21	
Overseer (overlooker)	1		2 00	
Overseer's assistant	1		1 70	
Packers	6		68	
Piecers	36		1 08	
Rovers		20		66
Rovers		a16		42
Slubbers		9		72
Speeders		9		72
Spinners, mule	34		1 47	

a Youth.   b Children.   c Weavers not reported.

OCCUPATIONS AND WAGES.

OCCUPATIONS, WITH NUMBER AND WAGES OF EMPLOYÉS, BY INDUSTRIES—Cont'd.

NOTE.—This table is *not* a complete exhibit for industries or states, but covers only establishments investigated by the Bureau. See page 91, also summaries, page 143 to 226.

COTTON GOODS (YARN), GREAT BRITAIN.—ESTAB. No. **204**.

Time, 10 hours per day; — days the past year.

Occupations.	Number.		Daily wages.	
	Male.	Fem.	Male.	Fem.
Carders	10		$0 72	
Drawers	9		65	
Engineer	1		2 00	
Fireman	1		96	
Lappers	3	1	90	$0 64
Mixers	3		80	
Oiler	1		96	
Openers		3		64
Overseers	2		2 00	
Overseers' assistants	3		1 20	
Piecers	41		76	
Piecers, little	a41		47	
Rovers		27		63
Slubbers		10		61
Speeders		7		64
Speeders		a7		32
Spinners, mule	41		1 51	

COTTON GOODS (YARN), GREAT BRITAIN.—ESTAB. No. **205**.

Time, 10 hours per day; — days the past year.

Occupations.	Male.	Fem.	Male.	Fem.
Carder	1		$1 60	
Carder	1		1 20	
Card grinders and strippers	12		96	
Drawers		13		$0 72
Lappers	4	2	88	68
Mixers	4		80	
Overseer (overlooker)	1		2 00	
Piecers	a28		68	
Piecers	a18		60	
Piecers	a28		52	
Piecers, little	a18		44	
Railway hands		a2		39
Rovers	25	13	80	63
Scutchers		5		64
Speeders		4		73
Speeders		a16		40
Spinners, mule	28		1 60	
Spinners, mule	18		1 44	
Slubbers		12		72

COTTON GOODS (YARN), ITALY.—ESTAB. No. **206**.

Time, 12 hours per day; 292 days the past year.

Occupations.	Male.	Fem.	Male.	Fem.
Attendants	8		$0 39	
Belt lacers	2		$0 48	
Belt lacers	a2		16	
Bobbin carriers		2		44
Box makers	6		62	
Carders	9		44	
Carders	23		35	
Card cleaners	12		44	
Card cleaners	3		30	
Card grinders	9		63	
Carpenters and blacksmiths	20		53	
Coal-carriers	2		44	
Cylinder maker	1		97	
Drawers		27		29
Drawers		a13		16
Elevator tenders	2		42	
Engineer	1		97	
Engineers	4		58	

COTTON GOODS (YARN), ITALY.—ESTAB. No. **206**—Concluded.

Time, 12 hours per day; 292 days the past year.

Occupations.	Number.		Daily wages.	
	Male.	Fem.	Male.	Fem.
Firemen	7		$0 58	
Firemen	2		30	
Jack-frame tenders		0		$0 29
Jack-frame tenders		44		27
Jack-frame tenders		44		20
Laborers	18		48	
Laborers	25		44	
Laborers	9		39	
Loom fixer	1		48	
Masons	2		53	
Oilers	4		48	
Oilers	9		44	
Oilers' assistants	a4		24	
Openers	12		44	
Overseer (overlooker)	1		1 40	
Overseer (overlooker)	1		67	
Overseer (overlooker)	1		62	
Overseers (overlookers)	2		58	
Overseer (overlooker)	1		48	
Overseers (overlookers)		10		25
Piecers	112		34	
Reelers		260		24
Scutchers	6		41	
Spinners, mule	32		73	
Spinners, other		a44		16
Spoolers		a140		10
Sweepers		7		20
Sweepers		a4		16
Tester	1	1	48	25
Twisters	6	15	67	27
Twisters		64		24
Verifier	1		44	
Waste carriers	4		39	
Watchmen	2		48	
Weigher	1		39	
Weighers	a10		25	
Winders		40		24
Wrappers		5		27

COTTON GOODS (SHEETING), MAINE.—ESTAB. No. **207**.

Time, 11 hours per day; — days the past year.

Occupations.	Male.	Fem.	Male.	Fem.
Apprentices, machinists	6		$1 25	
Back boys	b24		35	
Baler	1		1 33	
Baler	1		90	
Band boys	b2		40	
Beamers	2		90	
Bell man	2		1 53	
Blacksmith	1		1 75	
Bobbin boys	a4		90	
Bobbin boys	b2		45	
Card grinder	4		1 50	
Card grinders	4		1 23	
Card strippers	a12		80	
Carpenters	5		2 00	
Carpenters	1		1 75	
Casting man	1		1 15	
Color mixer	1		1 50	
Doffers	a10	a14	50	$0 55
Doffers		a28		42
Doubler boys	a2		70	
Drawers		15		85
Drawers		a3		65
Drawers		a8		60

a Youth.   *b* Children.

338 REPORT OF THE COMMISSIONER OF LABOR.

OCCUPATIONS, WITH NUMBER AND WAGES OF EMPLOYÉS, BY INDUSTRIES—Cont'd.

NOTE.—This table is *not* a complete exhibit for industries or states, but covers only establishments investigated by the Bureau. See page 91, also summaries, pages 143 to 226.

COTTON GOODS (SHEETING), MAINE.—ESTAB. No. **207**—Concluded.
Time, 11 hours per day; — days the past year.

Occupations.	Number.		Daily wages.	
	Male.	Fem.	Male.	Fem.
Drawers-in		3		$1 32
Drawers-in		3		90
Dyer	1		$1 80	
Elevator tenders	4		1 00	
Finishers	2		1 10	
Finishers	a2		90	
Folder	1		1 10	
Fly-frame tenders		34		1 00
Gas maker	1		1 50	
Harness repairers	1	2	2 50	80
Inspectors		11		75
Laborers	10		1 40	
Machinists	11		1 75	
Mason	1		1 75	
Oilers	4		1 37	
Oilers	5		1 00	
Oilers	a4		80	
Oilers	a2		60	
Openers	9		90	
Packer	1		1 00	
Painters	2		1 60	
Pattern maker	1		1 75	
Pickers	a15		85	
Piper	1		1 75	
Railway hands		a2		70
Reeler	a1		72	
Rovers	a8	11	65	1 20
Rovers	a2		45	
Scrubbers		6		50
Scrubbers		5		40
Second hand	1		2 25	
Second hands	8		1 15	
Second hands	8		1 60	
Second hands	4		1 33	
Section hands	11		1 75	
Section hands	16		1 50	
Section hands	11		1 00	
Sewing-machine operators		6		1 00
Shafting man	1		1 10	
Sizer	a1		85	
Slashers	4		1 40	
Slubbers		12		1 00
Spare hand	1		1 25	
Spare hand	1		90	
Spare hands	a2		65	
Spare hands	b2		40	
Speeders		9		98
Spinners, mule	23		1 44	
Spinners, other		25		75
Spinners, other		a72		50
Spoolers		54		70
Spool carrier	a1		42	
Stamper	1		1 10	
Sweepers	a12		40	
Teamsters	2		1 50	
Trimmers	a4		80	
Twisters	a5		85	
Undesignated	2		1 75	
Undesignated	1		1 15	
Undesignated	1		90	
Undesignated	a4		55	
Undesignated	a10		50	
Warpers	5	6	99	80
Waste hand	1		1 25	
Waste hand	1		90	
Waste hands	a2	a1	50	50
Watchman	5		1 35	
Weavers	34	50	1 16	1 11
Weavers	60	60	1 06	1 06
Weavers	45	32	1 00	1 00
Winders	2		72	

COTTON GOODS (SHEETING, SHIRTING, ETC.), MAINE.—ESTAB. No. **208**.
Time, 11 hours per day; — days the past year.

Occupations.	Number.		Daily wages.	
	Male.	Fem.	Male.	Fem.
Back boys	a44		$0 40	
Blacksmiths	2		1 79	
Blacksmith's helper	1		1 20	
Bobbin boy	a1		42	
Brush boys	a3		37	
Carpenter	1		2 25	
Carpenters	7		1 68	
Card clothiers	3		91	
Card grinders	12		1 33	
Card strippers	20		85	
Cleaners	b10		30	
Cloth-room hands	2		1 00	
Cloth-room hands	2		95	
Doffers	a2		72	
Doffers	a2		63	
Doffers	a2		46	
Doffers	b36		40	
Doublers	a2	54	80	$0 40
Drawers	4	36	92	90
Elevator tenders	4		1 05	
Filling hands	a3		80	
Firemen	2		1 15	
Foremen	2		2 75	
Harness repairers	5		1 00	
Inspector		1		1 00
Inspectors		32		68
Laborers	2		1 55	
Laborers	22		1 05	
Lappers	a2		75	
Machinist	1		2 25	
Machinists	9		1 87	
Machinists' apprentices	2		90	
Oilers	15		90	
Oilers	b6		30	
Overseers	5		4 50	
Overseers	5		3 00	
Painters	3		1 77	
Pickers	2		1 25	
Pickers	11		85	
Piecers-in		5		65
Piper	1		1 58	
Pressmen	3		1 08	
Rovers	a2		80	
Rovers	a5		50	
Rovers	b12		35	
Scrubbers	3	4	70	65
Scrubber	a1		55	
Second hand	1		2 10	
Second hands	2		1 90	
Second hand	3		1 87	
Section hands	24		1 60	
Section hands	11		1 38	
Slashers	5		1 50	
Slashers' helpers	a2		75	
Slubbers & spoolers	13		1 00	
Spinners, mule	28		1 50	
Spinners, other		31		85
Spinners, other		a96		50
Spinners, other		14		63
Spoolers		44		70
Stampers	3		1 08	
Sweepers	b1	a6	60	46
Sweepers	b8		25	
Teamsters	2		1 12	
Undesignated	2		75	
Undesignated	b1		40	
Warpers		10		87
Watchman	4		1 25	
Weavers	117	225	90	89
Weigher	1		1 37	
Winders	a3		55	

a Youth.   *b* Children.

OCCUPATIONS AND WAGES.

OCCUPATIONS, WITH NUMBER AND WAGES OF EMPLOYÉS, BY INDUSTRIES—Cont'd.

NOTE.—This table is *not* a complete exhibit for industries or states, but covers only establishments investigated by the Bureau. See page 91, also summaries, pages 143 to 226.

COTTON GOODS (GINGHAM), MAINE.—ESTAB. No. **209.**
Time, 11 hours per day; 308 days the past year.

COTTON GOODS (GINGHAM), MAINE.—ESTAB. No. **209**—Concluded.
Time, 11 hours per day; 308 days the past year.

Occupations.	Number.		Daily wages.		Occupations.	Number.		Daily wages.	
	Male.	Fem.	Male.	Male.		Male.	Fem.	Male.	Male.
Back boys	a11		$0 85		Rovers	b4		$0 48	
Balers	b9		67		Scrubbers	b3	b15	44	$0 44
Band boy	b1		60		Second hand	1		2 75	
Beamers	17		2 24		Second hands	2	57	2 10	95
Beamers	3	5	1 48	$1 48	Second hands	13		1 92	
Belt maker	1		2 50		Second hands	3		1 45	
Blacksmith	1		2 18		Section hands	17		1 80	
Blacksmith's helper	1		1 10		Section hands	10		1 63	
Bobbin boys	b7		62		Sewing-machine operators	1		1 19	
Bobbin boys	b3		90		Shearer	1		1 58	
Bolt cutter	1		1 28		Slasher	1		1 58	
Card clothier	1		1 56		Slashers	3		1 40	
Card fixer	1		1 09		Slasher's helper	1		85	
Card fixer	b1		80		Slubbers		2		97
Card grinders	8		1 37		Slubbers		2		87
Card strippers	b15		80		Slubbers		3		80
Calenderer	1		1 19		Slubbers	b2		43	
Carpenters	7		1 80		Spare hands	1	2	1 16	1 16
Cleaners	a10		45		Spare hands	b21		80	
Cleaners	a11		33		Spare hands	b1		53	
Cloth room hand		1		83	Spare hands	a3		37	
Cloth room hand		1		95	Spinners, mule	7		1 60	
Cloth room hands		2		75	Spinner, mule	1		1 50	
Doffer	b1		80		Spinners, other	b8	16	73	73
Doffers	b3		73		Spoolers		9		84
Doffer	b1	b29	54	45	Spoolers		25		71
Doffers	a9	a2	39	36	Sweeper	b1		60	
Doubler boys	b4		62		Sweepers	a23		30	
Drawers	b3	b8	42	55	Teamsters	4		1 18	
Drawers	7		91		Ticketer	1		2 50	
Dyers	25		1 50		Ticketers	b2	1	81	99
Dyers	11		90		Tool maker	1		1 80	
Elevator tender	1		1 05		Twisters	2		1 50	
Filling hand	1		1 53		Twister		1		1 70
Filling hands	2		95		Twister		1		1 42
Filling hands	b10		70		Twisters	1	1	1 26	1 42
Finisher	1		1 66		Warper	1		1 08	
Firemen	2		1 61		Warpers	8		1 13	
Folders	2		1 58		Waste hand	1		1 12	
Gas maker	1		1 36		Waste hand		b1		44
Gate tender	1		75		Watchmen	6		1 36	
Harness repairer		1		73	Weavers	385	73	1 18	1 38
Inspectors		10		90	Weavers	90	25	1 11	1 20
Laborers	2		1 58		Weavers		103		1 17
Laborers	13		1 35		Winders	52		1 15	
Laborers	13		1 05		Yarn sorter	1		95	
Laborers	59		90						
Machinist	1		2 03						
Mason	1		1 13						
Oiler	1		1 05						
Oilers	7		95						
Oiler	b1		64						

COTTON GOODS (SHEETING, DRILLING), MARYLAND.—ESTAB. No. **210.**
Time, 11 hours per day; 300 days the past year.

Occupations.	Number.		Daily wages.	
	Male.	Fem.	Male.	Male.
Overseer	1		6 44	
Overseer	1		4 75	
Overseers	4		3 15	
Overseer	1		2 75		Beamers	2		$1 25	
Overseer	1		2 37		Bobbin boys	b6		40	
Overseer	1		2 00		Carders	3		80	
Painter	1		2 03		Card grinders	4		1 50	
Painter	1		1 58		Doffers	b4		50	
Pattern maker	1		2 03		Doffers	a6	a10	30	$0 30
Picker	1		1 58		Drawers		5		75
Picker	1		1 19		Engineer	1		1 50	
Pickers	12		80		Filling hands	b4		50	
Piper	1		2 03		Laborers	6		1 25	
Piper's helper	1		1 80		Loom fixers	6		1 25	
Presser	1		1 58		Overseers	3		2 25	
Quillers	b23		67		Packers	6		1 25	
Railway hands	b2		64		Pickers	6		1 10	
Railway hands	b2		52		Railway hands	b4		60	
Reelers	5		2 21		Repair hands	6		1 75	

a Children.   *b* Youth.

OCCUPATIONS, WITH NUMBER AND WAGES OF EMPLOYES, BY INDUSTRIES—Cont'd.

NOTE.—This table is not a complete exhibit for industries or states, but covers only establishments investigated by the Bureau. See page 91, also summaries, pages 143 to 226.

COTTON GOODS (SHEETING, DRILLING), MARYLAND.—ESTAB. No. 210—Concluded.

Time, 11 hours per day; 300 days the past year.

Occupations.	Number.		Daily wages.	
	Male.	Fem.	Male.	Fem.
Rover	a1		$0 75	
Second hands	3		1 75	
Slubbers		6		$0 75
Speeders		8		75
Speelers	a2		60	
Spinners		40		67
Spoolers		12		75
Sweepers	b0		28	
Twisters	a7		50	
Undesignated	b4		35	
Undesignated		b15		35
Warpers	15		1 30	
Weavers		85		80

COTTON GOODS (SHEETING, DRILLING), MARYLAND.—ESTAB. No. 211.

Time, 11 hours per day; — days the past year.

Occupations.	Number.		Daily wages.	
	Male.	Fem.	Male.	Fem.
Blacksmith	1		$1 50	
Carders	15	15	70	$0 70
Carpenter	1		1 60	
Dressers		10		80
Engineer	1		1 75	
Folder	a1		1 00	
Loom fixers	2		1 75	
Machinist	1		2 13	
Overseers	3		2 25	
Packer	1		2 25	
Packers	a2		60	
Spinners		55		70
Watchman	1		1 50	
Watchman	1		1 25	
Weavers		60		84

COTTON GOODS (DUCK), MARYLAND.—ESTAB. No. 212.

Time, 11 hours per day; 300 days the past year.

Occupations.	Number.		Daily wages.	
	Male.	Fem.	Male.	Fem.
Carders	18	17	$0 70	$0 70
Card boys	a9		45	
Dressers	3	12	80	80
Engineer	1		1 75	
Fireman	1		1 25	
Laborers	19		1 00	
Packers	6		1 50	
Repair hands	5		1 05	
Spinners		41		70
Spinners	a12	a20	45	45
Undesignated	a2		45	
Watchmen	2		1 25	
Weavers	14	48	84	84

COTTON GOODS (DUCK), MARYLAND.—ESTAB. No. 213.

Time, 11 hours per day; 305 days the past year.

Occupations.	Number.		Daily wages.	
	Male.	Fem.	Male.	Fem.
Beamers	12		$0 71	
Card boys	a11		66	
Card grinders	6		1 54	
Doffers	b12	b23	42	$0 40
Drawers		8		71
Filling hands	b19		45	
Loom fixers	6		1 75	

COTTON GOODS (DUCK), MARYLAND.—ESTAB. No. 213—Concluded.

Time, 10 hours per day; 208 days the past year.

Occupations.	Number.		Daily wages.	
	Male.	Fem.	Male.	Fem.
Oilers	a10		$0 50	
Overseers	6		2 25	
Overseers	3		1 75	
Packers	7		1 47	
Pickers	11		1 27	
Railway hands	a2		77	
Slubbers		12		$0 79
Spare hands	a9		54	
Speeders		20		84
Spinners		20		79
Spoolers		6		79
Spoolers		38		75
Sweepers	b5	b6	33	30
Twisters	a4	28	75	85
Undesignated	13		2 10	
Undesignated	12		1 64	
Undesignated	a6	a14	64	42
Weavers		86		92

COTTON GOODS (SHEETING), MASSACHUSETTS.—ESTAB. No. 214.

Time, 10 hours per day; 308 days the past year.

Occupations.	Number.		Daily wages.	
	Male.	Fem.	Male.	Fem.
Back boys	a35		$0 58	
Belt maker	1		2 12	
Brush boys	a8		45	
Card clothier	1		1 90	
Card grinders	15		1 84	
Card strippers	29		91	
Cleaners		a12		$0 40
Cloth-room hands	11		1 29	
Doffers		a26		50
Drawers		12		61
Drawers-in		19		80
Elevator tenders	2		1 20	
Filling hands	11		1 14	
Foremen	2		1 47	
Laborers	8		1 00	
Lappers	2		1 18	
Oiler	1		1 20	
Oilers	4		1 03	
Overseers	5		4 00	
Pickers	2		59	
Railway hands		a7		50
Repair hands	27		1 75	
Rovers	a5		78	
Rovers	a5		66	
Scrubbers		16		55
Second hands	13		1 98	
Section hands	2		1 70	
Section hands	25		1 45	
Section hands	3		1 05	
Sizer	1		1 20	
Slashers	6		1 38	
Slashers	2		1 05	
Slubbers		18		55
Spare hands		7		1 01
Speeders		39		84
Spinners, mule	33		1 27	
Spinners, other		58		67
Spoolers	3	62	96	72
Tie-overs		4		87
Undesignated		16		69
Warpers		8		92
Watchmen	6		1 50	
Weavers		382		83

a Youth. b Children.

OCCUPATIONS AND WAGES.

OCCUPATIONS, WITH NUMBER AND WAGES OF EMPLOYÉS, BY INDUSTRIES—Cont'd.

NOTE.—This table is not a complete exhibit for industries or states, but covers only establishments investigated by the Bureau. See page 91, also summaries, pages 143 to 226.

COTTON GOODS (SHEETING), MASSACHUSETTS.—ESTAB. No. 215.

Time, 10 hours per day; 302 days the past year.

Occupations.	Number.		Daily wages.	
	Male.	Fem.	Male.	Fem.
Card grinders	4		$1 00	
Card strippers	6		75	
Carpenters	5		1 25	
Doffers	a10		60	
Drawers-in		16		$0 67
Dressers	2		1 75	
Engineers	3		1 17	
Firemen	4		1 00	
Laborers	20		93	
Machinists	10		1 25	
Overseers	4		3 00	
Painters	4		1 25	
Rovers	a25		40	
Second hands	4		1 25	
Slubbers		5		84
Speeders		27		67
Spinners, mule	20		1 00	
Spinners, other	a50	a44	43	43
Spoolers		b34		42
Trimmers		4		67
Warpers		5		72
Weavers	13	49	1 42	1 17
Weavers	44	4	1 17	92
Weavers	14		92	
Watchmen	6		1 00	

COTTON GOODS (SHEETING), MASSACHUSETTS.—ESTAB. No. 216.

Time, 10 hours per day; 305 days the past year.

Occupations.	Male	Fem	Male	Fem
Back boys	b8		$0 38	
Card boys	b2		38	
Card grinders	2		1 25	
Card strippers	2		1 00	
Carpenters	5		1 67	
Doffers	a8	b2	70	$0 38
Drawers-in		6		83
Engineer	1		1 59	
Laborers	14		1 25	
Laborers	2		90	
Laborers	4		83	
Loom fixers	4		1 50	
Machinists	3		1 50	
Masons	2		1 50	
Overseer	1		3 00	
Overseers	3		2 75	
Overseer	1		1 50	
Painters	3		1 25	
Pickers	2		1 00	
Railway hands	a2		63	
Second hand	1		1 50	
Second hand	1		1 29	
Second hands	2		95	
Slasher	1		1 50	
Spare hands		6		1 00
Speeders	2	16		95
Spinners, mule	7		1 42	
Spinners, other	b3	a5	45	45
Spinners, other	a4	a5	50	50
Spoolers		b1		50
Sweeper				
Sweepers	b2		29	
Undesignated	a6		63	
Warpers		2		83
Warper		1		74
Watchmen	4		1 00	
Weavers	3		1 50	
Weavers	11	1	1 44	1 46
Weavers	29	24	1 25	1 25
Weavers	1	4	1 04	1 04
Weavers	4	4	84	84

COTTON GOODS (SHEETING), MASSACHUSETTS.—ESTAB. No. 217.

Time, 10 hours per day; 301 days the past year.

Occupations.	Male.	Fem.	Male.	Fem.
Blacksmith	1		$1 50	
Card grinders	2		1 00	
Card strippers	3		1 00	
Carpenter	1		2 50	
Carpenters	1		1 50	
Carpenters	2		1 29	
Doffers	a5	a2	59	$0 50
Drawers	a7		60	
Engineer	1		2 77	
Fireman	1		1 50	
Laborers	12		1 25	
Laborers	4		1 00	
Loom fixers	4		1 75	
Machinist	1		2 50	
Machinists	2		1 50	
Overseers	3		3 00	
Rovers	a7		60	
Second hand	1		1 58	
Second hands	2		1 50	
Section hands	6		75	
Speeders		13		1 00
Spinners, mule	10		1 25	
Spinners, other		26		70
Warpers	2		1 00	
Watchman	1		1 63	
Weavers	4		1 39	
Weavers	18	2	1 21	1 20
Weavers	31	18	1 06	1 06
Weavers	1	1	87	87
Weavers	8	7	69	69

COTTON GOODS (SHEETING), MASSACHUSETTS.—ESTAB. No. 218.

Time, 10 hours per day; 307 days the past year.

	Male	Fem	Male	Fem
Card grinders	4		$0 90	
Card strippers	2	3	1 17	$0 75
Carpenters	5		1 50	
Doffers	a9		45	
Engineer	1		2 00	
Fireman	1		1 84	
Laborers	9		80	
Loom fixers	5		1 08	
Overseers	2		3 25	
Overseers	3		3 00	
Painters	2		1 25	
Second hands	5		1 50	
Spare hands	6		82	
Speeders		14		92
Spinners, mule	6		1 29	
Spinners, other	a21	a30	50	50
Weavers	10	12	1 54	1 50
Weavers	25	10	1 34	1 25
Weavers	13	18	1 17	1 08

COTTON GOODS (PRINT CLOTH), MASSACHUSETTS.—ESTAB. No. 219.

Time, 10 hours per day; 308 days the past year.

	Male	Fem	Male	Fem
Back boys	a22		$0 44	
Band boys	a3		67	
Beam fixer	1		1 90	
Card boys	a3		75	
Card boys	a7		40	
Card grinders	7		1 42	
Card strippers	7		95	
Chainer	a1		60	
Cleaners	a2	a3	75	$0 45
Doffers	a6	a25	89	73
Drawers		9		1 17½

a Youth.   *b* Children.

OCCUPATIONS, WITH NUMBER AND WAGES OF EMPLOYÉS, BY INDUSTRIES—Cont'd.

NOTE.—This table is not a complete exhibit for industries or states, but covers only establishments investigated by the Bureau. See page 91, also summaries, pages 143 to 226.

COTTON GOODS (PRINT CLOTH), MASSACHUSETTS.—ESTAB. No. 219—Concluded.

Time, 10 hours per day; 308 days the past year.

Occupations.	Number.		Daily wages.	
	Male.	Fem.	Male.	Fem.
Drawers		a3		$0 65
Filling hands	2		$1 25	
Folders	2		82	
Harness brusher	1		75	
Harness repairers		4		83
Inspectors	1	4	1 00	1 00
Laborers	4		1 18	
Laborer	1		69	
Lapper	1		95	
Machinist	1		2 15	
Oiler	1		1 35	
Oilers	6		1 00	
Oiler	1		80	
Oilers	a3		50	
Overseers	3		6 00	
Overseer	1		5 00	
Overseer	1		2 50	
Overseer	1		1 45	
Pickers	5		1 06	
Quillers	2		90	
Railway hands	a3		65	
Reed fixer	1		1 25	
Repair hand	1		1 85	
Repair hand	1		1 50	
Rovers	a2		70	
Rovers	a2		50	
Scrubbers	a1	a1	75	75
Scrubbers		a2		70
Second hand	1		4 00	
Second hand	1		2 05	
Second hand	1		2 48	
Second hands	3		2 00	
Section hands	5		2 20	
Section hands	22		1 91	
Section hands	1	4	1 60	1 16
Section hands	3		1 45	
Shafter	1		1 45	
Slashers	6		1 66	
Slashers' helpers	2		1 20	
Slubber	1		1 21	
Spoolers		8		91
Spinners, mule	27		1 51	
Spinners, other		18		1 00
Spinners, other		41		83
Spoolers		42		80
Sweepers and scrubbers	a3		47	
Sweepers	a4		70	
Teamsters	4		1 10	
Trimmer		1		85
Twister	1		1 80	
Twisters	1	3	1 24	78
Undesignated	a2		70	
Warpers	2	8	1 13	1 13
Warpers	5		85	
Waste hand	1		1 08	
Weavers	3	1 23	1 08	1 09
Weavers		99		1 00
Weavers		1 59		91
Weavers	a13	8	76	85
Weigher	1		1 10	

COTTON GOODS (PRINT CLOTH), MASSACHUSETTS.—ESTAB. No. 220.

Time, 10 hours per day; — days the past year.

Occupations.	Number.		Daily wages.	
	Male.	Fem.	Male.	Fem.
Carders	21	a50	$1 17	$0 75
Cloth-room hands	1	7	1 67	79
Drawers and dressers	9	8	1 33	92

COTTON GOODS (PRINT CLOTH), MASSACHUSETTS.—ESTAB. No. 220—Concluded.

Time, 10 hours per day; — days the past year.

Occupations.	Number.		Daily wages.	
	Male.	Fem.	Male.	Fem.
Overseers	15		$1 25	
Scrubbers		2		$0 62
Spinners, mule	60		95	
Spinners, other	a16	15	48	76
Spoolers and warpers		a33		70
Undesignated	20		1 81	
Weavers	66	97	93	93

COTTON GOODS (PRINT CLOTH) MASSACHUSETTS.—ESTAB. No. 221.

Time, 10 hours per day; — days the past year.

Occupations.	Number.		Daily wages.	
	Male.	Fem.	Male.	Fem.
Back boys	a46		$0 35	
Band boy	a1		55	
Bobbin boy	a1		72	
Card grinders	8		1 25	
Card strippers	9	3	95	$0 95
Cleaners	b5		35	
Doffers	a18		60	
Doffers		a11		50
Doublers		2		87
Drawers		17		75
Drawers	a6	2	75	75
Elevator tender	1		1 00	
Elevator tenders	2		82	
Filling hands	a3		75	
Fly-frame tenders	7	18	1 07	1 00
Oiler	1		1 25	
Oilers	3		90	
Overseers	3		3 25	
Overseers	4		1 75	
Pickers	3		85	
Rovers	a1		80	
Scrubbers		5		80
Scrubbers		3		55
Second hands	3		1 65	
Second hands	6		1 60	
Second hands	2		1 50	
Second hands	2		1 45	
Section hands	13		1 50	
Section hands	2		1 03	
Sizer	1		95	
Slashers	6		1 45	
Slubbers		8		1 12
Spare hands	2		1 12	
Spoolers		17		87
Spinners, mule	42		1 65	
Spinners, other		24		80
Spinners, other		a7		45
Spoolers		30		70
Spoolers		23		55
Sweepers		b4		22
Tubers	a10		23	
Undesignated		6		75
Warpers	6	4	1 13	1 06
Weavers		3 50		95
Yarn hand	1		95	

COTTON GOODS (CALICO), MASSACHUSETTS.—ESTAB. No. 222.

Time, 10 hours per day; 266 days the past year.

Occupations.	Number.		Daily wages.	
	Male.	Fem.	Male.	Fem.
Back tenders	a11		$1 20	
Back tenders	a7		1 02	
Back tenders	a5		72	
Back tenders	b8		45	

a Youth.   *b* Children.

OCCUPATIONS AND WAGES.

OCCUPATIONS, WITH NUMBER AND WAGES OF EMPLOYÉS, BY INDUSTRIES—Cont'd.

NOTE.—This table is *not* a complete exhibit for industries or states, but covers only establishments investigated by the Bureau. See page 91, also summaries, pages 143 to 226.

COTTON GOODS (CALICO), MASSACHUSETTS.—ESTAB. No. 222—Continued.

Time, 10 hours per day; 266 days the past year.

Occupations.	Number.		Daily wages.	
	Male.	Fem.	Male.	Fem.
Back boys	a25		$0 37	
Beamers		8		$1 00
Belt fixers	3		1 71	
Blacksmiths	2		2 06	
Blacksmith	1		2 00	
Bleachers	5		1 00	
Bleachers	b8		63	
Bobbin boys	b4		75	
Card grinders	10		1 25	
Carpenters	2		1 96	
Carpenters	14		1 54	
Color mixer	1		3 00	
Color hands	16		1 05	
Doffers	b11	b70	60	60
Drawers	b12	b18	52	52
Dyers	7		1 25	
Dyers	16		1 17	
Dyers	20		1 00	
Dyers	b10		52	
Engineer	1		3 75	
Engineers	2		1 90	
Engravers	8		4 00	
Filling hands	7		92	
Fireman	1		1 65	
Firemen	11		1 33	
Folders	2		90	
Folders	b2		62	
Folders and packers	7		1 65	
Folders and packers	7		1 25	
Folders and packers	26		1 00	
Harness brushers		13		63
Inspectors		7		08
Laborers	10		1 25	
Laborers	20		95	
Machinists	10		1 57	
Machinists	7		1 47	
Machinists	6		1 37	
Machinists' helpers	b7		1 08	
Machinists' helpers	b2		82	
Mason	1		2 17	
Mason's helper	1		1 15	
Nappers	6		1 05	
Overseer	1		5 50	
Overseer	1		5 33	
Overseers	7		3 75	
Overseer	1		3 50	
Overseers	2		3 33	
Overseers	3		3 00	
Oilers	53		90	
Oilers	b15		50	
Packers	b2		72	
Painter	1		2 00	
Painters	7		1 42	
Pantographers	1	8	1 47	1 00
Printers	8		4 83	
Printer	1		1 90	
Reelers		2		75
Rovers	b2		80	
Scrubbers		10		60
Second hands	2		2 00	
Second hands	12		1 80	
Second hands	3		1 60	
Second hands	17		1 50	
Section hands	21		1 46	
Section hands	6		1 30	
Section hands	14		1 10	
Selectors and stampers	4		1 20	
Shearers	b6		54	
Sketch makers	3		5 00	
Sketch maker	1		2 50	

COTTON GOODS (CALICO), MASSACHUSETTS.—ESTAB. No. 222—Concluded.

Time, 10 hours per day; 266 days the past year.

Occupations.	Number.		Daily wages.	
	Male.	Fem.	Male.	Fem.
Slashers	11		$1 35	
Slashers' helpers	10		1 05	
Spare hands	b14		60	
Spoolers		32		$0 68
Spinners, mule	48		1 37	
Spinners, other		125		71
Spoolers		67		71
Steamer and starcher	1		2 00	
Steamers and starchers	3		1 27	
Steamers and starchers	23		1 00	
Steamers and starchers	b7		75	
Steamers and starchers	b38		50	
Sweepers		13		60
Teamsters	4		1 10	
Ticketers		12		72
Undesignated	6	72	1 46	83
Warpers		12		79
Watchmen	14		1 46	
Weavers	8	31	1 20	1 02
Weavers		70		96
Weavers		72		89
Weavers	3	300	74	81
Weavers		20		66
Weavers		17		52

COTTON GOODS (CHECK), MASSACHUSETTS.—ESTAB. No. 223.

Time, 10 hours per day; 308 days the past year.

Occupations	Male	Fem	Male	Fem
Carders	15	36	$1 01	$0 75
Cloth-room hands	4	4	1 41	70
Drawers-in	1	14	75	83
Spinners, mule	36		1 03	
Spinners, other	b22	b18	57	53
Spoolers and warpers	6	24	1 18	75
Weavers	70	108	1 16	1 21

COTTON GOODS (THREAD), MASSACHUSETTS.—ESTAB. No. 224.

Time, 10 hours per day; — days the past year.

Occupations	Male	Fem	Male	Fem
Beamer	b1		$0 90	
Boiler tenders	2		2 42	
Boiler tender	1		1 50	
Cardor	1		1 50	
Carders	50		1 37	
Doffers	b17	b10	45	$0 45
Drawers		60		1 00
Drawers		5		67
Dressers	3		2 00	
Dyers and bleachers	10		1 60	
Engineer	1		3 00	
Grinders	9		1 37	
Laborers	4		1 50	
Laborers	15		1 28	
Packers and measurers		b5		54
Painter	1		2 50	
Painter	1		1 75	
Piecers	5		77	
Pickor	1		1 50	
Pickers	5		1 00	

a Children.   *b* Youth.

OCCUPATIONS, WITH NUMBER AND WAGES OF EMPLOYÉS, BY INDUSTRIES—Cont'd.

NOTE.—This table is not a complete exhibit for industries or states, but covers only establishments investigated by the Bureau. See page 91, also summaries, pages 143 to 226.

COTTON GOODS (THREAD), MASSACHUSETTS.—ESTAB. No. 224—Concluded.

Time, 10 hours per day; — days the past year.

Occupations.	Number.		Daily wages.	
	Male.	Fem.	Male.	Fem.
Repair hands	16		$2 50	
Scrubbers and sweepers		20		$0 60
Second hands	12		2 25	
Section hands	13		1 16	
Spinners, mule	15		1 40	
Spinners, other		82		95
Spoolers		11		1 00
Spoolers		26		75
Spoolers		49		54
Spool turners	4		2 25	
Teamsters	2		1 50	
Third hands	5		1 50	
Ticket cutters	2		1 25	
Ticketers		1		60
Twisters		7		1 05
Twisters		47		90
Warpers		4		1 50
Watchmen	3		1 50	
Weavers		28		1 10
Winders		25		1 25
Winders		3		1 15

COTTON GOODS (THREAD), MASSACHUSETTS.—ESTAB. No. 225.

Time, 10 hours per day; — days the past year.

Occupations.	Male.	Fem.	Male.	Fem.
Dressers	4		$1 88	
Engineer	1		2 00	
Inspector	1		1 00	
Machinist	1		1 25	
Overseer	1		3 00	
Overseers	2		2 50	
Overseer	1		1 25	
Packer	a1		75	
Spoolers		10		$1 00
Undesignated	a1	a5	75	50
Winders		16		1 00
Wrapper	1		1 00	

COTTON GOODS (SHEETING), NEW HAMPSHIRE.—ESTAB. No. 226.

Time, 10¼ hours per day; 309 days the past year.

Occupations.	Male.	Fem.	Male.	Fem.
Bleachers	5		$1 50	
Carders	47	117	96	$0 87
Cloth-room hands	35	39	1 73	1 08
Dressers	25	93	96	93
Harness repairers	5		82	
Laborers	30		1 30	
Spinners	a95	118	95	72
Spinners	a102	a185	69	69
Spoolers		53		75
Twisters		a53		66
Weavers	127	52	86	93
Weavers		158		87

COTTON GOODS (PRINT CLOTH), NEW HAMPSHIRE.—ESTAB. No. 227.

Time, 10¼ hours per day; 308 days the past year.

Occupations.	Male.	Fem.	Male.	Fem.
Band boys	a2		$0 57	
Band boys	b2		40	
Back boys	b29		39	
Card boys	a4		50	
Card clothier	1		1 50	
Card grinders	13		1 37	
Card strippers	11		90	

COTTON GOODS (PRINT CLOTH), NEW HAMPSHIRE.—ESTAB. No. 227—Concluded.

Time, 10¼ hours per day; 308 days the past year.

Occupations.	Number.		Daily wages.	
	Male.	Fem.	Male.	Fem.
Doffers	a9	a8	$0 80	
Doffers	a3		65	$0 75
Doffers	a2	a21	50	50
Drawers	1	4	1 17	1 00
Drawers	a2	6	62	62
Elevator tenders	2		1 00	
Elevator tenders	a2		75	
Elevator tenders	a2		50	
Filling hand	a1		42	
Fly-frame tenders		40		1 16
Fly-frame tenders		2		1 00
Inspectors	1		83	
Intermediates		5		87
Intermediates		6		70
Laborer	1		83	
Laborer	a1		67	
Lappers	3		96	
Lapper	1		65	
Oilers	5		1 00	
Oilers	3		85	
Overseers	15		4 00	
Overseers	2		3 00	
Pickers	2		1 12	
Pickers	4		96	
Pickers	7		87	
Railway hand	a1		62	
Rovers	6	2	96	96
Rovers	4		80	
Rovers	4		75	
Scrubbers		4		1 00
Scrubbers		a10		45
Second hands	14		2 00	
Second hands	2		1 75	
Second hands	4		1 50	
Section band	1		2 00	
Section hands	10		1 50	
Section hands	2		1 15	
Slashers	7		1 60	
Slubbers	2	3	96	87
Spare hand	1		1 25	
Spare hands	5	1	1 00	96
Spare hand	1		87	
Spoolers	8		1 00	
Spinners, mule	16		1 62	
Spinners, mule	16		1 25	
Spinners, other		30		92
Spinners, other	a12	36	70	73
Spoolers		20		67
Spoolers		43		54
Sweepers	a2		50	
Sweepers		a7		45
Undesignated	2		1 08	
Undesignated	6	10	91	71
Undesignated	1		83	
Warpers		10		1 17
Warpers		3		87
Waste hands	a4	a8	45	45
Weavers		418		95
Weavers	47	63	93	91
Yarn carrier		1		50

COTTON GOODS (CALICO), NEW HAMPSHIRE.—ESTAB. No. 228.

Time, 10¼ hours per day; 309 days the past year.

Occupations.	Male.	Fem.	Male.	Fem.
Carders		76		$0 94
Overseers	19		$4 39	
Second hands	31		2 12	
Spinners	a45	143	62	74
Weavers	67	704	1 55	1 65

a Youth.   *b* Children.

OCCUPATIONS AND WAGES.

OCCUPATIONS, WITH NUMBER AND WAGES OF EMPLOYÉS, BY INDUSTRIES—Cont'd.

NOTE.—This table is *not* a complete exhibit for industries or states, but covers only establishments investigated by the Bureau. See page 91, also summaries, pages 142 to 226.

COTTON GOODS (SHEETING), NEW JERSEY.—ESTAB. No. **229**.

Time, 10 hours per day; 300 days the past year.

Occupations.	Number.		Daily wages.	
	Male.	Fem.	Male.	Fem.
Drawers		8		$0 70
Dressers	2		$1 54	
Engineer	1		2 00	
Fireman	1		1 35	
Loom fixers	6		1 50	
Machinists	3		2 35	
Pickers	3		1 25	
Speeders		20		90
Spinners, mule	14		1 40	
Spinners, other		a30		60
Spoolers and warpers		a20		60
Undesignated	6		1 00	
Weavers		125		85
Weavers		5		65

COTTON GOODS (SHEETING), NEW YORK.—ESTAB. No. **230**.

Time, 11 hours per day; 298 days the past year.

Occupations.	Number.		Daily wages.	
	Male.	Fem.	Male.	Fem.
Back boys	b11		$0 42	
Bobbin boy	a1		55	
Beamers	2		1 25	
Card grinder	1		1 50	
Card grinders	5		1 37	
Card strippers	6		1 31	
Carpenter	1		2 75	
Carpenter	1		1 50	
Doffers	56	a12	45	$0 45
Drawers		6		67
Drawers-in		3		1 00
Engineer	1		2 88	
Fillers	a2		75	
Firemen	3		1 44	
Folders	4		1 25	
Frame spinning tenders	2		1 25	
Harness repairer	1		1 50	
Laborers	6		1 25	
Lappers	a2		67	
Lappers	58		45	
Loom fixers	7		1 75	
Machinist	1		2 75	
Machinist	1		2 00	
Machinists	2		2 25	
Oiler	1		1 50	
Oiler	1		1 00	
Oilers	a2		62	
Overseers	4		3 00	
Overseer	1		1 87	
Picker	1		1 56	
Picker	1		1 00	
Pickers	3		1 12	
Second hands	4		2 00	
Sizer	1		1 00	
Slashers	2		1 87	
Slasher	1		1 37	
Spare hands	2		1 00	
Speeders		5		75
Speeders		12		90
Spinners, mule	8		1 75	
Spinners, other		7		87
Spinners, other		4		75
Spinners, other		5		67
Spoolers		8		70
Trimmers		6		1 00
Twisters	5		1 25	
Undesignated		b7		40
Warpers		8		75

COTTON GOODS (SHEETING), NEW YORK.—ESTAB. No. **230**—Concluded.

Time, 11 hours per day; 298 days the past year.

Occupations.	Number.		Daily wages.	
	Male.	Fem.	Male.	Fem.
Waste hand	1		$1 00	
Watchmen	2		1 38	
Weavers	56	55	1 04	$1 04
Weavers	17	3	1 00	75

COTTON GOODS (SHEETING), NEW YORK.—ESTAB. No. **231**.

Time, 11 hours per day; 305 days the past year.

Occupations.	Number.		Daily wages.	
	Male.	Fem.	Male.	Fem.
Back boys	a9		$0 42	
Carpenter	1		2 50	
Carpenter	1		1 87	
Card boys	a2		67	
Card grinder	1		1 67	
Card grinders	2		1 56	
Card strippers	7		1 25	
Doffers	a2	a10	50	$0 45
Drawers		3		62
Drawers-in		8		90
Engineer	1		2 00	
Fireman	1		1 37	
Firemen	2		1 50	
Inspector		1		1 12
Laborers	2		1 25	
Laborer	1		83	
Loom fixers	3		1 75	
Machinist	1		2 25	
Mule fixer	1		1 67	
Overseers	2		4 50	
Overseers	2		2 12	
Overseer	1		1 50	
Pickers	b7		45	
Piecers		2		75
Rover	b1		42	
Second hand	1		1 33	
Second hands	2		2 00	
Slasher	1		1 87	
Slasher	a1		87	
Sizer		1		1 00
Speeders		2		1 00
Speeders		8		90
Spinners, mule	8		1 67	
Spinners, other		8		75
Spinners, other		2		70
Spinners, other		2		62
Spoolers		a9		62
Teamster	1		1 31	
Trimmers		4		93
Twisters	5		1 12	
Undesignated		b9		45
Warper		1		1 00
Warper		1		83
Watchman	1		1 37	
Waste hand	1		1 25	
Waste pickers		a2		45
Weavers	51	43	1 00	1 00
Weavers	11	12	75	75

COTTON GOODS (SHEETING, SHIRTING), NEW YORK.—ESTAB. No. **232**.

Time, 11 hours per day; 276 days the past year.

Occupations.	Number.		Daily wages.	
	Male.	Fem.	Male.	Fem.
Baler	1		$1 00	
Bobbin boy	b1		37	
Boiler tender	1		1 33	
Brush boy	a1		50	

a Youth.   *b* Children.

346   REPORT OF THE COMMISSIONER OF LABOR.

OCCUPATIONS, WITH NUMBER AND WAGES OF EMPLOYÉS, BY INDUSTRIES—Cont'd.

NOTE.—This table is *not* a complete exhibit for industries or states, but covers only establishments investigated by the Bureau. See page 91, also summaries, pages 143 to 226.

COTTON GOODS (SHEETING, SHIRTING), NEW YORK.—ESTAB. No. 232—Concluded.

Time, 11 hours per day; 276 days the past year.

Occupations.	Number.		Daily wages.	
	Male.	Fem.	Male.	Fem.
Card grinder	1		$1 00	
Card stripper	1		1 00	
Carpenter	1		2 00	
Doffer	a1		75	
Doffers	a1	b7	50	$0 37
Drawers-in	a2		55	
Drawer	a1		65	
Elevator tender	1		1 00	
Engineer	1		2 50	
Feeder	a1		1 00	
Folder	1		1 50	
Foreman	4		2 25	
Intermediates		2		1 00
Lapper	a1		50	
Laborers	4		1 25	
Laborers	3		1 00	
Laborer	1		75	
Machinist	1		2 00	
Rovers	b4	a3	87	75
Second hand	1		1 62	
Second hands	2		1 50	
Second hands	2		1 25	
Slasher	1		1 80	
Slubber	1		1 13	
Spinners, mule	3		1 50	
Spinners, other	3		95	
Spinners, other	a12		75	
Spoolers		6		80
Store room hand	1		1 50	
Twisters	2		1 00	
Undesignated	1		1 00	
Undesignated	a1		60	
Warpers		3		80
Watchman	1		1 35	
Weavers		52		1 12

COTTON GOODS (SHEETING, SHIRTING), NEW YORK.—ESTAB. No. 233.

Time, 11 hours per day ; 300 days the past year.

Occupations.	Male.	Fem.	Male.	Fem.
Back boys	b13		$0 44	
Blacksmith	1		2 25	
Blacksmiths	2		1 75	
Card boys	a3	a3	62	$0 52
Card grinders	5		1 12	
Card strippers	2		94	
Card strippers	5		81	
Carpenter (foreman)	1		2 50	
Carpenters	4		1 87	
Carpenters	3		1 50	
Doffers	b8	b9	33	33
Drawers		6		75
Drawers		b4		45
Dressers	3		1 25	
Dressers	2		1 00	
Engineer	1		2 12	
Firemen	1		1 37	
Foreman	1		3 00	
Inspectors	2		1 56	
Laborers	9		1 12	
Laborers	6		1 00	
Laborers	3		75	
Machinists	8		1 87	
Machinists	1		1 25	
Machinist's helper	1		1 00	
Masons	2		1 87	
Oilers	2		1 00	
Overseers	3		2 50	

COTTON GOODS (SHEETING, SHIRTING), NEW YORK.—ESTAB. No. 233—Concluded.

Time, 11 hours per day; 300 days the past year.

Occupations.	Number.		Daily wages.	
	Male.	Fem.	Male.	Fem.
Overseers	1		$2 25	
Painter	1		2 25	
Painter	1		2 12	
Painter	1		1 87	
Painter	1		1 12	
Picker	1		1 25	
Pickers	a5		60	
Scourers	9		1 00	
Second hands	11		1 56	
Slubbers		7		$0 75
Smash mender	1		1 12	
Spare hands		b1		42
Speeders		8		75
Spinners, mule	13		1 33	
Spinners, other		15		75
Spinners, other		10		55
Spoolers		a12		50
Teamster	1		1 12	
Twisters		a6		50
Undesignated	b5		50	
Undesignated	b8		44	
Watchmen	3		1 25	
Weavers	10	135	86	88

COTTON GOODS (SHEETING, BUNTING), NEW YORK.—ESTAB. No. 234.

Time, 11 hours per day ; 302 days the past year.

Baler	1		$1 25	
Brush boy	a1		1 00	
Carpenter	1		2 00	
Card grinders	2		1 12	
Card strippers	2		1 00	
Doffers	b2	a5	52	$0 42
Doffers	b5		45	
Doffers		b5		33
Drawers		2		60
Drawers-in		3		60
Engineer	1		2 50	
Firemen	2		1 16	
Folder	1		1 25	
Intermediates		3		62
Laborer	1		1 25	
Loom fixers	3		1 25	
Machinist	1		1 65	
Overseer	1		2 18	
Overseers	2		1 75	
Overseer	1		1 62	
Picker	1		1 12	
Picker	1		90	
Second hand	1		1 50	
Second hands	a2		67	
Slasher	1		1 62	
Slubbers		2		60
Spare hands	a2		60	
Speeder		1		75
Speeders		4		65
Spinners	a8	2	70	67
Spinners	a2	a6	62	53
Spinners		b2		40
Spoolers		4		71
Spoolers		4		67
Undesignated		a1		50
Warper	1			83
Warper	1			67
Weavers		45		80

a Youth.   *b* Children.

OCCUPATIONS AND WAGES. 347

OCCUPATIONS, WITH NUMBER AND WAGES OF EMPLOYÉS, BY INDUSTRIES—Cont'd.

NOTE.—This table is *not* a complete exhibit for industries or states, but covers only establishments investigated by the Bureau. See page 91, also summaries, pages 143 to 226.

COTTON GOODS (CALICO), NEW YORK.—ESTAB. No. 235.
Time, 11¼ hours per day; 304 days the past year.

Occupations.	Number.		Daily wages.	
	Male.	Fem.	Male.	Fem.
Back boys	a116		$0 31	
Back tenders	b44	b49	42	$0 42
Bobbin boys	a97		38	
Carders		349		67
Card grinders	12		92	
Card strippers	6		69	
Carpenters	14		1 46	
Designer	1		5 00	
Designer's assistants	2		1 92	
Doffers	b14		40	
Drawers	b21	b18	45	45
Drawers	a119	b119	38	38
Dressers, machine	7		1 68	
Folders	b22		69	
Foremen	2		2 17	
Foremen	14		1 87	
Intermediates	a14	165	35	70
Laborers	75		1 04	
Lappers		b10		50
Loom fixers	13		1 92	
Machinists	12		1 92	
Overseers	24		2 62	
Overseers	7		2 31	
Overseers	5		1 85	
Painters	9		1 83	
Pickers	10		1 00	
Printers	75	88	1 21	1 00
Rovers		b175		50
Second hands	28		1 92	
Second hands	29		1 45	
Sizers	65		48	
Slashers	14		1 21	
Slashers	28		92	
Slashers' helpers	a29		35	
Slashers' helpers		a18		25
Slubbers		b336		55
Slubbers	77		1 00	
Speeders		b214		50
Spinners, mule	116		1 23	
Spinners, other	400		88	
Spinners, other		189		59
Spinners		a1,078		35
Spoolers		b120		56
Sweepers		b8		50
Teamsters	18		1 92	
Undesignated	21		1 04	
Warpers	b88		48	
Watchmen	14		1 15	
Weavers	90	324	1 29	92
Weavers	b110	b60	44	35
Weighers	7		1 89	
Wheelwright	1		2 31	

COTTON GOODS (YARN), NEW YORK.—ESTAB. No. 236.
Time, 11 hours per day; 304 days the past year.

Occupations.	Number.		Daily wages.	
	Male.	Fem.	Male.	Fem.
Box maker	1		$1 25	
Carders	6		1 20	
Card grinders	2		1 50	
Engineer	1		2 00	
Fireman	1		1 67	
Oiler	1		1 25	
Overseers	2		3 00	
Packers	3		1 15	
Pickers	2		1 25	
Rovers	2		1 25	
Second hands	2		1 87	

COTTON GOODS (YARN), NEW YORK.—ESTAB. No. 236—Concluded.
Time, 11 hours per day; 304 days the past year.

Occupations.	Number.		Daily wages.	
	Male.	Fem.	Male.	Fem.
Spare hand	1		$1 25	
Speeders		4		$1 05
Speeders		3		75
Speeders' helpers		a6		32
Spinners, mule	9		1 75	
Sweepers		b2		50
Undesignated		3		1 00
Undesignated		11		70
Undesignated	a26		42	
Waste hand	1		1 25	

COTTON GOODS (SHEETING), NORTH CAROLINA.—ESTAB. No. 237.
Time, 11¼ hours per day; — days the past year.

Occupations.	Number.		Daily wages.	
	Male.	Fem.	Male.	Fem.
Card boys	a2		$0 40	
Card grinder	1		1 00	
Doffers	a8		35	
Drawers	b2		60	
Engineer	1		1 50	
Filling hands	a4		35	
Fireman	1		1 00	
Laborers	2		75	
Loom fixers	3		1 50	
Oilers	b2		50	
Overseers	3		1 75	
Packers	2		75	
Packer	1		1 25	
Picker	1		1 25	
Picker	c1		35	
Second hand	1		75	
Slashers	2		1 00	
Slubbers		2		$0 60
Speeders		9		60
Spinners		b20		45
Spoolers		7		50
Sweepers	a2		35	
Warpers	b3		60	
Watchman	1		75	
Weavers	16	34	75	75

COTTON GOODS (SHEETING), NORTH CAROLINA.—ESTAB. No. 238.
Time, 11¼ hours per day; 262 days the past year.

Occupations.	Number.		Daily wages.	
	Male.	Fem.	Male.	Fem.
Beamer	1		$0 75	
Carders	3		75	
Card grinder	1		75	
Doffers		a10		$0 30
Drawer	b1		50	
Drawers-in	b2		65	
Elevator tender	1		75	
Filling hand	b1		50	
Loom fixers	3		1 00	
Oilers	a2		40	
Overseers	3		2 50	
Packers	2		75	
Packer	c1		40	
Picker	1		75	
Picker	c1		25	
Rover	1		75	
Slasher	1		90	
Slubbers		2		60
Speeders		7		60

a Children.   *b* Youth.   *c* Child.

348　REPORT OF THE COMMISSIONER OF LABOR.

OCCUPATIONS, WITH NUMBER AND WAGES OF EMPLOYÉS, BY INDUSTRIES—Cont'd.

NOTE.—This table is not a complete exhibit for industries or states, but covers only establishments investigated by the Bureau. See pages 91, also summaries, pages 143 to 226.

COTTON GOODS (SHEETING), NORTH CAROLINA.—ESTAB. No. 238—Concluded.

Time, 11¼ hours per day ; 202 days the past year.

Occupations.	Number.		Daily wages.	
	Male.	Fem.	Male.	Fem.
Spinners		a10		$0 45
Spinners		a2		50
Spoolers		3		55
Sweepers	b2	b2	$0 30	30
Warpers		a2		50
Weavers		25		70

COTTON GOODS (PLAID), NORTH CAROLINA.—ESTAB. No. 239.

Time, 11¼ hours per day ; 225 days the past year.

Occupations	Male	Fem	Male	Fem
Beamers	3		$0 75	
Carders	4		80	
Card grinders	2		1 00	
Doffers	b8		40	
Drawers		2		$0 60
Dyers	7		75	
Fireman	1		1 00	
Lappers	2		90	
Lapper	1		60	
Loom fixers	4		1 13	
Overseer	1		3 00	
Overseer	1		1 75	
Overseer	1		1 00	
Packers	2		75	
Pickers	3		90	
Quillers		a14		50
Reelers		16		60
Railway hands	a1	a1	60	60
Second hands	2		75	
Slubbers		6		60
Spare hand		1		60
Speeders		7		60
Spinners		a60		45
Spoolers		10		60
Sweepers	b2		30	
Warpers	a6		60	
Watchman	1		90	
Weavers	40	40	67	67

COTTON GOODS (PLAID), NORTH CAROLINA.—ESTAB. No. 240.

Time, 11¼ hours per day ; 300 days the past year.

Occupations	Male	Fem	Male	Fem
Baler	1		$1 25	
Beamers	2		1 67	
Card grinders	3		1 00	
Carders	4		75	
Carpenter	1		1 50	
Doffers	a10		40	
Doffers	b4		30	
Drawers		2		$0 55
Dyers	3		75	
Fireman	1		75	
Loom fixers	3		1 50	
Machinist	1		2 00	
Oilers	3		75	
Opener	1		75	
Overseers	5		2 00	
Packers	2		1 13	
Packers' helpers	b2		35	
Pickers	2		1 00	
Quillers	b2		35	
Railway hand	a1		50	
Reelers		5		55

COTTON GOODS (PLAID), NORTH CAROLINA.—ESTAB. No. 240—Concluded.

Time, 11¼ hours per day ; 300 days the past year.

Occupations.	Number.		Daily wages.	
	Male.	Fem.	Male.	Fem.
Sizer	1		$0 75	
Slubbers		4		$0 60
Spare hands		2		50
Speeders		8		50
Spinners		a24		50
Spoolers		14		55
Spool carrier	a1		40	
Sweeper	a1		40	
Twisters	a2	a5	60	50
Warpers	5	1	1 00	60
Watchman	1		1 00	
Weavers	18	48	90	90
Winders		10		75

COTTON GOODS (PLAID, TOWELS, AND BAGS), NORTH CAROLINA.—ESTAB. No. 241.

Time, 11¼ hours per day; 306 days the past year.

Occupations	Male	Fem	Male	Fem
Baler	1		$1 00	
Beamer	1		2 50	
Beamers	3		1 00	
Carders	2		80	
Card grinders	1		1 50	
Doffers	b10		30	
Doffers	b2		40	
Drawers		3		$0 50
Drawers-in	4		75	
Dyers	7		75	
Engineers	3		1 00	
Folder	1		1 00	
Loom fixers	2		1 00	
Oilers	a3		50	
Overseers	2		2 50	
Overseers	5		1 50	
Pickers	2		75	
Quillers	b8	a3	40	40
Reelers		5		50
Slubbers		3		60
Speeders		5		60
Spinners		a30		45
Spoolers		5		50
Sweepers	b5		25	
Teamster	1		1 00	
Twisters		a2		40
Warpers	2		1 25	
Watchmen	2		1 00	
Weavers	2		1 00	
Weavers	26	61	75	75
Winders	4		75	

COTTON GOODS (YARN), NORTH CAROLINA.—ESTAB. No. 242.

Time, 11¼ hours per day ; 302 days the past year.

Occupations	Male	Fem	Male	Fem
Baler	1		$0 90	
Baler	a1		40	
Carders	3		75	
Card grinders	2		95	
Doffers	a5	a3	42	$0 42
Drawers		3		60
Engineer	1		2 50	
Fireman	1		1 00	
Loom fixer	1		1 00	
Oilers	a2		45	
Overseers	2		2 50	
Pickers	2		80	

a Youth.　　b Children.

OCCUPATIONS AND WAGES. 349

OCCUPATIONS, WITH NUMBER AND WAGES OF EMPLOYÉS, BY INDUSTRIES—Cont'd.

NOTE.—This table is *not* a complete exhibit for industries or states, but covers only establishments investigated by the Bureau. See page 91, also summaries, pages 143 to 226.

COTTON GOODS (YARN), NORTH CAROLINA.—ESTAB. No. 242—Concluded.

Time, 11½ hours per day; 302 days the past year.

Occupations.	Number.		Daily wages.	
	Male.	Fem.	Male.	Fem.
Railway hands	a1		$0 55	
Reelers		3		$0 60
Second hand	1		85	
Slubbers		2		60
Spare hand		1		60
Speeders		5		60
Spinners		a16		45
Spoolers		11		55
Sweeper	a1		40	
Teamster	1		80	
Twisters		a5		55
Warpers	4		1 00	
Watchman	1		1 00	

COTTON GOODS (GINGHAM), PENNSYLVANIA.—ESTAB. No. 243.

Time, 10 hours per day; 302 days the past year.

Occupations.	Male.	Fem.	Male.	Fem.
Beamers	12		$2 00	
Card boys	a3		78	
Card grinders	2		1 54	
Doffers		a19		$0 50
Drawers		a2		67
Dyers	10		1 67	
Dyer boys	a5		97	
Engineers	2		2 43	
Finishers	a8	2	63	93
Oilers	a3		90	
Overseers	15		2 25	
Packers	2		2 18	
Pickers	2		94	
Reelers		12		90
Repair hand	1		2 17	
Slubbers		2		1 12
Spare hands		a5		75
Speeders		9		1 12
Spinners		28		88
Spoolers		15		90
Sweepers	a2		50	
Undesignated	a4		50	
Warpers	5		1 85	
Watchman	4		1 67	
Weavers	40	134	1 12	1 12
Winders	49		66	

COTTON GOODS (DRILLING), SOUTH CAROLINA.—ESTAB. No. 244.

Time, 11 hours per day; 306 days the past year.

Occupations.	Male.	Fem.	Male.	Fem.
Carders	42		$0 85	
Cloth-room hands	7		1 00	
Dressers and spoolers		44		$0 90
Laborers	15		85	
Repair hands	8		2 00	
Spinners		80		65
Watchmen	5		1 10	
Weavers	91		92	

COTTON GOODS (PRINT CLOTH), VERMONT. ESTAB. No. 245.

Time, 11 hours per day; 290 days the past year.

Occupations.	Number.		Daily wages.	
	Male.	Fem.	Male.	Fem.
Card grinders	2		$1 50	
Card strippers	2		1 00	
Carpenter	1		2 00	
Doffers	a8	a7	42	$0 42
Drawers-in		6		90
Elevator tenders	5		87	
Engineer	1		4 33	
Fireman	1		1 50	
Folder	1		1 10	
Folder	a1		75	
Inspector	1		1 50	
Loom fixers	5		1 50	
Oiler	1		90	
Overseers	5		2 75	
Pickers	4		1 00	
Piecers	a11		75	
Roll coverer	1		1 00	
Rovers and back boys	a20		50	
Slasher	1		1 50	
Slasher	1		90	
Second hands	4		1 50	
Slubbers		6		88
Spare hands		6		82
Speeders	14		82	
Spinners, mule	12		1 20	
Spinners, other		a25		65
Sweepers		a8		42
Teamsters	2		1 25	
Undesignated		4		95
Weavers	65	50	1 00	82

COTTON GOODS (SHEETING), VIRGINIA.—ESTAB. No. 246.

Time, 11 hours per day; 285 days the past year.

Occupations.	Male.	Fem.	Male.	Fem.
Beamers	3		$0 83	
Carders	3		70	
Card grinders	2		97	
Doffers	a11		33	
Drawers		2		$0 50
Engineer	1		1 13	
Filling hands	1		94	
Laborers	8		79	
Machinists	2		1 88	
Overseers	6		1 50	
Packers	5		80	
Pickers	3		80	
Railway hands	1		70	
Second hands	2		1 25	
Slubbers	a4		44	
Speeders	a7		42	
Spinners	a13	a14	44	38
Spoolers		a7		35
Teamsters	2		85	
Undesignated	a2		67	
Undesignated	a3		47	
Warpers		a4		45
Weavers		55		78

a Youth.   *b* Children.

OCCUPATIONS, WITH NUMBER AND WAGES OF EMPLOYÉS, BY INDUSTRIES—Cont'd.

NOTE.—This table is not a complete exhibit for industries or states, but covers only establishments investigated by the Bureau. See page 91, also summaries, pages 143 to 226.

COTTON GOODS (SHEETING), VIRGINIA.—ESTAB. No. 247.

Time, 11 hours per day; 296 days the past year.

Occupations.	Number.		Daily wages.	
	Male.	Fem.	Male.	Fem.
Card boys	a2		$0 70	
Carders	2		90	
Card grinders	2		1 00	
Doffers	b8		40	
Drawers		2		$0 55
Foreman	1		1 12	
Loom fixers	3		1 20	
Machinist	1		2 00	
Overseers	3		2 25	
Overseer	1		1 25	
Overseers	2		1 12	
Packer	1	2	1 60	55
Pickers	2		1 00	
Picker	a1		65	
Railway hands		1		55
Slasher	1		1 70	
Slubbers		3		55
Spare hand	1	2	00	55
Spare hands		a3		45
Speeders		10		55
Spinners		a21		45
Spoolers		5		55
Sweepers	b2		40	
Sweepers	b4		30	
Warpers		2		75
Watchmen	2		1 15	
Weavers		58		75

COTTON GOODS (SHEETING), VIRGINIA.—ESTAB. No. 248.

Time, 11 hours per day; 302 days the past year.

Occupations.	Number.		Daily wages.	
	Male.	Fem.	Male.	Fem.
Carders	2		$0 75	
Card grinders	2		90	
Doffers	b10		40	
Drawer		1		$0 83
Fireman	1		1 00	
Laborers	2		1 21	
Machinist	1		2 00	
Oilers	a3		50	
Overseers	3		2 50	
Packers	2		1 60	
Packers		a2		55
Pickers	2		1 00	
Railway hand	a1		50	
Second hands	3		1 25	
Slubbers		3		63
Speeders		6		63
Spinners		a35		55
Spoolers		a6		55
Sweepers	b2		40	
Warpers		a4		55
Watchman	1		1 25	
Weavers		64		75

COTTON GOODS (PLAID), VIRGINIA.—ESTAB. No. 249.

Time, 11 hours per day; 306 days the past year.

Occupations.	Number.		Daily wages.	
	Male.	Fem.	Male.	Fem.
Baler	1		$1 00	
Card boys	b2		30	
Card grinder	1		1 75	
Doffers	a3		50	
Drawers		3		$0 50
Drawer-in		1		1 10
Drawer-in		1		75

COTTON GOODS (PLAID), VIRGINIA.—ESTAB. No. 249—Concluded.

Time, 10 hours per day; 300 days the past year.

Occupations.	Number.		Daily wages.	
	Male.	Fem.	Male.	Fem.
Dresser	a1		$0 75	
Dresser	a1		50	
Dyers	7		1 00	
Elevator tender	1		83	
Fireman	1		1 10	
Folder	1		1 00	
Inspectors	a2		75	
Loom fixers	2		1 50	
Machinist	1		2 75	
Oiler	a1		1 00	
Overseers	3		2 50	
Overseers	2		2 00	
Overseer	1		1 75	
Overseer	1		1 25	
Packer	a1		75	
Picker	1		1 00	
Picker	b1		30	
Quillers	b4	b6	30	$0 50
Railway hands	a2		75	
Reelers		2		75
Slubber		1		75
Spare hands	a2	a2	60	60
Speeders		3		75
Spinners	a4	a5	50	50
Spoolers		12		67
Undesignated	b1		30	
Warpers		3		90
Waste hand	1		1 00	
Watchman	1		1 00	
Weavers	25	24	1 10	1 10

ENGRAVING AND PRINTING, NEW JERSEY.—ESTAB. No. 250.

Time, 11 hours per day; 308 days the past year.

Occupations.	Number.		Daily wages.	
	Male.	Fem.	Male.	Fem.
Artists	6		$4 87	
Carpenters	2		2 78	
Cutters	10		2 72	
Electrotypers	6		2 92	
Engravers	8		5 52	
Glossers	6		1 62	
Lithograph printers	37		3 24	
Machinists	2		2 92	

FOOD PREPARATIONS (REFINED BEET SUGAR), CALIFORNIA.—ESTAB. No. 251.

Time, 10 hours per day; 217 days the past year.

Occupations.	Number.		Daily wages.	
	Male.	Fem.	Male.	Fem.
Battery men	2		$2 00	
Beet-room men	20		2 00	
Bone-black men	10		1 15	
Chemist	1		4 00	
Coal passers	2		1 25	
Engineers	15		5 00	
Engineer	1		3 00	
Evaporator men	2		1 00	
Firemen	2		2 50	
Firemen's helpers	10		1 00	
Foreman	1		2 00	
Foreman	1		1 50	
Laborers	6		1 00	
Liquor men	2		1 75	
Osmosier men	2		1 25	
Sugar packer	1		1 25	
Teamster	1		3 00	
Watchman	1		1 00	

a Youth.   b Children.

OCCUPATIONS AND WAGES. 351

OCCUPATIONS, WITH NUMBER AND WAGES OF EMPLOYÉS, BY INDUSTRIES—Cont'd.

NOTE.—This table is *not* a complete exhibit for industries or states, but covers only establishments investigated by the Bureau. See page 91, also summaries, pages 143 to 226.

FOOD PREPARATIONS (FLOUR), CALIFORNIA.—ESTAB. No. 252.

Time, 24 hours per day (two turns); 300 days the past year.

Occupations.	Number.		Daily wages.	
	Male.	Fem.	Male.	Fem.
Engineer	1		$3 50	
Fireman	1		2 50	
Laborer	1		2 50	
Millers	3		5 00	
Packer	1		3 00	
Packers	2		2 50	
Teamsters	3		2 60	
Undesignated	a2		1 75	
Watchman	1		2 50	
Wheat dumpers	4		2 50	

FOOD PREPARATIONS (FLOUR), CALIFORNIA.—ESTAB. No. 253.

Time, 24 hours per day (two turns); — days the past year.

Occupations.	Number.		Daily wages.	
	Male.	Fem.	Male.	Fem.
Engineer	1		$5 00	
Laborers	2		2 50	
Millers	2		4 00	
Packers	2		3 50	
Teamsters	2		3 33	
Watchman	1		2 50	
Wheat dumper	1		3 50	

FOOD PREPARATIONS (FLOUR), ILLINOIS.—ESTAB. No. 254.

Time, 24 hours per day (two turns); 300 days the past year.

Occupations.	Number.		Daily wages.	
	Male.	Fem.	Male.	Fem.
Engineers	2		$3 58	
Firemen	2		2 33	
Laborers	10		1 50	
Millers	5		2 50	
Packers	2		2 00	
Packers	4		1 75	
Roll tender	1		1 75	
Sweeper	1		1 50	
Watchmen	2		2 00	

FOOD PREPARATIONS (FLOUR), ILLINOIS.—ESTAB. No. 255.

Time, 24 hours per day (two turns); 260 days the past year.

Occupations.	Number.		Daily wages.	
	Male.	Fem.	Male.	Fem.
Cleaner	1		$1 50	
Engineers	2		2 50	
Fireman	2		2 00	
Laborers	4		1 50	
Miller, head	1		5 00	
Millers	2		3 00	
Packers	4		1 60	
Teamster	1		1 60	

FOOD PREPARATIONS (FLOUR), ILLINOIS.—ESTAB. No. 256.

Time, 24 hours per day (two turns); 250 days the past year.

Occupations.	Number.		Daily wages.	
	Male.	Fem.	Male.	Fem.
Cleaners	2		$1 50	
Engineers	2		2 00	
Laborers	6		1 50	
Miller, head	1		5 00	
Millers	2		2 00	
Packers	2		1 50	
Sweepers	2		1 50	
Teamsters	3		1 50	

FOOD PREPARATIONS (FLOUR), ILLINOIS.—ESTAB. No. 257.

Time, 24 hours per day (two turns); 275 days the past year.

Occupations.	Number.		Daily wages.	
	Male.	Fem.	Male.	Fem.
Engineer	1		$2 00	
Engineer	1		1 50	
Laborers	2		1 00	
Millers, head	2		3 00	
Millers	2		2 31	
Teamsters	2		1 83	

FOOD PREPARATIONS (FLOUR), ILLINOIS.—ESTAB. No. 258.

Time, 24 hours per day (two turns); 300 days the past year.

Occupations.	Number.		Daily wages.	
	Male.	Fem.	Male.	Fem.
Engineers	3		$2 50	
Firemen	3		2 00	
Laborers	28		1 75	
Millers	5		2 75	
Packers	3		2 00	
Sweepers	4		1 75	
Watchmen	2		2 00	

FOOD PREPARATIONS (FLOUR), ILLINOIS.—ESTAB. No. 259.

Time, 24 hours per day (two turns); 250 days the past year.

Occupations.	Number.		Daily wages.	
	Male.	Fem.	Male.	Fem.
Engineer	1		$3 00	
Engineer	1		2 00	
Laborers	8		1 50	
Miller, head	1		5 75	
Millers	2		2 00	
Oiler	1		2 00	
Packers	2		1 75	
Teamsters	2		1 75	
Watchman	1		1 50	

a Youth.

OCCUPATIONS, WITH NUMBER AND WAGES OF EMPLOYÉS, BY INDUSTRIES—Cont'd.

NOTE.—This table is *not* a complete exhibit for industries or states, but covers only establishments investigated by the Bureau. See page 91, also summaries, pages 143 to 226.

FOOD PREPARATIONS (FLOUR), ILLINOIS.—ESTAB. No. 260.

Time, 24 hours per day (two turns); 280 days the past year.

Occupations.	Number.		Daily wages.	
	Male.	Fem.	Male.	Fem.
Cleaner	1		$3 20	
Engineer	1		3 00	
Engineer	1		2 00	
Laborers	4		1 00	
Miller, head	1		5 20	
Miller	1		1 92	
Miller	1		2 31	
Sweepers	3		1 50	
Teamsters	2		1 92	

FOOD PREPARATIONS (FLOUR), ILLINOIS.—ESTAB. No. 261.

Time, 24 hours per day (two turns); 275 days the past year.

Occupations.	Male.	Fem.	Male.	Fem.
Cleaners	2		$1 73	
Engineer	1		2 88	
Engineer	1		1 92	
Firemen	2		1 50	
Laborers	4		1 25	
Miller, head	1		5 00	
Millers	2		2 31	
Packers	4		1 92	
Sweepers	2		1 50	
Teamsters	3		1 50	

FOOD PREPARATIONS (FLOUR), ILLINOIS.—ESTAB. No. 262.

Time, 12 hours per day; 225 days the past year.

Occupations.	Male.	Fem.	Male.	Fem.
Barrel nailer	1		$1 33	
Engineer	1		2 17	
Fireman	1		1 25	
Laborers	2		1 17	
Miller	1		2 70	
Packer	1		1 50	
Sweeper	1		1 25	
Spoutsman	1		1 50	
Teamster	1		1 67	
Watchman	1		1 25	

FOOD PREPARATIONS (FLOUR), ILLINOIS.—ESTAB. No. 263.

Time, 24 hours per day (two turns); 247 days the past year.

Occupations.	Male.	Fem.	Male.	Fem.
Barrel nailer	1		$1 00	
Engineer	1		3 00	
Laborers	3		1 40	
Miller	1		3 25	
Packer	1		1 66	
Packer	1		1 50	
Roll tender	1		1 50	
Spoutsman	1		1 50	
Sweeper	1		1 25	
Teamsters	3		1 50	
Watchman	1		1 25	

FOOD PREPARATIONS (FLOUR), INDIANA.—ESTAB. No. 264.

Time, 24 hours per day (two turns); 300 days the past year.

Occupations.	Number.		Daily wages.	
	Male.	Fem.	Male.	Fem.
Cleaners	2		$1 80	
Engineers	3		2 40	
Laborers	4		1 80	
Miller, head	1		6 00	
Millers	2		2 40	
Millwright	1		3 00	
Packers	2		1 80	
Sweepers	2		1 80	
Teamsters	2		2 00	

FOOD PREPARATIONS (CURED AND PACKED MEATS), INDIANA.—ESTAB. No. 265.

Time, 10 hours per day; 300 days the past year.

Occupations.	Male.	Fem.	Male.	Fem.
Butchers	75		$2 50	
Laborers	420		1 50	
Mechanics	45		2 25	
Undesignated	a32	a60	75	$0 75

FOOD PREPARATIONS (FLOUR), MINNESOTA.—ESTAB. No. 266.

Time, 24 hours per day (two turns); 313 days the past year.

Occupations.	Male.	Fem.	Male.	Fem.
Laborers	23		$2 50	
Laborers	85		1 62	
Machinists	14		2 37	
Millers	83		2 50	
Millwrights	21		2 02	
Oilers	30		2 12	
Packers	28		2 00	
Sweepers	50		1 62	

FOOD PREPARATIONS (FLOUR), MISSOURI—ESTAB. No. 267.

Time, 24 hours per day (two turns); — days the past year.

Occupations.	Male.	Fem.	Male.	Fem.
Engineers	2		$3 00	
Firemen	2		2 00	
Laborers	30		1 50	
Miller, head	1		6 92	
Miller	1		3 84	
Millers	2		2 88	

FOOD PREPARATIONS (FLOUR), MISSOURI.—ESTAB. No. 268.

Time, 12 hours per day; — days the past year.

Occupations.	Male.	Fem.	Male.	Fem.
Barrel nailers	2		$1 65	
Cleaners	2		1 65	
Engineer	1		4 80	
Firemen	2		2 85	
Laborers	15		1 50	
Miller, head	1		4 80	
Millers	2		2 85	
Millers' helpers	2		2 50	

a Youth.

OCCUPATIONS AND WAGES.

OCCUPATIONS, WITH NUMBER AND WAGES OF EMPLOYÉS, BY INDUSTRIES—Cont'd.

NOTE.—This table is *not* a complete exhibit for industries or states, but covers only establishments investigated by the Bureau. See page 91, also summaries, pages 143 to 226.

FOOD PREPARATIONS (FLOUR), MISSOURI.—ESTAB. No. 268—Concluded.

Time, 12 hours per day; — days the past year.

Occupations.	Number.		Daily wages.	
	Male.	Fem.	Male.	Fem.
Oilers	2	......	$1 85	......
Packers	2	......	2 00	......
Packers	2	......	1 65	......
Sweepers	2	......	1 65	......
Undesignated	1	......	1 65	......
Wheat inspectors	2	......	2 00	......

FOOD PREPARATIONS (FLOUR), MISSOURI.—ESTAB. No. 269.

Time, 24 hours per day (two turns); 300 days the past year.

Occupations.	Male.	Fem.	Male.	Fem.
Engineer	1	......	$1 92	......
Engineer	1	......	1 58	......
Laborers	2	......	1 00	......
Miller	1	......	2 90	......
Miller	1	......	1 58	......

FOOD PREPARATIONS (FLOUR), MISSOURI.—ESTAB. No. 270.

Time, 24 hours per day (two turns); — days the past year.

Occupations.	Male.	Fem.	Male.	Fem.
Engineers	2	......	$3 00	......
Firemen	2	......	2 00	......
Foreman	1	......	6 92	......
Laborers	30	......	1 50	......
Miller, head	1	......	3 83	......
Millers	2	......	2 88	......

FOOD PREPARATIONS (FLOUR), NEW HAMPSHIRE.—ESTAB. No. 271.

Time, 24 hours per day (two turns); 275 days the past year.

Occupations.	Male.	Fem.	Male.	Fem.
Cleaner	1	......	$0 85	......
Miller, head	1	......	3 85	......
Millers	2	......	3 08	......
Miller	1	......	2 69	......
Miller	1	......	2 31	......
Packers	2	......	1 65	......
Sweeper	1	......	1 25	......

FOOD PREPARATIONS (FLOUR), OHIO.—ESTAB. No. 272.

Time, 11 hours per day; 250 days the past year.

Occupations.	Male.	Fem.	Male.	Fem.
Engineer	1	......	$1 50	......
Miller	1	......	1 75	......
Packer	1	......	1 25	......
Porter	1	......	1 00	......
Teamster	1	......	1 25	......

FOOD PREPARATIONS (FLOUR), OHIO.—ESTAB. No. 273.

Time, 24 hours per day (two turns); — days the past year.

Occupations.	Number.		Daily wages.	
	Male.	Fem.	Male.	Fem.
Engineers	2	......	$3 50	......
Firemen	2	......	2 33	......
Laborers	8	......	1 67	......
Millers	6	......	2 65	......
Packers	7	......	1 92	......
Sweepers	2	......	1 67	......

FOOD PREPARATIONS (FLOUR), OHIO.—ESTAB. No. 274.

Time, 24 hours per day (two turns); — days the past year.

Occupations.	Male.	Fem.	Male.	Fem.
Coopers	7	......	$1 50	......
Engineers	2	......	1 50	......
Laborers	6	......	1 50	......
Millers	5	......	2 50	......
Packers	2	......	1 75	......
Teamsters	3	......	1 25	......

FOOD PREPARATIONS (SALT), OHIO.—ESTAB. No. 275.

Time, 24 hours per day (two turns); 300 days the past year.

Occupations.	Male.	Fem.	Male.	Fem.
Ash hauler	1	......	$1 25	......
Brine tender	1	......	1 25	......
Bromine maker	1	......	2 00	......
Coopers	12	......	1 25	......
Engineers	2	......	1 25	......
Firemen	4	......	1 25	......
Furnace boss	1	......	3 00	......
Salt lifters	8	......	1 00	......
Salt maker	1	......	2 00	......
Salt packers	5	......	1 25	......

FOOD PREPARATIONS (SALT), OHIO.—ESTAB. No. 276.

Time, 24 hours per day (two turns); 163 days the past year.

Occupations.	Male.	Fem.	Male.	Fem.
Barrel nailers	2	......	$1 00	......
Coopers	12	......	1 25	......
Drivers	2	......	1 25	......
Engineers	2	......	1 25	......
Firemen	4	......	1 25	......
Furnace boss	1	......	2 00	......
Laborer	1	......	1 00	......
Mine boss	1	......	2 00	......
Miners a	15	......	1 50	......
Salt lifters	7	......	1 00	......
Salt maker	1	......	1 25	......
Salt packers	5	......	1 00	......

a This establishment mines its own coal.

OCCUPATIONS, WITH NUMBER AND WAGES OF EMPLOYÉS, BY INDUSTRIES—Con'td.

NOTE.—This table is not a complete exhibit for industries or states, but covers only establishments investigated by the Bureau. See page 91, also summaries, pages 143 to 226.

FOOD PREPARATIONS (SALT), OHIO.—ESTAB. No. **277**.

Time, 24 hours per day (two turns); 300 days the past year.

Occupations.	Number.		Daily wages.	
	Male.	Fem.	Male.	Fem.
Brine tender	1	......	$1 25	......
Coopers	12	......	1 00	......
Cooper	1	......	1 33	......
Driver a	1	......	1 25	......
Drivers a	2	......	1 00	......
Engineers	2	......	1 25	......
Fireman	1	......	1 50	......
Firemen	3	......	1 25	......
Mine boss a	1	......	1 67	......
Miners a	16	......	1 25	......
Salt lifters	8	......	1 10	......
Salt maker	1	......	2 00	......
Scaffold man	1	......	1 00	......
Well tender	1	......	1 50	......

FOOD PREPARATIONS (FLOUR). WEST VIRGINIA.—ESTAB. No. **278**.

Time, 11 hours per day; 300 days the past year.

Occupations.	Male.	Fem.	Male.	Fem.
Engineer	1	......	$2 00	......
Laborer	1	......	1 42	......
Miller, head	1	......	3 53	......
Miller	1	......	1 87	......
Packer	1	......	1 67	......
Weigher	1	......	1 07	......

FURNITURE (CHAIRS), INDIANA.—ESTAB. No. **279**.

Time, 10 hours per day; 300 days the past year.

Occupations.	Male.	Fem.	Male.	Fem.
Cabinet makers	25	......	$2 00	......
Chair makers	2	......	2 00	......
Engineer	1	......	2 50	......
Foremen	4	......	3 00	......
Laborers	5	......	1 50	......
Laborers	5	......	1 00	......
Machine men	14	......	1 50	......
Machine men	1	......	2 50	......
Turners	3	......	2 00	......
Varnisher	1	......	1 50	......
Varnishers	21	......	1 25	......

FURNITURE (CHAIRS), INDIANA.—ESTAB. No. **280**.

Time, 10 hours per day; 300 days the past year.

Occupations.	Male.	Fem.	Male.	Fem.
Chair maker	1	......	$2 50	......
Chair makers	6	......	2 00	......
Finishers	10	......	1 50	......
Finishers	10	......	1 00	......
Laborers	10	......	1 25	......
Laborers	5	......	80	......
Machine men	2	......	2 50	......
Machine men	28	......	1 50	......
Upholsterers	5	......	2 00	......

a This establishment mines its own coal.

FURNITURE (SEWING-MACHINE FURNITURE), INDIANA.—ESTAB. No. **281**.

Time, 10 hours per day; 265 days the past year.

Occupations.	Number.		Daily wages.	
	Male.	Fem.	Male.	Fem.
Cabinet makers	118	......	$1 50	......
Engineer	1	......	3 33	......
Firemen	5	......	1 50	......
Gate keeper	1	......	1 25	......
Laborers	23	......	1 00	......
Machine men	25	......	2 00	......
Machine men	20	......	1 75	......
Machine men	10	......	1 50	......
Machine men	35	......	1 35	......
Machine men	12	......	1 00	......
Machine men	b18	......	75	......
Machine men	b40	......	50	......
Packer	1	......	1 75	......
Packers	3	......	1 40	......
Packers	20	......	1 10	......
Varnishers	30	......	1 50	......
Watchmen	5	......	1 50	......

FURNITURE (BEDROOM, PARLOR, ETC.), KENTUCKY.—ESTAB. No. **282**.

Time, 9 hours per day; 253 days the past year.

Occupations.	Male.	Fem.	Male.	Fem.
Cabinet makers	27	......	$1 80	......
Carvers	6	......	2 25	......
Laborers	8	......	1.13	......
Machine men	32	......	1 50	......
Packers	3	......	1 35	......
Teamsters	3	......	1 35	......
Upholsterers	5	......	1 50	......
Varnishers	33	......	1 26	......

FURNITURE (CENTRE TABLES). MICHIGAN.—ESTAB. No. **283**.

Time, 10 hours per day; 295 days the past year.

Occupations.	Male.	Fem.	Male.	Fem.
Apprentices	b2	......	$0 67	......
Cabinet maker	1	......	2 25	......
Cabinet makers	7	......	1 55	......
Cabinet makers	2	......	1 25	......
Engineer	1	......	2 00	......
Finishers	2	......	1 90	......
Finishers	7	......	1 50	......
Finishers	4	......	1 20	......
Finishers	2	......	1 00	......
Fireman	1	......	1 25	......
Foreman	1	......	3 34	......
Foremen	2	......	3 00	......
Laborers	2	......	4 50	......
Laborer	1	......	1 25	......
Machine man	1	......	2 50	......
Machine men	3	......	2 25	......
Machine men	7	......	2 00	......
Machine men	4	......	1 75	......
Machine men	4	......	1 55	......
Machine man	1	......	1 15	......
Machine-man's helper	b1	......	50	......
Teamster	1	......	2 50	......
Trimmer	1	......	2 00	......
Trimmers	3	......	1 75	......
Trimmers	2	......	1 25	......
Watchman	1	......	1 50	......

b Youth.

OCCUPATIONS AND WAGES.

OCCUPATIONS, WITH NUMBER AND WAGES OF EMPLOYÉS, BY INDUSTRIES—Cont'd.

NOTE.—This table is *not* a complete exhibit for industries or states, but covers only establishments investigated by the Bureau. See page 91, also summaries, pages 143 to 226.

FURNITURE (BEDROOM), MICHIGAN.—ESTAB. No. 284.

Time, 10 hours per day; 300 days the past year.

Occupations.	Number.		Daily wages.	
	Male.	Fem.	Male.	Fem.
Carver	1		$3 00	
Carver	1		2 50	
Elevator tenders	a2		40	
Engineer	1		2 75	
Finishers	2		1 75	
Finishers	2		1 50	
Finishers	8		1 25	
Finishers	17		1 15	
Finishers	a4		75	
Fireman	1		1 25	
Foreman	1		3 25	
Foreman	1		2 25	
Foreman	1		2 00	
Foreman	1		1 75	
Foreman	1		1 50	
Laborers	4		1 25	
Machine man	1		2 50	
Machine man	1		2 00	
Machine men	2		1 75	
Machine men	10		1 50	
Machine men	8		1 25	
Machine men	4		1 00	
Packers	5		1 10	
Planers	b2		40	
Sanders	b2		35	
Sawyers	b2		35	

FURNITURE, MICHIGAN.—ESTAB. No. 285.

Time, 10 hours per day; 290 days the past year.

Occupations.	Number.		Daily wages.	
	Male.	Fem.	Male.	Fem.
Cabinet makers	3		$3 00	
Cabinet makers	15		2 50	
Cabinet makers	14		2 25	
Cabinet makers	12		2 00	
Cabinet makers	11		1 67	
Cabinet makers	4		1 50	
Cabinet makers	12		1 25	
Cabinet makers	5		1 00	
Cabinet makers	a6		50	
Carvers	12		2 60	
Carvers	2		2 25	
Carvers	2		1 60	
Carvers	2		1 25	
Carvers	a2		80	
Carvers	a4		60	
Engineer	1		3 25	
Engineer	1		2 75	
Finisher	1		2 50	
Finishers	3		2 25	
Finishers	5		2 00	
Finishers	2		1 80	
Finishers	17		1 55	
Finishers	21		1 25	
Finishers	24		1 05	
Firemen	2		2 00	
Fireman	1		1 25	
Foreman	1		4 50	
Foremen	3		4 00	
Foremen	2		3 50	
Foremen	1		2 75	
Foremen	3		2 50	
Foreman, assistant	1		1 75	
Laborer	1		2 50	
Laborer	1		2 00	

FURNITURE, MICHIGAN.—ESTAB. No. 285—Concluded.

Time, 10 hours per day; 299 days the past year.

Occupations.	Number.		Daily wages.	
	Male.	Fem.	Male.	Fem.
Laborers	6		$1 67	
Laborers	2		1 50	
Laborers	12		1 25	
Laborer	a1		55	
Machine man	1		3 00	
Machine men	2		2 75	
Machine men	5		2 50	
Machine men	6		2 25	
Machine men	18		2 00	
Machine men	17		1 75	
Machine men	7		1 55	
Machine men	7		1 20	
Machine men	5		1 00	
Machine men	a2		80	
Machine men	a16		55	
Packer	1		2 50	
Packers	2		1 75	
Packers	6		1 55	
Packers	6		1 25	
Trimmers	2		2 25	
Trimmers	3		2 00	
Trimmers	8		1 75	
Trimmers	3		1 50	
Trimmer	1		1 25	
Upholsterers	3		2 00	
Upholsterers	2		1 75	
Upholsterers	3		1 50	
Upholsterers	2		1 00	

FURNITURE, MICHIGAN.—ESTAB. No. 286.

Time, 10 hours per day; 280 days the past year.

Occupations.	Number.		Daily wages.	
	Male.	Fem.	Male.	Fem.
Apprentice	a1		$0 50	
Apprentices	a5		93	
Cabinet makers	11		2 50	
Cabinet makers	11		1 83	
Cabinet makers	10		1 25	
Carver	1		2 75	
Carvers	10		2 25	
Engineer	1		2 00	
Finishers	2		1 80	
Finishers	39		1 50	
Finishers	21		1 25	
Finishers	8		1 00	
Finisher	a1		75	
Finisher	a1		50	
Laborer	1		2 00	
Laborers	2		1 75	
Laborers	2		1 50	
Laborers	15		1 25	
Laborers	2		1 00	
Laborers	10		75	
Laborers	2		65	
Lumbermen	2		1 75	
Lumbermen	4		1 25	
Lumbermen	2		1 00	
Machine men	23		2 00	
Machine men	10		1 75	
Machine men	4		1 50	
Machine men	9		1 40	
Machine men	6		1 25	
Machine-men's helpers	5		1 10	

a Youth.   *b* Children.

OCCUPATIONS, WITH NUMBER AND WAGES OF EMPLOYÉS, BY INDUSTRIES—Cont'd.

NOTE.—This table is not a complete exhibit for industries or states, but covers only establishments investigated by the Bureau. See page 91, also summaries, pages 143 to 226.

FURNITURE, MICHIGAN.—ESTAB. No. 286—Concluded.

Time, 10 hours per day; 289 days the past year.

Occupations.	Number.		Daily wages.	
	Male.	Fem.	Male.	Fem.
Machine-men's helpers	3	......	$1 00	......
Machine-men's helper	a1	......	65	......
Machine-men's helpers	a13	......	50	......
Packers	2	......	1 75	......
Packers	6	......	1 50	......
Packer	1	......	1 25	......
Packer	1	......	80	......
Trimmers	2	......	1 75	......
Trimmers	6	......	1 50	......
Upholsterers	2	......	3 00	......
Upholsterers	3	......	2 50	......
Upholsterer	1	......	2 00	......
Upholsterers	3	......	1 00	......
Veneerer	1	......	3 00	......
Veneerers	4	......	2 00	......
Veneerer	1	......	1 75	......
Veneerers	7	......	1 50	......
Veneerer	1	......	1 25	......
Watchman	1	......	1 75	......

GLASS (GREEN BOTTLES), CALIFORNIA.—ESTAB. No. 287.

Time, 10 hours per day; 230 days the past year.

Occupations.	Male.	Fem.	Male.	Fem.
Blowers	28	......	$4 33	......
Carrying boys	a40	......	50	......
Demijohn coverers	15	......	1 50	......
Engineer	1	......	2 50	......
Gatherers	a14	......	1 25	......
Laborers	15	......	1 75	......
Machinists and blacksmiths	3	......	3 00	......
Mixers	3	......	2 50	......
Oven boys	a8	......	1 25	......
Packers	8	......	2 25	......
Pot makers	2	......	3 00	......
Teamsters	3	......	3 00	......
Tenser	1	......	4 00	......
Teasers	2	......	2 50	......
Undesignated	5	......	2 25	......

GLASS (WINDOW GLASS), ILLINOIS.—ESTAB. No. 288. b

Time, 10 hours per day; 240 days the past year. c

Occupations.	Male.	Fem.	Male.	Fem.
Blowers	16	......	$6 25	......
Cutters	6	......	5 55	......
Flatteners	4	......	6 25	......
Gatherers	16	......	4 00	......

GLASS (GREEN BOTTLES), KENTUCKY.—ESTAB. No. 289.

Time, 10 hours per day; — days the past year.

Occupations.	Male.	Fem.	Male.	Fem.
Blacksmith	1	......	$2 25	......
Blowers	20	......	4 00	......
Foreman	1	......	3 00	......

GLASS (GREEN BOTTLES), KENTUCKY.—ESTAB. No. 289—Concluded.

Time, 10 hours per day; — days the past year.

Occupations.	Number.		Daily wages.	
	Male.	Fem.	Male.	Fem.
Foreman, assistant	1	......	$1 67	......
Laborers	3	......	1 25	......
Laborers	18	......	1 00	......
Mixer	1	......	2 00	......
Packer	1	......	2 25	......
Packers	a2	......	75	......
Teamster	1	......	1 25	......
Teasers	2	......	1 40	......
Tender boys	a5	......	83	......
Tender boys	a12	......	33	......
Watchman	1	......	1 15	......

GLASS (GREEN BOTTLES), NEW JERSEY.—ESTAB. No. 290.

Time, 9 hours per day; 240 days the past year.

Occupations.	Male.	Fem.	Male.	Fem.
Blacksmiths	4	......	$3 00	......
Blowers	132	......	4 50	......
Clay grinders	2	......	1 50	......
Engineers	3	......	1 75	......
Gatherers	a24	......	1 00	......
Laborers	10	......	1 25	......
Leersman	1	......	1 50	......
Mixers	4	......	2 50	......
Packers	12	......	1 75	......
Pot maker	1	......	3 50	......
Shearers	8	......	1 75	......
Snap-up boys	a216	......	50	......
Teamsters	10	......	1 50	......
Treaders	4	......	1 25	......
Waremen	3	......	1 40	......

GLASS (WINDOW GLASS, GREEN BOTTLES), NEW JERSEY.—ESTAB. No. 291.

Time, 9 hours per day; 260 days the past year.

Occupations.	Male.	Fem.	Male.	Fem.
Blacksmith	1	......	$2 62	......
Blowers	46	......	4 77	......
Blowers	8	......	4 00	......
Box makers	2	......	1 64	......
Cutters	4	......	4 00	......
Engineers	2	......	1 57	......
Foreman	1	......	4 87	......
Gatherers	8	......	2 97	......
Laborers	20	......	1 17	......
Master shearer	1	......	4 50	......
Master shearers	2	......	3 32	......
Mixers	2	......	1 97	......
Packer	1	......	1 80	......
Packers	6	......	1 17	......
Pot maker	1	......	2 70	......
Shearers	3	......	1 80	......
Undesignated	a52	......	68	......

GLASS (GREEN BOTTLES), NEW JERSEY.—ESTAB. No. 292.

Time 8 hours per day; 260 days the past year.

Occupations.	Male.	Fem.	Male.	Fem.
Blowers	21	......	$4 16	......
Box makers	2	......	1 33	......
Gatherers	a2	......	1 00	......

a Youth. b Other occupations not reported. c Blowers, gatherers, and flatteners worked 180 days.

OCCUPATION AND WAGES.

OCCUPATIONS, WITH NUMBER AND WAGES OF EMPLOYÉS, BY INDUSTRIES—Cont'd.

NOTE.—This table is *not* a complete exhibit for industries or states, but covers only establishments investigated by the Bureau. See page 91, also summaries, pages 143 to 226.

GLASS (GREEN BOTTLES), NEW JERSEY.—ESTAB. No. 292—Concluded.

Time, 8 hours per day; 200 days the past year.

Occupations.	Number. Male.	Number. Fem.	Daily wages. Male.	Daily wages. Fem.
Laborers	2		$1 17	
Leersmen	2		1 50	
Master shearer	1		3 00	
Mixer	1		1 33	
Shearers	2		1 50	
Snap-up boys	a16		60	
Wareman	1		1 66	

GLASS (WINDOW GLASS), NEW JERSEY.—ESTAB. No. 293.

Time, 7½ hours per day; 260 days the past year.

Occupations.	Male.	Fem.	Male.	Fem.
Blacksmiths	2		$2 00	
Blowers	32		4 50	
Box makers	6		1 33	
Clay grinder	2		1 10	
Cutters	16		4 16	
Engineers	4		1 33	
Flatteners	8		4 80	
Flatteners	2		4 00	
Gatherers	32		3 00	
Laborers	4		1 17	
Leersmen and shovers	16		2 06	
Master shearers	4		3 33	
Mixers	4		1 33	
Packers	4		1 16	
Pot maker	1		2 50	
Shearers	8		1 33	
Teamsters	8		1 33	
Treader	1		1 25	

GLASS (GREEN BOTTLES), OHIO.—ESTAB. No. 294.

Time, 9 hours per day; 210 days the past year.

Occupations.	Male.	Fem.	Male.	Fem.
Blacksmith	1		$3 00	
Blowers	16		4 50	
Box maker	1		1 66	
Chippers	3		1 80	
Engineer	1		1 66	
Gatherers	a8		1 25	
Grinder	a1		83	
Inspector	1		1 33	
Laborer	1		1 50	
Laying-up boys	a4		1 25	
Master teaser	1		5 00	
Mixers	2		1 75	
Packers	4		1 50	
Piler	a1		50	
Roller boys	b8		25	
Teasers	3		1 50	
Waremen	2		1 25	
Washers	2		1 00	
Water boys	a2		50	

GLASS (WINDOW GLASS), OHIO.—ESTAB. No. 295.

Time, 10 hours per day; 180 days the past year.

Occupations.	Male.	Fem.	Male.	Fem.
Blowers	8		$6 08	
Cutters	4		5 04	
Flatteners	2		6 31	
Gatherers	8		4 01	
Undesignated	24		2 25	

GLASS (WINDOW GLASS), OHIO.—ESTAB. No. 296.

Time, 10 hours per day; (c) 168 days the past year.

Occupations.	Male.	Fem.	Male.	Fem.
Blowers	18		$5 00	
Cutters	7		4 50	
Flatteners	4		5 50	
Gatherers	18		3 00	
Laborers	40		2 00	

GLASS (WINDOW GLASS), OHIO.—ESTAB. No. 297.

Time, 11 hours per day; 220 days the past year.

Occupations.	Male.	Fem.	Male.	Fem.
Blacksmith	1		$2 00	
Blowers	11		4 50	
Box makers	2		2 00	
Coal wheeler	1		2 00	
Cutters	4		4 50	
Fillers-in	2		2 00	
Flatteners	3		4 50	
Gatherers	10		3 00	
Laborers	3		1 50	
Layers-out	3		2 00	
Leersmen	2		2 00	
Lime sifter	1		2 00	
Mixer	1		2 00	
Packer	1		2 00	
Roller boys	a4		75	
Teaser, master	1		4 00	
Teaser	4		2 00	

GLASS (TABLE WARE), OHIO.—ESTAB. No. 298.

Time, 10 hours per day; 240 days the past year.

Occupations.	Male.	Fem.	Male.	Fem.
Assorters		a18		$0 50
Blacksmith	1		$2 25	
Blowers	4		4 00	
Cutters	3		2 00	
Engravers	2		3 00	
Finishers	3		3 50	
Gatherers	10		3 00	
Laborers	2		1 25	
Leersmen	2		1 50	
Mixers	2		1 65	
Mould makers	7		4 00	
Packers	5		1 50	
Pressers	10		4 00	
Teasers	2		2 50	
Tender boys	a40		60	
Watchman	1		1 50	

GLASS (TABLE WARE), OHIO.—ESTAB. No. 299.

Time, 10 hours per day; — days the past year.

Occupations.	Male.	Fem.	Male.	Fem.
Carry-in boys	a19		$0 70	
Finishers, bowl	19		3 50	
Finishers, foot	19		2 50	
Gatherers	19		2 20	
Pressers	19		4 00	
Turn-out boys	a19		90	
Warming-in boys	a95		50	

a Youth.   *b* Children.   *c* Blowers, gatherers, and flatteners worked 140 days.

358

OCCUPATIONS AND WAGES.

OCCUPATIONS, WITH NUMBER AND WAGES OF EMPLOYÉS, BY INDUSTRIES—Cont'd.

NOTE.—This table is *not* a complete exhibit for industries or states, but covers only establishments investigated by the Bureau. See page 91, also summaries, pages 143 to 226.

GLASS (FLINT BOTTLES), PENNSYLVANIA.—ESTAB. No. **300**.

Time, 8 hours per day ; 250 days the past year.

Occupations.	Number.		Daily wages.	
	Male.	Fem.	Male.	Fem.
Blowers	45		$4 00	
Laborers	12		1 50	
Mixers	2		2 00	
Mould cleaners	2		1 00	
Packers	5		1 50	
Teamsters	2		1 66	
Teasers	4		2 00	
Tender boys	a100		41	

GLASS (FLINT BOTTLES), PENNSYLVANIA.—ESTAB. No. **301**.

Time, 10 hours per day; 251 days the past year.

Blacksmith	1		$2 00	
Blowers	30		4 50	
Engineer	1		2 25	
Laborers	4		1 25	
Mixers	2		2 00	
Mould cleaners	2		1 25	
Packers	6		1 67	
Pot maker	1		2 25	
Teamsters	2		2 00	
Teasers	2		1 71	
Tender boys	a60		50	
Waremen	2		1 25	

GLASS (FLINT BOTTLES), PENNSYLVANIA.—ESTAB. No. **302**.

Time, 10 hours per day ; 260 days the past year.

Blacksmith	1		$2 50	
Blowers	51		4 00	
Carpenter	1		2 00	
Carpenter's helper	1		1 50	
Engineer	1		2 25	
Foremen	2		3 00	
Gatherers	a2		66	
Laborers	12		1 25	
Mixers	8		1 50	
Mould makers	3		3 00	
Mould-makers' helpers	1		1 50	
Packers	11		1 50	
Pot maker	1		3 00	
Pot-maker's helpers	3		1 50	
Pressers	2		3 00	
Stopper maker	1		7 00	
Stopper-maker's helpers	9		1 25	
Stopper-maker's helpers	6		80	
Teamsters	2		1 50	
Teasers	6		2 00	
Tender boys	a110		50	
Watchman	1		1 43	

GLASS (FLINT BOTTLES), PENNSYLVANIA.—ESTAB. No. **303**.

Time, 10 hours per day ; 304 days the past year.

Blacksmith	1		$2 66	
Blowers	21		4 75	
Mixers	2		1 66	

GLASS (FLINT BOTTLES), PENNSYLVANIA.—ESTAB. No. **303**—Concluded.

Time, 10 hours per day ; 304 days the past year.

Occupations.	Number.		Daily wages.	
	Male.	Fem.	Male.	Fem.
Mould cleaners	1		$1 25	
Packers	3		1 50	
Pot maker	1		5 00	
Teamsters	2		2 00	
Teasers	2		2 15	
Tender boys	a45		60	
Watchmen	2		2 15	

GLASS (FLINT BOTTLES), PENNSYLVANIA.—ESTAB. No. **304**.

Time, 10 hours per day; 285 days the past year.

Blacksmith	1		$2 00	
Blowers	12		4 50	
Carpenter	1		2 25	
Laborers	2		1 25	
Mixer	1		2 75	
Mould cleaner	1		1 25	
Packers	3		2 00	
Teaser	1		2 75	
Tender boys	a24		60	

GLASS (GREEN BOTTLES), PENNSYLVANIA.—ESTAB. No. **305**.

Time, 10 hours per day; 208 days the past year.

Blacksmith	1		$2 00	
Blowers	22		4 36	
Engineer	1		2 00	
Fillers-in	3		2 00	
Gatherers	a11		1 00	
Grinders	a6		70	
Laborers	3		1 25	
Master teaser	1		4 00	
Mixer	1		2 00	
Mould cleaner	1		1 50	
Packers	4		2 00	
Sand burner	1		2 00	
Teamster	1		2 00	
Teasers	3		2 00	
Tender boys	a40		65	
Waremen	2		1 10	
Watchman	1		1 50	

GLASS (GREEN BOTTLES), PENNSYLVANIA.—ESTAB. No. **306**.

Time, 10 hours per day; 234 days the past year.

Blacksmith	1		$3 00	
Blowers	24		3 98	
Carpenter	1		2 50	
Engineers	2		2 83	
Foreman	1		5 00	
Laborers	6		1 25	
Mixers	2		1 67	
Packers	3		2 00	
Pot maker	1		3 00	
Pot-maker's helper	1		1 67	
Shearers	4		2 50	
Teasers	3		2 00	
Tender boys	a35		65	

a Youth.

OCCUPATIONS AND WAGES.

OCCUPATIONS, WITH NUMBER AND WAGES OF EMPLOYÉS, BY INDUSTRIES—Cont'd.

NOTE.—This table is *not* a complete exhibit for industries or states, but covers only establishments investigated by the Bureau. See page 91, also summaries, pages 143 to 226.

GLASS (GREEN BOTTLES) PENNSYLVANIA.—ESTAB. No. 307.

Time, 10 hours per day; 208 days the past year.

Occupations.	Number.		Daily wages.	
	Male.	Fem.	Male.	Fem.
Blacksmith	1		$2 00	
Blowers	42		4 75	
Fillers-in	2		2 00	
Foreman	1		5 00	
Gatherers	16		1 00	
Laborers	6		1 25	
Master teaser	1		5 00	
Mixers	2		2 00	
Packers	7		2 00	
Teasers	3		2 00	
Tender boys	a50		66	
Watchmen	1		1 66	

GLASS (WINDOW GLASS) PENNSYLVANIA.—ESTAB. No. 308.

Time, 10 hours per day; 235 days the past year.b

Blowers	16		$5 46	
Box maker	1		2 50	
Carpenter	1		2 50	
Coal wheelers	2		1 50	
Cutters	6		4 16	
Fillers-in	6		1 66	
Flatteners	5		4 55	
Gatherers	16		3 55	
Laborers	2		1 50	
Layers-out	4		1 66	
Leersmen	4		1 66	
Mixers	2		1 61	
Packers	2		1 66	
Pot maker	1		2 50	
Sand burner	1		1 50	
Teamster	1		1 66	
Teasers	6		1 43	

GLASS (WINDOW GLASS), PENNSYLVANIA.—ESTAB. No. 309.

Time, — hours per day; 234 days the past year.c

Blacksmith	1		$2 00	
Blowers	11		5 50	
Cutters	5		4 17	
Fillers-in	2		2 40	
Flatteners	3		4 33	
Gatherers	10		3 57	
Glass picker	1		1 25	
Laborers	2		1 25	
Layers-out	3		1 83	
Leersmen	2		1 83	
Master teaser	1		4 28	
Mixer	1		2 00	
Packer	1		2 66	
Roller carrier	1		2 00	
Sand burner	1		2 00	
Teamster	1		2 00	
Teasers	3		1 71	
Watchman	1		1 57	

GLASS (PLATE GLASS), PENNSYLVANIA.—ESTAB. No. 310.

Time, 10 hours per day; 300 days the past year.

Occupations.	Number.		Daily wages.	
	Male.	Fem.	Male.	Fem.
Bricklayers	2		$3 00	
Bricklayers' helpers	4		2 00	
Carpenters	2		2 00	
Cutters	6		3 00	
Engineers	2		2 50	
Firemen	2		2 00	
Foremen	5		4 00	
Furnacemen	4		2 50	
Laborers	226		1 75	
Laborers	150		1 50	
Mixers	4		2 50	
Packers	2		3 00	
Packers' helpers	6		1 75	
Pot-makers	3		3 00	
Pot-makers' helpers	6		1 75	

GLASS (LAMP CHIMNEYS, GLOBES), PENNSYLVANIA.—ESTAB. No. 311.

Time, 10 hours per day; 276 days the past year.

Banders		2		$1 00
Blacksmith	1		$2 50	
Blowers	74		4 00	
Carrying-in boys	a3		80	
Cleaning-off boys	a3		1 00	
Crimping boys	a72		1 00	
Cutters	3		2 50	
Decorators	15	15	5 00	2 50
Drivers	2		2 00	
Gatherers	78		2 00	
Ground layers		4		1 50
Hold-mould boys	a3		1 00	
Laborers	2		1 50	
Leersmen	2		2 00	
Mixer	1		2 50	
Mould cleaners	a2		75	
Mould maker	1		2 50	
Packers	8		2 50	
Papering boys	a5		1 25	
Snapping-up boy	a1		1 00	
Teasers	2		2 50	
Washers	1	6	1 00	75
Washer	a1		50	
Watchmen	2		1 50	

GLASS (LAMP CHIMNEYS), PENNSYLVANIA.—ESTAB. No. 312.

Time, 10 hours per day; 300 days the past year.

Blowers	29		$5 00	
Finishers	43		5 00	
Gatherers	43		3 00	
Laborers	2		1 25	
Leersmen	5		1 25	
Mould cleaners	3		1 25	
Mould makers	6		4 00	
Packers	5		2 00	
Pressers	14		5 00	
Teasers	4		2 35	
Tender boys	a40		60	

a Youth.
b Blowers and gatherers worked 196 days.
c Blowers and gatherers worked 195 days; teasers, 273 days.

OCCUPATIONS, WITH NUMBER AND WAGES OF EMPLOYÉS, BY INDUSTRIES—Cont'd.

NOTE.—This table is *not* a complete exhibit for industries or states, but covers only establishments investigated by the Bureau. See page 91, also summaries, pages 143 to 226.

GLASS (TABLE WARE), PENNSYLVANIA.—ESTAB. No. **313.**

Time, 10 hours per day; 300 days the past year.

Occupations.	Number.		Daily wages.	
	Male.	Fem.	Male.	Fem.
Assorters		a10		$0 60
Blacksmith	1		$2 33	
Cutters	3		2 50	
Engravers	4		4 00	
Finishers	10		5 00	
Gatherers	15		2 20	
Laborers	6		1 25	
Mixers	3		2 16	
Mould makers	6		3 33	
Packers	7		2 00	
Pressers	15		5 00	
Tender boys	a46		80	
Watchmen	2		1 71	

GLASS (TABLE WARE), PENNSYLVANIA.—ESTAB. No. **314.**

Time, 10 hours per day; 300 days the past year.

Occupations	Male	Fem	Male	Fem
Blacksmith and engineer	1		$2 66	
Carrying-in boys	a13		66	
Finishers, bowl	3		2 00	
Finisher, foot	1		1 66	
Furnaceman	1		2 21	
Gatherers	11		1 66	
Leersmen	4		1 66	
Mixers	2		1 71	
Mould cleaners	4		1 00	
Mould makers	7		3 83	
Packers	7		2 00	
Papering boys	a3		54	
Pressers	10		3 00	
Sticking-up boys	a6		91	
Teamsters	2		1 83	
Warehouse man	1		2 16	
Watchmen	2		1 71	

GLASS (FLINT BOTTLES), WEST VIRGINIA.—ESTAB. No. **315.**

Time, 10 hours per day; 258 days the past year.

Occupations	Male	Fem	Male	Fem
Blacksmith	1		$2 25	
Blowers	18		4 90	
Carrying-in boys	a6		50	
Carrying-over boys	a6		60	
Cleaning-off boys	a6		80	
Cutters	2		2 25	
Engravers	6		2 25	
Etchers	2		2 00	
Fire-in boys	a6		50	
Foreman	1		4 00	
Leersmen	2		1 66	
Mixers	2		1 66	
Mould boys	a6		60	
Packers	5	a1	1 50	$0 50
Snap boys	a6		60	
Stopper maker	1		2 00	
Teamsters	2		1 66	
Tossers	2		1 75	
Undesignated	3		1 66	
Washer		a1		50
Watchmen	1		1 60	

JUTE GOODS (BAGS, BAGGING), CALIFORNIA.—ESTAB. No. **316.** b

Time, 10¼ hours per day; 300 days the past year.

Occupations.	Number.		Daily wages.	
	Male.	Fem.	Male.	Fem.
Batcher	1		$1 75	
Batcher	1		1 00	
Batchers	5		90	
Bobbin boys	a55		60	
Drawers	a7		50	
Engineer	1		4 40	
Fireman	1		2 40	
Laborer	1		1 04	
Machinists	3		2 50	
Machinist	1		2 20	
Machinists' helpers	2		1 00	
Overseers	2		3 60	
Overseer	1		2 25	
Repair hand	1		2 20	
Sewing-machine operators		24		1 00
Spinners		11		1 00
Sweeper	1		85	
Watchman	1		2 20	
Weavers		27		1 00
Wheelwright	1		4 20	

JUTE GOODS (JUTE, FLAX THREAD), NEW JERSEY.—ESTAB. No. **317.**

Time, 10 hours per day; 300 days the past year.

Occupations	Male	Fem	Male	Fem
Batchers	7		$1 30	
Carders		4		$0 83
Carders	a25		70	
Doffers		a20		43
Drawers		12		76
Engineer	1		1 50	
Fireman	1		1 50	
Oilers	2		1 00	
Overseers	2		2 25	
Pressers	7		1 25	
Reelers		18		59
Rovers		8		79
Spinners		20		90
Tinsmith	a1		1 00	

JUTE GOODS (BAGGING), NEW YORK.—ESTAB. No. **318.**

Time, 10 hours per day; 302 days the past year.

Occupations	Male	Fem	Male	Fem
Band sewer	a1		$0 67	
Batchers	7		1 50	
Bobbin boys	a3		67	
Bobbin boys	a3		50	
Breakers	3		1 17	
Bundler	1		2 00	
Calenderer	1		2 00	
Calenderers' helpers	a2		50	
Carders	9	9	83	$0 83
Carpenter	1		2 50	
Carrier, cloth	1		1 00	
Carriers, cloth	a4		67	
Carrier, cloth	a1		50	
Carrier, spool	a1		67	
Cutters	2		1 67	

a Youth.   *b* This does not include 150 Chinese, consisting of weavers, spinners, spoolers, and laborers, at an average of 80 cents per day.

OCCUPATIONS AND WAGES. 361

OCCUPATIONS, WITH NUMBER AND WAGES OF EMPLOYÉS, BY INDUSTRIES—Cont'd.

NOTE.—This table is *not* a complete exhibit for industries or states, but covers only establishments investigated by the Bureau. See page 91, also summaries, pages 143 to 226.

JUTE GOODS (BAGGING), NEW YORK.—ESTAB. No. **318**—Concluded.

Time, 10 *hours per day*; 302 *days the past year.*

Occupations.	Number.		Daily wages.	
	Male.	Fem.	Male.	Fem.
Darners		5		$0 67
Doffers	a5	a23	$0 67	50
Drawers		18		75
Drawers-in		2		75
Drawers-in helpers		a2		42
Dresser	1		2 25	
Elevator tender	1		1 00	
Engineer	1		3 50	
Firemen	2		1 83	
Foremen	5		3 00	
Foremen	3		2 50	
Foreman, assistant	1		2 17	
Foremen, assistant	2		2 00	
Foremen, assistant	3		1 50	
Handler, jute	1		1 33	
Handlers, jute	2		1 17	
Inspectors	2	3	1 58	83
Loom-fixers	4		2 25	
Machinist	1		3 00	
Machinist	1		2 50	
Machinist	1		2 33	
Machinist	1		1 83	
Machinists' helpers	a3		67	
Mangler	1		2 25	
Mangler's helpers	2		1 17	
Mangler's helper	1		1 00	
Measurer		1		1 00
Measurer	1		1 25	
Oiler	1		1 33	
Oilers	2		1 00	
Packers		2		1 21
Piecers		a4		58
Pressors	2		1 50	
Pressers' helpers	a3		67	
Reelers	10		1 17	
Rovers		8		1 00
Sewing-machine operators		9		92
Spare hands		a2		83
Spinners	23		1 17	
Spinners	6		83	
Strippers	2		1 33	
Sweepers	a2		58	
Sweepers	a4		50	
Trimmers		a3		58
Turners	2		1 33	
Twisters		a2		58
Warehouse men	3		1 75	
Warper	1		1 33	
Warpers	2		1 17	
Warpers		5		1 00
Warper	1		1 00	
Warper	1		83	
Watchman	1		2 58	
Weavers		95		75
Winders		20		75
Winders		a19		58

LEATHER (SOLE LEATHER), CALIFORNIA.—ESTAB. No. **319**.

Time, 10 *hours per day*; 300 *days the past year.*

Occupations	Male	Fem	Male wage	Fem wage
Bark grinder	1		$1 20	
Beamsmen	6		1 60	
Engineer	1		1 40	
Foreman	1		3 00	
Foreman, assistant	1		1 00	

LEATHER (SOLE LEATHER), CALIFORNIA.—ESTAB. No. **319**—Concluded.

Time, 10 *hours per day*; 300 *days the past year.*

Occupations.	Number.		Daily wages.	
	Male.	Fem.	Male.	Fem.
Laborers	8		$1 20	
Roller	1		1 80	
Watchman	1		1 00	

LEATHER (SOLE LEATHER), CALIFORNIA.—ESTAB. No. **320**.

Time, 10 *hours per day*; 300 *days the past year.*

Bark grinders	2		$2 00	
Beamsmen	11		2 40	
Curriers	15		2 40	
Engineer	1		4 00	
Engineer's assistant	1		2 75	
Foremen	2		2 75	
Laborers	14		2 00	
Rollers	2		2 75	
Teamster	1		2 25	
Watchman	1		2 25	

LEATHER (SOLE LEATHER), CALIFORNIA.—ESTAB. No. **321**.

Time, 10 *hours per day*; — *days the past year.*

Beamsmen	5		$2 17	
Brushers	2		2 00	
Dampener	1		2 00	
Engineer	1		2 66	
Finisher	1		2 66	
Laborers	5		2 00	
Oiler	1		2 00	
Undesignated	a2		1 83	

LEATHER (SOLE LEATHER), CALIFORNIA.—ESTAB. No. **322**.

Time, 10 *hours per day*; 300 *days the past year.*

Beamsmen	8		$2 25	
Curriers	10		2 50	
Engineer and fireman	1		3 00	
Laborers	10		2 00	
Pullers	25		2 00	
Pullers' helpers	12		1 50	

LEATHER (MOROCCO), DELAWARE.—ESTAB. No. **323**.

Time, 10 *hours per day*; 288 *days the past year.*

Beamsmen	23		$1 67	
Colorers	12		1 66	
Engineer	1		2 00	
Finishers	156		1 66	
Finishers	a27		67	
Stock-room hands	8		2 00	
Sewers		11		$1 17
Shavers	13		3 33	
Tanners	23		1 67	

a Youth.

OCCUPATIONS, WITH NUMBER AND WAGES OF EMPLOYÉS, BY INDUSTRIES—Cont'd.

NOTE.—This table is *not* a complete exhibit for industries or states, but covers only establishments investigated by the Bureau. See page 91, also summaries, pages 143 to 226.

LEATHER (MOROCCO), DELAWARE.—ESTAB. No. 324.

Time, 10 hours per day; 288 days the past year.

Occupations.	Number.		Daily wages.	
	Male.	Fem.	Male.	Fem.
Beamsmen	5		$1 75	
Colorers	2		1 58	
Colorer	a1		75	
Engineer	1		1 67	
Finishers	20		1 83	
Finishers	a19		62	
Shavers	3		2 42	
Shaver	a1		67	
Sewers		3		$1 00
Teamster	1		1 33	
Tanners	7		1 69	
Tanner	a1		75	

LEATHER (PATENT LEATHER), DELAWARE.—ESTAB. No. 325.

Time, 10 hours per day; — days the past year.

Occupations.	Male	Fem	Male	Fem
Beamsmen	7		$2 50	
Curriers	7		3 50	
Finishers	8		2 50	
Laborers	37		1 50	

LEATHER (MOROCCO), MASSACHUSETTS.—ESTAB. No. 326.

Time, 10 hours per day; 308 days the past year.

Occupations.	Male	Fem	Male	Fem
Beamsmen	10		$1 60	
Finishers	6		2 50	
Finishers	6		2 25	
Finishers	15		2 00	
Finishers	13		1 83	
Tanners	10		1 53	
Undesignated	65		1 25	

LEATHER (SOLE LEATHER), PENNSYLVANIA.—ESTAB. No. 327.

Time, 12 hours per day; 300 days the past year.

Occupations.	Male	Fem	Male	Fem
Beamsman	1		$1 33	
Beamsman	1		1 25	
Tanner	1		2 00	
Undesignated	7		1 00	

LEATHER (MOROCCO), PENNSYLVANIA.—ESTAB. No. 328.

Time, 10 hours per day; 300 days the past year.

Occupations.	Male	Fem	Male	Fem
Apprentices	7		$1 25	
Beamsmen	28		2 15	
Finishers	45		2 58	
Foreman	1		4 50	
Foreman			3 80	
Sewers		10		$1 66
Shavers	9		3 75	
Tanners	8		2 15	
Tanners	10		1 66	
Teamster	1		2 00	

LEATHER (MOROCCO), PENNSYLVANIA.—ESTAB. No. 329.

Time, 10 hours per day; 280 days the past year.

Occupations.	Number.		Daily wages.	
	Male.	Fem.	Male.	Fem.
Beamsmen	10		$2 15	
Colorer	1		1 70	
Finishers	32		2 50	
Pebblers	5		1 70	
Putters-out	2		1 70	
Sewers		4		$1 25
Shavers	5		3 00	
Tanners	8		1 80	
Valve boy	a1		67	

LEATHER (HARNESS LEATHER), PENNSYLVANIA.—ESTAB. No. 330.

Time, 10 hours per day; 300 days the past year.

Occupations.	Male	Fem	Male	Fem
Beamsmen	5		$1 80	
Engineer	1		2 00	
Finishers	31		1 60	
Foremen	3		3 75	
Laborers	24		1 20	
Liquor man	1		1 50	
Shavers	3		3 00	
Stock-room hands	2		1 50	
Teamster	1		2 00	
Watchman	1		1 50	

LINEN (YARN, NUMBER 36 ENGLISH), BELGIUM.—ESTAB. No. 331.

Time, 12½ hours per day; — days the past year.

Occupations.	Male	Fem	Male	Fem
Beamers and fillers	36		$0 50	
Bundlers	10		66	
Carders, tow		35		$0 40
Dressers	40		52	
Dryers	15		66	
Engineers and firemen	12		66	
Hacklers	b72		22	
Overseers (overlookers)	16		1 00	
Overseers' assistants (overlookers)	15		66	
Overseers' assistants		14		38
Preparers		b94		30
Preparers		b10		20
Reelers		140		40
Reelers		b20		20
Rovers		48		40
Spinners		270		40
Spinners		a110		31
Spinners		b103		20
Spreaders		30		33
Undesignated	17	23	50	35
Warehouse hands	29		48	
Warehouse hands	a17		43	
Warehouse hands	b8		20	
Workshop hands	60		50	
Workshop hands	a12		28	

a Youth. *b* Children.

OCCUPATIONS AND WAGES.

OCCUPATIONS, WITH NUMBER AND WAGES OF EMPLOYÉS, BY INDUSTRIES—Cont'd.

NOTE.—This table is *not* a complete exhibit for industries or states, but covers only establishments investigated by the Bureau. See page 91, also summaries, pages 143 to 226.

LINEN (DAMASK), GREAT BRITAIN.—Estab. No. 332.

Time, 10 hours per day; 302 days the past year.

Occupations.	Number.		Daily wages.	
	Male.	Fem.	Male.	Fem.
Beamers and warpers	2	11	$0 80	$0 40
Card cutters	4	11	38	40
Inspectors and pickers	7	17	65	30
Designers	4	1	1 60	32
Drawers	1	4	46	29
Dressers	10	......	75	......
Finishers and lappers	21	10	71	30
Firemen	3	......	87	......
Harness repairers	13	......	43	......
Joiners	4	......	1 05	......
Repair hands	12	......	84	......
Tenters	29	......	82	......
Undesignated	16	9	51	43
Weavers	1	422	74	36
Winders	3	114	80	39

LIQUORS AND BEVERAGES (MALT LIQUORS), ILLINOIS.—Estab. No. 333.

Time, 12 hours per day; 300 days the past year.

Bottlers	6	......	$1 72	......
Brewers	30	......	2 30	......
Cooper	1	......	2 50	......
Engineers	2	......	3 20	......
Firemen	2	......	1 92	......
Foreman	1	......	6 00	......
Laborers	3	......	1 72	......
Stablemen	2	......	1 54	......
Teamsters	12	......	2 12	......

LIQUORS AND BEVERAGES (MALT LIQUORS) ILLINOIS.—Estab. No. 334.

Time, 12 hours per day; 300 days the past year.

Brewers	2	......	$2 50	......
Brewer	1	......	2 13	......
Engineer	1	......	1 92	......
Foreman	1	......	4 00	......
Maltsters	2	......	1 92	......
Teamsters	2	......	1 73	......

LIQUORS AND BEVERAGES (MALT LIQUORS) ILLINOIS.—Estab. No. 335.

Time, 12 hours per day; 313 days the past year.

Bottlers	10	......	$1 25	......
Brewers and maltsters	20	......	2 00	......
Engineer	1	......	3 00	......
Engineer	1	......	2 00	......
Firemen	2	......	1 50	......
Foreman	1	......	5 00	......
Teamsters	5	......	1 75	......

LIQUORS AND BEVERAGES (DISTILLED LIQUORS), ILLINOIS.—Estab. No. 336.

Time, 12 hours per day; 300 days the past year.

Occupations.	Number.		Daily wages.	
	Male.	Fem.	Male.	Fem.
Ash wheeler	1	......	$1 50	......
Cooper	1	......	3 00	......
Coopers	4	......	2 15	......
Engineers	3	......	2 85	......
Firemen	4	......	2 00	......
Maltsters	6	......	1 75	......
Mash hands	3	......	2 00	......
Miller	1	......	3 00	......
Rectifier	1	......	2 00	......
Stablemen	12	......	1 50	......
Watchmen	2	......	2 00	......
Yard hands	3	......	1 50	......
Yeast maker	1	......	5 00	......

LIQUORS AND BEVERAGES (DISTILLED LIQUORS), ILLINOIS.—Estab. No. 337.

Time, 12 hours per day; 313 days the past year.

Beer runner	1	......	$2 00	......
Carpenter	1	......	2 25	......
Charcoal hand	1	......	1 67	......
Coopers	2	......	1 83	......
Engineer	1	......	4 17	......
Firemen	4	......	2 00	......
Foreman	1	......	3 00	......
Laborers	6	......	1 67	......
Mash hands	3	......	1 75	......
Meal man	1	......	1 75	......
Miller	1	......	3 00	......
Mill hand	1	......	1 67	......
Spirit runners	2	......	2 91	......
Watchman	1	......	1 71	......
Yeast maker	1	......	2 33	......

LIQUOR AND BEVERAGES (DISTILLED LIQUORS), ILLINOIS.—Estab. No. 338.

Time, 12 hours per day; 284 days the past year.

Beer runners	2	......	$3 00	......
Carpenters	2	......	2 50	......
Charcoal hand	1	......	2 33	......
Coopers	6	......	1 83	......
Dry ganger	1	......	3 67	......
Firemen	10	......	2 00	......
Foremen	2	......	3 67	......
Foreman	1	......	3 00	......
Laborers	4	......	2 00	......
Maltsters	3	......	1 83	......
Millers	3	......	2 67	......
Mill hands	10	......	2 17	......
Spirit runners	2	......	3 50	......
Teamster	1	......	2 50	......
Watchman	1	......	1 71	......

LIQUORS AND BEVERAGES (MALT LIQUORS), OHIO.—Estab. No. 339.

Time, 12 hours per day; 300 days the past year.

Brewers	45	......	$2 10	......
Teamsters	25	......	3 04	......

OCCUPATIONS, WITH NUMBER AND WAGES OF EMPLOYÉS, BY INDUSTRIES—Cont'd.

NOTE.—This table is *not* a complete exhibit for industries or states, but covers only establishments investigated by the Bureau. See page 91, also summaries, page 143 to 229.

LIQUORS AND BEVERAGES (MALT LIQUORS), OHIO.—ESTAB. NO. 340.

Time, 12 hours per day; 300 days the past year.

Occupations.	Number.		Daily wages.	
	Male.	Fem.	Male.	Fem.
Brewers	6		$2 28	
Engineer	1		3 84	
Engineer	1		2 88	
Engineer	1		2 26	
Firemen	3		2 28	
Laborers	30		2 00	
Teamsters	10		2 88	

LIQUORS AND BEVERAGES (MALT LIQUORS), OHIO.—ESTAB. NO. 341.

Time, 12 hours per day; — days the past year.

Bottlers	66		$0 83	
Brewers	20		2 00	
Engineer and fireman	1		2 00	
Foreman	1		2 00	
Teamsters	8		2 00	

LIQUORS AND BEVERAGES (DISTILLED LIQUORS), OHIO.—ESTAB. NO. 342.

Time, 12 hours per day; 300 days the past year.

Beer runner	1		$1 50	
Corn sheller	1		1 25	
Distiller	1		6 00	
Dry gauger	1		1 50	
Engineer	1		2 00	
Fireman	1		1 50	
Fermenting-room hand	1		1 00	
Maltster	1		2 00	
Mash hand	1		1 50	
Meal man	1		1 25	
Miller	1		2 00	
Teamsters	2		1 25	

LIQUORS AND BEVERAGES (MALT LIQUORS), PENNSYLVANIA.—ESTAB. NO. 343.

Time, 10 hours per day; 300 days the past year.

Brewers	6		$2 50	
Foreman	1		3 00	
Laborers	6		2 00	
Laborers	4		1 66	
Laborers	50		1 50	
Laborers	25		1 25	
Maltsters	6		2 00	
Teamsters	4		2 00	

LUMBER (STAVES, HEADINGS), ARKANSAS.—ESTAB. NO. 344.

Time, 10 hours per day; 291 days the past year.

Engineers	2		$3 00	
Foreman	1		2 00	
Jointers	4		2 25	
Laborers	20		1 50	
Sawyers	2		2 25	

LUMBER (SAWED LUMBER), ILLINOIS.—ESTAB. NO. 345.

Time, 11 hours per day; 220 days the past year.

Occupations.	Number.		Daily wages.	
	Male.	Fem.	Male.	Fem.
Edgers	2		$3 12	
Engineers	3		3 39	
Filers	4		3 25	
Firemen	6		1 50	
Laborers	80		1 40	
Machinists	2		2 62	
Millwrights	4		2 85	
Pilers and wheelers	80		1 50	
Sawyers	4		3 00	
Setters	2		2 00	
Trimmers	8		1 65	

LUMBER (SAWED AND PLANED LUMBER, LATHS, SHINGLES), ILLINOIS.—ESTAB. NO. 346.

Time, 11 hours per day; 220 days the past year.

Blacksmiths	4		$2 25	
Edgers	3		2 50	
Engineers	2		3 50	
Filers	5		2 50	
Firemen	6		1 75	
Foremen	2		4 00	
Foreman	1		2 00	
Loaders	63		1 34	
Laborers	95		1 56	
Laborers	30		1 45	
Laborers	60		1 25	
Millwrights	2		3 50	
Millwright	1		3 00	
Oiler	1		1 75	
Planers	17		1 00	
Sawyers	5		3 60	
Shingle and lath makers	33		1 37	
Truckers and pilers	66		1 36	

LUMBER (SAWED LUMBER), MAINE.—ESTAB. NO. 347.

Time, 10¼ hours per day; — days the past year.

Laborers	30		$1 50	
Loggers	5		2 00	
Log pilers	10		1 75	
Mill men	12		1 75	
Mill men	13		2 00	
Rafters	15		2 00	
Saw filers	3		2 50	
Sawyers	2		3 00	
Sawyers	5		2 00	

LUMBER (SAWED LUMBER), MICHIGAN.—ESTAB. NO. 348.

Time, 11 hours per day; 175 days the past year.

Blacksmith	1		$2 25	
Boom men	2		1 50	
Edgers	2		1 75	
Engineer	1		4 75	
Engineer	1		2 25	
Fireman	1		2 25	
Fireman	1		2 00	
Laborers	55		1 40	
Log jacker	1		1 62	

a Youth.

OCCUPATIONS AND WAGES.

OCCUPATIONS, WITH NUMBER AND WAGES OF EMPLOYÉS, BY INDUSTRIES—Cont'd.

NOTE.—This table is *not* a complete exhibit for industries or states, but covers only establishments investigated by the Bureau. See page 91, also summaries, pages 143 to 226.

LUMBER (SAWED LUMBER), MICHIGAN.—ESTAB. No. 348—Concluded.

Time, 11 *hours per day;* 175 *days the past year.*

Occupations.	Number.		Daily wages.	
	Male.	Fem.	Male.	Fem.
Millwright	1		$2 25	
Saw filers	2		4 50	
Sawyers	2		3 25	
Sawyer	1		2 75	
Sawyer	1		2 00	
Sawyers	5		1 75	
Teamster	1		1 60	
Trimmers	5		1 75	
Watchman	1		1 63	

LUMBER (SAWED LUMBER), WEST VIRGINIA.—ESTAB. No. 349.

Time, 10 *hours per day;* — *days the past year.*

Occupations.	Male.	Fem.	Male.	Fem.
Choppers	4		$1 10	
Dust roller	1		1 00	
Edger	1		1 25	
Fireman and engineer	1		1 25	
Loaders	2		1 10	
Loggers	6		1 10	
Lumber bearers	2		1 10	
Ratchet worker	1		1 25	
Road makers	2		1 10	
Sawyer	1		2 75	
Stackers	2		1 10	

LUMBER (SAWED LUMBER), WEST VIRGINIA.—ESTAB. No. 350.

Time, 10 *hours per day;* 300 *days the past year.*

Occupations.	Male.	Fem.	Male.	Fem.
Edgers	2		$1 25	
Fireman	1		1 25	
Laborers	4		1 25	
Lumber pilers	3		1 25	
Sawyer	1		2 00	
Watchman	1		1 00	

MACHINES AND MACHINERY (BOILERS, ENGINES), CALIFORNIA.—ESTAB. No. 351.

Time, 10 *hours per day;* 300 *days the past year.*

Occupations.	Male.	Fem.	Male.	Fem.
Blacksmiths	6		$3 75	
Blacksmiths' helpers	6		2 25	
Boiler makers	15		3 25	
Boiler-makers' helpers	10		2 00	
Laborers	10		2 00	
Machinists	5		2 00	
Moulders	20		3 50	
Moulders' helpers	10		2 15	
Pattern makers	8		3 50	

MACHINES AND MACHINERY (BOILERS, ENGINES), CALIFORNIA.—ESTAB. No. 352.

Time, 10 *hours per day;* — *days the past year.*

Occupations.	Male.	Fem.	Male.	Fem.
Boiler makers	3		$4 25	
Boiler-makers' helpers	4		2 00	
Carpenter	1		3 50	

MACHINES AND MACHINERY (BOILERS, ENGINES), CALIFORNIA.—ESTAB. No. 352—Concluded.

Time, 10 *hours per day;* — *days the past year.*

Occupations.	Number.		Daily wages.	
	Male.	Fem.	Male.	Fem.
Engineer	1		$3 00	
Laborers	2		2 00	
Machinists	4		3 00	
Watchman	1		1 75	

MACHINES AND MACHINERY (BOILERS, ENGINES), CALIFORNIA.—ESTAB. No. 353.

Time, 10 *hours per day;* — *days the past year.*

Occupations.	Male.	Fem.	Male.	Fem.
Apprentices	a10		$1 33	
Apprentice	a1		1 50	
Apprentices	a10		1 00	
Apprentices	a30		67	
Belt fixer	1		2 00	
Blacksmiths	4		3 50	
Blacksmith	1		3 25	
Blacksmiths	3		3 00	
Blacksmith	1		2 50	
Blacksmith	1		2 00	
Blacksmiths' helper	1		2 50	
Blacksmiths' helpers	15		2 25	
Blacksmiths' helpers	10		1 67	
Boiler makers	2		3 50	
Boiler makers	8		3 25	
Boiler maker	1		3 00	
Boiler makers	3		2 75	
Carpenters	2		3 50	
Carpenter	1		3 00	
Carpenters	2		2 50	
Carpenter	1		2 25	
Caulkers	2		3 25	
Core makers	2		3 75	
Core maker	1		3 50	
Core makers	2		2 75	
Core makers	3		2 50	
Chipper	1		2 50	
Chippers	2		2 25	
Chipper	1		2 00	
Chippers	3		1 75	
Cranemen	4		2 00	
Cranemen	2		1 75	
Draughtsman	1		4 50	
Draughtsman	1		4 25	
Draughtsmen	2		4 00	
Draughtsman	1		3 50	
Draughtsmen	3		2 50	
Draughtsman	1		1 33	
Engineer	1		3 00	
Foreman	1		8 00	
Foreman	1		6 00	
Foremen	3		5 50	
Foremen	2		4 50	
Foreman	1		4 25	
Foremen	3		4 00	
Foreman	1		3 00	
Foreman	1		2 50	
Flange turner	1		3 50	
Laborers	5		2 00	
Laborers	54		1 75	
Laborer	1		1 50	
Machinists	2		4 00	
Machinists	3		3 75	
Machinists	6		3 50	
Machinists	20		3 25	
Machinists	8		3 00	
Machinists	10		2 75	

a Youth.

OCCUPATIONS, WITH NUMBER AND WAGES OF EMPLOYÉS, BY INDUSTRIES—Cont'd.

NOTE.—This table is *not* a complete exhibit for industries or states, but covers only establishments investigated by the Bureau. See page 91, also summaries, pages 143 to 226.

MACHINES AND MACHINERY (BOILERS, ENGINES), CALIFORNIA.—ESTAB. No. 353—Concluded.

Time, 10 hours per day; — days the past year.

Occupations.	Number.		Daily wages.	
	Male.	Fem.	Male.	Fem.
Machinists	7		$2 50	
Machinists	8		2 00	
Machinists' helpers	3		2 50	
Machinists' helpers	7		2 25	
Machinists' helpers	3		2 00	
Machinists' helpers	13		1 67	
Machinists' helpers	15		1 33	
Machinists' helpers	13		1 00	
Machinists' helpers	a12		67	
Melter	1		3 00	
Moulders	2		3 75	
Moulders	4		3 50	
Moulders	23		3 25	
Oiler	1		2 50	
Painter	1		2 25	
Pattern maker	1		4 00	
Pattern makers	3		3 50	
Pattern makers	12		3 25	
Pattern maker	1		2 50	
Pattern-makers' helpers	2		2 50	
Plate worker	1		3 50	
Plate workers	6		3 25	
Plate workers	4		3 00	
Plate-workers' helper	1		2 50	
Plate-workers' helpers	11		2 25	
Plate-workers' helpers	8		2 00	
Riggers	5		2 00	
Sweeper	1		2 00	
Sweepers	3		1 75	
Ship carpenters	5		4 00	
Ship carpenter	1		3 75	
Ship carpenter	1		3 50	
Ship carpenter	1		2 50	
Teamsters	2		3 00	
Teamster	1		2 25	
Teamsters	2		2 00	
Watchman	1		2 75	
Watchman	1		2 25	
Watchmen	9		2 00	
Weigher	1		2 75	

MACHINES AND MACHINERY (SEWING MACHINES), ILLINOIS.—ESTAB. No. 354.

Time, 10 hours per day; 285 days the past year.

Occupations.	Male	Fem.	Male	Fem.
Adjuster	1		$3 00	
Adjuster	1		2 50	
Adjusters	2		2 00	
Fitters	14		1 95	
Fitters	8		1 75	
Fitters	4		1 45	
Fitters	a2		1 00	
Fitters	a3		60	
Foreman	1		3 25	
Foreman	2		2 25	
Japanner	1		3 00	
Japanners	2		2 25	
Japanner	1		1 00	
Japanners	a3		75	
Laborer	1		1 75	
Laborers	10		1 50	

MACHINES AND MACHINERY (SEWING MACHINES), ILLINOIS.—ESTAB. No. 354—Concluded.

Time, 10 hours per day; 285 days the past year.

Occupations.	Number.		Daily wages.	
	Male.	Fem.	Male.	Fem.
Laborers	4		$1 00	
Laborers	a5		75	
Laborers	a3		50	
Machine hands	3		1 75	
Machine hands	9		1 50	
Machine hands	14		1 25	
Machine hands	3		1 00	
Machine hands	a4		60	
Nickel plater	1		1 85	
Polishers	3		2 25	
Polisher	1		2 00	
Polisher	a1		1 15	
Screw maker	1		3 00	
Tool makers	2		3 25	
Tool makers	6		2 40	
Tool makers	2		1 75	
Tool maker	a1		1 15	

MACHINES AND MACHINERY (BOILERS), INDIANA.—ESTAB. No. 355.

Time, 10 hours per day; 120 days the past year.

Apprentice	a1		$0 75	
Boiler makers	4		2 50	
Boiler-makers' helpers	2		1 25	

MACHINES AND MACHINERY (BOILERS, ENGINES), INDIANA.—ESTAB. No. 356.

Time, 10 hours per day; 300 days the past year.

Blacksmiths	15		$2 50	
Boiler makers	100		2 00	
Carpenters	3		2 00	
Laborers	67		1 40	
Machinists	298		2 50	
Moulders	15		2 50	
Pattern makers	4		3 50	

MACHINES AND MACHINERY (ENGINES, SHAFTING, ETC.), INDIANA.—ESTAB. No. 357.

Time, 10 hours per day; 300 days the past year.

Apprentices, moulders	a2		$0 75	
Apprentice, moulders	a1		1 25	
Blacksmiths	2		2 75	
Blacksmiths' helper	1		1 50	
Cupola man	1		1 50	
Engineer	1		1 50	
Laborer	1		1 50	
Machinists	10		2 00	
Machinist	a1		1 00	
Millwrights	4		2 50	
Moulders	3		2 40	
Pattern makers	2		2 50	

a Youth.

OCCUPATIONS AND WAGES. 367

OCCUPATIONS, WITH NUMBER AND WAGES OF EMPLOYÉS, BY INDUSTRIES—Cont'd.

NOTE.—This table is *not* a complete exhibit for industries or states, but covers only establishments investigated by the Bureau. See page 91, also summaries, pages 143 to 226.

MACHINES AND MACHINERY (PORTABLE ENGINES, FARM MACHINERY), INDIANA.—ESTAB. No. **358**.

Time, 10 *hours per day*; 300 *days the past year*.

Occupations.	Number.		Daily wages.	
	Male.	Fem.	Male.	Fem.
Blacksmiths	8	......	$2 20	......
Blacksmiths' helpers	8	......	1 35	......
Boiler makers	10	......	2 00	......
Burr makers	2	......	2 80	......
Draughtsmen	3	......	3 50	......
Engineer	1	......	2 19	......
Grinders	2	......	1 50	......
Laborers	32	......	1 15	......
Laborers	a14	......	50	......
Machinists	43	......	2 30	......
Millwrights	12	......	2 10	......
Moulders	15	......	2 20	......
Pattern makers	4	......	3 00	......
Pipe cutters	3	......	1 75	......
Sheet-iron workers	4	......	2 00	......

MACHINES AND MACHINERY (MISCELLANEOUS MACHINERY), INDIANA.—ESTAB. No. **359**.

Time, 10 *hours per day*; 300 *days the past year*.

Occupations.	Male.	Fem.	Male.	Fem.
Blacksmiths	4	......	$2 60	......
Carpenters	4	......	2 50	......
Laborers	10	......	1 30	......
Machinists	22	......	2 20	......
Moulders	12	......	2 20	......
Pattern makers	3	......	2 50	......

MACHINES AND MACHINERY (ENGINES), KENTUCKY.—ESTAB. No. **360**.

Time, 10 *hours per day*; 300 *days the past year*.

Occupations.	Male.	Fem.	Male.	Fem.
Apprentices	a2	......	$1 00	......
Apprentices	a4	......	80	......
Blacksmiths	2	......	3 00	......
Blacksmiths	4	......	2 50	......
Blacksmiths' helpers	8	......	1 35	......
Blacksmiths' helpers	2	......	1 00	......
Cupolaman	1	......	2 50	......
Iron breakers	2	......	1 50	......
Laborers	20	......	1 35	......
Machinists	2	......	3 50	......
Machinists	3	......	3 00	......
Machinists	3	......	2 75	......
Machinists	20	......	2 00	......
Machinists	15	......	1 75	......
Machinists' helpers	10	......	1 00	......
Moulders	5	......	2 75	......
Moulders	5	......	2 00	......
Moulders' helpers	6	......	1 00	......
Pattern makers	6	......	2 50	......

MACHINES AND MACHINERY (STATIONARY ENGINES), MAINE.—ESTAB. No. **361**.

Time, 10 *hours per day*; — *days the last year*.

Occupations.	Male.	Fem.	Male.	Fem.
Apprentices	a5	......	$0 85	......
Blacksmiths	2	......	2 25	......
Blacksmith's helper	1	......	1 33	......

MACHINES AND MACHINERY (STATIONARY ENGINES), MAINE.—ESTAB. No. **361**—Concluded.

Time, 10 *hours per day*; — *days the past year*.

Occupations.	Male.	Fem.	Male.	Fem.
Engineer	1	......	$1 75	......
Furnace man	1	......	2 00	......
Machinists	10	......	2 50	......
Machinists' helpers	2	......	1 33	......
Moulders	13	......	2 50	......
Moulders	5	......	2 00	......
Moulders' helpers	8	......	1 33	......
Mounters	6	......	1 40	......
Pattern maker	1	......	2 25	......
Undesignated	1	......	85	......
Wood workers	2	......	2 25	......

MACHINES AND MACHINERY (TEXTILE MACHINERY), MASSACHUSETTS.—ESTAB. No. **362**.

Time, 10 *hours per day*; 308 *days the past year*.

Occupations.	Male.	Fem.	Male.	Fem.
Machinists	150	......	$2 25	......
Machinists' helpers	100	......	1 25	......
Wood workers	50	......	2 25	......

MACHINES AND MACHINERY (WOOD-WORKING MACHINES), MASSACHUSETTS.—ESTAB. No. **363**.

Time, 10 *hours per day*; 308 *days the past year*.

Occupations.	Male.	Fem.	Male.	Fem.
Engineer	1	......	$2 50	......
Laborers	5	......	1 50	......
Machinists	20	......	2 50	......
Watchmen	2	......	1 75	......
Wood workers	3	......	2 50	......

MACHINES AND MACHINERY (STATIONARY ENGINES), NEW JERSEY.—ESTAB. No. **364**.

Time, 10 *hours per day*; 300 *days the past year*.

Occupations.	Male.	Fem.	Male.	Fem.
Blacksmiths	3	......	$3 06	......
Laborers	45	......	1 45	......
Machinists	65	......	2 35	......
Moulders	30	......	2 64	......
Pattern makers	14	......	2 44	......

MACHINES AND MACHINERY (TEXTILE MACHINERY), PENNSYLVANIA.—ESTAB. No. **365**.

Time, 10 *hours per day*; — *days the past year*.

Occupations.	Male.	Fem.	Male.	Fem.
Apprentices	a40	......	$0 66	......
Foremen	6	......	3 00	......
Laborers	75	......	1 25	......
Laborers	25	......	1 10	......
Machinists	25	......	2 50	......
Machinists	100	......	2 00	......
Machinists	150	......	1 66	......
Undesignated	a50	......	50	......

a Youth.

OCCUPATIONS, WITH NUMBER AND WAGES OF EMPLOYÉS, BY INDUSTRIES—Cont'd.

NOTE.—This table is not a complete exhibit for industries or states, but covers only establishments investigated by the Bureau. See page 91, also summaries, pages 143 to 226.

METALS AND METALLIC GOODS (PIG IRON), ALABAMA.—ESTAB. No. 366.

Time, 24 hours per day (two turns); — days the past year.

Occupations.	Number.		Daily wages.	
	Male.	Fem.	Male.	Fem.
Breakers and loaders	10	......	$1 40	......
Cast-house men	13	......	1 10	......
Cindermen	10	......	1 40	......
Engineers	2	......	2 00	......
Fillers, top	4	......	1 50	......
Firemen	5	......	1 25	......
Foremen	2	......	3 00	......
Foremen	2	......	1 50	......
Iron carriers	4	......	1 50	......
Stock-house men	40	......	1 10	......
Stovemen	2	......	1 50	......
Teamsters	2	......	1 25	......
Weighers	2	......	1 50	......

METALS AND METALLIC GOODS (PIG IRON), BELGIUM.—ESTAB. No. 367.a

Time, 24 hours per day (two turns); — days the past year.

Occupations.	Male.	Fem.	Male.	Fem.
Blacksmiths	4	......	$0 60	......
Builders-up	b50	......	39	......
Calciners	30	......	70	......
Chargers	15	......	65	......
Chargers	......	21	......	$0 34
Carpenters	4	......	60	......
Coal carriers	2	......	48	......
Drivers	22	......	44	......
Dirt movers	5	......	52	......
Engineers	5	......	80	......
Fillers, bottom	......	12	......	32
Fillers, top	12	......	65	......
Firemen	5	......	61	......
Gallery cutters	25	......	71	......
Keepers	6	......	1 00	......
Keepers' helpers	18	......	64	......
Laborers	17	......	55	......
Laborers	12	......	45	......
Lamp carriers	b8	......	21	......
Lamp tenders	8	......	38	......
Loaders	15	......	54	......
Miners	55	......	73	......
Miners	75	......	40	......
Roadmen	75	......	59	......
Screeners	2	......	45	......
Sorters	3	......	45	......
Stock-house men	24	......	62	......
Undesignated	b32	......	32	......
Weighers	12	......	60	......

METALS AND METALLIC GOODS (BAR IRON), BELGIUM.—ESTAB. No. 368.

Time, 24 hours per day (two turns) c; — days the past year.

Occupations.	Male.	Fem.	Male.	Fem.
Foreman	1	......	$1 30	......
Foremen	2	......	1 00	......
Foremans' assistant	1	......	50	......
Machinists	4	......	40	......
Machinists' helpers	6	......	22	......
Masons	2	......	59	......
Puddlers	28	......	1 20	......

METALS AND METALLIC GOODS (BAR IRON), BELGIUM.—ESTAB. No. 368—Concluded.

Time, 24 hours per day (two turns) c; — days the past year.

Occupations.	Male.	Fem.	Male.	Fem.
Puddlers' helpers	56	......	$0 89	......
Rollers	2	......	85	......
Rollers' helpers	8	......	60	......
Rollers' helpers	b16	......	24	......
Shinglers	6	......	1 00	......
Weighers and laborers	15	......	56	......

METALS AND METALLIC GOODS (STEEL INGOTS), BELGIUM.—ESTAB. No. 369.

Time, 10½ hours per day; — days the past year.

Occupations.	Male.	Fem.	Male.	Fem.
Chemist	1	......	$0 65	......
Chemist's assistant	1	......	40	......
Foreman	1	......	1 10	......
Laborers	30	......	75	......
Laborers	b10	......	27	......
Melter	1	......	1 10	......
Melters' helpers	4	......	52	......

METALS AND METALLIC GOODS (STEEL PLATES), BELGIUM.—ESTAB. No. 370.

Time, 10½ hours per day; — days the past year.

Occupations.	Male.	Fem.	Male.	Fem.
Firemen	3	......	$0 70	......
Foreman	1	......	1 80	......
Foreman	1	......	1 00	......
Hammerman	1	......	1 50	......
Hammerman's helper	1	......	80	......
Heaters	3	......	1 40	......
Heaters' helpers	3	......	1 00	......
Heaters' helpers	3	......	70	......
Hookers-up	2	......	70	......
Laborers	6	......	60	......
Machinist	1	......	60	......
Machinist	1	......	50	......
Marker	1	......	1 20	......
Roller, chief	1	......	1 40	......
Roller, second	1	......	1 10	......
Roller, third	1	......	85	......
Rollers, fourth	2	......	70	......
Shearman	1	......	1 20	......
Shearman's helper	1	......	80	......
Shearmen's helpers	2	......	70	......
Shearmen's helpers	7	......	60	......
Shearmen's helpers	b3	......	34	......
Sweeper	1	......	52	......
Sweeper's helper	1	......	30	......

METALS AND METALLIC GOODS (STEEL RAILS), BELGIUM.—ESTAB. No. 371.

Time, 10½ hours per day; — days the past year.

Occupations.	Male.	Fem.	Male.	Fem.
Buggymen	4	......	$0 60	......
Foreman	1	......	1 00	......
Firemen	3	......	70	......
Firemen's helpers	2	......	30	......

a This establishment mines its own coal and makes coke. c The actual working time of employés is 10½ hours per day.
b Youth.

OCCUPATIONS AND WAGES.

OCCUPATIONS, WITH NUMBER AND WAGES OF EMPLOYÉS, BY INDUSTRIES—Cont'd.

NOTE.—This table is *not* a complete exhibit for industries or states, but covers only establishments investigated by the Bureau. See page 91, also summaries, pages 143 to 226.

METALS AND METALLIC GOODS (STEEL RAILS), BELGIUM.—ESTAB. No. **371**—Concluded.

Time, 10½ hours per day; — days the past year.

Occupations.	Number.		Daily wages.	
	Male.	Fem.	Male.	Fem.
Heaters	3		$1 40	
Heaters' helpers	3		1 00	
Heaters' helpers	3		70	
Hookers-up (crocheteurs)	6		70	
Machinist	1		64	
Machinist	1		60	
Machinist	1		50	
Roller, chief	1		1 40	
Rollers, second	2		1 00	
Rollers, third	2		90	
Roll turner	1		64	
Straightener	1		80	
Straighteners	4		60	

METALS AND METALLIC GOODS (ELECTROTYPES), CALIFORNIA.—ESTAB. No. **372**.

Time, 10 hours per day; 300 days this year.

Occupations.	Male	Fem	Male	Fem
Engineer	1		$2 00	
Finisher	1		3 33	
Finishers' helpers	11		1 25	
Moulders	3		3 00	

METALS AND METALLIC GOODS (IRON AND STEEL BARS AND RAILS), CALIFORNIA.—ESTAB. No. **373**.

Time, 10 hours per day; 280 days the past year.

Occupations.	Male	Fem	Male	Fem
Blacksmiths	18		$3 25	
Carpenters	6		3 25	
Forgemen	18		3 00	
Machinists	67		3 25	
Mill hands	58		2 75	
Steel workers	41		2 75	
Yard hands	82		1 75	

METALS AND METALLIC GOODS (BARBED WIRE, OTHER WIRE GOODS), CALIFORNIA.—ESTAB. No. **374**.

Time, 10 hours per day; — days the past year.

Occupations.	Male	Fem	Male	Fem
Barb-fence maker	1		$3 50	
Barb-fence makers	3		2 00	
Barb-fence makers	7		1 15	
Carpenters	5		3 00	
Carpenters' helpers	6		1 75	
Foreman	1		4 00	
Galvanizers	13		2 02	
Machinists	12		2 75	
Machinists' helpers	4		1 00	
Wire drawers	12		3 25	
Wire drawers	12		2 75	
Wire drawers	11		2 00	
Wire workers	20		3 00	
Wire-workers' helpers	20		1 25	

METALS AND METALLIC GOODS (SHEET IRON), DELAWARE.—ESTAB. No. **375**.

Time, 10 hours per day; 268 days the past year.

Occupations.	Number.		Daily wages.	
	Male.	Fem.	Male.	Fem.
Annealer	1		$1 85	
Annealer's helper	1		1 50	
Bundler	1		1 70	
Catchers	6		1 77	
Drag-outs	2		1 35	
Engineers	2		1 80	
Foreman	1		4 00	
Furnacemen	4		2 00	
Heaters	2		3 00	
Heaters' helpers	2		1 70	
Hookers-up	2		1 25	
Laborers	2		1 40	
Laborers	10		1 05	
Puddlers	6		2 50	
Puddlers' helpers	6		1 30	
Rollers	4		2 75	
Rollers	2		2 15	
Scrap man	1		1 50	
Spanner men	4		2 00	
Trimmer	1		3 00	

METALS AND METALLIC GOODS (PIG IRON), GREAT BRITAIN.—ESTAB. No. **376**.

Time, 24 hours per day (two turns); — days the past year.

Occupations.	Male	Fem	Male	Fem
Blacksmiths	2		$1 04	
Boiler cleaners	2		1 32	
Boiler makers	4		1 28	
Brakesmen	6		92	
Bricklayers	2		1 20	
Bymen	10		84	
Carpenters	2		1 04	
Engine cleaners	2		60	
Engineers	3		1 20	
Engineers	6		84	
Engineers	3		1 13	
Fillers	22		1 26	
Fillers	30		1 08	
Fillers	8		84	
Fillers	6		76	
Firemen	5		80	
Hoistmen	6		76	
Iron carriers	10		1 20	
Iron samplers	2		96	
Keepers	10		1 56	
Keepers' helpers	10		1 28	
Laborers	90		68	
Machinists	2		1 08	
Machine men	8		84	
Masons	2		1 20	
Moulder	1		1 08	
Ore dischargers	80		76	
Plate layers	6		72	
Road cleaners	2		64	
Slag tippers	4		84	
Spare brakemen	2		70	
Spare keepers	6		72	
Steam-crane men	2		84	
Stove cleaners	4		84	
Stovemen	4		96	
Sweepers	6		60	
Tube cleaners	4		96	

12854 LAB——24

OCCUPATIONS, WITH NUMBER AND WAGES OF EMPLOYÉS, BY INDUSTRIES—Cont'd.

NOTE.—This table is *not* a complete exhibit for industries or states, but covers only establishments investigated by the Bureau. See page 91, also summaries, pages 143 to 226.

METALS AND METALLIC GOODS (PIG IRON), GREAT BRITAIN.—ESTAB. No. 377.

Time, 24 hours per day (two turns); — days the past year.

Occupations.	Number.		Daily wages.	
	Male.	Fem.	Male.	Fem.
Barrow runners	4		$0 96	
Boilerman	1		1 00	
Dropman	1		98	
Dumpers	2		82	
Engineer	1		1 08	
Engineers	8		98	
Engineers	2		1 08	
Fillers, bottom	4		96	
Fillers, top	2		1 20	
Firemen	2		80	
Foreman	1		2 40	
Gasman	1		1 00	
Iron carriers	2		1 16	
Keepers	2		1 56	
Keepers' helpers	2		72	
Laborers	3		72	
Ore cleaner	1		00	
Slaggers	2		96	
Table loaders	2		1 00	
Table loader	1		98	
Truck emptiers	4		98	

METALS AND METALLIC GOODS (BAR IRON), GREAT BRITAIN.—ESTAB. No. 378.

Time, 12 hours per day; — days the past year.

Ashmen	8		$0 96	
Ash-lift driver	1		96	
Bankmen	2		1 12	
Bar carriers	8		1 12	
Bar drawers	6		1 36	
Blacksmiths	7		1 20	
Blacksmiths' helpers	7		88	
Blooming men	4		80	
Boiler men	2		1 08	
Bricklayers	6		1 20	
Bricklayers' helpers	6		72	
Catchers, muck	12		1 20	
Catchers, rail	3		1 32	
Coal tippers	4		1 20	
Cutters-down	12		1 32	
Donkey man	1		1 12	
Drag-outs	2		1 20	
Engineers	3		1 08	
Engineers	9		96	
Fillers	2		1 12	
Firemen	3		80	
Foreman	1		3 20	
Foreman	1		2 40	
Foreman	1		2 00	
Foreman	1		1 92	
Foremens' assistants	2		1 44	
Furnace men	14		1 60	
Laborers	20		72	
Loaders	4		1 44	
Metal tippers	3		1 20	
Millwrights	10		90	
Painters	3		96	
Pilers, iron	4		1 08	
Puddlers	240		2 43	
Riggers	5		1 32	
Roll turners	2		1 26	
Rollers, forge	2		2 16	
Roller, rail	1		4 80	
Roughers, forge	12		1 36	

METALS AND METALLIC GOODS (BAR IRON), GREAT BRITAIN.—ESTAB. No. 378—Concluded.

Time, 12 hours per day; — days the past year.

Occupations.	Number.		Daily wages.	
	Male.	Fem.	Male.	Fem.
Roughers, rail	3		$1 60	
Sawmen	2		1 20	
Scaler	1		1 20	
Shingler	1		3 60	
Shinglers, level hand	2		2 88	
Shinglers' helpers	9		1 92	
Straighteners	10		80	
Watchman	1		1 20	
Wheelers, coal	17		88	
Wheelers, fettling	6		88	
Wheelers, metal	17		1 12	
Wheelers, slag	6		88	

METALS AND METALLIC GOODS (CAST NAILS), GREAT BRITAIN.—ESTAB. No. 379.

Time, 10 hours per day; — days the past year.

Annealer	1		$1 30	
Cupola men	2		1 60	
Foreman	1		2 90	
Journeymen	12		2 20	
Scourer	a1		90	
Sorters		a2		$0 50
Underhands	12		1 00	

METALS AND METALLIC GOODS (STEEL PLATES), GREAT BRITAIN.—ESTAB. No. 380.b

Time, 24 hours per day (two turns); — days the past year.

Melters	10		$1 41	
Melters	16		1 08	
Melters' first helpers	10		85	
Melters' first helpers	10		67	
Melters' second helpers	16		76	
Melters' second helpers	10		58	
Pit men	10		85	
Pit men	16		67	
Weighers	3		72	

METALS AND METALLIC GOODS (BRASS CASTINGS), GREAT BRITAIN.—ESTAB. No. 381.

Time, 10 hours per day; — days the past year.

Castors	2		$2 40	
Finishers	6		1 20	
Finishers	12		85	
Finishers	a6		45	
Foremen	3		2 00	
Foremen	3		2 00	
Lacquerors		3		$0 70
Moulders	2		1 30	
Moulder's helper	1		85	
Moulders' helpers	a2		45	
Wrappers-up		2		45

a Youth.
b Employés in this establishment are not all reported.

OCCUPATIONS AND WAGES.

OCCUPATIONS, WITH NUMBER AND WAGES OF EMPLOYÉS, BY INDUSTRIES—Cont'd.

NOTE.—This table is *not* a complete exhibit for industries or states, but covers only establishments investigated by the Bureau. See page 91, also summaries, pages 143 to 226.

METALS AND METALLIC GOODS (BRASS CASTINGS), GREAT BRITAIN.—ESTAB. No. 382.

Time, 10 *hours per day;* — *days the past year.*

Occupations.	Number.		Daily wages.	
	Male.	Fem.	Male.	Fem.
Adjuster	1		$2 20	
Burnishers	2		1 77	
Caster	1		4 80	
Chaser	1		1 75	
Dipper	1		1 33	
Finishers	a3		80	
Finisher	a1		53	
Foremen	3		2 40	
Lacquerers		2		$0 80
Lathe men	3		1 55	
Moulder	1		1 70	

METALS AND METALLIC GOODS (BRASS CASTINGS), GREAT BRITAIN.—ESTAB. No. 383.

Time, 10 *hours per day;* — *days the past year.*

Occupations.	Male.	Fem.	Male.	Fem.
Adjusters	b2		$0 25	
Casters	3		2 30	
Core maker	1	1	1 05	$0 70
Foreman	1		3 33	
Lathe men	4		2 20	
Lathe men	3		1 33	
Lathe men	5		95	
Moulders, brass	3		1 25	
Moulders' helper, brass	c1		30	
Moulders' helper, brass	a1		62	
Moulders' helper, brass	a1		80	
Vise boys	a6		33	

METALS AND METALLIC GOODS (NAILS), ILLINOIS.—ESTAB. No. 384.

Time, 10 *hours per day;* — *days the past year.*

Occupations.	Male.	Fem.	Male.	Fem.
Annealer	1		$1 25	
Blacksmith	1		3 70	
Blacksmiths	2		2 75	
Blacksmiths' helpers	3		1 30	
Bluers	2		2 30	
Bluer helpers	a2		85	
Buggymen	2		1 90	
Buggymen	2		1 35	
Bricklayer	1		2 60	
Carpenters	2		1 75	
Catchers, plate	d2		6 30	
Catchers, slab	2		2 00	
Chargers	10		1 40	
Engineers	4		1 65	
Firemen	4		1 55	
Furnace-door tenders	a4		70	
Heaters, plate	4		6 25	
Heaters, old rail	6		4 15	
Heaters' helpers, plate	4		2 50	
Heaters' helpers, old rail	6		1 80	
Hookers-up, plate	2		2 00	
Hookers-up, slab	4		1 50	
Laborers	32		1 25	
Machinists	5		1 65	
Machine tenders	4		2 00	

METALS AND METALLIC GOODS (NAILS), ILLINOIS.—ESTAB. No. 384—Concluded.

Time, 10 *hours per day;* — *days the past year.*

Occupations.	Male.	Fem.	Male.	Fem.
Machine tenders	9		$1 50	
Master mechanic	1		3 70	
Nailers	d9		11 15	
Nailers	d10		9 20	
Nailers	d20		6 70	
Nail feeder	d1		4 50	
Nail feeders	d6		3 50	
Nail feeders	d12		2 25	
Nail feeders	d78		1 70	
Packer	d1		10 85	
Packer's helpers	d5		1 55	
Packer boys	a15		50	
Picker boys	b18		35	
Pilers, old rail	4		1 30	
Pilers, scrap	b4		50	
Rollers, plate	2		11 65	
Rollers, slab	d2		6 30	
Rollers' helpers, plate	d4		4 20	
Scrapers, plate	a2		85	
Shearman, plate	d1		12 00	
Shearman's helpers	2		2 75	
Shearman's helpers	15		1 50	
Shovers-under, plate	2		2 45	
Shovers-under, plate	4		1 87	
Telegraphmen	2		1 75	
Tenders, self-feeders	a57		85	
Warehouse men	3		1 35	
Watchmen	2		1 40	

METALS AND METALLIC GOODS (SPIKES, T RAILS), ILLINOIS.—ESTAB. No. 385.

Time, 10 *hours per day;* 250 *days the past year.*

Occupations.	Male.	Fem.	Male.	Fem.
Blacksmiths	4		$2 80	
Blacksmiths' helpers	4		1 80	
Bolt cutters	6		1 75	
Carpenter	1		2 00	
Catchers	4		3 50	
Engineers	6		2 80	
Firemen	6		1 80	
Foreman	1		4 33	
Foremen	2		3 00	
Gas makers	2		2 15	
Heaters	10		5 50	
Heaters' helpers	14		2 75	
Hookers-up	8		1 75	
Laborers	139		1 85	
Machinist	1		4 00	
Machinists	10		2 80	
Mason	1		5 00	
Nut cutters	2		1 50	
Nut maker	1		5 00	
Pattern maker	1		8 10	
Puddlers	6		4 00	
Puddlers' helpers	10		2 25	
Rollers	7		7 00	
Roll turners	3		3 30	
Roughers	11		3 50	
Scrapmen	4		1 25	
Shearmen	6		2 25	
Spike makers	6		2 50	
Strandsmen	8		2 00	
Teamsters	3		1 60	
Watchmen	3		1 55	

a Youth.   *b* Children.   *c* Child.   *d* All nail mill employés work only 5½ days per week.

OCCUPATIONS, WITH NUMBER AND WAGES OF EMPLOYÉS, BY INDUSTRIES—Cont'd.

NOTE.—This table is *not* a complete exhibit for industries or states, but covers only establishments investigated by the Bureau. See page 91, also summaries, pages 143 to 226.

METALS AND METALLIC GOODS (BAR AND PIG IRON), INDIANA.—Estab. No. 386.

Time, 10 hours per day; 269 days the past year.

Occupations.	Number.		Daily wages.	
	Male.	Fem.	Male.	Fem.
Blacksmiths	2		$2 00	
Blacksmiths' helpers	2		1 25	
Carpenters	2		1 80	
Catchers	2		3 75	
Crane tenders	2		1 60	
Engineers	6		1 75	
Fillers	10		1 35	
Firemen	2		1 20	
Gatemen	2		1 25	
Hammermen	2		4 00	
Heaters	4		4 50	
Heaters' helpers	9		1 60	
Keepers	2		1 85	
Keepers' helpers	2		1 40	
Laborers	53		1 20	
Machinists	2		3 00	
Masons	2		1 75	
Puddlers	32		4 00	
Puddlers' helpers	32		2 00	
Roller, guide	1		10 00	
Roller, bar	1		7 00	
Roller, muck	1		4 50	
Rollers' helpers	16		1 50	
Roll turner	1		3 00	
Roughers	6		3 75	
Shearmen	4		4 00	
Shearmen's helpers	7		1 50	
Teamsters	5		1 40	
Watchmen	2		1 35	
Warehouse men	3		1 50	

METALS AND METALLIC GOODS (STEEL RAILS), INDIANA.—Estab. No. 387.

Time, 10 hours per day; 200 days the past year.

Occupations.	Male.	Fem.	Male.	Fem.
Blacksmiths	3		$2 00	
Blacksmiths' helpers	3		1 50	
Carpenters	3		2 25	
Engineers	3		2 50	
Firemen	4		1 60	
Heaters	8		4 00	
Laborers	70		1 50	
Laborers	30		1 00	
Machinists	17		2 00	
Moulders	11		2 25	
Pattern makers	2		2 25	
Roll hands	11		3 50	

METALS AND METALLIC GOODS (BAR AND PLATE IRON), KENTUCKY.—Estab. No. 388.

Time, 10 hours per day; 150 days the past year.

Occupations.	Male.	Fem.	Male.	Fem.
Hammerman	1		$6 00	
Heaters, bar	2		5 00	
Heaters, bloom and scrap	2		5 50	
Heater, 8-inch	1		4 75	
Heater, plate	1		5 00	
Heater, sheet	1		5 25	
Heater, slat	1		5 00	
Laborers	100		1 25	
Puddlers	60		3 75	
Puddlers' helpers	40		2 00	

METALS AND METALLIC GOODS (BAR AND PLATE IRON), KENTUCKY.—Estab. No. 388—Concl'd.

Time, 10 hours per day; 150 days the past year.

Occupations.	Number.		Daily wages.	
	Male.	Fem.	Male.	Fem.
Roller, bar	1		$7 00	
Roller, 8-inch	1		6 00	
Roller, muck	1		4 00	
Roller, muck	1		3 50	
Roller, plate	1		9 00	
Roller, sheet	1		9 00	
Rollers' helpers, bar	10		2 00	
Rollers' helpers, eight-inch	6		2 25	
Rollers' helpers, muck	6		2 00	
Rollers' helpers, plate	7		2 25	
Rollers' helpers, sheet	5		2 25	

METALS AND METALLIC GOODS (BAR AND PLATE IRON), KENTUCKY.—Estab. No. 389.

Time, 10 hours per day; 213 days the past year.

Occupations.	Male.	Fem.	Male.	Fem.
Blacksmith	1		$3 00	
Blacksmith	1		2 50	
Blacksmiths' helpers	2		1 50	
Bricklayer	1		3 50	
Bricklayer's helper	1		1 50	
Bundler	1		3 00	
Bundler's helper	1		1 25	
Carpenter	1		1 65	
Cart driver	1		2 50	
Catcher, bar	1		4 00	
Catcher, plate	1		3 00	
Catcher, sheet	1		2 75	
Catchers' helpers	3		2 00	
Catchers' helpers	2		1 40	
Engineer	1		2 25	
Engineers	4		1 60	
Firemen	3		1 50	
Hammermen	3		3 50	
Hammermen's helpers	3		2 00	
Heater, plate	1		8 00	
Heater, 10-inch	1		7 00	
Heater, 8-inch	1		6 00	
Heater, sheet	1		6 00	
Heater, bar	1		4 25	
Heater's helper	1		2 75	
Heater's helper	1		2 50	
Heater's helper	1		1 65	
Knobblers	5		4 00	
Laborers	14		1 50	
Laborers	23		1 25	
Laborers	5		1 00	
Laborers	a3		75	
Laborers	a7		55	
Machinist	1		2 50	
Millwright	1		5 00	
Millwright's helper	1		1 50	
Pattern maker	1		2 50	
Piler, plate	1		4 00	
Piler, plate	1		1 50	
Pilers, plate	2		1 25	
Puddlers	22		3 25	
Puddler	1		2 50	
Puddlers' helpers	22		2 00	
Puddlers' helpers	22		1 25	
Roller, sheet	1		9 25	
Roller, plate	1		8 50	

a Youth.

OCCUPATIONS AND WAGES. 373

OCCUPATIONS, WITH NUMBER AND WAGES OF EMPLOYÉS, BY INDUSTRIES—Cont'd.

NOTE.—This table is not a complete exhibit for industries or states, but covers only establishments investigated by the Bureau. See page 91, also summaries, pages 143 to 226.

METALS AND METALLIC GOODS (BAR AND PLATE IRON), KENTUCKY.—Estab. No. 389—Concl'd.

Time, 10 hours per day; 213 days the past year.

Occupations.	Number.		Daily wages.	
	Male.	Fem.	Male.	Fem.
Roller, 10-inch	1		$3 50	
Roller, 8-inch	1		3 50	
Rollers, muck	2		5 00	
Roller, bar	1		4 25	
Rollers' helpers	10		2 00	
Roll turner	1		7 00	
Rougher, plate	1		3 00	
Rougher, sheet	1		3 00	
Rougher, bar	1		2 75	
Roughers, 10-inch	4		2 50	
Roughers, 8-inch	2		2 50	
Roughers, 8-inch	2		1 75	
Rougher's helper	1		2 00	
Scrappers	4		1 75	
Scrappers' helpers	a8		50	
Scrapmen	4		1 30	
Scrapmen	a2		50	
Shearman, plate	1		7 00	
Shearman	1		2 00	
Shearman	1		1 85	
Shearmen	2		1 65	
Shearmen	6		1 30	
Shearmen	2		1 10	
Shearmen's helpers	2		2 00	
Shearmen's helpers	2		1 65	
Shearman's helper	1		1 10	
Straighteners	5		1 60	
Watchmen	2		2 00	
Weighers	2		2 50	
Weighers	4		1 50	
Yard hand	1		2 50	

METALS AND METALLIC GOODS (WIRE GOODS), KENTUCKY.—Estab. No. 390.

Time, 10 hours per day; 300 days the past year.

Occupations.	Number.		Daily wages.	
	Male.	Fem.	Male.	Fem.
Cage framers	10		$2 00	
Cage makers	a5		75	
Cage wirers	10		1 50	
Engineer	1		1 50	
Iron workers	35		2 00	
Loaders	3		1 75	
Machine hands	10		1 00	
Sieve and riddle workers	5		1 00	
Wire workers (heavy)	10		1 50	
Wire weavers	8		1 25	
Wire workers (fancy)	a11		75	
Wire-workers' helper	a1		50	

METALS AND METALLIC GOODS (PIG IRON), MARYLAND.—Estab. No. 391.

Time, 24 hours per day (two turns); 201 days the past year.

Occupations.	Number.		Daily wages.	
	Male.	Fem.	Male.	Fem.
Breakers, ore	3		$1 25	
Cart drivers	3		1 17	
Cart drivers	4		1 25	
Coal burners	4		1 71	
Engineers	2		2 57	
Fillers	8		1 50	
Firemen	3		2 14	

METALS AND METALLIC GOODS (PIG IRON), MARYLAND.—Estab. No. 391—Concluded.

Time, 24 hours per day (two turns); 291 days the past year.

Occupations.	Number.		Daily wages.	
	Male.	Fem.	Male.	Fem.
Gutter men	6		$1 35	
Keepers	3		1 50	
Loaders	8		1 25	
Ore drawers	4		1 25	
Ore roasters	6		1 25	
Rakers	4		1 42	
Teamsters	4		1 30	
Watchman	1		1 07	
Wood fillers	10		1 50	
Wood loaders	2		1 50	

METALS AND METALLIC GOODS (PIG IRON), MARYLAND.—Estab. No. 392.

Time, 24 hours per day (two turns); 312 days the past year.

Occupations.	Number.		Daily wages.	
	Male.	Fem.	Male.	Fem.
Blacksmith	1		$1 75	
Blacksmiths' helper	1		1 00	
Brakeman	1		1 30	
Breakers, limestone	4		1 25	
Carpenter	1		1 75	
Cinder men	4		1 25	
Engineers	4		1 45	
Fillers	12		1 25	
Gutter men	4		1 27	
Keepers	4		1 50	
Keepers' helpers	7		1 25	
Laborers	25		1 25	
Machinist	1		2 30	
Machinist's helper	1		1 37	
Stable man	1		1 00	

METALS AND METALLIC GOODS (PIG IRON), MARYLAND.—Estab. No. 393.

Time, 24 hours per day (two turns); — days the past year.

Occupations.	Number.		Daily wages.	
	Male.	Fem.	Male.	Fem.
Blacksmiths	2		$1 50	
Charcoal burners	2		1 50	
Engineers	2		1 50	
Foundry man	1		3 00	
Keepers	2		1 50	
Keepers' helpers	2		1 25	
Laborers	77		95	

METALS AND METALLIC GOODS (BRASS GOODS), MASSACHUSETTS.—Estab. No. 394.

Time, — hours per day; — days the past year.

Occupations.	Number.		Daily wages.	
	Male.	Fem.	Male.	Fem.
Blacksmiths	4		$2 40	
Brass moulder	1		3 60	
Carpenters	5		2 25	
Foreman	1		3 20	
Laborers	18		1 20	
Machinists	40		2 20	
Moulders	19		2 00	
Pattern makers	2		2 80	

a Youth.

374 REPORT OF THE COMMISSIONER OF LABOR.

OCCUPATIONS, WITH NUMBER AND WAGES OF EMPLOYÉS, BY INDUSTRIES—Cont'd.

NOTE.—This table is not a complete exhibit for industries or states, but covers only establishments investigated by the Bureau. See page 91, also summaries, pages 143 to 226.

METALS AND METALLIC GOODS (PIG LEAD), MISSOURI.—ESTAB. No. 395.

Time, 8 hours per day; — days the past year.

Occupations.	Number.		Daily wages.	
	Male.	Fem.	Male.	Fem.
Blacksmiths	6		$2 00	
Carpenters	12		2 25	
Drillers	200		1 25	
Engineers	12		2 00	
Laborers	362		1 25	
Machinists	2		2 50	
Machinists' helpers	10		1 10	
Miners a	200		1 25	

METALS AND METALLIC GOODS (PIG LEAD), MISSOURI.—ESTAB. No. 396.

Time, 8 hours per day; — days the past year.

Occupations.	Male.	Fem.	Male.	Fem.
Blacksmith	1		$2 00	
Carpenter	1		2 50	
Carpenters	2		1 50	
Drillers	45		1 25	
Engineers	2		2 00	
Engineers	7		1 35	
Foremen	10		2 00	
Laborers	50		1 25	
Machinist	1		2 50	
Machinists' helpers	6		1 10	
Miners a	100		1 10	

METALS AND METALLIC GOODS (BUILDERS' HARDWARE), NEW HAMPSHIRE.—ESTAB. No. 397.

Time, 10 hours per day; — days the past year.

Occupations.	Male.	Fem.	Male.	Fem.
Fitters	50		$1 50	
Laborers	100		1 25	
Machinists	5		2 25	
Moulders	25		2 00	
Pattern makers	7		2 50	

METALS AND METALLIC GOODS (PIPE CASTINGS), NEW JERSEY.—ESTAB. No. 398.

Time, 9 hours per day; 300 days the past year.

Occupations.	Male.	Fem.	Male.	Fem.
Blacksmiths	3		$2 10	
Cupola men	2		2 10	
Laborers	12		1 35	
Machinists	4		2 00	
Moulders	8		2 50	
Moulders	30		2 37	
Moulders' helpers	38		1 41	
Pattern makers	4		2 40	
Teamsters	9		1 37	
Undesignated	1		1 66	

METALS AND METALLIC GOODS (PIG IRON), NEW YORK.—ESTAB. No. 399.

Time, 24 hours per day (two turns); — days the past year.

Occupations.	Male.	Fem.	Male.	Fem.
Blacksmith	1		$2 25	
Blacksmith's helper	1		1 25	
Brakemen	4		1 33	
Breakers, ore	6		1 33	
Carpenter	1		2 50	
Cindermen	2		1 33	

METALS AND METALLIC GOODS (PIG IRON), NEW YORK.—ESTAB. No. 399—Concluded.

Time, 24 hours per day; — days the past year.

Occupations.	Male.	Fem.	Male.	Fem.
Engineers	4		$1 66	
Fillers, top	2		1 50	
Fillers, bottom	12		1 33	
Foreman	1		2 81	
Keepers	2		1 67	
Keepers' helpers	4		1 50	
Machinist	1		3 00	
Machinist	1		2 00	
Machinist's helper	1		1 32	
Stable man	1		1 15	
Stove men	2		1 95	
Watchman	1		2 00	
Waterers, iron	2		1 32	
Weighers	2		1 33	
Yard hands	22		1 00	

METALS AND METALLIC GOODS (PIG IRON), NEW YORK.—ESTAB. No. 400.

Time, 24 hours per day (two turns); 365 days the past year.

Occupations.	Male.	Fem.	Male.	Fem.
Blacksmith	1		$2 00	
Blacksmith's helper	1		1 70	
Engineer	1		3 20	
Engineers	2		2 50	
Fillers, top	4		1 60	
Fillers, bottom	20		1 60	
Iron carriers	2		1 60	
Keepers	4		1 85	
Keepers' helpers	4		1 65	
Laborers	25		1 35	

METALS AND METALLIC GOODS (BAR IRON), NEW YORK.—ESTAB. No. 401.

Time, 10 hours per day; — days the past year.

Occupations.	Male.	Fem.	Male.	Fem.
Blacksmith	1		$1 91	
Blacksmith's helper	1		1 48	
Bundlers	2		1 55	
Carpenter	1		1 50	
Engineer	1		1 70	
Engineers	2		2 00	
Heaters	3		4 00	
Heaters	2		3 50	
Heaters' helpers	1		2 00	
Heaters' helpers	4		1 75	
Laborers	14		1 00	
Machinist	1		1 51	
Master mechanic	1		3 25	
Mason	1		2 95	
Masons' helpers	1		1 10	
Piler, iron	1		1 50	
Puddlers	21		3 15	
Puddlers' helpers	21		1 57	
Puddlers, level hand	6		2 96	
Pull-ups	52		56	
Rollers	3		6 00	
Rollers	2		5 25	
Roll turner	1		3 65	
Scrapman	1		1 75	
Scrapman	1		1 00	
Shearman	1		1 80	
Squeezer tender	1		1 50	
Watchman	1		1 20	
Waterers	2		1 60	
Wheelers	9		1 07	

a This establishment mines its own ore.   *b* Youth.

OCCUPATIONS AND WAGES. 375

OCCUPATIONS, WITH NUMBER AND WAGES OF EMPLOYÉS, BY INDUSTRIES—Cont'd.

NOTE.—This table is *not* a complete exhibit for industries or states, but covers only establishments investigated by the Bureau. See page 91, also summaries, pages 143 to 226.

METALS AND METALLIC GOODS (STEEL RAILS), NEW YORK.—ESTAB. No. **402**.

Time, 24 hours per day (two turns); — days the past year.

Occupations.	Number.		Daily wages.	
	Male.	Fem.	Male.	Fem.
Blacksmiths	8		$1 67	
Brakemen	6		1 75	
Buggymen	10		2 50	
Carpenters	2		1 67	
Catchers	6		2 60	
Chargers	23		2 07	
Cinder men	10		1 25	
Converters	8		2 08	
Cupola men	8		2 25	
Drag-outs	8		1 62	
Drillers	6		1 80	
Drop men	10		2 00	
Engineers	12		1 77	
Finishers	4		1 80	
Firemen	18		1 34	
Foremen	15		2 70	
Gaggers	8		2 52	
Gate men	2		1 54	
Hammermen	7		2 75	
Heaters	5		5 00	
Heaters' helpers	5		2 50	
Hookers-up	6		2 87	
Hookers-up	2		2 52	
Hookers-up, tumble	4		3 58	
Hydraulic men	8		1 50	
Laborers	36		1 38	
Ladlemen	6		2 14	
Leverman	1		2 10	
Loaders	16		1 35	
Machinists	12		2 00	
Melters	4		4 31	
Mould men	12		1 98	
Pit men	22		2 12	
Punchers	4		2 52	
Rollers	2		5 67	
Roughers	2		3 15	
Roughers	6		3 00	
Sawmen	2		2 39	
Scrapmen	2		1 25	
Shovers-up	6		1 77	
Stockers	26		1 95	
Straighteners	10		2 57	
Tableman	1		2 50	
Teamsters	4		1 00	
Tool-room men	2		1 27	
Trimmers	8		2 54	
Undesignated	10		2 12	
Watchmen	2		1 54	
Wheelers, coke	4		1 25	
Wheelers, limestone	2		1 25	

METALS AND METALLIC GOODS (HORSESHOES), NEW YORK.—ESTAB. No. **403**.

Time, 10 hours per day; — days the past year.

Occupations	Male	Fem	Male	Fem
Blacksmiths	2		$2 90	
Blacksmiths	18		2 50	
Blacksmiths	3		1 95	
Blacksmiths' helpers	13		1 37	
Ballers	16		3 50	
Bundlers	8		1 80	
Carpenters	3		2 25	
Catchers	22		1 72	
Chargers	3		2 00	
Engineers	4		3 00	

METALS AND METALLIC GOODS (HORSESHOES), NEW YORK.—ESTAB. No. **403**—Concluded.

Time, 10 hours per day; — days the past year.

Occupations.	Number.		Daily wages.	
	Male.	Fem.	Male.	Fem.
Engineers	8		$1 90	
Firemen	4		1 50	
Fitter feeders	100		3 00	
Fixers	2		1 50	
Foreman	1		5 50	
Foremen	2		4 50	
Foremen	4		4 00	
Foremen, assistant	3		3 00	
Furnace men	4		1 90	
Furnace men	86		1 50	
Gate men	2		1 25	
Heaters	32		4 23	
Heaters' helpers	32		1 75	
Hookers-up	3		2 40	
Hookers-up	4		1 50	
Hookers-up	18		1 30	
Horseshoe finishers	200		2 40	
Horseshoe nailers	50		2 25	
Horseshoe punchers	53		2 57	
Horseshoe runners	14		3 00	
Iron carriers	9		1 50	
Laborers	1,014		1 25	
Laborers	354		1 00	
Master mechanics	2		4 00	
Machinists	22		2 15	
Machinists	244		1 90	
Machinists' helpers	27		1 50	
Masons	3		2 50	
Masons' helpers	2		1 13	
Millwrights	2		2 15	
Moulders	7		2 50	
Mounters	3		2 25	
Nail-rod heaters	50		2 00	
Oilers	2		1 00	
Pilers, iron	5		1 40	
Puddlers	164		2 80	
Puddlers' helpers	147		1 50	
Rollers	26		4 84	
Rollers, muck	8		4 40	
Roll turners	4		3 60	
Roughers	18		2 50	
Scrapmen	150		1 50	
Shearmen	9		1 40	
Squeezer tenders	6		1 30	
Straighteners	13		1 67	
Straighteners, cold	3		1 50	
Undesignated	16		1 30	
Undesignated	a242		88	
Watchmen	2		1 25	
Watchmen	2		1 00	
Waste gatherers	2		1 00	
Waterers, iron	4		1 60	
Wheelers, coal	22		1 50	

METALS AND METALLIC GOODS (MERCHANT BRASS), NEW YORK.—ESTAB. No. **404**.

Time, 10 hours per day ; 290 days the past year.

Occupations	Male	Fem	Male	Fem
Annealers	2		$2 00	
Annealers' helpers	5		1 12	
Blacksmith	1		2 48	
Brass melter	1		3 00	
Brass-melters' helpers	3		1 62	
Brass workers	a4		85	

a Youth.

OCCUPATIONS, WITH NUMBER AND WAGES OF EMPLOYÉS, BY INDUSTRIES—Cont'd.

NOTE.—This table is *not* a complete exhibit for industries or states, but covers only establishments investigated by the Bureau. See page 91, also summaries, pages 143 to 226.

METALS AND METALLIC GOODS (MERCHANT BRASS), NEW YORK.—ESTAB. No. 404—Concluded.

Time, 10 hours per day; 290 days the past year.

Occupations.	Number.		Daily wages.	
	Male.	Fem.	Male.	Fem.
Brazier	1		$1 50	
Braziers	3		1 25	
Braziers	6		1 00	
Braziers	a2		75	
Brazier	a1		50	
Carpenter	1		1 80	
Coppersmith	1		3 00	
Engineer	1		2 40	
Foreman	1		4 78	
Foreman	1		4 00	
Foremen	2		3 00	
Foreman, assistant	1		1 62	
Laborers	8		1 00	
Laborers	8		1 12	
Machinist	1		3 00	
Machinist	1		1 75	
Packer	a1		50	
Pickler	1		1 62	
Pickler's helpers	2		1 12	
Press hands	4		1 05	
Press hands	a2		67	
Rivet maker	1		1 50	
Rollers	2		2 67	
Rollers' helpers	2		2 00	
Rollers' helpers	7		1 12	
Slitter	1		1 62	
Teamster	1		1 48	
Watchman	1		2 00	
Watchman	1		1 40	
Waterer	a1		75	
Wire drawers	2		2 40	
Wire drawers	3		1 85	
Wire drawers	2		1 50	
Wire drawers	5		1 25	

METALS AND METALLIC GOODS (PIG IRON), OHIO.—ESTAB. No. 405.

Time, 24 hours per day (two turns); — days the past year.

Occupations.	Number.		Daily wages.	
	Male.	Fem.	Male.	Fem.
Blacksmith	1		$2 00	
Blacksmith's helper	1		1 50	
Coal cleaners	3		1 25	
Engineer	1		2 77	
Engineer	1		1 75	
Fillers, bottom	12		1 25	
Fillers, top	2		1 35	
Gutterman (contractor)	b1		4 97	
Hot-blast men	2		1 25	
Keepers	2		1 75	
Keepers' helpers	2		1 35	
Laborer, boss	1		1 98	
Laborers	12		1 00	
Loaders	2		1 40	
Screeners and carters	3		1 25	
Unloaders	3		1 25	
Watchman	1		1 66	
Weighers	2		1 00	

METALS AND METALLIC GOODS (PIG IRON), OHIO.—ESTAB. No. 406.

Time, 25 hours per day (two turns); 232 days the past year.

Occupations.	Number.		Daily wages.	
	Male.	Fem.	Male.	Fem.
Blacksmith	1		$1 50	
Breakers, limestone	2		1 25	
Breakers, ore	2		1 50	
Carpenter	1		1 35	
Cindermen	2		1 15	
Engineers	2		1 75	
Engineers	2		1 15	
Fillers, top	2		1 05	
Fillers, bottom	2		1 05	
Gutter men	2		1 15	
Keepers	2		1 35	
Keepers' helpers	2		1 10	
Laborers	4		1 00	
Ore setter	1		1 25	
Stable man	1		1 25	
Watchman	1		1 50	

METALS AND METALLIC GOODS (PIG IRON), OHIO.—ESTAB. No. 407.

Time, 24 hours per day (two turns); 359 days the past year.

Occupations.	Number.		Daily wages.	
	Male.	Fem.	Male.	Fem.
Breakers, limestone	2		$1 25	
Carpenter	1		1 30	
Cart drivers	2		1 15	
Engineer	1		1 75	
Engineer	1		1 15	
Fillers, top	2		1 20	
Fillers, bottom	6		1 10	
Firemen	2		1 00	
Foundery man	1		2 70	
Iron carriers	2		1 15	
Keepers	2		1 40	
Keepers' helpers	2		1 10	
Laborers	10		1 00	

METALS AND METALLIC GOODS (PIG IRON), OHIO.—ESTAB. No. 408.

Time, 24 hours per day (two turns); 340 days the past year.

Occupations.	Number.		Daily wages.	
	Male.	Fem.	Male.	Fem.
Blacksmith	1		$2 10	
Breakers, iron	2		1 50	
Breakers, ore	4		1 20	
Cindermen	8		1 35	
Engineers	2		1 80	
Engineers	2		1 40	
Fillers, bottom	18		1 35	
Fillers, top	6		1 50	
Firemen	2		1 65	
Foundery man	1		5 56	
Iron carriers	3		1 30	
Keepers	2		1 60	
Keepers' helpers	9		1 35	
Laborers	13		1 10	
Machinist	1		2 00	
Overseer, night	1		2 17	
Sand man	1		1 10	
Waterers, iron	4		90	

a Youth.   b Included in this sum are the wages of two assistants.

OCCUPATIONS AND WAGES. 377

OCCUPATIONS, WITH NUMBER AND WAGES OF EMPLOYÉS, BY INDUSTRIES—Cont'd.

NOTE.—This table is *not* a complete exhibit for industries or states, but covers only establishments investigated by the Bureau. See page 91, also summaries, pages 143 to 226.

METALS AND METALLIC GOODS (PIG IRON), OHIO.—ESTAB. No. 409.

Time, 24 hours per day (two turns); 350 days the past year.

Occupations.	Number.		Daily wages.	
	Male.	Fem.	Male.	Fem.
Blacksmith	1		$1 50	
Blacksmith's helper	1		1 00	
Breakers, limestone	2		1 00	
Cagers	2		1 12	
Carpenter	1		1 50	
Cart drivers	4		1 08	
Cart drivers	2		1 25	
Cinder men	2		1 12	
Crib tender	1		1 12	
Engineers	2		82	
Fillers, top	4		1 10	
Fillers, bottom	12		1 12	
Firemen	2		1 00	
Guttermen	3		1 90	
Hot-blast man	1		1 00	
Keepers	2		1 40	
Keepers' helpers	2		1 15	
Loaders	3		1 08	
Overseer, night	1		1 75	
Screeners	4		1 00	

METAL AND METALLIC GOODS (PIG IRON), OHIO.—ESTAB. No. 410.

Time, 24 hours per day (two turns); 285 days the past year.

Occupations.	Male.	Fem.	Male.	Fem.
Blacksmith	1		$2 00	
Blacksmith's helper	1		1 25	
Boiler cleaners	2		1 32	
Brakeman	1		1 50	
Carpenters	2		1 87	
Cinder men	14		1 35	
Conductor	1		1 75	
Clay mixer	1		1 32	
Dock-brake boys	2		1 00	
Engineer	1		2 25	
Engineers	2		1 83	
Engineers	2		1 75	
Engineers	2		1 20	
Fillers, top	6		1 65	
Fillers, bottom	24		1 32	
Firemen	4		1 35	
Foremen	2		2 25	
Hot-blast men	2		1 48	
Iron carriers	14		1 75	
Keepers	2		1 76	
Keepers' helpers	10		1 48	
Laborers	20		1 10	
Machinist	1		1 75	
Sailor	1		1 65	
Scrapman	1		1 10	
Watchman	1		1 25	
Yard hands	21		1 32	

METALS AND METALLIC GOODS (PIG IRON), OHIO.—ESTAB. No. 411.

Time, 24 hours per day (two turns); — days the past year.

Occupations.	Male.	Fem.	Male.	Fem.
Breakers, iron	2		$1 20	
Cindermen	3		1 10	
Coal cleaner	1		1 10	
Fillers	8		1 10	
Foundry man	1		4 00	
Keepers	2		1 60	
Keepers' helpers	2		1 10	
Laborers	6		1 00	

METALS AND METALLIC GOODS (PIG IRON), OHIO.—ESTAB. No. 412.

Time, 24 hours per day (two turns); 285 days the past year.

Occupations.	Number.		Daily wages.	
	Male.	Fem.	Male.	Fem.
Blacksmith	1		$2 50	
Blacksmith's helper	1		1 25	
Boiler maker	1		1 75	
Brakemen	2		1 80	
Breakers, limestone	5		1 25	
Breakers, ore	5		1 30	
Carpenter	1		1 85	
Cinder men	10		1 32	
Dock-brake boys	2		1 00	
Engineers	3		2 25	
Engineers	2		1 83	
Fillers, bottom	24		1 35	
Fillers, top	6		1 55	
Firemen	6		1 40	
Iron carriers	10		1 60	
Keepers	4		1 60	
Keepers' helpers	8		1 35	
Laborers	29		1 20	
Laborers	14		1 10	
Machinist	1		1 75	
Pipe fitter	1		1 50	
Sailor	1		1 65	
Scrapmen	3		1 10	
Screeners	2		1 25	
Screeners	2		1 10	
Stockman	1		1 35	
Track repairer	1		1 50	
Watchman	1		1 30	
Weighers	4		1 10	

METALS AND METALLIC GOODS (PIG IRON), OHIO.—ESTAB. No. 413.

Time, 24 hours per day (two turns); 225 days the past year.

Occupations.	Male.	Fem.	Male.	Fem.
Blacksmith	1		$2 00	
Blacksmith's helper	1		1 15	
Breakers, limestone	2		1 25	
Breakers, ore	4		1 20	
Cagers	2		1 40	
Carpenters	2		1 75	
Cart drivers	2		1 20	
Cart drivers	4		1 40	
Engineers	3		2 00	
Fillers, top	8		1 50	
Fillers, bottom	12		1 40	
Fireman	1		1 30	
Iron carriers	6		1 32	
Keepers	2		2 00	
Keepers' helpers	4		1 40	
Laborers	12		1 15	
Overseer, night	1		2 50	
Overseer	1		2 50	
Scrapman	1		1 20	
Teamster	1		1 25	

METALS AND METALLIC GOODS (PIG IRON), OHIO.—ESTAB. No. 414.

Time, 24 hours per day (two turns); — days the past year.

Occupations.	Male.	Fem.	Male.	Fem.
Blacksmith	1		$2 00	
Blacksmith's helper	1		1 00	
Breakers, limestone	2		1 00	
Cagers	2		1 25	
Cart drivers	3		1 00	
Cinder men	2		1 25	
Engineers	2		1 75	

OCCUPATIONS, WITH NUMBER AND WAGES OF EMPLOYÉS, BY INDUSTRIES—Cont'd.

NOTE.—This table is not a complete exhibit for industries or states, but covers only establishments investigated by the Bureau. See page 91, also summaries, pages 143 to 226.

METALS AND METALLIC GOODS (PIG IRON), OHIO.—ESTAB. No. 414—Concluded.

Time, 24 hours per day (two turns); — days the past year.

Occupations.	Number.		Daily wages.	
	Male.	Fem.	Male.	Fem.
Fillers, top	2		$1 25	
Fillers, bottom	8		1 12	
Firemen	2		1 00	
Iron breakers and carriers	3		1 25	
Keepers	2		2 00	
Keepers' helpers	2		1 25	
Laborers	4		1 00	
Scrapmen	2		1 05	
Screeners	4		1 00	

METALS AND METALLIC GOODS (PIG AND BAR IRON), OHIO.—ESTAB. No. 415.

Time, 24 hours per day (two turns); 275 days the past year.

Occupations.	Number.		Daily wages.	
	Male.	Fem.	Male.	Fem.
Ash man	1		$2 00	
Blacksmith	1		2 50	
Blacksmith	1		2 00	
Blacksmiths' helper	1		1 75	
Blacksmiths' helpers	2		1 40	
Blacksmiths' helper	1		1 25	
Bricklayer	1		3 60	
Bricklayers' helper	1		1 25	
Bundlers	4		1 35	
Cagers	2		1 50	
Carpenter	1		2 25	
Cast-house men	8		1 35	
Catchers, bar	2		4 00	
Catchers, muck	2		2 50	
Catchers, 9-inch	2		2 50	
Catchers, 8-inch	2		1 50	
Catcher, butt	1		1 25	
Catchers' helpers	2		1 15	
Chargers	2		1 20	
Cinder men	2		1 70	
Cinder snappers	3		1 35	
Drag-outs, muck	2		2 65	
Drag-out, butt	1		1 20	
Engineer	1		2 50	
Engineer	1		2 25	
Engineers	3		1 80	
Engineers	2		1 75	
Engineer	1		1 10	
Fillers	8		1 35	
Fillers	8		1 25	
Finishers	2		2 25	
Firemen	4		1 60	
Foreman	1		6 00	
Foremen	2		2 25	
Heaters, 8-inch	2		7 00	
Heaters, 9-inch	4		5 00	
Heaters, bar	4		4 00	
Heater, butt	1		3 00	
Heater's helper, butt	1		2 00	
Heaters' helpers, bar	4		1 62	
Heaters' helpers, 8-inch	2		1 62	
Hookers-up, bar	1		1 55	
Hookers-up, bar	2		1 35	
Hookers-up, bar	2		1 10	
Hookers-up, muck	2		1 00	
Hookers-up, butt	a1		70	
Hot-blast men	2		1 35	
Keepers	2		1 60	

METALS AND METALLIC GOODS (PIG AND BAR IRON), OHIO.—ESTAB. No. 415—Concluded.

Time, 24 hours per day (two turns); 275 days the past year.

Occupations.	Number.		Daily wages.	
	Male.	Fem.	Male.	Fem.
Keepers' helpers	4		$1 25	
Laborer, boss	1		1 75	
Laborers	17		1 50	
Laborers	20		1 30	
Laborers	4		1 10	
Machinist	1		2 25	
Machinist's helper	1		1 35	
Millwright	1		3 60	
Pilers, iron	2		1 70	
Pilers, iron	2		1 50	
Pilers, iron	4		1 10	
Puddle bosses	2		1 75	
Puddlers	32		3 85	
Puddlers' helpers	44		1 95	
Rollers, 9-inch	2		12 00	
Roller, 8-inch	1		12 00	
Rollers, 8-inch	1		5 00	
Rollers, bar	2		4 00	
Rollers, muck	2		3 85	
Roller, butt	1		2 25	
Rollers' helper, muck	2		2 25	
Rollers' helpers, bar	2		1 80	
Roll turner	1		3 60	
Roll turner	1		2 00	
Roll turner	1		1 50	
Roughers, bar	2		2 96	
Roughers, bar	2		2 10	
Roughers, 8-inch	4		3 50	
Roughers, 9-inch	6		3 35	
Shearmen	4		2 10	
Shearmen	4		1 50	
Shearmen's helper	2		1 20	
Stickers-in, 8-inch	2		1 75	
Straightener, cold-bar	1		5 00	
Straighteners, hot-bar	4		1 44	
Straighteners, 8-inch	a4		70	
Straighteners, 9-inch	4		1 40	
Strandsmen	4		1 25	
Teamsters	4		1 70	
Unloaders	5		1 50	
Watchman	1		1 50	
Weighers	5		1 35	
Wheelers, coal	3		1 70	
Wheelers, coal	2		1 40	
Wheelers, iron	3		1 10	

METALS AND METALLIC GOODS (BAR IRON), OHIO.—ESTAB. No. 416.

Time, 10 hours per day; 269 days the past year.

Occupations.	Number.		Daily wages.	
	Male.	Fem.	Male.	Fem.
Blacksmith	1		$3 75	
Blacksmith's helper	1		1 65	
Carpenter	1		2 25	
Engineers	3		2 25	
Finishers	10		1 50	
Firemen	2		1 40	
Heaters	4		5 25	
Heaters' helpers	4		1 75	
Laborer, boss	1		2 50	
Laborers	28		1 12	
Millwright	1		2 75	
Puddlers	8		3 25	
Puddlers' helpers	8		2 25	
Rollers	5		6 00	

OCCUPATIONS AND WAGES.

OCCUPATIONS, WITH NUMBER AND WAGES OF EMPLOYÉS, BY INDUSTRIES—Cont'd.

NOTE.—This table is *not* a complete exhibit for industries or states, but covers only establishments investigated by the Bureau. See page 91, also summaries, pages 143 to 226.

METALS AND METALLIC GOODS (BAR IRON), OHIO.—ESTAB. No. 416—Concluded.

Time, 10 hours per day; 269 days the past year.

Occupations.	Number.		Daily wages.	
	Male.	Fem.	Male.	Fem.
Roughers	10		$3 60	
Shearmen	2		1 65	
Shearmen's helpers	2		1 40	
Straighteners	a10		80	
Watchmen	2		1 60	

METALS AND METALLIC GOODS (HOOP IRON, COTTON TIES), OHIO.—ESTAB. No. 417.

Time, 10 hours per day; 225 days the past year.

Occupations.	Male	Fem	Male	Fem
Blacksmiths	3		$2 25	
Breakers, iron	3		1 25	
Breakers, ore	2		2 00	
Bundlers	16		1 53	
Catchers	4		2 50	
Drag-outs	6		3 00	
Engineers	2		2 50	
Firemen	4		1 33	
Heaters	7		(b)	
Heaters' helpers	13		1 70	
Laborers	12		1 30	
Laborers	25		1 10	
Machinists	2		2 00	
Masons	2		4 00	
Millwrights	2		1 60	
Puddlers	42		4 00	
Puddlers' helpers	42		1 33	
Rollers	8		(c)	
Roll turners	5		3 00	
Roughers	14		4 00	
Straighteners and drag-outs	50		(d)	
Warehouse men	3		1 40	
Waterers	2		1 20	

METALS AND METALLIC GOODS (STEEL RAILS, RODS, INGOTS), OHIO.—ESTAB. No. 418.

Time, 10 hours per day; — days the past year.

Occupations.	Male	Fem	Male	Fem
Blacksmith	1		$2 50	
Blacksmiths	8		1 95	
Blowers	2		2 25	
Boiler makers	11		1 76	
Boiler-makers' helpers	12		1 50	
Boiler-makers' helper	1		1 36	
Bottom man	1		2 75	
Brakemen	8		1 60	
Bricklayer	1		1 50	
Brickmakers	2		3 00	
Brickmaker's helper	1		1 25	
Bulldog men	2		2 20	
Bullhead men	12		2 25	
Buggymen	0		1 22	
Bundlers	8		2 00	
Bundlers	4		1 20	
Buttmen	2		1 00	
Catchers	12		2 50	
Catchers	6		2 15	
Catchers	4		1 69	
Catchers	a2		1 25	
Catchers' helpers	4		75	

METALS AND METALLIC GOODS (STEEL RAILS, RODS, INGOTS), OHIO.—ESTAB. No. 418—Concluded.

Time, 10 hours per day; — days the past year.

Occupations.	Number.		Daily wages.	
	Male.	Fem.	Male.	Fem.
Chargers	24		$1 73	
Chargers	46		1 32	
Chippers	6		1 25	
Cinder men	12		1 85	
Core maker	1		1 30	
Cupola men	18		1 74	
Drag-outs	12		1 05	
Drillers	8		1 30	
Electric-light man	1		1 89	
Engineers	6		2 30	
Engineers	7		1 97	
Engineers	30		1 77	
Engineers	2		1 46	
Engineers	4		1 06	
Engineers	11		1 09	
Firemen	63		1 15	
Foreman	1		9 00	
Foremen	2		6 90	
Foremen	3		4 66	
Foreman	1		4 00	
Foreman	1		3 66	
Foremen	9		2 77	
Foreman	1		2 20	
Gas men	10		1 23	
Hammermen	2		2 50	
Heaters	10		5 00	
Heaters	4		4 50	
Heaters	10		3 60	
Heaters	8		3 29	
Heaters	12		2 65	
Heater	1		2 00	
Heaters' helpers	4		2 25	
Heaters' helpers	67		1 64	
Heaters' helpers	8		1 35	
Heaters' helpers	15		1 26	
Hookers-up	6		1 80	
Hookers-up	8		1 57	
Hookers-up	14		1 35	
Hookers-up	8		1 10	
Hot-bed men	6		1 25	
Laborers	4		1 50	
Laborers	27		1 31	
Laborers	309		1 01	
Ladlemen	12		2 11	
Ladlemen	4		1 41	
Large crab men	2		1 65	
Lead-outs	6		1 30	
Lever men	2		2 00	
Machinist	1		2 70	
Machinists	18		2 05	
Machinist	1		1 55	
Machinists' helpers	7		1 50	
Machinists' and blacksmiths' helpers	19		1 23	
Melter	1		4 00	
Melter	1		1 70	
Melters' helpers	2		1 40	
Moulder	1		2 30	
Moulders	3		2 07	
Moulders	10		1 70	
Moulders' helpers	7		1 38	
Pit men	18		2 12	
Pit men	4		1 80	
Rail runners	16		1 00	
Reelers	14		1 57	
Reversers	2		1 70	
Rollers, hoop	2		12 00	
Rollers, rod	2		10 00	
Rollers, rod	6		7 00	

a Youth.   *b* $5 to $8 per day.   *c* $5 to $10 per day.   *d* 50 cents to $1 per day.

380   REPORT OF THE COMMISSIONER OF LABOR.

OCCUPATIONS, WITH NUMBER AND WAGES OF EMPLOYÉS, BY INDUSTRIES—Cont'd.

NOTE.—This table is *not* a complete exhibit for industries or states, but covers only establishments investigated by the Bureau. See page 91, also summaries, page 143 to 226.

METALS AND METALLIC GOODS (STEEL RAILS, RODS, INGOTS), OHIO.—ESTAB. No. 418—Concluded.

Time, 10 hours per day; — days the past year.

Occupations.	Number.		Daily wages.	
	Male.	Fem.	Male.	Fem.
Rollers, guide	2		$6 00	
Rollers, muck	2		4 25	
Rollers, 18-inch	2		3 60	
Rollers	4		2 17	
Rollers' helpers	2		3 00	
Roll turners	13		2 25	
Roughers	12		2 78	
Roughers	6		2 63	
Roughers	16		2 29	
Roughers	4		1 62	
Runnersmen	12		1 84	
Saw men	2		1 80	
Screw men	4		1 67	
Shearmen, scrap	29		1 02	
Shearmen	4		1 52	
Shearmen	14		1 14	
Slatters	3		1 90	
Small crab boys	a2		60	
Splice finishers	3		2 00	
Stockers	22		1 28	
Speigel scalesmen	2		1 20	
Steel watchers	a2		75	
Stickers-in	12		2 50	
Stickers-in	2		1 82	
Stickers-in	4		1 30	
Stockmen	6		1 27	
Strandsmen	2		1 25	
Straighteners	4		4 00	
Straighteners, cold	2		2 00	
Straighteners	a8		1 08	
Telegraph men	28		1 77	
Telegraph men	13		1 24	
Throw-overs	2		1 50	
Tongsmen and hookers	20		3 12	
Tongsmen	2		2 60	
Undesignated	8		1 25	
Undesignated	a12		1 02	
Undesignated	a24		85	
Undesignated	a36		63	
Undesignated	b19		45	
Undesignated	b13		32	
Unloaders, coal	15		1 20	
Vessel men	6		2 00	
Watchman	1		1 20	
Waterers	4		1 20	
Weighers	2		1 20	
Weigher	1		2 40	
Weigher	1		2 00	
Weighers	2		1 80	
Weighers	9		1 15	
Wheelers, coal and ash	82		1 03	

METALS AND METALLIC GOODS (PLATE IRON, PLATE STEEL), OHIO.—ESTAB. No. 419.

Time, 10 hours per day; 280 days the past year.

Occupations.	Number.		Daily wages.	
	Male.	Fem.	Male.	Fem.
Blacksmith	1		$3 08	
Blacksmith	1		1 92	
Blacksmith's helpers	2		1 35	
Buggymen	2		3 14	
Carpenters	3		2 30	
Catchers, muck	2		4 84	
Catcher's helpers	2		2 42	

a Youth.
b Children.
c This sum includes wages of 12 assistants.

METALS AND METALLIC GOODS (PLATE IRON, PLATE STEEL), OHIO.—ESTAB. No. 419—Concluded.

Time, 10 hours per day; 280 days the past year.

Occupations.	Number.		Daily wages.	
	Male.	Fem.	Male.	Fem.
Cinder men	2		$1 50	
Cinder men	1		1 29	
Cold roller	1		1 54	
Cold rollers' helpers	a2		69	
Drag-outs, muck	6		1 78	
Drag-onts, plate	2		2 65	
Drag-out, helper	a1		90	
Engineer	1		2 80	
Engineer	1		2 60	
Engineers	3		2 12	
Firemen	3		1 70	
Fireman	1		1 10	
Furnace-door tenders	a2		50	
Galvanizer	c1		46 15	
Heaters	d4		6 13	
Heaters, plate	3		6 80	
Heaters, sheet	4		4 70	
Heater's helpers, plate	3		2 33	
Heater's helpers	3		2 03	
Heater's helpers	3		1 49	
Heater's helpers, sheet	8		2 05	
Heater's helpers	4		1 70	
Holster	1		1 10	
Hookers-up	a4		1 24	
Knobblers	e17		5 44	
Laborers	100		1 00	
Machinist	1		3 46	
Machinists	3		2 50	
Mason	1		3 09	
Marker	1		1 38	
Marker's helpers	a2		39	
Matchers	4		1 54	
Oiler	1		1 34	
Pack openers	2		1 67	
Painter	1		3 85	
Pilers, iron	8		1 35	
Piler, plate	d1		13 27	
Puddlers	16		3 35	
Puddlers' helpers	16		2 22	
Roller, plate	f1		27 88	
Rollers, sheet	4		6 67	
Rollers, muck	2		3 43	
Rollers' helpers, muck	4		2 09	
Roll turner	1		3 85	
Scrapmen	a4		80	
Screwman	1		2 80	
Scorer	1		1 55	
Shearman	1		4 60	
Shearman, plate	1		3 27	
Shearman, muck	1		3 08	
Shearmen, scrap	6		1 73	
Shearmen's helpers, plate	5		1 92	
Shearman's helper, muck	1		1 79	
Shearman's helper	1		1 67	
Shearman's helper	1		1 10	
Shinglers	2		7 54	
Shinglers' helpers	2		3 92	
Stocker	1		1 50	
Watchmen	4		1 50	
Wolghor	1		2 15	
Weighers	5		1 85	
Wheelers, coal	3		1 46	
Wheelers, coal	2		1 35	

d This sum includes the wages of 4 helpers.
e Includes wages of assistants.
f This sum includes wages of helpers.

OCCUPATIONS AND WAGES.

OCCUPATIONS, WITH NUMBER AND WAGES OF EMPLOYÉS, BY INDUSTRIES—Cont'd.

NOTE.—This table is *not* a complete exhibit for industries or states, but covers only establishments investigated by the Bureau. See page 91, also summaries, pages 143 to 226.

METALS AND METALLIC GOODS (STEEL WIRE), OHIO.—ESTAB. NO. 420.

Time, 10 hours per day; — days the past year.

Occupations.	Number.		Daily wages.	
	Male.	Fem.	Male.	Fem.
Blacksmiths	8		$1 06	
Bundlers	63		1 18	
Carpenters	8		1 86	
Cleaners	210		1 28	
Die reamers	27		1 67	
Engineers	5		1 67	
Firemen	14		1 08	
Foremen	20		3 89	
Furnace men and potsmen	43		1 18	
Galvanizers	95		1 08	
Laborers	400		1 08	
Machinists	7		2 25	
Mufflers	54		1 18	
Pointers	43		1 23	
Tiners	20		1 38	
Wheelers	62		1 18	
Wire drawers	375		2 10	

METAL AND METALLIC GOODS (CRUCIBLE STEEL), OHIO.—ESTAB. NO. 421.

Time, 10 hours per day; — days the past year.

Occupations.	Number.		Daily wages.	
	Male.	Fem.	Male.	Fem.
Foremen	2		$3 09	
Hammermen	4		4 16	
Hammermen's helpers	6		1 44	
Heaters	5		2 75	
Laborers	26		1 25	
Machinists	4		2 16	
Melters	3		4 80	
Melters' helpers	10		1 84	
Rollers	3		8 00	
Roughers and finishers	17		1 87	
Straighteners	a16		75	

METALS AND METALLIC GOODS (NAILS), OHIO.—ESTAB. NO. 422.

Time, 10 hours per day; — days the past year.

Occupations.	Number.		Daily wages.	
	Male.	Fem.	Male.	Fem.
Blacksmith	1		$3 25	
Blacksmiths	2		2 50	
Blacksmiths' helpers	2		1 75	
Bluer	1		4 65	
Bluer's helper	1		1 50	
Catchers	2		4 80	
Cropper	1		2 75	
Cropper's helper	a1		75	
Engineer	1		3 50	
Engineers	2		2 50	
Engineer	1		2 00	
Firemen	6		1 50	
Heaters, plate	8		5 62	
Heaters' helpers	8		2 50	
Hookers-up	2		2 70	
Laborers	15		1 15	
Machinist	1		3 60	
Machine tenders	8		2 50	
Nailers	27		8 48	.●
Nail feeders	51		2 04	
Packer	1		1 00	
Pilers, iron	a8		1 00	
Pull-overs	2		2 25	

METALS AND METALLIC GOODS (NAILS), OHIO.—ESTAB. NO. 422—Concluded.

Time, 10 hours per day; — days the past year.

Occupations.	Number.		Daily wages.	
	Male.	Fem.	Male.	Fem.
Rollers	2		$9 25	
Roughers	2		3 50	
Shearman, plate	1		6 15	
Shearman's helper	1		3 25	
Shearmen's helpers	6		2 40	
Shovers-under	4		3 20	
Tenders, self-feeders	a74		75	

METALS AND METALLIC GOODS (NAILS), OHIO.—ESTAB. NO. 423.

Time, 10 hours per day; — days the past year.

Occupations.	Number.		Daily wages.	
	Male.	Fem.	Male.	Fem.
Bluer	1		$4 00	
Bluer's helpers	a2		50	
Catchers, muck	3		2 50	
Catchers, plate	2		3 20	
Drag-outs	3		2 00	
Engineers	2		3 00	
Firemen	3		1 50	
Heaters	6		5 00	
Heater's helpers	6		2 00	
Hookers-up, plate	2		1 60	
Hookers-up, muck	3		1 50	
Hot-machine tenders	5		2 50	
Laborers	5		1 10	
Nailers	23		6 50	
Nail feeders	81		1 50	
Packer	1		6 00	
Packer's helpers	a17		50	
Pilers, iron	2		1 25	
Puddlers	42		8 00	
Puddlers' helpers	42		2 00	
Puddlers' helpers	42		1 25	
Rollers, muck	3		5 00	
Rollers, plate	2		7 00	
Roughers, plate	2		3 00	
Shearman, muck	2		1 35	
Shearman, plate	1		7 00	
Shearmen's helpers	5		1 60	
Shovers-under, plate	4		2 00	
Wheelers, ash	2		1 35	
Wheelers, iron	3		1 50	

METALS AND METALLIC GOODS (PIG IRON), PENNSYLVANIA.—ESTAB. NO. 424.

Time, 24 hours per day (two turns); 365 days the past year.

Occupations.	Number.		Daily wages.	
	Male.	Fem.	Male.	Fem.
Blacksmith	1		$2 50	
Blacksmith's helper	1		1 50	
Breakers, iron	16		1 30	
Carpenter	1		2 75	
Carpenter	1		2 00	
Cindermen	6		1 45	
Engineers	2		2 20	
Fillers, top	4		1 90	
Fillers, bottom	16		1 55	
Firemen	2		1 45	
Iron carriers	10		1 80	
Keepers	2		3 25	
Keepers' helpers	6		1 70	
Laborers	20		1 20	
Loaders	2		1 80	

a Youth.

OCCUPATIONS, WITH NUMBER AND WAGES OF EMPLOYÉS, BY INDUSTRIES—Cont'd.

NOTE.—This table is not a complete exhibit for industries or states, but covers only establishments investigated by the Bureau. See page 91, also summaries, pages 143 to 226.

METALS AND METALLIC GOODS (PIG IRON), PENNSYLVANIA.—ESTAB. No. 425.

Time, 24 hours per day (two turns); 185 days the past year.

Occupations.	Number.		Daily wages.	
	Male.	Fem.	Male.	Fem.
Engineers	2	......	$2 20	......
Fillers	10	......	1 65	......
Firemen	2	......	1 50	......
Keepers	2	......	2 00	......
Laborers	5	......	1 30	......
Laborers	40	......	1 15	......

METALS AND METALLIC GOODS (PIG IRON), PENNSYLVANIA.—ESTAB. No. 426.

Time, 24 hours per day (two turns); 150 days the past year.

Occupations.	Male.	Fem.	Male.	Fem.
Blacksmith	1	......	$2 00	......
Blacksmith's helper	1	......	1 35	......
Brakemen	3	......	1 85	......
Breaker, ore	1	......	1 65	......
Breaker, ore	1	......	1 25	......
Cart driver	1	......	2 25	......
Cinder snappers	2	......	1 35	......
Dumper	1	......	1 30	......
Engineer	1	......	2 65	......
Engineers	4	......	1 60	......
Fillers, bottom	18	......	1 35	......
Fillers, top	3	......	1 65	......
Hot-blast men	2	......	1 25	......
Incline brakeman	1	......	2 25	......
Keepers	2	......	1 80	......
Keepers' helpers	4	......	1 35	......
Laborer	1	......	1 70	......
Laborers	10	......	1 10	......
Stock-house men	2	......	1 20	......
Wheelers, ore	2	......	1 52	......

METALS AND METALLIC GOODS (BAR IRON), PENNSYLVANIA.—ESTAB. No. 427.

Time, 10 hours per day; 260 days the past year.

Occupations.	Male.	Fem.	Male.	Fem.
Blacksmith	1	......	$3 50	......
Blacksmiths' helpers	3	......	1 70	......
Carpenter	1	......	2 00	......
Catcher, bar	1	......	4 00	......
Catchers, 8-inch	2	......	3 00	......
Catchers, 10-inch	2	......	3 00	......
Catchers, muck	5	......	2 50	......
Catchers' helper	1	......	2 50	......
Cindermen	3	......	1 66	......
Drag-outs, 10-inch	2	......	2 00	......
Drag-out, bar	1	......	1 85	......
Engineer	1	......	3 50	......
Engineers	3	......	2 00	......
Firemen	2	......	1 05	......
Greaser	1	......	2 00	......
Grease distributer	1	......	1 15	......
Heaters, 8-inch	2	......	6 00	......
Heaters, 10-inch	2	......	6 00	......
Heaters, bar	2	......	5 00	......
Heaters' helper, bar	1	......	1 35	......
Laborer	1	......	1 45	......
Laborers	5	......	1 35	......
Laborers	6	......	1 25	......
Millwright	1	......	3 15	......

METALS AND METALLIC GOODS (BAR IRON), PENNSYLVANIA.—ESTAB. No. 427—Concluded.

Time, 10 hours per day; 260 days the past year.

Occupations.	Number.		Daily wages.	
	Male.	Fem.	Male.	Fem.
Pilers and chargers, bar	2	......	$1 58	......
Pilers and chargers, 10-inch	2	......	1 58	......
Puddlers	68	......	3 50	......
Puddle bosses	2	......	4 00	......
Puddlers' helpers	68	......	2 00	......
Rollers, 8-inch	2	......	8 00	......
Rollers, 10-inch	2	......	7 00	......
Roller, bar	1	......	6 00	......
Rollers, muck	3	......	3 50	......
Roughers, 8-inch	2	......	3 00	......
Roughers, 10-inch	2	......	3 00	......
Roughers, bar	1	......	3 25	......
Roughers, muck	5	......	2 50	......
Roughers' helpers	3	......	2 00	......
Shearman	1	......	1 75	......
Shearmen	5	......	1 65	......
Shearmen	6	......	1 85	......
Stocker	1	......	3 00	......
Stocker's helpers	4	......	2 00	......
Straighteners	2	......	2 00	......
Straighteners	3	......	1 00	......
Watchmen	3	......	1 65	......

METALS AND METALLIC GOODS (BAR IRON, NAILS, ETC.), PENNSYLVANIA.—ESTAB. No. 428.a

Time, 10 hours per day; 250 days the past year.

Occupations.	Male.	Fem.	Male.	Fem.
Blacksmiths and helpers	202	......	$1 75	......
Bricklayers	33	......	3 00	......
Cold-roll men	130	......	2 00	......
Engineers	25	......	2 40	......
Firemen	22	......	1 70	......
Laborers	45	......	2 00	......
Laborers	120	......	1 25	......
Laborers	300	......	1 12	......
Machinists	135	......	2 40	......
Millwrights and carpenters	40	......	2 30	......
Moulders	90	......	2 80	......
Pattern makers	20	......	2 40	......
Puddlers	152	......	3 35	......
Puddlers' helpers	152	......	2 13	......

METALS AND METALLIC GOODS (WROUGHT IRON PIPE), PENNSYLVANIA.—ESTAB. No. 429.

Time, 10 hours per day; 300 days the past year.

Occupations.	Male.	Fem.	Male.	Fem.
Blacksmiths	15	......	$2 00	......
Boiler makers	30	......	2 00	......
Carpenters	20	......	2 25	......
Engineers and firemen	35	......	2 00	......
Heaters and welders	450	......	3 00	......
Laborers	700	......	1 15	......
Machinists and helpers	157	......	2 00	......
Masons	6	......	3 50	......
Moulders	45	......	2 25	......
Pattern makers	10	......	2 50	......

a Rollers, heaters, catchers, nailers, etc., were not reported.

OCCUPATIONS AND WAGES.

OCCUPATIONS, WITH NUMBER AND WAGES OF EMPLOYÉS, BY INDUSTRIES—Cont'd.

NOTE.—This table is *not* a complete exhibit for industries or states, but covers only establishments investigated by the Bureau. See page 91, also summaries, pages 143 to 226.

METALS AND METALLIC GOODS (IRON SAFES), PENNSYLVANIA.—ESTAB. No. 430.

Time, 10 hours per day; 300 days the past year.

Occupations.	Number.		Daily wages.	
	Male.	Fem.	Male.	Fem.
Carpenters	2		$2 50	
Iron workers	101		1 80	
Laborers	9		1 25	
Painters	2		3 00	
Teamster	1		2 00	

METALS AND METALLIC GOODS (PIPE IRON), PENNSYLVANIA.—ESTAB. No. 431.

Time, 10 hours per day; 300 days the past year.

Occupations.	Male.	Fem.	Male.	Fem.
Blacksmiths	4		$2 45	
Bricklayers	7		8 25	
Carpenters	4		2 30	
Cupola man	1		5 00	
Engineers	6		2 00	
Firemen	4		1 50	
Heaters	18		6 00	
Heaters' helpers	36		1 85	
Laborers	300		1 15	
Machinists	7		2 90	
Pilers, iron	12		1 80	
Puddlers	98		3 62	
Puddlers' helpers	98		2 24	
Refiners	2		5 00	
Rollers, plate	2		10 00	
Rollers, muck	4		5 00	
Rollers' helpers	28		2 20	
Shearmen	2		5 10	
Shearmen	12		3 00	
Shearmen's helpers	2		1 86	
Shinglers	a2		12 00	

METALS AND METALLIC GOODS (CRUCIBLE STEEL), PENNSYLVANIA.—ESTAB. No. 432.

Time, 10 hours per day; — days the past year.

Occupations.	Male.	Fem.	Male.	Fem.
Blacksmith	1		$2 25	
Blacksmiths' helpers	2		1 70	
Bricklayers	3		3 50	
Bricklayers' helpers	2		2 00	
Bricklayers' helpers	3		1 65	
Carpenters	6		1 95	
Charcoal grinder	1		1 30	
Engineers	2		3 25	
Engineers	5		1 96	
Engineers	8		1 30	
Firemen	3		1 70	
Foreman	1		5 00	
Foremen	4		4 00	
Foremen	2		3 50	
Foreman	1		3 00	
Foreman	3		2 50	
Foreman	1		2 00	
Hammermen	7		4 50	
Inspectors	17		1 75	
Laborers	9		1 35	
Laborers	15		1 00	
Laborers	b3		75	
Machinists	4		2 37	
Medicine man	1		1 20	
Millwright	1		4 00	

METALS AND METALLIC GOODS (CRUCIBLE STEEL), PENNSYLVANIA.—ESTAB. No. 432—Concluded.

Time, 10 hours per day; — days the past year.

Occupations.	Number.		Daily wages.	
	Male.	Fem.	Male.	Fem.
Millwright's helpers	4		$1 70	
Rollers	a5		30 00	
Testers	2		1 45	
Watchman	1		2 25	
Watchmon	2		1 35	
Weighers	3		1 70	
Weigher	1		1 30	
Wire drawer	1		3 70	

METALS AND METALLIC GOODS (CRUCIBLE STEEL), PENNSYLVANIA.—ESTAB. No. 433.

Time, 10 hours per day; 296 days the past year.

Occupations.	Male.	Fem.	Male.	Fem.
Blacksmiths	8		$3 00	
Carpenter	1		2 75	
Die grinder	1		1 70	
Engineer	1		5 75	
Foreman	1		5 75	
Foreman	1		1 50	
Greaser	1		1 58	
Hammermen	20		3 00	
Laborers	46		1 50	
Laborers	100		1 25	
Melters	a4		31 23	
Millwright	1		3 75	
Millwright's helper	1		2 48	
Plumber	1		3 50	
Roller, 18-inch	a1		173 52	
Roller, bar	a1		112 75	
Roller, 22-inch	a1		71 85	
Roller, bloom	a1		82 99	
Roller, bar	a1		12 40	
Roller, muck	a1		9 00	
Roll turner	1		5 08	
Stockman	1		1 35	
Watchmen	7		1 90	
Weigher	1		1 35	

METALS AND METALLIC GOODS (STEEL RAILS), PENNSYLVANIA.—ESTAB. No. 434.

Time, 24 hours per day (two turns); — days the past year.

Occupations.	Male.	Fem.	Male.	Fem.
Blacksmiths	7		$2 10	
Blacksmiths' helpers	9		1 25	
Blowers	2		2 80	
Brakemen	5		1 60	
Bricklayers	10		2 70	
Buggymen	18		2 48	
Buggyman	1		1 65	
Carpenters	7		2 30	
Catchers	9		2 80	
Catchers	3		2 07	
Chargers	9		2 93	
Chippers and filers	12		1 80	
Cinder men	21		2 25	
Cleaners-up	6		1 35	
Converter bottom builders	9		3 40	
Converter hands	9		2 85	
Door h nds	6		99	

a Pay helpers out of earnings.   *b* Youths.

OCCUPATIONS, WITH NUMBER AND WAGES OF EMPLOYÉS, BY INDUSTRIES—Cont'd.

NOTE.—This table is *not* a complete exhibit for industries or states, but covers only establishments investigated by the Bureau. See page 91, also summaries, pages 143 to 226.

METALS AND METALLIC GOODS (STEEL RAILS), PENNSYLVANIA.—Estab. No. 434—Concluded.

Time, 24 hours per day (three turns); — days the past year.

Occupations.	Number.		Daily wages.	
	Male.	Fem.	Male.	Fem.
Door hands	66		$0 72	
Door hand	a1		62	
Drag-outs	6		1 15	
Drawers	15		2 30	
Drillers	2		2 25	
Drillers	12		1 88	
Engineers	2		2 10	
Engineers	41		1 60	
Foremen	1		5 20	
Foremen	2		2 50	
Foremen	2		1 87	
Forgeman	1		2 70	
Hammerman	1		2 70	
Hammermen	12		1 98	
Heaters	3		4 68	
Heaters' helpers	10		2 25	
Heaters' helpers	4		1 50	
Hookers-up	2		1 80	
Hot-bed hands	12		2 50	
Hot clippers	3		2 32	
Hydraulic hands	a3		60	
Hydraulic hoisters	a3		60	
Inspectors	2		2 40	
Laborers	50		1 35	
Laborers	160		1 20	
Ladle men and pit men	61		2 85	
Lever men	3		1 35	
Machinists	35		2 07	
Machinists' helpers	10		1 25	
Markers	2		1 62	
Masons	2		2 15	
Monkey	1		1 15	
Rail loaders	18		2 60	
Recorders	2		2 34	
Recorders	2		1 62	
Regulators	12		1 60	
Rollers	3		4 32	
Rollers' helpers	3		2 07	
Roughers	6		4 00	
Runner hands	15		1 05	
Shearmen	6		2 89	
Spiegel melters	3		3 55	
Stockers	24		2 12	
Straighteners, cold	12		3 22	
Straightening-press hands	18		1 35	
Strikers	3		1 53	
Telegraph men	30		1 67	
Undesignated	90		90	
Waterers	9		1 80	
Waterers	2		1 35	
Weighers	2		1 80	

METALS AND METALLIC GOODS (PIG IRON), TENNESSEE.—Estab. No. 435.

Time, 24 hours per day (two turns); 350 days the past year.

Occupations.	Number.		Daily wages.	
	Male.	Fem.	Male.	Fem.
Blacksmith	1		$1 35	
Blacksmith's helper	1		90	
Breakers, ore	4		90	
Engineer	1		2 10	
Engineer	1		1 80	
Engineer	1		1 35	
Fillers, top	2		1 30	
Fillers, bottom	10		1 10	

METALS AND METALLIC GOODS (PIG IRON), TENNESSEE.—Estab. No. 435—Concluded.

Time, 24 hours per day (two turns); 350 days the past year.

Occupations.	Number.		Daily wages.	
	Male.	Fem.	Male.	Fem.
Foundery men	2		$3 00	
Keepers	2		1 80	
Keepers' helpers	2		1 35	

METALS AND METALLIC GOODS (SCALES), VERMONT.—Estab. No. 436.

Time, 10 hours per day; 300 days the past year.

Occupations.	Number.		Daily wages.	
	Male.	Fem.	Male.	Fem.
Blacksmiths	8		$2 10	
Engineers	5		2 30	
Foremen	13		3 50	
Laborers	62		1 10	
Machinists	10		1 75	
Metal workers	52		2 20	
Moulders	31		2 25	
Painters	15		1 50	
Scalers	17		1 75	
Wood workers	24		1 90	

METALS AND METALLIC GOODS (PIG IRON), VIRGINIA.—Estab. No. 437.

Time, 24 hours per day (two turns); 300 days the past year.

Occupations.	Number.		Daily wages.	
	Male.	Fem.	Male.	Fem.
Blacksmith	1		$1 50	
Breakers, ore	4		1 00	
Cinder men	4		1 00	
Engineers	2		1 50	
Fillers	12		1 10	
Foundery man	1		5 00	
Keepers	2		1 50	
Keepers' helpers	2		1 15	
Iron carriers	2		1 00	
Laborers	5		90	
Watchman	1		90	

METALS AND METALLIC GOODS (PIG IRON), VIRGINIA.—Estab. No. 438.

Time, 24 hours per day (two turns); 320 days the past year.

Occupations.	Number.		Daily wages.	
	Male.	Fem.	Male.	Fem.
Blacksmith	1		$3 05	
Blacksmith's helper	1		90	
Cart drivers	2		1 13	
Cart drivers	a2		50	
Cindermen	6		1 13	
Dumpers	2		1 08	
Engineers	2		1 65	
Fillers, bottom	16		1 13	
Fillers, top	4		1 30	
Firemen	2		1 08	
Foundery man	1		4 00	
Gutter men	2		1 17	
Iron carriers	15		1 10	
Keepers	2		2 00	
Keepers' helpers	6		1 45	
Laborers	8		95	
Machinist	1		2 50	
Stableman	1		1 13	
Unloaders	12		1 00	
Weighers	2		1 85	

a Youth.

OCCUPATIONS AND WAGES.

OCCUPATIONS, WITH NUMBER AND WAGES OF EMPLOYÉS, BY INDUSTRIES—Cont'd.

NOTE.—This table is *not* a complete exhibit for industries or states, but covers only establishments investigated by the Bureau. See page 91, also summaries, pages 143 to 226.

METALS AND METALLIC GOODS (PIG IRON), VIRGINIA.—ESTAB. No. **439**.

Time, 24 hours per day (two turns); 360 days the past year.

Occupations.	Number.		Daily wages.	
	Male.	Fem.	Male.	Fem.
Blacksmith	1		$2 00	
Blacksmith's helper	1		1 50	
Brakemen	2		1 40	
Carpenter	1		2 13	
Carpenters	2		1 75	
Carpenter	1		1 40	
Cart drivers	2		1 05	
Cindermen	10		1 10	
Engineers	3		2 00	
Fillers, top	4		1 30	
Fillers, bottom	30		1 10	
Firemen	3		1 40	
Foreman	1		2 35	
Foreman	1		2 00	
Foreman	1		1 40	
Graders	13		1 00	
Iron carriers	8		1 15	
Keepers	2		2 30	
Keepers' helpers	6		1 50	
Laborer	1		95	
Ore cleaner	1		1 10	
Ore cleaners	4		95	
Scrapmen	4		1 00	
Stove men	2		1 70	
Unloaders	6		95	
Weigher	1		1 60	
Weighers	2		1 40	

METALS AND METALLIC GOODS (BAR IRON, NAILS), VIRGINIA.—ESTAB. No. **440**.

Time, 10 hours per day; — days the past year.

Occupations.	Male.	Fem.	Male.	Fem.
Apprentices	a10		$0 50	
Blacksmiths	2		2 00	
Blacksmiths' helpers	2		1 10	
Furnace men	2		1 50	
Foremen	3		3 60	
Heater, bar	1		3 50	
Heaters, plate	2		3 50	
Heater's helper, bar	1		1 25	
Heaters' helpers, plate	3		1 25	
Laborers	25		1 10	
Machinist	1		2 75	
Machinist's helper	1		1 50	
Millwright	1		2 25	
Nailers	6		4 50	
Nail feeders	22		1 30	
Puddlers	20		2 35	
Puddlers' helpers	20		1 40	
Roll hands, muck	10		1 50	
Roll hands, plate	8		2 50	
Roll hands, bar	8		3 00	
Shearmen	4		1 10	
Wheelers	2		1 10	

METALS AND METALLIC GOODS (BAR IRON, NAILS), VIRGINIA.—ESTAB. No. **441**.

Time, 10 hours per day; 260 days the past year.

Occupations.	Male.	Fem.	Male.	Fem.
Catchers	20		$1 60	
Heaters, plate	15		4 00	
Heaters, bar	16		3 45	
Heaters' helpers	15		1 60	

METALS AND METALLIC GOODS (BAR IRON, NAILS), VIRGINIA.—ESTAB. No. **441**—Concluded.

Time, 10 hours per day; 260 days the past year.

Occupations.	Number.		Daily wages.	
	Male.	Fem.	Male.	Fem.
Nailers	37		$4 40	
Nail feeders	146		1 20	
Puddlers	79		2 35	
Puddlers' helpers	159		1 40	
Rollers, plate	6		4 25	
Rollers, bar	8		3 75	
Roughers	24		1 60	
Undesignated	a30		30	

METALS AND METALLIC GOODS (SPIKES, BAR IRON), VIRGINIA.—ESTAB. No. **442**.

Time, 8 hours per day; 275 days the past year.

Occupations.	Male.	Fem.	Male.	Fem.
Blacksmiths	6		$1 90	
Boiler maker	1		1 84	
Carpenters	10		1 50	
Carpenters' helpers	10		85	
Catchers, guide	20		1 38	
Foremen	2		2 25	
Heaters, 18-inch	8		3 50	
Heaters, guide	10		3 02	
Heaters, guide	2		2 43	
Heaters' helpers, guide	10		1 50	
Heaters' helpers, guide	2		1 23	
Laborers	300		90	
Machinists	15		2 00	
Masons	4		3 00	
Millwrights	2		2 25	
Moulders	25		2 00	
Pattern makers	3		2 00	
Puddlers	25		2 40	
Puddlers' helpers	25		1 10	
Roller, guide	1		4 50	
Rollers, 18-inch	4		3 60	
Rollers, guide	5		3 50	
Rollers	4		3 20	
Rollers, muck	2		2 30	
Roll turners	2		3 25	
Roughers, 18-inch	5		2 50	
Roughers, guide	20		2 25	
Roughers, guide	4		2 05	
Scrap men	20		1 50	
Spike catchers	14		2 25	
Spike feeders	10		1 35	

METALS AND METALLIC GOODS (NAILS), WEST VIRGINIA.—ESTAB. No. **443**.

Time, 10 hours per day; — days the past year.

Occupations.	Male.	Fem.	Male.	Fem.
Blacksmiths	2		$2 50	
Bluer	1		4 00	
Bluer's helpers	a2		1 00	
Catchers, plate	2		2 50	
Engineers	2		2 50	
Heaters	7		4 50	
Heaters' helpers	7		1 75	
Hookers-up, plate	2		1 50	
Hot-machine tenders	5		2 50	
Laborers	15		1 25	
Masons	2		3 50	

a Youth.

OCCUPATIONS, WITH NUMBER AND WAGES OF EMPLOYÉS, BY INDUSTRIES—Cont'd.

NOTE.—This table is *not* a complete exhibit for industries or states, but covers only establishments investigated by the Bureau. See page 91, also summaries, pages 143 to 226.

METALS AND METALLIC GOODS (NAILS), WEST VIRGINIA.—ESTAB. No. 443—Concluded.

Time, 10 hours per day; — days the past year.

Occupations.	Number.		Daily wages.	
	Male.	Fem.	Male.	Fem.
Nailers	32		$6 00	
Nail feeders	126		1 50	
Packer	1		7 00	
Packer's helpers	a23		50	
Puddlers	36		2 75	
Puddlers' helpers	36		1 75	
Puddlers' helpers	36		1 25	
Rollers, muck	2		5 00	
Rollers, plate	2		7 00	
Rollers' helpers, muck	6		2 00	
Rollers' helpers, plate	2		2 50	
Shearman	1		8 00	
Shearman's helpers	3		2 00	
Shovers-under	5		2 00	

MUSICAL INSTRUMENTS AND MATERIALS (ORGANS), MAINE.—ESTAB. No. 444.

Time, 10 hours per day; 308 days the past year.

Occupations.	Male.	Fem.	Male.	Fem.
Action maker	1		$1 50	
Action maker	1		1 00	
Bench-room hands	11		1 62	
Box-room hand	1		1 50	
Box-room hand	1		1 10	
Engineer	1		1 50	
Finishers	8		1 12	
Fly finisher	1		1 50	
Fly finisher	1		1 25	
Foreman	1		2 00	
Machinists	8		1 62	
Teamster	1		1 62	
Tuner	1		3 00	
Turner	1		2 50	
Turner's helper	1		1 50	
Watchman	1		1 35	

MUSICAL INSTRUMENTS AND MATERIALS (ORGANS), NEW HAMPSHIRE.—ESTAB. No. 445.

Time, 10 hours per day; 250 days the past year.

Occupations.	Male.	Fem.	Male.	Fem.
Action maker	4		$2 00	
Case makers	5		1 75	
Engineer	1		1 66	
Fly finishers	3		2 00	
Laborer	1		1 75	
Mill hands	5		2 00	
Packers	2		2 50	
Tuner	1		2 50	
Tuner	1		1 25	
Varnisher	1		2 00	

MUSICAL INSTRUMENTS AND MATERIALS (PIANOS), NEW YORK.—ESTAB. No. 446.

Time, 10 hours per day; 300 days the past year.

Occupations.	Male.	Fem.	Male.	Fem.
Belly men	10		$3 26	
Box-room hands	2		2 50	
Cabinet makers	8		2 75	
Case makers	13		3 33	

MUSICAL INSTRUMENTS AND MATERIALS (PIANOS), NEW YORK.—ESTAB. No. 446—Concluded.

Time, 10 hours per day; 300 days the past year.

Occupations.	Number.		Daily wages.	
	Male.	Fem.	Male.	Fem.
Case makers	6		$2 91	
Case makers	4		2 50	
Engineer	1		3 00	
Finishers	15		3 33	
Fireman	1		1 66	
Fly finishers	7		3 33	
Foremen	14		3 30	
Key makers	14		2 66	
Kiln drier	2		2 66	
Laborers	2		1 58	
Machinists	2		2 66	
Piano movers	2		2 58	
Polishers	8		2 58	
Porters	3		1.64	
Regulators	13		3 26	
Sawyer	1		3 00	
Stringers	5		2 75	
Teamsters	3		2 33	
Tuners	6		3 33	
Tuners and fitters	2		2 66	
Undesignated	a5		71	
Varnishers	26		2 33	
Watchman	1		1 50	
Wrappers	2		1 16	

MUSICAL INSTRUMENTS AND MATERIALS (PIANOS), NEW YORK.—ESTAB. No. 447.

Time, 10 hours per day; 300 days the past year.

Occupations.	Male.	Fem.	Male.	Fem.
Action adjusters	2		$2 16	
Alloy man	1		3 66	
Belly men	6		3 83	
Belly men	43		2 97	
Blacksmiths	4		2 57	
Blacksmiths' helpers	10		1 53	
Blockers-out	2		3 00	
Blockers-out	4		1 66	
Blockers-out	25		1 50	
Bolt and nut maker	1		1 79	
Carpenters	7		2 00	
Cart drivers	3		1 50	
Carvers	7		3 00	
Case makers	71		2 50	
Case makers	32		2 00	
Casting cleaners	2		1 66	
Cupola men	2		2 29	
Drillers	2		2 21	
Dowel makers	2		2 33	
Engineer	1		3 33	
Engineers	2		2 50	
Engineers	3		2 25	
Finishers	16		3 31	
Finishers	35		2 91	
Finishers	10		2 66	
Finishers	19		3 25	
Firemen	4		1 66	
Firemen	5		1 50	
Fitters	4		2 50	
Fitters	12		2 16	
Fly finishers	7		2 63	
Foreman	1		6 66	
Foremen	21		4 00	
Foremen	3		3 33	
Foremen	9		2 72	
Foundery hands	12		1 66	
Frame makers, steel	6		2 41	
Fraisers	2		2 16	
Gluer	1		3 66	

a Youth.

OCCUPATIONS AND WAGES.

OCCUPATIONS, WITH NUMBER AND WAGES OF EMPLOYÉS, BY INDUSTRIES—Cont'd.

NOTE.—This table is *not* a complete exhibit for industries or states, but covers only establishments investigated by the Bureau. See page 91, also summaries, pages 143 to 226.

MUSICAL INSTRUMENTS AND MATERIALS (PIANOS), NEW YORK.—ESTAB. No. 447—Concluded.

Time, 10 hours per day; 300 days the past year.

Occupations.	Number.		Daily wages.	
	Male.	Fem.	Male.	Fem.
Gluers	10	......	$1 75	......
Hammer maker	1	......	2 16	......
Ivory cutters	3	......	2 50	......
Japanners	2	......	2 33	......
Joiners	12	......	2 00	......
Key makers	20	......	1 83	......
Kiln driers	10	......	1 50	......
Laborers	15	......	1 83	......
Laborers	47	......	1 43	......
Locksmiths	25	......	1 66	......
Lumber handlers	44	......	1 54	......
Machinists	9	......	3 00	......
Machinists	8	......	2 50	......
Melters	2	......	2 21	......
Moulders, composition	2	......	4 00	......
Moulders	6	......	3 29	......
Oilers	3	......	1 50	......
Ornamenters	3	......	2 00	......
Painter	1	......	2 33	......
Pattern maker	1	......	3 00	......
Planers	2	......	2 00	......
Plate grinders	2	......	1 66	......
Polishers	24	......	2 31	......
Polishers	18	......	1 62	......
Porters	11	......	2 16	......
Pressmen	6	......	1 83	......
Repairers	7	......	2 00	......
Regulators	2	......	5 00	......
Regulators	6	......	3 00	......
Regulators	5	......	2 55	......
Sawyers	14	......	2 16	......
Saw-mill hands	18	......	1 66	......
Scrapers	4	......	2 16	......
Sounding-board binders	2	......	2 00	......
Sounding-board makers	6	......	2 16	......
Steamers	2	......	1 66	......
Stringers	12	......	2 55	......
Teamsters	24	......	2 14	......
Tone-pulsator makers	2	......	2 46	......
Top makers	4	......	2 16	......
Top makers	6	......	2 00	......
Tuners	3	......	4 66	......
Tuners	12	......	2 79	......
Turners	2	......	2 05	......
Undesignated	67	......	1 37	......
Undesignated	a108	......	66	......
Varnishers	47	......	2 00	......
Varnish mixer	1	......	2 00	......
Veneer cutters	5	......	2 00	......
Watchmen	4	......	2 00	......
Watchmen	4	......	1 62	......
Windlass tenders	2	......	1 83	......

MUSICAL INSTRUMENTS AND MATERIALS (PIANOS), NEW YORK.—ESTAB. No. 448.

Time, 10 hours per day; 300 days the past year.

Occupations.	Number.		Daily wages.	
	Male.	Fem.	Male.	Fem.
Belly men	4	......	$3 88	......
Belly men	4	......	2 96	......
Belly-man's helper	1	......	1 00	......
Box-room hands	3	......	2 37	......
Cabinet makers	9	......	2 72	......

MUSICAL INSTRUMENTS AND MATERIALS (PIANOS), NEW YORK.—ESTAB. No. 448—Concluded.

Time, 10 hours per day; 300 days the past year.

Occupations.	Number.		Daily wages.	
	Male.	Fem.	Male.	Fem.
Case makers	12	......	$3 00	......
Case makers	6	......	2 54	......
Case makers	2	......	2 29	......
Case makers	4	......	2 04	......
Case maker	1	......	1 67	......
Engineer	1	......	3 00	......
Finishers	3	......	3 99	......
Finishers	7	......	3 33	......
Finishers	16	......	2 85	......
Fitters	5	......	2 67	......
Foremen	2	......	4 00	......
Foremen	12	......	3 37	......
Foreman	1	......	2 17	......
Key makers	15	......	2 66	......
Kiln driers	2	......	3 00	......
Laborers	9	......	1 50	......
Laborers	3	......	1 33	......
Machinist	1	......	2 67	......
Piano movers	2	......	2 50	......
Polishers	11	......	2 52	......
Porters	9	......	1 63	......
Regulators	3	......	4 49	......
Regulators	10	......	3 33	......
Regulators	3	......	3 17	......
Regulator	1	......	2 19	......
Sawyer	1	......	3 00	......
Stringers	6	......	2 63	......
Sweeper	1	......	96	......
Teamsters	4	......	2 37	......
Tuners	7	......	3 23	......
Tuner	1	......	2 90	......
Turners	4	......	2 67	......
Undesignated	1	......	2 50	......
Undesignated	1	......	1 62	......
Undesignated	2	......	1 25	......
Varnishers	32	......	2 24	......
Watchman	1	......	1 83	......
Wrapper	1	......	1 00	......

MUSICAL INSTRUMENTS AND MATERIALS (PIANOS), NEW YORK.—ESTAB. No. 449.

Time, 10 hours per day; 300 days the past year.

Occupations.	Number.		Daily wages.	
	Male.	Fem.	Male.	Fem.
Belly men	25	......	$2 63	......
Box-room hands	2	......	1 50	......
Case makers	22	......	2 37	......
Fly finishers	16	......	2 41	......
Foremen	3	......	2 67	......
Key makers	10	......	2 00	......
Piano movers	2	......	2 17	......
Regulators	6	......	3 00	......
Teamsters	3	......	2 00	......
Undesignated	a13	......	76	......
Varnishers	20	......	2 00	......

MUSICAL INSTRUMENTS AND MATERIALS (PIANOS), NEW YORK.—ESTAB. No. 450.

Time, 10 hours per day; 300 days the past year.

Occupations.	Number.		Daily wages.	
	Male.	Fem.	Male.	Fem.
Assorters	8	......	$1 50	......
Assorters' helpers	a4	......	50	......
Blacksmiths	2	......	2 00	......

a Youth.

388 REPORT OF THE COMMISSIONER OF LABOR.

OCCUPATIONS, WITH NUMBER AND WAGES OF EMPLOYÉS, BY INDUSTRIES—Cont'd.

NOTE.—This table is *not* a complete exhibit for industries or states, but covers only establishments investigated by the Bureau. See page 91, also summaries, pages 143 to 226.

MUSICAL INSTRUMENTS AND MATERIALS (PIANOS), NEW YORK.—ESTAB. No. 450—Concluded.

Time, 10 hours per day; 300 days the past year.

Occupations.	Number.		Daily wages.	
	Male.	Fem.	Male.	Fem.
Carders		18		$1 50
Carpenters	4		$2 00	
Carvers	7		2 50	
Driers	4		1 50	
Finishers		a10		1 25
Firemen	2		2 00	
Foremen	2		3 00	
Foreman	1		2 33	
Foremen	4		2 00	
Foresters	10		1 00	
Fullers	20		1 50	
Layers-out	4		2 00	
Layers-out	6		1 50	
Loggers	4		1 50	
Loggers	2		1 26	
Lumbermen	39		1 44	
Lumbermen	40		1 20	
Lumber handlers	8		2 00	
Lumber handlers	a12		50	
Machinists	3		2 00	
Overseers	2		3 20	
Overseer's assistant	1		2 00	
Sawyers and planers	9		1 50	
Sawyers and planers	10		1 00	
Sawyers' helpers	2		1 00	
Saw filer	1		3 00	
Saw filer	1		2 00	
Sewers, hand	60		1 50	
Spare hand	1		1 25	
Teamsters	8		1 50	
Undesignated	11		1 26	
Undesignated	a4		50	

OILS AND ILLUMINATING FLUIDS (LINSEED OIL), NEW YORK.—ESTAB. No. 451.

Time, 10 hours per day; 304 days the past year.

Occupations.	Number.		Daily wages.	
	Male.	Fem.	Male.	Fem.
Barrellers, oil	3		$1 25	
Boilers, oil	2		1 25	
Barrel washers	2		1 25	
Cake moulders	12		1 33	
Carpenter	1		2 00	
Coopers	4		2 00	
Engineers	2		1 50	
Laborers	39		1 25	
Machinist	1		2 00	
Packers	6		1 25	
Painters	2		1 25	
Pressmen	12		1 66	
Seed-room hands	10		1 25	
Spare hands	3		1 25	
Teamsters	2		1 60	
Trimmers	12		1 33	
Watchmen	2		1 25	

OILS AND ILLUMINATING FLUIDS (REFINED OIL, 110° TEST), PENNSYLVANIA.—ESTAB. No. 452.

Time, 10 hours per day; 304 days the past year.

Occupations.	Number.		Daily wages.	
	Male.	Fem.	Male.	Fem.
Coopers	32		$1 75	
Firemen	2		1 92	
Foreman	2		2 86	
Laborers	7		1 50	

OILS AND ILLUMINATING FLUIDS (REFINED OIL, 110° TEST), PENNSYLVANIA.—ESTAB. No. 452—Concluded.

Time, 10 hours per day; 304 days the past year.

Occupations.	Number.		Daily wages.	
	Male.	Fem.	Male.	Fem.
Painter	1		$2 50	
Stillmen	4		2 37	
Undesignated	3		2 16	

OILS AND ILLUMINATING FLUIDS (REFINED OIL, 110° TEST), PENNSYLVANIA.—ESTAB. No. 453.

Time, 10 hours per day; 310 days the past year.

Occupations.	Number.		Daily wages.	
	Male.	Fem.	Male.	Fem.
Coopers	15		$1 75	
Gluer	1		2 00	
Laborers	6		1 50	
Stillmen	2		2 25	
Teamsters	2		1 66	
Treater	1		2 50	

PAPER (PRINTING PAPER), CALIFORNIA.—ESTAB. No. 454.

Time, 24 hours per day (two turns); 286 days the past year.

Occupations.	Number.		Daily wages.	
	Male.	Fem.	Male.	Fem.
Engineer	1		$4 00	
Foreman	1		3 00	
Machine-room hands	3		2 00	
Pickers	9		1 35	
Pulp makers	3		2 00	
Rag-room hands	18		1 35	

PAPER (PRINTING PAPER), DELAWARE.—ESTAB. No. 455.

Time, 24 hours per day (two turns); 292 days the past year.

Occupations.	Number.		Daily wages.	
	Male.	Fem.	Male.	Fem.
Blacksmiths and millwrights	5		$2 50	
Calenderers	6		1 70	
Engineers	6		1 80	
Finishers	7		2 30	
Foreman	1		4 00	
Foreman	1		1 90	
Laborers	6		1 50	
Machine tenders	13		1 70	
Machine-room hands		10		$0 90
Rag cutters	6	17	1 50	70
Washers	17		1 60	

PAPER (PRINTING PAPER), DELAWARE.—ESTAB. No. 456.

Time, 24 hours per day (two turns); 300 days the past year.

Occupations.	Number.		Daily wages.	
	Male.	Fem.	Male.	Fem.
Engineers	4		$3 00	
Finishers	6		3 00	
Foreman	1		3 54	
Laborers	3		1 50	
Machinists	2		2 50	
Machine tenders	6		2 75	
Machine tenders	7		1 80	

a Youth.

OCCUPATIONS AND WAGES. 389

OCCUPATIONS, WITH NUMBER AND WAGES OF EMPLOYÉS, BY INDUSTRIES—Cont'd.

NOTE.—This table is *not* a complete exhibit for industries or states, but covers only establishments investigated by the Bureau. See page 91, also summaries, pages 143 to 226.

PAPER (PRINTING PAPER), DELAWARE.—ESTAB. No. 456—Concluded.

Time, 24 hours per day (two turns); 300 days the past year.

Occupations.	Number.		Daily wages.	
	Male.	Fem.	Male.	Fem.
Machine tenders	12	......	$1 00	......
Rag cutter	1	......	2 00	......
Rag cutters	5	......	1 50	......
Rag-engine tenders	6	......	2 33	......
Rag-engine tenders	2	......	1 83	......
Rag-engine tenders	8	......	1 50	......
Rag-room hands	a2	6	66	$0 70

PAPER (WRAPPING PAPER), DELAWARE.—ESTAB. No. 457.

Time, 24 hours per day (two turns); 300 days the past year.

Occupations.	Number.		Daily wages.	
	Male.	Fem.	Male.	Fem.
Engineers	2	......	$1 50	......
Laborers	8	......	1 65	......
Machine tenders	4	......	1 80	......
Machine-room hands	......	6	......	$1 75
Rag-engine tenders	3	......	1 75	......

PAPER (PRINTING PAPER), MAINE.—ESTAB. No. 458.

Time, 24 hours per day (two turns); — days the past year.

Occupations.	Number.		Daily wages.	
	Male.	Fem.	Male.	Fem.
Engineers	8	......	$2 00	......
Finishers	4	......	2 00	......
Foremen	10	......	1 35	......
Foreman	1	......	4 00	......
Laborers	20	......	1 25	......
Machine tenders	8	......	2 40	......
Machine tenders' helpers	8	......	1 40	......
Rag cutters	......	25	......	$0 90
Rag-room hands	a11	......	70	......
Warehouse men	6	......	1 75	......

PAPER (WRAPPING PAPER), MAINE.—ESTAB. No. 459.

Time, 24 hours per day (two turns); — days the past year.

Occupations.	Number.		Daily wages.	
	Male.	Fem.	Male.	Fem.
Beaters	2	......	$1 90	......
Beaters	4	......	1 50	......
Bleacher	1	......	1 75	......
Bleachers	3	......	1 50	......
Cutters	......	8	......	$0 75
Engineer	1	......	2 50	......
Finisher	1	......	2 00	......
Finisher	1	......	1 50	......
Finisher	......	1	......	1 00
Fireman	1	......	1 75	......
Machinist	1	......	2 50	......
Machine tenders	2	......	2 50	......
Machine tenders	2	......	1 30	......
Machine tender	1	......	1 25	......
Teamsters	3	......	1 50	......
Wheelwright	1	......	2 50	......
Wheelwright	1	......	1 75	......
Yard hands	3	......	1 50	......

PAPER (PRINTING PAPER), MASSACHUSETTS.—ESTAB. No. 460.

Time, 24 hours per day (two turns); 300 days the past year.

Occupations.	Number.		Daily wages.	
	Male.	Fem.	Male.	Fem.
Finishers	28	12	$1 64	$1 08
Finisher	a1	......	48	......
Machine tenders	5	......	3 90	......
Machine tenders	6	......	1 64	......
Rag-engine tenders	4	......	3 00	......
Rag-engine tenders	2	......	1 62	......
Rag-room hands	17	......	1 32	......
Rag-room hands	......	52	......	90
Repair hand	1	......	4 20	......
Repair hands	4	......	2 70	......

PAPER (WRITING PAPER), MASSACHUSETTS.—ESTAB. No. 461.

Time, 24 hours per day (two turns); — days the past year.

Occupations.	Number.		Daily wages.	
	Male.	Fem.	Male.	Fem.
Calenderers	......	12	......	$1 30
Counters and folders	......	2	......	1 50
Engineers	2	......	$3 00	......
Finishers	9	......	2 00	......
Foreman	1	......	2 25	......
Foremen	3	......	1 50	......
Jogglers	2	......	1 25	......
Laborers	4	......	1 25	......
Machine tenders	2	......	3 50	......
Machine-tenders' helpers	2	......	1 80	......
Overlookers	......	6	......	90
Platers	......	6	......	90
Rag-room hand	1	......	2 75	......
Rag-room hands	7	......	1 25	......
Rag-room hands	......	20	......	1 00
Rulers	......	5	......	1 00
Repair hands	2	......	2 25	......
Sorters	......	7	......	1 00
Sorters	......	4	......	1 25
Stamper and sealer	......	1	......	1 50
Watchman and fireman	2	......	2 40	......

PAPER (WRITING PAPER), MASSACHUSETTS.—ESTAB. No. 462.

Time, 24 hours per day (two turns); — days the past year.

Occupations.	Number.		Daily wages.	
	Male.	Fem.	Male.	Fem.
Bleachers	4	......	$1 64	......
Boiler tenders	2	......	2 40	......
Boiler tenders	2	......	1 98	......
Calenderers	3	......	2 10	......
Calenderer	1	......	3 60	......
Calenderer	1	......	2 70	......
Calenderer	1	......	1 80	......
Calenderers	11	......	1 64	......
Calenderers	18	......	1 50	......
Cutter	1	......	2 10	......
Cutter	1	......	1 80	......
Cutter	1	......	1 64	......
Cutters	3	16	1 50	$1 08
Finishers	3	......	2 70	......
Finishers	2	......	1 98	......
Finishers	4	......	1 80	......
Finishers	2	......	1 64	......
Laborer	1	......	2 40	......

OCCUPATIONS, WITH NUMBER AND WAGES OF EMPLOYÉS, BY INDUSTRIES—Cont'd.

NOTE.—This table is not a complete exhibit for industries or states, but covers only establishments investigated by the Bureau. See page 91, also summaries, pages 143 to 226.

PAPER (WRITING PAPER), MASSACHUSETTS.—ESTAB. No. 462—Concluded.

Time, 24 hours per day (two turns); — days the past year.

Occupations.	Number.		Daily wages.	
	Male.	Fem.	Male.	Fem.
Laborers	10		$1 64	
Machine tenders	6		3 60	
Machine tenders	2		1 80	
Machine tenders	4		1 64	
Machine tenders	6		1 50	
Rag-engine tenders	4		2 70	
Rag-engine tenders	2		1 80	
Rag-engine tenders	19		1 64	
Rag-room hand	1		3 30	
Rag-room hands	12		1 50	
Rag-room hands	6	60	1 20	$1 08
Repair hand	1		3 60	
Repair hand	1		3 00	
Repair hands	4		2 40	
Repair hand	1		1 64	
Watchman	1		1 50	

PAPER (WRITING PAPER), MASSACHUSETTS.—ESTAB. No. 463.

Time, 24 hours per day (two turns); 300 days the past year.

Occupations.	Number.		Daily wages.	
	Male.	Fem.	Male.	Fem.
Finisher	1		$2 75	
Finisher	1		2 50	
Finishers	2		1 60	
Finishers	7		1 50	
Finishers	11		1 00	
Finishers	a2	12	80	$0 80
Laborer	1		2 00	
Laborers	8		1 10	
Machine tender	1		3 90	
Machine tenders	4		3 60	
Machine tenders	4		1 50	
Machine tenders	4		1 20	
Rag-engine tenders	2		3 00	
Rag-engine tenders	2		1 80	
Rag-engine tenders	4		1 50	
Rag-engine tenders	12		1 38	
Rag-room hands	10	48	1 40	80
Rag-room hands	a5		75	
Repair hand	1		5 00	
Repair hand	1		3 50	
Repair hands	3		2 50	
Repair hand	1		2 25	
Ruler	1		5 00	
Ruler	1		3 50	
Rulers	6		1 50	
Rulers	2	16	1 40	1 20
Rulers		10		1 05

PAPER (WRITING PAPER), MASSACHUSETTS.—ESTAB. No. 464.

Time, 24 hours per day (two turns); 300 days the past year.

Occupations.	Number.		Daily wages.	
	Male.	Fem.	Male.	Fem.
Boiler tenders	2		$2 40	
Box maker	1		2 00	
Calenderer	1		2 75	
Calenderers	2		1 50	
Engineers	4		3 00	
Engineers' helpers	4		1 37	
Foreman	1		4 50	

PAPER (WRITING PAPER), MASSACHUSETTS.—ESTAB. No. 464—Concluded.

Time, 24 hours per day (two turns); 300 days the past year.

Occupations.	Number.		Daily wages.	
	Male.	Fem.	Male.	Fem.
Foreman	1		$3 00	
Foreman	1		2 00	
Jogglers	3		1 50	
Laborers	4		1 64	
Laborers	4		1 25	
Machine tenders	4		3 30	
Machine-tenders' helpers	4		1 50	
Rag-room hands	10	75	1 37	$0 90
Repair hand	1		3 50	
Repairer's helpers	2		2 00	
Ruler	1		3 00	
Ruler's helper	1		1 50	
Sealer	1		1 50	
Trimmers	2		3 00	
Trimmer	1		2 00	
Undesignated	7		1 50	
Undesignated	60		1 00	
Warehouse men	2		1 50	
Yardmen	2		1 25	

PAPER (ENAMELLED AND FANCY PAPER), MASSACHUSETTS.—ESTAB. No. 465.

Time, 10 hours per day; — days the past year.

Occupations.	Number.		Daily wages.	
	Male.	Fem.	Male.	Fem.
Engineer	1		$2 50	
Finishers		4		$1 10
Fireman	1		1 50	
Foremen	2		2 50	
Laborers	6		1 50	
Packers	3		1 40	

PAPER (ENVELOPES), MASSACHUSETTS.—ESTAB. No. 466.

Time, 10 hours per day; — days the past year.

Occupations.	Number.		Daily wages.	
	Male.	Fem.	Male.	Fem.
Cutters	2		$1 75	
Foremen	3		1 40	
Machine tenders	30		1 25	
Packers	2		1 50	
Watchman	1		1 50	

PAPER (PRINTING PAPER), NEW HAMPSHIRE.—ESTAB. No. 467.

Time, 24 hours per day (two turns); — days the past year.

Occupations.	Number.		Daily wages.	
	Male.	Fem.	Male.	Fem.
Finishers	8		$2 00	
Foremen	3		3 00	
Foreman	2		2 25	
Grinders	25		1 40	
Machine tenders	30		2 00	
Rag-engine tenders	30		1 50	
Rag-room hands	30	36	1 40	$1 00
Repair hands	10		2 00	
Woodmen	11		1 40	
Yard hands	25		1 40	

a Youth.

OCCUPATIONS AND WAGES.

OCCUPATIONS, WITH NUMBER AND WAGES OF EMPLOYÉS, BY INDUSTRIES—Cont'd.

NOTE.—This table is *not* a complete exhibit for industries or states, but covers only establishments investigated by the Bureau. See page 91, also summaries, pages 143 to 226.

PAPER (WRAPPING PAPER), OREGON.—ESTAB. NO. 468.

Time, 24 hours per day (two turns); — days the past year.

Occupations.	Number.		Daily wages.	
	Male.	Fem.	Male.	Fem.
Cutters	a5	......	$0 87	......
Engineers	5	......	2 25	......
Finishers	......	5	......	$1 75
Laborers	15	......	1 75	......
Machine tenders	5	......	2 75	......
Rag-room hands	......	10	......	1 00

PAPER (CARD, PRINTING, WRAPPING PAPER), VERMONT.—ESTAB. NO. 469.

Time, 24 hours per day (two turns); — days the past year.

Occupations	Male	Fem	Male	Fem
Finishers	10	......	$2 00	......
Foremen	4	......	3 00	......
Machine tenders	35	......	2 00	......
Rag-engine tenders	48	......	1 50	......
Rag-room hands	30	25	1 40	$0 75
Repair hands	20	......	2 00	......
Yard hands	30	......	1 40	......

PRINT WORKS (PRINTING), MASSACHUSETTS.—ESTAB. NO. 470.

Time, 10 hours per day; — days the past year.

Occupations	Male	Fem	Male	Fem
Ageing and steaming hands	31	......	$1 05	......
Back tenders	a24	......	75	......
Bleachers	21	......	1 15	......
Bleachers	a31	......	65	......
Colorers	36	......	1 20	......
Colorers	a2	......	80	......
Die makers	2	......	4 50	......
Die-maker's helpers	2	......	2 20	......
Dyers	58	......	1 15	......
Dyers	a34	......	70	......
Engravers	7	......	4 30	......
Engravers	3	......	3 80	......
Engraver's helpers	a6	......	1 60	......
Finishers	30	......	1 20	......
Finishers	a14	......	85	......
Finishers	25	......	65	......
Folders	14	......	1 60	......
Folders	6	......	1 10	......
Iron workers	27	......	1 80	......
Masons	2	......	2 40	......
Overseers	3	......	6 90	......
Overseers	3	......	5 50	......
Overseers	4	......	4 00	......
Overseers	2	......	3 50	......
Overseers	3	......	3 00	......
Overseers	6	......	2 75	......
Overseer	1	......	2 35	......
Overseers	7	......	2 00	......
Overseers	5	......	1 70	......
Overseer	1	......	1 40	......
Packers	18	......	1 20	......
Packers	a4	7	65	$0 90
Painter	1	......	1 60	......
Polishers	2	......	1 40	......
Printers	19	......	4 80	......
Printers' helpers	6	......	1 70	......
Rollers	4	......	4 30	......
Rollers' helpers	4	......	1 20	......

PRINT WORKS (PRINTING), MASSACHUSETTS.—ESTAB. No. 470—Concluded.

Time, 10 hours per day; — days the past year.

Occupations.	Male.	Fem.	Male.	Fem.
Singeing-room hands	18	......	$1 10	......
Sketchers	5	......	4 50	......
Sketchers' helpers	a3	......	1 50	......
Undesignated	12	......	1 40	......
Undesignated	70	......	1 10	......
Undesignated	a24	......	75	......
Washers	30	2	1 05	$0 90
Washers	a17	......	65	......
White-room hands	30	......	1 10	......
White-room hands	a28	......	80	......
Wood workers	19	......	1 60	......

PRINT WORKS (PRINTING), MASSACHUSETTS.—ESTAB. NO. 471.

Time, 10 hours per day; — days the past year.

Occupations	Male	Fem	Male	Fem
Ageing and steaming hands	6	......	$1 25	......
Back tenders	4	......	1 33	......
Bleachers	3	......	1 00	......
Calenderers and finishers	10	......	2 00	......
Calenderers and folders	......	14	......	$1 00
Colorers	6	......	1 33	......
Driers	a8	......	1 00	......
Engravers	4	......	4 00	......
Pantographers	......	3	......	91
Platform boys	a4	......	75	......
Printers	4	......	2 50	......
Shearers and winders	6	......	1 16	......

PRINT WORKS (PRINTING), NEW HAMPSHIRE.—ESTAB. NO. 472.b

Time, 10 hours per day; 300 days the past year.

Occupations	Male	Fem	Male	Fem
Ageing and steaming hands	2	......	$1 60	......
Ageing and steaming hands	23	......	1 20	......
Ageing and steaming hands	a8	......	75	......
Back tenders	12	......	1 25	......
Bleacher	1	......	2 00	......
Bleacher	1	......	2 00	......
Bleachers	28	......	1 25	......
Bleachers	a9	......	95	......
Bleachers	a16	......	75	......
Carpenters	3	......	1 60	......
Carpenters' helpers	8	......	1 35	......
Clammer	1	......	4 00	......
Clammer's helper	1	......	1 00	......
Colorer	1	......	2 75	......
Colorer	1	......	2 25	......
Colorers' helpers	31	......	1 20	......
Colorers' helper	a1	......	1 00	......
Die cutter	1	......	4 66	......
Die-cutter's helper	1	......	1 00	......
Dyers	7	......	1 50	......
Dyers	28	......	1 25	......
Dyers' helpers	a7	......	85	......
Dyers' helpers	a3	......	60	......

a Youth.
b This establishment is connected with No. 305.

OCCUPATIONS, WITH NUMBER AND WAGES OF EMPLOYÉS, BY INDUSTRIES—Cont'd.

NOTE.—This table is *not* a complete exhibit for industries or states, but covers only establishments investigated by the Bureau. See page 91, also summaries, pages 143 to 226.

PRINT WORKS (PRINTING), NEW HAMPSHIRE.—ESTAB. No. 472—Concluded.

Time, 10 hours per day; 300 days the past year.

Occupations.	Number.		Daily wages.	
	Male.	Fem.	Male.	Fem.
Engineer	1		$3 00	
Engravers	2		3 91	
Engravers	2		4 66	
Engravers' helper	1		2 00	
Finishers	30		1 80	
Finishers	a5	34	95	$0 90
Firemen	7		1 50	
Foreman	1		4 16	
Laborer	1		2 25	
Laborer	1		1 80	
Laborers	22		1 10	
Machinists	12		2 15	
Machine setter	1		2 00	
Machine-setter's helper	1		1 80	
Machine-setter's helpers	6		1 25	
Mangler	1		1 50	
Mangler's helpers	7		1 20	
Mangler's helpers	a3		60	
Pantographer	1	20	1 25	1 00
Pantograph setter	1		3 50	
Pantograph-setter's helper	1		1 66	
Plate cutters	4		4 33	
Plate-cutter's helper	1		1 66	
Printers	11		4 83	
Printer	1		3 50	
Printers	2		1 75	
Shearer	1		2 00	
Shearers	3		1 10	
Shearers' helpers	a6	4	55	91
Sketchers	5		4 66	
Sketcher's helper	1		1 66	
Sketcher's helper	1		1 33	
Sketcher's helper	a1		75	
Undesignated	a3		83	
Undesignated	a22		66	
Undesignated	a13		54	
Watchmen	5		1 50	
White-room hand	1		1 50	
White-room hands	6	1	1 15	91
Yardmen	10		1 20	

PRINT WORKS (PRINTING), NEW JERSEY.—ESTAB. No. 473.

Time, 10 hours per day; 300 days the past year.

Occupations	Male	Fem	Male	Fem
Bleachers	30		$1 00	
Colorers and dyers	40		1 25	
Engravers	25		2 00	
Finishers	60		1 00	
Laborers	40		1 00	
Printers	10		4 00	

PRINT WORKS (BLEACHING), NEW YORK.—ESTAB. No. 474.

Time, 11 hours per day; 300 days the past year.

Occupations	Male	Fem	Male	Fem
Bleachers	7		$1 17	
Expresser	1		2 50	
Folders	3	26	1 50	$0 83
Foremen	2		3 00	
Packer	1		2 00	
Undesignated	a3		87	

PRINT WORKS (PRINTING), PENNSYLVANIA.—ESTAB. No. 475.

Time, 10 hours per day; — days the past year.

Occupations.	Number.		Daily wages.	
	Male.	Fem.	Male.	Fem.
Engravers	19		$3 33	
Foremen	5		5 83	
Foremen	5		4 17	
Foremen	10		3 00	
Laborers	74		1 50	
Laborers	200		1 25	
Machinists	19		2 00	
Printers	14		4 16	
Undesignated	a97	37	83	$0 83
Undesignated	a100	28	58	1 00
Undesignated	b149		45	

RAILROAD CONSTRUCTION (FREIGHT AND PASSENGER CARS), NORTH CAROLINA.—ESTAB. No. 476.

Time, 10 hours per day; 300 days the past year.

Carpenter	1		$2 25	
Carpenters	2		1 75	
Carpenters	4		1 50	
Carpenters	4		1 25	
Carpenters	a2		75	
Engineer	1		1 25	
Fireman	1		80	
Laborers	13		80	
Laborers	a2		50	
Sawyer, machine	1		2 25	
Sawyers, machine	4		1 25	

RAILROAD CONSTRUCTION (LOCOMOTIVE AND FREIGHT CARS), NORTH CAROLINA.—ESTAB. No. 477.

Time, 10 hours per day; 300 days the past year.

Apprentices	a13		$0 50	
Blacksmiths	2		2 35	
Blacksmiths	2		1 75	
Blacksmiths' helpers	7		1 00	
Carpenters	2		2 00	
Carpenters	4		1 75	
Engineers, locomotive	27		2 88	
Firemen	27		89	
Laborers	15		1 00	
Machinists	3		2 38	
Machinists	3		1 75	
Moulders	2		2 35	
Painter, decorative	1		2 50	
Painters	3		1 50	

RAILROAD CONSTRUCTION (FREIGHT CARS AND CAR WHEELS), TENNESSEE.—ESTAB. No. 478.

Time, 10 hours per day; — days the past year.

Blacksmith	3		$2 10	
Blacksmiths' helpers	3		1 00	
Carpenters	3		1 56	
Core maker	1		1 85	
Cupola man	1		1 85	
Engineer	1		1 25	
Foremen	2		3 25	

a Youth.   *b* Children.

OCCUPATIONS AND WAGES. 393

OCCUPATIONS, WITH NUMBER AND WAGES OF EMPLOYÉS, BY INDUSTRIES—Cont'd.

NOTE.—This table is *not* a complete exhibit for industries or states, but covers only establishments investigated by the Bureau. See page 91, also summaries, pages 143 to 226.

RAILROAD CONSTRUCTION (FREIGHT CARS AND CAR WHEELS), TENNESSEE.—ESTAB. No. **478**—Concluded.

Time, 10 hours per day ; — days the past year.

Occupations.	Number.		Daily wages.	
	Male.	Fem.	Male.	Fem.
Foreman	1	......	$2 50	......
Laborers	3	......	1 50	......
Laborers	5	......	90	......
Machinists	2	......	2 25	......
Machinists' helpers	4	......	1 00	......
Moulders	3	......	2 25	......
Moulders' helpers	3	......	1 00	......
Pattern makers	2	......	2 50	......

RAILROAD CONSTRUCTION (PASSENGER CARS), VERMONT.—ESTAB. No. **479**.

Time, 10 hours per day ; — days the past year.

Occupations.	Male.	Fem.	Male.	Fem.
Apprentices	2	......	$1 13	......
Blacksmiths	6	......	1 50	......
Blacksmiths' helper	4	......	1 12	......
Boiler maker	1	......	1 80	......
Engineer	1	......	1 90	......
Foreman	1	......	2 48	......
Foreman	1	......	2 25	......
Foreman	1	......	2 16	......
Laborers	9	......	1 12	......
Machinist	1	......	3 46	......
Machinists	15	......	2 25	......
Machinists' helpers	6	......	1 65	......
Painters	4	......	2 00	......
Pattern maker	1	......	2 25	......
Repair hand	1	......	1 80	......
Repair hands	32	......	1 25	......
Tinsmith	1	......	1 98	......
Tinsmith's helper	1	......	1 25	......
Undesignated	1	......	2 45	......
Watchmen	2	......	1 12	......
Wood workers	14	......	1 50	......

RAILROAD CONSTRUCTION (FREIGHT AND PASSENGER CARS), VIRGINIA.—ESTAB. No. **480**.

Time, 10 hours per day; 300 days the past year.

Occupations.	Male.	Fem.	Male.	Fem.
Apprentices	a14	......	$0 70	......
Blacksmiths	17	......	2 30	......
Blacksmiths' helpers	19	......	1 30	......
Boiler makers	12	......	2 30	......
Boiler-makers' helpers	12	......	1 30	......
Bricklayer	1	......	3 00	......
Carpenters	38	......	2 10	......
Engineer, stationary	7	......	1 80	......
Laborers	68	......	1 10	......
Machinists	41	......	2 30	......
Moulders	22	......	2 20	......
Painters	7	......	1 80	......
Pattern makers	3	......	2 70	......
Planers	3	......	2 30	......
Pipe fitters	7	......	2 30	......
Shop hands	25	......	1 40	......
Tinsmiths	6	......	2 10	......

RUBBER (RUBBER BOOTS, SHOES, ARCTICS), MASSACHUSETTS.—ESTAB. No. **481**.

Time, 10 hours per day ; 300 days the past year.

Occupations.	Number.		Daily wages.	
	Male.	Fem.	Male.	Fem.
Boot makers	200	......	$2 30	......
Cutters	100	......	2 40	......
Cutters	75	......	1 30	......
Dyer	1	......	2 75	......
Engineers	4	......	2 50	......
Firemen	11	......	1 75	......
Grinders	150	......	1 25	......
Heaters	4	......	2 50	......
Laborers	47	......	1 35	......
Machinists and carpenters	12	......	2 25	......
Shoemakers	......	600	......	$1 16
Teamster	1	......	2 25	......
Varnishers	20	......	1 83	......

RUBBER (RUBBER BOOTS, SHOES, ARCTICS), NEW JERSEY.—ESTAB. No. **482**.

Time, 10 hours per day ; 292 days the past year.

Occupations.	Male.	Fem.	Male.	Fem.
Boot makers	47	......	$1 50	......
Box makers	7	......	1 50	......
Cutters	55	......	1 75	......
Mill hands	82	......	1 25	......
Packers	6	......	1 75	......
Packers	a10	......	65	......
Shoemakers	a65	......	1 25	......
Shoemakers	......	141	......	$1 00
Varnishers	16	......	1 75	......

RUBBER (RUBBER BOOTS, SHOES, ARCTICS), NEW JERSEY.—ESTAB. No. **483**.

Time, 10 hours per day; 292 days the past year.

Occupations.	Male.	Fem.	Male.	Fem.
Boot makers	45	......	$1 60	......
Boot makers	a22	......	1 00	......
Cutters	55	......	1 67	......
Cutters	a17	......	60	......
Mill hands	36	......	1 25	......
Mill hands	a4	......	67	......
Packers	9	9	1 84	$0 84
Shoemakers	42	194	1 25	1 00
Varnishers	16	......	2 00	......

RUBBER (RUBBER BELTING, HOSE), NEW JERSEY.—ESTAB. No. **484**.

Time, 10 hours per day ; 300 days the past year.

Occupations.	Male.	Fem.	Male.	Fem.
Hose makers	20	......	$1 75	......
Laborers	96	......	1 33	......
Mill hands	14	......	1 75	......

a Youth.

OCCUPATIONS, WITH NUMBER AND WAGES OF EMPLOYÉS, BY INDUSTRIES—Cont'd.

NOTE.—This table is not a complete exhibit for industries or states, but covers only establishments investigated by the Bureau. See page 91, also summaries, pages 143 to 226.

SILK (MACHINE TWIST, SEWING), CONNECTICUT.—ESTAB. No. 485.

Time, 10 hours per day; 300 days the past year.

Occupations.	Number.		Daily wages.	
	Male.	Fem.	Male.	Fem.
Doublers		10		$1 00
Dyers	2		$2 00	
Dyers	2		1 50	
Engineer	1		2 62	
Engineer	1		2 00	
Matchers		2		1 00
Overseers	2		4 00	
Overseers	2		2 50	
Rulers		3		1 00
Spare hands		2		1 00
Spare hands		2		75
Spoolers		25		1 00
Stretchers	3		75	
Twisters	2		1 17	
Twisters	3		80	
Watchman	1		2 00	
Winders		36		1 00

SILK (RIBBONS, DRESS GOODS), NEW JERSEY.—ESTAB. No. 486.

Time, 10 hours per day; 292 days the past year.

Occupations.	Number.		Daily wages.	
	Male.	Fem.	Male.	Fem.
Blockers	4		$1 50	
Foremen	4		5 00	
Pickers		30		$1 43
Spinners	a60		1 00	
Warpers		20		1 06
Weavers	60	180	2 33	2 00
Weavers	60	16	2 66	2 00
Winders		75		1 00
Winders		75		84

SILK (RIBBONS, DRESS GOODS), NEW JERSEY.—ESTAB. No. 487.

Time, 10 hours per day; 260 days the past year.

Occupations.	Number.		Daily wages.	
	Male.	Fem.	Male.	Fem.
Blockers		30		$1 00
Dyers	30		$2 00	
Machinists	20		2 25	
Pickers	10	30	2 00	1 12
Warpers	50	30	2 50	1 66
Weavers	75	300	2 50	1 50
Winders		50		1 00

SILK (RIBBONS, PIECE GOODS), NEW YORK, ESTAB. No. 488.

Time, 10 hours per day; 302 days the past year.

Occupations.	Number.		Daily wages.	
	Male.	Fem.	Male.	Fem.
Carpenter	1		$2 00	
Engineer	1		2 50	
Finishers	5		1 50	
Finishers		20		$0 75
Foreman	1		3 33	
Hemmers		3		1 17
Machinist	1		2 00	
Overseer	1		2 50	
Overseers	2		2 00	
Pickers	2		2 00	
Ribbon cleaners		7		0 83
Spare hands	a6		60	
Spoolers and doublers		17		75

SILK (RIBBONS, PIECE GOODS), NEW YORK.—ESTAB. No. 488—Concluded.

Time, 10 hours per day; 302 days the past year.

Occupations.	Number.		Daily wages.	
	Male.	Fem.	Male.	Fem.
Twisters	3		$1 50	
Warpers	2	28	1 67	$0 80
Watchman	1		1 43	
Weavers	57	51	1 70	1 11
Winders		6		92

SILK (TWIST), NEW YORK.—ESTAB. No. 489.

Time, 11 hours per day; 211 days the past year.

Occupations.	Number.		Daily wages.	
	Male.	Fem.	Male.	Fem.
Bundler	1		$2 33	
Bundler	a1		87	
Carpenter	1		1 50	
Doublers	a4	11	56	$0 77
Drier		1		1 00
Foremen	2		2 08	
Heater and steamer	1		1 50	
Machinist	1		2 50	
Preparer		1		92
Reelers	a7		1 06	
Reelers	a9		86	
Sorter and sizer		1		1 00
Spinners	a5		79	
Watchman	1		1 50	
Weigher		1		79
Winders	a5	16	46	81
Winders		8		61

SILK (TWIST), NEW YORK.—ESTAB. No. 490.

Time, 11 hours per day; 302 days the past year.

Occupations.	Number.		Daily wages.	
	Male.	Fem.	Male.	Fem.
Foreman	1		$2 00	
Machinist	1		2 00	
Spare hands	a10		$0 50	
Spinners	6			92
Spinners	10			83
Spinners	20			75
Spoolers	6			83
Twisters	4			83
Watchman	1		1 29	
Winders		6		75

STONE (GRANITE MONUMENTS), MAINE.—ESTAB. No. 491.

Time, 10 hours per day; — days the past year.

Occupations.	Number.		Daily wages.	
	Male.	Fem.	Male.	Fem.
Architect	1		$3 25	
Blacksmith	5		2 25	
Blacksmiths	6		1 75	
Engineer	1		1 75	
Foreman	1		3 50	
Foremen	3		3 00	
Laborers	12		1 65	
Polishers	2		1 75	
Quarrymen	70		1 60	
Stonecutters	25		3 75	
Stonecutters	50		2 50	
Stonecutters	13		1 75	
Teamsters	4		1 73	
Teamster	1		1 00	

a Youth.

OCCUPATIONS AND WAGES. 395

OCCUPATIONS, WITH NUMBER AND WAGES OF EMPLOYÉS, BY INDUSTRIES—Cont'd.

NOTE.—This table is *not* a complete exhibit for industries or states, but covers only establishments investigated by the Bureau. See page 91, also summaries, pages 143 to 226.

TOBACCO (CIGARS), CONNECTICUT.—ESTAB. NO. 492.

Time 10 hours per day; 300 days the past year.

Occupations.	Number.		Daily wages.	
	Male.	Fem.	Male.	Fem.
Cigar makers	15	......	$2 25	......
Laborer	1	......	2 00	......
Packer	1	......	3 33	......
Stripper	......	1	......	$1 17
Stripper	......	1	......	83
Strippers	......	2	......	58

TOBACCO (CIGARS), ILLINOIS.—ESTAB. NO. 493.

Time, 10 hours per day; 288 days the past year.

Bunch breakers	......	3	......	$1 33
Bunch breakers	......	17	......	1 00
Cigar makers	......	10	......	2 00
Cigar makers	......	45	......	1 33
Packers	6	......	$3 00	......
Stripper	a1	b13	83	33

TOBACCO (CIGARS), ILLINOIS.—ESTAB. NO. 494.

Time, 10 hours per day; 300 days the past year.

Bunch breakers	......	9	......	$1 33
Cigar makers	30	......	$2 17	......
Packers	2	......	3 00	......
Strippers	a8	......	75	......

TOBACCO (CIGARS), ILLINOIS.—ESTAB. NO. 495.

Time, 10 hours per day; — days the past year.

Bunch breakers	......	30	......	$1 05
Foremen	2	......	$2 91	......
Packers	8	......	2 50	......
Rollers	70	......	1 22	......
Strippers	......	a38	......	48

TOBACCO (CIGARS), ILLINOIS.—ESTAB. NO. 496.

Time, 10 hours per day; 275 days the past year.

Cigar makers	8	......	$2 00	......
Packer	1	......	2 67	......
Strippers	a3	......	50	......

TOBACCO (CIGARS), ILLINOIS.—ESTAB. NO. 497.

Time, 8 hours per day; 250 days the past year.

Cigar makers	10	......	$2 00	......
Packers	2	......	2 00	......
Strippers	a5	......	42	......

TOBACCO (CHEWING TOBACCO), ILLINOIS.—ESTAB. NO. 498.

Time, 10 hours per day; 300 days the past year.

Occupations.	Number.		Daily wages.	
	Male.	Fem.	Male.	Fem.
Foremen	3	......	$3 00	......
Laborers	5	......	1 50	......
Leaf sorters	4	......	1 20	......
Pressmen	15	......	1 50	......
Strippers	a10	a40	60	$0 60
Watchman	1	......	1 50	......
Wrappers	20	......	2 00	......

TOBACCO (CHEWING AND SMOKING TOBACCO), ILLINOIS.—ESTAB. NO. 499.

Time, 10 hours per day; 300 days the past year.

Carpenter	1	......	$2 00	......
Cutters	4	......	2 00	......
Cutters	4	......	1 83	......
Dressers	3	......	1 83	......
Engineer	1	......	2 50	......
Laborers	2	......	1 67	......
Laborers	5	......	1 25	......
Leaf sorters	......	6	......	$0 92
Packers	4	......	1 50	......
Packers	......	15	......	63
Printers	2	......	1 67	......
Strippers	......	5	......	1 00
Undesignated	......	8	......	67
Watchman	1	......	1 57	......

TOBACCO (CHEWING AND SMOKING TOBACCO), ILLINOIS.—ESTAB. NO. 500.

Time, 10 hours per day; 300 days the past year.

Cutters	2	......	$2 25	......
Dressers	8	......	1 75	......
Dresser	1	......	1 25	......
Dressers	a3	......	75	......
Foremen	2	......	3 00	......
Leaf sorters	......	a7	......	$0 75
Packers	10	......	1 50	......
Pressmen	2	......	1 50	......
Strippers	b20	b30	33	33
Watchman	1	......	1 50	......

TOBACCO (CHEWING TOBACCO), KENTUCKY.—ESTAB. NO. 501.

Time, 10 hours per day; 310 days the past year.

Cutters	3	......	$1 50	......
Dressers	......	6	......	$1 20
Foremen	3	......	2 50	......
Laborers	22	......	1 20	......
Leaf sorters	6	......	1 40	......
Pressman	1	......	1 80	......
Pressmen	4	......	1 50	......
Strippers	......	6	......	1 00
Strippers	a10	a36	80	80
Undesignated	a5	......	70	......
Undesignated	......	a7	......	80
Wrappers	2	4	2 00	2 00

a Youth.   *b* Children.

OCCUPATIONS, WITH NUMBER AND WAGES OF EMPLOYÉS, BY INDUSTRIES—Cont'd.

NOTE.—This table is *not* a complete exhibit for industries or states, but covers only establishments investigated by the Bureau. See page 91, also summaries, pages 143 to 226.

TOBACCO (CHEWING TOBACCO), KENTUCKY.—ESTAB. No. **502.**

Time, 10 *hours per day;* 300 *days the past year.*

Occupations.	Number.		Daily wages.	
	Male.	Fem.	Male.	Fem.
Laborers	4	......	$1 50	......
Laborers	2	......	1 35	......
Lump makers	2	......	1 67	......
Lump tagger	a1	......	67	......
Stemmers	......	10	......	$0 83
Wringer	1	......	1 00	......

TOBACCO (CHEWING AND SMOKING TOBACCO), MICHIGAN.—ESTAB. No. **503.**

Time, 10 *hours per day;* 309 *days the past year.*

Occupations.	Male.	Fem.	Male.	Fem.
Cutters	6	......	$2 00	......
Dressers	12	4	1 50	$1 00
Foremen	5	......	2 00	......
Laborers	4	......	1 25	......
Leaf sorters	13	......	1 50	......
Packers	23	......	1 00	......
Strippers	a4	a51	80	80
Teamster	1	......	2 67	......
Undesignated	a6	a28	60	60
Watchman	1	......	2 00	......

TOBACCO (CHEWING AND SMOKING TOBACCO), MISSOURI.—ESTAB. No. **504.**

Time, 10 *hours per day;* — *days the past year.*

Occupations.	Male.	Fem.	Male.	Fem.
Box makers	44	......	$1 62	......
Foremen	2	......	5 93	......
Lump makers	69	......	1 88	......
Pressmen	80	......	1 24	......
Pressmens' helpers	224	......	1 20	......
Porters	23	......	1 47	......
Repair hands	8	......	2 99	......
Stemmers	310	......	93	......
Wrappers	24	......	96	......

TOBACCO (CHEWING AND SMOKING TOBACCO), MISSOURI.—ESTAB. No. **505.**

Time, 10 *hours per day;* — *days the past year.*

Occupations.	Male.	Fem.	Male.	Fem.
Cutters	10	......	$2 33	......
Dressers	12	......	2 00	......
Engineer	1	......	5 33	......
Engineer	1	......	2 50	......
Foremen	5	......	2 66	......
Forewoman	......	1	......	$1 45
Laborers	......	35	......	80
Packers	6	30	2 00	1 10
Sewers	......	4	......	1 15
Sorters and mixers	6	......	1 50	......
Spreaders	15	......	2 00	......
Stringers	......	15	......	80
Strippers	a30	......	1 00	......
Undesignated	2	......	2 75	......

TOBACCO (CIGARS), NEW JERSEY.—ESTAB. No. **506.**

Time, 9½ *hours per day;* — *days the past year.*

Occupations.	Number.		Daily wages.	
	Male.	Fem.	Male.	Fem.
Cigar maker	1	......	$3 40	......
Cigar makers	13	......	1 86	......
Cigar makers	5	......	1 83	......
Cigar makers	8	......	1 66	......
Cigar makers	4	......	1 50	......
Laborer	1	......	1 00	......

TOBACCO (CIGARS), NEW JERSEY.—ESTAB. No. **507.**

Time, 9 *hours per day;* 300 *days the past year.*

Occupations.	Male.	Fem.	Male.	Fem.
Bunch breakers	......	20	......	$0 75
Foreman	1	......	$2 00	......
Laborers	4	......	1 16	......
Packers	6	......	1 50	......
Rollers	......	30	......	1 00
Strippers	......	a10	......	66

TOBACCO (CHEWING AND SMOKING TOBACCO), NEW YORK.—ESTAB. No. **508.**

Time, 10 *hours per day;* 304 *days the past year.*

Occupations.	Male.	Fem.	Male.	Fem.
Cutters	12	......	$2 00	......
Dressers	2	3	2 00	$1 33
Driers	5	......	2 00	......
Engineer	1	......	3 33	......
Finishers	3	......	2 00	......
Firemen	2	......	2 00	......
Lump makers	2	6	1 67	1 33
Packers	5	......	2 00	......
Packers	......	50	......	1 33
Pressmen	5	......	2 00	......
Stampers	......	a28	......	67
Stemmers	......	100	......	75
Teamsters	2	......	2 00	......

TOBACCO (CHEWING TOBACCO), NORTH CAROLINA.—ESTAB. No. **509.**

Time, 10 *hours per day;* 296 *days the past year.*

Occupations.	Male.	Fem.	Male.	Fem.
Foreman	1	......	$1 25	......
Laborers	3	......	75	......
Laborers	a4	......	40	......
Lump makers	12	......	1 00	......
Mixers	2	......	1 12	......
Picker, wrapper	1	......	1 00	......
Pickers, wrapper	a7	......	67	......
Pressmen	4	......	1 50	......
Stemmers	b20	b21	35	$0 25

a Youth.   *b* Children.

OCCUPATIONS AND WAGES.

OCCUPATIONS, WITH NUMBER AND WAGES OF EMPLOYÉS, BY INDUSTRIES—Cont'd.

NOTE.—This table is *not* a complete exhibit for industries or states, but covers only establishments investigated by the Bureau. See page 91, also summaries, pages 143 to 226.

TOBACCO (CHEWING TOBACCO), NORTH CAROLINA.—ESTAB. No. 510.

Time, 11½ hours per day; 300 days the past year.

Occupations.	Number.		Daily wages.	
	Male.	Fem.	Male.	Fem.
Carpenter	1	......	$2 25	......
Finishers	a8	5	60	$0 60
Fireman	1	......	1 00	......
Laborers	9	......	83	......
Leaf sorters	......	56	......	55
Lump makers	40	......	1 50	......
Pressmen	12	......	1 00	......
Stemmers	2	3	60	45
Stemmers	b10	b10	25	25
Strippers	a58	......	45	......
Teamster	1	......	75	......
Watchmen	2	......	1 00	......
Wrappers	......	3	......	75
Wrappers	......	50	......	67

TOBACCO (SMOKING TOBACCO), NORTH CAROLINA.—ESTAB. No. 511.

Time, 10 hours per day; 285 days the past year.

Occupations.	Number.		Daily wages.	
	Male.	Fem.	Male.	Fem.
Box makers, paper	6	......	$1 00	......
Box makers, wood	10	......	90	......
Box makers' helpers	5	......	67	......
Carpenter	1	......	1 50	......
Carpenters	8	......	1 33	......
Cutters	24	......	67	......
Driers	7	......	1 00	......
Engineer	1	......	1 50	......
Feeder, mill	1	......	60	......
Foremen	3	......	4 00	......
Foreman	1	......	3 00	......
Foremen	3	......	2 50	......
Foremen	8	......	2 00	......
Foremen	5	......	1 50	......
Laborers	12	......	60	......
Laborers	12	......	67	......
Machinist	1	......	3 50	......
Machinists	6	......	1 75	......
Mixers	7	......	60	......
Packers	4	......	75	......
Packers	40	......	60	......
Packers	6	......	50	......
Packers	a19	......	35	......
Printer	1	......	1 25	......
Printer	1	......	1 00	......
Stablemen	14	......	60	......
Stampers and labelers	2	......	83	......
Stampers and labelers	12	10	67	$0 50
Stampers and labelers	a35	a30	35	35
Watchmen	2	......	1 00	......

TOBACCO (CIGARS), OHIO.—ESTAB. No. 512.

Time, 9 hours per day; 300 days the past year.

Occupations.	Number.		Daily wages.	
	Male.	Fem.	Male.	Fem.
Bunch breakers	25	......	75	$1 44	$1 44
Foremen	4	......	3 00	......
Laborers	7	......	1 50	......
Packers	14	......	2 16	......
Rollers	75	75	1 44	1 44
Strippers	......	a40	......	54

TOBACCO (CIGARS), OHIO.—ESTAB. No. 513.

Time, 10 hours per day; — days the past year.

Occupations.	Number.		Daily wages.	
	Male.	Fem.	Male.	Fem.
Bunch breakers	32	33	$1 08	$1 08
Foremen	2	......	3 00	......
Packers	11	......	2 67	......
Rollers	58	27	1 58	1 58
Strippers	......	a22	......	54

TOBACCO (CIGARS), OHIO.—ESTAB. No. 514.

Time, 10 hours per day; 295 days the past year.

Bunch breakers	29	38	$1 50	$1 00
Packers	16	1	2 25	2 00
Rollers	115	30	1 50	1 00
Strippers	a15	a9	40	33
Wrapper bookers	8	58	1 00	70

TOBACCO (CIGARS), OHIO.—ESTAB. No. 515.

Time, 9 hours per day; 270 days the past year.

Bunch breakers	5	5	$1 00	$1 00
Packers	4	......	2 00	......
Rollers	15	15	1 50	1 50
Strippers	......	a10	......	60

TOBACCO (CIGARS), OHIO.—ESTAB. No. 516.

Time, 10 hours per day; — days the past year.

Cigar makers	60	......	$1 73	......
Foremen	3	......	2 50	......
Packers	5	......	2 50	......
Strippers	......	a10	......	51

TOBACCO (CIGARS), OHIO.—ESTAB. No. 517.

Time, 10 hours per day; 300 days the past year.

Bunch breakers	25	25	$1 12	$1 12
Foremen	2	......	3 00	......
Packers	7	......	2 50	......
Rollers	25	......	1 26	......
Rollers	......	25	......	1 26
Strippers	......	a15	......	42

TOBACCO (STOGIE CIGARS), OHIO.—ESTAB. No. 518.

Time, 8½ hours per day; 300 days the past year.

Bunch breakers	......	a50	......	$0 33
Caser	1	......	$1 25	......
Forewoman	......	1	......	1 67
Packer	......	1	......	58
Rollers	......	50	......	58
Strippers	......	a5	......	21

a Youth. *b* Children.

OCCUPATIONS, WITH NUMBER AND WAGES OF EMPLOYÉS, BY INDUSTRIES—Cont'd.

NOTE.—This table is *not* a complete exhibit for industries or states, but covers only establishments investigated by the Bureau. See page 91, also summaries, pages 143 to 226.

TOBACCO (CIGARS), RHODE ISLAND.—ESTAB. No. 519.

Time, 10 hours per day; 300 days the past year.

Occupations.	Number.		Daily wages.	
	Male.	Fem.	Male.	Fem.
Apprentice	a1		$1 50	
Apprentice	a1		1 00	
Cigar makers	8		2 33	
Cigar makers	7		2 17	
Cigar makers	4		1 83	
Laborer	1		1 50	
Packer	1		2 17	
Strippers		4		$1 00

TOBACCO (CHEWING TOBACCO), VIRGINIA.—ESTAB. No. 520.

Time, 10 hours per day; 300 days the past year.

Occupations.	Male.	Fem.	Male.	Fem.
Branders	7		$0 90	
Brander	1		75	
Carpenters	4		2 33	
Carpenters	5		1 83	
Carpenters' helpers	a9		67	
Engineer	1		2 33	
Firemen	2		1 45	
Foremen	11		1 42	
Laborers	105		75	
Lump makers	30		1 43	
Lump makers	44		1 00	
Pressmen	62		1 10	
Pressmen	6		1 00	
Pressmen's helpers	b23		30	
Stemmers	a8	163	70	$0 55
Stemmers	b25	b125	25	25
Strippers	a32		50	
Strippers	b15		40	
Strippers	b13		30	
Wrapper	1		80	
Wrappers		15		50

TOBACCO (CHEWING TOBACCO), VIRGINIA.—ESTAB. No. 521.

Time, 10 hours per day; 296 days the past year.

Occupations.	Male.	Fem.	Male.	Fem.
Foreman	1		$2 50	
Foremen, assistant	2		1 25	
Laborers	15		1 00	
Lump makers	12		1 20	
Lump makers	8		1 00	
Pickers, wrapper	5		1 00	
Pressmen	15		1 75	
Pressmen's helpers	a4		43	
Receiver	1		1 33	
Stemmers	b8	b19	33	$0 25
Stemmers	b18	75	25	50
Wrappers		12		80

TOBACCO (CHEWING TOBACCO), VIRGINIA.—ESTAB. No. 522.

Time, 10 hours per day; 300 days the past year.

Occupations.	Male.	Fem.	Male.	Fem.
Brander	1		$1 50	
Brander	1		80	
Engineer	1		2 00	

TOBACCO (CHEWING TOBACCO), VIRGINIA.—ESTAB. No. 522—Concluded.

Time, 10 hours per day; 300 days the past year.

Occupations.	Male.	Fem.	Male.	Fem.
Finishers		4		$0 50
Fireman	1		$1 00	
Foremen	3		2 00	
Laborers	15		85	
Lump makers	85		1 10	
Pressmen	20		1 15	
Pressmen's helpers	a2		50	
Stemmers	a40	45	50	50
Undesignated		25		50
Watchmen	2		1 28	

TOBACCO (CHEWING TOBACCO), VIRGINIA.—ESTAB. No. 523.

Time, 10 hours per day; 300 days the past year.

Occupations.	Male.	Fem.	Male.	Fem.
Foremen	3		$3 00	
Foremen	3		2 00	
Laborers	20		1 00	
Laborers	a10		50	
Lump makers	58		1 00	
Pressmen	20		1 00	
Pressmen's helpers	a10		50	
Stemmers	b25	25	25	$0 50
Watchman	1		1 67	
Wrappers	a125		50	

TOBACCO (CHEWING TOBACCO), VIRGINIA.—ESTAB. No. 524.

Time, 10 hours per day; 300 days the past year.

Occupations.	Male.	Fem.	Male.	Fem.
Engineer	1		$1 50	
Fireman	1		1 00	
Foremen	3		1 50	
Laborers	8		90	
Laborers	a25		40	
Lump makers	7		1 20	
Pressmen	4		1 60	
Pressmen's helpers	2		60	
Pressmen's helpers	a4		40	
Stemmers		70		$0 50
Strippers	a5	5	50	50
Wrappers		14		1 00

TOBACCO (CHEWING TOBACCO), VIRGINIA.—ESTAB. No. 525.

Time, 10 hours per day; 300 days the past year.

Occupations.	Male.	Fem.	Male.	Fem.
Laborers	15		$0 90	
Lump makers	70		1 30	
Lump makers	12		1 10	
Pressmen	40		1 25	
Stemmers	a65	61	50	$0 60
Strippers	a20	5	50	60

a Youth. *b* Children.

OCCUPATIONS AND WAGES.

OCCUPATIONS, WITH NUMBER AND WAGES OF EMPLOYÉS, BY INDUSTRIES—Cont'd.

NOTE.—This table is *not* a complete exhibit for industries or states, but covers only establishments investigated by the Bureau. See page 91, also summaries, pages 143 to 226.

TOBACCO (CIGARETTES), VIRGINIA.—ESTAB. No. 526.

Time, 10 hours per day; 302 days the past year.

Occupations.	Number.		Daily wages.	
	Male.	Fem.	Male.	Fem.
Box makers, paper ..	a3	29	$0 83	$0 83
Cigarette makers		a590		67
Cutters	25	......	1 00	......
Engineer	1	......	1 67	......
Finisher	1	......	1 67	......
Finishers	a2	25	83	83
Foremen	2	......	3 00	......
Laborers	37	......	1 00	......
Operator, cigarette-machine	1	......	2 00	......
Operator's helpers ..	......	2	......	83
Package makers	......	16	......	1 00
Packers	......	75	......	83
Stemmers	......	100	......	55
Undesignated	a3	......	50	......

TOBACCO (STOGIE CIGARS), WEST VIRGINIA.—ESTAB. No. 527.

Time, 10 hours per day; 300 days the past year.

Occupations.	Male.	Fem.	Male.	Fem.
Cigar makers	48	......	$1 50	......
Foreman	1	......	2 50	......
Packers	......	2	......	$0 60
Strippers	......	a10	......	50

VESSELS (STEAMSHIPS), DELAWARE.—ESTAB. No. 528.

Time, 10 hours per day; 300 days the past year.

Occupations.	Male.	Fem.	Male.	Fem.
Blacksmiths	28	......	$2 25	......
Car builders	286	......	2 00	......
Carpenters, ship ...	66	......	2 50	......
Casting cleaners ...	8	......	1 50	......
Chippers and caulkers	51	......	1 50	......
Core makers	4	......	1 50	......
Cupola men	2	......	1 75	......
Fitters	62	......	2 00	......
Flangers	6	......	3 00	......
Holders-on	57	......	1 40	......
Joiners, ship	201	......	2 00	......
Laborers	403	......	1 20	......
Machinists	76	......	2 37	......
Mill hands	19	......	2 60	......
Millwrights	6	......	2 50	......
Moulders	35	......	2 50	......
Painters	140	......	1 75	......
Pattern makers	14	......	2 50	......
Riggers	12	......	1 62	......
Riveters	113	......	1 75	......
Teamsters	7	......	1 50	......
Upholsterers	20	......	2 00	......

VESSELS (STEAMSHIPS), DELAWARE.—ESTAB. No. 529.

Time, 10 hours per day; 300 days the past year.

Occupations.	Male.	Fem.	Male.	Fem.
Apprentices	a29	......	$0 75	......
Blacksmiths	23	......	2 30	......
Blacksmiths' helpers	35	......	1 17	......
Boat callers	3	......	1 25	......

VESSELS (STEAMSHIPS), DELAWARE.—ESTAB. No. 529—Concluded.

Time, 10 hours per day; 300 days the past year.

Occupations.	Number.		Daily wages.	
	Male.	Fem.	Male.	Fem.
Brace fitters	7	......	$1 67	......
Carpenters	30	......	2 27	......
Chippers and caulkers	7	......	1 50	......
Core makers	8	......	1 95	......
Cupola man	1	......	1 67	......
Draughtsmen	8	......	4 00	......
Drillers	2	......	1 17	......
Engineers	3	......	1 78	......
Fireman	1	......	1 25	......
Fitters	32	......	1 67	......
Furnace men, shaft	5	......	3 25	......
Furnace man, scrap	1	......	3 25	......
Furnace men, angle	5	......	2 50	......
Furnace-men's helpers	4	......	1 42	......
Heater boys	a18	......	59	......
Holders-on	12	......	1 30	......
Joiners	87	......	2 00	......
Laborers	172	......	1 14	......
Millwrights	7	......	2 25	......
Moulders	2	......	2 33	......
Moulders	35	......	2 25	......
Painters	30	......	1 75	......
Passer boys	a15	......	67	......
Pattern makers	10	......	2 50	......
Pinchers	5	......	1 25	......
Riveters	38	......	1 50	......
Riggers	5	......	1 50	......
Rollers	2	......	1 50	......
Sawyer	1	......	1 83	......
Sawyer's helper ...	1	......	1 33	......
Teamsters	4	......	1 17	......

VESSELS (SAILING VESSELS), MAINE.—ESTAB. No. 530.

Time, 10 hours per day; — days the past year.

Occupations.	Male.	Fem.	Male.	Fem.
Blacksmiths	6	......	$1 75	......
Carpenters, ship ...	4	......	1 75	......
Fasteners	20	......	1 62	......
Foremen	4	......	2 00	......
Joiners	15	......	1 75	......
Painters	3	......	1 50	......
Spar makers	4	......	1 75	......

VESSELS (SAILING VESSELS), MAINE.—ESTAB. No. 531.

Time, 10 hours per day; — days the past year.

Occupations.	Male.	Fem.	Male.	Fem.
Blacksmiths	10	......	$2 50	......
Blacksmiths' helper	1	......	1 25	......
Caulkers	50	......	1 75	......
Carpenters, ship ...	90	......	1 62	......
Fasteners	20	......	1 62	......
Foreman	1	......	4 50	......
Foreman	1	......	4 00	......
Foreman	1	......	3 25	......
Foreman, assistant..	1	......	2 50	......
Joiners	35	......	1 62	......
Mill hand	1	......	2 00	......
Mill hands	9	......	1 37	......
Painters	8	......	1 87	......

a Youth.

400 REPORT OF THE COMMISSIONER OF LABOR.

OCCUPATIONS, WITH NUMBER AND WAGES OF EMPLOYÉS, BY INDUSTRIES—Cont'd.

NOTE.—This table is *not* a complete exhibit for industries or states, but covers only establishment investigated by the Bureau. See page 91, also summaries, pages 143 to 226.

VESSELS (SAILING VESSELS), MAINE.—ESTAB. No. 532.

Time, 10 hours per day; — days the past year.

Occupations.	Number.		Daily wages.	
	Male.	Fem.	Male.	Fem.
Draughtsman	1		$1 50	
Engineer	1		1 50	
Foundery men	5		2 00	
Laborer	1		1 50	
Machinists	6		2 00	
Pattern makers	2		2 25	
Teamster	1		1 50	

WOODEN GOODS (BARRELS), CALIFORNIA.—ESTAB. No. 533.

Time, 10 hours per day; 275 days the past year.

Occupations.	Male.	Fem.	Male.	Fem.
Coopers	60		$2 50	
Engineer	1		6 00	
Fireman	1		2 25	
Foreman	1		4 00	
Foreman	1		3 00	
Foreman	1		2 25	
Laborers	a6		75	
Machine hands	2		3 00	
Machine hands	5		2 50	
Machine hands	4		2 00	
Nailers and liners	a17		85	
Oiler	1		2 00	
Raisers	8		2 40	
Shaver	1		2 60	
Sorter	1		2 25	
Teamster	1		2 50	
Tressers	3		2 25	
Trimmers	2		2 50	
Watchmen	2		2 00	
Yard hands	8		1 75	

WOODEN GOODS (SASH, DOORS, BLINDS), INDIANA.—ESTAB. No. 534.

Time, 10 hours per day; 300 days the past year.

Occupations.	Male.	Fem.	Male.	Fem.
Carpenters	37		$2 25	
Engineer	1		2 00	
Laborers	5		1 50	
Machine hands	10		2 00	
Painters	5		2 20	

WOODEN GOODS (WOODENWARE), VIRGINIA.—ESTAB. No. 535.

Time, 10 hours per day; 300 days the past year.

Occupations.	Male.	Fem.	Male.	Fem.
Bottomers	7		$1 50	
Bottomers' helpers	a5		50	
Driers	6		1 00	
Engineer	2		2 00	
Fireman	2		1 25	
Laborers	18		1 00	
Machinists	5		1 88	
Machinists' helpers	a2		63	
Matchers	a64		75	
Packers	9		1 10	
Packers	a10		83	
Planers	4		1 25	
Sawyers	20		1 00	
Turners	47		1 60	
Watchman	2		1 25	

WOOLLEN GOODS (CLOTH), CALIFORNIA.—ESTAB. No. 536.

Time, 10 hours per day; 300 days the past year.

Occupations.	Number.		Daily wages.	
	Male.	Fem.	Male.	Fem.
Carders	9		$1 75	
Dresser	1		3 75	
Dyers	4		1 87	
Engineer	1		2 75	
Finishers	8		1 00	
Firemen	1		1 50	
Fuller	1		2 00	
Fullers	8		1 12	
Laborers	6		1 00	
Loom fixer	1		1 75	
Overseer	1		3 87	
Overseer	1		3 50	
Overseer	1		2 50	
Scourer	1		1 00	
Shearer	1		1 16	
Spinners	6		1 00	
Spoolers	a3		75	
Watchman	1		1 67	
Weavers	39		1 50	
Weavers	7		1 00	
Wool sorters	2		1 25	

WOOLLEN GOODS (WOMEN'S DRESS GOODS), CONNECTICUT.—ESTAB. No. 537.

Time, 11¼ hours per day; 275 days the past year.

Occupations.	Male.	Fem.	Male.	Fem.
Burlers		4		$0 90
Carders	8		$1 25	
Carpenter	1		2 00	
Drawers-in		1		1 20
Dressers	2		1 50	
Driers	a2		75	
Dyer	1		3 00	
Dyer	1		2 00	
Dyers	3		1 25	
Finisher	1		1 25	
Finishers	6		90	
Firemen	2		1 50	
Fullers	2		1 10	
Hander-in		b1		40
Machinist	1		2 60	
Overseers	3		3 00	
Overseer	1		2 00	
Second hands	2		1 75	
Sewing-machine operator		1		75
Spinners, mule	12		1 50	
Spoolers		5		75
Watchman	1		1 30	
Weavers		25		1 16
Weave-room hands	4		1 00	

WOOLLEN GOODS (WOMEN'S DRESS GOODS), CONNECTICUT.—ESTAB. No. 538.

Time, 11 hours per day; 300 days the past year.

Occupations.	Male.	Fem.	Male.	Fem.
Burlers		9		$0 60
Carders	7		$1 15	
Carders	a9		57	
Carpenter	1		1 50	
Drawers-in		1		1 15
Dressers	4		1 30	
Driers	c3		43	
Dyer	1		3 00	
Dyer	1		1 87	

a Youth.   *b* Child.   *c* Children.

OCCUPATIONS, WITH NUMBER AND WAGES OF EMPLOYÉS, BY INDUSTRIES—Cont'd.

NOTE.—This table is *not* a complete exhibit for industries or states, but covers only establishments investigated by the Bureau. See page 91, also summaries, pages 143 to 226.

WOOLLEN GOODS (WOMEN'S DRESS GOODS), CONNECTICUT.—ESTAB No. 538—Concluded.

Time, 11 hours per day; 300 days the past year.

Occupations.	Number.		Daily wages.	
	Male.	Fem.	Male.	Fem.
Dyers	4	......	$1 00	......
Finishers	7	......	1 00	......
Fireman	1	......	2 00	......
Fuller	1	......	1 35	......
Handers-in	......	a2	......	$0 40
Laborer	1	......	1 25	......
Loom fixer	2	......	1 35	......
Machinist	1	......	1 75	......
Overseer	1	......	2 50	......
Overseer	1	......	2 25	......
Overseer	1	......	2 10	......
Overseer	1	......	2 00	......
Swing-machine operator	......	1	......	75
Spinners, mule	17	......	1 15	......
Spoolers	......	4	......	70
Second hands	4	......	1 00	......
Teamster	1	......	1 25	......
Watchman	1	......	1 25	......
Weavers	......	18	......	1 26
Weavers	......	18	......	70

WOOLLEN GOODS (CLOTH), DELAWARE.—ESTAB. No. 539.

Time, 10 hours per day; 308 days the past year.

Occupations.	Number.		Daily wages.	
	Male.	Fem.	Male.	Fem.
Burlers	......	b10	......	$0 66
Carder	1	......	$3 00	......
Carders	2	......	1 50	......
Carder	1	......	1 25	......
Carders	b6	......	1 00	......
Carpenter	1	......	2 25	......
Doffers	2	......	1 00	......
Doffers	b2	......	70	......
Doublers	......	b8	......	66
Drawers-in	3	......	1 25	......
Drawers-in	b2	......	50	......
Dyer	1	......	3 00	......
Engineer	1	......	1 83	......
Finisher	1	......	3 00	......
Finishers	5	......	1 25	......
Fireman	1	......	1 16	......
Foreman	1	......	3 33	......
Foreman	1	......	2 66	......
Fullers	2	......	1 33	......
Inspector	1	......	1 83	......
Laborers	7	......	1 25	......
Loom fixers	2	......	2 00	......
Overseer	1	......	1 50	......
Packer	1	......	1 25	......
Picker	1	......	2 00	......
Presser	1	......	1 33	......
Shearers	......	2	......	1 00
Spinner, mule	1	......	2 50	......
Spinner, mule	2	......	2 00	......
Spinner, mule	1	......	1 66	......
Spoolers	......	3	......	1 00
Spool carriers	a10	......	50	......
Teamsters	3	......	1 50	......
Time keeper	1	......	1 50	......
Twisters	......	3	......	75
Warpers	2	......	2 00	......
Watchmen	2	......	1 42	......
Weavers	35	5	2 00	2 00
Wool sorters	3	......	1 25	......

WOOLLEN GOODS (CLOTH), DELAWARE.—ESTAB. No. 540.

Time, 10 hours per day; 300 days the past year.

Occupations.	Number.		Daily wages.	
	Male.	Fem.	Male.	Fem.
Bobbin carrier	1	......	$1 35	......
Burlers	......	b15	......	$0 58
Carders	3	......	1 33	......
Carders	3	......	1 00	......
Carders	b3	......	72	......
Carpenter	1	......	2 00	......
Carpenters	2	......	1 50	......
Cloth carriers	6	......	1 00	......
Drawer and twister	1	......	3 00	......
Drawers and twisters	b2	......	41	......
Engineer	1	......	2 00	......
Fullers	2	......	1 50	......
Giggers	3	......	1 33	......
Inspector	1	......	1 83	......
Laborer	1	......	1 50	......
Laborers	8	......	1 16	......
Laborer	b1	......	50	......
Loom fixers	3	......	2 25	......
Machinist	1	......	3 00	......
Measurer	1	......	1 60	......
Overseer	1	......	2 70	......
Pattern starter	1	......	2 00	......
Pickers	5	......	1 50	......
Piecers	b10	......	45	......
Presser and breaker	1	......	1 33	......
Presser and breaker	b1	......	84	......
Scourers	2	......	1 83	......
Shearer	1	......	1 33	......
Shearer's helper	b1	......	83	......
Spinners, mule	2	......	2 70	......
Spool carrier	b1	......	72	......
Spoolers	......	b6	......	50
Undesignated	b6	b10	72	58
Warpers	3	......	1 66	......
Watchman	1	......	1 66	......
Weavers	22	30	1 25	1 25
Weigher	1	......	1 25	......
Wool sorters	3	......	1 66	......

WOOLLEN GOODS (CLOTH), GREAT BRITAIN.—ESTAB. No. 541.

Time, 10 hours per day; — days the past year.

Occupations.	Number.		Daily wages.	
	Male.	Fem.	Male.	Fem.
Beamers	3	......	$0 73	......
Burlers	b30	......	44	......
Card cleaners	80	......	80	......
Doublers	......	16	......	$0 44
Dyers	6	......	92	......
Finishers	37	......	87	......
Finishers	b32	......	36	......
Layers-on	......	6	......	44
Loom fixers	6	......	1 33	......
Loom-fixers' helpers	4	......	50	......
Menders	......	20	......	40
Piecers	b36	......	40	......
Repair hands	6	......	1 15	......
Scourers	7	......	80	......
Scourer and dyer	1	......	80	......
Scourers and fullers	8	......	92	......
Spinners, mule	12	......	86	......
Tenters	3	......	1 58	......
Tenters	4	......	18	......
Warpers	b7	4	56	40
Weavers	3	176	83	50
Wool sorter	1	......	1 20	......

a Children. b Youth.

OCCUPATIONS, WITH NUMBER AND WAGES OF EMPLOYÉS, BY INDUSTRIES—Cont'd.

NOTE.—This table is not a complete exhibit for industries or states, but covers only establishments investigated by the Bureau. See page 91, also summaries, pages 143 to 220.

WOOLLEN GOODS (CASSIMERE), ILLINOIS.—ESTAB. No. 542.

Time, 10½ hours per day; 300 days the past year.

Occupations.	Number.		Daily wages.	
	Male.	Fem.	Male.	Fem.
Carders	a4	a5	$0 58	$0 58
Dressers	......	a5	......	44
Dyers	4	......	1 35	......
Engineer	1	......	2 88	......
Finishers	9	14	1 40	72
Machinist	1	......	2 12	......
Overseers	5	......	2 88	......
Overseer	1	......	2 40	......
Overseer	1	......	1 92	......
Overseer	1	......	1 44	......
Pickers	a2	......	48	......
Second hand	1	......	1 68	......
Spinners	4	5	1 02	1 02
Watchman	1	......	1 50	......
Weavers	2	......	2 12	......
Weavers	26	......	1 47	......
Wool sorters	3	......	1 92	......

WOOLLEN GOODS (JEANS), INDIANA.—ESTAB. No. 543.

Time, 11 hours per day; 300 days the past year.

Occupations.	Number.		Daily wages.	
	Male.	Fem.	Male.	Fem.
Burlers	......	2	......	$0 75
Carders	a12	......	$0 75	......
Drawers-in	......	a3	......	74
Dyers	3	......	1 25	......
Engineer	1	......	2 00	......
Finishers	2	......	1 25	......
Overseers	4	......	3 00	......
Overseer	1	......	2 50	......
Pickers	2	......	1 25	......
Spinners	......	20	......	75
Watchman	1	......	1 80	......
Weavers	......	20	......	1 00
Weavers	......	30	......	83
Wool sorters	2	......	1 25	......

WOOLLEN GOODS (JEANS, FLANNEL), INDIANA.—ESTAB. No. 544.

Time, 11 hours per day; 300 days the past year.

Occupations.	Number.		Daily wages.	
	Male.	Fem.	Male.	Fem.
Carder	a1	......	$0 58	......
Carders	b5	......	42	......
Dyer	1	......	2 50	......
Engineer	1	......	2 00	......
Finisher	1	......	2 50	......
Finishers	5	......	1 25	......
Laborers	6	......	1 00	......
Overseer	1	......	3 00	......
Overseer	1	......	2 00	......
Second hand	1	......	1 50	......
Spinners	a2	a4	58	$0 42
Weavers	14	......	1 08	......
Wool sorter	1	......	1 25	......

WOOLLEN GOODS (FLANNEL, BLANKETS), INDIANA.—ESTAB. No. 545.

Time, 11 hours per day; 300 days the past year.

Occupations.	Number.		Daily wages.	
	Male.	Fem.	Male.	Fem.
Carder	1	......	$1 00	......
Carders	a2	......	83	......
Carders	a2	......	75	......
Carders	a11	......	67	......
Carders	a4	......	58	......
Card cleaner	1	......	1 50	......
Card cleaners	4	......	1 16	......
Card cleaners	2	......	1 09	......
Carpenter	1	......	2 50	......
Carpenter	1	......	1 75	......
Drawers-in	3	2	92	$0 34
Drawer-in	......	1	......	67
Drawers-in	......	4	......	50
Dresser	1	......	1 75	......
Dresser	1	......	1 50	......
Dresser	1	......	1 33	......
Dyers	4	......	1 67	......
Dyers	3	......	1 50	......
Dyers	5	......	1 33	......
Dyers	11	......	1 25	......
Dyer	1	......	1 16	......
Dyers	4	......	1 00	......
Dyers' helpers	5	......	67	......
Dyers' helpers	a3	......	60	......
Engineer	1	......	1 50	......
Finisher	1	1	1 50	1 21
Finisher	1	......	1 16	......
Finisher	1	......	1 12	......
Finishers	4	......	1 00	......
Finishers	2	......	84	......
Finishers	a3	......	75	......
Finishers	a20	......	67	......
Finisher	a1	......	58	......
Firemen	4	......	1 50	......
Fuller	1	......	1 33	......
Fuller	1	......	1 25	......
Fullers	5	......	1 17	......
Fullers	6	......	1 00	......
Fuller	a1	a2	83	67
Fullers	a3	......	58	......
Laborer	1	......	1 33	......
Laborer	1	......	1 17	......
Laborers	6	......	1 00	......
Laborer	a1	......	85	......
Loom fixers	2	......	2 00	......
Loom fixer	1	......	1 75	......
Loom fixer	1	......	1 67	......
Loom fixers	2	......	1 50	......
Machinist	1	......	3 25	......
Machinist	1	......	2 50	......
Machinists	3	......	2 25	......
Oiler	1	......	1 25	......
Overseer	1	......	4 50	......
Overseers	2	......	4 00	......
Overseer	1	......	3 67	......
Overseer	1	......	3 33	......
Overseer	1	......	3 00	......
Overseers	2	......	2 50	......
Overseer	1	......	1 75	......
Pickers and driers	2	......	1 16	......
Pickers and driers	16	......	1 00	......
Picker and drier	a1	......	64	......
Pickers and driers	a2	......	50	......
Second hand	1	......	2 00	......
Second hands	2	......	1 67	......

a Youth.   b Children.

OCCUPATIONS, WITH NUMBER AND WAGES OF EMPLOYÉS, BY INDUSTRIES—Cont'd.

NOTE.—This table is not a complete exhibit for industries or states, but covers only establishments investigated by the Bureau. See page 91, also summaries, pages 143 to 226.

WOOLLEN GOODS (FLANNEL, BLANKETS), INDIANA.—ESTAB. No. 545—Concluded.

Time, 11 hours per day; 300 days the past year.

Occupations.	Number.		Daily wages.	
	Male.	Fem.	Male.	Fem.
Second hand	1	......	$1 33	......
Second hand	1	......	1 16	......
Spinner	1	......	1 00	......
Spinners	a15	......	75	......
Spinners	a6	......	63	......
Spinners	a17	a2	67	$0 67
Spinners	a3	a3	58	50
Spinners	a12	......	50	......
Spinners	a6	a2	46	46
Spinners	a6	a7	42	42
Spinner	a1	......	29	......
Spooler	1	a7	1 50	50
Watchman	1	......	1 67	......
Watchman	1	......	1 00	......
Weavers	......	107	......	1 07
Wool sorter	1	......	2 00	......
Wool sorters	4	......	1 50	......
Wool sorter	1	......	1 25	......
Wool sorters	5	......	1 00	......
Wool sorter	a1	......	83	......
Wool sorters	a4	......	75	......

WOOLLEN GOODS (FLANNEL, YARN), INDIANA.—ESTAB. No. 546.

Time, 10 hours per day; 200 days the past year.

Occupations.	Male.	Fem.	Male.	Fem.
Carders	1	......	$2 00	......
Dyers	2	......	2 00	......
Engineer	1	......	1 50	......
Finisher	1	......	2 50	......
Laborers	4	......	1 00	......
Overseer	1	......	2 00	......
Picker	1	......	1 00	......
Spinners, male	4	......	1 25	......
Weavers	......	10	......	$1 00
Wool sorter	1	......	2 00	......

WOOLLEN GOODS (FLANNEL, BLANKETS), IOWA.—ESTAB. No. 547.

Time, 10 hours per day; — days the past year.

Occupations.	Male.	Fem.	Male.	Fem.
Carders	3	......	$1 25	......
Carders	a4	......	75	......
Dyer	1	......	1 50	......
Engineer	1	......	3 00	......
Finishers	2	*g	1 50	$0 75
Foreman	1	......	4 00	......
Foremen	2	......	2 75	......
Foreman	1	......	2 50	......
Laborers	3	......	1 50	......
Packers	3	......	1 50	......
Spinners, male	1	......	1 25	......
Spinners	......	3	......	75
Twisters	......	a5	......	60
Weavers	2	15	1 25	1 20
Wool sorter	1	......	2 00	......

WOOLLEN GOODS (JEANS), KENTUCKY.—ESTAB. No. 548.

Time, 11 hours per day; 310 days the past year.

Occupations.	Number.		Daily wages.	
	Male.	Fem.	Male.	Fem.
Carders	4	a17	$1 75	$0 66
Dyers	10	......	1 54	......
Engineer	1	......	2 97	......
Finishers	a16	......	72	......
Fireman	1	......	1 56	......
Laborer	1	......	1 00	......
Loom fixers	5	......	1 75	......
Overseers	2	......	3 52	......
Overseers	3	......	2 97	......
Pickers	4	......	1 20	......
Spinners	a4	a44	68	60
Watchman	1	......	1 50	......
Weavers	......	1 60	......	60
Wool sorters	5	......	1 54	......

WOOLLEN GOODS (JEANS), KENTUCKY.—ESTAB. No. 549.

Time, 11 hours per day; 310 days the past year.

Occupations.	Male.	Fem.	Male.	Fem.
Carders	......	4	......	$1 10
Carders	5	a3	......	66
Dyers	5	......	$1 10	......
Engineer	1	......	3 00	......
Finishers	b14	......	33	......
Finisher	1	......	1 43	......
Fireman	1	......	1 65	......
Laborers	2	......	1 87	......
Laborers	12	......	1 25	......
Overseers	5	......	3 00	......
Picker	1	......	1 65	......
Pickers	5	......	99	......
Spinners	......	36	......	75
Undesignated	b2	......	33	......
Watchmen	1	......	1 80	......
Weavers	......	1 00	......	1 10
Wool sorter	1	......	1 65	......
Wool sorters	a7	......	44	......

WOOLLEN GOODS (CASSIMERE), MAINE.—ESTAB. No. 550.

Time, 11 hours per day; — days the past year.

Occupations.	Male.	Fem.	Male.	Fem.
Carders	......	2	......	$0 75
Engineers	1	......	$1 50	......
Finisher	1	......	1 50	......
Foreman	1	......	3 00	......
Picker	......	1	......	50
Spinner	1	......	1 00	......
Washer and scourer	1	......	1 50	......
Weavers	......	2	......	75

WOOLLEN GOODS (CLOTH), MAINE.—ESTAB. No. 551.

Time, 11 hours per day; — days the past year.

Occupations.	Male.	Fem.	Male.	Fem.
Carders	......	3	......	$0 67
Designer	1	......	$2 00	......
Dresser	1	......	1 60	......

a Youth.   *b* Children.

OCCUPATIONS, WITH NUMBER AND WAGES OF EMPLOYÉS, BY INDUSTRIES—Cont'd.

NOTE.—This table is not a complete exhibit for industries or states, but covers only establishments investigated by the Bureau. See page 91, also summaries, pages 143 to 220.

WOOLLEN GOODS (CLOTH), MAINE.—ESTAB. No. 551—Concluded.

Time, 11 hours per day ; — days the past year.

Occupations.	Number.		Daily wages.	
	Male.	Fem.	Male.	Fem.
Machinist	1		$2 00	
Overseers	2		2 75	
Overseer	1		2 50	
Overseer	1		2 25	
Picker	1		80	
Second hands	3		1 45	
Second hands	4		1 15	
Spinners	9		1 00	
Undesignated		4		$0 75
Weavers		13		1 30
Wool sorter	1		1 75	

WOOLLEN GOODS (WOMEN'S DRESS GOODS), MAINE.—ESTAB. No. 552.

Time, 11 hours per day ; — days the past year.

Occupations.	Male.	Fem.	Male.	Fem.
Brush boy	1		$0 80	
Carders	a8		60	
Dyers	2		1 25	
Drier	1		1 10	
Fireman	1		1 50	
Fuller	1		1 50	
Fuller's helper	1		1 25	
Giggers	2		1 10	
Inspectors	2	6	80	$0 75
Loom fixers	2		1 75	
Overseers	3		3 00	
Overseers	3		2 25	
Picker	1		1 50	
Presser	1		1 35	
Scourers	3		1 20	
Second hand	1		1 75	
Second hands	3		1 50	
Sewing machine operators		2		80
Shearers	2		1 25	
Spare hand	1		1 25	
Spinners, mule	8		1 60	
Strippers	2		1 25	
Twister	1		80	
Watchman	1		1 25	
Weavers	50		1 40	
Wool sorters	2		1 75	

WOOLLEN GOODS (FLANNEL), MAINE.—ESTAB. No. 553.

Time, 11 hours per day ; — days the past years.

Occupations.	Male.	Fem.	Male.	Fem.
Carders	a6		$0 85	
Carpenter	1		2 00	
Drawers	2		1 00	
Dyer	1		2 00	
Dyers	1		1 25	
Fuller	1		1 50	
Laborers	30		1 20	
Loom fixer	1		1 60	
Machinist	1		2 00	
Overseer	1		3 00	
Overseer	1		2 75	
Overseer	1		2 50	
Overseer	1		2 25	
Picker	1		1 33	
Second hand	1		2 00	

a Youth.

WOOLLEN GOODS (FLANNEL), MAINE.—ESTAB. No. 553—Concluded.

Time, 11 hours per day ; — days the past year.

Occupations.	Number.		Daily wages.	
	Male.	Fem.	Male.	Fem.
Second hand	1		$1 75	
Spinners, mule	13		1 50	
Spoolers	5		1 00	
Teamster	1		1 25	
Warpers	2		2 00	
Weavers	35		1 15	
Wool sorters	6		1 50	

WOOLLEN GOODS (CLOTH), MARYLAND.—ESTAB. No. 554.

Time, 11 hours per day; 302 days the past year.

Occupations.	Male.	Fem.	Male.	Fem.
Baler	1		$1 25	
Beamers	4		1 50	
Box boys	b2		40	
Burlers		4		$0 90
Carpenter	1		2 50	
Carpenter	1		1 90	
Carpenters	2		1 75	
Carpenters	4		1 50	
Creel boys	a6		52	
Drawers-in		2		80
Drawers-in helpers		b4		37
Dyers	13		1 25	
Engineers	2		2 00	
Finishers	a2		80	
Finishers	a3		56	
Foreman	1		3 00	
Foremen	5		2 50	
Foremen	2		2 00	
Fuller	1		1 75	
Fullers	4		1 35	
Inspector	1		1 25	
Laborers	4		1 25	
Loom fixers	2		1 75	
Machinists	2		3 00	
Pickers	12		1 30	
Pickers	a4		80	
Pickers		9		68
Pieceers	b31		45	
Scourers	4		1 25	
Shearer	1		1 50	
Speckers		8		67
Spinners, mule	4		1 35	
Spool carriers	2		1 25	
Spoolers		9		1 00
Sweepers	b2		40	
Tenters	6		1 25	
Teamsters	2		1 50	
Teamster	1		1 15	
Waste grinder	1		1 00	
Weavers	3	50	1 10	1 10
Weavers	1	39	90	90
Wool sorter	1		2 20	
Wool sorters	a2		80	

WOOLLEN GOODS (CASSIMERE), MASSACHUSETTS.—ESTAB. No. 555.

Time, 10 hours per day ; — days the past year.

Occupations.	Male.	Fem.	Male.	Fem.
Carders	5	3	$0 85	$0 85
Dyers	4		1 00	
Finishers	7		1 15	
Fullers	3		1 00	

b Children.

OCCUPATIONS AND WAGES.

OCCUPATIONS, WITH NUMBER AND WAGES OF EMPLOYÉS, BY INDUSTRIES—Cont'd.

NOTE.—This table is not a complete exhibit for industries or states, but covers only establishments investigated by the Bureau. See page 91, also summaries, pages 143 to 226.

WOOLLEN GOODS (CASSIMERE), MASSACHUSETTS.—ESTAB. No. 555—Concluded.

Time, 10 hours per day; — days the past year.

Occupations.	Number.		Daily wages.	
	Male.	Fem.	Male.	Fem.
Giggers	10	......	$1 00	......
Overseers	6	......	2 60	......
Pickers	3	......	1 00	......
Repair and watch hands.	6	......	1 80	......
Second hands	8	......	1 66	......
Speckers	......	20	......	$0 80
Spinners, mule	14	......	1 10	......
Spinners	......	2	......	65
Undesignated	25	18	1 25	70
Undesignated	a13	......	75	......
Weavers	20	45	1 15	1 00
Weavers	......	a5	......	50

WOOLLEN GOODS (CASSIMERE), MASSACHUSETTS.—ESTAB. No. 556.

Time, 10 hours per day; — days the past year.

Occupations.	Number.		Daily wages.	
	Male.	Fem.	Male.	Fem.
Bobbin carriers	a2	......	$0 70	......
Boiler man	1	......	1 37	......
Drawers	......	3	......	$1 25
Drawer-in	......	1	......	1 37
Dresser	1	......	1 50	......
Filling carrier	1	......	1 25	......
Fuller	1	......	1 50	......
Gigger	1	......	1 50	......
Loom fixers	4	......	1 75	......
Machinist	1	......	2 00	......
Overseers	2	......	3 50	......
Overseer	1	......	3 00	......
Overseer	1	......	2 50	......
Overseer	1	......	2 00	......
Presser	1	......	1 00	......
Second hand	1	......	1 25	......
Second hands	5	......	1 00	......
Shearer	1	......	1 25	......
Speckers	......	8	......	65
Spinners, mule	2	......	1 37	......
Spoolers	a3	a3	67	67
Tenters	2	......	1 00	......
Undesignated	14	......	1 00	......
Undesignated	a8	......	67	......
Washer	1	......	1 25	......
Watchman	1	......	1 50	......
Weavers	27	29	1 25	1 25
Wool sorter	1	......	1 50	......

WOOLLEN GOODS (CASSIMERE), MASSACHUSETTS.—ESTAB. No. 557.

Time, 10 hours per day; — days the past year.

Occupations.	Number.		Daily wages.	
	Male.	Fem.	Male.	Fem.
Burlers	......	2	......	$1 25
Burlers	......	2	......	1 05
Carders	3	......	$1 23	......
Dressers	2	1	1 65	75
Dressers	......	8	......	60
Dyers	9	......	1 15	......
Finishers	8	2	1 25	1 12
Finishers	......	8	......	75
Machinists	4	......	1 75	......
Overseer	1	......	5 00	......
Overseer	1	......	3 15	......
Overseers	3	......	2 75	......

WOOLLEN GOODS (CASSIMERE), MASSACHUSETTS.—ESTAB. No. 557—Concluded.

Time, 10 hours per day; — days the past year.

Occupations.	Number.		Daily wages.	
	Male.	Fem.	Male.	Fem.
Overseers	3	......	$2 00	......
Railway hands	a4	......	63	......
Speckers	......	14	......	$0 60
Spinners, mule	3	......	1 25	......
Undesignated	4	......	2 00	......
Undesignated	7	......	1 50	......
Undesignated	a3	......	50	......
Weavers	24	25	1 35	1 35
Winders	a2	18	50	75

WOOLLEN GOODS (CLOTH), MASSACHUSETTS.—ESTAB. No. 558.

Time, 10 hours per day; 308 days the past year.

Occupations.	Number.		Daily wages.	
	Male.	Fem.	Male.	Fem.
Carders	a57	......	$0 78	......
Cloth-room hands	......	77	......	$0 87
Drawers-in	......	6	......	1 12
Dressers	12	3	1 33	00
Driers	11	......	1 00	......
Dyers	37	......	1 08	......
Finishers	21	......	1 01	......
Firemen	3	......	1 58	......
Fullers	14	......	1 01	......
Giggers	29	......	94	......
Laborers	7	......	1 03	......
Laborers	17	......	96	......
Laborers	a7	......	69	......
Pickers	9	......	1 06	......
Pressers	4	......	1 02	......
Scourers	7	......	1 16	......
Scrubbers	......	a7	......	65
Second hand	1	......	3 00	......
Second hands	6	......	2 25	......
Second hands	2	......	1 85	......
Second hands	4	......	1 70	......
Second hand	1	......	1 50	......
Shearers	5	......	87	......
Spinners, mule	41	......	1 26	......
Spinners	......	3	......	98
Spoolers	......	a25	......	55
Teamsters	3	......	1 51	......
Teasel setters	2	......	1 27	......
Undesignated	17	......	1 85	......
Undesignated	3	......	1 05	......
Watchmen	3	......	1 15	......
Weavers	14	158	1 35	1 10
Wool sorters	17	......	1 86	......

WOOLLEN GOODS (WORSTED FABRIC), MASSACHUSETTS.—ESTAB. No. 559.

Time, 10 hours per day; 308 days the past year.

Occupations.	Number.		Daily wages.	
	Male.	Fem.	Male.	Fem.
Carders	3	......	$0 95	......
Dyers	4	......	1 00	......
Engineer	1	......	1 35	......
Finishers	15	......	75	......
Gate keeper	1	......	1 00	......
Loom fixers	6	......	2 00	......
Overseers	6	......	2 50	......
Spinners, mule	4	......	1 25	......
Watchman	1	......	1 35	......
Weavers	40	40	1 45	$1 45

a Youth.

OCCUPATIONS, WITH NUMBER AND WAGES OF EMPLOYÉS, BY INDUSTRIES—Cont'd.

NOTE.—This table is *not* a complete exhibit for industries or states, but covers only establishments investigated by the Bureau. See page 91, also summaries, pages 143 to 226.

WOOLLEN GOODS (FLANNEL), MASSACHUSETTS.—ESTAB. No. 560.

Time, 10 hours per day; 300 days the past year.

Occupations.	Number.		Daily wages.	
	Male.	Fem.	Male.	Fem.
Carders	7	......	$1 50	......
Carpenter	1	......	2 75	......
Drawers	a7	......	92	......
Dressers	3	......	1 75	......
Dyers	2	......	1 50	......
Engineer	1	......	2 17	......
Machinist	1	......	2 75	......
Overseers	2	......	3 00	......
Overseers	3	......	2 50	......
Pickers	3	......	1 42	......
Roving carrier	1	......	1 17	......
Scourer	1	......	1 75	......
Scourers and dyers	4	......	1 50	......
Second hands	2	......	1 50	......
Spinners, mule	10	......	1 65	......
Spoolers	a5	......	75	......
Twisters	3	......	1 42	......
Weavers	36	......	1 10	......
Wool sorters	4	......	1 75	......

WOOLLEN GOODS (FLANNEL), MASSACHUSETTS.—ESTAB. No. 561.

Time, 10 hours per day; — days the past year.

Occupations.	Number.		Daily wages.	
	Male.	Fem.	Male.	Fem.
Drawers	a2	......	$0 75	......
Dresser	1	......	2 00	......
Dyer	1	......	2 50	......
Engineer	1	......	2 50	......
Overseer	1	......	3 00	......
Overseer	1	......	2 75	......
Overseer	1	......	2 62	......
Picker	1	......	1 50	......
Roving carrier	1	......	1 00	......
Scourer	1	......	1 67	......
Scourers	2	......	1 50	......
Second hands	2	......	1 50	......
Spinners, mule	6	......	1 42	......
Spoolers	......	a3	......	$0 50
Teamster	1	......	1 83	......
Watchman	1	......	1 66	......
Weavers	......	15	......	1 30
Wool sorter	1	......	1 75	......

WOOLLEN GOODS (FLANNEL), MASSACHUSETTS.—ESTAB. No. 562.

Time, 10 hours per day; 300 days the past year.

Occupations.	Number.		Daily wages.	
	Male.	Fem.	Male.	Fem.
Carders	a8	......	$0 62	......
Drawers-in	......	2	......	$1 00
Dressers	......	3	......	1 50
Engineer	1	......	1 75	......
Overseer	1	......	2 75	......
Overseers	2	......	2 55	......
Overseers	2	......	2 00	......
Scourers	5	......	1 25	......
Second hands	4	......	1 37	......
Second hands	7	......	1 25	......
Second hands	4	......	1 00	......
Speckers	......	a8	......	65
Spinners, mule	8	......	1 50	......
Spoolers	......	5	......	60
Twister	1	......	1 25	......
Watchman	1	......	1 50	......
Weavers	......	28	......	1 00
Wool sorter	1	......	1 50	......

WOOLLEN GOODS (BLANKET, FLANNEL, YARN), MISSOURI.—ESTAB. No. 563.

Time, 10 hours per day; 200 days the past year.

Occupations.	Number.		Daily wages.	
	Male.	Fem.	Male.	Fem.
Carders	17	......	$1 25	......
Dyers	11	......	1 25	......
Engineer	1	......	2 50	......
Finishers	9	13	2 00	$2 00
Laborers	3	......	1 25	......
Machinist	1	......	2 50	......
Overseer	1	......	3 75	......
Overseer	1	......	3 50	......
Overseers	2	......	3 00	......
Overseer	1	......	2 50	......
Packers	6	......	1 50	......
Spinners, mule	18	......	1 25	......
Twisters	......	4	......	1 00
Weavers	17	7	1 50	1 50
Wool sorters	9	......	1 50	......

WOOLLEN GOODS (CASSIMERE), NEW HAMPSHIRE.—ESTAB. No. 564.

Time, 11 hours per day; 305 days the past year.

Occupations.	Number.		Daily wages.	
	Male.	Fem.	Male.	Fem.
Bobbin tenders	5	......	$1 25	......
Burlers	......	30	......	$0 90
Carders	......	19	......	80
Card strippers	7	......	1 25	......
Carpenters	4	......	2 37	......
Dressers	6	......	1 75	......
Driers	2	......	1 15	......
Dyers and scourers	16	......	1 25	......
Engineer	1	......	3 00	......
Fireman	1	......	1 75	......
Fireman	1	......	1 37	......
Fullers	8	......	1 25	......
Laborers	12	......	1 37	......
Laborers	26	......	1 25	......
Loom fixers	6	......	1 90	......
Machinists	3	......	2 00	......
Menders	......	7	......	1 35
Overseers	5	......	3 50	......
Overseers	5	......	3 00	......
Overseer	1	......	2 50	......
Overseer	1	......	2 25	......
Overseers	4	......	2 00	......
Overseers	2	......	2 75	......
Overseers	3	......	2 00	......
Packers	4	......	1 25	......
Painters	2	......	1 25	......
Pattern maker	1	......	1 50	......
Pickers and driers	7	......	1 20	......
Second hands	7	......	1 80	......
Second hand	1	......	1 50	......
Second hand	1	......	1 25	......
Shearers	5	......	1 50	......
Shearer	1	......	1 15	......
Spinners, mule	18	......	1 75	......
Spoolers	......	14	......	85
Teamsters	2	......	1 50	......
Warpers	......	4	......	1 50
Warpers	......	4	......	1 00
Watchmen	3	......	1 37	......
Weavers	50	45	1 50	1 50
Wool sorters	18	......	1 37	......
Wool sorters	2	......	1 00	......

a Youth.

OCCUPATIONS AND WAGES.

OCCUPATIONS, WITH NUMBER AND WAGES OF EMPLOYÉS, BY INDUSTRIES—Cont'd.

NOTE.—This table is *not* a complete exhibit for industries or states, but covers only establishments investigated by the Bureau. See page 91, also summaries, pages 143 to 226.

WOOLLEN GOODS (CLOTH, BLANKETS), NEW JERSEY.—ESTAB. No. 565.

Time, 10 hours per day; 300 days the past year.

Occupations.	Number.		Daily wages.	
	Male.	Fem.	Male.	Fem.
Carders	10	1	$1 13	$0 90
Carders	a6		45	
Dyers	8		1 00	
Finishers	24	24	75	66
Fullers and giggers	18		1 00	
Fullers and giggers	a4		75	
Laborers	18		1 00	
Loom fixers	12		1 88	
Overseers	18		2 50	
Pickers	18		1 00	
Repair hands	7		2 00	
Repair hands	7		1 50	
Spinners	18	6	1 00	1 00
Spinners	a4		55	
Spinners	a8		37	
Weavers	a12	a10	50	50
Weavers	50	30	1 00	1 00
Wool sorters	1	12	80	67

WOOLLEN GOODS (CLOTH), NEW YORK.—ESTAB. No. 566.

Time, 11 hours per day; 300 days the past year.

Occupations.	Number.		Daily wages.	
	Male.	Fem.	Male.	Fem.
Back boys	a10		$0 66	
Back boys	a14		42	
Blacksmith	1		2 00	
Bobbin carriers	a4		67	
Brush boys	a3		67	
Burlers		66		$0 70
Card boys	a7		70	
Card stripper	1		1 54	
Card strippers	6		1 21	
Carders			a17	68
Carpenter	1		2 25	
Carpenter	1		1 75	
Chain builder	1		1 32	
Chain builders	3		94	
Designers	8		1 65	
Designers	a3		60	
Drawer	1		3 00	
Drawers-in		6		1 40
Dressers	2		1 40	
Drier	1		1 25	
Driers	18		1 10	
Drier	1		75	
Dyer	1		1 50	
Dyers	6		1 25	
Dyers	21		1 15	
Engineer	1		2 00	
Finishers	2		1 25	
Fireman	1		1 38	
Fireman	1		1 10	
Foreman	1		4 00	
Foreman	1		3 00	
Foremen	2		2 30	
Foreman	1		1 65	
Fuller	1		1 50	
Gigger	1		1 50	
Laborers	2		1 21	
Machinist	1		3 25	
Machinist	1		2 25	
Machinist	1		2 00	
Overseer	1		3 00	
Overseer	1		2 20	
Painter	1		1 54	
Picker	1		1 60	

a Youth.

WOOLLEN GOODS (CLOTH), NEW YORK.—ESTAB. No. 566—Concluded.

Time, 11 hours per day; 300 hours the past year.

Occupations.	Number.		Daily wages.	
	Male.	Fem.	Male.	Fem.
Picker	1		$1 21	
Pickers	6		1 05	
Pressers	3		1 25	
Rovers	2		1 32	
Scourers	22		1 15	
Scrubber	1		1 10	
Second hands	3		2 00	
Section hands	9		1 88	
Section hand	1		1 65	
Sewers		30		$1 10
Sewers		7		1 00
Sewers		5		83
Shearers	6		1 15	
Spinners, mule	9		1 10	
Spinners, mule	a11		75	
Spoolers	a10	a17	50	50
Teamster	1		1 33	
Twisters		a12		75
Twisters		a12		67
Undesignated		1		2 00
Undesignated	a2		55	
Warpers	7		1 75	
Warper	1		1 32	
Warpers' helpers	a2		67	
Watchman	1		1 25	
Watchmen	2		1 50	
Weavers	84	52	1 02	1 02
Wool sorters	15		1 40	
Yarn hand	1		1 43	

WOOLLEN GOODS (CLOTH), NEW YORK.—ESTAB. No. 567.

Time, 11 hours per day; 266 days the past year.

Occupations.	Number.		Daily wages.	
	Male.	Fem.	Male.	Fem.
Back boys	a8		$0 72	
Burlers		a19		$0 62
Card boys	b18		50	
Carders	16		1 08	
Carpenters	4		1 55	
Designer	1		6 09	
Designer	1		2 50	
Drawers-in	2		1 50	
Dressers	3		1 02	
Dyers	12		1 12	
Engineer	1		1 75	
Filling carriers	8		1 00	
Firemen	2		1 32	
Foreman	1		5 00	
Foremen	2		3 41	
Foremen, assistant	3		96	
Fullers	9		1 05	
Gas maker	1		1 25	
Gigger	1		1 75	
Giggers	13		1 03	
Gigger	a1		75	
Laborers	10		1 00	
Loom fixers	6		2 16	
Machinists	3		1 75	
Measurers	2		1 19	
Overseer	1		4 50	
Overseer	1		4 00	
Percher	1		1 50	
Pressers	3		1 25	
Second hands	5		2 50	
Sewers-in	4		1 00	
Shearers	5		1 15	
Spare hands	3		1 50	

b Children.

408 REPORT OF THE COMMISSIONER OF LABOR.

OCCUPATIONS, WITH NUMBER AND WAGES OF EMPLOYÉS, BY INDUSTRIES—Cont'd.

NOTE.—This table is not a complete exhibit for industries or states, but covers only establishments investigated by the Bureau. See page 91, also summaries, pages 143 to 226.

WOOLLEN GOODS (CLOTH), NEW YORK.—ESTAB. No. 567—Concluded.

Time, 11 hours per day; 266 days the past year.

Occupations.	Number.		Daily wages.	
	Male.	Fem.	Male.	Fem.
Speckers	a21		$0 87	
Spinners, mule	7		1 75	
Spinners, mule	17		1 40	
Spoolers		14		$1 00
Spoolers	a10			60
Spoolers	b8			50
Teamsters	2		1 37	
Twisters		b17		55
Undesignated	a1	a1	62	63
Undesignated	b2		50	
Watchmen	2		1 41	
Weavers	3		1 57	
Weavers	39	53	1 20	1 20
Weavers	a2		81	
Wool sorters	11		1 84	

WOOLLEN GOODS (WORSTED YARN), NEW YORK.—ESTAB. No. 568.

Time, 10 hours per day; 300 days the past year.

Occupations.	Number.		Daily wages.	
	Male.	Fem.	Male.	Fem.
Carders	a18		$0 83	
Comb fixer	1		2 08	
Doffers	b12		37	
Drawers		a14		$0 58
Engineer	1		3 67	
Fireman	1		1 33	
Foreman	1		3 00	
Foremen	2		2 75	
Foreman	1		2 50	
Foreman	1		2 25	
Foreman	1		1 67	
Foreman	1		1 50	
Machinist	1		2 50	
Reelers		16		67
Spinners		a41		50
Twisters		a26		58
Undesignated	1		83	
Wool sorters	18		1 75	

WOOLLEN GOODS (CLOTH), NORTH CAROLINA.—ESTAB. No. 569.

Time, 11¼ hours per day; 300 days the past year.

Occupations.	Number.		Daily wages.	
	Male.	Fem.	Male.	Fem.
Back boys	b3		$0 40	
Beamers	2		75	
Burler		1		$0 50
Carders	b2		50	
Carders	b2		38	
Dyers	4		75	
Engineer	1		1 83	
Finisher	1		85	
Finishers	4	3	75	50
Fireman	1		85	
Loom fixers	3		85	
Loom fixer	1		75	
Overseer	1		2 25	
Overseers	4		1 75	
Pickers	2		75	
Spinners, mule	3		1 25	
Undesignated	b4		45	
Weavers		17		75
Wool sorters	2		1 00	

WOOLLEN GOODS (CLOTH), PENNSYLVANIA.—ESTAB. No. 570.

Time, 10 hours per day; 304 days the past year.

Occupations.	Number.		Daily wages.	
	Male.	Fem.	Male.	Fem.
Band boy	1		$1 00	
Bobbin carriers	a6		75	
Bobbin winders		55		$1 17
Burlers and speckers	105		1 17	
Carders	2		2 50	
Carders' assistants	4		$1 67	
Card feeders	5		1 05	
Card grinder	1		2 50	
Card strippers	10		1 60	
Carpenter	1		2 25	
Cloth-room hands	9		2 00	
Condensers and winders	5		1 03	
Creel winders	10		1 67	
Drawers and twisters	12		2 83	
Drawers' and twisters' helpers	a21		67	
Dressers	a10		67	
Dye house hands	30		1 67	
Electrician	1		2 00	
Engineer	1		2 50	
Filling carriers	6		1 75	
Fireman	1		1 67	
Fullers and washers	28		1 75	
Giggers	20		1 50	
Harness repairers	8		1 75	
Inspectors	10		2 00	
Inspector	1		1 00	
Laborers	26		1 50	
Laborers	7		1 33	
Laborers	5		1 10	
Loom fixers	19		2 67	
Machinists	2		2 33	
Mechanics, engineers, and firemen	21		2 50	
Menders	75		1 25	
Oiler	1		1 50	
Overseers	2		5 00	
Overseers	2		3 33	
Overseers	3		2 30	
Overseers	3		3 00	
Overseers	2		2 00	
Overseer	1		1 50	
Packers	4		1 67	
Packers	8		62	
Piecers	a51		67	
Reelers	12		1 00	
Scourer	1		2 33	
Shearers	10		1 50	
Spinners, mule	10		1 50	
Spoolers	28	7	1 25	83
Spool carriers	2		1 50	
Spool carriers	1		1 25	
Spool stripper	1		83	
Stock carriers	3		1 44	
Twisters	25		1 00	
Warehouse man	1		3 00	
Warehouse-man's assistant	1		2 00	
Warpers	16		2 33	
Warpers' helpers	a14		83	
Waste hands	4		2 00	
Watchmen	3		2 33	
Weavers	350		1 92	
Wool sorters		13		75
Yarn hand	1		83	

a Youth.   *b* Children.

OCCUPATIONS AND WAGES.

OCCUPATIONS, WITH NUMBER AND WAGES OF EMPLOYÉS, BY INDUSTRIES—Cont'd.

NOTE.—This table is *not* a complete exhibit for industries or states, but covers only establishments investigated by the Bureau. See page 91, also summaries, pages 143 to 226.

WOOLLEN GOODS (CLOTH), PENNSYLVANIA.—ESTAB. No. 571.
Time, 10 hours per day; — days the past year.

Occupations.	Number.		Daily wages.	
	Male.	Fem.	Male.	Fem.
Burlers	......	25	......	$0 63
Carders	8	......	$2 69	......
Card feeders	a40	......	83	......
Dyers	20	......	1 33	......
Fullers and giggers	20	......	1 37	......
Fullers' and giggers' helpers	30	......	1 00	......
Laborers	15	......	1 17	......
Piecers	25	......	96	......
Piecers	a62	......	62	......
Pickers	50	......	1 00	......
Spinners, mule	25	......	1 83	......
Weavers	150	150	1 71	1 33
Wool sorters	25	......	1 50	......

WOOLLEN GOODS (CLOTH), PENNSYLVANIA.—ESTAB. No. 572.
Time, 10 hours per day; 300 days the past year.

Occupations.	Male.	Fem.	Male.	Fem.
Burlers	......	104	......	$1 00
Carders and spinners	28	......	$1 00	......
Carpenters	2	......	2 50	......
Dressers	8	......	2 00	......
Dyers	29	......	1 25	......
Engineers	1	......	2 50	......
Finishers	31	......	1 50	......
Fireman	1	......	1 75	......
Foreman	1	......	5 00	......
Laborers	5	......	1 75	......
Machinists	2	......	2 50	......
Spoolers and winders	......	10	......	95
Teamster	1	......	2 00	......
Warehouse man	1	......	2 00	......
Watchmen	2	......	1 66	......
Weavers	224	......	1 87	......

WOOLLEN GOODS (YARN, BLANKET), PENNSYLVANIA.—ESTAB. No. 573.
Time, 10 hours per day; 230 days the past year.

Occupations.	Male.	Fem.	Male.	Fem.
Card tenders	......	2	......	$0 73
Engineer	1	......	$2 25	......
Foreman	1	......	4 00	......
Laborers	3	......	1 25	......
Overseer	1	......	3 00	......
Overseer	1	......	2 00	......
Piecers	......	6	......	60
Spoolers	......	20	......	70
Twisters	......	2	......	60
Weavers	12	......	1 33	......
Wool sorters	2	......	1 66	......

WOOLLEN GOODS (CLOTH), VERMONT.—ESTAB. No. 574.
Time, 11 hours per day; 270 days the past year.

Occupations.	Male.	Fem.	Male.	Fem.
Back boys	69	......	$0 45	......
Blacksmiths	2	......	1 69	......
Bobbin carrier	a1	......	50	......
Box maker	1	......	1 81	......
Burlers	......	a173	......	$0 59
Carders	14	a31	1 00	61
Card grinders	5	......	1 00	......

WOOLLEN GOODS (CLOTH), VERMONT.—ESTAB. No. 574—Concluded.
Time, 11 hours per day; 270 days the past year.

Occupations.	Number.		Daily wages.	
	Male.	Fem.	Male.	Fem.
Card strippers	4	......	$1 00	......
Carpenters	8	......	1 92	......
Doffers	a2	......	60	......
Doubler	1	......	1 00	......
Doublers	......	a7	......	$0 60
Drawers	......	5	......	1 13
Drawers	......	5	......	80
Dressers	4	......	1 29	......
Driers	4	......	1 02	......
Dyers	24	......	1 02	......
Dyer boys	55	......	53	......
Firemen	2	......	1 40	......
Filling carriers	8	......	1 10	......
Flockers	a2	......	70	......
Fullers	16	......	1 00	......
Gas maker	1	......	1 15	......
Giggers	22	......	1 10	......
Inspector	1	......	2 75	......
Inspector	1	......	2 02	......
Inspectors' assistants	2	......	1 25	......
Inspectors	16	......	1 00	......
Lappers	3	......	1 00	......
Laborer	1	......	1 10	......
Laborer	a1	......	50	......
Loom fixers	8	......	1 86	......
Machinists	6	......	1 78	......
Marker	......	1	......	1 41
Mason	1	......	2 25	......
Master mechanic	1	......	5 50	......
Menders	......	a11	......	77
Overseers	5	......	5 00	......
Overseers	10	......	2 50	......
Overseers	8	......	1 25	......
Packers	3	......	1 50	......
Painter	1	......	1 75	......
Picker	1	......	1 25	......
Pickers	12	......	1 00	......
Picker	a1	......	55	......
Piper	1	......	2 00	......
Presser	1	......	1 50	......
Pressers	4	......	1 02	......
Pressers	a15	......	79	......
Rovers	2	7	90	90
Reelers	......	3	......	62
Scourers	8	......	1 02	......
Second hands	6	......	2 00	......
Second hands	7	......	1 40	......
Second hands	4	......	1 00	......
Slubbers	......	3	......	80
Spare hands	2	......	1 00	......
Speeders	......	6	......	90
Spinners, mule	44	......	1 30	......
Spoolers	......	a12	......	47
Steamers	17	......	1 00	......
Stock keepers	2	......	1 25	......
Sweepers	a3	......	60	......
Teamsters	4	......	1 22	......
Teasel setter	1	......	1 25	......
Undesignated	20	......	94	......
Undesignated	......	55	......	25
Waste sorters	b15	......	50	......
Watchmen	2	......	1 40	......
Weavers	43	100	1 17	1 17
Weavers' helpers	b1	......	85	......
Winders	......	52	......	43
Wool sorter	1	......	4 00	......
Wool sorters	14	......	1 67	......
Wool sorter	1	......	1 00	......
Yard hand	1	......	1 25	......
Yard hands	11	......	1 10	......

a Youth.   *b* Children.

OCCUPATIONS, WITH NUMBER AND WAGES OF EMPLOYÉS, BY INDUSTRIES—Cont'd.

NOTE.—This table is not a complete exhibit for industries or states, but covers only establishments investigated by the Bureau. See page 91, also summaries, pages 143 to 226.

MISCELLANEOUS (BUTTONS), GREAT BRITAIN.—ESTAB. NO. 575.

Time, 10 hours per day; — days the past year.

Occupations.	Number.		Daily wages.	
	Male.	Fem.	Male.	Fem.
Carders		3		$0 55
Drillers		3		55
Foreman	1		$2 80	
Tool sharpener	1		2 20	
Turners	20		1 40	
Sawyers	6		1 60	
Scourer	1		1 20	
Stainer	1		2 40	

MISCELLANEOUS (STARCH), MAINE.—ESTAB. NO. 576.

Time, 12 hours per day; — days the past year.

Occupations.	Number.		Daily wages.	
	Male.	Fem.	Male.	Fem.
Driers	20		$2 25	
Foremen	7		3 50	
Laborers	80		1 50	

MISCELLANEOUS (BUTTONS), MASSACHUSETTS.—ESTAB. NO. 577.

Time, 10 hours per day; 300 days the past year.

Occupations.	Number.		Daily wages.	
	Male.	Fem.	Male.	Fem.
Button cutters	15		$1 50	
Carpenter	1		2 50	
Engineer	1		3 00	
Foremen	6		3 00	
Machine tenders		250		$0 80
Machinists	12		2 50	
Teamster	1		2 00	
Watchman	1		2 40	

MISCELLANEOUS (MATCHES), NEW HAMPSHIRE.—ESTAB. NO. 578.

Time, 10 hours per day; — days the past year.

Occupations.	Number.		Daily wages.	
	Male.	Fem.	Male.	Fem.
Boiler men	2		$1 50	
Dippers	2		1 75	
Laborer	1		1 50	
Laborer	1		1 25	
Laborers	4		90	
Packers		a10		$0 90
Packers		a5		75
Undesignated	a4		75	

MISCELLANEOUS (CHINA DECORATIONS), NEW JERSEY.—ESTAB. NO. 579.

Time, 10 hours per day; 300 days the past year.

Occupations.	Number.		Daily wages.	
	Male.	Fem.	Male.	Fem.
Decorator	1		$5 00	
Decorators	4		3 33	
Decorator	1		3 00	
Decorators	2		2 50	
Decorator	1		2 33	
Decorator		1		$2 00
Decorators	3		2 00	
Decorator		1		1 66
Decorators	2		1 66	
Decorators		2		1 50

MISCELLANEOUS (CHINA DECORATIONS), NEW JERSEY.—ESTAB. NO. 579—Concluded.

Time, 10 hours per day; 300 days the past year.

Occupations.	Number.		Daily wages.	
	Male.	Fem.	Male.	Fem.
Decorator	1		$1 50	
Decorators	a3		1 33	
Decorator		1		$1 16
Decorator		a3		83
Decorator	a1		83	
Decorators	a2	a3	66	66
Decorators	a2	a3	50	50
Decorators	b2	b4	33	33

MISCELLANEOUS (QUEENSWARE), NEW JERSEY.—ESTAB. NO. 580.

Time, 9½ hours per day; 300 days the past year.

Occupations.	Number.		Daily wages.	
	Male.	Fem.	Male.	Fem.
Decorators		51		$0 78
Engineer	1		$2 33	
Engineer	1		2 17	
Jiggers	19		3 66	
Jiggers' helpers	57		1 05	
Kiln men	22		2 00	
Laborers	18		1 25	
Mould makers	2		3 05	
Mould-makers, helpers	2		1 81	
Packers	4		2 16	
Pressers	25		2 27	
Pressers' helpers	a25		1 50	
Sagger maker	2		5 00	
Sagger-makers' helper	a1		1 33	
Slip-house men	7		1 52	

MISCELLANEOUS (TRUNKS, SATCHELS), NEW JERSEY.—ESTAB. NO. 581.

Time, 10 hours per day; 300 days the past year.

Occupations.	Number.		Daily wages.	
	Male.	Fem.	Male.	Fem.
Box makers	40		$2 00	
Engineer	1		2 50	
Foremen	6		2 66	
Laborers	20		1 33	
Trunk makers	40		2 33	
Trunk-makers' helpers	a40		1 17	
Satchel makers	20		2 00	
Satchel-makers' helpers	a3		75	

MISCELLANEOUS (TRUNKS, SATCHELS), NEW JERSEY.—ESTAB. NO. 582.

Time, 9½ hours per day; 293 days the past year.

Occupations.	Number.		Daily wages.	
	Male.	Fem.	Male.	Fem.
Box makers	45		$2 33	
Engineer	1		2 16	
Fireman	1		1 83	
Foreman	1		4 16	
Satchel makers	70		2 16	
Satchel-makers' helpers	a15	50	1 00	$0 83
Trunk makers	120		1 75	
Trunk-makers' helpers	a45		1 66	

a Youth. *b* Children.

APPENDIX B.

EARNINGS AND EXPENSES OF WAGE RECEIVERS IN EUROPE.

NOTE.—With reference to these family budgets, etc., see page 242.

ITALY.

REMARKS.—The condition of the laboring class in Italy, especially in the southern portion of the state, is one of extreme poverty and hardship. The habitation of the laborer and the mechanic is generally a room in a damp, ill-smelling building, on a street ten or fifteen feet wide, and rarely visited by the sun by reason of the height of the buildings on either side. Economy is practised such as prevails in few other countries. The coffee grounds from the wealthy man's kitchen are dried and resold to the poor. In a similar way oil is twice and sometimes three times used, the drippings, after successive fryings, being gathered from the pan and sold to the poor. There are markets of second-hand articles of food and clothing. Old shoes, hats, clothes, candle-ends, dried coffee grounds, second-hand oil, etc., are spread out upon the broad stones of the plaza, or square of a town, and it is in such places, to a considerable extent, that the workingman buys his supplies. In Lombardy and Tuscany a slightly better condition is becoming apparent. The general character of the workman's surroundings is superior to that of the workman in other sections of the state. Some of the manufacturers of Milan have recently taken a step toward the improvement of the habitations of their operatives.

Owing to the high octroi, or gate tax, prevailing in all cities and towns, the cost of living is from 20 to 25 per cent. greater in towns than in villages and in the country without the walls of towns. On this account a considerable portion of hand-machine manufacturing (such as weaving, spinning, etc.), is carried on in villages and rural districts. To bring a quart of wine into Milan costs the laborer 2 cents; a chicken or goose, 3 cents; bread is taxed about 20 per cent., and milk and some other articles of food at a similar rate. The tax at the gates of other cities will average the same as that at Milan. The making of iron bedsteads is an occupation constantly encountered. These bedsteads are in almost universal use among the lower classes, and also to a great extent among the middle and upper classes. The beds are manufactured, as a rule, in the dwelling of the workman—usually a room from 15 to 20 feet square, level with the street, with no windows, the insufficient light coming in through the door opening into a narrow street. In favorable weather the workman sets his tools and bench upon the street in front of his room, and works there.

No. 1. IRON-BEDSTEAD MAKER—NAPLES.

Condition.—Family numbers six: Parents, son aged 18, son aged 16, children aged 12 and 7.

Diet.—Breakfast: Coffee or wine, black bread. Dinner: Macaroni, beef stew, or tripe, potatoes, funnochio (*a*), wine, bread. Supper: Coffee or wine, and bread; sometimes macaroni.

---

a **Funnochio** is a kind of rank or coarse celery, very much in favor with Southern Italians.

Earnings of father				$168 00
Earnings of oldest son				130 00
Earnings of rest of family				178 75
Total				476 75

Cost of Living.

Coffee, sugar, and milk	$32 85	Rent		$18 00
Macaroni	80 30	Incidentals		18 75
Bread and flour	73 00			
Potatoes, funnochio, etc	73 00	Expenditures		425 60
Wine	65 70	Earnings		476 75
Clothing, towels, sheets, etc.	52 00			
Shoes	12 00	Surplus		51 15

No. 2. Iron-Bedstead Maker—Naples.

Condition.—Single man, about 25; is skilled workman. Sleeps in a lodging house with from fifteen to twenty others in the room; surroundings damp; no window; has never been to school, but can read a little; gets his meals at cheap macaroni eating houses.

Diet.—Breakfast: Bread and oil, or funnochio, eaten on the way to work. Dinner: Macaroni, tripe, or beef hash, red wine, and bread. Supper: Wine or coffee, and bread.

Average cost of breakfast	$0 06
Average cost of dinner	14
Average cost of supper	6
Cost of food per day	26
Earnings	$150 00

Cost of Living.

Lodging	$14 60	Clothing		$16 00
Bread	21 90	Incidentals		15 00
Oil	10 95			
Macaroni	29 20	Expenditures		148 80
Wine	24 20	Earnings		150 00
Coffee	10 95			
Shoes	6 00	Surplus		1 20

No. 3. Iron-Bedstead Maker—Naples.

Condition.—Family of five: Parents, brother of wife, and two children, aged 4 and 5. Occupy a room in dingy house on a dark, narrow street. A cheap curtain divides it into one large and one small compartment; brother occupies small compartment, parents and children sleep in large part. During the day the beds are rolled up and stacked in one corner, and work carried on in sleeping room. The father is a good workman and earns on an average 70 cents per working day. The mother cooks, cares for the children, and does a little washing. Family are saving to emigrate to the United States.

Diet.—Breakfast: Coffee, milk, bread. Dinner: Wine, macaroni or rice, tomatoes, bread, occasionally dried figs, chestnuts, onions, tripe, fish, etc. Supper: Coffee, milk, bread.

Earnings of father	$203 00
Earnings of wife's brother	145 00
Earnings of mother	29 00
Total	377 00

		Cost of Living.	
Rent	$12 00	Clothing, including shoes	$51 60
Bread	80 30	Incidentals	4 75
Coffee, milk, and sugar	73 00		
Macaroni	36 50	Expenditures	360 65
Vegetables, pork, cheese, etc.	66 00	Earnings	377 00
Wine	36 50		
		Surplus	16 35

No. 4. WEAVER—SIENA.

Condition.—Family of four: Parents, wife's sister, and child, aged 6. Work is carried on in a large basement, poorly lighted. Twelve hand looms, earth floor. Habitation of family consists of one room in tenement house, up one flight of crooked stairs; paved with brick, with large open chimney in which cooking is done. Principal fuel is brushwood gathered by child, and at odd hours and on Sundays by the mother. The family all sleep in one room. The husband and wife and sister work at looms, making each from ten to twelve yards per day, and earning each from 25 to 35 cents per day. Child gathers brushwood, also begs.

Earnings of father	$105 00
Earnings of mother	72 50
Earnings of sister	72 50
Total	250 00

		Cost of Living.	
Rent	$12 00	Shoes	$6 50
Bread	58 40	Incidentals	10 20
Macaroni	29 20		
Coffee and milk	29 20	Expenditures	246 70
Vegetables, cheese, wine, etc	69 20	Earnings	250 00
Clothing	32 00		
		Surplus	3 30

No. 5. WEAVER—RACIGLIONE.

Condition.—Family of five: Parents, two children, 5 and 6 years of age, and mother of the father. Parents work at hand looms, the grandmother spins (at home), attends to the children, and to two goats, the milk of the goats being sold at 4 cents per quart. Occupy a room with earth floor, on a level with the ground; room divided into two compartments. Weaving room on same street, up a steep hill; only six looms; level of room three feet below level of the street; no windows, lighted by the door.

Earnings of father	$126 00
Earnings of mother	97 50
Earnings of grandmother (spinning)	48 75
Earnings of grandmother (sale of milk)	43 80
Total	316 05

		Cost of Living.	
Rent	$14 40	Clothing	$19 65
Bread	53 00	Iron bedstead, chairs, etc	8 70
Macaroni	69 40		
Groceries, funnochio, olives, eggs	72 50	Expenditures	313 40
Wine	51 00	Earnings	316 05
Coffee *a*	17 25		
Wooden clogs and leather shoes	7 50	Surplus	2 65

a Item for coffee always includes the milk and sugar used in coffee. The Italian laborer uses a good deal of milk in his coffee. The sugar used is mostly beet sugar imported from France or Germany.

No. 6. WEAVER—ACQUAPENDENTE, CENTRAL ITALY.

Condition.—Young woman aged 18, engaged to marry a stone mason, and both stinting themselves to save money to emigrate to South America. Lives with parents, who are field hands; room on narrow street, two windows, brick floor; girl works ten to twelve hours per day at loom in a cellar, earth floor, poor light; earns from 20 to 30 cents per day; makes from nine to eleven yards of cloth per day.

Diet.—Breakfast: Bread and wine, or coffee. Dinner: Artichokes, onions, or macaroni, and bread, and occasionally salt pork or eggs. Supper: Bread and coffee, or wine.

Average cost of breakfast	$0 04
Average cost of dinner	7
Average cost of supper	4
Cost of food per day	15
Earnings	$81 25

Cost of Living.

Rent *a*	$00 00	Clothing, including shoes	$12 40
Bread	18 25		
Coffee	7 48	Expenditures	70 63
Wine	6 95	Earnings	81 25
Macaroni	10 95		
Artichokes, pork, eggs, finnochio, eaten only on extra occasions, feast days, etc	14 60	Surplus	10 62

REMARKS.—The basement-like rooms in which weaving is done are not provided with stoves or fire places. Each operator has a small bucket or jug of hot ashes or coals. This the women put under their dresses; the men place them at their feet. There is also, in quite cold weather, a large pan of coals set in the middle of the room. The weavers quit their work occasionally to sit for a few minutes around this pan and warm their hands and feet.

The fuel for this primitive heating arrangement consists to some extent of brushwood, clippings from old grapevines, etc. Coal is imported from England. Price per ton at West Mediterranean ports, $5 to $6. Price in interior, but on railroads, $7 to $10. Price in towns distant from sea and railroads, $10 to $15 per ton.

No. 7. OSTERIA KEEPER—MONTE ROSA.

Condition.—Family of eight: Parents; son aged 22; three daughters, aged 14, 15, and 21; boy aged 10, and girl aged 9. Father keeps an osteria, or place where wine is sold, and lodging house for peasants. Lodgers pay 4 cents per night per bed. Several beds to the room. Wife spins wool, milks goats, washes bed clothing, linen, etc., cooks, and cares for silk worms. Daughter aged 21, weaves; daughter aged 15, weaves; daughter aged 14, assists her mother in housework, care of the silk worms, etc. The boy and girl pick brushwood from the roads and gather mulberry leaves for the silk worms. Son, aged 22, works at odd jobs, in fields, etc. Occupy house of six rooms, not including entrance room, used as wine and eating room, on ground floor opening on the street. To the back of this entrance room is an open court through which the rear half of the house is reached. Lower part of rear half of house used as stable for goats and asses. Five rooms on second floor—two used by family, one for care of silk worms, and two rooms, several beds each, for transient lodgers. House of stone, floors of brick, windows looking on open court Surroundings better than in large cities, but street is narrow and crooked, and location, on the whole, not pleasant.

---

a Lives with parents, paying no rent, hence not included in this, an individual estimate.

Diet.—Breakfast: Bread, coffee or wine, and occasionally pork or cheese. Dinner: Beef stew, or macaroni, beans, bread, wine, sometimes cheese, eggs, or beef. Supper: Bread, coffee or wine; sometimes cheese, onions or funnochio.

Earnings of father	$311 00
Earnings of wife, spinning	41 00
Earnings of daughter, aged 21	91 80
Earnings of daughter, aged 15	79 30
Earnings of son, laborer (not steadily at work)	71 00
Earnings of boy, aged 10	25 00
Sale of silk cocoons	99 00
Sale of goats' milk	73 00
Total	791 10

Cost of Living.

Rent	$84 00	Incidentals	$58 50
Clothing, including bedding, etc.	93 50		
Wine	116 80	Expenditures	767 80
Coffee	58 40	Earnings	791 10
Bread and flour	146 00		
Groceries, etc.	187 60	Surplus	23 30
Shoes (leather)	23 00		

No. 8. Salesman—Naples.

Condition.—Family of four: Parents and two small children. Father is salesman in glove store; mother works in glove manufactory. Occupy two rooms, one large, the other quite small. Large room used for sleeping and living in; small room for cooking. Sleeping room has two windows, brick floor, but partly covered with mats; no conveniences of gas or water. Water closet in house very offensive; otherwise habitation tolerable. Factory room, where mother sews gloves on machines, small and crowded; bad air and poor light.

Diet.—Breakfast: Goats' milk, bread, and figs; occasionally onions or cheese. Dinner. Macaroni, onions, bread, and wine, and on occasions eggs or fish or salt meat. Supper: Bread, coffee or milk; sometimes chestnuts, figs, or similar food.

Earnings of father	$180 40
Earnings of mother	90 00
Total	270 40

Cost of Living.

Rent	$24 00	Incidentals	$19 20
Bread	43 80		
Macaroni	43 80	Expenditures	269 90
Coffee	20 00	Earnings	270 40
Wine	29 20		
Groceries	37 90	Surplus	50
Clothes, including shoes	52 00		

No. 9. Stone Mason—Pozzuoli, Southern Italy.

Condition.—Family of six: Parents, boy aged 15, girl aged 14, boy aged 9, and baby. Son aged 15 assists his father; boy of 9 carries stones; mother cares for baby, sews, cooks, etc. Occupy room on level with street, keep goat and kid and dog in room; pan of coals for heating and cooking; surroundings dingy and unpleasant. Father works on a building short distance from his habitation. The stone used is a kind of porous, pumice stone, quarried not far from the building. Sand obtained from wells in vicinity.

Diet.—Breakfast: Bread and oil or coffee. Dinner: Boiled chestnuts, or macaroni, onions, funnochio, bread and wine; sometimes salt pork. Supper: Bread and coffee, or cheese.

Earnings of father	$183	60
Earnings of sons	132	20
Total	315	80

Cost of Living.

Rent	$15	00	Incidentals	$20	00
Bread	65	70			
Macaroni	43	80	Expenditures	330	20
Coffee	21	90	Earnings	315	80
Wine	43	80			
Groceries	61	00	Deficit	14	40
Clothing	59	00			

REMARKS.— Building trades in Italy are conducted on a very solid basis, but not with much push or rapidity. There is no steam elevator to shoot up half a ton of bricks or stones at one time to the mason, and not even a hod carrier. The blocks of stone are carried by boys and girls, either one block at a time, on their backs, or, when the stones are small (about one and one-half times the size of an ordinary brick), in baskets. Girls carry sand and mortar in buckets. When the stone and mortar carriers are delayed the mason waits, idling. As a result of this method of procedure, the laying of 500 to 600 stones (size about 6 inches by 6 inches by 5 inches) is considered a good day's work for an average mason.

The pay of a mason ranges from 40 to 70 cents per day of ten to twelve hours. He is able to exist upon this sum, and nothing more. A family of father and mother and half a dozen children will inhabit one room, with an earth or brick floor, damp, and even though having windows looking on a street, yet poorly lighted on account of the narrowness of the street and the great height of the surrounding buildings. During the day the beds, that at night cover perhaps every inch of the floor, are rolled up and piled in a corner. The workman's breakfast is often but a pone of black bread, eaten on the way to work; a plate of macaroni, onions, boiled chestnuts, wine, and bread is considered a good dinner. The bricklayer's food may be computed to cost on an average 15 to 25 cents per day; his room costs $12 to $15 per year; a suit of clothes $2 to $6 (or second-hand, $1.50); shoes from 20 cents to $1.50.

Boys who carry mortar, sand, or blocks of stones receive from 10 to 20 cents per day of ten to twelve hours.

No. 10. SKILLED SHOEMAKER—FLORENCE.

Condition.—Family of four: Parents and two babies. Works in cellar, pursuing his business on Sundays as well as week days.

Diet.—Breakfast: Bread and onions, or coffee. Dinner: Macaroni, sometimes pork—black bread, salad, funnochio, etc. Supper: Bread and coffee—sometimes cheese.

Earnings	$195 00

EARNINGS AND EXPENSES OF WAGE RECEIVERS IN EUROPE. 417

Cost of Living.

Rent	$12 00	Incidentals	$24 00
Bread	43 80		
Macaroni	43 80	Expenditures	193 40
Groceries	33 80	Earnings	195 00
Clothing (including shoes)	36 00	Surplus	1 60

No. 11. SHOEMAKER—FLORENCE.

Condition.—Young man about 21; ordinary workman; without family. Lodges in crowded lodging house, a dozen or more in one room; workshop is on narrow street, poorly lighted, and bad air.

Diet.—Breakfast: Coffee and bread. Dinner: Macaroni, bread, wine; sometimes funuochio, onions, or other vegetable. Supper: Coffee and bread; or black bread and one-third to one-half pound dried figs.

Average cost of breakfast	$0 03
Average cost of dinner	9
Average cost of supper	4
Average cost of food per day	16
Earnings	$110 00

Cost of Living.

Lodging	$14 60	Incidentals	$15 00
Bread	18 25		
Macaroni	18 25	Expenditures	99 40
Wine	7 30	Earnings	110 00
Onions, figs, chestnuts, etc.	6 00		
Clothing, etc	16 00	Surplus	10 60
Shoes	4 00		

No. 12. SHEPHERD IN THE ROMAN CAMPAGNA.

Condition.—Man about 50 years of age; lives in haystack-like hovel; leads a solitary life; cannot read; possesses but a slight degree of intelligence.

Diet.—Breakfast: Black bread, oil, water. Dinner: Black bread, oil, water. Supper: Black bread, oil, water. This meagre and monotonous diet is varied at infrequent intervals by a very small piece of bacon, salt pork, or macaroni, an onion, or a little funnochio; on great fête days by a little wine.

Earnings, at 7 cents a day	$25 55

Cost of Living.

Bread	$14 60	Clothing and incidentals	$3 66
Oil	5 47		
Other food supplies	1 82	Expenditures	25 55
		Earnings	25 55

No. 13. SHEPHERD IN THE ROMAN CAMPAGNA.

Condition.—Family of four: Parents, boy 9 and girl 8 years of age. Occupy a squalid hovel in open field. Parents herd sheep; boy and girl attend to drove of hogs. All knit socks or similar articles. Shoes consist of pieces of raw cowhide bound, sandal-like, to the feet by strings.

Earnings of family	$87 60

Cost of Living.

Bread	$58 40	Clothing and incidentals	$7 30
Other food (mostly oil)	21 90		
		Expenditures	87 60
		Earnings	87 60

No. 14. Shepherd in the Roman Campagna.

Condition.—Single man; earns 2 cents per day; bread and oil found for him. Has herded sheep ten years. Very low order of intelligence; cannot read, and has never been to Rome, although not above twenty miles distant.

Earnings per year	$7 30
Expenditures (clothing, etc.)	7 30

Remarks.—The shepherds of Italy, especially those in the campagna surrounding Rome, are among the lowest and most miserable of mankind. Their condition is hardly better than that of the North American Indian, sleeping in a tepee by night and roaming the plains by day. The Roman shepherd's habitation is constructed in a fashion similar to the Indian tepee. A dozen or so poles, each 20 to 25 feet long, are bunched together, forming a conical frame work on which a thatching of straw is put to protect from heat and cold and wind and rain. A bundle of straw is the shepherd's bed; his furniture consists usually of a three-legged stool; and the fire to warm him, made of scanty brushwood, burns in a hole scooped out for the purpose in the center of the earth floor of the apartment. While herding sheep the shepherd knits stockings; his clothing often consists of goat or sheepskins, and one suit lasts for years. The wages of a shepherd, he finding his own food, are from 7 to 8 cents per day. When food is found for him, the pay is from 2 to 3 cents per day. No rent is paid for the thatched hovel, and usually when a new sheep or goatskin is needed for a jacket or pair of trowsers, it is furnished by the employer gratis.

No. 15. Stonecutter.

Condition.—Family of seven: Parents, son aged 15, boy aged 11, girl aged 14, two children. Occupy two brick-floored rooms; fair amount of comfort and tidiness; two windows and good light in front room. Father is a skilled stonecutter; son helps; boy learning. The mother and daughter dress neatly—do sewing, cooking, and general household work.

Diet.—Breakfast: Bread, coffee, milk. Dinner: Bread, soup, macaroni, vegetables, sometimes wine. Supper: Bread, coffee, milk, occasionally figs or chestnuts or bit of pork.

Earnings of father	$250 00
Earnings of son	83 30
Earnings of daughter	40 00
Earnings of boy	52 00
Total	425 30

Cost of Living.

Rent	$24 00	Fuel and incidentals	$19 00
Bread	106 85		
Coffee	18 15	Expenditures	422 70
Milk	33 85	Earnings	425 30
Macaroni	36 50		
Vegetables, etc	113 15	Surplus	2 60
Clothing, etc	71 20		

No. 16. STONECUTTER.

Condition.—Family of three: Parents and child. Father is an ordinary stonecutter. Mother is cook in private family; family saving to emigrate to South America. Occupy single room in lodging house; damp, badly lighted, generally uninviting.

Diet.—Breakfast: Bread and onions, coffee and milk, occasionally salami or a little cheese. Dinner: Soup, macaroni, vegetables, bread, sometimes salt pork or salami or cheese, wine. Supper: Bread, coffee, milk.

Earnings of father	$150 80
Earnings of mother, including board	60 00
Total	210 80

Cost of Living.

Bread	$32 85	Fuel and incidentals	$15 00
Coffee and milk	21 90		
Groceries, etc	73 00	Expenditures	193 15
Rent	12 00	Earnings	210 00
Clothing	38 40		
		Surplus	16 85

No. 17. STONECUTTER.

Condition.—Family of four: Father, son aged 20, daughter, and a little girl. Expert chiseller; puts all but the finishing touches to statues and delicate marble work. Occupy two rooms, plank floor; has windows in front room looking on street and one window in back room overlooking court. Both rooms plain but neat—look comfortable. Family can read; dress neatly and generally respectable in appearance and mode of life.

Diet.—Breakfast: Coffee, milk, bread. Dinner: Macaroni, vegetables (as onions, beans, potatoes, etc.), bread and wine, and sometimes a little salami or pork; cheese, chestnuts, etc. Supper: Coffee, milk, bread or macaroni.

Earnings of father	$480 00
Earnings of son	174 00
Total	654 00

Cost of Living.

Rent	$28 00	Clothing and bedding	$87 00
Bread and flour	54 75	Fuel and incidentals	66 56
Coffee	10 95		
Milk	29 20	Expenditures	540 71
Macaroni	25 55	Earnings	654 00
Meats	19 80		
Vegetables, fruits, etc	218 90	Surplus	113 29

REMARKS.—For fine stonecutting, such as chiselling the sculptor's statue from the rough block, long apprenticeship is necessary. A man 25 years of age who has been apprenticed ten to twelve years can earn $5 per week; higher than this he will not go unless unusual skill be developed. If, in addition to the skill imparted by years of practice, the workman has a quick eye and natural talent, he may become a "finisher," earning from $1.80 to $2 per day. Men of this class are generally intelligent, saving, and industrious, and many of them have considerable amounts laid by in savings banks. Boys of 13 to 15 years of age get from $1.30 to $1.60 per week.

No. 18. GLASS WORKER—VENICE.

Condition.—Family of four: Parents and two children. Occupy third-floor room; one window in room, overlooking canal. Father is a skilled worker in glass; makes delicate articles, as glass eyes, colored vases, etc. Mother attends to home and babies. Both father and mother can read.

Earnings of father $275 40

Cost of Living.

Rent	$15 00	Fuel, lights, etc	$13 00
Bread	36 50		
Coffee and milk	36 50	Expenditures	252 49
Meat	14 40	Earnings	275 40
Groceries, etc	105 95		
Clothing	31 14	Surplus	22 91

No. 19. GLASS WORKER—MURANO, DISTRICT OF VENICE.

Condition.—Family of five: Parents, son aged 19, son aged 18, girl aged 12. Occupy two small rooms, no ornamentation or comforts. Father ordinary glass maker, son the same, mother and girl also work in glass manufactory.

Diet.—Breakfast: Bread and milk or coffee or sometimes dried fruit, as figs, etc. Dinner: Soup—macaroni or rice, onions, sometimes fish, tripe, or salt pork, eggs, salad or funnochio, wine. Supper: Bread, milk, and coffee.

Earnings of father	$145 25
Earnings of sons	146 00
Earnings of mother	90 00
Earnings of girl	25 00
Total	406 25

Cost of Living.

Rent	$16 00	Religion and incidentals	$18 00
Bread	62 05		
Milk and coffee	47 45	Expenditures	365 26
Fish	10 95	Earnings	406 25
Meats	9 36		
Groceries	142 45	Surplus	40 99
Clothing and shoes	47 00		
Fuel and light	12 00		

No. 20. WEAVER—PIEDMONT.

Condition.—Family of three: Parents and child. Father and mother are weavers. Father can read a little; otherwise no education. Live in one room—not well furnished.

Earnings of father	$120 00
Earnings of mother	87 00
Total	207 00

Cost of Living.

Rent	$12 00	Fuel and light	$15 00
Bread	32 85		
Coffee and milk	25 55	Expenditures	215 60
Cheese	10 95	Earnings	207 00
Groceries, etc	91 25		
Clothing	28 00	Deficit	8 60

EARNINGS AND EXPENSES OF WAGE RECEIVERS IN EUROPE. 421

Following is a general statement deduced from the preceding examples and from others not reproduced here :

AVERAGE DAILY WORKING TIME AND RATES OF WAGES IN ITALY—1885.

Occupation.	Number of hours.	Daily wages.
Tailor	10 to 12	$0 70 to $1 00
Stonemasons	10 to 12	50 to 70
Carpenters	10 to 12	40 to 60
Boys 12 to 15, working as hod carriers		10 to 20
Mechanics:		
skilled	10 to 12	50 to 80
ordinary	10 to 12	40 to 60
Weavers:		
hand-loom men	10 to 12	25 to 40
hand-loom women	10 to 12	20 to 30
steam-loom women	10 to 12	25 to 40
Shoemaker:		
skilled	10 to 12	50 to 80
ordinary	10 to 12	40 to 60
Shepherds	11 to 14	a02 to b07
Day laborers	10 to 12	20 to 35
Cook :		
man		c30 to 33½
woman, wealthy family		c20 to 25
man, in ordinary family		c12 to 16½
Lady's maid, in wealthy family		c10 to 12
Servant of officer in army		d03 to 05½
Soldier in army		e01 to 02
Soldier, in Vatican (Pope's Guard)		e14½ to ......
Glass maker:		
skilled		80 to 1 00
ordinary		50 to 60
Stonecutter :		
after not less than six years' apprenticeship		80 to 1 00
ordinary		50 to 60
Printer		50 to 70

   a With board.
   b Without board.
   c With board and lodging.
   d In addition to army pay, uniform, and rations.
   e With board, lodging, and uniform.

PRICES OF COMMODITIES IN ITALY—1885.

Article.	Price.	Article.	Price.
Milk, per quart	$0.04 to $0.06	New potatoes, per pound	$0.02 to $0.03
Wine, per quart	.08 to .16	Butter, ordinary, per pound	.16 to .20
Eggs, in winter, per dozen	.24	good, per pound	.20 to .40
summer, per dozen	.12 to .14	Coal, at seaport towns, per ton	5.00 to 6.00
Bread, common, per pound	.02 to .03	in interior, on railroads, per ton	5.00 to 8.00
superior, per pound	.03 to .04	off railroads, per ton	8.00 to 15.00
Figs, dried	.02 to .06	Mutton, per pound	.16 to .18
Strawberries (in season), per pound	.05 to .10	One sheep	3.00
Cherries (in season), per pound	.03 to .05	Pork, salted, per pound	.13 to .15
Cheese, Swiss, inferior	.08	fresh, per pound	.15 to .18
good	.13	Macaroni, first grade, per pound	.05 to .06
very best	.18	second grade, per pound	.03 to .04

Cost of Clothing.—A suit made to order by a fashionable tailor can be had: No. 1 wool; durable, stout cloth; stylish cut and appearance, for $10. No. 2 wool (Italian manufacture), neat in appearance and good in wear, $7.50. A laborer's suit, consisting of breeches, jacket, vest, flannel shirt, underwear, socks, neck tie, costs from $4.45 up; to which must be added for shoes, if leather, $1.25 to $1.50; if wooden, 20 cents. A bricklayer's clothing outfit comprising breeches, jacket, vest, shirt, underwear, hat, handkerchiefs, shoes, costs at a minimum, $10 to $12.50.

Diet.—Articles in most general consumption—onions, macaroni, funnochio, tomatoes, oil, bread, milk, coffee, wine; when any meat, most generally salami (a kind of sausage), salt pork, tripe—rarely beef, mutton, or fresh meat. In Southern Italy, to the list of articles in very general use should be added, dried figs, chestnuts, and dried fruits of various kinds.

A laborer expending 20 cents per day for food would divide it about thus:

Bread	$0.04
Milk and coffee	4
Macaroni (or tripe) and onions	8
Wine	4
Total	20

TAXES AND TARIFFS IN ITALY.

Raw material, hides, silk cocoons, wool, hemp, flax, jute are duty free. Dutiable articles are taxed at the following rate, according to make, color, and quality:

Wool manufactures, per 224 lbs	$10 00 to $60 00
Woven goods, per 224 lbs	4 60 to 60 00
Blankets, per 224 lbs	22 00
Velvet, per kilogram (about 2¼ lbs)	1 60
Silk manufactures, per kilogram	1 20
Leather, tanned hides, per 224 lbs	5 00
Furs, per 224 lbs	12 00

Total importations into Italy were valued for 1877, at $230,244,556.80.; for 1882, at $269,080,235.60.

Income on importations into Italy amounted in 1882 to $28,508,016.40.

MUNICIPAL TAXATION—MILAN.[a]

Awnings, per year	$6 00
Houses, per year, per room	6 00
Servants, per year	1 00
Wine, octroi duty, per quart	2
Geese, chickens, etc., octroi duty, per head	3
Bread, per kilogram	1 cent to 2
Milk, per quart	1
Vegetables and eggs	free

Income tax, 13⅛ per cent.

CONCLUDING REMARKS.

As dark a coloring as this report may seem to give, the general condition of the laboring classes in Italy is better to-day than for years past. It must be remembered that the climate is genial and mild, and that what in other lands might be extreme hardship is in Italy at most a mere inconvenience. Except among the high lands of the Appenines, and in Lombardy and Piedmont, and the northern section of the state, inability to purchase fuel does not occasion suffering or even hardship. In most large places, as Naples, Rome, Florence, etc., there exist what may be termed public kitchens, whither the frugal housewife takes a pound of macaroni to be cooked, or a quart of

---

[a] The Municipal Government of Milan pays to the General Government, from its receipts from octroi duties, in round numbers, per year $120,000. Naples, Rome, Genoa, and other cities pay to the General Government a similar tax, the amount being proportioned to the size of the city, and the sum received from octroi duties.

chestnuts to be boiled, or a pound of pork to be fried, so that lack of fuel is little deprivation for the Italian laborer's family, independent both of cold and cooking.

Very simple and primitive methods yet prevail in most parts of the country. A large amount of the manufactures is still the product of hand looms and hand machinery. Agricultural implements are of the oldest and simplest makes. A change, however, is becoming apparent. American machinery, notably improved agricultural implements, as reapers, ploughs, etc., is being introduced, and woollen and silk manufactories, especially in Lombardy and Piedmont, are using improved machinery and employing skilled workmen.

A general and radical change in the entire method of labor may be looked for within the next few years.

BELGIUM.

REMARKS.— The Belgian laborer is as industrious, perhaps, as the laborer of any other country in the world; two circumstances, however, operate to lessen the results which his energy and labor should produce. First, the extreme density of population, and consequent great amount of competition, and secondly, his habits of intemperance.

Beer, among the Germans, and light wines among the French and Italians, are consumed almost to the exclusion of other beverages; but in Belgium the workingman drinks not only a very unwholesome and inferior quality of wine and beer, but, to a considerable extent, rum and gin as well. Rum and gin drinking are on the increase, and many workmen lose Mondays through their Saturday night and Sunday dissipations.

In the matter of habitations the standard is considerably better than that in Italy. A moderately thrifty workman will rent a tenement house of from two to four rooms, the rent of such a house ranging from $3 to $6 per month, depending upon locality and other circumstances. In rural districts houses are generally provided with a small plot of ground for gardening. In the large cities this is wanting; the houses in Antwerp and Brussels, are built solidly together; the hallways opening into the houses are generally dark and narrow, and the stairs leading to the upper stories exceedingly crooked and steep. Often a rope is provided to hold to when going up the steps, it being impossible, or at least dangerous, to ascend otherwise. The system of "Bauer-dorfs," or "peasant villages," so universal in Germany and some other European states, does not prevail in Belgium. The peasant's house is usually detached, is one story high, and thatched. In addition to gardening, the peasant generally raises a little poultry, a pig or two, and cows, all these animals being housed either in one of the rooms of the peasant's house or in small sheds adjoining. The women treat animals under their charge with the greatest care. In cold or rainy weather they are particular to put a kind of rough blanket on the cows; they give them warm food, and in many ways care for small details which in other countries are more neglected.

In some of the large glass-manufacturing establishments expert glass blowers earn as much as $3 per day; others engaged in making large glass vessels or other work requiring particular skill earn from $1.50 to $2 per day. Men of this class frequently own their own homes, or, if not, rent comfortable tenement houses of the better class, costing from $10 to $15 per month. The number, however, who receive the above-mentioned wages bear but a small proportion to the whole. Skilled paper makers, iron workers, woollen weavers, and similarly engaged workmen, will not average more than 50 to 65 cents per day.

Some of the larger manufacturers are taking steps toward the betterment of the habitations of their operatives, such as founding or encouraging social clubs, reading rooms, furnishing plain, wholesome dinners in large dining halls, etc.

Women engage in work quite as arduous as men; their pay, however, is always from 10 to 30 per cent. less.

No. 21.—PAPER MAKER—VICINITY OF ANTWERP.

Condition.—Family of three: Parents and small child. The parents both work in paper mill, earning together, on an average, 80 cents per day. Rent small house in common with another family; occupy the two rooms on upper floor. Rooms small, but tolerably comfortable; decorated with curtains and a few cheap pictures. During the day child is left in care of occupants of lower floor. The father is a young man, rather more intelligent than the average; reads and writes; belongs to workman's club; does not drink gin or rum.

Diet.—Breakfast: Rye bread, coffee, milk. Dinner: Beef soup, potatoes, bread, and occasionally sausage or pork, salad or other vegetable. Supper: Bread, coffee, milk, sometimes prunes or other cheap dried fruit.

Earnings of father	$183 60
Earnings of mother	75 00
Total	258 60

Cost of Living.

Rent	$24 00		Shoes (leather)	$8 00
Bread	41 94		Religion and incidentals	13 00
Coffee, with milk	18 25			
Beer and sour wine	11 00		Expenditures	264 85
Rice, prunes, etc. (for Sundays)	8 32		Earnings	258 60
Sausage, corned meat, pork	47 32			
Groceries	55 67		Deficit	6 25
Clothing	37 35			

No. 22.—PAPER MAKER—VICINITY OF ANTWERP.

Condition.—Family of five: Parents, son aged 14, boy aged 11, and girl aged 8; father and mother work in paper mill, the father earning on an average about 51 cents per day; the mother, 25 cents. Son aged 14, working in paper mill, averages 25 cents per day. The boy and girl work in cigar factory, making centers, putting on inner wrappers, etc.; boy averages 17 to 20 cents per day, girl averages 10 to 15 cents per day. Occupy tenement of three rooms, crowded, dirty locality, not pleasant, offensive smells from canal. Not much furniture in house and but little attempt at decoration. Front room used as dining and sitting room and kitchen, cooking being done upon a kind of fireplace stove. Parents work in factory along with about 200 other hands. In busy seasons factory runs day and night. Mother complains of night work as hard on eyes. Boy and girl in cigar factory in delicate health, say work is too confining and unwholesome; can read a little, but not much.

Diet.—Breakfast: Bread, coffee, or sometimes beer, and cheese. Dinner: Meat soup, potatoes, onions, rice, bread, and often beer, occasionally sausage, corned meat, etc.; on rare occasions, fresh beef. Supper: Bread and coffee.

Earnings of father	$147 90
Earnings of mother	72 50
Earnings of son of 14	54 00
Earnings of boy of 11	45 00
Earnings of girl of 8	29 90
Total	349 30

EARNINGS AND EXPENSES OF WAGE RECEIVERS IN EUROPE. 425

Cost of Living.

Rent	$28 80	Shoes	$11 00
Bread and flour	73 00	Religion and incidentals	12 00
Coffee or chicory	18 20		
Groceries, etc.	62 92	Expenditures	337 52
Meat, salted, corned, and fresh	15 60	Earnings	349 30
Beer and liquors	36 40		
Fuel and lights	15 60	Surplus	11 78
Clothing, including table linen, sheets, etc	64 00		

No. 23. WEAVERS—ANTWERP.

Condition.—Family of seven: Parents, daughter aged 20, husband and children of daughter; daughter aged 15. Father weaves silk, earning about $5 per week. Married daughter weaves, earning 30 cents per day; daughter aged 15 also weaves. Husband of daughter stone mason, but not steadily at work. The mother stays at home, sewing, cooking, caring for children, etc. Occupying tenement house of four rooms; neat and comfortable; matting on floors, curtains and other evidences of neatness; father belongs to workman's club; older members of family can all read.

Diet.—Breakfast: Bread, coffee, milk. Dinner: Meat soup, salt pork or sausages, vegetables (as potatoes, cabbage, etc.), and on fête days, or Sundays, beer or wine. Supper: About same as breakfast.

Earnings of father	$249 70
Earnings of married daughter	77 00
Earnings of unmarried daughter	61 00
Earnings of daughter's husband	130 00
Total	517 70

Cost of Living.

Rent	$36 00	Clothing	$63 96
Bread	109 50	Fuel	12 00
Coffee	51 10	Incidentals	24 00
Groceries	109 50		
Meats	25 50	Expenditures	466 56
Wine and beer	14 00	Earnings	517 70
Furniture, etc	21 00	Surplus	51 14

No. 24. WEAVERS—ANTWERP.

Condition.—Family of four: Parents and two small children. Occupy lodgings in upper part of tenement house. Two rooms. Front room has window and closet; back room small, used for kitchen and dining room. Father and mother both weavers; children too small to work.

Earnings of father	$174 00
Earnings of mother	105 00
Total	279 00

Cost of Living.

Rent	$18 66	Fuel and lighting	$12 00
Bread	54 75	Furniture, etc	7 20
Coffee, milk, etc	29 20	Incidentals	17 00
Meat (about once a week)	10 40		
Groceries	64 53	Expenditures	276 64
Beer and tobacco	21 90	Earnings	279 00
Clothing and shoes	41 00	Surplus	2 36

No. 25. Collier—Liege.

Condition.—Family of six: Parents, daughter aged 15, boy aged 11, two girls aged 9 and 8. The father is a coal collier, mother shovels coal, girl of 15 carries coal on her back, the two children sweep manure off the streets. Occupy small house with three rooms—dingy, dirty locality—no effort at ornamentation. Family illiterate. Father gets drunk. A poor quality beer is the ordinary drink, but a considerable amount of gin is also consumed. The mother is coarsened by hard work, the daughter becoming so, while the two manure sweepers, living in the slums, rapidly lose whatever little refinement of nature they may have originally possessed. Father works twelve hours per day—six hours on and six hours off.

Diet.—Breakfast: Rye bread and coffee, and occasionally a little cheese. Dinner: Soup, beans, bread; sometimes varied with potatoes or rice, cabbage, etc. About once a week bacon or salt pork and beer. Supper: Rye bread and coffee or beer.

Earnings of father	$156 00
Earnings of mother	87 00
Earnings of daughter	58 00
Earnings of two children	72 50
Total	373 50

Cost of Living.

Rent	$24 00	Fuel and light	$15 00
Bread	87 60		
Meats	18 25	Expenditures	371 10
Coffee, milk, etc.	43 80	Earnings	373 50
Beer and spirituous liquors	43 80		
Groceries	76 65	Surplus	2 40
Clothing and shoes	62 00		

No. 26. Cannon Founder—Liege.

Condition.—Family of three: Parents and child. Occupy three rooms of tenement house; carpet in bedroom, which is also used as parlor or receiving room; kitchen and dining room are one and the same. The third room very small, used as pantry. The father is a good workman; belongs to workman's club, and does not drink gin or rum. The mother works in a cloth manufactory. Both mother and father can read, and child is learning; air of neatness about the house above the ordinary.

Diet.—Breakfast: Coffee, milk, bread sometimes in addition, cheese, or a little dried fruit. Dinner: Soup, beans and pork, and bread—sometimes cabbage (sauerkraut), eggs or bacon, etc. Supper: Coffee, milk, bread.

Earnings of father	$241 00
Earnings of mother	116 00
Total	357 00

Cost of Living.

Rent	$36 00	Furniture, etc	$30 00
Bread and flour	65 70	Incidentals	7 50
Coffee and milk	25 55		
Meats	36 50	Expenditures	348 48
Groceries	91 23	Earnings	357 00
Clothing	41 00		
Fuel and lights	15 00	Surplus	8 52

No. 27. WINDOW-GLASS BLOWER—DISTRICT OF CHARLEROI.

Condition.—Family of six: Parents, son aged 18, daughter aged 17, boy aged 15, girl aged 7. Father is an expert blower; son, glass flattener, boy of 15 works in glass, daughter same. The mother is occupied only with household duties. Occupy house of five rooms, a small garden attached; clean, tidy appearance. Floors scrubbed and polished, mats in parlor and large bedroom. All the family, excepting small girl, can read and write. Father saving and thrifty; has money in savings bank.

Diet.—Breakfast: Coffee, milk, bread; sometimes eggs or bacon. Dinner: Vegetable or beef soup, potatoes, sauerkraut; occasionally beef, more often pork, bacon or similar meat, rice or bread pudding. Supper: Coffee, milk, bread; occasionally prunes, dried fruit, or honey.

Earnings of father	$639 00
Earnings of son	210 10
Earnings of daughter	99 00
Earnings of boy	75 00
Total	1,023 10

Cost of Living.

Rent	$75 00	Fuel and light	$52 00
Clothing	121 60	Incidentals	25 90
Bread	65 70		
Coffee	18 25	Expenditures	770 65
Milk	29 20	Earnings	1,023 10
Meats	62 50		
Vegetables and groceries	255 50	Surplus	252 45
Furniture, etc.*a*	65 00		

No. 28. WINDOW-GLASS MAKER—DISTRICT OF CHARLEROI.

Condition.—Family of five: Parents, boy aged 9, boy aged 8, girl aged 6. All but child work in glass manufactory. Occupy part of tenement house, two rooms—about 15 feet by 12, and one small room or pantry. Rooms clean but bare and unattractive. Family save money and have a small sum in savings bank.

Diet.—Breakfast: Coffee, rye bread. Dinner: Soup, potatoes, beets, cabbage, or similar vegetable, sometimes pork or bacon, on feast days occasionally fresh meat. Supper: Coffee, rye bread.

Earnings of father	$193 00
Earnings of mother	130 00
Earnings of two sons	120 00
Total	443 00

Cost of Living.

Rent	$36 00	Fuel and light	$31 20
Bread	54 75	Religion and incidentals	24 00
Coffee	14 60		
Milk	32 75	Expenditures	416 35
Meats	9 60	Earnings	443 00
Beer, wine, etc	18 25		
Groceries, etc	146 00	Surplus	26 65
Clothing and shoes	49 20		

a This item extraordinary; not expended every year.

No. 29. STONE MASON—BRUSSELS.

Condition.—Family numbers three: Parents and small child. Father is a stone mason, mother works in linen manufactory. The father begins work in summer at 5.30 a. m. and works until 7 p. m., with two hours rest during the day. In winter begins at 7 a. m. and quits at 5.30 p. m., stopping during the day for rest and meals about one hour. Occupy lodgings, two rooms in crowded house—sleep and live in one room, cook and eat in the other. Rooms plain and bare. Father can read and write, but does not belong to any club; drinks too much.

Diet.—Breakfast: Rye bread, coffee, milk. Dinner: Soup, beans, cabbage, bread, cheese, occasionally beer, bacon, salt pork, or fresh meat, cheese, rice pudding, etc. Supper: Rye bread, coffee, milk, sometimes dried stewed fruit.

Earnings of father (290 days)	$261 00
Earnings of mother	130 50
Total	391 50

Cost of Living.

Rent	$28 00	Bedding, etc.	$12 33
Bread	32 85	Fuel and light	15 71
Coffee and chicory	10 95	Religion and incidentals	15 00
Milk	14 60		
Meats	7 30	Expenditures	357 04
Beer and spirits	21 75	Earnings	391 50
Groceries	153 30		
Clothing	39 00	Surplus	34 46
Shoes	6 25		

No. 30. WEAVER AND SUGAR REFINER—LILLE.

Condition.—Family of four: Parents and two children. Occupy two rooms in tenement house. First room used for bedroom and parlor—looks neat. Second room used as kitchen—small and uncomfortable. The father works in the sugar refinery; the mother is a weaver in a manufactory of cotton cloth. Neither have much education. Children are being sent to school.

Diet.—Breakfast: Rye bread, coffee, occasionally some potatoes. Dinner: Soup, vegetables (as beans, potatoes or cabbage, sauerkraut, etc.), bread, and occasionally salt pork or bacon, cheese, beer or buttermilk. Supper: Rye bread, coffee or beer.

Earnings of father	$188 50
Earnings of mother	116 00
Total	304 50

Cost of Living.

Rent	$36 00	Clothing and shoes	$36 40
Bread	54 75	Fuel and incidentals	20 80
Potatoes	21 90		
Coffee, milk, etc	43 80	Expenditures	311 22
Lard, butter, pig's fat, etc.	10 92	Earnings	304 50
Meats, groceries, etc.	58 40		
Beer and spirituous liquors	28 25	Deficit	6 72

No. 31. LACE MAKER AND FURNITURE JOINER—BRUSSELS.

Condition.—Family of seven: Parents, daughter aged 16, daughter aged 15, boy aged 12, girl aged 10, girl aged 9. Occupy three-room tenement house. Pleasant locality. The front room is used as dining room and parlor, and is carpeted. Room to rear of parlor used for kitchen, bedroom upstairs. The father is a furniture maker. The mother makes lace; two oldest daughters work with mother. Family dress neatly; older members can read; drink a good deal of beer, but manage to save money; have an account in savings bank.

Diet.—Breakfast: Bread, coffee. Dinner: Vegetables, as sauerkraut, potatoes, beets, beans, etc., occasionally pork or sausage, cheese, bread, and beer. Supper: Bread, coffee, occasionally some sort of stewed dried fruit.

Earnings of father	$211 25
Earnings of mother	146 25
Earnings of other members of family	174 25
Total	531 75

Cost of Living.

Rent	$45 00	Light and fuel	$22 97
Bread	91 25	Incidentals	36 00
Coffee, milk, etc.	51 10		
Meats	17 66	Expenditures	481 42
Groceries and vegetables	129 69	Earnings	531 75
Spirits, beer, etc.	26 50		
Clothing	61 25	Surplus	50 33

No. 32. Puddler—Seraing.

Condition.—Family numbers three: Parents and small child. Occupy tenement house, four rooms—kitchen, parlor or dining room, and two rooms on second floor; one large room used for sleeping apartment, one small room used as closet or store room. Parlor or dining room is carpeted, looks neat and cheerful. Bedroom plain but comfortable. Mother was formerly a woollen weaver, is occupied now only by sewing and general household duties. Father is a puddler in iron works.

Diet.—Breakfast: Bread, coffee, sometimes potatoes, or cheese. Dinner: Meat soup, vegetables, as beans, rice, potatoes, cabbage, etc.; sometimes pork, fresh meat, or eggs, bread and wine or beer. Supper: Rye bread, coffee, milk, sometimes a little stewed dried fruit.

Earnings of father	$450 00

Cost of Living.

Bread	$54 60	Light and fuel	$18 00
Meats	24 44	Incidentals	21 00
Coffee and milk	25 55		
Groceries and vegetables	171 55	Expenditures	413 14
Clothing	39 00	Earnings	450 00
Shoes	11 00		
Rent	48 00	Surplus	36 86

REMARKS.—At this place are works comprising every branch of industry connected with the manufacture of iron, as coal mines, iron-stone mines, puddling furnaces, cast-steel works, engine factories, etc. In these various departments of iron and mining industries, from nine to eleven thousand workmen are employed. The employés of the "Cockerill Works" at Seraing enjoy in every way comforts and conveniencies greater than the ordinary. The hospital erected for the employés of the works is kept up at a cost of from $9,000 to $10,000 per year. There are savings banks, sick funds, good elementary schools, public kitchens and dining halls for such as desire to use them, and generally an air of thrift and well-being in gratifying contrast to the less favorable condition of the workman elsewhere.

No. 33. Laborer in Rolling Mill—Seraing.

Condition.—Family numbers five: Parents, son aged 15, son aged 14, girl aged 10. Occupy tenement house of three rooms—two bedrooms and one small room; use both as kitchen and dining room; the house is not well furnished, but is clean and neat. Father is considered a good laborer, but not skilled.

Diet.—Breakfast: Rye bread, coffee, sometimes potatoes or beans. Dinner: Soup (sometimes meat soup, sometimes vegetable), potatoes, onions or cabbage, occasionally salt pork or bacon; on some Sundays and fête days, fresh meat or eggs; some kind of pudding, beer. Supper: Rye bread, coffee, milk.

Earnings of father	$171 00
Earnings of mother	105 00
Earnings of other members of the family	153 00
Total	429 00

Cost of Living.

Rent	$39 00	Light and fuel	$15 00
Bread	73 00	Incidentals	21 90
Coffee and milk	36 50		
Meats	32 85	Expenditures	411 42
Potatoes	23 72	Earnings	429 00
Groceries, vegetables, etc	112 20		
Clothing	57 25	Surplus	17 58

No. 34. Workman in Machine Shops—Seraing.

Condition.—Single man, aged about 26. Hires lodgings and boards out. Several lodgers in one room, but condition nevertheless fairly good. He is reckoned to be a good mechanic. Is thrifty. Has money in bank.

Diet.—Breakfast: Rye bread, coffee, sometimes sausage or cheese. Dinner: Soup, meat, and potatoes, or other vegetables, as sauerkraut, onions, rice, etc., bread and pudding, or occasionally stewed dried fruit, and bread, beer, sometimes wine. Supper: Rye bread, coffee, milk.

Earnings	$191 40

Cost of Living.

Lodging and fuel	$18 00	Expenditures	$159 66
Board	87 36	Earnings	191 40
Clothing	25 35		
Beer and spirits	10 95	Surplus	31 74
Religion and incidentals	18 00		

Itemized Cost of Workman's Dinner.

Piece of bread	$0 01
Soup	03
Meat and potatoes	04
Dessert of rice, or bread pudding, or dried fruit	02
Beer	02
Total	12

No. 35. Collier—Seraing.

Condition.—Family numbers four: Parents and two children. Occupy tenement house containing three rooms—house bare, but clean and neat; no carpets, but front room, used as parlor and dining room, is provided with mats. The two children go to elementary school. Father works on an average ten hours per day.

Diet.—Breakfast: Bread, coffee, sometimes potatoes or onions. Dinner: Soup, vegetables (as beans, cabbage, potatoes, or rice), sometimes sausage, pork, or bacon; once or twice a week a pudding of bread or rice; bread and beer. Supper: Bread, coffee, and milk.

Earnings of father	$225 00
Earnings of mother	90 00
Total	315 00

Cost of Living.

Rent	$36 00	Clothing and shoes	$43 75
Bread	51 10	Incidentals	21 25
Potatoes	18 25		
Coffee and milk	40 15	Expenditures	322 62
Meats	12 77	Earnings	315 00
Fuel and light	16 00		
Groceries and beer	83 35	Deficit	7 62

ENGLAND.

REMARKS.—The following figures, condensed by Sir John Lubbock, M. P., from the latest official statistical report of the United Kingdom, are given as showing in a general way the comparative state of affairs in England in 1860 and in 1885. Amounts are given in round numbers.

Population in 1860 was under	29,000,000
Population in 1885 was over	36,000,000
Paupers in 1860	850,000
Paupers in 1885	780,000
Criminals convicted in 1860	14,000
Criminals convicted in 1885	11,000
Savings banks deposits in 1860	£40,000,000
Savings banks deposits in 1885	90,000,000
Income tax, schedule D, in 1860	120,000,000
Income tax, schedule D, in 1885	291,000,000
National debt in 1860	822,000,000
National debt in 1885	740,000,000
Exports in 1860	165,000,000
Exports in 1885	296,000,000
Imports in 1860	210,000,000
Imports in 1885	390,000,000
Shipping in 1860, tons	4,600,000
Shipping in 1885, tons	7,400,000

Notwithstanding the evidence of these figures that affairs are more prosperous now than formerly, and notwithstanding the fact that the condition of the English workman is undoubtedly superior to that of his brother on the continent, much is yet to be desired, and in many ways his condition is in a far from prosperous state. Certainly a not unimportant cause of this is the extent to which the evil of intemperance prevails. The inquiry into the itemized expenses of laborers' families showed in some instances that 36 per cent. of the earnings of the head of the family (from 10 to 15 shillings out of a wage of from 25 to 30 shillings) went for beer, ale, or spirituous drink. Expenditures under this head of from 10 to 20 per cent. appeared quite the rule.

In most of the manufacturing cities and centers, workmen's clubs have been organized. These clubs are provided with reading rooms, lecture halls, billiards, etc., and inquiry upon the subject provoked a common opinion that they have exerted and are exerting a considerable influence for good.

The detailed statements of earnings and expenditures which immediately follow are for the families of some employés of two mills at Halifax. These mills, employing 800 operatives, are the largest cotton mills in Yorkshire. Raw cotton from Egypt and America is converted into hanks and warps at the rate of 60,000 pounds of yarn per week—or about five hundred miles of yarn per minute. The machinery used is of the most approved patterns, and for the most part is made in Lancashire, not above thirty miles distant. Three engines give an indicated power of 1,600 horse. The steam is generated in five large boilers fed by mechanical stokers, consuming 5,000 tons of coal per year (wholesale price per ton, $1.80 to $1.92). A large quantity of the products of these mills is sold and manufactured into cloth in the vicinity of Halifax. A considerable proportion, however, is exported to Germany, Austria, and Italy, notwithstanding the high tariffs existing in those lands. In Germany the tariff on every pound of full-worsted yarn is 2½ cents. The other countries mentioned have similar or higher tariffs upon this article.

Before going into the details of receipts and expenditures, a few words regarding wages of factory operatives at the time these inquiries were made (December, 1885), may not be out of place.

The rule is to pay by amount of work done. Taking the number of hours at 56½ per week, the weekly earnings of a young woman (16 years of age and upward) of ordinary ability will average $2.40; one of extra ability will average $3.60. A young man (14 to 17 years of age) will earn, depending on skill and industry, from $2.88 to $3.12 per week. Mule minders earn from $7.20 to $8.16 per week. This work in England is considered unfit for women, a woman's skirt being apt to become caught in the machinery. In Scotland, however, in some mills women wear bloomers and fill the positions of mule minders, it is said, as satisfactorily as men.

Children are, by act of Parliament, forbidden to work before the age of 10. Between the ages of 10 and 13 they are required to attend school half the day. If, at the close of his thirteenth year, the pupil fails to pass the examination fixed by law, he is required to continue another year at school. If attendance at school be missed one day the child must make up for it by attending the whole of the next day, instead of one-half. Thus, up to the age of 10 the English laborer's children are not permitted to work at all; and from 10 to 13, and sometimes 14, the maximum number of hours he is permitted to work per week is thirty.

Wages of child just turned 10 years, 28¼ hours	$0 42
Wages of child 12 to 13 years, 28¼ hours	84
Wages of child just turned 13 years, 56½ hours	1 80
Wages of child just turned 13 years, 56½ hours	2 44

Overlookers who understand machinery earn from $6 to $9.60 per week. In the two mills under consideration there are ten overlookers, or slightly over 1 per cent. of the total number of hands employed.

Superintendents, one to each mill, average per week $14.58.

PRICES IN HALIFAX, ENGLAND, DECEMBER, 1885.

Flour:				
No. 1	per pound	$0 02½	to	$0 03
No. 2	per pound	02⅞	to	02¼
Eggs	per dozen	24		
Eggs (in summer)	per dozen	12	to	18
Beef:				
No. 1	per pound	20		
No. 2	per pound	12	to	16

EARNINGS AND EXPENSES OF WAGE RECEIVERS IN EUROPE. 433

Sugar:
White granulated	per pound	$0 05¼
Brown granulated	per pound	03 to $0 04
Coal	per ton	3 60
House rent, two to three rooms	per week	88
Gas	per 1,000 cubic feet	54
Shoes		1 92
Stout working suit		6 00 to 8 75

No. 36. SPINNER—HALIFAX.

Condition.—Family numbers three: Parents and child. Occupy tenement house containing parlor and one bedroom, each about 15 by 12 feet, one small bedroom, and one kitchen or wash room. Parlor is also used for dining room, has window opening on street, is carpeted, and looks clean and comfortable. The grate is adapted for baking bread and simple cooking, saving expense of extra fires. Father reads and writes, and is generally intelligent. Wife was formerly weaver, but does not work now. She has a brother in the army, and sister emigrated to New Zealand. Family are saving, have small account in savings bank. The father belongs to a social and reading club. On Saturdays work stops at 1 p. m. afternoon spent at foot ball, cricket, or other outdoor sport. Family dress well, look contented and cheerful.

Diet.— Breakfast: Tea or coffee, bread and butter, sometimes bacon or eggs. Dinner: Piece of beef or chop, bread, butter and potatoes, sometimes other vegetables and cheese, and several times a week pudding. Supper: Bread and butter, tea or coffee, occasionally dried fruit.

Earnings of father $411 32

Cost of Living.

Rent	$45 76	Gas, or other light	$5 51
Bread	32 95	Fuel	14 25
Meats	43 80	Club dues	1 44
Coffee and tea	14 56	Incidentals	11 96
Milk	21 90		
Vegetables	25 55	Expenditures	412 23
Fruit	7 30	Earnings	411 32
Groceries	149 65		
Clothing	37 60	Deficit	91

No. 37. MULE SPINNER—HALIFAX.

Condition.—Family numbers four: Parents and two children. Occupy four-room tenement house. Fairly comfortable. Father is a good workman; but drinks too much, and often loses Mondays. Children go to school; mother is a weaver.

Diet.—Breakfast: Tea, bread and butter, sometimes pork or bacon. Dinner: Soup, roast beef or chop, potatoes, pickle, ale or beer, sometimes rice or plum pudding. Supper: Bread and butter, tea, coffee and milk, and what is left over from dinner.

Earnings of father	$312 00
Earnings of mother	218 40
Total	530 40

Cost of Living.

Rent	$54 75	Groceries	$29 20
Bread and flour	69 45	Educational, amusements, etc.	12 77
Meats	62 05	Clothing	53 25
Lard, butter, and cheese	69 45	Furniture, etc.	31 00
Milk	18 25		
Coffee	7 30	Expenditures	527 91
Tea	9 12	Earnings	530 40
Eggs	10 95		
Light (gas and oil)	5 47	Surplus	2 49
Beer, spirits, and tobacco	94 90		

No. 38. SPINNER—HALIFAX.

Condition.—Family numbers five: Parents and three children. Occupy house of three rooms, not including kitchen or wash room; parlor used also as dining room; is carpeted and looks neat. Two bedrooms on second floor; one about 12 by 14 feet, the other smaller, occupied by the children.

Diet.—Breakfast: Tea or coffee, bread and butter, sometimes potatoes and bacon. Dinner: Meat or fish, vegetables, ale or beer, occasionally pudding. Supper: Bread and butter, tea or coffee, occasionally dried stewed fruit.

Earnings of father	$374 40
Earnings of mother	187 20
Earnings of boy of 11 and girl of 12	64 48
Total	626 08

Cost of Living.

Rent	$41 60	Fuel and light	$23 44
Bread	76 65	Incidentals	29 50
Coffee and tea	20 07		
Meat and fish	98 55	Expenditures	607 52
Vegetables	32 95	Earnings	626 08
Milk	27 37		
Groceries	186 15	Surplus	18 56
Clothing	71 24		

No. 39. MULE SPINNER—HALIFAX.

Condition.—Single man, aged about 23. Boards with family of mill operatives—four others in same room, which is, however, large and well ventilated, having two windows looking on the street. Young man has average skill and industry. Belongs to Liberal club. Spends a good deal on billiards and ale.

Diet.—Breakfast: Bread and butter; sometimes bacon or pork, tea or coffee. Dinner: Soup, roast beef and potatoes, occasionally rice or cabbage, or other vegetable, and once or twice a week some sort of pudding. Supper: Bread, coffee, tea; sometimes potatoes warmed over; dried fruit.

Earnings	$344 30

Cost of Living.

Board, light and fuel	$182 52	Incidentals	$11 00
Beer, ale, and tobacco	50 96		
Clothing	21 75	Expenditures	300 59
Amusements, club dues, etc	29 60	Earnings	344 30
Shoes	4 76		
		Surplus	43 71

No. 40. Overlooker—Halifax.

Condition.—Family numbers seven: Parents, girl aged 17, girl aged 15, three children from 5 to 12. Two oldest girls work in mills,. the one as a spinner, the other as twister. Occupy tenement house of two floors, three rooms to the floor. The parlor is carpeted and the walls papered; looks neat and inviting. Bedrooms are comfortably furnished, and two of them have windows looking on the street. The family dress well; go to church. The father is member of a social club, is thrifty, and has money in the bank. Children go to school. The mother attends to household work, sewing, cooking, etc.

Diet.—Breakfast: Bread and butter, tea or coffee, occasionally potatoes, or remnants of dinner of day before, as piece of cold meat, beef, or bacon. Dinner: Chop with bread and potatoes, one other kind of vegetable, pudding. Supper: Bread, tea or coffee.

Earnings of father	$468 00
Earnings of two daughters	260 00
Total	728 00

Cost of Living.

Rent	$62 40	School fees	$6 24
Bread	91 25	Furniture *a*	39 25
Meats	94 90	Incidentals	31 60
Coffee and tea	16 42		
Milk	18 25	Expenditures	727 25
Vegetables	45 62	Earnings	728 00
Beer and tobacco	74 82		
Groceries	175 00	Surplus	75
Clothing	71 50		

No. 41. Spinner—Halifax.

Condition.—Family numbers four: Parents, two children. Occupy tenement house, containing on second floor one bedroom, size 14 by about 12 feet; one small room, or rather large closet, over hall. On the first floor, one room with window looking on street, used as parlor and dining room, and small kitchen or washroom. Both the bedroom and parlor are neatly and comfortably furnished. The children go to school. The father is skilful and industrious. The mother is a twister in cotton mill.

Diet.—Breakfast: Coffee or tea, bread, and butter, sometimes bacon or pork. Dinner: Vegetables, as potatoes, cabbage and onions, meat (salted, or, several times a week, fresh beef, or chop), bread, and sometimes pudding, ale or beer. Supper: Bread, tea or coffee.

Earnings of the father	$405 60
Earnings of the mother	202 80
Total	608 40

Cost of Living.

Rent	$49 92	Light and fuel	$23 86
Bread	58 40	Clothing and shoes	52 00
Meats	73 00	Incidentals	21 40
Coffee and tea	20 81		
Vegetables	32 85	Expenditures	567 48
Groceries	185 92	Earnings	608 40
Beer and tobacco	38 37		
Fruit (green and dried)	10 95	Surplus	40 92

a Extraordinary expenses, not incurred every year.

No. 42. MILL SUPERINTENDENT—HALIFAX.

Condition.—Family numbers five: Parents, three children from 4 to 8 years old. Occupy tenement house of five rooms; pleasant locality; house is kept clean; well furnished; is supplied with water and gas. Parlor is carpeted; oil cloth in kitchen. Oldest child goes to school. Family dress well; possess more than average intelligence. The father earns about $14 per week.

Diet.—Breakfast: Bread and butter, tea or coffee; occasionally potatoes and fried bacon or eggs. Dinner: Soup, roast beef, chop, or veal cutlet, vegetables (potatoes generally, though sometimes rice, cabbage, onions, etc.), bread, and several times a week pudding. Supper: Bread and butter, coffee or tea, dried stewed fruit.

Earnings of father $719 72

Cost of Living.

Rent and water rates	$62 40	Fuel	$23 40
Bread	73 00	Clothing	76 00
Meat and fish	89 43	Incidentals	39 25
Lard, butter, cheese, etc	65 70		
Fruits (dried and fresh)	33 80	Expenditures	629 62
Coffee and tea	27 37	Earnings	719 72
Milk	20 07		
Groceries, etc	112 00	Surplus	90 10
Gas and other light	7 20		

No. 43. SPINNER—HALIFAX.

Condition.—Family numbers eight: Parents, wife's sister, five children 6 to 15 years of age. Occupy tenement house of four rooms. Rather dingy locality, house not well furnished. Parents and younger children occupy second-floor bedroom, size about 11 by 13 feet. Wife's sister and eldest daughter occupy small hall room adjoining. On the first floor one room, 11 by 13 feet, used as parlor and dining room, and in the rear a small room used as kitchen and washroom. The family dress poorly. Father drinks too much and often loses Mondays. The eldest daughter, aged 15, and wife's sister also work in cotton mill.

Earnings of father $322 40
Earnings of wife's sister 187 20
Earnings of daughter 104 52

Total 614 12

Diet.—Breakfast: Bread, tea or coffee, sometimes American bacon. Dinner: Bacon or pork, once or twice a week fresh meat, potatoes, etc.; on Sundays a pudding, ale or beer, and bread. Supper: Bread and butter, coffee or tea; occasionally a little cheese.

Cost of Living.

Rent	$44 20	Fuel and light	$18 75
Bread and flour	116 80	Education and incidentals	13 40
Vegetables	65 00		
Meats	46 50	Expenditures	623 76
Groceries	182 00	Earnings	614 12
Beer, ale, and tobacco	87 60		
Clothing	49 51	Deficit	9 64

No. 44. CARPET WEAVER—HALIFAX.

Condition.—Family numbers four: Parents and two small children. Occupy two-story house, two rooms to each floor. House plain but clean. The family dress neatly

EARNINGS AND EXPENSES OF WAGE RECEIVERS IN EUROPE. 437

and live well. The father is sober and industrious. Can save money ordinarily, but is cramped now because children are very young and the mother is not able to work.

Diet.—Breakfast: Bread, coffee, milk. Dinner: Soup, bacon, cheese, several times a week fresh meat, as beef or chops, potatoes, rice or beans, bread, and beer. Supper: Bread and butter, tea or coffee, sometimes potatoes, cold meat, or other remnant of dinner.

Earnings $364 00

Cost of Living.

Rent	$42 12	Fuel and light	$17 25
Bread	47 45	Incidentals	32 40
Milk	18 25		
Coffee and tea	21 90	Expenditures	389 22
Groceries	133 05	Earnings	364 00
Meats	31 20		
Beer, ale, and spirits	14 60	Deficit	25 22
Clothing	31 00		

No. 45. CARPET WEAVER—HALIFAX.

Condition.—Family numbers six: Parents, three children, and mother of the father. Occupy tenement house of four rooms; unattractive locality. The rooms are bare and poorly furnished. The mother also is a carpet weaver. The father averages fifty-six and one-half hours per week; the mother is delicate and unable to work full time.

Diet.—Breakfast: Bread, coffee or tea, occasionally molasses. Dinner: Lentils, potatoes, pork or bacon, or several times per week beef, bread, ale, or beer; Sundays a bread, rice, or other pudding. Supper: Bread, tea or coffee.

Earnings of father	$374 40
Earnings of mother	144 00
Earnings of boy	31 20
Total	549 60

Cost of Living.

Rent	$41 60	Light and fuel	$21 16
Bread and flour	87 60	Education and incidentals	22 37
Coffee and tea	23 72		
Milk	21 90	Expenditures	542 67
Groceries, ale, beer, and tobacco	223 60	Earnings	549 60
Meats	41 32		
Clothing, shoes, and hats	59 40	Surplus	6 93

No. 46. WOOL SORTER—HALIFAX.

Condition.—Family numbers eight: Parents, five children, aged from 3 to 13 years, and girl aged about 17, sister of the father. Occupy four-room tenement house, plainly furnished and altogether too small for the family. Three rooms are used for sleeping apartments; the fourth room serves for kitchen, dining and wash room. The sister and two eldest children work in the same mill, which produces carpets.

Diet.—Breakfast: Bread and butter, coffee or tea. Dinner: Meat and potatoes, rice or lentils, bread and butter, beer; sometimes bread, rice or other pudding. Supper: Bread, butter, tea or coffee; occasionally dried fruit, or leavings of dinner.

Earnings of father	$312 00
Earnings of sister	209 04
Earnings of two children	66 58

Cost of Living.

Rent	$46 28	Groceries	$189 76
Bread and flour a	105 85	Clothing	57 50
Beer, spirits, and tobacco	54 38	Incidentals, etc.	22 50
Tea and coffee	19 24		
Milk	23 12	Expenditures	614 96
Gas and other light	6 24	Earnings	587 64
Fuel	13 40		
Vegetables	26 77	Deficit	27 32
Meats	49 92		

No. 47. Carpet Weaver—Halifax.

Condition.—Family numbers three: Parents and child. Occupy upper half of tenement house of four rooms. The father is industrious and thrifty; has small sum in savings bank; is a member of reading and social club. The mother dresses neatly, and works half time.

Diet.—Breakfast: Bread, butter, sometimes bacon, coffee or tea. Dinner: Soup, bacon, pork, or often fresh meat (mutton or beef), potatoes, rice, ale or beer; Sundays, a pudding. Supper: Bread, tea or coffee, occasionally potatoes warmed over, or cheese.

Earnings of father	$375 00
Earnings of mother	113 36
Total	488 36

Cost of Living.

Rent	$24 96	Fuel and light	$16 50
Bread and flour a	49 27	Clothing	37 40
Meats	73 00	Carpet	1 55
Lard, butter, etc.	40 15	Incidentals	23 30
Tea and coffee	18 20		
Milk	19 42	Expenditures	474 57
Beer and ale	23 73	Earnings	488 36
Groceries	145 65		
Club dues	1 44	Surplus	13 79

No. 48. Spinner—Leeds.

Condition.—Family numbers five: Parents, and three children from 4 to 11 years of age. Occupy tenement house of three good-sized rooms, and one hall room. First floor front room used as dining room and parlor; is carpeted and looks cheerful and inviting. Family dress well; seem saving and industrious. Two older children go to school.

Diet.—Breakfast: Bread, bacon, sometimes cheese, coffee or tea. Dinner: Beef, vegtables, bread, and beer; once or twice a week, pudding. Supper: Bread, coffee or tea, occasionally molasses, or remnants of dinner.

Earnings of father	$395 20
Earnings of mother	172 80
Earnings of boy, half time	23 40
Total	591 40

a The mother bakes her own bread, and frequently has for breakfast or supper "scones," a kind of hot bread or cake.

Cost of Living.

Rent	$51 40	Clothing	$49 75
Bread and flour	80 30	Fuel and light	21 05
Milk	18 25	Religion and incidentals	19 70
Tea and coffee	22 88		
Cheese	9 90	Expenditures	568 88
Meats	76 65	Earnings	591 40
Spirits and tobacco	36 50		
Groceries	182 50	Surplus	22 52

REMARKS.—The same general conditions prevail here as at Halifax. The workman's home consists ordinarily of a tenement house containing three to six rooms. There is no material difference in the wages of this district and of Halifax. An industrious man weaver may average 30 shillings ($7.20) per week; a woman weaver from $3.60 to $5 per week, according to skill and industry. A bricklayer averages 5 to 6 shillings ($1.20 to $1.44) per day, and generally wages are about as stated in the figures for Halifax.

No. 49. Engineer in Woolen Mill—Leeds.

Condition.—Family numbers seven: Parents, three children 5 to 10 years of age, and two girls aged 12 and 13. Occupying comfortable cottage containing four rooms and a small kitchen or wash room. The bedrooms are comfortably furnished; two of them have windows looking on street. Family dress well and go to church. The father does not absolutely need the assistance of the two older children, but prefers that they grow up industrious. They go to school half of each day and work in mills the other half, excepting on Saturdays and Sundays, when they neither work nor attend school. The father is industrious and saving, has account in savings bank, is member of club, and does not drink to excess.

Diet.— Breakfast: Bread, tea or coffee; sometimes bacon and potatoes. Dinner: Soup, and the meat of the soup (several times a week fresh meat), rice or lentils, potatoes, bread, ale or beer. Supper: Bread and butter, coffee, tea, milk, and occasionally a little dried fruit.

Earnings of father	$386 88
Earnings of mother	192 40
Earnings of two girls	64 48
Total	643 76

Cost of Living.

Rent	$62 40	Fuel and light	$23 50
Bread and flour	87 60	House ornaments, etc.	17 50
Meats	91 25	Incidentals	31 40
Tea and coffee	20 02		
Milk	16 47	Expenditures	618 14
Vegetables	33 85	Earnings	643 76
Groceries	164 25		
Clothing	69 90	Surplus	25 62

No. 50. Bricklayer—Leeds.

Condition.—Family numbers six: Parents, son aged 16, girl about 15, and two children. Occupy cottage with four rooms, not including small wash room or kitchen. House is not well furnished, and general appearance is not inviting. The father is a good bricklayer, but drinks a good deal and does not work full time. The son and oldest daughter work in woollen mills. Family dress poorly.

Earnings of father	$288 00		
Earnings of son	162 24		
Earnings of daughter	156 00		
Total	606 24		

Diet.—Breakfast: Bread, bacon, coffee. Dinner: Bacon or pork, or occasionally ham or beef, potatoes, ale or beer, bread; on Sundays a pudding of some sort. Supper: Bread, tea or coffee; sometimes potatoes warmed over, or other remnant of dinner.

Cost of Living.

Rent	$49 92	Light and fuel	$19 75
Bread and flour	91 25	Bedding, etc	12 49
Coffee and tea	17 68	Education and incidentals	18 20
Milk	14 60		
Meats	52 86	Expenditures	624 10
Beer, ale, gin, and tobacco	102 20	Earnings	606 24
Groceries	193 45		
Clothing	40 20	Deficit	17 86
Shoes	11 50		

No. 51. DOCK-YARD LABORER—LIVERPOOL.

Condition.—Family numbers five: Parents and three children. Occupy two small rooms in large tenement house. Surroundings are uncomfortable and uncleanly. The family dress miserably. All drink too much, and their general condition is one of hardship and poverty. The father is a "substitute" dock-yard laborer. When working earns 10 cents an hour, but does not average above five or six hours per working day. The mother goes out house cleaning, scrubbing, etc. The children for the most part left to care for themselves are growing up, apparently, to become either beggars or criminals.

Diet.—Breakfast: Bread and coffee. Dinner: Bread, potatoes or beans, sometimes bacon or soup and soup meat. Supper: Bread and coffee; occasionally potatoes or beans warmed over, or a little cheese.

Earnings of father	$155 95		
Earnings of mother	100 00		
Total	255 95		

Cost of Living.

Rent	$24 96	Beer and spirits	$22 00
Bread and flour	76 65	Clothing	21 90
Coffee and chicory	13 00	Light, fuel, and incidentals	17 00
Milk	10 95		
Meats	16 42	Expenditures	273 21
Cheese	8 34	Earnings	255 95
Potatoes	12 72		
Groceries	49 27	Deficit	17 26

REMARKS.—This class of labor is as poorly paid, and is in as miserable a condition, as perhaps any class of labor in the kingdom. Though the absolute sum received by the regularly employed navvy is greater than the wage of a laborer or even a skilled mechanic in Italy, yet the former has a more inclement and trying climate, his wants, fancied or real, are more numerous, and he is less able to maintain health and happiness on 80 cents a day than is done in Italy on half that sum.

EARNINGS AND EXPENSES OF WAGE RECEIVERS IN EUROPE. 441

The condition of the irregularly employed navvy is, of course, even more deplorable. The docks of London, Liverpool, and the other large ports are crowded with these miserable men awaiting the uncertain chance of a few hours' employment. Through the fogs and drizzling rains of the long English winters they stand around shivering, and when a vessel arrives to be unloaded a hundred men apply where perhaps only ten are needed. In short, this class of men, though willing, even anxious to work, may be regarded as in a state little short of beggary.

Within the last five years charitable societies have turned their attention in some degree toward this large and needy class, and now, at many places, especially the London docks, stands have been established where are furnished at nominal prices plain but nourishing meals, consisting ordinarily of hot soup, beef hash, coffee, bread, and, when any desert, a piece of pie or bit of pudding. Were it not for this charity, it would be difficult to understand how many of the London and Liverpool and other dock-yard navvies succeed in existing.

No. 52. NAVVY—LIVERPOOL.

Condition.—Family numbers six: Parents, boy aged 14, and three children 7 to 11 years of age. Occupy two rooms on third floor of large lodging house; one room has a window looking on dim court; other room opens on hallway at head of steps and has no window; bad light and bad air; general appearance unfavorable. The father is "first hand" navvy, that is, is regularly employed when there is work; boy of 14 works in a grocery store; the mother does some washing, cooks, and attends to household.

Diet.—Breakfast: Bread and butter; occasionally cheese, molasses, coffee. Dinner: Bread and potatoes, pork or bacon, and sometimes soup and the meat of the soup. Supper: Bread and coffee.

Earnings of father	$223 00
Earnings of mother	99 84
Earnings of boy	62 40
Total	385 24

Cost of Living.

Rent	$31 20	Beer, ale, and tobacco	$26 30
Bread and flour	87 60	Education and incidentals	23 55
Coffee and tea	15 42		
Milk	10 95	Expenditures	385 91
Meats	43 80	Earnings	385 24
Vegetables	31 02		
Groceries	76 17	Deficit	67
Clothing and shoes	39 90		

No. 53. DOCK-YARD LABORER—LIVERPOOL.

Condition.—Family numbers four: Parents, child, and mother of the husband. Occupy two rooms looking on court. The rooms are rather bare, but are kept neat and clean. The father works at the docks, the wife sews on rough work for ready-made clothing firms. The grandmother, who is feeble, looks after the house and child. The head of this family may be considered doing as well as the average industrious navvy.

Diet.—Breakfast: Bread, coffee or tea. Dinner: Bread, potatoes, salt pork, and beans, or sometimes soup and soup meat, or fresh meat, coffee or beer. Supper: Bread and butter, tea or coffee.

Earnings of father	$225 36
Earnings of mother	180 54
Total	405 90

Cost of Living.

Rent	$31 20	Fuel and light	$17 25
Bread and flour	65 70	Incidentals	20 95
Coffee, chicory, and tea	16 60		
Meats	44 75	Expenditures	403 66
Cheese, butter, and eggs	21 86	Earnings	405 90
Groceries	142 35		
Clothing	43 00	Surplus	2 24

No. 54. BRICKLAYER—LIVERPOOL.

Condition.—Family numbers five: Parents, and three children from 1 to 5 years of age. Occupy small cottage of four rooms; surroundings good. The father is industrious; ordinarily could save money, but with present large young family is just able to make both ends meet. Family dress neatly; the mother, in addition to caring for the children, cooks and does all household work.

Diet.—Breakfast: Bread and butter, coffee or tea, sometimes cheese or molasses. Dinner: American bacon, or, several times per week, fresh beef, potatoes, or beans, beer; Sundays a pudding. Supper: Bread, tea or coffee, and occasionally meat or potatoes left from dinner.

Earnings of father $384 40

Cost of Living.

Rent	$53 04	Clothing (including shoes)	$39 50
Bread and flour	63 61	Incidentals, including medical attendance	29 20
Meat	54 38		
Groceries, beer, and ale	95 45		
Tea and coffee	15 62	Expenditures	384 40
Milk	15 16	Earnings	384 40
Fuel and light	18 44		

No. 55. BRICKLAYER—MANCHESTER.

Condition.—Family numbers four: Parents and two children. Occupy cottage of three rooms and small kitchen; pleasant locality; general air of the place, one of comfort. The family dress neatly; mother attends to house and children and sews; the father is a good and industrious bricklayer, making on an average 32 shillings 6 pence ($7.80) per week.

Diet.—Breakfast: Bread, butter, coffee or tea; sometimes bacon and molasses. Dinner: Bread, potatoes, rice or beans, pork or beef, ale; once or twice a week (generally Sundays) a pudding. Supper: Bread, tea or coffee, now and then cheese, or remnants of dinner, as potatoes warmed over, etc.

Earnings of father $405 60

Cost of Living.

Rent	$62 40	Fuel	$14 40
Bread and flour	49 32	Beer, tobacco, etc	18 72
Meats	51 66	Clothing	42 00
Coffee and tea	14 60	Religion and incidentals	24 96
Milk	12 77		
Vegetables	18 25	Expenditures	405 60
Groceries	92 87	Earnings	405 60
Oil and other light	3 65		

EARNINGS AND EXPENSES OF WAGE RECEIVERS IN EUROPE. 443

No. 56. CARPENTER—DISTRICT OF MANCHESTER.

Condition.—Family numbers seven: Parents, and five children from 3 to 14 years of age. Occupy five-room tenement. House plainly but comfortably furnished. The parlor, used also for dining room, has carpet and a few cheap pictures. This room is also used for light cooking, the "fireplace stove" being arranged for that purpose. There is, however, a small room used as kitchen and wash room. The boy of 14 works in cotton mill, though not full time. The father is a good carpenter; averages $1.44 per day, or $8.64 per week.

Diet.—Breakfast: Bread and butter, tea or coffee; occasionally cheese or bacon or potatoes. Dinner: Soup, meat of the soup, several times a week fresh meat, potatoes, bread, and beer, and Sundays rice or other pudding. Supper: Bread, butter, tea or coffee, and occasionally cheese or molasses.

Earnings of father	$432 00	
Earnings of son	93 00	
Total	525 00	

Cost of Living.

Rent	$67 60	Butter	$9 95	
Bread and flour	101 92	Other groceries	103 85	
Meats	57 67	Light and fuel	21 75	
Coffee and tea	20 87	Clothing and shoes	63 45	
Milk	11 52	Incidentals	13 75	
Sugar and molasses	14 79			
Vegetables	24 28	Expenditures	525 00	
Cheese	6 30	Earnings	525 00	
Lard	7 30			

No. 57. BLACKSMITH—DISTRICT OF BIRMINGHAM.

Condition.—Family numbers five: Parents and three children. Occupy cottage containing three rooms. House is passably comfortable, though rather too small for the size of the family. Two rooms are used for sleeping; the third room serves as dining room, kitchen, and parlor. The father is a horseshoer.

Diet.—Breakfast: Bread and butter, or cheese, tea or coffee. Dinner: Pork and beans, potatoes, or rice; sometimes fresh meat and pudding; bread. Supper: Bread, tea or coffee, occasionally molasses, or potatoes or other food warmed over from dinner.

Earnings of father	$364 00	

Cost of Living.

Rent	$44 20	Groceries	$106 49	
Bread and flour	69 45	Clothing	34 56	
Meats	31 07	Incidentals	9 60	
Coffee and tea	12 77			
Milk	18 85	Expenditures	379 65	
Vegetables	19 90	Earnings	364 00	
Cheese and butter	16 16			
Oil and other light	3 12	Deficit	15 65	
Fuel	13 48			

No. 58. SHOEMAKER—DISTRICT OF LEEDS.

Condition.—Single man, aged about 23. Boards with workman's family in tenement house. Is a "cutter," and earns per day, on an average, 4 shillings and 5 pence ($1.06).

Cost of Living.

Board, with light and fuel	$149 24	Incidentals	$30 60
Clothing	16 09		
Shoes	3 84	Expenditures	252 69
Other clothing (shirts, underwear, etc.)	9 12	Earnings	330 72
Beer and billiards	43 80	Surplus	78 03

No. 59. SHOEMAKER—LONDON.

Condition.—Family numbers five: Parents and three children. Occupy two rooms in a large tenement house; crowded, unpleasant locality. The water pipes in this house are constantly out of repair, causing an offensive smell. The father is a sewing-machine operator on shoes, works in factory where best machinery is in use. A good article of shoe is made to order and finished in an afternoon for 7s. 11d. ($1.90).

Diet.—Breakfast: Bread and coffee, sometimes bacon or cheese. Dinner: Bread, potatoes, bacon or occasionally fresh pork or beef, lentils—sometimes dried fruit or pudding, beer or ale. Supper: Bread and butter, coffee.

Earnings $424 32

Cost of Living.

Rent and water rates	$74 88	Light and fuel	$19 68
Bread and flour	69 35	Clothing	48 50
Meats	32 85	Incidentals	24 55
Coffee and tea	17 90		
Milk	10 95	Expenditures	424 32
Groceries and beer	125 66	Earnings	424 32

REMARKS.—Several years ago there was established in London what was called a "vegetarian" restaurant. This restaurant is still in operation. The bill of fare contains ordinarily such dishes as oatmeal or crushed wheat, with sugar and milk, various kinds of vegetable soups, potatoes, lentils, other sorts of vegetables, puddings of rice or bread, stewed fruit, pie, bread, tea, coffee, or milk. For 6d. (12 cents) any three of these dishes are served; for 4d. (8 cents) any two are served. Each course is liberal in quantity, and for 6d., or even 4d., a very substantial and nourishing meal may be had. This style of restaurant is steadily growing in favor, especially with young men and women not living with their families. Where not long ago there was but one such vegetarian restaurant, there are now a dozen or more scattered in various parts of the metropolis. In London very few housewives bake bread, that article being almost always obtained at the bake shops. This is not so much the rule in provincial cities (as Bradford, Halifax, Leeds). In such cities a large proportion of workmen's families do their own baking, and in particular seem fond of a kind of light bread called "scone," made with soda and eaten hot.

GERMANY.

REMARKS.—It would be impossible to convey a true idea of the condition of the laboring class in Germany without first considering the question of beer. Beer is so universally used and its consumption forms so large a part of the workman's expenditures, that a full understanding of this subject is necessary in order to obtain an insight into the German workman's true condition and mode of life.

In 1870 there were in Prussia alone 120,000 saloons and 40,000 public houses where liquors were sold. In 1880 the German census showed an increase of 38 per cent., or from 160,000 saloons and public houses the figures had risen to, in round numbers, 200,000, and the average daily consumption for every man, woman, and child was four glasses. Twenty-seven per cent. of the male lunacy in Prussian asylums is attributed to drink. Almost every workman belongs to a beer *kneiper* or club.

A *kneiper* is formed by a dozen or so men, fellow workmen, or neighbors, agreeing to meet at the nearest public house certain nights of the week, there to drink beer and smoke. One man orders a round of beer. The glasses hold each a pint, but they drink the last drop, and another of the party returns the first man's treat. A second round comes and goes. Number three next treats, and so on until sometimes as many as a dozen pint glasses have been emptied at one sitting per man.

Leaving aside the question of health this custom is attended by two unfortunate results : it lessens or destroys the love for domesticity and home, and consumes a very considerable portion of the family's earnings.

At many of the large cotton and woollen mills, in addition to the beer consumed at the regular meals, extra allowances are deemed necessary, and at 11 in the morning and at 4 in the afternoon the wagon and driver of the public house may be seen in the court of the mills dispensing hundreds of glasses of beer to the hands, who are allowed 10 minutes for the purpose.

While the custom of living exclusively in cities or villages, prevailing even among the agricultural classes, may originally have arisen in the middle ages from fear of marauders and robbers, the maintenance of that custom in the present day is not improbably due in a measure to this very fact of the German's love of beer *kniepers* and sociability. And here, again, two ill results ensue: First, a loss of time resulting from having to walk, sometimes considerable distances, to and from the fields; and secondly, less perfect health from living in crowded villages instead of in cottages, in the open fields, with fresh and pure air around them. The German "*Bauerdorf,*" or "Peasant village," is usually a mere bunch of low, two-story houses, huddled close together, and the narrow, crooked streets invariably decorated on both sides with stacks of ill-smelling manure. For the sake of having company to drink beer with in the evening, the German farm laborer lives amid such unclean and unwholesome surroundings rather than in a farm cottage, without company and beer *kneipers*, but with cleanliness, pure air, and health.

In the early morning the agricultural laborer starts for the fields, sometimes two or three miles distant, armed with a jug of beer, a pound of black bread, and, if in good circumstances, with a piece of bacon or sausage. Wages are low and every member of the family is compelled to work. Young infants are carried to the fields and set under the trees, there to care for themselves while the mothers do their share in producing the families' earnings.

The class of wandering journeymen—*Handwerksbursch*—though not so numerous as formerly, still exists, and members of that class are constantly met with on the highways, strolling from town to town, not so much with the expectation of making anything as of seeing the world and rubbing off their "corners" before settling down. At the age of 19 or 20 they are put into the army, and their abilities for a further period of three years turned in non-productive directions. It will be seen, therefore, that immediately after the close of his apprenticeship, say at the age of 17 or 18, the average mechanic or laborer, if a "*Handwerksbursch,*" is little more than a journeyman vagabond, barely supporting himself; and at the close of his two or three years' vagabondage he is pressed into the army, so that it is not until his twenty-fourth or twenty-fifth year that he begins to be able to help his own family, or to marry and care for children.

This lateness in becoming producers, and their inordinate consumption of beer, are, in the opinion of many, two very important causes of the unsatisfactory condition of German labor.

Cotton Mills—South Würtemberg.

These mills, employing 700 operatives, are pleasantly situated among the hills, in a healthy locality, several miles off the railroad, and twelve miles from any town.

Around a small park, forming a hollow square, are built a number of plain two-story houses, which form the habitations of the 700 hands. Each house has two floors, four rooms to the floor. Families of five to seven persons may occasionally be found occupying a whole floor; none enjoy the luxury of an entire cottage, and the majority content themselves with two rooms, making four families to the cottage. In front of each cottage is a small plat of ground, planted with vegetables, which are shared in common by the inmates of the cottage, both lower and upper floors. The park or hollow square is planted with shade trees and provided with long tables, on which, in summer, the operatives eat their dinners between the hours of 12 and 1.

Wages and Expenses.—Work begins at 6 a. m. and continues until 7 p. m., with rests during the day amounting to one hour and forty minutes. The number of work hours per week averages from sixty-six to sixty-eight.

Daily wages of spinner (man)	$0 60
Daily wages of spinner (woman)	37.5 to 40.8

The average wages of weavers is about the same. Boys and girls from 8 to 12 years work but half time.

Boys and girls 8 to 12 years of age, working half time, thirty-three to thirty-four hours per week, earn per week from 54 cents to $1.08.

A weaver's or spinner's working suit costs $7.20; Sunday suit for the same, from $8.64 to $9.60.

Rent.

Two rooms, per week	$0 36 to $0 43
Two rooms, per year	18 12 to 24 96
Floor of three to four rooms, per week	72 to 96
Floor of three to four rooms, per year	37 44 to 49 92

Board.—The mill company boards such of its employés as desire for 60 pfennigs (15 cents) per day, the following food being furnished: Breakfast: Two pieces of rye bread and coffee. Dinner: Soup, meat of the soup and one kind of vegetable, generally either cabbage or potatoes. Supper: Bread (two pieces) and coffee.

At these mills 2,500 pint glasses of beer are drank per day, giving an average for each man, woman, and child of 3½ pints, costing (at 2½ cents per pint) 8¾ cents.

A singing class, to which many of the hands belong, meets twice a week in the hall of the public house. Baths and laundry facilities are furnished the employés free of charge.

No. 60. WEAVER—SOUTH WÜRTEMBERG.

Condition.—Family numbers four: Parents, child, and grandmother. Occupy two rooms on second floor of cottage; parents work in mills; the grandmother looks after the house and child; family dress very plainly; general condition only passable.

Diet.—Breakfast: Bread and coffee. Dinner: Soup and soup meat, or occasionally sausage; potatoes or cabbage, bread, and beer. Supper: Rye bread and coffee.

Earnings of father	$180 00
Earnings of mother	122 40
Total	302 40

Cost of Living.

Rent	$18 12	Beer	$25 50
Bread	43 80	Clothing	41 76
Meats	29 20	Fuel and light	12 77
Coffee	13 55		
Milk	11 99	Expenditures	311 96
Potatoes and cabbage	14 60	Earnings	302 40
Groceries	100 67	Deficit	9 56

No. 61. WEAVER—SOUTH WÜRTEMBERG.

Condition.—Family numbers six: Parents, boy aged 13, three children from 5 to 12 years of age. Occupy one-half of lower floor of cottage; rooms are kept clean, but are bare and not well furnished; are too small for size of the family. The father is a good weaver.

Diet.—Breakfast: Bread and coffee. Dinner: Vegetable or meat soup, meat of soup, or occasionally pork, sausage, etc.; potatoes or cabbage, bread and beer. Supper: Bread and coffee, or beer.

Earnings of father	$187 20
Earnings of mother	112 50
Earnings of boy, aged 13	39 00
Earnings of girl, aged 12	31 20
Total	369 90

Cost of Living.

Bread and flour	$63 88	Clothing	$41 20
Meats	32 85	Fuel and light	9 60
Coffee and milk	34 67	School tax and incidentals	10 91
Potatoes	21 90		
Cabbage and other vegetables	18 25	Expenditures	370 00
Groceries	73 00	Earnings	369 90
Beer	45 62		
Rent	18 12	Deficit	10

No. 62. OPERATIVE IN COTTON MILL—SOUTH WÜRTEMBERG.

Condition.—Single man, aged about 22. Occupies attic room over public house; quarters small and uninviting; boards with mill company.

Diet.—Breakfast: Two pieces of bread and a bowl of coffee. Dinner: Soup, soup meat, or sometimes pork or sausage; potatoes or cabbage; bread and half quart of beer. Supper: Bread and coffee and often beer.

Earnings	$171 00

Cost of Living.

Lodging	$11 52	Incidentals	$12 00
Board	54 75		
Beer	34 68	Expenditures	142 23
Clothing	22 08	Earnings	171 00
Light and fuel	7 20		
		Surplus	28 77

No. 63. ENGINEER IN COTTON MILL—SOUTH WÜRTEMBERG.

Condition.—Family numbers five: Parents and three children, the oldest just 11. Occupy two rooms on lower floor of cottage. Surroundings clean and neat. The wife evidences some taste for improvement. Girl of 11 goes half time to school and works in mill half time. The other children are too small to do anything. The father drinks rather less than the average; tries to lay by money. The mother is a weaver.

Diet.—Breakfast: Bread and coffee. Dinner: Soup, potatoes, cabbage, sometimes bacon, salt pork, or sausage; on rare occasions veal or beef; bread and beer. Supper: Bread and coffee and cabbage.

Earnings of father	$199 68
Earnings of mother	124 80
Earnings of girl	37 44
Total	361 92

Cost of Living.

Bread	$56 57	Beer	$18 25
Coffee	16 42	Clothing	48 00
Milk	18 25	School tax and incidentals	14 40
Meats	32 85		
Potatoes, cabbage, beans, etc	35 04	Expenditures	361 47
Groceries	80 30	Earnings	361 92
Rent	24 96		
Fuel and light	16 43	Surplus	45

No. 64. OPERATIVE IN COTTON MILL—SOUTH WÜRTEMBERG.

Condition.—Gray-haired old man, aged 62, without family. Occupies small attic room, very bare and scantily furnished. This man is an Englishman; left his native place, district of Manchester, about twenty-four years ago, when the American civil war was causing depression in England. He has been steadily employed in these mills since 1863. Since 1883, having been in the employ of the mills twenty years and passed his 60th year, he has drawn from the company a stipend, or pension, of 19 pfennigs (about 5 cents) per day. The old man is not very spry, and does not average much more than half time. The mill company boards him for 15 cents per day and gives him his lodging free.

Diet.—Breakfast: Two pieces of bread and bowl of coffee. Dinner: Soup, soup meat, potatoes, bread, and beer. Supper: Bread and coffee.

Earnings	$93 60
Pension	16 64
Total	110 24

Cost of Living.

Board	$54 75	Incidentals	$6 66
Fuel and light	4 30		
Beer	26 28	Expenditures	110 24
Clothing and shoes	18 25	Earnings	110 24

No. 65. WEAVER—SOUTH WÜRTEMBERG.

Condition.—Single woman. Boards with a family occupying three rooms of a cottage; sleeps in room with three other girls.

Earnings	$124 68

Cost of Living.

Board, lodging, lights, and fuel	$67 05	Incidentals	$8 90
Clothing	16 20		
Beer	17 52	Expenditures	109 67
		Earnings	124 68
		Surplus	15 01

No. 66. SHOEMAKER—DISTRICT OF GÖPPINGEN.

Condition.—Family numbers seven: Parents, five children from 5 to 13 years of age. Occupy two rooms in a large lodging house; poorly furnished; too crowded; condition generally inferior and mean. The wife has a cart and dog, and harnesses herself to the cart alongside of the dog and delivers milk throughout the town. Several of the children go to school. The oldest (boy aged 13) works in shoe factory.

EARNINGS AND EXPENSES OF WAGE RECEIVERS IN EUROPE. 449

Diet.—Breakfast: Bread and coffee. Dinner: Potatoes or cabbage, bread and beer, occasionally sausage and dumpling. Supper: Bread and coffee. At 4 o'clock a light meal of bread and beer is generally eaten.

Earnings of father	$156 00
Earnings of mother	112 32
Earnings of boy	43 68
Total	312 00

Cost of Living.

Bread and flour	$79 08	Light and fuel	$8 75
Coffee	16 64	Religion and incidentals	18 20
Milk and sugar for coffee	24 96	Expenditures	327 65
Vegetables	37 44	Earnings	312 00
Groceries	74 88		
Rent	28 40	Deficit	15 65
Clothing	39 30		

No. 67. BRICKLAYER—GÖPPINGEN.

Condition.—Family numbers seven: Parents, wife's sister, aged about 16; four children from 1 to 7 years of age. Occupy two small and miserably furnished rooms. Unpleasant locality, poor light, and bad air. The mother and sister work in the fields.

Diet.—Breakfast: Bread and coffee. Dinner: No regular dinner; the father takes lunch to work; the women carry food to the fields; consists usually of rye bread, beer, occasionally bit of sausage. Supper: Rye bread, beer, potatoes, or cabbage in various forms (sauerkraut, etc.), sometimes cheese, egg cakes, or sausage.

Earnings of father	$168 48
Earnings of mother and sister	190 20
Total	358 68

Cost of Living.

Bread and flour	$65 70	Fuel and light	$16 43
Coffee and chicory	18 72	Luxuries (beer and tobacco)	52 56
Milk	16 16	Incidentals	5 73
Potatoes and cabbage	36 40	Expenditures	368 68
Groceries, etc	89 16	Earnings	358 68
Rent	25 92		
Clothing	41 90	Deficit	10 00

No. 68. MASON—DISTRICT OF COLOGNE, PRUSSIA.

Condition.—Family numbers seven: Parents and five children. Occupy two rooms on narrow street. The rooms are bare, but clean. Family seem thrifty and industrious. Father is a good workman; the mother averages about 30 cents a day, sewing in shirt factory.

Diet.—Breakfast: Black bread and coffee. Dinner: Soup, soup meat, bread and beer, and potatoes. At 4 o'clock bread and beer. Supper: Bread, beer or coffee, sometimes potatoes (left over from dinner).

Earnings of father	$262 08
Earnings of mother	108 00
Total	370 08

Cost of Living.

Bread	$52 56	Clothing	$44 79
Vegetables (mostly sauerkraut)	49 92	Furniture	7 20
Coffee	15 60	Fuel and light	12 65
Milk	12 48	Incidentals	19 28
Meats	24 96		
Groceries	49 92	Expenditures	352 47
Beer	28 25	Earnings	370 08
Rent	34 56	Surplus	17 61

No. 69. CARPENTER—COLOGNE.

Condition.—Family numbers six: Parents and four children. Occupy two rooms; poor light and bad air; rooms most meagerly furnished. The father is an industrious carpenter, gets fair wages, and condition would be better were his family not so young, and were not the mother in too feeble health to do steady work.

Diet.—Breakfast: Bread and coffee. Dinner: Soup, soup meat, potatoes or cabbage, bread and beer. Occasionally, instead of soup, bacon or sausage. At 4 o'clock, lunch of bread and beer. Supper: Rye bread and beer.

Earnings of the father	$268 32
Earnings of the mother	31 20
Total	299 52

Cost of Living.

Bread	$51 10	Rent	$28 80
Coffee and chicory	13 52	Clothing	36 50
Milk	15 60	Incidentals	20 08
Eggs	6 24		
Meats	17 47	Expenditures	314 06
Potatoes, cabbage, etc.	37 44	Earnings	299 52
Groceries	34 96		
Beer	36 75	Deficit	14 54
Fuel and light	15 60		

No. 70. CARPENTER—HEIDELBERG.

Condition.—Family numbers four: Parents and two small children. Occupy one large room with window looking on street. A screen divides the room in two unequal parts; the larger part is used for living and sleeping; the smaller part is used as kind of store, where the wife sells milk, eggs, and butter. The husband is an average fairly good carpenter; could live a little better than they do, but are trying to save money to emigrate to America.

Diet.—Breakfast: Bread, milk, and coffee. Dinner: Bread, beer, potatoes or other vegetables, egg cakes, and sometimes bacon or sausage; occasionally a dumpling of some sort. Supper: Rye bread, coffee, and milk.

Earnings of father	$224 64
Income from sale of milk, eggs, etc., and from all other sources	87 60
Total	312 24

EARNINGS AND EXPENSES OF WAGE RECEIVERS IN EUROPE. 451

Cost of Living.

Rent	$18 72	Clothing	$42 50
Bread	28 03	Fuel and lights	12 22
Coffee	9 36	Incidentals	18 00
Milk	24 46		
Potatoes	16 08	Expenditures	281 41
Cabbage, onions, etc	12 84	Earnings	312 24
Meats	20 80		
Groceries	54 60	Surplus	30 83
Beer	23 80		

No. 71. BROOM MAKER—VICINITY OF HEIDELBERG.

Condition.—An old man. Lives in lodgings, paying 15 pfennigs (about 3½ cents) per night. In summer he gets up at 3.30 a. m., goes to the woods, cuts twigs which he makes into brooms and sells at 9 pfennigs apiece. By working hard he can make and sell ten brooms per day. This man is so hardened and dulled by drudgery he does not even think of a better state.

Diet.—Breakfast: Bread, coffee, and sugar. Dinner: Beer, bread, potatoes, cheese, etc. Supper: Bread, coffee, and sugar.

Earnings $68 64

Cost of Living.

Lodging	$12 16	Incidentals	$2 44
Bread	10 95		
Coffee and sugar	7 30	Expenditures	69 25
Beer	7 30	Earnings	68 64
Potatoes and sauerkraut	10 95		
Groceries	10 95	Deficit	61
Clothing	7 20		

No. 72. NAILMAKERS—VICINITY OF FRANKFORT-ON-THE-MAIN.

Condition.—Family numbers eight: Parents, boy aged 15, boy aged 14, and four children from 4 to 12 years of age. Occupy one close, unventilated room in a miserable, ill-smelling house. At night straw mattresses are spread on the floor. General condition is one of abject poverty. Hours of labor vary from thirteen to fourteen and even fifteen per day.

Earnings of father	$126 88
Earnings of boy of 14	50 04
Earnings of all other members of family	59 28
Total	236 10

Cost of Living.

Bread	$85 78	Fuel and incidentals	$9 00
Potatoes and cabbage	31 02		
Coffee and milk	25 51	Expenditures	241 75
Meats	10 95	Earnings	236 10
Groceries and beer	45 36		
Rent	14 88	Deficit	5 65
Clothing	19 25		

No. 73. MINER—SALZBURG, AUSTRIA, NEAR BAVARIAN FRONTIER.

Condition.—Family numbers three: Parents and baby. Live in one room in tenement house, in village not far from salt mines. The father works in six-hour shifts, earning per shift on an average of 50 to 60 kreutzers (20 to 24 cents). The mother works a little on hand loom, weaving, but much of her time she has to attend to the house and baby.

Diet.—Breakfast: Black bread and coffee. Dinner: Black bread and beer, potatoes, or sometimes cabbage. Supper: Black bread and coffee or beer. Meat is seldom or never used by this family.

Earnings of father	$140 40
Earnings of mother	60 40
Total	200 80

Cost of Living.

Rent	$14 40	Light and fuel	$8 00
Bread	32 85	Incidentals	5 60
Coffee	9 12		
Milk	9 12	Expenditures	204 09
Beer	25 55	Earnings	200 80
Potatoes	18 25		
Groceries	52 40	Deficit	3 29
Clothing	28 80		

SWITZERLAND.

No. 74. MUSIC-BOX MECHANIC—GENEVA.

Condition.—Family numbers five: Parents and three small children. Occupy two rooms, one with a window looking on court. Rooms are plain and clean. The oldest child goes to school. The father and mother both work in music-box factory; father is mechanic of only ordinary skill, but is industrious and thrifty and manages to lay by money. Average earnings per day amount to $1.

Diet.—Breakfast: Bread, milk, and coffee; sometimes whey or cheese. Dinner: Rye-bread, sausage, bacon or pork, or cheese, potatoes, milk or coffee. Supper: Bread and milk or coffee; occasionally a little honey.

Earnings of father	$288 00
Earnings of mother	124 80
Total	412 80

Cost of Living.

Bread	$59 95	Fuel and lights	$16 40
Milk	29 21	School tax and books	3 25
Eggs	2 60	Soap and starch	3 18
Coffee	9 36	Incidentals	21 30
Vegetables	33 80		
Cheese	9 88	Expenditures	359 64
Groceries, beer, and wine	98 63	Earnings	412 80
Rent	31 20		
Clothing	40 88	Surplus	53 16

REMARKS.—The manufacture of music-boxes requires workmen of considerable skill. According to statements of managers of music box factories in Switzerland, an apprenticeship of from twelve to fifteen years must be undergone before a "marker," or man who marks the music on the cylinders, can be considered completely master of his trade. The apprenticeship begins very early, so that if one have the natural ability he may be a good marker at the age of 25 or 30, receiving as high wages as $2 per day.

Men who put pegs in the holes marked by the marker, and mechanics in other lines requiring no unusual skill, average from 90 cents to $1.10 per day. Three weeks of each year the workman must perform military service, camping, drilling, etc.; one week more may be counted for holidays and sickness, so that even with the strongest and most healthy, forty-eight weeks per year is a good average.

The habitation of the workman in Geneva consists generally of one or two rooms in a large tenement house. There are stores which sell meat, steaks, ham, etc., ready cooked. Cooked potatoes, peas, and sauerkraut may be purchased in the same way, and many workingmen's families, buying from these stores, do little or no cooking at their homes.

No. 75. Music-box "Marker"—Geneva.

Condition.—Family numbers seven: Parents and five children. Occupy two rooms and kitchen on third floor of tenement house. Surroundings are close and cramped, but quite up to, if not above, the average. Rooms are comfortably furnished and kept very tidy and clean. The father is a skilled workman; averages from $1.90 to $2 per day. The eldest boy, aged 15, works in music-box factory. The mother looks after the household and children; also works a little at home on watches. Four children go to school. The family dress neatly and seem thrifty.

Diet.—Breakfast: Coffee, milk, bread, and butter, sometimes honey. Dinner: Bread and butter, cabbage, potatoes, pork or bacon, or sometimes beef, wine, coffee or milk; occasionally pudding or dried fruit of some sort. Supper: Bread, milk or coffee, sometimes cheese or honey.

Earnings of father	$547 20
Earnings of son	104 00
Earnings of mother	67 40
Total	718 60

Cost of Living.

Bread	$83 95	Clothing	$61 50
Milk	32 85	Light and fuel	22 50
Coffee	14 40	Incidentals	70 00
Vegetables	38 80		
Meats	51 10	Expenditures	533 63
Cheese	9 12	Earnings	718 60
Wine	15 64		
Groceries	85 77	Surplus	184 97
Rent	48 00		

No. 76. Skilled Mechanic (Music-box Factory)—Geneva.

Condition.—Family numbers five: Parents and three children. Occupy three rooms in tenement house. The father is a first-rate mechanic; arranges the delicate mechanism of music boxes (the springs for turning cylinders, the accompaniments, as drum, flute, bells, etc.). Earns on an average $2 per day. Children go to school. The mother works in factory part time. Family dress and live better than the average.

Diet.—Breakfast: Bread and butter, cheese, coffee, and milk. Dinner: Soup, soup meat, sometimes beef or mutton, ham, bacon or pork, potatoes, bread, and wine; on

Sundays dessert of pudding and fruit. Supper: Bread and butter, coffee or milk; sometimes dried fruit, cheese, potatoes left over from dinner, etc.

Earnings of father	$576 00
Earnings of mother	124 80
Total	700 80

Cost of Living.

Bread and flour	$74 82	Light and fuel	$19 75
Milk	25 55	Rent	46 80
Coffee	14 60	School fees	7 25
Vegetables	36 50	Incidentals	36 10
Meats	43 80		
Cheese	10 95	Expenditures	492 07
Wine	22 40	Earnings	700 80
Groceries	76 65		
Clothing	76 90	Surplus	208 73

No. 77. ORDINARY MECHANIC (MUSIC-BOX FACTORY)—GENEVA.

Condition.—Family numbers six: Parents and four children, the oldest 8 years. Occupy one room and small kitchen in tenement house; not well furnished. Family dress and live only passably. Parents both work in music-box factory.

Diet.—Breakfast: Bread, coffee, and milk. Dinner: Bread, cheese, potatoes, sometimes salt pork or sausage, whey, wine. Supper: Bread, coffee—occasionally cheese, whey, or potatoes.

Earnings of father	$192 40
Earnings of mother	156 00
Total	348 40

Cost of Living.

Bread	$67 52	Fuel and lights	$12 50
Milk	23 72	School and other taxes	6 25
Coffee	10 95	Incidentals	33 40
Vegetables	29 20		
Meats and cheese	32 85	Expenditures	366 43
Wine	12 77	Earnings	348 40
Groceries	66 57		
Rent	31 20	Deficit	18 03
Clothing	39 50		

No. 78. WATCHMAKER—GENEVA.

Condition.—Single man, aged about 30. Boards in tenement house. The room has window looking on street, but is low, dingy, and uninviting. Man is good ordinary mechanic, averages about 80 cents per working day.

Diet.—Breakfast: Bread and coffee. Dinner: Soup, soup meat or sausage, potatoes, bread and butter, wine, beer, or coffee. Supper: Bread, cheese, milk, or coffee.

Earnings	$230 40

Cost of Living.

Board	$109 20	Expenditures	$194 85
Wine, spirits, and tobacco	31 20	Earnings	230 40
Clothing	29 75		
Incidentals, etc	24 70	Surplus	35 55

No. 79. AGRICULTURAL LABORER—DISTRICT BETWEEN VEVAY AND MARTIGNY.

Condition.—Family numbers eight: Parents, and six children from 3 to 15 years of age. Occupy small chalet or cottage of four rooms. Surroundings are clean and comfortable, although the house is rather small for size of family. Have three cows and a small flock of sheep. Girl of 15 watches the cows and knits socks for self and brothers. A small garden is planted with a few vegetables, and flax and hemp. The mother spins and weaves, makes cheeses, and performs general household work. The father cultivates farm, raising rye and oats and some tobacco.

Diet.—Breakfast: Rye bread, milk, honey. Dinner: Rye bread, potatoes, milk, whey, cheese, sometimes bacon or salt pork. Supper: Rye bread, milk or coffee; occasionally eggs or cheese.

REMARKS.—The Swiss peasant frequently owns the hut and land on which he lives; while the cow, farming utensils, etc., are often only rented. The peasant is economical and temperate in most respects; his principal weakness is love of wine, beer, and tobacco, especially the latter. In the long winter evenings, when sitting around the fireside, carving in wood, or performing other indoor work, he is seldom separated from his pipe; and when watching his cows, he knits and smokes at the same time. His bill of fare rarely embraces more than rye bread, potatoes, whey, and cheese.

They make their own clothes. Around each chalet, or cottage, is a small patch of flax and hemp. They have a few sheep, and in the winter, when not carving, they spin flax, weave cloth from the wool of their sheep, and, in short, are quite independent of outside markets. In the fall, merchants from Berne and Geneva go into the mountain districts and ride from one house to another buying cheeses, which are ultimately exported to various parts of the world. Thus, at the beginning of winter the Swiss peasant has a small sum of ready money in his box, and when the deep snows and mountain storms keep him at home, he and his wife and children sit around the fire, carve wood, spin flax and wool, and do other similar indoor work.

They live simply and frugally and work very hard, but they seem to have all the necessaries of life, and with the purity of air and independence which is theirs, the Swiss peasant may, on the whole, be considered to be in a superior condition to the Italian, German, or other European peasant. It is impossible to estimate in dollars and cents the earnings of this class of labor. They keep no account of the amount of the produce of the farm, and this much only can be stated with certainty: that the rye bread, milk, whey, cheese, potatoes, and other vegetables, which form their chief diet, are entirely, or almost entirely, produced by the farmer at home; that the greater part of the clothing is home spun and home woven; and that the sale of cheeses and wood carvings balances and sometimes a little more than balances the expenditures for taxes, rent, school fees, and general incidentals.

These remarks should be understood as applying mainly to that portion of the agricultural class either slightly or considerably removed from towns and railroads.

No 80. ITINERANT COBBLER.

Condition.—A Single man. He goes about from one farm house to another, takes the old cowhides that have been laid aside waiting his arrival and converts them into rough shoes and leggings, for which work he gets his lodgings, meals, and about 15 cents per day in money.

Earnings, board and lodging estimated at 15 cents per day, $1.05 per week	$54 60
Two hundred and ninety days, at 15 cents	42 50
Total	97 10

456   REPORT OF THE COMMISSIONER OF LABOR.

Cost of Living.

Food	$54 60	Incidentals	$5 34
Rent and lodging gratis			
Clothing	17 26	Expenditures	97 10
Tobacco and other luxuries	19 90	Earnings	97 10

No. 81. FEMALE CIGARETTE MAKERS—ZÜRICH.

Condition.—Family consists of two, an old maid and her mother. Occupy one room on fourth floor of tenement house; room is clean and neat; plainly though comfortably furnished; both mother and daughter work at home making cigarettes; earn together on an average 3½ francs, or 70 cents, per day of twelve hours.

Diet.—Breakfast: Bread and coffee; occasionally cheese or eggs. Dinner: Soup, soup meat, potatoes, bread, and beer or coffee. Supper: Bread and butter, coffee, or milk; sometimes potatoes warmed over from dinner.

Earnings of mother and daughter $218 40

Cost of Living.

Bread and flour	$27 37	Clothing	$29 60
Milk	9 12	Fuel and light	8 12
Coffee	7 03	Incidentals	13 29
Vegetables	10 95		
Cheese	9 12	Expenditures	212 27
Meats	16 42	Earnings	218 40
Wine, beer, etc	14 60		
Groceries	47 45	Surplus	6 13
Rent	19 20		

No. 82. OPERATIVES IN SILK-RIBBON MANUFACTORY—ZÜRICH.

Condition.—Family numbers eight: Parents, husband's mother, five children, the oldest 14 years of age. Occupy three rooms in tenement house, not very pleasantly situated. Two rooms are used for sleeping; the third room serves as kitchen, dining and living room. Parents and eldest daughter work in silk mills. The husband's mother cooks, washes, and attends to the children.

Diet.—Breakfast: Bread, coffee, and milk. Dinner: Soup, soup meat, or occasionally sausage, potatoes or cabbage, bread and beer, sometimes wine. Supper: Bread, coffee, occasionally cheese, or egg cakes.

Earnings of father	$208 00
Earnings of mother	145 60
Earnings of girl, aged 14	62 30
Total	415 90

Cost of Living.

Bread and flour	$91 25	Clothing	$47 60
Milk	29 29	Light and fuel	13 00
Coffee	16 02	Incidentals	15 25
Bacon	3 30		
Meats and cheese	24 51	Expenditures	423 13
Vegetables	26 66	Earnings	415 90
Groceries	76 65		
Beer, wine, and tobacco	48 40	Deficit	7 23
Rent	31 20		

APPENDIX C.

SYNOPSIS OF LABOR LEGISLATION IN THE UNITED STATES.

CALIFORNIA.

Title 15, chapter 1, section 651, paragraph 13651, Code of 1876, provides that persons employing minor children as wards or apprentices shall not work them over eight hours a day except in vinicultural or horticultural pursuits.

Title 7, chapter 10, section and paragraph 3244, provides that eight hours are a legal day's work in the absence of a special contract. The next section forbids such special contract in all work done for the state.

By Acts of March 13, 1872 (Acts of 1871-72, p. 413), and March 27, 1874 (Acts of 1873-74, p. 726), constituting paragraphs 15638 to 15642, Code of 1876, laws were passed for the protection of the health and lives of minors similar in detail to those of other states herein more fully set forth.

COLORADO.

Employers of females in manufacturing, mechanical, or mercantile establishments must provide suitable seats for their use when not engaged in the active duties of their employment, under a penalty of from $10 to $30 for each offense. (Act of April 2, 1885; Laws of 1885, p. 297.)

Owners or agents of coal mines employing ten or more men must make map or plan showing workings of mine, not over 100 feet to the inch, and showing also the general inclination of the strata and the boundary lines, map to be kept at mine office in the county where the mine is situated, and a copy must be filed with the mine inspector. Map must be kept up every three months, and by January 10 in each year the workings of the mine up to the close of the preceding December, so that the inspector can mark the changes on his map. If owner or agent neglect to make map or correction, or inspector believe either to be incorrect, he may have work done at owner's expense, but at his own, if owner's map or correction be accurate. Six months after passage of act, unlawful to employ in mines where 15,000 square yards have been excavated more than fifteen workers, except in opening shafts or outlets, unless there are two separate outlets to every seam separated by natural strata, not less than 100 feet in breadth, by which distinct means of ingress and egress are always available, air shafts in which there are ladder ways being considered as escape shafts. Both outlets need not belong to the same mine, and the second need not be made until 15,000 square yards are excavated.

To all other mines worked by shafts, slopes, or drifts there must be two openings twelve months after 15,000 square yards are excavated, but two need not be provided where there are not more than fifteen persons at work at once. Where owner has not sufficient land for second outlet he may condemn adjoining land by direction of the proper court. Communication with contiguous mines must be constructed in connection with every vein or stratum of coal worked. When human voice cannot be heard throughout mine, owner must maintain metal tube from top to bottom of slope or shaft, or a telephone, so that conversation may be had all over the mine. The top of the shaft must have an approved safety gate and catch, and a cover overhead on every carriage for persons, and sufficient flanges or horns on the sides of every drum of machines, as well as adequate brakes. The main link of the swivel must be of wire rope, of the best quality of iron, and tested by weights satisfactory to the inspector. There must be bridle chains to the main link for the cross-pieces of the carriage. No single chain can be used for the hoisting or lowering of persons, and not more than five persons for each ton of capacity of the machine can be hoisted or lowered.

In mines operated by shaft, slope, or drift there must be ventilation of not less than 100 cubic feet, and such additional number of cubic feet as may be ordered by the mine inspector, per minute per person employed, and also an amount of ventilation of not less than 500 cubic feet per minute for each horse or mule used, which shall be circulated throughout the mine so as to drive away or render harmless noxious gases from working-places. Airways are to be driven when the mine inspector orders, and all except those made last near working places must be closed up air-tight so that air currents may sweep into the interior of the mine. Mines must be provided with artificial means of producing ventilation by fanning, suction fans, exhaust steam furnaces, and other appliances so as to keep an abundant supply of air. If furnace be used, the upcast must be lined with incombustible material. Mines generating firedamp must be kept free from combustible material, and their working places must be examined every morning by a competent person with a safety lamp before miners are allowed to enter. Doors must be so hung that they will not stay open.

There must be employed a "mining boss," whose duty is to exercise supervision over the interior of the mine; to see that the miners advance their excavations, that all loose coal, slate, and rock are made secure, and that for the purpose a sufficient amount of timber of suitable length and size is placed in the working places of the mine; to measure ventilation once a week at the inlet and outlet and at or near faces of all entries; results to be noted on blanks furnished by the mine inspector, to be sent him once a month, and copies to be filed in mine office subject to the inspection of the miners. Competent engineers must be employed. No person shall ride on loaded wagon in any shaft or slope.

No young person under 12 years of age, or woman or girl of any age shall be permitted to enter any coal mine to work therein, nor any minor under the age of 16 years, unless he can read and write. Safety lamps in mines must belong to the immediate proprietor. All boilers must be provided with proper steam and water gauges and safety valves. All underground self-acting planes or gangways on which cars or persons are moved must have proper wires signalling between the ends of the planes and the stopping places. There must be sufficient places of refuge at the sides not more than fifty feet apart; also a travelling way cut in the side of the hoisting shaft at the bottom sufficiently high and wide for persons to pass the shaft without going over or under the cage or hoisting apparatus.

If loss of life or personal injury occur by explosion or accident, the owner or agent must notify the mine inspector and, if death has happened, the coroner of the county. The mine inspector must visit the mine, render all necessary assistance to insure safety for the men, and file coroner's testimony and such other as he may see fit to take, as a record in his office.

Miners and land owners shall have at all proper times access to and examination of the scales, machinery, and apparatus, to determine the quantity of coal mined and to test the machinery, and they may designate competent persons to have access to the mines and machinery at all proper times, and to see the weights and measures of all coal mined and the accounts as kept. There shall be only one representative for the owners and but two for the miners, the latter being appointed once a month, to inspect mines and machinery and measure ventilating current. Owners may accompany miners or their agents, and they must afford every facility for investigation, while the miners must not interrupt ordinary work. Miners or other workmen wilfully injuring shafts, lamps, instruments, air courses, or brattices, or obstructing or throwing open airways, or opening and not closing doors, or carrying matches or lighted pipes where safety lamps are used, or handling or disturbing machinery, or entering any place against caution, or wilfully neglecting or refusing to securely prop roof of working place, or disobeying any proper order, or doing any other act endangering the lives or health of persons or the security of mines or machinery, are guilty of a misdemeanor punishable by fine of from $25 to $200, or by imprisonment of from thirty days to one year in the county jail.

Upon application to the proper court, owners or agents of mines who employ more than twelve miners underground during each twenty-four hours may be enjoined from work until the statute is complied with, and this remedy is cumulative.

The owner, agent, lessee, or operator of mines is liable in direct damages to person on account of a violation of the statute, and in case of death to the injured party the widow or lineal heirs may equally as well bring suit. This act does not apply to mines employing not more than twelve persons, but upon application of owner or miners, or when mine inspector deems it necessary, the latter may make suitable regulations for such mines. Four months after passage of act, judges of district courts are to appoint four reputable coal miners and the governor one practical engineer, to constitute a board of examiners to inquire into the character and qualifications of candidates for mine inspector. The first meeting of the board was at Denver, July 20, 1883, when they certified to the governor all candidates approved by four of their number. Such candidates must be citizens of the United States, of temperate habits, 30 years of age, one year's experience in Colorado coal mines, five years' experience in United States mines, and a practical knowledge of mining engineering and the different systems of working and ventilating mines, and the nature and properties of noxious and poisonous gases, especially firedamp. From the number certified the governor selects a mine inspector for four years, at a salary of $2,000 a year, who must reside in the state and keep his office at the capital, and who may be reappointed. A vacancy must be filled from the other names sent up, and the board of examiners, themselves newly appointed by the district judges, keep the lists of candidates full.

The inspector qualifies by taking oath of office and giving a $5,000 bond, but no person can be an inspector who is a manager or agent of a mine or a mining engineer for any company, or interested in operating any mine. The inspector shall devote his whole time to his duties, shall examine once a quarter mines in which more than twenty men work, to see that the statute is carried out, and he may visit any coal mine and its works and machinery at all reasonable times, day or night, but not to unnecessarily obstruct or impede its working. The owner must furnish necessary means for inspection, of which the inspector makes an office record, showing the number of mines, their development, number of persons employed, the extent to which the law is obeyed, the progress in the improvements sought to be effected by the law, the number of accidents and deaths from injuries, the output of coal and development made annually, with all facts concerning the production and transportation of coal to market, etc., the record to be filed on or before the first Monday in November preceding the biennial meeting of the legislature, in the office of the secretary of state, who must include it in his biennial report.

The owner or agent of a mine working ten or more men close to an abandoned mine containing inflammable gas or firedamp must bore holes twelve feet in advance of the coal face of the working places, and, when directed by the mine inspector, on both sides. The mining boss or other competent person must examine mine daily and make a record in a book kept at the mine. The fire boss must make a daily record of defects in ventilating apparatus and any standing gas, designating entry and room in which gas is found, which record is open at all times for examination by the inspector and miners.

Persons violating act are guilty of a misdemeanor, punishable by fine from $100 to $500. (Chapter 16, General Statutes: act of February 24, 1883, Acts of 1883, p. 106; act of April 8, 1885, Acts of 1885, p. 134.)

Chapter 15, section 12, General Statutes of 1877, provided that children under 14 years of age should not work in coal mines. Owners, etc., violating statute were liable to a fine of from $100 to $500.

CONNECTICUT.

No child under 14 years of age who has resided in the United States nine months can be employed at labor unless he has attended a public or other day school in which instruction is regularly given in the branches of education required in public schools during twelve weeks or sixty full school days of the twelve months next preceding the month in which the child is employed, nor unless six weeks' attendance has been consecutive. Any person employing such a child contrary to law is liable to a fine not exceeding $60.

Parent or guardian of child under 14 years of age must furnish employer with a certificate signed by teacher, school visitor, or committee of school, showing lawful school attendance of minor. Employer must require certificate, keep it while the child is employed, and show it during business hours to school visitor or secretary or agent of the state board of education, and the certificate is evidence. Parent or controller of child falsifying as to age or residence in the United States, or instructing child to make false statements, may be fined as much as $7 or imprisoned as many as thirty days. (Laws of 1882, chapter 80, p. 162.)

Every story above the second story, not including the basement, in any workshop, manufactory, hotel, or building occupied on such story as assembly or lodge room by any literary, benevolent, or other society, or boarding house accommodating over twelve lodgers, or tenement house arranged for or occupied by more than five families, must be provided, within six months, with more than one way of egress by stairways on the inside or fire escapes on the outside of the building, and such stairways and fire escapes shall be kept free from obstruction and accessible from each room in said story. It is the duty of first selectman of town, or fire marshal of city, or warden of borough, in which such buildings are situated, to examine same and give certificates if they be lawfully equipped. Violation of statute by owner subjects him to $50 fine. (Laws of 1883, chapter 120, p. 305; act of May 3, 1883, repealing chapter 72, Laws of 1881, p. 39.)

Parent or controller of child between 8 and 16 years of age, of good physical and mental condition, must cause child to attend school, while school is in session, in the district of its residence. This does not apply to children under 14 who have attended school twelve weeks of the preceding twelve months, according to chapter 80, Acts of 1882, and children over 14 not subject when properly employed at labor at home or elsewhere. (Act of April 16, 1885, chapter 90, Laws of 1885, p. 456.)

Persons or corporations employing laborers and requiring from them, under penalty of a forfeiture of a part of the wages earned by them, a notice of intention to leave such employment, are liable to the payment of a like forfeiture, to be recovered in an action on this statute, if employés are discharged without similar notice, except for incapacity or misconduct, or in case of a general suspension of labor by the employer. (Act of April 10, 1885, chapter 72, Laws of 1885, p. 445.)

No person in charge of any mechanical or manufacturing business or establishment can employ or suffer to be employed any minor under 15 years of age more than ten hours a day or fifty-eight hours a week. Violation subjects offender to a forfeit of $50, half to complainant and half to the town. Parent or guardian compelling or permitting employment liable to a fine of $10. Eight hours' work in any day lawful day's labor, unless otherwise agreed. (Title 14, chapter 6, sections 9 and 10, General Statutes of 1875, p. 194, enacted in 1867.)

By General Statutes of 1875, p. 127, it is provided that school visitors of towns must examine, once or more every year, the condition of children employed in factories to see if the law relating to such employment is complied with, and report violations to grand jurors.

DAKOTA.

Every person who, by force, threats, or intimidation, prevents or attempts to prevent any employé from continuing in employment or from accepting employment, or induces employé to quit work or to return any work before it is finished, is guilty of a misdemeanor, punishable by a fine up to $500 or imprisonment up to one year, or both. Every person intimidating employers and preventing them from hiring any person or compelling such hiring, or forcing them to alter their ways of doing business or to increase or decrease their force, is guilty of a misdemeanor. Any two or more associating together, who enter on mining property or, being near enough to be heard, use threats, gestures, etc., to intimidate workers or those who may desire to work, are guilty of a misdemeanor and subject to imprisonment from thirty days to six months and to a fine not more than $250; the fine if not paid to be discharged by imprisonment, each day to count for $2.50. (Civil Code of 1883, including acts of 1885, sections 733, 734, and 735, pp. 1260 and 1261.)

Every owner, stockholder, overseer, employer, clerk, or foreman of any manufactory, workshop, or other place used for mechanical or manufacturing purposes who, having control, shall compel any woman or any child under 18 years of age, or permit any child under 14, to labor in any day exceeding ten hours is guilty of a misdemeanor and subject to a fine of from $10 to $100. (Ibid, section 739, p. 1261.)

DELAWARE.

Owners of buildings, now or hereafter erected, more than two stories in height, used in third or higher story, in whole or part, as factory, workshop, or tenement house, must have sufficient fire escapes from third story and those above, by stairways or ladders outside of building, or stairways in separate towers or structures, furnished with safe and easy communication with such buildings. Act not to apply to buildings already supplied with two or more independent stairways from highest to lowest story, if not nearer than sixty feet.

Duty of chief engineer of city, town, or borough, or, if no such officer, mayor or chief officer, to examine fire escapes as to suitableness and sufficiency, whether quality, location, or number, and give owner a certificate good for two years.

Owner, whether person or corporation, failing to comply punishable by fine up to $200. (Chapter 546, title 20, Laws of 1881, p. 713.)

GEORGIA.

Section 1885, Code of 1882, being act of 1853-54, p. 37, provides that hours of labor shall be from sunrise to sunset for persons under 21 in all manufacturing establishments and machine shops. The next section abolishes corporal punishment and makes owners of establishments violating liable in an action.

ILLINOIS.

All buildings of four or more stories, except exclusively private houses, must have one or more metallic ladders or stair fire escapes from near the ground to the uppermost story, with platforms near windows, the number, location, and material subject to approval of board of supervisors or board of county commissioners. All buildings over two stories used for manufacturing purposes must have at least one escape for each fifty people having working accommodations above the second story. After six months from passage of act, and upon thirty days' notice, owners must have buildings fitted up in accordance with act or be liable to fine of from $25 to $200, and $50 for each week's neglect. Buildings erected in the future must have necessary fire escapes before completion. (Act of June 29, 1885, chapter 55a, Hurd's Revised Statutes, 1885, p. 644.)

The owner, agent, or operator of coal mine must furnish upon railroad track adjoining mine a "track scale," upon which shall be weighed all coal hoisted before or at the time of loading on cars or wagons. If output does not justify purchase of "track scale," or it cannot be used, a platform scale may be substituted. A record must be kept at the owner's expense of all coal weighed, open to the inspection of miners, operators, carriers, land owners, adjacent land owners, and all others interested. The person weighing must make affidavit of true weights, a false affidavit being perjury. A record must be filed with the inspector of the district.

Miners may furnish at their own expense a check weighman to balance scales and see that coal is properly weighed, who must keep a correct account and shall have access to the beam box while the coal is being weighed. He must be a citizen of Illinois and of the county in which the mine is situated, and must make affidavit of true weights, etc., falsity therein being perjury. Owner, etc., of mine must give him a permit, not transferable, to remain in weigh room while coal is being weighed. The first violation of this statute is punishable by fine up to $50, the second by fine up to $200, the third by fine up to $500 or imprisonment up to six months, but the statute applies only to mines shipping coal by railroad or water. Mining contracts dispensing with this mode of weighing coal are void. (Acts of June 14, 1883, Laws of 1883, p. 113, and June 29, 1885, Laws of 1885, p. 221; Hurd's Revised Statutes of 1885, p. 827.)

An act providing for the health and safety of coal miners, approved May 28, 1879, slightly amended by acts of 1883 and 1885, above quoted, provides for maps, escapement shafts, ventilation, safety lamps, bore holes, signals, hoistways, examination of boilers, etc. First violation punishable by fine from $50 to $200; second, from $100 to $500. No person under 14 or female of any age permitted to work in any mine. The state is divided into five inspection districts. Upon the recommendation of a board of examiners, appointed by the bureau of labor statistics, consisting of two practical coal miners, two coal operators, and one mining engineer, the governor shall appoint an inspector of coal mines for each district for two years, who must have a practical mining experience of ten years, be 30 years old, and not interested in any mine. He shall give a $5,000 bond, have a salary of $1,800 a year, must make a personal examination of each mine in his district, and make an annual report to the bureau of labor statistics. Upon complaint of three coal operators or ten coal miners, the bureau of labor statistics may, on fifteen days' notice to him, investigate each inspector, and, if advisable, remove him. Board of examiners must make additional recommendations whenever notified by bureau. Miners must use copper needles in preparing blasts, and not less than nine inches of copper on the iron bars used for tamping blasts of powder. Engine and boiler houses to be roofed and sided with fire-proof material in mines hoisting coal by steam power, where no other means of ingress and egress are provided. (Hurd's Revised Statutes of 1885, p. 820.)

Eight hours a legal day's labor in all mechanical employments, except on farms and when otherwise agreed; does not apply to service by day, week, or month, or prevent contracts for longer hours. (Act of March 5, 1867; Hurd's Revised Statutes, chapter 48, p. 592.)

INDIANA.

Owner, agent, overseer, or foreman of any cotton or woollen factory employing or permitting to be employed any person, male or female, under the age of 18 years in such factory for a longer period than ten hours in any day, shall be fined from $50 to $100. (Revised Statutes of 1881, section 2125.)

Whoever, by threats, intimidation, or force, prevents or seeks to prevent any person from doing work for or furnishing materials to any other person, firm, or corporation engaged in any lawful business shall be liable to a fine of from $20 to $100, to which may be added imprisonment in the county jail from ten days to six months. Whoever unlawfully, by threats, intimidation, or force, prevents or attempts to prevent any railroad company or its agents, servants, and employés from moving, running, and operating locomotives, cars, and trains of such railroad, or from transporting or carrying passengers and freight on its line of road, or attempts to or does prevent any express company, common carrier, or person engaged in transporting or carrying passengers or freight for hire, from so transporting or carrying either passengers or freight, shall be fined from $50 to $1,000, to which may be added imprisonment in the state's prison from two to twenty-one years, and such offender shall be disfranchised and rendered incapable of holding any office of trust or profit for any determinate period. (Ibid, sections 2126 and 2127.)

At the request of a mine owner, miner, or other person interested in a coal mine, the mine inspector must have map made on a scale not less than one inch to 100 feet, to be certified to by him and kept in his office. The governor, with the advice of the senate, must appoint a mine inspector for two years, who must be a resident and practical miner, not pecuniarily interested in any mine in Indiana, and shall take oath of office and give bond in the sum of $1,000. He shall have his office in the central part of the mining district and receive a salary of $1,500 a year. This act is not to apply to mines employing less than ten men. The inspector must examine scales, and, if they be incorrect, notify owner or agent. The user of incorrect scales, after notice, is liable to a fine of from $10 to $100 for each day's use. (Ibid, sections 5460, 5473, and 5474, act of March 5, 1881.)

No boy under 14 years of age can be employed in any mine. Violation punishable by fine up to $500, but act not to apply to mines employing less than ten men. (Ibid, section 5477.)

Mine inspector must examine all scales in coal mines, which must be tested by sealed weights furnished by the state auditor. Using false scales is punishable by fine of from $10 to $100 a day. When coal mining is paid by weight, miners have a right to a check weighman in the weigh office, who shall inspect the weighing and be selected and paid by them. (Ibid, section 6794, amending section 5480; act of March 3, 1883, chapter 59, Laws of 1883, p. 1692.)

Ropes used for hoisting and lowering in coal mines must be of wire, and shall be examined every morning before the miners descend. When gas is known to exist a competent fire boss must be at the bottom of every mine each day to inform each man of the state of his room or entry, and every such mine must be examined every morning by a competent person with a safety lamp before miners are allowed to enter. (Ibid, section 6793.)

Companies, corporations, or associations shall be required, in the absence of a written contract to the contrary, to settle with and pay their employés, engaged in mechanical or manual labor, in money at least once a month. Employés, in case of refusal so to pay, may demand such payment from their employers, who, if they then neglect to pay for thirty days thereafter, are liable in a suit by employés for the amount due, reasonable attorney's fees, and a penalty of $1 a day for each succeeding day: *Provided*, That such penalty shall not exceed twice the amount due and withheld. (Laws of 1885, chapter 21, p. 36.)

Owners, agents, or operators of coal mines not to allow more than ten persons to work in any mine, shaft, slope, or drift, in every twenty-four hours, after 5,000 square yards have been excavated, until a second outlet is made, which must be separated from hoisting shaft by at least 100 feet of natural strata and be accessible to employés at all times.

Stairways, at an angle of not more than 65°, must be provided for every shaft used as a manway, with landings at convenient distances, and guard rails from top to bottom.

Gangways to outlet shall be at least four feet high and three wide, and shall be kept as free from water as average hauling roads. Water from the surface or from strata must be so conducted as not to wet persons on stairway or shaft.

Breaks through, or airways, shall be made in every room at least every seventy-five feet, and all except those made near working faces shall be made air-tight by brattice, trap doors, or otherwise. Doors used in assisting ventilation must be so adjusted as to close themselves and not stand open, and no person must prop them open.

Air courses must be driven adjoining entries and as nearly parallel thereto as possible, not to exceed such width as will render them safe, with a sufficient pillar of coal between them to secure the roof.

Owners, agents, or operators must keep a sufficient supply of timber at mines and deliver props and timbers of proper lengths to the rooms of the workmen when needed.

Approved safety catches shall be attached to every cage used for carrying persons.

Miners' bosses must visit their miners in their working places at least once every day, where between ten and fifty are employed, and once in two days where more than fifty.

Violations of act punishable by fine of from $10 to $500. (Laws of 1885, chapter 34, p. 65.)

Children under 12 years of age are not to be employed in the business of manufacturing iron, steel, nails, metals, machinery, or tobacco. Children under 12 years of age must not be employed over eight hours a day by those permitted by law to employ them. Violation is punishable by fine of from $10 to $100. (Laws of 1885, chapter 88, p. 219.)

No railroad company shall exact from its employés without their written consent in each case any portion of their wages for any hospital, reading room, library, gymnasium, or restaurant.

Officer of company violating act publishable by fine of from $100 to $500. (Laws of 1885, chapter 31, p. 123.)

IOWA.

This state has a law relative to mine inspections and the appointment and duties of a mine inspector similar to that in force in Colorado. The mine inspector has a salary of $1,700 annually, with not to exceed $500 annually for disbursements. He begins his term on April 1 of every odd-numbered year, and his regular reports must be filed biennially on or before August 15 in years preceding a session of the legislature. There must be in coal mines, to every seam of coal worked, two outlets separated by natural strata of not less than 100 feet in breadth. In no case shall a furnace shaft be used as an escape-shaft. All escape-shafts must have stairs at an angle of not more than 60°. No boy under 12 years of age is allowed to work, and where there is any doubt as to his age, parents or guardians must furnish affidavit. Persons violating act after notice from inspector are liable to a fine up to $500 or imprisonment up to six months. The act applies to all mines. (Act of March 18, 1884, chapter 21, Laws of 1884, p. 23; repealing act of March 30, 1880, chapter 202, Laws of 1880, p. 196).

KANSAS.

This state has a law relative to mine inspections and the appointment and duties of a mine inspector similar to that in force in Colorado. Map of mine must be revised by July 10 of each year. When a mine is abandoned or worked out the map must be corrected and a report thereof made to the inspector. The two openings must be separated by natural strata of not less than eighty feet in breadth if mine be worked by shaft or slope, and not less than fifty feet if by drift. If coal mine exceeds 100 feet in depth six months additional time shall be allowed for completing the second opening for each additional 100 feet of depth or fractional part thereof. Number of men employed in any mine limited to twenty-five until the second opening is perfected. All shafts must be case-lined or otherwise made secure, and all escapement shafts must be provided with ladders securely fastened so as to bear at least ten men, and where ladders cannot be conveniently used, other safe means for hoisting miners must be provided independent of the regular hoisting shaft or its machinery. Man holes on underground planes must not be over thirty feet apart when same are worked by machinery, and where coal is drawn by animals, or persons travel, not more than sixty feet apart.

Governor, with advice of council, appoints inspector, who must be a citizen and resident of Kansas for two years, 30 years old, at least five years in or about coal mines, with theoretical and practical knowledge; must have office near mining districts, and not be interested in operating mines; holds office for two years at a salary of $2,000 a year, with a bond for $3,000. He must examine each mine at least twice a year. Coal operators must make quarterly statements of coal mined and the number of miners and other persons employed, which are to be embodied in the annual report, on February 1 of each year, of the inspector to the governor. Violation of statute by owner, agent, lessee, or operator is a misdemeanor punishable by fine of from $100 to $1,000, or imprisonment up to twelve months, or both.

No person under 12 years of age shall be employed, and none between 12 and 16 unless the latter can read and write and show by teacher's certificate school attendance at least three months in the previous year. (Act of February 28, 1883, chapter 117, Laws of 1883, p. 172, as amended by acts of 1885, chapter 143, p. 228.)

MAINE.

Every building in which trade, manufacture, or business is carried on requiring workmen above the first story, must have fire-escapes, outside stairs, or ladders from each story, or gallery above the ground, easily accessible and to be satisfactory to the board of fire engineers, if there be an organized fire department; otherwise, to town officers. Engineers and officers may specify alterations, additions, or repairs, giving sixty days' written notice to owners, who, failing to comply, forfeit from $5 to $50 a day for each day's neglect, and they may be punished for maintaining a common nuisance, upon no other proof than the occupancy of building. The use of such building for public purposes may be forbidden by officers until compliance with order. Owner using or letting property after notice and before compliance therewith, forfeits from $20 to $50 for each offense. Officers, upon compliance, must give certificate good for one year, and occupant of building refusing to pay $2 for a certificate or to post it up in the building, forfeits $10 for each week's delay. Town officers neglecting their duty forfeit $50. Town may proceed civilly or criminally for violations. (Chapter 121, Acts of 1883, being chapter 26, Revised Statutes, p. 297.)

By chapter 82, section 43, p. 750, Revised Statutes, ten hours of actual labor is a day's work, except in monthly labor, or where a longer time is stipulated, or in agricultural employment. By chapter 48, sections 13, 14, and 15, p. 439, Revised Statutes, being acts of 1880, chapter 221, no child can be employed in a cotton or woollen factory without attending a public or private school for four months during the year preceding employment if under 12 years of age, and for three months if between 12 and 15, the necessary evidence of such schooling being a sworn teacher's certificate filed with the employer. Violation on part of employer subjects him to a fine of $100, half to informer and half to town school fund. No one under 16 years of age shall be employed over ten hours a day. Violation subjects employer to fine of $100, half to employé and half to the town.

MARYLAND.

All employers of females in Baltimore city, in mercantile or manufacturing business, shall provide seats for employés when not employed, under penalty of $150. (Chapter 35, Acts of 1882, p. 68.)

To protect the health of employés, all factories, manufacturing establishments, and workshops must be kept in cleanly condition and free from effluvia arising from drain, privy, or other nuisance; and no factories shall be so overcrowded as to be injurious to health, and they shall be well lighted and ventilated so as to render as harmless as possible gases, vapors, dust, and other impurities. Violation subjects offender to a fine of $150. (Chapter 265, Acts of 1884, p. 365.)

Any five or more engaged in the same or similar occupation, a majority being citizens of Maryland, may incorporate as a "trades union" to promote their well-being and for mutual assistance. (Chapter 267, Acts of 1884.)

An agreement or combination by two or more to do or procure to be done any act in contemplation or furtherance of a trade dispute between employers and workingmen shall not be indictable as a conspiracy if such act by one person would not be an offense. (Chapter 366, Acts of 1884.)

The employment of workingmen in the mines of Alleghany and Garrett counties shall not exceed ten hours a day, from 7 o'clock a. m., unless by special contract. (Chapter 427, Acts of 1884.)

By Chapter 125, acts of 1876, Revised Code 1878, p. 820, children under 16 years of age must not be empoyed in any manufacturing establishment over ten hours a day. Violation by employer, parent, or guardian punishable by fine up to $50.

Chapter 379, Acts of 1878, provides for arbitration between employers and employés.

MASSACHUSETTS.

Inspectors of factories and public buildings, being two or more of the district police designated by the governor, must enforce the various provisions of law relating to the inspection of buildings and the employment of women and minors in manufacturing and mercantile establishments, and for this purpose may enter all buildings used for public or manufacturing purposes, examine the methods of protection from accident, the means of escape from fire, and make investigations as to the employment of women and children. (Chapter 266, section 6, Acts of 1882; amending preceding acts.)

Openings of hoistways, hatchways, elevators, and well holes, upon every floor of a factory or mercantile or public building, shall be protected by good and sufficient trap doors or self-closing hatches and safety catches, or such other safeguards as the inspectors direct; and all due diligence shall be used to keep such trap doors closed at all times, except when in actual use by the occupant of the building having the use or control of the same. All elevator cabs or cars, whether used for freight or passengers, shall be provided with some suitable mechanical device, to be approved by the said inspectors, whereby the cars or cabs will be securely held in the event of accident to the shipper rope or hoisting machinery, or from any similar cause. (As amended, Acts of 1882, Chapter 208, section 1.)

All factories and manufacturing establishments, three or more stories in height, in which forty or more persons are employed, unless supplied with a sufficient number of tower stairways, shall be provided with sufficient fire escapes, properly constructed upon the outside thereof, and connected with the interior by doors or windows, with suitable landings at every story above the first, including the attic, if the same be used for work rooms. Fire escapes must be kept in good repair, free from obstruction. Fire escapes existing on July 1, 1877, need not be changed in accordance with this section unless change is necessary for the protection of life. Cities may by ordinance provide that the provisions of this section relating to fire escapes shall apply to all buildings, three or more stories in height, within their limits.

Every building three or more stories in height, in whole or in part used, occupied, leased, or rented for a tenement to be occupied by more than four families, or a lodging house, shall be provided with a sufficient means of escape in case of fire, to be approved by inspector of factories and buildings.

Owner, lessee, or occupant of a manufacturing establishment, factory or workshop, or owning or controlling the use of any tenement house mentioned in last section shall, for violation of any inspection law, be liable to a fine of from $50 to $500, as well as for damages suffered by an employé through such violation, but no criminal prosecution shall begin until four weeks after written notice from inspector of necessary changes has been delivered or sent by mail, and not then if changes have been made. Notice to one of a firm, or clerk, or treasurer of a corporation is sufficient to bind firm or corporation. This section is not to prohibit an injured person from bringing an action for damages.

Inspectors' authority not to extend to Boston or any other city which has officers specially appointed to enforce inspection laws.

District police detailed as inspectors, failing to perform inspection duties faithfully shall be immediately discharged from their office. (Chapter 266, sections 1, 2, 3, 4, and 5, Acts of 1882, amending preceding acts.)

No explosive or inflammable compound shall be used in any factory in such place or manner as to obstruct or render hazardous the egress of operatives in case of fire. (Chapter 137, Acts of 1881.)

Persons or corporations employing females in manufacturing, mechanical, or mercantile establishments, must provide suitable seats and permit their use by such females when not necessarily engaged in their active duties. Violations punishable by fine of from $10 to $30 for each offense. (Chapter 150, Acts of 1882.)

Municipal officers may designate time and hours and fix size and weight of bells, whistles, and gongs which employers of workmen may use for their benefit. (Chapter 84, Acts of 1883.)

The act forbidding the employment of minors under 18 years of age, and women, more than ten hours a day, except when necessary to make repairs in the machinery to insure its ordinary running, or where hours are differently apportioned for the sole purpose of making one day's work shorter, and which provides that in no case shall the week's work exceed sixty hours, is amended by making the act apply to "mechanical and mercantile" as well as "manufacturing" establishments on and after July 1, 1883. (Chapter 157, Acts of 1883; but by chapter 275, Acts of 1884, amendatory act does not apply to "mercantile" establishments.)

Inspectors of factories and public buildings, or the inspector of buildings, in Boston, believing any freight or passenger elevator unsafe, dangerous to use, or unlawfully constructed, shall put a notice of its dangerous condition upon the door prohibiting its use until made safe to their satisfaction. Removing notice, or operating elevator while notice is affixed, without consent of inspector, punishable by a fine of from $10 to $50 for each offense. (Chapter 173, Acts of 1883.)

Chapter 52, section 1, Acts of 1876, being chapter 48, section 1, of the Public Statutes, which prohibited the employment of children under 10 years of age in any manufacturing, mechanical, or mercantile establishment under a forfeiture by parent or guardian permitting such employment of from $20 to $50 for the use of the public schools, is amended by adding, subject to the same forfeiture, a clause declaring that "no child under 12 years of age shall be so employed during the hours in which the public schools are in session in the city or town in which it resides," which was to take effect July 1, 1883. (Chapter 224, Acts of 1883.)

Outside or inside doors of buildings where operatives are employed shall not be locked, bolted, or otherwise fastened during labor hours, as to prevent free egress. Owners, lessees, or occupants of such buildings, neglecting or refusing to comply with this act after five days' written notice from an inspector, forfeit from $10 to $50. Inspectors of factories and public buildings shall enforce this act. (Chapter 52, Acts of 1884.)

No minor under 18 years of age shall be employed in laboring in any mercantile establishment more than sixty hours in any one week. Employers must post in conspicuous places where such persons are employed a notice printed, stating the number of hours required, not exceeding ten in any one day. Longer employment, unless to make up lost time, is a violation of this act. Persons or corporations having in their employment persons in violation of this act, or failing to post notice, and parents or guardians permitting such employment are liable to a fine of from $50 to $100 for each offense. On trials for wrongful employment a sworn statement by minor, and his parent or guardian, made by him at the time of entering employment, as to his age, shall be *prima facie* evidence of the fact. Section 4, chapter 74, Public Statutes, as amended by chapter 157, Acts of 1883, is so far repealed as not to apply to mercantile establishments. (Chapter 275, Acts of 1884.)

Chapter 224, Acts of 1883, which amends chapter 52, section 1, Acts of 1876, being chapter 48, section 1, Public Statutes, is itself amended by forbidding the employment of children under 12 years of age "at any time during the days" instead of "during the hours" when the public schools are in session. (Chapter 222, Acts of 1885.)

Chapter 48, sections 2 to 7, Public Statutes, inclusive, provides that no child under 14 years of age shall be employed in any manufactory, mechanical or mercantile establishment, except during the vacations of the public schools, unless during the year preceding such employment he has for at least twenty weeks attended some public or private day school; nor shall such employment continue unless such child in each and every year attends school as aforesaid; and no child shall be so employed who does not present a certificate, made by or under the direction of the school committee, of his attendance at school as provided. Employers shall require and keep on file a certificate of the age and place of birth of every child under 16 years of age employed, and the amount of his school attendance during the year next preceding such employment. The penalty for employment of children contrary to these provisions is not less than $20 nor more than $50. Truant officers are obliged to visit establishments and inquire into the situation of the children employed, and may demand the names of children and the certificates of age and school attendance. Children under 14 years of age who cannot read and write are not to be employed while public schools are in session; parents or guardians permitting such employment are subject to a fine of not less than $20 nor more than $50.

Chapter 74, section 1, provides that employers requiring from employés, under penalty of forfeiture of wages earned, a notice of intention to leave employment, shall be liable to like forfeiture if employé be discharged without similar notice, except for incapacity or misconduct, unless in case of a general suspension of labor by such employers.

Sections 2 and 3 provide that whoever, by intimidation or force, prevents or seeks to prevent a person from entering into or continuing in the employment of a person or corporation, shall be punished by fine of not more than $100; and that employers are not to contract with employés for exemption from liability for injuries resulting from employers' own negligence.

Chapter 104, sections 13, 15, and 16, provides that the belting, shafting, gearing, and drums of all factories, when so placed as to be dangerous to persons employed therein while engaged in their ordinary duties, shall be as far as practicable securely guarded. No machinery, other than steam-engines, in a factory shall be cleaned while running, if objected to in writing by an inspector.

All factories shall be well ventilated and kept clean.

Every room above the second story in factories or workshops in which five or more operatives are employed shall be provided with more than one way of egress by stairways on the inside or outside of the building, and such stairways shall be, as nearly as may be practicable, at opposite ends of the room. Stairways on the outside of the building shall have suitable railed landings at each story above the first, and shall connect with each story of the building by doors or windows opening outwardly, and such doors, windows, and landings shall be kept at all times clear of obstruction. All main doors, both inside and outside, must open outwardly, and each story must be amply supplied with means for extinguishing fires.

MICHIGAN.

No child under 14 years of age shall be employed in any business unless he has attended a public or private day school, taught by a person qualified in primary branches, at least four months out of the twelve next preceding the month of employment, except in districts where there is only a three months' school. A certificate of attendance from a superintendent of school, or a school director, is sufficient if acted upon by the employer in good faith. Making a false certificate is a misdemeanor. Certificates must be deposited with the employer at the time of the employment and kept on file subject to inspection.

No child under 10 years of age shall be employed in any factory, warehouse, or workshop where goods are manufactured or prepared for manufacture.

No child or young person under 18 years of age, and no woman shall be employed over ten hours a day or sixty hours a week, and at least one hour shall be allowed in the labor period for dinner.

Persons employing females in any factory, workshop, store, or hotel, shall provide seats for them to use when not necessarily engaged in their employment. Violation of this act is a misdemeanor, punishable by a fine of $50.

Chief officer of police in cities and supervisors of towns must inspect, report, and prosecute violations, and directors of corporations wilfully violating act are each liable. This act is not to apply to penal, reformatory, or benevolent institutions. (Acts of 1885, No. 39, p. 37, amending and additional to Acts of 1883, No. 144, p. 149.)

Owner, proprietor, or lessee of a building, factory, mill, warehouse, or workshop more than two stories high, where male and female help is employed above the second story, shall provide suitable ladders or such other fire escapes as may be neccessary for the escape of employés. The board of building inspectors shall examine buildings at least once a year and report to township or village boards, or the common council of cities, who may notify in writing owner, proprietor, or lessee to provide needful alterations or additions. A refusal to alter or add subjects person refusing to a penalty of from $25 to $100 a month. (Acts of 1883, No. 170, p. 182.)

Ten hours are a legal day's work, unless there be an agreement to the contrary, in factories, workshops, salt mills, saw mills, logging, or lumber camps, booms, or drives, mines, or other places used for mechanical, manufacturing, or other purposes, where men and women are employed. Employers requiring more work shall pay per diem rates for overtime. Employers taking advantage of the poverty or misfortune of employé or one seeking employment, are guilty of a misdemeanor and liable to a fine of from $5 to $50 for each offense. This act does not apply to domestic or farm laborers. (Acts of 1885, No. 137, p. 154.)

Formation of corporations is authorized of five or more persons in the interest of trade or labor "for the improvement of their several social and material interests, the regulation of their wages, the laws and conditions of their employment, the protection of their joint and individual rights in the prosecution of their trades or industrial vocations, the collection and payment of funds for the benefit of sick, disabled members, etc., and all existing associations may become corporate." (Acts of 1885, No. 145, p. 163.)

MINNESOTA.

On all railroad lines the labor of locomotive engineers and firemen shall not exceed eighteen hours in one day, provided that no engineer or firemen shall desert his engine in case of accident or other unavoidable delay. Officer, director, superintendent, master mechanic, foreman, agent or employé compelling such labor, except as herein provided, or in cases of urgent necessity, may be fined from $25 to $100. (Acts of 1885, Chapter 206, p. 277.)

Chapter 24, Statutes of 1878, provides that children under 18 years of age and women shall not work over ten hours a day in any manufactory or workshop. Any person compelling such work is liable to a fine of from $10 to $100. In any manufacturing or mechanical business ten hours shall be a day's work in the absence of a special contract.

MISSOURI.

An act similar to the Colorado act provides for the health and safety of miners. Copy of owner's map to be deposited with the clerk of the county court where mine is situated, as well as at mine office. Map to be corrected in January. Mines employing ten or more men must have two outlets, to be completed in one year if mine be under 100 feet deep, in two years if between 100 and 200, in three years if between 200 and 300, in four years if between 300 and 500, and in five years if over 500. Where working force has been driven up to another mine the respective owners while working must keep an open roadway at least two and one-half feet high and four feet wide as a communication. Escapement shaft must be separated from main shaft by natural strata of a width at the discretion of the mine inspector. The ventilation must be at the rate of 100 cubic feet of air per man per minute, to be measured at the foot of the downcast.

No male person under 12 years of age, or female of any age, is permitted to work in a coal mine, nor is any boy under 14 years of age, unless he can read and write. Engineers employed must not be under 18 years of age. No more than twelve persons shall ride at once, and the number to ascend or descend in one cage may be from four to twelve, as the mine inspector may direct, and the rate of speed shall not exceed 500 feet a minute. Places of refuge at the sides of underground gangways must not be over twenty feet apart.

County court of county where coal mine is situated appoints qualified mining or civil engineer to be mine inspector—must be one year a resident of county, and not interested in any mine—at a bond of $500. Court fixes compensation, and may unite offices of "mining inspector" and "county engineer." The inspector must collect facts relating to mines and miners, and make an annual report to the commissioner of labor statistics and inspection. Violations of this act are punishable by fine from $50 to $200 for first offense, and $200 to $500 for subsequent offense. (Act of March 23, 1881, p. 165, as amended by Acts of 1885, p. 206.)

The owner, lessee, operator, or manager of any mine, factory, workshop, warehouse, elevator, foundry, machine shop, or other manufacturing establishment, shall not put at work, or place therein for the purpose of labor or service, more persons in any one room or place than hygienic laws will warrant with safety to the health of such persons. All such rooms or places of employment shall have sufficient ventilation to carry off all foul or impure air, and to reduce the air of such room or place of employment to the standard of fresh air as near as may be practicable. Such rooms or places shall also have a sufficient number of doors, stairways, and fire escapes for the ready egress and escape of the maximum number of employés therein, and it is the duty of the commissioner of labor statistics and inspection to include in his annual report any non-observance of the requirements and regulations which come to his knowledge, together with the facts in relation thereto and such recommendations as seem proper. Persons controlling places mentioned refusing the commissioner admission for inspection, or neglecting or refusing to furnish information, are liable to a fine of from $25 to $100. (Acts of 1883, p. 192, repealing acts of 1879, p. 174; Revised Statutes, p. 1419.)

Railroad, mining, express, telegraph, and manufacturing companies must give thirty days' notice of a reduction of wages, by posting written or printed bills specifying parties and the amount of reduction, in a conspicuous place where employés are at work, or mailing same to each employé. For a violation the injured party may recover $50 and costs. (Acts of 1885, p. 82.)

Persons or corporations engaged in manufacturing or mining are not to issue, pay out, or circulate for payment of wages of labor any order, check, memorandum, token, or evidence of indebtedness payable in whole or part otherwise than in lawful money of the United States, unless negotiable and redeemable at face value without discount, in cash or goods, at the option of the holder, at the place of business of such persons or corporations, or at the store of any other person on whom the paper is drawn where goods are kept for sale, and the issuer within thirty days from date or delivery shall redeem the same in goods at the market price or lawful money, at the option of the holder. If employers have pay days every thirty days, they are not obliged to redeem in cash until the next pay day. Violation of this act is punishable by fine from $10 to $500 for each offense. (Acts of 1885, p. 83; amending Acts of 1881, p. 73.)

Employers of females in any mercantile business must provide suitable seats for their use at or beside their counters or work benches and permit the use of such seats by such females to a reasonable extent for the preservation of their health. Violation of this act is punishable by fine not to exceed $25 for each offense; and it is the duty of the commissioner of labor statistics and inspection to see that the act is observed. (Acts of 1885, p. 150.)

It is forbidden mine owners, agents, or operators employing miners at bushel or ton rates, or other quantity, to pass output mined by miners over screen or device which takes any part from the value thereof before it has been weighed and duly credited to the employé sending it to the surface and accounted for according to legal weights. There must be a weighman at each mine, sworn to do. justice between employer and employé, and weigh output of coal as above required. He must take oath and post same in weigh-room, and a violation of its provisions is punishable by fine of from $25 to $100, or imprisonment for thirty days, or both, for each offense. Persons having or using scales for the purpose of weighing output, so arranged or constructed that fraudulent weighing can be done, or knowingly resorting to any means whereby coal is not properly weighed, may be punished by fine from $200 to $500, or imprisonment for sixty days, or both, for each offense. All contracts between operators and miners militating against this act are void, and all coal sent to the surface shall be weighed in accordance with their provisions. This act applies to the class of persons known as loaders, engaged in mines where work is done by machinery; where workmen are under contract to load coal by the bushel, ton, or any other quantity, and where settlement is had by weight, the output must be weighed in accordance with this act. (Acts of 1885, p. 207.)

When no special agreement has been made, measurements of earth work, stone masonry, brick, stonecutting, plastering, or roofing work, must be made in accordance with this act to secure a basis for payment of labor. (Acts of 1885, p. 198.)

NEBRASKA.

Employers of female help in stores, offices, or schools, to provide chairs, stools, or seats for such employés, upon which they shall be allowed to rest when their duties will permit, or when such position does not interfere with the faithful discharge of their duties. Violation forfeits $10 to $50 to employé whose health has been injured by neglect of employer to provide a suitable seat. (Acts of 1883, chapter 45; Compiled Statutes, section 245; Criminal Code, p. 808.)

Chapter 90, p. 621, Compiled Statutes, makes ten hours a day's labor, so far as it concerns laborers and mechanics.

NEW HAMPSHIRE.

Truant officers, when required by school committees and boards of education, must enforce the laws regarding children in manufacturing establishments. (Chapter 42, Laws of 1881, p. 464.)

No child under 16 years of age shall be employed in a manufacturing establishment unless he has attended a public school, or private day school taught by a person competent to teach common-school branches, at least twelve weeks during the preceding year. No child under that age can be so employed except in vacation of the schools in his district, who can not write legibly and read fluently in readers of the grade usually classed as Third Reader. (Chapter 56, Laws of 1881, p. 475; amending sections 11 and 12, Chapter 91, General Laws of 1878.)

Mayor and aldermen of cities and selectmen of towns, by themselves, or inspectors appointed by them, shall superintend and direct the construction of buildings used for factories, etc., and inspecting officers shall examine all buildings in use or hereafter erected.

If buildings be unsafe, or so managed as to be unhealthful, or not provided with suitable fire escapes, they may be closed until alterations prescribed by inspecting officers be made.

Persons using buildings after order from inspecting officers closing them (unless prescribed alterations be made), are liable to a fine up to $100, for the use of the city or town. (Chapter 94, Laws of 1883, p. 61.)

An act in amendment of section 1 of chapter 269 of the General Laws, and to aid and protect the laboring and manufacturing interests of the state, adds at the end of the section: "Nor shall any person address to any person passing along any street to, from, or about his lawful business or occupation, any offensive, derisive, or annoying word or words, or call such person by any derisive or offensive name; nor shall any person make any noise or exclamation in the presence or hearing of such person so passing with intent to deride, offend, or annoy such person, or to prevent him from pursuing his lawful business or occupation." Violation of this act is a misdemeanor. (Chapter 76, Laws of 1885, p. 274.)

Chapter 91, General Laws, section 13, p. 222, provides that persons employing in factories children under the age of 15 without certificate of necessary schooling, are liable to a fine of $20 for each offense. Chapter 187, General Laws, section 14, provides that no person shall be compelled to work more than ten hours a day, which, in the absence of a special contract, are a legal day's work. Section 15 provides that no minor under the age of 15 shall be employed more than ten hours a day in any manufacturing establishment without the written consent of parent or guardian. Employer violating may be fined $100. Chapter 21, Laws of 1879, p. 340, provides that no child under the age of ten years shall be employed by any manufacturing company under a penalty of from $20 to $100, one-half to go to the complainant and one-half to the state.

NEW JERSEY.

Employers who own or control stores for the sale of general store goods and merchandise in connection with their manufacturing or other business, shall not attempt to control their own employés or laborers in the purchase of store goods or supplies at said stores by withholding payment of wages longer than the usual time of payment, whereby employés are compelled to purchase supplies at said stores. Violation punishable by fine up to $100 and costs. (Public Laws 1881, chapter 190, p. 239.)

Employers of females in any mercantile business must provide suitable seats for their use at or beside counters or work benches where such females are employed, and must permit them to use such seats to the extent necessary for the preservation of their health. Violation is punishable by fine up to $100. (Public Laws 1882, chapter 159, p. 227.)

Corporations or persons employing females in any manufacturing, mechanical, or mercantile establishment must provide suitable seats for the use of female employés, and permit such use when such employés are not necessarily engaged in active duty. Violation is punishable by fine of from $10 to $25. (Public Laws 1884, chapter 137, p. 200.)

Persons owning, leasing, or controlling * * * factories, manufactories, or workshops of any kind in which employés or operatives to the number of thirty or more are steadily or casually at work, such factories, etc., being three or more stories high, such persons employing shall provide such buildings with safe external means of escape, so arranged that in case of fire the ground can be readily reached from the third or higher floors.

Fire inspectors must designate the number and kind of and the manner in which said external fire escapes are to be erected, and give notice of the same to such employers.

Failure or refusal to comply with notice after ninety days after receipt thereof is punishable by fine up to $300, and the violator is liable in damages for death or personal injury from fire. (Public Laws 1882, chapter 110, p. 142.)

No boy under 12 or girl under 14 years of age shall be employed in any factory, mine, workshop, or establishment where the manufacture of any kind of goods whatever is carried on. No child between 12 and 15 years of age shall be so employed unless such child has attended public day or night school, or well-recognized private school, at least five days or evenings in each week for at least twelve consecutive weeks in the twelve months next preceding employment; such attendance may be divided into two terms of six consecutive weeks each, so far as the arrangements of school terms will permit, and unless such child or his parent or guardian shall have presented to the employer a certificate, to be signed by the teacher, giving the name of the parent or guardian, the name and number of schools attended, and number of weeks' attendance: *Provided*, That if age be not known, teacher may certify to the best of his ability; and, *Provided*, That in case of orphan children, where necessity may require, the inspector may permit employment upon the application of the guardian.

This act does not apply, so far as hours of employment are concerned, to persons engaged in preserving perishable goods in fruit-canning establishments.

Governor, with advice of senate, shall appoint a "factory and workshop inspector," who must report annually to the governor by or before October 31. He shall appoint, with the governor's approval, two "deputy inspectors." His salary is $1,800 a year, with the right to travel free on railroads. The salaries of his deputies are fixed at $1,000 each annually. It is the duty of these officers to enforce this act and all laws relating to the sanitary conditions of factories and workshops, and the employment, safety, protection, and compulsory attendance at school of minors, and to institute suits in the name of the inspector. They have power to demand from physicians certificates of the physical condition of minors, and may prohibit the employment of minors who cannot obtain such certificates. They may require parents and guardians to furnish certificates from the registry of births, or an affidavit of the age of minors, false swearing in which is perjury. Employers violating act forfeit $50 for each offense, recoverable in an action of debt. Parents or guardians knowingly permitting wrongful employment forfeit $50 in an action by the inspector, execution in which to run against the person. Affidavits of parents and guardians as to age conclusive in trials against employers. Inspector or deputies finding minor working under false certificate may compel him to desist. (Public Laws of 1884, chapter 137, p. 200, supplementary to Public Laws of 1883, chapter 57, p. 59.)

It is not unlawful for any two or more persons to unite, combine, or bind themselves by oath, covenant, agreement, alliance, or otherwise, to persuade, advise, or encourage, by peaceable means, any person to enter into any combination for or against leaving or entering into the employment of any person or corporation. (Public Laws of 1883, chapter 28, p. 36.)

Manufacturers requiring from employés, under forfeiture of wages, notice of intention to quit, shall be liable to like forfeiture if they discharge employés without similar notice, unless in case of a general suspension of business.

Accidents in workshops, mines, and factories must be at once reported to workshop inspector at Trenton and city or district physician.

Belting, shafting, gearing, and drums in factories and workshops dangerous to employés to be securely guarded when possible, otherwise notice of danger to be conspicuously posted.

No minor under 18, or woman, shall clean gearing or machinery when in motion, or work between traversing part of any machine while in motion by mechanical power.

Openings of hoistways, etc., on floors in factories and mercantile buildings must be protected by trap doors, self-closing hatches, or guard rails three feet high.

Explosives or inflammable compounds not to be used so as to render hazardous egress in case of fire.

No minor under 16 employed more than ten hours a day or sixty hours a week in any manufacturing, mercantile, or mechanical establishment.

Suitable places to be provided, where females perform unclean work, for them to wash and dress, and stairways used by them must be screened.

Separate water closets for the sexes must be provided.

Inspector may have power to prohibit overcrowding in factories when he, supported by a physician's opinion, believes it to exist.

Inspector may order fan or mechanical apparatus to prevent the inhalation of dust in establishments where dust is generated by the work.

Factories and mines must be ventilated, to be as near harmless as possible.

Provision is made for the construction and ventilation of bake houses.

Workmen and others must not sleep where bread is made.

Violation of act subjects offender to a penalty of $50 for each offense in an action of debt, execution to run against the body. (Public Laws of 1885, chapter 188.)

Parents, guardians, or other persons controlling children from 12 to 16 years old, temporarily discharged from employment to receive instruction, must send them to school while so out of employment, unless excused by inspector or school board, under fine of from $10 to $25 for first offense, and a fine of $25 or imprisonment from one to three months for each subsequent offense, fines to go to the school fund.

When no school within two miles of factory or shop where child under 15 is employed, or of his residence, attendance at school temporarily approved by inspector is compliance with the law. (Public Laws of 1885, chapter 217.)

By Public Laws of 1880, chapter 138, page 170, provisions were made for the arbitration of labor disputes before an arbitrator selected by employers, another by employés, and a third by the other two. Arbitration is voluntary, but after submission the award is binding. Other legislation was adopted up to 1880, but it is mainly covered by subsequent enactments.

NEW MEXICO TERRITORY.

An act similar to the Colorado act provides for the safety and health of miners and the inspection of coal mines. There must be at least two shafts, slopes, or outlets separated by natural strata of 150 feet in breadth.

The amount of ventilation required is not less than fifty-five cubic feet per second of pure air, or 3,300 feet per minute, for every fifty men working, and as much more as circumstances may require.

There is no mine inspector, but his duties are performed by an inside overseer for every mine, appointed by the owner or agent thereof. Any neglect on the part of the overseer wilfully is a misdemeanor, and if death ensue he is guilty of manslaughter. (Compiled Laws of 1884, sections 1575 to 1585, inclusive; Laws of 1882, chapter 57.)

By Compiled Laws of 1884, section 1568, Laws of 1876, chapter 38, it is provided that in estimating the worth of labor required to be performed upon any mining claims to hold the same by the laws of the United States, in the regulation of mines, the value of a day's labor is fixed at $4, provided that in the sense of this statute eight hours of labor actually performed upon a mining claim shall constitute a day's labor.

NEW YORK.

Employers of females in any mercantile or manufacturing business or occupation must provide and maintain suitable seats for the use of such female employés to such an extent as may be reasonable for the preservation of their health. Violation is a misdemeanor. (Revised Statutes, p. 1089; Laws of 1881, chapter 298.)

No conspiracy is punishable criminally unless it is one of those enumerated in the last two sections, and the orderly and peaceable assembling or coöperation of persons employed in any calling, trade, or handicraft for the purpose of obtaining an advance in the rate of wages, or compensation, or of maintaining such rate is not a conspiracy. (Laws of 1882, chapter 384, amending section 170, Penal Code.)

Nothing in this code shall be so construed as to prevent any person from demanding an increase of wages, or from assembling and using all lawful means to induce employers to pay such wages to all persons employed by them as shall be a just and fair compensation for services rendered. (Laws of 1882, chapter 384, amending section 675, Penal Code.)

The manufacture of cigars or the preparation of tobacco in any form on any floor or in any part of any floor in any tenement house is forbidden in cities having over 500,000 population, if such floor, or any part of such floor, be by any person occupied as a home or residence for the purpose of living, sleeping, cooking, or doing any household work therein.

Any house, building, or portion thereof occupied as the home or residence of more than three families living independently of one another, and doing their own cooking upon the premises, is a tenement house.

The first floor, if cigars or tobacco be there sold, is exempt from the provisions of this act.

Violation of act is a misdemeanor punishable by fine of from $10 to $100, or by imprisonment from ten days to six months, or both. (Laws of 1884, chapter 272, superceding Laws of 1883, chapter 93.)

A person employing or directing another to perform labor in the erection, repairing, altering, or painting of any house, or building, or other structure, who shall knowingly or negligently furnish and erect, or cause to be furnished for erection, for or in the performance of such labor, such unsuitable or improper scaffolding, hoists, stays, ladders, or other mechanical contrivances as will not give proper protection to the life and limb of any person so employed, is guilty of a misdemeanor and may be fined up to $500, or be imprisoned from thirty days to six months, or both. (Laws of 1885, chapter 314).

By Revised Statutes, page 2354, Laws of 1870, chapter 385, it is provided that eight hours shall be a day's work for mechanics, workingmen, and laborers, except in farm or domestic labor, but overwork for extra pay is permitted. This act applies to those employed by the state or municipality, or employed by persons contracting for state work. Violation of act by officers subjects them to removal, and violation or evasion by contractors is punishable by fine of from $100 to $500, and, at option of the state, a forfeiture of the contract.

By Revised Statutes, page 1206, Laws of 1874, chapter 421, no child of less than 14 years of age shall be employed during school hours, unless such child has attended a public or private day school or been satisfactorily instructed at home for fourteen of the preceding fifty-two weeks of every year. The usual certificate of attendance is provided for, and a fine of $50 is made the penalty for each violation of the act.

OHIO.

It is the duty of the owners or agents of factories or workshops, if more than two stories high, to provide convenient exits from the different upper stories, easily accessible in case of fire. Mayors of cities or villages must require owners or agents of such factories or workshops to provide such exits within sixty days after receipt of written notice from them.

Owners or agents refusing compliance with such notice forfeit from $50 to $300 a month, recoverable by action for the use of the city or village where building is situated.

Mayors, or chiefs, or other heads of police, as inspectors of fire escapes, must examine buildings covered by this act once a year and report to city councils. (Laws of 1883, p. 187, amending sections 2573, 2574, and 2575 of the Revised Statutes.)

An act similar to the Colorado act provides for the inspection of mines. The following is the legislation thereon since 1880:

All safety lamps in coal mines must be property of mine owner and in charge of mine agent; in all mines doors used for assisting ventilation must shut of their own accord and not be able to stand open; mining boss must keep careful watch over ventilation and measure it once a week at the inlets, outlets, and faces of all entries; measurements must be recorded and furnished mine inspector monthly. (Laws of 1881, p. 80, amending section 301, Revised Statutes.)

Miners and land owners shall have access to mines and examine machinery and scales and apparatus to test their accuracy; may designate persons, one for each, to see weights, measures, and accounts; and miners may appoint two of their number to inspect once a month mines and machinery and measure ventilating current; owners shall afford every facility, and committee must report within ten days to mine inspector. (Laws of 1881, p. 129, amending section 305, Revised Statutes.)

Ventilation of all coal mines shall be not less than 100 cubic feet per minute, per person employed, so circulated as to render harmless gas in working places, and no working place shall be driven more than 120 feet in advance of a break-through, all which, except those last made, shall be closed up air tight, so that air currents shall sweep through the mine; artificial means of producing ventilation must be provided, such as suction fans, exhaust-steam furnaces, etc.; mines generating firedamp must be kept free from standing gas and examined every morning by competent persons with safety lamps before workmen are allowed to enter. (Laws of 1881, page 148, amending section 298, Revised Statutes.)

Owners or agents of mines having excavation 15,000 yards wide must make map, 200 feet to the inch, showing actual condition of mines, lines of adjoining lands and names of owners, to be annually improved to show changes of condition during preceding year, or semi-annually when mine inspector directs; map to be kept at mine office and a copy filed, when requested by inspector, at Columbus; inspector makes map at owner's cost when owner refuses; owner refusing, after sixty days' notice from inspector may be fined $5 a day until map or addition is made; when mines are exhausted or abandoned, maps must be made, before pillars are drawn, showing the last workings, to be filed with the county recorder within ninety days, with sworn certificate of its correctness from engineer making map and mining boss. (Laws of 1883, p. 57, amending section 296, Revised Statutes).

The state is divided into three mining districts, governor to appoint a chief inspector for four years at $5,000 bond, and the latter three district inspectors for three years at $2,000 bond. Chief must have knowledge of chemistry, mineralogy, and the geology of Ohio, so far as such knowledge relates to mining, and a practical knowledge of mining engineering, the different systems of working and ventilating mines, and the nature and property of noxious gases. Inspectors must give their whole time to their duties, examine the condition of all mines as often as possible, and make a record of the date of examination, condition of mines, extent to which laws are observed, progress in improvement, and in security of life and health sought to be secured by this chapter, number of accidents, injuries received, and deaths. Loss of life occurring, inspector and coroner hold inquest. Former files record monthly and has free access to mines. Chief inspector makes rules and regulations and annual reports to the governor; has office in statehouse, and keeps maps and plans of all mines in the state, and records of his work. District inspector has office in the central part of the district, and keeps maps and records. Where the voice cannot be heard throughout mine the owner must provide a metal speaking tube to carry sound from top to bottom. He must provide an approved safety catch and sufficient cover overhead on all carriages used for hoisting or lowering persons, and at top of shaft an approved safety gate and an adequate brake to every drum or machine used for hoisting or lowering persons in shafts or slopes, and in every shaft a passage way from one side to the other, so that persons do not have to pass under descending cages. (Laws of 1884, p. 153, amending sections 290, 291, 292, 293, 294, 295, and 299, Revised Statutes.)

No minor under 12 years of age shall be employed in any factory, workshop, or establishment where goods are manufactured, nor under 18 years of age more than ten hours a day, and in no case shall hours of labor exceed sixty a week. Employers must post in every room notices stating the number of hours labor required each day. Violation punishable by fine of from $50 to $100, or imprisonment not less than thirty nor more than sixty days, to be prosecuted by inspector of shops and factories for the benefit of the school funds. (Laws of 1885, April 27, repealing original section 6986, Revised Statutes.)

Persons or corporations employing female employés in any manufacturing, mechanical, or mercantile establishment shall provide suitable seats for their use, and permit them to use such seats when not necessarily engaged in the active duties for which they are employed. Violation punishable by fine from $10 to $20 for each offense. (Laws of 1885, April 16.)

The chief inspector and the district inspectors of workshops and factories shall carefully inspect the sanitary condition of all workshops and factories in their respective districts; examine the system of sewerage in connection therewith, the situation and condition of water closets or urinals in and about the same, the system of heating, lighting, and ventilating all rooms therein where persons are employed at daily labor, the means of exit in case of fire or other disaster, and all belting, shafting, gearing, elevators, drums, and machinery of every kind and description in and about the same, and see that they are not located so as to be dangerous to employés when at work, and that they are, so far as practicable, securely guarded, and that every vat, pan, or structure filled with molten lead or hot liquid shall be surrounded with proper safeguards for preventing accident or injury to those employed, and that all such shops and factories are in a proper sanitary condition, and adequately provided with means of escape in case of fire or other disaster.

Inspectors, if they find upon such inspection that the heating, lighting, ventilation, or sanitary arrangement of such shop or factory is such as to be injurious to the health of persons employed or residing therein, or that the means of egress, in case of fire or other disaster, is not sufficient, or that the belting, shafting, gearing, elevators, drums, and machinery therein are dangerously located, or that structures filled with hot metal or liquid are not surrounded with proper safeguards for preventing accident, shall notify owners or agents of such shops or factories to make necessary alterations within thirty days, or some reasonable time. Failure to make alterations is a misdemeanor punishable by fine of from $10 to $200.

District inspectors must make a record of all examinations, showing date, condition of shops and factories, changes ordered, number of shops and factories, number of men, women, and children employed in each, with such other facts as they think proper, which record must be filed weekly with the chief inspector, to be by him recorded, and so much as is of public interest to be included in his annual report. (Laws 1885, amending and repealing sections 2573a, 2573b, 2573c, supplementary to section 2573, Revised Statutes, being Laws of 1884, p. 153.)

By sections 297, 300, 302, 303, 304, and 306, Revised Statutes, it is provided that in mines worked by shaft where 15,000 square yards have been excavated, no person shall work unless to every seam of coal there are two separate outlets separated by 100 feet of natural strata, and in all other mines after 15,000 square yards of excavation there must be two such outlets within twelve months after such excavation and until second outlet be made no more than ten persons shall work at once. There must be sober and competent engineers, and no more than ten persons shall ride on a cage at once, and no one on loaded cage in any shaft or slope. No boy under 12 shall be allowed to work in any mine, nor any minor between the ages of 12 and 16 unless he can read and write. Inspector may enjoin mine owner from employing over ten miners until second outlet is completed. On written charges of gross neglect or malfeasance against an inspector, signed by fifteen miners or one operator, a board of examiners appointed by governor, consisting of two practical coal miners, one chemist, one mining engineer, and one operator, hear the case, take testimony, and report to the governor. This chapter does not apply to mines with no more than ten employés, but the inspector may make regulations for them upon the application of the owners.

Section 4024, Revised Statutes, forbids employment of children under 14, residing in the state during preceding school year, under control of parent or guardian, not dependent upon their own resources for support, during school hours, unless they have attended school twelve weeks of preceding school year. A certificate of attendance is required. Such employment must not be over forty weeks in the year unless such children furnish employers with certificates showing their exemption from this section, which section does not apply when the nearest school is over two miles from residence.

Section 4029, Revised Statutes, makes two weeks attendance at half-time or night school equal to one week at day school.

Section 6986, Revised Statutes, fines from $5 to $50 employers compelling women, or children under 18, or permitting any child under 14, to work more than ten hours a day in any place used for mechanical or manufacturing purposes.

Section 7015 fines from $5 to $100 employers who issue in payment of wages orders payable in anything but money, or by intervention of such orders pays wages in goods at higher prices than cash rates, or sell goods to laborers on orders issued by employers, or do any other thing by which wages are paid in goods at higher prices than cash rates.

Section 7016 fines from $20 to $100, or imprisons not more than sixty days, or punishes in both ways, those compelling or attempting to coerce employés to purchase goods from particular firms or corporations.

Section 4365 makes ten hours a legal day's work in any manufacturing or mechanical business, when the contract is silent, and all contracts shall be so construed.

Sections 307, 308, 309, and 310 provide for the appointment by the governor of a commissioner of statistics of labor for two years, with the usual powers and duties; with $2,000 allowed for annual salary, by section 1284, and $500 for annual expenses, by section 1296.

OREGON.

By sections 670, General Statutes, Acts of 1864, sections 655, it is provided that persons preventing or endeavoring to prevent, by threats, force, or intimidation, employés from continuing or performing work, or accepting new work, or preventing or endeavoring to prevent employers from employing any person, or compelling them to employ any person, or forcing or inducing them to alter their modes of carrying on business, or limiting or increasing employés' wages or term of services, may be fined from $20 to $300, or be imprisoned from one to six months. There has been no labor legislation since 1880.

PENNSYLVANIA.

Presiding justices of common pleas courts, upon petition or agreement, shall issue license for the establishment of tribunals to settle disputes in iron, steel, glass, textile fabrics and coal trades. Petition must be signed by fifty workman or five separate firms, individuals, or corporations, within county of petitioners, or by five employers each employing at least ten men, or by the representatives of a firm, individual, or corporation employing not less than seventy-five men, and the agreement shall be signed by both of said specified numbers and persons: *Provided*, That if there be a strike or dispute at the time, and suspension exists, or is probable, the judge shall require testimony as to the representative character of petitioners, and if they do not represent at least half each party in dispute license may be denied. Workmen signing must be resident of judicial district one year, engaged in branch of trade they represent for two years, and be citizens of the United States. Employers signing must also be citizens, and engaged in some branch of the different business mentioned for one year, must each employ ten workmen of such branch and each may be a firm, individual, or corporation. Petition must be sworn to by at least two signers.

If petition be correct and contain names of an equal number of arbitrators on each side, and of an umpire mutually chosen, the judge shall issue a license authorizing the existence of a tribunal, and fixing the time and place of meeting, which shall be recorded in the court of common pleas. If petition have sufficient number of signers on one, but not both sides, license may issue conditioned on assent of delinquent side in writing, with names of arbitrators, umpire, etc.; if no assent within sixty days, petition to be dismissed.

One tribunal may be created in each judicial district for each of the trades named, to continue for one year, and take jurisdiction of any dispute between employers and workingmen, who have petitioned, or been represented in petition, for tribunal, or who submit disputes in writing. Vacancies in tribunal are to be filed by the judge from three names presented by remaining members of same class. Removal to adjoining county creates no vacancy in arbitrators or umpire, and disputes in one county may be referred to tribunal in adjoining county.

The position of umpire can only be filled by the mutual choice of all the representatives of both employers and workingmen, and he acts only after failure of tribunal to agree in three meetings. His award is final only upon what is submitted to him in writing signed by all members of the tribunal, or by parties submitting the same, and upon questions affecting the price of labor. It shall in no case be binding upon either employer or workmen, save as they may acquiesce or agree therein after such award.

Tribunal shall consist of not less than two employers, or their representatives, and two workmen, the exact number being inserted in the petition or agreement, and they shall be named in license. There shall be a chairman and secretary. Tribunal shall receive no compensation from city or county, but expenses, other than fuel, light, and the use of room and furniture, which are furnished by city or county, may be paid by voluntary subscriptions, which tribunal may receive.

When there is no umpire a chairman chosen administers oaths, signs subpœnas, etc., as umpires do when acting. No lawyers or agents are to appear on either side, and the proceedings are voluntary. Umpire's decision as to admission of evidence is final. Committees from the tribunal, an equal number from each side, may unanimously decide questions. Rules are to be made by tribunal a ndumpire to govern proceedings. Umpire shall be sworn and make his award within ten days, which is made a matter of record by producing same to the judge within thirty days, who approves it. The act is to be cited, "Voluntary trade-tribunal act of 1883," and forms are given for petition, license, submission, and award. (Brightley's Purdon's Digest, 1883; Public Laws of 1886, p. 15.)

Persons mining and manufacturing, or either, coal ore or other mineral shall pay their employés in lawful money, or by order redeemable at its face value in lawful money by the issuer within thirty days. Violation a misdemeanor, punishable by fine up to $100, to go to school fund. Employers interested in merchandising are not to make a greater profit on goods than outside dealers in like articles. Violation makes the debt uncollectible from employé. Employers refusing for twenty days to pay employés regularly or to redeem orders shall pay 1 per cent. a month if suit be brought for amount due. (Public Laws of 1881, p. 147, June 29.)

Miners are to be paid for the quantity of coal mined, whether nut or lump coal, seventy-six pounds being a bushel and 2,000 pounds a ton, but other contracts may be made. Cars are to be of uniform capacity and branded by mine inspector. No unbranded cars can enter mine longer than three months without being branded; this provision not to apply to mines using no more than ten cars.

At every bituminous mine the miners have a right to employ a check weighman and measurer, who has the right to examine scales, measure cars, and to be always present at weighing and measuring, examinations and measurements to be at seasonable hours, so as not to interfere with work. Interference with him is punishable by fine of from $20 to $100, or imprisonment. He shall credit each miner with merchantable coal mined by him in a book kept for the purpose. Disputes between him and owner to be settled by the mine inspector, and cheating by him is punishable with three months' imprisonment.

Misdemeanor for owner to switch cars before dumping. Violation is punishable by fine of $100, and restitution must be made to miner for sums lost. (Public Laws of 1883, p. 52, June 1.)

Unlawful for persons or corporations engaged in mining or manufacturing coal, or both, to employ or permit to be employed female labor or laborers in or about any coal mine or manufactory. Violation punishable by fine of from $100 to $500, or imprisonment up to six months, or both, one half of fine to go to informer and one half to the school fund of the district. The act does not affect the employment of females in office, or clerical work. (Public Laws of 1885, No. 165, p. 202, June 30.)

In addition to fire escapes provided by the act of June 11, 1879, Public Law 128, which must be safe, permanent, and external, and satisfactory to fire commissioners, it is made the duty of owners of buildings used for factories, manufactories, work shops, or tenement houses more than two stories high, to provide and cause to be securely affixed to a bolt through the wall over the window head inside of at least one window in each room on the third or higher floor a chain at least ten feet long, with a rope at least one inch in diameter fastened thereto long enough to reach the ground, or such other appliances as may be approved by fire or county commissioners. When third or higher floor is not subdivided into rooms, at least six windows on a floor must be provided with chains and ropes or other appliances. Whenever rooms on third or higher floor have more than three windows each, at least one out of three windows must have chain and rope, and these articles must be kept in an unlocked box near the inside sill of the window.

In all places mentioned in this act hallways and head and foot of stairways must be kept lighted at night with a red lamp, and alarms and gongs, easy of access and ready for use, shall be kept in such buildings. Penalty for violation is a fine up to $300 and imprisonment from one to twelve months, and in case of fire resulting in death or personal injury, persons or corporations violating act are liable additionally in an action for damages. (Public Laws of 1885, No. 41, p. 65, June 3.)

Fire escapes provided by act of June 11, 1879, Public Laws 128, for buildings in which employés are usually employed in the third or higher stories, must be independent of internal stairways, number and location to be governed by the size of the building and the number of inmates, and arranged so as to be readily accessible, safe, and adequate. They must consist of outside, open, iron stairway of not more than 45° slant, with steps not less than six inches wide and twenty-four inches long. Buildings accommodating more than 100 persons shall have two such escapes, and more if necessary. Owners may put up other escapes subject to official approval. Fire marshals and fire commissioners, or, where there are none, school directors, must examine fire escapes, and, if approved, give certificates. Violation of act punishable by fine up to $300 and by imprisonment from one to two months. In case of fire, in the absence of escapes, resulting in death or personal injury, violators subject to imprisonment from six to twelve months and civilly liable in an action for damages.

Act not to apply to approved fire escapes now in use. (Public Laws of 1885, No. 42, p. 68, June 3.)

No boy under 12 years shall be employed in any bituminous coal mine, or under fourteen years in any anthracite coal mine, nor shall women or girls of any age be employed in either class of mines, or in or about the outside workings. No boy under 10 years shall be employed in or about the outside workings of a bituminous mine, or under 12, of an anthracite mine; but all such boys, women, or girls may be employed in office and clerical work. (Public Laws of 1885, No. 169, p. 217, June 30; No. 170, p. 233, June 30.)

Persons controlling bituminous coal mines must keep at mouth of drift, shaft, or slope, or wherever mine inspector directs, properly-constructed stretchers to carry away injured employés. (Public Laws of 1885, No. 169, p. 217.)

Engineer of breaker engine in anthracite mines must be 18 years old. No person under 15 years of age shall be appointed to oil machinery. (Public Laws of 1885, No. 170, p. 229, June 30.)

Persons controlling anthracite coal mines must keep at each mine an ambulance, and at least two stretchers, to carry injured persons to their homes. Each ambulance must have easy springs, windows on sides or ends, large enough for two persons with two attendants, and provided with mattresses or bedding or roller frames, with sufficient covering. Stretchers must be of such material and construction as to afford the greatest comfort to injured persons. Injured persons unable to walk must be sent home or to a hospital. No ambulance necessary if workmen live within radius of a half mile. Two mines within one mile of each other, connected by telegraph or telephone, need have but one ambulance, nor need any mine employing less than twenty persons. Conveyance of injured persons may be by railroad, but under cover if more convenient. (Public Laws of 1885, No. 170, p. 230, June 30.)

No. 169, Public Laws of 1885, page 205, June 30, relates to bituminous coal mines, and provides for the lives, health, safety, and welfare of persons employed therein. No. 170, Public Laws of 1885, page 218, June 30, provides for the health and safety of persons employed in and about anthracite coal mines and the protection and preservation of property connected therewith, and relates to mines employing more than ten persons. Specific sections of both acts are quoted above. They are similar to acts of other states elsewhere mentioned, and contain provisions, besides those quoted, relating to arbitration between mine inspectors and owners; boards of examiners of candidates for inspectors; regulations for boilers; deaths in or about mines; inspection districts; qualifications, appointments, duties of inspectors; qualifications and duties of foremen; injunctions to restrain workings of mine; regulations for machinery; maps, plans, and surveys of mines; openings, outlets, and slopes; props and timbers for miners; notices in case of accidents or deaths; ventilation and regulations connected therewith; making openings on adjoining lands; wash houses for miners, etc.

By Public Laws of 1872, p. 1175, Brightley's Purdon's Digest, 442, it is made lawful for employés, as individuals or members of associations, to refuse to work whenever, in their opinion, wages are insufficient or treatment offensive or further labor would be contrary to the rules of their society, without subjecting them to prosecution for perjury; but act not to apply to members of organizations not in strict conformity to Federal or state constitutions, nor does it prevent prosecution of those who hinder others from working or seeking work.

By Public Laws of 1849, p. 672, Brightley's Purdon's Digest, 771, ten hours are made a day's work in cotton, woollen, silk, paper, bagging, and flax factories, and no minor under 13 to be employed therein under penalty of $50 each offense—half to person suing and half to county. No minor between 13 and 16 to be employed more than nine months in the year, or who has not attended school three consecutive months in same year. Parents and guardians permitting employment of children contrary to act, forfeit $50 as above.

By Public Laws of 1855, p. 472, no operative under 21 can be employed more than ten hours a day or sixty hours a week in cotton, silk, woollen, flax, bagging, or paper factory. Persons so employing forfeit $50 to school fund.

By Public Laws of 1879, p. 128, Brightley's Purdon's Digest, 813, every building of any kind in which work is done above the second story must have permanent, safe, external means of escape in case of fire satisfactory to fire commissioners and fire marshal of the district. In case of injury or death an action accrues for damages and a penalty is incurred of $300.

By Public Laws of 1868, p. 99, Brightley's Purdon's Digest, 1009, eight hours between rising and setting of the sun are made a day's work in the absence of an agreement for longer time, which any person may make. Act does not apply to farm labor or service by the year, month, or week.

RHODE ISLAND.

No child under 10 years of age shall be employed in any manufacturing or mechanical establishment; parent or guardian permitting employment being liable to a fine up to $20.

No child under 14 years of age shall be so employed except during the vacation of the public schools, unless during preceding year he has attended some public or private day school for at least twelve weeks, nor shall such employment continue unless there shall be a like attendance each year; but no child can be employed who does not present certificate of such attendance made by or under direction of the school committee. Owners, superintendents, and overseers must require and keep on file certificates of place and date of birth of children under 15 years of age, as nearly accurate as may be, so long as employment of such children continues, and the amount of school attendance for the year preceding employment. The form of the certificate is determined by the state board of education, and it is made by the school committee.

Owner, superintendent, or overseer employing, or parent or guardian permitting employment of children under 14 years of age, contrary to this act, are liable to a fine up to $20.

Truant officers, at least once every school term, must visit all establishments to see if the law be carried out. They must demand the names of children under 15 years of age employed in their towns and require certificates to be produced.

Owner, superintendent, or overseer permitting employment of children under 15 years of age while public schools are in session, who cannot write their names, ages, and places of residence, are liable to a fine up to $20. (Chapter 363, Acts of January, 1883.)

Town and city councils may make, regulate, and pass ordinances in reference to the construction and location of stairways, and the putting up of fire escapes upon buildings where workmen are employed, and provide for punishment for violation of ordinances not to exceed $10 for each day's continuance. They may also pass ordinances and make regulations as to the construction, location, and operation of elevators and hoistways, and the approaches thereto, used for the carriage of persons and merchandise; penalty incurred for violation being $5 for each day's continuance. (Chapter 340, Acts of January, 1883.)

By title 20, chapter 69, section 26, Public Statutes, labor performed in any manufacturing establishment and all mechanical labor during ten hours is a legal day's work, unless otherwise agreed by the parties.

By same chapter, section 23, no minor between 12 and 15 can be employed in any manufacturing establishment more than eleven hours a day, nor before 5 a. m., nor after 7.30 p. m. Violation by owner, employer, or agent of factory, or parent, or guardian of child, punished by fine of $20 for each offense, one-half to complainant and one-half to school fund.

By title 30, chapter 141, section 8, Public Statutes, every person who alone, or in concert with others, attempts by force, violence, threats or intimidation to or does prevent another from entering upon or pursuing any employment upon satisfactory terms to employé, may be fined up to $100, or be imprisoned up to ninety days.

The statutes quoted since 1880 do not differ in very many particulars from others relating to the same subjects recently before adopted.

TENNESSEE.

An act providing for the ventilation and operation of coal mines is similar in its general tenor to those heretofore quoted. Alterations in maps are to be made by the 1st of January and July of each year. The two shafts, slopes, or outlets, must be separated by natural strata of not less than 150 feet. Ventilation to be not less than fifty-five cubic feet per second of pure air, or 3,300 cubic feet, per minute for every fifty men at work, and as much more as circumstances may require. Owners or agents must have "inside boss" to take charge of mine.

No boy under 12 years of age shall work in or enter any mine. Proof of his age must be given by certificate or otherwise before he shall be employed, and no father, or other person, shall knowingly conceal or misrepresent the age of any boy.

No person is allowed to ride on a loaded cage, and no more than ten persons at one time on any cage.

All machinery in and about mines, especially in coal breakers where boys work, must be properly fenced off, and tops of shafts must be so fenced by vertical or flat gates, covering area of shafts.

Duties of inspector to be performed by the geologist of the bureau of agricultural statistics and mines, who has his office at Chattanooga, employs such assistants as may be necessary, and is allowed yearly $600 for salary as inspector and $1,000 for expenses. He must examine all coal mines in the state at least once in six months. (Chapter 170, Acts of 1881, p. 234.)

The following note appears to section 2370 of the Code of 1884: "The act of 1881, chapter 170, regulating the ventilation and operation of coal mines is omitted, because it is adapted to mines entered by shafts, whereas, with a single exception, the mines in this state are drift mines."

TEXAS.

By title 9, chapter 1, article 289, Penal Code, it is made unlawful for persons to the number of three or more to assemble for the purpose of preventing any person from pursuing any labor, occupation, or employment, or to intimidate any person from following his daily vocation, or to interfere in any manner with the labor or employment of another. Persons violating are subject to a fine up to $500, and if they cause a riot, to imprisonment from six months to one year.

VERMONT.

By section 673, Revised Laws, Acts of 1867, No. 35, it is provided that no child between 10 and 14 years of age, who has resided in the state one year, shall be employed in a mill or factory unless such child has attended a public school three months during the preceding year. A person employing a child in violation of this section shall forfeit from $10 to $20, one-half to go to the complainant and one-half to the town.

Section 4320 Revised Laws, acts of 1867, No. 36, provides for the punishment of owners, superintendents, or overseers of manufacturing and mechanical establishments, who knowingly employ, or permit to work, children under 10 years of age, or employ children under 15 more than ten hours a day, by a fine of $50. Parents or guardians consenting to such employment, punishable in like manner.

Section 4226 Revised Laws, acts of 1877, No. 6, provides for the punishment of persons who threaten violence and injury to others with intent to prevent their employment in a mill, manufactory, shop, quarry, mine, or railroad by imprisonment up to three months, or a fine up to $100.

Section 4227 Revised Laws, acts of 1877, No. 6, provides for the punishment of persons who, by threats, intimidation, or force, affright, drive away, and prevent other persons from accepting, undertaking, or prosecuting such employment, with intent to prevent the prosecution of work in such mill, shop, manufactory, mine, quarry, or railroad by imprisonment up to five years, or a fine up to $500.

WASHINGTON TERRITORY.

The act providing for the inspection and ventilation of coal mines, and securing the health and safety of miners, is much the same as those of states heretofore referred to. The inspector of mines is appointed by the governor for two years, at a yearly salary of $1,800, to be paid, so far as it will go, out of the mining fund, which is raised by a tax of four mills a ton of coal, to be paid quarterly by operators into the territorial treasury. Workings of mines up to date to be reported every four months. Ventilation in mines worked by shaft, slope, drift, or tunnel, to be not less than 100 feet per minute per person employed, and as much more as the inspector may direct. Inspector is empowered to make all needful regulations for the security of the health and lives of miners. (Laws of 1883, p. 25.)

WEST VIRGINIA.

The act providing for the appointment of a mine inspector and the inspection of coal miners has the same general provisions as those heretofore quoted. The governor appoints a mine inspector for two years, at a yearly salary of $1,200, and a yearly allowance of $500 for expenses. Owners of mines employ fifteen or more men, to make map. Workings of mines up to date to be reported the 1st of January and July of each year. Inspector must make an examination once a year, or oftener, if necessary. There must be a proper and sufficient system of ventilation by pure air, so that mines shall be kept in healthy condition for men working therein.

Owner must have practical overseer, or mining boss to keep careful watch over the mines and their working, especially as to the ventilation and supports overhead. Owners, agents, lessees, or operators, being themselves competent, may be their own "mining bosses."

Inspector must make a special examination when requested by owner, operator, etc., or ten miners, and if mine be not properly drained, or ventilated, or found otherwise in bad condition, he suggests remedies, which the owner, operator, etc., must apply, subject to a fine of from $20 to $100. Inspector must report to the governor annually by January 1 the condition of every mine in the state in operation two months previous to the report, stating particularly the number of persons employed, the number of accidents, injuries, and deaths, if any, with suggestions as to the proper legislation necessary to remedy any defects in the law. He may be removed by the governor for any good cause. (Acts of 1883, chapter 70).

WISCONSIN.

In all manufactories, workshops, or other places used for mechanical or manufacturing purposes, the time of labor of children under the age of 18 and of women employed therein shall not exceed eight hours in one day and every stockholder, employer, director, officer, overseer, clerk, or foreman who shall compel any woman or any such child to labor exceeding eight hours or who shall permit any child under 14 years of age to labor more than ten hours in any one day in any such place, if he have control over such child sufficient to prevent it, or who shall employ at manual labor any child over 12 and under 14 years of age in any such factory or workshop for more than seven months in any one year, is liable to a fine of from $5 to $50 for each offense. (Acts of 1883, chapter 135, supplement to Revised Statutes, p. 375, amending section 1728, Revised Statutes. Amendment consists in changing penalty from a forfeiture to a fine.)

Any person, persons, or body corporate owning, occupying, or controlling any factory, workshop, or structure three or more stories high, in which several persons are employed in any kind of labor on or above the third story or floor shall provide and keep connected with the same one or more good and substantial metallic fire-proof ladders, stairs, or stairways, ready for use at all times, reaching from the cornice to the ground on the outside of such building, and placed in such position as to be easy of access to the occupants of such building in case of fire, and sufficient to furnish reasonable means of escape to the persons employed therein from each and every floor and story. Failure to provide and keep such means of escape from fire punishable by fine up to $100 or imprisonment up to three months. (Chapter 50, acts of 1885, p. 42, amending section 4575a, Revised Statutes).

Churches, public and private school houses, hotels, factories, or other manufacturing establishments hereafter constructed must have doors so hung as to swing outward or both in and out. (Chapter 190, Acts of 1885, p. 165.)

The commissioner of labor statistics, deputy, or factory inspector shall have power to enter any factory or workshop where labor is employed for the purpose of gathering facts and statistics, or of examining the means of escape from fire, and the provisions made for the health and safety of operatives therein, and in case the officer examining shall discover any violations of, or neglect to comply with, the law in respect to child labor, hours of labor for women and children, fire escapes and similar enactments now or hereafter to be made, he shall notify the owner or occupant of such factory or workshop in writing of the offense or neglect, and if such offense or neglect be not corrected or remedied within thirty days after service of the notice, he shall lodge formal complaint with the district attorney of the county in which the offense is committed or the neglect occurs, whereupon that officer shall proceed at once against offenders according to law.

Factory inspector, or other officer, may post in any factory or workshop examined by him, the laws in respect to child labor, hours of labor, fire escapes, or other matters pertaining to the health and safety of artisans, the mutilation, destruction, or removal of which is punishable by a fine of $50 for each offense.

Commissioner of labor statistics furnishes blank forms to employers, who must fill them out under oath, and return them to commissioner within a reasonable time, to be prescribed by him. Owner, occupant, or agent, refusing to admit a bureau officer to factory or workshop, forfeits $10 for each offense, and for neglecting to fill out blanks, swear to same, and return at proper times, $10 for each day's delay, forfeiture suit by district attorney, upon complaint of bureau officer, or citizen, for the benefit of the school fund. (Chapter 247, Acts of 1885, p. 212, amending chapter 319, Acts of 1883.)

By section 1729, Revised Statutes, p. 504, in all engagements to labor in any manufacturing or mechanical business where there is no express contract to the contrary, a day's work shall consist of eight hours, and all engagements or contracts for labor in such cases shall be so construed; but the act does not apply to contracts for labor by the week, month, or year.

INDEX.

Agricultural implements, cost of production of, 92, 93.
    summary of selected occupations, 143, 168.
    all employés, by states, 220.
    with per cent., 175, 176.
Agricultural products, value of leading, exported from the United States, 1866-85, 242.
Agriculture, foreign-born engaged in, 1870 and 1880, 245.
Alsace, cost of spinning one pound of cotton yarn in, 182.
Arbitration, establishment of boards of, 274-276.
Arms and ammunition, cost of production of, 92, 93.
    summary of all employés, etc., by states, 220.
Artisans' tools, cost of production of, 92, 93.
    summary of all employés, etc., by states, 220.
Bank of England, contraction in circulation of the, 1846-47, 18.
Banks, postal, number of, in the United Kingdom, 1873-84, 34.
Banks, savings, depositors and deposits in, in France, 1835-83, 43.
    deposits in, in Saxony, 1845-70, 52.
    decrease in deposits in, under trustees in the United Kingdom, 1847-48, 20.
    exhibit of, in the United States, 1874-85, 75.
    number of depositors, etc., in, in Prussia, 1839-81, 51.
    under trustees in the United Kingdom, 1873-84, 34.
    1846-56, 19.
    1857-85, 22.
    1862-72, 26.
    in post-office, of the United Kingdom, 1866-72, 28.
Belgium, average cost of production of a ton of coal in, 141.
    earnings and expenses of wage receivers in, 428-431.
    industrial depressions in, 44-47.
    production and value of coal in, 1831-83, 47, 48.
    iron in, 1840-83, 48.
    steel in, 1840-83, 48.
    share of labor and capital in coal mining, Province of Hainault, 1869-82, 148.
Boards of arbitration, establishment of, 274-276.
Boots and shoes, cost of production of, 92-97.
    production of, in Massachusetts, 1859-85, 71.
    summary of selected occupations, 143-145, 168.
    all employés, by states, 220.
    with per cent., 176-178.
Boxes, summary of all employés, etc., by states, 220.
Bricks, cost of production of, 96, 97.
    summary of all employés, etc., by states, 220.
Brooms, summary of selected occupations, 145.
    all employés, by states, 220.
    with per cent., 179.
California, synopsis of labor legislation in, 457.
Carpetings, cost of production of, 96, 97.
    summary of selected occupations, 145-147, 168.
    all employés, by states, 220.
    with per cent., 179, 180.
Carriages and wagons, cost of production of, 96, 97.
    summary of selected occupations, 147.
    all employés, by states, 220, 221.
    with per cent., 180, 181.

Causes of present depression, 291, 292.
    depressions as elicited by committees of Congress, 61–63.
        agents of the Bureau, 76, 78.
Clocks and watches, cost of production of, 98, 99.
    summary of all employés, etc., by states, 221.
Clothing, cost of production of, 98, 101.
    summary of selected occupations, 148, 169.
    all employés, by states, 221.
    with per cent., 181, 182.
Coal, average cost of a ton of, in Belgium, 141.
    production and value of, in Belgium, 1831–83, 47, 48.
    cost of, in France, 1853–83, 135.
    yearly, in France, 1829–83, 42.
    five mines in France, 1883, 137.
    largest producing districts in France, 1883, 136.
    and value of, in Germany, 1848–82, 53.
    of anthracite, in the United States, 1882–85, 70.
    bituminous, in the United States, 1882–85, 70.
    share of labor and capital in mining, Province of Hainault, Belgium, 1860–83, 146.
Coal, coke, and ore, cost of production of, 100–103.
    summary of selected occupations, 149, 150.
    all employés, by states, 221.
    with per cent., 182–184.
Colorado, synopsis of labor legislation in, 457–459.
Commercial and mercantile conditions, 276, 277.
Connecticut, synopsis of labor legislation in, 460.
Consuming power, crippled, 243–250.
Contraction of credit, 276.
Cooking and heating apparatus, cost of production of, 104, 105.
    summary of selected occupations, 150, 151.
    all employés, by states, 221.
    with per cent, 185, 186.
Corporations, restriction of land grants to, 271.
Cotton, employés and wages in spinning and carding in the Rhine district of Germany, 1855–85, 238, 239
    weaving, in the Rhine district of Germany, 1855–85, 240, 241.
    importations of, into the United Kingdom, 1861–3, 21.
    compressing, summary of all employés, etc., by states, 221.
    goods, analysis of labor cost of, 126–129.
    cost of production of, 104–111.
    summary of selected occupations, 151–155, 170–172.
    all employés, by states, 221.
    with per cent., 186–195.
    value of exported from Great Britain, 30.
    and cotton goods, average currency prices of, in New York, 1847–84, 74.
    manufactures, value of, of Great Britain, 30.
    yarn, analysis of cost of producing, at Oldham, England, 134.
    cost of producing, at Oldham, England, 134.
    system of payment for spinning, at Oldham, England, 227, 228.
    cost of spinning one pound of, in Alsace, 132.
    England, 133.
    variation in market price of, in Great Britain, 1867–72, 25.
    1873–85, 31.
Credit, contraction of, 276.
Currency, 276.
Dakota, synopsis of labor legislation in, 461.
Delaware, synopsis of labor legislation in, 461.
Depressions, modern industrial, 15, 16.
    alleged causes of, as gathered by agents of the Bureau, 76–78.
    causes of present, 291, 292.
    as elicited by committees of Congress, 61–63.
    contemporaneousness and severity of, 290, 291.
    in Great Britain, 16–34.
        France, 35–43.
        Belgium, 44–48.
        Germany, 49–54.
        the United States, 1837–86, 55–64.

INDEX.

Depressions, remedies for, suggested, 292, 293.
　　　　　as elicited by agents of the Bureau, 269, 270.
　　　　　　committees of Congress, 264-268.
　　years of, 290.
Distribution of products, 277-279.
Domestic products, export price of, in currency, 1855-85, 74, 75.
Employés, occupation of, with number and wages, by industries—
　　agricultural implements, 295-299.
　　arms and ammunition, 299.
　　artisans' tools, 299.
　　boots and shoes, 299-309.
　　boxes, 309, 310.
　　bricks, 310.
　　brooms, 310, 311.
　　carpetings, 311-315.
　　carriages and wagons, 315-317.
　　clocks and watches, 317, 318.
　　clothing, 318-322.
　　coal, coke, and ore, 322-327.
　　cooking and heating apparatus, 327-332.
　　cotton compressing, 333.
　　cotton goods, 333-350.
　　engraving and printing, 350.
　　food preparations, 350-354.
　　furniture, 354-356.
　　glass, 356-360.
　　jute goods, 360, 361.
　　leather, 361, 362.
　　linen, 362, 363.
　　liquors and beverages, 363, 364.
　　lumber, 364, 365.
　　machines and machinery, 365-367.
　　metals and metallic goods, 368-386.
　　musical instruments and materials, 386-388.
　　oils and illuminating fluids, 388.
　　paper, 388-391.
　　print works, 391, 392.
　　railroad construction, 392, 393.
　　rubber, 393.
　　silk, 394.
　　stone, 394.
　　tobacco, 395-399.
　　vessels, 399, 400.
　　wooden goods, 400.
　　woollen goods, 400-409.
　　miscellaneous, 410.
　　summary of all, with per cent.—
　　　　　agricultural implements, 175, 177.
　　　　　boots and shoes, 176-178.
　　　　　brooms, 179.
　　　　　carpetings, 179, 180.
　　　　　carriages and wagons, 180, 181.
　　　　　clothing, 181, 182.
　　　　　coal, coke, and ore, 182-184.
　　　　　cooking and heating apparatus, 185, 186.
　　　　　cotton goods, 186-195.
　　　　　food preparations, 195, 196.
　　　　　furniture, 196, 197.
　　　　　glass, 197-199.
　　　　　leather, 199, 200.
　　　　　liquors and beverages, 200.
　　　　　machines and machinery, 200, 201.
　　　　　metals and metallic goods, 201-208.
　　　　　musical instruments and materials, 208.
　　　　　paper, 208, 209.
　　　　　print works, 210.

Employés, summary of, all, with per cent.—
    tobacco, 210–213.
    woollen goods, 213–219.
    with wages and time, by industries, 226.
  summary of all, with wages and time, by states—
    agricultural implements, 220.
    arms and ammunition, 220.
    artisans' tools, 220.
    boots and shoes, 220.
    boxes, 220.
    bricks, 220.
    brooms, 220.
    carpetings, 220.
    carriages and wagons, 220, 221.
    clocks and watches, 221.
    clothing, 221.
    coal, coke, and ore, 221.
    cooking and heating apparatus, 221.
    cotton compressing, 221.
    cotton goods, 221.
    engraving and printing, 222.
    food preparations, 222.
    furniture, 222.
    glass, 222.
    jute goods, 222.
    leather, 222.
    linen, 222.
    liquors and beverages, 222.
    lumber, 222, 223.
    machines and machinery, 223.
    metals and metallic goods, 223.
    musical instruments and materials, 223.
    oils and illuminating fluids, 223.
    paper, 223, 224.
    print works, 224.
    railroad construction, 224.
    rubber, 224.
    silk, 224.
    stone, 224.
    tobacco, 224.
    vessels, 224.
    wooden goods, 224, 225.
    woollen goods, 225.
    miscellaneous, 225.
Employers, organization of, of workmen, 286–289.
England, cost of spinning one pound of cotton yarn in, 133.
    reeled yarn in the Bolton district, 233.
    twist in the Bolton district, 231.
    weft in the Bolton district, 232.
  discounts from the lists in the Bolton district, 232.
  revolutions per spindle, etc., in the Bolton district, 233.
  earnings and expenses of wage receivers in, 431–444.
  price per yard of Leeds woollen and mixed goods, duties, etc., 261.
  wages per hour in the manufacture of machinery in Birmingham, 1885, 394.
  contraction in the circulation of the Bank of, 1846–47, 18.
Engraving and printing, summary of all employés, etc., by states, 222.
Europe, earnings and expenses of wage receivers in—
    Belgium, 423–431.
    England, 431–444.
    Germany, 444–452.
    Italy, 411–423.
    Switzerland, 452–456.
Exports and imports, value of, for the United Kingdom, 1860–84, 72.
    of merchandise of the United States, 1825–85, 71, 72.
    all, from the United States, 1860, 1870, 1875–85, 248.
Failures, number of, in the United States, and amount of liabilities, 1857–85, 67.
Food preparations, cost of production of, 110–113.

INDEX. 491

Food preparations, summary of selected occupations, 155, 156.
   all employés, by states, 222.
     with per cent., 195, 196.
France, industrial depressions in, 35-43.
 production, etc., of coal in, 1858-83, 135.
 yearly production of coal in, 1829-83, 42.
 production of coal in largest producing districts in, 1883, 136.
   five coal mines in, 1883, 137.
   the department of Pas-de-Calais, 1883, 136.
   illuminating gas, coke, and tar in certain departments of, 139.
   and average market price of merchant iron in, 1874-83, 41.
 yearly production of iron in, 1829-83, 42.
 production and average market price of pig-iron in, 1874-83, 41.
 cost of production, etc., of iron ore in, 1853-83, 138.
   1883, 138.
 production and average market price of steel in, 1874-83, 41.
 miles of railroads in operation and miles built each year in, 1840-84, 43.
 daily wages in Paris, 1844, 1853, 1860, 1871, 1875, 1881, and 1882, 236.
   principal cities of, not including Paris, 1853, 1857, 1871, 1875, 1881, and 1882, 237.
 depositors and deposits in savings banks in, 1835-83, 43.
 value of imports and exports for, 1860-84, 73.
Furniture, summary of selected occupations, 156, 172.
  all employés, by states, 222.
   with per cent., 196, 197.
Gas, coke, and tar, production of, in certain departments of France, 139.
Georgia, synopsis of labor legislation in, 461.
Germany, cost of production of bar iron in Westphalia, 1878, 140.
 production of rolled iron in Westphalia, 1878, 139.
 employés, and wages in weaving cotton in the Rhine district of, 1855-85, 240, 241.
   spinning and carding cotton in the Rhine district of, 1851-85, 238, 239.
 earnings and expenses of wage receivers in, 444, 452.
 yearly production and value of coal in, 1848-82, 53.
   pig-iron in, 1863-82, 58.
 industrial depressions in, 49-54.
German Empire, miles of railroad in operation in the, 1835-81, 58.
Glass, cost of production of, 112, 113.
 analysis of material cost of, 130, 131.
 summary of selected occupations, 156, 157, 172.
  all employés, by states, 222.
   with per cent., 197-198.
Great Britain, wheat acreage of, 1870-84, 28.
  average price of wheat in, 1835-39, 16.
   1846-50, 18.
   gazette prices of wheat, in 1870-84, 29.
 importation of wheat into, 1880-84, 248.
 value of cotton manufactures of, 30.
 variation in market price of cotton yarns in 1867-72, 25.
   1873-85, 31.
 value of exported cotton goods of, 30.
 land system of, 29.
 wages per hour in iron moulding in, 1885, 234, 235.
 industrial depressions in, 16-34.
Hours of labor, reduction of and uniformity in, through organization, 257, 258.
Illinois, synopsis of labor legislation in, 461, 462.
Immigration, restriction of, 271-273.
 into the United States, 1821-85, 245.
Importation of wheat into Great Britain and Ireland, 1880-84, 248.
Imports and exports, value of, for France, 1860-84, 73.
   the United Kingdom, 1860-84, 73.
   United States, 1860-84, 73.
   of merchandise of the United States, 1885-85, 71, 72.
   for the United Kingdom, 1860-84, 73.
   of merchandise of the United States, 1835-85, 71, 72.
   all, from the United States, 1860, 1870, 1875-85, 248.
Indiana, synopsis of labor legislation in, 462-464.
Industries, occupations, with number and wages of employés in various, 295-410.
  summary of all employés, with wages and time, by, 226.

492   INDEX.

Iowa, synopsis of labor legislation in, 464.
Iron, production and value of, in Belgium, 1844-83, 48.
    yearly production of, in France, 1829-83, 42.
    bar, cost of production of, in Westphalia, Germany, 1878, 140.
    pig, average monthly prices for, at Philadelphia, 1870-75, 69.
        yearly production of, according to fuel used in the United States, 1870-85, 69.
    rolled, production of, in Westphalia, Germany, 1878, 139.
    ore, cost of production, etc., of, in France, 1853-83, 138.
        1883, 138.
    moulding, wages per hour in, in Great Britain, 1885, 234, 235.
Ireland, importation of wheat into, 1880-84, 248.
Italy, average run of wages in, 1885, for various occupations, 421.
    earnings and expenses of wage receivers in, 411-423.
    prices of commodities in, in 1885, 421.
    taxes and tariffs in, 422.
Joint stock companies, number of, registered in the United Kingdom, 1873-84, 33.
Jute goods, cost of production of, 113.
    summary of all employés, etc., by states, 222.
Kansas, synopsis of labor legislation in, 464, 465.
Labor, reduction and uniformity in hours of, through organizations, 287, 288.
Land grants, restriction of, to corporations, 271.
Laws, enactment of, to stop speculation, 273, 274.
Leather, cost of production of, 114, 115.
    summary of selected occupations, 158, 172.
        all employés, by states, 222.
            with per cent., 199, 200.
Linen, summary of all employés, etc., by states, 222.
Liquors and beverages, cost of production of, 114, 115.
    summary of selected occupations, 158.
        all employés, by states, 222.
            with per cent., 200.
Locomotives, number of, in the United States, 87.
Lumber, cost of production of, 114, 115.
    summary of all employés, etc., by states, 222, 223.
Machinery, displacement of muscular labor by, in the manufacture of agricultural implements, 81.
    arms and ammunition, 81.
    bricks, 81.
    boots and shoes, 81-82.
    brooms, 82.
    carriages and wagons, 82.
    carpets, 82-83.
    clothing, 83.
    cotton goods, 83.
    flour, 83.
    furniture, 84.
    glass, 84.
    leather, 84.
    lumber, 84.
    machines and machinery, 84.
    metals and metallic goods, 84.
    musical instruments, 84.
    mining, 85.
    oil, 85.
    paper, 85.
    pottery, 86.
    railroad supplies, 86.
    rubber boots and shoes, 86.
    saws, 86.
    silk, 86.
    soap, 86.
    tobacco, 86.
    trunks, 86.
    vessels, 86.
    wine, 86.
    wooden goods, 86.
    woollen goods, 86, 87.

Machinery, wages per hour in the manufacture of, in Birmingham, England, 1885, 236.
Machines and machinery, cost of production of, 114, 115.
    summary of selected occupations, 158, 172.
        all employés, by states, 223.
            with per cent., 200, 201.
Michigan, synopsis of labor legislation in, 468, 469.
Minnesota, synopsis of labor legislation in, 469.
Miscellaneous, summary of all employés, etc., by states, 225.
Missouri, synopsis of labor legislation in, 469-471.
Modern industrial depressions, 15.
Musical instruments and materials, cost of production of, 118, 119.
    summary of selected occupations, 162, 172.
        all employés, by states, 223.
            with per cent., 206.

Maine, synopsis of labor legislation in, 465.
Manufactures, foreign-born engaged in, 1870 and 1880, 245.
Manufacturing nations considered as a group, 254-263.
Maryland, synopsis of labor legislation in, 465, 466.
Massachusetts, production of boots and shoes in, 1850-85, 71.
    synopsis of labor legislation in, 466-468.
Merchant iron, production and average market price of, in France, 1874-83, 41.
Metals and metallic goods, cost of production of, 116-119.
    analysis of material cost of, 128-131.
    summary of selected occupations, 159-162, 173.
        all employés, by states, 223.
            with per cent., 201-206.

Nebraska, synopsis of labor legislation in, 471.
New Hampshire, synopsis of labor legislation in, 471, 472.
New Jersey, synopsis of labor legislation in, 472-474.
New Mexico Territory, synopsis of labor legislation in, 474.
New York, average currency prices of cotton and cotton goods in, 1847-84, 74.
    synopsis of labor legislation in, 474, 475.
Occupations, summary of selected—
    agricultural implements, 143, 168.
    boots and shoes, 143-145, 168.
    brooms, 145.
    carpetings, 145-147, 168.
    carriages and wagons, 147.
    clothing, 148, 169.
    coal, coke, and ore, 149, 150.
    cooking and heating apparatus, 150, 151, 169.
    cotton goods, 151-155, 170-172.
    food preparations, 155, 156.
    furniture, 156, 172.
    glass, 156, 157, 172.
    leather, 158, 172.
    liquors and beverages, 158.
    machines and machinery, 158, 172.
    metals and metallic goods, 159-162, 173.
    musical instruments and materials, 162, 173.
    paper, 163, 173.
    print works, 163, 173.
    tobacco, 164, 173.
    woollen goods, 165-167, 174.
    with number and wages of employés, by industries, 295-410.
Ohio, synopsis of labor legislation in, 475-478.
Oils and illuminating fluids, cost of production of, 118, 119.
    summary of all employés, etc., by states, 223.
Oldham (England), analysis of cost of producing cotton yarn at, 134.
    clauses of agreement between employés and operatives' associations at, 230, 231.
    cost of producing cotton yarn at, 134.
    spinners' wages at, 1885, 229.
    increase of wages of spinners at, for quicker speed, 229.
    system of payment for spinning cotton yarn at, 227, 228.
Oregon, synopsis of labor legislation in, 478.

Paper, cost of production of, 120, 121.
 summary of selected occupations, 163, 173.
  all employés, by states, 223, 224.
   with per cent., 208, 209.
Pennsylvania, synopsis of labor legislation in, 478-482.
Philadelphia, average monthly prices for pig-iron at, 1870-75, 68.
Pig-iron, average price of Scotch, per ton, 1866-72, 24.
 production and average market price of, in France, 1874-82, 62.
 yearly production and value of, in Germany, 1863-82, 59.
Postal banks, number of, in the United Kingdom, 1873-84, 34.
Print works, cost of production of, 120, 121.
 summary of selected occupations, 163, 173.
  all employés, by states, 224.
   with per cent., 210.
Production, cost of, of agricultural implements, 92, 93.
 arms and ammunition, 92, 93.
 artisans' tools, 92, 93.
 boots and shoes, 92-97.
 bricks, 96, 97.
 carpetings, 96, 97.
 carriages and wagons, 96, 97.
 clocks and watches, 96, 99.
 clothing, 98-101.
 coal, coke, and ore, 100-103.
 cooking and heating apparatus, 104, 105.
 cotton goods, 104-111.
 food preparations, 110-113.
 glass, 112, 113.
 jute goods, 112, 113.
 leather, 114, 115.
 liquors and beverages, 114, 115.
 lumber, 114, 115.
 machines and machinery, 114, 115.
 metals and metallic goods, 116-119.
 musical instruments, 118, 119.
 oils and illuminating fluids, 118, 119.
 paper, 120, 121.
 print works, 120, 121.
 rubber goods, 120, 121.
 silk, 120, 121.
 tobacco, 120-123.
 woollen goods, 122-125.
Production, variation in the cost of, 90, 91.
Products, distribution of, 277-279.
Profit-sharing, 279-286.
Prussia, number of depositors and amount of deposits in savings banks in, 1839-81, 53.
 number of miles of railroad in operation in, 1838-81, 54.
Railroad construction, summary of all employés, etc., by states, 224.
Railroads, amount invested in the, of the United Kingdom December 31, 1882, 18.
 cost per annum of operating the, of the country with steam power, 87.
 horse and man power necessary to perform the work of, 87, 88.
 miles of, in operation and miles built each year in France, 1840-84, 43.
   the United States, 1830-85, 62.
  opened in the United Kingdom, 1843-52, 19.
   1853-63, 21.
   1864-72, 25.
   1873-84, 32.
  in divisions of the United Kingdom, 1884, 32.
   Prussia, 1838-81, 54.
  operation in the German Empire, 1835-81, 52.
 speculative building of, 242, 243.
Rails, iron, yearly production of, in the United States, 1874-85, 68.
 steel, yearly production of, in the United States, 1874-85, 68.
Rates of wages, variation in the, 141, 142.
Reeled yarn, cost of spinning, in the Bolton district, England, 232.

INDEX. 495

Remedies suggested for depressions, 292, 293.
      as elicited by agents of the Bureau, 269, 270.
        committees of Congress, 264-269.
Restriction of immigration, 271-273.
Rhode Island, synopsis of labor legislation in, 482, 483.
Rubber goods, cost of production of, 120, 121.
 summary of all employés, etc., by states, 234.
Savings banks, depositors and deposits in, under trustees, in the United Kingdom, 1846-56, 19.
   number of depositors, etc., in, under trustees, in the United Kingdom, 1857-65, 22.
        1866-72, 26.
        1873-84, 34.
   decrease in deposits in, under trustees, in the United Kingdom, 1847-48, 20.
   number of depositors, etc., in post-office, of the United Kingdom, 1862-72, 26.
     in France, 1835-83, 43.
      in Prussia, 1839-81, 51.
      in Saxony, 1845-70, 52.
   exhibit of, in the United States, 1874-85, 75.
Saxony, classes of depositors in savings banks in, 1845-81, 52.
 deposits in savings banks in, 1845-70, 52.
Silk, cost of production of, 120, 121.
 summary of all employés, etc., by states, 234.
Speculation, enactment of laws to stop, 273, 274.
Steel, production and value of, in Belgium, 1840-83, 48.
 yearly production of, in France, 1829-83, 42.
 production and average market price of, in France, 1874-83, 41.
 Bessemer, yearly production of, in the United States, 1874-85, 67.
Stone, summary of all employés, etc., by states, 234.
Switzerland, earnings and expenses of wage-receivers in, 453-456.
Tariff inequalities, 250-252.
Tennessee, synopsis of labor legislation in, 483.
Texas, synopsis of labor legislation in, 483.
Tobacco, cost of production of, 120-123.
 summary of selected occupations, 164, 173.
  all employés, by states, 224.
   with per cent., 210-213.
Twist, cost of spinning, in the Bolton district, England, 231.
Under-consumption, 243-250.
United Kingdom, amount invested in railroads in the, December 31, 1852, 18.
   railroads opened in the, 1843-52, 18.
     1853-63, 21.
     1864-72, 25.
     1873-84, 33.
   miles of railroads in divisions of the, 1884, 33.
   capital invested in railroads of the, December 31, 1872, 25.
   depositors, etc., in savings banks under trustees in the, 1846-56, 19.
     1857-65, 22.
     1866-72, 26.
     1873-84, 34.
   decrease in deposits in savings banks under trustees in the, 1847-48, 20.
   number of depositors, etc., in post-office savings banks in the, 1862-72, 26.
     1873-84, 34.
   joint-stock companies in the, 1866-72, 25.
    number of, registered in the, 1873-84, 33.
   value of imports and exports for the, 1860-84, 73.
   importation of cotton into the, from the United States, 1861-63, 21.
United States, export price in currency of domestic products of the, 1855-85, 74, 75.
  immigration into the, 1820-85, 245.
  industrial depressions in the, 1837-36, 55-64.
    1882-86, 65-70.
  miles of railroad in operation and built each year in the, 1830-85, 68.
  number of failures in the, and amount of liabilities, 1857-85, 67.
   locomotives in the, 87.
  production of anthracite coal in the, 1882-85, 70.
   bituminous coal in the, 1882-85, 70.
  yearly production of pig-iron, according to fuel used, in the, 1870-85, 69.
   iron rails in the, 1874-85, 68.

United States, yearly production of steel rails in the, 1874-85, 68.
　　　　　　　　　　Bessemer steel ingots in the, 1874-85, 77.
　　　　　savings banks in the, exhibit of, 1873-85, 75.
　　　　　synopsis of labor legislation in the—
　　　　　　　　　　　　　California, 457.
　　　　　　　　　　　　　Colorado, 457-459.
　　　　　　　　　　　　　Connecticut, 460.
　　　　　　　　　　　　　Dakota, 461.
　　　　　　　　　　　　　Delaware, 461.
　　　　　　　　　　　　　Georgia, 461.
　　　　　　　　　　　　　Illinois, 461, 462.
　　　　　　　　　　　　　Indiana, 462-464.
　　　　　　　　　　　　　Iowa, 464.
　　　　　　　　　　　　　Kansas, 464, 465.
　　　　　　　　　　　　　Maine, 465.
　　　　　　　　　　　　　Maryland, 465, 466.
　　　　　　　　　　　　　Massachusetts, 466-468.
　　　　　　　　　　　　　Michigan, 468, 469.
　　　　　　　　　　　　　Minnesota, 469.
　　　　　　　　　　　　　Missouri, 469-471.
　　　　　　　　　　　　　Nebraska, 471.
　　　　　　　　　　　　　New Hampshire, 471, 472.
　　　　　　　　　　　　　New Jersey, 472-474.
　　　　　　　　　　　　　New Mexico Territory, 474.
　　　　　　　　　　　　　New York, 474, 475.
　　　　　　　　　　　　　Ohio, 475-478.
　　　　　　　　　　　　　Oregon, 478.
　　　　　　　　　　　　　Pennsylvania, 478-482.
　　　　　　　　　　　　　Rhode Island, 482, 483.
　　　　　　　　　　　　　Tennessee, 483.
　　　　　　　　　　　　　Texas, 483.
　　　　　　　　　　　　　Vermont, 483, 484.
　　　　　　　　　　　　　Washington Territory, 484.
　　　　　　　　　　　　　West Virginia, 484.
　　　　　　　　　　　　　Wisconsin, 484, 485.
　　　value of imports and exports of the, 1835-85, 71, 72.
　　　　　　　　　　for the, 1860-84, 73.
　　　value of wheat exported from the, 1878-85, 249.
　　　　　　　leading agricultural products exported from the, 1860-85, 249.
　　　　　　　etc., of all products exported from the, 1860, 1870, 1875-85, 248.
Vermont, synopsis of labor legislation in, 483, 484.
Vessels, summary of all employés, etc., by states, 224.
Wages, daily, in Paris, France, 1844, 1853, 1860, 1871, 1875, 1881, and 1882, 236.
　　　principal cities of France, not including Paris, 1853, 1857, 1871, 1875, 1881, and 1882, 237.
　　　of spinners at Oldham, England, 1885, 229.
　　　increase of, of spinners, for quicker speed, at Oldham, England, 229.
　　　variation in the rates of, 141, 142.
Washington Territory, synopsis of labor legislation in, 484.
Weft, cost of spinning, in the Bolton district, England, 232.
West Virginia, synopsis of labor legislation in, 484.
Wheat, average price of, in Great Britain, 1835-39, 16.
　　　　　　　　　　1846-50, 18.
　　　gazette prices of British, 1870-84, 29.
　　　acreage of, in Great Britain, 1870-84, 28.
　　　importation of, into Great Britain and Ireland, 1880-84, 248.
　　　value of, exported from the United States, 1878-85, 249.
Wisconsin, synopsis of labor legislation in, 484, 485.
Wooden goods, summary of all employés, etc., by states, 224, 225.
Woollen goods, cost of production of, 122-125.
　　　summary of selected occupations, 165-167, 174.
　　　　　　　all employés, by states, 225.
　　　　　　　　　　with per cent., 213-219
Woollen and mixed goods, price of, Leeds (England), duties, etc., 251.
Workmen, organization of, of employers, 286-289.

www.ingramcontent.com/pod-product-compliance
Lightning Source LLC
Chambersburg PA
CBHW021415300426
44114CB00010B/500